HANDBOOK OF LATIN AMERICAN STUDIES: No. 46

A Selective and Annotated Guide to Recent Publications
in Art, Folklore, History, Language, Literature, Music,
and Philosophy

VOLUME 47 WILL BE DEVOTED TO THE SOCIAL SCIENCES:
ANTHROPOLOGY, ECONOMICS, EDUCATION, GEOGRAPHY, GOVERNMENT AND
POLITICS, INTERNATIONAL RELATIONS, AND SOCIOLOGY

EDITORIAL NOTE: Comments concerning the *Handbook of Latin American Studies* should be sent directly to the Editor, *Handbook of Latin American Studies*, Hispanic Division, Library of Congress, Washington, D.C. 20540.

HANDBOOK OF LATIN AMERICAN STUDIES: NO. 46

HUMANITIES

Prepared by a Number of Scholars
for the Hispanic Division of The Library of Congress

Edited by DOLORES MOYANO MARTIN

1984

UNIVERSITY OF TEXAS PRESS   *Austin*

International Standard Book Number 0-292-73035-7
Library of Congress Catalog Card Number 36-32633
Copyright © 1986 by the University of Texas Press
Printed in the United States of America

Requests for permission to reproduce material from this work should be sent to
Permissions, University of Texas Press,
Box 7819, Austin, Texas 78713-7819.

First Edition, 1986

CONTRIBUTING EDITORS

HUMANITIES

Earl M. Aldrich, Jr., *University of Wisconsin, Madison*, LITERATURE
Joyce Bailey, *New Haven, Conn.*, ART
Jean A. Barman, *University of British Columbia*, HISTORY
Roderick J. Barman, *University of British Columbia*, HISTORY
Judith Ishmael Bissett, *Miami University, Ohio*, LITERATURE
David Bushnell, *University of Florida*, HISTORY
D. Lincoln Canfield, *Southern Illinois University at Carbondale*, LANGUAGES
Donald E. Chipman, *North Texas State University, Denton*, HISTORY
S. L. Cline, *Harvard University*, HISTORY
Don M. Coerver, *Texas Christian University*, HISTORY
Michael L. Conniff, *University of New Mexico, Albuquerque*, HISTORY
René de Costa, *University of Chicago*, LITERATURE
Edith B. Couturier, *National Endowment for the Humanities*, HISTORY
Ethel O. Davie, *West Virginia State College*, LITERATURE
Lisa E. Davis, *Hunter College*, LITERATURE
Ralph E. Dimmick, *Organization of American States*, LITERATURE
Roberto Etchepareborda, *Organization of American States*, HISTORY
Leonard Folgarait, *Vanderbilt University*, ART
Fernando García Núñez, *University of Texas at El Paso*, LITERATURE
Magdalena García Pinto, *University of Missouri, Columbia*, LITERATURE
Naomi M. Garrett, *West Virginia State College*, LITERATURE
Jaime Giordano, *State University of New York at Stony Brook*, LITERATURE
Cedomil Goić, *University of Michigan*, LITERATURE
Roberto González Echevarría, *Yale University*, LITERATURE
Richard E. Greenleaf, *Tulane University*, HISTORY
Oscar Hahn, *University of Iowa*, LITERATURE
Michael T. Hamerly, *Dumbarton Oaks Collection, Washington*, HISTORY
John R. Hébert, *Library of Congress*, BIBLIOGRAPHY AND GENERAL WORKS
Carlos R. Hortas, *Hunter College*, LITERATURE
Regina Igel, *University of Maryland, College Park*, LITERATURE
Randal Johnson, *University of Florida*, FILM
Djelal Kadir, *Purdue University*, LITERATURE
Norma Klahn, *Columbia University*, LITERATURE
Franklin W. Knight, *Johns Hopkins University*, HISTORY
Pedro Lastra, *State University of New York at Stony Brook*, LITERATURE
Asunción Lavrin, *Howard University*, HISTORY
Maria Angélica Guimarães Lopes, *University of South Carolina, Columbia*, LITERATURE
William Luis, *Dartmouth College*, LITERATURE
Murdo J. MacLeod, *University of Arizona*, HISTORY
Wilson Martins, *New York University*, LITERATURE
Robert J. Mullen, *University of Texas at San Antonio*, ART
José Neistein, *Brazilian American Cultural Institute, Washington*, ART

Julio Ortega, *University of Texas at Austin*, LITERATURE
José Miguel Oviedo, *University of California, Los Angeles*, LITERATURE
Margaret Sayers Peden, *University of Missouri*, LITERATURE
Vincent C. Peloso, *Howard University*, HISTORY
Richard A. Preto-Rodas, *University of South Florida, Tampa*, LITERATURE
Daniel R. Reedy, *University of Kentucky*, LITERATURE
James D. Riley, *Catholic University of America*, HISTORY
Rubén Ríos Avila, *University of Puerto Rico*, LITERATURE
Frank Salomon, *University of Wisconsin, Madison*, HISTORY
Rebecca Scott, *University of Michigan*, HISTORY
Nicolas Shumway, *Yale University*, LITERATURE
Merle E. Simmons, *Indiana University*, FOLKLORE
Susan M. Socolow, *Emory University*, HISTORY
Saúl Sosnowski, *University of Maryland, College Park*, LITERATURE
Robert Stevenson, *University of California, Los Angeles*, MUSIC
Juan Carlos Torchia-Estrada, *Organization of American States*, PHILOSOPHY
Kathryn Waldron, *New York City*, HISTORY
George Woodyard, *University of Kansas*, LITERATURE
Thomas C. Wright, *University of Nevada*, HISTORY
Winthrop R. Wright, *University of Maryland, College Park*, HISTORY
George Yudice, *Emory University*, LITERATURE

SOCIAL SCIENCES

Michael B. Anderson, *Inter-American Development Bank*, ECONOMICS
Roderic Ai Camp, *Central College, Pella, Iowa*, GOVERNMENT AND POLITICS
Lyle Campbell, *State University of New York at Albany*, ANTHROPOLOGY
William L. Canak, *Tulane University*, SOCIOLOGY
Charlotte Jones Carroll, *The World Bank*, ECONOMICS
Thomas F. Carroll, *George Washington University*, ECONOMICS
Manuel J. Carvajal, *Florida International University*, ECONOMICS
Donald V. Coes, *University of Illinois, Urbana*, ECONOMICS
Lambros Comitas, *Columbia University*, ANTHROPOLOGY
David W. Dent, *Towson State College*, GOVERNMENT AND POLITICS
Clinton R. Edwards, *University of Wisconsin, Milwaukee*, GEOGRAPHY
Everett Egginton, *University of Louisville*, EDUCATION
Robert C. Eidt, *University of Wisconsin, Milwaukee*, GEOGRAPHY
Gary S. Elbow, *Texas Tech University*, GEOGRAPHY
Yale H. Ferguson, *Rutgers University, Newark*, INTERNATIONAL RELATIONS
Michael J. Francis, *University of Notre Dame*, INTERNATIONAL RELATIONS
William R. Garner, *Southern Illinois University*, GOVERNMENT AND POLITICS
Dennis Gilbert, *Hamilton College*, SOCIOLOGY
George W. Grayson, *College of William and Mary*, INTERNATIONAL RELATIONS
Norman Hammond, *Rutgers University, New Brunswick*, ANTHROPOLOGY
Kevin Healy, *Inter-American Foundation*, SOCIOLOGY
John R. Hébert, *Library of Congress*, BIBLIOGRAPHY AND GENERAL WORKS
Mario Hiraoka, *Millersville State College*, GEOGRAPHY
John M. Hunter, *Michigan State University*, ECONOMICS
John M. Ingham, *University of Minnesota*, ANTHROPOLOGY
W. Jerald Kennedy, *Florida Atlantic University*, ANTHROPOLOGY
Waud H. Kracke, *University of Illinois at Chicago Circle*, ANTHROPOLOGY
Thomas J. La Belle, *University of California, Los Angeles*, EDUCATION
Robert Malina, *University of Texas at Austin*, ANTHROPOLOGY

CONTENTS

INDEXES

EDITOR'S NOTE

I. GENERAL AND REGIONAL TRENDS

Despite the economic crisis that is affecting Latin America, from Cuba's socialist experiment to Chile's free market economy, as noted in *HLAS 45* (p. xv), the publishing business has suffered much less than expected and, on the contrary, appears to be thriving in a number of countries. For example, young poets have "greater access to print" thanks to government-sponsored publications in Argentina, Mexico, Nicaragua, and Venezuela (p. 461). In Brazil, Congress led the way by issuing an anthology of short fiction written by members of both houses, suggestively entitled *Horas vagas* (*Leisure time*, p. 514), once again proving that the Brazilian publishing business is not only the most active in Latin America but, as stated in a major study of the subject by Lawrence Hallewell, well on the way to becoming "the premier book industry of the Third World" (item **3461**, p. 435).

The growing interest of extra-hemispheric scholars in Latin America noted in previous volumes is evident once again in Swedish, Italian, West and East German studies of the region that are itemized in several bibliographies (items **2a, 7a, 10, 12,** and **75**). The extraordinary growth of the field in the Soviet Union observed in *HLAS 45* (p. xvi) continues in this volume (item **106**) as does serious interest in Latin American studies in India (item **89**), the third Asian nation, in addition to Japan and China.

The continuing internationalization of Latin American scholarship is exemplified by *The New Grove Dictionary of Music* (p. 567), the first worldwide encyclopedia in one field to devote that much space to Latin America: 250 composers and 70 dances, song types and instruments (p. 567). That hemispheric topics are no longer the purview of specialists in the region is exemplified by the fact that a recent article on Brazilian slavery (item **3620**) is commented on in this volume by two leading experts on North American slavery (item **3567**). Again, the professionalization of Latin American history as a field is especially evident in Brazil where, our contributors point out, the historical community has evolved "from a collection of amateur authors, often specialists in traditional fields like law or medicine, to a full-fledged profession" (p. 322). This transformation is most evident in the proceedings of two important historical congresses (items **3478** and **3514**).

Concurrent with the internationalization of Latin American studies is the desire among scholars to ground their theories and methodologies on Latin American rather than "European or North American social and cultural realities" (p. 55). Thus, concern in determining what constitutes "Latin American culture" is evident throughout the region. In Brazil, for example, there is keen interest in *literatura de cordel*, a genre perceived as a manifestation of the nation's ethos as well as the end result of a singularly creative popular culture (p. 55). In that vein, the search for a definition of what constitutes folk art or popular art in Latin America is also apparent in the art section of this volume (items **279, 281, 283, 287, 288, 315** and **316**). Concurrent with such concerns is enthusiasm for the concept of *lo andino*, defined by a contributor to this volume as "enduring cultural fundamentals that allegedly pervade all centuries of Andean life" (p. 90). Attempts at such "native-oriented historiographies" (items **1695, 1721** and **1724**) are on the increase as exemplified by writers of *historia andina* who scrutinize "native polities into the 17th, 18th and 19th centuries—periods which, despite the immense colonial document record," remain "ethnohistorically darker" than Inca times (p. 90). We observe a similar fascination with what is meant by "the indigenous" in the literature section of this volume where the astonishing upsurge of interest in José María Arguedas is equivalent to that accorded the two major figures of the Andean region, Gabriel García Márquez and Mario Vargas Llosa. Mostly sociolinguistic and anthropological, these studies of Arguedas (items **5403, 5404, 5405, 5409, 5410, 5417, 5418, 5420, 5421, 5422, 5424, 5426,** and **5428**) attest to the influence of the social sciences noted in *HLAS 42* (p. xiv). No longer the exclusive province of anthropologists and linguists, indigenous languages now command the interest of both literary critics and the reading public, an interest exemplified by the publication of "an unusually comprehensive trilingual anthology" (p. 463), issued in Bolivia, that includes poetry in Quechua and Aymara (item **5641**). Indeed, interest in what are the "local and indigenous elements" of Latin American poetry is also evident in *Revista de Crítica Literaria Latinoamericana*, a journal published in Lima, which "contains several thought-provoking articles" (items **5804, 5810** and **5811**) that "are really part of a much larger and as yet unannounced debate seeking to formulate a new concept" of the nature of an avant-garde that is "less Eurocentric" (p. 463).

Interest in what can be defined as specifically Latin American is also reflected in the PHILOSOPHY section which as of this volume, *HLAS 46*, will be subtitled "Latin American Thought" and cover only works about Latin American thinkers (p. xvii). Studies by Latin American authors about philosophical topics extraneous to the region will be mentioned in the introduction to the section wherein this change of policy is explained in more detail (pp. 601–605). One of the reasons for such a change is the unprecedented increase in the number of works about the thought and thinkers of Latin America, exemplified most dramatically by the deluge of publications on the Peruvian José Carlos Mariátegui, so evident in previous volumes and continuing unabated in this one (items **7586, 7587, 7588, 7590, 7591, 7592, 7593, 7594, 7595, 7596, 7598, 7599, 7602, 7603, 7605, 7606,** and **7609**).

On the subject of women, recent developments are the publication of several reference aids on the topic (items **66, 69a,** and **79**) as well as the appearance of "significant new works by established women poets, most of which go beyond the usual themes of love and loss" (p. 462 and items **5679, 5705, 5743, 5749, 5762,** and **5782**).

The preponderance of Mexican authors and the sophistication of Mexican scholarship in the fine arts is evident once again in this volume (p. 36). Moreover, Mexican topics are being selected more and more by US art historians who are not Latin Americanists (p. 36).

The evils of urbanization, a dominant theme in the social sciences (see *HLAS 41*, p. xiii) and a persistent concern of many Latin American poets and writers (see *HLAS 42*, p. xiv), is especially noticeable in Mexican fiction. It is expected that by the year 2000 Mexico City will have 30 to 35 million inhabitants concentrated into its 925 square miles, making it the most populous city in the world. The violence and corruption engendered by such inhuman crowding already pervades much Mexican narrative where the monster city is portrayed as the "center of arbitrary power" (p. 395).

Another observable trend in this volume is the rising interest in contemporary topics. Historians of Venezuela, for example, have produced an "unprecedented number" of works on 20th-century subjects (p. 252). In Argentina, contemporary affairs also command a great deal more attention than in previous *Handbooks*, with interest in the Radical Party, the party in power, having temporarily displaced *rosismo* as a leading subject (p. 287). Likewise, historians of Chile, concerned with the "dilemma and the promise of contemporary Chile" (p. 273), have turned more and more to the early decades of the century in their search for the roots of the Chilean predicament, a search that is reflected in the volume of historiography on the nitrate period (items **3065, 3068, 3073, 3087, 3092, 3097, 3115, 3116, 3120** and **3147**). Research on foreign relations continues most markedly in Mexico and Venezuela, reflecting the increasingly important roles of both nations in this continent and in the world at large (p. 152 and 252).

The publication and republication of sources is another development of this biennium most evident in Mexico, Venezuela and Peru. In Mexico the quantification of primary materials for long-term historical analysis is being conducted by the Seminar on the History of Mentalities in "the most intensive use of ecclesiatical sources" (p. 134). In Venezuela, the publication of colonial documents is exemplified by the massive set on the Capuchin missions of Guayana (item **2635**) as well as by the abstracts of Caracas' ecclesiastical archives (item **2637**). And in Peru, the reedition of out-of-print sources, carefully annotated and introduced by scholars, has stimulated research into the impact and significance of native thought (p. 91).

As observed in previous volumes, regional studies continue to thrive. Examples are the proliferation of Argentine local histories (p. 289), the growing concern of Brazilian historians with the southern regions of their country (p. 321), the recent interest in the history of Yucatan's economic development and the continuing examination of the US-Mexican Borderlands and of Mexican migration therein (p. 153).

The flow of histories of immigration to Argentina and Brazil continues unabated (p. 289 and 321) and coincides with the first scholarly study of the portrayal of immigration in 19th-century Argentine literature (item **5112**) and the emergence of the immigrant as a figure in Brazilian prose fiction (p. 509).

As noted in previous *Handbooks*, sociopolitical topics continue to appeal to historians (p. 251, 261, 287, and 322) as well as to fiction writers and poets annotated in this volume. This is especially the case in Brazil where novelists concerned with "sociopolitical phenomena" and the explication of social problems in terms of "abuse of power" (p. 509) focus on subjects such as "the anguish of political exile, oppression and repression" (p. 508). In the same vein, "more and more" Brazilian short story writers "are writing about the 1964 coup and its ugly ramifications of political oppression, torture and murder" (p. 515). Such recent short stories, writes one critic, "grapple painfully with the numerous incidents . . . that destroyed the Brazilian illusion that we are a people incapable of habitual cruelty" (p. 516). Brazilian plays also "reflect a continuing interest in political and social problems" (p. 537) as do Brazilian *crônicas*, traditionally light and humorous, but which now ponder serious issues such as the "worrisome state of international affairs" (p. 524). And finally, "political and social protest" has become "an increasingly frequent theme" in Brazilian poetry (p. 529).

Several anniversaries are commemorated in the history and literature sections of this volume. The bicentennial of the birth of Andrés Bello (1781–1981) has resulted in several excellent publications which illuminate the significance and impact of this figure on the history and literature of Latin America (items **3066, 3068, 3083, 3103, 5101, 5103,** and **5117**). The combined anniversaries of the bicentennial of Simón Bolívar's birth (1783–1983) and sesquicentennial of his death (1830–1980) have resulted in a proliferation of books on the Liberator that are grouped and annotated under the subheading "Bolivariana" (p. 241). Another important centennial commemorates the emergence of Argentina's generation of the 1880s, a crucial group of intellectuals, writers and politicians caught up in heated debate about the meaning of democracy, liberalism, populism and elitism (p. 387 and items **5095, 5109,** and **5138**). Scholarly interest in the centennial of the War of the Pacific (1883–1983) noted in *HLAS 44* (p. 282 and 298) continues as far as Chile and Peru are concerned but "has been surprisingly slight in Bolivia" (p. 272).

Another significant event of the biennium was the death of Argentine writer Julio Cortázar in 1984. His death ends what must be considered "a golden age of Latin American literature in English translation" (p. 555), an era which began with the publication of *Hopscotch* in 1966 and ended with Gregory Rabassa's translation of an anthology of Cortázar stories in 1984 (item **6467**). This span (1966–84) closes a "20-some year period characterized by the enthusiastic reception of a literature that until the 1960s was virtually invisible to North American readers" (p. 555).

And finally, the most notable development of the last biennium is, without a doubt, the extraordinary upsurge of interest in the colonial period evident in the history and literature sections of this volume. One historian observes that "the number of quality items in the colonial subsection is perhaps the most significant change from the last volume" (p. 114), and another notes that the quality of "virtually all books and articles" on colonial Spanish South America is "high, regardless of whether the approach or theme is traditional or new" (p. 214). In literary criticism, an equal increase in the quantity and quality of colonial studies is proof to one scholar that "Latin American criticism is becoming more scholarly and specialized" (p. 375). Examples of the trend are the outstanding quality of some works of criticism on the period (items **5064** and **5085**) and the historical interest commanded by such figures as Felipe Guamán Poma de Ayala who is no longer regarded merely as an "informant on Inca realities" but rather as an "exemplar of colonial Andean innovation" (p. 91 and items **1578, 1590, 1626, 1658,** and **1686**). Although the conquest/early colonial and late colonial periods continue to attract more historians than the 17th century (p. 215), one study of a 17th-century figure is unquestionably the critical event of recent years. Octavio Paz's *Sor Juana Inés de la Cruz o las trampas de la fe* (item **2011**) is, in the words of one contributor, not only a "monumental" work but "the best and most complete study ever done of Sor Juana, her life, her writings and her times," in addition to being "a work of one great literary figure about another, of one poet on another, of one Mexican who keenly perceives the enduring worth of a fellow Mexican" (p. 379). While this literary critic welcomes the fact that Paz's study is not "obscured by a ponderous mass of historical information" (p. 379), the historian's comment is that it is "likely to remain a much discussed biography" (p. 135).

II. CHANGES IN VOLUME 46

Art

Leonard Folgarait, Vanderbilt University, was responsible for preparing the section on Spanish-American art of the 19th and 20th centuries.

Folklore

In *HLAS 42* (p. xvii) we explained the reasons for alternating Folklore and Film in the humanities volume of *HLAS*. As noted therein, this volume carries the Folklore section and *HLAS 48*, the next humanities volume, will carry the next Film section.

History

S.L. Cline, Harvard University, prepared the section on the ethnohistory of Meso-america. Frank Salomon, University of Wisconsin, Madison, annotated the litera-ture on the ethnohistory of South America. Rebecca Scott, University of Michigan, collaborated with Franklin W. Knight in compiling the section on the history of the Caribbean and The Guianas. Kathryn Waldron, New York City, and Susan M. Socolow, Emory University, collaborated with Michael T. Hamerly in covering the colonial history of Spanish South America.

Literature

Fernando García Núñez, University of Texas at El Paso, prepared the section on Mexican prose fiction of the 20th century. Spanish American poetry of the 20th century was annotated by several new contributors who collaborated with Pedro Lastra, responsible for Colombia and Venezuela as of this *Handbook*, and Oscar Hahn who covers Chile. René de Costa, University of Chicago, served as general editor and the following contributors covered the poetry of the indicated countries: Magdalena García Pinto, University of Missouri: Uruguay and Paraguay; Jaime Giordano, State University of New York at Stony Brook: Argentina; Norma Klahn, Columbia University: Mexico; Julio Ortega, University of Texas, Austin: Peru, Bolivia and Ecuador; Rubén Ríos Avila, University of Puerto Rico: the Hispanic Caribbean; and George Yudice, Emory University: Central America.

Richard A. Preto-Rodas, University of South Florida, prepared the section on *crô-nicas* for Brazilian literature. Judith Ishmael Bissett, Miami University, Oxford, Ohio, annotated all materials on Brazilian drama.

Philosophy

As of this volume, *HLAS 46*, this section will be subtitled "Latin American Thought." The change is already noted on p. xiv of this Editor's Note and the reasons for the new policy are spelled out in more detail by the contributor to this section, Juan Carlos Torchia Estrada, on pp. 601–605.

Subject Index

As stated in previous volumes, the policy of the *Handbook* Subject Index is to use the Library of Congress Subject Headings as much as possible but when neces-sary to adapt them to terms that predominate in the literature as familiar and useful ones to Latin Americanists. In this volume, *HLAS 46*, geographic index terms that are smaller than those at the country level are indexed separately when appropriate but are not cross-referenced to the particular country as in, for example, *Buenos Aires, Argentina* (city) which is a separate entry but not listed next to the entry *Argentina*.

Other Changes

Changes in the editorial staff of the *Handbook*, the administrative officers of the Library of Congress, and membership in the Advisory Board are reflected in the title pages of the present volume.

Dolores Moyano Martin

HANDBOOK OF LATIN AMERICAN STUDIES: No. 46

A Selective and Annotated Guide to Recent Publications in Art, Folklore, History, Language, Literature, Music, and Philosophy

BIBLIOGRAPHY AND GENERAL WORKS

JOHN R. HEBERT, *Assistant Chief, Hispanic Division, The Library of Congress*

A LARGE NUMBER OF wide-ranging publications of interest to this *HLAS* section were canvassed sometime between January and August 1984. Among them were national, subject, personal, and general bibliographies; guides to collections; significant reference works; noteworthy contributions in the area of general studies in Latin America and area studies; useful new journals; and articles and monographs on the development of libraries, archives, and collections in the region. Several works encompassing broad themes, facilitating the study of a segment of Latin American culture, or enhancing areas of research are cited in this essay.

The problem of lack of or infrequent publication of national bibliographies for the nations of Latin America persists, although there are exceptions. They include the *Anuario Bibliográfico Dominicano* (item 3), covering 1980–82, and generated by the National Library of the Dominican Republic, and the *Bibliografía Costarricense: 1937–45* (item 4), a retrospective catalog of imprints for these years, produced by the National Library of Costa Rica. One should also note the pioneering effort of George Elmendorf who is currently compiling retrospective national bibliographies for the entire national period of Nicaragua and El Salvador.

There are a number of bibliographies, research guides, and other publications scattered below under different headings that ought to be noted collectively here because of their concern for specific subjects (e.g., women in Latin America, armed struggle, individuals, etc.). One such instance is the study of women in Latin America, a dominant theme in preceding volumes of *HLAS*, exemplified below by some noteworthy publications: *Diccionario biográfico de la mujer en el Uruguay* (item 69a); Elsa Chaney's *Women of the world: Latin America and the Caribbean* (item 66), a work providing a variety of statistical data on the region's women; Doreen Goyer's *The handbook of national population censuses: Latin America and the Caribbean, North America, and Oceania* (item 77), a compilation of population census data; and June Hahner's essay, "Researching the History of Latin American Women: Past and Future Directions" (item 79) in *Revista Interamericana de Bibliografía*, a survey of women's studies in Latin America showing they are in their infancy and that many more researchers are needed to further the task.

Armed struggle as a bibliographical topic is not unique but two interesting items have appeared recently: Margarita Kallsen's *Referencias bibliográficas de la Guerra del Chaco* (item 26) which contains over 450 items and Louis A. Pérez's article, "Armed Struggle and Guerrilla Warfare in Latin America" (item 33), a bibliography based on Cuban journals covering the period 1959–79, that appeared in *Revista Interamericana de Bibliografía*.

An excellent personal bibliography is Roberto González Echevarría's and Klaus Müller-Bergh's *Alejo Carpentier* (item 38), which provides a useful guide to the writings by and criticism of the noted Cuban author.

Reference aids and indexes that facilitate the location of journals and other periodicals as well as their holdings are invaluable sources of information for researchers. The Brazilian National Library has produced such a guide to Brazilian periodicals on microform: *Periódicos brasileiros em microformas: catálogo coletivo* (item **47b**); the Costa Rican Consejo Nacional de Investigaciones Científicas y Tecnológicas (CONICYT) has come out with an impressive second edition, of nearly 15,000 titles, of the *Catálogo colectivo de publicaciones periódicas existentes en Costa Rica* (item **54**); and the Inter-American Center for Documentation and Agricultural Information (Turrialba, Costa Rica) lists more than 5000 journal titles in agriculture and selected scientific fields in *Catálogo colectivo de publicaciones periódicas de las bibliotecas del CIDIA* (item **83**).

Works of bibliography and reference related to the arts are always welcome. Listed below are Joyce Bailey's long awaited *Handbook of Latin American art* (item **2**) and Julianne Burton's excellent *The New Latin American cinema* (item **16**), an annotated bibliography of sources in English, Spanish, and Portuguese for 1960–80.

The study of Latin America and area studies in general is a continuing interest of this *HLAS* section. In recent years, we have noted the rising interest in Latin American studies in Europe and Asia and, from time to time, we have referred to area and foreign language studies and the continuing concern for their funding in the US and other regions outside of Latin America. A number of worthwhile works on this topic have been issued this year: Alexander Sizonenko's brief overview of Latin American studies in the Soviet Union, "La Latinoamericanística en las Repúblicas Federadas en la URSS" (item **106**); Karl-Christian Goethner's article, "Research at GDR Universities in Latin America" (item **75**), which describes East German scholars and institutions interested in the field; and R. Narayanan's article, "Latin American Studies in India" (item **89**). These works along with Enrique Bernales' *El desarrollo de las ciencias sociales en el Perú* (item **60**) are especially useful for documenting developments in the study of the social sciences and of the humanities in specific countries. These particular works are supplemented by publications providing information on Swedish, Italian, and German research on varied Latin American themes: the Swedish *Latinamerikana i Svensk bibliografi 1977–80* (item **2a**); Aldo Albonico's *Bibliografia della storiografia e pubblicistica italiana sull'America latina, 1940–80* (item **7a**); Giuseppe Bellini's *Bibliografia dell ispanoamericanismo italiano* (item **10**), listing mainly works on Hispanic American literature; and *Die Beziehungen zwishen Lateinamerika und der Bundesrepublik Deutschland* (item **12**).

It is clear from the works noted above, that the study of regional areas has emerged as a lively topic of discussion and one is encouraged that the theme commands that much interest, especially in view of the recommendations of the US Presidential Commission on Foreign Language and Area Studies. Another view of the capabilities of US universities to provide advanced training and research in foreign languages and area studies is presented in an important study by Richard Lambert, *Beyond growth: the next stage in language and area studies* (item **103**). A similar discussion that occurred in Japan is reported by Mikota Usui in "The Labyrinth of Foreign Area Studies: Problems and Promises" (item **107**).

As this brief overview of the literature demonstrates, the number of publications that provide bibliographic and research access to materials on Latin America as well as a rich assortment of opportunities to scholars remains as varied and constant as in previous years.

GENERAL BIBLIOGRAPHY

1 Delorme, Roberto. Latin America, 1979–1983: a social science bibliography. Santa Barbara, Calif.: ABC-Clio Information Services, 1984. 1 v.: bibl., index.

Sequel to *Latin America: Social Science Information Sources, 1967–1979* (see *HLAS 43:1*). Contains titles of books and articles, mainly in English, that have been published since the publication of previous volume through Sept. 1983.

Findlay, James A. Modern Latin American art: a bibliography. See item **380.**

2 Handbook of Latin American art = Manual de arte latinoamericano. v. 1, General references and art of the nineteenth & twentieth centuries. pt. 1, North America; pt. 2, South America. General editor, Joyce Waddell Bailey. Volume/regional editor, Brazil, Aracy Abreu Amaral. Volume editor, Southern Cone, Ramón Gutierrez. Regional editor, Southern Cone, Alberto S.J. De Paula. Santa Barbara, Calif.: ABC-Clio Information Services, 1984. 1195 p.: indexes.

Vol. 1, in three-vol. project, reviews Latin American art in 19th and 20th centuries. Subsequent volumes will provide coverage for colonial and precolumbian periods. Contains general bibliographic section and artist's bibliography for each Latin American country (e.g., Cuba-Painting, Drawing). Provides extensive art coverage for Brazil and Argentina. Includes abbreviations, serials, symbols, and author indexes. For art historian's comment, see item **381.**

2a Latinamerikana i svensk bibliografi, 1977–1980 = America latina en la bibliografía sueca, 1977–1980. Utarbetad av Jan Grammar *et al.* Under handledning av Miguel Benito. Stockholm: Latinamerika-Institutet i Stockholm, 1982. 80 p. (Latinamericana; nr. 12)

Lists publications in Swedish on Latin America, that appeared 1977–80. Also includes general works and publications on individual countries.

NATIONAL BIBLIOGRAPHIES

3 *Anuario Bibliográfico Dominicano.* Biblioteca Nacional. 1984– . Santo Domingo.

Lists Dominican publications issued primarily 1980–82 as well as much earlier works not included in previous compendia. Citations appear in alphabetical order by subject. Provides separate author and subject indexes.

4 Bibliografía Costarricense: 1937– 1945. San José: Centro de Documentación y Bibliografía, Dirección General de Bibliotecas y Biblioteca Nacional, Ministerio de Cultura, Juventud y Deportes, 1984. 75 p.

Listing in chronological order by date of imprint, works published 1937–45 on Costa Rica. Supplements *Indice Bibliográfico de Costa Rica* by Luis Dobles Segreda for 1927–36 period and *Boletín Bibliográfico Costarricense* for 1946–56 period published by the National Library. Works appear in alphabetical order by author. Includes separate listing of newspaper and journal titles.

5 *Boletim Bibliográfico da Biblioteca Nacional.* Biblioteca Nacional, Vol. 26, No. 1, 1981 [and] Vol. 26, No. 2, 1981– . Rio de Janeiro.

Publications appear in order by decimal classification (i.e., discipline). Includes author index.

6 ——. Biblioteca Nacional, Vol. 27, No. 1/4, 1982– . Rio de Janeiro.

This publication, which appeared in May 1984, includes listing of publications in classified order, author index, and list of journal titles received.

7 Tardieu, Patrick D. Bibliographie haitienne: 1981–1982 (IFH/C, 160, jan. 1984, p. 53–76, tables)

Lists by subject 160 titles on or by Haitians that appeared 1981–1982. Also includes dissertations from US institutions.

SUBJECT BIBLIOGRAPHIES

7a Albónico, Aldo. Bibliografia della storiografia e pubblicistica italiana sull'America latina, 1940–1980. Milano, Italy: Cisalpino-Goliardica, 1981. 146 p.: index.

Publications, monographs and articles from Italy on Italians in Latin America. Lists general works and publications on individual countries. Includes author index.

Alcalde Cardoza, Javier. Bibliografía anotada sobre aspectos políticos de la integración andina. See *HLAS 45:2755.*

Alzamora C., Lucía. Bibliografía, planificación regional en América Latina. See *HLAS 45:2757.*

8   Argueta, Mario R. Algunas obras de referencia hondureña en el campo de las ciencias sociales (Boletín del Sistema Bibliotecario de la UNAH [Biblioteca Nacional Autónoma de Honduras, Tegucigalpa] 13:2, abril/julio 1984, p. 3–10)
Brief bibliographical essay on general as well as individual themes (e.g., economics, agrarian reform, legal sciences, history, geography).

9   ———. Guía para el investigador de la historia colonial hondureña: un ensayo temático bibliográfico (Boletín del Sistema Bibliotecario de la UNAH [Universidad Nacional Autónoma de Honduras, Tegucigalpa] 12:4, oct./dic. 1983, p. 3–17, plate)
Provides useful subject bibliographical essay on period. Argueta's review is selective at best but filled with commentary on particular attributes of each work chosen for consideration.

10   Bellini, Giuseppe. Bibliografia dell ispanoamericanismo italiano. Milano: Cisalpino-Goliardica, 1982. 144 p.: index (Letterature e culture dell'America latina; 3)
Lists publications by Italians or printed in Italy on Hispanic American literature, appearing since 1970. Includes some works in the social sciences as well as separate listing of translations into Italian. Provides separate subject and author indexes.

11   Berg, Hans van den. Material bibliográfico para el estudio de los aymaras, callawayas, chipayas, urus. Cochabamba, Bolivia: Universidad Católica Boliviana, Facultad de Filosofía y Ciencias Religiosas, 1980. 3 v.: bibl.
Exhaustive partially annotated compilation of works on subject. First two volumes provide bibliographic listing; final contains indexes. This is a major study of the four native groups.

12   Die Beziehungen zwischen Lateinamerika und der Bundesrepublik Deutschland = Las Relaciones América Latina—República Federal de Alemania.
2. aktuail-sierte un erg. Aufl. Hamburg: Institut für Iberoamerika-Kunde, Dokumentations-Leitstelle Lateinamerika, 1980. 47 p. (Dokumentationsdienst Lateinamerika. Kurzbibliographie = Documentación latinoamericana. Introducción bibliográfica)
Provides citations on the topic of West German-Latin American relations. Subjects such as economics, nuclear energy, history, and technological transfer are represented.

Bibliografía anotada sobre fonología, dialectología y ortografía naua. See *HLAS 45:1503.*

13   Bibliografía de Bahía Blanca. Obra realizada en adhesión al sesquicentenario de la ciudad y financiada por la Municipalidad de Bahía Blanca. Bahía Blanca, Argentina: Universidad Nacional del Sur, Biblioteca Central, 1979. 103 p.: indexes.
Lists nearly 1200 unannotated entries by author in alphabetical order. Includes subject and chronological indexes as well as earliest work listed (i.e., published 1824).

14   Bibliografía del café. Turrialba, Costa Rica: PROMECAFE: IICA, Centro Interamericano de Documentación e Información Agrícola, División de Servicios de Información, 1982. 542 p.: bibl., indexes (Documentación e información agrícola; no. 111)
Lists 6700 citations related to the study of coffee (e.g., cultivation, ecology, general works, diseases, technology). Computerized compilation contains key word, author, and institutional indexes.

Bibliography of Mayan languages and linguistics. See *HLAS 45:1504.*

15   Blanes Jiménez, José. Bibliografía referida al trópico cochabambino. La Paz: Ediciones CERES, 1982. 163 p.: bibl., indexes (Serie Estudios regionales; no. 4. Serie Documentos CERES)
This first work to attempt to collectively identify publications on tropical Cochabamba was also a project of the Centro de Estudios de la Realidad Económica y Social (CERES), La Paz. Lists 687 publications in alphabetical order by author. Includes subject and geographic indexes.

16   Burton, Julianne. The new Latin American cinema: an annotated bibliography of sources in English, Spanish, and

Portuguese, 1960–1980. New York: Smyrna Press, 1983. 80 p.: bibl.

Research guide to historical, theoretical, and critical works on Latin American cinema. Describes nearly 150 articles on the subject and film production in nine Latin American countries (Argentina, Bolivia, Brazil, Chile, Cuba, Mexico, Nicaragua, Jamaica, and Venezuela). Also includes Puerto Rican and US Hispanic cinema.

Castillo, Margarita and **María José Galrão.** Bibliografía agrícola de Costa Rica. See *HLAS 45:3102.*

17   **Castro, Manuel de.** Bibliografía de las bibliografías franciscanas españolas e hispanoamericanas. Nota preliminar de Víctor Sánchez Gil. Presentación de José Simón Díaz. Madrid: Cisneros, 1982. 242 p.: bibl., index (Publicaciones de Archivo Ibero-Americano)

Lists works by Franciscans from earliest printed works. Covers themes such as history of the Americas, missions, music, descriptions of various orders, and dictionaries. Introduction sketches evolution of Franciscan bibliography and provides information on major Franciscan writers, literature, and Franciscan bibliography. Includes general names index.

Collazo, Alberto and **Jorge Glusber.** Guía bibliográfica de las artes visuales en la Argentina: siglo XX. See item **420.**

Cordero Iñigüez, Juan. Bibliografía ecuatoriana de artesanías y artes populares. See item **308.**

18   **Dannemann, Manuel.** Bibliografía de la artesanía tradicional chilena. Editada por la Comisión Nacional Chilena del Instituto Andino de Artes populares del Convenio Andrés Bello. Elaborada por Manuel Dannemann, con la colaboración de Joyce Fuhrimann. Santiago: La Comisión, 1983. 96 p., 1 leaf of plates: bibl., indexes, port.

A selected listing of 210 citations related to the study of the traditional folk art in Chile. Bibliography is divided into four segments: general works, special works on folk art and craft, works on the application of traditional art, and the relationship of traditional art and craft to other subjects.

19   **Documentação paranaense:** catálogo bibliográfico. Biblioteca Pública do Paraná, Divisão de Documentação Paranaense. Curitiba, Brasil: Secretaria da Cultura e do Esporte, 1980–1983. 2 v.: index.

Lists works published about Paraná or by individuals from Paraná and located at Paraná's Public Library. Vol. 2, a supplement, lists and indexes works completed between 1979–82. Vol. 1 is not indexed. Entries appear in alphabetical order by author.

Erickson, Frank A. and **Elizabeth B. Erickson.** An annotated bibliography of agricultural development in Jamaica. See *HLAS 45:3204.*

20   **Etchepareborda, Roberto.** Interpretaciones recientes del pasado argentino (Cuadernos del Sur [Universidad Nacional del Sur, Bahía Blanca, Argentina] 16, enero/dic. 1983, p. 99–116, table)

Primary purpose of article is to discuss recent publication about Argentine history (i.e., articles, books, and theses) that have not appeared in Spanish. Useful work of historiography describes each contribution for a Spanish-speaking audience.

21   **Flores Colombino, Andrés.** Catálogo latinoamericano de publicaciones sexológicas. Redactor, Andrés Flores Colombino. Montevideo: Federación Latinoamericana de Sociedades de Sexología y Educación Sexual, 1982. 1 v.

Lists 1913 citations on the subject by country.

22   **Genossenschaftswesen in Lateinamerika** = Cooperativismo en América Latina. Hamburg: Institut für Iberoamerika-Kunde, Dokumentations-Leitstelle Lateinamerika, 1981. 28 leaves: bibl. (Dokumentationsdienst Lateinamerika. Kurzbibliographie = Documentación latinoamericana. Introducción bibliográfica)

Contains citations to recent articles and monographs on the theme of cooperatives and cooperative societies in Latin America. Separate sections are devoted to individual countries. Also provides information on library sources in Germany.

23   **Gordon, Sara.** América Central: bibliografía (Iztapalapa [Universidad Autónoma Metropolitana, División de Ciencias Sociales y Humanidades, Iztapalapa, México] 2:3, julio/dic. 1980, p. 228–235)

Selected, unannotated listing of 161 publications, primarily contemporary works, on the general theme of politics in Central

America, with separate listings for each country.

24 Howe, Robert. A bibliographic guide to Latin American and Caribbean government publications on foreign investment, 1965–1981 (Government Publications Review [Pergamon Press, New York] 10:5, Sept./Oct. 1983, p. 459–477)

Bibliographic guide to official publications dealing with foreign investments between 1965–81. Briefly describes roles of government and intergovernmental organizations in the economic sector. Separate sections cover current serial titles that serve as information sources for the latest investment laws and regulations; publications of relevant international and intergovernmental organizations; and literature on the various regulatory agencies, central banks, planning departments, and statistical services.

25 Ibarra, Hernán. Ecuador, bibliografía analítica agraria, 1900–1982. Quito?: Ediciones CIESE con el auspicio de ILDIS, 1982. 419 p.: indexes.

Provides annotated citations to over 950 publications on Ecuador concerning the following topics: agrarian history, reform and legislation; local history; statistics; ethnic questions; haciendas; worker organizations; credit; and agrobusiness. Also includes separate library, author, and subject indexes.

Jiménez, Dina. Bibliografía retrospectiva sobre política agraria en Costa Rica, 1948–1978. See HLAS 45:3122.

26 Kallsen, Margarita. Referencias bibliográficas de la Guerra del Chaco. 2a ed. actualizada. Asunción: Centro de Publicaciones de la Universidad Católica Nuestra Señora de la Asunción, 1982. 68 p.: bibl., indexes (Serie Bibliografía paraguaya; 1)

Unannotated listing, in alphabetical order by author, of over 450 monographs and pamphlets on the Chaco War.

27 Kupfer, Monica E. A bibliography of contemporary art in Latin America: books, articles, and exhibition catalogs in the Tulane University Library, 1950–1980. New Orleans, La.: Center for Latin American Studies and Howard-Tilton Memorial Library, Tulane University, 1983. 97 leaves.

Catalog is based on holdings of Tulane University's Howard-Tilton Library. Lists publications of a general nature and by individual countries.

Lifschitz, Edgardo. Bibliografía analítica sobre empresas transnacionales = Analytical bibliography on transnational corporations. See HLAS 45:2879.

Lizano, Eduardo and **Maritza Huertas.** Bibliografía sobre el Mercado Común Centroamericano. See HLAS 45:3084.

27a López Rosado, Diego G. Bibliografía económica de la Revolución Mexicana, 1910–1930. México: Universidad Nacional Autónoma de México, 1982. 362 p. (Serie bibliografías; 10)

Lists publications in alphabetical order by author within separate categories (e.g., demography, agriculture, cattle, land, mining, petroleum, industrial development, communications, money, credit, foreign commerce, work, public finances, and foreign exchange). Includes general bibliography and subject index.

28 Lovera De-Sola, R.J. Catálogo de libros de historia colonial de Venezuela compilado en 1950–1978 (in Congreso Venezolano de la Historia, 4th, 1980. Memoria [see item 2621] v. 2, p. 191–291)

Provides unannotated listing of monographs and pamphlets on subject. Items appear in alphabetical order by author. Lacks indexes.

29 Lowenstein, Pedro et al. Bibliografia e índice da geologia da Amazônia legal brasileira, 1965–1975. Belém, Brazil: Conselho Nacional de Desenvolvimento Científico e Tecnológico, Instituto Nacional de Pesquisas da Amazônia, Museu Paraense Emílio Goeldi, 1980. 176 p.: indexes (Publicações avulsas do Museu Goeldi; no. 35)

Lists 1247 citations to works on geology of the Amazon region, subdivided into 17 sections, with author and geographic names indexes. Includes only works published between 1965–75; a 1969 work in same series covered materials appearing between 1941–64.

30 Meier, Matt S. Bibliography of Mexican American history. Westport, Conn.: Greenwood Press, 1984. 1 v.: indexes.

Partially annotated bibliography of nearly 5,000 entries on Mexican American history divided into 12 sections within two broad categories: chronological and topical. Works appear in sections on: Colonial, Mexican, Post-1848, and 20th Century History as well as in general sections on Culture, Labor, Civil Rights, Bibliography, and Archives.

Multinational corporations and international investment in Latin America: a selected and annotated bibliography with an annotated film bibliography. See *HLAS 45:2898.*

31 Municípios baianos: bibliografia. Governo do Estado da Bahia, Secretaria do Planejamento, Ciência e Tecnologia, Fundação Centro de Pesquisas e Estudos (CPE). Salvador: Edições CPE, 1980. 191 p.: index (Publicações CPE. Série Bibliografias; 6)

List of publications on state of Bahia's local government includes works on municipal administration, agriculture, history of municipal workers, tourism, economics, geography, etc. Provides subject index and library locations of publications listed.

32 Muñoz de Linares, Elba and **Alicia Céspedes de Reynaga.** Bibliografía sobre indigenismo y ciencias sociales. v. 1/2. Lima: Instituto Indigenista Peruano, Centro Interamericano de Administración del Trabajo, 1983. 2 v. (733 p.) (Serie bibliográfica; 4)

Provides listing, by discipline, of theses completed on the subject and submitted at Peruvian universities. Largest number of theses concern fields of anthropology, social sciences, law, education, medicine and social work. Includes indexes for author, subject, ethnic group, geography, and institutions.

33 Pérez, Louis A., Jr. Armed struggle and guerrilla warfare in Latin America: a bibliography of Cuban sources, 1959–1979 (RIB, 33:4, 1983, p. 507–544, bibl.)

Contains citations from Cuban publications since Castro (i.e., *Bohemia, Juventud Rebelde, Granma, Obra Revolucionaria,* and *Verde Olivo*). Bibliography is divided into general and separate country sections.

Petersen, Silvia Regina Ferraz. O movimento operário brasileiro: bibliografia. See *HLAS 45:6491.*

Ramírez, Axel. Bibliografía comentada de la medicina tradicional mexicana: 1900–1978. See *HLAS 45:1889.*

34 Ramos Guédez, José Marcial. Bibliografía del Estado Miranda. Caracas: Gobernación del Estado Miranda, 1981. 286 p. (Biblioteca de autores y temas mirandinos. Colección Cristóbal Rojas; no. 1)

Lists 1900 publications related to themes on state of Miranda. Includes official publications on and by the state as well as books, pamphlets, documents, and periodicals. Provides onomastic and toponymic indexes.

35 Rauls, Martina. Die Beziehungen des Karibischen Raumes zu Afrika = Las Relaciones entre el area del Caribe y Africa: introducción bibliográfica = Relations between the Caribbean area and Africa: introductory bibliography. Hamburg: Institut für Iberoamerika-Kunde, Dokumentations-Leitstelle Lateinamerika, 1980. 24 leaves (Dokumentationsdienst Lateinamerika. Kurzbibliographie)

Lists selected current titles of 264 entries on politics, economics and social relations of Africa and the Caribbean. Provides German library locations for items cited.

Reátegui G., Mirca. Bibliografía sobre antropología y arqueología de la selva del Perú. See *HLAS 45:1305.*

36 Salas S., Margarita *et al.* Bibliografía sobre identidad cultural en el Perú. Lima: Instituto Indigenista Peruano, Centro Interamericano de Administración del Trabajo, 1982. 126 p.: bibl. (Serie bibliográfica; 2).

Lists contemporary, post–1960, studies of cultural identity in Peru as well as separate studies of ethnicity, cosmography, folklore, language, literature and socialization. Provides library location of each publication.

COLLECTIVE AND PERSONAL BIBLIOGRAPHIES

36a Brazil. Biblioteca Nacional. Seção de Promoções Culturais. José Lins do Rêgo, 1901–1975: catálogo da exposição. Apresentação de Plinio Doyle. Prefácio de Josué Montello. Rio de Janeiro: A Biblioteca, 1981. 95 p.: ill.

Catalog and bibliography of publications by and about José Lins do Rêgo (d. 1957) in honor of his 80th birthday.

36b ———. ———. ———. Paulo Barreto, 1881–1921: catálogo da exposição comemorativa do centenário de nascimento. Apresentação de Plinio Doyle. Prefácio de Homero Sena. Rio de Janeiro: A Biblioteca, 1981. 47 p.: 12 leaves of plates: bibl., ill.

Lists publications by and about the late 19th and early 20th century Brazilian journalist Paulo Barreto (b. João Paulo Alberto Coelho Barreto). Provides brief biographical sketch.

37 Galbis, Ignacio R. M. Hugo Rodríguez-Alcalá: a bibliography, 1937–1981. Syracuse, N.Y.: Centro de Estudios Hispánicos, Syracuse University, 1982? 45 p. (Bibliotheca hispana novissima; 6)

Useful compilation of publications by and about the noted Paraguayan author.

38 González Echevarría, Roberto and **Klaus Müller-Bergh.** Alejo Carpentier: bibliographical guide = Alejo Carpentier: guía bibliográfica. Westport, Conn.: Greenwood Press, 1983. 271 p.: index.

Annotated bibliography devoted to writings by and criticism of Carpentier. Includes all of Carpentier's books, translations, and journalistic output, including his columns in *El Nacional* of Caracas. Also covers studies of the Cuban writer, including monographs, dissertations, articles, notes and reviews. Provides names index.

38a Naranjo de Castillo, Cira and **Elke Nieschulz de Stockhausen.** El libertador en su centenario: una bibliografía. Caracas: Auspiciada por la Fundación J. Boulton, 1983. 94 p.: bibl., ill., indexes.

Lists publications that appeared at the time of Simón Bolívar's birth centennial in 1883. Identifies nearly 200 items. Introductory article describes 1883 commemoration and includes title, imprint, and city of imprint indexes.

39 Perdomo, Omar. Bibliografía martiana de Angel Augier. Compilación, prólogo y cronología de Omar Perdomo. La Habana: Casa Natal de José Martí, 1980. 46 p.: indexes.

Lists 214 books, pamphlets, and articles written by the prodigious Cuban writer. This is the largest compilation of Martí's works to appear since 1961. Also includes title and onomastic indexes.

LIBRARY SCIENCE AND SERVICES

40 Bartone, Carl R. Planning regional document-delivery services for the water decade: the Latin American and Caribbean region (UNESCO/JIS, 4:4, Oct./Dec. 1982, p. 253–262)

Provides brief description of objectives, scope, structure and operations of the Regional Network for Information and Documentation in areas of water supply, sanitation and environmental health. Includes report on development of a regional document-delivery service.

41 Congresso Latino Americano de Biblioteconomia e Documentação, 1st, *Salvador, Brasil, 1980.* Anais. Patrocínio editorial, Ministério da Educação e Cultura. Coordenação do Aperfeiçoamento de Pessoal de Nível Superior (CAPES). Salvador, Brasil: FEBAB, 1980. 3 v.: bibl., ill.

Contains congress' working papers whose main theme was the automated transfer of information and the transfer of technology.

42 Couto, Luiz Mário Marques and **Marco Antônio P. Werneck Rodrigues.** Aplicação de sistemas de informação na área acadêmica (Revista de Biblioteconomia de Brasília [Asociados de Bibliotecarios do Distrito Federal and Departamento de Biblioteconomia de Universidade de Brasília] 11:1, jan./junho 1983, p. 55–64)

Provides brief historical account (since 1970) of development of the University of Brasília's automated information system.

43 Lizcano de García, Gloria. Lista básica especializada para escuelas de bibliotecología de América Latina y criterios mínimos para la formación de colecciones. Bogotá: Federación Internacional de Documentación, Comisión Latinoamericana: Instituto Colombiano para el Fomento de la Educación Superior, 1980. 218 p.

Lists 1546 unannotated basic works useful for library and information science libraries in Latin American higher education. Provides author index.

44 Martínez Baeza, Sergio. El libro en Chile. Santiago: Biblioteca Nacional, 1982. 427 p.: ill., indexes.

Introductory history to the book in Chile contains chapters on: book in Spain and the Americas; foundation of Chile's National Library in 1813; directorship of Francisco García Huidobro (1825–52); National Library and University of Chile (1852–79); National Library and the Council of Public Instruction (1879– 1929); National Library and the Direction of Libraries, Archives and Museums (1929–77); and current administration of the National Library. Includes list of library directors and names index.

45 National Council on Libraries, Archives, and Documentation Centres, *Barbados.* Final report. Bridgetown: The Council, 1982. 19 p.

Calls for establishment of the Barbados Library, Archive and Information Centre Network (BLAIN) which will coordinate all phases of library network development vis-à-vis the island's governmental sources.

46 Sambaquy, Lydia de Queiroz. A eletrônica nas bibliotecas e arquivos (Forum Educacional [Instituto de Estudos Avançados em Educação, Fundação Getúlio Vargas, Rio de Janeiro] 7:3, julho/set. 1983, p. 14–30, bibl.)

Author emphasizes the need for more cooperation in the development of networks in the Brazilian library and archives system.

47 Seminário Nacional de Bibliotecas Universitárias, 2nd, *Brasília, Brasil, 1981.* Anais. Brasília: CAPES, 1981. 378 p.: ill.

Discusses themes of planning, architecture, acquisitions of materials, and automation of service in Brazil's academic libraries.

47a Silva, Ivani Pires da *et al.* Guía nacional de bibliotecas para deficientes visuais (Revista Brasileira de Biblioteconomia e Documentação [Federação Brasileira de Associações de Bibliotecários, São Paulo?] 14:3/4, julho/ dez. 1981, p. 139–152)

Lists by region, libraries for visually impaired in Brazil as well as location, hours of service, size of collection, services and capacity of facilities provided.

ACQUISITIONS, COLLECTIONS AND CATALOGS

47b Brazil. Biblioteca Nacional. Periódicos brasileiros em microformas: catálogo colectivo. Rio de Janeiro: A Biblioteca, 1981. 296 p. (Coleção Rodolfo Garcia; v. 18. Série B, Catálogos e bibliografias)

Lists periodicals and locations in Brazil as well as in selected libraries abroad. Publications appear in alphabetical order within state sections. Includes separate listings of titles in microfilm and special collec-

tion of *Relatórios provinciais e ministeriais* during period of empire.

48 Duque Peláez, Isabel *et al.* Guía del Archivo Municipal de Ocoyoacac, Edo. de Méx. Producto de las experiencias del servicio social y prácticas de campo de un grupo de alumnos del Departamento de Historia de la Universidad Iberoamericana. México: Universidad Iberoamericana, Departamento de Historia, 1979. 49 p., 2 leaves of plates: bibl., ill., maps (Cuaderno de trabajo; 2)

Provides access to community archives, including materials from 19th and 20th centuries. Includes references to all local activities.

49 Fernandes, Antônia Régia Mendonça and **Hilda de Sena Correa Wiederhecker.** Catálogo coletivo dos periódicos brasileiros relacionados com educação. Brasília: Conselho de Reitores das Universidades Brasileiras, 1982. 483 p.

Identifies relevant titles and locations of such serials in over 700 Brazilian academic institutions (i.e., central libraries, faculty libraries and other research bodies). Indicates serial holdings.

50 Figueres, Myriam. Catálogo de la colección de la literatura cubana en la Biblioteca Colón. Prólogo de Rosa M. Cabrera. Washington: Organización de los Estados Americanos, Biblioteca Colón, 1984. 114 p.: indexes, plates (Serie de Documentación e Información; 9. OEA/SG/o.1/IV/III.9)

Lists works in the OAS' Columbus Library on the theme. Organized into sections on anthologies, stories, essays, drama, history and criticism, memoirs, novels and poetry. Provides author and title indexes. Unannotated citations are arranged in alphabetical order by author.

51 García Blásquez, Raúl and **César Ramón Córdova.** Bibliografía de los estudios y publicaciones del Instituto Indigenista Peruano: 1961–1969. Lima: Instituto Indigenista Peruano, Centro Interamericano de Administración del Trabajo, 1982. 123 p.: indexes (Serie bibliográfica; 1)

Provides annotated listing in alphabetical order by author of Instituto studies. They cover those completed both within and independent of the project on the development and integration of Peru's indigenous population. Includes author, geographic and subject indexes.

52 Garritz, Amaya. Guía del Archivo Amado Aguirre. México: Universidad Nacional Autónoma de México, Instituto de Investigaciones Históricas, 1982. 291 p.: index (Serie bibliográfica; 6)

Provides access to the collection's 11 boxes and 39 *expedientes*. Large proportion of Aguirre's papers are related to his professional career (i.e., military, political and civilian when he worked as engineer). A participant in Mexico's revolution on Obregón's side, he had an active career during 1913–33.

53 Liehr, Reinhard. El Fondo Quesada en el Instituto Ibero-Americano de Berlín (LARR, 18:2, 1983, p. 125–133)

Describes Quesada Collection at Berlin Institute. Consists primarily of papers of Argentine writer-diplomat Vicente Quesada (1830–1913) and Argentine writer-historian Ernesto Quesada (1858–1934). Collection also includes Argentine newspapers and journals of 19th and early 20th centuries.

54 López de Badilla, María del Rocío. Catálogo colectivo de publicaciones periódicas existentes en Costa Rica, 1982. San José: Consejo Nacional de Investigaciones Científicas y Tecnológicas, 1982. 750 p.

Second ed. of 1976 union list of serials (see *HLAS 40:82*) covers nearly 15,000 serial titles and constitutes impressive addition to literature on research resources. Provides location and holdings of serial titles as well as information culled from 76 libraries.

55 Nueva hemerografía potosina, 1828–1978. Introducción y coordinación de Rafael Montejano y Aguiñaga. Investigaciones de A. Alcocer Andalón *et al*. México: Universidad Nacional Autónoma de México (UNAM), 1982. 373 p. (Serie Hemerografías. UNAM, Instituto de Investigaciones Bibliográficas, Biblioteca Nacional, Hemeroteca Nacional. Serie Documentos. Academia de Historia Potosina, Biblioteca de Historia Potosina; 6)

Lists, in alphabetical order, the collection's nearly 1400 periodical titles, journals and newspapers. Provides pertinent information on each publication (i.e., title, establishment date, editor, location, holdings, and general subjects of content).

REFERENCE WORKS AND RESEARCH

56 Alayón, Norberto. Monografías y tesis de trabajadores sociales. Miraflores, Perú: Centro Latinoamericano de Trabajo Social, 1981. 186 p.: index (Cuadernos Celats; no. 34)

Lists 2457 monographs and theses on the subject of "social workers" produced in 25 centers of learning in 12 countries of Latin America (i.e., Argentina, Brazil, Colombia, Costa Rica, Chile, Ecuador, El Salvador, Guatemala, Mexico, Peru, Dominican Republic and Venezuela). Brazilian and Peruvian publications represent over 57 percent of total number of monographs listed.

58 Batista, Geraldo Nogueira. Habitat, guia de bibliotecas e centros de documentação. Brasília: SEPLAN, Conselho Nacional de Desenvolvimento Científico e Tecnológico, Coordenação Editorial, 1982. 95 p.: indexes.

Provides information on 79 libraries and documentation centers in Brazil with collections related to housing and urban development. Provides name, address, telephone number, and brief description of collections for each entity. Includes geographic and subject indexes.

59 Bendfeldt Rojas, Lourdes. Tesario universitario, 1980 (Cultura de Guatemala [Universidad Rafael Landivar, Guatemala] 2:1, enero/abril 1981, p. 99–251)

Complete description of 94 theses, including their tables of content, presented as the National University in 1980, on themes related to Guatemala.

60 Bernales B., Enrique. El desarrollo de las ciencias sociales en el Perú. Lima: Centro de Investigación de la Universidad del Pacífico, 1981. 126 p.

Considers history, current state, and future prospects of social science studies in Peru. Carefully examines the ability of universities to sponsor research and discusses specific problems that arise from dependence on a university structure. Offers suggestion for creating research center.

61 Bettiol, Osmar and **Francisco Bahia Margalho.** Guia das bibliotecas de ciências agrárias: ensino superior. 2a. ed., rev. e ampliada. Brasília: Ministério da Educação e Cultura, Secretaria de Ensino Superior, 1982. 134 p.: ill., indexes.

Augmented edition provides listing by region of Brazilian libraries with collections related to agricultural sciences. Also includes indexes to institutions and subject strength.

62 Bilindex: a bilingual Spanish-English subject heading list of Spanish equivalents to Library of Congress Subject Headings = Bilindex: una lista bilingüe en español e inglés de encabezamientos de materia, equivalentes en español de los encabezamientos de la Biblioteca del Congreso de Estados Unidos de Norteamérica. Oakland: California Spanish Language Data Base, 1984. 501 p.

Useful tool for those seeking equivalent terminology in Spanish and English.

63 Block, David and **Howard L. Karno.** A directory of vendors of Latin American library materials. Madison: Secretariat, Seminar on the Acquisition of Latin American Library Materials, Memorial Library, University of Wisconsin-Madison, 1983. 38 p.: index (SALALM bibliography and reference series; 9)

Lists information on 97 book dealers providing location, stock and services offered. Also includes list of vendors by country.

64 Buenos Aires, Argentina **(city). Municipalidad. Instituto Histórico de la Ciudad de Buenos Aires. Sección Archivo Histórico.** Indice temático general, 1856–1866: Corporación Municipal. Dirección del trabajo: Estela Pagani. Ejecución: Marta Celis de Molina and Estela Pagani. Buenos Aires: 1981. 58 p.: index.

Provides information on holdings of city government archives. Items appear in subject categories. Includes reference subject term index.

65 ——. ——. ——. ——. Indice temático general, 1880–1887: Gestión Torcuato de Alvear. Dirección del trabajo: Estela Pagani. Ejecución: Marta Celis de Molina and Estela Pagani. Colaboración: Luis A. Alvarez. Buenos Aires: 1983. 205 p.

Identifies official papers generated by the Municipal Corporation of Buenos Aires during the period when Argentine President Torcuato de Alvear (1927–29) served as President of the City's Municipal Commission (1880–83) and also as Mayor of the City of Buenos Aires (1883–87).

66 Chaney, Elsa M. Women of the world: Latin America and the Caribbean. Washington: US Department of Commerce, Bureau of the Census, 1984. 173 p.: ill., map, tables (WID; 1)

This handbook is part of Women in the world handbook series produced by the National Statistics on Women Project of the Office of Women in Development, US Agency for International Development. Presents and analyzes statistical data on women in Latin America and the Caribbean. Provides separate chapters on population distribution and change; literacy and education; women in economic activity; marital status and living arrangements; and fertility and mortality.

67 Chatman, James R. Dissertations in the Hispanic and Luso-Brazilian languages and literatures: 1982 (AATSP/H, 66, 1983, p. 271–299)

Identifies 278 dissertations in the fields of Hispanic and Luso-Brazilian languages and literatures, 244 completed in 1982 alone, in US and Canadian institutions. Also lists total of 243 dissertations in preparation.

67a Alonso, Vicenta Cortés. Fuentes documentales españolas para la historia de los Estados Unidos (PAIGH/H, 94, julio/dic. 1982, p. 151–174, bibl.)

Provides useful information on various sources in Spain that contain information on present-day US including areas obviously related to Spanish lands along the Gulf of Mexico and US Southwest. Identifies guides as well as public and private archives.

68 Costa, Francisco Augusto Pereira da. Dicionário biográfico de Pernambucanos célebres. Prefácio de José Antonio Gonsalves de Mello. Facsimilar de 1a. ed. de 1882. Recife, Brasil: Prefeitura da Cidade do Recife, Secretaria de Educação e Cultura, Fundação de Cultura Cidade do Recife, 1982. 804 p., 1 leaf of plates (Coleção Recife; v. 16)

Facsimile of 1882 ed. was produced in honor of 100th anniversary of publication of the Diário de Pernambuco. Features over 200 Pernambucan notables during colonial and empire periods.

69 Cueto, Emilio C. A short guide to old Cuban prints (UP/CSEC, 14:1, Winter 1984, p. 27–42)

Presents outline of most significant

graphics depicting Cuban landscapes and people during four colonial centuries. Lists over 200 entries in alphabetical order, and discusses interrelationships between prints and printmakers. Notes reproductions and locations for originals.

69a Diccionario biográfico de la mujer en el Uruguay. Osvaldo A. Fraire, editor. Montevideo: Impr. Rosgal, 1983. 163 p.

First publication of its type in Uruguay provides biographical information on more than 80 Uruguayan women. They hold prominent positions in government, arts, academia, and private business. Criteria for selection is not indicated.

Documentación socioeconómica centroamericana. See *HLAS 45:3076.*

70 Editores oficias brasileiros de publicações periódicas. Brasília: Associações dos Bibliotecários do Distrito Federal (ABDF), Comissão de Publicações Oficiais Brasileiras, 1983. 137 p.

Lists, in alphabetical order, 645 publishers of Brazilian official publications. Lacks index.

71 Estudios fronterizos México-Estados Unidos: directorio de investigadores. Tijuana, México: Centro de Estudios Fronterizos del Norte de México, 1982. 282 p.: indexes.

Provides information on individual research projects on the subject including name of investigator, institution, area of interest, project, and description. Entries are divided according to researcher's geographical location (i.e., country and state). Includes investigator and institutional indexes.

72 Etchepareborda, Roberto. La bibliografía reciente sobre la cuestión Malvinas: pts. 1/2 (RIB, 34:1, 1984, p. 1–52; 34:2, 1984, p. 227–288)

Two-part extensive bibliographic essay on recent publications related to the Falkland/Malvinas controversy between England and Argentina. Pt. 2 contains a thematic bibliography on the question.

73 FEPA: an Argentine Research Foundation (LARR, 19:3, 1983, p. 185–192)

Brief description of Fundación para el Estudio de los Problemas Argentinos (FEPA) established in 1977 as a result of concern for Argentina's position of leadership in Latin America. In addition to a description of the

research institute's functions, work includes list of its publications and projects.

74 García Belsunce, César A. Latin American archives (UNESCO/JIS, 5:1, Jan./March 1983, p. 36–40, ill.)

Examines situation vis-à-vis archives and related problems in four countries: Argentina, Brazil, Colombia and Costa Rica. Although these Latin American institutions are moving towards the objective of creating modern, professional archives, they are blocked in this endeavor by lack of resources (i.e., professional staff, technicians) as well as by lack of understanding among the general population of the role archives play and their importance.

75 Goethner, Karl-Christian. Research at GDR universities on Latin America (LARR, 19:3, 1983, p. 165–178)

Describes East German scholars, universities and institutions interested in Latin American studies. Of value are descriptions of academic entities in the cities of Rostock: Institute of Latin American Studies, Wilhelm Pieck University and programs at University of Rostock; Leipzig: Karl Marx University; and Berlin: Universities of Humboldt and of Economy. While prior to World War II there was interest in Latin America in the GDR, studies in the Latin American social sciences expanded after 1960.

76 González Echenique, Javier. Archivo Nacional. Santiago: Dirección de Bibliotecas, Archivos y Museos, Ministerio de Educación Pública, 1983. 143 p.: ill. (some col.), map (Colección Chile y su cultura. Serie Museos nacionales; 5)

Provides brief description of history of Chile's National Archives accompanied by many illustrations of documents in the collections.

77 Goyer, Doreen S. and **Eliane Domschke.** The handbook of national population censuses: Latin America and the Caribbean, North America, and Oceania. Westport, Conn.: Greenwood Press, 1983. 711 p.: bibl., index, maps.

Handbook is designed to facilitate working with population census data. Provides comparative study of censuses of every country: how they are taken, definitions and concepts used, general content, special features, and locations of copies. Each national and territorial entry includes map, name of capital city, name of the official statistical agency, national and US repositories of data, and chronological description of census. Each post–1945 entry includes information on availability of unpublished data and computer tapes, languages of publication, and list of national statistical publications.

78   Guía nacional de tesis. v. 1, 1960–
1977. v. 2, 1978–1982. Ministerio de Planeamiento y Coordinación, Sistema y Fondo Nacional de Información para el Desarrollo (SYFNID), Centro Internacional de Investigaciones para el Desarrollo (CIID-Canada). La Paz: SYFNID, 1982. 2 v.: indexes.

Theses from 10 Bolivian universities, completed 1960–82, are listed and arranged by university and discipline within each university. Includes subject and author indexes.

79   Hahner, June E. Researching the history of Latin American women: past and future directions (RIB, 33:4, 1983, p. 545–552, bibl.)

Author thinks that the study of women in Latin America has just begun and many more workers are needed to continue the task. Article's footnotes contain valuable bibliography.

80   Henderson, Donald C. Indice general del *Anuario de Estudios Americanos* de 1964 a 1973 (EEHA/AEA, 34, 1977, p. 819–902, bibl.)

Offers chronological, author, subject and geographic indexes for journal's 1964–73 period. Includes total of 184 articles, 31 bibliographies, 83 critical and 994 informative reviews.

81   Index to articles in *The New York Times* relating to Puerto Rico and Puerto Ricans between 1899 and 1930. New York: CUNY Centro de Estudios Puertorriqueños, 1981. 94 p.

Contains over 1000 articles and editorials that appeared in *The New York Times* between 1899–1930, concerning Puerto Rico and Puerto Ricans on the island and in US. Entries, listed in order by date, are based on their appearance in *The New York Times Index*.

82   Indice bibliográfico de la revista *Anales de la Sociedad de Geografía e Historia de Guatemala*: 1924–1977 (SGHG/A, 54, 1980, p. 25–280)

Lists references to over 1700 articles

with access provided through separate author, title and subject indexes.

83   Inter-American Center for Documentation and Agriculture Information. Biblioteca y Terminal de Servicios. Catálogo colectivo de publicaciones periódicas de las bibliotecas del CIDIA. Turrialba, Costa Rica: Centro Interamericano de Documentación e Información Agrícola, Biblioteca y Terminal de Servicios, 1981. 520 p. (Documentación e información agrícola; no. 96)

Lists 5040 titles from most important journals in agricultural science and related fields found in collections of the Inter-American Center for Documentation and Agricultural Information, Turrialba, Costa Rica. Notes holdings for each journal.

84   Kaspar, Oldrich. Fuentes para el estudio del descubrimiento y la conquista de América conservadas en las bibliotecas checoslovacas (UO/R, 48, dic. 1982, p. 9–22)

Brief historiographical essay on early works concerning late 15th-century European discoveries found in Czech libraries. Nicolás Bakalár's *Tratado de las nuevas tierras y del Nuevo Mundo* (ca. 1506) was published in Pilsen and borrowed heavily from Vespucci's *Mundus novos.*

85   Luján Muñoz, Jorge. Guía del Archivo General de Centro América. Guatemala: Ministerio de Educación, Archivo General de Centro América, 1982. 48 p.: bibl., map.

Briefly describes history of archive, its classification scheme, and number of *legajos*, by country. Bibliography lists additional works on the collections.

86   Mesoamérica, directorio y bibliografía, 1950–1980. Alfredo Méndez-Domínguez, editor. Guatemala: Universidad del Valle de Guatemala, 1982. 313 p.

Biobibliographic guide to European and American Mesoamericanists. Of particular interest are the work's extensive bibliographic citations provided by each entrant. Includes separate journal and country-discipline lists.

87   Mexique. Paris: Centre français du commerce extérieur, Direction des marchés étrangers, 1981. 318 p.: ill. (Dossier d'informations de base)

Contains current statistical information on the Mexican economy of interest to exporters and investors. Data appeared prior to 1982 economic crisis.

88 Muñoz de Linares, Elba; Clara Cárdenas Timteo; and Alicia Céspedes de Reynaga. Indices y resúmenes de *Perú indígena* y *Perú integral.* Lima: Instituto Indigenista Peruano, Centro Interamericano de Administración del Trabajo, 1983? 259 p.: facsim., indexes, tables (Serie bibliográfica; 5)

Contains abstracted listings of articles that appeared in two journals: *Perú indígena* (1948–67) and *Perú integral* (1958–59). Items are arranged by subject of content. Includes separate author, institution, subject, geography and ethnic groups indexes as well as index to 1943–66 legislation.

89 Narayanan, R. Latin American studies in India (LARR, 19:3, 1983, p. 179–184)

Describes recent development (only within past decade) of Indian scholarly interest in Latin American studies, mostly centered at Jawaharlal Nehru's School of International Studies (New Delhi).

89a Orovio, Helio. Diccionario de la música cubana: biográfico y técnico. La Habana: Editorial Letras Cubanas, 1981. 442 p.: ill.

Provides descriptions of musicians and composers, types of music, and instruments from Cuba. Useful biographical source.

90 Porto Alegre, Aquiles. Homens ilustres do Rio Grande do Sul. Porto Alegre, Brazil: ERUS, 1981? 235 p. (Estante Riograndense União de Seguros-ERUS)

Reproduction of 1917 ed. of work containing approximately 175 biographical sketches of notable citizens of Rio Grande do Sul. Reedition includes corrections to faulty historical data. Useful historical piece.

91 Producción bibliográfica de la USAC, 1945–1977: Seminario B–211. Idalia González Dubon, directora. Universidad de San Carlos de Guatemala, Facultad de Humanidades, Escuela de Bibliotecología. Guatemala: Editorial Universitaria de Guatemala, 1981. 569 p.

Lists theses in chronological order and within each academic faculty. Separate author indexes follow each discipline. Also includes alphabetical listing by author of

articles appearing in *Revista de la Universidad de San Carlos* (1965–75).

92 Quién es quién en la sociedad argentina. Buenos Aires: Ediciones Elites, 1982. 753 p.

Provides brief biographical descriptions of Argentine professionals, artists, scientists, and businessmen. Information is as recent as 15 Jan. 1982. Also includes section on institutional (i.e., business) data.

93 Recent doctoral dissertations (RIB, 33:4, 1983, p. 650–655)

Lists doctoral dissertations completed at US and Canadian institutions, 1982–83.

93a Resources for Latin American Jewish studies. Judith Laikin Elkin, editor. Ann Arbor, Mich.: Latin American Jewish Studies Association, 1984. 59 p. (LAJSA publication; 1)

Proceedings of first research conference held by Latin American Jewish Studies Assn., Hebrew Union College, Jewish Institute of Religion, Cincinnati, Ohio, 30 Oct.–1 Nov. 1982, contain papers on various aspects of the study of Jews in Latin America (i.e., US library collections on Latin American Jews, archival resources, loss of Jewish records in Latin America, reference sources for study of the theme, etc.).

94 Salvador, Nélida and Elena Ardissone. Bibliografía de tres revistas de vanguardia. Buenos Aires: Universidad de Buenos Aires, Facultad de Filosofía y Letras, Instituto de Literatura Argentina Ricardo Rojas, 1983. 73 p.: indexes (Guías bibliográficas; 12)

Provides separate subject bibliographies for contents of three Argentine literary journals: *Prisma* (1921–22); *Proa* (1922–23); and *Proa* (1924–26). Includes illustration and author indexes.

Schroeder, Susan. Cuba: a handbook of historical statistics. See *HLAS 45:8205.*

95 Thomas, Jack Ray. Biographical dictionary of Latin American historians and historiography. Westport, Conn.: Greenwood Press, 1984. 1 v.: appendices, bibl., index.

Provides biobibliographical sketches of Latin American historical writers. Introduction offers overview of Latin American historiography from colonial period to present. Includes four appendices which list and cross reference historians by birthplace, year of birth, career, and subjects researched.

96   University of Texas, *Austin.* **Institute of Latin American Studies.** Latin American area specialists at the University of Texas at Austin. Austin: The Institute, 1983. 22 p.

Lists 117 academics at Univ. of Texas, Austin, with Latin American interests. Also provides information on current research, country or countries of specialization and recent publications.

97   Vervuert, Klaus Dieter. Information und Dokumentatin in Brasilien. Frankfurt am Main: IDD Verlag für Internationale Dokumentation W. Flach, 1983. 56 p.: bibl. (Aktuelle Beiträge und Berichte; Heft 13)

Briefly describes main information sources in Brazil and opportunities for research in the country.

GENERAL WORKS

98   Bonnet, Juan A. and **Modesto Iriarte.** Perspectivas para una red de comunicación de enlace vía satélite entre las universidades de Latinoamérica y del Caribe (AI/I, 8:5, Sept./Oct. 1983, p. 284–288, bibl., ill.)

Article proposes that increased use of computers and improved communication linkages among hemispheric universities will be important factors in promoting academic excellence and reducing economic and social problems of higher education. Development of computerized library information system is essential.

Chang, Ligia and **María Angélica Ducci.** Realidad del empleo y la formación profesional de la mujer en América Latina. See *HLAS 45:2788.*

99   Encuentro Nacional de Investigadores Bibliográficos, *1st, Caracas, Venezuela, 1981.* Anales. Caracas: Instituto Autónomo Biblioteca Nacional y de Servicios de Bibliotecas, Programa Biblioteca Nacional, Dirección de Estudios e Investigaciones, 1982? 107 leaves.

Documents results of meeting convened to discuss bibliographic developments in Venezuela. Meeting was dedicated to Agustín Millares Carlo's memory and presentations in his honor were made. Themes of meeting were: actual state of bibliographic

studies in Venezuela; determination of subject priorities for bibliographies; study and adoption of international norms for bibliographic description; study and adoption of norms for bibliographies of official publications; funding of a Venezuelan Bibliographical Society; and training of human resource specialists in bibliography and bibliographic investigation. Includes list of participants.

100   Fomento del libro en República Dominicana. Preparado por Raymundo Amaro Guzmán. Santo Domingo: Publicaciones ONAP (Oficina Nacional de Administración y Personal, 1982. 42 p. (Colección Guías informativas; no. 5)

Contains discussion of government's participation in book industry and trade in the Dominican Republic. Briefly discusses government's book production and legal deposit programs.

101   Fondo de Cultura Económica, *México.* Libro conmemorativo del 45 aniversario. México: FCE, 1980. 210 p.: bibl., ill.

Provides overview of Fondo de Cultura Económica's activities since its inception in 1934. Includes information on publications produced, by year and discipline, and pithy bibliographical essays on topics covered.

101a   Fundação Joaquim Nabuco. 30 [i.e. Trinta] anos do Instituto Joaquim Nabuco de Pesquisas Sociais. Recife, Brazil: Editora Massangana, 1981. 343 p.: ill. (Série Documentos; 15)

Chronicle of Institute activities since its foundation in 1951.

102   Hope, Margaret. Journey in the shaping: report of the First Symposium on Women in Caribbean Culture, July 24, 1981. Cave Hill, Barbados: Women and Development Unit, University of the West Indies, 1981. 59 p.

Reports on symposium held at Carifesta, 1981, Barbados. Topics discussed at length are: Caribbean women and art, dance, music, literature, and theater. ·

103   Lambert, Richard D. *et al.* Beyond growth: the next stage in language and area studies. Washington: Association of American Universities, 1984. 436 p.: bibl., tables.

Report concentrates on present capacities of nation's universities for advanced training and research in foreign language and area studies. Prepared by Working Group on Foreign Language and Area Studies, Department of Defense/University Forum, it concludes that relationship between Dept. of Defense needs and those of the academic community is not perfect. Documents condition of university programs in language and area studies and recommends strategies for strengthening them.

104 Paredes Cruz, Joaquín. Colombia al día, síntesis de la realidad nacional. 2a. ed. Bogotá: Plaza & Janés, 1982. 527 p., 24 p. of plates: bibl., ill., index.

Provides general overview of Colombia from historical and geographic perspectives. Sections on economy, transportation, communication, health, education and tourism are particularly useful.

Roldán, Eduardo. La economía mexicana: auge, crisis y perspectivas; hermerografía internacional. See *HLAS 45:3048.*

105 Ross, Stanley R. An interview with Nettie Lee Benson (HAHR, 63:3, Aug. 1983, p. 431–447)

Provides informative capsule review of the career of Nettie Lee Benson, noted Latin American collections librarian and historian at Univ. of Texas. Her ideas on national patrimony in collecting research materials and her insights into Mexican historical research are especially valuable.

106 Sizonenko, Alexandr. La latinoamericanística en las Repúblicas Federadas en la URSS (URSS/AL, 12:60, dic. 1982, p. 39–44)

Brief description of Latin American studies programs and interests in Soviet republics. Although interest in the subject began in 1920s, it is evident from the article that research on the subject did not begin until the late 1950s.

107 Usui, Mikoto. The labyrinth of foreign area studies: problems and promises (Latin American Studies [University of Tsukuba, Special Research Project on Latin America, Sakura-Mura, Japan] 5, 1983, p. 1–28)

Resumé of 1982 symposium held at Univ. of Tsukuba on overseas area study in Japan. Latin America's long interest in Japanese studies is acknowledged.

108 Visión de Belice. Traducción, Blanca Acosta. La Habana: Casa de las Américas, 1982. 149 p.: ill. (Colección Nuestros países. Serie Resumen)

General work on Belize at the time of independence. Discusses subjects of current interest as well as its history.

NEW SERIAL TITLES

109 *Encuentro.* Revista trimestral. El Colegio de Jalisco. Vol. 1, No. 1, oct./ dic. 1983– . Guadalajara, México.

First issue of trimestral journal with articles on the humanities and social sciences with special emphasis on Jalisco and western Mexico. Subscription is available for US$25.00 per year from El Colegio de Jalisco, Avenida de las Rosas 543, Colonia Chapalita, 45000 Guadalajara, Jalisco, México.

110 *HISLA.* Revista latinoamericana de historia económica y social. No. 1, 1. semestre 1983– . Lima.

Semestral journal edited by Centro Latinoamericano de Historia Económica y Social whose objective is to promote thought and research on Latin America's economic and social processes. Initial articles include research on foreign investment in Brazil; Encomienda Coquera in Los Yungas de La Paz (1560–66); and colonial Mexico and the new economic history. Journal is available for US$20.00 through HISLA, Heraclio Bonilla (Editor), Apartado 31058, Administración Postal Ingeniería, Lima 31, Perú.

Journal of Mayan Linguistics. University of Iowa, Anthropology Department. See *HLAS 45:1526.*

111 *Temas Americanistas.* Universidad de Sevilla, Cátedra de Historia de América [and] Unidad Estructural de Investigación de Historia Social, Escuela de Estudios Hispanoamericanos. No. 1, 1982– . Sevilla, Spain.

First issue of four already published (latest in 1984) of irregular bulletin concerning colonial Latin America. Designed to provide a publishing outlet for faculty and other researchers attached to the Universidad de Sevilla and the Escuela de Estudios Hispanoamericanos. Issues of the work are available from Secretaría de Publicaciones de la Universidad de Sevilla, C/. San Fernando 4,

Sevilla or from Escuela de Estudios His-panoamericanos, C/. Alfonso XII, 16, Sevilla.

Temas de Economía Mundial. Centro de Investigaciones de la Economía Mundial. See *HLAS 45:3527.*

JOURNAL ABBREVIATIONS BIBLIOGRAPHY AND GENERAL WORKS

AATSP/H Hispania. University of Cincinnati, American Association of Teachers of Spanish and Portuguese. Cincinnati, Ohio.

AI/I Interciencia. Asociación Interciencia. Caracas.

EEHA/AEA Anuario de Estudios Americanos. Consejo Superior de Investigaciones Científicas [and] Universidad de Sevilla, Escuela de Estudios Hispano-Americanos. Sevilla, Spain.

HAHR Hispanic American Historical Review. Duke University Press *for the* Conference on Latin American History of the American Historical Association. Durham, N.C.

IFH/C Conjonction. Institut français d'Haïti. Port-au-Prince.

LARR Latin American Research Review. University of North Carolina Press *for the* Latin American Studies Association. Chapel Hill.

PAIGH/H Revista de Historia de América. Instituto Panamericano de Geografía e Historia, Comisión de Historia. México.

RIB Revista Interamericana de Bibliografía (Inter-American Review of Bibliography). Organization of American States. Washington.

SGHG/A Anales de la Sociedad de Geografía e Historia de Guatemala. Guatemala.

UNESCO/JIS UNESCO Journal of Information Science, Librarianship and Archives Administration. United Nations Educational, Scientific and Cultural Organization. Paris.

UO/R Revista de la Universidad de Oriente. Santiago, Cuba.

UP/CSEC Cuban Studies/Estudios Cubanos. University of Pittsburgh, Center for International Studies, Center for Latin American Studies. Pittsburgh, Pa.

URSS/AL América Latina. Academia de Ciencias de la URSS (Unión de Repúblicas Soviéticas Socialistas). Moscú.

ART

Ancient Art, Popular Art, Folk Art

JOYCE WADDELL BAILEY, *Director, Handbook of Latin American Art*

THE SEARCH FOR A DEFINITION of popular art or folk art continues in the publications reviewed here (items **279, 281–283, 287–288, 305,** and **315–316**). These discussions range from Marxist interpretations of the artistic production of an oppressed class, to European art historical analogies, to historical and eye-witness accounts. Stastny's study is the most thorough, and although he falls into the European analogy trap, his historical approach with careful analysis of the objects has the most promise (item **316,** ch. 3).

At the same time a number of valuable surveys of folk and popular art have been published, making more materials available for analysis (items **280, 289–290, 293–294,** and **296**). Many of the surveys include important technical information and three texts are devoted entirely to the subject (items **301** and **313**).

One unfortunate matter, on which all authors agreed, is the destructive effect of commercialization on traditional artistic production (items **285** and **297–298**). Commercial centers in the US and tourism are the primary offenders cited.

Publications in the ancient area follow the usual pattern of picture books and exhibitions (items **254, 256, 258, 262–263, 271, 273,** and **275**) stylistic and iconographic studies of sites and cultures (items **253, 260, 267–269, 270, 274,** and **278**) and anthologies (items **259, 264,** and **266**). The exhibition catalog entitled *Between continents/between seas: precolumbian art of Costa Rica* (item **254**) is of exceptional quality, visually and textually. Terence Grieder has added another synthetic study to the literature on the origins of ancient art in the Western Hemisphere (item **261**).

Several research tools (items **251–252** and **381**) and national or subject bibliographies (items **255, 308,** and **420**) have been produced during this period, which will ameliorate research in this field of study.

GENERAL

251 Arntzen, Etta and **Robert Rainwater.**
Guide to literature of art history. Chicago: American Library Association, 1980. 616 p.: indexes.

Immensely valuable reference for any art historian. Its lack of many Latin American titles attests to the difficulty in finding them, not to the compilers' competence. One standard practice grouping ancient art of the Americas under "primitive" should be changed to "ancient" in future editions.

252 Hoffberg, Judith A. and **Stanley W. Hess.** Directory of art libraries and visual resource collections in North America. Compiled for the Art Libraries Society of North America (ARLIS/NA). New York: Neal-Schuman Publishers, 1978. 298 p. (supplement, 36 p.): indexes.

This directory is of special interest to students of Latin American art in all three chronological periods because there is an "Index to Collection Emphases," both by collection and by subject (e.g., Architecture-Meso-America, Decorative Arts-Andean) and a separate "Subject Index to Special Collections." Only lacking for student of Latin American art is a guide to works of art in public and private collections.

ANCIENT ART
General

253 Arellano, Jorge Eduardo. Introducción al arte precolombino de Nicaragua (BNBD, 40, marzo/abril 1981, p. 1–36, bibl., facsm., ill., plates, tables)
Survey of the subject; useful overview.

254 Between continents/between seas: precolumbian art of Costa Rica. Text by Suzanne Abel-Vidor *et al.* Photographs by Dirk Bakker. New York: H.N. Abrams; Detroit: Detroit Institute of Arts, 1981. 240 p.: bibl., ill. (some col.)
Beautiful exhibition catalog contains excellent essays on the archaeology, ethnohistory and art of the ancient cultures of Costa Rica. Marvelous color plates!

255 Bibliografía básica comentada sobre la pintura mural prehispánica de Mesoamérica. Sonia Lombardo de Ruiz, coordinadora. México: Dirección de Estudios Históricos, Instituto Nacional de Antropología e Historia, 1979. 131 p.: indexes (Cuaderno de trabajo / Seminario de Estudios de Historia del Arte; no. 2)
A bibliography of 246 items on the subject, annotated by various members of the Seminario de Estudios de Historia del Arte de la Dirección de Estudios Históricos of INAH. Most entries include the library (in Mexico) and the call number (typescript).

257 Culturas precolombinas: Chavin, formativo. Lima: Banco de Crédito del Perú en la Cultura, 1981. 171 p.: ill. (some col.) (Arte y tesoros del Perú)
Excellent photographs (many in color), with summary text on subject.

258 Dickey, Thomas; John Man; and **Henry Wiencek.** The kings of El Dorado. Chicago: Stonehenge, 1982. 176 p.: bibl., ill. (some col.) index (Treasures of the world)
Color plates are beautiful but bombastic prose adds little to the literature and nothing to scholarship.

259 Falsifications and misreconstructions of precolumbian art: a conference at Dumbarton Oaks, October 14th and 15th, 1978. Elizabeth P. Benson, organizer. Elizabeth H. Boone, editor. Washington: Dumbarton Oaks, Trustees for Harvard University, 1982. 142 p.: bibl., ill.
Publications of selected papers from the conference (for archaeologist's comment, see *HLAS 45:255*). "The consensus of the conference was that forgeries can most efficiently be detected . . . through an experienced comparison with objects known to be authentic" (p. vi).

260 Gasparini, Graziano and **Luise Margolies.** Inca architecture. Translated by Patricia J. Lyon. Bloomington: Indiana University Press, 1980. 350 p.: bibl., ill., index.
English translation of *HLAS 42:1639;* good text and photographs.

260a Grass, Antonio. Los rostros del pasado: diseño prehispánico colombiano = The faces of the past: prehispanic Colombian design. Translation, Debra McKinney. Bogotá: A. Grass, 1982. 341 p.: ill.
Two-dimensional study of design in masks from the ancient cultures of Mexico, Colombia, Ecuador, Peru and Brazil.

261 Grieder, Terence. Origins of precolumbian art. Austin: University of Texas Press, 1982. 1 v: bibl., index (The Texas Pan American series)
Proposes evolutionary theory of culture, which author terms "genetic." Theory's intellectual structure conforms more closely to principles of natural selection (Darwinism) than to those of heredity (Mendelism). Outlines three waves of cultural difussion and shows ancient American cultures as integrated, rather than isolated from other world cultures.

262 Oro del Perú: Palacio de la Virreina, Barcelona, abril-mayo 1982: exposición. Organizada por el Instituto de Cooperación Iberoamericana *et al.* Madrid: s.n., 1982? 60 p.: ill. (some col.)
Exhibition catalog with nine excellent color plates of the gold objects.

263 Oro prehispánico de Colombia: exposición temporal. Museo del Hombre Dominicano, Banco Central de la República Dominicana, septiembre/octubre, 1979.

Santo Domingo: Ediciones Museo del Hombre Dominicano, 1979, 44 p., 6 leaves of plates: ill. (some col.) (Serie Catálogos y memorias; no. 12)

Exhibition catalog with some useful illustrations.

264 Pre-Columbian art history: selected readings. Alana Cordy-Collins, editor. Palo Alto, Calif.: Peek Publications, 1982. 343 p.: bibl., ill.

Reissue (2.ed.) of selected readings (see *HLAS 41:252; HLAS 42:251*, intended as pedagogic aids for the art history of ancient cultures. Consists of 19 articles.

ANCIENT ART
Mexico

265 Angulo V., Jorge. El Museo Cuauhnahuac en el Palacio de Cortés: recopilación histórico-arqueológica del proceso de cambio en el Edo. de Morelos. Chappie Angulo, fotos y dibujos. México: SEP, Instituto Nacional de Antropología e Historia, 1979. 250 p., 2 folded leaves of plates: bibl., ill. (some col.), facsims., maps, ports.

History of construction of Palacio de Cortés and its conversion to Museo Cuauhnahuac. Includes guide to the new museum inaugurated Feb. 1974.

266 The Art and iconography of late post-classic central Mexico: a conference at Dumbarton Oaks, October 22nd and 23rd, 1977. Elizabeth P. Benson, organizer. Elizabeth Hill Boone, editor. Washington: Dumbarton Oaks, Trustees of Harvard University, 1982. 254 p.: bibl., ill.

Although there are some original contributions in this collection of papers from the 1977 Dumbarton Oaks conference, chairman Nicholson's arguments for the Mixteca-Puebla culture should be laid to rest—after 25 years. As the chairman (Nicholson) states in his article on the topic: "The situation with regard to the spatial aspect of the Mixteca-Puebla genesis problem is hardly more satisfactory than the chronological" (p. 245). He also cites difficulties in stylistic and iconographic definitions of artistic configurations to match his concept. Reader is left pondering same question posed by the author: ". . . does the Mixteca-Puebla concept still have methodological validity?" (p. 246,

for archaeologist's comment, see *HLAS 45:268*).

267 Bonifaz Nuño, Rubén. El arte en el Templo Mayor: México-Tenochtitlan. Fotografías por Fernando Robles. México: Instituto Nacional de Antropología e Historia, SEP, 1981. 188 p.: col. ill.

Well illustrated account of subject with excellent color plates of Coyolxauhqui, a carved stone uncovered in 1978.

Foncerrada de Molina, Marta. Mural painting in Cacaxtla and Teotihuacan cosmopolitanism. See *HLAS 45:421*.

——— and **Sonia Lombardo de Ruiz.** Vasijas pintadas mayas en contexto arqueológico: catálogo. See *HLAS 45:422*.

268 Fuente, Beatriz de la. El homocentrismo en la escultura maya (EEHA/AEA, 37, 1980, p. 435–442, ill.)

Discussion of varied treatment of the human form at four classic Maya cities: Tikal, Piedras Negras, Palenque and Copán.

269 ———. Temas principales en la escultura Huasteca (IIE/A, 50:1, p. 9–18, bibl., ill.)

In this formal analysis (for archaeologist comment, see *HLAS 45:427*), author proposes two categories for Huastec sculpture: 1) free standing forms, usually of individuals; and 2) relief forms usually involving various images. Material studied (436 objects) dates from the early post-classic period (10th-12th centuries).

270 Gutiérrez Solana, Nelly and Susan K. Hamilton. Las esculturas en terracota de El Zapotal, Veracruz. México: Universidad Nacional Autónoma de México, 1977. 251 p.: ill. (Cuadernos de historia del arte; 6)

Careful and interesting study of the most significant of the 400 terracotta items found at El Zapotal. Feminine figures are related to those from El Cocuite. Late classic date is assigned to the group.

271 Hambleton, Enrique. La pintura rupestre de Baja California. México: Fomento Cultural Banamex, 1979 (1980 printing). 157 p.: bibl., chiefly col. ill., maps.

Pictorial essay with brief text on a fascinating subject that has just begun to receive scholarly attention. Excellent color plates.

Hartung, Horst. La arquitectura en Oaxaca de sus inicios hasta el posclásico. See *HLAS 45:304.*

Heikamp, Detlef. Mexico und die Medici-Herzöge. See *HLAS 45:307.*

272 Mastache de Escobar, Alba Guadalupe. Técnicas prehispánicas del tejido. México: Instituto Nacional de Antropología e Historia, 1971. 142 p., 3 folded leaves of plates: ill. (Serie Investigaciones; 20)

Analysis of textiles found at four sites in excavations at El Vaso de la Presa, Morelos, Río Balsas basin preceded by summary of textiles found at other archaeological sites in Mesoamérica.

273 Museo de Santa Cecilia Acatitlán. Catálogo de la escultura mexicana del Museo de Santa Cecilia Acatitlán. Felipe R. Solís Olguín, compiler. Santa Cecilia Acatitlán, México: Instituto Nacional de Antropología e Historia, 1977. 41, 3 p.: bibl., ill.

Catalog of Mexican (Aztec) sculpture in the museum from various locations including Santa Cecilia Acatitlán. Photographs of each item.

274 Piña Chán, Román. Chichén Itzá, la ciudad de los brujos del agua. México: Fondo de Cultura Económica, 1980. 156 p., 2 folded leaves of plates: bibl., ill. (Sección de obras de antropología)

Summary of the history and development of the site with an interesting chart listing the principal stylistic characteristics of some monuments (ranges from Puuc-Chenes characteristics to Late Yucatec-Maya features). Fair photographs.

275 Stierlin, Henri. L'art aztèque et ses origines: de Teotihuacan à Tenochtitlan. Plans, cartes et dessins in-texte par José Conesa. Fribourg, Suisse: Office du livre, 1982. 220 p.: ill.

Picture book on the subject with short, textual summary. Excellent color plates. plates.

276 ———. Art of the Maya: from the Olmecs to the Toltec-Maya. Translated from the French by Peter Graham. New York: Rizzoli, 1981. 211 p.: bibl., ill. (some col.), index.

Another picture book with many excellent color photographs by the author.

277 Stresser-Péan, Guy. Joyas de oro desconocidas de la antigua colección Bellón, en Oaxaca (UNAM/AA, 19, 1982, p. 187–190, bibl., ill.)

Publication of very poor photograph of gold objects (necklace, pendants) from former Bellón collection. Items appear to be ancient in date and possibly Mixtec.

278 von Winning, Hasso. La procesión de los teomamaque: notas sobre la iconografía de la cerámica moldeada de Veracruz (IIE/A, 13:51, 1983, p. 5–11, ill.)

Description and iconography of some 40 mould-made vessels with figures in relief. Provenance of only three vessels is known (Las Colinas, Tlaxcala; Huachín, Veracruz); others are from private collections. Author dates group (Complejo Río Blanco AD 600-700).

FOLK ART AND POPULAR ART
General

279 Albizu, Edgardo. Dialéctica del arte popular (ESME/C, 66/67, julio/dic. 1979, p. 101–123, ill.)

Another attempt to define popular art—this time by contrasting the dialectical processes of *arte culto* and *arte popular.*

280 Arte popular de América. Fotografías, F. Català Roca. Barcelona: Editorial Blume, 1981. 320 p.: bibl., col. ill., index.

Review of popular art throughout the Western Hemisphere, from Canada to Argentina. Excellent color plates.

281 Castrillón Vizcarra, Alfonso. Historia del arte y arte popular: notas para una teoría del arte popular (*in* Congreso Peruano: El Hombre y la Cultura Andina, 3d, 1977. El hombre y la cultura andina [see *HLAS 43:253*] v. 5, p. 909–916)

Discusses imprecision of terminology in addressing popular art and argues against a class-based (socioeconomic) or biased intepretation.

282 Díaz Castillo, Roberto. El arte popular: un problema conceptual (IPGH/FA, 31, junio 1981, p. 21–16)

Another attempt at defining popular art by citing the varied definitions in the international literature on the subject.

283 ———. Lo esencial en el concepto del arte popular (CDLA, 21:124, enero/feb. 1981, p. 83–89)

Another Marxist interpretation of the origins of popular art in oppressed classes—in Guatemala, Cuba, Vietnam.

284 **El Diseño en una sociedad en cambio.** C. Malo *et al.* Cuenca, Ecuador: CIDAP; s.l.: Ecuador-OEA, 197? 252 p.: ill.

Proceedings, with essays, from the 2d. National Seminary on Design. Of interest to students of folk art and its development.

285 **García Canclini, Néstor.** Del mercado a la boutique: las artesanías en el capitalismo (ECO, 47[3]:243, enero 1982, p. 241–262)

Brief discussion of the interrelationships of popular cultures and capitalism.

287 **Rojas Mix, Miguel** and **Rubén Bareiro Saguier.** Arte popular, folclore, arte culto: la expresión estética de las culturas latinoamericanas (GEE/NA, 4, 1981, p. 335–361, bibl.)

Authors conclude that there are no strict definitions for *arte popular* and *arte culto*—they have to be understood in terms of dialectical processes involving the artist, product and audience.

FOLK ART AND POPULAR ART
Mexico

288 **Alberto Beltrán:** el arte popular mexicano es una expresión colectiva (URSS/AL, 9:33, 1980, p. 112–119, ill.)

Interview with well-known graphic artist on the topic.

Díaz y de Ovando, Clementina. Viaje a México: 1844. See item **389.**

289 **Islas Carmona, Roberto.** La indumentaria (ARMEX, 23:200, marzo 1976, p. 30–47, ill.)

Charro costume and iconography in Mexico.

290 **Lackey, Louana.** The pottery of Acatlán: a changing Mexican tradition. Norman: University of Oklahoma Press, 1982. 164 p.: bibl., some col. ill., index.

Ethnographic study of the pottery of Acatlán, Puebla, Mexico which author suggests may have merit beyond itself as an instrument of ethnographic analogy for archaeologists.

291 **Mauricio Salazar, Abraham.** El ciclo mágico de los días: testimonio de un poblado indígena mexicano. Texto, Antonio Saldívar. Fotografía, Marianne Yampolsky. s.l.: Departamento Editorial de Salvat Mexicana de Ediciones, 1979. 76 p.: ill. (some col.)

This delightful book consists of illustrations (many in color) of the work of the folk artist, Abraham Mauricio Salazar, about the town and life in San Agustín, Guerrero, Mexico.

292 **O'Gorman, Patricia.** Tradition of craftsmanship in Mexican homes. Photos by Bob Schlkwijk. New York: Architectual Book Pub. Co., 1980. 258 p.: ill.

Interesting tour of homes which incorporate popular art forms in the architecture and decor.

293 **Pettit, Florence Harvey** and **Robert M. Pettit.** Mexican folk toys: festival decorations and ritual objects. New York: Hastings House Publishers, 1978. 191 p., 16 leaves of plates: bibl., ill., index.

Popular account of subject, useful photographs.

294 **Velázquez, Gustavo G.** El rebozo en el Estado de México. México: Biblioteca Enciclopédica del Estado de México, 1981. 93 p., 3 p. of plates: bibl., ill. (some col.) (Biblioteca enciclopédica del Estado de México; 111)

Discussion of origin, production and commercialization of the *rebozo* in Mexico state. Fair photographs.

295 **Wroth, William.** Christian images in Hispanic New Mexico: the Taylor Museum Collection of santos. Colorado Springs, Colo.: The Museum, 1982. 215, 32 p. of plates: bibl., ill. (some col.)

Rare masterful account offers many insights into the "folk art" of the Southwest. Meaning of Christian images and their popular use precedes detailed description of paintings and sculptures in New Mexico (1700–1860). Appendices provide terminology, dating techniques, glossary of saints. Extensive bibliography. Each of 191 plates (mostly b/w, some in color) give sharp reproductions, detailed descriptions and stylistic comments. [R.J. Mullen]

FOLK ART AND POPULAR ART
Central America and The Caribbean

296 Aguilar Arrivillaga, Eduardo. Estudio de la vivenda rural en Guatemala. Guatemala: Editorial Universitaria, 1980. 211 p.: bibl., ill. (Colección Aula; 22)
Survey of subject with many sketches, typology and maps.

297 Díaz Castillo, Roberto. Artes y artesanías populares en Guatemala (Tradiciones de Guatemala [Universidad de San Carlos de Guatemala, Centro de Estudios Folklóricos, Guatemala] 14, 1980, p. 7–16)
General discussion of centers of production of popular art in Guatemala and the destructive effects of US commercial centers and duty-free shops on native artistic traditions.

298 Gaitán Lara, Dalilia and **Lesbia A. Ortiz.** La pintura popular de Camalapa como reflejo de la problemática socioeconómica de este municipio (Tradiciones de Guatemala [Universidad de San Carlos de Guatemala, Centro de Estudios Folklóricos, Guatemala] 14, 1980, p. 125–148, bibl.)
Reviews effect of commercialization of area's popular art; includes list of 13 popular artists with short biographies.

299 García de Cuevas, Natalia. El arte popular de la cerería en Guatemala. Fotos, Félix González Valdez, Brenda Penados de Leal y Antonio Tobar. Guatemala: Sub-Centro Regional de Artesanías y Artes Populares, 1983. 46 p., 38 p. of plates: col. ill. (Colección Artesanías populares; 1)
Study of candle-making in Guatemala from Conquest—when Spaniards taught the Indians the technique—to present.

300 Lara Figueroa, Celso A. Síntesis histórica de las cerámicas populares de Guatemala. Fotografías, Mauro Calanchina. Guatemala: Dirección General de Antropología e Historia, 1981. 180 p.: bibl., ill. (Publicación extraordinaria / Dirección General de Antropología e Historia. Serie: Cultura popular)
Synthetic study of the development of popular ceramics in Guatemala, using ancient expressions as point of departure. Fair photographs.

301 López López, Agustín. Tejeduría artesanal: manual. Guatemala: Sub-Centro Regional de Artesanías y Artes Populares, 1982. 163 p., 3 leaves of plates: bibl., ill. (some col.) (Colección Tierra adentro; 2)
Technical manual on weaving, with special reference to Guatemala.

Luján Muñoz, Luis. Notas sobre la pintura mural en Guatemala. See item 409.

302 Morales Hidalgo, Italo. Cerámica tradicional del Oriente de Guatemala. Dibujos, Oscar Barrientos, Fernando Alvarez A. Mapas, Hugo A. Ordoñez Chocano. Guatemala: Sub-Centro Regional de Artesanías y Artes Populares, 1980. 108 p., 1 leaf of plates: ill. (Colección Tierra adentro; 1)
Survey with maps and mineral analyses of subject.

303 O'Neale, Lila Morris. Tejidos de los altiplanos de Guatemala. 2a ed. Guatemala: Editorial J. de Pineda Ibarra, 1979. 2 v. (951 p.) bibl., ill. (Publicación / Seminario de Integración Social Guatemalteca; no. 17)
Spanish translation of 1945 English edition (See *HLAS 11:266*).

304 Rodríguez San Pedro, María del Carmen. La artesanía en Cuba socialista (BNJM/R, 70[21]:2, 3. época, mayo/agosto 1979, p. 103–118)
Outlines the revolutionary government's efforts to encourage native crafts in the country and urges more efforts in this direction.

Sertima, Ivan van. The voodoo gallery: African presence in the ritual and art of Haiti. See *HLAS 45:1135*.

FOLK ART AND POPULAR ART
South America

305 Araújo, Iaperí. Elementos da arte popular. Natal: s.n., 1978. 71 p., 6 leaves of plates: ill.
Author tries to identify the most important elements of Popular Art and relate these to the cultural life in Northeastern Brazil.

306 Arte popular, la talla popular en piedra de Huamanga. Lima: Banco de Crédito del Perú, 1980. 176 p.: chiefly ill. (some col.) (Colección Arte y tesoros del Perú)
Survey of carved stone sculpture from Huamanga, Peru, from 18th and 19th centuries. Fair to excellent color plates.

307 **Berg Salvo, Lorenzo.** Artesanía tradicional de Chile. Fotografías, Peter Hirsch *et al*. Santiago: Departamento de Extensión Cultural del Ministerio de Educación, 1978. 77 p.: bibl., ill. (some col.) (Serie El Patrimonio cultural chileno. Colección Historia del arte chileno; libro 7)

Author divides Chile into 10 regions and illustrates contemporary crafts from each. Illustrations are useful but text lacks map of these regions.

308 **Cordero Iñigüez, Juan.** Bibliografía ecuatoriana de artesanías y artes populares. Cuenca, Ecuador: Centro Interamericano de Artesanías y Artes Populares, 1980. 373 p., 1 leaf of plates: index, map.

Indispensable bibliography for the study of folk and popular art in Ecuador. Compilation contains 999 items as well as map of areas covered and subject index.

Dannemann, Manuel. Bibliografía de artesanía tradicional chilena. See item **18.**

310 **Guarda, Gabriel.** Provincia de Osorno, arquitectura en madera, 1850–1928. Santiago: Ediciones Universidad Católica de Chile, 1981. 128 p.: ill.

Survey of wooden architecture of Osorno province, Chile; well illustrated.

311 **Instituto Nacional de Antropología.** 1000 [i.e. Mil] años de tejido en la Argentina: 24 de mayo al 18 de junio de 1978. Buenos Aires: El Instituto, 1978. 86 p.: ill.

Catalog for historical exhibition of weaving from ancient to modern times in Argentina. Fascinating subject with each item carefully catalogued but without enough illustrations.

312 **Legast, Anne.** La fauna mítica tairona (MOBR/B, 5, enero/abril 1982, p. 1–18, bibl., photos, tables)

Study of Tairona animal iconography (northern Colombia) from collection of the Museo del Oro.

313 **Moreno Aguilar, Joaquim.** El ikat. Cuenca, Ecuador: Centro Interamericano de Artesanías y Artes Populares, 1982. 32 p.: ill. (Cuadernos de arte popular; no. 3)

Short description of method of tying and dyeing threads before weaving in order to create a design. The word *ikat* comes from the Malayan *mengikat*.

314 **La Navidad.** Colaboradores, Susana González de Vega, Jorge Dávila Vázquez. Cuenca, Ecuador: Centro Interamericano de Artesanías y Artes Populares, 1981. 39 p.: ill. (Cuadernos de arte popular; no. 1 [Dic. 1981])

Description of fiesta and related popular art in Ecuador.

315 **Sabogal Wiesse, José.** Artesanos y artesanías en el Perú (III/AI, 41:2, abril/junio 1981, p. 339–345)

Concludes that true popular art (*artesanías*) depends on craftsman's attitude. Thus, the 10,000 identical *ponchos* shipped to US or Japan do not constitute art, popular or otherwise.

316 **Stastny, Francisco.** Las artes populares del Perú. Madrid: Edubanco, 1981? 254 p.: ill. (some col.)

Pt. 1 of well-illustrated book addresses problem of definition of this art form; pt. 2, is review of the art form in Peru.

317 **Wilbert, Johannes.** Warao basketry: form and function. Los Angeles: University of California at Los Angeles, Museum of Cultural History, 1975. 86 p.: bibl., ill. (some col.) (Occasional papers of the Museum of Cultural History, University of California, Los Angeles; no. 3)

Careful study of Warao basketry from the Orinoco Delta, Venezuela. Includes technology, ethnography and typology.

SPANISH AMERICA: Colonial

ROBERT J. MULLEN, *Associate Professor of Art History, The University of Texas at San Antonio*

THE NUMBER OF BOOKS and articles annotated for this section increased dramatically to over 100 in comparison with *HLAS 44*. Area coverage was equally impressive with 17 countries represented. As usual Mexico has the greatest number but Peru shows a remarkable increase. Coverage is widespread and scholarship is high. Even Florida and the Canary Islands are represented below.

Several works are outstanding not merely for their scholarship but for their artistry as books. The beautifully rendered account of the *santos* of New Mexico (item **295**) deserves special mention. A pleasure to behold, this work is also a masterpiece of sensitive interpretation of a very rare subject. The interpretation of Christian images in their particular role as "folk art" is classic. Another excellent book on images (item **361**) portrays, in superb color plates, some of the finest sculptures created in Mexico. What makes this publication so unusual is the fact that the pieces illustrated belong to private collections and hence are "firsts" to the world at large. Works by many Mexican authors cover a wide range of topics. Unusual and absolutely delightful is the facsimile of a study originally published in 1923 (item **356**) illustrating in rich color a particular form of folk art that originated in Michoacan: lacquered objects. In what must be regarded as the definitive account, the story of Mexico City from its origins until today is superbly narrated and illustrated in a three volume set (item **347**). A transliteration of payments made to those engaged in whatever capacity on the construction of the "new" cathedral in Mexico in 1584–85 (item **370**) will serve scholars seeking information on that critical construction period. Another aid to researchers is the study (item **349**) of the now extinct Colegio Apostólico and the Franciscan churches and houses established by its graduates in the northern reaches of Mexico. A publication of unusual quality in bookmaking (item **362**) illustrates with remarkable color precision selected examples of Puebla's *talavera*. One also welcomes the annotated bibliography (item **366**) of all known and available works by that *maestro* art historian, Francisco de la Maza. Vol. 50 of the *Anales del Instituto de Investigaciones Estéticas* contains, as usual, a number of fine articles. Of particular merit is the one (item **321**) showing how facial images in religious paintings changed from the idealized to the natural (native) following the canonization of the first American saint, Rose of Lima.

Scholars working on Peru produced many unusual studies. The Gisberts again made a major contribution with a complete revision of their 1962 work on Cuzco painters (item **375**). They note how spending many ensuing years in Cuzco and discovering much additional documentation compelled them to revise the first edition. A fascinating revelation concerns the "mestiza" façade of the little known church of Coporaque near Cuzco (item **373**). Also revealing are recent excavations made at San Francisco in Lima, preparatory to its restoration (item **376**). There are a number of worthwhile works on several other Latin American countries. On Ecuador, for example, there is a rare study of five haciendas near Quito (item **344**) and those indefatigable researchers, José and Teresa Gisbert, have partly lifted the veil of obscurity that hid "the most important" Quito sculptor of the 17th century, Padre Carlos (item **342**). On Chile there are two notable studies, one consisting of an extensive and detailed account of the unusual past and present architecture of Valdivia, a southern port on which little is written (item **323**), and the other relating and depicting the story of the lonely homesteads/haciendas that developed in the central region (item **325**). A study of some 20 rarely seen Carmelite convents in Argentina focuses both on their architecture and the many images of their patroness, Saint Teresa of Jesus (item **324**).

There are four exceptional works on Venezuela. The first, an urban study of La Guaira, Caracas' port, combines the extraordinary talents of a great historian and art historian (item **342**). It includes 378 illustrations consisting of maps, plans, aerial photos, and a host of sharp details in a most satisfying and complete visual projection. The second work is another notable example of bookmaking, a selection of chinaware and ceramics found in several private collections in Venezuela (item **340**). The third book serves as an introduction to an unknown "naif" artist and his haunting sculptures (item **309**). And finally, the fourth is a fine urban study of Cartagena's "historic zone" filled with data and excellent illustrations (item **343**).

From Guatemala we have a complete account of the life and works of one of its most productive architects, Diego de Porres (item **335**). From Panama there is a pleasant surprise in the full account of the restoration of the small church of Veraguas (item **336**), particularly of its altars, built by indigenous artists. A most unusual book is one depicting a large number of "paintings" made from mother-of-pearl which are at the Museo de América in Madrid (item **318**).

The bibliography below includes a number of fine articles from the *Anuario de Estudios Americanos*. That this journal is becoming a good medium for articles on art and architecture is evident in vol. 51 which includes three articles on painting: 1) on portraits and self portraits: 2) on a painting by Luis Juárez in Quebec: and 3) on newly discovered works by Antonio Rodríguez.

GENERAL

318   García Saiz, María Concepción. La pintura colonial en el Museo de América. v. 1, La escuela mexicana. v. 2., Los enconchados. Madrid: Ministerio de Cultura, Dirección General del Patrimonio Artístico, Archivos y Museos, Patronato Nacional de Museos, 1980. 2 v.: bibl., ill. (some col.)

Catalog consists of illustrations (b/w) and descriptions of 69 "paintings" made from mother of pearl (*los enconchados*) in this Madrid Museum. Color plates (12) focus on details. Organized by themes: Conquest, Life of Mary, Life of Christ, others. Bibliography.

319   González Galván, Manuel. Influencia, por selección, de América en su arte colonial (IIE/A, 50:1, 1982, p. 43–54, ill.)

Another attempt to explain distinctive quality of so much of colonial art in Latin America, particularly that of the pueblos. Distinguishes "formal" influence from "indirect through selection."

320   Montêquin, François-Auguste de. El proceso de urbanización en San Agustín de la Florida, 1565–1821: arquitectura civil y militar (EEHA/AEA, 37, 1980, p. 583–647, ill.)

Well known author (*Maps and plans of cities and towns of colonial New Spain*) brings additional archival material to study of Saint Augustine (Florida) focusing on its civil and military architecture.

321   Vargas Lugo, Elisa. La expresión pictórica religiosa y la sociedad colonial (IIE/A, 50:1, 1982, p. 61–76, ill.)

Examines impact of several New Spain Church Councils on religious painting. Concentrates on effect of canonization of first American saint, Rosa of Lima, on imagery. Notes change from idealized to actual, indigenous, facial images. These disappear in 18th century when Church guidelines regain ascendancy. Profusely illustrated.

ARGENTINA, BOLIVIA AND CHILE

322   Catedral de La Paz. Museo. La Paz: Universidad Boliviana, Universidad Mayor de San Andrés, Instituto de Estudios Bolivianos, 1981. 30 p., 32 p. of plates: ill.

Brief description of colonial treasures housed in the Cathedral Museum (e.g., statues, paintings, silverwork, furniture, vestments). Includes 32 excellent b/w photos.

323   Guarda, Gabriel. Conjuntos urbanos, históricos, arquitectónicos: Valdivia, siglos XVIII-XIX. s.l.: Ediciones Nueva Universidad, 1980. 83 p.: bibl., ill.

Extensively detailed pictorial, graphic and textual account of 18th, 19th (particularly) and 20th-century architecture in this southern city of Chile, once known for its massive fortifications. High quality photos and drawings. Excellent, most professional work. City is surprisingly modern, à-la-early 20th-century Europe (many German immigrants).

324   Sánchez Márquez, Manuel. Santa Teresa en la Argentina. Investigación artística y relevamiento fotográfico de Iris Gori y Sergio Barbieri. Buenos Aires: Ediciones de Arte Gaglianone, 1982. 200 p.: ill. (some col.)

Strong cult of Saint Teresa of Jesus which originated in Argentina in 17th century, resulted in some 20 Carmelite convents. These structures, plus paintings of her life (eight from Cuzco alone) and numerous statues, constitute many well illustrated art treasures (heretofore scarcely known) devoted to her. Many are modern. Rare combination of historical text and devotional scholarship.

325 Trebbi del Trevigiano, Rómolo. Desarrollo y tipología de los conjuntos rurales en la zona central de Chile, siglos XVI-XIX. Santiago: Ediciones Nueva Universidad, 1980. 174 p.: bibl., ill.

Outstanding account (16th-19th centuries) of lonely homesteads/haciendas in central Chile (which for more than a century lacked nucleated centers). Free hand sketches, plans and details enhance book's attractiveness. Twelve chapters examine every aspect. Good "explanatory" photos. Noteworthy contribution.

THE CARIBBEAN

Cueto, Emilio C. A short guide to old Cuban prints. See item **69.**

326 Dobal, Carlos. La verdad sobre Jacagua. Santiago, República Dominicana: UCMM, 1979. 140 p.: ill. (Colección "Estudios" / Universidad Católica Madre y Maestra; 32)

Jacagua was the second settlement of today's Santiago. Author provides new interpretation after studying ruins of its church, at variance with that of Walter Palm.

327 Rodríguez Demorizi, Emilio. Lugares y monumentos históricos de Santo Domingo. Santo Domingo: Editora Taller, 1980. 279 p.: bibl., chiefly ill.; index (Biblioteca dominicana de geografía y viajes; v. 15)

Consists of some 400 reproductions (fair quality) of drawings, paintings, prints and photos of Santo Domingo (1861–1940). Index makes for easy accounting. Based on extraordinary amount or research. No text.

328 Torres Oliver, Luis J. Breve historia del Convento Porta Coeli o Ermita de Porta Coeli (ICP/R, 21:79, abril/junio 1978, p. 1–8, bibl., ill., plates)

Documentary account of Dominican convent church in Puerto Rico (1520s–present).

329 Ugarte, María. Monumentos coloniales. Santo Domingo: Museo de las Casas Reales, 1977. 291 p.: bibl., ill. (some col.)

Sensitive depiction in word and picture of colonial structures in Santo Domingo that have been restored or stabilized. A "before and after" approach, professionally done.

330 Venegas Fornias, Carlos. Dos etapas de colonización y expansión urbana. La Habana: Editora Política, 1979. 175 p.: bibl., ill.

Account of urban growth of Havana is accompanied by many illustrations (fair) including aerials, plans, drawings, photos. Covers two growth periods: 1515–1658 and 1659–1878.

CENTRAL AMERICA

331 Alvarez Arévalo, Miguel. Algunas esculturas de la Virgen María en el arte guatemalteco. Guatemala: Impresos industriales, 1982. 105 p.: bibl., ill. (Colección Imágenes de Guatemala; v. 3)

Provides story and style analyses of images (mostly sculpture) of Mary as venerated in Guatemala under her various titles. Only fair quality reproductions. Bibliography.

332 Castillero Calvo, Alfredo. El casco viejo de Panamá y el Convento de Santo Domingo. Panamá: Instituto Panameño de Turismo: Instituto Nacional de Cultura, 1981. 30 p.: ill.

Account of research undertaken prior to restoration of Casco Viejo and the stabilization of Santo Domingo convent, immediately adjacent. Includes many plans of Panama City.

333 ———. La Iglesia de San Francisco y la Plaza Bolívar. Panamá: Impresora de la Nación, 1980. 24 p.: bibl., ill.

Reproduces rare photos of Church of San Francisco, Panama, in its colonial attire which bears no resemblance to that seen today (modified 1918). Plaza Bolívar was dedicated in 1926. Includes two colonial town plans and one of 1850.

334 **Gallo, Antonio.** Pintura guatemalteca del siglo XVIII: José Balladares; 1710–1775 (Cultura de Guatemala [Universidad Rafael Landívar, Guatemala] 3:2, sept./dic. 1981, p. 91–134)

Earthquake of 1976 destroyed much in Guatemala but also instigated preservation of colonial patrimony. One consequence of such interest was this full scale study of an 18th-century painter and a look at the values of that age.

335 **Luján Muñoz, Luis.** El arquitecto mayor Diego de Porres, 1677–1741. Guatemala: Editorial Universitaria, 1982. 433 p., 1 folded leaf of plates: ill. (some col.); indexes (Colección Monografías; vol. no. 15)

Complete investigation of life, works and style of a most productive Guatemalan architect. Includes plans, photos (fair), reconstructions, detailed documentation, indexes by name, place, and architectural detail. Impressive and definitive work.

336 **San Francisco de la Montaña,** joyel del arte barroco americano. Reina Torres de Araúz et al. Panamá: Instituto Nacional de Cultura, Dirección Nacional del Patrimonio Histórico, 1980. 103 p.: bibl., ill.

Full account of restoration and its altars of a small parroquia in Veraguas, outside Panamá. Altars (18th century) were made on site. Includes numerous detailed shots in good b/w photography. Fine restoration of beautiful and rare (for Panama) indigenous sculpture.

337 **Swezey, William R.** Los entierros del Hermano Pedro y la Capilla de la Tercera Orden: una revisión arqueo-histórica (Mesoamérica [Revista del Centro de Investigaciones Regionales de Mesoamérica, Antigua, Guatemala] 3:4, dic. 1982, p. 365–386, ill.)

Reinternment excavations reveal foundations of San Francisco, Guatemala, from origin through many modifications. Well documented.

338 **Velarde, Oscar A.B.** Breves notas sobre la arquitectura colonial en Panamá (LNB/L, 303/304, junio/julio 1981, p. 127–140, bibl.)

Good reference on colonial structures of Panama City.

COLOMBIA, VENEZUELA AND ECUADOR

339 **Bermúdez Bermúdez, Arturo E.** Materiales para la historia de Santa Marta. Bogotá: Banco Central Hipotecario, 1981. 339 p., 20 leaves of plates: ill.

Invaluable study of this Colombian strategic port. Documents urban growth, churches, religious houses, hospitals, homes, military structures, water supplies, even attacks by pirates. Includes facsimiles of plans.

340 **Duarte, Carlos F.** and **María L. Fernández.** La cerámica durante la época colonial venezolana. Fotos de Mariano U. de Aldaca. Caracas: E. Armitano Editor, 1980. 309 p.: col. ill. (Serie Venezuela)

Displays and describes best pieces of chinaware and ceramics from several private collections in Venezuela. Important to realize these objects, not produced there, were mostly from Spain (16th-18th centuries). Superb bookmaking with exquisite color plates.

341 **Gasparini, Graziano** and **Manuel Pérez Vila.** La Guaira: orígenes históricos: morfología urbana. Capítulo sobre "Las artes en el puerto de La Guaira durante la época colonial" por Carlos Duarte. Caracas: Centro Simón Bolívar, Ministerio de Información y Turismo,1981. 421 p.: bibl., ill. (some col.)

Three-part volume focuses on this all important Caracas port. Pérez Vila (p. 9–128) covers history of founding, early difficulties and economic viability reached by La Guaira in early 17th century. Gasparini (p. 129–379) examines its urban growth from 17th to end of 18th century with exhaustive study of its fortifications. Duarte (p. 380–400) focuses on the colonial visual heritage of the port's non-military architecture. Sharp, beautiful illustrations (378) include maps, plans, photos (aerial). A dozen color plates strikingly portray its personality. Extraordinary and felicitous combination of talents.

342 **Mesa, José de** and **Teresa Gisbert.** Marcos Guerra y el problema del escultor quiteño Padre Carlos (EEHA/AEA, 37, 1980, p. 685–695, ill.)

In their usual masterful manner authors link works of well known Jesuit sculptor, Marcos Guerra, with shadowy Padre Carlos, the "most important sculptor in

Quito during the seventeenth century." Authors attribute some of Guerra's statues to latter. Excellent photos.

343 Téllez, Germán and **Ernesto Moure.**
Repertorio formal de arquitectura doméstica: Cartagena de Indias, época colonial. Bogotá: Corporación Nacional de Turismo, 1982. 256 p., 1 folded leaf of plates: ill.

Thorough examination of homes (only) in Cartagena's large "historic zone." Replete with data, drawings, plans and photos, all executed professionally and sharply reproduced (b/w). Compiled (1969–71) by faculty of Bogotá's architectural school. Result is an architectural historian's dream. Extra large format (13"x14") permits unusual detailing. Model work.

344 Wurster, Wolfgang W. Aportes sobre la arquitectura de haciendas coloniales del Ecuador (EANH/B, 10, dic. 1977, p. 61–101, ill., plates)

Provides description, documentation, photos (good), plans, elevations, and details of five haciendas near Quito. Thorough and professional contribution on rarely treated subject.

MEXICO

345 Alvarez Noguera, José Rogelio. El patrimonio cultural del Estado de México: primer ensayo. México: Biblioteca Enciclopédica del Estado de México, 1981. 584 p.: ill. (Biblioteca Enciclopédica del Estado de México; 110)

Catalog of patrimony of *State* of Mexico constitutes third (after Hidalgo and Yucatán) to continue 1940s program to inventory each state. Consists of six parts: pts. 1/3) general overview including prehispanic period; pts. 4/5) civil architecture (p. 47–88); and pt. 6) religious architecture (mostly colonial) in over 100 communities (p. 89–575). Remarkable work contains excellent text and sharp illustrations but no new research (dates given are those published).

346 Báez Macías, Eduardo. El retablo de Fray Miguel de Herrera en la Iglesia de Santa Catarina, Estado de México (IIE/A, 49, 1979, p. 73–78, ill.)

Good study and very fine detailed photos of this great retablo.

347 Benítez, Fernando. La Ciudad de México, 1325–1982. México: Salvat, 1981. 1 v.: ill. (some col.)

The "ultimate" in depicting the history of the city of Mexico. Vol. 1 covers (briefly) Tenochtitlán and 16th-17th centuries; Vol. 2, 18th and 19th centuries; Vol. 3, 20th. Remarkably rich in sources, varying viewpoints and superb illustrations, mostly color, including seldom seen manuscripts and maps. Large format (13"x10"). Incomparable research and presentation.

348 Carrillo y Pérez, Ignacio. Lo máximo en lo mínimo: la portentosa imagen de Nuestra Señora de los Remedios, conquistadora y patrona de la Imperial Ciudad de México. Ed. facsimilar de la de 1808. México: Patrimonio Cultural y Artístico del Estado de México, Gobierno del Estado de México, FONAPAS, 1979. 153, 50 p.: bibl., ill. (Biblioteca enciclopédica del Estado de México; 87)

Title is that of 1808 publication here reproduced as facsimile. Introduction brings history of this highly venerated (since mid-16th century) statue of Mary up to date. The Virgen de los Remedios is found in Tlalnepantla, State of Mexico. Illustrations (fair) depict statue and her church.

349 Chauvet, Fidel de Jesús. La Iglesia de San Fernando de México y su extinto Colegio Apostólico. México: Centro de Estudios Bernardino de Sahagún, 1980. 165 p., 32 p. of plates: ill. (Publicación; no. 2)

San Fernando and its now extinct Colegio Apostólico (Mexico City) are both carefully analyzed by a distinguished Franciscan historian. Also describes in detail work of Colegio's graduates (called *fernandinos*) in mission fields of California (1767–1854) and Sierra Gorda (1744–70), State of Querétaro. Includes very good and rare photos of Concá, Tilaco, Jalpan, Landa. Excellent match of research and graphics.

350 Colín, Mario. Retablos del Señor del Huerto que se venera en Atlacomulco. México: Patrimonio Cultural y Artístico del Estado de México; s.l.: Gobierno del Estado de México, FONAPAS, 1981. 147 p.: ill. (some col.) (Biblioteca enciclopédica del Estado de México; 50)

Santuario in Atlacomulco (State of Mexico) is principal of many shrines devoted to El Señor del Huerto, a particular image of the suffering Christ. Retablos are mostly *votivos* (small oils on various materials.) Includes illustrations (fair to good) of more than 75. Brief explanatory text.

351 Díaz, Marco. La arquitectura de los jesuitas en Nueva España: las instituciones de apoyo, colegios y templos. México: Universidad Nacional Autónoma de México, Instituto de Investigaciones Estéticas, 1982. 289 p.: bibl., ill. (some col.)

Thorough analysis of Jesuit churches and colegios (erected 1572–1767). Manrique's introduction stresses importance to Mexico of this Order yet carefully distinguishes between buildings "constructed by Jesuits" (correct) and "Jesuit architecture" (incorrect). Based on full archival research. Includes numerous illustrations, excellent photos (many in color). Marred by lack of index and somewhat random placement of illustrations. Lengthy bibliography.

352 ———. Retablo salomónico en Puebla (IIE/A, 50:1, 1982, p. 103–110, ill.)

Studies many 17th and 18th-century retablos in State of Puebla and concludes their development followed independent routes. Provides interesting (and rare) examination of original retablo in Cathedral of Puebla. (The one seen today is a 19th-century transformation.) Well illustrated.

353 Estudio de conservación y desarrollo de áreas y edificios patrimoniales. Direction and supervision by José Manuel Gómez Vázquez A. Realization and coordination by Jorge González Clarverán. Guadalajara, México: Ayuntamiento Ciudad de Guadalajara, COPLAUR: Universidad de Guadalajara, 1978. v. : ill.

Proposal for restoring/conserving historic areas in Guadalajara. Emphasizes urban context. Good reference with many, but very small photos.

354 Fraga González, Carmen. Esculturas de la Virgen de Guadalupe en Canarias: tallas sevillanas y americanas (EEHA/AEA, 37, 1980, p. 697–707, ill.)

Examines Spanish and Mexican origins of several statues of the Virgin of Guadalupe now in the Canary Islands.

355 Kubler, George. Arquitectura mexicana del siglo XVI. México: Fondo de Cultura Económica, 1982. 639 p.: 468 ill., maps.

Obra clásica que no ha sido superada, a pesar de ciertos adelantos en el conocimiento del tema desde la edición original inglesa en 1948. Es más que una historia del arte arquitectónico: constituye también una contribución fundamental a la historia de las órdenes mendicantes así como del urbanismo en el siglo XVI mexicano. La presente edición es simplemente magnífica. [Lino Gómez Canedo]

356 León, Francisco de P. Los esmaltes de Uruapan. Ed. facsimilar del ms. original. Presentación de Porfirio Martínez Peñaloza. México: Fomento Cultural Banamex, 1980. 119 p., 72 leaves of plates: bibl., col. ill.

First publication (color facsimile) of work completed by León in 1923. Text (119 p.), handwritten and embellished like an illuminated manuscript, describes Michoacan's particular form of popular art—lacquered objects— from prehispanic times to 1920s. Exquisite color reproductions illustrate 72 such objects. Bibliography.

357 Manrique, Jorge Alberto. La estampa como fuente del arte en la Nueva España (IIE/A, 50:1, 1982, p. 55–60)

Examines key role played by prints in development of painting and sculpture in New Spain.

358 Mendiola Quezada, Vicente. Arquitectura del Estado de México: siglos XVI, XVII, XVIII, y XIX. t. 1, Textos. México: Biblioteca Enciclopédica del Estado de México, 1982. 1 v. (Biblioteca enciclopédica del Estado de México; 112)

Goes well beyond inventory (see item **345**) in analysis of architecture in this State. Formal elements of four centuries (16th through 19th) are followed by detailed accounts of structures, mostly religious, in some 75 locales. Components (e.g., convento, church, nave, facade) are analyzed. Brings Kubler and McAndrew up to date. Entirely descriptive (no plans, no illustrations). Vocabulary.

359 Monterrosa Prado, Mariano. Bibliografía sobre arte colonial de Justino Fernández. México: Dirección de Estudios Históricos, Instituto Nacional de Antropología e Historia, Seminario de Estudios de Historia del Arte, 1978. 39 leaves (Cuaderno de trabajo; no. 4)

Annotated bibliography in typescript consists of 95 items. [J.W. Bailey]

360 ——. Manual de símbolos cristianos. México: Instituto Nacional de Antropología e Historia, Dirección de Estudios Históricos, 1979 [i.e. 1980]. 170 p.: bibl.

Dictionary of religious symbols (no illustrations) of colonial Mexico and of how they relate to theological concepts, saints, virtues, vices. Unique and very useful.

361 **Moyssén Echeverría, Xavier.** Estofados en la Nueva España. México: Grupo Multibanco Comermex, 1978. 82 p.: bibl., col. ill. (Ediciones de arte Comermex; 8)

One of finest publications available on polychrome wood sculptures of colonial Mexico. Many from private collections are "firsts" to the public. Excellent text highlights four major schools in the Americas. Clearly distinguishes technical aspects of polychrome, *encarnación* and *estofado* and the particular roles of several categories of artisans. Excellent scholarship and bookmaking. Notable color illustrations (27). Bibliography. Another outstanding contribution from the "private" sector (Grupo Multibanco Comermex).

362 **Peón Soler, Alejandra** and **Leonor Cortina Ortega.** Talavera de Puebla. México: Ediciones Comermex, 1973. 81 p.: bibl., col. ill.

Text covers technical and stylistic aspects from 16th century to present. Superb color plates (26) illustrates distinctive "Talavera" ceramics from Puebla. Bibliography. A work of unusual quality.

363 **Romero Quiroz, Javier** and **José Luis Medrango García.** Corpus Christi Tlalnepantla. Tlalnepantla de Baz, México: H. Ayuntamiento, 1981. 205 p.: ill. (some col.)

Sequence of 16th-century construction of convento in Tlalnepantla (Mexico state) with its open air chapel is accompanied by fairly good photographs. Summarizes available information. Several chapters deal with prehispanic conditions and architecture. Cites various 19th- and 20th-century laws pertaining to its elevated legal status.

364 **Ruiz Gomas, José Rogelio.** Rubens en la pintura novohispana de mediados del siglo XVII (IIE/A, 50:1, 1982, 87–101, bibl., ill.)

Cites certain works (eight ill.) by Arteago, Juárez, Ramírez and Echave Ibia as being influenced by Rubens. First noticed ca. 1640, his influence was transmitted primarily by prints.

365 **Salas Cuesta, Marcela.** La Iglesia y el Convento de Huejotzingo. México: Universidad Nacional Autónoma de México, Instituto de Investigaciones Estéticas, 1982. 144 p., 20 p. of plates: bibl., ill. (Cuadernos de historia del arte; 18)

In spite of edifice's importance in 16th-century architecture, this is the first monograph on it. Text is composite of many published sources. Illustrations (20) are only fair.

366 **Talavera Solórzano, Elsa Leticia.** Bibliografía sobre arte colonial de Francisco de la Maza. México: Seminario de Estudios de Historia del Arte, Dirección de Estudios Históricos, Instituto Nacional de Antropología e Historia, Departamento de Investigaciones Históricas, 1978. 87 p., (Cuaderno de trabajo; no. 5)

Annotated bibliography of all known and available works by the great *maestro* art historian Francisco de la Maza consists of 23 books and more than 200 other publications (minus 18 writings not located). Arranged chronologically (1939–74).

367 **Testimonios barrocos:** Pinacoteca Marqués del Jaral de Berrio, enero/abril de 1978. México: Fomento Cultural Banamex, between 1978 and 1981. 40 p.: ill. (some col.)

Catalog of possessions of well known colonial family of Mexico City, Condes de San Mateo de Valparaíso y Marqueses del Jaral de Berrio, (Palacio de Iturbide). Genealogy, title, furnishings, oils, statues, all 18th century, are handsomely illustrated. Another Fomento Cultural Banamex accomplishment.

368 **Toussaint, Manuel.** Claudio de Arciniega: arquitecto de la Nueva España. México: Universidad Nacional Autónoma de México, 1981. 78 p., 9 p. of plates: ill. (Monografías de arte; 5)

It is something of a mystery why this exhaustive study by the dean of Mexican art historians on one of the most influential architects active in Mexico during 16th century had its publication delayed until 1981. (It is not a facsimile.) Several archival sources indicate that Arciniega was associated with over a dozen buildings mostly in Mexico and Puebla. Includes a few selective, high quality photos.

369 Victoria, José Guadalupe. Sobre las nuevas consideraciones en torno a Andrés de la Concha (IIE/A, 50:1, 1982, p. 77–86)

Uses new data to resolve controversy as to dates in which Concha was active in Mexico (1570–1612).

370 Zavala, Silvio Arturo. Una etapa en la construcción de la Catedral de México, alrededor de 1585. México: Colegio de México, Centro de Estudios Históricos, 1982. 216 p.: bibl., ill, index (Jornadas; 96)

Transliteration of documents (1584–85) of payments made to host of persons involved with "new" (more or less present) Cathedral in Mexico. Index reveals many names and makes meaningful this vast compendium of financial accounts. Researchers can glean much from this "raw data."

PERU

371 Bernales Ballesteros, Jorge. Esculturas de Roque de Balduque y su círculo en Andalucía y América (EEHA/AEA, 34, 1977, p. 349–371, ill.)

Several sculptures in Lima are shown as closely related to works of the well known 16th-century Andalusian sculptor.

372 La Casa cusqueña. Ramón Gutiérrez et al. Corrientes?, Argentina: Departamento de Historia de la Arquitectura, Universidad Nacional del Nordeste, 1981. 197 p.: bibl., ill.

Urban development of Cuzco from Spanish to present times. Thoroughly researched and documented. Detailed analysis of urban design, structures, materials, individual houses. Many (fair quality) illustrations. Exemplary.

373 Gutierrez, Ramón; Idilio Santillana; Graciela M. Viñuales; and Amaya Yrarrazábal. Coporaque: la trayectoria de un poblado andino (EEHA/AEA, 37, 1980, p. 565–581, ill.)

Careful and complete examination of this fascinating 17th-18th century church in Coporaque (San Juan Bautista) in Cuzco Dept. Façade is described as "mestiza."

374 Inventario y evaluación del patrimonio turístico del Departamento de la Libertad. Lima?: Ministerio de Industria, Comercio, Turismo e Integración, Dirección General de Turismo, Dirección de Desarrollo, 1978. 315 p., 9 leaves of plates: bibl., ill. (some col.)

Examines this coastal department north of Lima for its tourism potential. Written for internal use it is filled with "infrastructure" data. Section on cultural assets (p. 100–125) provides basic information on churches and principal homes.

375 Mesa, José de and Teresa Gisbert. Historia de la pintura cuzqueña. Lima: Fundación A.N. Wiese: Banco Wiese, 1982. 2 v. (830 p., 99 p. of plates): bibl., ill. (some col.), index (Biblioteca peruana de cultura)

Complete revision of 1962 work necessitated by author's subsequent years in Cuzco and discovery of additional (50 percent plus) documentation. Vol. 1 is text with 61 color plates. Five chapters treat: artists up to 1700; native artists (mostly anonymous); 18th-century artists; murals; and lastly, aesthetics, techniques and themes. Vol. 2 contains 615 b/w photos (good quality), captioned but without text. Extensive bibliography. Prodigious undertaking and another outstanding work by this celebrated team. Yet humbly they state "it is only a preliminary work." Sponsored by Banco Wiese, Peru. An absolute *must.*

376 Nakandakari Shimabukuro, Ernesto. Convento e Iglesia de San Francisco de Lima: investigación arqueológica. Lima: Instituto Nacional de Cultura, Centro de Investigación y Restauración de Bienes Monumentales, 198? 68 p., 37 leaves of plates: ill. (Serie Histórico-artístico; no. 2)

Factual account of excavations made during restoration of this very significant convento in Lima, begun in 1546. Typed ms. with many drawings. Photos (17) detail excavation progress.

377 Stastny, Francisco. El manierismo en la pintura colonial latinoamericana. Lima: Universidad Nacional Mayor de San Marcos, 1981. p. 17–45, 20 p. of plates: bibl., ill.

Concentrates on European mannerist painters in Latin America, particularly those in Peru. European antecedents appear in 20 photos. One of many papers delivered at international colloquium on Mannerism in Latin America, Oaxtepec, Mexico, 1976.

19th and 20th Centuries

LEONARD FOLGARAIT, *Assistant Professor of Fine Arts, Vanderbilt University*

THIS FIRST CONTRIBUTION TO *HLAS,* following James B. Lynch Jr.'s 15 year tenure as editor of this section, gives me the opportunity to acknowledge his importance to scholars and students alike. His authoritative yet fair judgements presented in annotations that were invariably clear, elegant and concise were of immense help to all of us who sought to identify significant works from among the growing literature in the field.

Of all entries annotated below, the following are especially noteworthy for their overall excellence. Most concern important topics and reach provocative conclusions via ambitious and sound methodologies. They should serve as models for further study as well as open up new areas of research. The works in question are: Hayden Herrera's, *Frida: a biography of Frida Kahlo* (item **395**); Gaspar Galaz and Milan Ivelic's, *La pintura en Chile desde la colonia hasta 1981* (item **427**); Esther Acevedo *et al's Bibliografía comentada sobre el arte del siglo XIX* (item **384**); José Luis Cuevas', "La Creación Artística es Ajena a la Alegría de Vivir" (item **388**); and Esther Acevedo and Eloísa Uribe's, *La escultura del siglo XIX* (item **392**).

It is not surprising that most of the literature in this section is by Mexican authors or on Mexican topics. The rapid advance of Mexican scholarship in the fine arts, especially with regard to methodologies, is becoming an established trend. Increasingly American scholars are selecting Mexican topics for research. This nation's leadership not withstanding, there are a great number of worthwhile works concerning and emerging from Central and South America as well.

Insofar as other aspects of research in Latin American art are concerned, such as symposia and graduate degree programs, they continue on the same steady rise as over the last five years. As of now, there seems to be no peak in sight, a positive sign and an additional incentive for continued work.

With world attention fixed firmly on Latin America, especially on its political and economic development, one looks forward to the region's art scholarship over the next few years and to how ideological influences will affect it. In times of flux and upheaval such as these, undoubtedly new art forms will emerge as well as the need to study them. Whether these studies will turn partisan or strive for objectivity will provide an interesting test of the region's future.

GENERAL

378   Anuario Latinoamericano de las Artes Plásticas. Correo Editorial. 1981– Buenos Aires.

Wealth of visual, critical, and documentary information about the making, promotion, and selling of art in Latin America (late 1970s–1981). Short essays highlight situations in Argentina, Brazil, Chile, Mexico, and Uruguay. Important information on sales and critics.

379   IV [i.e. Cuarta] Bienal Americana de Artes Gráficas= IV [Fourth] American Biennial of Graphic Arts. Cali, Colombia: Museo de Arte Moderno La Tertulia, 1981. 154 p.: ill. (some col.)

Over 200 high-quality illustrations demonstrate drawings and graphics from almost every country of North and South America. No essays or criticism.

380   Findlay, James A. Modern Latin American art: a bibliography. Westport, Conn.: Greenwood Press, 1983. 301 p.: index (Art reference collection, 0193–6867; no. 3)

This bibliography (2,384 items) was compiled from holdings of N.Y's Museum of Modern Art Library in *A guide to the art of Latin America* (see *HLAS 14:649*), from the art sections of *HLAS 1–40*, and the working paper of the *Handbook of Latin American Art* (see item **381**)—but only first of these sources is acknowledged by compiler. "Contents" page does not reflect organization of bibliographic materials, there are 16 numbered *blank* pages in bibliography, and editing has all the signs of a "rush job." Not for the serious student of the subject. [J.W. Bailey]

381 Handbook of Latin American art= Manual de arte latinoamericano: a bibliographic compilation. v. 1, General references and art of the nineteenth & twentieth centuries: pt. 1, North America. General editor, Joyce Waddell Bailey. Volume/regional editor—Brazil, Aracy Abreu Amaral. Volume editor—Southern Cone, Ramón Gutiérrez. Regional editor—Southern Cone, Alberto S.J. De Paula. Santa Barbara, Calif.: ABC-Clio Information Services, 1984. 579 p.: indexes.

Pt. 1 of 11,000 entry compilation for general reference and art of 19th and 20th centuries. Preceded by complete subject classifications by geographic region and country. Includes books, anthologies, literature from periodicals, exhibition catalogs, published and unpublished reports, and reviews. Codes at end of entries refer user to *HLAS* annotations (i.e., volume and item number), or to library in which work is located. There are separate categories for monographic studies of artists by country. Artists are listed alphabetically in Index 6 ("Index of Artists from Monographic Studies"), and other indexes consist of personal authors, institutional authors, periodicals, abbreviations for periodicals, and symbols. Multilingual basic research tool. For bibliographer's comment, see item **2**. [J.W. Bailey]

382 Kassner, Lily S. de. Notas en torno a la expresividad de la figura humana en cuatro pintores latinoamericanos. Ciudad Universitaria, México: Universidad Nacional Autónoma de México, 1980. 45 p.: bibl., ill. (some col.)

Does not contribute new scholarship on the subject, but gives Oswaldo Guayasamin of Ecuador and Cándido Portinari of Brazil deserving critical attention, in the company of the Mexicans Siqueiros and Orozco.

Kupfer, Monica E. A bibliography of contemporary art in Latin America: books, articles and exhibition catalogs in the Tulane University Library, 1950–1980. See item **27**.

383 Latin America in its architecture. Roberto Segre, editor. Fernando Kusnetzoff, editor of the English ed. Translated from the Spanish by Edith Grossman. New York: Holmes & Meier, 1981. 216 p.: bibl., index (Latin America in its culture; 2)

Collection of eight essays of high scholarship. Subjects range from questions of technology to those of social and historical context. Essays are critical and analytical, as typified by Ramón Vargas Salguero and Rafael López Rangel, who on p. 136 write "the essential result is that the density of Latin American architecture is ultimately tied to the historical destiny of the classes in power."

MEXICO

384 Bibliografía comentada sobre arte del siglo XIX. Esther Acevedo *et al.* México: Seminario de Estudios de Historia del Arte, Dirección de Estudios Históricos, Instituto Nacional de Antropología e Historia, 1978. 210 leaves (Cuaderno de trabajo / Dirección de Estudios Históricos, INAH; 6)

Essential research and reference tool for 19th-century Mexican art historians of all media. Lists hundreds of bibliographic references, annotated, abstracted, and cross-referenced. Intelligent introduction and efficient indexes complete this comprehensive and invaluable study aid.

385 Cardoza y Aragón, Luis. José Clemente Orozco: dos apuntes para un retrato. México: Universidad Nacional Autónoma de México, 1981. 39 p.

Short account of career and work of author, major Mexican intellectual figure, introduces book. Main text more concerned with author's sensitive and poetically evocative prose than with its subject. Too much emphasis on subjective and fantastic reverie. Not a useful contribution to Orozco studies.

386 Chávez Morado, José. José Chávez Morado: imágenes de identidad mexicana. Por Raquel Tibol. México: Coordinación de Humanidades, Universidad Nacional

Autónoma de México, 1980. 158 p.: ill. (some col.) (Colección de Arte; 36)

Essay (43 p.) precedes lavish spread of excellent photographs (100 p. plus). Combination of insightful and expert criticism and representative illustrations enhances Chavez Morado's importance. Complete biography. Successfully places subject in mainstream of Mexican art and social history.

387 Chávez Vega, Guillermo. Desarrollar las tradiciones de la pintura mural (URSS/AL, 3[39], 1981, p. 97–104, ill.)

Useful biographical data and personal interview with contemporary Mexican muralist on question of mural aesthetics. Includes references to viability of muralism after movement's classic years.

388 Cuevas, José Luis. La creación artística es ajena a la alegría de vivir (UY/R, 23:143, nov./dic. 1982, p. 91–118)

Major statements by Mexico's best known figurative artist, in response to intelligent and provocative questions. Lengthy and comprehensive interview is crucial addition to Cuevas literature. Artist's conversation ranges from aspects of his work to technical and historical questions and from aesthetics to ideology. Most useful and clear document on artist's premises and autobiography.

389 Díaz y de Ovando, Clementina. Viaje a México: 1844 (IIE/A, 50:2, 1982, p. 159–191, ill.)

Noteworthy study. Frenchman Mathieu de Fossey documented an 1844 tour of Mexico. This edited translation is full of observation about the country entering modernity, its folk art, architecture, and city planning.

390 Eder, Rita. Gironella. México: Universidad Nacional Autónoma de México, 1981. 158 p., 47 p. of plates: ill. (some col.)

Ambitious book combines biographical and critical essays, documents, artist's writings, many excellent illustrations, and short essays of appreciation by Rufino Tamayo, Juan Rulfo, and Octavio Paz. Author emphasizes Gironella's important role in the post-1950 reaction to nationalism of previous artists. Key source for Mexican art of the 1950s and 1960s.

391 ———. Las mujeres artistas en México (IIE/A, 50:2, 1982, p. 251–260)

Essay fills long-neglected gap even if only as introduction to the subject. As preparation and incentive for further research, it raises provocative questions and proposes interesting methods to pursue the study of Mexican women artists, whose names and accomplishments are otherwise scattered.

392 Escuela Nacional de Bellas Artes, México. La escultura del siglo XIX: catálogo de colecciones de la Escuela Nacional de Bellas Artes. Manuscrito de Manuel G. Revilla, 1905. Anotaciones al catálogo por Rubén M. Campos. Editado por Esther Acevedo de Iturriaga, Eloisa Uribe. México: Secretaría de Educación Pública, Instituto Nacional de Bellas Arte, 1980. 117 p.: bibl., ill. (Cuadernos de arquitectura y conservación del patrimonio artístico; no.9. Serie Documentos)

Fully documented and illustrated catalog of Mexican 19th-century sculpture. Original documents and photographs are indexed and annotated. Essays by the editors are fully researched, clear, and persuasive. Major publication on the topic.

393 Exposición homenaje nacional a Emiliano Zapata en el centenario de su nacimiento: 1879–1979; Nov. 15, 1980-Feb. 21, 1981. Museo Biblioteca Papel. Responsables de la exposición, Víctor Sandoval et al. Monclova, Mexico: El Museo, 1980. 19 p.: ill. (some col.), ports.

Catalog of comprehensive exhibit of documents and images connected with Zapata. Important contribution because of the number of documents and reproductions of the rebel leader's image (i.e., 200 illustrations).

394 Flores, Edmundo. Chapingo, los murales de Diego Rivera y las gringas (Vuelta [Revista mensual, México] 7:76, marzo 1983, p. 20–23)

Excerpts from memoirs of student at Chapingo's National School of Architecture (1923–26) when Rivera painted his murals therein. Anecdotal and chatty, memoirs provide otherwise unavailable information about the murals' context.

Gormsen, Erdmann. Die Städte im Spanischen America. See *HLAS 45:5099.*

395 Herrera, Hayden. Frida, a biography of Frida Kahlo. New York: Harper & Row, 1983. 507 p., 48 leaves of plates: bibl., ill., index.

Book of singular importance, this

biography offers the first comprehensive treatment of a major Mexican artist. Kahlo emerges as a forceful individual with complex motives and unstoppable drive to assert herself and her art in spite of numerous obstacles; professional, personal, and physical. The result of much patient original research, this work is thoroughly documented. Serious flaws are a tendency toward anecdotal and chatty dialogue, imprecise language in the formal description and analysis of paintings, and an odd lack of dimension in the presentation of the greater social and historical context. Good and important biography in need of sounder methodology as art history.

396 Jodidio, Philip. Zúñiga and the Mexican soul (CA, 21, Oct. 1981, p. 85–89, plates)

Brief account of sculptor's career and aesthetic views. Most interesting are Zúñiga's extreme statements against modernism and his belief in a Pan-American aesthetic. Provocative essay that is not fully developed.

397 Martín Hernández, Vicente. Arquitectura doméstica de la Ciudad de México, 1890–1925. México: Universidad Nacional Autónoma de México, Escuela Nacional de Arquitectura, 1981. 262 p., 2 p. of plates: bibl., ill.

Important treatment of subject, this is architectural and urban history of real value, fully documented and richly illustrated with plans and photographs. Ambitious text attempts to place subject in context as much as possible, offering ideological arguments.

398 Mérida, Carlos. Carlos Mérida en sus 90 años. Editor, Mario de la Torre. México: Cartón y Papel de México, 1981. 173 p., 11 p. of plates: ill. (some col.) (Colección CPM)

Spanish and English essays of appreciation imbued with nostalgia and bias. Book's value lies in a wealth of documentary photographs and biographical material. Only Mérida's graphic works are illustrated, over 100 in inmaculate color, including complete technical data.

399 Moliner, José María. Raíces de la pintura expresionista mejicana (CH, 379, enero 1982, p. 130–140)

Brief account traces roots of Expressionism in 19th-century European intel-

lectual history. Treats its development in Mexico by going through a list of dozen contributors to this "style", rather than by coherent analysis. Useful for its documentary value.

400 Moyssén, Xavier. Los dibujos de Orozco para el mural Onmisciencia (IIE/A, 50:2, 1982, p. 214–249, ill.)

Very deliberate and thoroughly documented essay incorporates much of the literature on the subject. Example of good detective work in piecing together the mural's final look. Very descriptive, considers only visual evidence.

401 Museo Nacional de Historia, México. Catálogo del retrato del siglo XIX en el Museo Nacional de Historia. Esther Acevedo de Iturriaga, compiladora. México: Instituto Nacional de Antropología e Historia, 1982. 168 p.: bibl., ports.

Key reference tool illustrates, describes, and analyzes central concerns and characteristics of 19th-century portraiture in this major Mexican collection. Model of sound scholarship for such catalogs.

402 Ortiz Monasterio, Luis. Ricardo Romero, dibujante, 1903–1929. México: Universidad Nacional Autónoma de México, 1981. 54 p., 56 p. of plates: ill. (Cuadernos de historia del arte; 14)

Monograph on important Mexican draftsman. Useful and well researched short essay concentrates on artist's training and aesthetics. Real treat is wealth of b/w illustrations of Romero's drawings and their astonishing technical and conceptual virtuosity.

403 Prieto Castillo, Daniel. El arte y el anarquismo mexicano (IPGH/RHI, 3, 1982, p. 93–124)

Valuable and important work traces relationship between anarchism and aesthetics in Mexico since the 19th century. Includes wealth of documentation and excellent analyses. Implications for contemporary situation are provocative and stimulating.

404 Rivas Mercado, Antonieta. 87 [i.e. Ochenta y siete] cartas de amor y otros papeles. Correspondencia y escritos ordenados, revisados y anotados por Isaac Rojas Rosillo. 2a ed. Xalapa, México: Editorial UV, 1980, 1981. 177 p., 4 p. of plates: port (Biblioteca Universidad Veracruzana)

Selected letters and short pieces of fiction by rich patroness of the arts who lived during important period of cultural development (1900–31). She was intimately connected with painter Manuel Rodríguez Lozano (1895–1971). Includes three portraits by Tina Modotti, important contemporary photographer.

405 Vanderwood, Paul J. Agustín Casasola in context: an introduction to his photographs (PCCLAS/P, 8, 1981/1982, p. 127–140, bibl., ill.)

Important introduction to the photographer who most successfully captured the drama and imagery of the Revolutionary period. Author's clear and persuasive text places Casasola's work in its historical context. Valuable essay.

406 Vega V., Marta de la. El fenómeno del arte y los procesos de cambio social: reflexiones en torno a García Canclini (ECO, 41[2]:236, junio 1981, p. 147–175)

Essay on the social historical method in art history. Argues against any sort of "reductionism," especially strict formalism. Repeats previous positions of European and American scholars but does not offer specific examples. Noteworthy for the clarity of its theoretical writing.

407 Villarreal Macías, Rogelio and **Juan Mario Pérez Oronoz.** Fotografía, arte y publicidad. México: Federación Editorial Mexicana, 1979. 110 p.: bibl., ill. (Serie Arte, ciencia y sociedad; 1)

Important work by Mexican writers on largely neglected subject. Authors have succeeded in reaching their goal, "a materialist interpretation" of photography. Rather heavy-handed defense of photography as "real" art is followed by conclusion that some photographs, such as those used in advertising, are not. Briefly and persuasively presents ideological function of advertising in general. Provocative book ends with diverse selection of works by 25 contemporary Mexican photographers.

CENTRAL AMERICA

408 Arellano, Jorge Eduardo. Documental sobre la escultura en Nicaragua (BNBD, 34, marzo/abril 1980, p. 57–108, bibl., photos)

Thorough documentary essay offers complete history of sculpture in Nicaragua.

Many good illustrations, extensive bibliography. Most interesting section concerns contemporary sculptors addressing questions of aesthetics and purpose.

409 Luján Muñoz, Luis. Notas sobre la pintura mural en Guatemala (IAHG/AHG, 2:2, 1980, p. 197–213, plates)

Short but useful survey of mural painting in Guatemala from preconquest to modern times. Also includes helpful orderings into distinct categories such as "popular " or "folk" murals. Few but key illustrations.

410 Noriega, Enrique. Carlos Mérida, una expresión americana. Guatemala: Ediciones Acento, 1981. 112 p.: ill.

Useful reference book on important Guatemalan/Mexican abstract painter. Full biography is followed by critical accounts and list of major works. Very few b/w illustrations, all of poor quality.

THE CARIBBEAN

(Except Cuba)

411 Lerebours, Michel-Philippe. Haiti et ses peintres: une esthétique nouvelle (IFH/C, 149, fév. 1981, p. 7–49)

Well researched and documented essay on the question of "primitive" vs. modern art in Haiti. Traces histories of these terms both in Haiti and in Europe. Stimulating account of impact of modern aesthetics in a Third World context.

412 Miller, Jeannette. Arte dominicano contemporáneo. Curadora invitada, Jeannette Miller = Contemporary Dominican art: October 6–November 6, 1981; guest curator, Jeannette Miller. Artistas, Gaspar Mario Cruz *et al.* Translation, Edison Antigua. New York: Signs Gallery, 1981. 27 p.: ill.

Catalog essay for exhibit of eight artists makes good case for the unique character of Dominican art. Gives as main reason for this uniqueness island's political and cultural isolation from its neighbors during Trujillo regime.

CUBA

413 Havana. Museo Nacional. The National Museum of Cuba painting: the Fayum portrait, Western European painting,

Cuban painting. Translated from the Russian by Yury Nemetsky. Edited by Ricardo González Jane *et al.* Havana: Letras Cubanas, 1978. 20 p., 123 leaves of plates: ill. (some col.)

Short but informative essay on Cuban painting introduces what is essentially a catalog of Museum's collection. Full page reproductions of 123 paintings, mostly in color also serve book's documentary purpose. Comprehensive visual display not found elsewhere.

414 Medina, Alvaro. La *Revista de Avance* y la plástica cubana de los años 20 (*in* Cuba, les étapes d'une liberation. Hommage à Juan Marinello et Noël Salomon: actes du Colloque International des 22, 23 et 24 novembre 1978. Toulouse, France: Centre d'études cubaines, Université de Toulouse-Le Mirail, 1980, v. 2, p. 15–31)

Using as focus debate on art and politics in journal *Revista de Avance*, author describes Cuban art world in 1920s as motivated and structured by strong reactions to politics of 1910 and 1917 Mexican and Russian revolutions. Clearly and forcefully argued, essay advances scholarship on Latin American *avant-garde* and modernism as response to political questions.

415 Mosquera, Gerardo. Nuevas expresiones de la plástica cubana (AR, 8:30, 1982, p. 31–35, plates)

Despite tone of celebratory subjectivity, short essay provides valuable updating of current Cuban art, including conceptualist installations. Includes numerous quotes of government officials.

416 ——. La pintura cubana a través del prisma de la Revolución (URSS/AL, 2:62, feb. 1983, p. 85–99, ill.)

Concise set of statements in interview format between Cuban artist Manuel Mendive and critic Mosquera. Includes explicit and productive discussion of important questions such as what were the stylistic and ideological adjustments established in Cuba after the Revolution.

SOUTH AMERICA
ARGENTINA

417 Alva Negri, Tomás. Arte argentino y crítica europea, con versión inglesa.

Buenos Aires: Ediciones Bonino, 1975. 178 p., 9 leaves of plates: bibl., ill. (some col.)

Designed to prove positive impact of recent Argentine art on European critics, much of book seems self-congratulatory. Of real value are data on artists themselves and marketing strategies they are subject to.

418 Areán González, Carlos Antonio. La pintura en Buenos Aires. Buenos Aires: Municipalidad de la Ciudad de Buenos Aires, 1981. 243 p.: ill.

Traces history of painting in Buenos Aires from early 19th century to present. Subdivides period into concrete units of study, to which author devotes separate chapters. Well researched and convincingly argued study which nevertheless tends toward facile formalism.

419 Caride, Vicente P. Carlos Filevich, obra gráfica. Buenos Aires: Ediciones Dead Weight, 1981. 96 p.: ill. (Colección La Barca gráfica. Arte)

Useful book on graphic work of Filevich (1929–63). Includes over 70 good illustrations, introductory essay, and five critical essays by different authors. However, lacks biographical and historical data.

420 Collazo, Alberto and Jorge Glusber. Guía bibliográfica de las artes visuales en la Argentina: siglo XX. Buenos Aires: Centro de Arte y Comunicación (CAYC), 1983. 99 p.: index.

Bibliography (1060 items and addendum of 36 from 1982) is mandatory for study of contemporary art in Argentina, especially current situation in Buenos Aires. [J.W. Bailey]

421 Documentos para una historia de la arquitectura argentina. Coordinación general, Marina Waisman. Ramón Gutiérrez *et al.* Buenos Aires: Ediciones Summa, 1978. ca. 250 p.: bibl., ill.

Consists of essays by 30 architects and one archaeologist which cover subject from pre-colonial period to present. Generously illustrated with fair-to-poor photographs. Book includes very valuable documentation accompanied by straightforward commentary as well as highly didactic pronouncements. Important contribution even if of mixed quality.

422 Kosice, Gyula. Arte Madí. Buenos Aires: Ediciones de Arte Gaglianone, 1982. 198 p.: ill. (some col.)

Important account of Madí art movement active in 1940s Buenos Aires. Author, one of its original founders, gave it its name. Provides history of Madí updated manifesto, and illustrates and documents this movement as thoroughly as possible. Also includes long bibliography. Key source for modernism in Argentina.

423 Mario J. Buschiazzo, su obra escrita. Buenos Aires: Universidad de Buenos Aires, Facultad de Arquitectura y Urbanismo, Instituto de Arte Americano-Mario J. Buschiazzo, 1981. 56 p.: index, port. (Colección Publicaciones de apoyo a la investigación; 1)

Lists more than 300 works on and by this contemporary Argentine architectural/historian. [R.J. Mullen]

424 Pagano, José León. El arte de los argentinos. Buenos Aires: Editorial y Librería Goncourt, 1981. 231 p.: bibl., index.

New edition of 1937 text, updated by author's son. Organized as an encyclopedia, it is a useful and accurate reference tool. No illustrations.

425 Running, Thorpe. Enrique Molina: an Argentine's alliance with Dalí (ASU/LAD, 15:1, 1980, p. 4–5, 20, ill.)

Useful account of Molina's methods as a surrealist in both poetry and painting, as well as brief history of surrealism in Argentina and its relationship to the European source.

426 Schiaffino, Eduardo. La evolución del gusto artístico en Buenos Aires. Recopilado por Godofredo E.J. Canale. Buenos Aires: F.A. Colombo, 1982. 159 p.: ill.

Mixed presentation consists of encyclopedic entries on individual figures and longer essays on subjects related to the rise and development of aesthetic theory and practice in 19th- and 20th-century Buenos Aires. Of some documentary interest.

CHILE

427 Galaz, Caspar and **Milan Ivelíc.** La pintura en Chile desde la colonia hasta 1981. Valparaíso, Chile: Universidad Católica de Valparaíso, Ediciones Universitarias de Valparaíso, 1981. 393 p., viii p. of plates: bibl., ill. (some col.) index (El Rescate)

Massive and comprehensive treatment of modern painting in Chile. Authors cover ground with refreshing and straightforward expertise, presenting a complex period with coherence and clarity. Book is treasurehouse of illustrations, all excellent, many in color. Includes good bibliography and useful index which makes book an indispensable tool on its subject.

Guarda, Gabriel. Conjuntos urbanos, históricos, arquitectónicos: Valdivia, siglos XVIII-XIX. See item **323.**

428 Munizaga Vigil, Gustavo. Cronología sobre urbanismo y diseño urbano en Chile, 1870–1970 (Revista Latinoamericana de Estudios Urbanos Regionales: EURE [Pontificia Universidad Católica de Chile, Instituto de Planificación del Desarrollo Urbano y Regional, Santiago] 6:18, agosto 1980, p. 69–90)

Very useful and exhaustive listing of studies and buildings, as part of city planning in Chile. Commentary is concise and well researched.

COLOMBIA

429 Nel Gómez, Pedro. Pedro Nel Gómez. Bogotá: Benjamín Villegas & Asociados: OP Gráficas, 1981. ca. 200 p.: chiefly ill. (some col.)

Lavish picture book documents major works of important Colombian muralist as well as his works in other media. Includes useful and straightforward short critical essay and autobiographical comments by the artist.

430 Roda, Juan Antonio. Juan Antonio Roda, obra gráfica, 1970–1981. Bogotá: C. Valencia Editores, 1982. 161 p.: ill.

Major Colombian printmaker is given lavish treatment. Includes more than 30 finely printed reproductions, essay by artist explaining his additive method of composition which he illustrates with 10 stages of one work; and short essay of appreciation. Well-rounded treatment, although not scholarly in intention.

ECUADOR

431 Benavides Solís, Jorge. El conflicto urbano: crónicas. Quito: Facultad de Arquitectura y Urbanismo de la Universidad

Central, 1979. 121 p., 16 leaves of plates: ill.

Native Ecuadorian architect presents 22 short critical essays on subjects ranging from precolumbian architecture to lack of recreational urban spaces in modern Quito. His methods encompass the sociological to the psychological. Important meditations by a practitioner/critic.

432 Esteban Mejía, Manuel. La pintura abstracta y neofigurativa en 150 años de vida republicana (*in* Arte y cultura, Ecuador, 1830–1980. Fernando Tinajero Villamar *et al.* Quito: Corporación Editora Nacional, 1980, p. 475–488 [Libro del sesquicentenario; 2])

Essay traces ongoing debate between supporters of abstraction and figuration in 19th- and 20th-century Ecuadorian art. Explanations are clearly organized and should encourage further study.

433 Vargas, José María. Visión global de las artes plásticas en ciento cincuenta años de vida republicana (*in* Arte y cultura: Ecuador, 1830–1980. Fernando Tinajero Villamar *et al.* Quito: Corporación Editora Nacional, 1980, p. 421–430 [Libro del sesquicentenario; 2])

Very short but good synthesis of 19th- and 20th-century Ecuadorian art. Writing is descriptive rather than critical, listing only major names and trends.

VENEZUELA

434 Anuario de Arquitectura. Proimagen Editores. 1981– . Caracas.

Excellent resource, this annual publication includes historical and critical essays. Illustrated with many photographs, some in good color, and dozens of plans and drawings. Premise is documentary, rather than didactic, and succeeds in presenting a generous cross-section of national production for 1981.

435 Boulton, Alfredo. Narváez. Caracas: Macano Ediciones, 1981. 136 p.: ill.

Documentary photo-journal of important Venezuelan sculptor. Excellent b/w photographs and complete biography traces key works and events of his life. Major mistake is lack of bibliography.

436 Calzadillas, Juan. Notas para una formación social del arte venezolano

(CONAC/RNC, 41:247, abril/dic. 1981, p. 91–110)

Essay delivers more than title promises. Includes short and useful history of collectors, patrons, criticism, galleries, museums, and art organizations during last two centuries, all of them thoroughly researched. Nevertheless, more useful as documentary source than as analysis.

437 Delgado, Sonia and **Rafael Delgado.** Fuentes de las artes plásticas en Venezuela. Caracas: E. Armitano, 1981. 231 p., l folded leaf: col. ill., index.

Very valuable treatment of modernism in Venezuelan art covers major developments since late 19th century and traces them to European sources. Authors have marshalled an impressive volume of material, both documentary and visual, and present it in such a persuasive way that it could serve as a model on the subject.

438 Dorronsoro, Josune. Significación histórica de la fotografía. Reproducción de fotografías, Vladimir Sersa. Caracas: Equinoccio, Editorial de la Universidad Simón Bolívar, 1981. 139 p.: ill. (Colección Rescate)

Essential book for the study of the subject in Venezuela; author places development of photography therein (ch. 2) in an international and historical context (ch. 1). [J. W. Bailey]

438a Grupo Cinco, *Caracas.* Juan Félix Sánchez. Alberto Arvelo, escritor. Sigfrido Geyer, fotógrafo. Caracas: Fundación La Salle de Ciencias Naturales, 1981. 190 p.: col. ill.

Author of introduction exhorts critics not simply to tolerate "naif" artists but to understand and promote them. Hence this beautiful book presents the intensely personal world of a contemporary village sculptor to a sophisticated audience. His life is hauntingly portrayed with simple snapshots. Exemplary, unforgettable. [R.J. Mullen]

439 Jait, Vladimir. Arquitectura moderna de Venezuela (URSS/AL, 9:45, p. 105–116, plates)

Short but ambitious article traces roots of modernism in Venezuelan architecture. Raises many questions of client's needs, urban development, and social impact of buildings. Although mediocre, illustrations serve his purpose well.

440 Noriega, Simón. La crítica de arte en Venezuela. Mérida, Venezuela: Universidad de los Andes, Facultad de Humanidades y Educación, Escuela de Letras, Departamento de Arte, 1979. 230 p. (Colección Actual. Serie Arte)

Useful synthesis and analysis of criticism and historiography in 19th and 20th centuries. Devotes most attention to 20th century by highlighting six critics of painting. Includes separate chapter on architecture and long bibliography.

441 ———. La pintura de Héctor Poleo. Mérida, Venezuela: Talleres Gráficos Universitarios, 1983. 116 p.: bibl., ill.

Important new source for the study of the artist. Includes developmental analysis of artist's style (1930 to present); chronology, bibliography, with fair b/w illustrations. [J.W. Bailey]

442 Nunes, Jorge. Rengifo. Caracas: E. Armitano, 1981. 184 p.: bibl., ill. (some col.) (Serie Pintores venezolanos)

Short biographical essay is followed by useful bibliography and excellent reproductions of over 100 paintings. Both generalist and specialist will appreciate essay's content. It shows Rengifo as an able and intriguing recorder of social and intimate life in Venezuela.

443 Pineda, Rafael. Narváez, la escultura hasta Narváez. Caracas: E. Armitano, 1980. 293 p.: bibl., ill. (some col.) index.

Essentially an argument for the "greatness" and "inevitability" of the sculptor Narváez. Half of book is devoted to 19th-century Venezuelan sculpture which prepared the ground for Narváez. Includes very useful illustrations and documentation, but text tends toward the congratulatory.

444 Rodríguez, Bélgica. Breve historia de la escultura contemporánea en Venezuela. Caracas: FUNDARTE, 1979. 75 p., 14 p. of plates: bibl., ill. (En Venezuela; 9)

Brief introduction to subject is well written, researched, and illustrated. Seeks roots of Venezuelan modernism in a Latin American rather than European context. Lucid critical commentary.

445 Sheleshniova, Natalia. La pintura en busca de la expresión nacional (URSS/AL, 12, 1980, p. 106–113)

Short but informative account of Venezuelan painters of this century who have been concerned with question of a "national" style.

BRAZIL

JOSÉ NEISTEIN, *Executive Director, Brazilian-American Cultural Institute*

AMONG WORKS SELECTED for this section, there are some theoretical studies and reference aids that deserve special mention: the most complete iconography of the Northeast by Clarival do Prado Valladares (item **461**); an original theoretical contribution by Fayga Ostrower (item **456**); a study that establishes the typology of the art book in Brazil (item **452**); several works that meticulously account for the historical patrimony of many Brazilian regions (items **451** and **458–460**); and a compilation of essays by one of the keenest critics to write on Brazil (item **457**).

Other contributions describe lesser known aspects of colonial art (items **466** and **469**). A study of Brazilian furniture design makes an excellent contribution (item **463**) and another work commemorates 400 years of the Saint Benedict Monastery in Bahia (item **467**).

On the 19th century there is one outstanding survey by Quirino Campofiorito (item **471**) and some interesting monographs on the period (items **472–474**).

Works on the 20th century are as numerous in this volume as in *HLAS 44* and include some important catalogues and monographs (items **479–481, 486, 488,** and **490–493**). There are also some worthwhile studies of folk art (items **496–497**).

Several books on photography merit special attention for their high standards and overall quality (items **498** and **500–501**).

Works on city planning and architecture make a stimulating, varied and rich subsection below. There are some notable monographs on cities (items **502** and **508–510**) and others on aspects on Brazilian architectural history (items **503–505**, **511**, and **513**), including an informative polemic (item **512**).

Two books in the Miscellaneous subsection are original contributions to their respective fields (items **516–517**).

REFERENCE AND THEORETICAL WORKS

446   Bardi, Pietro Maria. Arte da cerâmica no Brasil. São Paulo: Banco Sudameris Brasil, 1980. 148 p.: bibl., col. ill. (Arte e cultura; 3)

In spite of many books and essays on the art of clay in Brazil, this is the first attempt at offering an overall view that includes pre- and post-colonial Indian artifacts and folk ceramics. Examines Portuguese, Oriental, French, English, Dutch, Italian and other influences, along with contributions of 20th-century creative artists. Excellent photographs taken mostly from private collections in São Paulo.

447 ———. Mestres, artífices, oficiais e aprendizes no Brasil. São Paulo: Banco Sudameris Brasil, 1981. 173 p.: ill. (some col.), facsims., ports. (Arte e cultura; 4)

Studies how craftsmanship developed throughout Brazilian history in the form of guilds or corporations. Examines materials used such as wood, iron, leather, fabrics and gold; describes skills, design, and technology; and notes relevance of fishing, cooking, clothing, jewelry and naive art. Many appropiate b/w illustrations.

448   Brancante, Eldino da Fonseca. O Brasil e a cerâmica antiga. São Paulo: E.F. Brancante, 1981. 730 p.: ill. (some col.)

This book is a general history of both ceramics found in Brazil but produced elsewhere as well as those produced in Brazil or expressly for Brazil. Fine reference work. Comprehensive text and wealth of photographs.

449   Costa, Maria Heloisa Fénelon. A arte e o artista na sociedade karajá. Brasília: Fundação Nacional do Indio, Departamento Geral de Planejamento Comunitário, Divisão de Estudos e Pesquisas, 1978. 196 p.: bibl., ill. (some col.)

Survey of Karajá Indian art and artists of Santa Isabel (southwest of Ilha do Bananal, Goiás) which is now the Parque Nacional do Araguaia. Includes body-painting, textiles, ceramics, children's drawings and designs. [J.W. Bailey]

450   Gullar, Ferreira. Sobre arte. Rio de Janeiro: Avenir Editora; São Paulo: Palavra e Imagem Editora, 1982. 66 p.

Consists of speculative essays on art in general and Brazilian art written 1975–80 by Gullar, avant-garde artist, poet and one of the most influential intellectuals of his generation. Subjects include: meaning of art, art in an industrial society, art and merchandise, art and the influence of mass culture, design, and naive art. Original contribution.

451   IPAC-BA: Inventário de Proteção do Acervo Cultural da Bahia. v. 3, Monumentos e sítios da Serra Geral e Chapada Diamantina. v. 4, Monumentos e Sítios do Recôncavo. Salvador: Secretaría da Indústria e Comércio, 1982. 2 v. (386 p., 393 p.): bibl., ill.

Two more volumes of invaluable survey of Bahia historic structures. Vols. 3/4 meticulously describe each house or church of historical interest. They give current use, plan, photographic record and suggest possible future uses after restoration. Complete inventory includes streets, furniture, implements and religious art. Standard work for art historians.

452   Knychala, Catarina Helena. O livro de arte brasileiro. v. 1, Teoria, história, descrição, 1808–1980. Rio de Janeiro: Presença, 1983– . 1 v.: bibl., ill.

Defines and establishes what is an art book and describes and classifies Brazilian production in this regard. Considers only works of aesthetic value and examines paper quality, typeset, layout, binding, etc., whether illustrated or not. Probably the first systematic history of Brazilian art books.

453 Maia, Isa. Realidade do artesão e do artesanato da região Sul (PUC/V, 28:109, março 1983, p. 82–88, bibl.)

Brief survey of crafts and artisans in three southern states, Paraná, Santa Catarina and Rio Grande do Sul. [J.W. Bailey]

454 Marino, João. Coleção de arte brasileira. São Paulo: Raízes Artes Gráficas, 1983. 319 p.: ill. (some col.)

Unique, splendid book, written by one of Brazil's major collectors of Brazilian art. Both collection and book cover religious imagery from 16th-19th centuries: painting, furniture, folk carvings, naive painting, silver, pewter, and metalwork. Comprehensive look at Brazilian art throughout its history. Special section devoted to indigenous art before discovery by Portuguese.

455 Museu Nacional de Belas Artes, *Brasil.* Museu Nacional de Belas Artes. Texto, seleção das obras reproduzidas, pesquisa, normalização de texto e revisão, Edson Motta e equipe do Museu Nacional de Belas Artes. Rio de Janeiro: Ministério da Educação e Cultura, Fundação Nacional de Arte, Instituto Nacional de Artes Plásticas, 1979. 193 p.: bibl., ill. (some col.), index, 1 plan, ports. (Coleção Museus brasileiros; 1)

One of Brazil's major art museums, the MNBA is particularly important for its collection of works by Brazilian painters from colonial times to present. Includes history of museum and extensive description of collection. Color reproductions are fair.

456 Ostrower, Fayga. Universos da arte. Rio de Janeiro: Editora Campus, 1983. 358 p.: ill. (some col.)

One of Brazil's foremost artists, Fayga has been teaching theory of art for over 20 years. In this book she discusses work and personality, space structure and expressivity of form, perception and intuition in the creative process, art and life fulfillment. Rich, complex text developed from course given to workers in a Rio factory. Very appropriate illustrations. Original theoretical contribution.

457 Pedrosa, Mário. Dos murais de Portinari aos espaços de Brasília. Organização, Aracy A. Amaral. São Paulo: Editora Perspectiva, 1981. 421 p. (Coleção Debates; 170)

Mario Pedrosa, a humanist, was one of Brazil's sharpest art critics. Complementing previous collection of his essays "Mundo, Homem, Arte em Crise." Editora Perspectiva now publishes vol. 2 devoted both to Brazil's finest artists (1930–70s) and to Brasília's architecture, including historical, cultural and artistic features. Indispensable.

458 Plano de preservação dos sítios históricos: região metropolitana do Recife. Recife: Governo do Estado de Pernambuco, Secretaria de Planejamento, Fundação de Desenvolvimento da Região Metropolitana do Recife, 1978. 391 p.: bibl., ill. (some col.)

Provides detailed plan for the preservation of historical—and in many cases artistic—sites of Recife, including background on and "diagnosis" of present structural condition, maps and floor plans. Standard reference book.

459 Plano de preservação dos sítios históricos do interior (PPSHI). pt. 1, Municípios do litoral e do circuito de Fazenda Nova. Governo do Estado de Pernambuco, Secretaria de Planejamento, Fundação de Desenvolvimento Municipal do Interior de Pernambuco/FIAM. Recife: FIAM, 1982. 1 v.: bibl., ill.

Pt. 1 of plan for the preservation of historical—and in many instances also artistic—sites in Pernambuco's interior. Standard reference book includes maps, plans, analytical charts, and considers topography, environment, historical background, etc.

460 Souza, Oswaldo Câmara de. Acervo do património histórico e artístico do Estado do Rio Grande do Norte. Natal: Edição Fundação José Augusto, 1981. 427 p.: ill.

Description and photographs of civilian, military and religious architecture of Rio Grande do Norte as well as 17th-19th century religious imagery, both before and after restoration. One of the best inventories of Rio Grande do Norte.

461 Valladares, Clarival do Prado. Nordeste histórico e monumental. v. 1, O descobrimento, a catequese, os jesuitas, as entradas, a natureza, a caminho do sertão, Piauí, Maranhão, Ceará, Rio Grande do Norte, Paraíba, Pernambuco. v. 2, Temas nordestinos na música erudita contemporânea. Salvador: Odebrecht, 1982. 2 v.: bibl., col. ill.; index, 1 sound disc (33⅓ rpm, stereo; 12 in.)

Most comprehensive, rigorous, and beautiful work of its kind. Covers all Northeastern states and virtually all art forms, including iconography of music, from colonial times to present. It is the late Valladares' last major work and will remain the standard for years to come. English-Portuguese bilingual edition.

462 Wagner, Renato. Jóia contemporânea brasileira = Brazilian contemporary jewelry. São Paulo: R. Wagner, 1980. 267 p.: bibl., ill. (some col.) index.

Some of Brazil's most representative creative jewelry designers are included in this deluxe book. Introduction covers precolumbian to 20th-century Brazilian jewelry. Provides biographical sketch and brief analysis of each artist.

COLONIAL PERIOD

463 Canti, Tilde. O móvel no Brasil: origens, evolução e características. Rio de Janeiro: Cândido Guinle de Paula Machado, 1980. 340 p.: bibl., ill. (some col.), plans.

Not the first but probably the most comprehensive study of Brazilian furniture, from first half of 15th to mid-19th century. Provides preliminary study of Portuguese furniture. Also analyzes English and Dutch influences. Richly illustrated with photographs and drawings. Includes glossary and bibliography.

464 Ferreira, Delson Gonçalves. O Aleijadinho. Belo Horizonte: Editora Comunicação em convênio com a Secretaria de Cultura, Turismo e Esportes da Prefeitura de Belo Horizonte, 1981. 156 p.: bibl., ill.

Both a personal and historical approach to Aleijadinho, this dynamic essay relates the artist to political and economic issues of his day and discusses Aleijadinho's mysticism, his hands, figures of Christ, even his Latin and handwriting. Also considers Germain Bazin's approach. Ultimately a study of the mulatto's contribution to Brazilian intellectual and artistic expression. Won the 1981 Cidade de Belo Horizonte Prize.

465 Lambru, Dimitri. Jóias da arte sacra brasileira. 126 fotografias de Dimitri Lambru. Textos de Walmir Ayala. Rio de

Janeiro: Colorama, 1981? 154 p.: bibl., col. ill.

Representative selection of Brazil's religious art from 17th and 18th centuries, basically from Bahia, Pernambuco and Minas Gerais. Brief introductory notes. Very good photographs.

466 Levy, Hannah and **Luiz Jardim.** Pintura e escultura I. São Paulo: Ministério da Edução e Cultura, Instituto do Patrimônio Histórico e Artístico Nacional: Universidade de São Paulo, Faculdade de Arquitetura e Urbanismo, 1978. 230 p.: bibl., ill. (Textos escolhidos da Revista do Instituto do Patrimônio Histórico e Artístico Nacional; 7)

Painting, although less consequential than Brazilian colonial architecture and sculpture, is also important, albeit less studied. This work, by including portraits which are very little known, enhances the importance of these texts. Welcome contribution.

467 400 [i.e. Quatrocentos] anos do Mosteiro de São Bento da Bahia, The Monastery of Saint Benedict of Bahia: its 400 years. Paulo Rocha *et al.* Salvador: O Mosteiro: Construtora Norberto Odebrecht, 1982. 164 p.: bibl., ill. (some col.)

In order to commemorate the fourth centennial of Bahia's Monastery of Saint Benedict, oldest of its kind in the New World, this trilingual publication reassesses the religious, historical and artistic significance of that monastery in Bahian and Brazilian history. Particularly underscores importance of colonial sculptors Friars Agostinho da Piedade and Agostinho de Jesus and architect Friar Macário de São João.

468 Salles, Fritz Teixeira de. Vila Rica do Pilar. Ilustrações, Haroldo Matos. Belo Horizonte: Editora Itatiaia; São Paulo: Editora da Universidade de São Paulo, 1982. 235 p.: bibl., ill. (Coleção Reconquista do Brasil; nova sér. vol. 71. Biblioteca de estudos brasileiros; 1)

Historical essay along with artistic and intellectual appreciation of founding, development and decadence of Ouro Preto, originally known as Vila Rica do Pilar. Insightfully analyzes its splendor and major artists. Also considers principal political issues. Fine contribution. Illustrated with pen and ink drawings.

469 Smith, Robert Chester. Igrejas, casas e móveis: aspectos da arte colonial brasileira. Recife: Ministério da Educação e

Cultura, Universidade Federal de Pernambuco, Instituto do Patrimonio Histórico e Artístico Nacional, 1979. 383 p.: 31 leaves of plates: bibl., ill.

First Brazilian one-volume compilation of Robert C. Smith's studies of his beloved Pernambuco, many never before available in Portuguese. Pays tribute to the foreign art historian and critic who best understood Brazilian colonial art.

470 Valladares, Clarival do Prado. Aspectos da arte religiosa no Brasil: Bahia, Pernambuco, Paraíba. Salvador: Odebrecht; Rio de Janeiro: Spala Editora, 1981. 388 p.: bibl., chiefly col. ill., index. ill., index.

Meticulously describes main churches and all types of religious iconography produced in Bahia, Pernambuco and Paraíba during 16th-19th centuries. Includes beautiful color photographs of 221 items. Deluxe edition.

19TH CENTURY

471 Campofiorito, Quirino. História da pintura brasileira no século XIX. s.l.: Edições Pinakotheke, 1983. 291 p.: ill. (some col.) (Série Ouro; SO–3)

Analyzes major trends: what remained from colonial times; French Artistic Mission and followers; Dom Pedro II's protection of painters during Second Empire; Republic and decadence of neoclassical discipline. Good period. Many b/w reproductions, some very good in color.

472 Ferrez, Gilberto. O álbum de Luís Schlappriz: memória de Pernambuco: álbum para os amigos das artes, 1863. Recife: Fundação de Cultura Cidade do Recife, 1981. 90 p.: bibl., ill.

Swiss artist L. Schlappriz produced 33 lithographs (1863–65) of vistas and street scenes of Recife and surroundings. G. Ferrez puts this set of photographs together for first time. Others by other artists were produced in Europe, but this set, the first one produced locally, is a rare piece of Brasiliana.

473 Levy, Carlos Roberto Maciel. Antônio Parreiras (1860–1937), pintor de paisagem: gênero e história. Rio de Janeiro: Edições Pinakotheke, 1981. 204 p.: bibl., ill. (some col.) index.

Probably best scholarly study yet published on Parreiras, book includes biography, excerpts of previously published texts, comparative chronology, bibliography, scientific considerations, historical and dialectical discussions, and inventory of Parreiras' output. His integrity and creative perspectives are text's main concern. Many documentary b/w photographs and adequate color ones.

474 Mello Júnior, Donato. Facchinetti. São Paulo: Art Editora; Rio: Editora Record, 1982. 45 p., 6, 98 p. of plates: bibl., ill. (some col.)

Brazilian art historians and critics have rediscovered Facchinetti in recent years. He grew up and developed as landscape painter in Rio de Janeiro during Second Empire. Strongly influenced by realism and impressionism, he reached his peak during the Republic's first years, specializing in Brazilian landscape.

475 Pintores da paisagem paranaense. Curitiba: Secretaria de Estado da Cultura e do Esporte, 1982. 120 p.: bibl., col. ill., index.

Paraná's landscape and seascape is seen here chiefly through canvases and drawings of Alfredo Andersen (1860–1936)—considered the father of "paranaense" painting—as well as those of his disciples, followers of Lange de Morretes, and foreign and Brazilian artists of later generations. Many artistic tendencies are represented. Excellent reproductions.

476 Pires, Fernando Tasso Fragoso. Antigas fazendas de café da província fluminense. Rio de Janeiro: Editora Nova Fronteira, 1980. 111 p.: bibl., ill. (Memória brasileira)

State of Rio's coffee plantations were the first in Brazil. They spanned the 19th century, from colony's end to Empire's last days. Rio's manors represent a wealth of architecture beautifully portrayed in this book, in both the historical text and its good photographs. Art history, however, is somewhat lacking.

20TH CENTURY

477 Amaral, Aracy A. Arte e meio artístico: entre a feijoada e o x-burguer, 1961–1981. São Paulo: Nobel, 1982. 423 p.: bibl., index.

Compilation covers great variety of

subjects researched or reviewed in essays conceived for very different occasions and purposes (e.g., coordinates of Brazilian modern art from folk art to avant-garde experiments to São Paulo's Biennial, other institutions, their implications in Brazil itself and repercussions abroad).

478   Andrade, Mário de. Cartas de trabalho: correspôndencia com Rodrigo Mello Franco de Andrade, 1936–1945. Brasília: Ministério da Educação e Cultura, Secretaria do Patrimônio Histórico e Artístico Nacional, Fundação Nacional Pró-Memória, 1981. 191 p.: ill. (Publicações da Secretaria do Patrimônio Histórico e Artístico Nacional; no. 33)

This correspondence reflects the self-awareness of modern Brazil as two seminal personalities discuss the creation of SPHAN, an agency charged with the protection of the nation's artistic treasures, a task of major importance. Edition enhanced by drawings, photographs and notes. A must.

479   Araújo, Olívio Tavares de. Thomaz. São Paulo: Editora Grifo, 1980. 88 p.: ill. (some col.)

Frederico Morais once defined contemporary Brazilian painter Thomaz Ianelli as being "a path between Volpi and Klee." Incisive study covers his apprenticeship years; describes color, texture, signs and style, transfigured reality, search for the absolute; and includes critical anthology and short biography. Many good color reproductions.

480   Bento, Antônio. Portinari. Rio de Janeiro: L. Christiano Editorial, 1980. 366 p.: bibl., ill. (some col.), index.

Bento, dean of Brazilian art critics, covers the entire output of Portinari, one of Brazil's major painters. Main proposals and single works are covered in 72 chapters, eight appendices and 212 reproductions both in color and b/w. Colors do not always do justice to originals.

481   Bianco, livro-documento. Rio de Janeiro: Léo Christiano Editorial, 1982. 284 p.: ill. (some col.), index, port.

This book-document is the standard work on Enrico Bianco (b. Rome 1918) who emigrated to Brazil at 18, and developed his skills as an artist with Portinari. Book reviews and reproduces major paintings and drawings. Many essays on his output include those by Mário de Andrade, Sérgio Milliet, P.M. Bardi, Lourival Gomes Machado and Carlos Drummond de Andrade.

482   Do modernismo à Bienal. Apresentação do Museu de Arte Moderna, Luiz Seráphico de Assis Carvalho. Apresentação da exposição, Ilsa Kawall Leal Ferreira. Textos, Marta Bastista Rosseti, Fábio Magalhães, Radhá Abramo. Colaboradores, Carmem Maria M.M. Maldi *et al.* Fotos, Rômulo Fialdini, Paulo Vasconcelos. São Paulo: Museu de Arte Moderna de São Paulo, 1982. 167 p.: ill. (some col.)

Catalogue is worthwhile less for the short and generalized introductory texts than for the iconography of the period. Illustrates main trends of Brazilian art from 1920s to 1950s, including lesser known examples as well as established ones.

483   Giorgi, Bruno. Bruno Giorgi. Editor, Marcos Antônio Marcondes. Fotógrafo, Rômulo Fialdini. São Paulo: Art Editora; Rio de Janeiro: Editora Record, 1980. 30 p., 64 leaves of plates: bibl., chiefly ill. (some col.)

Most important living Brazilian sculptor does not belong to any "schools" as currently established. Therefore, text tries to determine his uniqueness. Includes chronology and photographs. Reproductions provide an account of his aesthetic trajectory.

484   Gonçalves, Luiz Felipe. Sigaud, o pintor dos operários. Rio de Janeiro?: L.F. Editorial Independente, 1980. 137 p.: bibl., ill. (some col.) index.

Sigaud (1899–1979) has been consistently influential in Brazil, as exemplified by this book. From among his many subjects, those related to the working class and religious history are the most important. His development goes from academicism to constructivism and expressionism.

485   Gullar, Ferreira. Newton Rezende. Rio de Janeiro: Edições Galeria Bonino, 1980. 127 p.: bibl., chiefly col. ill.

Paintings and drawings of this contemporary Brazilian painter of surrealism, humor and social criticism are preceded by studies of his "semantics" by author Gullar, Antônio Houaiss, Otto Maria Carpeaux and Mauro Villar. Good color reproductions.

486   ———; Mário Pedrosa; and Lygia Clark. Lygia Clark. Rio de Janeiro:

Funarte, 1980. 58 p.: ill. (some col.) (Arte Brasileira contemporânea)

Lygia Clark was a consistent participant in Rio de Janeiro's avant-garde movements that followed the 1959 "Exposição Neoconcreta." Her many ideas, media and creative processes are evident here in word and image. Two texts about her are already classics: Gullar's "Uma Experiência Radical" and Pedrosa's "Significação de Lygia Clark."

487   Klintowitz, Jacob. A cor na arte brasileira: 27 artistas representativos = Colour in Brazilian art. s.l.: Volkswagen do Brasil, 1982. 218 p.: ill. (some col.)

Author chose period 1917–present to show multiplicity of expression in Brazilian painting through color, from naive and intuitive artists to the very sophisticated. Beautifully varied reproductions are stunningly printed and text is short. Author preferred to let these images speak for themselves.

488   A Modernidade em Guignard. s.l.: Empresas Petróleo Ipiranga, 198?. 179 p.: ill. (some col.) (Curso de especialização em história da arte no Brasil)

Collection of essays attempts to encompass implications of Alberto da Veiga Guignard's oeuvre in modern Brazil both as artist and teacher. Includes reproductions, statements, photographs, documents, biography, and bibliography. Successful enterprise.

489   Morais, Frederico. Núcleo Bernardelli: arte brasileira nos anos 30 a 40. Rio de Janeiro: Edições Pinakotheke, 1982. 136 p.: bibl., ill. (some col.), index, ports.

Young artists who worked with Bernardelli brothers (1931–42) contributed much to the arts in Rio de Janeiro of that period. Their work was one of the consequences but also an alternative to propositions of São Paulo's 1922 Week of Modern Art. Text underscores political and social issues of the day in order to situate the resulting art.

490   Museu Nacional de Belas Artes, *Brasil.* Carlos Oswald no Museu Nacional de Belas Artes do Rio de Janeiro, 1982. Orlando Dasilva. Rio de Janeiro: O Museu, 1982. 102 p.: ill. (some col.)

Carlos Oswald (1882–1971) was Brazil's pioneer in etchings. This catalog of the master's posthumous Rio show covers most of the best he produced in that medium. Also

includes paintings, bibliography, and English/French résumés.

491   Oswaldo Goeldi. Rio de Janeiro: Solar Grandjean de Montigny-PUC/RJ, 1981? 130 p.: bibl., ill.

One of the leading masters in Brazilian printmaking, Oswaldo Goeldi was influenced by the expressionists and active 1920s–50s when he exerted a strong influence on Brazilian art. Collection of essays protrays him as illustrator and describes his technique, drawings, and uniqueness. Also includes letters from Kubin to Goeldi.

492   Valladares, Clarival do Prado. Alberto Valença: um estudo biográfico e crítico. Salvador: Construtora Norberto Odebrecht, 1980. 359 p.: bibl., col. ill., index.

Standard work on Alberto Valença, Bahia's best landscape painter. His seascapes, portraits, architecture and interior canvases are also highly regarded by peers and critics. These excellent 132 color reproductions are preceded by detailed biobibliography and sharp critical appraisal. Brazilian "veristic" painter was a third generation disciple of Corot.

493   Volpi, Alfredo. Volpi a construção da catedral. Ensaio introdutório de Olívio Tavares de Araújo. Projeto editorial de Ladi Biezus. São Paulo: MAM-Museu de Arte Moderna de São Paulo: Logos Engenharia, 1981. 101 p.: col. ill.

Sharp text discusses how Volpi intuitively "reinvented" certain forms in modern art by creating his own secularized cathedrals through subtle use of color and constructivistic modes of the triangle. Point is well illustrated with appropriate examples. Well printed edition.

494   Zilio, Carlos. A querela do Brasil: a questão da identidade da arte brasileira: a obra de Tarsila, Di Cavalcanti e Portinari, 1922–1945. Rio de Janeiro: Edição Funarte, 1982. 139 p.: bibl., ill. (some col.), index (Temas e debates / MEC/FUNARTE; 1)

Book seeks a Brazilian cultural identity, a "Brazilian space," through a study of paintings by Tarsila, Di Cavalcanti and Portinari. Draws sharp comparisons with Picasso, Matisse, Duchamp, Magritte, and Russian modern art. Study's ultimate concerns are art and intellectual activity in modern Brazil.

FOLK ART

495 O Artesão tradicional e seu papel na sociedade contemporânea = The traditional artisan and his role in contemporary society. Berta G. Ribeiro *et al.* Rio de Janeiro: FUNARTE/Instituto Nacional do Folclore, 1983. 253 leaves: bibl., ill.

Essays by seven authors question the significance and cover many aspects of crafts today: for whom and for what their traditions and social change, theoretical inquiries, the beauty of everyday objects, and a study on ethnozoology among the Karajá. Bibliography.

496 Coimbra, Silvia Rodrigues; Flávia Martins; and Maria Letícia Duarte. O reinado da lua: escultores populares do Nordeste. Rio de Janeiro: Editora Salamandra, 1980. 305 p.: bibl., ill., ports.

Studies principal folk sculptors of Brazil's Northeast whether secular or religious. Includes artists from nine states. Excellent photographs of wood and clay pieces. Objective, descriptive texts. Includes many personal statements and bibliography.

497 Dansot, Edmond. Arte popular pernambucana. Edmond Dansot, fotografías. Ricardo Ramos, textos. s.l.: Sistema Financeiro Francês e Brasileiro-Credibanco, 1982. 124 p.: chiefly col. ill.

First class source of information on the wealth and variety of Pernambucan folk art primarily because the photographs sharp observation, careful selection, and an artistic approach. Illustrates all possible forms and materials with commentaries.

PHOTOGRAPHY

498 Bahia. Mário Cravo Neto, fotografia. Jorge Amado, texto. São Paulo: Raízes, 1980. 129 p.: bibl., chiefly col. ill.

One of the finest books of color photographs of Bahia ever produced. Images are perceptive, sensitive, and revealing. Uniqueness of Bahia's capital, Salvador, is brought to bear through her architecture, Baroque traditions, current city life, ethnicity, folk traditions. A document and a work of art.

499 Brasília ano 20: depoimento de 35 fotógrafos de Brasília. Brasília: Agil, 1980. 92 p.: ports.

Covers 20 years of Brasília's history to show how, in many respects, its further development diverged from the original plan. Perceives such divergence as reflecting Brazilian "humanity" in its many contrasts. A document for the future insofar as much of it concerns the recent past.

500 Henrique, Pedro. Impressão do Brasil. Fotografía, Pedro Henrique. Projeto gráfico/roteiro, Ziraldo. São Paulo: Olivetti, 1981. 124 p.: col. ill.

Henrique's color photographs capture the beauty of Brazil and the soul of her people: landscape, past and present architecture, variety of faces. Very successful artistic project.

501 Krajcberg, Frans. A cidade de São Luis do Maranhão. Fotos, Frans Krajcberg. Texto, Luiz Seráphico. São Paulo: Rhodia, 1981. 141 p.: col. ill.

It is said that São Luis do Maranhão is the Ouro Preto of Northern Brazil and justifiably so. Krajcberg's color photographs do full justice to São Luis stunning beauties. Text discusses origin, history, the Jesuits' presence, and the black African contribution, as well as the city's celebrated tiles.

CITY PLANNING AND ARCHITECTURE

502 Belo Horizonte: de Curral del Rei à Pampulha. Apresentação, coordenação de textos e assessoria geral, Paulo Mendes Campos. Programação gráfica de Ronald Andrade. Belo Horizonte: Centrais Elétricas de Minas Gerais, 1982. 126 p.: ill., ports.

Remarkable collection of photographs and statements from a variety of personalities attest to many changes undergone by Belo Horizonte, still a village towards the end of the 19th century. Covers turn of the century, city planning, 1920s, 1930s and 1940s, and many aspects of public and private life. Good reference work and exercise in nostalgia as well.

503 Carvalho, José Antônio. O colégio e as residências dos jesuítas no Espírito Santo. Rio de Janeiro: Expressão e Cultura, 1982. 302 p.: bibl., ill., index.

Important role played by Jesuits in the development of Brazil's first settlements is exemplified by Espírito Santo, a captaincy when they arrived in 1549. This monograph provides a wealth of information and illustrations of the city's Jesuit architecture.

504 Uma Cidade em questão I: Grandjean de Montigny e o Rio de Janeiro. Realização do Departamento de Artes da Pontifícia Universidade Católica do Rio de Janeiro. Rio de Janeiro: PUC, 1978? 274 p.: bibl., ill.

At the invitation of Dom João VI, Grandjean de Montigny introduced French neo-classicism in Rio from where it spread throughout Brazil. Comprehensive treatment of this superimposition of cultures. Includes several very good essays as well as chronology, documents and many illustrations.

505 Guia dos bens tombados. Coordenação de pesquisa, Maria Elisa Carrazzoni. Ilustrações, Jimmy Scott e Sussy. Rio de Janeiro: Expressão e Cultura: Pedidos pelo reembolso postal, EXPED-Expansão Editorial, 1980. 517 p.: bibl., ill.

Comprehensive coverage of all of Brazil's civilian, military and religious architecture, including all structures registered as cultural, historical or artistic landmarks, state-by-state and county-by-county. Major monuments are illustrated with minute pen-and-ink drawings. Includes accurate historical introduction, description, summary and bibliography for each individual landmark. Very important reference book.

506 Guimarães, Carlos Rafael. Rio Grande do Sul histórico. Porto Alegre: Painel Editora, 1980. 179 p.: ill. (some col.) (Série Raízes gaúchas; v. 1)

Reviews history of Rio Grande do Sul from archaeological evidence to Getúlio Vargas' era including the discovery, colonial times, Empire and Republic. Succinct overall view. Articulate text. Includes varied iconography: old maps, prints, paintings, drawings, photographs, and documents.

507 O Livro de São Paulo. Coordenação geral, Luiz Seráphico. Fotos, Dulce Soares et al. Texto, Julita Scarano. São Paulo: Rhodia, 1979. 177 p.: bibl., chiefly ill.

Fine photographic study of São Paulo offers subtle interpretation of the city. Eloquent use of the camera and poetry to portray its past and present architecture, monuments, interiors, and people. Includes several studies and city's itinerary.

508 Loureiro, Maria Amélia Salgado. A evolução da casa paulistana e a arquitetura de Ramos de Azevedo. São Paulo: Voz do Oeste, 1981. 117 p.: ill., plans.

City of São Paulo's houses from 16th through 20th centuries, of which few still exist, are chiefly portrayed through documents and drawings. Finest section is devoted to the unique contribution of Engineer-Architect Francisco de Paula Ramos de Azevedo, who designed some of the city's finest buildings (e.g., Municipal Theatre, Teachers College, Palaces of Justice and Industry, Arts and Crafts School, Main Post Office).

509 Niemeyer, Oscar. Rio, de província a metrópole. Rio de Janeiro: Avenir Editora, 1980. 76 p.: ill.

Critical as well as self-critical memoirs of the city of Rio de Janeiro by Brazil's foremost architect. Central issues of these reminiscences are the redesigning of much of Rio and the contrast between demands of middle as opposed to upper-class housing. Compares the old and the new and includes many relevant drawings by the author.

510 Rio deco. Idealizado e programado por Luciano Figueiredo e Oscar Ramos. Com textos do arquiteto Sérgio Bernardes e do poeta Décio Pignatari. Fotografado por Ivan Cardoso. Rio de Janeiro: Edições Achiamé, 1980. 100 p.: chiefly ill. (some col.)

Describes how the international style introduced at the Exposition Internationale des Arts Décoratifs affected Rio's high-rises, private homes, cafés, railway stations, sculptures, sidewalk design, etc. Discusses materials, forms and color. Décio Pignatari's essay "Um Neolítico de Consumo" provides the historical context.

511 Salmoni, Anita and Emma Debenedetti. Arquitetura italiana em São Paulo. São Paulo: Editora Perspectiva, 1981. 192 p.: ill. (Coleção Debates; 173. Arquitetura)

Examines role played by Italian architecture in modern and contemporary São Paulo (e.g., contributions of G. Warchawschik, a Russian who studied in Rome after 1917, Rio Levi, Lina Bò Bardi, and lesser known architects such as T.G. Bezzi, Luigi Pucci, Chiappori Palanti, as well as Ramos de Azevedo's collaborators). Includes many appropriate photographs.

512 II [i.e. Segundo] Inquérito Nacional de Arquitetura: depoimentos. Acácio Borsói et al. Coordenadores, Eliane Faerstein,

Jorge Castro, Sandra Monarcha. Rio de Janeiro: Instituto de Arquitetos do Brasil, Departamento do Rio de Janeiro: Projeto Editores Associados, 1982. 182 p.: ill., ports.

Consists of 15 interviews with architects, city planners, and art critics on main issues confronting Brazilian contemporary architecture. Questions are standard but answers vary and include polemics on theoretical and practical problems and cover international, national, and regional questions. Includes curricula and many photos. Good reference aid.

513 Souza, Sara Regina Silveira de. A presença portuguesa na arquitetura da Ilha de Santa Catarina: séculos XVIII e XIX. Florianópolis: Fundação Catarinense de Cultura, 1981. 220 p.: bibl., ill.

In-depth study draws technical as well as artistic comparisons: (e.g., role played by Azorian settlers, military, religious and civilian architecture). Includes plans, maps and photographs from both sides of the Atlantic as well as glossary, bibliography, and iconographical sources.

514 Telles, Leandro Silva. Porto Alegre antigo. Porto Alegre: Painel Editora, 1980. 117 p.: ill. (some col.) (Série Raízes gaúchas; v. 2)

This fine collection of old maps, prints and paintings as well as old photographs makes a good supplement to the study of old times in Rio Grande do Sul's capital, changed greatly since then.

515 Toledo, Benedito Lima de. São Paulo, três cidades em um século. São Paulo: Livraria Duas Cidades, 1981. 179 p.: bibl., ill.

São Paulo, which had a colonial look one century ago, has since been rebuilt three times over, so that little of the past remains. How will it look towards the end of this century when there are 25 million inhabitants? At present, leaving the city is most difficult. While reminiscing about the past, author suggests changes in methods to rebuild the city. But how? Includes rich photographical material and bibliography.

MISCELLANEOUS

516 Araújo, Adalice Maria de. Mito e magia na arte catarinense. Florianópolis: Estado de Santa Catarina, Secretaria da Educação e Cultura, 1979. 436 p.: bibl., ill.

First of its kind, book presents rigorous analysis of myth and magic both at universal and individual levels. Focuses on many folk and learned artists of Santa Catarina state. Many appropriate illustrations (monochromatic only, unfortunately) and rich bibliographical sources. High analytical quality.

517 Brinquedos tradicionais brasileiros. Serviço Social do Comércio, Conselho Regional no Estado de São Paulo. São Paulo: O Conselho, 1983. 99 p.: ill. (some col.), port.

Book intermingles images of creative toys produced in Brazil with poetry and sociology. Traditional *homo sapiens* is here seen as *homo felix, homo festus, homo ludicus,* in their Brazilian variations. Successful project, beautifully printed book, excellent reproductions in color.

JOURNAL ABBREVIATIONS
ART

AR Areíto. Areíto, Inc. New York.

ARMEX Artes de México. México.

ASU/LAD Latin American Digest. Arizona State University, Center for Latin American Studies. Tempe.

BNBD Boletín Nicaragüense de Bibliografía y Documentación. Banco Central de Nicaragua, Biblioteca. Managua.

BNJM/R Revista de la Biblioteca Nacional José Martí. La Habana.

CA Critica d'Arte. Studio Italiano di Storia dell'Arte. Vallecchi Editore. Firenze, Italy.

CH Cuadernos Hispanoamericanos. Instituto de Cultura Hispánica. Madrid.

CONAC/RNC Revista Nacional de Cultura. Consejo Nacional de Cultura. Caracas.

EANH/B Boletín de la Academia Nacional de Historia. Quito.

ECO Eco. Librería Bucholz. Bogotá.

EEHA/AEA Anuario de Estudios Americanos. Consejo Superior de Investigaciones Científicas [and] Universidad de Sevilla, Escuela de Estudios Hispano-Americanos. Sevilla, España.

ESME/C Cultura. Ministerio de Educación. San Salvador.

GEE/NA Nova Americana. Giulio Einaudi Editore. Torino, Italy.

IAHG/AHG Antropología e Historia de Guatemala. Instituto de Antropología e Historia de Guatemala. Guatemala.

ICP/R Revista del Instituto de Cultura Puertorriqueña. San Juan.

IFH/C Conjunction. Institut Français d'Haïti. Port-au-Prince.

IIE/A Anales del Instituto de Investigaciones Estéticas. Universidad Nacional Autónoma de México. México.

III/AI América Indígena. Instituto Indigenista Interamericano. México.

IPGH/RHI Revista de Historia de las Ideas. Instituto Panamericano de Geografía e Historia. Editorial Casa de la Cultura Ecuatoriana. Quito.

LNB/L Lotería. Lotería Nacional de Beneficencia. Panamá.

MOBR/B Boletín. Museo del Oro [and] Banco de la República. Bogotá.

PCCLAS/P Proceedings of the Pacific Coast Council on Latin American Studies. University of California. Los Angeles.

PUC/V Veritas. Pontifícia Universidade Católica do Rio Grande do Sul. Pôrto Alegre, Brasil.

UNAM/AA Anales de Antropología. Universidad Nacional Autónoma de México, Instituto de Investigaciones Históricas. México.

URSS/AL América Latina. Academia de Ciencias de la Unión de Repúblicas Soviéticas Socialistas. Moscú.

FOLKLORE

MERLE E. SIMMONS, *Professor of Spanish, Indiana University*

THE BIBLIOGRAPHY I PUBLISH below lists approximately 200 *selected* entries. While all are, without exception, worthy of attention, I have been careful to see that all geographic areas of Latin America are represented. This means that the quality of items listed varies from country to country. Not all publications from very large and productive countries like Brazil could be included, while items listed from smaller countries are sometimes of relatively modest worth.

Since the Folklore section of *HLAS* appears at four-year intervals, the present work surveys materials I have examined since late 1979 when I submitted my last contribution to *HLAS 42*.

Perhaps the most noteworthy development in Latin American folklore research has been the appearance of various excellent bibliographical guides. Although my own annual folkore bibliographies terminated with the volume for 1976 listed below (item **964**) several excellent specialized bibliographies have appeared. Among these are the contributions of Luyten on Brazil (item **961**); Szwed and Abrahams on the Greater Antilles (item **965**); Colonelli on Brazil (item **994**); Vieira Filho on Brazil (item **1039**); Cordero Iñíguez on Ecuador (item **1085**); Sánchez Romeralo *et al.* on Latin America (item **963**); and the bibliography of Guatemalan folklore published by the Universidad de San Carlos de Guatemala (item **1047**). These estimable works, along with numerous good bibliographies that appeared with increasing frequency as integral parts of books, monographs, and articles provide impressive proof that the scholarly level of folklore research in Latin America is rising rapidly.

This conclusion is corroborated by the increasing attention that the best Latin American scholars are giving to folklore theory. Already prestigious folklorists like Aretz (item **952**) and Dannemann *et al.* (item **966**) continue their long-standing efforts, as does Lara Figueroa (items **1053–1059**), but it is most gratifying to find challenging theoretical essays written by younger professionals like Blache and Magariños (item **953**) and Jiménez de Báez (item **959**). All are engaged in efforts to ground folklore research in their part of the world upon theory based on Latin American, not European or North American, social and cultural realities.

In the whole area of folklore studies perhaps the most striking phenomenon of the last five or 10 years has been the rapid rise in Brazil of interest in *literatura de cordel*. Although *cordel* is by definition printed broadsides or pamphlets containing versified narratives by known popular poets or singers—and most definitions of folklore generally question whether *printed* materials by *known* authors qualify— the fact is that interest in *cordel* as a manifestation of Brazilian culture, whether "folk" or "popular," has swelled in recent years. Brazilians on different social, cultural, and intellectual levels have discovered in *cordel* a multi-faceted symbol of Brazilian creativity and cultural uniqueness, and as a consequence innumerable books and articles about it have been published, many of the latter in journals of folklore and anthropology. Some 20 of them are listed in this bibliography. Several of the best works in the field have been done by North Americans like Slater in no less than five entries! (items **1026–1031**), Curran (item **996**), and Hulet (item **1003**).

As always, certain individual works or scholars deserve special commendation. Lara Figueroa and his productive group of folklorists at the Universidad de San Carlos de Guatemala continue to impress with numerous books and articles and the regular appearance of their periodical publications, *Tradiciones de Guatemala* and *La Tradición Popular*. Lara Figueroa also excels as the extremely energetic editor of *Folklore Americano* (item **958**) published in Mexico by the Instituto Panamericano de Geografía e Historia. In a similar way the continuing appearance of the new series *Cadernos de Folclore* (item **989**), published by the Ministério da Educação in Rio de Janeiro, is a bright spot in the folklore picture. Among individual studies marked by superior scholarship are Vidal de Battini's three volumes on Argentine stories and legends (item **977**); Wilbert's three books on the folk literature of two Indian groups in Argentina (items **970** and **973**) and one in Brazil (item **1000**); List's fine study of music and poetry in a Colombian village (item **1082**); Tavares de Lima's excellent book on the folklore of São Paulo (item **999**); and vol. 3 of the superb *cancionero* of Mexican *coplas* compiled by Frenk de Alatorre and her collaborators (item **1106**). Finally, I note that during the period covered here an unusual number of excellent works on Hispanic-Mexican folklore from the US Southwest have also been published. I should mention particularly the outstanding contributions by Campa (item **1104**), Robb (item **1121**), and Trotter (item **1124**).

GENERAL

951 *América Indígena*. Instituto Indigenista Interamericano. Vol. 41, No. 2, abril/junio 1981– . México.

Special issue contains eight articles by various authors about handicrafts in several Latin American countries. Though contributors focus primarily on modern-day production of articles for commercial market, not upon process' traditional aspects, folklorists interested in material lore will find this issue of interest.

952 Aretz, Isabel. Qué es el folklore. Caracas: CONAC: Instituto Interamericano de Etnomusicología y Folklore, 1977. 67 p.: ill. (Cuadernos INIDEF; 1)

Using many charts and schematic drawings, one of Spanish America's outstanding folklorists sets forth her ideas about what folklore is, how it should be studied, and uses it can serve. Although highly personal, and sure to evoke arguments among specialists, her exposition is clear and unequivocal. Excellent introduction to the field.

953 Blache, Martha and Juan A. Magariños de Morentín. Síntesis crítica de la teoría del folklore en Hispanoamérica. Buenos Aires: Tekné, 1980. 76 p.: bibl., charts.

Critical synthesis of multiple points of view about many problems inherent in study of folklore *as a scientific discipline* in Spanish America. Cites practically all distinguished scholars in the field in order to document differing authoritative approaches. Important survey of statements about folklore theory.

954 Carvalho Neto, Paulo de. Folklore y educación. Guatemala: Editorial Piedra Santa, 1980. 104 p.: bibl., ill.

Sets forth ideas of author, one of Latin America's most able folklorists, concerning use of folklore by teachers in classroom. Offers suggestions for applying folklore to education and gives many specific examples.

955 Chang Vargas, Giselle and Fernando González Vásquez. Cultura popular tradicional: fundamento de la identidad cultural. San José: Editorial Universidad Estatal a Distancia: Departamento de Antropología, Ministerio de Cultura, Juventud y Deportes, 1981. 100 p.: ill.

Useful basic manual about cultural studies (i.e., anthropology, folklore, and related fields) which deals with both theory and history of such disciplines.

956 Crumrine, N. Ross. Folk drama in
Latin America: a ritual type characterized by social group unification and cultural
fusion (NS, 6:12, 1981, p. 103–125, diagram)

Describes and analyzes in compara-
tive and quite scholarly way ritual, syntactic,
semantic, and pragmatic aspects of Lenten
folk dramas in three different locales (i.e.,
Mayo community of northern Mexico; Cara-
caos region near Piura, Peru; and Marinduque
prov. south of Manila, the Philippines).

957 Espinosa, J. Manuel. Additional Hispanic versions of the Spanish religious ballad "Por el Rastro de la Sangre"
(UNM/NMHR, 56:4, Oct. 1981, p. 349–367,
bibl., ill.)

Surveys history of "Por el Rastro de la
Sangre," Spanish ballad about Passion of
Christ widely known in Spanish America.
Presents new version that author recently
discovered in Peña Blanca, N.M., and also reprints several versions Gisela Beutler collected in Colombia.

958 *Folklore Americano*. Instituto Panamericano de Geografía e Historia.
Nos. 26/31, 1979/1981– . México.

Since the very able Guatemalan folklorist, Celso A. Lara Figueroa, took over the
editorship of *Folklore Americano* in 1975, he
has overseen publication of no fewer than 14
issues of this best of all journals in the field
of Latin American folklore. Articles published are generally of good quality (though
sometimes they treat subjects that are more
anthropological or ethnographic than folkloric in nature) and any person interested in
studying Latin American folklore must read
Folklore Americano. In *HLAS 42* (p. 75–125),
we annotated articles published in *Folklore
Americano* through No. 25 (June 1978). However, in order to hold the number of entries
in this *HLAS 46* to around 200, there are no
annotations of articles that appear in No. 26
(Dec. 1978) through No. 31 (June 1981). Instead, the more noteworthy articles in these
issues are listed below:

No. 26 (Dec. 1978): Susana Chertudi
"Cuentos Populares de la Cordillera de
Neuquén, Argentina" (p. 23–36); Kenneth W.
Smith "*Todos los santos*: Spirits, Kites, and
Courtship in the Guatemalan Maya High-
lands" (p. 49–58); J. Manuel Juárez Toledo
"Música Tradicional de los Yucpa-Irapa del
Estado Zulia, Venezuela" (p. 59–81); Paulo de
Carvalho-Neto "Historias de Tramposos"
(p. 105–148); Abdón Ubídia "Sobre el Pro-
blema del Estudio del Cuento Popular en el
Ecuador" (p. 149–176).

No. 27 (June 1979): Silvia Perla García
and Sara Josefina Newbery "Formas Tradi-
cionales de la Medicina Vigentes en el Area
Pampeana" (p. 97–119); Catalina Saugy "Los
Espectáculos de Destreza Campera en el
Tuyú, Argentina" (p. 121–148); Martha
Blache "Dos Aspectos de la Tradición en San
Antonio de Areco" (p. 163–194); Ercilia Mo-
reno Chá "El Término: Aportes Musicoló-
gicos para su Estudio" (p. 195–209).

No. 28 (Dec. 1979): Alvaro Fernaud
Palares "Folklore y Educación: ¿Conceptos
Antagónicos?" (p. 23–43); Ofelia C. Deleón
Meléndez "Tradiciones Populares Guate-
maltecas y su Aplicación en la Enseñanza"
(p. 45–68); J. Arturo Chamorro E. "Uso y
Función del Teponaztle en el Medio Rural
Tlaxcalteca, México" (p. 69–83); Celso A.
Lara Figueroa "La Décima y la Copla en la
Poesía Popular de Guatemala" (p. 85–111);
Martha Blache "El Mensaje de una Leyenda
Mítica: El Tesoro Escondido" (p. 113–138);
Sebastião Geraldo Breguêz "A Religião e
Poder: um Estudo sobre a Religiosidade Popu-
lar no Brasil" (p. 139–144); Silvia Perla
García "Algunas Consideraciones sobre la
Fiesta de San Juan en Misiones y Formosa,
Argentina" (p. 145–157); Abraham Caycho
Jiménez "Sistemática Nosográfica del Folk-
lore Médico en el Perú" (p. 159–191).

No. 29 (June 1980): Ronny Velásquez
"Notas sobre Rafael María Avila, Cantor
Popular de Zulia, Venezuela" (p. 5–29); Luis
Ibérico Más "Antropología de la Religión:
Notas sobre el Nacimiento de un Santo"
(p. 31–39); Manuel Dannemann "Conferen-
cia Internacional con Motivo del Centenario
de la Sociedad de Folklore de Inglaterra,
1878–1978" (p. 41–45); Paulo de Carvalho-
Neto "Los Cuentos Folklóricos del Ecuador"
(p. 47–51); Roberto Díaz Castillo "Lo Esen-
cial en el Concepto de Arte Popular"
(p. 53–58); Inés Dölz Blackburn, "Relación
entre la Poesía Tradicional Hispana del
Sudoeste de los Estados Unidos y la Poesía
Popular Chilena" (p. 63–72); Yolando Pino
Saavedra "Cuentos Recogidos de Boca de
Mapuches" (p. 73–117).

No. 30 (Dec. 1980): Ana María Dupey
"El Culto Popular a Ceferino Namuncurá en
la República Argentina" (p. 5–16); Luis

Ibérico Más "Estudio sobre la Presencia de los Animales en el Folklore de Cajamarca, Perú" (p. 29–70); Martha Blache "Exégesis Literaria de las Travesuras del Mbopipucu en el Paraguay" (p. 71–76); Luis Luján Muñoz "Breve Estudio sobre el Léxico del *Caló* de Guatemala" (p. 99–102); Dora P. de Zárate "En Torno a los Cuentos Folklóricos de *Tío Conejo* en Panamá" (p. 109–114).

No. 31 (June 1981): Martha Blache "Enunciados Fundamentales Tentativos para la Definición del Concepto de Folklore" (p. 5–13); Manuel Dannemann "La Cultura y la Simetría: el Viejo Thoms y el Nuevo Folklore" (p. 15–20); Inés Dölz Blackburn "Alonso de Ovalle y su Visión del Folklore Chileno Colonial del Siglo XVII" (p. 27–31); Celso A. Lara Figueroa "El Subtipo *Cuentos del compadre pobre y el compadre rico* en la Literatura Popular de Guatemala" (p. 33–47); Félix Coluccio "El Tema del Diablo en la Poesía Tradicional Argentina e Iberoamericana" (p. 49–56); E. Mildred Merino de Zela "Apuntes sobre la Conceptualización del Mito dentro del Folklore" (p. 57–60); Paulo de Carvalho-Neto "El Folklore Infantil Lúdico y los Conflictos del Niño" (p. 61–69); Martha Crivos and Amalia Eguía "Dos Estudios Antropológicos sobre Medicina Tradicional de los Valles Calchaquíes, Argentina" (p. 71–76).

959 Jiménez de Báez, Yvette. . . . . Y otra vez lo popular (CM/D, 111, marzo/junio, 1983, p. 40–48, ill.)

Reexamines with great care and subtlety whole concept of what *popular* literature (mostly popular poetry and song) really is. Some challenging new perceptions result. Draws primarily upon examples from Hispanic world, with special emphasis on Spanish America. Important article.

960 Lara Figueroa, Celso A. Contribución del folklore al estudio de la historia. Guatemala: Editorial Universitaria, 1977. 254 p.: bibl., ill. (Colección Problemas y documentos; v. 7)

Studies systematically relationship of history to folklore. Chap. 1 discusses historical research as a science. Chap. 2 analyzes folklore as subject for scientific study. Chap. 3 evaluates possibilities for using folkloric materials as source for studying Latin American history. Stimulating and very well documented study.

961 Luyten, Joseph Maria. Bibliografia especializada sobre literatura popular em verso. São Paulo: Universidade de São Paulo, Escola de Comunicações e Artes, 1981. 104 p.

Unannotated listing of some 1200 books and articles about popular and traditional poetry, mostly in Luso-Hispanic world. Useful reference work, though the lack of annotation is unfortunate. Especially good for *literatura de cordel* and other Brazilian genres.

962 Ramón y Rivera, Luis Felipe. Fenomenología de la etnomúsica latinoamericana. Caracas: Corporación Marca, 1980. 169 p.: indexes, music (Biblioteca INIDEF; 3)

Identifies, describes, and comments upon innumerable musical phenomena that are found in folk and aboriginal music throughout Latin America (e.g., scales, expressive elements, rhythms, structures, etc.). Provides many musical examples and works of numerous songs.

Román de Silgado, Manuel; Alejandro Ortiz; and Juan Ossio. Educación y cultura popular: ensayo sobre las posibilidades educativas del folklore andino. See *HLAS 45:4498.*

963 Sánchez Romeralo, Antonio; Samuel G. Armistead; and Suzanne H. Petersen. Bibliografía del romancero oral. Madrid: Cátedra Seminario Ménendez Pidal, 1980. 1 v.: indexes (Romancero y poesía oral; 5)

Best general bibliography available on Spanish ballad (i.e., *romance*) tradition in both Spanish and Spanish America. Lists 1624 items with very brief indications of area or areas of oral tradition referred to, archives or libraries which own the work, etc. Includes indexes of authors, journals, places, areas, archives and libraries, and ballad titles.

964 Simmons, Merle E. Folklore bibliography for 1976. Philadelphia: Institute for the Study of Human Issues, 1981. 223 p.: index (Indiana University Folklore Institute monograph series; 33)

Annotated bibliography of 1275 items covers books and articles about any aspect of folklore published in US and Latin America; also publications specifically about US or Hispanic folklore that appeared anywhere in the world. Items grouped according to genres.

965 Szwed, John F. and Roger D. Abrahams. Afro-American folk culture: an annotated bibliography of materials from North, Central, and South America, and the West Indies. With Robert Baron *et al.* Philadelphia: Institute for the Study of Human Issues, 1978. 2 v.: indexes (Publications of the American Folklore Society, Bibliographical and special series; v. 31–32)

Pt. 1 (488 p.) is about North America; pt. 2 (416 p.) covers West Indies, Central, and South America. Valuable annotated bibliography of Afro-American folk culture. Includes useful indexes.

966 Teorías del folklore en América Latina. Manuel Dannemann *et al.* Caracas: CONAC, 1975. 297 p.: bibl., port. (Biblioteca INIDEF; 1)

Belatedly I note this important reprinting of a series of articles about folklore theory written over the years by some of the most authoritative folklorists of Latin America: Manuel Dannemann of Chile, August Raúl Cortazar of Argentina, Darío Guevara of Ecuador, Luis da Câmara Cascudo and Renato Almeida of Brazil, Dora P. de Zárate of Panama, Ildefonso Pereda Valdés of Uruguay, Guillermo Abadía Morales of Colombia, and Isabel Aretz of Venezuela. Though not new, these are all basic theoretical statements.

ARGENTINA

967 Alvarez, Gregorio. El tronco de oro: folklore del Neuquén. 2a. ed. Neuquén, Argentina: Siringa Libros, 1981. 324 p.: bibl., ill.

New ed. of work first published 1968. Extremely rich source of information about practically all kinds of folklore from Neuquén, Patagonia. Though modern methodology is not used, author's scholarly instincts are sound and his knowledge vast. Contains innumerable texts of tales, songs, proverbs, beliefs, examples of regional speech, etc. Valuable contribution.

968 Chertudi, Susana. Folklore literario argentino. Buenos Aires: Centro Editor de América Latina, 1982. 113 p. (Capítulo. Biblioteca argentina fundamental; 167. Serie complementaria sociedad y cultura; 19)

Brings together four previously published folktake studies by one of Argentina's best folklorists: "El Cuento Folklórico" (p. 7–47); "Las Especies Literarias en Prosa"

(p. 49–73); "Cuentos de Animales en el Folklore Argentino" (p. 75–94); "'Antes Fuí Hija/ Ahora Soy Madre'" (p. 95–113).

969 —— and **Sara Josefina Newbery.** La difunta Correa. Buenos Aires: Editorial Huemul, 1978. 240 p.: bibl., ill. (Colección Temas de antropología; 1)

Scholarly study of La Difunta Correa as legendary figure around whom there has developed a complex of beliefs and a cult that is widely diffused in Argentina. Background information about popular canonization of "saints" other than La Difunta Correa is also of value. Includes some texts of legends, poems, prayers, etc.

970 Folk literature of the Mataco Indians. Johannes Wilbert and Karin Simoneau, editors. Contributing authors, Domenico Del Campana *et al.* Los Angeles: UCLA Latin American Center Publications, University of California, Los Angeles, 1982. 507 p., 1 p. of plates: bibl., ill., indexes, map (Folk literature of South American Indians. UCLA Latin American studies; v. 52)

Vol. 5 in excellent series on South American Indian narrative folklore. Deals with Mataco people of Argentina's Gran Chaco region. Offers sections with very detailed motif analyses (Thompson system) of narratives about star mythology and cosmogony, origins, cataclysms, the trickster, animals, and unclassified stories; also, a general introduction by Niels Fock. Includes excellent motif indexes.

971 Formas culturales tradicionales en el área pampeana. Buenos Aires: Instituto Nacional de Antropología, 1978. 1 v.: bibl. (Informes del Instituto Nacional de Antropología; 0325–5948)

More in the tradition of folklore than of ethnology, this monograph includes three principal works: Silvia Perla García "Una Leyenda de Creencia en el Oeste de la Provincia de Buenos Aires: las Luces Malas;" Sara Josefina Newbery "Vigencia de las Antiguas Formas de Curar en Tres Partidos de la Provincia de Buenos Aires: Ayacucho, General Madariaga y Rauch;" and Jesús María Pereyra and Emilia Altomare de Pereyra "El Cancionero de los Pagos de Cañada de la Cruz." [W.E. Carter]

972 Franco, Arturo. Folklore de Catamarca: Belén 1930. Ilustración de tapa y texto,

Gladys Montaldo. Fotografía, Enrique Lobo. Tucumán, Argentina: Editorial América, 1980. 217 p.: ill.

Evokes and describes many aspects of regional life in Catamarca, including much folklore (e.g., songs—many *copla* texts are given—dress, tales, fiestas, beliefs and superstitions, dances, proverbs, riddles, cures, games). Not a work of scholarship, it nevertheless contains much useful information.

973 Gusinde, Martin. Folk literature of the Yamana Indians: Martin Gusinde's collection of Yamana narratives. Johannes Wilbert, editor. Berkeley: University of California Press, 1977. 308 p.: bibl., ill., indexes (UCLA Latin American studies series; v. 40)

Translations into English of tale-texts taken from Martin Gusinde's *Die Feuerland-Indianer*, study of the Yamana Indians of Tierra del Fuego. Editor alters Gusinde's work by some rewriting and makes changes in order of texts. Also provides useful summaries and motif indexes. The Yamanas died out several decades ago.

974 Oberti, Federico. Historia y folklore del mate. Buenos Aires: Edición del Fondo Nacional de las Artes, 1979. 386 p.: ill.

About *yerba mate* tea in Argentina, Uruguay, Paraguay, and Brazil. Deals with its history, customs and practices surrounding its use, the receptacles (also called *mates*) in which it is served, etc.

975 Quereilhac de Kussrow, Alicia Cora. La fiesta de San Baltasar: presencia de la cultura africana en El Plata. Buenos Aires: Ediciones Culturales Argentinas, Ministerio de Cultura y Educación, Secretaría de Estado de Cultura, 1980. 241 p.: bibl., ill.

Monograph about fiesta celebrated in Corrientes prov., northeastern Argentina. Describes whole region and its people; then studies exhaustively history and present status of fiesta in honor of San Baltasar, black Magi king. Includes attention to music, choreography, etc. Excellent bibliography.

976 Vega, Carlos. Apuntes para la historia del movimiento tradicionalista argentino. Buenos Aires: Secretaría de Cultura de la Presidencia de la Nación, Instituto Nacional de Musicología Carlos Vega, 1981. 161 p., xvi p. of plates: ill., ports.

Reprints material that appeared origi-

nally 1963–65, but includes six hitherto unpublished chapters. Traces mainly history of nationalism and traditionalism in Argentine arts and letters, with special emphasis on music and related fields. Deals with musical folklore.

977 Vidal de Battini, Berta Elena. Cuentos y leyendas populares de la Argentina. Cartografía de María Teresa Grondona. Buenos Aires: Ediciones Culturales Argentinas, Secretaría de Estado de Cultura, Ministerio de Cultura y Educación, 1980. 3 v.: bibl., maps.

First three of 10 projected volumes of Argentine folktales are devoted to animal tales exclusively. Together they offer so far 841 tale-texts collected in the field, most with numerous variants. Includes data about informants, comprehensive introduction, and maps. Very important basic work in the field.

BOLIVIA

Aguiló, Federico. Los cuentos: ¿tradiciones o vivencias? See *HLAS 45:1386.*

978 Bustillos V., Freddy and **Shiguemi Sato.** Fiesta de la Virgen del Carmen en Charazani (Revista Boliviana de Etnomusicología y Folklore [Instituto Nacional de Antropología, La Paz] 11:2, 1981, p. 1–16, bibl., facsim., maps)

Reports on fieldwork concerning fiesta celebrated in community north of La Paz, mostly of Spanish and Quechua speakers. Traces fiesta's history and describes its processions, music, dances, musical groups, products sold in the market, etc.

979 Chávez, Dunia. Sondeo de opinión: ¿qué se sabe sobre folklore? (Revista Boliviana de Etnomusicología y Folklore [Instituto Nacional de Antropología, La Paz] 1:3, 1980, p. 1–25, tables)

Reports on poll taken among fourth-year students in middle cycle at six randomly chosen La Paz schools in order to determine how much they know about folklore, their attitude toward it and Bolivia's national heritage, musical preference, etc.

980 Díaz Villamil, Antonio. Leyendas de mi tierra. La Paz: Librería Editorial Juventud, 1980. 148 p.: ill.

Republication of some literarily retold

legends of Bolivia, mostly Indian tales or narratives about Bolivian history. Unfortunately, no sources are indicated. Early work of Díaz Villamil (d. 1948).

Kimura, Hideo. La mitología de los ese ejja del Oriente Boliviano: el dueño imaginario de los animales silvestres. See *HLAS* 45:1391.

981 Paredes Candia, Antonio. Brujerías, tradiciones y leyendas. v. 1/4. Ilustraciones de Pedro Shimose. La Paz: Difusión, 1969/1979. 4 v.: ill. (Colección Cíclope; 2)
Historical tales and legends, stories about witchcraft, etc., retold in highly literary style. A few are from genuine oral tradition.

982 ———. Cuentos kjuchis: folklore secreto. La Paz: Ediciones ISLA, 1978. 82 p.: ill. (Colección Folklore secreto; 5)
Consists of 15 obscene jokes collected from oral tradition by one of Bolivia's most competent folklorists. Only place of origin is noted for each joke.

983 ———. Folklore de Potosí: algunos aspectos. La Paz: Ediciones ISLA, 1980. 250 p., 20 p. of plates: bibl., ill.
Miscellany that contains brief descriptions of customs, beliefs, regional recipes, material folklore (e.g., dress, utensils, etc.), fiestas, dances, and songs. Also includes section of literarily retold folktales, words without music of some songs, riddles, tonguetwisters, nicknames, and other verbal lore. Offers finally a few pages of miners' lore in dictionary format.

BRAZIL

984 Antologia do folclore cearense. Organização de Florival Seraine. 2a. ed. Fortaleza: Edições UFC (Universidade Federal do Ceará), 1983. 356 p.: bibl.
Revised and enlarged ed. of 1968 work. Reprints 25 articles about wide range of folkloric subjects by various Ceará authors. Also includes texts of eight poems of *literatura de cordel*. Disorganized miscellany, but some individual articles are of interest and value.

Araújo, Adalice Maria de. Mito e magia na arte catarinense. See item **516.**

985 Azevedo, Teófilo de. Cultura popular do norte de Minas. São Paulo: s.n., 1979. 174 p. (Série Folclore)
Azevedo, professional street singer from northern Minas Gerais, publishes in this unusual book many of his songs (words only, no music). Practically all genres of songs are represented. Also of great interest are some of his explanatory commentary, definitions of terms, brief personal autobiography, etc.

986 Basso, Ellen B. A "musical view of the universe": Kalapalo myth and ritual as religious performance (AFS/JAF, 94:373, July/Sept. 1981, p. 273–291, tables)
Defines myth and ritual as found among the Kalapalo Indians of central Brazil and analyzes in considerable detail relationship between myth (i.e., certain narratives author considers to be myths) and ritual, which is primarily musical in character.

987 Braga, Júlio Santana. Contos afrobrasileiros. Salvador: Fundação Cultural do Estado da Bahia, 1980. 58 p. (Coleção Antônio Vianna; v. 3)
Offers 44 texts of tales that have been preserved orally or in writing by groups who practice Afro-Brazilian popular religions.

988 Cabral, Alfredo do Vale. Achegas ao estudo do folclore brasileiro. Organização, introd., e notas de José Calasans Brandão da Silva. Rio de Janeiro: Ministério da Educação e Cultura, Departamento de Assuntos Culturais, Fundação Nacional de Arte, Campanha de Defesa do Folclore Brasileiro, 1978. 150 p.: bibl.
Brandão da Silva has organized a new and expanded edition of Cabral's pioneering 19th-century work on Bahia's folklore. There are sections on songs, supernatural beings, children's games, proverbs, riddles, superstitions, prayers, etc. Silva also provides introduction to Cabral and his work.

989 Cadernos de Folclore. 1– . Rio de Janeiro: Ministério de Educação e Cultura, Departamento de Assuntos Culturais, Fundação Nacional de Arte (FUNARTE), 1975–
Continuing series contains brief monographs (usually 25 to 70 p.) concerning various aspects of Brazilian folklore broadly defined. Some of Brazil's best folklorists contribute to the series, though some studies

are written by less renowned scholars. Quality of contributions is usually quite good, and most monographs contain useful bibliography, numerous photographs or drawings, and other desirable features. Since my last bibliography was completed for *HLAS 42* (p. 75–125), I have seen the following titles: No. 14, Beatriz G. Dantas *Chegança* (1976); No. 15, Raul Giovanni Lody *Pano da costa* (1977); No. 16, Zaide Maciel de Castro and Aracy do Prado Couto *Folias de Reis* (1977); No. 17, Raul Giovanni Lody *Samba de Caboclo* (1977); No. 18, Roberto Benjamin *Congos da Paraíba* (1977); No. 19, José Loureiro Fernandes *Congadas paranaenses* (1977); No. 20, Carlos Rodrigues Brandão *A folia de Reis de Mossámedes* (1977); No. 21, Soffiati Neto *O jogo das bolinhas* (1977); No. 22, Sérgio Ferretti, Valdelino Cécio and Joila Moraes *Dança do Lelé* (1978); No. 23, Fernando Corréa de Azevedo *Fandango do Paraná* (1978); No. 24, Théo Brandão *Cavalhadas de Alagoas* (1978); No. 25, Altimar de Alencar Pimentel *Barca da Paraíba* (1978); No. 26, Osvaldo Meira Trigueiro and Roberto Benjamin *Cambindas da Paraíba* (1978); No. 27, Doralécio Soares *Boi-de-mamáo catarinense* (1978); No. 28, Théo Brandão *Quilombo* (1978); No. 29, Paulo Pardal *Carrancas do São Francisco* (1979); No. 30, Guilherme Santos Neves *Bandas de Congos* (1980); and No. 31, Sérgio Ferretti, Valdelino Cécio, Joila Moraes, and Roldão Lima *Tambor de Crioula* (1981).

990 Cárdenas, Carmela Oscanoa de. O uso do folclore na educação: o frevo na didática pré-escolar. Recife: Fundação Joaquim Nabuco-Editora Massangana, 1981. 116 p.: ill. (Série Monografias; 19)
Studies dance as a genre of folklore and discusses the uses of dancing as a pedagogical aid. Concentrates on the *frevo* found in the region of Recife, particularly at Carnival time.

991 Cascudo, Luís da Câmara. Dicionário do folclore brasileiro. 4. ed., rev. e aumentada. São Paulo: Edições Melhoramentos, 1979. 811 p.
Huge dictionary, first published in 1954, is basic reference source for study of Brazilian folklore, and is indeed, useful aid for study of folklore in general.

992 Chilcote, Ronald H. The politics of conflict in the popular poetry of North-

east Brazil (UCLA/JLAL, 5:2, Winter 1979, p. 205–231, tables)
From systematic interviews with many singers, poets, and publishers of *literatura de cordel*, author synthesizes overview of their personal backgrounds, perception of their role in society, ideologies and attitudes toward political events, view of politicians, presidents, and messianic religious leaders, and importance of *literatura de cordel* as social protest.

993 Cláudio, Affonso. Trovas e cantares capixabas. Introdução e notas de Guilherme Santos Neves. 2a. ed. Rio de Janeiro: Ministério da Educação e Cultura, Secretaria de Assuntos Culturais, Fundação Nacional de Arte (FUNARTE), Instituto Nacional do Folclore; Vitória: Secretaria de Estado da Cultura e do Bem Estar Social, Fundação Cultural do Espírito Santo, 1980. 120 p.
New edition of 1923 work. Offers words without music of several songs, texts of some popular poetry, and a few folktales from Espírito Santo region, Brazil.

994 Colonelli, Cristina Argenton. Bibliografia do folclore brasileiro. São Paulo: Conselho Estadual de Artes e Ciências Humanas, 1979. 294 p.: index (Coleção Folclore; 20)
Lists 4919 unannotated items arranged alphabetically by authors' names. Subject index of entire bibliography at end (p. 271–294). Most complete and up-to-date bibliography of Brazilian folklore currently available.

995 Corrêa, Iracema França Lopes. A congada de Ilhabela na Festa de São Benedito. São Paulo: Escola de Folclore, Editorial Livramento, 1981. 150 p.: ill., map, music, photos.
Detailed monographic study of Festival of São Benedito on Island of Ilhabela, São Paulo, and particularly of dance-drama that blacks perform as part of celebration. Includes words of many songs, some music, dance diagrams, etc.

996 Curran, Mark J. Literatura de Cordel today: the poets and publishers (UCLA/JLAL, 6:1, Summer 1980, p. 55–75)
Reports results of questionnaire answered by 30 poets and publishers of *literatura de cordel*. Designed to elicit answers concerning *present-day* status of *literatura*

de cordel as well as poets' view of their role in society, effects of mass media upon such literature, expectations for the future, etc.

997 Damante, Hélio. Folclore brasileiro: São Paulo. Rio de Janeiro: Ministério da Educação e Cultura, Secretaria de Assuntos Culturais, Fundação Nacional de Arte (FUNARTE), Instituto Nacional do Folclore, 1980. 65 p., 14 p. of plates: bibl., ill. (Folclore brasileiro; 11)

No. 11 in series of volumes devoted to individual states. Historico-geographic introduction about São Paulo state is followed by chapters on subjects such as popular speech, oral literature, dances, folk arts and crafts, a calendar of festivals, regional food, etc.

998 Edelweiss, Frederico G. Apontamentos de folclore. Salvador: Centro Editorial e Didático da UFBa, 1979. 112 p.: bibl.

Notes (written 1947) were recently discovered among papers of deceased author. Now published for first time, they are a kind of general manual of Brazilian folklore as understood by Edelweiss over 35 years ago. Systematically presented, his ideas are of historical interest, though, of course, dated.

999 O Folclore do litoral norte de São Paulo. Rossini Tavares de Lima *et al.* Rio de Janeiro: Ministério da Educação e Cultura, Secretaria de Assuntos Culturais, Fundação Nacional de Arte (FUNARTE), Instituto Nacional do Folclore; São Paulo: Secretaria de Estado da Cultura de São Paulo, Universidade de Taubaté, 1981. 317 p.: ill.

Exemplary study based on fieldwork by team which investigated certain important features of folklore of São Sebastião, Ubatuba, Caraguatatuba, and Ilhabeia regions of São Paulo. Mainly in-depth studies of several dance-dramas such as *Congada de São Francisco*, *Reis*, etc. Impressive documentation of literary texts and music. Also includes cursory attention to narratives and some material lore (ceramics, etc.).

1000 Folk literature of the Gê Indians. Johannes Wilbert, editor, with Karin Simoneau. Contributing editors, Horace Banner *et al.* Los Angeles: UCLA Latin American Center Publications, University of California, Los Angeles, 1978. 653 p.: bibl. (UCLA Latin American studies; v. 44)

Presents 177 narratives collected 1914–68, from Gê Indians of central Brazil.

Collection is divided into origin, animal, and adventure categories. Each narrative is analyzed for its motif content. Introduction briefly treats Gê cosmology and worldview.

1001 França, Basileu Toledo. Romanceiro & trovas populares: esparsos de Americano do Brasil. Goiânia: U.F.G. Editor, 1979. 223 p.: ill. (Coleção Documentos goianos; no. 2)

Reprints two previously published works by Antonio Americano do Brasil: *O romanceiro* (1929) and *Mil e uma trovas luzianas* (1932–33). Contains texts of considerable interest, though so-called *romances* actually belong to other genres. The 1001 *trovas*, mostly quatrains, are of value and interest. França provides long and verbose introduction.

1002 Galeno, Cândida Maria S. Ritos fúnebres no interior cearense. Fortaleza: Editora H. Galeno, 1977. 72 p.

Observant and well-informed nonfolklorist describes, step-by-step, burial customs she is acquainted with in the interior of Ceará state.

1003 Hulet, Claude L. *Literatura de cordel*: the thematic dynamics of its narrative deep structure (UCLA/JLAL, 6:1, Summer 1980, p. 77–86)

Attempts to analyze thematic dynamics of deep structure of one *literatura de cordel* narrative. Uses method that involves primarily identification of its "motifemes" and employment of five-step analysis that moves from "The Story Line" through three intermediate stages which lead finally to "Identification of the Plot-Motivating/Stage-Setting/Deep Thesis."

1004 Instituto Nacional do Folclore, *Brazil.* Atlas folclórico do Brasil: artesanato, danças e folguedos: Espírito Santo. Rio de Janeiro: Edições FUNARTE (Fundação Nacional do Arte), 1982. 93 p.: ill.

First of proposed series of *Folklore atlases* for various states of Brazil. Based on fieldwork and careful assembling of data, volume surveys three aspects of folklore in Espírito Santo: handcrafts, dances, and popular dramas.

1005 Karasch, Mary. Central African religious tradition in Rio de Janeiro (UCLA/JLAL, 5:2, Winter 1979, p. 233–253, bibl., tables)

Sets forth thesis that Central African slaves who entered Rio de Janeiro in 19th century did not really convert to Roman Catholicism or to religions from other parts of Africa such as Candomblé; they merely changed their symbols, as they had done for centuries in Africa, by taking over Catholic saints as mainstays of their folk religion.

1006 Laytano, Dante de. A cozinha gaúcha na história do Rio Grande do Sul. Porto Alegre: Escola Superior de Teologia São Lourenço de Brindes, 1981. 188 p.: bibl. (Coleção Temas gaúchos; 22)

Book about gaucho cooking in Rio Grande do Sul. Traces its history and discusses foreign influences upon regional dishes. Gives many recipes for traditional dishes made of milk products, meat, rice, coffee, sugar, etc. Also includes vocabulary of linguistic terms related to cooking.

1007 Lenko, Karol and **Nelson Papavero.** Insetos no folclore. São Paulo: Conselho Estadual de Artes e Ciências Humanas, 1979. 518 p.: bibl., index (Coleção Folclore; 18)

Lenko, an entymologist, authored this exhaustive study of insects in Brazilian folklore, though it was completed only after his death by Papavero. Based on fieldwork and impressive library research, it treats each insect or family of insects in separate chapters (28 in all). Draws upon songs, tales, beliefs, sayings, etc.

1008 Lewin, Linda. Oral tradition and elite myth: the legend of Antônio Silvino in Brazilian popular culture (UCLA/JLAL, 5:2, Winter 1979, p. 157–204, bibl., maps)

Studies Antônio Silvino (1875–1944) as *literatura de cordel* outlaw folk hero of Brazil's Northeast. Focuses more upon what his legend says about popular culture, regional values, and popular poets than about bandit-heroes or class antagonisms. Excellent study of many aspects of *literatura de cordel*.

1009 Lubatti, Maria Rita da Silva. O folclore na vivência atual de Açu, Marreca e Quixaba, Campos RJ. São Paulo: Escola de Folclore: Editorial Livramento, 1979 or 1980. 73 p., 3 leaves of plates: bibl., ill.

Describes life in towns of Açu, Marreca, and Quixaba in Campos area, Rio de Janeiro state. Based on fieldwork. Deals briefly with many aspects of folklore (e.g., festivals, customs and practices, folk medicine, superstitions, beliefs, games).

1010 Luyten, Joseph Maria. O japonês na literatura de cordel (USP/RA, 24, 1981, p. 85–95, bibl.)

Studies roles played by Japanese in *literatura de cordel* before World War II to present. Finds that Brazil's popular poets generally denigrate the Japanese.

1011 ———. A literatura de cordel em São Paulo: saudosismo e agressividade. São Paulo: Edições Loyola, 1981. 203 p.: bibl. (Série Comunicação; 23)

Scholarly study of *literatura de cordel* and creators of this kind of popular literature in city of São Paulo. Focuses especially on ways in which a genre, originally cultivated in Brazil's Northeast, has been adapted to urban conditions. Cites many texts and provides information about authors.

1012 Machado, Franklin de C. O que é literatura de cordel? Rio de Janeiro: Codecri, 1980. 143 p.: bibl., ill. (Coleção Alternativa; v. 04)

Seeks to trace history of *literatura de cordel* and similar song-narratives in Brazil and elsewhere. Discusses their present place in Brazilian tradition, characteristics of the genre, themes treated, poets who compose such narratives, etc. Good treatment of subject.

1013 Machado, Paulo de Tarso Gondim. O Padre Cícero e a literatura de cordel: fenomenologia da devoção ao Padre Cícero. Fortaleza: Gráfica Editorial Cearense, 1982. 230 p.: ill.

Sets forth conflict between official religion and popular religion as represented by Father Cícero, revered leader of politico-religious movement centered around poor in Brazil's Northeast. Based upon innumerable poems about Father Cícero and persecutions he suffered as related by popular poets who wrote *literatura de cordel*.

1014 Maia, Tom and **Thereza Regina de Camargo Maia.** O folclore das tropas, tropeiros e cargueiros no Vale do Paraíba. Rio de Janeiro: Ministério da Educação e Cultura, Secretaria de Assuntos Culturais, Fundação Nacional de Arte (FUNARTE), Instituto Nacional do Folclore, 1981. 125 p.: bibl., ill., 1 map, ports.

Studies way of life, customs, folklore, etc., of muleteers who until recently were common in Valley of Paraíba, São Paulo. Based on fieldwork with numerous informants. Among types of folklore treated: popular speech, proverbs, tales, and material lore (e.g., equipment used by muleteers).

1015 Megale, Nilza Botelho. Cento e sete invocações da Virgem Maria no Brasil: história, iconografia, folclore. Petrópolis: Vozes, 1980. 372 p.: bibl., ill.

Offers historical and iconographic information about 107 different Brazilian manifestations of the Virgin Mary. Sometimes touches on legends, beliefs, and other folklore related to her various images.

1016 Mélo, Veríssimo de. Folclore infantil: acalantos, parlendas, adivinhas, jogos populares, cantigas de roda. Rio de Janeiro: Livraria Editora Cátedra em convênio com o Instituto Nacional do Livro, Ministério da Educação e Cultura, Brasília, 1981. 301 p.: bibl., ill.

Contains five previously published articles on children's games, songs, dances, riddles, and other folklore: "Acalantos" (1949); "Parlendas" (1949); "Adivinhas" (1948); "Jogos Populares do Brasil" (1956); and "Rondas Infantis Brasileiras" (1953). Contains words of many songs with music and extended commentaries.

1017 Menezes, Eduardo Diatahy B. de. Estrutura agrária: protesto e alternativas na poesia popular do Nordeste (UPR/RCS, 11:1/2, 1980, p. 29–61)

Offers along with running commentary two complete texts of *literatura de cordel* that voice social and political protest. One is from 1924; the other appeared a few years later.

1018 Merheb, Alice Inês Silva. "Sol e chuva ... casamento de viúva:" contribução ao estudo da astronomia e meteorologia popular. Viçosa, Brasil: Universidade Federal de Viçosa, Assessoria de Assuntos Culturais, 1976. 77 p.: bibl.

Discourses on various aspects of oral lore collected in Ponte Nova, Minas Gerais, and offers many examples of beliefs (mostly weather lore and magic beliefs), some riddles, popular sayings, etc.

1019 Pimentel, Altimar de Alencar. Chuva e sol: ritos e tradições. Brasília: Thesaurus, 1980. 116 p.

Miscellany of weather lore from the Northwest of Brazil and other places: beliefs, rituals, proverbs, riddles, legends, etc.

1020 Pontes, Mário. Doce como o diabo: demônio, utopia e liberdade na poesia de cordel nordestina. Rio de Janeiro: Editora Codecri, 1979. 70 p.: ill. (Coleção Alternativa; v. 2)

First section studies the devil's intervention in songs of *literatura de cordel* from Ceará state. Second article deals with some utopian locals found in such literature. Still a third article addresses some problems related to *literatura de cordel* evoked by author's childhood memory of visit to his home by the famous wandering singer, O Cego Aderaldo.

1021 Queiroz, Jeová Franklin de. Cultura popular: sertão só se informa bem quando o cordel aparece (Interior [Ministerio do Interior, Brasília] 7:38, maio/junho 1981, p. 36–44, ill.)

Though unpretentious and poorly organized, this general overview of *literatura de cordel* in Brazil's Northeast contains much useful information about this type of popular literature, poets, publishers, and illustrators who produce it, place of such literature in society, etc.

1022 Rassner, Ronald M. The transmission of the oral narrative from Africa to Brazil (Research in African Literatures [University of Texas Press, Austin] 13:3, Fall 1982, p. 327–358)

Discourses on diverse aspects of transmission of oral narratives between Africa and Brazil (actually there is evidence of some influence passing from Brazil *to* Africa). Analyzes structural features of various tales in order to arrive at challenging conclusions that are at variance with some previously accepted theories.

1023 Reis, José Ribamar Sousa dos. Bumba meu boi, o maior espetáculo popular do Maranhão. Recife: Fundação Joaquim Nabuco; Editora Massangana, 1980. 61 p.: ports. (Série Monografias; 18)

Studies traditional dance-drama

known as *Bumba-meu-boi* as it exists in Maranhão region, Brazil. Traces its history, describes present status, and compares Maranhão version with those of other areas.

1024 Roderjan, Roselys Vellozo. Folclore brasileiro: Paraná. Rio de Janeiro: Ministério Nacional da Educação e Cultura, Secretaria da Cultura, Fundação National de Arte (FUNARTE), Instituto Nacional de Folclore, 1981. 87 p., 25 p. of plates: bibl., ill. (Folclore brasileiro)

General survey of folklore of Paraná state. Contains chapters on popular speech, oral literature, dances, drama, crafts, regional food, etc.

1025 Simpósio de Comunicações sobre Pesquisas em Folclore, 2nd, *Belo Horizonte, Brazil, 1980.* Síntese. Belo Horizonte: Secretaria de Estado do Governo, Coordenadoria de Cultura do Estado do Minas Gerais, 1981. 122 p., 1 leaf of plates: bibl., ill

Collection of papers and round-table commentaries presented at symposium held in Belo Horizonte (19–21 Aug. 1980). Contributions by 28 authors of varying length and quality discuss diverse aspects of folklore in Brazil and elsewhere.

1026 Slater, Candace. Cordel and canção in today's Brazil (LARR, 17:3, 1982, p. 29–53)

Defines differences and similarities in the canção and *literatura de cordel* in terms of content, structure, mode (i.e., lyrical or narrative), context, function in society, attitudes of authors towards their work, etc. Cites many texts as documentation.

1027 ———. *The hairy leg strikes*: the mass media and the Brazilian literatura de cordel (AFS/JAF, 95:375, Jan./March 1982, p. 51–89, ill.)

Analyzes and interprets four related narratives about a fearsome hairy leg that portends the end of the world. Originally a tongue-in-cheek newspaper story, this account has inspired three *literatura de cordel* adaptations. Provides original news story and three *cordel* texts in both Portuguese and English.

1028 ———. Joe Bumpkin in the wilds of Rio de Janeiro (UCLA/JLAL, 6:1, Summer 1980, p. 5–53, ill., plates, tables)

Analysis of two *literatura de cordel*

narratives about country bumpkins and their troubles in big cities leads to observations about changing social attitudes and differences between southern and northern *literatura de cordel*. Also treats poets who wrote pamphlets and their public. Includes texts with English translations.

1029 ———. The *romance* of the warrior maiden (*in* El romancero hoy: 2° Coloquio Internacional, University of California, Davis. v. 3, Historia, comparatismo, bibliografía crítica. Edición a cargo de Antonio Sánchez Romeralo, Diego Catalán, Samuel G. Armistead, con la colaboración de Jesús Antonio Cid *et al.* Madrid: Cátedra Seminario Menéndez Pidal, 1979, p. 167–182 [Romancero y poesía oral; 4])

Analyzes themes and plots found in seven versions of old Hispanic ballad, *A donzela que vai à guerra*, that were orally collected in Brazil. Main theme revolves around masculine and feminine sex roles played by young woman who passes as male in order to go to war.

1030 ———. Setting out for São Paulo: internal migration as a theme in Brazilian popular literature (UCSD/NS, 8, 1982, p. 245–256)

Examines love songs and poetry contained in *literatura de cordel* produced by and for transplanted Northeast migrants who go to live in São Paulo and other southern regions. Notes psychological attitudes of migrants, particularly social protest they voice in such compositions.

1031 ———. Stories on a string: the Brazilian *literatura de cordel*. Berkeley: University of California Press, 1982. 313 p.: appendices, bibls., indexes, map, tables.

General study of *literatura de cordel*, best there is in English and probably the best that exists in any language. Treats historical background of *cordel* (i.e., versified popular narrative), its present status, theoretical approaches to its study, relationship between *cordel* poets and their public, etc. Analyzes many texts. Includes excellent appendices and exhaustive bibliographies.

1032 Soler, Luís. As raízes árabes, na tradição poético-musical do sertão nordestino. Recife: Universidade Federal de Pernambuco, Editora Universitária, 1978. 99 p.: bibl.

Studies Arabic-Iberic influence on popular singers of Brazil's Northeast, mostly from historical point of view.

1033 Sousa, Manoel Matusalém. Cordel, fé e viola. Petrópolis: Vozes, 1982. 86 p.

Priest discourses on human, social, religious, and cultural values inherent in *literatura de cordel*. Considers it a "prophetic" genre of popular literature.

1034 Tavares Júnior, Luiz. O mito na literatura de cordel. Rio de Janeiro: Tempo Brasileiro, 1980. 80 p.: bibl., diagrams.

Analyzes two *literatura de cordel* texts employing structural methods of analysis: 1) *Os martirios de Genoveva de Brabante*, and 2) *Historia do rapaz que botou a sela na mãe e amigou-se com a irmã*. Finds that structurally they are archetypical models of the Myth of Persecuted Innocence and Myth of Evil Punished.

1035 Teixeira, Fausto. Crendices & superstições. Vitória: Fundação Cultural do Espírito Santo, 1975. 123 p.: map.

Dictionary of 1399 beliefs, superstitions, magic practices, etc. grouped according to subjects (e.g., human life, animal world, supernatural world) and collected (1958–67) by teachers and students in Espírito Santo state. Also includes glossaries of regional speech.

1036 Terra, Ruth Brito Lemos. O ermita e o anjo no Nordeste (USP/RIEB, 23, 1981, p. 7–26, bibl.)

Scholarly analysis of versified narrative in pamphlet form (published 1917) with title *Historia de um homem que teve uma questão com Santo Antônio*. Traces its origin to medieval exemplum about hermit and angel, a narrative that gave rise to folktales in many places.

1037 Verger, Pierre Fatumbi. Orixás: deuses iorubás na Africa e no Novo Mundo. Tradução, Maria Aparecida da Nóbrega. Salvador: Editora Corrupia Comércio, 1981. 295 p.: bibl., ill., index, photos.

Although I usually exclude in *HLAS* the torrent of books published about Brazilian popular religions, I include this work because its 259 superb b/w photos set it apart. Author is student of Brazilian popular religions with roots in Africa. Folklorists interested in popular religions would do well to consult the volume.

1038 Vianna, Hildesgardes. Folclore brasileiro: Bahia. Rio de Janeiro: Ministério da Educação e Cultura, Instituto Nacional do Folclore, 1981. 79 p.: bibl., ill., music (Folclore brasileiro; 12)

No. 12 in series devoted to individual states of Brazil. Historico-geographic introduction leads into separate chapters on various aspects of Bahian folklore (e.g., popular speech, oral literature, dances, popular cults, arts and crafts, regional foods).

1039 Vieira Filho, Domingos. Populário maranhense: bibliografia. Rio de Janeiro: Civilização Brasileira em convênio com a Secretaria de Cultura do Maranhão, 1982. 72 p., 3 leaves of plates: bibl., ill., index (Série Inéditos)

Useful listing of 438 books, articles, and recordings having to do with Maranhão's folklore. Arranged according to subject matter, most entries have brief annotations. Includes good subject index.

1040 Vila Nova, Sebastião. Literatura de cordel e sociedade de massa (Folclore [Associação de Folclore e Artesanato de Guarujá, São Paulo] 7, 1982, p. 10–11)

Thought-provoking observations about invention of term *literatura de cordel* by elite classes of society to identify in a pejorative way the "literature" of non-elite groups. Notes that industrialization has broken down social stratification and also made obsolete distinctions formerly made between literatures of the different clearly defined social classes.

1041 Vilela, Aloísio. O coco de Alagoas: origem, evolução, dança e modalidades. 2a. ed. Maceió: Museu Théo Brandão-UFAL, 1980.

Descriptive commentary about dance of Northeastern Brazil by well informed layman who writes without scholarly pretensions. First presented in 1951 Congress of Folklore, it contains words without music of many songs.

1042 Von der Weisheit des Volkles: Sprichwörter, Rätsel und Kinderreime (IA/ZK, 33:1, 1983, p. 71–74)

Translates into German some proverbs, popular sayings, riddles, word games, etc. Includes brief introduction.

CENTRAL AMERICA

1043 Acevedo, Jorge Luis. La música en
Guanacaste. San José: Editorial de la
Universidad de Costa Rica, 1980. 199 p.:
charts, ill., music.
Beautifully printed book about music
in Costa Rica. In text, photographs, dance
diagrams, and musical transcriptions, it deals
with practically all aspects of folk and traditional music (i.e., music itself, musical instruments, songs, dances, fiestas). Includes
several brief contributions by authors other
than Acevedo.

Ajmac Cuxil, Concepción. Ritual del matrimonio tradicional y moderno en Tecpán.
See *HLAS 45:8098.*

1044 Arosemena Moreno, Julio. Geografía
de las danzas folklóricas panameñas
(*in* Simposium Nacional de Antropología, Arqueología y Etnohistoria de Panamá, 5th,
Panamá, 1974. Actas. Panamá: Universidad
de Panamá, Centro de Investigaciones Antropológicas e Instituto Nacional de Cultura,
Dirección Nacional de Patrimonio Histórico,
1978, p. 425–445, bibl., maps, tables)
Indicates through brief introductory
comment, chart, and series of maps the geographical distribution of some of the main
folkloric dances known today in Panama.

1045 ———. Máscaras de diablos: su con-
fección (*in* Simposium Nacional de
Antropología, Arqueología y Etnohistoria de
Panamá, Panamá, 1974. Actas. Panamá: Universidad de Panamá, Centro de Investigaciones Antropológicas e Instituto Nacional
de Cultura, Dirección Nacional del Patrimonio Histórico, 1978, p. 399–423, plates)
Describes in detail the process of
making zoomorphic or anthropomorphic
devils' mask as observed in Panama. Photographs illustrated the process.

1046 Berríos Mayorga, María. La adivinanza
en Nicaragua. Managua: Papelera Industrial de Nicaragua, 1979. 187 p.
Offers 664 riddles along with introduction that deals with the riddle in general and
particularly the present collection.

**1047 Bibliografía del folklore de Guatemala,
1892–1980.** Universidad de San Carlos
de Guatemala, Facultad de Humanidades, Escuela de Bibliotecología. Guatemala: Direc-

ción General de Antropología e Historia,
1980. 174 p.: indexes (Colección Antro-
pología. Serie Cultura popular)
Contains over 700 annotated items di-
vided into following sections: "Folklore Ma-
terial o Ergológico;" "Folklore Social;"
"Folklore Espiritual-Mental;" "Folklore en
General;" "Folklorología;" "Calendarios y
Listas sobre distintas Actividades de Indole
Folklórica;" "Proyección Folklórica;" and
"Folklore Aplicado." Also includes index of
authors and titles. Excellent reference tool.

1048 Carvalho-Neto, Paulo de. Viajeros in-
gleses y norteamericanos del siglo XIX
y el folklore de Centroamérica y México.
Traducción de textos, Delina Anibarro
Halushka. Guatemala: Editorial Universitaria, 1981. 112 p.: bibl., ill. (Colección Problemas y documentos; v. 9)
Calls attention to observations about
folklore written by 45 19th-century English
and North American travelers in Central
America and Mexico. In most cases, pertinent passages are offered in Spanish
translation.

1049 Chacón Polanco, Mario Roberto.
Los barriletes gigantes de Santiago
Sacatepéquez: una aproximación histórica,
social y artística (USCG/TP, 15, 1981,
p. 71–104, bibl., ill.)
Systematic study of custom of flying
huge colored kites to celebrate Day of the
Dead in Santiago Sacatepéquez, Guatemala.
Treats practice's historic, social, and artistic
aspects. Studies specifically certain folkloric
features of celebration.

1050 Dary Fuentes, Claudia. Literatura
popular de los caribes negros de Guatemala (USCG/TP, 34, 1981, p. unnumbered
ill., maps, photos)
Provides brief but quite informative
introduction about history of blacks in
Guatemala, then offers seven tale-texts
that were orally collected from informants
of black-Carib ethnic stock in town of
Livingston, Guatemala's eastern coast.

1051 Díaz Castillo, Roberto. En el XIII
aniversario del Centro de Estudios
Folklóricos de la Universidad de San Carlos
de Guatemala (USCG/TP, suplemento extraordinario, 1980, p. 3–47, photos)
Brief but informative history of very
active Centro de Estudios Folklóricos from

1967 founding until 1980. Discusses purposes and goals, notes activities, lists publications issued by Centro, etc.

1052 Facio, Sara. Actos de fe en Guatemala. Fotos, Sara Facio y María Cristina Orive. Textos, Miguel Angel Asturias. Traducción al francés, André Camp. Traducción al inglés, Gerald Martin. Buenos Aires: La Azotea, 1980. 97 p.: chiefly col. ill.

Handsome art book features superb color photographs of scenes of non-urban life in Guatemala. Some of these would be of interest to folklorists studying Guatemalan customs, rural dress, dances, processions, etc. Texts by Miguel Angel Asturias in Spanish, English, and French.

1053 Lara Figueroa, Celso A. Las andanzas de Pedro Urdemalas en Guatemala (USCG/TG, 9/10, 1978, p. 73–169, ill., map)

Presents texts and analyses for each of 18 orally collected Guatemalan folktales about the *pícaro* of Hispanic tradition, Pedro de Urdemalas. Briefly traces history of Urdemalas from medieval Spain to present and comments upon the character as he appears in contemporary Guatemalan folklore. Provides informant data.

1054 ———. Los cuentos de adivinanza en la literatura guatemalteca de tradición oral (IAHG/AHG, 2 : 3, 1981, p. 171–188, bibl.)

Careful transcriptions of four orally collected folktales, from eastern Guatemala, having to do with riddles. Includes some useful synopses of tales and data about informants.

1055 ———. Los cuentos de animales en el folklore de Guatemala (IAHG/AHG, 2 : 2, 1980, p. 81–103, bibl.)

Offers eight carefully transcribed animal tales from oral tradition that deal with Uncle Rabbit and Uncle Coyote. Includes brief introduction, good notes, and data about informants.

1056 ———. Los cuentos de nunca acabar en el folklore guatemalteco (USCG/TP, 35, 1981, p. unnumbered, ill., photos)

Brief introduction provides basic information about folktale scholarship and methodology used by professional folklorists in studying folktales. Examples of some orally collected Guatemalan tale-texts follow. They are formula tales, mostly cumulative tales.

1057 ———. Por los viejos barrios de la Ciudad de Guatemala. Con fotos de Mauro Calanchina. Guatemala: Centro de Estudios Folklóricos, Universidad de San Carlos de Guatemala, 1977. 265 p.: bibl., ill. (Colección Proyección folklórica; v. 1)

Pt. 1 of book (p. 13–34) discusses, in theoretical and historical terms, concept of *projections* of folklore into literature. Pt. 2 (p. 35–201) publishes 11 literary pieces by the author, based on such projections. He writes them for sociopolitical reasons in order to contribute toward the formation of a genuinely national culture and literature in Guatemala.

1058 ———. Tío Conejo y Tío Coyote en la literatura popular guatemalteca (USCG/TP, 25, 1979, p. 2–22, ill.)

Offers eight orally collected animal tales about the hare and the coyote along with commentary that interprets their conflicts in terms of class struggle.

1059 ———. Los trovadores del pueblo: poesía popular de Guatemala (USCG/TP, 20, 1978, p. 2–27, ill., map, music)

Briefly describes number of lyric and narrative genres of folk poetry as found in eastern Guatemalan folklore. Genres under consideration are *coplas, décimas, romances, romancillos,* and *corridos.*

1060 Luján Muñoz, Luis. Tradiciones navideñas de Guatemala. Guatemala: Esso Central America, 1981. 199 p.: appendix, bibl., ill. (some col.) (Cuadernos de la tradición guatemalteca; v. 1)

Describes Guatemalan Christmas customs beginning with burning of the devil (Dec. 7) through celebration of the day of Virgin of Candelaria (Feb. 2). Appendix contains many texts of songs (only a few with music), folk drama, small glossary, etc.

1061 Marina Villatoro, Elba. Vida y obra de los curanderos del El Petén, Guatemala (USCG/TP, 38, 1981, p. 1–18, ill., map, photos)

Sketches briefly history and geography of El Petén region, then reports on several *curanderos,* or healers, who were interviewed there. Photographs by author supplement descriptive and analytical material.

1062 Morales Hidalgo, Italo Amilcar. Breve estudio sobre el Baile de Tun en San Bernardino Suchitepéquez desde su orígenes

hasta nuestros días (SGHG/A, 51:51, enero/
dic. 1978, p. 51–66, bibl.)

Good study of Corpus Christi dance-
drama that displays vestiges of pre-conquest
sacrificial dance, the *Baile del Tun*. Presents
considerable historical data along with ethnographic description of dance as performed
today in San Bernardino Suchitepéquez,
Guatemala.

1063 Núñez Meléndez, Esteban. Plantas me-
dicinales de Costa Rica y su folclore.
2. ed. Ciudad Universitaria Rodrigo Facio:
Editorial Universidad de Costa Rica, 1978.
318 p.: bibl., index.

Studies geographically and historically
the medicinal use of various plants in Costa
Rica, and then offers detailed descriptions of
plants and indications of how they are used.

1064 Palen, Roberta R. Weaving and traditional costume in Guatemala: a selective bibliography (RIB, 31:1, 1981, p. 17–26)

Surveys books and articles about traditional dress and weaving methods in Guatemala. Comments upon each work and evaluates it critically.

1065 Portillo Figueroa, José Víctor. Salu-
dando con sombrero ajeno: recopilación de dichos simples y de refranes. Guatemala: Impreofset O. de León Palacios, 1981.
107 p. (Colección En busca de autores; 4)

Offers 1102 "Dichos Simples o Frases
hechas que aun no Llegan a Refranes"
(p. 13–57); then 1252 "Refranes o Frases
Proverbiales" (p. 59–107). They are not alphabetized or grouped according to subject,
nor are they defined. No sources are indicated.
Author provides very brief introduction.

1066 Reyes Prado, Anantonia. Aportes para
el estudio de la historia del nacimiento guatemalteco (USCG/TB, 13, 1980,
p. 125–175, bibl., photos)

Informative history of Christmas
crèches (i.e., *nacimientos*) in Guatemala
from their beginnings in Spanish and European tradition to present. Cites many sources
of information such as early chronicles and
other written documents. Includes some
good photographs.

1067 Rowe, Ann Pollard. A century of
change in Guatemalan textiles. New
York: Center for Inter-American Relations,
1981. 151 p.: bibl., ill., map, photos.

Published on the occasion of an ex-

hibition organized by the Center for Inter-
American Relations, this catalog-study of traditional Guatemalan textiles is an excellent
treatment of subject. Besides informative
commentary based on good notes and copious bibliography, there are superb photographs, many in color.

1068 Sánchez de Duarte, Eloísa. Refranes de
mi tierra: poesías de América y de
otros países. San Salvador: Editorial Ercilla,
1978. 348 p.

Pt. 1 of work (p. 1–243) lists several
hundred sayings and proverbs in alphabetical
order, but it gives no sources or any explanations. Pt. 2 (p. 245–348) has nothing to do
with folklore; it is an anthology of poetry by
various poets of North and South America.

1069 Schultze Jena, L. Mitos y leyendas de
los pipiles de Izalco. Translated
by Gloria Menjívar Rieken and Armida Pa-
rada Fortín. San Salvador: Ediciones Cuscat-
lán, 1977. 163 p.

Translation into Spanish of *Indiana II:
Mythen in Muttersprache der pipil von
Izalco in El Salvador* (1935), pioneer study of
myths and legends of the Pipil Indians of El
Salvador. Contains more than 50 texts in
Pipil and Spanish.

1070 Smith, Ronald R. The Society of Los
Congos of Panamá: Afro-American
dance theatre (*in* The Role of Afro-American
folklore in the teaching of the arts and the
humanities. Edited by Adrienne Lanier
Seward. Bloomington, Ind.: s.n., 1979,
p. 118–164, bibl., charts, ill., map)

Describes and analyzes a black dance-
drama (performed in Colón) with roots in
16th century when black slaves were brought
to Panama.

Williams, Barbara J. and **Carlos A. Ortiz-
Solorio.** Middle American folk soil taxonomy. See *HLAS 45:5122.*

CHILE

1071 Agosín, Marjorie. Bibliografía de
Violeta Parra (RIB, 32:2, 1982,
p. 179–190, bibl.)

Introduction evaluates very highly
Violeta Parra's work as collector of Chilean
folksongs, superb singer of such songs, and
herself composer of many excellent songs

and poems based on folk tradition. Carefully annotated bibliography of works by and about Parra follows.

1072 Cánepa-Hurtado, Gina. La canción de lucha en Violeta Parra y su ubicación en el complejo cultural chileno entre los años 1960 a 1973: esbozo de sus antecedentes socio-históricos y categorización de los fenómenos culturales atingentes (RCLL, 9 : 17, 1983, p. 147–170)

Seeks to interpret, from Marxist perspective, Violeta Parra's songs of social struggle (i.e., *canciones de lucha*) as based upon a "folkloric culture" which is never precisely defined. Moves from Parra to a general discussion of such songs as Chilean expressions of resistance to imperialism and foreign values not only in musical tastes but in other areas as well.

1073 Cárdenas Tabies, Antonio. Usos y costumbres de Chiloé. Santiago: Editorial Nascimento, 1978. 222 p.: bibl.

Gives some basic information about the island of Chiloé and its people. Describes in brief passages, each with its own heading, a multitude of customs, practices, beliefs, ceremonies and rituals, folk cures, etc.

1074 Jijena Sánchez, Rafael. La alforja del peregrino. Estudio preliminar, notas y vocabulario, Silvia Elena Palomar. Buenos Aires: Editorial Huemul, 1978. 180 p.: bibl. (Colección Clásicos Huemul; 98)

Jijena Sánchez gathers from oral tradition some texts of *coplas* and other types of popular songs, also some tales and legends. Provides commentary but no indication of sources. Palomar's preliminary study surveys and evaluates life and works of pioneer folklorist Jijena Sánchez.

1075 Parra, Violeta. Cantos folklóricos chilenos. Santiago: Editorial Nascimento, 1979. 134 p.: ill., music.

With a chapter for each individual singer, Parra relates in the first person her collecting encounters with 15 folksingers. Provides words and music (transcriptions are by Luis Gaston Soublette) of over 50 songs of many types gathered from these singers.

1076 Plath, Oreste. Folklore chileno. Santiago: Editorial Nascimento, 1979. 492 p.: bibl.

Panoramic survey of many types of Chilean folklore arranged in 11 chapters on such subjects as sayings and expressions, legends, traditions, customs and superstitions, games, children's songs and sayings, religious folklore, musical folklore, etc. Each chapter has its own bibliography.

1077 ———. Folklore lingüístico chileno: paremiología. Santiago: Editorial Nascimento, 1981. 150 p.

Offers various popular sayings, proverbs, comparisons, etc. found in Chilean tradition and explains their meaning and usage.

1078 ———. Folklore médico chileno: antropología y salud. Santiago: Editorial Nascimento, 1981. 331 p.: bibl.

Surveys and discusses multiple aspects of Chilean folk medicine of both Indian and Hispanic origin. Includes chapters on topics such as cures having to do with colors, planets, music, the sea and tides, etc.; and others on specific ailments such as pregnancy, menstruation, dental problems, etc.

1079 La Sabiduría de un pueblo. Recopilación de Miguel Jordá. Santiago: Ediciones Mundo, 1975. 223 p. (La Fe de un pueblo; 1)

Offers large collection of poems on religious subjects (i.e., *canto a lo divino*), mostly quatrains glossed by *décimas*. Groups texts according to subject matter.

1080 Uribe Echevarría, Juan. Villancicos hispanos y chilenos (SCHG/R, 148, 1980, p. 7–67, ill., music)

Offers first an excellent survey of the history of the Spanish *villancico* (i.e., a Christmas song) replete with many literary texts from medieval times to present. Then focuses on Christmas in Chile and again offers words of many *villancicos* (some with music). Only a few texts are genuine folklore, but all are closely related to folk tradition.

COLOMBIA

1081 León Rey, José Antonio. Juegos infantiles del Oriente Cundinamarqués. Bogotá: Instituto Caro y Cuervo, 1982. 125 p.: map.

Drawing mostly upon his own memory, author describes 103 traditional games played in Oriente prov., Cundinamarca dept.

Includes many songs and verses that accompany such games, but no music.

1082 List, George. Music and poetry in a Colombian village: a tri-cultural heritage. Bloomington: Indiana University Press, 1983. 601 p.: bibl., ill., maps, music.

Exemplary study of music and sung poetry (and everything related to these) of small town near the Atlantic coast of northern Colombia. No other single Latin American community's traditional music has ever been studied so thoroughly. Based on years of field study and extensive library research.

1083 McDowell, John H. Beyond iconicity: ostention in Kamsá mythic narrative (IU/JFI, 19:2/3, May/Dec. 1982, p. 119–139)

Challenging theoretical discussion which questions analysis of folk narratives based upon use of synopsized texts. In calling attention to weaknesses of this procedure, author cites evidence drawn from his own analysis of narratives gathered among Kamsá Indians of Andean Colombia.

ECUADOR

1084 Carvalho Neto, Paulo de. Historias a lo Divino: 24 historias a lo Divino, populares y tradicionales en el Ecuador. Ciudad Universitaria: División Editorial, Dirección General de Extensión Universitaria, Universidad de San Carlos de Guatemala, 1979. 342 p.: ill. (Colección Proyección folklórica; v. 2)

Offers 24 Ecuadorian stories retold in literary style by professional folklorist and able writer who knows his craft. Twelve concern supernatural beings and 12 deal with charms and magic. Author also provides brief introduction.

1085 Cordero Iñíguez, Juan. Bibliografía ecuatoriana de artesanías y artes populares. Cuenca, Ecuador: Centro Interamericano de Artes Populares (CIDAP), 1980. 373 p.: index, maps, tables.

Excellent bibliography that contains 999 entries, most of them annotated. Its scope is much broader than title indicates since it covers not only handicrafts and popular art but other kinds of folklore as well.

1086 Sacha Pacha: el mundo de la selva: relatos bilingües. Recogidos y redactados por Juan Santos Ortiz de Villalba. Dibujos

originales de Vicente Etxarte. Quito: CICAME (Centro de Investigaciones Culturales de la Amazonía Ecuatoriana), 1976. 159 p.: ill.

Collection of legend or folktale texts from Ecuador and northern Peru that were orally collected in Quichua and here published in Quichua with Spanish translations. Includes seven legends about places, six about animals, 25 about people, and 16 about devils. Also includes a few proverbs and interpretations of dreams.

Salomon, Frank. La "yumbada:" un drama ritual quechua en Quito. See *HLAS 45 : 1425.*

GREATER ANTILLES

1087 Abrahams, Roger D. Storytelling events: wake amusements and the structure of nonsense on St. Vincent (AFS/JAF, 95 : 378, Oct./Dec. 1982, p. 389–414)

Describes body of folktales employed in *wake* or *nine-night* as celebrated in Afro-American community of Richland Park, St. Vincent. Addresses question of how folktales achieve cultural meaning as they are performed within such a traditional event. Includes many orally collected texts.

1088 Antología literaria dominicana. v. 1, Poesía. v. 2, Cuento. v. 3, Teatro. v. 4, Discursos, semblanzas, ensayos. v. 5, Folklore; Indice acumulativo. Editado por Margarita Vallejo de Paredes. Colaboradores: Lilia Portalatín Sosa, Pedro Pablo Paredes V., Jorge Max Fernández. Santo Domingo: Instituto Tecnológico de Santo Domingo, 1981. 5 v.: bibl., indexes.

Vol. 5, *Folklore e índice acumulativo,* contains 30 articles by 20 different writers. Most, but not all, are about literary or musical folklore (e.g., songs, tales, dances, prayers, etc.) and many are classics of their kind (e.g., Pedro Henríquez Ureña's "Romances en América"). Important compendium of articles that have withstood the test of time. Should be consulted by anyone interested in Dominican folklore.

1089 Beck, Jane C. To windward of the land: the occult world of Alexander Charles. Bloomington: Indiana University Press, 1979. 309 p.: bibl., ill.

In-depth study of an informant from

islands of St. Lucia, primarily a fisherman-obeah man (i.e., sorcerer and healer). Investigates his biographical background, system of beliefs, obeah practices, etc. Most of the book is first-person narration taken from field recordings.

1090 Cabanillas de Rodríguez, Berta. El folklore en la alimentación puertorriqueña. Río Piedras: Editorial de la Universidad de Puerto Rico, 1983. 180 p., 15 p. of plates: bibl., ill., index, ports.

Book about food lore in Puerto Rico. Surveys songs, poems, games, riddles, sayings, proverbs, street cries, beliefs, etc., having to do with foods. Offers innumerable texts, useful bibliography, and good index.

1091 Cahier de folklore et des traditions orales d'Haïti. Edited by Max Benoit. Port-au-Prince: Imprimerie des Antilles, 198? 1 v.: ill.

Ethnohistory professor at Université de l'Etat de'Haïti, Benoit publishes collection of research papers based on fieldwork done by his students of folklore over period of several years: Jean Osner Alsain "Le Phenomene de la Morte et la Mentalité Paysanne" (1971–71, p. 11–24); Joseph Charles "Le Jardin Secret de l'Haitien" (1969–70, p. 25–48, about folk beliefs); August Henri-Claude "La Superstition dans les Jeux de Hasard" (1974–75, p. 49–60); Bellard Philome "'Les Expéditions': Essai sur la Magie Offensive" (1973–74; p. 61–83); Georges Chery "Les Proverbes et les Croyances Créoles: Ont-ils une Influence sur le Comportement de l'Haitien?" (1973, p. 85–97); Calixte Clerisme "Aperçu sur Nos Contes" (1970, p. 99–111); Enel Clerisme "Le Symbolisme des Couleurs dans le Culte Vaudou et Son Emprunt au Catholicisme" (1969, p. 113–127); Jean Rosier Descardes "La Vengeance des Loas" (1978, p. 129–149, about folk religion); and Paul Antoine "Place du Palma-Christi dans la Culture Populaire" (no date given, p. 151–172).

1092 Davis, Martha Ellen. Voces del purgatorio: estudio de la salve dominicana. Santo Domingo: Museo del Hombre Dominicano, 1981. 106 p.: bibl., ill., map, music.

Studies the *salve*, a religious-secular song with European and African roots that is today one of the most cultivated genres of traditional music in the Dominican Re-public. Focuses mostly on socioreligious aspects of the *salve*, but includes some musical examples.

1093 Espina Pérez, Darío. Alma de Haiti: leyendas, narraciones y fantasías. Sevilla: Editorial Católica Española, 1978. 203 p.

Collection of personal literary sketches about life in Haiti that touches on many local traditions, legends, stories, beliefs, etc. Of little value to folklorists except perhaps as background for placing knowledge gained from other sources in a vital context.

1094 Ferére, Gérard A. Haitian voodoo: its true face (UWI/CQ, 24:3/4, Sept./Dec. 1978, p. 37–47, bibl.)

Seeks to rescue Haitian voodoo from misunderstandings of outsiders that have long plagued it. Considers it a primitive form of religion that "educated Haitians more and more appreciate . . . as one of the most genuine expressions of their folklore." Examines voodoo's origins, some of its beliefs and practices, and ceremonies.

1095 Flowers, Helen L. A classification of the folktale of the West Indies by types and motifs. New York: Arno Press, 1980. 660 p.: bibl.

Photoreproduction of doctoral dissertation done at Indiana University in 1952. Classifies West Indian folktales using Thompson system of classification.

1096 Folklore infantil de Santo Domingo. Recogido y anotado por Edna Garrido de Boggs. Transcripciones musicales de Ruth Crawford Seeger. Ilustrado por Gloria Gastón. Santo Domingo: Editora de Santo Domingo, 1980. 664 p.: ill., music

New edition of 1955 classic in the field. Exemplary in its scholarship because of exhaustive fieldwork and library research. Includes sections on songs, games, word formulas, jokes, tongue-twisters, tales, riddles, etc. Ruth Crawford Seeger made the musical transcriptions and Gloria Gastón the line drawings.

1097 Lizardo, Fradique and **José Porfirio Muñoz Victoria.** Fiestas patronales y juegos. Santo Domingo: Ediciones Fundación García-Arévalo, 1979. 318 p.: bibl., ill. (Serie Investigaciones; no. 11)

Studies fiestas that celebrate various saints and identifies and describes games associated with them. Classifies games, provides calendar of fiestas, lists communities studied, and gives informant information. Profusely illustrated.

1098 Moodie, Sylvia. Some superstition and beliefs of Hispano-Trinidadians (*in* Conference of Hispanists, 5th, University of the West Indies, Mona Campus, Jamaica, 1982. Myth and superstition in Spanish-Caribbean literature. Mona, Jamaica: University of the West Indies, Department of Spanish, 1982, p. 220–268, appendices)

Discusses relationship between folk religion and superstitions of various kinds; then cites examples of superstitions found in Trinidad (e.g., prayers, spells, use of plants for magical purposes, folk cures, evil eye, supernatural beings, etc.). Provides many texts of prayers and cites many bibliographical sources.

1099 Orta Ruiz, Jesús. Décima y folclor: estudio de la poesía y el cantar de los campos de Cuba. La Habana: Unión de Escritores y Artistas de Cuba, 1980. 241 p. (Colección La décima)

Studies the *décima* and other popular songs and poetry of Cuba through texts author gathered from folkloric and literary sources. Stresses their relationship to Cuban history and their importance in reflecting the patriotic and revolutionary fervor of the people.

1100 Wolkstein, Diane. The magic orange tree, and other Haitian folktales. Collected and told by Diane Wolkstein. Drawings by Elsa Henríquez. New York: Schocken Books, 1980. 212 p.: ill, music.

Offers 27 literarily retold folktales, each with introductory commentary. Also provides words (in English or Creole) and music of a few songs that accompany certain tales.

MEXICO

1101 Aiken, Riley. Mexican folktales from the borderlands. Dallas, Tex.: Southern Methodist University Press, 1980. 159 p.: ill.

Literary versions of 49 tales from both sides of the Texas-Mexican border. Almost no information is given about sources or informants. Texts were earlier printed in

various publications of the Texas Folklore Society.

1102 Beutler, Gisela. Adivinanzas españolas de la tradición popular actual de México, principalmente de las regiones de Puebla-Tlaxcala: contribución al estado presente de la investigación de adivinanzas latinoamericanas = Spanische Rätsel aus der heutigen Volkstradition Mexikos, hauptsächlich aus den Gebieten von Puebla-Tlaxcala. Trad. al español por Vera Zeller. Wiesbaden: Steiner, 1979. 106 p.: bibl., 2 maps (Das Mexiko-Projekt der Deutschen Forschungsgemeinschaft = El Proyecto México de la Fundación Alemana para la Investigación Científica; 16)

Offers 333 riddle texts along with detailed notes and analysis, introductory discussion, comparative bibliographical references, etc. Excellent work.

1103 Bock, Philip K. Tepoztlán reconsidered (UCLA/JLAL, 6:1, Summer 1980, p. 129–150, ill., tables)

Written primarily to make up-to-date observations about Mexican community studied in 1920s by Robert Redfield and in 1940s by Oscar Lewis. Author's reassessment of certain aspects of life in Tepoztlán contains data of interest to folklorists about religious and other fiestas, including Carnival celebrations.

1104 Campa, Arthur L. Hispanic culture in the Southwest. Norman: University of Oklahoma Press, 1979. 316 p.: bibl., ill., index, map.

General survey of regional Hispanic culture in the Southwest with stress on Colorado and New Mexico. Focuses on social life (i.e., customs) with particular attention to music, dancing, and other kinds of folklore. Excellent illustrations.

1105 Castillo Romero, Pedro. Calendario folklórico de las fiestas en Nayarit. s.l.: Editorial del Magisterio Benito Juárez, 1979. 266 p.: port.

Interesting calendar of fiestas of Nayarit state. Gives not only date and place of each fiesta but in many cases offers fairly lengthy descriptions of what takes place, tells something of history of each festival, etc.

1106 Coplas que no son de amor: textos. Recopilados y editados por investigadores del Centro de Estudios Lingüísticos y Literarios de El Colegio de México. Bajo la dirección de Margit Frenk Alatorre. México: El Colegio de México, 1980. 440 p.: bibl., indexes (Cancionero folklórico de México; t. 3)

Vol. 3 of *Cancionero folklórico de México*. Vols. 1/2 dealt with coplas about love (see *HLAS 38: 1517* and *HLAS 42: 1311*). This volume offers texts Nos. 5717–8567, which are *coplas* about animals, humorous *coplas*, *coplas* about suffering, etc.

1107 Dickey, Dan William. The Kennedy corridos: a study of the ballads of a Mexican American hero. Austin: Center for Mexican American Studies, University of Texas at Austin, 1978. 127 p.: bibl., ill. (Mexican American monographs; no. 4)

Traces briefly the historical development of the *corrido* tradition and provides some interesting information about recordings of *corridos*. Then analyzes texts of 24 commercial recordings about John F. Kennedy's death.

1108 Edson, Gary. Mexican market pottery. New York: Watson-Guptil Publications, 1979. 168 p.: ill., index, maps.

Examines pre- and posthispanic pottery tradition in Mexico. Describes contemporary traditional processes of pottery-making, as well as traditions and innovations in pottery shape and ornamentation. Discusses characteristics of pottery tradition of each of major pottery centers in Mexico.

Frederich, Barbara E. Folk remedies in modern pharmacies: examples from Tijuana, Mexico. See *HLAS 45: 5096.*

1109 Griego y Maestas, José. Cuentos: tales from the Hispanic Southwest; based on stories originally collected by Juan B. Rael. Selected by and adapted in Spanish by José Griego y Maestas. Retold in English by Rodolfo A. Anaya. Santa Fe: Museum of New Mexico Press, 1980. 174 p.: ill.

Texts of 23 folktales collected from oral tradition by Juan B. Rael and published first in *Cuentos españoles de Colorado y Nuevo México*. Here they are offered in Spanish with English translations on facing pages. Translators provide brief introduction to volume.

1110 Herrera-Sobek, María. The acculturation process of the chicana in the corrido (PCCLAS/P, 9, 1982, p. 25–34)

Surveys some Mexican songs (i.e., *corridos*) about life in US which suggest that Mexican women are more progressive and forward-looking than are their menfolk. Latter show themselves to be conservative and to view with alarm their women's acceptance of North American ways.

1111 ——. The bracero experience: elitelore versus folklore. With an introduction by James W. Wilkie. Los Angeles: UCLA Latin American Center Publications, University of California, 1970. 142 p.: bibl., discography, index (UCLA Latin American studies; v. 43. A Book on lore)

Contrasts life of *braceros* in the US as depicted in literature (i.e., elitelore) with experiences reflected in *corridos* of braceros themselves. Braceros express much more favorable attitude toward US than do novelists and other literati who have not shared the *bracero* experience.

1112 Hispanic legends from New Mexico: narratives from the R.D. Jameson collection. Edited with an introduction and notes by Stanley L. Robe. Berkeley: University of California Press, 1980. 548 p.: bibl. (Folklore and mythology studies; 31)

Edits from R.D. Jameson Collection 730 legend texts translated into English. Includes informant notes and motif numbers. Texts were collected 1951–57 from Spanish speakers in northeastern New Mexico. Editor's preface discusses historical and ethnic context of collection and of legend scholarship in general.

1113 Jiménez, Luz. Los cuentos en náhuatl de Doña Luz Jiménez. Recopilación de Fernando Horcasitas y Sarah O. de Ford. México: Universidad Nacional Autónoma de México, 1979. 172 p.: bibl. (Serie antropológica / Instituto de Investigaciones Antropológicas; 27. Etnología/lingüística)

Offers in Náhuatl with Spanish translation texts of 44 orally collected narratives taken 1948–65 from one informant in Milpa Alta, Federal District. Tales and stories are of various types (e.g., etiological tales, supernatural tales, moralizing stories, narratives about local happenings, humorous tales).

1114 Jones, Oakah L., Jr. Hispanic traditions and improvisations on the *frontera septentrional* of New Spain (UNM/NMHR, 56:4, Oct. 1981, p. 333– 348, bibl., ill.)

Good brief survey of introduction of many Hispanic customs into frontier areas of northern New Spain during colonial period. Drawing upon archival and printed sources, article treats such subjects as fiestas, religious processions and practices, and folk art (e.g., carving of saints' images, folk dramas, dances, trade fairs).

1115 Kofman, Andrei. Tradiciones españolas y mexicanas en el folklore lírico de México (URSS/AL, 8:44, 1981, p. 108–122, ill., plate)

Seeks to define Mexican culture and psychology of Mexicans by comparing traditional Mexican *coplas* and other popular songs with Spanish counterparts. Treats such subjects as changes in poetic symbols, the loss of "feminine" lyric songs in Mexico, the "macho" complex, the Mexican preoccupation with death, etc.

1116 Laughlin, Robert M. Of cabbages and kings: tales from Zinacantán. Washington: Smithsonian Institution Press, 1977. 427 p.: bibl., ill. (Smithsonian contributions to anthropology; no. 23)

Offers 173 traditional myth, tale, and legend texts that were orally collected in Tzotzil community, Chiapas. Texts are in Tzotzil with English translations. Provides background material, data about informants, comparative notes, and other explanations (see also item **1117**).

1117 ———. Of shoes and ships and sealing wax: sundries from Zinacantán. Washington: Smithsonian Institution Press, 1980. 285 p.: bibl., ill. (Smithsonian contributions to anthropology; 25)

Companion work to author's *Of cabbages and kings* (see item **1116**). Sec. 1 contains no folklore, but sec. 2, "At Home," provides orally collected texts of prayers, ritual formulas, and songs (no music) in Tzotzil and English.

1118 Martínez López, Enrique. Corrido, bibliografía y abreviaturas (*in* El Romancero hoy: 2° Coloquio Internacional, University of California, Davis. v. 2, Poética. Edición a cargo de Antonio Sánchez Romeralo, Diego Catalán, Samuel G. Armistead, con la colaboración de Jesús Antonio Cid *et al.* Madrid: Gredos, 1979, p. 373–377 [Romancero y poesía oral; 3])

Recent listing of books and articles about ballads (i.e., *corridos*) in Mexico and US.

1119 Olivera de Bonfil, Alicia. La tradición oral sobre Cuauhtémoc. México: UNAM, Instituto de Investigaciones Históricas, 1980. 183 p.: bibl., ill. (Dictámenes Ichcateopan; 3)

Systematic and extremely valuable report of effort by team of specialists from Instituto de Investigaciones Históricas to separate historical facts from local oral tradition concerning supposed burial of Cuauhtémoc, Mexico's national hero, in town of Ichcateopan, Guerrero. Few oral traditions have ever been studied so thoroughly. Folklorists will find methodology and findings most fascinating.

1120 Quevedo, Francisco. Lírica popular tabasqueña: cantares yucatecos, estudios folklóricos. 2a. ed. México: Consejo Editorial del Gobierno del Estado de Tabasco, 1980. 129 p.: ill. (Serie Literatura; 20)

New ed. of 1916 work. Quevedo, newspaperman whose pseudonym was "Quico," comments on various aspects of Yucatecan folklore, mostly popular songs. Though dated, his articles contain useful and interesting information and a number of song texts (no music).

1121 Robb, John Donald. Hispanic folk music of New Mexico and the Southwest: a self-portrait of a people. Norman: University of Oklahoma Press, 1980. 891 p.: appendices, bibl., discography, ill., indexes, music.

Huge collection of orally collected Hispanic folksongs of many types that were gathered in New Mexico and the Southwest. Both words (Spanish texts with English translations) and music are provided. Also studies dances. Includes informative general introduction and excellent indexes. A basic work in the field.

1122 Serrano Martínez, Celedonio. El Coyote: corrido de la Revolución. Acapulco: Ediciones Municipales, 1978. 333 p., 2 fold. leaves of plates: ill.

New ed. of 1951 long narrative poem. Although not folklore, work is projection of Mexico's traditional *corridos* into realm of art poetry. One of the best examples of literature of this type.

1123 Taggert, James M. Animal metaphors in Spanish and Mexican oral tradition (AFS/JAF, 95 : 377, July/Sept. 1982, p. 280–303, bibl.)

Attempts to show how in three texts of Hispanic tale of "Juanito el Oso," one collected in Spain and two in Mexico, Spanish and Indian narrators develop different animal metaphors to fit their contrasting views of the universe. Draws some sweeping conclusions from fairly limited data.

1124 Trotter, Robert T., II and Juan Antonio Chavira. Curanderismo. Athens: University of Georgia Press, 1981. 204 p.: appendix, bibl., ill., index.

Very sympathetic ethnographic study of healers (i.e., *curanderos*) and their practices as researched mostly in the Lower Rio Grande Valley of Texas and Mexico. Deals with history, attitudes, theories of healing, various levels of treatment (i.e., material, spiritual, and mental), future of curanderismo, etc. Basic book for anyone interested in folk medicine.

1125 ¡Vivan los artesanos!: Mexican folk art from the Collection of Fred and Barbara Meiers. La Jolla, Calif.: Mingel International Museum of World Folk Art, 1980? 48 p.: ill.

Catalog-guide to exhibition of Mexican folk art presented, it appears, in 1980. Notable for its illustrations, many in dazzling color. On exhibit were art objects of all kinds.

1126 Whitaker, Irwin and Emily Whitaker. A potter's Mexico. Albuquerque: University of New Mexico Press, 1978. 136 p.: bibl., ill., index, photos.

Handsome book with innumerable photographs, some in color, about pottery-making in Mexico. Deals with clays used, techniques of manufacture, designs employed in everyday pottery as well as decorative pieces, etc.

1127 Wroth, William. The chapel of Our Lady of Talpa. Colorado Springs: The Taylor Museum of The Colorado Springs Fine Arts Center, 1979. 103 p.: appendices, bibl., ill., maps, photos.

Fine study of family chapel built in village of Talpa, New Mexico, in 1830s. Treats its history, architectural characteristics, details of construction, and folk art associated with it (e.g., carved saints' images, altars, religious paintings, etc.). Includes excellent photographs, many in color.

PARAGUAY

1128 Bejarano, Ramón César. Caraí vosá: elementos para el estudio del folklore paraguayo. 2a. ed., corr. y ampliada. Asunción: Editorial Toledo, 1982. 144 p.: bibl., ill. (some col.) (Serie Estudios antropológicos; no. 1)

Extensively revised ed. of 1960 work. A general manual of Paraguayan folklore, it deals with theory, history of folklore, its uses, classification of materials, and techniques of study.

1129 Blache, Martha. Análisis estructural de una creencia de la zona guaranítica: el lobisón (AINA/C, 8, 1972/1978, p. 21–42, tables)

Analyzes belief in werewolves among Guaraní Indians on iconic, connotative, and symbolic levels.

1130 ———. Yasy Yateré: un personaje contradictorio (MEMDA/E, 29/30, enero/dic. 1979, p. 1–10)

Interesting and quite original analysis of 26 versions of Paraguayan myth-legend gathered from Paraguayan informants living in Buenos Aires. Arrives at some conclusions concerning legend's meaning and function based on rigorous global analysis of the texts using methodology developed by French semiologist A.J. Greimas.

1131 González Torres, Dionisio M. Folklore del Paraguay. Asunción: Editorial Comuneros, 1980. 602 p.: bibl., ill., index.

Large miscellany divided into three main parts: 1) "Folklore Espiritual" (i.e., songs, legends, myths, tales, beliefs, superstitions, magic, religion, popular medicine, music, song, dance, etc.); 2) "Folklore Social o Sociológico" (i.e., language, proverbs, games, fiestas, etc.); and 3) "Folklore Material o Ergológico" (i.e., dress, regional dishes, crafts, etc.). All this is preceded by brief section on generalities.

1132 Granda, Germán de. El romancero tradicional español en el Paraguay: razón de una, aparente, anomalía (ICC/T, 37 : 1, enero/abril, 1982, p. 120–147)

Reports success in collecting a few oral ballad (i.e., *romance*) texts which prove that, contrary to previous assumptions, Paraguay did not lack totally a Spanish *romance* tradition. Proceeds, however, to ponder various social and historical circumstances which explain why the Hispanic ballad tradition was weak in Paraguay.

1133 Martínez-Crovetto, Raúl. Folklore toba oriental: relatos fantásticos de origen chamánico (USCNSA/SA, 10:1/2, dic. 1975, p. 177–205, ill.)

Consists of 36 texts of myths and legends of various kinds told by shamans of Paraguay's Toba people. They were collected second hand from informants who, though not shamans themselves, had heard them from shamans. Most deal with fantastic occurrences or episodes where shamans take part.

1134 Micó, Tomás L. Leyendas y mitos del Paraguay. Asunción: T.L. Micó, 1980. 141 p., 16 leaves of plates: bibl., col. ill.

Surveys beliefs about some mythological and legendary animals, goblins, supernatural beings, etc., from Guaraní tradition and shows in photographs some representations of such figures as created by Ramón Elías, a Paraguayan sculptor.

1135 ———. Motivos mitológicos y legendarios del Paraguay en el centenario de Narciso R. Colmán (Rosicrán). Asunción: Instituto Paraguayo de Ciencia del Hombre, 1981. 93 p., 1 leaf of plates: bibl., ill.

Extended commentary on work of Colmán (pseudonym "Rosicrán") who wrote poetry and legends based on Guaraní tradition. Micó surveys some legendary and mythological figures found there. His commentary is subjective and diffuse, but contains much informative data about a fairly esoteric field of study.

PERU

Aku parlanakuypachi: cuentos folklóricos de los quechua de San Martín. See *HLAS* 45:1559.

Bertrand-Rousseau, Pierrette. Cinco fábulas shipibo. See *HLAS* 45:1566.

1136 Castañeda León, Luisa. Vestido tradicional del Perú = Traditional dress of Peru. Lima: Museo Nacional de la Cultura Peruana, 1981. 197 p.: bibl., ill., index., map.

Surveys, in text written in Spanish with English translation, the history of Peruvian dress from Inca times to present. Deals mostly with regional dress of Indians and mestizos on lower social levels. Excellent drawings and paintings, mostly in color, illustrate text.

1137 Ibérico Más, Luis. El folklore agrario de Cajamarca. Ilustraciones, Enrique Guerrero C. Cajamarca: Dirección de Investigación y Proyección Social de la Universidad Nacional de Cajamarca, 1981. 209 p., 4 leaves of plates: bibl., ill.

Provides ethnographic information about rural life in Cajamarca prov., then surveys various beliefs and customs associated with it (e.g., omens, weather, lore, texts of tales and legends, proverbs, beliefs about animals, riddles, regional vocabulary).

1138 ———. El folklore literario de Cajamarca. Cajamarca: Universidad Nacional de Cajamarca, 1976. 176 p.: bibl.

Surveys different genres of literary folklore (i.e., tales and legends, proverbs, riddles, and popular sayings) by presenting useful theoretical discussion of each genre followed by interesting illustrative texts collected in Cajamarca. Unfortunately, provides no information about sources. Bibliography is also deficient.

1139 Leyendas ancashinas. Marcos Yauri Montero, compilador. Lima: P.L. Villanueva, 1979. 121 p.

Collection of 80 literarily retold legends and folktales from Ancash area. Orally collected, but informant data are lacking.

1140 Mendizábal de Roel, Margarita. Un personaje mítico de la selva: el *chullachaki* (in Congreso Peruano: El Hombre y la Cultura Andina, 3d, 1977. El hombre y la cultura andina [see *HLAS 43:253*] v. 5, p. 933–945, bibl.)

Gathers together various beliefs and two tale-texts about the *chullachaki*, a malignant being or spirit who is said to live in the jungle area of Peru. Some data come from oral informants, others from printed sources.

1141 Merino de Zela, E. Mildred. Bibliografía del folklore peruano: 1956–1975 (in Congreso Peruano: El Hombre y la Cultura Andina, 3d, 1977. El hombre y la cultura andina [see *HLAS 43:253*] v. 5, p. 973–976)

Preliminary report on work done

on bibliography of Peruvian folklore for
1956–75 that is being prepared by Seminario
de Folklore, Instituto Riva Agüero, Universidad Católica, under auspices of Comité
Interamericano de Folklore.

Osterling, Jorge P. San Agustín de Pariác: su
tradición oral. See *HLAS 45:1471.*

1142 Psiquiatría folklórica. Carlos Alberto
Seguín, editor. Mario Chiappe Costa,
Marlene Dobkin de Ríos, Max Silva Tuesta,
autores. Lima: Ediciones Ermar, 1979. 156 p.,
3 leaves of plates: bibl., ill.

Collection of articles by authors indicated above dealing with psychiatric aspects
of *curanderismo,* folk medicine, hallucinogens, etc.

1143 Sabogal Wiesse, José R. Literatura oral
andina: problemática y pronuncia-
miento (*in* Congreso Peruano: El Hombre y la
Cultura 3d, 1977. El hombre y la cultura andina [see *HLAS 43:253*] v. 5, p. 957–967)

Exalts merits of oral narratives found
in Peru's Andean region and notes their great
wealth of themes. Although it appears that
folk narratives are probably uppermost in author's mind, one example reproduced here is
only a well told personal narrative, not a traditional tale.

1144 Santa Cruz, Nicomedes. La décima en
el Perú. Lima: Instituto de Estudios
Peruanos, 1982. 453 p.: bibl., discography.

Comprehensive collection of 259 Peruvian *décima* texts (no music) from both literary and oral traditions preceded by historico-
literary study of genre in Peru. Important
contribution.

Textos capanahua. See *HLAS 45:1616.*

URUGUAY

1145 Hidalgo, Bartolomé. Obra completa.
Prólogo y notas de Walter Rela. Montevideo: Editorial Ciencias, 1979. 95 p.: bibl.

Publishes 11 poems in gaucho dialect
and five in cultured language. Hidalgo was
important early 19th-century precursor of
late 19th-century "gaucho" literature in Río
de la Plata region. His use of folk speech and
popular themes ties him to folk tradition.
Rela offers good brief introduction.

1146 Selección de paremias. Montevideo:
Academia Nacional de Letras, 1981.
199 p.: bibl., index (Biblioteca de la Academia
Nacional de Letras. Serie II, Vocabularios)

Offers 300 Uruguayan popular sayings
and proverbs along with definitions and documentation of their use in oral or written tradition. Representative of collection 10 times
their number gathered in archive of Academia Nacional de Letras. Excellent work.

VENEZUELA

1147 Castellón, Hello. La brujería y es-
piritismo en Venezuela. 2a. ed. Caracas: Publicaciones Seleven, 1980. 181 p.: ill.

General book about occult sciences in
Venezuela (e.g., witchcraft, *curanderismo,*
cult of María Lionza, spiritism, seers). Deals
historically with Indian, black, and Hispanic
elements that enter into such practices
and discusses their present-day status in
Venezuela.

1148 Domínguez, Luis Arturo. Breve historia del Instituto Nacional de Folklore (VANH/B, 62:246, abril/junio 1979,
p. 419–427)

Traces history of folklore research in
Venezuela from 1946 founding of Seminario
de Investigaciones Folklóricas Nacionales
through 1971 establishment of Instituto Nacional de Folklore and down to present. Surveys scholars, journals, groups involved in
folklore research, etc.

1149 Márquez Carrero, Andrés. Folklore del
Estado Mérida. Mérida, Venezuela:
Universidad de Los Andes, Facultad de Humanidades y Educación, Instituto de Investigaciones Literarias Gonzalo Picón Febres,
1978. 102 p.: bibl., ill.

Sets down some examples of various
kinds of folklore from Mérida state, Venezuela (e.g., beliefs, practices, superstitions,
words of songs, games, riddles, many proverbs and sayings).

1150 Pollak-Eltz, Angelina. Aportes
indígenas a la cultura del pueblo venezolano. Caracas: Universidad Católica
Andrés Bello, Instituto de Investigaciones
Históricas, 1978. 173 p.: bibl.

Excellent manual that draws together
much widely dispersed information derived

from many studies of indigenous contribution to daily life, customs, folklore, etc., of rural Venezuela. Touches on such things as crafts, regional foods, popular medicine, musical instruments, fiestas, songs, folktales, myths, legends, beliefs, superstitions, etc. Includes excellent bibliography.

———. Magico-religious movements and social change in Venezuela. See *HLAS 45:1471*.

1151 Reyes, Abilio. La fiesta. Caracas: Universidad Central de Venezuela, Facultad de Humanidades y Educación, Instituto de Investigaciones Literarias, 1980. 59 leaves (Colección Prepublicaciones)

Supplementary title found on p. l: "La Fiesta como Fundamento Social de las Expresiones Folklóricas." Describes Venezuelan fiestas, particularly fiestas of Saint Peter, as celebrated in Miranda state, which feature dances and singing. Provides words of many songs, but no music.

JOURNAL ABBREVIATIONS
FOLKLORE

AFS/JAF Journal of American Folklore. American Folklore Society. Austin, Tex.
AINA/C Cuadernos del Instituto Nacional de Antropología. Secretaría de Estado de Cultura y Educación, Dirección General de Institutos de Investigación. Buenos Aires.
CM/D Diálogos. Artes/Letras/Ciencias humanas. El Colegio de México. México.
IA/ZK Zeitschrift für Kulturaustausch. Institut für Auslandsbeziehungen. Stuttgart, FRG.
IAHG/AHG Antropología e Historia de Guatemala. Instituto de Antropología e Historia de Guatemala. Guatemala.
ICC/T Thesaurus. Instituto Caro y Cuervo. Bogotá.
IU/JFI Journal of the Folklore Institute. Indiana University. Bloomington, Ind.
LARR Latin American Research Review. University of North Carolina Press *for the* Latin American Studies Association. Chapel Hill.
MEMDA/E Etnía. Museo Etnográfico Municipal Dámaso Arce. Olavarría, Argentina.
NS NS NorthSouth/NordSud/NorteSur/NorteSul. Canadian Journal of Latin American Studies. Canadian Association of Latin American Studies. University of Ottawa.
PCCLAS/P Proceedings of the Pacific Coast Council on Latin American Studies. University of California. Los Angeles.
RCLL Revista de Crítica Literaria Latinoamericana. Latinoamericana Editores. Lima.
RIB Revista Interamericana de Bibliografía (Inter-American Review of Bibliography). Organization of American States. Washington.
SCHG/R Revista Chilena de Historia y Geografía. Sociedad Chilena de Historia y Geografía. Santiago.
SGHG/A Anales de la Sociedad de Geografía e Historia de Guatemala. Guatemala.
UCLA/JLAL Journal of Latin American Lore. University of California, Latin American Center. Los Angeles.
UCNSA/SA Suplemento Antropológico. Universidad Católica de Nuestra Señora de la Asunción, Centro de Estudios Antropológicos. Asunción.
UCSD/NS The New Scholar. University of California, Center for Iberian and Latin American Studies [and] Institute of Chicano Urban Affairs. San Diego.
UNM/NMHR New Mexico Historical Review. University of New Mexico [and] Historical Society of New Mexico. Albuquerque.
UPR/RCS Revista de Ciencias Sociales. Universidad de Puerto Rico, Colegio de Ciencias Sociales. Río Piedras.
URSS/AL América Latina. Academia de Ciencias de la URSS (Unión de Repúblicas Soviéticas Socialistas). Moscú.
USCG/TG Tradiciones de Guatemala. Universidad de San Carlos de Guatemala, Centro de Estudios Folklóricos. Guatemala.
USCG/TP La Tradición Popular. Universidad de San Carlos de Guatemala, Centro de Estudios Folklóricos. Guatemala.
USP/RA Revista de Antropologia. Universidade de São Paulo, Faculdade de Filosofia, Letras e Ciências Humanas [and] Associação Brasileira de Antropologia. São Paulo.
USP/RIEB Revista do Instituto de Estudos Brasileiros. Universidade de São Paulo, Instituto de Estudos Brasileiros. São Paulo.
UWI/CQ Caribbean Quarterly. University of the West Indies. Mona, Jamaica.
VANH/B Boletín de la Academia Nacional de la Historia. Caracas.

HISTORY

ETHNOHISTORY: Mesoamerica

S. L. CLINE, *Assistant Professor, Department of History, Harvard University*

PUBLICATION IN MESOAMERICAN ethnohistory continues to be of two basic types: codices and documentary sources, and analytical works. In the first category, there have been a number of remarkable and beautifully produced volumes. These include full-color fascimile editions of the *Historia tolteca chichimeca* (item **1542**), the *Matrícula de tributos* (item **1558**), and the reedition in color of *Codex Xolotl* (item **1525**). Sahaguntine studies have been forwarded by the appearance of the three-volume, full-color facsimile of the *Florentine Codex* (item **1571**), the publication of the final volume of Anderson and Dibble's translation of the *Florentine Codex* (item **1570**), and finally an English translation by Klor de Alva of the Colloquios (item **1569**). Also notable is a black and white facsimile of Codex Aubin (item **1536**), with a translation of the Nahuatl text to German. Documentary sources of archival materials have also appeared including a representative collection of local level Nahuatl documents (see *HLAS 40: 1953*), documents from Mexico's AGN on Coyoacan (item **1522**), and materials from Spain's AGI on Guatemala (item **1521**).

Several major monographs have also been published. Offner's study of the pre-hispanic Aztec legal system (item **1563**) and Borah's thorough examination of the General Indian Court of colonial Mexico (item **1507**) are vital to understanding the changes brought to Indian society by Spanish colonial policies. Anawalt's visually appealing and intellectually rigorous study of Indian clothing is a welcome addition to the literature (item **1501**). Another notable contribution is Bricker's readable and enlightening monograph on Mayan myth, ritual and history (item **1510**). Interesting work is being done on pictorials. Boone created a remarkable reconstruction of the lost prototype of the *Codex Magliabechiano* (item **1506**). Galarza and Yoneda have begun to systematize the study of local-level native pictorials (items **1531–1532** and **1574**).

Recent conferences have not only promoted exchanges of ideas and information, but have resulted in a number of high quality publications. These include volumes from a Stanford conference on the Aztec and Inca states (item **1544**); an American Society for Ethnohistory symposium on Guatemalan historical demography (item **1543**); an International Congress of Americanists session on late prehispanic and early colonial Aztecs (item **1530**); and a New York Academy of Sciences conference on ethnoastronomy and archaeoastronomy (item **1529**). The need for more exchanges between scholars is highlighted by the recent completion of two editions of Ruiz de Alarcón's 17th-century Nahuatl incantations by teams of translators not aware of the others' existence. Only one (item **1527**) was available for review, the other by J. Richard Andrews and Ross Hassig is to appear later in 1984, published by University of Oklahoma Press.

A number of trends in the field continue. The evolution of the state, social and economic structures during the preconquest period are enduring subjects of scholarly concern. Studies of native societies in the colonial era are making increasing use of local-level native language documentation (e.g., items **1524** and **1552**). These have a great potential for yielding new insights, though we should heed Borah's recent warning (item **1508**) to evaluate *all* documents for biases and distortions.

Finally, this section of the *HLAS* has a new editor. Overall I am impressed by both the quality and quantity of the work being done. The number of items forwarded to me for review unfortunately far exceeded the number which could be included in this volume.

Aguilera, Carmen. Algunos datos sobre el chapopote en las fuentes documentales del siglo XVI. See *HLAS 45:541.*

1501 Anawalt, Patricia Rieff. Indian clothing before Cortés: Mesoamerican costumes from the codices. Charts prepared by Jean Cuker Sells. Norman: University of Oklahoma Press, 1981. 232 p.: bibl., ill., index, maps.

Outstanding contribution, careful examination of costume; significantly shows clothing's importance in sociopolitical and religious-ritual spheres. Fine reproductions from the codices, many in color. For archaeologist's comment, see *HLAS 45:543.*

1502 Anderson, Arthur J.O. Sahagún's sources for Book II (UNAM/ECN, 15, 1982, p. 73–88)

Close reading of Book II indicates there were more differences in the Nahuatl and Spanish texts than in other books of the *Historia general*; some differences were explanations to non-Aztec speakers.

1503 Arenas, Pedro de. *Vocabulario manual de las lenguas castellana y mexicana*: edición facsimilar de la publicada por Henrico Martínez en la Ciudad de México, 1611. Con un estudio introductorio de Ascensión H. de León-Portilla. México: Universidad Nacional Autónoma de México, 1982. 5, 160 p., 12 p. of plates: bibl., facsims. (Facsímiles de lingüística y filología nahuas; 1)

Facsimile of first ed. Excellent introductory essay discusses history of the manuscript and its philological importance.

1504 Baudot, Georges. Los *Huehuetlatolli* en la cristianización de México: dos sermones en lengua náhuatl de Fray Bernardino de Sahagún (UNAM/ECN, 15, 1982, p. 125–145)

Transcription and translation of two sermons in Nahuatl written by Sahagún. Interesting textual and conceptual transformations of huehuetlatolli to Catholic sermons.

1505 Bernal, Ignacio and **Miguel León-Portilla.** Vida y obra de Fray Bernardino de Sahagún: dos cartas de Paso y Troncoso a García Icazbalceta (UNAM/ECN, 15, 1982, p. 247–290)

Previously unpublished correspondence concerning Sahagún; indicates state of Sahaguntine studies in 19th century.

1506 Boone, Elizabeth Hill. The *Codex Magliabechiano* and the lost prototype of the Magliabechiano group. Berkeley: University of California Press, 1983. 250 p.: bibl., ill., index (Biblioteca nazionale centrale di Firenze. Manuscript. Codex Magliabecchi XIII; 11/3)

Outstanding study of the codex and related documents; these are seen as copies of lost prototype which Boone has painstakingly reconstructed.

1507 Borah, Woodrow. Justice by insurance: the General Indian Court of colonial Mexico and the legal aids of the Half-Real. Berkeley: University of California Press, 1983. 479 p.: appendix, bibl., charts, index, maps.

Masterly study; not just a major contribution to Spanish administrative history but a perceptive analysis of transformation in the Indian world as natives adapted to the Spanish legal system. Destined to become a classic in the literature.

1508 ———. Some problems of sources (*in* Explorations in ethnohistory: Indians of Central Mexico in the sixteenth century [see item **1530**] p. 23–39, bibl.)

Excellent discussion of problems of using ethnohistorical sources including forgery and unattributed copying. Cautions that no ethnohistorical source be accepted without evaluation of the circumstances in which it was produced.

1509 ———. The Spanish and Indian law: New Spain (in The Inca and Aztec states, 1400–1800: anthropology and history [see item **1544**] p. 265–288, bibl.)

Succinct and lucid discussion of Indians' interactions with the Spanish legal system, how it shaped colonial policy and changed Indian customs.

1510 Bricker, Victoria Reifler. The Indian Christ, the Indian King: the historical substrate of Maya myth and ritual. Austin: University of Texas Press, 1981. 368 p.: bibl., index, maps, photos.

Important contribution to ethnohistory: traces a number of modern Maya rituals to colonial myths and history rather than precolumbian; analysis of major events in Maya history such as the Tzeltal Rebellion and the Caste War; especially valuable inclusion of Maya texts with author's translations.

1511 Broda, Johanna. Aspectos socioeconómicos e ideológicos de la expansión del Estado Mexica (RUC, 28:117, enero 1979, p. 73–94, bibl.)

Examination of the "problematic" of the Mexica state with emphasis on aspects of ideology legitimating it. Short discussion of human sacrifice.

1512 Brotherston, Gordon. Year 13 reed equals 3113 BC: a clue to Mesoamerican chronology (UCSD/NS, 8, 1982, p. 75–84, bibl., ill.)

Argues that the Thompson correlation for the Maya-area texts can also be used for "Aztec-Mixtec" manuscripts.

1513 Brumfiel, Elizabeth M. Aztec state making: ecology, structure, and the origins of the State (AAA/AA, 85:2, June 1983, p. 261–284, bibl.)

Argues that the formation of the Aztec state cannot be accounted for solely in terms of ecological variables and suggests that there is an interplay of political and ecological factors.

1514 Brundage, Burr Cartwright. The phoenix of the Western world: Quetzalcoatl and the sky religion. Drawings by Jeanne Meinke. Norman: University of Oklahoma Press, 1982. 349 p.: bibl., ill., index, map (The Civilization of the American Indian series; no. 160)

Extended, speculative essay on Quetzalcoatl and positing a "sky religion" distinct from "terrene concepts" which constituted a separate religion.

1515 Calnek, Edward E. Patterns of empire formation in the Valley of Mexico: late postclassic period, 1200–1521 (in The Inca and Aztec states, 1400–1800: anthropology and history [see item **1544**] p. 43–62, bibl.)

Traces the development of political structures with the growth of population; deals with questions concerning legitimacy, shifts in economic and political power, and the development of bureaucracy. For archaeologist's comment, see *HLAS 45:550*.

———. Tenochtitlan in the early colonial period. See *HLAS 45:282*.

1516 Carmack, Robert M. New Quichean chronicles from Highland Guatemala (CEM/ECM, 13, 1981, p. 83–103, bibl., ill., maps)

Brief description of important, newly accessible colonial manuscripts including the original Quiché text of the *Título Totonicapan* and previously unknown pictorials.

1517 Carrasco, David. Quetzalcoatl and the irony of empire: myths and prophecies in the Aztec tradition. Chicago: University of Chicago Press, 1982. 233 p.: bibl., ill., index.

Links the symbols of Quetzalcoatl to legitimation of power and authority in six prehispanic urban centers. For archaeologist's comment, see *HLAS 45:283*.

1518 Carrasco Pizana, Pedro. La aplicabilidad a Mesoamérica del modelo andino de verticalidad (RUC, 28:117, enero 1979, p. 237–243, bibl.)

Gives examples of control of diverse ecological zones in the Nahua region. Stresses non-commercial nature of this direct exploitation. Considers the "Andean model" not particular to that zone.

1519 ———. The political economy of the Aztec and Inca states (in The Inca and Aztec states, 1400–1800: anthropology and history [see item **1544**] p. 23–40, bibl.)

Stresses similarities of the two states

ethnohistory: Indians of Central Mexico of the sixteenth century [see item **1530**] p. 83–102, bibl.)

Modifies a number of generalizations held about land tenure, especially property transfers; valuable observations about modern Tepetlaoztoc land tenure indicating customary procedures are often more important than the formal legal system.

1538 —— and **B.J. Williams.** Aztec arithmetic: positional notation and area calculation (Science [American Association for the Advancement of Science, Lancaster, Mich.] 210:31, Oct. 1980, p. 499–505, bibl., ill.)

Demonstrates that the Aztec notation system had a symbol for zero and "used position to ascribe values."

1539 Hellbom, Anna-Britta. The life and role of women in the Aztec culture (UNESCO/CU, 8:3, 1982, p. 55–65)

Outlines women's role in Aztec society; based primarily on information in *Codex Mendoza* and Sahagún. Sees women's roles as typical of highly stratified societies; functions determined by class.

1540 Hicks, Frederic. Rotational labor and urban development in prehispanic Tetzcoco (*in* Explorations in ethnohistory: Indians of Central Mexico in the sixteenth century [see item **1530**] p. 147–174, bibl., chart)

Outlines extensive nature of rotational labor; suggests that it was a means of uniting the political unit, allowed for flexibility of labor use, and hindered dichotomy between urban and rural sectors.

1541 Hidalgo, Mariana. La vida amorosa en el México antiguo. México: Editorial Diana, 1979. 118 p.: bibl., ill.

Useful summary treatment of topics such as prostitution, homosexuality, incest, and concubinage.

1542 Historia tolteca-chichimeca. Edited by Paul Kirchhoff, Lina Odena Güemes, and Luis Reyes García. México: Instituto Nacional de Antropología e Historia, 1976. 287 p.: bibl., ill., indexes, maps, tables.

Magnificent full color facsimile of mid-16th century manuscript from Cuauhtinchan (published in 1976 but not annotated in *HLAS*). Includes careful transcription and translation of the Nahuatl text. Also contains many native pictorial elements: maps and glyphs. Treats mythical-legendary background of the Toltecs as well as annals of the people of Cuauhtinchan.

1543 The Historical demography of Highland Guatemala. Robert M. Carmack, John Early, and Christopher Lutz, editors. Albany: State University of New York at Albany, Institute of Mesoamerican Studies, 1982. 202 p. (Publication; no. 6)

Consists of papers, originally presented at a symposium, by archaeologists, historians, and anthropologists: Murdo J. MacLeod "An Outline of Central American Colonial Demography: Sources, Yields and Possibilities;" Thomas T. Veblen "Native Population Decline in Totonicapan, Guatemala;" W. George Lovell "Collapse and Recovery: a Demographic Profile of the Cuchumatan Highlands of Guatemala, 1520–1821;" Christopher Lutz "Population History of the Parish of San Miguel Dueñas, Guatemala, 1530–1770;" and Robert M. Carmack "Social and Demographic Patterns in an Eighteenth-Century Census from Tecpanaco, Guatemala."

1544 The Inca and Aztec states, 1400–1800: anthropology and history. Edited by George A. Collier, Renato Rosaldo, and John D. Wirth. New York: Academic Press, 1982. 475 p.: index, maps (Studies in anthropology)

Collection of papers from 1978 Stanford conference. Those on Mesoamerican topics are annotated separately in this section: Borah (item **1509**); Calnek (item **1515**); Carrasco (item **1519**); Karttunen (item **1545**); Klor de Alva (item **1548**); Lockhart (item **1552**); and Rounds (item **1568**).

Jiménez, Alfredo. Política española y estructuras indígenas: el área maya en el siglo XVI. See item **1990.**

1545 Karttunen, Frances. Nahuatl literacy (*in* Inca and Aztec states, 1400–1800: anthropology and history [see item **1544**] p. 395–417, bibl.)

Excellent summary of the evolution of Nahuatl in the colonial period; cogent analysis of the implications of literacy for native society.

1546 Klein, Cecelia F. Who was Tlaloc? (UCLA/JLAL, 6:2, Winter 1980, p. 155–204, bibl., ill.)

Traces the role of Tlaloc from lord of the underworld, to acquisition of calendrical significance and ultimately to his representation as a concept of antiquity.

1547 Klor de Alva, J. Jorge. La historicidad de los *Coloquios* de Sahagún (UNAM/ECN, 15, 1982, p. 147–184, bibl.)

Concludes that first book is a reconstruction of conversations which occurred in 1524 and that second book concerns events which occurred after first contacts between the friars and the Indians.

1548 ———. Spiritual conflict and accommodation in New Spain: toward a typology of Aztec responses to Christianity (*in* The Inca and Aztec states, 1400–1800: anthropology and history [see item **1544**] p. 345–366, bibl.)

Well reasoned reappraisal of the "spiritual conquest;" stresses natives' resistance to Christianity and the incompleteness of their conversion due to lack of understanding of basic doctrine.

1549 Knorozov, Yurii. Maya hieroglyphic codices. Translated from the Russian by Sophie D. Coe. Albany: State University of New York at Albany, Institute for Mesoamerican Studies, 1982. 429 p.: bibl. (Publication; no. 8)

Translation of the Russian *Ieroglificheskie Rukopisi Maiia;* description and commentary on the glyphs in the *Dresden Codex*, the *Madrid Codex*, and the *Paris Codex*. For anthrolinguist's comment, see *HLAS 45:1528*.

1550 León-Portilla, Miguel. México-Tenochtitlán: su espacio y tiempo sagrados. México: Instituto Nacional de Antropología e Historia, 1978. 79, 8 p.: charts, photos.

Important contribution to the understanding of Nahua ideas of the sacred; Tenochtitlan as a mythic conception and the reality of the prehispanic metropolis.

1551 ———. Los nombres de lugar en Náhuatl: su morfología, sintaxis y representación glífica (UNAM/ECN, 15, 1982, p. 37–72, bibl., ill.)

Useful linguistic analysis of Nahuatl

locatives and placenames with selective glyphic representations.

1552 Lockhart, James. Views of corporate self and history in some Valley of Mexico towns: late seventeenth and eighteenth centuries (*in* The Inca and Aztec states, 1400–1800: anthropology and history [see item **1544**] p. 367–393)

Careful examination of Nahuatl primordial titles; provides insight into the evolution of native concepts of ethnic identity during the colonial period; especially interesting translations of some portions of the titles.

1553 Loera y Chávez de Esteinou, Margarita. Calimaya y Tepemaxalco: tenencia y transmisión hereditaria de la tierra en dos comunidades indígenas: época colonial. México: Instituto Nacional de Antropología e Historia, 1977. 138 p.: bibl., charts, graphs, maps (Cuadernos de trabajo del Departamento de Investigaciones Históricas; 18)

Preliminary study of colonial-era native inheritance patterns based on general information in wills.

1554 López Austin, Alfredo. Cuerpo humano e ideología: las concepciones de los antiguos nahuas. v. 1/2. México: Universidad Nacional Autónoma de México, Instituto de Investigaciones Antropológicas, 1980. 2 v.: bibl., ill. (Serie antropológica; 39. Etnología/historia)

Exhaustive discussion of Nahua thought concerning the human body and its more general ideological implications.

1555 Macazaga Ordoño, César. El juego de pelota. México: Editorial Innovación, 1982. 93 p.: bibl., ill., index.

Study of the sacred ball game, well chosen illustrations accompany the text. Argues that the ballgame is a fertility rite.

1556 ———. Mitología de Coyolxauhqui. 3a. ed. México City: Editorial Innovación, 1981. 79 p.: bibl., ill., index (Colección Religión del México antiguo; 3)

Preliminary iconographic study of the Mexica earth goddess Coyolxauhqui suggesting equivalence with other deities.

1557 Manrique Castañeda, Leonardo. Fray Andrés de Olmos: notas críticas sobre su obra lingüística (UNAM/ECN, 15, 1982, p. 27–35)

Contains a summary of Olmos' biography, brief outline of some linguistic features of the texts, and a listing of known works and those attributed to him.

1558 Matrícula de tributos: *Códice de Moctezuma.* Kommentar: Frances F. Berdan und Jacqueline de Durand-Forest. Graz, Austria: Akademische Druck- und Verlagsanstalt, 1980. 44 p., 34 p. of plates: bibl., ill. (some col.) (Codices selecti phototypice impressi; v. 68)

Beautiful color facsimile ed. of this major pictorial manuscript depicting towns and tributes of *Moctezuma's* empire; useful introduction and an essay on the Aztec economy.

1559 Melgarejo Vivanco, José Luis. El *Códice Vindobonensis.* Xalapa, México: Instituto de Antropología, Universidad Veracruzana, 1980. 156 p.: bibl., ill.

Brief analysis of the codex; includes localization of toponymic glyphs; extended discussion of calendrical glyphs.

1560 Mexico. Archivo General de la Nación. Documentos mexicanos: cachiqueles, mayas, matlatzincas, mixtecos y nahuas. t. 1/2 . Elaborado por Cayetano Reyes García *et al.* México: El Archivo, 1982. 332 p.: indexes (Serie Guías y catálogos; 72)

Two-part catalog of native language documents in Mexico's AGN. Sections are divided by language group. Listings include date, place, subject matter, pictorial content of each document; citation by ramo, volume, expediente, and folio; indexes make the work particularly accessible. Important tool for scholars.

Miller, Arthur G. On the edge of the sea: mural painting at Tancah-Tulum, Quintana Roo, Mexico. See *HLAS 45:481.*

Montolíu, María. Los dioses de los cuatro sectores cósmicos y su vínculo con la salud y enfermedad en Yucatán. See *HLAS 45:1885.*

Münch G., Guido. La religiosidad indígena en el Obispado de Oaxaca durante la colonia y sus proyecciones actuales. See item **1920.**

Oberem, Udo and **Roswith Hartmann.** Zur Seefahrt in den Hochkulturen Alt-Amerika. See item **1683.**

1561 Oettinger, Marion, Jr. and **Fernando Horcasitas.** The lienzo of Petlacala: a pictorial document from Guerrero, Mexico. Philadelphia: American Philosophical Society, 1982. 71 p.: ill. (some col.) (Transactions of the American Philosophical Society; v. 72, pt. 7)

Reproduction and analysis of iconography and written text of colonial lienzo; description of its modern ritual use.

1562 Offner, Jerome A. Household organization in the Texcocan heartland: the evidence in the *Codex Vergara* (*in* Explorations in ethnohistory: Indians of Central Mexico in the sixteenth century [see item **1530**] p. 127–146, bibl., charts, ill.)

Examination of household and ward organization as found depicted in *Codex Vergara*; special reference to legal and political aspects of calpulli organization.

1563 ———. Law and politics in Aztec Texcoco. New York: Cambridge University Press, 1983. 337 p.: bibl., ill., index, maps.

Solid contribution. Thoroughgoing analysis of the Aztec legal system; in-depth discussion of aspects of Aztec society regulated by law such as land tenure, inheritance, kinship relations, trade. Comprehensive history of prehispanic Texcoco.

1564 Ortiz de Montellano, Bernardo R. El canibalismo azteca: ¿una necesidad ecológica? (UNAM/AA, 16, 1979, p. 15–182, bibl., tables)

Translation from the English; contribution to the debate on cannibalism arguing that the diet contained adequate protein without human flesh.

Pohl, Mary. Ritual continuity and transformation in Mesoamerica: reconstructing the ancient Maya *cuch* ritual. See *HLAS 45:580.*

1565 Prem, Hanns J. Early Spanish colonization and Indians in the Valley of Atlixco, Puebla (*in* Explorations in ethnohistory: Indians of Central Mexico in the sixteenth century [see item **1530**] p. 205–228, bibl.)

Study of settlement process in Puebla area stresses patterns which actually evolved and compares these to the Audiencia's guidelines for Spanish settlement.

1566 Reyes García, Luis. Cuauhtinchán del siglo XII al XVI: formación y desarrollo histórico de un señorío prehispánico. Wiesbaden: Steiner, 1977. 127 p., 21 leaves of plates (1. fold.): bibl., ill. (El Proyecto México de la Fundación Alemana para la Investigación Científica; 10)

Based on extensive archival research. Examines internal situation of Cuauhtinchan rather than its alliances and conquests. Includes material on various ethnic groups which settled this polity and their interrelations; rich data on *teccalli*.

1567 Rojas Rabiela, Teresa. Agricultural implements in Mesoamerica (*in* Explorations in ethnohistory: Indians of Central Mexico in the sixteenth century [see item **1530**] p. 175–204, bibl., ill.)

Well illustrated discussion of native agricultural tools. Suggests that agriculture's success came from highly organized work and careful resource management.

1568 Rounds, J. Dynastic succession and the centralization of power in Tenochtitlan (*in* The Inca and Aztec states, 1400–1800: anthropology and history [see item **1544**] p. 63–89, bibl.)

Argues that "changes in the succession practices of Tenochtitlan were closely associated with changes in the power relationships between the dispersed traditional elite and the centralized dynastic elite."

1569 Sahagún, Bernardino de. The Aztec-Spanish dialogues of 1524. Translated by J. Jorge Klor de Alva (Alcheringa [Ethnopoetics, Association of Australian Paleontologists, Sidney] 4:2, 1980, p. 52–193)

Transcription of Nahuatl text of the *Colloquios y doctrina christiana* and first English translation of the work. Valuable introductory material.

1570 ———. General history of the things of New Spain. pt. 1, Introductions and indices. Translated with notes and illus. by Arthur J.O. Anderson and Charles E. Dibble. Santa Fe, N.M.: School of American Research, 1982. 1 v.: bibl. (Monographs of the School of American Research; no. 14, pt. 1)

Final volume of monumental translation of the *Florentine Codex*. Contains translations of Sahagún's various prologues and interpolations; introductions by the translators; especially valuable are the indexes to subject matter, places, persons and deities for the whole 12-volume project (for other vols.

of translation, see *HLAS 40:2011; HLAS 42:5119; HLAS 44:1559*).

1571 ———. Historia general de las cosas de Nueva España: *Codice Florentino*. México: Secretaría de Gobernación, 1979. 3 v.: ill. (some col.)

Magnificent full-color facsimile ed. of the single most important colonial codex. Includes fine reproduction of the nearly 2000 drawings.

Spores, Ronald. New World ethnohistory and archaeology, 1970–1980. See *HLAS 45:585*.

Taladoire, Eric. Les terrain de jeu de balle: Mésoamérique et sud-ouest des Etats- Unis. See *HLAS 45:360*.

Torre Villar, Ernesto de la. Los señores del México antiguo en la obra de Diego García Panes. See item **2028**.

1572 Trautmann, Wolfgang. The impact of Spanish conquest on the development of the cultural landscape in Tlaxcala, Mexico (*in* Explorations in ethnohistory: Indians of Central Mexico in the sixteenth century [see item **1530**] p. 253–276, bibl., charts)

Creates a model to show development of spatial processes in Tlaxcala, based on the concept of center-periphery.

Turner, B.L., II. La agricultura intensiva de trabajo en las tierras mayas. See *HLAS 45:5118*.

Wilhemy, Herbert. Welt und Umwelt der Maya: Aufstieg und Untergang einer Hochkultur. See *HLAS 45:5121*.

1573 Williams, Barbara J. Mexican pictorial cadastral registers: an analysis of the *Códice de Santa María Asunción* and the *Codex Vergara* (*in* Explorations in ethnohistory: Indians of Central Mexico in the sixteenth century [see item **1530**] p. 103–125, bibl., ill.)

Analysis of pictorial land records of the Texcoco region, focusing on two distinct native conventions of cadastral depiction; particularly useful illustrations and discussion of glyphs.

1574 Yoneda, Keiko. Los mapas de Cuauhtinchán y la historia cartográfica prehispánica. México: Archivo General de la Nación, 1981. 285 p.: appendices, bibl., ill., photos.

Valuable study focuses on pictorials as historical documents. Through stylistic analysis, attempts to determine standard forms used by the native authors. Fine attempt to introduce more standard methods of analysis.

1575 Zamora Acosta, Elías. El control vertical de diferentes pisos ecológicos: aplicación del modelo al Occidente de Guatemala (RUC, 28:117, enero 1979, p. 245–272, bibl., map)
Examines control by cabeceras of different ecological zones and how they acquired products necessary for economic development, especially cacao.

1576 Zantwijk, Rudolf van. La entronización de Acampichtli de Tenochtitlán y las características de su gobierno (UNAM/ECN, 15, 1982, p. 17–26)
Examination of historicity and role of Acampichtli, based on evidence in *Codex Azcatitlan, Codex Izhuatepec,* and *Codex Mendoza,* among others.

ETHNOHISTORY: South America

FRANK SALOMON, *Associate Professor of Anthropology, University of Wisconsin, Madison*

ENTHUSIASM FOR THE IDEA OF *LO ANDINO*—enduring cultural fundamentals that allegedly pervade all centuries of Andean life—was one of the motives fueling recent ethnohistoric research, but the very success of the effort seems to undercut the original construct. A decade ago, when only the 16th and 20th centuries were in focus, it was tempting to highlight likenesses between them as evidence for essentials withstanding exogenous change. Fast-growing knowledge of then unknown periods and transitions now points out sources of change as much within the native orbit as outside it.

Where prehispanic studies are concerned, this shift accompanied a change of focus from the Inca state and its abrupt end, to smaller but more enduring polities whose internal dynamics begin to appear as forces shaping both Incaic and colonial reality. Julien's *Hatunqolla* (item **1651**) combines ethnohistoric with archaeological research in a detailed case study. Also worth noting are two works by Caillavet (items **1596** and **1597**). The 1979 Stanford conference which gathered new work on subimperial units, edited by Collier, Rosaldo and Wirth and published as *The Inca and Aztec states, 1400–1800* (item **1544**), ratifies a turn away from cataclysmic images of these units' encounter with European power. Warrants for collating pre- and post-conquest regional data encouraged efforts at topical summation over long chronologies, such as the May 1983 Wenner-Gren Symposium on variation in ecological complementarity.

Efforts at a native-oriented historiography reaching beyond conquest times outpaced late-horizon studies. Proponents of "historia andina" pressed the history of native polities into the 17th, 18th, and 19th centuries— periods which, despite the immense colonial document record, had remained ethnohistorically darker than Inca times. Spalding's *Huarochiri . . .* (item **1721**) and Stern's *Peru's Indian peoples and the challenge of Spanish conquest* (item **1724**), a runner-up for the American Historical Association's Bolton Prize, greatly broaden the path pointed out by Spalding's earlier studies of post-Toledan native politics. For the same and later periods Celestino and Meyers' *Las Cofradías . . .* (item **1604**) provides basic data on intracommunal institutions (see also Barragan's item **1586** ; Oberem's item **1681** ; and Varón's item **1739**). Reexamination of Andean participation in the market, a prime agenda for the mid-colony, was the object of an as-yet unpublished 1983 SSRC conference at Sucre, Bolivia.

Rebellion continues to dominate all other themes in 18th-century research; new work shows increasing attentiveness to intra-indigenous processes behind it as against exterior pressures. Jan Széminski's *Los objetivos de los tupamaristas* (item **1729**) concentrates on ideological underpinnings (see also Burga's and Flores Galindo's item **1593**; Hidalgo's item **1648**; Cajías item **1600**; and item **1711**). The SSRC conference "Resistencia y Rebelión en el Mundo Andino, Siglos XVII–XX" (April 1984) harvested some of this research. Broader themes of ethnogenetic process (see Saignes' items **1709** and **1710**) as well as local cultural data including a rare source on ritual combat (see Hopkins' item **1650**) suggest the feasibility of more varied eventual treatments.

Platt's *Estado boliviano y ayllu andino* (item **1695**) breaks almost completely new ground in ethnohistoricizing the 19th century. It retrieves the record of a south-Andean activism that affected modern land tenure regimen (see also Broadbent's item **1591** and Carrasquilla's item **1602**). But the 19th century remains a difficult and inviting research frontier.

The study of indigenous thought took a turn away from the abstracting of mental structures and toward locating native ideas in the historical contexts they addressed or affected. The evidential base for such work expanded through republication of major established sources with improved apparatus and contextual research—Urioste's new edition of the Huarochiri manuscript (item **1735**, and see also Hartmann's item **1645** and *HLAS 42:1589*) being a prime example. Rostworowski's *Estructuras andinas del poder* (item **1704**) puts the structuralist distillates of old and new sources into diachronic context by exploring their correlates in military and political organization (see also Urbano's item **1734**).

In this emerging history of native ideas the appropriation of Christian thought by Andeans got the lion's share of research attention. Felipe Guaman Poma de Ayala still occupies the limelight, no longer as an informant on Inca realities, but as a human exemplar of colonial Andean innovation (see items **1578**, **1590**, **1626**, **1658**, and **1686**). Some concerns parallel to those of Guaman Poma studies arise in works on the history of popular religion and belief. Seventeenth-century and later worship began to count as a field of study in its own right rather than an echo of Inca belief (see items **1665**, **1670**, **1696**, **1699**, and **1717**).

Two new journals mark improvements in format and scope: *Revista Andina*, published by the Centro de Estudios Rurales Andinos Bartolomé de las Casas of Cuzco, shows a strong pan-Andean and ethnohistorical emphases, and *HISLA*, from the Centro Latinoamericano de Historia Económica y Social, Lima, sets Andean studies in a broadly Latin American context. Both offer *Current Anthropology*-style debate formats.

The section editor requests communications and reprints useful for enlarging coverage of non-Andean South America.

1577 Adorno, Rolena. Bartolomé de Las Casas y Domingo de Santo Tomás en la obra de Felipe Wamán Puma (IILI/RI, 120/121, julio/dic. 1982, p. 673–679, bibl.)

The great native chronicler apparently had some knowledge of Dominican pro-indigenous writings. His chap. "Pregunta Su Magestad" echoes a Dominican *memorial* of 1560 asking for limitation of encomiendas. Part of chap. "Consideraciones," "sigue

punto por punto los argumentos propuestos por Las Casas en su *Tratado de las doce dudas.*"

1578 ——. On pictorial language and the typology of culture in a New World chronicle (Semiótica [Association Nationale de Semiotique, La Hague] 36:1/2, 1981, p. 51–106, bibl., ill., table)

How should one interpret visual symbols whose sense depends on orientation to creator's or viewer's differing cultures? Test cases are Guaman Poma's use of clothing and interior/exterior space. "Thorough fusion of Christian values and Andean culture results from the former being pulled away from identification with the European colonial sphere."

1579 Albó, Xavier and **Félix Layo** . Ludovico Bertonio, 1557–1625: fuente única al mundo aymara temprano (Revista Andina [Instituto de Estudios Rurales Bartolomé de las Casas, Cuzco, Perú] 3, 1984, p. 223–264, bibl., tables)

In addition to renowned Aymara grammar (1603) and dictionary (1612), Bertonio wrote a little-known *Silva de phrases* (phrasebook) in Aymara and Spanish, and several religious works of interest for study of colonial linguistics. Essay analyzes Bertonio's social and linguistic perspective, supplies key to sound values of his Aymara orthography.

1580 Alcina Franch, José. Tomebamba y el problema de los indios cañaris de la sierra sur del Ecuador (EEHA/AEA, 37, 1980, p. 403–433, bibl., ill.)

Ethnohistorical prologue to forthcoming publications of 1974–75 Spanish archaeological mission to Ecuador's largest Inca site. Synthesizing colonial sources and modern studies, describes Incaic city Tomebamba as namesake of larger province located between two other ethnically Cañari provinces, Hatun Cañar (modern Cañar prov.) and Cañaribamba (south of Nudo de Portete).

Arellano López, Jorge and **Eduardo E. Berberián.** Mallku: el Señorío post-Tiwanaku del altiplano sur de Bolivia: provincias Nor y Sur López. See *HLAS 45:705.*

Arenas, Pastor. Etnobotánica lengua-maskoy. See *HLAS 45:1561.*

Arnaud, Expedito. Os índios Mirânia e a espansão luso-brasileira: Médio Solimões-Japurá, Amazonas. See *HLAS 45:1152.*

1581 Azevedo, Eliane S. Sobrenomes no Nordeste e sus relações com a heterogeneidade étnica (IPE/EE, 13:1, jan./abril 1983, p. 103–116, bibl., maps, tables)

Surnames with religious connotation are statistically associated with blacks, names related to plants and animals with In-

dian descent, and "other" names with European descent. Diachronic sample of death records and sample of current names in 60 localities indicate that changes in name frequency allow projections of ethnic change.

1582 Baldinger, Kurt. Cieza de León, Die Eroberung von Perú, Zum neu entdeckten Original der *Chronik* von Cieza de León (ZRP, 99:3/4, 1983, p. 367–377)

Critical essay on the newly discovered original texts of *Crónica del Perú* by Cieza de León, recovered in Italy by Francesca Cantú (see item **1708**).

1583 Ballesteros Gaibrois, Manuel. La caída del imperio de los incas. Madrid: Forja, 1982. 155 p.: bibl., ill. (Biblioteca del saber inmediato; 6. Serie de historia)

Vest-pocket summary of Spanish invasion with a curtsy to the "vision of the vanquished" but no citation of any research postdating 1928.

1584 Barendse, João Adolfo. Preliminares históricos indispensáveis para localização das tribos indígenas na época das reduções jesuíticas em Guairá (*in* Simpósio Nacional de Estudos Missioneiros, 2nd, Santa Rosa, Brazil, 1977. Anais. Santa Rosa: Faculdade de Filosofia, Ciências e Letras, 1978, p. 158–170, bibl.)

Brief summary of 1673 work by Nicolás del Techo, *Historia de la provincia del Paraguai de la Compañía de Jesús.*

1585 Barnadas, Josep. Panorama historiográfico de estudios recientes sobre Charcas colonial (Revista Andina [Centro de Estudios Rurales Andinos Bartolomé de las Casas, Cuzco, Perú] 1:2, dic. 1983, p. 475–543, bibl.)

Compendious bibliographic essay on contributions since approximately 1970, covers archive guides, bibliographies, and editions of primary sources as well as monographic literature; emphasizes native societies in all centuries. Expresses optimism about fast-growing literature: "por convergencia de problemáticas sectoriales, empezamos a vislumbrar sus encrucijadas fundamentales." Valuable reference work.

1586 Barragan R., Rossana. Etnicidad y verticalidad ecológica de Sicasica, Ayo-Ayo y Calamarca, siglos XVI-XVII: el acceso y el nacimiento de la hacienda en Palca,

1596–1644. La Paz: Museo Nacional de Etnografía y Folklore, 1982. 51 p., 11 leaves of plates: ill. (Avances de investigación; no. 1)
Under Inca rule, land use in southeast of modern La Paz dept. showed mono-ethnic nuclei only on tuber lands; *quirua* (Aymara equivalent of *chaupi yunga*) shows outliers of Tiahuanaco, etc. Depopulation facilitated Spanish appropriation of non-tuber lands, but nuclei resisted well. Communal land regimen and reproduction of Andean staples still held steady ca. 1644.

1587 Becker, Itala Irene Basile and **Juana Paris de Cabey.** Os índios da Banda Oriental do Uruguai. Os Charrua e Minuano: seu histórico abastecimento e assentamento; sua relação com as frentes expansionistas (*in* Simpósio Nacional de Estudos Missioneiros, 2nd, Santa Rosa, Brazil. Anais. Santa Rosa: Faculdade de Filosofia, Ciências e Letras Dom Bosco, 1978, p. 61–76, bibl., maps)
Concerns Chaná-Timbu, Charrua, and Guaraní. Compressed tertiary treatment, follows Darcy Ribeiro's "contact" scheme and divides period from 1510s to 19th century, extinction into three eras. Focuses on impact of catechization, introduction of horse and cattle, imposition of sedentarism.

Beckerman, Stephen. Datos etnohistóricos acerca de los bari, motilones. See *HLAS 45:1216.*

1588 Berchanski, Juan Carlos; Jaime Luis Oliver; and **Oswaldo Juan Piuzzi.** Algunas concepciones de la historia vigentes en la historiografía indiana del siglo XVI (PUCP/H, 4:2, dic. 1980, p. 137–174, bibl.)
Focuses in part on 16th-century writers' disagreements on "verifiability" versus "memorability" as criteria for inclusion of events, but concentrates chiefly on their attachment to reigning and nascent ideas about meaning of historic change.

1589 Bixler, Ray H. Comment on the incidence and purpose of royal sibling incest (AES/AE, 9:3, Aug. 1982, p. 580–582, table)
Briefly reviews Inca data from Cobo, John Rowe, and Maria Rostworowski de Díez Canseco as support for position that "full-sibling marriage was very uncommon and succession by an offspring of such a union was extremely rare."

1590 Bravo, María Concepción. Polo de Ondegardo y Guaman Poma, dos mentalidades ante un problema: la condición del indígena en el Perú del siglo XVI (*in* América y la España del siglo XVI: homenaje a Gonzalo Fernández de Oviedo cronista de Indias en el V centenario de su nacimiento, Madrid, 1478. Edición preparada por Francisco de Solano y Fermín del Pino. Madrid: CSIC, Instituto Gonzalo Fernández de Oviedo, 1983, v. 2, p. 275–289, bibl.)
Essay contrasting two approaches to single problem: foreseeable crisis that would be caused by extinction of native Peruvians. Both take preservation of nuclear communities to be crucial, with Poma emphasizing expulsion of interlopers, and Polo urging elimination of tribute laws which weaken local collectivity.

1591 Broadbent, Sylvia. The formation of peasant society in central Colombia (ASE/E, 28:3, Summer 1981, p. 259–277, bibl.)
Peasant social structure of the Bogotá region today shows few traces of multilayered, matrilineally organized Chibcha political hierarchy. How was it demolished? Initial Spanish conquest preserved and used old sociopolitical units. Abolition of Indian tribute from 1832 and 1810 legal dissolution of communal *resguardo* titles, decisively transformed Chibcha collectivities.

Brochado, José Proenza. Tradição cerâmica tupiguarani na América do Sul. See *HLAS 45:721.*

1592 Buechler, Judith-María. Trade and market in Bolivia before 1953: an ethnologist in the garden of ethnohistory (ASE/E, 30:2, 1983, p. 107–119, bibl.)
Reviewing literature on precolumbian through modern highland markets, places La Paz-area marketing carried on by *colonos*, migrants, and *comunarios* in context of prereform economy. Ends with brief life history of a trader, demonstrating coexistence of native and imported exchange institutions.

1593 Burga, Manuel and **Alberto Flores Galindo.** La utopía andina (IPA/A, 17:20, 1982, p. 85–101, bibl.)
Emphasizes multicentury "diálogo" between aristocratic written ideology and the "oral utopia" of peasant rebels, noting especially insurgencies of 1868–1923. Does not

write off the possible persistence of nativist thinking.

1594 Busto Duthurburu, José Antonio del.
La conquista del Perú. Fotografías, Abraham Guillén, Teresa Guérin del Busto. 2a. ed. Lima: Librería Studium Editores, 1981. 335 p.: ill.

Old-fashioned hispanocentric history (1513–46) with military emphasis; coverage is thorough but there are no citations or bibliography.

1595 ———. José Gabriel Túpac Amaru antes de su rebelión. Fotografías, Juan Ossio Acuña. Lima: Pontificia Universidad Católica del Perú, Fondo Editorial, 1981. 134 p., 25 leaves of plates: bibl., ill. (some col.)

Interestingly chiefly for color illustrations of Tupac Amaru's homeland, tertiary work gathers data from Carlos Daniel Valcárel and others about rebel's family as part of rural society, about Micaela Bastidas' genealogical connection to her husband, and about his early career as transport entrepreneur and *kuraka*.

1596 Caillavet, Chantal. Caciques de Otavalo en el siglo XVI: Don Alonso Maldonado y su esposa (Miscelánea Antropológica Ecuatoriana [Museos del Banco Central de Ecuador, Guayaquil] 2:2, 1983, p. 38–55)

Testament of Alonso Maldonado (d. 1609), grandson of *ango* who ruled during Spanish invasion, gives clues to resource base of his office: *"fuente de pescado,"* feather regalia, musical instruments, fields in subtropical and high-altitude zones. His wife Lucía Coxilaguango testated about her collection of prehispanic jewelry. Original documents reproduced.

1597 ———. Ethno-histoire équatorienne: un testament indien inédit du XVIe siécle (UTIEH/C, 41, 1983, p. 5–23, bibl., ill. map)

Diego Collín, lord of Panzaleo (near Quito), left 1598 will revealing much of private and ceremonial life. Emphasizes credit links to far-flung net of aboriginal nobles, command of delegated specialists allotted by Incas, insistence on norms of inheritance that may well be preincaic, and many objects designed as insignia of rank. Short but important document reproduced.

1598 ———. La sal de Otavalo, Ecuador: continuidades indígenas y rupturas coloniales (Sarance [Instituto Otavaleño de Antropología, Otavalo, Ecuador] 9, 1981, p. 47–81, bibl., ill.)

Spanish translation of 1979 article (see *HLAS 42:1600*).

1599 ———. Toponomía histórica, arqueología y formas prehispánicas de agricultura en la región de Otavalo, Ecuador (IFEA/B, 12:3/4, 1983, p. 1–21, bibl.)

Holds that pre- or non-Quechua toponyms of northern Ecuador contain elements which correlate with archaeologically known works of intensive agriculture. For example, ending *-pigal* is said to occur at sites of raised fields called *camellones* by Spanish. Novel, though incomplete, attack on old and difficult problem.

1600 Cajías, Fernando. Los objetivos de la revolución indígena de 1781: el caso de Oruro (Revista Andina [Centro de Estudios Rurales Andinos Bartolomé de las Casas, Cuzco, Perú] 1:2, dic. 1983, p. 407–427, bibl.)

Studies testimony of people imprisoned for participating in native invasion of Oruro. After collapse of alliance with criollos, more radical goals favored by landless *yanaconas* emerged: seizure of haciendas, attack on Church, cultural nativism, independence under a neo-Inca king, and frankly genocidal hostility to "europeos americanos."

1601 Calzavarini, Lorenzo-Giuseppe. Nación chiriguana, grandeza y ocaso. Presentación de Gunnar Mendoza. Cochabamba: Editorial Los Amigos del Libro, 1980. 320 p., 12 p. of plates: bibl., ill., index, maps (Enciclopedia boliviana)

Despite claim of study in six Bolivian archives, relies entirely on secondary sources (especially B. Susnik's works) and aims chiefly at interpretation: "La especificidad de la respuesta chiriguana será la de colocarse en la historia occidental como anti-historia."

Cardale de Schrimpff, Marianne. Las Salinas de Zipaquirá: su explotación indígena. See *HLAS 45:799*.

Cardim, Fernão. Tratados da terra e gente do Brasil. See *HLAS 45:1229*.

Carrasco Pizana, Pedro. The political economy of the Aztec and Inca states. See item **1519.**

1602 Carrasquilla, Juan. Los piscos: caciques de Bogotá (ACH/BHA, 48:733, abril/junio 1981, p. 461–473)

Luis Pisco assumed Funzá cacicazgo in 1696. Descendent Ambrosio Pisco was tried 1781 for usurping it and for his part in comunero rebellion. In 1824, it fell to Miguel Pisco to protect dynastic stake following liquidation of *mayorazgos* (estates entailed to first-born heirs) by Republican regime.

Casanova V., Jorge. Migraciones aido-paï: Secoya, Pioje. See *HLAS 45:1235.*

Cea Egaña, Alfredo. Embarcaciones de la antigua Isla de Pascua, con especial referencia a las canoas con flotador lateral, Vaka Ama. See *HLAS 45:764.*

1604 Celestino, Olinda and **Albert Meyers.** Las cofradías en el Perú: región central. Frankfurt: Verlag Klaus Dieter Vervuert, 1981. 552 p.: bibl., maps, tables (Editionen der Iberoamericana Reihe; 3)

Extensive study of Church sodalities in urban (Lima, Jauja) settings and rural parishes, from medieval antecedents to 1970s. Based largely on fresh documentation, details role of durable associations in articulating native society with colonial regime and in managing resource base for local welfare and ritual life.

1605 Chang-Rodríguez, Raquel. Coloniaje y conciencia nacional: Garcilaso de la Vega Inca y Felipe Guaman Poma de Ayala (UTIEH/C, 38, 1982, p. 29–43)

Interprets Garcilaso Inca as proponent of Inca-Spanish-African *mestizaje* and as precursor of nationalist ideology. Guaman Poma, by contrast, is treated as opponent of mixing peoples. Nonetheless, both share common concept of *patria* as more inclusive than one's immediate birthplace. Each considers himself linked through patrimony to all Tawantinsuyu.

1606 ———. A forgotten Indian chronicle: Titu Cusi Yupanqui's *Relación de la conquista del Perú* (UP/LAIL, 4:2, Fall 1980, p. 87–95, bibl.)

Contends that 1570 text given by neo-Inca lord Titu Cusi to Friar Marcos García,

transcends transient political aims and constitutes "revolutionary subversive" claim for the continuing rights of "natural sovereigns" as against Spaniards.

1607 ———. Sobre los cronistas indígenas del Perú y los comienzos de una escritura hispanoamericana (IILI/RI, 120/121, julio/dic. 1982, p. 533–548, ill.)

Short overview of Titu Cusi Yupanqui, Juan de Santa Cruz Pachacuti Yamqui Salcamaygua and Felipe Guaman Poma de Ayala. Act of undertaking "escritura, símbolo de la cultura hegemónica" embodies at the same time acculturation and resistance, and gives rise to "visión contradictoria y polémica de los hechos."

1608 Chaumeil, J.P. Historia y migraciones de los yagua de finales del siglo XVIII hasta nuestros días. Traducción, María del Carmen Urbano. Lima: Centro Amazónico de Antropología y Aplicación Práctica, 1981. 209 p.: bibl., ill., indexes (Serie antropológica; no. 3)

Yagua, a macro-Cariban people, responded to threats with frequent documented migration. "Siphon" economies in rubber, lumber, etc., overpowered "los brazos más baratos de Loreto," but in recent times missionization has again become crucial as fundamentalists, Franciscans, Peruvian government functionaries, and tourist operators vie for control. For ethnologist's comment, see *HLAS 45:1238.*

Chaves Mendoza, Alvaro. Los animales mágicos en las urnas de Tierradentro. See *HLAS 45:801.*

1609 Choque Canqui, Roberto. El papel de los capitanes de indios de la provincia Pacajes "en el entero de la mita" [sic] de Potosí (Revista Andina [Centro de Estudios Rurales Andinos Bartolomé de las Casas, Cuzco, Perú] 1:1, 1983, p. 117–125, bibl.)

Local lords deputed two levels of *mita* captains to round up quotas of forced mine laborers. Manuscript sources (17th-18th centuries) show that higher-level *mita* captains spent own resources to fill quotas, and commoners liable to service did likewise to avoid it.

1610 Clarac de Briseño, Jaqueline. Algunas consideraciones acerca de la metodología etnohistórica: su aplicación a la Cordillera de los Andes, Venezuela (Boletín Antropológico [Universidad de los Andes, Departamento de Antropología y Sociología, Museo Arqueológico, Centro de Investigaciones, Mérida, Venezuela] 1, sept./oct. 1982, p. 7–14, bibl., maps)

Discursive essay on ethnologist's experience in ethnohistory, from initial frustration to discovery of useful correspondences between contemporary magical practice and trials of 18th-19th century *mojanes* (shamans). Theoretical discussion concerns reasons for persistence and "reestructuración" of European, native, and African practices.

1611 Collier, George A. In the shadow of empire: new directions in Mesoamerican and Andean ethnohistory (*in* Inca and Aztec states, 1400–1800: anthropology and history [see item **1544**] p. 1–20, bibl.)

Inca-Aztec comparison promises test case for theories of the rise of empires because of independence from Old World, but it has proven elusive precisely because comparisons using Old World concepts sacrifice richest meanings of American data. Recent findings allow progress with regard to relations between empires and persisting subimperial units. For archaeologist's comment, see *HLAS 45:556.*

1612 Cordero Palacios, Octavio. El Azuay histórico: los cañaris y los incocañaris. Cuenca, Ecuador: Consejo Provincial del Azuay, Departamento de Cultura, 1981. 146 p.: ill. (Biblioteca azuaya; 4)

Local indigenist lore of south-Ecuadorian highlands, mostly from *Relaciones geográficas de Indias.* Reproduces Jesús Arriaga's scheme for interpreting archaeological abacus, and contains possibly useful lists of Cañari place names, botanical terms, and native *apellidos.*

1613 Cordy-Collins, Alana. Ancient Andean art as explained by Andean ethnohistory: an historical review (*in* International Congress of Americanists, 44th, University of Manchester, England, 1982. The Americas, a compendium of recent studies: proceedings. Edited by John Lynch. Manchester, England: Manchester University Press, 1983, p. 181–196, bibl.)

Resumé of recent research in which various authors applied ethnohistoric sources to problems of prehispanic iconography or design, with emphasis on Peruvian north coast.

1614 Costales, Alfredo and **Piedad Costales.** Amazonia: Ecuador-Perú-Bolivia. Quito: Mundo Shuar, 1983. 331 p., 4 leaves of plates: bibl., ill., tables.

Only chap. 1 explicitly concerns ethnohistory; attempts an overview of "grupos étnicos" inhabiting 22 river systems of Amazonia (1534–50), with population estimates and degree to which extinction overtook them by 1873. Other chapters, however, also contain historic data especially with regard to governance, land use, and land tenure.

1615 ——— and ———. Centuria: 1534–1634. Riobamba, Ecuador: Casa de la Cultura Benjamín Carrión, Núcleo de Chimborazo, 1982. 200 p.: ill., maps, tables.

Regional study of Riobamba area, Ecuador's central highlands, homeland of preincaic Puruhá. Includes rare data on first or pizarran encomiendas, with names of aboriginal polities and chiefs in 1530s, and verbatim extracts of later legal testimonies by Puruhá lords involved in land and succession disputes.

1616 ——— and ———. Relaciones geográficas de la Presidencia de Quito, 1776–1815. Quito: Mundo Shuar, 1980? 155 p.: ill.

Nine late-colonial primary sources (from Archivo Nacional de la Historia, Quito) on Ecuadorian Amazonia, including territory of Bracamoros, Xíbaro (i.e., Shuara), and Quijos peoples. Bulk of information concerns inroads of extractive economy, notably "canela" and quinine.

1617 ———; ———; and Fernando Jurado Noboa. Los señores naturales de la tierra [by Alfredo Costales and Piedad Costales]. Las coyas y pallas del Tahuantinsuyo: su descendencia en el Ecuador hasta 1900 [by Fernando Jurado Noboa]. Quito: Edición Xerox del Ecuador, 1982. 681 p.: diagrams, ill., maps, tables.

These are two separate works bound together: the Costales' *Los señores . . .* (p. 1–256); and Jurado Noboa's *Las coyas . . .* (p. 257–681). *Los señores . . .* attempts to reconstruct from mythological and documentary sources plan of both preincaic and incaic Quito. Jurado Noboa's *Las coyas* . . ., a compendious genealogical study, includes biographical sketches and many portraits of persons identified as Ecuadorian descendants of Inca royal women. Virtually all appear to be non-Andean in dress and social position. Insufficient citations of sources to permit verification.

1618 Dantas, Beatriz Góis and **Dalmo de Abreu Dallari.** Terra dos índios xocó: estudos e documentos. São Paulo: Comissão Pró-Indio/São Paulo, 1980. 186 p.: facsims.

In 1979, native land claimants were ordered off the lands of Ilha San Pedro, Sergipe; rebuff to their multi-century claim was motive of this venture in applied ethnohistory. Authors have combined sources from Portuguese and Brazilian archives (mostly 19th century) supporting Xocó claim with two essays. Sources reproduced.

1619 Demarest, Arthur. Viracocha: the nature and antiquity of the Andean high god. Cambridge, Mass.: Harvard University, Peabody Museum of Archaeology and Ethnology, 1981. 88 p.: ill. (Peabody Museum monographs; 6)

Wira Qocha (Viracocha, etc.) is name or epithet of widely attested but poorly understood Inca deity. Reexamining familiar sources, author holds that "Viracocha" of Inca state religion is a single facet of multifarious sky god dating from Middle Horizon. "Viracocha" embodies "mature" sun crucial to state-fostered maize agriculture.

1620 Denevan, William M. La población aborigen de la Amazonia en 1492 (CAAAP/AP, 3:5, junio 1980, p. 3–42, bibl., maps, tables)

Translation of 1976 article (see *HLAS* 40:2279). Argues for large prehispanic population (6,800,000 persons in "la gran Amazonia") based on prorating of known densities for different ecological zones.

1621 Dieterich, Heinz. Some theoretical and methodological observations about the Inca empire and the Asiatic mode of production (LAP, 9[4]:35, Fall 1982, p. 111–132, bibl.)

Argues that Inca evidence, far from demanding revision or broadening concept

"Asiatic mode of production," vindicates with "ideal-typical" clarity existence and development of this formation exactly as propounded by Marx: "something like the missing link in historical-materialist interpretation of the universal historical evolution." See also items **1694, 1730** and *HLAS 42:1678*.

1622 Dillon, Paul H. The Chancas of Angaráes: 1450(?)-1765 (*in* Investigations of the Andean past: papers from the First Annual Northeast Conference on Andean Archaeology and Ethnohistory. Edited by Daniel H. Sandweiss. Ithaca, N.Y.: Cornell University, Latin American Studies Program, 1983, p. 268–290, bibl., maps, tables [Cornell Latin American series])

Based on manuscripts in Lima archives documenting persistence to 1765 of Chanca enclave amid Angaráes. Disputes Espinoza Soriano's portrayal of them as *mitmaqkuna*. Unlike others within orbit of Huancavelica mercury mines, Chanca resisted demographic collapse in early colony and partly evaded *mitas*.

1623 Duviols, Pierre. Albornoz y el espacio ritual andino prehispánico (Revista Andina [Centro de Estudios Rurales Andinos Bartolomé de las Casas, Cuzco, Perú] 3, 1984, p. 169–222)

Republication of *Instrucción para descubrir todas las guacas del Piru,* short guidebook for persecutors of Andean religion. Corrects errors of 1967 ed. Introductory essay assigns date of 1583–84 and explores Guaman Poma's reasons for praising Albornoz while damning his fellow-*extirpador* Avila.

1624 ———. Algunas reflexiones acerca de las tesis de la estructura dual del poder incaico (PUCP/H, 4:2, dic. 1980, p. 183–196, bibl.)

Duviols reviews basis of Zuidema's 1964 "dual monarchy" thesis in testimonies of Polo de Ondegardo, Acosta, and Gutiérrez de Santa Clara. Affirms that second through fifth names of conventional king list are those of sixth through ninth, Incas' lower-moiety co-sovereigns.

1625 ———. El *Contra idolatriam* de Luis de Teruel y una versión primeriza del mito de Pachacámac, Vichama (Revista

Andina [Centro de Estudios Rurales Andinos Bartolomé de las Casas, Cuzco, Perú] 1:2, dic. 1983, p. 385–392)

Jesuit Teruel finished his book on Andean religion after 1620. Never adopted as official handbook for destroyers of Andean worship, it was lost and we have only an excerpt used by Calancha. Reproduces from Jesuit letter of 1617 a Teruel text retelling coastal myth of Vichama.

1626 ———. Guaman Poma, historiador del Perú antiguo: una nueva pista [Revista Andina [Centro de Estudios Rurales Andinos Bartolomé de las Casas, Cuzco, Perú] 1:1, 1983, p. 103–115, bibl.)

Scheme of four prehispanic ages, presented by Guaman Poma as Andean idea appears in Fray Buenaventura de Salinas y Córdova's 1630 work, apparently as transposition of Daniel's prophecy. Duviols holds both authors learned scheme from earlier source, possibly as-yet undiscovered notebooks of Francisco Fernández de Córdova, high-born Huánuco criollo.

1627 ———. Révisionisme historique et droit colonial au 16ème siècle: la thème de la tyrannie des incas (in Indianité, ethnocide, indigenisme en Amérique latine. GRAL, Centre interdisciplinaire d'études latino-américaines, Toulouse-le Mirail. Paris: Centre national de la recherche scientifique, 1982, p. 11–22, bibl. [Amérique latine. Pays ibériques])

Legalistic debate on legitimacy of Inca rule employed Aristotelian-derived concept of "natural lord" and its opposite, "tyrant," frequently. Traces accusation of tyranny as used in pro-indigenous positions of Victoria and las Casas, anti-Inca apologetics of the Pizarran group, and chronicles of Gómara, Zárate, and Cieza and Toledan writings.

1628 Espinoza Soriano, Waldemar. El curaca de los Cayambes y su sometimiento al imperio español, siglos XV y XVI (IFEA/B, 9:1/2, 1980, p. 89–119, bibl.)

Jerónimo Puento, grandson of Nasacota Puento who led north-Ecuadorian resistance to Incas, presented *probanzas* in 1579 and 1583 about his services in the repression of Amazonian Quijos revolt and in administering colonial tribute. Reproduces testimony with essay scolding Puento for "servilismo."

1629 ———. Los fundamentos lingüísticos de la etnohistoria andina y comentarios en torno al anónimo de Charcas de 1604 (UM/REAA, 10, 1980, p. 149–181, bibl.)

Pt. 1 concerns methods for interpreting toponyms and quarrying old lexicons, emphasizing phenomena such as hispanizing of native words, hybrid words, and use of native words for imported meanings. Pt. 2 restores credit for central-highland and coastal theories of origin of Quechua to Riva Agüero and González de la Rosa (both ca. 1910). Pt. 3 concerns former extent of Puquina speech, documented with 1604 list of Charcas parishes classified by languages (reproduced). Same article also published in *Aula quechua* (Edited by Rodolfo Cerrón Palomino. Lima: Ediciones Signo, 1982, p. 163–202, bibl.).

1630 ———. Los mitmas plateros de Ishma en el país de los ayarmaca, siglos XV–XIX (Boletín de Lima [s.n.] 30:5, 1983, p. 38–52)

Memorial of *Don Juan Coxco, cacique principal y gobernador del ayllu Erbay Izma de los yungas plateros* (1712) gives lead for study of Lima-area population stationed in Picoy to make luxury metalware. Postconquest litigation allows one to trace their evolution as members of growing urban Indian sector.

1631 Etnohistoria del Corregimiento de Chimbo: 1557–1820. Edited by Ximena Costales. Quito: Mundo Andino, 1983. 463 p.: bibl.

Compendium of primary sources, extracts, and summaries, mostly 18th century, about important Quechua-speaking region near modern Guaranda, Ecuador. Arranged by classificatory categories of Archivo Nacional de la Historia, Quito, selection has ethnohistoric material under "cacicazgos," "indígenas," and "obrajes" including *visita* fragments, succession lawsuits, etc.

1632 La Fiesta religiosa campesina: Andes ecuatorianos. Investigación dirigida por Marco Vinicio Rueda. Quito: Ediciones de la Universidad Católica, Departamento de Antropología, 1982. 395 p., 26 p. of plates: bibl., ill.

Results of team fieldwork by M.V. Rueda and 19 students in 1978–79 among several highland Ecuadorian groups. Ethnohistoric data appear in chap. 4, "Raíces Históricas," synthesized along lines of Marzal's studies of Peruvian folk Catholicism. Extended quotes of primary sources (notably Cieza, Gutiérrez de Sta. Clara, and Acosta) appear in "Apéndice."

1633 Figueiredo, Ariosvaldo. Enforcados: o índio em Sergipe. Rio de Janeiro: Paz e Terra, 1981. 139 p. (Coleção Estudos brasileiros; v. 52)

Substantial tertiary synthesis of four-century antecedents of recent Xocó land claim controversy. Heavy on missionary, governmental, and commercial aspects but not attentive to native society as such (see item 1618).

1634 Flores, Moacyr. Cultura missioneira (PUC/V, 26:104, dez. 1981, p. 447–452)

Regarding many central traits of Guaraní culture as diabolical errors, Jesuits from Anchieta onward sought to substitute distinctive new "missionary culture" through schooling of Guaraní children. Expulsion of Jesuits ended propagation of "missionary culture" but as late as 1858 Indians were observed practicing some of its elements in ruined missions.

1635 Flores Ochoa, Jorge A. Causas que originaron la actual distribución espacial de las alpacas y llamas (in El Hombre y su ambiente en los Andes centrales: ponencias presentadas en el Cuarto Simposio Internacional, Museo Nacional de Etnología, Osaka, 1980. Edited by Luis Millones and Hiroyasu Tomoeda. Suita, Japan: National Museum of Ethnology, 1982, p. 63–92, ill., tables [Senri Ethnological Studies; no. 10])

Spots in which modern camellid herds concentrate cover only small part of archaeologically attested range. Early-colonial and recent documentation from Valley of Cuzco, Titicaca high plains, Pisaq district, and Pampa de Anta shows that their displacement into highest tiers of original pasture belt is direct result of policy favoring sheepherding.

1636 Fresco, Antonio and **Wania Cobo.** Consideraciones ethnohistóricas acerca de una tumba de pozo y cámara de Ingapirca, Ecuador (UM/REAA, 8, 1978, p. 147–161, bibl., ill.)

Excavations at Inca "castillo" of In-gapirca, Cañar prov., Ecuador, yielded shaft tomb with multiple burial of female leader and her attendants. Comparison with *Relaciones geográficas* and extirpation data suggests that she was priestess of same cult Incas appropriated in building the "castillo."

1637 Fuenzalida V., Fernando. Los gentiles y el origen de la muerte (Revista de la Universidad Católica [Lima] 5, agosto 1979, p. 213–222)

The pan-Andean myth of *gentiles* (living dead) expresses realization that death is a precondition for continuation of life. *Gentiles* were incestuous and incapable of ordering society by marital alliance; incest taboo is the alternative to chaos. Conclusion echoes Leach: "inmortalidad es a muerte, como incesto a exogamia."

1638 Gade, Daniel and **María Escobar.** Village settlement and the colonial legacy in southern Peru (AGS/GR, 27:4, 1982, p. 430–449, bibl., ill., maps)

In southern half of Cuzco dept., 70 percent of 119 *reducción* villages built by decree in 16th century still exist, but modern settlement patterns reflect re-dispersion from their ill-adapted mediterranean town plans. Today, "satellite settlements" formed by Independence-era herders, not *reducción* villages, are the predominantly Andean settlements. Complements Málaga Medina's 1974 article (see HLAS 38:2127).

1639 Glave, Luis Miguel. Trajines: un capítulo en la formación del mercado interno colonial (Revista Andina [Centro de Estudios Rurales Andinos Bartolomé de las Casas, Cuzco, Perú] 1:1, 1983, p. 9–76, bibl., ill., tables)

The 16th-century Peruvian economic system, far from being a Spanish transplant, remained operationally based on native organization. Case in point: long-distance transport yielding colonial wealth through exploitation of Andean *tambo* and road-*mita* systems. Manuscript sources (partly reproduced) depict wine *trajín* between Arequipa-Moquegua and coca *trajín* to Cuzco.

1640 Golte, Jürgen. Cultura y naturaleza andinas (IPA/A, 15:17/18, 1981, p. 119–132)

Andean technology created distinctive consciousness: domestication of many species and niches required complex forms of cooperation which are experienced as part and parcel of the nature to which they respond. Modern setting offers challenges "indisolubles en términos de la cultura andina." Anthropologists must accept need for technical contributions from outside.

1641 González Carré, Enrique and **Fermín Rivera Pineda.** La muerte del Inca en Santa Ana de Tusi (IFEA/B, 11:1/2, 1982, p. 19–36, bibl., ill., plates)

In Quebrada de Chaupihuaranga annual dramatization of Inca's death portrays him as "hijo o 'súbdito preferido'" of Apu or "divinidad andina." Pizarro and the Inca fight at six *tambos* representing Quito-Cuzco road; Inca gives audience prophecy before being captured and "killed." Text reproduces fragment of mixed Quechua-Spanish ritual speech.

1642 Guillén Guillén, Edmundo. El enigma de las momias incas (Boletín de Lima [s.n.] 28:5, julio 1983, p. 29–42, bibl.)

Polo, Sarmiento, and other chroniclers seemingly account for loss of Inca kings' mummified remains, but close reading leaves room for doubt whether Polo and the rest obtained real royal mummies. Author thinks hiding places in Cuzco or Vilcabamba dominion may yet yield as many as five royal mummies.

Guss, David M. Historical incorporation among the Makiritare: from legend to myth. See *HLAS 45:1258.*

1643 Haro Alvear, Silvio Luis. Mitos de origen de Reino del Quito (IGME/RG, 18, abril 1983, p. 76–93, ill.)

Relates various archaeological objects (petroglyphs, figurines, etc.) with their alleged correlates in the mythologies of many American peoples.

1644 ———. Mitos y cultos del Reino de Quito. Quito: Editora Nacional, 1980 [i.e. 1981]. 446 p., 16 p. of plates: bibl., ill.

Attempts to reconstruct religions of preincaic Ecuador, and vindicate Velascan tradition, by applying ideas from Morgan, Tylor, Frazier, and Uhle, to vast assortment of chronicle data, folklore, and homemade linguistic inference. Main focus is on celestial bodies and mountains. Local details include little-known petroglyphs and fragments on indigenous ritual.

1645 Hartmann, Roswith. El texto Quechua de Huarochirí: una evaluación crítica de las ediciones a disposición (PUCP/H, 5:2, dic. 1981, p. 167–208, bibl.)

Detailed review essay on Gerald Taylor's 1980 Quechua-French bilingual ed. of the "Huarochirí Manuscript" (see *HLAS 42:1529*). Disputes Taylor's contentions as to relation between Huarochirí ms. and Francisco de Avila's 1608 *Tratado de los falsos dioses.* Although technical, the discussion is acute and of general interest.

——— and **Olaf Holm.** La "romana" en tiempos prehispánicos y su uso actual en la costa del Ecuador. See *HLAS 45:820.*

1646 Heath, Shirley Brice and **Richard Laprade.** Castilian colonization and indigenous languages: the cases of Quechua and Aymara (*in* Language spread: studies in diffusion and social change. Edited by Robert L. Cooper. Bloomington: Indiana University Press; Washington: Center for Applied Linguistics, 1982, p. 118–147, bibl., map)

Summary of published colonial documentation and recent sociolinguistic evidence. Despite Peninsular objections to Quechua, Crown policies formulated 1580–1680, and continued until 1768, amounted to an "additive" program promoting Quechua to *lingua franca* role. Under more discriminatory late-colonial and modern conditions, Aymara retained greater potency as symbol of group unity.

1647 Herrera, Aída de. Literatura incaica. Caracas: Librería Editorial Salesiana, n.d. 222 p.

Author has rounded up the usual suspects (Ollantay, songs from Guaman Poma, songs collected by Jesús Lara, etc.) for scrapbook of translations with extensive but elementary comments.

1648 Hidalgo Lehuede, Jorge. Amarus y cataris: aspectos mesiánicos de la rebelión indígena de 1781, en Cusco, Chayanta, La Paz y Arica (Chungara [Universidad del Norte, Departamento de Antropología, Arica, Chile] 10, marzo 1983, p. 117–138, bibl., table)

Great rebellions arose in a climate of popular prophecy; rebel ideology included calls for an end to Christianity and return to mummified ancestors. Perceived as rebel Messiah, Tupac Amaru II was thought to live on in Paitití. Reproduces brief document indicating diffusion of such ideas as far as Atacama by 1782.

1649 Hijos de Paria Qaqa: la tradición oral de Waru Chiri: mitología, ritual y costumbres. Edited and translated by George L. Urioste. Syracuse, N.Y.: Syracuse University, Maxwell School of Citizenship and Public Affairs, 1983. 2 v.: appendices, bibl., indexes (Foreign and Comparative Studies Program. Latin American series; no. 6)

New bilingual (Quechua-Spanish) critical ed. of the great *Runa yndio ñiscap* manuscript dubiously attributed to Avila. Includes historical introduction, variorum notes covering earlier transcriptions and translations, index to names of places and persons, and bibliography. Translation is meticulous but vivid and conveys some of the style of original. Important study and reference ed. (see item **1645** and *HLAS 42:1589*).

1650 Hopkins, Diane. Juego de enemigos (IPA/A, 17:20, 1982, p. 167–188, bibl.)

Ritual battle is widely reported in highland ethnography but ethnohistoric data are extremely scarce. Reports discovery of significant 1772 trial in which defendents took part in lethal "play" combat between moieties of Langui, in Cañas y Canchis.

The Inca and Aztec state, 1400–1800: anthropology and history. See item **1544**.

1651 Julien, Catherine J. Hatunqolla: a view of Inca rule from the Lake Titicaca region. Berkeley: University of California Press, 1983. 286 p.: bibl., ill., maps, tables (University of California publications in anthropology; v. 15)

Author undertook separate ethno-historical and archaeological inquiries into Inca impact on Aymara-Uru-Puquina society. Ethnohistorical data suggest that during a century of Inca rule, administrative structures partly respected pre-Inca arrangements. Episodes of rebellion also suggest Qolla institutions proved durable. Yet archaeological findings indicate marked acculturation toward Inca norms.

1652 ———. Inca decimal administration in the Lake Titicaca region (*in* The Inca and Aztec states, 1400–1800: anthropology and history [see item **1544**] p. 19–151, bibl., tables)

Knot-recorded prehispanic census of Lupaqa embedded in 1567 *visita* contains indirect evidence of decimal regimen. Symmetric and nearly round numbers governed by moiety (*saya*) lords at province level equates them to *hunu* (10,000-tributary) authorities in Inca scheme. *Ayllus* they commanded look like *pachakas* (100-tributary units).

1653 Kus, James S. La agricultura estatal en la costa norte del Perú (III/AI, 40:4, oct./dic. 1980, p. 713–729, bibl., ill.)

How well does ethnohistoric testimony of Inca state agriculture describe pre-Inca modes? Correspondence between field boundaries and ceremonial axes, the likelihood that they were built by state labor gangs, and other indicators suggest widespread state management during at least 1,500 years.

1654 Lazzarotto, Danilo. Encomiendas e povos das missões (*in* Simpósio Nacional de Estudos Missioneiros, 2nd, Santa Rosa, Brazil, 1977. Anais. Santa Rosa: Faculdade de Filosofia, Ciências e Letras Dom Bosco, 1978, p. 42–49)

Summarizes resistance of Jesuits in Guairá (Paraguay, southeast of Asunción) facing encomenderos, hostile bishops, *bandeirantes*, predatory traders; defends Jesuits against accusations that *reducciones* constituted a virtual Jesuit encomienda.

1655 León, Leonardo. Expansión inca y resistencia indígena en Chile, 1470–1536 (Chungara [Universidad del Norte, Departamento de Antropología, Arica, Chile] 10, marzo 1983, p. 95–115, bibl., ill.)

Reexamines chronicles for evidence on degree to which aboriginal resistance conditioned Inca policy; argues that geographic advantage in holding passes, and "marcada tendencia . . . a formar alianzas territoriales" made it possible for small native numbers to hold off Inca armies. Battle of Maule and building of forts interpreted in this light.

1656 Llanos Vargas, Héctor. Los cacicazgos de Popayán a la llegada de los conquistadores. Bogotá: Banco de la República, Fundación de Investigaciones Arqueológicas Nacionales, 1981. 95 p., 1 leaf of pages: ill. (some col.) (Publicación de la Fundación de Investigaciones Arqueológicas Nacionales; no. 10)

Using *visitas* of 1559, 1569, 1582, and 1606, author frames question of "tribal" or "chiefdom" oganization. Concludes that around Popayán (e.g., Guambía, Coconuco, Timbío, etc.) "no se dio una jerarquía de clases sociales, sino una sectorización, donde los jefes tuvieron ciertos privilegios de acuerdo a sus funciones de líderes . . .". For archaeologist's comment, see *HLAS 45:807*.

1657 —— and **Roberto Pineda Camacho.** Etnohistoria del Gran Caquetá, siglos XVI–XIX. Bogotá: Banco de la República, Fundación de Investigaciones Arqueológicas Nacionales, 1982. 126 p.: bibl., ill. (some col.), maps (some col.) (Publicación de la Fundación de Investigaciones Arqueológicas Nacionales; no. 15)

Amazonian Colombia (Caquetá, Amazonas) experienced penetration from Brazilian and Pacific sides a century before rubber boom. Using Bogotá and Popayán archives, sorts out numerous groups in early sources. Ethnographic fragments on missionary diffusion of Quechua in Amazonia, hallucinogens, captivity and cannibalism are of interest. Reproduces 18th-century maps, demographic data.

1658 López Baralt, Mercedes. La crónica de Indias como texto cultural: articulación de los códigos icónico y lingüístico en los dibujos de la *Nueva Corónica* de Guaman Poma (IILI/RI, 48:120/121, julio/dic. 1982, p. 461–531, ill.)

Written elements are typed by their relation to images. Some clarify or "anchor" images, while others complete their sense by offering additional meanings. Omnipresent appropriation of foreign linguistic code into a less alien pictorial one is paralleled by Guamán Poma's program for development of a literate Andean culture (see item **1578**).

1659 López Sebastián, Lorenzo Eladio. Las marcas en los "keros:" hipótesis de interpretación (UM/REAA, 10, 1980, p. 21–41, bibl., ill.)

Some *keros* (wooden beer vases) have symbols incised on their bases. Author studied 22 marked *keros* from Madrid and Paris museums. Drawings hypotheses from studies in other continents—that they are either makers' or owners' marks— they opt for the latter.

1660 Lyon, Patricia J. An imaginary frontier: prehistoric highland-lowland interchange in the southern Peruvian Andes (*in* Networks of the past: regional interaction in archaeology. Proceedings of the 12th Annual Conference of the Archaeological Association of the University of Calgary. Edited by Peter D. Francis, F.J. Kense, and P.G. Duke. Calgary, Canada: University of Calgary Archaeological Association, 1981, p. 3–18)

Study of documentation and remains from Vilcabamba, Cosñipata, and Marcapata, Inambari, and Tambopata River valleys, all in the rainforests east of Cuzco. Incas treated area much as other regions, establishing alliances and defensive posts "staffed largely by *mitimaes*." . . . Inca presence ended where river navigation began.

1661 McNaspy, Clement J. Pueblos de guaraníes en las selvas río-platenses: una visita a las ruinas jesuíticas. Asunción: Ediciones Loyola, 1981. 68 p., 12 p. of plates: ill.

Approach to *reducciones* via ecclesiastical and architectural history, perhaps useful as context for Guaraní ethnohistory.

Marcato, Sonia de Almeida. A repressão contra os Botocudos em Minas Gerais. See *HLAS 45:1162*.

1662 Marsh, Charles R. Recent studies on Guaman Poma de Ayala (UP/LAIL, 6:1, Spring 1982, p. 27–32)

Describes Rolena Adorno's work on European ingredients of Guaman Poma's thought and on his visual imagery; George Urioste's commentary on his Quechua; Regina Harrison's study of oral traditional elements; Mercedes López-Baralt's study of the drawings; and Sara Castro-Klarén's characterization of Guaman Poma's ideological proposals.

Martin de Nantes, *père.* Relação de uma missão ao no Rio São Francisco. See item **3497**.

1663 Martini de Vatausky, Yoli Angélica. Los franciscanos de Río IV, los indios ranqueles y otros temas de la vida en la frontera (PF/AIA, 41, 1981, p. 321–388)

Río Cuarto, ciudad argentina, fue sede de colegio de misiones (fundado 1856) para cristianizar los indios de la Pampa. Autor utiliza archivo del colegio y demuestra que el gobierno se interesó más en la sumisión o exterminio de los indios que en su conversión al cristianismo. Trabajo notable. [Lino Gómez Canedo]

1664 Marzal, Manuel María. Garcilaso y la antropología peruana (PUCP/DA, 5, julio 1980, p. 1–24)

Noting Valcárcel's observation that some 70 percent of Garcilaso's chapters are more ethnographic than historical, author summarizes Garcilaso's viewpoints on three "edades" of history, on Inca religion, and on acculturation after 1532 with special attention to Andean perception of European livestock. Sees in Garcilaso a precursor of "conciencia nacional."

1665 ———. Religión católica e identidad nacional (in Perú: identidad nacional. Lima: Ediciones CEDEP, 1979, p. 123–168)

In practice, as opposed to doctrine, Peruvian Catholicism is the composite product of four centuries' stressful relations between Andean, African, Amazonian, and European belief systems. Despite heterogeneity, Peruvian religious subcultures have a common core. Sketches historical context.

1666 Mathewson, Kent. Bridging the Guayas River gap: legend and landscape archaeology in coastal Ecuador (Andean Perspectives [Urbana, Ill.] 4, 1982, p. 15–20, maps)

Legend widely discussed in Guayaquil's historiography concerns a "paso de Guaynacapa" across Guayas River. Author reports 1980 find of remains of stone causeway, probably built by pre- or non-Inca population to improve access to raised fields, which could be the sort of "paso" thus mythified.

1667 Mayer, Enrique. A tribute to the household: domestic economy and the encomienda in colonial Peru. Austin: Institute of Latin American Studies, University of Texas, 1982. 37 p.: bibl. (A Special publication of the Institute of Latin American Studies. Working paper)

Unusual thought-experiment: ethnologist rereads the 1562 testimony of householder Agostín Luna Capcha in Ortiz de Zuñiga's Huánuco visita and seeks to reconstruct economic reasoning behind it. Chief focus is the problem of satisfying Spanish tribute without disrupting subsistence; sheds light on local impact of tribute laws.

1668 Melia, Bartolomeu. El "modo de ser" guaraní en la primera documentación jesuítica, 1594–1639 (USP/RA, 24, 1981, p. 1–24, bibl.)

Studied with aid of ethnographic analogy, Jesuit missionary letters yield information about concept of teko ("ser, estado de vida, condición, estar, costumbre, ley, hábito") and its elaboration in Guaraní culture under stress of "reduction." Foci include territoriality, migration, defense of polygamy, and role of "dancers" in propagating anti-European millenarist resistance.

1669 Mesa, Carlos E. Creencias religiosas de los pueblos indígenas que habitaban en el territorio de la futura Colombia (ISTM/MH, 37: 109/111, enero/dic. 1980, p. 111–142)

Extensive summary of data on Chibcha rites and beliefs, and less full coverage on Cariban peoples, based on chronicles of Fray Alonso de Zamora O.P., Fray Pedro de Simón, and Lucas Fernández de Piedrahita. Theoretical framework is unmodified Tylorian notion of totemism.

1670 Millones, Luis. Brujerías de la costa/brujerías de la sierra: estudio comparativo de dos complejos religiosos en el área andina (in El Hombre y su ambiente en los Andes centrales: ponencias presentadas en el Cuarto Simposio Internacional, Museo Nacional de Etnología, Osaka, 1980. Edited by Luis Millones and Hiroyasu Tomoeda. Suita, Japan: National Museum of Ethnology, 1982, p. 229–274, ill. [Senri Ethnological Studies; no. 10])

Holds that same process which relegated folk religion to stigma of "witchcraft" in Europe—namely conflict with state-backed priesthoods—also operated in prehispanic Peru. In both highland Tawantinsuy and coastal Chimor, such "folk" functions of religion as curing, love magic, etc., accrued to lower sphere of religious practice.

1671 ———. Los dioses de Santa Cruz. Lima: Pontificia Universidad Católica del Perú, Departamento de Ciencias Sociales, 1978? 47 p.: bibl.

Discusses Pachacuti Yamqui's Relación de antigüedades as moralizing chronicle centered on one central antithesis: cult of the high god Huiracocha. Santa Cruz Pachacuti Yamqui identifies "Huiracocha" cult with Inca state, legitimacy, and a natural religion approximating Christian revelation while opposing innumerable shrine cults or huacas, which he associates with local lords, illegitimacy, and idolatry. In Pachacuti's view reigns of triumphant Incas coincide with former's ascendancy.

1672 ———. Sociedad indígena e identidad nacional (in Perú: identidad nacional. Lima: Ediciones CEDEP, 1979, p. 57–77)

Synthesizing secondary literature on Andean political movements, essay proposes that at three historic junctures, Andean ideology transcended kinship-based and locality-based group definition in ways that promoted "identidad nacional:" 1) Inca empire, self-defined through political "citizenship;" 2) millenarian Taki Onqoy movement of 1560s; and 3) Tupac Amaru II 1780 revolt, which proposed "national" development of "Republic of Indians."

1673 ———; **Max Hernández;** and **Virgilio Galdo G.** Amores cortesanos y amores prohibidos: romance y clases sociales en el antiguo Perú (IGFO/RI, 42 : 16[170] julio/dic. 1982, p. 669–688)

Sources ca. 1600 yield various putatively Inca love stories. Essay examines two in which lovers follow courtly strictures of estate privilege, and two that involved "prohibited" love transgressing it. Analysis leads to conclusions on an Andean sexual double standard.

1674 ———; **Virgilio Galdo G.;** and **Anne Marie Dussault.** Reflexiones en torno al romance en la sociedad indígena: seis relatos de amor (RCLL, 7 : 14, 1981, p. 7–28, bibl.)

In stories of Acoitapia and Chuquillanto, or Sayre Tupa and Cusi Huarcai (both set down by Murúa), as well as in Pachacuti Yamqui's and Cabello's love tales embroidered onto Incaic oral histories, there are data on "guacanques" (love charms), aphrodisiacs, and concepts about licit and illicit love.

Moncaut, Carlos Antonio. Reducción Jesuítica de Nuestra Señora de la Concepción de los Pampas, 1740–1753: historia de un pueblo desaparecido a orillas del Río Salado bonaerense. See item **2789.**

Morey, Robert V. A joyful harvest of souls: disease and the destruction of the Llanos Indians. See *HLAS 45 : 1289.*

1675 Morris, Craig. The infrastructure of Inka control in the Peruvian central highlands (in The Inca and Aztec states, 1400–1800: anthropology and history [see item **1544**] p. 153–171, bibl., maps, tables)

Applies archaeological evidence from Inca administrative center Huánuco Pampa to question pioneered by ethnohistorians: "How did (the Inca installation) mediate between the seat of ultimate authority in Cuzco and the people it ruled in the countryside?" Military and bureaucratic means appear less salient or developed than feasting and redistribution.

1676 Murra, John V. Andean societies (Annual Reviews in Anthropology [Annual Reviews Inc., Palo Alto, Calif.] 13, 1984, p. 119–141, bibl.)

Retrospective essay on Andean studies tradition. Synopsis of ethnohistoric sources plays down traditional Inca studies and highlights more durable local systems as key research areas. Synopsis of 20th-century research emphasizes genesis of pro-Andean consciousness among urbanite intellectuals exposed to international currents in anthropology.

1677 ———. La *mit'a* al Tawantinsuyu: prestaciones de los grupos étnicos (Chungara [Universidad del Norte Departamento de Antropología, Arica, Chile] 10, marzo 1983, p. 77–94, bibl.)

Spanish version of item **1678.**

1678 ———. The *mit'a* obligations of ethnic groups to the Inka state (in The Inca and Aztec states, 1400–1800: anthropology and history [see item **1544**] p. 237–262, bibl.)

In 1549, "pacifier" La Gasca ordered 72 teams of researchers to look into rural society, and known fragments of this venture (covering Chupaychu, Canta, and Caraveli), together with later data, allow comparisons of tributary regimes as seen from below. No drastic overhaul of local regimen seems to be involved.

1679 ———. El tráfico de *mullu* en la costa del Pacífico (in Simposio de Correlaciones Antropológicas Andino-Mesoamericanas, 1st, Salinas, Ecuador, 1971. Simposio. Edited by Jorge G. Marcos and Presley Norton. Guayaquil, Ecuador: Escuela

Superior Politécnica del Litoral [ESPOL], 1982, p. 265–273, bibl.)

Restored to its intended context after 11-year publication delay, well-known essay on prehispanic deepwater traffic in processed Spondylus shell now fits into archaeological literature on long-distance contacts. Also published in Murra's 1975 anthology *Formaciones económicas y políticas del mundo andino* (see *HLAS 38:2135*).

1680 Oberem, Udo. Un documento inédito del siglo XVII sobre Guamanga (PUCP/H, 5:1, julio 1981, p. 113–118, bibl.)

Summary of *memorial* tendered to the Council of the Indies in 1664 brings to light one of Atahualpa Inca's descendants: "Don Juan Crisóstomo Chilingano Atagualpa Ynga . . . cacique y governador" in Guamanga, a colonial noble whose testimony bore on little-known native militias of the 17th century. Reproduces texts.

1681 ——. Un ejemplo de autovaloración social entre la alta nobleza indígena del Quito colonial (Miscelánea Antropológica Ecuatoriana [Museos del Banco Central del Ecuador, Guayaquil] 2, 1983, p. 125–134)

Doña Bárbara Atagualpa Ynga sent Crown letters (1610–13) claiming share of subsidies accorded descendants of last prehispanic Inca king. Oberem interprets them as expressing royal self-concept. Doña Bárbara's servitors included "yanacunas incas," seemingly Inca-by-privilege transplanted into Quito. Reproduces original documents.

1682 ——. "Etnohistoria" e "historia folk:" un ejemplo de Sudamérica (Historia Boliviana [Amatu Books, Cochabamba] 2:1, 1982, p. 1–10, bibl.)

Translation of 1974 article. Numerous definitions of "ethnohistory" allude to "folk history;" examples from the Quijos of eastern lowland Ecuador show that the relation between them is intelligible in terms of "la sedimentación de las experiencias históricas en relatos etiológicos." Mythifications point to significance of events in Quijos culture.

1683 —— and Roswith Hartmann. Zur Seefahrt in den Hochkulturen Alt-Amerikas (*in* Kolloquien zur Allgemeinen und Vergleicheden Arzhaeologie. Bd. 2. München, FRG: Verlag C.H. Beck, 1982, p. 121–157, bibl., ill., maps)

Synthesis of ethnohistoric and archae-

ological sources on seafaring in both Meso-america and Andean South America; for the latter, colonial data of all centuries and some ethnographic analogies are used in discussing ship design, including Ecuadorian data not found in other works on subject.

1684 Oberti R., Italo. Cusco arqueológico y etnohistórico: una introducción bibliográfica (Revista Andina [Centro de Estudios Rurales Andinos Bartolomé de las Casas, Cuzco, Perú/ 1:2, dic. 1983, p. 443–474, charts, tables)

Substantial bibliographic essay concentrates on major contributors from Squier onward, listing only one work for each but characterizing their contributions more than cursorily. Emphasizes city's role as Inca capital. Useful for novice Andeanists and scholarly travelers.

1685 Ossio, Juan. Relaciones interétnicas y verticalidad en los Andes (PUCP/DA, 2, mayo 1978, p. 1–23, bibl.)

Characterizes Andean ethnology as polarized between "culturalista" views, which treat Andean mental structures in isolation from institutional relations, and "empiricist"views, which concentrate on "domination" at expense of cultural study. Argues that a more authentic approach requires showing how actions which constitute and preserve institutional relations are framed upon ethnoclassificatory schemes.

1686 Padilla Bendezú, Abraham. Huamán Poma, el indio cronista dibujante. México: Fondo de Cultura Económica, 1979. 191 p., 57 p. of plates: ill. (Colección Tierra firme)

Affirms Guaman Poma's claim of royal descent, judges his acquaintance with chronicles to be substantial (including possible service as secretary to Cabello), argues against his being a native of Huánuco, and identifies his death place not as Lima but as Santiago de Chipao.

1687 Parkerson, Phillip T. The Inca coca monopoly: fact or legal fiction? (APS/P, 127:2, April 1983, p. 107–123)

Disputes Toledan testimony of royal coca monopoly. *Visitas* of Chucuito, Jauja, and Zongo show coca lands under control of ethnic lords and households. If commoners used coca more after Spanish invasion, reason lies more in peculiarities of mining economy than in collapse of Inca sumptuary law. Review of well-known sources.

1688 Pease G.Y., Franklin. The formation of Tawantinsuyu: mechanisms of colonization and relationships with ethnic groups (*in* The Inca and Aztec states, 1400–1800: anthropology and history [see item **1544**] p. 173–198, bibl.)

Far from monolithic, Inca state varied widely in ways it articulated vassal societies to large-scale institutions. Polities which had built centralized, regimes before conquest (case studies: Lapaqa, Chimor) entered without wholesale transformation, but stateless societies (case study: Chachapoyas) seem to have been supplied with prosthetic sovereigns dependent on Cuzco. Translation of *HLAS 42:1698.*

1689 ———. Relaciones entre los grupos étnicos de la sierra sur y la costa: continuidades y cambios (*in* El Hombre y su ambiente en los Andes centrales: ponencias presentadas en el Cuarto Simposio Internacional, Museo Nacional de Etnología, Osaka, 1980. Edited by Luis Millones and Hiroyasu Tomoeda. Suita, Japan: National Museum of Ethnology, 1982, p. 107–122, bibl. [*Senri Ethnological Studies*; no. 10])

Andean lords drew on privileges in two economic systems. Pease finds that one mechanism which facilitated such dual integration was newly introduced dowry. Utilizes materials from recently opened archives at Moquegua to document links in colonial times between polities on altiplano and coast.

1690 Piana, Ernesto Luis. Toponimia y arqueología del siglo XIX en La Pampa. Buenos Aires: Editorial Universitaria de Buenos Aires, 1981. 294 p., 1 leaf of plates: bibl., facsims., ill.

Author collected non-Spanish toponyms. Despite admitted unfamiliarity with Araucanian language, addresses such matters as spread of Quechua toponyms along rail lines built by workers from Andean northwest. Includes facsimile documents about 1870s-80s Indian wars.

1691 Pino Díaz, Fermín del. Contribución del Padre Acosta a la constitución de la etnología: su evolucionismo (IGFO/RI, 38:153/154, julio/dic. 1978, p. 507–546)

Amplifies O'Gorman's (1940) and

Rowe's (1964) suggestions that Acosta prefigures cultural evolutionism. Acosta's modernity consists not merely in his postulate of a three-staged sequence, but in the "establecimiento de una correlación causal entre los niveles de evolución religiosa, económica, y política, al modo como lo hará luego la escuela funcionalista."

1692 ———. Los estudios etnográficos y etnológicos de la Expedición Malaspina (IGFO/RI, 42:169/170, julio/dic, 1982, p. 393–465, bibl., ill.)

Malaspina expedition visited *patagones* of Puerto Deseado, Argentina in 1789, and in 1790, the *huiliches* of Isla Chiloé, Chile. Ethnographic content of these only partly published explorations centers on hunting and other economic bases. Essay includes detailed historical background, plates.

1693 Pino Zapata, Ricardo. Pacificación y colonización de la frontera y la Araucania (UC/AT, 446, 1982, p. 89–118, map)

Wars and guerrillas against Mapuche and other natives, as seen from viewpoint of local Hispanic settlers in Chilean south (1821–86). Chief sources are provincial newspapers, summarized and briefly quoted.

1694 Pla, Alberto J. Modo de producción asiático y las formaciones económicosociales inca y azteca. México: Ediciones El Caballito, 1979. 213 p.: bibl., ill. (Colección Fragua mexicana; 34)

Claims to dissociate "Asiatic mode" from unilineal dogma and use it critically vis-à-vis works of Godelier, Murra, Wachtel. Affirms Inca and Aztec states were similar in economic structure, adducing comparisons much like those formulated by Carrasco (item **1519**), and holds that "Asiatic mode" predominated in both (see also items **1621** and **1730**).

1695 Platt, Tristan. Estado boliviano y ayllu andino: tierra y tributo en el norte de Potosí. Lima: Instituto de Estudios Peruanos, 1982. 197 p.: bibl., map, tables (Historia andina; 9)

In south highland Bolivia at the dawn of the Republic, native *ayllus* practiced "cacical" version of mercantile capitalism: local lords met tribute quotas by marketing wheat grown with communal labor prestations. Payments were interpreted by natives as guarantees of communal land rights, and Republican attempts to substitute a regimen of individual private tenure with corresponding taxes (*exvinculación*, called "la primera reforma agraria") provoked largely successful resistance from 1870s. Innovative study based on novel sources.

1696 Poole, Deborah. Los santuarios religiosos en la economía regional andina: Cusco (IPA/A, 16:19, 1982, p. 79–116, bibl., maps, tables)

In making pilgrimages to the shrines of Misk'a, Sankha, and Pampak'ucho, highlanders perpetuate boundaries of "ciertas categorías sociales y territoriales de la economía precolonial centradas y delimitadas en santuarios." These include well-documented emplacement of *mitmaq* and Inca-by-privilege *ayllus*. Summarizes extensive archive and field research.

1697 Rabinowitz, Joel. La lengua pescadora: the lost dialect of Chimú fishermen (*in* Investigations of the Andean past: papers from the First Annual Northeast Conference on Andean Archaeology and Ethnohistory. Edited by Daniel H. Sandweiss. Ithaca, N.Y.: Cornell University, Latin American Studies Program, 1983, p. 243–267, bibl., tables [Cornell Latin American studies series])

Four sources attest that fishermen on the Peruvian north coast spoke their own language. Contends that "la pescadora" was divergent dialect related to Muchic and Quingnam, most evident in the Chicama valley. It evolved from occupational jargon to separate tongue in context of a caste-like speech community.

1698 Ramírez-Horton, Susan. Retainers of the lords or merchants: a case of mistaken identity (*in* El Hombre y su ambiente en los Andes centrales: ponencias presentadas en el Cuarto Simposio Internacional, Museo Nacional de Etnología, Osaka, 1980. Edited by Luis Millones and Hiroyasu Tomoeda. Suita, Japan: National Museum of Ethnology, 1982, p. 123–136, bibl., charts [Senri Ethnological Studies; no. 10])

Documents of Peruvian north coast show apparent trader complex among natives. Were they real "merchant Indians" (i.e. status traders), or bearers of goods from *mitmaq* outliers, or was trading a colonial inno-

vation? Suggests second hypothesis may be valid.

Ravines, Rogger. Chanchán: metrópoli chimú. See *HLAS 45:878.*

1700 Regalado de Hurtado, Liliana. La *Relación* de Titu Cusi Yapanqui: valor de un testimonio tardío (PUCP/H, 5:1, julio 1981, p. 45–61, bibl.)

As source for Inca thought, 1570 *Relación* has obvious shortcomings; author was neither eyewitness nor adult at time of the events he narrates. Moreover, his testimony appears twice biased: by its partisan role as a negotiating position, and by the hispanicized rhetoric. Nonetheless, Regalado holds that, if read "between the lines," the *Relación* yields significant information on Inca institutions. (See also item **1606**).

1701 Rivera Cusicanqui, Silvia. Rebelión e ideología: luchas del campesinado aymara del Altiplano Boliviano, 1910–1920 (Historia Boliviana [Amauta Books, Cochabamba] 1/2, 1981, p. 83–99)

Argues against the unlineal approach to peasant movements; suggests allegedly "prepolitical" rebellions of Pacajes (1914) and Achacachi (1920) anticipated "modern" revolutionism. They did so, however, in ways ill-interpreted by social science: re-emergence of "caciques" and communal officers, remobilization of colonial land titles, and expression of reform goals in partly mythic terms.

Rivera Dorado, Miguel. Arqueología y etnohistoria de la costa norte del Ecuador. See *HLAS 45:831.*

1702 Rodicio García, Sara. El sistema de parentesco inca (UM/REAA, 10, 1980, p. 183–254, bibl., charts)

Holds that at root of terminological problem studied by Lounsbury lies a "proceso evolutivo que a partir de una estructura matrilineal desemboca en la patrilineal" leaving behind lexical residues. Leaves out of account Zuidema's model of Inca kinship, and 1972 reply to Lounsbury in which he modified it.

1703 Rodríguez, Juan Evangelista. Historia de Cochasquí. Quito: Consejo Provincial de Pichincha, 1983. 1 v.: facsims. (Programa de Cochasquí)

Facsimile memoir by literate peasant, with facing transcription. Recalls agrarian life ca. 1930, apparently in a "cholo" milieu (there is little Quichua) as struggle of a morally superior but "desamparado" community to get attention of government agencies.

1704 Rostworowski de Díez Canseco, María. Estructuras andinas del poder: ideología religiosa y política. Lima: Instituto de Estudios Peruanos, 1983. 202 p.: bibl., ill. (Historia andina; 10)

Dualism—the pairing of complementary, opposed halves—pervades Andean religious thought and political organization. Religious half of book marshals data on lessknown dual deities as well as famous Inca gods. Political part approaches "diarchy" and the motif of paired kings via data on dual and tripartite military command as well as dual ethnic authorities. Asserts Incas imposed such patterns on conquered peoples.

1705 ———. Los pescadores del litoral peruano en el siglo XVI *Yunga Guaxme* (GEE/NA, 4, 1981, p. 11–42, bibl.)

Condenses much material from author's study of little-known coastal sources (see *HLAS 44:1666*) to demonstrate a widespread pattern of complementarity and barter between specialized fishing *ayllus* and other producers. For the north coast native, terminologies of specialization are known. Detailed treatment of fishing and sailing technology.

Rowe, John Howland. An account of the shrines of ancient Cuzco. See *HLAS 45:882.*

1706 ———. Inca policies and institutions relating to the cultural unification of the empire (*in* The Inca and Aztec states, 1400–1800: anthropology and history [see item **1544**] p. 93–118, bibl.)

"Cultural unification was probably not a primary goal of the Inca government." Nonetheless, Inca policy in education and language, management of *yana* servitors, resettlement of *kamayuq* specialists, demographic transplanting of *mitmaq*, prestation of "chosen women," and promulgation of imperial religious cults, did leave pan-Andean legacies which remained important under Spanish rule. Revises author's earlier (1946) interpretation of *yana* status.

1707 ———. Una relación de los adoratorios del antiguo Cusco (PUCP/H, 5:2, dic. 1981, p. 209–261, bibl.)

Discovery (1974) of Bernabé Cobo's manuscript *Historia del Nuevo Mundo*

(1653) yields better text for study of Cuzco's *ceque* system (radial organization of shrines). According to introductory essay, Cobo based his account on unidentified source written between 1560–71. Earlier authorship, attributed to Polo de Ondegardo and (by Rowe) to Molina "Cuzqueño," must now be considered unknown.

1708 Sáenz de Santa María, Carmelo. Un manuscrito de Cieza localizado en la Biblioteca Apostólica Vaticana (IGFO/RI, 41:16 3/164, enero/junio 1981, p. 31-?)

Long known only through use which Herrera y Tordesillas made of it, full text of pt. 3 of Cieza de León's *Crónica del Perú* is now available thanks to Francesca Cantú's discovery of manuscript. Author describes and evaluates Cantú's ed., highlighting marginal notes made by Cieza himself and elucidating Cieza's "lascasian" views (see item **1582**).

1709 Saignes, Thierry. Politiques ethniques dans la Bolivie coloniale: XVIe-XIXe siècles (*in* Indianité, ethnocide, indigenisme en Amérique Latine. GRAL, Centre interdisciplinaire d'études latino-americaines, Toulouse-le Mirail. Paris: Centre national de la recherche scientifique, 1982, p. 23–52, bibl., ill., maps [Amérique latine. Pays ibériques])

Concise synthesis of what is known about colonial transformation of south-Andean peoples (including "Chunchos" of sub-Andean Amazonia) with special focus on changes in internal organization. Argues against notion that colonial policy of "isolating" natives was succeeded by an "integrating" republican policy. Both tendencies existed in tension in all periods. But ethnic groups in diverse regions felt their effects unequally and reacted differently.

1710 ———. ¿Quiénes son los Kallawaya?: nota sobre un enigma etnohistórico (Revista Andina [Centro de Estudios Rurales Andinos Bartolomé de las Casas, Cuzco, Perú] 1:2, 1983, p. 357–384, bibl., charts, map, tables)

When and how did Bolivian curers acquire esoteric herbalist lore and language? Specialty appears as of 1767, in document record. Saignes thinks it resulted from a "lenta cristalización" of relations with forest peoples. Based on newly-found archival sources.

1711 Salomon, Frank. Shamanism and politics in late-colonial Ecuador (AES/AE, 10:3, Aug. 1983, p. 413–428, bibl.)

Four trials of native *brujos* (1703–86) demonstrate that weaknesses of jural institutions gave scope for illegal initiatives by shamans. Conflicts they exploited were specifically colonial (e.g., expansion of cattle-ranching into native zones), but Spanish authorities prosecuted on demonological, not political, grounds, and in so doing, accredited shamans' magical powers.

Sanoja, Mario. De la recolección a la agricultura. See *HLAS 45:685.*

1713 Schmitz, Pedro Ignacio. Os primitivos habitantes do Rio Grande do Sul (*in* Simpósio Nacional de Estudos Missioneiros, 2nd, Santa Rosa, Brazil, 1977. Anais. Santa Rosa, Brazil: Faculdade de Filosofia, Ciência e Letras Dom Bosco, 1978, p. 50–60, bibl., maps)

At conquest, three aboriginal groups inhabited Rio Grande do Sul: the "planalto" housed the Guianas, later called Kaingang; the "campanha" was home of Charrua and Minuano, fishers and hunters; and cultivable zones housed Tupi-Guaranian villagers. Colonial evidence includes mission records for the Tupians, numerous in 17th century.

1714 Sempat Assadourian, Carlos. Dominio colonial y señores étnicos en el espacio andino (HISLA Revista [Centro Latinoamericano de Historia Económica y Social, Lima] 1, 1983, p. 7–20, bibl.)

Programmatic essay directed at historians. Argues that evidence on diversity of Andean local leadership groups, and their varied roles during and after Spanish invasion crisis, require their equal inclusion with *encomenderos* and Crown in defining colonial process. For further comment see *HISLA Revista* (3, 1983, p. 101–113).

1715 Sherbondy, Jeanette. El regadío, los lagos y los mitos de origen (IPA/A, 17:20, 1982, p. 3–32, bibl., maps)

Surveys cosmological thought associated with Inca water management, emphasizing idea that ancestors arise from ocean via tunnels, that highland lakes extend ocean, and that foundation of settlements at lakes accordingly expresses primordial legitimacy. Association of "higher" moieties with upstream position reflects such ideas.

1716 Silva, Deonisio da. Do indio, pelo jesuita, ao Rei: o enigma da República dos Guaranis (PUC/V, 28:109, março 1983, p. 74–81)

Karl Kautsky thought the Jesuit "República Guaraní" belonged in the prehistory of communism; essay considers paradox of an alleged classless society engendered by mercantalist expansion.

Silva, J. Romão da. Os bororos: família etnolinguística. See *HLAS 45:1613.*

1717 Silverblatt, Irene. Dioses y diablos: idolatrías y evangelización (IPA/A, 16:19, 1982, p. 31–48, bibl.)

In 17th century, some Andean women confessed to witchcraft by diabolic pact. Argues their behavior derives neither from prehispanic "manichaean" belief, nor from Andean disposition to blame women, but from power of conquest to force a reinterpretation of native ideas onto natives themselves.

1718 Silverblatt, Irene. The evolution of witchcraft and the meaning of healing in a colonial Andean society (Culture, Medicine, and Psychiatry [D. Reidel, Dordrecht, The Netherlands] 7, 1983, p. 413–427, bibl., ill.)

Argues that Spanish identification of the health-giving mountain and earth deities as devils had, by 1620s, caused some native healers to identify their art as witchcraft and to connect ethnic patriotism with contraband beliefs. Based on *extirpación* documents from Archbishopric of Lima. Claims such phenomena primarily affected women.

Smith, Richard Chase. Liberal ideology and indigenous communities in post-independence Peru. See *HLAS 45:1480.*

1719 Soldi, Ana María. La agricultura tradicional en hoyas. Lima: Pontificia Universidad Católica del Perú, Fondo Editorial, 1982. 104 p.: bibl., ill., maps.

Hoyas are sunken fields allowing crop roots to reach water table; author details cases from northern Peru to northern Chile, some in modern use. Paracas area yields freshest data thanks to 1576–1624 data in land suit. Hoya building requires surprisingly modest labor input and may date to pre-state societies.

1720 Spalding, Karen. Exploitation as an economic system: the state and the extraction of surplus in colonial Peru (*in* The Inca and Aztec states, 1400–1800: anthropology and history [see item **1544**] p. 321–343, bibl.)

Colonial economy was "integrated," not "dual." But "integration" of natives who still had access to subsistence occurred through no marketplace magic and resulted from compulsion (e.g., tribute, *corvée*, forced sales). State stopped short of creating open labor market because protecting labor base from rival exploiters proved overriding necessity.

1721 ———. Huarochirí: an Andean society under Inca and Spanish rule. Stanford, Calif.: Stanford University Press, 1984. 364 p.: bibl., ill., maps, tables.

For Huarochirí in Lima highlands, as for no other part of the Andes, abundant sources allow reconstruction of both the "believed" and the "behaved" versions of Andean culture. Major synthesis of regional history traces survival and transformation of local polities through Inca and Spanish colonial era up to 1750s, with emphasis on economy, forms of leadership, and forms of resistance.

1722 ———. Resistencia y adaptación: el gobierno colonial y las élites nativas (IPA/A, 15:17/18, 1981, p. 5–21)

Colonial ethnic lords, even those who ostensibly collaborated with Church authorities, often protected both communal productive organization and their own political interests by sheltering non-Christian shrine and mummy cults. Two case studies concern Quispe Ninavilca lords of Huarochirí (ca. 1660 and 1723) and prosecution of Francisco Julcarilpo in nearby Carampoma.

Spores, Ronald. New World ethnohistory and archaeology, 1970–1980. See *HLAS 45:585.*

1723 Stein, William. Myth and ideology in a nineteenth-century Peruvian peasant uprising (ASE/E, 29:4, 1982, p. 237–264, bibl.)

Record of 1885 Atusparia uprising, in which peasants of Ancash, Peru, attacked tribute levies, has been shaped by townsmen's stereotypes and fictionalized accounts. Essay seeks to reconstruct rebels' thinking,

in part, though analysis of "Rey Inca" myths collected in 1952.

1724 Stern, Steve J. Peru's Indian peoples and the challenge of Spanish conquest: Huamanga to 1640. Madison: University of Wisconsin Press, 1982. 295 p.: bibl., ill., index, maps.

Extensive study of Ayacucho area shows that until 1560s, "post-Incaic alliances" between non-Inca ethnic lords and Spanish elites regulated local power balance. Conflicts arising from miners' need to exploit natives more directly undercut alliances; and native rulers seized on litigation as means of countering consequent hypertrophy of *mita*. Andean self-rule was partially preserved, but at cost of binding it to colonial exploitation. Substantial effort to integrate cultural data (for example, on *Taki Onqoy* nativist movements) with economic and political history using large array of new sources.

1725 ———. The social significance of judicial institutions in an exploitative society: Huamanga, Peru, 1570–1640 (*in* The Inca and Aztec states, 1400–1800: anthropology and history [see item **1544**] p. 289–320, bibl., ill.)

Editors' summary: ". . . in the short run Indians used judicial politics to lessen the exploitation of their labor. They played state bureaucrats concerned with the supraregional distribution of *mita* labor for mining, against colonials who had more regionally concentrated interests. . . . Yet, in the long run, indigenous litigation weakened capacities for independent resistance.

1726 ———. El *Taki Onqoy* y la sociedad andina: Huamanga, siglo XVI (IPA/A, 16:19, 1982, p. 49–77, bibl.)

The millenarist outbreaks of 1560s can be understood as expressing desperation at the consequences of an interethnic order built up during period of "postincaic alliances," but turned to Andean disadvantage as mining advanced. Detailed Ayacucho-area research.

1727 Stocks, Anthony. Native enclaves in the upper Amazon: a case of regional non-integration (ASE/E, 30:2, 1983, p. 77–92, bibl.)

Cocamilla, acculturated Tupían people

of the lower Huallaga, had by 1680s been decisively separated from "pagan" Amazonians, but effectively maintained autonomy by series of adaptations servicing river traffic. Since 1978, land tenure incentives have encouraged explicitly Cocamilla self-organization.

1728 Susnik, Branislava. Los aborígenes del Paraguay. v. l, Etnología del Chaco Boreal y su periferia: siglos XVI y XVII. v. 2, Etnohistoria de los guaraníes: época colonial. v. 3, Etnohistoria de los chaqueños, 1650–1910. Asunción: Museo Etnográfico Andrés Barbero, 1978/1981. 3 v.: bibl., maps.

Forming part of multivolume compendium (for vols. l/2, see *HLAS 42:1742*) this dense synthetic compilation classifies Chaco peoples into: 1) "ecuestres" (Abipones, Toba, Lengua, Mbayá, etc.); 2) "canoeros;" 3) "cazadores marginales;" and 4) "cultivadores neolíticos." Chief foci are political relations among native peoples and with Europeans; productive bases; territoriality; and migration. Useful reference work, with large bibliography.

1729 Szemiński, Jan. Los objetivos de los tupamaristas: las concepciones de los revolucionarios peruanos de los años 1780–1783. Wrocław: Zkaład Narodowy Im. Ossolinskich, 1982. 202 p.: ill.

By applying structuralist principles to testimony of many accused Tupamaristas and their captors, author seeks to separate Andean ideological motifs from later nationalist concepts which have adhered to the data. Argues Andean rebels sought casteless, Catholic, multi-ethnic, independent society under Inca dynastic rule.

1730 Tantaleán Arbulú, Javier. Modo de producción asiático: estado y sociedad inka (PUCP/H, 5:1, julio 1981, p. 63–103, bibl.)

Based as it is on European stereotypes about "despotism," and on inadequate 19th-century generalizations about non-western states, "Asiatic" model has severe shortcomings in explaining origin and dynamism of precapitalist (e.g. Inca) polities. Useful contribution to the debate recorded in Espinoza Soriano's anthology (see *HLAS 42:1678*) and articles such as Dieterich's (item **1621**) and Pea's (item **1694**).

Taussig, Michael. Folk healing and the structure of conquest in southwest Colombia. See *HLAS 45:1328*.

1731 Troconis de Veracoechea, Ermila. Venezuela: indígenas, siglo XVII (VANH/B, 64:255, julio/sept. 1981, p. 609–617, bibl.)

Broad summary of institutions affecting natives of Venezuela's Oriente, based on secondary sources and incompletely identified documents in Archivo Nacional de Historia. Illegal and informal variant of encomienda, called *apuntamiento*, and the *encomienda por data* (a legal but ill-supervised trusteeship associated with expeditionary conquests), arose from scramble for scarce native manpower.

1732 Troll, Carl. Las culturas superiores andinas y el medio geográfico (IPA/A, 14:15, 1980, p. 3–55, graphs, ill., maps, photos)

Useful republication of Carlos Nicholson's translation of influential 1931 essay. Key south-Andean adaptive techniques facilitate central management of production and exchange. They are freeze-drying of tubers, herding of camellids, and irrigation of arable highlands.

1733 Urbano, Henrique. Representaciones colectivas y arqueología mental en los Andes (IPA/A, 17:20, 1982, p. 33–83, bibl.)

Essay on state of research in Andean rite, thought, and belief, severely criticizing academic traditions associated with Rowe, Murra, Pease, etc. Useful for bibliography and for insights into lines of controversy in Peruvian anthropology.

1734 ———. Wiracocha y Ayar, héroes y funciones en las sociedades andinas. Cuzco, Perú: Centro de Estudios Rurales Andinos Bartolomé de las Casas, 1981. 185 p.: bibl. ill. (Biblioteca de la tradición oral andina; 3)

Argues that myths should be read neither as historic data nor as mystifications but as "teoría de la sociedad" cast in symbolic terms. Author holds that despite hispanizing distortions in the surviving texts one can detect a consistent Dumézilian tri-functionality of ritual, political, and agricultural realms. In mythic cycles of the four deities called Wiracocha and the four brothers Ayar, the fourth figure is relegated to an antistructural role.

1735 Urioste, George L. Hijos de Pariya Qaqa: la tradición oral de Waru Chiri; mitología ritual y costumbres. Manuscript No. 3169 in Spanish and Quechua, Biblioteca Nacional, Madrid. Syracuse, N.Y.: Syracuse University, Maxwell School of Citizenship and Public Affairs, 1983. 2 v. (332 p.): bibl.; index (Foreign and Comparative Studies Program. Latin American series; no. 6)

New bilingual (Quechua-Spanish) critical edition of Huarochiri *Runa yndio ñiscap* manuscript with full apparatus: variorum of translations, indices to places and persons, bibliography, and introduction. Important study and reference edition (see item **1645** and *HLAS 42:1529*). Translator is native Bolivian Quechua speaker.

1736 Valencia Espinoza, Abraham. Pesas y medidas inkas: continuidad en los mercados de canas. Cuzco, Perú: Centro de Estudios Andinos-Cuzco, 198? 77 p., 5 leaves of plates: ill.

Some measures documented in González Holguín (1608) are still in use near Cuzco; most derive from body dimensions (e.g., *wiqawi*), a pile that fits in a circle equal to head circumference. Interesting example of ethnographic analogy solution to source problems.

1737 Valiente, Teresa. Universo andino en el siglo XVI: detrás de los nombres personales quechua (IAI/I, 9, 1984, p. 341–350, bibl.)

Quechua meanings of 930 personal names recorded in the 1562 *visita* of Chupaychu (Huánuco) display semantic clustering within age-sex categories. For example, adolescent girls' names refer to plants of the heights, boys' to valley species. Argues (without statistics) that ecological order is dominant motif.

1738 Vallée, Lionel. El discurso mítico de Santa Cruz Pachacuti Yamqui (IPA/A, 17:20, 1982, p. 103–126, bibl.)

The Quechua word *pacha* means "space" but also "time." Discusses origin myths in Pachacuti Yamqui's *Relación*, in order to uncover formal congruence of cyclical time and circular space. Also discusses ideas from Urbano and Millones about transition from chaos to order.

1739 Varón, Rafael. Cofradías de indios y poder local en el Perú: Huaraz, siglo XVII (IPA/A, 17:20, 1982, p. 127–146, bibl.)

San Sebastián de Huaraz in later 17th century saw proliferation of native sodalities and a few ethnically mixed ones. They partly reflected native organization in *warankas*, also functioning as moieties; in 1643 case, moieties disputed possesssion of a saint. *Cofradía* leadership was normally in hands of local lords or close kin.

1740 Vega, Juan José. La guerra de los viracochas. Lima: Ediciones PEISA, 1982. 167 p.: bibl. (Biblioteca peruana; 61)

Spanish invasion and Inca resistance to 1542. Popularization based on narrow selection of familiar sources, with lip service to the "vision of the vanquished."

Villalobos R., Sergio. Revisita de los indios del Corregimiento de Arica en 1753. See item **2752.**

1741 Wachtel, Nathan. The mitimas of the Cochabamba valley: the colonization policy of Huayna Capac (*in* The Inca and Aztec states, 1400–1800: anthropology and history [see item **1544**] p. 199–235, bibl., maps, tables)

English version of important study published in French (see *Journal de la Société des Américanistes*, 66, 1981) and in Spanish (*Historia Boliviana*, 1, 1981). Giant Inca colony in maize-growing valley expelled most aborigines to create a land-use pattern of "stripes" across the valley, assigned to contingents from many ethnic groups. Both permanently transplanted people and *corvée* workers were needed to operate it.

1742 Zapater E., Horacio. Una nueva fuente para la etnohistoria chilena: la crónica de Jerónimo de Quiroga (SCHG/R, 149, 1981, p. 24–40, bibl.)

First full published text of Quiroga's *Memorias de los sucesos de la Guerra de Chile* appeared in Chile in 1979. Essay highlights ethnographic relevance to 17th-century Araucanian household organization, military formations, territorial organizations, and selective appropriation of Hispanic religion.

1743 Zavalía Matienzo, Roberto. Los Valles Calchaquíes: síntesis de una historia desconocida; los menhires felínicos y petrografías inéditas (ANH/IE, 29, julio/dic. 1980, p. 267–294)

Valle de Tafí (Tucumán prov., Argentina) in old Diaguita region, has numerous *menhires* or steles. Describes (no illustrations) stele and petroglyph adorned, respectively, with feline images and warrior figures. Imagery is interpreted through ethnohistoric and secondary sources as reflecting Inca influences and conflict between region's native and intrusive non-Inca peoples.

1744 Zelenka, Georg. El guarda-maíz: una institución incaica (Boletín de Lima [s.n.] 27:5, mayo 1983, p. 33–41, bibl., ill)

Six chronicle sources mention the *pariana*, watchman of maize fields against vermin and thieves. Author holds that it was a state-assigned office, but its characteristic insignia—a fox headdress—was not incaic. Adducing Chimú ceramics, he connects it with coastal cult that revered female foxes.

1745 Zuidema, R. Tom. Bureaucracy and systematic knowledge in Andean civilization (*in* The Inca and Aztec states, 1400–1800: anthropology and history [see item **1544**] p. 419–458, bibl., ill., maps)

Argues against Goody's idea that it is literacy which, by making knowledge fully cumulative, gives scope to formal science. Holds that in nonliterate Andean society, formal reasoning involved in using sight-lines for calendrical computing, as well as elaboration of knot records for bureaucratic ends, grew within religious practice of observing nature and not from administrative recording functions.

1746 ———. Hierarchy and space in Incaic social organization (ASE/E, 30:2, 1983, p. 49–75, bibl., ill., tables)

Treats hierarchical structures of ancient Cuzco, with emphasis on paired kings and on role of *panacas*. Argues that *panacas*, organized around royal mummies, were voluntary groups articulating sectarian, factional or class interests and not corporate descent groups.

1747 ———. The lion in the city: royal symbols of transition in Cuzco (UCLA/JLAL, 9:1, 1983, p. 38–100, bibl., ill.)

Famous metaphor "Cuzco is a puma" reaches us through Betanzos, Sarmiento, and later explicators of street plan. Puma's body and the body politic were likened in ritual action as well. "Puma-men" figure as guardians of order and of political transition (e.g., successions, initiations, conferral of honors).

1748 ———. Masks in the Incaic solstice and equinoctial rituals (*in* The Power of symbols: masks and masquerade in the Americas. Edited by N. Ross Crumrine and Marjorie Halpin. Vancouver, Canada: University of British Columbia Press, 1983, p. 149–162, bibl.)

"Masks represented forces from the night, from the underworld, and from outside the border of a civilized political unit." Face-painting centered on decoration with sacrificial blood; masking often employed images of beings from the world's boundaries. Evidence includes modern myth, chronicles, guesswork etymologies.

1749 ———. El primer *Nueva corónica y buen gobierno* (UP/LAIL, 6:2, Fall 1982, p. 126–132, bibl., ill.)

Review essay of 1980 Murra-Adorno-Urioste ed. of Guaman Poma (see *HLAS 44:5092*) contends that some of new ed.'s glossary translations are inadequate.

1750 ——— and **Deborah Poole.** Los límites de los cuatro Suyus incaicos en el Cuzco (IFEA/B, 11:1/2, 1982, p. 83–89, bibl., tables)

Disputes Espinoza Soriano's interpretation of 1577 document in which ethnic lords of Cuzco region described their affiliation to the four *suyus* or "quarters" of Inca territorial organization (see *HLAS 40:2047*). Poole's fieldwork yields identification of many toponyms not localized previously and allows more precise mapping of *suyu* boundaries. "Quarters" do not divide the 360° of radial space equally. Their orientations nearly coincide with the processional lines of Incaic *Citua* festival, and their termini (as markers of Cuzco's local organization) coincide with the ecological boundaries of "vertical" zonation in such a way that Cuzco's local organization penetrates neither puna nor subtropical valleys.

HISTORY: GENERAL

DONALD E. CHIPMAN, *Professor of History, North Texas State University*
JAMES D. RILEY, *Professor of History, The Catholic University of America*

OVERALL, THE NUMBER OF WORKS annotated in this section has stabilized. The downward slide so apparent in *HLAS 40* (p. 90) and *HLAS 42* (p. 159) has not continued. In fact, the aggregate total is up slightly from *HLAS 44* (p. 121).

In the General sub-section, no trends are readily visible. A number of pieces are theoretical in character, intellectual history seems to have made something of a comeback, and a wide variety of subjects are covered. The items worthy of note include Pike's article on the psychological states of intellectuals (item **1782**), and Hardoy and Langdon's statistical study of urbanization (item **1766**) which, though quite long and appearing in a very obscure journal, merits the effort necessary to obtain it. There is also an outstanding interpretive work by Chevalier (item **1757**), masquerading as a textbook. Other items of interest are Bravo's study of merchant marines (item **1754**), which opens a new field for study; Eltis' comparison of free and coerced immigration (item **1761**), which is noteworthy for his analysis of the two types rather than the presence of new information on either; and in the realm of methodology, Mörner's piece on the use of travelers' accounts (item **1771**).

The number of quality items in the Colonial sub-section is perhaps the most significant change from the last volume. The outstanding works here are bench-mark studies of the Carrera de Indias. Utilizing an enormous corpus of documentation and statistical data, Lorenzo Sanz has produced a two-volume monograph on trans-Atlantic traffic (item **1840**), during the reign of Philip II. It has important implications for both European and Latin American history. Revisionist studies of commerce in the last half of the 17th century, again based on impressive documentation and statistical data, are by García Fuentes (items **1820** and **1821**). These items present evidence of a significant turn around in Spanish commercial activity beginning in the 1660s, and continuing throughout the reign of Charles II. They are also a major contribution to the historiography of the late Hapsburg era. For the early 18th century, Hilton's summary of Anglo-Spanish commercial conflicts after the Treaty of Utrecht (item **1829**) deserves attention. This sub-section also includes a number of books and articles of unusual quality dealing with widely disparate topics. In alphabetical order, they are: Aparicio's study of efforts to free Christian slaves in North Africa (item **1794**); Borah's assessment of where we stand on demographic studies (item **1799**); Israel's fine monograph on the Dutch Republic and the Hispanic World (item **1830**); Lockhart's historiographical essay on the status of social history (item **1839**); Marchena Fernández's excellent study of the Spanish army in the colonies (item **1841**); Mörner's call for regional studies to sharpen generalizations about social stratification (item **1844**); Ramo's major work on Columbus' second voyage (item **1863**); Schwartz's analysis of aristocracy in Luso-Hispanic colonies (item **1869**); and Villalta's account of the fate of Portuguese commercial interests in the aftermath of their nation's revolt against Spanish captivity (item **1875**).

In the sub-section Independence and 19th Century listed below, the quality of the works is disappointing relative to *HLAS 44*, wherein the outstanding contributions in the History: General section lay within the late colonial and independence periods. Notable exceptions to this general assessment are Anna's third book on Latin American independence (item **1880**); Costeloe's article on the impact of American rebellions on Spanish trade (item **1882**); and Pérez Guilhou's work on public reaction in Spain to American insurgent movements (item **1893**).

Given the small number of total pieces in the 20th Century sub-section, the fact that more than half dwell on dependency or Marxist themes should not be taken as particularly significant. Surprisingly though, there is nothing on international relations. In past years, this category was a staple. Of special merit and usefulness to scholars is Halperin-Donghi's article on dependency theory (item **1908**). A collection of essays by Falcoff and Pike on the Spanish Civil War holds together as a monograph because of the interrelatedness of the pieces (item **1913**). The best of the book-length monographs is Frederick Nunn's widely reviewed work on military attitudes in the 20th century (item **1911**).

Chipman wishes to acknowledge the continuing support of the Faculty Research Committee and the Department of History of North Texas State University, and the professional assistance of Olga Paradis and Beth Broyles Honeycutt.

GENERAL

1751 Andújar, Manuel. Andalucía e Hispanoamérica: crisol de mestizajes. Sevilla: EdiSur, 1982. 119 p.: ill. (Colección Cuadernos de cultura popular; 4)

Rambling, unfocused effort by journalist who worked in Latin America, to try to explain the region to Spaniards. Compares process of *mestizaje* in Latin America to same process in Andalusia and tells Spaniards that if they want to understand Latin America, look at Andalusia. [JDR]

1752 Azevedo, Israel Belo de. As cruzadas inacabadas: introdução à história da Igreja na América Latina. Rio de Janeiro: Editora Gêmos, 1980. 175 p.: bibl., ill.

Brief popular account of history of Christianity in Latin America. Very much outline treatment which emphasizes names and dates but has some value because of surprising emphasis given in later sections to work of Protestant missions and establishment of Protestant churches during 19th and 20th centuries. [JDR]

1753 Bello, Francisco R. El proceso latinoamericano: la grande y la pequeña historia. Buenos Aires: Libros de Hispanoamérica, 1982. 168 p.: ill.

Essay by retired Argentine diplomat reflects on variety of subjects ranging from Ferdinand's and Isabella's character to recent Malvinas War. Presentation rambles but generally stays on theme of cultural unity of Latin American nations. Argues that cultural integration must come before political integration. [JDR]

1754 Bravo, Oscar. Transporte marítimo y marina mercante en América Latina: su desarrollo histórico. Stockholm: Institute of Latin American Studies, 1979. 73 p.: bibl., ill. (Research paper series; paper no. 20)

Valuable contribution on relatively untouched topic. Explains sorry state of today's Latin American merchant marines by providing brief analysis of colonial and early republican commercial policy and case studies of evolution of concern for a merchant marine in Colombia and Chile. [JDR]

1755 Carmagnani, Marcello. La política en el estado oligárquico latinoamericano (Historias [Dirección de Estados Históricos del Instituto de Antropología e Historia, México] 1, julio/sept. 1982, p. 5–14)

Translation of chap. from author's book (published 1981, in Italian). Describes how electoral system functioned in late-19th century states with nominally representative institutions, and how elites handled intragroup conflicts and developed consensus necessary to control the population. [JDR]

1756 Castro, Manuel de. Bibliografía de las bibliografías franciscanas españolas e hispanoamericanas (PF/AIA, 41:161/162, enero/junio 1981, p. 3–222)

Major compilation of works by and about Spanish and Spanish American Franciscan Order. Introduction is divided into bibliographic essays on Franciscan writers, literature about the Order, and Franciscan publications. Total of 1146 entries are cataloged, ranging from general bio-bibliographical information to specialized topics. For bibliographer's comment on this same work published as monograph, see item 17. [DEC]

1757 Chevalier, François. América Latina de la independencia a nuestros días. Barcelona: Labor, 1979. 504 p.: bibl., ill., index, maps (Nueva Clio; 44)

Interesting interpretive history of Latin America from Independence to 1940s. Emphasizes economic, social, and intellectual developments, and practically ignores the political. For 1977 French original, see *HLAS 40:2148.* [JDR]

1758 Chiaramonte, José Carlos. Supuestos conceptuales en los intentos de periodización de la historia latinoamericana (UNAM/RMS, 44:1, enero/marzo 1982, p. 217–262)

Dry exegesis on Marx's theory of historical periodization based on "modes of production." Says nothing specifically about its application to Latin America. [JDR]

1759 Cuenca Toribio, José Manuel. Iglesia y estado a fines del antiguo régimen: la elección del episcopado hispano-americano, 1789–1824 (EEHA/AEA, 33, 1976, p. 105–143)

Scholarly examination of trends in Spanish policy and practice regarding episcopal appointments, in late colonial period and at different stages of American rebellion. With expository footnotes almost equaling article in length, also makes contribution to general study of Church in independence period. [D. Bushnell]

1760 Dussel, Enrique D. A history of the Church in Latin America: colonialism to liberation, 1492–1979. Translated and revised by Alan Neely. Grand Rapids, Mich.: Eerdsman, 1981. 360 p.: bibl., ill.

English translation of third ed. (see *HLAS 36:1475*). [JDR]

1761 Eltis, David. Free and coerced transatlantic migrations: some comparisons (AHA/R, 88:2, April 1983, p. 251–280, graphs, tables)

Very interesting synthetic demographic study comparing "push-pull" factors affecting two types of migration to the hemisphere, total size of the groups, conditions of passage and experience in their new homes. Covers period after 1520, but emphasizes 1820–60, and regions of Brazil and Cuba. [JDR]

1762 Figueroa Marroquín, Horacio. Trabajos de investigación histórica. Guatemala: Editorial Universitaria, 1981. 175 p.: bibl., facsims., ill. (Obras del Dr. Horacio Figueroa Marroquín; vol. 2)

Assorted studies by Guatemalan medical historian, covering medical history of Simón Bolívar, colonial epidemiology (*Enfermedad de Robles*, smallpox), and career of Manuel Avalos y Porras, 18th-century Guatemalan acclaimed as "El Harvey de América." [D. Bushnell]

Gormsen, Erdmann. Die Städte im Spanischen Amerika. See *HLAS 45:5099.*

Hahner, June E. Researching the history of Latin American women: past and future directions. See item 46.

1763 Halperín-Donghi, Tulio. La cuantificación en historia: trayectoria y problemas (*in* Botana, Natalio R. *et al.* Ciencias sociales: palabras y conjeturas [see *HLAS 45:8309*] p. 183–211, bibl.)

Reprint of *HLAS 44:1826.* [JDR]

———. "Dependency theory" and Latin American historiography. See *HLAS 45:2845.*

1764 ———. Intelectuales, sociedad y vida pública en Hispanoamérica a través de la literatura autobiográfica (UNAM/RMS, 44:1, enero/marzo 1982, p. 315–333)

Discusses various ideas regarding definition of an intellectual and his task, and then examines how specific 19th-century individuals tried to interact with, and lead the societies in which they lived, as shown through their autobiographies. [JDR]

1765 Hanke, Lewis. La Conferencia José Gil Fortoul de 1981: ¿como debería celebrarse el medio milenio del descubrimiento de América? (VANH/B, 44:256, oct./dic. 1981, p. 821–837)

Offers suggestions regarding how quincentennial of America's discovery should be observed. Calls for multi-national effort over next decade with emphasis on development of historical sources, clear definitions of what is to be done and how, and especially, instruction. Among suggestions is the creation of a fully integrated history of the Americas. [DEC]

1766 Hardoy, Jorge Enrique and **María Elena Langdon.** Análisis estadístico preliminar de la urbanización de América Latina entre 1850–1930 (CPES/RPS, 15:42/43, mayo/dic. 1978, p. 115–173, tables)

Very interesting and valuable companion piece to *HLAS 43:1710* by same authors. Examines country-by-country process of urbanization, based on exhaustive compilation of non-census sources identified in bibliography. Essential source for demographers and urban historians. [JDR]

1767 Hernández de Torres, Eduardo. Episcopado agustiniano en América Latina. Santiago de Chile: Ediciones Agustinianas, 1981. 93 p.: bibl., port.

Brief biographical sketches of 61 Agustinian friars who became Catholic bishops in Latin America from Conquest to present. [JDR]

1768 Liehr, Reinhard. Orígenes, evolución y estructura socioeconómica de la hacienda hispanoamericana (EEHA/AEA, 33, 1976 [i.e. 1979] p. 527–577)

General descriptive essay on hacienda as institution, based on studies appearing prior to 1977. Defines "hacienda" so as to exclude plantations. Offers no really novel interpretations and is somewhat derivative of Magnus Mörner's work. [JDR]

Lombardi, Cathryn L.; John V. Lombardi; and **K. Lynn Stoner.** Latin American history: a teaching atlas. See *HLAS 45:50.*

1769 Míguez Bonino, José; Carmelo Alvarez; and **Roberto Craig.** Protestantismo y liberalismo en América Latina. San José: Coedición del Departamento Ecuménico de Investigaciones y el Seminario Bíblico Latinoamericano, 1983. 91 p.: bibl. (Colección Aportes)

Three popular essays on development of Protestantism in Latin America discuss: 1) historic mission and need for reorganizing future efforts; 2) historic links between Liberalism and Protestantism; and 3) role of Protestantism in Costa Rica. [JDR]

1770 Mörner, Magnus. Buy or breed?: alternative sources of slave supply in the plantation societies of the New World: report for the session on "Plantation Economies in North and South America in the Eighteenth-Nineteenth Centuries" at the XV International Congress of Historical Sciences in Bucarest, August 1980. Stockholm: Institute of Latin American Studies, 1980. 51 p.: bibl., il. (Research paper series; paper no. 23)

Brief study on question of why slaveholders in specific regions decided either to purchase new slaves from Africa to meet their needs, or to breed those they already possessed. Was purchase more economically efficient than breeding? Reaches no conclusions, but analyzes variables involved. [JDR]

1771 ———. European travelogues as sources to Latin American history from the late eighteenth century until 1870 (PAIGH/H, 93, enero/junio 1982, p. 91–149, bibl.)

Technical study of pitfalls inherent in use of travel accounts and some ideas on how to use them intelligently are illustrated by using accounts of European travelers. Contains a useful bibliography. [JDR]

1772 ———. Los problemas estructurales del agro latinoamericano: perspectivas históricas (*in* Mörner, Magnus *et al.* El sector agrario en América Latina: estructura económica y cambio social. Stockholm: Instituto de Estudios Latinoamericanos de Estolcolmo, 1979, p. 9–22)

Essay argues for more historical research into agrarian conditions as precondition for successful agrarian reform programs. Considers research which has already been done, and insights gained, on such topics as the relationship of population to resources, internal migration patterns, labor systems and land tenure. Suggests areas where much research is needed, including agricultural technology, productivity, and distribution of income. [JDR]

1773 ———; **Julia Fawaz de Viñuela;** and **John D. French.** Comparative approaches to Latin American history (LARR, 17:3, 1982, p. 55–89, bibl.)

Considers scope, methodology, and problems involved in comparative studies and provides critical analysis of recent research using a comparative approach. Ends with explanation of benefits of such an approach exemplified by insights authors gained in their own collective study of Cuzco region since colonial times. [JDR]

1774 Morón, Guillermo. América: 500 años de historia (PAIGH/H, 93, enero/junio 1982, p. 7–14)
Speech delivered upon completion of 30-year project for the writing of a general history of the Americas, sponsored by the Pan American Institute of Geography and History. [JDR]

1775 Morse, Richard M. La cultura política iberoamericana de Sarmiento a Mariátegui (Vuelta [s.n., México] 5:58, sept. 1981, p. 4–16, ill.)
Fascinating semi-popular essay on the way Latin American political thinkers received foreign political ideas and modified them to fit Latin America's deeper political culture. Wide-ranging, but gives particular attention to Sarmiento's analysis of Europe and US, and Mariátegui's formulation of "Indian Marxism." [JDR]

1776 Mott, Luiz R.B. A revolução dos negros do Haiti e o Brasil (MAN, 13:145, jan. 1982, p. 3–10, bibl.)
Paper delivered at 1981 conference on *quilombo* of Palmares. Argues that blacks were not isolated but communicated among different plantations, regions, and even continents. Uses as examples how, in 18th century, information was transmitted about quilombo of Palmares, and in 19th, about slave revolts in Northeastern Brazil. [JDR]

1777 Ocampo López, Javier. Historia de las ideas de integración de América Latina. Tunja, Colombia: Editorial Bolivariana Internacional, 1981. 321 p.: bibl., ill., indexes, ports (Serie Fundamentos y doctrina; v. 1)
Study of ebb and flow of idea of continental unity between late 18th and 20th centuries, as seen in writing of intellectuals and politicians. Uses standard works and takes standard approach to question. [JDR]

1778 Oliver, Lilia V. La población de América Latina (Boletín del Instituto de Estudios Sociales [Universidad de Guadalajara, México] 1, enero/marzo 1980, p. 27–37)
Weak and very superficial study of demographic trends since the Conquest. [JDR]

1779 Parsons, James J. The migration of Canary Islanders to the Americas: an unbroken current since Columbus (AAFH/TAM, 39:4, April 1983, p. 447–481, map)
Well done study of changing character of immigration from the islands of America since the discovery and its impact on various American regions, particularly Cuba and Venezuela. [JDR]

1780 Pereira Larraín, Teresa. El pensamiento de una generación de historiadores hispanoamericanos: Alberto Edwards, Ernesto Quesada y Laureano Vallenilla Lanz. Santiago: Instituto de Historia, Pontificia Universidad Católica de Chile, 197?. 103 p.: bibl. (Estudios históricos; no. 2)
Study of intellectual character of writings by Chilean, Argentine, and Venezuelan historians of late 19th and early 20th centuries. Compares and contrasts influences on them, their ideas about history and society, and their political values. [JDR]

1781 Pérez Amuchástegui, Antonio J. *et al.* América Latina: hacia la integración. Prólogo, J.L. Salcedo-Bastardo. Caracas: Comité Ejecutivo del Bicentenario de Simón Bolívar, 1980. 291 p.: bibl., ill., ports.
Results of conference of Latin American scholars (Caracas, 1978). Contains 19 semi-scholarly essays outlining key individuals and events in specific countries linked to the idea of integration promoted by Simón Bolívar and Andrés Bello. [JDR]

1782 Pike, Frederick B. The psychology of regeneration: Spain and America at the turn of the century (UND/RP, 43:2, April 1981, p. 218–241)
Unusual essay which uses evidence from writings of North American and Spanish intellectuals at turn of the century regarding each other, to show how attitudes can be the result of "personal psychic factors." Particularly concerned with the clash in men's minds between desire to preserve traditions and need for modernization. [JDR]

1783 Pirez, Pedro. Estado y configuración espacial en el período de la organización nacional en América Latina (CSUCA/ESC, 8:23, mayo/agosto 1979, p. 85–101)
Rather confused and simplistic theoretical article considering the State's role in

the reorientation of populations subsequent to economic expansion in late 19th century. [JDR]

1784 Prieto, Alberto. Categorismo periodizador para la historia América Latina (UO/R, 48, dic. 1982, p. 23–42) Applies Marx's ideas of historical periodization to the history of Latin America. [JDR]

1785 Proceso sociohistórico de América Latina: sistema de hipótesis. Equipo Sociohistórico, coordinador, Germán Carrera Damas. Investigadores, Josefina Ríos de Hernández *et al.* Caracas: Centro de Estudios del Desarrollo, Universidad Central de Venezuela, 1977. 212 p.: bibl. (CENDES; 9) Proposal for a methodology and perspective to be used in writing a general social and economic history of Latin America. Prepared by team of social scientists including some historians who generally follow a dependency approach. [JDR]

1786 Rangel, Carlos. La inestable Latinoamérica (Vuelta [s.n., México] 6:69, agosto 1982, p. 42–45) Critical essay by noted Venezuela journalist on reasons why Latin America has not been able to develop "durable and legitimate" constitutional systems, or to successfully incorporate democratic ideas into the region's culture. [JDR]

1787 Romero, Luis Alberto. Los estudios históricos y la integración latinoamericana (UNAM/L, 14, 1981, p. 447–461) Interesting discussion of effort of historians to find a middle ground between weak global synthesis and monographs in describing region's history. Suggests scholarship would be best served by a comparative approach analyzing reactions to series of shocks region has received from "European-Western" world since the discovery. [JDR]

1788 Saint-Lu, André. Bolívar et Martí, "figures de l'indépendance" (*in* Cuba, les étapes d'une libération: hommage à Juan Marinello et Noël Salomon; actes du colloque international des 22, 23 et 24 1978. Toulouse: Centre d'études cubaines, Université de Toulouse-Le Mirail, 1979, v. 2, p. 85–88) Brief and superficial consideration of the glorification surrounding Bolívar and Martí among intellectuals. [JDR]

1789 Sobre la idiosincrasia histórico-cultural de América Latina: pts. 1/2 (URSS/AL, 4[40], 1981, p. 73–124, ill.; 6[42], 1981, p. 65–116, ill.) Speeches by 11 Russian and two Latin American scholars (i.e., Leopoldo Zea and Volodia Teitelboim), given at round-table discussion sponsored by Moscow's Institute for Latin America. Most concern special character of Latin American literature and the reception of political and economic ideas. [JDR]

Temas Americanistas. Universidad de Sevilla, Cátedra de Historia de América (and) Unidad Estructural de Investigación de Historia Social, Escuela de Estudios Hispanoamericanos. See item **111.**

1790 Torres-Rivas, Edelberto. Estado y nación en la historia latinoamericana (Socialismo y Participación [Centro de Estudios para el Desarrollo y la Participación, Lima] 16, dic. 1981, p. 85–101) Weak theoretical article examines, from Marxist perspective, motivations and interests behind Independence and formation of nation-states in 19th and 20th centuries. [JDR]

1791 O Tráfico de escravos negros: sécs. XV–XIX: documentos de trabalho e relatório da reunião de peritos organizada pela UNESCO em Port-au-Prince, Haiti, de 31 de janeiro a 4 de fevereiro de 1978. Tradução de Antônio Luz Correia. Lisboa: Edições 70, 1981. 422 p.: bibls. (Biblioteca de estudos africanos; 6) Collection of 10 articles and 11 short reports on the African slave trade by Third World, European, and Russian scholars, presented at UNESCO-sponsored conference (Haiti, 1978). Most concern Africa proper, but two articles pertain to Santo Domingo and four to Atlantic slave trade. [JDR]

Velázquez, María del Carmen. Situación de la investigación historiográfica en América. See *HLAS 45:4354.*

1793 Winson, Anthony. The formation of capitalist agriculture in Latin America and its relationship to political power and the State (CSSH, 25:1, 1983, p. 84–104) Interpretive article which attempts to assess impact of establishment of market-oriented agricultural economy on late 19th-century politics. Informed by a Marxian theoretical perspective, concludes that export-oriented elites used the State for their own purposes. [JDR]

COLONIAL

1794 Aparicio, Severo. Contribución de las Provincias Mercedarias de América a la redención de cautivos (ISTM/MH, 37:109/11, enero/dic. 1980, p. 143–173, bibl., tables)

Well researched study of contributions from the American provinces of the Orden de la Merced which were earmarked for freeing Christian captives in North Africa. As author notes, donations of this nature were long-standing part of order's constitution. Focus is on Cuzco and Lima provinces with century-by- century summations. [DEC]

1795 Ballesteros Gaibrois, Manuel. Escritores de Indias (PMNH/HC, 13/14, 1981, p. 217–226)

Analyzes motives and literary merits of writers on the Indies. Author provides precise definitions of chroniclers, historians, and antiquarians; comments on remarkable breadth of interest exhibited by writers; and draws attention to foreign observers such as Stephens and von Humboldt. [DEC]

1796 Bannon, John Francis. The colonial world of Latin America. Maps by Dan Irwin. St. Louis, Mo.: Forum Press, 1982. 89 p.: bibl., index, maps (The World of Latin America series)

Author provides cursory treatment of history of Latin America from precolumbian period to 1820s. Includes brief description of economic, political, social, religious, and cultural institutions of colonial period. Book concludes with independence movements throughout Latin America. [DEC]

1797 Bauer, A.J. Jesuit enterprise in colonial Latin America: a review essay (AHS/AH, 57:1, Jan. 1983, p. 90–104)

Solid article which goes beyond review of recent studies of Jesuit landowning by Conrad and Cushner, to look at state of knowledge on Jesuit *haciendas* and *haciendas* in general. Specific topics include investment patterns, land management, labor force utilization, extent to which Jesuits enjoyed competitive advantage over other procedures,

and agricultural innovation or lack thereof. [S. Socolow]

1798 Bianchi Aguirre, Claudio. Fray Bartolomé de las Casas o de la ciencia: el hombre y la liberación americana (NOSALF/IA, 8/9:2[1/2] 1980, p. 102–122, bibl.)

Author appeals for consideration of Bartolomé de las Casas as pioneer and exponent of political humanism. Las Casas' essays, cataloging crimes of his countrymen against Indians, are also viewed as applicable to the American struggle to attain democracy, equality, social justice, human rights, and individual liberty. [DEC]

1799 Borah, Woodrow. Demographic and physical aspects of the transition from the aboriginal to the colonial world (ISA/CUR, 8:1, 1980, p. 41–70, bibl.)

Within context of what has been done and what remains to be done, Borah addresses complex issues such as criteria for determining urban centers or cities in aboriginal America, relationship between native population and degree of urbanization, continuity between Indian and Spanish urban communities, and relocation of ordered communities. [DEC]

1800 Bronner, Fred. Tramitación legislativa bajo Olivares: la redacción de los arbitrios de 1631 (IGFO/RI, 41:165/166, julio/dic. 1981, p. 411–443, tables)

Detailed treatment of efforts of *arbitristas* to change course of New World fiscal policy, especially as followed by Conde-Duque Olivares in early 1630s. Due to variety of causes, proposals for reforms and improved efficiency, which were aired before juntas and councils, proved to be ineffectual. [DEC]

1800a Bry, Theodor de. Escenas de América de Bry; Grabadores, Francfort del Meno, 1601. Editor, Mario de la Torre. Textos de Miguel Angel Fernández. México: Cartón y Papel de México, 1981. 96 p., 5 folded leaves of plates: bibl., ill., (some col.)

Handsome ed. contains facsimile reproductions of most famous works of Theodor de Bry and his descendants. Parallel columns of Spanish and English text outline life and works of de Bry family and provide translations of German captions which accompany engravings. [DEC]

1801 Cardoso, Ciro Flamarion S. Escravismo e dinâmica da população escrava nas Américas (IPE/EE, 13:1, 1983, p. 41–53)

Although it may be true, as Marx said, that every historic mode of production has its own law of population, Cardoso argues that a law of population for American slavery is now yet possible because of lack of information for areas other than the American South and British West Indies. [L. Huddleston]

1802 Castañeda, Paulino. Facultades de los obispos indianos para dispensar de ilegitimidad (ISTM/MH, 38:113, mayo/agosto 1981, p. 227–247)

Case studies of individuals, such as mestizos, mulattos, or natural children, who sought dispensation of their illegitimate status in order to achieve social or career advancement. Recounts instances in which New World bishops exercised power to grant such requests without referral to Rome. [DEC]

1803 Castro Seoane, José and Ricardo Sanlés Martínez. Aviamiento y catálogo de misioneros a Indias y Filipinas en el siglo XVI, según los libros de la Casa de la Contratación: expediciones agustinianas (ISTM/MH, 37:109/111, enero/dic. 1980, p. 5–56)

Part of continuing compilation of Agustinian missionaries dispatched to the New World and the Orient. This segment (1580–1600) completes the 16th century. Includes names of missionaries and their destination, power and titles granted to them, and their accounterment of office. [DEC]

1804 ⸻ and ⸻. Aviamiento y catálogo de misioneros a Indias y Filipinas en el siglo XVI, según los libros de la Casa de la Contratación: expediciones de dominicos (ISTM/MH, 38:113, mayo/agosto 1981, p. 129–170)

Pt. 1 (1526–1550) of compilation which will include names of Dominican missionaries dispatched to the New World and the Orient in 16th century, powers and titles granted to them, and their accouterment of office. [DEC]

1805 Clément, Jean-Pierre. El nacimiento de la higiene urbana en la América española del siglo XVIII (IGFO/RI, 43:171, enero/junio 1983, p. 77–95)

Summarizes growing concern for healthfulness and quality of life in urban centers. Topics include purity of air, food, and water; disposal of garbage and sewage; and hygienic interment of the dead. [DEC]

1806 ⸻. La place de l'Amérique hispanique dans les écrits espagnols durant XVIII siècle (in Bénassy, Marie-Cécile et al. Etudes sur l'impact culturel du Nouveau Monde. Séminaire interuniversitaire sur l'Amérique espagnole coloniale. Paris: Editions L'Harmattan, 1982, v. 2, p. 59–95)

Compares quality and quantity of 18th-century writing on Spanish America by Spanish and French authors. Clément sees French writers as having a significant edge in quality which he attributes to the "bourgeoisie spirit" in France as well as to less censorship there. [W. Painter]

1807 Cocca, Aldo Armando. Orígenes y desarrollo de las fundaciones del derecho antiguo al derecho indiano (UNL/H, 22, 1981, p. 337–360)

As title implies, Cocca summarizes historic antecedents of *derecho indiano*— ranging from proto-history and classical civilizations to medieval and modern times. Pious foundations, schools of Indians, rights of mayorazgo, and other legacies fall within the purview. [DEC]

1808 Colosía Rodrígues, María Isabel P. de and Joaquín Gil Sanjuan. El tráfico de Málaga con las Indias en tiempos de Carlos I (IGFO/RI, 38:153/154, julio/dic. 1978, p. 563–592, facsims.)

Examines an attempt by Charles V to increase commercial traffic with the Indies by including Málaga as a royally sanctioned port. This relatively brief experiment met determined opposition, and was not of great consequence as it failed to reorient traditional Malagueñan commerce from the Mediterranean. [DEC]

1809 Contreras Miguel, Remedios. Conocimientos técnicos y científicos del descubridor del Nuevo Mundo (IGFO/RI, 39:155/158, enero/dic. 1979, p. 89–104, map)

By analyzing materials which Columbus owned and annotated as well as those which he had access to, author examines extent of the discoverer's technical and scientific information, his miscalculations, and misinformations. Contends that Columbus had more valid information prior to voyage of 1492 than is generally accepted. [DEC]

1810 Cortés Alonso, Vicenta. La mano de obra negra en el Virreinato: siglo XVI (RUC, 28 : 117, enero 1979, p. 489–502, graphs, tables)

Vicenta Cortés, one of the foremost authorities on Spanish archives, offers here a brief assessment of where research stands on black labor in the Iberian nations and their overseas possessions, and what needs to be done. In the latter area, fruitful avenues of investigations are suggested. [DEC]

1811 Crouch, Dora; Daniel J. Garr; and Axel I. Mundingo. Spanish city planning in North America. Foreword by George Kubler. Cambridge, Mass.: MIT Press, 1982. 298 p.: bibl., plates.

Laws of the Indies issued by Philip II in 1573, which governed city planning in the New World are presented as well as commentary on them. Authors note disparities between laws and compliance, and they use three cities—Santa Fe, N.M., Los Angeles, and St. Louis—as examples of principles embodying 16th-century laws. [DEC]

1812 Delgado Ribas, Josep M. Fiscalidad y comercio con América: los resguardos de rentas de Catalunya, 1778–1799 (UB/BA, 22 : 30, 1980, p. 69–88, tables)

Contends that while Bourbon reforms in trade and commerce are widely regarded as beneficial to the economic growth of Spain, custom's officials assigned to the newly opened ports were notoriously corrupt, lazy, and incompetent. Case study of functionaries assigned to the port of Barcelona is used to document the assertion. [DEC]

1813 Destombes, Marcel. Astrolabios náuticos del siglo XVI: a propósito de un astrolabio náutico de la Casa de la Contratación, Sevilla, 1563 (IGFO/RI, 41 : 165/166, julio/dic. 1981, p. 359–394, ill.)

Encyclopedic article which locates (in world museums) and describes 21 16th and early 17th-century nautical astrolabes. Roughly half have been museum pieces for many years, while the other half have been acquired more recently from sunken vessels. The last word on astrolabes. [DEC]

1814 Engstrand, Iris H. Wilson. Spanish scientists in the New World: the eighteenth-century expeditions. Seattle: University of Washington Press, 1981. 220 p., 18 leaves of plates: bibl., ill., index.

Well researched account of two major scientific expeditions to the New World organized by Charles III, for the purpose of recording and cataloging zoological, botanical, and geographical information. Much material collected was later lost or misplaced due to Charles' death and loss of his patronage. [DEC]

1815 Ezquerra Abadía, Ramón. En torno a la memoria de Aranda (EEHA/AEA, 33, 1976 [i.e. 1979] p. 273–307)

Reviews historical controversy surrounding authenticity of the 1783 *Memoria* of the Conde de Aranda. No attempt is made to resolve that issue, rather the presumed intent behind the document's publication in 1827 is addressed. [DEC]

1817 Fernández Marchena, Juan. El Ejército de América: el componente humano (SHM/RHM, 25 : 51, 1981, p. 119–154, graphs, tables)

Excellent study of composition and deployment of Spanish army in the colonies. Charts clearly depict percentages of troops in various units such as cavalry and infantry as well as by military rank and by classes in society. Data are primarily available for latter half of 18th century. [DEC]

1818 Flynn, Dennis O. Fiscal crisis and the decline of Spain: Castile (Journal of Economic History [North Carolina State University, Economic History Association, Raleigh] 42 : 1, March 1982, p. 139–147, tables)

Flynn's article supports, from different viewpoint, earlier thesis that the primary external cause of decline of Spain was due to increased world supply of silver from American mines. [DEC]

1819 Galdón, María Victoria. Pretensiones a intereses locales en pro de la habilitación de Málaga para el comercio con Indias, 1776–1778 (IGFO/RI, 43 : 171, enero/junio 1983, p. 183–202)

Traces concerted and ultimately successful efforts waged by prominent Malagueñans for inclusion of their port in

Carrera de Indias. Cabildo of Málaga employed agents and writers to advance cause before the Crown, and a local fund for development of agriculture was created. Campaign was further aided by the favorable recommendation of José de Gálvez. [DEC]

1820 García Fuentes, Lutgardo. El comercio español con América, 1650–1700. Prólogo de Luis Navarro García. Sevilla: Escuela de Estudios Hispano-Americanos, Consejo Superior de Investigaciones Científicas, 1980. 574 p.: bibl., ill., index (Publicaciones de la Escuela; no. general 265)

Important revisionistic study of trans-Atlantic commerce in last half of 17th century. Numerous appendices, graphs, and tables buttress general conclusions such as absence of commercial rivalry between Seville and Cádiz, symptoms of economic recovery in early 1660s, and increasing incidence of voyages to and from New Spain vis-à-vis Tierra Firme. A major work. [DEC]

1821 ———. En torno a la reactivación del comercio indiano en tiempos de Carlos II (EEHA/AEA, 36, 1979, p. 251–286, bibl., tables)

Presents evidence that Spanish commercial activity experienced a significant turn-around beginning in 1660s, and continued throughout Charles II's reign. Discusses factors influencing the change, such as reduction of *avería* and increased involvement of Cádiz in Carrera de Indias. [DEC]

1822 García García, Calixto. Las leyes agrarias en el contexto de las *Leyes de Indias* (IEAS/R, 119, abril/junio 1982, p. 117–174, facsim., tables)

Useful compilation of laws of an agrarian nature, which have been extracted from the *Recopilación de las leyes de Indias*. In all there are 56 laws arranged into 10 categories spanning years 1513–1646. Of interest is paucity of such legislation pertaining to agriculture. [DEC]

1823 García Regueiro, Ovidio. Ilustración e intereses estamentales: la versión castellana de la "historia" de Raynal (*in* Coloquio Ilustración Española e Independencia de América, Bellaterra, Spain, 1978: homenaje a Noël Salomon. Edición preparada por Alberto Gil Novales. Barcelona: Universidad Autónoma de Barcelona, 1979, p. 165–205)

Author offers speculation on why 18th-century Castilian translations of Raynal's *Historia . . . de las dos Indias* by the Duke of Almodóvar was neither accurate nor completed. Explores motives such as irreconcilable philosophical differences between Raynal and his translator, political climate of late 1700s, and lack of resources to finish project. [DEC]

1824 Garica-Abasolo, Antonio Francisco. La expansión mexicana hacia el Pacífico: la primera colonización de Filipinas, 1570–1580 (CM/HM, 32:1, julio/sept. 1982, p. 55–88, bibl., tables)

Addresses 1570s populating and provisioning of Philippines from New Spain. Acapulco-Manila connection witnessed transfer of soldiers, priests, and merchandise— all necessary due to reasons of security, missionary impulse, subsistence level economy of natives—and lack of readily exploitable wealth. [DEC]

1825 Gil-Bermejo García, Juana. La Iglesia y defensa de las Indias (EEHA/AEA, 33, 1976 [i.e. 1979] p. 343–383, tables)

Examines contributions of Roman Catholic Church toward defense of the Indies against 17th-century attacks by pirates. Concludes that voluntary contributions were insignificant. Assesses involuntary collections by means of *subsidio* and *escusado*. [DEC]

1826 Gómez Alfaro, Antonio. La polémica sobre la deportación de los gitanos a las colonias de América (CH, 386, agosto 1982, p. 308–336)

Traces controversy surrounding proposed deportation of gypsies during reigns of Ferdinand VI and Charles III. Explores previous decisions regarding Spain's unwanted minorities, legal ramifications of transportation, and circumstances which thwarted project. [DEC]

1827 Gorender, Jacob. Questionamentos sobre a teoria econômica do escravismo colonial (IPE/EE, 13:1, 1983, p. 7–39)

Agreeing with Engels that every mode of production requires its own economic theory, Gorender attempts to establish parameters for a theory of colonial slavery. Contends that colonial slavery cannot be subsumed under capitalist theory, nor was it feudal, and argues that "sparetime" economic activities by slaves were integral to a slave economy. [L. Huddleston]

1828 Hernández Ruigómez, Manuel. Un sermón pronunciado ante el Consejo de Indias en vísperas de la ruptura de hostilidades entre las coronas española y británica (IGFO/RI, 42:167/168, enero/junio 1982, p. 203–221)

Analyzes text of 1739 sermon delivered before Indies Council by Carmelite friar Juan de la Concepción, in order to gauge Spanish temper immediately prior to War of Austrian Succession. Fray Juan justified impending conflict on several grounds, including his view of Great Britain as Spanish Catholicism's ancient enemy. [DEC]

1829 Hilton, Sylvia Lyn. En conflicto anglo-español sobre derechos de navegación en mares americanos, 1729–50 (IGFO/RI, 38:153/154, julio/dic. 1978, p. 671–713)

Good summary of Anglo-Spanish commercial conflicts from Treaty of Utrecht to 1750. Views English commercial concessions incorporated in the *asiento* as source of irritation to Bourbon reformers who regarded them as inimical to Spain's welfare as well as a dangerous entrée into illicit commerce. [DEC]

1830 Israel, Jonathan Irvine. The Dutch Republic and the Hispanic world, 1606–1661. Oxford: Clarendon Press; New York: Oxford University Press, 1982. 478 p.: bibl., ill., index.

Superb analysis of second phase of war between Dutch Republic and Spanish Empire. Israel attempts to explain why a "prolonged and exhaustive struggle should have taken place" after Spain had clearly acknowledged the inevitability of Dutch political and religious independence. Answer, he thinks, rises from contradictory political and economic circumstances in both countries. [DEC]

1831 Izard, Miquel. Algunas notas sobre el comercio colonial atlántico: los intercambios del Reino Unido con América, 1772–1808 (IGFO/RI, 159/162, enero/dic. 1980, p. 425–439, graphs, tables)

Statistical study of value of contraband goods flowing between United Kingdom and the Indies during last half of 18th century. [DEC]

1832 Jornadas de Andalucía y América, 1st, *Universidad de la Rábida, Spain, 1981?* Primeras Jornadas de Andalucía y América. Huelva, Spain: Instituto de Estudios Onubenses, 1981? 2 v.: bibl., ill.

Brief treatment of efforts to acclimatize indigo plants from Yucatan into southern regions of Spain during Philip II's reign. [DEC]

1833 Kaspar, Oldrich. Fuentes para el estudio del descubrimiento y la conquista de América conservadas en las bibliotecas checoslovacas (UO/R, 48, dic. 1982, p. 9–22)

Traces earliest references in Czech literature to the discovery and conquest of the New World. Of interest are a surprising number of works, earliest of which is ca. 1506. Suggests that Central Europe was not isolated from news concerning the activities of Atlantic nations. [DEC]

1834 Lavalle, Bernard. Las "doctrinas" de frailes como reveladoras del incipiente criollismo sudamericano (EEHA/AEA, 36, 1979, p. 447–465)

Examines disputes between religious orders and secular priests over control of Indian doctrines in regions of Quito and Santa Fe de Bogotá, using them as illustration of growing Americanism in late-16th and early-17th centuries. [DEC]

1835 Lavrin, Asunción. Women and religion in Spanish America (*in* Women and religion in America. v. 2., The colonial and revolutionary periods. Rosemary Radford Ruether and Rosemary Skinner Keller, editors. San Francisco, Calif.: Harper & Row, 1983, p. 42–78, ill.)

Excerpts from 14 documents by and about women which illuminate the role of religion in their lives. Includes author's explanations and brief introduction. Intended for student audience, but almost all are previously unpublished pieces and so scholars will find the citations of interest. [JDR]

1836 Leal, Ildefonso. Un fragmento del libro prohibido de Raynal: *Historia de las Indias* (PAIGH/H, 92, julio/dic. 1981, p. 127–194)

Good discussion of why Raynal's six-volume *Historia . . . dans les deux Indes* was banned by royal provision in Spain and the Indies. Raynal's broad condemnation of European methods of conquest, especially those of Spain, made his work anathema in several European countries. Examines portions of work that are most critical of Spain. [DEC]

1837 Lechner, J. El concepto de *policía* y su presencia en la obra de los primeros historiadores de Indias (IGFO/RI, 41:165/166, julio/dic. 1981, p. 395–409)

Discusses widely varying concepts of *"policía"* as Spanish historians and royal officials applied it to New World civilizations. In that conceptual framework, *"policía"* (policy, not police) seems to have connoted a mixture of Christian values, rationality, and civility. [DEC]

1838 Llombart, Vicente. Mercantilismo tardío, "liberalización" comercial, y explotación colonial americana: las reflexiones sobre el comercio español a Indias, 1762, del conde de Campomanes (*in* Coloquio Ilustración Española e Independencia de América, Bellaterra, Spain, 1978: homenaje a Noël Salomon. Edición preparada por Alberto Gil Novales. Barcelona: Universidad Autónoma de Barcelona, 1979, v. 1, p. 333–343)

Brief discussion of unedited manuscript of Conde de Campomanes, discovered by the author in late 1970s. In it Campomanes, who admired the British model, proposed changes in Spanish mercantilism which antedate Charles III's commercial reforms. [DEC]

1839 Lockhart, James. La historia social de Hispanoamérica colonial: evolución y posibilidad (ECO, 45[1]:241, nov. 1981, p. 1–60)

Wide-ranging historiographical essay on the current status of social history of colonial Hispanic America. Author sees topic as more advanced in American possessions of the Iberian nations than in metropolises. Among suggestions for the future are second generation studies of developed topics, biographical works, and analysis of social upheavals. [DEC]

1840 Lorenzo Sanz, Eufemio. Comercio de España con América en la época de Felipe II. t. 1, Los mercaderes y el tráfico indiano. t. 2, La navegación, los tesoros y las perlas. Valladolid, Spain: Servicio de Publicaciones de la Diputación Provincial, 1979/1980. 2 v.: bibl., ill., index (Publicaciones de la Excma. Diputación de Valladolid)

Two-part work utilizes immense volume of documentation, primarily from AGI, Simancas, and Casa Ruiz of Valladolid, in order to analyze trans-Atlantic traffic during 1555–1660: 1) meticulously discusses, charts, and graphs commerce to and from Indies, both legal and illegal; and 2) enormous quantity of precious metals and gems registered in Spain. Landmark study in economic history with important implications for both European and Latin American history. [DEC]

1840a Lunardi, Ernesto di. La travagliata nascita dell'America Ispana (AISA/TA, 41, dic. 1980, p. 5–24, facsim., ill., plate)

Interpretive survey of interpenetration of European and American cultures in context of second Columbian expedition and Granadine war. Views Hispanic component (e.g., encomienda) and surveys indigenous institutions. Stresses motivating ideas of spiritual patrimony and material culture, and speculates on Creole culture and caudillismo. [V.C. Peloso]

1841 Marchena, Juan. La financiación militar en Indias: introducción a su estudio (EEHA/AEA, 36, 1979, p. 81–110)

Calls for detailed study of cost of military defenses for the Spanish American empire in 18th century, and relationship of those expenses to overall budgetary considerations. Reviews available data for selected sites in earlier centuries. [DEC]

1841a Marcus, Raymond. Bartolomé de Las Casas: un discepolo di Savonarola (AISA/TA, 41, dic. 1980, p. 39–43, facsim., plate)

Argues that Las Casas in Spain was less the uncompromising opponent of the Spanish conquest than a politically astute Dominican reformer whose life resembles that of the Florentine Dominican political genius Girolamo Savonarola. Las Casas' finest contribution was establishing a vigorous Christian community in the New World respectful of the laws and faithful to principles of the gospel. [V.C. Peloso]

1842 Martínez Shaw, Carlos. Cataluña y el comercio con América: el fin de un debate (UB/BA, 22:30, 1980, p. 223–236)

Author seeks to end misconception that Catalonia was excluded from Carrera de Indias, until Charles III's liberalized commercial policies promoted free trade in 1778. Cites involvement of Catalonians in commerce. Views free trade *Reglamento* as administrative acknowledgement of economic exigencies rather than as corrective to three centuries of discrimination. [DEC]

1843 Mesa, Carlos E. Real Patronato y regio vicariato (ACH/BHA, 67:730, julio/sept. 1980, p. 445–468, bibl.)
Superficial review of the origins and implications of the Patronato Real. Contains examples of conflict between secular and religious persons in New World as well as problems of application. [DEC]

1844 Mörner, Magnus. Economic factors and stratification in colonial Spanish America, with special regard to elites (HAHR, 63:2, May 1983, p. 335–369)
Mörner contends that current generalizations about social stratification of colonial Spanish America are probably suspect. For example, we can as easily postulate that power and status led to wealth as the opposite. Regards systematic regional studies through time in economic and social terms at different societal levels as especially fruitful approaches to increased understanding of the relationship "between economic dynamics and social structure and change." [DEC]

1845 ———. La emigración española al Nuevo Mundo antes de 1810: un informe del estado de la investigación (EEHA/AEA, 32, 1975, p. 43–131, bibl., tables)
Another of this prolific scholar's excellent surveys on state of research in fields of social history. Spanish translation of piece in *HLAS 40:2276.* [JDR]

1846 ———. Estratificación social hispanoamericana durante el período colonial: versión preliminar de un capítulo preparado para la *Historia general de América.* Stockholm: Institute of Latin American Studies, 1980. 128 p.: bibl. (Research paper series; no. 28)
Examines wide range of factors influencing social stratification. Concludes that overall colonial Hispanic society was arranged along lines of Castilian patterns transplanted to New World, but nevertheless

influenced locally and regionally by multiracial, economic, and political realities. Variations were so numerous as to preclude study from single perspective. [DEC]

1847 ———. Evolución demográfica de Hispanoamérica durante el período colonial. Stockholm: Institute of Latin American Studies, 1979. 77 p.: bibl., ill. (Research paper series: no. 14)
Broad-bush treatment of colonial demographic patterns. Topics include precolumbian population, post-conquest decline, European and African immigration, and internal population changes. [DEC]

1848 Muro Orejón, Antonio and **Fernando Muro Romero.** Los libros impresos y manuscritos del Consejo de Indias (EEHA/AEA, 33, 1976 [i.e. 1979] p. 713–854)
Extensive compilation of printed works and manuscripts consulted by members of the Council of the Indies as they formulated day-by-day policy for the New World. Materials requested by Council members as well as general topics under consideration are arranged alphabetically. Books and manuscripts are referenced to known inventories of Council materials. [DEC]

1852 ———. La Ilustración y el clero mestizo en América (ISTM/MH, 33:97/99, enero/dic. 1976, p. 165–179)
Traces exclusion of Indians and mestizos from religious orders in early colonial times to their initial acceptance at turn of 18th century. [DEC]

1853 ———. Las universidades hispanas de América y el indio (EEHA/AEA, 33, 1976 [i.e. 1979] p. 855–874)
Extolls record of Spain in founding 19 universities throughout her American kingdoms as well as liberal charters of those institutions as they applied to admission of Indians and mestizos. Recounts difficulties in educating Indian commoners, and creation of schools for caciques' sons. [DEC]

1854 Ortega y Medina, Juan Antonio. El conflicto anglo-español por el dominio oceánico: siglos XVI y XVII. México: Universidad Nacional Autónoma de México, Instituto de Investigaciones Históricas, 1981. 298 p., 45 p. of plates: bibl., ill. (some col.), index (Serie de historia general; no. 12)
Broad treatment of struggle for Atlan-

tic dominance between missionary and imperial goals of Catholic Spain and those of Protestant England. Views Spain's loss of naval supremacy as portentous in ensuing contest between traditional values of Hispanic world in America and political-economic power of Anglo-America. [DEC]

1855 Otte, Enrique. La última voluntad de Diego de Ordás (EEHA/AEA, 34, 1977, p. 137–147)

Brief treatment of last days of Conquistador Diego de Ordaz. Notes Ordaz's obsession with obtaining admission to the Order of Santiago and disposition of his estate in 1532. [DEC]

1856 Pagden, Anthony. Cannibalismo e contagio: sull'importanza dell'antropofagia nell'Europa preindustriale (QS, 17[50]:2, agosto 1982, p. 533–550)

Consideration of how European theologians and other writers analyzed cannibalism and justified its censure. Deals only in part with cannibalism among native American cultures. [JDR]

1857 Pérez, Héctor J. Spain, Great Britain and Spanish America: a study of international relations, 1788–1808 (UCPR/H, 25:49, oct. 1981, p. 43–58, bibl.)

Superficial and badly written study of relations between Britain and Spain after 1788. Based on published documents. [JDR]

1858 Pérez Fernández, Isacio. Inventario documentado de los escritos de Fray Bartolomé de las Casas. Revisado por Helen Rand Parish. Bayamón, Puerto Rico: Centro de Estudios de los Dominicos del Caribe, 1981. 928 p.: bibl., ill., index (Estudios monográficos; v. l)

Massive inventory of Las Casas' works. Includes, aside from materials which Las Casas authored, writings of others which he translated, copied, or edited. Materials are arranged chronologically from 1512 to bishop's death in 1566. Original compilation of Pérez Fernández (1978) was revised and expanded by Helen Rand Parish (1979). [DEC]

1859 Pietschmann, Horst. Burocracia y corrupción en Hispanoamérica colonial: una aproximación tentativa (GEE/NA, 5, 1982, p. 11–37)

Presents evidence that corruption at all levels of colonial bureaucracy was persistent and pervasive throughout entire colonial era. Notes four categories of illicit activities: 1) illegal commerce; 2) bribes and subordination; 3) favoritism; and 4) sale of bureaucratic services to the public. [DEC]

1860 Pino, Fermín del. Los Reinos de México y Cuzco en la obra del Padre Acosta (RUC, 28:117, enero 1979, p. 13–43, bibl., tables)

Regards José de Acosta's *Historia natural y moral de las Indias* as one of first systematic comparisons of Aztec and Inca religion and civilization. Acosta's ethnohistorical observations of both cultures, along nearly parallel lines which stress similarities much more than differences, are lauded for their breadth and vision. [DEC]

Pupo-Walker, Enrique. La vocación literaria del pensamiento histórico en América: desarrollo de la prosa ficción, siglos XVI, XVII, XVIII y XIX. See item **5066.**

1861 Quesada, Carlos. Histoire hypothétique et idéologie anti-indienne au XVIII siècle: pt. 2 (in Bénassy, Marie-Cécile et al. Etudes sur l'impact culturel du Nouveau Monde. Seminaire interuniversitaire sur l'Amérique espagnole coloniale. Paris: Editions L'Harmattan, 1982, v. 2, p. 97–109)

Discusses contrast between Jean Jacques Rousseau's perception of the American Indian and that of Cornelius de Pauw. Contrary to Rousseau's idealized noble savage, de Pauw regarded the Indian as intellectually, culturally, and physiologically inferior to Europeans, and believed America's climate, terrain, flora, and fauna made for an evil environment. [DEC]

1862 Ramos Pérez, Demetrio. Castilla del Oro: el primer nombre dado oficialmente al continente americano (EEHA/AEA, 37, 1980, p. 45–67)

Traces rise and demise of "Castilla del Oro" to connote entire American continent. Based on discoveries of Balboa and appointment of Pedrarias Dávila in 1513, the Crown rejected America in favor of "Castilla del Oro," but subsequent discoveries and appointments to nearby geographic areas restricted its designated confines by early 1530s to Panama. [DEC]

1863 ———. Colón y el enfrentamiento de los caballeros: un serio problema del segundo viaje, que nuevos documentos ponen al descubierto (IGFO/RI, 39:155/158, enero/dic. 1979, p. 9–87)

Superbly documented treatment of problems encountered by Columbus with Spanish noblemen in his second voyage's recruitment, provisioning, and aftermath. Ramos points to multiple and burdensome responsibilities of Columbus, bitter disappointments of colonists on Española, and defection of Spanish peerage under leadership of Pedro Margarit and Padre Buil. Major work using new documentation. [DEC]

1864 Rea, Robert R. A distant thunder: Anglo-Spanish conflict and the Americas in the eighteenth century (*in* Cardinales de dos independencias: Noroeste de México-Sureste de los Estados Unidos: memoria del simposio celebrado en la Universidad Iberoamericana, con la colaboración de la Universidad de Florida, los días 29 y 30 de noviembre de 1976, con motivo del Bicentenario de la Independencia de los Estados Unidos. México: Fomento Cultural Banamex, 1978, p. 175–195)

Broad view of Anglo-French diplomacy in 18th century, especially as it applied to Spain in her role as a French satellite. Author sees the Americas' commercial wealth as the prize, and calls for increased attention to Spanish-French relations in Europe during 1714–63. [DEC]

1865 Rech, Bruno. Las Casas und das *Alte Testament* (JGSWGL, 18, 1981, p. 1–30)

Examines in broad context the *Old Testament*'s influence on Las Casas' work. In his debate with Juan Ginés de Sepúlveda, both men interpreted the *Bible* to buttress their respective positions. Las Casas, however, appears to have made better use of scriptures in censuring the nature of the conquest. [DEC]

1866 Retamal Favereau, Julio. Diplomacia anglo-española durante la Contrarreforma. Santiago: Ediciones Universidad Católica de Chile, 1981. 252 p.: bibl., facsims.

Revisionist study of Anglo-Spanish diplomacy during reigns of Philip II and Elizabeth I. Diplomatic assignments of John Man to Madrid and Guerau de Spes to London are carefully analyzed from Spanish and English state papers. While acknowledging ambassadors' superficial failure to promote peace and amnesty, attributes severing of diplomatic ties to Counter-Reformation forces beyond their control. [DEC]

1867 Rodríguez Vicente, María Encarnación. Los cargadores a Indias y su contribución a los gastos de la monarquía: 1550–1750 (EEHA/AEA, 34, 1977, p. 211–232, bibl., tables)

Uses printed pamphlet and *representación*, both issued by Consulado de Cádiz and housed in AHN (Madrid), to present and analyze statistical data regarding carriers' contribution to Real Hacienda (1555–1750). Contains useful tables and supportive appendices. [DEC]

1869 Schwartz, Stuart B. La nobleza del Nuevo Mundo: movilidad y aspiraciones sociales en la conquista y colonización de la América hispánica (UNCR/R, 4:8, enero/julio 1979, p. 7–29, tables)

Good analysis of circumstances which underlay creation of aristocracy in Luso-Hispanic colonies. Means of qualifying for noble status—control of land, mines, Indian labor, and commerce—remained the same throughout colonial era, but success in attaining titles was clearly tied to economic straits of later Hapsburgs. [DEC]

1870 Solano, Francisco de. La tenencia de la tierra en Hispanoamérica: proceso de larga duración: el tiempo virreinal (IGFO/RI, 43:171, enero/junio 1983, p. 9–26)

Calls for research and writing directed toward comprehensive study of tenancy extending over some 300 years. Defends validity of such a work. Recounts land policy as broadly defined in the *Recopilación* and in sources for post-1681 years. [DEC]

1871 Tengwall, David. A study in military leadership: Portuguese South Atlantic empire (AAFH/TAM, 40:1, July 1983, p. 73–94)

Discusses role of *sargento mor* in Portuguese military conquest and acquisition of colonies in South Atlantic from 1570 to early 1700s. Discusses establishment of *sargento mor* position, its reponsibilities, selection process, and geographical locations of services. Concludes that *sargento mor* "brought some semblance of order and stability to Portuguese South Atlantic empire." [DEC]

1871a TePaske, John J. New World silver: Castille and the Phillipines, 1590–1800 (*in* Precious metals in the later medieval and early modern worlds. Edited by J.F. Richards. Durham: Carolina Academic Press, 1983, p. 425–445)

Bullion, especially silver was one dimension of complex and farflung Spanish trading system, especially under Phillip II, in which political considerations rivaled economic ones in the formulation of trade policy. Focusing on official receipts, TePaske arrives at conclusion that differs from Harry Cross' (item) on levels and impact of American silver in the Spanish world. Notes that after 1660 Mexico became supplier of bullion, accounting for some 65 percent of official Spanish revenues, with increasing proportions remaining in the Indies for local defense and administration. [F.W. Knight]

1872 Thompson, Alvin O. Race and colour prejudices and the origin of the Transatlantic slave trade (UPR/CS, 16:3/4, Oct. 1976/Jan. 1977, p. 29–59)

Contends that European race and color prejudices against Africans had deep historical roots, extending in some instances to the Graeco-Roman period. A corollary, therefore, is that social, moral, and intellectual "justifications" for the trade antedated its inception, rather than flowed from the nature and characteristics of the human cargo. [DEC]

1873 Unceín Tamayo, Luis Alberto. El humanismo y las Indias (PAIGH/H, 92, julio/dic. 1981, p. 71–97)

Defines humanism in broader Christian context, and emphasizes many intellectual cross currents which flowed across Western European boundaries in late 15th and early 16th centuries. Inevitably, humanistic influences in Spain shaped and defined corpus of Spanish law as it was applied to governing aboriginal societies in the Spanish kingdoms. [DEC]

1873a Varela Marcos, Jesús. Aranda y su sueño de la independencia suramericana (EEHA/AEA, 37, 1980, p. 351–368, ill.)

Reviews Count of Aranda's 1786 utopian proposal for restructuring Iberian world on basis of exchanging Peru for Portugal and making Río de la Plata an independent monarchy. Placed in context of evolution of Aranda's views on American questions and defeatist climate of opinion that spawned other such proposals as well. While at it, casts doubt on Aranda's authorship of 1783 secret memorial which is perhaps best known example of this genre. [D. Bushnell]

1874 Varner, John Grier and **Jeannette Johnson Varner.** Dogs of the conquest. Norman: University of Oklahoma Press, 1983. 238 p.: bibl., ill., index.

Examines role of dogs in Spanish conquest of the New World. While topic has been neglected in historiography, authors' approach is unfortunately anecdotal and uncritical. [DEC]

1875 Villalta, Collado. El embargo en bienes de los portugueses en la flota de tierra firme de 1641 (EEHA/AEA, 36, 1979, p. 169–207)

Interesting study of embargo of property consigned to Portuguese nationals in first year after their nation's revolt against Spanish captivity. It further reveals favored position and power which Portuguese merchants had come to enjoy in the Carrera de Indias before the sudden reversal of their fortunes. [DEC]

1876 Zorraquín Becú, Ricardo. Esquema del derecho internacional de las Indias (EEHA/AEA, 32, 1975, p. 573–597)

Development of international law as applied to New World is related sequentially to Alexandrine Bulls of 1493, Spain's physical occupation of Indies with attendant juridical implications, and international conventions which emerged from mid-1600s to wars of independence. [DEC]

1877 Zorrilla Concha, Enrique. Gestación de Latinoamérica: la posesión del mundo americano por los ibéricos. Santiago de Chile: Ediciones Nuestramérica, 1982. 382 p.: bibl., ill.

Textbook treatment of colonial Iberoamerica. Somewhat old fashioned since it ignores 1970s research in social and economic history. [JDR]

INDEPENDENCE AND 19TH CENTURY

1878 Aguirre Elorriaga, Manuel. El abate de Pradt en la emancipación hispanoamericana: 1800–1830. Caracas: Universidad

Católica Andrés Bello, Instituto de Investigaciones Históricas, 1983. 377 p.

Reedición de tesis doctoral (Universidad Gregoriana, Roma, 1937; impresa Caracas 1941) que sigue siendo el mejor estudio acerca del prelado francés y sus actividades en favor de la emancipación de la América española. Muy bien documentado y escrito. [L. Gómez Canedo]

1879 Andrés Bello: the London years. Edited by John Lynch. Richmond, England: Richmond Pub. Co., 1982. 167 p.: bibl.

Selection of contributions that appeared in symposium proceedings entitled *Bello y Londres* (Caracas: Fundación La Casa Bello, 1980/1981), on London cultural scene and British policy as they affected Spanish America, as well as on specific activities in London during independence era of Andrés Bello. John Lynch's essay "Great Britain and Spanish American Independence, 1810–1830," is a very nice synthesis. [D. Bushnell]

1880 Anna, Timothy E. Spain and the loss of America. Lincoln: University of Nebraska Press, 1983. 343 p.: bibl., index.

Highly readable and well-researched study of American question from standpoint of imperial Spain, emphasizing "systemic dysfunctions" that made adequate response to insurrection so difficult. These are perhaps lesser part of total story than Anna suggests, but nevertheless an important and all too often neglected part. Much of his argument can be found in summary form in *The Americas* (Washington, 38:4, April 1982, p. 481–495). [D. Bushnell]

1881 Bell, Samuel E. and James M. Smallwood. The Zona Libre, 1858–1905: a problem in American diplomacy. El Paso: Texas Western Press, University of Texas at El Paso, 1982. 88 p.: bibl. (Southwestern studies; monograph no. 69)

Established in 1858 by Mexican government to forestall demise of towns along US-Mexican border, the free trade zone quickly developed serious political, economic, and social overtones that plagued relations between both countries for over 50 years. Authors see abolition of free trade zone in 1905 as opening the way for improved relations. Also available as article in *Arizona and the West* (24:2, Summer 1982, p. 119–152). [DEC]

1882 Costeloe, Michael P. Barcelona mer- chants and the Latin American wars of independence (AAFH/TAM, 38:4, April 1982, p. 431–448)

Enlightening look at impact of American rebellions on Spanish trade: use of British and neutral flags, efforts to extract capital from colonies, role of Cuba in attenuating loss of mainland. Deals with Barcelona specifically, on basis of local records. [D. Bushnell]

1883 Cuenca Toribio, José Manuel. Iglesia y Estado a fines del antiguo régimen: la elección del episcopado hispano-americano, 1789–1824 (EEHA/AEA, 33, 1976 [i.e. 1979] p. 105–143, tables)

Examines selection of bishops to fill Spanish and New World dioceses as reflection of clergy's politicalization in turbulent regimes of Charles III, Joseph Bonaparte, and Ferdinand VII. [DEC]

1884 Felstiner, Mary Lowenthal. Family metaphors: the language of an independence revolution (CSSH, 25:1, Jan. 1983, p. 154–180)

Interesting attempt to apply analysis of symbolic language to independence movement. Uses writings of Chilean leaders to detect three dominant metaphors or images: Americans as rebellious Indians, oppressed slaves, and disinherited sons. Relates all three to pre-independence social reality and post-revolutionary policy. [S. Socolow]

1885 Ferrer Benimeli, José Antonio. La masonería y la independencia de América española: reflexiones metodológicas (EEHA/AEA, 35, 1978, p. 159–177)

Sensible observations concerning treatment—generally superficial or worse—of Masonic influences in existing literature, together with some representative data on Masonic activities. [D. Bushnell]

1886 Gallardo, Guillermo. Viaje a Buenos Aires del primer agente comercial de los Estados Unidos de Norteamérica (JEHM/R, 9:2, 1980, p. 383–404, ill., plate)

Annotated translation of part of Joel Roberts Poinsett's *Journal to Rio de Janeiro, Buenos Aires and Chili* written 1810–11. This section, referring to his journey from US to Buenos Aires passing through Brazil, was published before in Spanish but apparently not in English original. [D. Bushnell]

1887 Komissarov, Boris. Rusia y América Latina en los documentos diplomáticos rusos de 1818–1821: pts. 1/2 (URSS/AL, 11:59, nov. 1982, p. 105–118; 2:62, feb. 1983, p. 105–118)

Two-part article. Pt. 1 describes Russian diplomats and consular officials who reported from Spain, Portugal, and various parts of Western Hemisphere, as well as their reports concerning revolutionary movements in the Americas. Pt. 2 examines diplomatic issues concerning Russia's territorial presence in California, and commercial interests in Brazil. Both sections are based on documents from Russian diplomatic archives (quoted liberally, but with little interpretation) which have been published recently in multi-volume documentary source on Russian diplomatic history in the 19th century. [JDR]

1888 Lancha, Charles. El ideal unionista latinoamericano de Bolívar y Martí (*in* Cuba, les étapes d'une libération: hommage à Juan Marinello et Noël Salomon: actes du colloque international des 22, 23 et 24 novembre 1978. Toulouse: Centre d'études cubaines, Université de Toulouse-Le Mirail, 1979, v. 1, p. 197–219)

Comparison of the basis for Bolívar's and Martí's call for continental unity as well as their attitudes toward racial and political democracy. Concludes that although Martí revered Bolívar, the content of their ideas could not have been more different. [JDR]

1889 Lewin, Boleslao. Rousseau en la independencia de Latinoamérica. 2. ed. Buenos Aires: Ediciones Depalma, 1980. 157 p.

Identifies traces of Rousseau's thought in Latin America in independence era, at some length for Platine area, more sketchily for other countries. May at times overstate his importance but abundantly documents his presence. Slightly enlarged version of work first published 1967 (see *HLAS 30:1907*). [D. Bushnell]

1890 Malamud, Carlos D. Autonomía o dependencia: una falsa opción;en torno a la polémica entre D.C.M. Platt y Stanley y Barbara Stein (IGFO/RI, 41:163/ 164, enero/junio 1981, p. 281–285)

Simply restates terms of argument between Platt and the Steins (see *HLAS 44:1812*). [JDR]

1891 Mayo, John. The impatient lion: Britain's "official mind" and Latin America in the 1850s (IAA, 9:2, 1983, p. 197–223, bibl.)

Entry in a debate among English historians as to whether or not Britain used intimidation to gain commercial advantage in Latin America. Using the Barron, Forbes affair in Mexico and the Whitehead Affair in Chile, illustrates how, although Britain would never knowingly give aid to business for purely commercial ends, the subtlety of British motives and behavior was lost on Latin American nations who saw only actions and a great disparity of power. [JDR]

1892 Miller, Francesca. Tsarist initiatives in the New World: problems of interpretation (UCSD/NS, 8, 1982, p. 499–504)

While warmly praising Russell Bartley's work on Russia and Latin American independence (see *HLAS 42:1896*), argues that Russian interest in Latin America as a whole was less than Bartley suggests. [D. Bushnell]

1893 Pérez Guilhou, Dardo. La opinión pública española y las Cortés de Cádiz frente a la emancipación hispanoamericana, 1808–1814. Advertencia de Enrique M. Barba. Buenos Aires: Academia Nacional de la Historia, 1982. 206 p.: bibl. (Biblioteca de historia argentina y americana; t. 18)

Best work yet on Spain's reaction to American outbreaks and handling of American representation and related questions at Cádiz. Though based on extensive research in Spanish newspapers and Cortes records, its importance lies less in new facts or interpretation than in clarity and systematic approach. [D. Bushnell]

1894 Pérotin-Dumon, Anne. Course et piraterie dans le Golfe du Mexique et la Mer des Antilles (SHG/B, 53/54, 1982, p. 49–71, bibl.)

Effort to bring some order to very confusing topic by distinguishing phases and varieties of corsair activities in support of (and also against) Spanish American independence. At same time, seeks to underscore importance of phenomenon concerning which no adequate "vision globale" has yet appeared. [D. Bushnell]

1895 Rodríguez, Mario. The presence of the American Revolution in the contemporaneous Spanish world (PCCLAS/P, 6, 1977/1979, p. 15–24)

Cites evidence that Spanish officials in Charles III's reign did not, as commonly assumed, censor publication of books and newspaper articles detailing events of the American Revolution for the Spanish-reading public. [DEC]

1896 Salcedo-Bastardo, J.L. Bello y los "simposiums" de Grafton Street (CONAC/RNC, 41:247, abril/dic. 1981, p. 15–47)

Discusses encounter of Andrés Bello with Miranda in 1810—when he, along with Bolívar, went to London on diplomatic mission for Caracas patriots—and argues that Bello's subsequent dedication to Spanish American independence on continental scale reflected lasting influence of Precursor. [D. Bushnell]

1897 Shulgovski, Anatoli. Simón Rodríguez: hombre y pensador (URSS/AL, 12:48, 1981, p. 4–23, plate)

Along with biographical and historiographical details on Rodríguez, properly emphasizes his importance as a Latin American representative of utopian socialism. [D. Bushnell]

1898 Soto Cárdenas, Alejandro. Influencia de la independencia de los Estados Unidos en la constitución de las naciones latinoamericanas. Washington: Secretaría General, Organización de los Estados Americanos, 1979. 202 p.

Study of impact of US independence movement on Latin American political culture. Mostly study of Latin Americans who wrote about the Declaration of Independence and the American Constitution. Reveals general unawareness of 1970s scholarship. [JDR]

1899 Tanzi, Héctor José. El pensamiento europeo y su influencia en la emancipación americana (PAIGH/H, 92, julio/dic. 1981, p. 99–126)

Clear, brief, documented statement of thesis that traces theoretical basis of American governing juntas to Spanish "populist" political thought. Nothing Tanzi (and others) had not said before, but a convenient summary. [D. Bushnell]

1900 Zeuske, Max. Sobre el carácter del campesinado y los movimientos cam-

pesinos latinoamericanos en el siglo XIX (UCLV/I, 70, sept./dic. 1981, p. 195–202)

Outline treatment of changes in land tenancy and land use in 19th century and tensions this created among "peasantries." Author's definition of "peasant" is so flexible, his discussion includes both slaves and immigrant sharecroppers, and their protests. [JDR]

20TH CENTURY

1901 Baev, Iordan. Jorge Dimitrov y la lucha revolucionaria en América Latina (URSS/AL, 10:58, oct. 1982, p. 4–20)

Description of Bulgarian Communist who worked with party and union leaders from Latin America during 1920s and 1930s, and later became president of the Bulgarian Council of Ministers in 1946. [JDR]

1902 Bartley, Russell H. Acerca de la historia de las corrientes ideológicas en la Latinoamericanística (URSS/AL, 1:61, enero 1983, p. 31–37)

Sees close link between development of Latin Americanists in the US, topics they study, and US foreign policy interest in the area. [JDR]

1903 Bollinger, William and **Daniel Manny Lund.** Minority oppression: toward analyses that clarify and strategies that liberate (LAP, 9:2[33], Spring 1982, p. 2–28)

Intended as introduction of journal issue dealing with minority group oppression in the Americas from Marxian perspective. Examines difficulties inherent in a consideration and analysis of differences between "national oppression," oppression of socially defined racial groups, and oppression of indigenous peoples in the 20th century. [JDR]

1904 Elkin, Judith Laikin. A demographic profile of Latin American Jewry (AJA, 34:2, Nov. 1982, p. 231–248, tables)

Recounts efforts to estimate size of Jewish population in various Latin American countries during 20th century, and describes demographic characteristics of Jewish population based on the limited number of scientific studies which have been done. [JDR]

1905 García G., Rigoberto. La urbanización latinoamericana en la primera mitad del siglo XX. Stockholm: Institute of Latin

American Studies, 1979. 39 leaves: bibl., map (Research paper series; no. 15)

Very brief explanation of character of urban development in Latin America as reflecting the region's "ties of dependency." [JDR]

1906 Guerra Vilaboy, Sergio. Orígenes del movimiento obrero y comunista latinoamericano (Universidad de La Habana [Departamento de Actividades Culturales] 211, abril 1979/dic. 1980, p. 166–185)

Superficial study of beginnings of trade unions in Latin America, and regional confederations which emerged from them (1900–36). Solely based on secondary sources. [JDR]

1907 ———and **Alberto Prieto.** Cronología del movimiento obrero y de las luchas por la revolución socialista en América Latina y el Caribe, 1917–1939. La Habana: Casa de las Americas, 1980. 106 p.: bibl. (Colección Nuestros países. Serie Resumen)

Very brief study of attempts to form socialist unions in Latin America during the 1920s and 1930s. More than half is simple, country-by-country, chronology. [JDR]

1908 Halperin-Donghi, Tulio. "Dependency theory" and Latin American historiography (LARR, 17:1, 1982, p. 115–130)

Very intelligently written, brief analysis of intellectual origins of ideas of Gunder Frank and the Steins, and reception given their formulations by historians in Latin America, North America, and Europe. [JDR]

1909 Jeifets, Lazar. Para contar la verdad sobre la URSS (URSS/AL, 12:60, dic. 1982, p. 106–117)

Recounting of delegations from Latin America who visited the Soviet Union during 1920s to attend international congress, and their impressions of it. Entirely based on writings of some of these individuals and on Russian newspapers. [JDR]

1910 Manrique Castro, Manuel. De apóstoles a agentes de cambio: el trabajo social en la historia latinoamericana. Lima: Ediciones CELATS, 1982. 186 p.: bibl.

History of social work profession in Latin America. Sections discuss importance of Papal encyclicals of Leo XIII and Pius XI in the beginnings of the profession; establishment of Catholic schools of social work in Chile, Brazil, and Peru; and consequences of doctrine of "community development" transmitted from England to US. [JDR]

1911 Nunn, Frederick M. Yesterday's soldiers: European military professionalism in South America, 1890–1940. Lincoln: University of Nebraska Press, 1983. 365 p.: bibl., index.

Excellent study concerning the attitude of military men toward civilians and needs of the nation. Based on study of military journals and what their writings reveal about officers' thought and self-perceptions. Concludes that officers believe they have a universal role in their societies, are very uncomfortable with the present and idealize the past and tradition. [JDR]

1912 Scalabrini, Giovanni Battista. A emigração italiana na América. Tradução, notas e introdução de Redovino Rizzardo. Apresentação de Rovílio Costa. Porto Alegre: Escola Superior de Teologia São Lourenço de Brindes, 1979. 232 p.: ports. (Coleção Imigração italiana; 31)

Republication of writings of early 20th-century Italian bishop who promoted concern for the welfare of Italian immigrants in the Western Hemisphere. Not a great deal specifically on the life of immigrants in Latin America. [JDR]

1913 The Spanish Civil War, 1936–39: American hemispheric perspectives. Edited by Mark Falcoff and Frederick B. Pike. Lincoln: University of Nebraska Press, 1982. 357 p.: bibl., index.

Collection of six articles and introduction detail reactions to Spanish Civil War in the Americas. Countries covered include the US, Mexico, Cuba, Colombia, Peru, Chile, and Argentina. Articles are uniformly scholarly and provide a great deal of new information. [JDR]

MEXICO: General and Colonial Period

ASUNCION LAVRIN, *Associate Professor, Howard University*
EDITH B. COUTURIER , *National Endowment for the Humanities*

IN THIS VOLUME we can report a growing interest in special topic monographs. No major new work on any general topic covering the entire history of Mexico appeared during the period 1981–84. Most titles listed under the General Section are, therefore, indexes to documents, compilation of documentary sources, etc., which suggest a marked interest in making primary sources and bibliographical tooks accessible to scholars and students of history (see items **1914** and **1918**).

The new historical journal *Encuentro* (item **1917**) made its appearance in 1983, published by the Colegio de Jalisco, and devoted to the study of the region of Jalisco.

Similar interest in making sources available to historians is evident in the section covering works of general interest for the colonial period (i.e., Colonial Period: General). The task of cataloging sections of the National Archives of the Nation continues apace, and several indexes have appeared during this biennium (items **1925, 1926, 1927,** and **1942**). Other research centers and regional historical institutions are also moving in that direction. In addition to their work, there is that of scholars such as Torre Villar and Schwaller (see, for example, items **1923, 1940, 1947, 1949,** and **1950**). Of special interest is the collection of documents on the agricultural crisis of 1785–86, which puts in the hands of the researcher over 300 documents on that topic (item **1930**).

A noteworthy project concerned with quantifying sources for long-term trend analysis is being carried out by the Seminar on the History of Mentalities, at the Department of Historical Research in Mexico, under the direction of Solange Alberro. Several publications and working papers appearing since 1980, identify and statistically categorize the incidence of ecclesiastical control of expressions of sexual behavior, marriage, and family matters. The transgressions of the faithful, as recorded in the Inquisition's books are also included in these works (items **1922, 1935, 1936,** and **1943**). These works identify trends up to 1700, but do not analyze the meaning of the data, with the exception of Serge Gruzinki's, as mentioned below, and Solange Alberro's two works of inquisitorial control of bigamy and solicitation, and the Holy Office's activities in Zacatecas (items **1956** and **2036**). To this date these studies constitute the most intensive use of ecclesiastical sources.

Other inquiries into the history of the Church are represented by an institutional history of the Church in Oaxaca in the 18th century (item **1964**), the only attempt to cover an ecclesiastical topic in a broad manner. Works within a narrower focus, but of significance, are the following: Moreno de los Arcos (item **1919**); Burrus and Zubillaga (item **2043**); Martínez Rosales (item **2003**); Canterla (item **1929**); Brading (item **1961**); Churruca Peláez (item **1968**); and Inga Clendinen (item **1969**). A very sensitive treatment of the contrasts between precolumbian and colonial religious matrimonial norms and practices is that of Serge Gruzinski, whose works on religious mentalities are noteworthy (item **1983**). The 1982 Conference on The Church and Society, sponsored by the Tulane University Center for Latin American Studies, spurred a number of works on confraternities, reform of the clergy, evangelization, and others (items **1971, 1979, 1996, 2013,** and **2023**).

Institutional history was best represented by several studies of educational institutions (items **1928** and **1966**); a study on the municipal government of the city of Mexico (item **2014**); and one on the Accounting Tribunal (item **2021**). However, the best work in this category is that of Woodrow W. Borah, on the General Indians Court of Mexico, the result of many years of research (item **1924**).

Social historians continue to explore themes such as ethnic groups, labor, the family, and women, with noteworthy results. Specific studies on indigenous groups were not numerous this biennium, but a study of Indians in colonial Yucatán by Farriss set high standards of interpretation (item **1972**). Focusing on Yucatán's and Oaxaca's indigenous populations, other authors have written on migration patterns, landownership and social power, and the utilization of economic resources (items **1965, 2006,** and **2019**).

Several authors have successfully blended the study of labor and ethnic groups (items **2017, 2020,** and **2024**). The institution of the family was mostly studied in its elite manifestation by John Kicza (items **1991** and **1992**), and John Tutino (item **2030**). A short but pithy work is that of Thomás Calvo (item **1962**). On women, Muriel has provided us with a comprehensive survey of feminine culture, which is largely the culture of religious women (item **1941**). Sor Juana Inés de la Cruz inspired the latest work penned by Octavio Paz, which is likely to remain a much discussed biography (item **2011**). Also of interest are works by Lavrin and Clendinnen (items **1970** and **1995**).

Hacienda studies have largely concentrated on single units (items **1933, 1999,** and **2029**). However, Martin and García Bernal set their own works on the broader contexts of the development of large estates and the socioeconomic problems with indigenous communities (items **1974** and **2002**). Although difficult to categorize, the work by W. Trautmann, is an interesting attempt to tie the main threads of the geography and the history of one region (item **1951**). Of interest to economic historians were studies on copper mining, cattle entrepreneurs, and the exportation of capital to Spain (items **1934, 1959,** and **1963**). The most detailed study in this field was undoubtedly that of Linda Greenow, which successfully tied the study of credit to the study of society (item **1980**). A paucity of works on the independence period points to a lull in this area (items **1984, 1985,** and **1986**).

The most distinguished work on the North is the extensive study of Durango's settlement by Michael Swann, a very good example of the application of quantification to socioeconomic history (item **2057**). Ecclesiastical studies focused on missionary activities and indigenous acculturation, but no new ground was broken in this biennium (items **2038, 2042, 2051,** and **2058**). It is to be hoped that the noticeable decrease in studies on the northern frontiers will be superseded in the future.

GENERAL

1914 Aguilar Zarandona, Irene; Marcela Pellón Caballero; and **Alejandra Vigil Batista.** Indice del Archivo Parroquial de Zacualpan de Amilpas. México: Universidad Iberoamericana, Departamento de Historia, 1978. 110 p.: bibl., ill. (Cuadernos de trabajo; 1)

First in series of papers from history seminar of Iberoamericana University. Contains baptismal, matrimonial, and death records of town of Zacualpan Amilpas (Morelos) from the 16th through 20th centuries. Earliest baptismal record dates back to 1587. Also includes confraternity and religious organizations' records as well as civil birth registry begun in 1839. Well done archival guide. [AL]

1915 Arrigunaga Peón, Joaquín de. Demography and parish affairs in Yucatán, 1797–1897: documents from the Archivo de la Mitra Emeritense = Demografia y asuntos parroquiales en Yucatán, 1797–1897: documentos del Archivo de la Mitra Emeritense. Edited by Carol Steichen Dumond and Don E. Dumond. Eugene, Or.: Department of Anthropology, University of Oregon, 1982. 453 p.: bibl., ill. (University of Oregon anthropological papers; no. 27)

Censuses and statistical data from Campeche, Tabasco, Quintana Roo, and Yucatán for 1797–1897 period. Extremely useful for social history. [AL]

1916 Castillo, Gustavo del *et al.* La comarca lagunera: su historia. v. 1, Fuentes documentales y estudios. v. 2, Las haciendas algodoneras. v. 3, Análisis de su problemática. México: Centro de Investigaciones Superiores del INAH, 1979. 3 v.: maps (Cuadernos de la Casa Chata; 17/19)

Three volumes contain variety of primary and secondary sources for the study of the Lagunera region. For example, vol. 1 includes 1766 report of Nicolás Lafora and 1880 report. Vols. 2/3 consist of studies of cotton industry, ejido system, and other socioeconomic topics. [AL]

1917 Encuentro. Ciencias sociales y humanidades. Revista trimestral. El Colegio de Jalisco. Vol. 1, No. 1, oct./dic. 1983- . Guadalajara, México.

New journal published by El Colegio de Jalisco, devoted to interdisciplinary studies of Jalisco region. Accepts articles on literature, social sciences, and humanities, and will offer book review section. Among first contributors are Luis González, François Chevalier, Jean Meyer, and Thomas Calvo. [AL]

1918 Huerta, María Teresa *et al.* Balance y perspectivas de la historiografía social en México. Seminario de Historiografía Social, Departamento de Investigaciones Históricas, DEH-INAH. México: SEP, Instituto Nacional de Antropología e Historia, 1980. 2 v. (532 p.) (Colección Científica; 84. Fuentes Historia social)

Bibliographical essays on six themes of social history: historical demography, labor, education, welfare, social movements, and indigenismo. Essays survey material published up to 1973 only. Bibliography is largely in Spanish with sparse representation of works in English. [AL]

Kelsey, Harry. The Gregorian calendar in New Spain: a problem in sixteenth-century chronology. See item **2041.**

1919 Moreno de los Arcos, Roberto. Los territorios parroquiales de la ciudad arzobispal, 1325–1981 (Gaceta Oficial del Arzobispado de México [México] 5[22]:9/10, sept./oct. 1982, unpaged, maps)

Work deals with manner in which original spatial organization of Tenochtitlan affected religious division of Mexico City parishes. Includes process of confirmation, development, and secularization of parishes throughout 20th century. [AL]

1920 Münch G., Guido. La religiosidad indígena en el Obispado de Oaxaca durante la colonia y sus proyecciones actuales (UNAM/AA, 19, 1982, p. 185–205)

Traces the Church's relations with Oaxaca indigenous communities since conquest, highlighting persistence of aboriginal beliefs and practices, and role of religious confraternities in the community. Ends with description of contemporary confraternities, stressing continuity in area's cultural tradition. [AL]

COLONIAL PERIOD: GENERAL

1921 Aguirre, Carlos. La constitución de lo urbano: ciudad y campo en la Nueva España (Historias [Dirección de Estudios Históricos, Instituto Nacional de Antropología e Historia, México] 1, julio/sept. 1982, p. 30–40)

Inquiry into relationship between city and countryside. Argues that hegemony of former over latter was a consequence of postconquest socioeconomic forces channelled to serve the interest of dominant classes, invariably urban. [AL]

1922 Alberro, Solange B. de. La actividad del Santo Oficio de la Inquisición en Nueva España, 1571–1700. México: Instituto Nacional de Antropología e Historia, Departamento de Investigaciones Históricas, Seminario de Historia de las Mentalidades y Religión en el México Colonial, 1981. 272 p.: ill. (Colección Científica. Fuentes para la historia; 96)

Statistical measurement of incidence of transgressions recorded by the Inquisition from its inception through end of Hapsburg dynasty. Subjects covered are: heresy, idolatry, witchcraft, sexual crimes, bigamy, superstition, etc. Statistical information broken down according to: ethnic origin, geographical region, social status of accused, and incidence of occurrence. Useful analytical tool for those interested in social history. [AL]

1923 Alvarez, Víctor M. Diccionario de conquistadores. t. 1, Abarca-Laserna. t. 2, Ledesma-Zubia. México: Departamento de Investigaciones Históricas, INAH, 1975. 2 v. (612 leaves): bibl. (Cuadernos de trabajo; 8)

Biobibliographical dictionary of conquistadores arriving in New Spain between 1519–40. Information culled from archival and printed sources. Useful. [AL]

1924 Borah, Woodrow Wilson. Justice by insurance: the General Indian Court of colonial Mexico and the legal aids of the half-real. Berkeley: University of California Press, 1983. 479 p.: bibl., index.

In-depth study of the General Indian Court throughout colonial period. Surveys all court activities, paying special attention to its structure, procedures and policies. Firmly grounded in archival sources, work offers wealth of information and shows Borah's fine scholarship at its best. [AL]

1925 Bribiesca Sumano, María Elena. Catálogo de los Ramos Oficio de Soria y Oficio de Hurtado. México: Archivo General de la Nación, 1980. 84 leaves (Serie Guías y catálogos; 58)

Catalog of holdings of notarial offices of José I. Negreiros and Pedro Martínez de Soria covers 1732–1821 period. Most documents deal with collection of taxes (*alcabala*), but catalog also contains viceregal *bandos*, trade and mining documents, etc. [AL]

1926 ———; **Elisa Cruz Domínguez; Aurora Peña Alvarez;** and **Rosa María Navarrete.** Catálogo del Ramo Correspondencia de Virreyes, Marqués de Croix. v. 1/5. México: Archivo General de la Nación, 1980/1981. 5 v.: indexes (Serie Guías y catálogos; 56)

Index's volumes cover 1462 items of correspondence through 1771. [AL]

1927 ———; ———; and **Silva Ojeda Jiménez.** Indice del ramo alcaldes mayores. v. 1/7. México: Archivo General de la Nación, 1980/1981. 7 v. in 6: bibl., indexes (Serie Guías y catálogos; 53)

Index covers vols. 610-1578 of this

Ramo and a variety of themes: taxation, militias, appointment, reports, etc. Provides wealth of information on municipal administration. [AL]

1928 Canedo, Lino Gómez. La educación de los marginados durante la época colonial: escuelas y colegios para índios y mestizos en la Nueva España. México: Editorial Porrúa, 1982. 425 p.: bibl., index (Biblioteca Porrúa; 78)

Study of schools founded for the education of Indians and mestizos. Emphasizes 16th century and institutional history of these establishments. Thorough coverage based on a variety of primary and secondary sources. [AL]

1929 Canterla, Francisco. La Orden Hospitalaria de San Hipólito Mártir hasta la fecha de su reforma (EEHA/AEA, 37, 1980, p. 127–155)

Traces establishment and development of Bethlemite order through 1789, when process of internal reform was completed. Author is concerned with organizational problems faced by order, its relations with civil and religious authorities, and its eventual reform. [AL]

1930 La Crisis agrícola de 1785–1786: selección documental. v. 1/2. Enrique Florescano, compilador. Rodolfo Pastor, colaborador. México: Archivo General de la Nación, 1981. 2 v. (896 p.): bibl. (Colección Documentos para la historia; 1)

Consists of 311 documents from Mexico's National Archives and city's ex-ayuntamiento (city council) concerning 1785–86 agricultural crisis. Worthwhile contribution to social and economic history, this collection encompasses broad geographical coverage and impressive variety of documents. [AL]

1931 Crónicas de la conquista del Nuevo Reyno de Galicia. José Luis Razo Zaragoza y Cortés, compilador. Guadalajara, México: Gobierno del Estado de Jalisco, Instituto Jalisciense de Antropología e Historia, Universidad de Guadalajara, 1982. 343 p. (Colección histórica de obras facsimilares; 5)

Facsimile reproduction of collection of conquest chronicles first published 1963. Includes testimonies of Nuño de Guzmán and 10 participants in conquest of New Galicia (seven signed, three anonymous). [AL]

1932 Florescano Mayet, Enrique. Ensayos sobre la historiografía colonial de México. México: Departamento de Investigaciones Históricas, INAH, 1979. 77 p.: bibl. (Cuadernos de trabajo; 27)

Overview of development of colonial period historiography, starts with earliest chroniclers and ends with most recent researchers and interpreters. Bibliography is restricted to books. Author considers works in Spanish and English and includes a few works by other scholars. Useful survey with a sound critical base. [AL]

1933 García Morales, Soledad. Hacienda de Pacho (UV/PH, 45, enero/marzo 1983, p. 27–35, ill., tables)

Brief history of this hacienda, throughout colonial period, based on material found in notarial archives. Assessment of year 1780 has useful material. [AL]

1934 Garner, Richard L. Exportaciones de circulante en el siglo XVIII: 1750–1810 (CM/HM, 31:4, abril/junio 1982, p. 544–598, bibl., graphs, tables)

Revises data from several sources in effort to assess value of capital exported from Mexico to Spain in last half of 18th century. Appendices provide excellent comparative material. Concludes that the Mexican economy was negatively affected by drain of invaluable monetary resources. [AL]

1935 González Marmolejo, Jorge René. El delito de solicitación en los edictos del tribunal del Santo Oficio, 1576–1819 (*in* Alberro, Solange B. de et al. Seis ensayos sobre el discursos colonial relativo a la comunidad doméstica: matrimonio, familia y sexualidad a través de los cronistas del siglo XVI, el Nuevo Testamento y el Santo Oficio de la Inquisición. México: Departamento de Investigaciones Históricas, INAH, 1980, p. 169–211, appendix, graphs [Cuadernos de trabajo; 35])

Supplies data on number of inquisitorial edicts condemning solicitations of confessors while performing their spiritual tasks. Identifies periods of greater enactment of such edicts throughout colonial period, but does not analyze data in terms of social meaning. [AL]

1936 ——— and José Abel Ramos Soriano. Discurso de la Inquisición sobre el matrimonio, la familia y la sexualidad a través de los edictos promulgados por el tribunal del Santo Oficio, 1576–1819 (*in* Alberro, Solange B. de et al. Seis ensayos sobre el discurso colonial relativo a la comunidad doméstica: matrimonio, familia y sexualidad a través de los cronistas del siglo XVI, el Nuevo Testamento y el Santo Oficio de la Inquisición. México: Departamento de Investigaciones Históricas, INAH, 1980, p. 105–165, graphs, ill., tables [Cuadernos de trabajo; 35])

Classifies and analyzes Inquisitorial edicts on marriage, the family, and sexual matters, establishing long-term tabular statistics on promulgation of such edicts. Does not address judicial action or personal behavior of transgressors. [AL]

1937 Hoberman, Louisa Schell. Hispanic American political theory as a distinct tradition (JHI, 41:2, April/June 1980, p. 199–218)

Reviews changes in Spanish political theory through 18th century, describing gulf between theory and system of consultative politics. Using 17th-century *desagüe* project as example of operation of government, author observes that the horizontal and vertical distribution of power, as well as decentralization and overlapping jurisdictions resulted in inability to carry through planned flood control projects. Previous theorists on Hispanic American political tradition have assumed a consistency and an authority which only partially describes it. [EBC]

1938 ———. Technological change in a traditional society: the case of the desagüe in colonial Mexico (Technology and Culture [Society for the History of Technology, University of Chicago Press] 21:1, Jan. 1980, p. 386–407)

Fresh look at both politics and technology of 17th-century *desagüe* project which also discusses scientific and intellectual ideas governing Enrico Martínez's, Friar Andrés de San Miguels' and Adrien Booss' remedies to persistent flooding of Mexico City. Concludes that this extraordinary public work was not expanded because of cost, factionalism, and "social conservatism." [EBC]

1939 Maya, Carlos. Estructura y funcionamiento de una hacienda jesuita: San José Acolman, 1740–1840 (IAA, 8:4, 1982, p. 329–359, bibl., tables)

Comparison of profitability of one Jesuit hacienda complex with a number of similar enterprises. Based on primary sources of San José Acolman, author makes critical use of rich secondary material in order to address significant issues in Mexico's agricultural history. [EBC]

1940 Las Minas de Nueva España en 1774. Alvaro López Miramontes, Cristina Urrutia de Stebelski, compiladores. México: SEP, Instituto Nacional de Antropología e Historia, Departamento de Investigaciones Históricas, 1980. 203 p.: bibl., ill. (Colección científica; 83. Fuentes Historia económica)

Vol. 2 of three on sources for history of mining in colonial Mexico. Contains reports ordered by Viceroy Bucareli on Mexican mines in 1772. Among 12 mines represented are Sombrerete, Pachuca, Bolaños, Guanajuato, and Parral. [AL]

1941 Muriel, Josefina. Cultura femenina novohispano. México: Universidad Nacional Autónoma de México, 1982. 548 p., 24 p. of plates: ill. (some col.) (Serie de historia novohispana; 30)

Comprehensive survey of feminine cultural activities in colonial Mexico. Largely literary in character, they were mostly carried out by nuns as chroniclers of their orders, poets, cultivators of theology and mystical prose. Includes useful, little known quotations from such writings by lay and religious women. [AL]

1942 Ramírez Montes, Guillermina. Ramo Aguardiente de Caña. México: Archivo General de la Nación, 1981. 51 leaves: indexes (Serie Guías y catálogos; 60)

Deals with documentation resulting from 1794 establishment of tax on this alcoholic beverage. Documents furnish information on taxes, appointment of officials, policing of clandestine factories and royal orders. The 189 items in this ramo cover 1794–1820. [AL]

1943 Ramos Soriano, José Abel. Libros prohibidos sobre matrimonio, familia y sexualidad en los edictos promulgados por la Inquisición, 1575–1819 (*in* Alberro, Solange B. de *et al.* Seis ensayos sobre el discurso colonial relativo a la comunidad doméstica: matrimonio, familia y sexualidad a través de los cronistas del siglo XVI, el Nuevo Testamento y el Santo Oficio de la Inquisición.

México: Departamento de Investigaciones Históricas, INAH, 1980, p. 185–211, appendix, graphs [Cuadernos de trabajo; 35])

Quantifies frequency of prohibition by Inquisition of books on marriage and sexuality. Stresses that period of great persecution was second half of 18th century. Focuses on reporting numbers rather than analyzing their significance. [AL]

1944 Rieu-Millan, Marie-Laure. Une lettre inédite de Fray Servando de Mier, 1810 (UTIEH/C, 39, 1982, p. 65–73)

Unpublished letter of Fray Servando Teresa de Mier (dated Feb. 3, 1810) found in Chamber of Deputies archives, Madrid. Apparently, Fray Servando listed his "merits" and services to the Crown in an effort to become eligible for election as a Creole representative to the Cortes. [AL]

1945 Rivera Marín de Iturbe, Guadalupe. La propiedad territorial en México, 1301–1810. México: Siglo Veintiuno Editores, 1983. 357 p.: bibl. (Historia)

Synthesis of history of land tenure in Mexico emphasizes legislation regulating land ownership. Covers, among other topics, Aztec and Hispanic backgrounds, legal bases of communal and ecclesiastic property, and for formation of large haciendas. [AL]

1946 Rodríguez de Lebrija, Esperanza. Guía documental del Archivo Histórico de Hacienda. v. 1., No title. v. 2, Indice analítico. México: Archivo General de la Nación, 1981. 2 v. (Serie Guías y catálogos; 61)

Includes material not appearing in 1940 guide on Jesuits, collateral posted for official positions, Audiencia appointments, merchandise remittances, etc. [AL]

1947 Rojas Rabiela, Teresa. Indice de documentos para la historia del antiguo señorío de Xochimilco. Presentación de Teresa Rojas Rabiela y Juan Manuel Pérez Zevallos. México: Centro de Investigaciones y Estudios Superiores en Antropología Social, 1981. 174 p.: ill., index (Cuadernos de la Casa Chata; 43)

Lists documents belonging to Xochimilco available in 15 different sections of the national archives of Mexico, as well as in four foreign repositories. [AL]

1948 Sánchez Bella, Ismael. Visitas de la Audiencia de México: siglos XVI y XVII (EEHA/AEA, 32, 1975, p. 375–402)

Straightforward account of *visitas*, or visitations by royal emissaries to supervise administration of viceroys in the Indies. Covers all 16th and 17th-century visitas carried out in New Spain, although not in depth. Reports describing these visitas are not included. [AL]

1949 Schwaller, John Frederick and **Anne C. Taylor Schwaller.** Partidos y párrocos bajo la Real Corona en la Nueva España, siglo XVI. México: Instituto Nacional de Antropología e Historia, Departamento de Investigaciones Históricas, 1981. 614 p.: ill. (Colección científica. Fuentes Historia económica de México; 104)

Lists of all pay vouchers for parish priests in 16th-century Mexico available at Archives of the Indies, Seville. Provides information on personal priests, maps, parishes, etc. Efficiently indexed and organized. [AL]

1950 Testimonios históricos guadalupanos. Compilación, prólogo, notas bibliográficas e índices de Ernesto de la Torre Villar y Ramiro Navarro de Anda. México: Fondo de Cultura Económica, 1982. 1458 p.: bibl., index (Sección de obras de historia)

La más copiosa y autorizada compilación de escritos sobre la aparición de Nuestra Señora de Guadalupe. Testimonios precedidos de notas historiográficas redactadas con objetividad y conocimiento. La bibliografía guadalupana (47 p.) comprende libros y artículos notables. Valiosa guía para futuros análisis. [L. Gómez Canedo]

1951 Trautmann, Wolfgang. Las transformaciones en el paisaje cultural de Tlaxcala durante la época colonial: una contribución a la historia de México bajo especial consideración de aspectos geográfico-económicos y sociales. Wiesbaden: F. Steiner, 1981. 279 p.: ill. (Das Mexiko-Projekt der Deutschen Forschungsgemeinschaft = El Proyecto México de la Fundación Alemana para la Investigación Científica; 17)

Regional study of Tlaxcala area throughout colonial period. Use of ecological resources by several sectors of population forms understructure of this work. Themes such as landownership, crop production, town settlement, roads and communications, etc., provide a global perspective of the region. By stressing breadth rather than depth,

offers satisfactory overview that integrates geography and history. [AL]

1952 Trexler, Richard C. Alla destra di Dio: organizzazione della vita attraverso i Santi Morti in Nuova Spagna (QS, 17[50]:2, agosto 1982, p. 498–531)

Using ecclesiastical chronicles of Torquemada, Motolinia, Pérez Ribas, and Mendieta, Trexler interprets symbolic relation between life and death (including death rites) of missionaries who died "in odor of sanctity." This exploration of new territory in the history of religious beliefs is an interesting exercise in *mentalité* history. [AL]

1953 Van Young, Eric. Mexican rural history since Chevalier: the historiography of the colonial hacienda (LARR, 19:3, 1983, p. 5–61, bibl.)

Somewhat theoretical attempt to analyze studies of Mexican hacienda system published since 1952, especially since 1965. Discusses issues such as feudal vs. capitalist nature of hacienda system, debt peonage, rural laborer, regional differences, entrepreneurial histories, as well as sources used. By cumulating recent works, author contributes to a needed synthesis of Mexican rural history. [EBC]

1954 Wobeser, Gisela von. La formación de la hacienda en la época colonial: el uso de la tierra y el agua. México: Universidad Nacional Autónoma de México, Instituto de Investigaciones Históricas, 1983. 216 p., 1 leaf of plates: bibl., ill. (some col.), maps.

General survey of history of the hacienda's development in colonial Mexico. Its best part are its illustrations, handsomely printed and culled from the National Archives' rich map collection. [AL]

1955 Zavala, Silvio Arturo. Libros de asientos de la gobernación de la Nueva España: período del virrey don Luis de Velasco, 1550–1552. México: Archivo General de la Nación, 1982. 510 p.: bibl., facsims., indexes (Colección Documentos para la historia; 3)

Printed version makes accessible to all interested researchers manuscript collection of Viceroy Luis de Velasco's administrative legislation during 1550–52. Originals are part of Kraus Collection (Library of Congress, Manuscript Division, Washington). [AL]

CENTRAL AND SOUTH

1956 Alberro, Solange B. de. El discurso inquisitorial sobre los delitos de bigamia, poligamia y de solicitación (*in* Alberro, Solange B. de *et al.* Seis ensayos sobre el discurso colonial relativo a la comunidad doméstica: matrimonio, familia y sexualidad a través de los cronistas del siglo XVI, el Nuevo Testamento y el Santo Oficio de la Inquisición. México: Departamento de Investigaciones Históricas, INAH, 1980, p. 215–226 [Cuadernos de trabajo; 35])

Study of variety of punishments prescribed by the Inquisition in cases of bigamy and solicitation of women by their confessors. Stresses the Church's casuistic approach to such problems. [AL]

1956a Arnaldo y Sassi, Francisco. Demarcación y descripción de el Obispado de Mechoacán y fundación de su Iglesia cathedral: número de prebendas, curatos, doctrinas y feligrezes que tiene, y Obispos que ha tenido desde que se fundó [sic] (Bibliotheca Americana [Bibliotheca Americana, Inc., Coral Gables, Fla.] 1:1, Sept. 1982, p. 61–109, plate)

A 1649 description of Michoacán. Original manuscript is at Newberry Library, Chicago. Editorial annotations by Diego Rivero. [AL]

1957 Barba, Cecilia. Un acercamiento a la metodología de colonización: la primitiva obra hospitalaria de los franciscanos en la Nueva España (*in* The Church and society in Latin America. Edited by Jeffrey A. Cole. New Orleans: Center for Latin American Studies, Tulane University, 1984, p. 53–72)

Argues that hospitals designed by Franciscan missionaries served as centers of acculturation and Christianization. Contrasts precolumbian and Spanish concepts of disease, medicine, welfare, and religion in a *mentalité* analysis. [AL]

1958 Bargatzky, Thomas. Aguilar und Guerrero: zwei versprengte Spanier in Yukatan im Zeitalter der Conquista (DGV/ZE, 106:1/2, 1981, p. 161–175, bibl., map)

Describes itinerary of two shipwrecked Spaniards in Quintana Roo, evaluates innovations ascribed to one of them, and compares this data with early Polynesian contact history. [EBC]

1959 Barrett, Elinore M. Copper in New Spain's eighteenth-century economy: crisis and resolution (JGSWGL, 18, 1981, p. 73–96)

Well informed article on the role of copper in New Spain's mining industry. Furnishes data on location of mines, demand and supply, royal monopoly, technical problems, labor, etc. Most information refers to late 18th century. [AL]

1960 Brading, David A. The city in Bourbon Spanish America: elite and masses (ISA/CUR, 8:1, 1980, p. 71–85, bibl., tables)

Comparative look at 18th-century life in Mexico City and Lima. Examines urban industry, employment, social disorder, and religious life. Concludes that it was the lower strata of urban society rather than the apex which defined each city's individual characteristics. [Donald Chipman]

1961 ———. Tridentine Catholicism and enlightened despotism in Bourbon Mexico (JLAS, 15:1, May 1983, p. 1–22)

Offers examples of how late Bourbon kings carried out policy of religious reform by cutting down or restricting practices encouraged by Tridentine Catholicism. Discusses general policies of parish secularization, and restriction of popular practices such as processions, confraternity membership, etc. [AL]

1962 Calvo, Thomas. Familia y registro parroquial: el caso tapatío en el siglo XVIII (CM/RE, 3:10, primavera de 1982, p. 53–67)

Based on survey of the Guadalajara Sagrario's matrimonial records. Author assesses value of marriage institution, election of marital partner, and high rate of illegitimacy and concubinage, in order to shed light on the family as an institution of 17th-century New Galicia. Quantitative data base is not included in the study, which raises questions and answers them in a charming narrative style. [AL]

1963 ———. Le pré-capitalisme aux champs: un étrange "seigneur de troupeaux" mexicain (CDAL, 24, 1981, p. 167–183)

Utilizing a relatively unknown figure, that of Francisco Pareja y Rivera, author illustrates 18th-century career of cattle dealers in New Galicia, an entrepreneurial type neglected by historians. Uses notarial records as leading source of information. [AL]

1964 Canterla y Martín de Tovar, Francisco. La Iglesia de Oaxaca en el siglo XVIII. Sevilla: Escuela de Estudios Hispano-Americanos de Sevilla, Consejo Superior de Investigaciones Científicas, Caja Provincial de Ahorros de Huelva, 1982. 273 p., 11 leaves of plates: ill. (Publicaciones de la Escuela; 281)

History of the Church from the top down. Covers 18th century in chronological order, and deals with government of Bishops, tensions between regulars and seculars, secularization process, and general administration of the Bishopric. Based on sources available in Spain. [AL]

1965 Carmagnani, Marcello. Los recursos y los estrategias de los recursos en la reproducción de la sociedad india de Oaxaca (GEE/NA, 4, 1981, p. 263–280)

Study's main theme concerns survival strategies of Oaxaca's indigenous communities throughout colonial period. Stresses utilization of economic resources, dynamic relationship between domestic unities and communities, and role of institutions such as confraternities, community funds, and local markets. [AL]

1966 Castañeda Delgado, Paulino. El Colegio de San Juan de Letrán de México: apuntes para su historia (EEHA/AEA, 37, 1980, p. 69–126, ill.)

Succinct, mostly 16th-century history of school originally founded for educating mixed-blood boys, based largely on Archives of the Indies sources. [AL]

1967 Chiaramonte, José Carlos. En torno a la recuperación demográfica y la depresión económica novohispanas durante el siglo XVII (CM/HM, 30:4, abril/junio 1981, p. 561–604, bibl., tables)

Able discussion and synthesis of existing historical demography literature, and different interpretations offered by several authors of correlation between demographic and economic trends in 17th-century New Spain. [AL]

1968 Churruca Peláez, Agustín. Primeras fundaciones jesuitas en Nueva España, 1572–1580. México: Editorial Porrúa, 1980.

442 p., 14 p. of plates: bibl., ill., index (Biblioteca Porrúa; 75)

Comprehensive history of Company of Jesus' establishment in New Spain. Useful documentary appendices list names of Jesuits in New Spain and possessions of all the establishments in 1580. [AL]

1969 Clendinnen, Inga. Disciplining the Indians: Franciscan ideology and missionary violence in sixteenth-century Yucatán (PP, 94, Feb. 1982, p. 27–48)

Seeks explanation for Franciscan missionary violence as expressed in inquisitorial purges of idolatry (Yucatán, 1562). Examines ideology of 16th-century Franciscans and proposes that their unchallenged authority, strong zeal, and conception of Indians as children in a socio-religious context, help explain their unusual behavior. [AL]

1970 ———. Yucatec Maya women and the Spanish Conquest: role and ritual in historical reconstruction (Journal of Social History [University of California Press, Berkeley] Spring 1982, p. 427–442)

General delineation of meaning of everyday life for Yucatec Maya women in years after conquest. Author interprets meaning of daily rituals in order to contrast pre- and post-conquest situations, concluding that there was "subtle but real diminution in the status of the women of Yucatán" during period under study. [AL]

1971 Cummings, Victoria. An alternative path to success: careers in the sixteenth-century Church: a case study (in The Church and society in Latin America. Jeffrey A. Cole, editor. New Orleans: Center for Latin American Studies, Tulane University, 1984, p. 1–20)

Uses example of Archbishop Pedro Moya de Contreras in order to illustrate changing values of 16th-century Spanish bureaucracy which encouraged professionalization in an effort to consolidate royal power. Based on archival sources. [AL]

1972 Farris, Nancy M. Indians in colonial Yucatán: three perspectives (in Spaniards and Indians in southeastern Mesoamerica: essays on the history of ethnic relations. Edited by Murdo J. MacLeod and Robert Wasserstrom. Lincoln: University of Nebraska Press, 1983, p. 1–39 [Latin American studies series]

Overview of Maya society in colonial Yucatán emphasizes migration patterns and social organization. Underlies strength of indigenous cultural and political patterns, and their survival through slow adaptation to Spanish pressures, a process which may be unique to Yucatán. [AL]

1973 García-Abásolo González, Antonio Francisco. Resultados de una visita a Nueva Galicia en 1576 (EEHA/AEA, 36, 1979, p. 3–39)

Account of 1574 official visit to New Galicia mining area reveals province's socioeconomic fabric in late 16th century. Useful information on Chichimecs, administration of justice, and population. [AL]

1974 García Bernal, Manuela Cristina. Los comerciantes estancieros en Yucatán y la gran propiedad de Nohpat (Temas Americanistas [Universidad de Sevilla, Escuela de Estudios Hispanoamericanos] 4, 1984, p. 8–14)

Study of titles of large cattle property near Mérida indicates that by early 17th century, some merchants were already significant landowners and were incorporating themselves to encomendero elite. Based on archival sources. [AL]

1975 Garza, Mercedes de la. Palenque ante los siglos XVIII y XIX (CEM/ECM, 13, 1981, p. 46–65, bibl., ill.)

History of rediscovery of Palenque by many visitors and explorers who slowly unearthed the mysteries of this city. [AL]

1976 Gerhard, Peter. Un censo de la diócesis de Puebla en 1681 (CM/HM, 30:4, abril/junio 1981, p. 530–560, bibl., graphs, map)

Presents recently discovered 1681 census of Puebla in its entirety. Author's careful annotations and discussion of figures' meaning enhance work's value. [AL]

1977 Gómez Fregoso, José Jesús. Clavijero, aportaciones para su estudio y ensayo de interpretación. Guadalajara, México: Universidad de Guadalajara, 1979. 168, 13 p.: bibl.

Contains new translation of Clavijero's biography, written in Latin by his colleague Juan Luis Maneiro, several essays by author and documentary reprints of Clavijero's works. [AL]

1978 González Sánchez, Isabel. Tumulto de lost trabajadores eventuales de la hacienda de Santiago de Huamantla, Tlaxcala, 1796 (IAA, 8:4, 1982, p. 361–372, map)

Describes incident involving forced labor and concludes that protective legislation failed to prevent brutal treatment of villagers. Also includes descriptions of working conditions, based on interviews. [EBC]

1979 Greenleaf, Richard E. The Inquisition Brotherhood: Cofradía de San Pedro Mártir of colonial Mexico (AAFH/TAM, 40:2, Oct. 1983, p. 171–208)

Surveys confraternity's history from 1585 inception through 1837. By stressing institutional and financial structures of this elite institution, makes important contribution to New Spain's ecclesiastical and economic history. [AL]

1980 Greenow, Linda L. Credit and socioeconomic change in colonial Mexico: loans and mortgages in Guadalajara, 1720–1820. Boulder, Colo.: Westview Press, 1983. 249 p.: bibl., ill., index (Delplain Latin American studies; no. 12)

Study of credit network in Viceroyalty of Nueva Galicia. Surveys patterns of lending, interrelation of individuals, groups and institutions in credit market, and city-region relations, among other subjects. Based on period's mortgage records (*libros de hipotecas*), this is useful study which adds new dimension to colonial Mexico's economic history. [AL]

1981 Grunberg, Bernard. Las relaciones entre Cortés y sus hombres y el problema de la unidad en la conquista de México: febrero 1519-agosto 1521 (IGFO/RI, 43:171, enero/junio 1983, p. 301–314)

Analyzes personal, legal, socioeconomic factors that contributed to good relationship that existed between Cortés and his men, allowing him to exercise discipline and maintain unity among his forces during conquest of Mexico. [AL]

1982 ———. El universo de los conquistadores en la *Historia verdadera* de Bernal Díaz del Castillo (IGFO/RI, 39:155/158, enero/dic. 1979, p. 106–122)

By culling information from Bernal's narrative, author highlights personal daily experiences and values, making an interesting attempt to recreate the conquerors' personal universe. [AL]

1983 Gruzinski, Serge. Matrimonio y sexualidad en México y Texcoco en los albores de la conquista o la pluralidad de los discursos (in Alberro, Solange B. de et al. Seis ensayos sobre el discurso colonial relativo a la comunidad doméstica: matrimonio, familia y sexualidad a través de los cronistas del siglo XVI, el Nuevo Testamento y el Santo Oficio de la Inquisición. México: Departamento de Investigaciones Históricas, INAH, 1980, p. 19–74 [Cuadernos de trabajo; 35])

Surveys and interprets social and individual rules regulating several aspects of male-female relations among central Mexico's indigenous groups. Deals with topics such as moral codes of behavior, adultery, virginity, punishment for sexual transgressions, etc. Follows Foucault's interpretation of sexuality and society. Comprehensive and interesting study. [AL]

1984 Guedea, Virginia. José María Morelos y Pavón: cronología. México: Universidad Nacional Autónoma de México, Instituto de Investigaciones Históricas, 1981. 234 p., 2 folded leaves of plates: bibl., maps (Serie de historia moderna y contemporánea; 13)

Chronology of known events in José María Morelos' life. Includes relevant contemporary political and administrative data, which helps place Morelos in his times. Two maps of Morelos' maneuvers during his military campaigns complement work. Useful reference work. [AL]

1985 Hamnett, Brian R. Royalist counterinsurgency and the continuity of rebellion: Guanajuato and Michoacán, 1813–20 (HAHR, 62:1, Feb. 1982, p. 19–48)

Surveys strategies adopted by royalist army to pacify Michoacán area, highlighting the role of Iturbide. Concludes that royalist control was never total or effective. [AL]

1986 Hernández Ruigómez, Manuel. El primer paso del proceso independentista mexicana: el contragolpe de Gabriel de Yermo, 1808 (IGFO/RI, 41:165/166, julio/dic. 1981, p. 541–601)

Narrative of peninsular coup against Viceroy Iturrigaray. Attempts to see events through Gabriel Yermo's point of view. [AL]

1987 Herrejón Peredo, Carlos. Hidalgo: la justificación de la insurgencia

(CM/RE, 4:13, invierno de 1982, p. 31–53)

Traces roots of Hidalgo's ideology of 12th-century populism. [AL]

1988 Hordes, Stanley M. Historiographical problems in the study of the Inquisition and the Mexican crypto-Jews in the seventeenth century (AJA, 34:2, Nov. 1982, p. 138–152)

Surveys historical literature on 17th-century relations between crypto-Jews and Inquisition, noting interpretive problems caused by authors endorsing either black or white legend approaches to this historical issue. [AL]

1989 ———. The Inquisition as economic and political agent: the campaign of the Mexican Holy Office against the crypto-Jews in the mid-seventeenth century (AAFH/TAM, 39:1, July 1982, p. 23–38)

Interesting contribution to our knowledge of 1640s crisis explores Inquisition's motivations and activities in wake of Braganza rebellion. Concludes that although initial impetus towards persecution of crypto-Jews was political, desire for local profit from confiscated properties became chief incentive. [EBC]

1990 Jiménez, Alfredo. Política española y estructuras indígenas: el área maya en el siglo XVI (RUC, 28:117, enero 1979, p. 129–151, bibl.)

Argues for revision in methodological approach to study of colonial Maya society. Its many features were not destroyed by Spanish legal and religious policies. Processes of survival and adaptation to a new political situation merit further consideration from ethnohistorians. Recent ethnohistories of Mayan society are, in fact, using author's suggested new approach. [AL]

1991 Kicza, John E. Colonial enterpreneurs, families and business in Bourbon Mexico City. Albuquerque: University of New Mexico Press, 1983. 1 v.: bibl., ill., index.

Study of social composition and financial activities of merchants of Mexico City in 18th century's last decades. Covers broad spectrum of merchants and conveys realistic view of business community. Useful socioeconomic work based on archival sources. [AL]

1992 ———. The great families of Mexico: elite maintenance and business practices in late colonial Mexico City (HAHR, 62:3, Aug. 1982, p. 429–457, tables)

Composite portrait of Mexico City's elite families stresses socioeconomic underpinnings which allowed them to retain their preeminence. Examines political, familial, and social ties in detail. [AL]

1993 Kobayashi, José María. Dos empresas educativas en el México del siglo XVI (CM/RE, 3:9, invierno de 1982, p. 5–32)

General survey of establishment of educational centers for Indians in New Spain, with special reference to Santa Cruz, Tlatelolco, and San Nicolás, Michoacán. Based on author's book on education in New Spain (see *HLAS 38:2504*). [AL]

1994 Lameiras, José. Tuxpan y su vecindad en los primeros tiempos coloniales (CM/RE, 3:12, otoño de 1982, p. 5–43, bibl.)

Study stresses separateness of indigenous communities prior to Spanish colonization. Their unification after the conquest led to eventual internal homogeneization and separation from Spanish culture. Author uses Tuxpan's example to buttress argument. [AL]

1995 Lavrin, Asunción. Unlike Sor Juana?: the model nun in the religious literature of colonial Mexico (University of Dayton Review [Ohio] 16:2, Spring 1983, p. 75–92)

Compares Sor Juana's life and writings to those of other 17th and 18th-century nuns of New Spain, noting similarities and differences in their perception of religious life. [AL]

1996 ———. Worlds in contrast: rural and urban confraternities in Mexico at the end of the eighteenth century (in The Church and society in Latin America. Edited by Jeffrey A. Cole. New Orleans: Center for Latin American Studies, Tulane University, 1984, p. 99–124)

Surveys economic structure of rural confraternities in late 18th-century Archbishopic of Mexico, and contrasts it with much wealthier urban institutions. Examines confraternities of both Indians and whites in attempt to stress the economic significance of their social composition and geographical locations. [AL]

1998 López-Portillo y Weber, José. La rebelión de Nueva Galicia. México: Consorcio Minero Benito Juárez Peña Colorada,

1980. 637 p., 9 leaves of plates: ill. (some col.), indexes, maps, port. (Colección Peña Colorada)

Third ed. of 1939 work. Of historiographical interest. [AL]

1999 López Sarrelangue, Delfina. Una hacienda comunal indígena en la Nueva España: Santa Ana Aragón (CM/HM, 32:1, julio/sept. 1982, p. 1–38, bibl.)

Excellent study of Indian community hacienda. Discusses labor, internal administration, leases and other subjects with a wealth of information. Work based on broader study of Tlatelolco's indigenous community. [AL]

2000 McGovern-Bowen, Carolyn G. Mortality and crisis mortality in eighteenth-century Mexico: the case of Pátzcuaro, Michoacán. Syracuse, N.Y.: Department of Geography, Syracuse University, 1983. 50 leaves: bibl., ill. (Discussion paper; 82)

Demographic study of impact of several pandemics and famine outbreaks on 18th-century Pátzcuaro. Author furnishes mortality characteristics by race, sex, and age. Useful for local and comparative history. [AL]

2001 Marchetti, Giovanni. Hacia la edición crítica de la *Historia* de Sahagún (CH, 396, 1983, p. 1–36)

Critical analysis of writing process of Sahagún's *History* in its several versions. Of historiographical interest. [AL]

2002 Martin, Cheryl E. Haciendas and villages in late colonial Morelos (HAHR, 62:3, Aug. 1982, p. 407–428, tables)

Author dwells on antagonistic relationship between Indian villages and sugar *hacendados*. Pays special attention to labor issues. Sees conflict as essential feature of village-hacienda relations. [AL]

2003 Martínez Rosales, Alfonso. La Provincia de San Alberto de Indias de Carmelitas Descalzas (CM/HM, 31:4, abril/junio 1982, p. 471–543, bibl.)

Surveys establishment, development and decline of Carmelites in colonial Mexico, emphasizing their internal administration and their relations with Hapsburg and Bourbon dynasties. Useful synthesis based on primary sources. [AL]

2004 Mohar, Luz María. Modificaciones del tributo prehispánico en Oaxaca en el siglo XVI: el impacto de la conquista española. México: Centro de Investigaciones Superiores del INAH, 1979. 118 p.: ill. (Cuadernos de la Casa Chata; 16)

History of tribute in Oaxaca area based on printed summary source and secondary works. Offers global view of tribute during preconquest period and its evolution under the Spanish rule through end of 16th century. Informative, but does not supersede previous interpretations of tribute as an institution. [AL]

2005 Moreno, Roberto. La ciencia de la Ilustración mexicana (EEHA/AEA, 32, 1975, p. 25–41)

Periodization of development of late 18th-century science in New Spain. Moreno defines four periods: 1) background (1735–67); creole (1768–88); official (1788–1802); and synthesis (1803–21). Discussion of European interpretive models precedes the study. [AL]

2006 Münch, Guido. Tenencia de la tierra y organización social en Oaxaca durante la colonia (UNAM/AA, 17, 1980, p. 159–183)

Work's main argument is that kinship system of Oaxaca's socio-political power prior to conquest was substituted by another in which individuals used the land and paid taxes to Spanish Crown. Power base of pre-conquest elites was thus eroded with consequent reorganization of social classes. Author devotes special attention to cacicazgos, communal land use and role of the Marquesado in Oaxaca. [AL]

2007 Navarro García, Luis. El cambio de dinastía en Nueva España (EEHA/ AEA, 36, 1979, p. 111–168)

Detailed chronicle of New Spain's government administration during 1701–02 which marked transition from Hapsburg to Bourbon dynasty. [AL]

2008 ———. Los oficios vendibles en Nueva España durante la Guerra de Sucesión (EEHA/AEA, 32, 1975, p. 133–154)

Documents sales of office during Philip V's reign. Administrative reform planned by first Bourbon king did not succeed due to financial needs created by War of Succession. Includes detailed information on offices sold in New Spain during 18th century's first decade. [AL]

2009 O'Gorman, Edmundo. La incógnita de la llama *Historia de los indios de la Nueva España* atribuida a Fray Toribio Motolinía: hipótesis acerca de la fecha, lugar de composición y razón de ser de esa obra, y conjetura sobre quién debió ser el autor y cuál el manuscrito original. México: Fondo de Cultura Económica, 1982. 139 p.: bibl. (Colección Tierra firme)

Reiterates once again author's hypothesis and entangled conjectures about Motolinía's *Historia*, adding more of the same kind. Unfortunately, does not furnish proof. [L. Gómez Canedo]

2010 Palomo, Gerardo. Tributo y sociedad: notas en torno a una problemática del siglo XVI. México: Centro de Investigaciones y Estudios Superiores en Antropología Social, 1981. 88 p.: bibl. (Cuadernos de la Casa Chata; 38)

Monograph on labor, tribute, and use of natural resources in 16th-century New Spain. Argues that economic system of Spain and its colonies was precapitalist, with feudal tributary base. [AL]

2011 Paz, Octavio. Sor Juana Inés de la Cruz, o Las trampas de la fe. Barcelona: Seix Barral, 1982. 658 p., 32 p. of plates: ill., index (Biblioteca breve; 608)

Latest biography of notable poet-nun. Paz attempts to portray her life as representative of her period, and mixes historical and literary materials. Historical interpretation of 17th century is extremely subjective. Study's strength lies in its unsurpassed style rather than in its historical accuracy. For literary critic's comment, see item **5057**. [AL]

2012 Pérez Herrero, Pedro. Actitudes del Consulado de México ante las reformas comerciales borbónicas: 1718–1765 (IGFO/RI, 43:171, enero/junio 1983, p. 97–182)

Studies economic and ideological polemics over fleets, supply and demand of merchandise, and prices among different merchant groups involved in Spain-Mexico-Philippines trade. Seeks to establish correlation between commercial interests of those diverse groups and royal policies. Useful and well documented. [AL]

2013 Poole, Stafford. The Third Mexican
Provincial Council of 1585 and the reform of the Diocesan clergy (*in* The Church
and society in Latin America. Edited by
Jeffrey A. Cole. New Orleans: Center for
Latin American Studies, Tulane University,
1984, p. 21–37)

Study of Archbishop Moya de Con-
trera's role as a reformer of the clergy in late
16th-century New Spain, and efforts of Third
Mexican Council to institutionalize such reforms. [AL]

2014 Porras Muñoz, Guillermo. El gobierno
de la Ciudad de México en el siglo XVI.
México: Universidad Nacional Autónoma
de México, 1982. 515 p. (Serie de historia
novohispana; 31)

Study of anatomy of Mexico City's
municipal government in 16th century consists of two very useful sections comprising
over three-quarters of text: 1) chronology of
the cabildos and their members; and 2) biographical dictionary of municipal bureaucrats. [AL]

2015 Razo Zaragoza, José Luis. Crónica de
la Real y Literaria Universidad de
Guadalajara y sus primitivas constituciones.
Guadalajara, México: Universidad de Guadalajara: Instituto Jalisciense de Antropología
e Historia, 1980. 230 p., 23 leaves of plates:
bibl., facsims., ill. (some col.), ports. (Serie de
historia)

Second ed. of 1963 work. Its greatest
merit consists of providing ample quotations
from royal cédulas establishing the University and its complete Constitutions. [AL]

2016 Riccio, Alessandra. Due modi dell'es-
pressione Americana: Sor Juana Inés
de la Cruz e Fray Servando (Ecdotica e Testi
Ispanici [Atti del Convegno Nazionale della
Associazione Ispanisti Italiani, Verona] 18:2,
giugno 1981, p. 187–200)

Comparative study of lives and
thoughts of Sor Juana and Fray Servando as
examples of criollo consciousness in two
modes of expression. [AL]

2017 Riley, James D. Crown law and rural
labor in New Spain: the status of
gañanes during the eighteenth century
(HAHR, 64:2, May 1984, p. 259–286)

Surveys changing character of *gañanía*
labor system from late 17th century through
end of colonial period. Sees important

changes in legislation affecting gañanes, with
increased relaxation of forced Indian residence and labor in haciendas. Based on archival sources. [AL]

2019 Robinson, David J. Indian migration in
eighteenth-century Yucatán: the open
nature of the closed corporate community (*in*
Studies in Spanish American population history. Edited by David J. Robinson. Boulder,
Colo.: Westview Press, 1981, p. 149–173, ill.,
tables [Dellaplain Latin American studies;
no. 8])

Focuses on internal Indian migration
within 18th-century Yucatán. Based on data
from four communities and thousands of
cases found in parish church records.

Suggests migration expressed desire to
escape labor and tax exploitation. [AL]

2020 Salvucci, Richard J. Aspectos de un
conflicto empresarial: el obraje de
Balthasar De Sauto y la historia social de San
Miguel El Grande (EEHA/AEA, 36, 1979,
p. 405–443)

Using suit and official investigation of
administration of obraje and its owner, author draws rich picture of colonial society in
provincial town of San Miguel el Grande. Information on social and economic influence
of town's elite and meaning of obraje industry
are intertwined in narrative. [AL]

2021 Sánchez Bella, Ismael. El tribunal de
Cuentas de México (*in* Congreso Venezolano de la Historia, 4th, Caracas, 1980.
Memoria [see item 2621] v. 3, p. 63–121,
bibl.)

Thorough study of Accounting Office
in 16th-century New Spain. Discusses its internal organization, functions, bureaucrats,
and problems facing this governmental office
in discharge of duties. Based on Spanish archival sources. [AL]

2022 Schwaller, John Frederick. Heirs of
conquerors (Southeastern Latin Americanists [Southeastern Conference of Latin
American Studies, Gainesville, Fla.] 27:1,
June 1983, p. 1–9)

Contrary to previous assumptions that
conquistadors' heirs declined in wealth and
power in 16th century, it appears that they
retained a significant position in colonial society. Schwaller identifies a number of descendants of early conquistadors and settlers

as late 16th-century bureaucrats and explains process of retaining elite status. [AL]

2023 ———. The implementation of the Ordenanza del Patronazgo in New Spain (*in* The Church and society in Latin America. Edited by Jeffrey A. Cole. New Orleans: Center for Latin American Studies, Tulane University, 1984, p. 39–50)

Study of the structure and implementation of the Ordenanza del Patronazgo, set of rules devised by the Crown to recognize and secularize the Church, and improve quality of the clergy. Article highlights Archbishop Moya de Contreras' role in its enforcement. [AL]

2024 Seed, Patricia. Social dimensions of race: Mexico City, 1753 (HAHR, 62:4, Nov. 1982, p. 569–606, tables)

Survey of relationship between occupation and ethnic affiliation in 18th-century Mexico. Social perception of race was partly determined by patterns of employment. Breakdown of work-force data by sex and ethnic groups makes interesting analysis of 1753 census, the basis of this study. [AL]

2025 Soberanes Fernández, José Luis. El estatuto del Regente de la Audiencia de México: 1776–1821 (EEHA/AEA, 32, 1975, p. 415–446)

In-depth study of post of *regente*, administrative position in Audiencias, established in 16th-century Spain, but which reached its American possessions in late 18th century. Thoroughly covers the post's regulations, prerogatives and duties, and surveys Mexican *regentes* from 1776 through end of colonial period. [AL]

2026 Taylor, William B. Bandit gangs in late colonial times: rural Jalisco, Mexico, 1794–1821 (Bibliotheca Americana [Bibliotheca Americana, Inc., Coral Gables, Fla.] 1:2, Nov. 1982, p. 29–57, maps, plates, tables)

Deals with highway robbery and banditry in Guadalajara area in late colonial period (1790–1820). Devotes special attention to analysis of social composition of bandits such as age, marital status, previous occupation, and strategies used in their activities. [AL]

2027 Téllez Xirón, Diego. Exterminio de la embriaguez. Versión paleográfica de

Rafael Aguayo Spencer. México: M. Porrúa, 1981. 24, 30 p.: ill.

First printing of inquiry on drunkenness and decree to ban it with facsimile reproduction of original. Lacks introductory essay or historical apparatus. [AL]

2028 Torre Villar, Ernesto de la. Los señores del México antiguo en la obra de Diego García Panes (EEHA/AEA, 34, 1977, p. 665–694, appendix, ill.)

Introduction to work of Diego García Panes (1730–1811), bureaucrat and historian of precolumbian civilizations and conquest of Mexico. In this study, author assesses value of García Panes' contribution as source for succeeding historians. Appendix includes Panes' biographies of Aztec lords. [AL]

2029 Trautmann, Wolfgang. Genese und kolonialzeitliche Entwicklung der Hacienda in Tlaxcala, Mexiko (SJUG, 32:2, 1981, p. 117–129)

Contribution from German Tlaxcala-Puebla Project explores early years of hacienda organization. [EBC]

2030 Tutino, John. Power, class, and family: men and women in the Mexican elite, 1750–1810 (AAFH/TAM, 39:3, Jan. 1983, p. 359–382)

Maintains that noble women never wielded the extensive patriarchial power enjoyed by men. Cites examples from members of Reglas, Jalas, and Sánchez Espinosa's families, but discusses extensively special events in Counts of Santiago family, that permitted a younger daughter to control family estates (1797–1803). Points out limitations on her authority and its evanescent character. [EBC]

2031 Tyrakowski, Konrad. Aspekte einer angepassten touristischen inwertsetzung des kirchlich: archäologischen komplexes von San Miguel del Milagro und Cacaxtla im staat Tlaxcala, Mexiko (IAA, 8:4, 1982, p. 373–403, bibl., maps, plates)

Another German Puebla-Tlaxcala Project contribution which deals with internal migration and pilgrimage sites. Contains archaeological, ecological, and historical data. [EBC]

2032 Van Young, Eric. Conflict and solidarity in Indian village life: the Guadalajara region in the late colonial period (HAHR, 64:1, Feb. 1984, p. 55–80)

Study of inner strife within Indian villages and means used by communities to deflect such conflict to outside objects through litigation. Notes differences between elites and non-elites within villages. Uses sociological models and archival sources to buttress theoretical bases. [AL]

2033 Weckmann, Luis. Las esperanzas milenaritas de los Franciscanos de la Nueva España (CM/HM, 32:1, julio/sept. 1982, p. 89–105, bibl.)
Revisitation of subject of milleranism in the Franciscan Order. Surveys well known authors and sources. [AL]

2034 Zavala, Silvio. Hernán Cortés ante la justificación de su conquista (PAIGH/H, 92, julio/dic. 1981, p. 49–69)
Traces scholastic roots of legal arguments used by Cortés (among other conquistadors) to exact suzerainty from the Indians. Argues that by mid-17th century the Crown had switched to a "pacifist" explanation for its territorial expansion. [AL]

NORTH AND BORDERLANDS

2035 Alatriste, Oscar. Desarrollo de la industria y la comunidad minera de Hidalgo del Parral durante la segunda mitad del siglo XVIII, 1765–1810. México: Universidad Nacional Autónoma de México, 1983. 180 p.: ill. (Seminarios / Facultad de Filosofía y Letras)
Study of renaissance of wealthy mining district of Parral. Continues Robert West's work, and benefits from data available after Tribunal de Minería's establishment. Contains data on variety of economic issues, including technology, comparative production figures, labor, as well as defense. Concludes that royal policies were successful in regard to Parral. [EBC]

2036 Alberro, Solange B. de. Zacatecas, "zone frontière," d'après les documents d'Inquisition, XVᵉ et XVIIᵉ siècles (CDAL, 24:2, 1981, p. 185–219)
Article's thesis is that those seeking relief from period's ideological constrictions (largely 17th century) went to such frontier zones as Zacatecas, where distances and less effective surveyance was likely to produce greater freedom of expression and behavior. Based on Inquistorial records. [AL]

2037 Baegert, Jacob. The letters of Jacob Baegert, 1749–1761: Jesuit missionary in Baja California. Translated by Elsbeth Schulz-Bischof. Introduced and edited by Doyce B. Nunis, Jr. Los Angeles: Dawson's Book Shop, 1982. 236 p.: bibl., ill. (some col.) (Baja California travels series; 45)
Letters of Alsatian missionary written during his 12-year tenure in Baja California. His careful descriptions are useful source of information on indigenous cultures. [AL]

Cortés Alonso, Vicenta. Fuentes documentales españoles para la historia de los Estados Unidos. See item **67a.**

2038 Guest, Francis F. Cultural perspectives on California mission life (HSSC/SCQ, 65:1, Spring 1983, p. 1–65)
Discusses cultural heritage of Spanish missionaries in effort to create historical understanding of mission life. Dwells on concepts of patriarchal rule, spirituality, punishment, etc., as key for understanding missionary-Indian relationships. [AL]

2039 Hernández Aparicio, Pilar. Los viajes de Don Isidro de Atondo y Antillón a California, 1683–85 (EEHA/AEA, 37, 1980, p. 3–43)
Descriptive rather than analytical account of 17th-century exploration of California, utilizing AGI and other archival materials, as well as secondary works written on subject. [EBC]

2040 Jenkins, Myra Ellen. Some eighteenth-century New Mexico women of property (in Hispanic arts and ethnohistory in the southwest: new papers inspired by the work of E. Boyd. Edited by Marta Weigle, Claudia Larcombe, and Samuel Larcombe. Santa Fe, N.M.: Ancient City Press, 1983, p. 335–345)
Mining New Mexico archives, author finds four women of property and influence and attempts short biographies comparing their business successes. [EBC]

Jones, Oakah L., Jr. Hispanic traditions and improvisations on the *frontera septentrional* of New Spain. See item **1114.**

2041 Kelsey, Harry. The Gregorian calendar in New Spain: a problem in sixteenth-century chronology (UNM/NMHR, 58:3, July 1983, p. 329–352, tables)
Change from Julian to Gregorian calendar in 1582 posed dating problems for his-

torians. Kelsey explains how change affected dating of Antonio de Espejo's and Diego Pérez de Luján's reports on New Mexico. [AL]

2042 McCarty, Kieran. A Spanish frontier in the Enlightened Age: Franciscan beginnings in Sonora and Arizona, 1767–1770. Washington: Academy of American Franciscan History, 1981. 116 p., 1 p. of plates: bibl., ill., index (Monograph series; v. 13)

History of process of replacement of Jesuit missionaries by members of Franciscan order after former were expelled from the Spanish colonies. Emphasizes problems faced by Franciscans in transition period as missionaries in area previously closed to them. [AL]

Meier, Matt S. Bibliography of Mexican American history. See item **30**.

2043 Misiones mexicanas de la Compañia de Jesús, 1618–1745: cartas e informes conservados en la "Colección Mateu." Edición preparada por Ernest J. Burrus y Félix Zubillaga. Madrid: J. Porrúa Turanzas, 1982. 349 p.: bibl., index (Colección Chimalistac de libros y documentos acerca de la Nueva España; no. 41)

Consists of 39 documents, fully annotated and indexed, on Jesuit missions in Sinaloa, Sonora, Chihuahua, Pimería Alta, Nayarit and California (1744–45). Original source is Coleción Mateu, Barcelona, most of which remained unpublished until now. [AL]

2044 Ortiz, Roxanne Dunbar. Roots of resistance: land tenure in New Mexico, 1680–1980. Los Angeles: Chicano Studies Research Center Publications, University of California: American Indian Studies Center, University of California, 1980. 202 p.: bibl., index (Monograph / Chicano Studies Research Center Publications; no. 10)

Popularly written book traces New Mexican social, economic, and population history, with discussions of policy and politics sometimes included. Based largely on secondary sources. [EBC]

2045 Portillo, Alvaro del. Descubrimientos y exploraciones en las costas de California, 1532–1650. Madrid: Ediciones Rialp, 1982. 538 p.: bibl., ill., indexes.

Reissue of original work published over 25 years ago. Author incorporates new materials and bibliographical references. Sur-

veys all discovery expeditions of California up to 1650. [AL]

2046 Prem, Hanns J. *Con mesa, aguijón y triangulo filar:* die kolonialzeitliche Grenze zwischen Huejotzingo und Tlaxcala (IAA, 7:1/2, 1981, p. 151–168, bibl., ill.)

Another German Puebla-Tlaxcala Project contribution which reconstructs the frontiers from historic documents of 1545 and 1762. Interesting contribution to historical geography of New Spain. [EBC]

2047 Radding, Cynthia. Las estructuras socioeconómicas de las misiones de la Pimería Alta, 1768–1850. Hermosillo, México: Instituto Nacional de Antropología e Historia, Centro Regional del Noroeste, 1979. 130 p., 18 leaves, 6 leaves of plates: ill., maps (Noroeste de México; no. 3)

Solid study of Pimería Alta missions. Author's thesis is that during period under study missions became mestizo towns based on private property, undergoing profound ethnic and socioeconomic change. [AL]

2048 Reinhard, Liehr. Staatsverschuldung und Privatkredit: die *Consolidación de vales reales* in Hispanoamerika (IAA, 6:2, Abr. 1980, p. 149–185, bibl.)

Claims that 1804–08 *Consolidación de vales reales* destroyed system of private credit and opened path for invasion of British capital. Based on newly discovered AGI documents in Patronato which give final details of monies shipped to Spain during these years. [EBC]

2049 Ribes Iborra, Vicente. Ambiciones estadounidenses sobre la Provincia Novohispana de Texas. México: Universidad Nacional Autónoma de México, 1982. 91 p.: bibl. (Cuadernos. Serie documental / Instituto de Investigaciones Históricas; no. 7)

Documentary selection from Spanish archives support author's thesis that US had expansionist thoughts on northern New Spain since early 19th century. Documents cover period 1803–20, and reflect Spanish perceptions of colonization in Texas and North American attitudes about Spanish colonies. [AL]

2050 Riley, Carroll L. and Joni L. Manson. The Cibola-Tiguex Route: continuity and change in the Southwest (UNM/NMHR, 58:4, Oct. 1983, p. 347–367)

Deals with precolumbian trade routes, as they established important human and trade connections, and continued to be used by Spaniards and by contemporary North Americans. [AL]

2051 Río, Ignacio del. Aculturación e integración socioeconómica de los chichimecas en el siglo XVI (UNL/H, 22, 1981, p. 255–268)

Highlights role of missionaries in weaning Chichimecs away from nomadism. Based on well known sources for general readership. [AL]

2052 Sánchez, Jane C. Spanish-Indian relations during the Otermín Administration, 1677–1683 (UNM/NMHR, 58:2, April 1983, p. 133–152)

Author uses Indian witnesses' depositions to assess the complex quality of Spanish-Indian relations after 1680 Pueblo revolt. [AL]

2053 Saravia, Atanasio G. Obras. v. 1/3, Apuntes para la historia de la Nueva Vizcaya. México: Universidad Nacional Autónoma de México, 1978/1980. 3 v.: bibl., ill. (some col.) (Nueva biblioteca mexicana; 66/72, 77)

Collection of 29 historical essays by Atanasio Saravia, historian of northern Mexico. Useful for potential history of historiography in Mexico. [AL]

2054 Snow, David H. A note on encomienda economics in seventeenth-century New Mexico (in Hispanic arts and ethnohistory in the Southwest: new papers inspired by the work of E. Boyd. Edited by Marta Weigle, Claudia Larcombe, and Samuel Larcombe. Santa Fe, N.M.: Ancient City Press, 1983, p. 347–357, tables)

Revisionist view of New Mexico's encomienda uses population estimates and relatively detailed information on wealth of encomiendas to conclude that tribute burden may not have been as onerous as previously

thought. Thorough and well researched contribution to encomienda studies. [EBC]

2055 Spiess, Lincoln Bunce. A group of books from colonial New Mexico (in Hispanic arts and ethnohistory in the Southwest: new papers inspired by the work of E. Boyd. Edited by Marta Weigle, Claudia Larcombe, and Samuel Larcombe. Santa Fe, N.M.: Ancient City Press, 1983, p. 359–377, ill.)

Catalog and description of 33 books dating from 15th to 19th centuries used by Franciscan missionaries. [EBC]

2056 Stoddard, Ellwyn; Richard L. Nostrand; and Jonathan P. West. Borderlands sourcebook: a guide to the literature on northern Mexico and the American Southwest. Norman: University of Oklahoma Press, 1983. 446 p.: bibl., ill., index, tables.

Extensive interdisciplinary bibliography. Includes 59 essays on archaeology, history, economics, geography, etc. Very useful. [AL]

2057 Swann, Michael M. Tierra adentro: settlement and society in colonial Durango. Boulder, Colo.: Westview Press, 1982. 444 p.: bibl., ill., index (Dellplain Latin American studies; no. 10)

Throughly researched and analyzed study of Durango settlement and population. Devotes special attention to demographic matters but also examines socioeconomic aspects of growth and development. Highly commendable study. [AL]

2058 Zorrilla, Juan Fidel. Crónica de Tamaholipa (UNL/H, 22, 1981, p. 239–254)

Contribution to early history of northeastern Tamaulipas emphasizes important role of Fray Andrés Olmos and Luis de Carvajal, as well as reviewing the archaeological, ethnographic, and historical evidence on ethnic origins of the Huasteca's indigenous peoples. [EBC]

MEXICO: 19th Century, Revolution and Post-Revolution

RICHARD E. GREENLEAF, *Director, Center of Latin American Studies, Tulane University*
DON M. COERVER, *Associate Professor of History, Texas Christian University*

MAJOR STUDIES OF POLITICS and diplomacy in foreign relations appeared during the recent biennium. Among the most important were Freidrich Katz on European and North American influences on the Revolution (item **2221**); T.G. Powell on Mexican relations with Spain during the Spanish Civil War (item **2260**); and Donathan Olliff on US-Mexican relations during the Reform (item **2125**). The Archivo General de la Nación has published guides to three archival collections: *Archivo de Alfredo Robles Domínguez* (item **2239**); *Catálogo de la Serie Armas, Fondo Presidentes Alvaro Obregón, Plutarco Elías, 1920–1928* (item **2241**); and *Archivo de Genovevo de la O* (item **2240**). Also appearing were the long awaited English translation of Robert Potash's study of the Banco de Avío (item **2132**) and the final three volumes of *Fuentes de la historia contemporánea* compiled under the direction of Stanley R. Ross (item **2274**).

Comprehensive studies on the 19th century include Stuart Voss on regional developments in Sonora and Sinaloa (item **2161**); McAfee's and Robinson's source book on the Mexican War (item **2127**); Harold Sims' work on the expulsion of the Spanish (items **2144** and **2145**); Frank Samponaro on Santa Anna and the Federalists (item **2141**); Jean Meyer on the application of Ley Lerdo (item **2120**); D.C.M. Platt on British finances (item **2130**); Cathryn Thorup on US-British economic competition (item **2153**); and George Paulsen's articles on US mining claims (items **2128** and **2256**). Bell and Smallwood examine a major border problem in the second half of the 19th century in their discussion of the "Zona libre" (item **2066**). Regional and economic studies of the Porfiriato continue to be the focus of research. Among the best were Ian Jacobs' revisionist treatment of the revolt against Díaz in Guerrero (item **2218**); Thomas Benjamin on the plight of mahogany workers in Chiapas and Tabasco (item **2176**); William Bluestein on class relations in Morelos (item **2177**); and Donald Stevens on agrarian policy and pressures in San Luis Potosí (item **2149**). Also useful is John Coatsworth on the economic impact of railroad development (item **2078**). Solid historiographical studies on the Porfiriato include those by Enrique Florescano and Stuart Voss (items **2090** and **2161**).

The economic development of the Yucatán was the center of research and debate. Massively researched works include Gilbert Joseph's study of the Revolution (item **2110**) and articles by Joseph and Allen Wells on International Harvester's role in the economy based on documents from the company (item **2112**). Rejoinders to the articles were written by Brannon and Baklaoff (item **2179**) and Carstensen and Roazen-Parrillo (item **2074**). At issue in the debate is the extent to which Harvester controlled production of henequen. Also valuable is A.J. Graham Knox's analysis of agrarian reform in the Yucatán (item **2207**). Major economic studies of the 20th century include Clifford Trow on the protection of US properties (item **2292**); Stephen Kane on US-Mexican relations in the petroleum industry (item **2220**); Dale Story on industrial elites in Mexico (item **2287**); Ian Roxborough and Ilan Buzberg on union militancy during the recent economic crisis (item **2275**).

The state, political parties, and nationalism were the subject of attention in works by González Casanova (item **2204**), Tardanico (item **2291**), Hamilton (item **2211**), and Basáñez (item **2173**). David Levy, Donald Mabry, and Mary Kay Vaughan produced excellent studies on state-university relations (items **2227, 2228,** and **2296**). W. Dirk Raat has published an extensive research-guide to recent scholarship in Mexican history, 1876–1940 (item **2226**), as well as a comprehensive study of Mexican revolutionary exile activity in the early decades of the 20th century (item **2267**).

Studies of the Borderlands and issues in Mexican migration to the US have continued to attract scholars, but the quality of the works varied substantially in the last biennium. Some of the best studies of the Borderlands were David J. Weber on the American Southwest under Mexican rule (item **2164**); Harris and Sadler on revolutionary activities in El Paso (item **2213**); and Douglas W. Richmond on Carranza's border policies (item **2270**). Ellwyn Stoddard *et al.* have edited an extensive bibliography of source materials on the Borderlands (item **2068**). Studies of migration topics include Arnoldo de León on the attitudes of whites towards Mexicans in 19th-century Texas (item **2083**); Mario García on Mexican immigrants to El Paso (item **2094**); Niles Hanson on the effects of undocumented workers on the border economy (item **2212**); Francisco Balderrama on the protection of Mexicans in Los Angeles during the Great Depression (item **2172**); and Juan Ramón García on the deportation of Mexicans during Operation Wetback in 1954 (item **2201**). There was continuing emphasis on Mexican labor history. While Carrillo Azpéitia surveyed Mexican labor in the 19th century, there were new installments in the series *La clase obrera en la historia de México* dealing primarily with the 20th century (item **2185**).

The historiography of Mexican education grew with the publication of three major works. Vaughan offers a revisionist interpretation of the relationship between Porfirian and revolutionary education, focusing on the supposedly revolutionary education programs of the 1920s (item **2296**). Levy and Mabry are primarily concerned with the issue of university autonomy especially as it relates to UNAM (items **2227** and **2228**); both authors conclude that UNAM has enjoyed considerable success in maintaining its autonomy in the face of an "authoritarian" state.

David R. Lessard, Research Associate of the Center for Latin American Studies at Tulane University deserves major credit for screening literature and writing this section during 1983–84.

19TH CENTURY

2059 Aldana Rendón, Mario. Economía y política en Jalisco a fines del siglo XIX: pt. 1 (Boletín del Instituto de Estudios Sociales [Universidad de Guadalajara, México] 1, enero, marzo 1980, p. 17–26)

General sketch of events in Jalisco from Reform period until onset of Mexican Revolution.

2060 Ampudia M., José Enrique. La penitenciaría de México: 1882–1911 (MAGN/B, 5[4]:18/6[1]:18, oct./dic. 1981-enero/marzo 1982, p. 5–8, facsim., plates)

Brief sketch of creation and inauguration of penitentiary in Mexico City.

Arreola, Daniel D. Landscapes of nineteenth-century Veracruz. See *HLAS 45 : 5086.*

———. Nineteenth-century townscapes of eastern Mexico. See *HLAS 45 : 5087.*

2061 Atlacomulco: inventarios generales de los archivos municipal y parroquial. México: Biblioteca Enciclopédica del Estado de México, 1980. 150 p., 81 p.: ill.

Guide to municipal and Church archives. Documents cover 19th and 20th centuries. Church documents have references to colonial period.

Avila H., Julieta; Beatriz Cano S.; ad **María Eugenia Fuentes B.** Acolman: fuentes para su historia. See *HLAS 45 : 36.*

2062 Bakewell, Peter. An interview with Silvio Zavala (HAHR, 62:4, Nov. 1982, p. 553–568, bibl.)

Interview covers Zavala's views on his past and recent work, historiography of Mexican history, and teaching of history. Includes bibliography of Zavala's works.

2063 Baldwin, Deborah. Broken traditions: Mexican revolutionaries and Protestant allegiances (AAFH/TAM, 40:2, Oct. 1983, p. 229–258)

Study of growth of Protestantism in Mexico (1870–1910), social and economic characteristics of Protestant congregations, links between Protestant church establishment and revolutionaries, and role of Protestants in Revolution. Inclusion of Protestants in Revolutionary leadership created fear among Catholics. However, Protestant church organization offered some solutions to the rebels' problems.

2064 Bancos obreros (CEHSMO, 4:16, mayo 1979, p. 40)

Collection of articles on workers' banks in periodicals (1877–84).

2065 Beat, Guillermo and Domenico Sindico. The beginning of industrialization in northeast Mexico (AAFH/ TAM, 39:4, April 1983, p. 499–518, tables)

Study of first stage of industrialization in Monterrey (1890–1902) during which time area was dominated by US and Great Britain external markets. National and local governments favored large businesses and avoided protectionist policies.

2066 Bell, Samuel E. and James M. Smallwood. Zona libre: trade and diplomacy on the Mexican border, 1858–1905 (UA/AW, 24:2, Summer 1982, p. 119–152, map, plates)

Creation of free zone in 1858 had important social, economic, and political effects for both Mexico and the US. American border merchants argued it encouraged smuggling. It was an obstacle to Díaz's bid for recognition by US. Long conflict demonstrated the complexity of US-Mexican relations.

2067 Bellingeri, Marco and Enrique Montalvo. Lenin en México: la via junker y las contradicciones del Porfiriato (Historia [Instituto de Antropología e Historia, Dirección de Estudios Históricos, México] 1, julio/sept. 1982, p. 15–29)

Analysis and rejection of Lenin's theory of capitalist development in Mexico during Porfiriato. Authors offer alternative model.

2068 Borderlands sourcebook: a guide to the literature on northern Mexico and the American Southwest. Edited by Ellwyn R. Stoddard, Richard L. Nostrand, and Jonathan P. West. Norman: University of Oklahoma Press: Published under the sponsorship of the Association of Borderlands Scholars, 1983. 445 p.: bibl., index, maps.

Extensive work with sections and essays on Borderlands history, exploration, conquest, geography, anthropology, archaeology, social problems, water resources, drug policies, pollution, migration, and linguistics. Bibliography includes lists of dissertations, maps, photographs, and manuscript materials in Mexican archives.

2069 Bustamante, Carlos María de. Diario histórico de México. t. 1, v. 1, Diciembre 1822-junio 1823. Nota previa y notas al texto, Manuel Calvillo. Edición al cuidado de Rina Ortiz. México: SEP, Instituto Nacional de Antropología e Historia, 1980. 1 v.: col. port.

Daily accounts of political events in Mexico (1822–23 and 1821–61).

2070 Cabrera, José María. Cinco artículos de José María Cabrera (CEHSMO, 5:18, enero 1980, p. 24–36, facsims., photos)

Reproduction of articles in which Cabrera proposes methods to change mutual aid societies into workers' banks.

2071 ———et al. Documentos (CEHSMO, 4:16, mayo 1979, p. 11–39)

Collection of documents on cooperative societies, workers' banks, and worker's credit (1877–84).

2072 Cano Sánchez, Beatriz. Contribución bibliográfica para la historia económica del Estado de Tlaxcala: siglos XIX y XX (IAA, 8:4, 1982, p. 403–418)

Bibliography of 188 items. Topics include dictionaries, general works, theoretical works, land tenure, labor economic history, statistics.

2073 Carrillo Azpéitia, Rafael. Ensayo sobre la historia del movimiento obrero mexicano, 1823–1912. México: Centro de Estudios Históricos del Movimiento Obrero Mexicano, 1981. 1 v.: bibl.

Brief and general account of worker movements in Mexico. One-half of book deals with colonial labor conditions.

2074 Carstensen, Fred V. and **Diane Roazen-Parrillo.** International Harvester, Molina y Compañía, and the Henequen Market: a comment (LARR, 18:3, 1983, p. 197–203)

Reply to article by Gilbert Joseph and Allen Wells in *Latin American Research Review* (17:1, 1983, p. 69–99). Authors counter belief that North American buyers controlled henequen industry and that Harvester conspired to drive down sisal prices between 1902–11.

2075 Case, Robert. La frontera texana y los movimientos de insurrección en México, 1850–1900 (CM/HM, 30:3, enero/marzo 1981, p. 415–452)

Examines activities of border rebels in Mexico and failure of both governments to develop cohesive border policy.

2076 Cerutti, Mario. La formación de capitales preindustriales en Monterrey, 1850–1890: las décadas previas a la configuración de una burguesía regional (UNAM/RMS, 44:1, enero/marzo 1982, p. 81–117, tables)

Study of causes and actors in Monterrey's industrial development. Bankers, landowners, and merchants became tied with new national and international entrepreneurs.

2077 Chevalier, François. Nuevas aportaciones para el estudio de la Revolución mexicana (CAM, 244:5, sept./oct. 1982, p. 143–148)

Brief essay on economic and social problems of copper and silver mines in Mexico and their contribution to promoting the Revolution.

2078 Coatsworth, John H. Growth against development: the economic impact of railroads in Porfirian Mexico. DeKalb: Northern Illinois University Press, 1981. 249 p.: bibl., ill., index (The Origins of modern Mexico)

Based on extensive research in government publications and railroad company reports, author shows that railroads were essential to economic growth and that they contributed to population migration to new centers of economic activity. Finds that rail-

roads were more beneficial to export trade rather than domestic trade.

2079 Coffin, José. El General Gutiérrez. 2a. ed. México: Consejo Editorial del Gobierno del Estado de Tabasco, 1980. 186 p. (Serie Historia; 23)

First published 1912. Sympathetic portrayal of revolutionary leader from Tabasco.

2080 Creel de Müller, Lulú. El conquistador del desierto: biografía de un soldado de la república. Chihuahua: L. Creel de Müller, 1982. 592 p., 10 p. of plates: bibl., ports.

Favorable and popular biography of Gen. Luis Terrazas.

2081 Crespo, Horacio and **Herbert Frey.** La diferenciación social del campesinado como problema de la teoría y de la historia: hipótesis generales para el caso de Morelos, México (UNAM/RMS, 44:1, enero/marzo, 1982, p. 285–313, bibl., tables)

Study of "peasant differentiation" in Morelos chiefly in 19th century. Debates theories of Karl Kautsky and V.I. Lenin within historical context of Morelos' peasantry.

2082 Cuello, José. Beyond the "Borderlands" is the north of colonial Mexico: a Latin-Americanist perspective to the study of the Mexican north and the United States Southwest (PCCLAS/P, 9, 1982, p. 1–24)

Historiographical and theoretical treatment of Borderlands history. Argues that Borderlands history is not an integral part of Latin American history and as such must be conceived as a separate field of study. Extensive review of the literature.

2083 De León, Arnoldo. They called them greasers: Anglo attitudes toward Mexicans in Texas, 1821–1900. Austin: University of Texas Press, 1983. 153 p.: bibl., index, map.

Study of beliefs of whites in Texas, roots of attitudes, how attitudes were expressed, and how they became institutionalized in white society to the detriment of Mexicans. Reveals controversial conclusions in arguing that whites possessed a far greater degree of racism than ethnocentrism.

2084 ———— and **Kenneth L. Stewart.** Lost dreams and found fortunes: Mexican and anglo immigrants in South Texas, 1850–1900 (WHQ, 14:3, July 1983, p. 291–310, tables)

Part of larger quantitative study in progress, work describes differing economic fates of two sets of immigrants into South Texas. With pattern of Anglo political-military domination established in 1860, Anglos realized their economic dreams while rise of ethnic division of labor led to impoverishment of Mexican immigrants.

2085 Documentos básicos de la Reforma, 1854–1875. Investigación histórica, introducción, compilación y registro bibliográfico, Mario V. Guzmán Galarza. Edición y presentación, Humberto Hiriart Urdanivia. México: Partido Revolucionario Institucional, 1982. 4 v.: bibl., ill., ports.

Collection of documents compiled from primary archives and libraries.

2086 Dumas, Claude. *Nation et identité* dans le Méxique du XIXe siècle: essai sur une variation (UTIEH/C, 38, 1982, p. 45–69)

Study of formation of the national identity of Mexico from independence through Porfiriato. Examination of writings of Lucas Alamán, José María Luis Mora, and Silvio Zavala, and their efforts to create a national identity.

2087 Escobar Toledo, Saúl. La acumulación capitalista en el Porfiriato. México: Departamento de Investigaciones Históricas, INAH, 1980. 43 p.: bibl. (Cuadernos de trabajo; 31)

Capital accumulation during Porfiriato created oligarchy of manufacturing and banking interests that differed from dominant sectors in agriculture. Both had different economic interests.

2088 Fernández Tomás, Jorge B. Una ojeada al *Imparcial* de 1900–1901: la política porfirista contra el movimiento obrero (CEHSMO, 6:21, enero 1981, p. 2–6, photos)

List of articles published in *El Imparcial* (1900–01) that showed concern for the condition of workers.

2089 ———. Recopilación hemerográfica (CEHSMO, 5:17, sept. 1979, p. 2–13, photos)

Collection of brief articles on social problems of alcoholism among workers in Mexico in late 19th century.

2090 Florescano, Enrique. Notas sobre la historiografía económica del período 1870–1910. México: Departamento de Investigaciones Históricas, INAH, 1980. 41 p.: bibl. (Cuadernos de trabajo; 32)

Historiography of economic history covering demography, agriculture, industry, commerce, finance, and foreign trade and mining.

2091 Frome, Howard. The manuscript postal markings of Mexico, 1856–1878. Chatham, N.Y.: H. Frome, 1982. 57 p.: ill., index.

Collection of illustrations of postal markings found on Mexican stamps. Manuscript cancels were obtained from several collections. Includes brief explanatory text.

2092 Fuentes Mares, José. Poinsett, historia de una gran intriga. 7. ed. México: Ediciones Océano, 1982. 216 p., 6 p. of plates: bibl., facsims.

Seventh ed. of book with one major modification concerning debate over centralism and federalism in early years of independent Mexico.

2093 ———. Santa Anna, el hombre. 4a. ed. México: Editorial Grijalbo, 1982. 302 p., 16 p. of plates: ill. (Colección Autores mexicanos)

Originally published as *Aurora y ocaso de un comediante* (1956), this 4th ed. contains few textual modifications, but does eliminate notes and references.

2094 García, Mario T. Desert immigrants: the Mexicans of El Paso, 1880–1920. New Haven: Yale University Press, 1981. 316 p., 7 leaves of plates: bibl., ill., index (Yale Western Americana series; 32)

Study of immigration to and through El Paso in Porfirian and early revolutionary periods. Prior to 1910, most immigrants were lower-class workers; after the Revolution, middle, and upper-class elements became more important. Excellent blend of border, immigration, and urban studies.

2095 Gaxiola, Francisco Javier. Biografía del Señor General José Vicente Villada, Gobernador Constitucional del Estado de México. Ed. facsimilar de la de 1895. México: Patrimonio Cultural y Artístico del Estado de México, Gobierno del Estado de México, FONAPAS, 1979. 167 p. (Biblioteca enciclopédica del Estado de México, 92)

Facsimile ed. of 1895 publication. Biography of military and political career of governor during his second term of office beginning March 8, 1893.

2096 Gijón Barragán, Mario. La sociedad unionista del Ramo de la Sombrería (CEHSMO, 6:22, abril 1981, p. 2–18)

Discussion of creation, structure, and operation of the mutualist society for hat makers in Mexico City (1870–75).

2097 Gómez Quiñones, Juan. Porfirio Díaz, los intelectuales y la Revolución. México: Ediciones El Caballito, 1981. 231 p.: bibl. (Fragua mexicana; 40)

Study of intellectual discontent and the rise of nationalism in Mexico (1890–1911). Attempts to show that among intellectuals there were many ideas of reform prior to Revolution. Challenges notion that Revolution had no intellectual precursors.

2098 González Calzada, Manuel. Tabasco, hombres y nombres, historia y cultura. México: Consejo Editorial del Gobierno del Estado de Tabasco, 1981. 73 p. (Cuadernos del Consejo Editorial; 5)

Brief essay on personages, education, journalism, theatre, literature, and history in Tabasco. Includes additional essay on Manuel Mestre Ghigliazza as Revolution's precursor in Tabasco.

2099 González Loscertales, Vicente. Bases para el análisis socioeconómico de la colonia española de México en 1910 (IGFO/RI, 39:155/158, enero/dic. 1979, p. 267–295)

Socioeconomic analysis of Spanish residents in Mexico in 1910. Discusses demographic data, occupations in agriculture, industry, commerce, mining and banking, peasants, workers movement, and social and cultural organizations.

2100 González Navarro, Moisés. Tipología del liberalismo mexicano (CM/HM, 32:2, oct./dic. 1982, p. 198–225)

Text of speech which relates ideas of political factions with interest of dominant class in 19th-century Mexico. Discussion involves two types of liberalism: individual and social. While social liberalism triumphed with 1917 Constitution, individual liberalism continued to survive.

2101 Guedea, Virginia. José María Morelos y Pavón: cronología. México: Universidad Nacional Autónoma de México, Instituto de Investigaciones Históricas, 1981. 234 p., 2 folded leaves of plates: bibl., maps (Serie de historia moderna y contemporánea; 13)

Chronology and guide to events, letters, proclamations, and reports dealing with Morelos' priesthood, revolutionary career, trial, and death. Includes extensive bibliography.

2102 Haufe, Hans and **Konrad Tyrakowski.** Die hacienda Santa Agueda, Tlaxcala: zur genese eines mustergutes der porfiriatszeit (IAA, 7:1/2, 1981, p. 111–136, bibl., ill., plates)

Analysis of formation of an hacienda during late Porfiriato that demonstrated considerable success as major enterprise in milk industry.

Hernández Montemayor, Laura. Catálogo de fuentes para el estudio de la historia de Tamaulipas. See *HLAS 45:44*.

2103 Herrejón Peredo, Carlos. Hidalgo: la justificación de la insurgencia (CAM, 246:1, enero/feb. 1983, p. 162–180)

Study of history of insurrection and its relation to Hidalgo. Concludes that Hidalgo followed basic points of insurrection: to conserve one's own life, to defend lives of innocent, and, where war leads to a just victory, to preserve peace and common good.

2104 Heydenreich, Titus. Ein ubekannter Zeuge der intervention in Mexiko: Engelbert-Otto Freiherr von Brackel-Welda, 1830–1930 (JGSWGL, 18, 1981, p. 291–327)

Presentation of Baron Brackel's role during French Intervention in Mexico. Based on family letters. Baron finally came to condemn intervention.

2105 Hohenstein, Jutta. Politische, wirtschaftliche und soziale Verhältnisse in Mexiko im Spiegel deutschsprachiger Publikationen: 1821–1861 (JGSWGL, 18, 1981, p. 187–247)

Presentation of views of Germans on political, social, and economic conditions of independent Mexico. Early interest in Mexico involved precious metals and commerce, declined after Treaty of Guadalupe, and increased at onset of French Intervention.

2106 Houdart-Morizot, Marie-France. Du bon usage des mouvements indiens: rebelles et rébellions de la Sierra Gorda,

Mexique, 1847–1849 (CDAL, 23, 1981, p. 47–100)

Discussions of how external forces used rebellious Indians in Sierra Gorda for furthering political and economic ends.

2107 Invasión norteamericana en Tabasco, 1846–1847: documentos. Reunidos por Manuel Mestre Ghigliazza. 2a. ed., facsimilar. México: Consejo Editorial del Gobierno del Estado de Tabasco, 1981. 364 p., 4 leaves of plates: bibl., ill., index, ports. (Serie Historia; 33)

Chronological list of documents. Includes index. First published 1948.

2108 Irigoyen, Renán. La Constitución de Cádiz en 1812 y los sanjuanistas de Mérida (UY/R, 23:135/136, mayo/agosto 1981, p. 23–48)

Discussion of radical political ideas of society of San Juan in Yucatán and their relationship to 1812 Spanish Constitution and Mexican independence movement.

2109 Joachim, Benoit. Perspectivas hacia la historia social de Latinoamérica: Puebla en el México de los siglos XIX–XX. Puebla: Centro de Investigaciones Históricas y Sociales, Editorial Universidad Autónoma de Puebla, 1979. 102 p.: bibl.

Blueprint for writing social history. Author formulates plan to write regional history which includes study of regional politics, economics, infrastructure, and production; analysis of demographic changes; study of social classes and struggles. Includes valuable bibliography on methodology for writing social history.

2110 Joseph, Gilbert M. Revolution from without: Yucatán, Mexico, and the United States, 1880–1924. Cambridge: Cambridge University Press, 1982. 407 p.: bibl., ill., index (Cambridge Latin American series; 42)

Excellent contribution to regional study of the Revolution. Author's examination of regional political, social, and economic factors convincingly demonstrates why the Revolution had to come "from without," even though there existed abundant causes for revolution within Yucatán.

2111 ——— and **Allen Wells.** Collaboration and informal empire in Yucatán: the case for political economy (LARR, 18:3, 1983, p. 204–218)

Continuation of authors' earlier essay (item **2112**) and rejoinder to critical articles that appeared in the same issue of *Latin American Research Review* (see item **2178**). Joseph and Wells argue that critics merely introduced variations of earlier themes and that they do not rely on contemporary regional history nor local archival materials.

2112 ——— and ———. Corporate control of a monocrop economy: International Harvester and Yucatán's henequen industry during the Porfiriato (LARR, 17:1, 1982, p. 69–99)

Analysis of role of International Harvester, its effects on Yucatán's economy, and its relationship to local elites. Also examines Harvester's role as multinational enterprise in developing nation.

2113 Lemoine, Ernesto. Nueva Orleans, foco de propaganda y actividades de la insurgencia mexicana (*in* Cardinales de dos independencias: Noreste de México-Sureste de los Estados Unidos: memoria del simposio celebrado de la Universidad Iberoamericana, con la colaboración de la Universidad de Florida los días 29 y 30 de noviembre de 1976, con motivo del Bicentenario de la Independencia de los Estados Unidos. México: Fomento Cultural Banamex, 1978, p. 15–36)

Argues that the leaders of Mexico's independence movement were convinced that outside help was essential for victory. Studies role played by insurgents from New Orleans.

2114 López Espinoza, Rogelio. El estado de Yucatán y la explusión de españoles de 1827 (UY/R, 22:131/132, sept./dic. 1980, p. 23–25, ill.)

List of Spanish expelled from Yucatán in 1827 and those exempted. Includes applicable laws of occupations.

2115 López Reyes, Diógenes. Historia de Tabasco. México: Consejo Editorial del Gobierno del Estado de Tabasco, 1980. 541 p.: ill. (Serie Historia; 25)

General history from colonial times to 1959, mostly devoted to modern period. Author was surgeon by profession with strong interest in history.

2116 López Rosado, Diego G. Fuentes para el estudio de las obras públicas. México: Universidad Nacional Autónoma de México, 1981. 249 p.: bibl., index (Bibiografía

de historia económica y social de México;
10. Serie Bibliografías; 9)

Extensive compilation of materials
dealing with public works from prehispanic
time until 1925.

2117 Manzanilla L., Emilio. Las instituciones bancarias en la República Mexicana: 1864–1925 (UY/R, 21, nov./dic. 1979,
p. 10–24)

Discusses evolution of Mexican banking system from its genesis under international institutions to formation of Banco
Central de México in 1925.

2118 Mejía Zúñiga, Raúl. Valentin Gómez
Farías, hombre de México, 1781–1858.
México: Fondo de Cultura Económica, 1982.
334 p.: bibl. (SEP/80, 18)

Biased, poorly-documented biography
of prominent Liberal leader and Reforma precursor. Good biography of Gómez Farías is
much needed; unfortunately, this is not it.

**2119 Mexico, from independence to revolu-
tion, 1810–1910.** Edited with commentary by W. Dirk Raat. Lincoln: University
of Nebraska Press, 1982. 308 p.: bibl., index, maps.

Useful collection of essays divided
into four major sections: 1810–24; 1824–54;
1855–76; and 1876–1910. Porfirian section
is longest and almost uniformly critical
of Díaz.

2120 Meyer, Jean. La desamortización de
1856 en Tepic (CM/RE, 4:13, invierno
de 1983, p. 5–30, bibl., charts)

In-depth analysis of 1856 application
of Ley Lerdo in Tepic. Author concludes that
application did not cause specifically a local
uprising but gave the conservatives a military
leader, Manuel Lozada, of use in subsequent
civil war. Based largely on archival sources.

2122 ———. El ejército mexicano en el siglo
XIX (Vuelta [México] 5:51, feb. 1981,
p. 28–30, bibl., ill.)

Brief overview of formation and operation of Mexican Army from creation under
Bourbons to its role under Díaz.

2123 Negrete Salas, Martaelena. La frontera
tejana y el abigeato, 1848–1872
(CM/HM, 31:1, julio/sept. 1981, p. 79–100)

Examination of impact of rustling on
both sides of frontier based on 1873 report
by Comisión Pesquisidora del Norte and on

evidence developed by US-Mexican Mixed
Claims Commission (1868–74).

2124 Obregón, Arturo. Los proyectos de
mecanización en la industria del
tabaco y las empleadas de la fábrica de puros
y cigarros de la Ciudad de México, 1846
(CEHSMO, 6:22, abril 1981, p. 32–40, bibl.)

Discussion of attempts of workers in
tobacco industry in Mexico City to stop importation of machinery. Many workers were
women who depended on their jobs to support families. Includes reproduction of
manifesto addressed by employees to the
government.

2125 Olliff, Donathon C. Reforma Mexico
and the United States: a search for alternatives to annexation, 1854–1861. University: University of Alabama Press, 1981.
213 p.: bibl., index.

Examination of process by which economic goals of Liberals led them to desire an
"economic protectorate" for Mexico under
US. Failure to establish such a relationship
primarily resulted from US interest in acquiring territory rather than economic
domination.

2126 Olveda, Jaime. Gordiano Guzmán, un
cacique del siglo XIX. México: Centro
Regional de Occidente, SEP-INAH, 1980.
221 p.: bibl., maps.

Based on premises of François Chevalier and Max Weber, author studies rise to
power of 19th-century cacique from Jalisco.
Based on substantial archival research.

2127 Origins of the Mexican War: a documentary source book. Compiled by
Ward McAfee and J. Cordell Robinson. Salisbury, N.C.: Documentary Publications, 1982.
2 v.: bibl., ill. (U.S. relations with Latin
American nations; v. 1)

Collection of documents revealing
policies and objectives of both countries.
New documents from Mexican archives
demonstrate desire on part of Mexico to
negotiate a settlement.

2128 Paulsen, George E. Fraud, honor, and
trade: the United States-Mexico dispute over the claim of La Obra Company,
1875–1902 (UC/PHR, 52:2, May 1983,
p. 175–190)

Study of fraud committed by US
claimants of La Obra Mining Co. and attempts by Mexico to recover money it paid.

Dispute demonstrated changes in US attitude toward Mexico over 27 years it was debated. In end, US taxpayers assumed burden of re-paying Mexico and restoring American honor.

2129 Peña, Guillermo de la. A legacy of promises: agriculture, politics, and ritual in the Morelos highlands of Mexico. Austin: University of Texas Press, 1981. 289 p.: bibl., ill., index (The Texas Pan American series)

Argues that highlands of Morelos have been influenced by ties with lowlands to the south. Includes broad historical outline of agriculture economics and politics from colonial to modern times.

2130 Platt, D.C.M. Finanzas británicas en México, 1821–1867 (CM/HM, 32:2, oct./dic. 1982, p. 226–261)

Extensive analysis of vitality of Mexican economy of 19th century and role of British capital. During first three quarters of century finance in Mexico was mainly domestic and not foreign. Mexican products were not in demand abroad. Mexico promoted industrialization with its own resources.

2131 Pompa y Pompa, Antonio. Evaluación de la Revolución (UNL/H, 22, 1981, p. 303–310)

Analysis of evolution of Mexican Revolution in terms of three stages: 1) emancipation from the Spanish; 2) liberalism of the Reform period; and 3) Porfiriato. Concludes that Mexico has permanent revolution seeking to satisfy aspirations of the Mexican people.

2132 Potash, Robert A. Mexican government and industrial development in the early republic: the Banco de Avio. Amherst: University of Massachusetts Press, 1983. 251 p.: bibl., index.

Long awaited English version of 1959 ed. published by Fondo de Cultura Económica. This version contains new observations about cotton industry based on new research. Also contains historiographical essay on economic history of period written since 1960.

2133 Quintal Martín, Fidelio. Justo Sierra O'Reilly, el historiador (UY/R, 24:144, nov./dic. 1982, p. 55–64, bibl.)

Brief discussion of how Sierra conceived and wrote history.

2134 Rabiela, Hira de Gortari. La política en la formación del estado nacional (UNAM/RMS, 44:1, enero/marzo 1982, p. 263–284)

Analysis of effects of political and economic centralization on social groups in Mexico City during Porfiriato. Those who benefited from Díaz policies believed they had solved earlier problems of national disunity and had created new national maturity.

2135 Reyes, Cayetano. Las tierras creadas del noroeste de Michoacán (CM/RE, 3:9, invierno de 1982, p. 33–48, table)

Study of colonization projects in Michoacán at end of 19th century. Projects reinforced and modernized haciendas and were designed to promote peace, security, and economic progress in valley of Huaniqueo.

2136 Reyna, María del Carmen. Las condiciones del trabajo en las panaderías de la Ciudad de México durante la segunda mitad del siglo XIX (CM/HM, 31:3, enero/marzo 1982, p. 431–448)

Analysis of characteristics of bread shops in 19th-century Mexico. States that colonial trends in operation persisted until 20th century and that shops never moved toward full industrialization. Also studies labor, social, and economic problems associated with enterprises.

2137 Rublúo, Luis. Historia de la Revolución Mexicana en el Estado de Hidalgo. México: patronato del Instituto Nacional de Estudios Históricos de la Revolución Mexicana, 1983. 2 v.: bibl. (Biblioteca del Instituto Nacional de Estudios Históricos de la Revolución Mexicana; 92)

Discussion of political and economic events in Hidalgo as precursor to Revolution. Retraces activities of notable leaders of the movement.

2138 Salinas Cantú, Hernán. Biografía del Dr. Jesús María González (UNL/H, 22, 1981, p. 201–212, bibl.)

Brief, factual account of the 19th-century doctor and surgeon's medical career.

2139 Samponaro, Frank N. La alianza de Santa Anna y los federalistas, 1832–1834: su formación y desintegración

(CM/HM, 30:3, enero/marzo 1981, p. 358–390, bibl.)

Alliance between Santa Anna and federalists resulted from dissatisfaction with political centralization of interim president Anastasio Bustamante. Fallout between the two allies was related to fact that original arrangement was made only for convenience of both sides.

2140 ———. Mariano Paredes y el movimiento monarquista mexicano en 1846 (CM/HM, 32:1, julio/sept. 1982, p. 39–54)

Study of attitude and thinking of military leader concerning move to create a monarchy in Mexico. After extensive documentation and archival investigation, author concludes that Paredes was defender of constitutional monarchy for Mexico.

2141 ———. Santa Anna and the abortive anti-Federalist revolt of 1833 in Mexico (AAFH/TAM, 40:1, July 1983, p. 95–107)

Analysis of the reasons why Santa Anna did not support the anti-Federalist revolt of 1833. Confirms traditional view that Santa Anna was both shrewd and unprincipled politician.

2142 Sánchez García, Alfonso *et al.* Sumaria tolucense, siglo y medio. Ed. conmemorativa del sesquicentenario de la ciudad de Toluca como capital del Estado de México. Toluca: Departamento de Comunicación Social y Desarrollo Cultural del H. Ayuntamiento de la Ciudad de Toluca, 1980. 324 p., 4 leaves of plates: bibl., ill. (some col.)

Collection of essays on history, culture, art, economics, and journalism of Toluca since 1830.

2143 Santamaría, Francisco Javier. Memorias, acotaciones y pasatiempos. v. 7, 12, 14, 18–20. México: Consejo Editorial del Gobierno del Estado de Tabasco, 1981. 6 v. in 5: facsims. (Cuadernos del Consejo Editorial; 1–3, 7, 12)

Collection of author's writings, notes, and diary entries.

2144 Sims, Harold D. Descolonización en México: el conflicto entre mexicanos y españoles: 1821–1831. México: Fondo de Cultura Económica, 1982. 259 p.: appendices, bibl., tables.

Author traces the growing anti-Spanish sentiment which culminated in the expulsion laws of 1827 and 1929, concluding that the cost of expulsion was too high particularly in its economic impact.

2145 ———. Los exiliados españoles de México en 1829 (CM/HM, 30:3, enero/marzo 1981, p. 391–414, bibl., tables)

Discussion of social and economic role of Spanish in Mexico prior to their expulsion. Also discusses their travel to New Orleans and problems they encountered in US. Mexico lost considerable number of investors and merchants with the expulsion of the Spanish.

2146 Sindico, Domenico E. Ingresos y consumos de los trabajadores agrícolas en dos haciendas mexicanas a principios del siglo XIX (GEE/NA, 1981, p. 281–298, tables)

Presentation of income (monetary and in-kind) and consumption by peasants on haciendas in early 19th century. Argues that these patterns permit better understanding of Mexico's later agrarian economy.

2147 ———. Modernization in nineteenth-century sugar haciendas: the case of Morelos: from formal to real subsumption of labor to capital (LAP, 7[4]:27, Fall 1980, p. 83–99)

Study of an hacienda's transformation in Morelos, from Bourbon Reforms to 1910, and changes made toward development in a capitalist society. Author places study within debate over 19th-century's dominant mode of production.

2148 Singelmann, Peter; Sergio Quesada; and **Jesús Tapia.** Land without liberty: continuities of peripheral capitalist development and peasant exploitation among the cane growers of Morelos, Mexico (LAP, 11:3, Summer 1982, p. 29–45)

Argues that in case of Morelo's rural and cane growers there was an incomplete transition from feudalism to capitalism. Authors find that neither independence from colonial rule nor Porfiriato's fall nor post-revolutionary changes entailed a complete proletarianization of the rural labor force.

2149 Stevens, Donald Fithian. Agrarian policy and instability in Porfirian México (AAFH/TAM, 49:2, Oct. 1982, p. 153–166)

Analysis of agrarian movement, repression and stability in Huasteca region of San

Luis Potosí. Shows that Díaz did not have complete control over local pressures that attacked Indian lands. He realized, however, that political stability in countryside was essential and attempted moves to conciliate opposing forces.

2150 Tabasco, 27 de febrero de 1864. Recopilación y edición, Manuel González Calzada. México: Consejo Editorial del Gobierno del Estado de Tabasco, 1981. 157 p.: facsims. (Cuadernos del Consejo Editorial; 4)

Reproduction of documents relating to French invasion of Tabasco and efforts to repel it.

2151 Tanck de Estrada, Dorothy. Las Cortes de Cádiz y el desarrollo de la educación en México (UY/R, 23:137/138, sept./dic. 1981, p. 15–42)

Discusses how four concepts enacted by the Cortes would be applied to Mexico's education: 1) the State as coordinator of education; 2) the State as supervisor of clerical instruction; 3) the State as promoter of modern education; and 4) the *ayuntamiento* as promoter of primary education.

2152 Tavera Alfaro, Xavier. Juan José Martínez de Lejarza: un estudio de luz y sombra. México: SEP, Instituto Nacional de Antropología e Historia, Centro Regional México-Michoacán, 1979. 86 p.: bibl., ill. (Colección científica; 77. Historia)

Brief biography of Michoacán author and politician. Martínez wrote first statistical analysis of independent Mexico.

2153 Thorup, Cathryn. La competencia económica británica y norteamericana en México: 1887–1910 (CM/HM, 31:4, abril/junio 1982, p. 599–641, bibl.)

Modifies thesis that Mexico welcomed British investments in order to minimize US influence. Mexico did attempt to use British capital to neutralize North American influence but only after 1900. Between 1887–1910, US commerce and finance grew considerably in Mexico.

2154 Tullis, F. LaMond. Early Mormon exploration and missionary activities in Mexico (BYU/S, 22:3, Summer 1982, p. 289–301, facsims., plates)

Factual account of Mormon expeditions to Sonora and Mexico City in late 19th century and problems they encountered. Expeditions set out to colonize and carry out missionary activities.

2155 ———. Reopening the Mexican mission in 1901 (BYU/S, 22:4, Fall 1982, p. 441–453)

Discussion of accomplishments of Mormon leader in re-opening missions in southern Mexico and later efforts to establish missions in other parts of country. Creation of missions continued and prospered until economic and political discontent began to plague Mexico.

2156 Tutino, John. Rebelión indígena en Tehuantepec (CP, 24, abril/junio 1980, p. 89–101)

Explains Juchitec rebellion of 1848 as result of confrontation of local authorities (representing the State and white community's interests) and indigenous communities, over control of traditional, economic resources (e.g., salt in Tehuantepec). Indigenous rebellions elsewhere can also be explained by such mechanisms. [A. Lavrin]

2157 Tyler, Daniel. The Carrizal Archives: a source for the Mexican period (UNM/NMHR, 57:3, July 1982, p. 257–267)

Notes on contents of gaps of Carrizal municipal archives. Microfilmed at University of Texas, El Paso, collection constitutes important source for Borderlands history.

2158 Vanderwood, Paul J. Disorder and progress: bandits, police, and Mexican development. Lincoln: University of Nebraska Press, 1981. 264 p., 12 leaves of plates: bibl., ill., index.

Continuation of what Vanderwood has shown in previous articles: that *rurales* were old, inefficient, corrupt, and unable to provide defense when insurgents arose in 1910; that banditry consisted of rebels who sought upward mobility and were not necessarily popular protestors.

2159 Vásquez, Josefina. The beginning of a nation: the nineteenth century (*in* Mexico today. Edited by Tommie Sue Montgomery. Philadelphia: Institute for the Study of Human Issues, 1982, p. 35–38)

Brief description of 19th-century Mexico for popular consumption.

2160 Vaughan, Mary K. The State, education, and social class in Mexico, 1880–1928. DeKalb: Northern Illinois University Press, 1982. 316 p.: bibl., index (The Origins of modern Mexico)

Revisionist view of continuity in Mexican education from Porfirian to Revolutionary period. Author gives greater credit to porfiristas for their role in promoting public education while being more critical of so-called revolutionary education programs in 1920s. Most of study is on 1920s period.

2161 Voss, Stuart F. On the periphery of nineteenth-century Mexico: Sonora and Sinaloa, 1810–1877. Tucson: University of Arizona Press, 1982. 318 p.: bibl., index.

In his comparative political history of Sonora and Sinaloa, author focuses on activities of "urban notables," especially their struggle for the governorship. Somewhat weighted in Sonora's direction due to greater availability of sources.

2162 ———. The Porfiriato in time and space (LARR, 18:3, 1983, p. 246–254)

Review article concerns six authors and their efforts to confront issues of time and space in writing history of Porfiriato. Discusses how authors examine what is Mexican, who are Mexicans, when they became so, and what it has meant for them to be Mexicans.

2163 Wasserstrom, Robert. A caste war that never was: the Tzeltal conspiracy of 1848 (UP/PSN, 7:2, Spring 1978, p. 73–85, ill., map)

Analysis of Indian rebellion in Central Chiapas. Rebellion was caused by expansion of landholdings by local mestizos and by criticism of Indians' religious practices. Problems set stage for future unrest.

2164 Weber, David J. The Mexican frontier, 1821–1846: the American Southwest under Mexico. Albuquerque: University of New Mexico Press, 1982. 416 p.: bibl., ill., index (Histories of the American frontier)

Well written and researched account of Mexico's failure to retain possession of her northern frontier in early decades of independence. Inability of central authorities to formulate coherent frontier policy led to loss of economic and military control of region which Anglo-Americans quickly exploited.

2165 Wells, Allen. Family elites in a boom and bust economy: the Molinas and Peóns of Porfirian Yucatán (HAHR, 62:2, May 1982, p. 224–253, tables)

Major revisionist study of "henequen aristocracy" during Porfiriato. Using two case studies, author combines elite, kinship, and regional studies to demonstrate complex political, financial, and social forces at work within Yucatecan aristocracy. Concludes that economic cooperation was key to Porfirian power structure at the regional level (see item **2112**).

REVOLUTION AND POST-REVOLUTION

2166 La Agencia Confidencial y la Casa del Obrero Mundial (CEHSMO, 5:17, sept. 1979, p. 14–16)

Reprint of five documents showing how Secretaría de Gobernación during the Carranza period monitored the activities of the Casa and how relations between the Casa and the Revolution deteriorated.

2167 Aguilar, José Angel. La decena trágica. México: Patronato del Instituto Nacional de Estudios Históricos de la Revolución Mexicana, 1981–1982. 2 v.: bibl. (Biblioteca del Instituto; 89)

Brief, chronological account of the Ten Tragic Days. Includes limited bibliography.

2168 Aguilar Camín, Héctor. Saldos de la Revolución: cultura y política de México, 1910–1980. México: Editorial Nueva Imagen, 1982. 275 p.: bibl. (Serie Historia)

Text of speeches, essays, and articles on wide range of topics, all centering around continuing theme of whether Revolution has died.

2169 Aldana Rendón, Mario A. Margarito Ramírez: actividad política y administrativa de un régimen, 1919–1927. Guadalajara: Universidad de Guadalajara, Instituto de Estudios Sociales, 1980. 58 p.: bibl. (Colección Ensayos y monografías)

Brief sketch of military and political career of revolutionary leader from Jalisco.

2170 Alvarez, Mayda. Los jóvenes y el sistema político mexicano: elementos para una proposición (CAM, 248:3, mayo/junio 1983, p. 44–51)

Presentation of the student and youth activities primarily since 1968, and their relations with the government, guerrillas, press, and political parties. Argues that the

youth political movement needs its own organizations and programs that make demands
on the State.

2171 Amezcua, Jenaro. Biografía de Enrique
Flores Magón (CEHSMO, 5:17, sept.
1979, p. 24–32)
Brief and sympathetic sketch of revolutionary leader written in 1943.

2172 Balderrama, Francisco E. In defense of
la raza, the Los Angeles Mexican Consulate, and the Mexican community, 1929 to
1936. Tucson: University of Arizona Press,
1982. 137 p.: bibl., index.
Study of role of consulate in protecting
Mexicans during Great Depression. Consuls'
efforts to feed, clothe, shelter, and prevent
deportation of Mexican citizens represented
valuable assistance, but consuls may have
overstepped their diplomatic mission by
intervening in politics.

2173 Basáñez, Miguel. La lucha por la
hegemonía en México: 1968–1980.
México: Siglo Veintiuno Editores, 1981.
243 p.: bibl., ill. (Sociología y política)
Operating on basis that Mexico is a
"contradictory state" with both authoritarian and non-authoritarian features, author
analyzes three different sectors contending
for the formulation of public policy: public,
private, and "dissident." Some coverage of
1940–68 period.

2174 Beezley, William H. In search of everyday Mexicans in the Revolution (RIB,
33:3, 1983, p. 366–382)
Author wryly takes to task historians
of Mexican Revolution for their preoccupation with "the Revolution" and its leaders
while virtually ignoring the ordinary revolutionary. Maintaining that the Revolution's
history has been "doubled-crossed" by historiography and social statistics, author argues
that the new "social history" provides portrait of non-existent "average man" while
failing to provide insight into the Revolution's "everyday Mexican."

2175 Beltrán, Enrique. Cándido Bolívar
Pieltain y los biólogos españoles en
México (SMHN/R, 38, dic. 1976, p. 19–28)
Discusses arrival and careers of Span-
ish biologists who helped improve Mexican
scientific community during 20th century.

2176 Benjamin, Thomas. El trabajo en las
monterías de Chiapas y Tabasco:
1870–1946 (CM/HM, 30:4, abril/junio
1981, p. 508–529, bibl., tables)
Based on a number of novels by
B. Traven, author confirms that mahogany
workers in Chiapas and Tabasco were among
most brutally exploited of all workers during
the Porfiriato. Their plight extended well into
1920s and 1930s and ended when unions and
industry operated in the regions.

2177 Bluestein, William. The class relations
of the hacienda and the village in pre-
revolutionary Morelos (LAP, 11:3, Summer
1982, p. 12–28)
Attempts to develop understanding of
class relations on the hacienda and village
toward forming a class history of the Revolution. Argues that Zapata's movement was not
only anti-feudal but anti-capitalist. Article
does not uncover any new primary sources.

2178 Bodayla, Stephen D. Bankers versus
diplomats: the debate over Mexican
insolvency (SAGE/JIAS, 24:4, Nov. 1982,
p. 461–482, bibl.)
Description of disagreement between
Ambassador Dwight Morrow and international committee of bondholders. Morrow favored comprehensive plan to meet demands
of all of Mexico's creditors while international committee supported separate agreement for securities holders it represented.
Committee's view prevailed, but agreement
reached was undone by 1930s' Depression.

2179 Brannon, Jeffrey and Eric N. Baklanoff.
Corporate control of a monocrop economy (LARR, 18:3, 1983, p. 193–196)
Reply to article by Joseph and Wells
(see item **2112**). Brannon and Baklanoff argue
that International Harvester did not control
"production and price of raw henequen fiber
between 1902 and 1915 or that the agreement
between Molina changed the qualitative relationship between Yucatan's henequen
hacendados and major American consumers."

2180 Camp, Roderic A. Intellectuals: agents
of change in Mexico (SAGE/JIAS,
23:3, Aug. 1981, p. 297–320)
Examines explanations for increased
importance of intellectuals and whether they
could be essential to Mexico's future. Argues
that the Mexican intellectual will not be an
agent of change.

2181 Cárdenas de la Peña, Enrique. Tiempo y tarea de Luis Gonzaga Cuevas. México: s.n., 1982. 6 v. (folios)

Contiene biografía de Cuevas e ilumina de paso y poderosamente un período turbulento y triste de la historia de México. Basado principalmente en documentos del archivo privado de Cuevas (Centro de Estudios de la Historia de México, Condumex, México). Obra realmente valiosa. [L. Gómez Canedo]

2182 Carr, Barry. Marxism and anarchism in the formation of the Mexican Communist Party, 1910–1919 (HAHR, 63:2, May 1983, p. 277–305)

Analysis of evolution of socialist and Marxist thought prior to formation of the Mexican Community Party in 1919. Argues that social democracy had stronger effect on party's development than previously thought.

2183 Casasola, Gustavo. Anales gráficos de la historia militar de México, 1810–1980: los insurgentes, las guerras de intervención, asonadas, pronunciamientos, cuartelazos, la Revolución mexicana, anecdotas y biobrafías [sic]. v. 1–6. México: Editorial G. Casasola, 1980. 6 v.: chiefly ill., indexes (Hechos y hombres de México, 1810–1980 / Gustavo Casasola; t. 1–6)

Pictorial and chronological history of the Mexican military (1810–1980); illustrated biographies of Venustiano Carranza, Porfirio Díaz, Emiliano Zapata, Plutarco Elías Calles, Francisco Villa, and Lázaro Cárdenas. Includes brief text.

2183a Casasola, Miguel V. and Jesús Silva Herzog. La expropiación del petróleo, 1936–1938: álbum fotográfico. Fotografías de Miguel V. Casasola. Textos de Jesús Silva Herzog. México: Fondo de Cultura Económica, 1981. 109 p.: ill.

Collection of photographs of events surrounding 1938 oil expropriation. Includes text by Jesús Silva Herzog.

2184 Ceja Reyes, Víctor. Los cristeros: crónica de los que perdieron. México: Editorial Grijalbo, 1981. 2 v. (381 p., 195 p. of plates): ill.

Compilation of personal accounts of combatants during Cristero War. Focus is on how war started, why Church opposed the State, who directed movement, and who supported and opposed the war. Based on interviews with surviving cristeros.

2185 La Clase obrera en la historia de México. v. 12, De Adolfo Ruiz Cortines a Adolfo López Mateos: 1952–1964 [by] José Luis Reyna and Raúl Trejo Delarbe. v. 16, Al norte del Río Bravo: pasado lejano, 1600–1930 [by] Juan Gómez-Quiñones and David Maciel. v. 17, Al norte del Río Bravo: pasado inmediato, 1930- 1981 [by] David Maciel. Coordinador, Pablo González Casanova. México: Siglo Veintiuno Editores: Instituto de Investigaciones Sociales de la UNAM, 1980–1981. 3 v.: bibls.

Vol. 12 is an analysis of organized labor in relation to political economic changes, industrialization, and attempts to institutionalize the labor movement. Vols. 16–17 are studies of Mexican workers in the US in the context of colonialism, North American imperialism, and racism.

2186 Cockcroft, James D. Immiseration, not marginalization: the case of Mexico (LAP, 10:2/3, Spring/Summer 1983, p. 86–107)

Using Marx's theory of immiseration and relative surplus population, analyzes development of industrial capitalism in Mexico. Nation lacks adequate capital to generate sufficient employment which creates underemployment, unemployment, and increased poverty. The State regulates the immiserated, channels their economic activity, and organizes their political behavior.

2187 Colín, Mario. Guía de documentos impresos del Estado de México. t. 1, 1824–1835. t. 2, 1835–1860. t. 3, 1861–1911. t. 4, 1911–1972. México: Biblioteca Enciclopédica del Estado de México, 1976–1981. 4.v.: facsims., indexes (Biblioteca enciclopédica del Estado de México; 56–59)

Compilation of documents, letters, reports, decrees covering events in Mexico State (1911–72).

Cordero, Fernando. La influencia de los ferrocarriles en los cambios económicos y especiales de México, 1870–1910. See *HLAS 45:5090.*

2188 Cosío Villegas, Daniel. Llamadas. México: Colegio de México, Centro de Estudios Históricos, 1980. 251 p.: bibl. (Lecturas básicas)

Compilation of introductory remarks to volumes of *Historia moderna de México*.

2189 Davis, Charles L. and Kenneth M. Coleman. Electoral change in the one-party dominant Mexican polity, 1958–1973: evidence from Mexico City (JDA, 16:4, July 1982, p. 523–542, graphs)

Citing growing politicization and partisanship of Mexico City electorate, authors focus on PAN as vehicle for expression of opposition to PRI's dominance. Authors conclude that PAN gains during period came primarily from mobilization of nonaligned rather than conversion of PRI supporters.

2190 Dennis, Philip A. The anti-Chinese campaigns in Sonora, Mexico (ASE/E, 26:1, Winter 1979, p. 65–80, ill.)

Discussion of ethnic and racial campaigns against Sonora's Chinese leading to their expulsion in 1931. Problems are discussed in light of return of Mexicans from US during Depression. Mexican workers were unable to acquire jobs in US and found that Chinese controlled jobs and wealth in Sonora.

2191 Documentos de la relación de México con los Estados Unidos. v. 1, El mester político de Poinsett, noviembre de 1824-diciembre de 1829. v. 2, Butler en persecución de la Provincia de Texas, 31 de diciembre de 1829–29 de mayo de 1836. Compiled by Carlos Bosch García. México: Instituto de Investigaciones Históricas, Universidad Nacional Autónoma de México, 1983. 2 v.: bibl. (Serie documental; 13–14)

Ambos vols. contienen largas introducciones del editor, elaboradas principalmente a base de despachos de representantes americanos y de algunos funcionarios mexicanos, especialmente vol. 2. La obra será complementada por vol. 3, *El endeudamiento de México*, y vol. 4, *De las reclamaciones, la guerra y la paz* (en prensa). Se trata de un valioso instrumento de trabajo, muy bien presentado e impreso. [L. Gómez Canedo]

2192 Documents on the Mexican Revolution. v. 2, The Madero Revolution as reported in the confidential despatches of U.S. ambassador Henry Lane and the Embassy in Mexico City, June 1910 to June 1911. Salisbury, N.C.: Documentary Publications, 1976–1983. 1 v. in 2: indexes.

Vol. 2 contains reproductions of telegrams and correspondence in English concerning Madero's death. Materials presented support view that Ambassador Wilson did not know of plan, or assist in plot against Madero (vols. 1 and 3–8 not available at press time).

2193 Durán, Esperanza. Revolution and international pressures: the Mexican experience, 1910–1920 (SAGE/JIAS, 24:4, Nov. 1982, p. 483–495)

Review article discusses following works: Peter Calvert, *The Mexican Revolution, 1910–1914: the diplomacy of Anglo-American conflict*; Fredrich Katz, *The secret war in Mexico: Europe, the United States and the Mexican Revolution*; and Berta Ulloa, *La Revolución intervenida: relaciones diplomáticas entre México y los Estados Unidos, 1910–1914*; *Historia de la Revolución mexicana: período 1914–1917* (4 vols.); *La revolución escondida*; and *La encrucijada de 1915*. Works show importance of external influences on Revolution's internal dynamics and how Mexico itself influenced international events.

2194 Encuentro sobre Historia del Movimiento Obrero, *Universidad Autónoma de Puebla, 1978*. v. 1/3. Memorias. Puebla: Universidad Autónoma de Puebla, 1980. 2 v.: bibl., ill. (Colección Fuentes para el estudio de la historia del movimiento obrero y sindical)

Series of well documented essays on workers' movement in Mexico. Covers various industries and organizations.

2195 Esteves, José. Entrevista con Miguel Angel Velasco (CEHSMO, 6:22, abril 1981, p. 19–31)

Interview covers following topics: events of Revolution, workers' movement, Communist Party in Mexico, and Augusto César Sandino's struggle.

2196 Estudios de historia moderna y contemporánea de México. México: Universidad Nacional Autónoma de México, 1980. 252 p., 1 folded leaf of plates: map (Instituto de Investigaciones Históricas; v. 8)

Series of articles and book reviews covering politics, economics, history of 19th and 20th-century Mexico.

2197 Flores Vizcarra, Jorge and Otto Granados Roldán. Salvador Alvarado y la Revolución mexicana. Culiacán, México:

Universidad Autónoma de Sinaloa, 1980. 111 p.: bibl. (Colección Realidad nacional; 4)

Study of the general's political and military activities and his participation in the Mexican Revolution in Sonora, his influence in later years, and his military government in Yucatán.

2198 Florescano, Enrique. El poder y la lucha por el poder en la historiografía mexicana. México: Departamento de Investigaciones Históricas, INAH, 1980. 80 p.: bibl. (Cuadernos de trabajo; 33)

Study of how the governing classes have used the past to legitimize their power, defend their interests, and stabilize political order.

2199 Fray Gregorio de la Concepción— **Gregorio Melero y Piña:** toluqueño insurgente: su proceso, la relación de sus hazañas y otros apéndices. Introducción y notas por Dionisio Victoria Moreno. México: Biblioteca Enciclopédica del Estado de México, 1981. 158, 95 p.: bibl., ill. (Biblioteca enciclopédica del Estado de México; 109)

Documents, essays, and notes on life and revolutionary career of Carmelite priest from Toluca. Not complete biography but attempt to shed light on his activities during independence movement.

2200 Freebairn, Donald K. Agricultural interaction between Mexico and the United States (SAGE/JIAS, 25:3, Aug. 1983, p. 275–298)

Study of agricultural structures of US and Mexico and policies generated thereby. Emphasizes points of comparison and competition since 1950.

2201 García, Juan Ramón. Operation Wetback: the mass deportation of Mexican undocumented workers in 1954. Westport: Greenwood Press, 1980. 268 p.: bibl., ill., index (Contributions in ethnic studies; no. 2)

Based on US documents, presents overview of Mexican immigration to US, Bracero Program, migration policies, and "Operation Wetback." Discussion of 1954 campaign to apprehend undocumented Mexicans appears in later chapters.

2202 García Quintanilla, Alejandra. La formación de la estructura económica de Yucatán, 1850–1940 (UY/R, 24:139, enero/feb. 1982, p. 13–37)

Analysis of social and economic forces

of henequen haciendas and their relationship to external markets. Based on Marxist analysis with few additional sources.

2203 Garfias M., Luis. Verdad y leyenda de Pancho Villa: vida y hechos del famoso personaje de la Revolución mexicana. México: Panorama Editorial, 1981. 165 p.: ill. (Colección Panorama)

Another popular history of Villa.

2204 González Casanova, Pablo. El estado y los partidos políticos en México: ensayos. México: Ediciones Era, 1981. 178 p.: bibl. (Colección Problemas de México)

Collection of five essays published earlier on social and economic conditions in Mexico, political reforms, relations between the State and masses, and future of State and society.

2205 González y González, Luis. Los días del presidente Cárdenas. México: Colegio de México, 1981. 381 p.: bibl., ill., index (Historia de la Revolución Mexicana; t. 15. Período 1934–1940)

General narrative of Cárdenas presidency including bibliography.

2206 ———. Nuevo balance del cardenismo (Vuelta [s.n., México] 4:44, julio 1980, p. 4–8)

Brief review of the Cárdenas years. Based on secondary services. Covers general topics.

2207 Graham Knox, A.J. Henequen haciendas, Maya peones, and the Mexican revolutionary promises of 1910: reform and reaction in Yucatán, 1910–1940 (UPR/CS, 17:1/2, April/July 1977, p. 55–82)

Studies course of agrarian reform in Yucatán during Revolution and its effects upon plantation system and population dependent on plantations for livelihood. Agrarian reform in Yucatán was long process and its full effects were not felt until Cárdenas years. Agrarian struggles were not associated with violence as they were in other areas of Mexico. Hacendado class was bitter and strong enemy of reforms. Finally, agrarian reforms failed to improve condition of rural masses.

2208 Guadarrama, Rocío. Los sindicatos y la política en México: La CROM, 1918–1923. México: Ediciones Era, 1981. 239 p.: ill. (Colección Problemas de México)

Analysis of CROM's role in Mexican working-class movement during post-Revolution formative years. Focuses on struggle between surviving as independent organization within context of the State's consolidation. Based on CROM documents and major secondary sources.

2209 Guerra, François-Xavier. La Révolution mexicaine: d'abord une révolution minère? (AESC, 36 : 5, sept./oct. 1981, p. 785–814, maps, tables)

Regional study of Revolution. Emphasizes strength of unrest in mining centers as Revolution's initial focus.

2210 Gutiérrez Casillas, José. Jesuitas en México durante el siglo XX. México: Editorial Porrúa, 1981. 726 p., 61 p. of plates: bibl., ill., index (Biblioteca Porrúa; 77)

Chronological and factual account of Jesuit life and activities in Mexico during 20th century until 1979.

2211 Hamilton, Nora. The State and the national bourgeoisie in postrevolutionary Mexico: 1920–1940 (LAP, 11 : 4, Fall 1982, p. 31–54)

Focuses on relations between the State and private sector (1920–40) in order to understand conditions which have led to emergence of dominant coalition that shapes Mexico's development. Concludes that alliances between the State and dominant capitalist class were in place by 1940.

2212 Hansen, Niles M. The border economy: regional development in the Southwest. Austin: University of Texas Press, 1981. 225 p.: bibl., index, map.

Documents growth of US border states and shows that undocumented workers from Mexico pose no serious threat to Borderlands. Concludes that there is a symbiotic relationship between border area of Mexico and US.

2213 Harris, Charles H., III and Louis R. Sadler. The "underside" of the Mexican Revolution: El Paso, 1912 (AAFH/TAM, 39 : 1, July 1982, p. 69–84)

Study of Mexican activities and US citizens and government agencies involved in munitions traffic, intelligence, recruiting and filibustering in El Paso during Pascual Orozco's rebellion. Cooperation between US and Mexican governments in depriving Orozco of munitions ultimately led to re-

bellion's failure. Based on substantial archival research in US.

2214 Henderson, Peter V.N. Félix Díaz, the Porfirians, and the Mexican Revolution. Lincoln: University of Nebraska Press, 1981. 239 p.: bibl., index, port.

Excellent political biography of major figure during early revolutionary years. Concludes Díaz had more ambition than ability and was primarily important as symbol of old regime around which anti-revolutionary forces could rally.

2215 Historia documental del partido de la Revolución. t. 1, PNR, 1929–1932. t. 2, PNR, 1933. t. 3, PNR-PRM, 1934–1938. t. 4, PRM, 1938–1944. t. 5, PRM-PRI, 1945–1950. t. 6, PRI, 1951–1956. t. 7, PRI, 1957–1962. México: Partido Revolucionario Institucional, Instituto de Capacitación Política, 1981–1982. 7 v.: ill., indexes.

Collection of documents, speeches, and regulations on PRI's history (1929–62).

2216 Horn, James J. The Mexican Revolution and health care, or the health of the Mexican Revolution (LAP, 10 : 4, Fall 1983, p. 24–39)

Critical account of health care and health policies in Mexico. Studies morbidity, mortality, malnutrition, water, and sanitation. Patterns of health care reflect inequities and contradictions in society at large and show additional reason to doubt Revolution's success.

2217 Ibáñez Molto, María Amparo. La fase religiosa de la Revolución mexicana en la prensa de Valencia (CH, 370, abril 1981, p. 67–75)

Compares two Spanish newspapers, their reporting and opinions of anti-clericalism and Church-State relations in Mexico during Calles period.

2217a Informe de la compañía mexicana de Luz y Fuerza Motriz, S.A. (CEHSMO, 5 : 18, enero 1980, p. 20–23)

Reprint of 1915 document in which company explains to Gen. Pablo González its inability to grant workers' demands.

2218 Jacobs, Ian. Ranchero revolt: the Mexican Revolution in Guerrero. Austin: University of Texas Press, 1982. 234 p.: bibl., index, ill. (The Texas Pan American series)

Revisionist view of Revolution. Challenges notion that oppressed rural masses led revolt against Díaz by exploring role of rural middle class "ranchers" in Guerrero state. Based on substantial archival material.

2219 Joseph, Gilbert M. Revolution from without: Yucatán, Mexico, and the United States, 1880–1924. Cambridge: Cambridge University Press, 1982. 407 p.: bibl., ill., index (Cambridge Latin American studies; 42)

Regional study of Mexican Revolution in Yucatán where forces of Revolution were quite different from other areas. Interpretation is that Revolution in Yucatán was "made from above and imposed from without", and that it failed to achieve many of its goals of social and economic justice in the area.

2220 Kane, N. Stephen. The United States and the development of the Mexican petroleum industry, 1945–1950: a lost opportunity (IAMEA, 35 : 1, Summer 1981, p. 45–72)

Analysis of efforts attempted by US and Mexico to realign their relations in petroleum industry. Both countries had separate reasons for renewing ties but were unable to reach agreements because of problems concerning loans and investments.

2221 Katz, Friedrich. The secret war in Mexico: Europe, the United States, and the Mexican Revolution. Chicago: University of Chicago Press, 1981. 659 p.: bibl., index.

Outstanding study of efforts by major European powers and US to protect their interests during Revolution by conducting "secret war" to install a friendly government in Mexico. US policy is viewed as especially contradictory. Based on impressive array of archival sources from Mexico, Europe, and US.

2222 Kemper, Robert V. and **Anya Peterson Royce.** Mexican urbanization since 1821: a macro-historical approach (UA, 8 : 3/4, Winter 1979, p. 267–289)

Shows diversity of urbanization in Mexico as illustrated in cases of Mexico City, Oaxaca, Mérida, and Monterrey. Urbanization was slow throughout Mexico in early 19th century, increased during Porfiriato, declined between 1910–40, and increased following 1940. For ethnologist's comment, see *HLAS 45:978.*

2223 Labastida Martín del Campo, Julio. De la unidad nacional de desarrollo estabilizador: 1940–1970 (*in* América Latina: historia del medio siglo. v. 2, Centroamérica, México y el Caribe. Coordinación, Pablo González Casanova. México: Siglo Veintiuno Editores, 1981 p. 328–376, bibl.)

Exposition and anaylisis of political, social, economic, and international events in Mexico. Based mainly on secondary sources.

2224 LaFrance, David. The Madero Collection in Mexico's Archivo General de la Nación (RIB, 33 : 2, 1983, p. 191–197)

Useful description of Madero papers in Ramo de Presidentes in Mexico's AGN. While most material related to the Madero presidency, collection includes documents covering 1894–1940 period. Most helpful for researchers looking for political, military, or financial information.

2225 Lamartine Yates, Paul. Mexico's agricultural dilemma. Tucson: University of Arizona Press, 1981. 291 p.: bibl., ill., index.

Survey of Mexico's agricultural development problems since World War II. Believes agrarian institutions generated by Revolution, especially the *ejido,* are unable to meet Mexico's current agricultural needs and favors extension of full property rights to *ejidatarios.*

2226 Langle Ramírez, Arturo. Huerta contra Zapata: una campaña desigual. México: Universidad Nacional Autónoma de México, Instituto de Investigaciones Históricas, 1981. 115 p.: bibl. (Serie Historia moderna y contemporánea; 14)

Brief account of political and military battles between Huerta and Zapata which endangered the agrarian spirit of the Revolution. One-half of book contains documents. Limited bibliography.

2227 Levy, Daniel C. University and government in Mexico: autonomy in an authoritarian system. New York: Praeger, 1980. 173 p.: bibl., index, ill. (The Praeger special studies series in comparative education)

Study focuses on UNAM, although there is some attention to provincial public universities. In addition to examining question of autonomy, author also deals with issues of university freedom in personnel selection and of traditional concept of academic freedom. Conclusion is that Mexican public universities enjoy considerable autonomy despite "authoritarian" system (see also item **222**).

Longwell, A. Richard. The literature on Mexico's agrarian reform. See *HLAS 45:5105.*

2228 Mabry, Donald J. The Mexican University and the State: student conflicts, 1910–1971. College Station: Texas A&M University Press, 1982. 328 p.: bibl., index.

Description of evolving relationship between the State and university as seen through various student conflicts. "The Mexican University" in this case is literally UNAM. Status of university autonomy is constant theme with author, concluding that UNAM has generally been successful in maintaining its autonomy largely because there was no revolutionary student movement which threatened the government (see also item **2227**).

2229 Mac Donald Escobedo, Eugenio. Turismo, una recapitulación. México: Editorial Bodoni, 1981. 251 p.: bibl., ill., ports.

Collection of government pronouncements and declarations on tourism in Mexico (1823–1980).

2230 Macías, Anna. Against all odds: the feminist movement in Mexico to 1940. Westport: Greenwood Press, 1982. 195 p.: bibl., index (Contributions in women's studies; no. 30)

Analysis of feminist movement in Mexico dating from 1890. Discusses machismo, Church-State conflicts, feminist conferences, attitudes of government leaders, social and economic conditions, an antifeminist press. Includes valuable bibliographical essay containing guides and works on Mexican women.

2231 Maciel, David R. La clase obrera en la historia de México: al norte del Río Bravo; pasado inmediato, 1930–1981. México: Siglo Veintiuno Editores, 1981. 234 p.: bibl., tables.

Synthesis of unionizing activities by Chicano workers since 1930s in variety of fields, including agricultural, industrial, and mining.

2232 Magdaleno, Mauricio. Instantes de la Revolución. México: Instituto Na-

cional de Estudios Históricos de la Revolución Mexicana, 1981. 286 p. (Biblioteca del Instituto; 88)

General essays on wide range of individuals and events related to Revolution, including Villa, Zapata, Madero, Convention of Aguascalientes, *Los de abajo*, Carranza, Pershing Expedition. No bibliography.

2233 Martínez, Andrea and **Jorge Fernández Tomás.** Asambleísmo, "espontaneidad," huelga y maderismo: una ojeada y muchas preguntas sobre las movilizaciones de 1911 en el sector textil (CEHSMO, 5:20, sept. 1980, p. 27–44, photos)

Analysis of internal operation of textile workers and their movement. Includes documents from Archivo General de la Nación. Places strikes of textile workers within heart of Madero revolt.

2234 Martínez Assad, Carlos R.; Ricardo Pozas Horcasitas; and **Maro Ramírez Rancaño.** Revolucionarios fueron todos. México: Fondo de Cultura Económica, 1982. 341 p.: bibl.

Analysis of activities of revolutionary leaders, local caudillos, and politicians who made their fortunes from the Revolution. Emphasizes Adalberto Tejada, Saturnino Cedillo, Abelardo Rodríguez, and Juan Andrew Almazán.

2235 Medin, Tzvi. El minimato presidencial: historia política del maximato, 1928–1935. México: Ediciones Era, 1982. 170 p.: bibl., index (Colección Problemas de México)

Study of political development of Calles era (1928–35) and its extension to Cárdenas presidency. Analyzes period's political struggles, institutions, and political ideology. Includes useful bibliography.

2236 Menegus Bornemann, Margarita and **Juan Felipe Leal.** Las haciendas de Mazaquiahuac y El Rosario en los albores de la Revolución agraria: 1910–1914 (CM/HM, 31:2, oct./dic. 1981, p. 233–77, bibl., maps, tables)

Using microsocial-macrosocial framework, authors analyze impact of various revolutionary movements on two pulque haciendas in Tlaxcala state. Two haciendas functioned as economic unit and suffered little economically until 1914. Part of larger study covering 1910–40 period; extensive use of hacienda records.

2237 Menéndez, Iván. En defensa propia: México contra la guerra (CAM, 247:2, marzo/abril 1983, p. 26–30)

Brief exposition of Mexico's determination to adhere to principles of: 1) nonintervention; 2) peaceful solution to international conflict; 3) judicial equality among nations; 4) international cooperation for economic development; and 5) promotion of world peace. Shows when these points have been applied in its foreign policy.

2238 Mexican immigrant workers in the U.S. Edited by Antonio Ríos-Bustamante. Los Angeles: Chicago Studies Research Center Publications, University of California, Los Angeles, 1981. 178 p.: bibl., ill. (Anthology; no. 2)

Collection of 14 articles covering international labor migration from Mexico, human rights and public policy, Mexican women workers, and future trends in Mexican migration. Articles vary greatly in quality, and many notable experts are not included.

2239 Mexico. Archivo General de la Nación. Archivo de Alfredo Robles Domínguez. México: El Archivo, 1981. 2 v. (316 leaves) (Serie Guías y catálogos; 45)

Guide to archive of revolutionary figure, as governor of Federal District and military leader. Covers period 1909–16 in chronological order.

2240 ———.———. Archivo de Genovevo de la O. Elaborado por Laurentino Luna et al. México: Departamento de Publicaciones del Archivo, 1980. 8, 149 leaves (Serie Guías y catálogos; 36)

Guide to archive of zapatista leader including material on military activities. Documentation covers period of 1911–51 in chronological order.

2241 ———.———. Catálogo de la Serie Armas, Fondo Presidentes Alvaro Obregón, Plutarco Elías Calles, 1920–1928. México: El Archivo, 1980. 153 leaves: index (Serie Guías y catálogos; 34)

Pt. 1 of Serie Armas. Designed to indicate role of revolutionary armed forces in stabilization of Mexico following Revolution. Contains information relating to rebellions

sedition, contraband, purchases, and manufacturing of arms; military expenses, appointments, agreements, and construction; role of military in elections.

2242 Mexico today. Edited by Tommie Sue Montgomery. Philadelphia: Institute for the Study of Human Issues, 1982. 140 p.

Collection of essays by various Mexican writers, scholars, and politicians. Works offer criticism yet optimism for contemporary Mexico. Essay by Josefina Vásquez, "The Beginning of a Nation: the Nineteenth Century," reviewed in this section (item **2159**).

2243 Mexico's political economy: challenges at home and abroad. Edited by Jorge I. Domínguez. Beverly Hills: Sage, 1982. 239 p.: bibl., index (Sage focus editions; 47)

Study of implications of Mexico's internal affairs for its international relations. Contains four essays about problems and conditions of tomato growers, unionism in auto industry, PEMEX, and changes in Mexican economy which have constrained Mexico's freedom in foreign affairs.

2244 Meyer, Lorenzo. La Revolución mexicana y sus elecciones presidenciales: una interpretación, 1911–1940 (CM/HM, 32:2, oct./dic. 1982, p. 143–197)

Study of historical evolution of electoral process in Mexico. Emphasizes qualitative rather than quantitative aspects of process. Democratic electoral rights have not been exercised fully because of absence of democratic traditions, lack of organized forces, and manipulation of votes.

2245 Meyer, Michael C. Felix Sommerfeld and the Columbus Raid of 1916 (UA/AW, 25:3, Autumn 1983, p. 213–228, ill., table)

Revision of earlier article in *Historia Mexicana* (see *HLAS 44:2238*). Makes convincing case for link between Sommerfeld and Germans and for connection between these parties and Villa. German connection with Columbus raid, however, is "strong but circumstantial."

2246 Moreno García, Heriberto. Guaracha, tiempos viejos, tiempos nuevos. Morelia: FONAPAS Michoacán; Zamora: Colegio de Michoacán, 1980. 215, 1 p.: bibl., ill. (Serie de historia)

Regional study of land tenure and land reform of one hacienda and its transformation into an ejido.

2247 Muría, José María. Notas sobre la historiografía regional jalisciense en el siglo XX (CM/RE, 3:10, primavera de 1982, p. 69–85)

Brief discussion of 20th century historiography of Jalisco covering wide range of colonial and modern topics.

2248 Nalven, Joseph. Resolving the undocumented worker problem (UCSD/NS, 8, 1982, p. 473–481)

Review article discusses two works: G.C. and M.W. Kiser, *Mexican workers in the United States* (see *HLAS 44: 2235*), and Jonathan Power, *Migrant workers in Western Europe and the United States*. Both works are set within historical context of Mexican labor migration to US and current debates on undocumented workers.

2249 Neymet, Marcela de. Cronología del Partido Comunista Mexicano. México: Ediciones de Cultura Popular, 1981. 1 v.: bibl. (Historia)

General listing of events and activities of Mexican Communist Party.

2250 Niblo, Stephen R. British propaganda in Mexico during the Second World War: the development of cultural imperialism (LAP, 10:4, Fall 1983, p. 114–126)

Examines experience of British propaganda agents who were active in Mexico during early years of World War II. British were able to penetrate and manipulate the Mexican media by developing new techniques.

2251 Nikólskaia, Galina. Evolución regulada del ejido (URSS/AL, 2:62, feb. 1983, p. 32–46)

Analysis of 1981 Ley de Planeación y Fomento Agropecuario and its relation to ejido's history. Concludes that law helped to solidify private and state capitalism.

2252 Obregón, Arturo. El Banco Obrero: un proyecto histórico del artesanado inscrito en el proceso de modernización del país (CEHSMO, 4:16, mayo 1979, p. 2–10)

Discusses formation of workers' banks that would gather and increase workers' capital and try to maintain their equality in context of growth of economic crises and capital expansion.

2253 ———. La inauguración de la primera sucursal del Gran Círculo de Obreros (CEHSMO, 5:20, sept. 1980, p. 2–8, photos)

Reproduction of inaugural act of first workers' association established outside of Mexico City.

2254 Ortega, Carlos; Augusto Urteaga; and Francisco González Ayerdi. Los estudios económicos sobre el siglo XX. México: Departamento de Investigaciones Históricas, INAH, 1979. 63 p.: bibl. (Cuadernos de trabajo; 28)

Historiography covering economic history, finance, industrialization, regional development, political economy, commerce, investment, and agriculture.

2255 Parra, Manuel Germán. Historia del movimiento sindical de los trabajadores del estado. México: FSTSE, 1982 or 1983. 320 p.: bibl., ill. (some col.)

Pictorial history of Federación de Sindicatos de Trabajadores al Servicio del Estado. Work is divided into four periods from 1825–1982.

2256 Paulsen, George E. Reaping the whirlwind in Chihuahua: the destruction of the Minas de Corralitos, 1911–1917 (UNM/NMHR, 58:3, July 1983, p. 253–270)

Study of destruction of mines in Chihuahua and failure of American Special Mexican Claims Commission to obtain compensation for US investors. Based on Commission's archival sources.

2257 Peniche Vallado, Leopoldo. Don Jesús Silva Herzog: una inteligencia fuera de serie (CAM, 244:5, sept./oct. 1982, p. 59–70)

Brief essay praising Silva Herzog's contributions to Mexico and Mexican history.

2258 Pérez Castro, Ana Bella. Movimiento campesino en Simojovel, Chiapas, 1936–1978: problema étnica o de clases sociales (UNAM/AA, 19, 1982, p. 207–229, bibl., charts)

Analysis of class consciousness among group of Chiapas Indians as manifested in land conflicts. Shows that group does not live in colonial situation but within 20th-century Mexican capitalism.

2259 Plana, Manuel. El algodón y el riego en La Laguna: la formación de la propiedad agraria en una región económica del norte de México durante el Porfiriato:

1877–1910 (GEE/NA, 4, 1981, p. 211–262, ill., tables)

Study of origins, formation, and structure of land tenure in La Laguna with special emphasis on cotton haciendas.

2260 Powell, Thomas G. Mexico and the Spanish Civil War. Albuquerque: University of New Mexico Press, 1981. 210 p.: bibl., index.

Revisionist interpretation of efforts by Mexican government and individuals to aid Republican Spain, including activities to enlist support from governments in Latin America and Europe. President Cárdenas figures prominently in account, but author concludes that efforts to help were seriously undercut by communist partisanship in both Spain and Mexico.

2261 Pozas Horcasitas, Ricardo. La consolidación del Nuevo Orden Institucional en México: 1929–1940 (in América Latina: historia de medio siglo. v. 2, Centroamérica, México y el Caribe. Coordinación: Pablo González Casanova. México: Siglo Veintiuno Editores, 1981, v. 2, p. 259–327, bibl., tables)

Exposition and analysis of political, social, economic events during the consolidation of the Mexican state. Based mainly on secondary sources. For political scientist's comment, see *HLAS 45:6075*.

2262 Los Presupuestos en la época revolucionaria, 1912–1918. Prelim. study by Carlos J. Sierra. México: Secretaría de Programación y Presupuesto, Dirección General de Difusión y Relaciones Públicas, 1982. 147 p.

Compilation of budgets and debates during Madero's government and Carranza's constitutionalist period. Includes brief introductory study.

2263 Prieto Laurens, Jorge. Anécdotas históricas de Jorge Prieto Laurens. México: B. Costa-Amic Editor, 1977. 197 p., 16 p. of plates: ill.

Collection of personal accounts and events in Mexico from Huerta to Ruiz Cortines.

2264 Quiles Ponce, Enrique. Henríquez y Cárdenas, ¡presentes!: hechos y realidades en la campaña henriquista. 2a. ed. México: Costa-Amic Editores, 1980. 334 p.: facsims., ill.

Popular account of campaign of independent candidate for president (1952–58).

2265 Quirk, Robert E. The Mexican Revolution, 1914–1915: the Convention of Aguascalientes. Westport: Greenwood Press, 1981. 325 p., 2 leaves of plates: bibl., index, map.

Reprint of 1960 ed. published by Indiana University Press (see *HLAS 23:3313*).

2266 Raat, W. Dirk. The Mexican Revolution: an annotated guide to recent scholarship. Boston: G.K. Hall, 1982. 275 p.: index (Reference publications in Latin American studies)

Research guide covering Mexican history, 1876–1940. Wide range of topics includes historiography, methodology, regional studies, biographies, revisionism, and quantitative studies. For bibliographer's comment, see *HLAS 45:22*.

2267 ———. Revoltosos: Mexico's rebels in the United States, 1903-1923. College Station: Texas A&M University Press, 1981. 344 p., 4 leaves of plates: bibl., index.

Much needed study of Mexican revolutionary exile activity in US. Author shows how both US and Mexican governments have interest in controlling such activity and developing "binational police and espionage system." Emphasizes 1906–13 period and role of Mexican Liberal Party.

2268 Resoluciones del VI Congreso de la CGT de México celebrado los días 11 al 18 de junio de 1928 (CEHSMO, 5:17, sept. 1979, p. 17–23)

Reprint of congress' proceedings and resolutions covering worker and peasant movements, economic problems, working hours and conditions, and international labor movement.

2269 Richmond, Douglas W. Intentos externos para derrocar al régime de Carranza 1915–20 (CM/HM, 32:1, julio/sept. 1982, p. 106–132)

Analysis of attempts to overthrow Carranza by conservative exiles and North American investors. Attributes failure to oust Carranza to popular rejections of imperialism and sees his final downfall as result of political errors and failure to accelerate domestic reforms.

2270 ———. Mexican immigration and
border strategy during the Revolution,
1910–1920 (UMN/NMHR, 57:3, July 1982,
p. 269–288, plates)
Discusses Carranza's efforts in trying
to secure Mexico's northern border, improve
area's economic conditions, keep workers in
Mexico, and protect workers who were in
US. His policies reflected desire to improve
treatment of Mexican immigrants and to
strengthen Mexican economy within nationalist context.

2271 Rodman, Selden. A short history of
Mexico. New York: Stein and Day,
1982. 179 p., 18 p. of plates: bibl., ill.
First published as *The Mexican trav-
eler* (1969), this updated version adds brief
section on major current events (1969–80).

2272 Rodríguez Ozan, María Elena. La en-
señanza de la historia de las ideas en
México (IPGH/RHI, 3, 1982, p. 159–167)
Brief study of writing of philosophy
and history in Mexico and Latin America.
Largely descriptive treatment of writers.

2273 Romero Aceves, Ricardo. La mujer en
la historia de México. México: Costa-
Amic Editores, 1982. 750 p.: bibl
Brief biographical sketches of major
Mexican women from pre-colonial to modern
times.

2274 Ross, Stanley Robert. Fuentes de la
historia contemporánea de México: períodos y revistas. v. 3–5, 1959–1968. México: Universidad Nacional Autónoma de
México, 1976–78. 3 v.: bibl. (Instituto de Investigaciones Bibliográficas, Biblioteca Nacional. Serie Bibliografías; 4)
Comprehensive list of 46, 125 items
culled from 1958–68 newspapers and periodical articles. Each item annotated. Publication of these three volumes completes
quarter century project on sources for study
of the Mexican Revolution (1910–40).

2275 Roxborough, Ian and Ilan Buzberg.
Union locals in Mexico: the "new
unionism" in steel and automobiles (JLAS,
15:l, May 1983, p. 117–135)
Study of rise of militancy in industrial
unions within context of late 1970s and early
1980s economic crisis in Mexico. Authors argue, however, that there is little likelihood
that strong national movement will develop.

2276 Ruiz, Ramón Eduardo. The great
rebellion: Mexico, 1905–1924. New
York: Norton, 1980. 530 p.: bibl., index.
Interesting and often controversial interpretation of "The Revolution" as rebellion,
most of whose leaders were essentially conservative and concerned with renovating, not
revolutionizing, Mexican society. Contains
variety of biographical sketches and excellent data on the economy, especially for
Porfiriato's final years.

2277 Sánchez Lamego, Miguel A. Generales
de la Revolución: biografías. México:
Patronato del Instituto Nacional de Estudios
Históricos de la Revolución Mexicana,
1979–1981. 2 v. (Biblioteca del Instituto Nacional de Estudios Históricos de la Revolución Mexicana; 81)
Brief biographical sketches of 21 generals of the Revolution.

2278 Sanderson, Steven E. Agrarian populism and the Mexican state: the
struggle for land in Sonora. Berkeley: University of California Press, 1981. 290 p.: appendix, bibl., index.
Case study of agrarian politics in the
key state of Sonora. Author places his survey
within the broader themes of agrarian reform
versus developmentalism and the formulation of a national agrarian policy.

2279 St. Lüders. Agrarverhältnisse, Bevöl-
kerungsstruktur und Bauernbewegung
in Morelos und den benachbarten Bun-
desstaaten zur Zeit der mexikanischen revolution (UR/L, Spring 1980, p. 23–56, tables)
Discussion of Zapata movement dur-
ing Revolution and creation of agrarian plans,
committees, cooperatives, and new production techniques in sugar industry. Majority of
Zapata followers, however, desired to retain
their traditional way of life.

2280 Saxe-Fernández, John. Petróleo y es-
trategia: México y Estados Unidos en
el contexto de la política global. México:
Siglo Veintiuno Editores, 1980. 177 p.:
bibl., ill.
Argues that Mexico should not allow
US to exchange oil for aid and protection.
Believes that Mexico can use its oil to force
US to adopt less aggressive policies. Mexico's
recent economic crisis lessens book's value.

2281 Sayeg Helú, Jorge. La Revolución mexicana a través de sus documentos fun-

damentales, 1900–1913. México: Instituto Nacional de Estudios Históricos de la Revolución Mexicana, 1981. 1 v.: bibl. (Biblioteca del Instituto; 87)

Brief extracts and text of major documents on Porfiriato's fall and Revolution's early years.

2282 Schmidt, Henry C. The Mexican intellectual as political pundit, 1968–1976: the case of Daniel Cosío Villegas (SAGE/JIAS, 24:2, Feb. 1982, p. 81–103, bibl.)

Analysis of final stage in Cosío's "fifty-year meditation on postrevolutionary Mexico." Concludes that Cosío's most important contribution as critic was not his explanation of Mexican politics but his "expansion of the usable materials in Mexican political analysis."

2283 Seminario del Movimiento Obrero y la Revolución Mexicana de la Dirección de Estudios Históricas. Del Leviatán al viejo topo: historiografía obrera en México, 1920–1930 (Historias [s.n., México] julio/sept. 1982, p. 41–54)

Review and discussion of recent labor historiography within class-struggle context.

2284 Serna, María Luisa. Las luchas obreras en 1924 (CEHSMO, 6:21, enero 1981, p. 7–24)

Chronology of Mexican labor movement in 1924 based on archival sources.

2285 Shafer, Robert Jones and Donald Mabry. Neighbors: Mexico and the United States, wetbacks and oil. Chicago: Nelson-Hall, 1981. 241 p.: bibl., index.

Attempts to discuss two current issues affecting US-Mexican relations, but presents general overview of Mexican history. Addressed to general audience, book includes limited, deficient bibliography.

2286 Sovetsko-meksikanskie otnosheniia = Relaciones mexicano-soviéticas: 1917–1980: Sbornik dokumentov. Sostaviteli sbronika: Aleksandr I. Sizonenko, Lázaro Cárdenas. Moskva: Institut Latinskoi Ameriki AN SSSR, Ministerstvo inostrannykh del Meksiki, 1981. 111 p.: bibl.

Texts of official documents, from both Mexican and Soviet archives, on relations between Mexico and USSR (1917–80). Some items are noted as having been published for the first time. Four pages of notes provide useful identification of persons or events discussed. Emphasizes harmonious relations between both countries. [R.V. Allen]

2287 Story, Dale. Industrial elites in Mexico: political ideology and influence (SAGE/JIAS, 25:3, Aug. 1983, p. 351–376)

Examines whether industrial elites in Mexico show a unified ideology that represents a strong role for industrialists in their relation with domestic and international actors. Focuses on CANACINTRA (National Chamber of Manufacturing Industries) and CONCAMIN (Confederation of Industrial Chambers). While the industrialists may profess ideological unity and demonstrate an adversary approach to the government, they realize their inability to act as a unified political force.

2288 Taibo, Paco Ignacio. Las huelgas en la interinato de Adolfo de la Huerta, 1° junio-30 noviembre 1920 (CEHSMO, 5:20, sept. 1980, p. 9–18, tables)

List of strikes by industry, number of workers, and demands and results.

2289 Tamayo, Jorge L. Obras de Jorge L. Tamayo. v. 1–4, Escritos juaristas. v. 5–7, Realidades y proyecciones de México. v. 8, Realidades y proyecciones de Oaxaca. Edición prepara y dirigida por Boris Rosen. Colaboraron, Gerardo Camacho Suárez y Juan García Jímenez. México: Centro de Investigación Científica Jorge L. Tamayo, 1980–1982. 8 v.: bibl., ill., indexes.

Eight-volume collection of the works of noted Oaxaca geographer and engineer.

2290 Taracena, Alfonso. Historia de la Revolución en Tabasco. 3a. ed. México: Consejo Editorial del Gobierno del Estado de Tabasco, 1981. 1 v. (Serie Historia)

Recapitulation and interpretation of the Revolution in Tabasco. Lacks footnotes and bibliography.

2291 Tardanico, Richard. State, dependency, and nationalism: revolutionary Mexico, 1924–1928 (CSSH, 24:3, July 1982, p. 400–423, tables)

Analysis of development of the State during Calles era in context of Porfiriato's legacy, Revolution's natiionalism, and international development of capitalism.

2292 Trow, Clifford W. Tired of waiting: Senator Albert B. Fall's alternative to Woodrow Wilson's Mexican policies,

1920–1921 (UNM/NMHR, 57:2, April 1982, p. 159–182)

Study of Fall's activities in protecting American interests and property in Mexico. Fall was impatient with Wilson's diplomatic means of dealing with Mexico and argued for an intervention policy.

2293 Tuck, Jim. The holy war in Los Altos: a regional analysis of Mexico's Cristero rebellion. Tucson: University of Arizona Press, 1982. 230 p.: bibl., ill., index.

Chronicle of Cristero activities in Los Altos area of eastern Jalisco. While work provides good description of military actions and leadership problems, "analysis" is limited. There is little to connect region's uniqueness to its support of Cristero cause or regional uprising to Cristero revolt as a whole.

2294 Turner, Ethel Duffy. Revolution in Baja Calfornia: Ricardo Flores Magon's high noon. Edited and annotated y Rey Devis. Detroit: Blaine Ethridge Books, 1981. 119 p.: bibl., ill., index.

Brief account of magonista revolution in Baja California in 1911 by wife of John Kenneth Turner and associate of Ricardo Flores Magón.

2295 United States relations with Mexico: context and content. Edited by Richard D. Erb and Stanley R. Ross. Washington: American Enterprise Institute for Public Policy Research, 1981. 291 p.: bibl.

Collection of essays by scholars and public officials on immigration, health, trade, commerce, water, and general economic issues.

2296 Vaughan, Mary K. The State, education, and social class in Mexico, 1880–1928. DeKalb: Northern Illinois University Press, 1982. 316 p.: bibl., index (The Origins of modern Mexico)

Study of government's educational policy at federal level. Argues that from Porfirian era, there has been continuity in history of Mexican education which did not necessarily begin in 1920s. Also argues that 1920s educational policy failed not because of weakness of the needy but because society needed drastic transformations.

2297 Weigand, Phil C. The role of the Huichol Indians in the revolutions of

western Mexico (PCCLAS/P, 1977/1979, p. 167–176)

Analysis of role played by Indians in four major revolutions in Mexico from 1860s to 1950s. Indians were fierce fighters since colonial period and defended status quo of their communities. They joined rebellion only when authorities threatened their societies.

2298 Weston, Charles H., Jr. The political legacy of Lázaro Cárdenas (AAFH/TAM, 39:3, Jan. 1983, p. 383–405)

Detailed analysis of roles Cárdenas played in presiding over Revolution's radical phase and in launching conservative post-1940 era. Cárdenas' legacy indicates that corporatist administration "may promote stability and economic growth, but it does not promote effective political participation by the working class or an egalitarian distribution of wealth. . ."

2299 Yamada, Mutsuo. Mexico City: development and urban problems after the Revolution, 1910–1970 (Latin American Studies [University of Tsukuba, Sakura-Mura, Japan] 7, 1983, p. 49–75, maps, tables)

Broad discussion of ecological and environmental problems faced by Mexico City. Concludes that while improvements have been made in living conditions, much more investment must be provided. See also item **2300.**

2300 ———. Mexico City: development and urban problems before the Revolution (Latin American Studies [University of Tsukuba, Sakura-Mura, Japan] 7, 1983, p. 1–47, ill., maps, tables)

Survey of Mexico City's geographical, water, demographic, and environment problems. Concentrates on colonial period.

2301 Zapata, Emiliano. Documentos inéditos sobre Emiliano Zapata y el Cuartel General: seleccionados del Archivo de Genovevo de la O, que conserva el Archivo General de la Nación. México: Comisión para la Conmemoración del Centenaro del Natalicio del General Emiliano Zapata, 1979. 215 p.: facsims., indexes, port.

Collection of documents covering land problems, water rights, and requests for land. Also includes testimonies of abuses by soldiers and government officials, military strategies of Zapata, and conditions of revolutionary troops. Materials are located in Archivo de Genovevo la O and Fondo Correspondencia de Emiliano Zapata of Archivo General de la Nación.

2302 Zapata y el Plan de Ayala. México: Centro de Estudios del Agrarismo en México, 1981. 102 p.: bibl.

Brief sketch of Zapata's life and revolutionary activity. Includes bibliographies on Zapata and Zapatismo.

2303 Zavala, Estela. Los impuestos financieros de los primeros años de la Revolución (CM/HM, 31:3, enero/marzo 1982, p. 325–360)

Study of tax reforms during six years after Revolution's onset. Reforms took two different orientations: one designed to finance military enterprises, another to improve country's commercial life.

CENTRAL AMERICA

MURDO J. MACLEOD, *Professor of History, University of Arizona*

THE CIVIL WARS IN GUATEMALA and El Salvador, the radical and divisive transformations in Honduras, the state of siege imposed on the revolutionary government of Nicaragua by outside forces, and the deep economic crisis in Costa Rica, are beginning to affect the publishing rate of Central American history. The number of publications in the field has declined and, in several countries, it is becoming difficult to obtain published works. This student's impressionistic observations notwithstanding, the quality of historical research on Central America has improved, one of the few positive results of the upheavals in the region.

Another consequence of these troubled times has been a sharpening of focus. There is less research of a general nature and a decline in colonial studies. Writing on the national period still suffers from its adherence to three persistent, almost exhausted genres: studies of *próceres* and heroes of independence; biographies of this or that president, politician, lawyer or journalist; and collections of evocative essays, mood pieces which are seldom done well, and even when successful are, like the parson's egg, only good in places. In spite of these hoary relics, the writing on the recent period has quickened in pace, confidence, and direction. In most of the Central American nations—and here we would include Belize—historians and others are anxious to determine how Central America arrived at its present tragic state. Nor are they satisfied with impressionistic findings. These scholars, often Marxist in orientation, are willing to undertake painstaking research and assemble large quantities of data necessary to provide convincing evidence for their complex theoretical analyses. Notable in this regard are the works of Italo López Vallacillos (item **2413**) and Gabriel Zaid (item **2449**) on El Salvador, essays from a collection edited by Pablo González Casanova (item **2423, 2439, 2445, and 2446**), and the study of Mario Posas and Rafael del Cid on Honduras (item **2431**). These and other such works on the last century or so stress the role of Liberal Positivism as an agent that introduced foreign capital and dependency to the region.

On other specific areas of research, the following worthwhile works have made considerable advances: Omar Jáen Suárez on Panamanian demography (item **2318**); Manuel Rubio Sánchez on Guatemalan coffee (item **2326**); and Jeffrey Casey Gaspar on the Costa Rican banana industry (items **2393 and 2394**). Colonial research continues to be well served by such scholars as Gilbert Joseph (item **2345**), Christopher Lutz (item **2349**), Carlos Rosés Alvarado (item **2360**), Carmelo Sáenz de Santa María (items **2363, 2364, and 2365**), and André Saint-Lu (item **2366**). Historians of Belize such as Peter Ashdown have begun a skeptical reexamination of some local historical myths (item **2381**). Costa Rican scholars are still preoccupied with the revolution of 1948, but publications by Jorge M. Salazar Mora (item **2438**) and José Luis Vega Carballo (item **2446**) have raised the level of the debate. Panamanian historians are, as one might expect, absorbed in studies of the nation's peculiar independence struggles and its canal, with works by Baltazar Isaza Calderón (item **2403**) and María J. Meléndez (item **2418**) among the noteworthy. Political history in Nicaragua is still concerned with educating the people and rewriting its history to reflect the Sandinista struggle and victory, and leaders in this task have been writers such as Claribel Alegría and D.J. Flakoll (item **2374**), Gustavo Alemán Bolaños (item **2375**), and Ternot MacRenato (item **2416**).

What is remarkable about the small Central American corpus of writing of the last two years is how such a level of research and sophistication was attained amid clearly atrocious conditions.

GENERAL

2306 Barón Castro, Rodolfo. El centroamericano como sujeto histórico (UY/R, 24:143, 1982, p. 13–33)

Much revised public address, which attempts to give a geographical and political definition of Central America, and of a Central American. Author then searches for a Central American spirit and feeling of nationhood.

2307 Blanco Segura, Ricardo. Entre pícaros y bobos. San José: Editorial Universidad Estatal a Distancia, 1981. 149 p.

Attempt to create some Costa Rican "cuadros de costumbres" by Church historian. First essay is on Bishop Valdivieso's murder in Nicaragua; many essays deal with colonial events and characters and a few discuss topics and events of period shortly after independence.

2308 Cacua Prada, Antonio. Colombianos en Guatemala (ACH/BHA, 66:725, abril/junio 1979, p. 175–197, bibl.)

Colombian diplomat in Guatemala uses printed material and few documents from Guatemalan archives to research history of Colombians in Guatemala, from time of Chibchas to present. Slight essay.

2309 Díaz Rozzotto, Jaime. De la Ilustración del Reino de Granada a la independencia de Centroamérica (in Coloquio Ilustración Española e Independencia de América, Bellaterra, Spain, 1978. Homenaje a Nöel Salomon: ilustración española e independencia de América. Edición preparada por Alberto Gil Novales. Barcelona: Universidad Autónoma de Barcelona, 1979, p. 273–282)

Rambling public address on links between reason and science of Enlightenment and crumbling of colonial regime. Followed by brief discussion with others. Light fare.

2310 Diez Castillo, Luis A. Los cimarrones y los negros antillanos en Panamá. 2a. ed. Panamá: Impr. J. Mercado Rudas, 1981. 121 p.: bibl., ill.

Four chapters discuss evolution of slavery in colonial Panama, the first *cimarrones* and their ties to pirates, life and society in *cimarrón* villages, and contribution of Caribbean island blacks to Panamanian life.

2311 Documentos y estudios sobre Natá. Recopilados y ordenados por Baltasar Isaza Calderón. Panamá: Editora de la Nación, 1972. 324 p.: bibl., ill., facsims., maps, ports.

Collection to celebrate 450th anniversary of old but minor town, from founding *acta*, 1903 declaration of independence, to brief biographies of area historians.

2312 Expediente de Campos Azules: historia de Bluefields en sus documentos en el 75 aniversario de su erección en ciudad. Compilación, presentación y notas por Eduardo Pérez-Valle. Managua: s.n., 1978. 400 p.: bibl.

History of Bluefields (Campos Azules), and thorough study of this Nicaraguan port on Caribbean from Columbus, through years of English pirates and planters, reigns of Miskito kings and Prussian Company, to

Somoza regime. Incorporates many interesting documents into text. Good bibliography.

2313 Flores A., Francisco A. Breves notas sobre José Cecilio del Valle: 1777–1834 (IAHG/AHG, 2:2, 1980, p. 173–180, bibl., ill.)

Brief essay on much studied Central American patriot, writer, and politician.

2314 Gasteazoro, Carlos Manuel. Ricardo J. Alfaro y la semblanza de su generación (APL/B, 4, 5. época, mayo 1983, p. 11–23)

Acts and ideas of generation of Panamanian pioneer nationalists, who sought to strike a balance between local pride and nationalism and a debatable openness to an intrusive outside world.

2315 Gudmundson, Lowell. The expropriation of pious and corporate properties in Costa Rica, 1805–1860: patterns in the consolidation of a national elite (AAFH/TAM, 39:3, Jan. 1983, p. 281–303, map, tables)

Expropriation of Church property before and after independence resolved Church-State question relatively early in Costa Rica, and also led to consolidated elite. English version of *HLAS 44:2331.*

2316 Gutiérrez Braun, Hernán. La ingeniería en Costa Rica, 1502–1903: ensayo histórico. Cartago: Editorial Tecnológica de Costa Rica, 1981. 163 p.: bibl., ill.

History of notable construction activity in Costa Rica from 16th century to present, including churches, roads, railroads, docks, mines, public buildings, and electrical systems. No illustrations.

2317 Jaén Suárez, Omar. El estudio sobre la población del Istmo de Panamá del siglo XVI al XX (APL/B, 4, 5. época, mayo 1983, p. 57–66)

Synopsis of Paris *thèse* and of Spanish book published in Panama (1978) based upon it. See also *HLAS 44:2298.*

2318 ———. La población del Istmo de Panamá del siglo XVI al siglo XX: estudio sobre la población y los modos de organización de las economías, las sociedades y los espacios geográfics. 2a. ed. Panamá: O. Jaén Suárez, 1979. 603 p.: bibl., ill.

Massive, fact filled, pioneering study (2. ed.) on Panamanian history and demogra-phy. Impressive work, with full scholarly apparatus and complete bibliography.

2319 Jerez Alvarado, Rafael. Tegucigalpa, aporte para su historia. Tegucigalpa: s.n., 1981. 285 p.: bibl., ill.

More of guide book for future writer than geniune history. Volume contains lists, short essays, and documents about Honduran capital. Emphasizes places, buildings, and parks.

2320 *Journal of Latin American Studies.* Centers or Institutes of Latin American Studies at the Universities of Cambridge, Glasgow, Liverpool, London, and Oxford. Vol. 15, Pt. 2, Nov. 1983- . London.

Issue mostly devoted to Central American economic history. Significant, important collection of articles by: V. Bulmer-Thomas, Enrique A. Baloyra-Herp, Laurence Whitehead, Héctor Pérez Brignoli, David Browning, Lowell Gudmundson, Samuel Stone, and Christopher Abel.

2321 Lardé y Larín, Jorge. Historia de Centro América. San Salvador: Ministerio del Interior, 1981. 129 p., 10 leaves of plates: ports.

Basic university text for El Salvador by country's leading historian is bare bones, factual survey of little interest to working scholar.

2322 *Mesoamérica.* Centro de Investigaciones Regionales de Mesoamérica. Año 4, Cuaderno 5, junio 1983- . Antigua, Guatemala.

Special issue on colonial and national history of Chiapas, once part of Guatemala Audiencia, consists of historical essays by: Jan de Vos; Freiderike Baumann; Murdo J. MacLeod; Rodney C. Watson; Sidney D. Markman; Thomas T. Veblen; and Laura Gutiérrez-Witt.

Míguez Bonino, José; Carmelo Alvarez; and **Roberto Craig.** Protestantismo y liberalismo en América Latina. See item **1769.**

2323 Molina y Morales, Roberto. El precursor y fundador del periodismo en El Salvador: Pbro. Don Miguel José de Castro y Lara (ESME/C, 70, julio/dic. 1980, p. 113–121)

Brief biography of turbulent and paradoxical career of pioneering patriot, journalist and cleric (1775–1829).

Murga Frassinetti, Antonio. Economía primaria exportadora y formación del proletariado: el caso centroamericano, 1850–1920. See *HLAS 45:3088.*

2324 Naylor, Robert A. Documentos sobre Centroamérica en las archivos de Gran Bretaña (Mesoamérica [Revista del Centro de Investigaciones Regionales de Mesoamérica, Antigua, Guatemala] 3:4, dic. 1982, p. 443–455)

Useful review of manuscript sources, some of them little known to those who work in Central American history.

2325 Porras, Hernán F. Papel histórico de los grupos humanos de Panamá. Panamá: s.n., 1980? 47 p.: port.

Pamphlet briefly sketching history of various racial groups in Panama, with mention of other factors of importance such as the Portobelo fairs, railroad, and canal. By late Panamanian journalist, diplomat and historian.

2326 Rubio Sánchez, Manuel. Historia del comercio del café en Guatemala: siglos XVIII y XIX: pt. 2 (SGHG/A, 51:51, enero/dic. 1978, p. 123–216, facsims., tables)

Guatemala's leading economic historian of colonial period continues his well documented series on Guatemalan export industries, this one extending to late 19th century. Pt. 2 of three-part essay.

2327 Sáenz de Santa María, Carmelo. Inglaterra y el Reino de Goathemala (IGFO/RI, 42:167/168, enero/junio 1982, p. 109–201)

Two Guatemalan savants, Fernando de Echevers, who published his treatise in 1742, and Francisco de Paula García Peláez, who published various writings in years after independence, admire English commercial enterprise and companies, and political economy of Adam Smith.

2328 Setzekorn, William David. Formerly British Honduras: a profile of the new nation of Belize. Rev. ed. Chicago; Athens: Ohio University Press, 1981. 299 p.: bibl., index, maps, port.

Historical outline of new nation, since precolumbian times. In general author is favorable to George Price and PUP, somewhat anti-British, and very anti-Guatemalan.

Solórzano Fonseca, Juan C. Centroamérica en el siglo XVII: un intento de explicación económica y social. See *HLAS 45:3092.*

2330 Terga, Ricardo. Caccoh: donde brota el mar pequeño: un estudio histórico de la vida de San Cristóbal Caccoh (GIIN/GI, 14:1/2, enero/julio 1979, p. 1–147, bibl., graphs)

Study of village in northern Verapaz from precolumbian times to 20th century. Author, a cleric, is uncritical of Church activities in area, but there is much careful research and heavy use of oral history taken from local inhabitants.

2331 Vargas, Oscar René. El desarrollo del capitalismo en Nicaragua (CSUCA/ESC, 20, mayo/agosto 1978, p. 31–45, tables)

Marxist interpretation of underdevelopment in Nicaragua, based on premise that underdevelopment is result of second stage of world capitalism, its transformation of "natural" economies into underdeveloped ones. Author argues that such transformation occurred in second half of 19th century and closely links it to rise of Nicaragua's export sector. Conceptually clear arguments are backed by appropriate statistical charts.

2332 Vega Carballo, José Luis. San José, antecedentes coloniales y formación del estado nacional. San José: Instituto de Investigaciones Sociales, Facultad de Ciencias Sociales, Universidad de Costa Rica, 1981. 39 p.: bibl., ill. (Avance de investigación; no. 42)

History of San José growth and development since colonial period. Serious, well documented study with appropriate maps and charts.

2333 Wheelock, Jaime. Raíces indígenas de la lucha anticolonialista en Nicaragua: de Gil González a Joaquín Zavala, 1523 a 1881. 4a. ed. México: Siglo Veintiuno Editores, 1980. 123 p.: bibl.

Showing solid command of published literature, Sandinista leader argues that Nicaragua's struggle against oppression dates from Spanish conquest and colonial period. Narrative emphasizes Indians and peasants, concludes with 1881 war.

2334 Woodward, Ralph Lee, Jr. Los comerciantes y el desarrollo económico en las Américas: 1750–1850 (RCPC,

35 : 168/169, julio/sept. 1980, p. 17–20)
Translation of 1968 article (see *HLAS 32:1195*).

2335 ──────. Where to study Central America: a geography of historical materials (FIU/CR, 10 : 1, Winter 1981, p. 47–49, ill.)
Review of archives in Central America, Europe, and US useful to historian of Central America.

2336 Zilbermann de Luján, María Cristina.
El estanco de la nieve en Guatemala (IGFO/RI, 41 : 163/164, enero/junio 1981, p. 79–90)
Little studied colonial government monopoly, established in 1754 and leased to private individuals. Arrangement led to protests over high price of ice and adulteration of iced drinks. This *estanco*, and other minor monopolies, were extinguished by Cortes of Cádiz in 1813. Revived in 1819, it seems to have died in early national period (ca. 1840?).

COLONIAL

2337 Acuña Ortega, Víctor H. Capital comercial y comercio exterior en Centroamérica durante el siglo XVIII (Mesoamérica [Centro de Investigaciones Regionales de Mesoamérica, Antigua, Guatemala] 3 : 4, dic. 1982, p. 302–331)
Capital concentrated in Guatemala City dominated export trade in 18th century, and city developed at expense of indigo-producing provinces. Thus, ownership of center and means of exchange became greater source of wealth and power than ownership of such means of production as land and labor. For economist's comment, see *HLAS 45:3064*.

2338 Arellano, Jorge Eduardo. La Iglesia en Nicaragua durante la época colonial (CH, 367/368, enero/feb. 1981, p. 142–175, tables)
Survey of colonial Church activities, from early mass baptisms, through activities of Las Casas and Valdivieso and founding of first monastic houses, missionary expeditions of 17th and 18th centuries, and revivalist campaign of Friar Antonio Margil, to Episcopal activities and growth of folk Catholicism.

Argueto, Mario R. Guía para el investigador de la historia colonial hondureña: un ensayo temático bibliográfico. See item **9**.

2339 Bákit, Oscar. Garavito, nuestra raíz perdida. San José: Jiménez & Tanzi, 1981. 93 p.: ill.
Very romantic, but neverthless highly evocative account, from Indian point of view, of belated Spanish *entradas* and conquests of Costa Rica.

2340 Escalón, José. Aportación al estudio de la medicina centroamericana en la época hispánica: Doctor Don José Flores (ESME/C, 70, julio/dic. 1980, p. 171–196, bibl.)
Study of 18th-century Chiapan-Guatemalan physician and writer, of university and intellectual *ambientes* in which he flourished, and of his travels and writings.

2341 Fortune, Armando. Mestizaje en el Istmo de Panamá a comienzos del siglo XVII (LNB/L, 253, marzo 1977, p. 1–18, bibl.)
Based on demographic information in Juan Requejo Salcedo's published *relación* to the Crown (1640), author discusses size of various racial groups and racial mixing. Ideas are traditional and poorly conceived. Some evidence and arguments are drawn from other regions and carelessly applied to colonial Panama.

2342 Gavarrete Escobar, Juan. Anales para la historia de Guatemala: 1497–1811. Guatemala: Editorial José de Pineda Ibarra, 1980. 307 p. (Publicación extraordinario / Dirección General de Antropología e Historia)
Chronological narrative history from late precolumbian times until the last years of colonial period. Some serious gaps, and author is wont to take chroniclers' assertions uncritically, but useful as reference work.

2343 Guardia, Roberto de la. Participación melanoderma en la melexación (*in* Simposium Nacional de Antropología, Arqueología y Etnohistoria de Panamá, 5th, 1974, Panamá. Actas. Patrocinadores: Universidad de Panamá, Centro de Investigaciones Antropológicas e Instituto Nacional de Cultura, Dirección Nacional del Patrimonio Histórico. Panamá: Ediciones Instituto Nacional de Cultura, 1978, p. 43–71 [Colección Patrimonio histórico])
Attempt via documentary exegesis to

establish which African tribes and nations were among slaves brought to late colonial Panama.

2344 Jickling, David. Los vecinos de Santiago de Guatemala en 1604 (Mesoamérica [Centro de Investigaciones Regionales de Mesoamérica, Antigua, Guatemala] 3:3, junio 1982, p. 145–231, ill., tables)

First thorough discussion of often used *alcabala* census of *vecinos* of Santiago de Guatemala dated 1604.

2345 Joseph, Gilbert M. British loggers and Spanish governors: the logwood trade and its settlements in the Yucatán Peninsula (UPR/CS, 14:2, 1974, p. 7–37, ill., maps, tables)

Very thorough history of logging industry and trade, but mostly from the Jamaican and English point of view. Yucatán receives some mention; Central America hardly any. Interesting discussion of life within logging camps and colonies and important examination of England's rivals in this trade in New England, Holland, and elsewhere.

Lovell, W. George. The Cuchumatán highlands of Guatemala on the eve of the Spanish Conquest. See *HLAS 45:5069.*

2346 ——— and William R. Swezey. La población del sur de Guatemala al momento de la conquista española (IAHG/AHG, 2:3, 1981, p. 43–54, bibl., graphs, map)

Attempt to estimate population of Guatemala, excluding the Peten, at moment of Spanish contact. López de Cerrato count of 1549–51 is used extensively and checked against estimates of potential population density, and against findings of regional studies. Pioneering and much needed effort (for English version, see *Canadian Journal of Anthropology*, 3:1, Fall 1982, p. 71–84).

2347 ———; Christopher H. Lutz; and William R. Swezey. The Indian population of southern Guatemala: an analysis of López de Cerrato's *Tasaciones de tributos* (AAFH/TAM, 40:4, April 1984, p. 459–476)

An advance beyond article described above. Authors have now completed their analysis of evidence in the López de Cerrato *tasaciones.* Results are best we have so far on question of finding a "baseline" figure for population of Guatemala at Spanish contact.

2348 Luján Muñoz, Jorge. Los escribanos en pueblos de indios en el Reino de Guatemala durante la colonia: nuevas aportaciones (IAHG/AHG, 2:2, 1980, p. 163–170, bibl.)

Additional information, based on new documents, which author adds to his *Los escribanos en las Indias occidentales . . .* (see *HLAS 44:2336*). New material concerns role of Spanish scribes in Indian villages.

———. Nueva información sobre los terremotos de 1773. See *HLAS 45:5070.*

2349 Lutz, Christopher H. Historia sociodemográfica de Santiago de Guatemala, 1541–1773. Guatemala: Centro de Investigaciones Regionales de Mesoamérica, 1982. 499 p.: ill. (Serie monográfica; 2)

Based on dissertation, this exhaustive book is an outstanding modern history of a colonial city and first one on Santiago with modern concerns and demographic techniques. Significant contribution.

2350 MacLeod, Murdo J. Modern research on the demography of colonial Central America: a bibliographical essay (Latin American Population History Newsletter [New York University, Center for Latin American and Caribbean Studies, New York *jointly with* Conference on Latin American History (CLAH), Committee on Demographic History] 3:3/4, Spring/Fall 1983, p. 23–39)

Title is self-explanatory.

2351 ———. The primitive nation state, delegations of functions, and results: some examples from early colonial Central America (*in* Essays in the political, economic, and social history of colonial Latin America. Edited by Karen Spalding. Newark: University of Delaware, Latin American Studies Program, 1982, p. 53–68 [Occasional papers and monographs; no. 3])

Describes how weak colonial state arranged for various sectors of local elite to perform government functions and how they were rewarded.

2352 Meléndez Chaverri, Carlos. Conquistadores y pobladores: orígenes histórico-sociales de los costarricenses. San José: Editorial Universidad Estatal a Distancia, 1982. 286 p., 2 folded leaves of plates: bibl., ill.

Brief competent history based on sound knowledge of printed sources of first two centuries of Spanish rule. Valuable *anexo* consists of biographies and family members of leading conquistador-founders of elite Costa Rican colonial families.

2353 Newson, Linda A. Demographic catastrophe in sixteenth-century Honduras (*in* Studies in Spanish American population history. Edited by David J. Robinson. Boulder, Colo.: Westview Press, 1981, p. 217–241, map, tables [Dellplain Latin American studies; no. 8]

Reworking of data and of published literature on epidemics leads author to include that post-conquest decline in population was more severe than most have assumed.

2354 ———. The depopulation of Nicaragua in the sixteenth century (JLAS, 14:2, Nov. 1982, p. 253–286, map, tables)

Story of post-conquest decline, which, while using basically same sources, claims a more severe decline than previous students of subject.

2355 Oss, Adriaan C. van. El régimen autosuficiente de España en Centro América (Mesoamérica [Centro de Investigaciones Regionales de Mesoamérica Antigua, Guatemala] 3:3, junio 1982, p. 67–89, map, plate)

Rejects mercantilist views of colonial Central America which have emphasized long-distance trade and imperial connections. Suggests instead model of local self-sufficiency, unified by Church and by various forms of cultural adaptation.

2356 Panama. Archivo Nacional. Indice de los tomos I y II de *Reales cédulas* correspondientes a la Audiencia de Panamá, procedentes del Archivo de Indias de Sevilla, expedidas de 1573 a 1627. Confeccionado por Mercedes Figueroa. Panamá: Archivos Nacionales de Panamá, 1982. 2, 68 leaves (Archivos Nacionales de Panamá; v. 1, t. 1–2)

Index to *Reales cédulas* sent to Panama, 1573–1627. A few involve relations with Bogotá, Spain, Peru, and Guatemala.

2357 Pardo, J. Joaquín. Catálogo de los manuscritos existentes en la colección latino americana de la biblioteca de la Universidad de Texas relativos a la historia de Centro América (SGHG/A, 51:51, enero/dic. 1978, p. 231–278)

Reprint of 1958 catalog published in Guatemala by University's Faculty of Humanities.

2358 Peña, José F. de la and María Teresa López Díaz. Comercio y poder: los mercaderes y el Cabildo de Guatemala, 1592–1623 (CM/HM, 30:4, abril/junio 1981, p. 469–505, bibl., tables)

First-rate analysis of origins of merchant class during period of colonial transition. Authors compare this class with others in colonial capitals, especially with those of Mexico City.

2359 Relaciones geográficas del siglo XVI. Edición de René Acuña. México: Universidad Nacional Autónoma de México, Instituto de Investigaciones Antropológicas, 1982. 1 v.: bibl., ill., index (Serie antropológica; 45. Etnohistoria)

Long awaited transcription of two known surviving *Relaciones geográficas* from Guatemala. Excellent transcription, editing and commentary make this book invaluable to those working on early colonial period.

2360 Rosés Alvarado, Carlos. El ciclo del cacao en la economía colonial de Costa Rica: 1650–1794 (Mesoamérica [Centro de Investigaciones Regionales de Mesoamérica, Antigua, Guatemala] 3:4, dic. 1982, p. 247–278, graphs)

Careful study of Costa Rica's first small export boom, centered around Matina on Caribbean coast. Various phases and obstacles are well explained.

2361 Rubio Sánchez, Manuel. Historia del Puerto de la Santísima Trinidad de Sonsonate o Acajutla. San Salvador: Editorial Universitaria, 1977. 547 p.: bibl., facsims.

Author continues his valuable, thorough, well documented series of book on Central American colonial ports. For other vols. in series, see *HLAS 42: 2416–2417.*

2362 Ruiz de Villarías, Ana. Fuentes documentales y narrativas sobre el Venerable Pedro de San José Betancur y la congregación de los Bethlemitas (SGHG/A, 51:51, enero/dic. 1978, p. 27–49)

Documents from Paris, Rome, Madrid, Seville, Canaries, and Guatemala on founder of order which began in Guatemala. Also discusses some narrative sources. Many documents concern process of his beatification and canonization. He was declared Venerable in 1771 but since then his cause has advanced little.

2363 Sáenz de Santa María, Carmelo. La Compañía de Comercio de Honduras, 1714–1717 (IFGO/RI, 40:159/162, enero/dic. 1980, p. 129–157, appendix)

Study of the Marqués de Montesacro, founder of Honduras Company, of his contract with the Crown setting up the company, and of his only voyage with his fleet to the colony. Lengthy and valuable documentary appendix.

2364 ———. El *Libro viejo* de la fundación de Guatemala: su valor sentimental, su valor histórico (Cultura de Guatemala [Universidad Rafael Landívar, Guatemala] l:3, nov./dic. 1980, p. 11–44)

Distinguished historian of Guatemala decides that weight of evidence is that manuscript of *Libro viejo,* first book of *Actas de Cabildo* (Santiago de Guatemala, 1524–30) is authentic and, therefore, a valuable historical source. New transcription and edition by Sáenz is to appear.

2365 ———. Una revisión etnoreligiosa de la Guatemala de 1704: según Fray Antonio Margil de Jesús (IGFO/RI, 41:165:166, julio/dic. 1981, p. 445–497, map)

Document from hand of famous evangelist leads to information on Indian religious beliefs and practices in early 18th century. Author of manuscript was obsessed with idolatry, and thus, found it everywhere. Transcription of document is appended.

2366 Saint-Lu, André. Movimientos sísmicos, perturbaciones psíquicas y alborotos sociopolíticos en Santiago de Guatemala (IGFO/RI, 42:169/170, julio/dic. 1982, p. 545–558)

Social and political effects of earthquakes on capital city. Believed to be caused by divine wrath, earthquakes led to public outpourings of repentance, false revelations and prophecies, and various workings of the devil. They also led to civil disturbances, elite quarrels, looting, and jail breaks. Thus moments of crisis reveal much to researcher about mentalities in the past. Stimulating and innovative essay.

2367 Samayoa Guevara, Héctor Humberto. Aciertos y desaciertos de los cronistas

al interpretar los rasgos y complejos de la cultura indígena de Guatemala (IAHG/AHG, 2:2, 1980, p. 153–162, bibl.)

Critical exegesis, by late Guatemalan historian, of what some chroniclers said about Indian society. Preliminary glance at question suggests to author that history presented in colonial chroniclers must be tested against findings of ethnohistory and anthropology.

2368 ———. El régimen de intendencias en el Reino de Guatemala. Guatemala: Piedra Santa, 1978. 148 p. (Biblioteca centroamericana de las ciencias sociales)

Institutional brief history of setting up and functioning of the four Central American intendencies at end of colonial period.

2369 Sánchez Ochoa, Pilar. Cambio en la estructura familiar indígena: influencias de la Iglesia y la encomienda en Guatemala (RUC, 28:117, enero 1979, p. 169–191)

Disintegrating effects of post-conquest Spanish exploitation on structure of Indian family in Guatemala. Author adds that this early disaster was partly overcome because enormous recuperative powers of Guatemala's colonial Indian society.

2370 Spaniards and Indians in southeastern Mesoamerica: essays on the history of ethnic relations. Edited by Murdo J. MacLeod and Robert Wasserstrom. Lincoln: University of Nebraska Press, 1983. 291 p.: bibl., ill., index, maps (Latin American studies series)

Collection of eight essays on precolumbian, colonial, and modern history of Yucatán, Chiapas, and Guatemala, with special emphasis on ethnic relations.

2371 Suñe Blanco, Beatriz. El Corregidor del Valle de Guatemala: una institución española para el control de la población indígena (RUC, 28:117, enero 1979, p. 153–168, bibl.)

Follows history of colonial institution somewhat unique to area around Santiago (Antigua). Until mid 18th century, area was mostly administered by city's cabildo and its officers or appointees. This caused recurrent conflict with Audiencia's president and oidores.

2372 Watson, Rodney C. Nuevas perspectivas para las investigaciones geográfico-históricas en Chiapas (Mesoamérica [Centro de Investigaciones Regionales de Mesoamérica, Antigua, Guatemala] 3 : 3, junio 1982, p. 232–239)

Quick survey of present research on Chiapas and its future possibilities.

2373 Zilbermann Morales, María Christina and Jorge Luján Muñoz. Santiago de Guatemala en víspera de los terremotos de 1773 (EEHA/AEA, 32 1975, p. 541–571, ill.)

Evocation of Antigua and its history just before earthquakes which caused the move to Guatemala City's present site. Thorough, and appropriately illustrated.

NATIONAL

2374 Alegría, Claribel and D.J. Flakoll. Nicaragua, la Revolución sandinista: una crónica política, 1855–1979. México: Ediciones Era, 1982. 479 p. (Serie Popular Era; 80)

Account of over a century of Nicaraguan history. Emphasizes US interventions, Augusto César Sandino, Somoza dynasty, 1973 earthquake, formation of Frente Sandinista, and Somoza's overthrow. Much new material from interviews with leading protagonists and excerpts from hard-to-find newspapers and pamphlets yield previously little-known "inside" story of final years of struggle against Somoza.

2375 Alemán Bolaños, Gustavo. Sandino el libertador: la epopeya, la paz, el invasor, la muerte. San José: Editorial Nueva Década, 1980. 244 p.: ill. (Biografía del héroe americano)

Another detailed, informative history of Sandino's life, ideas, and death and of Somoza's rise to power.

2376 Andrews, Patricia A. El liberalismo en El Salvador a finales del siglo XIX (RCPC, 36 : 172/173, julio/dic. 1981, p. 89–93)

Liberal revolution of 1871 brought with it new ideas on the State's role, more State intervention in the economy, and infrastructural investment, all of which merely reinforced export monoculture. Few advances in social justice or equity were contemplated, elites remained in firm control, army was strengthened, and the Church and legislature both lost power to executive branch. By 1900,

a new tranquil stability had emerged, based not so much on positivism as on simple developmental pragmatism.

2377 Apuntes de historia de Nicaragua. León: Universidad Nacional Autónoma de Nicaragua, Departamento de Ciencias Sociales, Sección de Historia, 1980. 2 v. (435 p.): bibl., ill.

Two-volume textbook for Nicaraguan university students consists of essays on: 1) 19th-century imperialist expansion, rise of Liberal bourgeoisie under José Santos Zelaya, US domination and occupation; and 2) rise and decline of Somoza clan, resistance and rise of Sandinistas to power.

Araúz, Celestino Andrés. La independencia de Panamá en 1821: antecedentes balance y proyecciones. See item **2844** .

2378 Argueta, Mario. 1880–1980 [Mil ochocientos ochenta-mil novecientos ochenta]: cien años del enclave minero en Honduras (HUN/RU, 7 : 17/18, 1981, p. 59–68, tables)

Explanation of revival of Honduran mining industry in 1880s, and how circumstances surrounding it brought foreign control of industry, a phenomenon which has lasted until today.

2379 Arias de Blois, Jorge. La mortalidad en Guatemala hacia fines del siglo XIX (SGHG/A, 50 : 50, enero/dic. 197, p. 133–149, tables)

According to author, use of data pushed historians to study previously neglected fields, one being mortality rates and causes of death. Life expectancy at birth in 1880–81 was 32.2 years, increasing to 39.2 years peak somewhere between ages five and nine, crude signs of very high infant mortality and, no doubt, poor reporting. Pioneering study which, author hopes, will attract others to this neglected and revealing field.

2380 Arosemena, Bey Mario. La revolución de acción comunal y la gestión presidencial del Ingeniero Florencio H. Arosemena (LNB/L, 312/313, marzo/abril 1982, p. 1–14)

Biography of noted Panamanian president, Liberal politician and engineer, with emphasis on his overthrow in 1930s. Author is clearly supporter of him and his policies.

2380a Arosemena, Mariano et al. El ensayo en Panamá: estudio introductorio y antología. Estudio introductorio de Rodrigo Miró. Panamá: Presidencia de la República, 1981. 505 p.: bibl. (Biblioteca de la cultura panameña; t. 7)

Interesting and thoughtful introduction on Latin American essay as form of writing. Continues with selection, ranging from one by Mariano Arosemena (1833), to one by Raúl A. Leis (1980). Excellent bibliographical appendix about 37 authors, and their essays discuss such matters as land tenure, the presidency, demography, Panamanian independence, Teilhard de Chardin, Latin American positivism, blacks in Panama, and, of course, the Zone. An informative and enjoyable collection.

2381 Ashdown, Peter. The Belize elite (BISRA/BS, 10:1, 1982, p. 10–36)

Gov. Sir Roger Goldsworthy's 1880s policies changed the colony's balance of power and allowed the "propertied and educated elite" to share government with appointed officials of British Colonial Office.

2382 ——. Marcus Garvey, the UNIA, and the black cause in British Honduras, 1914–1949 (UWI/JCH, 15, 1981, p. 41–55)

Author debunks common notion of racially tolerant society in Belize. Examines growing discontent after 1914 which led to 1919 race riots, to organization of Belize branch of Universal Negro Improvement Association (UNIA), and to visits from Marcus Garvey. Unfortunately for local UNIA, its most effective leader, Samuel Haynes, left with Garvey, and UNIA withered thereafter over arguments on tactics and finances. It ended up as conservative ethnic group opposed to PUP.

2383 Bacigalupo, Leonard. The American Franciscan missions in Central America: three decades of Christian service. Andover, Mass.: Charisma Press, 1980. 483 p.: bibl., index.

History by Franciscan of new Franciscan missions to Central America (1944–75). Honduras receives most attention.

2384 Belausteguigoitia, Ramón de. Con Sandino en Nicaragua: la hora de la paz. Managua: Editorial Nueva Nicaragua, 1981. 244 p. (Biblioteca popular sandinista; 3)

Personal first-hand account of Sandino and his campaign, much of it based on camp observations and conversations with Sandino.

2385 Blanco Segura, Ricardo. Los que el obispo juzgare. San José: Editorial Costa Rica, 1981. 149 p., 10 leaves of plates: bibl., ill.

Antecedents, founding, and functioning of seminary in San José. Discusses daily life and conflict with Liberals.

Bolland, O. Nigel. Labour control in post abolition Belize. See *HLAS 45:1054.*

2386 Casal, Pío. Reseña de la situación general de Guatemala, 1863. Edición, introducción y notas por Jorge Luján Muñoz. Guatemala: Academia de Geografía e Historia de Guatemala, 1981. 102 p.: bibl., ill. (Publicación especial; no. 22)

General report on state of country first published serially in *La Semana* (1865). Presents Conservative Party view of events since independence, optimistic that with Carrera in power, future would be rosy. Especially useful details on public finance.

2387 Cerutti, Franco. Una fuente olvidada de la historia nicaragüense del siglo XIX: Pedro Ortiz (IGFO/RI, 41:165/166, julio/dic. 1981, p. 603–636)

Brief biography of Nicaraguan journalist and public official (1859–62). Exiled to Costa Rica, he was assassinated there the following year. His small literary production, Cerutti says, is valuable source for late 19th-century Nicaraguan history.

Conte-Porras, Jorge. Arnulfo Arias Madrid. See *HLAS 45:6177.*

2388 ——. Iconografía de Omar Torrijos H. (LNB/L, 305/309:2, agosto/dic. 1981, p. 817–841, photos)

Uninformative photo-biography of late Panamanian leader.

2389 ——. La rebelión de Las Esfinges: historia del movimiento estudiantil panameño. Panamá: LithoImpresora Panamá, 1978. 177 p.: bibl., ill., index.

History of student participation in Panamanian politics. Special attention to Federación de Estudiantes de Panamá, struggle over university reform, and student role in nationalist resistance to US and the Zone. Contains important documents on topic.

2390 Díaz Chávez, Filander. Carías, el último caudillo frutero. Tegucigalpa:

Editorial Guaymuras, 1982. 153 p.: bibl., ill. (Colección Códices)

Book characterizes dictator Tiburcio Carías Andino as regressive founder of Honduran neo-colonial state. Long on theory and short on data. A full analytical biography of Carías and his government is still needed.

2391 Dridzo, Abram. Yegor Sivers y su viaje a Nicaragua (URSS/AL, 5:53, 1982, p. 119–124)

Very brief study of first Russian travel account of Nicaragua (1851–61).

2392 García Carrillo, Eugenio. El hombre del Repertorio americano. San José: Universidad Autónoma de Centro América, Editorial STVDIVM, 1981. 138 p.: bibl., ill.

Adulatory biography of Costa Rican journalist and politician, Joaquín García Monge (1881–1958).

2393 Gaspar, Jeffrey Casey. La industria bananera en Costa Rica, 1880–1940: la organización social del trabajo (IGFO/RI, 38:153/154, julio/dic. 1978, p. 738–789, graphs, tables)

Solid study based on thorough knowledge of bibliography on subject. Relates labor systems to many other factors such as purchase contracts, prices, comparative production totals in other Caribbean areas, land tenure around Limón, United Fruit Co.'s policies and activities, labor struggles, legislation, immigrant labor, and race relations. Finds that social organization of labor was based on changing relationship among three groups: workers, private growers, and United Fruit Co., which monopolized exports. Important study.

2394 ———. Limón, 1880–1940: un estudio de la industria bananera en Costa Rica (CSUCA/ESC, 8:23, mayo/agosto 1979, p. 245–279)

Gradual economic transformation of section of Caribbean coast of Costa Rica under expanding impact of banana plantations and exports. Careful discussion backed by useful and little known source material. For economist's comment, see *HLAS 45:3116*.

2395 Gasteazoro, Carlos Manuel. Tabla cronológica de Omar Torrijos H. (LNB/L, 305/309:2, agosto/dic. 1981, p. 843–907)

Tabular and detailed chronological biography based on most notable events of Torrijos' life. Useful to historians of period as almanac.

2396 González Flores, Alfredo. Pensamiento. Prólogo y selección, Alberto Cañas. San José: Editorial Costa Rica, 1980. 355 p.: bibl. (Biblioteca Patria; 15)

Biography and writings of Costa Rican president (1914–17). Book contains: 1) messages to congress; 2) excerpts from his books on Costa Rican politics and economics; and 3) some shorter publications.

2397 Guardia, Carlos A. Historia y evolución de la ingeniería sanitaria en Panamá (LNB/L, 303/304, junio/julio 1981, p. 45–62)

Partial, undocumented general history more fully developed in item **2398**.

2398 ———. Saneamiento original en el área del Canal de Panamá (LNB/L, 312/313, marzo/abril 1982, p. 35–58, bibl., ill.)

Fine history of public health efforts and successes in Panama from 1850 until Canal's completion in 1915. Draws expertly on wealth of little known and technical material, both from Panama and US. Discussion of struggle to provide a potable water supply is especially notable.

Guerra Rivas, Tomás. El Salvador, octubre sangriento: itinerario y análisis del golpe militar del 15 de octubre de 1979. See *HLAS 45:6119*.

2399 Gurdián Guerrero, Francisco. La última noche del General Augusto César Sandino. 2a. ed., corr. y aum. Managua: Rapido-Graph, 197? 50 p., 3 leaves of plates: ill.

Second expanded ed. of pamphlet which gives a disorganized but graphic account of murder of Sandino and his followers.

2400 Hernández-Alarcón, Eduardo. Urbanization and modernization in Costa Rica during the 1880s (PCCLAS/P, 6, 1977/1979, p. 139–151, tables)

Economic factors, such as agricultural exports led by coffee, growth of internal trade, expanding government bureaucracy, and urban public works, all spurred urbanization during this crucial decade. As urbanization and coffee exports grew, so did dependency.

2401 Hunter, Yvonne. The Sisters of Mercy in Belize (BISRA/BS, 11:1, 1983, p. 1-15)
Brief history of Sisters of Mercy in Belize since arrival in 1883. Emphasizes education and poor relief.

2402 La Intervención de México en Nicaragua según la prensa norteamericana (MAGN/B, 4:1[11], enero/marzo 1980, p. 29-35, ill., plates)
Mexican archival documents about hostility of US Republican Party to Mexico's recognition of Nicaragua's Liberal government (1926). Mexican government and others obviously feared possibility of US intervention in Mexico.

2403 Isaza Calderón, Baltasar. Carlos A. Mendoza y su generación: historia de Panamá, 1821-1916. Panamá: Academia Panameña de la Historia, 1982. 360 p., 1 leaf of plates: bibl., ill.
Carlos Mendoza (1856-1916) was much influenced, as were those of his generation, by Colombia's radical Liberals. Traces party's fortunes, follows adherents in Panama, and their political role in "guerra de los mil días," and 1903 independence movement. Mendoza became a leading figure in these events, subsequently part of conciliatory mission to Colombia, and leader of President Ramón Valdés' opposition. With Mendoza's death began decline of Panamanian Liberals, according to Isaza Calderón.

2404 ———. Ernesto J. Castillero Reyes: el hombre, el educador, el historiador (LNB/L, 312/313, marzo/abril 1982, p. 15-33)
Brief favorable biography of Panamanian educator, librarian, and historian, with analysis of his writings and role in national politics. Appendix lists principal publications (1929-46).

2405 Jiménez, Ernesto Bienvenido. Ellos, los presidentes. Guatemala: Editorial José de Pineda Ibarra, 1981. 269 p.: bibl., ill.
Biographies of Guatemalan presidents from Gabino Gainza to Jacobo Arbenz. Useful as reference work. Author is generally in favor of Arévalo-Arbenz revolution, overthrown in 1954.

2406 Jones, Grant. Mayas, Yucatecans and Englishmen in the nineteenth century

fiesta system of Northern Belize (BISRA/BS, 10:3/4, 1982, p. 25-42)
Study of Mayan festival with Yucatecan and English visitors, and criminal trials following it facilitates understanding racial politics and economics, and regional power in mid 19th-century Belize. For ethnologist's comment, see HLAS 45:1090.

2407 Karnes, Thomas L. The family as multinational enterprise (PCCLAS/P, 6, 1977/1979, p. 153-166)
Brief history of Vaccaro family, of Standard Fruit Co., and of their success and failures. Generally favorable view of role of multinational corporations in Middle America.

2408 Kerr, Derek N. La edad de oro del café en El Salvador: 1863-1885 (Mesoamérica [Centro de Investigaciones Regionales de Mesoamérica, Antigua Guatemala] 3:3, junio 1982, p. 1-25, tables)
Coffee displaced indigo while Liberal positivism backed economic growth and importation of foreign developmental capital. This led, among other things, to suppression of *ejidos* and communal lands, thus allowing coffee culture to take over lands previously used for subsistence agriculture. Peasants became laborers on estates.

2409 Lainfiesta, Francisco. Mis memorias. Guatemala: Academia de Geografía e Historia de Guatemala, 1980. 638 p. (Publicación especial; no. 21)
Memoirs of a Guatemalan Liberal deputy, diplomat, and writer (1837-1912). Good picture emerges of everyday elite life, and of political intrigues in late 19th-century capital.

2410 Leistenschneider, Freddy. Administración del General Francisco Morazán. San Salvador: Ministerio del Interior, Impr. Nacional, 1982. 329 p.: bibl., ill. (some col.) (Publicaciones del Ministerio)
Detailed, favorable biography of hero of Central American unity. Book's organization is difficult to follow, but there are many useful documents on Morazán's life, decrees, battles, and death.

2411 Lemoine, Ernesto. Guatemala en 1838: a través de dos cartas remitidas desde Totonicapán por José Matías Quiñones a su amigo, el mexicano Carlos María de

Bustamante (IAHG/AHG, 2:2, 1980, p. 181–194, bibl.)

Author uses two descriptive letters from Guatemalan legislator and cleric in Totonicapán to Mexican friend, to discuss Guatemala in 1838. Letter writer was despondent about Guatemalan institutions and political leaders, guardedly in favor of new state of Los Altos but against the early Carrera whom he describes as a Nero leading an army of Bedouins and a Morazán supporter.

2412 Leonard, Thomas M. The 1977 Panama Canal treaties in historical perspective (*in* Journal of Caribbean Studies [Association of Caribbean Studies, Coral Gables, Fla.] 2:2/3, Autumn/Winter 1981, p. 190–209)

Historical background to main issues in 1977 Canal Treaty. Nothing much new in text, but there are extensive and useful notes.

2413 López Vallacillos, Italo. Trayectoria y crisis del estado salvadoreño: 1918–1981 (UJSC/ECA, 36:392, junio 1981, p. 499–528, ill., tables)

Discusses economic system of these years, and how elite managed various crises until present breakdown. Central hypothesis is that ruling class had two leading sectors: a traditional, agro-export one, and a more industrial and financial, modernizing one. Important polemic with excellent and useful notes.

2414 Luján Muñoz, Jorge. La Asamblea Nacional Constituyente Centroamericana de 1823–1824 (PAIGH/H, 94, julio/dic. 1982, p. 33–89)

Meeting of first constituent assembly after break with Mexico. Thorough, documented essay traces many of the region's later political features to tendencies first displayed at the assembly.

———. Situación de la enseñanza superior de la historia y de la investigación histórica en Guatemala. See *HLAS 45:4439.*

2415 MacCameron, Robert. Bananas, labor, and politics in Honduras, 1954–1963. Syracuse, N.Y.: Maxwell School of Citizenship and Public Affairs, Syracuse University, 1983. 166 p.: 1 leaf of plates; bibl., maps (Foreign and comparative studies. Latin American series; no. 5)

Discusses 1954 United Fruit Co. strike: historical background, strike itself, and results affecting labor development and politics in Honduras. Strike's aims were partly fulfilled under Ramón Villeda Morales' leadership, but author repeatedly points out wide gap between expectations for social and economic change and failures to carry them out.

2416 MacRenato, Ternot. The rise to power of Anastasio Somoza García (UCSD/NS, 8, 1982, p. 309–323)

Very detailed and well researched description of Somoza García's rise to power by participant in Sandinista Revolution.

2417 Martínez, Daniel. Panamá: 1821–1979 (*in* Socialismo y Participación [Centro de Estudios para el Desarrollo y la Participación, Lima] 7, junio 1979, p. 33–58, tables)

Interesting socialist account, backed by data and graphs, of Panama's political and economic history during those years.

Martínez G., Eric Jorge. Indices de archivos parroquiales: Tegucigalpa y Yuscarán. See *HLAS 45:51.*

2418 Meléndez, María J. Después de los franceses (LNB/L, 303/304, junio/julio 1981, p. 117–125)

In 1887 the French company decided to abandon idea of sea level canal, but it took its US successor two years (1904–06) to reach same conclusion and to begin to plan locks and dams. After several early reverses, US team moved rapidly ahead, with help of large quantities of abandoned French equipment. Writer does not wish to debunk US canal building feats, but points out that French accomplishments are too often ignored, and that final construction of canal was not without mistakes.

Menjívar, Rafael. Formación y lucha del proletariado industrial salvadoreño. See *HLAS 45:8121.*

2419 México, Estados Unidos y la guerra constitucionalista de Nicaragua (MAGN/B, 4:1[11], enero/marzo 1980, p. 15–28, plates)

Letters to Mexican government from ambassador in Nicaragua and others there describing political situation (1922–29). Important not only for understanding of Nicaragua, but also for those interested in US-Mexican relations at that time.

2420 Michaels, Albert L. and Ivan Jaksić.
José Figueres y la revolución de 1948 en Costa Rica: historia oral y fuentes escritas (CPU/ES, 24:2, 1980, p. 135–148)
Oral histories of 1948 events emphasize development of Figueres' political ideas. Adds little to existing record.

2421 Miranda, Hernany. Semblanzas de salvadoreños destacados. San Salvador: Imprenta National, 1982. 268 p.: port.
Alphabetical dictionary of biographies of distinguished Salvadorans, with average entry about half a page in length. Useful as almanac.

2422 Miró, Rodrigo. Nuestro siglo XIX: hombres y aconteceres. Panama City: Instituto de Investigaciones Históricas Ricardo J. Alfaro, Academia Panameña de la Historia, 1980. 227 p.
Anecdotal essays on people and events, most about Panama but others on subjects such as José Martí, Rubén Darío, and influence of French culture on Latin America. Some essays contain valuable documents on Panamanian-Colombian relations and other matters.

2423 Molina Chocano, Guillermo. Honduras: de la guerra civil al reformismo militar, 1925–1973 (*in* América Latina: historia de medio siglo. v. 2, Centroamérica, México y el Caribe. Coordinación: Pablo González Casanova. México: Siglo Veintiuno Editores, 1981, p. 223–256, bibl., tables)
One of essays on Central America from excellent collection edited by González Casanova. One of best reviews on recent Honduran history. Bibliography is judicious and useful.

2424 Morales, Carlos. El hombre que no quiso la guerra: una revolución en el periodismo de Costa Rica. San José: Ariel/Seix Barral, 1981. 270 p.: bibl., facsims., ill., ports.
Interesting attempt to write history and analysis of Costa Rica's popular press by journalist and educator. Uprising of 1889 receives extensive treatment, and was, author believes, beginning of nation's modern

journalism. Includes some valuable brief documents.

2425 Murga Franssinetti, Antonio. Estado y burguesía industrial en Honduras (CSUCA/ESC, 18, sept./dic. 1977, p. 9–23)
Study of roles of very small industrial section of Honduran bourgeoisie. Interviews by questionnaires were held with 57 industrialists, and questioning largely concerned industrialists' opinions on the State's role. These men believed that the State should support private enterprise, but otherwise stay out of it. They believe in restricting competition even if it means smaller market. While some sought to influence government decisions they seldom acted cohesively to achieve their aims.

2426 Newton, Velma. Recruiting West Indian labourers for the Panama Canal and Railroad construction projects (BMHS/J, 37:1, 1983, p. 9–19)
Driven out by poverty and attracted by exaggerated promises, thousands left Caribbean islands for American mainland after 1850. Panamanian Railroad and Canal Construction received largest number, well over 60,000 if one includes those who were smuggled in. Newton reviews recruitment practices and advertisements, and compares them with real conditions which migrants faced.

2427 Obregón Loría, Rafael. Hechos militares y políticos. Alajuela, Costa Rica: Museo Histórico Cultural Juan Santamaría, 1981. 419 p.: bibl., ill., index (De nuestra historia patria)
New ed. of, and a new title for, author's *Conflictos militares y políticos de Costa Rica*, first published over 30 years ago. This ed. contains new chapters on border problems with Nicaragua in 1960s and 1970s, and on strike conflicts in 1970s.

2428 Peña Hernández, Enrique. Síntesis histórica del amparo en Guatemala (Cultura de Guatemala [Universidad Rafael Landivar, Guatemala] 2:1, enero/abril 1981, p. 73–82, bibl.)
Discusses right of *amparo*, a Latin American variant of *habeus corpus*, in Guatemalan context, where it first achieved full recognition in 1879 Constitution.

2429 Peters, Gertrud. Fuentes para el estudio del comercio de los Estados Unidos con Costa Rica: siglos XIX y XX (UNCR/R, 4:8, enero/julio 1979, p. 83–107, bibl., tables)

Useful review of these sources in US, Europe, and Costa Rica, accompanied by several valuable graphs, and breakdown of US ports of entry and exit.

2430 Polo Sifontes, Francis. Nuestros gobernantes, 1821–1981. Guatemala: Editorial José de Pineda Ibarra, 1981. 215 p.: ports.

Photographs and potted description of accomplishments while in office of Guatemalan executives from Gabino Gainza to Fernando Romeo Lucas García.

2431 Posas, Mario and **Rafael del Cid.** La construcción del sector público y del Estado nacional de Honduras, 1876–1979. Ciudad Universidad Rodrigo Facio, Costa Rica: Editorial Universitaria Centroamericana, 1981. 254 p.: bibl. (Textos del Instituto Centroamericano de Administración Pública. Colección Rueda del tiempo)

Last report of Ford Foundation-funded project by Instituto Centroamericano de Administración Pública on evolution of area's public sector. Three chapters discuss: 1) agrarian capitalism and foreign domination of state apparatus in Honduras (1876–1948); 2) capitalist expansion and growth of role of Honduran State (1947–72); and 3) militarization of the State and military anti-reformism (1972–79).

2432 La Posición del gobierno mexicano frente a la intervención norteamericana en Nicaragua y la proposición sandinista de alianza latinoamericana 1926–1930 (MAGN/B, 4:1[11], enero/marzo 1980, p. 36–49, ill., plates)

Documents from Mexican archives. Includes several on Mexican government's opposition to US intervention in Nicaragua (1926–30), open letter from Augusto César Sandino to various governments of the Americas (published Veracruz, Nov. 1928) proposing a Latin American defensive alliance, a Sandinista proposal for a Latin American confederation of states (March 1929), and two letters from Sandino to President Emilio

Portes Gil (May and August 1929) thanking him for financial support and for permitting entry and residence in Mexico.

2433 Quintero, César. Aportes fundamentales del Dr. José D. Moscote al constitucionalismo panameño (LNB/L, 100, marzo 1981, p. 1–7)

Hagiographical brief biography of Panamanian jurist with interest in framing of constitutions, especially Panamanian one of 1904.

2434 Ramírez, Sergio. Sandino siempre. León: Universidad Nacional Autónoma de Nicaragua, 1980. 72 p.: ill. (Colección popular; no. 2)

Finds uncompromising anti-imperialism and Pan-Americanism in Sandino's writing. Warns against those who would use these writings for anti-revolutionary purposes. Treats José Santos Zelaya and Benjamín Zeledón as patriotic heroes. Brief biography of Sandino.

2435 Referencia en torno a la política de México hacia Centroamérica: 1923–1937 (MAGN/B, 4:1[11], enero/marzo 1980, p. 4–14, plates)

Documents on Mexico's new activism in Central American politics, 1923–37. From these documents it is obvious that US government became concerned at these policies and acted to prevent them from interfering with US aims.

Reina Valenzuela, José. Historia de la universidad. See *HLAS 45:4442.*

2436 Reys, Herasto. Historia de San Miguelito. Panamá: H. Reyes, 1981. 252 p.: ill. (Serie Historia de los pueblos)

Story of remarkable growth of Panamanian community from a handful of people in 1950 to 150,000 in 1980. Struggles for land and for their rights by people of this new town receive extensive and sympathetic attention. Series dedicated to Panamanian local history.

2437 Rosa, Ramón. Obra escogida. Introducción, selección y notas de Marcos Carías. Tegucigalpa: Editorial Guaymuras, 1980. 398 p., 1 leaf of plates: ill. (Colección Talanquera)

Selected writings of 19th-century Honduran co-president (1876–83), writer, and Liberal positivist (1848–93).

2438 Salazar Mora, Jorge Mario. Política y reforma en Costa Rica, 1914–1958. San José: Editorial Porvenir, 1981. 253 p.: bibl., port (Colección Debate)

Well researched and documented account of growth of reformist political movements in Costa Rica from Calderón Guardia through Picado Michalski to 1948 civil war, to moderate reformism of Liberación Nacional and Pepe Figueres. Concludes that no radical social change has yet taken place in Costa Rica and that reform movements have done little for rural poor.

2439 Salazar Valiente, Mario. El Salvador: crisis, dictadura, lucha, 1920–1980 (in América Latina: historia de medio siglo. v. 2, Centroamérica, México y el Caribe. Coordinación: Pablo González Casanova. México: Siglo Veintiuno Editores, 1981, p. 87–138)

Impressive, well argued socialist account of Salvadoran politics and economics since world crisis of 1930s. Period 1974–80 is treated as separate *anexo*. For political scientist's comment, see *HLAS 45:6130.*

2440 Salisbury, Robert V. The Middle American exile of Víctor Raul Haya de la Torre (AAFH/TAM, 40:1, July 1983, p. 1–15)

Haya's visits to Mexico, and especially to Guatemala, El Salvador, and Costa Rica, and description of his activities in these countries.

2441 El Sandinismo y la lucha de liberación nicaragüense (MAGN/B, 4:1[11], enero/marzo 1980, p. 50–62, ill., plates)

Documents from Mexican archives on Sandino's murder and Somoza's rise to power. Obvious that many pro-Sandino Nicaraguans hoped that President Lázaro Cárdenas would be of major help to them.

2442 Soler, Ricaurte. Justo Arosemena y la cuestión nacional panameña (Boletín de Antropología Americana [Instituto Panamericano de Geografía e Historia México] 6, dic. 1982, p. 67–74)

Role of early but forgotten pioneer of Panamanian nationalism in preparing local thinking for independence from Colombia and US influence.

2443 Solís R., Luis Guillermo. La dinastía de los colonizadores: *vecinismo* en San Isidro de Pérez Zeledón, Costa Rica (Mesoamérica [Centro de Investigaciones Regionales de Mesoamérica, Guatemala] 3:3, junio 1982, p. 90–106, tables)

What were political tendencies of migrants who entered area between 1880 and 1940? Author finds "dynasty" of peasant colonizers based on "vecinismo," endogamy, and extended family ties.

2444 Stansifer, Charles L. Cultural policy in the old and the new Nicaragua (UFSI/R, 41, 1981, p. 1–17, ill., maps)

Review of cultural history of Nicaragua designed to clarify new Sandinista cultural policies and preferences. For literary critic's comment, see item **5883.**

2445 Torres Rivas, Edelberto. Guatemala: medio siglo de historia política (in América Latina: historia de medio siglo. v. 2, Centroamérica, México y el Caribe. Coordinación: Pablo González Casanova. México: Siglo Veintiuno Editores, 1981, p. 139–173, bibl.)

Most poorly supported and argued of these essays, but nevertheless a useful synthesis of what has been written about Guatemala during these turbulent years.

2446 Vega Carballo, José Luis. Costa Rica: coyunturas, clases sociales y estado en su desarrollo reciente, 1930–1975 (in América Latina: historia de medio siglo. v. 2, Centroamérica, México y el Caribe. Coordinación: Pablo González Casanova. México: Siglo Veintiuno Editores, 1981, p. 1–37, bibl., tables)

Detailed discussion of 1930s economic crisis in Costa Rica, 1948 civil war, gradual loss of reformist drive on part of Liberación Nacional, and emergence of new national crisis in last few years. Important synthesis of published material.

———. Hacia una interpretación del desarrollo costarricense: ensayo sociológico. See *HLAS 45:8135.*

Villalobos Vega, Bernardo. Bancos emisores y bancos hipotecarios en Costa Rica 1850–1910. See *HLAS 45:3161.*

2447 Woodward, Ralph Lee, Jr. Pensamiento científico y desarrollo económico en Centroamérica: 1860–1920 (RCPC, 36:172/173, julio/dic. 1981, p. 73–86, tables)

Relation between changes in economic thinking generated by Liberal-Positivist revolutions of last third of 18th century, and types of economic development, including above all new colonialism of dependency, which came with it.

2448 ———. Population and development in Guatemala: 1840–1879 (Secolas Annals [Journal of the Southeastern Council on Latin American Studies, Macon, Ga.] 14, March 1983, p. 5–18, tables)

Preliminary and partial reevaluation of Carrera years. Finds evidence of population growth and economic activity in these years, in spite of many natural disasters. Growth, however, is of a markedly different kind to that of Liberal years which followed.

2449 Zaid, Gabriel. Colegas enemigos: una lectura de la tragedia salvadoreña (Vuelta [México] 5:56, julio 1981, p. 9–27)

Chronicle of strange and tragic twists and turns in Salvadoran politics in 1970s and early 1980s. Full of revealing personal details and descriptions of little known alliances, this fascinating essay is essential reading for scholars who wish to understand background of Salvadoran civil war. Contains appropriate documents within text. For political scientist's comment, see *HLAS 45:6131.* For English version, see *Dissent* (New York, Winter 1982, p. 13–40).

2450 Zeledón B., Sergio A. General Benjamín Zeledón, 1879–1912 (NMC/N, 2:4, enero/marzo 1981, p. 24–43, ill.)

Brief illustrated documentary biography by nephew of Nicaraguan official and military leader who is now being reevaluated as precursor of Sandinista movement. Documents from US Marine archives show complicity in his execution.

THE CARIBBEAN, THE GUIANAS AND THE SPANISH BORDERLANDS

FRANKLIN W. KNIGHT, *Professor of History, The Johns Hopkins University*
REBECCA J. SCOTT, *Assistant Professor of History, University of Michigan, Ann Arbor*

THE PROLIFERATION OF MATERIAL on the Caribbean noted in the biennium, 1980–82, continued with a great number of books spanning disciplines, providing geographical breadth, and illustrating that the region has continued to attract highly competent scholars in the humanities and social sciences. In the category of general reading, David Trask's *The war with Spain in 1898* (item **2482**) is an outstanding, balanced, well-written attempt to understand both the American and Spanish sides of the dispute which succeeds in analyzing a conflict, as well as examining two cultures. Peggy Liss' *Atlantic empires* (item **2469**) is an intellectual tour de force which integrates the separate elements of politics and commerce that fueled the rise of Atlantic empires during the 18th century.

The late colonial period has some very fine studies: Karl Watson's *The civilized island, Barbados* (item **2508**) provides a broad trajectory of Barbadian society, and nicely integrates political, social, economic and cultural history in a small readable book. David Geggus' *Slavery, war and revolution* (item **2501**) is by far the most reliable study of the Haitian Revolution, and is thoroughly documented. John

Clark's *La Rochelle and the Atlantic economy during the eighteenth century* (item **2496**) explores in detail the complex trading relationship of the French Antilles, and illuminates the nature of family trade and politics. Anne Pérotin-Dumon's fine article, "Témoignages sur la Guadeloupe en 1794" (item **2505**) demonstrates how difficult it is to capture, even in the medium of the novel, the variety, range and complexity of the revolution in the Antilles.

Slavery and slave society continue to be the most intellectually stimulating field. Kenneth and Virginia Kiple examine the relationship between diet and disease in the Caribbean slave population, in "Deficiency Diseases in the Caribbean" (item **2502**). Patrick Villiers explores the technological change in slave ships in his *Traite des noirs et navires négriers au XVIII° siècle* (item **2507**). Inés Roldán de Montaud's article on the Cuban *emancipados*, "Origen, Evolución y Supresión del Grupo de Negros Emancipados en Cuba" (item **2551**) is impressive. Also worthwhile are Edward Cox's studies *Free coloreds in the slave societies of St. Kitts and Grenada, 1763–1833* (item **2497**) and "The Struggle of the Free Coloreds in Grenada and St. Kitts" (item **2528**). Nigel Bolland argues in "Systems of Domination after Slavery" (item **2523**) that land/labor ratios are not the only, or best way of looking at labor disputes in the English Caribbean during the 19th century; while the slave rebellion in western Jamaica drew much attention from several scholars. Two articles by Rebecca Scott examine the causes and dynamics of slave emancipation in Cuba (items **2554** and **2555**).

Some excellent studies on Puerto Rico during the 19th century have been appearing both in the island and on the mainland. They include Francisco Scarano's *Sugar and slavery in Puerto Rico* (item **2553**); Laird Bergad's *Coffee and the growth of agrarian capitalism in nineteenth-century Puerto Rico* (item **2549**); Andrés Ramos Mattei's *La hacienda azucarera* (item **2549**) and *Azúcar y esclavitud* (item **2518**), the compilation edited by him; Guillermo Baralt's *Esclavos rebeldes* (item **2519**); the compilation edited by Francisco Scarano, *Inmigración y clases sociales en el Puerto Rico del siglo XIX* (item **2536**); Fernando Pico's *El amargo café* (item **2547**) and Teresita Martínez de Carrera's "The Attitudes of Influential Groups of Society toward the Rural Working Population in Nineteenth-Century Puerto Rico," (item **2541**). Mining and its social impacts in Cuba are discussed in two excellent articles by Vicente González Loscertales and Inés Roldan de Montaud, "La Minería del Cobre en Cuba" (item **2533**) and by Lisandro Pérez, "Iron Mining and Sociodemographic Change in Eastern Cuba: 1884–1940" (item **2600**). Louis Perez's *Cuba between empires, 1878–1902* (item **2476**) is readable, thoroughly documented, and detailed on the inherent problems of political and social change.

Amy Bushnell's study, *The King's coffer* (item **2510**), is a marvellous book, not only for the Spanish borderlands, but for the entire structure of Spanish American colonial society.

For the contemporary period, the most exciting publication is Robert Hill's initial two volumes of his projected ten volume collection of the *Marcus Garvey and the Universal Negro Improvement Association Papers* (item **2593**), the most complete collection of such papers yet published. Garvey is a major figure in 20th-century New World history, and the availability of this documentation will facilitate the writing of new biographies, as well as encourage much reevaluation of past work. Work on the labor movement in the Caribbean continues with the most outstanding publication being Ken Post's *Strike the iron* (item **2604**), a sequel to his brilliant *Arise ye starvelings* (*HLAS 42:2619*).

On the Grenada Revolution, Jorge Luna's *Granada, la nueva joya del Caribe* (item 2589), written before the overthrow of Maurice Bishop, provides insights as well as sensitivity. The *Memorias inéditas del censo de 1931* (item 2594) offers new comparisons for extending our understanding of Cuban society and demography serially. Bruce Calder's *The impact of intervention* (item 2572) provides a meticulous study of US involvement in the Dominican Republic.

Although relatively little attention has been given to the subject of migration in this issue, the great number of conferences, symposia and colloquia held during the past two years should result in many future publications. Moreover, the increasing political interest in the Caribbean Basin should begin to make an impact on the literature. One hopes that along with this output a narrower consensus on the definition of the Caribbean will emerge.

GENERAL

2451 Anthony, Michael. The making of Port-of-Spain. v. 1, 1757–1939, Port of Spain: Key Caribbean Publications, 1978. 1 v.: bibl., ill., index.

While far below the standard of Colin Carke's study of Kingston, this study fills a gap in information on Caribbean cities and towns. Interesting popular and anecdotal narrative. [FWK]

Báez Díaz, Tomás. La mujer dominicana. See *HLAS 45:8138.*

2452 Beckles, Hilary McD. The 200 years war: slave resistance in the British West Indies, an overview of the historiography (JHS/R, 13, 1982, p. 1–10)

Review of literature on slave revolts suggests need for "an analysis of the many 'common' plots which the planters and their recorders more or less considered to be unspectacular". [FWK]

2453 Boisrond, Tonnerre. Mémoires pour servir à l'histoire d'Haiti. Port-au-Prince: Editions Fardin, 1981. 108 p: bibl.

Facsimile reproduction of early 19th-century memoir on history of Haitian Revolution, previously published in 1852. Author was from prosperous free family of Afro-Haitians, educated in France, and participated in revolution alongside Dessalines. Reproduces letters and documents as well as recollections. [RJS]

2454 Bravo, Juan Alfonso. Azúcar y clases sociales en Cuba: 1511–1959 (UNAM/RMS, 43:3, julio/sept. 1981, p. 1189–1228, tables)

Based on limited and familiar secondary sources, shows that Cuban economy and society were influenced greatly by the vagaries of sugar production. For sociologist's comment, see *HLAS 45:8149.* [FWK]

2455 Bunker, Oscar L. Historia de Caguas. Caguas: s.n., 1975–1981. 2 v.: bibl., ill., index.

Detailed local history. [RJS]

2456 Camuñas Madera, Ricardo. Origen y desarrollo de Guayama (UCPR/H, 24:48, abril 1981, p. 91–102)

Narrative local history, based on printed primary and secondary sources. [RJS]

2457 Concepción, Mario. La Concepción de la Vega: relación histórica. Santo Domingo: Editora Taller, 1982. 279 p.: bibl., index (Biblioteca dominicana de geografía y viajes; v. 16)

Simple narrative of history and people of the town, from 1502 to present. [FWK]

Cueto, Emilio C. A short guide to old Cuban prints. See item 69.

2458 Dávila Santiago, Rubén. Algunas consideraciones sobre las primeras organizaciones obreras y la conciencia de clase (UPR/RCS, 22:3/4, sept./dic. 1980, p. 301–327, bibl., ill.)

Highly theoretical essay on labor, development of class consciousness and nature of early workers' organizations in Puerto Rico. Emphasizes role of artisan groups. [RJS]

2459 Dilla Alfonso, Haroldo. La evolución histórica dominicana y sus relaciones con Haití: 1492–1844 (UO/R, 48, dic. 1982, p. 65–119, table)

Emphasizes fundamental similarities between Haiti and the Dominican Republic, and history of anti-Haitian sentiment in the latter. Based on a range of secondary sources. [RJS]

2460 Fabre, Camille. St. Joseph des Vieux Habitants. Basse-Terre: Fabre, 1979. 158 p., 4 p. of plates: ill.

Narrative of Catholic Church in Guadeloupe (1636–1966). [FWK]

Fernández Rodríguez, Aura C. Origen y evolución de la propiedad y de los terrenos comuneros en la República Dominicana. See *HLAS 45:3175.*

2461 Fouchard, Jean. The Haitian Maroons: liberty or death. Translated from the French by A. Faulkner Watts. New York: E.W. Blyden Press, 1981. 386 p.: bibl., index, map.

Uses evidence of contemporary newspapers to draw a portrait of slaves, freedmen, and runaways, their motivations, circumstances and physical characteristics. Analyzes different forms of *marronage*, links *marronage* and Haitian revolution. For ethnologist's comment, see *HLAS 45 : 1078.* [RJS]

2462 Geggus, David P. Unexploited sources for the history of the Haitian revolution (LARR, 18:1, 1983, p. 95–103)

Describes archival sources in Spain, the Caribbean, Great Britain, and US, and suggests ways they might be used. Topics addressed include *marronage*, diplomacy, composition of the slave population, and British effort to conquer Saint Domingue. Useful. [RJS]

Guanche, Jesús. Hacia un enfoque sistémico de la cultura cubana. See *HLAS 45:1080.*

2463 Handler, Jerome S. and Robert S. Corruccini. Plantation slave life in Barbados: a physical anthropological analysis (JIH, 14, 1983, p. 65–90, ill.)

Analysis of skeletal evidence, particularly teeth, from a burial population of Barbadian slaves. Draws interesting inferences about nutrition, disease, and cultural practices. Evidence suggests "minimal and inadequate nutrition, periodic severe dietary deprivation, and occasional near starvation." [RJS]

2464 Hartog, Johannes. History of Sint Maarten and Saint Martin. Translation by A.H. Stronks. Philipsburg, Netherlands Antilles: Sint Maarten Jaycees, 1981. 176 p.: ill.

Continuation of series of delightfully illustrated works on the Netherlands Antilles, but in this case also including the island's French part. Useful social, economic and cultural data. [FWK]

Helms, Mary W. Black Carib domestic organization in historical perspective: traditional origins of contemporary patterns. See *HLAS 45:1082.*

2465 Higman, B.W. Slavery remembered: the celebration of emancipation in Jamaica (UWI/JCH, 12, 1979,, p. 55–74)

Interesting description demonstrating changes—subtle and otherwise—which characterized the celebrations, how they became secularized and Europeanized through time. [FWK]

2466 Lafleur, Gérard. Bouillante: l'histoire et les hommes (SHG/B, 53/54, 1982, p. 35–47, bibl., map)

Local history, based on archival sources. For ethnologist's comment, see *HLAS 45:1095.* [RJS]

2467 Laguerre, Michel S. The complete Haitiana: a bibliographic guide to the scholarly literature, 1900–1980. Millwood, N.Y.: Kraus International Publications, 1982. 2 v.: index.

Extensive bibliography prepared under auspices of Research Institute for the Study of Man. Includes natural sciences as well as humanities and social sciences, and theses as well as books, articles, and government documents. Covers works in many languages, including Haitian Creole. Follows the style of, and is intended as a complement to, Comitas' *The complete Caribbeana* (see *HLAS 41:1014*). Organized by subject. For ethnologist's comment, see *HLAS 45:1096.* [RJS]

2467a Le Riverend, Julio. Cuba: del semicolonialismo al socialismo: 1933–1975 (*in* América Latina: historia de medio siglo. v. 2, Centroamérica, México y el Caribe. Coordinación: Pablo González Casanova. México: Siglo Veintiuno Editores, 1981, p. 39–86, bibl., tables)

Actually a review of Cuban history between 1790 and 1979 with special emphasis on junctures of economic and political crises. [FWK]

Levine, Robert M. Race and ethnic relations in Latin America and the Caribbean: an historical dictionary and bibliography. See *HLAS 45:1099.*

2468 Lindsay, Louis. The myth of a civilizing mission: British colonialism and the politics of symbolic manipulation. Mona, Jamaica: Institute of Social and Economic Research, University of the West Indies, 1981. 40 leaves: bibl. (Working paper; no. 31)

Thoughtful and stimulating discussion of ways in which ideas are used to condition political responses towards England's role in imperialism both in England and throughout the empire. [FWK]

2469 Liss, Peggy K. Atlantic empires: the network of trade and revolution, 1713–1826. Baltimore: Johns Hopkins University Press, 1983. 348 p.: bibl., index (Johns Hopkins studies in Atlantic history and culture)

Impressive disentangling of the complex webs of trade, commerce, politics and national economies during the critical period when centrifugal forces were shattering the American empires. Important work for all students of New World history, complementing and superseding works by Ralph Davis, William Woodruff, and Richard Pares. [FWK]

2470 Lundahl, Mats. Haitian underdevelopment in a historical perspective: review article (JLAS, 14:2, Nov. 1982, p. 465–475)

Critical review by economist of five recent works on Haiti. Emphasizes links between external and internal factors in explaining underdevelopment, discusses what author views as peasant "myopia" in rejecting changes in agricultural practices. [RJS]

2471 Márquez Sterling, Carlos. José Martí, síntesis de una vida extraordinaria. México: Editorial Porrúa, 1982. 198 p., 16 p. of plates: ill., port. (Sepan cuantos; no. 367)

Elegantly written, chronological narrative of Martí's life. [FWK]

2472 Mir, Pedro. La noción de período en la historia dominicana. Santo Domingo: Universidad Autónoma de Santo Domingo, 1981/1983. 2 v.: bibl., ill. (Publicaciones; v. 295/320. Colección Historia y sociedad; no. 44/58)

Idiosyncratic work of synthesis and analysis by Dominican poet, traces selected historical themes. Traces popular responses to range of "devastations" in country's history. [RJS]

2473 Moreno Fraginals, Manuel. La historia como arma y otros estudios sobre esclavos, ingenios y plantaciones. Barcelona: Editorial Crítica, 1983. 178 p.: bibl. (Crítica/Historia; 25)

Valuable collection of essays, several quite recent, by distinguished Cuban social and economic historian. Contains provocative arguments concerning abolition, sugar industry crisis, and evolution of labor relations in Hispanic Caribbean. Based on extensive primary research, and a conviction of the importance of history to the reinterpretation of nationhood during a revolutionary process. [RJS]

2474 Nagelkerke, Gerard A. Netherlands Antilles, a bibliography, 17th century–1980. Leiden: Dept. of Caribbean Studies, Royal Institute of Linguistics and Anthropology; The Hague: Smits Drukkers-Uitgevers, 1982. 422 p.: bibl., indexes.

Comprehensive holdings of the Institute collection at Leiden. [FWK]

Olwig, Karen Fog. Finding a place for the slave family: historical anthropological perspectives. See *HLAS 45:1110.*

2475 Pérez, Lisandro. The political context of Cuban population censuses: 1899–1981 (LARR, 9:2, 1984, p. 143–161)

Perceptive essay that illuminates processes of census-taking, and larger political systems. Examines "imperial censuses" of 1899 and 1907, neocolonial census of 1919, Machado's politicized census of 1931, "progressive" censuses of 1943 and 1953, socialist censuses of 1970 and 1981. [RJS]

2476 Pérez, Louis A. Cuba between empires, 1878–1902. Pittsburgh: University of Pittsburgh Press, 1983. 490 p.: bibl., index (Pitt Latin American series)

Careful narrative based on correspondence, memoirs, government records, of interaction between US policy and Cuban domestic affairs. Argues convincingly that US intervention was "directed as much against Cuban independence as it was against Spanish sovereignty." Weaves account of interplay of classes, institutions, and individuals within Cuba together with evolving history of different groups representing US. Major contribution. [RJS]

2477 Polanco Brito, Hugo Eduardo. Salcedo y su historia. 2a. ed. Santiago, República Dominicana: Universidad Católica Madre y Maestra, 1980. 407 p.: bibl., index (Colección Estudios; 60)

Re-edition of 1954 doctoral thesis, traces local history of community in Dominican Republic using primary sources. [RJS]

2478 Rigaud, Nemours L. Petit Gôave: monographie. 2a. ed. Port-au-Prince: Editions de l'action sociale, 1980. 214 p., 1 leaf of plates: ill.

Local history of Haitian city includes discussion of current development projects. [RJS]

Römer, René A. Een volk op weg: un pueblo na kaminda. See *HLAS 45:3234.*

2480 Sánchez Tarniella, Andrés and Antonio Roopel. Sobre la identidad nacional. La política y la crisis por A. Sánchez Tarniella. La dialéctica de partidos por Antonio Roopel. Río Piedras: Ediciones Bayoán, 1981. 189 p.: bibl.

Interesting confrontation between opposing points of view, Sánchez Tarniella arguing that Puerto Rico has a history of liberty which it is losing owing to structural changes in the society and the economy. Roopel accepts the diagnosis but fails to see a connection between it and a confusion over identity, although he admits Puerto Ricans demonstrate multiple personalities. [FWK]

2481 Schnakenbourg, Christian. Recherches sur l'histoire de l'industrie sucrière à Marie-Galante. Nérac, France: Impr. J. Owen, 1981? 144 p.: bibl., ill.

Discusses history of sugar industry in one of Guadeloupe's islands, tracing growth, crisis, transformation of production. Pt. 1 discusses plantation (1664–1902),pt. 2 central mill (1845–1964). Detailed research based on archival sources. Contains population and production statistics. Also available as article in *Bulletin de la Société d'Histoire de la Guadeloupe* (48/50:2/4, 1981, p. 5–142). [RJS]

Schroeder, Susan. Cuba: a handbook of historical statistics. See *HLAS 45:8205.*

Sertima, Ivan van. The voodoo gallery: African presence in the ritual and art of Haiti. See *HLAS 45:1135.*

2482 Trask, David F. The war with Spain in 1898. New York: Macmillan; London: Collier Macmillan, 1981. 654 p.: bibl., index, maps (The Macmillan wars of the United States)

Most exhaustive account of the Spanish American war to date, based on research in US, Spain and Great Britain. More than military history, however, it analyzes political, diplomatic, military, cultural and social factors that led to war as well as conflicts that were so resolved. Trask's account differs from many recent ones in that he sees imperial and military power as the consequences of war rather than as causes of its outbreak. Makes outstanding reading. [FWK]

2483 Turnier, Alain. Avec Mérisier Jeannis: une tranche de vie jacmélienne et nationale. Port-au-Prince: Impr. Le Natal, 1982. 441 p., 13 leaves of plates (1 folded): bibl., ill.

Local history of Jacmel within context of Haitian events between 1844 and 1915 with emphasis on military narratives. [FWK]

2484 Zimmerling, Dieter. Die piraten der Karibik (WM, 10, Aug. 1982, p. 80–90, plates)

Popular text and lovely illustrations. [FWK]

EARLY COLONIAL

2485 Boria, Rubén. Fray Pedro de Córdoba, O.P., 1481–1521. Tucumán, Argentina: n.p., 1982. 190 p.

Pedro de Córdoba, first superior of Dominican Order in the Caribbean, was instrumental in Bartolomé de las Casas' "conversion" and author of important *Doctrina cristiana para instrucción de los indios*, published posthumously in 1544 in Mexico by Bishop Zumárraga. This is his only complete biography and the best, although somewhat on the apologetic side. [L. Gómez Canedo]

2486 Butel, Paul. Les Caraïbes au temps des flibustiers: XVIe–XVIIe siècles. Paris: Aubier Montaigne, 1982. 299 p.: bibl., map (Aubier-histoire)

Narrative history of Caribbean in 16th and 17th centuries based on secondary and primary printed sources. Emphasizes international rivalries, adventurers, and origins of sugar industry. [RJS]

2487 **Canabrava, Alice Piffer.** O açúcar nas Antilhas: 1697–1755. São Paulo: USP, Instituto de Pesquisas Econômicas, 1981. 257 p.: bibl. (Série Ensaios econômicos; v. 15)

Based on limited secondary sources, and does not challenge any of standard texts on period. Enhanced by illustrations (mainly from Du Tertre, Labat and Chambon) and figures on period's sugar trade, mainly for Barbados and Nevis. Woefully deficient bibliography. [FWK]

2488 **Crónicas francesas de los indios caribes.** Recopilación, traducción y notas, Manuel Cárdenas Ruiz. Introducción, Ricardo E. Alegría. Río Piedras: Editorial Universidad de Puerto Rico en colaboración con el Centro de Estudios Avanzados de Puerto Rico y el Caribe, 1981. 624 p.: bibl., ill.

Informative translations from French documents of early Indian inhabitants of eastern Caribbean islands. [FWK]

Cross, Harry E. South American bullion production and export: 1550–1750. See item **2622**.

2489 **Galenson, David W.** The Atlantic slave trade and the Barbados market: 1673–1723 (EHA/J, 42:3, Sept. 1982, p. 491–511, tables)

Uses records of Royal African Company in Barbados to show that rising slave prices in the Caribbean resulted in a larger proportion of children among the imported slaves thereby affecting the demographic history of populations both in Africa and the Americas. [FWK]

2490 **García Menéndez, Alberto A.** Los jueces de apelación de la Española y su residencia. Santo Domingo: Museo de las Casas Reales, 1981. 271 p.: appendix (Colección Monografía y ensayos; 2)

Study of early *juicio de residencia* in Española traces history of administration of justice and conflicts within island. Transcribes relevant documents in appendix. [RJS]

2491 **Hartog, Johannes.** José Díaz Pimienta: rogue priest (AJA, 34:2, Nov. 1982, p. 153–163)

First full account of Cuban priest (b. San Juan de los Remedios) burned at the stake in Seville auto da fe on 25 July 1720, having been tried and found guilty by In-

quisition for "theft, assault with a deadly weapon, forgery, piracy, extortion, sexual misconduct, not to mention a wide range of disciplinary infractions and personal eccentricities." [FWK]

2492 **Hilton, Sylvia-Lyn.** Ocupación española de Florida: algunas repercusiones en la organización sociopolítica indígena, siglos XVI y XVII (IGFO/RI, 42:167/168, enero/junio 1982, p. 41–70)

Describes indigenous Indian life and customs and their transformation after subjugation by the Spanish, including demographic disaster. [RJS]

2493 **Muñoz, Juan Bautista.** Santo Domingo en los manuscritos de Juan Bautista Muñoz. Transcripción y glosas por Roberto Marte. Santo Domingo: Ediciones Fundación García Arévalo, 1981. 573 p., 1 leaf of plates: bibl., ill., indexes (Serie documental Fundación García Arévalo; v. 1)

Transcription of documents of 18th-century Spanish scholar relevant to Santo Domingo. Includes valuable materials from the very early colonial period. Editor provides introduction and annotations. [RJS]

2494 **Otte, Enrique.** Los Jerónimos y el tráfico humano en el Caribe: una rectificación (EEHA/AEA, 32, 1975, p. 187–204, ill.)

Reconstructs background and probable contents of early correspondence of Jeronymites in Santo Domingo, corrects accounts of *Documentos inéditos de Indias* and Manuel Serrano Sanz, refutes assertions of Bartolomé de las Casas and Gonzalo Fernández de Oviedo, and shows economic interests overwhelmed humanitarian concerns for Indies' early indigenous inhabitants. [FWK]

2495 **Sánchez Ramírez, Antonio.** Notas sobre la Real Hacienda de Cuba: 1700–1760 (EEHA/AEA, 34, 1977, p. 465–486, graphs, tables)

Details period's income and expenditure. Weak on analysis. [FWK]

TePaske, John T. New World silver: Castille and the Philippines, 1500–1800. See item **1871a**.

O Tráfico de escravos negros sécs. XV–XIX: documentos de trabalho e relatório da reunião de peritos organizada pela UNESCO em Port-au-Prince, Haiti, de 31 de janeiro a 4 de fevereiro de 1978. See item **1791**.

LATE COLONIAL

2496 Clark, John Garretson. La Rochelle and the Atlantic economy during the eighteenth century. Baltimore: Johns Hopkins University Press, 1981. 286 p.: bibl., ill., index, tables.

Exhaustive analysis of political economy of La Rochelle, dealing with family structure, kinship patterns, business organization, and imperial and extra-imperial ramifications of trade and commerce in 18th century. Important for French Antillean trade to Martinique, Guadeloupe, and Saint-Domingue. [FWK]

2497 Cox, Edward L. Free coloreds in the slave societies of St. Kitts and Grenada, 1763–1833. Knoxville: University of Tennessee Press, 1984. 197 p.: bibl., ill., index.

Significant addition to historiography provides internal regional comparisons in cases of both islands and rest of Caribbean as well as experiences of this category of individual within context of New World societies. Extensive examinations of demography, economy, religion, and civil rights. [FWK]

2498 Debien, Gabriel. Guillaume Mauviel, évêque constitutionnel de Saint-Domingue, 1801–1805. Basse-Terre: Société d'histoire de la Guadeloupe, 1981. 112 p.: bibl. (Notes d'histoire coloniale; no. 105)

Travel and political travails of last appointed bishop to French colony of Saint-Domingue. [FWK]

2499 Foubert, Bernard. Les volontaires nationaux de l'Aube et de la Seine-inférieure à Saint-Domingue: octobre 1792– 1793 (SHG/B, 51, 1982, p. 3–56, maps, tables)

Military account supplemented by personal letters from the southwestern part of Saint-Domingue (1792–93). [RJS]

2500 Geggus, David Patrick. Jamaica and the Saint Domingue slave revolt, 1791–1793 (AAFH/TAM, 38:2, Oct. 1981, p. 219–233)

Examines reaction of different groups in Jamaica to French Revolution in nearby

French colony. Explains why Jamaica remained relatively tranquil. [FWK]

2501 ———. Slavery, war, and revolution: the British occupation of Saint Domingue, 1793–1798. Oxford: Clarendon Press; New York: Oxford University Press, 1982. 492 p.: bibl., index, maps.

Most outstanding study to date of Haitian Revolution and standard reference for this event and subject. Provides wealth of detail on colony's social and economic aspects and on difficulties of operating under conditions of war. Corrects previous assumptions and conclusions by Ott, James, and others. [FWK]

Hilhouse, William. Indian notices: or, sketches of the habits, characters, languages, superstitions, soil, and climate of the several nations; with remarks on their capacity for colonization, present government and suggestions for future improvement and civilization. See *HLAS 45:1084.*

Joseph, Gilbert W. British loggers and Spanish governors: the logwood trade and its settlements in the Yucatán Peninsula. See item **2345.**

2502 Kiple, Kenneth F. and Virginia H. Kiple. Deficiency diseases in the Caribbean (JIH, 11:2, Autumn 1980, p. 197–215, table)

Impressive both for its suggestive findings on relation between dietary deficiencies and diseases among slaves and for its superb bibliographical references. [FWK]

Kopytoff, Barbara Klamon. Colonial treaty as sacred charter of the Jamaican Maroons. See *HLAS 45:1094.*

2503 Marrero y Artiles, Leví. Cuba: economía y sociedad. v. 9, Azúcar, ilustración y conciencia: pt. 1, 1763–1868. Madrid: Editorial Playor, 1983. 318 p.: ill., maps.

Comprehensive, lavishly illustrated study based on extensive archival research. Part of continuing series that focuses on economy, population, society, and includes numerous transcriptions of documents. Particular attention paid to growth of cities and towns. Very useful. For vols. 6–8, see *HLAS 43:3222* and *HLAS 45:3245.* [RJS]

2504 Newson, Linda. Foreign immigrants in Spanish America: Trinidad's colonisation experiment (UPR/CS, 19:1/2, April/ July 1979, p. 133–151, graphs, tables)

Claims that Spanish concession of 1776 to promote immigration to Trinidad reversed a long-standing opposition to the encouragement of foreigners in the Spanish Americas. Tables give number and size of island's land grants. [FWK]

2505 Pérotin-Dumon, Anne. Témoignages sur la Guadeloupe en 1794 (SHG/B, 47, 1981, p. 5–34, plates)

Examines 1794 revolution in small island noting that while Alejo Carpentier's novel captures much of its essence, it fails to convey the full drama, trauma, and experience as well as internal conflicts which characterized this revolution. [FWK]

2506 Torres-Cuevas, Eduardo. Formación de las bases sociales e ideológicas de la Iglesia católica-criolla del siglo XVIII (UO/R, 48, dic. 1982, p. 153–188)

History of Cuban Church, including biographies of bishops and chronology of development of institutions. [RJS]

2507 Villiers, Patrick. Traite des noirs et navires négriers au XVIII° siécle. Grenoble: Editions des 4 seigneurs, 1982. 10, 162 p.: bibl., ill.

Offers well documented synthesis of French trade. Original documentation from naval archives (iconographic as well as written) illustrates ship designs for human cargoes. Complemented by the *Journal de Traite* (1787) of slave ship from Bordeaux, which reveals changes on eve of French Revolution with a triangular trade between French Mascareignes (Indian Ocean), East African Coast, and Saint Domingue. [A. Pérotin-Dumon]

2508 Watson, Karl S. The civilised island, Barbados: a social history, 1750–1816. Barbados: K. Watson, 1979. 149 p.: bibl., ill.

Intelligently conceived and written social analysis of Barbados during last years of slave society. Apart from demographic and social history, includes descriptions of education, drama, music, dance, and medical practices. Demonstrates eclectic nature of local cultural practices. [FWK]

SPANISH BORDERLANDS

2509 Acosta Rodríguez, Antonio. Crecimiento económico desigual en la Luisiana española (EEHA/AEA, 34, 1977, p. 735–757)

Asserts that colony's economic underdevelopment preceded its transfer to Spain, and that the relatively poor state of Spanish economy and industry merely perpetuated marginality and poverty. [FWK]

2510 Bushnell, Amy. The king's coffer: proprietors of the Spanish Florida treasury, 1565–1702. Gainesville: University Presses of Florida, 1981. 198 p: bibl., index.

A veritable gem of a study of Spanish colonial administration, economy, and society. Bushnell has carefully analyzed how empire's center and periphery compromised on their conflicting and often contradictory aims. Provides sharp contrast with main centers of empire like Mexico and Peru, since Florida was seen as outpost for missionaries, soldiers, and Indians. [FWK]

2511 Coker, William S. Una compañía privilegiada: John Forbes, en la Florida española durante la Guerra de 1812 (IGFO/RI, 40:159/126, enero/dic. 1980, p. 219–254)

Describes political and business acumen of Forbes and mixed fortune of having established his company in neutral Spanish territory and how it was eventually affected by the war. [FWK]

2512 ———. Religious censuses of Pensacola: 1796–1801 (FHS/FHQ, 61:1, July 1982, p. 54–63, tables)

Description of six religious censuses summarizes their data and describes conditions under which they were collected. [E.B. Couturier]

2513 Holmes, Jack D.L. Educational opportunities in Spanish West Florida: 1781–1821 (FHS/FHQ, 60:1, July 1981, p. 77–87)

Interesting description of apprenticeship and tutorial education for white youth based on variety of primary sources in Philadelphia, Baltimore, New Orleans, and London. [E.B. Couturier]

2514 Marchena Fernández, Juan. Guarniciones y población militar en Florida oriental: 1700–1820 (IGFO/RI, 41:163/164, enero/junio 1981, p. 91–142, tables)

Established initially to protect Spanish transatlantic shipping, the Florida colony became important by late 18th century because of its strategic location for trade. [FWK]

2515 Reilly, Stephen Edward. A marriage of expedience: the Calusa Indians and their relations with Pedro Menéndez de Avilés in southwest Florida, 1566–1569 (FHS/FHQ, 59:4, April 1981, p. 395–421)

Narrative of 16th-century Hispano-Indian politics focuses on marriage between a reluctant Menéndez de Avilés and sister of leading cacique. Provides information on various Indian groups and their inter-relations. [E.B. Couturier]

2516 Tornero Tinajero, Pablo. Estudio de la población de Pensacola: 1784–1820 (EEHA/AEA, 34, 1977, p. 537–561, ill., tables)

Based on material in Archivo General de Indias, updates examinations by Duvon C. Corbitt (1945) and Antonio Acosta Rodríguez (1979). Uses seven counts between 1784 and 1820. [FWK]

19TH CENTURY

2517 Adélaide-Merlande, Jacques. La commission d'abolition de l'esclavage (SHG/B, 53/54, 1982, p. 3–34)

Detailed discussion of composition and deliberations of 1848 commission to determine nature and circumstances of French abolition of slavery. [RJS]

2518 Azúcar y esclavitud. Edited by Andrés A. Ramos-Mattei. Río Piedras: Universidad de Puerto Rico, 1982. 129 p.: ill. (Faculty of the Humanities Publication series)

Useful collection of essays and comments by: Francisco Scarano, Gervasio García, José Curet, Guillermo Baralt, Andrés Ramos-Mattei, and María de los Angeles Castro. Themes include hacienda economy, abolition, role of *libertos* in Puerto Rico. Addresses questions of profitability of slavery, nature of the transition to free labor, reorganization of labor after emancipation. [RJS]

2519 Baralt, Guillermo A. Esclavos rebeldes: conspiraciones y sublevaciones de esclavos en Puerto Rico,

1795–1873. Río Piedras: Ediciones Huracán, 1982. 183 p.: bibl. (Colección Semilla)

Based on sources in municipal archives, study enumerates and analyzes series of over 20 slave revolts in Puerto Rico, primarily during period of increasing sugar production. Finds variety of triggers for these incidents, ranging from rumors of abolition to landing of foreign expeditions to hardship following drought and economic crisis. Also examines homicides committed by slaves (1850–73). [RJS]

2520 Barbosa, José Celso. José Celso Barbosa, pionero en el cooperativismo puertorriqueño, siglo XIX. Pilar Barbosa de Rosario, recopiladora. San Juan: Obra de José Celso Barbosa y Alcalá, 1982. 167 p.: bibl., ports. (La Obra de José Celso Barbosa. Parte 3, Documentos para la historia; vol. 1–2)

Writings of Celso Barbosa on political affairs as well as mutual aid groups (cooperatives) at end of 19th century. [FWK]

2521 Bellegarde-Smith, Patrick. Haitian social thought in the XIX century: class formation and Westernization (UPR/CS, 20:1, March 1980, p. 5–33)

Interesting intellectual tour de force interspersed with some fatuous statements such as calling C.L.R. James "the foremost West Indian historian." [FWK]

2522 Bergad, Laird W. Coffee and the growth of agrarian capitalism in nineteenth-century Puerto Rico. Princeton: Princeton University Press, 1983. 242 p.: bibl., ill., index.

Careful study of growth of coffee agriculture in Puerto Rico based on primary sources and focusing on Lares municipality. Emphasizes role of immigrant entrepreneurs, persistence of family holdings, and impact of export agriculture. Both a case study of transformation of systems of land and labor and a contribution to the analysis of dependency and underdevelopment. Major work. [RJS]

2523 Bolland, O. Nigel. Systems of domination after slavery: the control of land and labor in the British West Indies after 1838 (CSSH, 23:4, Oct. 1981, p. 591–619, bibl.)

Regards as too simplistic suggestion that post-emancipation conflicts revolved around man/land ratio and believes a better approach towards understanding such conflicts would consider varieties of labor control and transformation of systems of labor domination. Covers English Antilles from Guyana to Belize. For ethnologist's comment, see *HLAS 45:1055*. [FWK]

2524 Bosch, Juan. La guerra de la restauración. Santo Domingo: Editora Corripio: Distribuye Mateca, 1982. 261 p.
Bosch asserts that 1863–65 War of Restoration constitutes most important phase in Dominican history. His account rambles far and wide in space and time, lacks footnotes and index, but is quite readable. Makes some good points about Dominican society and economy in mid 19th as well as early 20th centuries. [FWK]

2525 Brathwaite, Edward Kamau. The slave rebellion in the Great River Valley of St. James, 1831–1832 (JHS/R, 13, 1982, p. 11–30)
Imaginative research and poetic reconstruction of western Jamaica's familiar slave rebellion. [FWK]

2526 Campbell, Carl. Ralph Woodford and the free coloureds: from a conquest society to a society of settlement: Trinidad, 1813–1828 (Journal of Caribbean Studies [Association of Caribbean Studies, Coral Gables, Florida] 2:2/3, Winter 1981, p. 238–249)
Contrary to Linda Newson's position, author thinks that Cédula of 1783 on land distribution was crucial to Trinidad's economic development. [FWK]

2527 Corso y piratería en el Caribe, siglo XIX. José Luciano Franco, editor. La Habana: Dirección de Publicaciones de la Academia de Ciencias de Cuba (ACC), 1980. 22 p. (Informe científico-técnico; no. 107)
Literal transcriptions of documents selected from Cuban archives dealing with early 19th-century Caribbean piracy. [FWK]

2528 Cox, Edward L. The struggle of the free coloreds in Grenada and St. Kitts for the removal of their political disabilities: 1813–1833 (PCCLAS/P, 8, 1981/1982, p. 25–34)
Emphasizes political activities. [FWK]

2529 De Verteuil, Anthony. The years before. Trinidad: Imprint Caribbean, 1981. 309 p., 1 folded leaf of plates: bibl., ill.
Readable narrative history with biographical sketches of 1829–1933 period before legal abolition of slavery in Trinidad. Focuses on changing relations between masters and slaves and unusual social and economic flux among various remnants of European groups therein as well as growing competition of cocoa farmers with sugar producers. Based on local archives, newspapers, family papers, and some secondary sources. [FWK]

2530 Documentos para la historia de la República Dominicana. Emilio Rodríguez Demorizi, compilador. Santo Dominto: Editora del Caribe, 1981. 4 v.: bibl., index (Academia Dominicana de la Historia; v. 55)
Continues series started in 1944 to select and publish documents. Covers 1844–61, with emphasis on Haitian relations. Context of selected documents is somewhat vague. [FWK]

2531 Dutton, Geoffrey. In search of Edward John Eyre. South Melbourne; New York: Macmillan, 1982. 152 p.: ill., index.
Extremely sympathetic account of Edward Eyre. Explains that George William Gordon, executed 1865 for Jamaica's Morant Bay rebellion, was "legally innocent but morally guilty." Readable, sometimes provocative, but lacks bibliography or footnotes. Several statements and facts disputed by Don Robotham's working paper (item 2550). Substantially similar to author's *The hero as murderer* (see *HLAS 32:2025*). [FWK]

2532 García Ochoa, María Asunción. La política española en Puerto Rico durante el siglo XIX. Río Piedras: Editorial de la Universidad de Puerto Rico, 1982. 697 p.: appendices, bibl., ill., index.
Emphasizes middle years of 19th century, documentation being mostly demographic and economic including trade figures. Contains some useful insights into overall changes of Spanish American imperialism during 19th century. [FWK]

2533 González Loscertales, Vicente and Inés Roldán de Montaud. La minería del cobre en Cuba: su organización, problemas administrativos y repercusiones sociales, 1828–1849 (IFGO/RI, 40:159/162, enero/dic. 1980, p. 255–299, tables)
Copper-mining in Cuba responded not only to international market conditions but also to presence in Cuba of experienced miners fleeing Spain's political conflicts, al-

though numbers of skilled were consistently insufficient to maintain mining impetus. Notes high use of rented and paid slaves in mines. [FWK]

2534 Historia del Pacto Sagastino a través de un epistolario inédito: el pacto produce el desconcierto, 1897–1898. Pilar Barbosa de Rosario, recopiladora. Río Piedras: Editorial Universitaria, Universidad de Puerto Rico, 1981. 218 p., 4 leaves of plates: bibl., facsims., ill., ports (La Obra de José Celso Barbosa. Pt. 3, Documentos para la historia política puertorriqueña; 11)

Collection of documents (1896–98) concerning Puerto Rican autonomist commission and its work. Includes letters, circulars, and newspaper reports. [RJS]

Hoetink, H. The Dominican people 1850–1900: notes for a historical sociology. See *HLAS 45:1086.*

2535 Holt, Thomas C. "An empire over the mind:" emancipation, race, and ideology in the British West Indies and the American South (*in* Region, race and reconstruction: essays in honor of C. Vann Woodward. Edited by J. Morgan Kousser and James M. McPherson. New York: Oxford University Press, 1982, p. 283–313)

Drawing on examples from both US and Jamaica, Holt examines process through which policy-makers attempted to define meaning of freedom for former slaves, and sought to shape emancipation to ensure continued estate labor. Author contrasts emancipators', planters', and freedmen's views of political economy, and relates their interaction to growth of racist thought in late 19th century. Excellent essay. [RJS]

2536 Inmigración y clases sociales en el Puerto Rico el siglo XIX. Francisco A. Scarano, *et al.* Francisco A. Scarano, editor. Río Piedras: Ediciones Huracán, 1981. 208 p.: bibl., ill. (Colección Semilla)

Excellent collection of essays on immigration, labor, planters, merchants, and politics in both sugar and coffee sectors of 19th-century Puerto Rico. Includes articles by Francisco Scarano, Astrid Cubano, Andrés Ramos Mattei, Laird Bergad, and Fernando Picó. [RJS]

2537 Joachim, Benoit. Les racines du sous développement en Haïti. Port-au-Prince: Imprimerie H. Deschamps, 1980. 257 p.: bibl.

Interpretive essay, with special focus on 19th century, traces underdevelopment in Haiti up to US occupation. Discusses class structure, economic situation, politics. Emphasizes dependency and what author sees as "neofeudal" agrarian structures. Based on manuscript as well as printed sources, but does not fully cite the former. [RJS]

2538 Leahy, Vincent. Bishop James Buckley, 1820–1828. Arima, Trinidad and Tobago: Dominic Press, 1980. 125 p., 1 leaf of plates: ill. (West Indian church history; 2)

Important for insights into Catholic religious dimension of slave society at crucial turning point in history of slavery and English Caribbean colonialism. First bishop appointed to vast region covering English and Danish islands from Jamaica to the Guianas, Buckley had many problems as spiritual head of important minority religion which, in Trinidad's case, represented majority of population. [FWK]

2539 Lidin, Harold J. History of the Puerto Rican independence movement. v. 1, 19th century. Hato Rey: Master Typesetting of Puerto Rico, 1981. 1 v.: bibl., index.

Narrative account by a journalist, based on secondary and some primary sources. [RJS]

2540 Maluquer de Motes Bernet, Jorge. El problema de la esclavitud y la revolución de 1868 (IJZ/H, 31:117, enero/abril 1971, p. 55–75)

Essentially a political discussion of considerations given question of slavery, based on Spanish newspaper and pamphlets with little attention to extensive secondary literature. [FWK]

2541 Martínez de Carrera, Teresita. The attitudes of influential groups of colonial society towards the rural working population in nineteenth-century Puerto Rico: 1860–73 (UWI/JCH, 12, 1979, p. 35–54, tables)

Sophisticated examination of problems of conflicting social, economic, intellectual, and political groups toward their island and how these groups cancelled themselves. Excellent example of the new social history emanating from Puerto Rico. [FWK]

2542 Matos González, Ramiro and José Soto Jiménez. Las campañas militares de la independencia dominicana, 1844–1856. 3a. edición corregida y aumentada. Santo Domingo: Edita-Libros, 1981. 202 p.: bibl., maps (some col.)

Military history at its most literal-minded. [RJS]

2543 Ottley, Carlton Robert. The Trinidad *callaloo*: life in Trinidad from 1851–1900. Diego Martin, Trinidad: Crusoe Pub. House, 1978. 152 p.: ill., index.

Popular, non-professional account reveals outrageous ethnic and cultural chauvinism as well as stereotyping. [FWK]

2545 Pérez, Louis A. Toward dependency and revolution: the political economy of Cuba between wars, 1878–1895 (LARR, 18:1, 1983, p. 127–142)

Traces 19th-century antecedents for American economic and political hegemony in 20th century, but author's data base is weak, his analysis weaker, and his point more asserted than proved. [FWK]

2546 Phillips, Glenn O. The beginnings of Samuel J. Prescod, 1806–1843: Afro-Barbadian civil rights crusader and activist (AAFH/TAM, 38:3, Jan. 1982, p. 363–378)

Based mainly on secondary sources, traces Prescod's early career and entry into local Barbadian politics. [FWK]

2547 Picó, Fernando. Amargo café: los pequeños y medianos caficultores de Utuado en la segunda mitad del siglo XIX. Río Piedras: Ediciones Huracán, 1981. 162 p. (Colección Semilla)

Detailed, gracefully written study based on notarial and other archives of small and medium coffee cultivators. Pt. 1 discusses landholding, credit, labor, production process in coffee economy; pt. 2 traces specific families. Very useful work of social and agricultural history which illuminates complementary roles of large and small landholdings. [RJS]

2548 Priego, Joaquín. Las batallas del 19 y 30 de marzo 1844. Santo Domingo: Publicaciones América, 1980. 198 p.: bibl., ill.

Military incidents and persons who rose against Haitians occupying the Dominican Republic since 1821. [FWK]

2549 Ramos Mattei, Andrés. La hacienda azucarera: su crecimiento y crisis en Puerto Rico, siglo XIX. San Juan: Cerep, 1981. 128 p.: bibl., ill.

Important analysis of sugar production, sugar trading, society, and economy in 19th-century Puerto Rico. [FWK]

2550 Robotham, Don. "The notorious riot:" the socio-economic and political base of Paul Bogle's revolt. Mona, Jamaica: Institute of Social and Economic Research, University of the West Indies, 1981. 95 p.: bibl. (Working paper; no.28)

Examines basic social and economic problems of lower orders of Jamaican society in 1860s. Concludes that neither Douglas Hall nor Edward Dutton presents fair estimate of Paul Bogle's contribution to important 1865 events at Morant Bay. [FWK]

2551 Roldán de Montaud, Inés. Origen, evolución y supresión del grupo de negros emancipados en Cuba: 1817–1870 (IGFO/RI, 42:169/170, julio/dic. 1982, p. 559–641)

Based on impressive archival and secondary documentation, shows that approximately 26,000 *emancipados* were found mostly in sugar-producing areas, and that their working and living conditions were comparable to those of slaves. Indicates that many local Cuban schemes were promoted for introducing free contract Africans similar to those then employed by English Antillean sugar producers, but since Great Britain opposed such schemes while slavery existed in Cuba they came to nought. [FWK]

2552 Sánchez Martínez, Guillermo. Días cubanos de Santiago Sawkins (UO/R, 48, dic. 1982, p. 137–146)

Describes 12-year stay in Cuba of North American painter, some of whose paintings, sketches, and engravings of early 19th-century Cuba survive. [RJS]

2553 Scarano, Francisco A. Sugar and slavery in Puerto Rico: the plantation economy of Ponce, 1800–1850. Madison: University of Wisconsin Press, 1984. 242 p.: bibl., ill., index.

Monographic study of specific plantation economy emphasizes continuing importance of slavery and magnitude of slave trade. Also analyzes structure of merchant and planter elite, reflects on role of immigrants and effects of that role on national consciousness. Solid and original. [RJS]

Schnakenbourg, Christian. Note sur l'histoire de l'usine du Galion: Martinique, 1865–1939. See *HLAS 45:1132*.

2554 Scott, Rebecca J. Explaining abolition: contradiction, adaptation, and challenge in Cuban slave society, 1860–1886 (CSSH, 26:1, Jan. 1984, p. 83–11)

Based on original national and regional archival sources, Scott establishes a very carefully argued and persuasive case that, contrary to general assumptions (most explicitly stated by Moreno Fraginals), slavery was not inherently incompatible with technological change. Most efficient Cuban estates reconciled slave with wage labor and new machines. Moreover, innovating planters were not necessarily abolitionist in outlook. Rather, abolition process was extremely complex with direction given by planters and the State in response to changing pressures from slaves and revolutionary insurgents. Crucial for understanding dynamics of 19th-century Cuban society. [FWK]

2555 ——. Gradual abolition and the dynamics of slave emancipation in Cuba, 1869–86 (HAHR, 63:3, Aug. 1983, p. 449–477, tables)

Based on impressive original research in Spain, Cuba, and US, Scott examines disintegration of slave society in one of its most successful New World cases. Her elaborate discussion challenges many of conclusions of Manuel Moreno Fraginals, Arthur Corwin, and Franklin Knight on the nature of slavery and its demise in Cuba. [FWK]

2556 Taylor, Bruce M. Our man in London: John Pollard Mayers, agent for Barbados, and the British Abolition Act, 1832–1834 (UPR/CS, 16:3/4, Oct. 1976/Jan. 1977, p. 60–84)

Reveals attempts by planters to counter or delay implementation of abolition of slavery, or failing that to get best terms possible for themselves. In early 1833, Mayers thought emancipation was inevitable. [FWK]

2557 Trade, government, and society in Caribbean history, 1700–1920: essays presented to Douglas Hall. Richard B. Sheridan *et al.* Edited by B.W. Higman. Kingston: Heinemann Educational Books

Caribbean, 1983. 172 p.: ill., index, maps, tables.

Interesting and varied collection of well researched articles that cover themes not usually dealt with in standard histories: Richard Sheridan on Jamaica slave trade; Neville Hall on urban slavery in Danish West Indies; Keith Lawrence on British colonial administration in Tobago; Carl Campbell on Crown Colony government in Trinidad; Bridget Brereton on emancipation celebration in Trinidad during late 19th century; Woodville Marshall on 1862 St. Vincent riots; Barry Higman on domestic service in Jamaica (1750–1971); Frank Taylor on tourist industry; and Patrick Bryan on Dominican Republic export trade (1900–16). Valuable addition to the historical literature. [FWK]

2558 Turner, Mary. The Baptist war and abolition (JHS/R, 13, 1982, p. 31–41)

Examines connections in Jamaica between slaves and masters and, in England, between Protestant missionaries and English abolitionists as well as political ferment over reform. Political acuity of abolitionists was to turn rumors of revolts and revolts to accusations of provocations by planting classes. [FWK]

2559 ——. Chinese contract labour in Cuba: 1847–1874 (UPR/CS, 14:2, 1974, p. 66–81, tables)

Shows that importation of more than 100,000 Chinese helped prolong slavery in Cuba. [FWK]

2560 Turu, Danielle. Consideraciones sobre el valor real del azúcar cubano vendido en el siglo XIX: contrabando y evaluaciones de aduana (EEHA/AEA, 34, 1977, p. 607–632, tables)

Recalculation of value of Cuban sugar exports in 19th century demonstrates that official figures obscured total, that taxes on exports represented very small proportion of income, and that since there was no direct taxation, profits from sugar trading were enormous. [FWK]

2561 United States. Department of State. Despachos de los cónsules norteamericanos en Puerto Rico. t. 1, 1818–1868. Río Piedras: Editorial de la Universidad de Puerto Rico, 1982. 1 v.: bibl.

Compendious volume, representing

enormous labor of transcription and editing, makes US consular dispatches from Puerto Rico far more accessible for research. Excellent source for study of economic activity, Spanish policy, commercial relations. [RJS]

2562 **Varas, Jaime.** La verdadera historia del cooperativismo boricua, 1800 a 1898. Hato Rey: Ramallo Bros. Print., 1982. 803 p: index, ports.

Rich data on neglected theme in Caribbean studies: rise of cooperative ventures in 19th century. Describes basic constitutions of these organizations but says nothing on rank and file membership. [FWK]

2563 **Vásquez, Pedro R.** Duarte, apóstol y libertador. Santo Domingo: Departamento de Publicaciones del Hogar del Niño Dominicano, 1980. 289 p.: bibl., ill.

Another example of fallout from the centennial of Duarte's death in 1876, being celebrated in print. [FWK]

2564 **Vilaplana Montes, Manuel.** Juan Valera y la guerra hispano-cubana (EEHA/AEA, 34, 1977, p. 589–605)

Spanish diplomat was far more aware than his government of implications of Cuban insurrection and attitudes in US. [FWK]

2565 **Wilmot, Swithin.** The peacemakers: Baptist missionaries and ex-slaves in western Jamaica, 1838–1840 (JHS/R, 13, 1982, p. 42–48)

Based on Colonial Office records, shows that despite assertions and opposition of planters, Baptist missionaries were moderate and tried to mediate wages and working conditions for ex-slaves rather than encourage them to abandon estate labor. [FWK]

2566 **Yacou, Alain.** L'expulsion des Français de Saint-Domingue réfugiés dans la région orentale de l'île de Cuba: 1808–1810 (UTIEH/C, 39, 1982, p. 49–64, table)

Based on archival research in Cuba and Spain as well as France, illustrates expansion of coffee culture in Eastern Cuba by French immigrants. [FWK]

20TH CENTURY

2567 **Albizu Campos, Pedro.** Pedro Albizu Campos: obras escogidas. t. 2, 1934–1935. Recopilación, introducción y notas por J. Benjamín Torres. San Juan: Editorial Jelofe, 1981?. 1 v.: ports.

Vol. 2 of Albizu Campos' selected works. Rather limited selection with no particular focus includes Albizu's declaration on Sandino's 1934 murder. [FWK]

2568 **Antoine, Jacques Carmeleau.** Jean Price-Mars and Haiti. Preface by Jean F. Brierre. Washington: Three Continents Press, 1981. 224 p.: bibl., ill., index.

Thorough, somewhat hagiographic biography of noted Haitian intellectual, politician, and ethnographer. Traces Price-Mars' career and writing, emphasizing his role in both Haitian public life and study of Afro-American culture. [RJS]

2569 **Arvelo, Tulio H.** Cayo Confite y Luperón: memorias de un expedicionario. Santo Domingo: Editora de la Universidad Autónoma de Santo Domingo, 1982. 295 p.: ill. (Publicaciones; v. 304. Colección Historia y sociedad; no. 51)

Interesting account of failure of anti-Trujillo forces in famous 1947 assault. Mentions Fidel Castro and Juan José Arévalo and many other participants, not all of whom were Dominican exiles. [FWK]

2570 **Barbosa de Rosario, Pilar.** Manuel F. Rossy y Calderón, ciudadano cabal: ensayo biográfico. San Juan: La Obra de José Celso Barbosa, 1981. 278 p.: bibl., ill.

Short bibliographical essay followed by annotated selections from Rossy's personal archive. Rossy was José Celso Barbosa's and author's family friend. [FWK]

2571 **Bellegarde Smith, Patrick.** Class struggle in contemporary Haitian politics: an interpretative study of the campaign of 1957 (Journal of Caribbean Studies [Association of Caribbean Studies, Coral Gables, Fla.] 2:1, Spring 1981, p. 109–127)

Aims to understand "Caribbean class struggle and elite ideological structure." Based on secondary sources and author's recollections. Analyzes coalition and process through which Duvalier assumed power, places them in world context. [RJS]

2572 **Calder, Bruce J.** The impact of intervention: the Dominican Republic during the U.S. occupation of 1916–1924. Austin: University of Texas Press, 1984.

334 p., 10 p. of plates: bibl., ill., index (The
Texas Pan American series)
Sophisticated, broad-ranging study of
US occupation of Dominican Republic and of
domestic reaction to it. Includes analysis of
US policy, rise of Dominican sugar industry,
development of nationalism. Based on extensive primary research. Highlights previously
ill-understood guerrilla opposition to occupation. Compares intervention to US involvement elsewhere in the Caribbean. Major
contribution. [RJS]

2573 Cassá, Roberto. Capitalismo y dictadura. Santo Domingo: Editora de la
Universidad Autonóma de Santo Domingo,
1982. 794 p.: appendices, bibl. (Publicaciones; v. 271. Colección Historia y sociedad; no. 36)
Structural analysis of dependent capitalism in Dominican Republic and its relationship to Trujillo dictatorship, from explicitly Marxist perspective. Examines agrarian
structures, industry, imperialism, capital accumulation, impact on world economy, class
struggle, the State, and ideological aspects of
dictatorship. Contains extensive statistical
appendices. [RJS]

2574 Chántez Oliva, Sara E. Condiciones de
vida de la clase obrera en le período
pre-revolucionario: 1952–1958 (UCLV/I, 69,
mayo/agosto 1981, p. 103–125, tables)
Standard Marxist argument that conditions for the working class deteriorated during 1950s decade. For sociologist's comment,
see *HLAS 45:8156.* [FWK]

2575 Crahan, Margaret E. Protestantism in
Cuba (PCCLAS/P, 9, 1982, p. 59–70)
Review of growth and activities of
Protestant sects (1898–1979) devotes attention to social and political conditions. Shows
that churches confused religious mission
with ideology and culture and US ethno-
centricity. Moreover, while missionaries accepted their own values as superior, none
fully understood their host society, nor had
the intellectual understanding or material
equipment to accomplish the appointed task.
[FWK]

2576 La Cuestión nacional: el Partido Nacionalista y el movimiento obrero
puertorriqueño: aspectos de las luchas económicas y políticas de la década de 1930–40.

Taller de Formación Política. Río Piedras:
Ediciones Huracán, 1982. 207 p.: bibl. (Colección Semilla)
Strong leftist analysis of Puerto Rican
National Party and labor organization has
weak factual background and fails to make
analysis comprehensible. [FWK]

2577 De Jesús Toro, Rafael. Historia económica de Puerto Rico. Cincinnati:
South-Western Pub. Co., 1982. 796 p.: bibl.,
ill., indexes.
Despite publication date, most of volume's statistics date before 1972. Emphasizes
manufacturing sector as prime instrument in
Puerto Rico's economic growth. [FWK]

2578 Documentos para la historia de Cuba.
v. 1–2; v. 4, pts. 1–2. Compiladora,
Hortensia Pichardo. 4a. ed., rev. La Habana:
Editorial de Ciencias Sociales, 1976–1980. 4
v.: ill. (Nuestra historia)
Covers period from 1935 to 1943 national census. Emphasizes development and
policies of Cuban Communist Party, anti-
government activities, letters and eulogies to
Pablo de la Torriente Brau, reorganization of
education, military reforms. [FWK]

2579 Dookhan, Isaac. The search for identity: the political aspirations and frustrations of Virgin Islanders under the United
States Naval administration, 1917–1927
(UWI/JCH, 12, 1979, p. 1–34, tables)
Thoroughly illustrated analysis of
often conflicting responses of various island
groups to assertion of US hegemony. [FWK]

2580 Dumpierre, Erasmo. J.A. Mella: biografía. Habana: Editorial de Ciencias
Sociales, 1977. 175 p., 13 leaves of plates:
bibl., ill.
Narrative and superficial, more than
analytical and exhaustive work that contributes to information on the acknowledged
founder of Cuba's Communist Party as well
as on general nature of student life and politics in Cuba and Latin America during early
20th century. [FWK]

2581 Ferreras, Ramón Alberto. Preso: 1960,
la cárcel bajo Trujillo. Santo Domingo
de Guzmán: Editorial de Nordeste, 1980.
320 p.: ill., ports.
Ex-prisoner provides rambling descriptions of political prisoners during Trujillo regime. [FWK]

2582 Gaillard, Roger. Charlemagne Péralte, Le Caco. Port-au-Prince: R. Gaillard, 1982. 375 p., 16 p. of plates: bibl., ill., index (Las Blancs débarquent; 6)

Vol. 6 in series on US intervention in Haiti and ensuing resistance. Covers period Oct. 1918–Nov. 1919. Focuses on guerrilla leader Charlemagne Peralte. Analyzes sources of conflict, compares earlier and later periods of *cacoisme*. Sees earlier movement as manipulated by local leaders, later movement as authentically patriotic. Based on primary sources, interviews, printed sources. Interesting study, filled with detail. [RJS]

2583 ———. Hinche mise en croix. Port-au-Prince: Imprimerie Le Natal, 1982. 262 p., 4 p. of plates: bibl., ill., index (Les Blancs débarquent; 5)

Impact of American invasion and occupation on small Haitian community (1917–18). [FWK]

2584 ———. Premier écrasement du cacoïsme. Port-au-Prince: Imprimerie Le Natal, 1981. 237 p., 14 p. of plates: bibl., ill., index (Les Blancs débarquent; 3)

Vol. 3 in series on US intervention in Haiti. Covers period July–Dec. 1915. Describes lack of initial resistance to US occupation, nature of US policy, increasingly bloody confrontation with Haitians, defeat of *cacos*. Traces biography of Charlemagne Peralte. Detailed, draws on interviews, newspapers. [RJS]

2585 Galván, William. Minerva Mirabal: historia de una heroína. Santo Domingo: Editora de la Universidad Autónoma de Santo Domingo, 1982. 357 p.: bibl., ill. (Publicaciones; v. 316. Colección Historia y sociedad; no. 56)

Biography of a brave young woman who defied the Trujillos and paid with her life. [FWK]

2586 García, Gervasio L. and Angel G. Quintero Rivera. Desafío y solidaridad: breve historia del movimiento obrero puertorriqueño. Río Piedras: Ediciones Huracán, 1982. 172 p.: bibl., ill. (Colección Semilla)

Complements works such as Blanca Silvestrini's, Fernando Picó's, and Miles Galvin's. Provides overall summary of workers and working conditions in Puerto Rico

from 19th century to present. Based mainly on secondary materials, but with good data and charts. [FWK]

2587 Julián de Nieves, Elisa. The Catholic Church in colonial Puerto Rico: 1898–1964. Río Piedras: Editorial Edil, 1982. 266 p.: bibl.

Despite its misleading title, an elegantly written and useful narrative of complex relationship between Church and State in period of transition from Spanish rule to North American influence. Based on newspapers, Church records, and secondary sources. [FWK]

2588 Kula, Marcin. Los estratos medios de la sociedad en el movimiento revolucionario: la revolución de 1933 en Cuba (UNAM/RMS, 43:3, julio/sept. 1981, p. 1229–1243)

Suggests that contrary to Marxists' expectations, middle sectors were crucial in elaboration and attempts to implement social change, a common pattern in Third World countries. For sociologist's comment, see *HLAS 45:8180*. [FWK]

Langley, Lester D. The United States and the Caribbean, 1900–1970. See *HLAS 45:3082*.

2589 Luna, Jorge. Granada, la nueva joya del Caribe. La Habana: Editorial de Ciencias Sociales, 1982. 234 p., 49 p. of plates: ill.

Intelligent and insightful account of first years (ends 1980) of Grenada's Revolution under Bishop, by senior editor at Prensa Latina who had extensive experience in Caribbean and Latin America. Title is play on words. [FWK]

2590 Lundahl, Mats. A note on Haitian migration to Cuba: 1890–1934 (UP/CSEC, 12:2, July 1982, p. 22–36, tables)

Views temporary and permanent migration as relieving population pressure in Haiti as well as contributing to labor availability in Cuba at point when sugar industry was expanding. Complements works by Juan Pérez de la Riva and Franklin W. Knight on Antillean migration to Cuba's sugar industry. [FWK]

2591 Machado y Morales, Gerardo. Ocho años de lucha. Edición a cargo de Mario Gajate. Miami: Ediciones Históricas Cubanas: Ediciones Universal, 1982. 224 p.: ill. (Serie Historia y biografías)

Presumably written by Machado before his death to clear his name and image, and published by descendant. Some dates are imprecise and other problems hinder historical use. [FWK]

2592 Malfan, Henri. Cinq décennies d'histoire du mouvement étudiant haïtien. Montréal: Jeune Clarté, 191. 140 p.: bibl., ill.

History of Haitian student movement (1915-present) based on secondary sources for early period, some original sources and interviews for modern period. Aimed at inspiring further student activism. [RJS]

2593 The Marcus Garvey and Universal Negro Improvement Association papers. v. 1, 1826–August 1919. v. 2, 27 August 1919–31 August 1920. Robert A. Hill, editor. Berkeley: University of California Press, 1983. 2 v.: bibl., ill., indexes.

Vols. 1–2 of projected 10 devoted to papers dealing with most controversial and astonishing Afro-American and the most remarkable black movement in the Americas' history. Papers and commentary provide basis for reexamining Garvey's paradoxical character and illustrates enormous shortcomings of some available biographies. Commendable job of compilation, identification, and contextual situation. Most important work. [FWK]

2594 Memorias inéditas del censo de 1931. Edited by Gladys Alonso y Ernesto Chávez Alvarez. La Habana: Editorial de Ciencias Sociales, 1978. 356 p. (Demografía)

Complete census data for 1931 demonstrates how by that time the collection process in Cuba had become sophisticated. Offers useful comparisons with 1899, 1907, and 1919 returns. [FWK]

2595 Mencía, Mario. Fidel Castro en el "Bogotazo:" abril 1984 (ACH/BHA, 49:736, enero/marzo 1982, p. 167–206)

Reprint of 1978 *Bohemia* article shows Fidel's high connections in Venezuela, importance of student politics in Latin America, and their traditional links with the labor movement. [FWK]

2596 Moncada: la acción. Compilación, Francisco Ramírez Sánchez, Carlos Morejón Cerra, María Dolores Díaz Alvarez. La Habana: Editora Política: Centro de Estudio de Historia Militar, Fuerzas Armadas

Revolucionarias de Cuba, 1981. 425 p., 24 p. of plates: ill., ports (Colección revolucionaria; t. 2 [1953])

Collection of interviews with Moncada survivors who recollect with graphic photographs the event's immediate aftermath. [FWK]

2597 Moncada: antecedentes y preparativos. Compilador, Carlos Morejón. 2a. ed. La Habana: Editora Política: Sección de Historia, Dirección Política Central de las Fuerzas Armadas Revolucionarias, 1980. 315 p.: ill. (Colección revolucionaria; t. 1 [1952–1953])

Odd assortment of documents from *Bohemia*, books, newspapers, speeches, and later reflections by the armed forces with the Revolution very much in mind. [FWK]

2598 Negrón-Portillo, Mariano. El autonomismo puertorriqueño: su transformación ideológica, 1895–1914. Río Piedras: Ediciones Huracán, 1981. 95 p.: ill. (Colección Semilla)

Study of autonomist reformism, based on content analysis of newspaper *La Democracia* (1895–1914). Examines Liberal (later Federal) Party ideology and its transformation under US rule. Sees initial desire for annexation to US, defensive effort to protect Puerto Rican cultivators, growing resentment of US economic influence, eventual bitterness and rejection of US domination. Sees party's position as one of "conservative, defensive, and anguished reformism." [RJS]

2599 Núñez Jiménez, Antonio. En marcha con Fidel. v. 1, 1959. La Habana: Editorial Letras Cubanas, 1982. 1 v.: bibl., ill.

Delightfully readable account by insider of the Revolution's first year. Covers glory, agonies, and slow consolidation of Fidel Castro's government. [FWK]

2600 Pérez, Lisandro. Iron mining and sociodemographic change in eastern Cuba: 1884–1940 (JLAS, 14:2, Nov. 1982, p. 381–405, table)

Nicely complements 1976 article by Robert Hoernel (see *HLAS 40:3032*). Indicates superordinate influence of sugar on other sectors of economy as well as on eastern Cuba's demographic profile. In 1914, Cuba ranked as world's ninth iron ore producer, exporting 60 percent of it to US and importing 91 percent of iron miners from Spain and Canary Islands. [FWK]

2601 Pérez, Louis A., Jr. The imperial design: politics and pedagogy in occupied Cuba, 1899–1902 (UP/CSEC, 12:2, July 1982, p. 2–19)

Dramatic emphasis on US attempt to use education as medium for imperial expansion. [FWK]

2602 Pierre-Charles, Gérard. Haiti, 1930–1975: la crisis ininterrumpida (*in* América Latina: historia de medio siglo. v. 2, Centroamérica, México y el Caribe. Coordinación: Pablo González Casanova. México: Siglo Veintiuno Editores, 1981, p. 174–222, bibl.)

Suggests that US occupation ended long period of political and economic conflicts among factions that could not establish local hegemony or stability. Occupation subordinated economy to US and established military domination of Haiti's political machine. [FWK]

———. El Caribe contemporáneo. See *HLAS 45:3089.*

2603 Plummer, Brenda Gayle. The Afro-American response to the occupation of Haiti: 1915–1934 (AU/P, 43:2, June 1982, p. 125–143)

Uses response of black Americans in 1920s to continued occupation of Haiti as indications of growing knowledge in world affairs as well as increase in their collective self-consciousness. Points out that lack of political influence meant that even critics could do very little to influence US policies. [FWK]

2604 Post, Ken. Strike the iron: a colony at war: Jamaica, 1939–1945. Atlantic Highlands, N.J.: Humanities Press; The Hague: Institute of Social Sciences, 1981. 2 v. (567 p.): bibl., index, map.

Sequel to *Arise ye starvelings* (see *HLAS 42:2619*) provides detailed analysis of rise of labor movement and politics in Jamaica. Research is outstanding; slant, liberal. Required reading for anyone interested in English Caribbean politics, labor, and society. [FWK]

2605 Seminario Domicano: Década del 80, *Santo Domingo, Dominican Republic, 1981.* República Dominicana, 1980–1990: perspectivas de una década. Santo Domingo: Instituto Tecnológico de Santo Domingo, 1982. 230 p.: bibl.

Conference papers attempt to assess economy, quality of life, education, and political prospects of Dominican Republic during 1980s. Despite title, most authors evaluate the 1970s. [FWK]

2606 Serna Herrera, Juan Manuel de la. Nacionalismo y socialismo en las Antillas, 1890–1970: el surgimiento del movimiento obrero y las ideas socialistas (IPGH/RHI, 3, 1982, p. 69–82, bibl.)

Descriptive, superficial treatment of English Antilles and rise of labor movement. No analysis of impact of socialist ideas. [FWK]

2607 Thomas, Hugh. The revolution on balance. Washington: The Cuban-American National Foundation, 1983. 19 p.: tables.

Despite use of late 1970s data, the thinking which accompanies this material is often flawed, and obsolete. Partisan study. [FWK]

2608 Ysalguez, Hugo A. El 14 de junio, la raza inmortal; invasión de Constanza, Maimón y Estero Hondo. Santo Domingo: Impresora Corporán, 1980. 142 p.: ill.

Memoirs of anti-Trujillo campaigner who participated in struggle against the dictator, working out of US, Cuba and Puerto Rico. First published in newspaper *Listín.* [FWK]

SPANISH SOUTH AMERICA: General

MICHAEL T. HAMERLY, *Precolumbian Studies, Dumbarton Oaks Research Library and Collection, Washington, D.C.*

2609 Celestino, Olinda and **Albert Meyers.** Las cofradías el en Perú: región central. Frankfurt: Vervuert, 1981. 351 p.: bibl., maps, tables. (Editionen der Iberoamericana; Reihe 3. Monographien u. Aufsatze; 6)

First in-depth study of religious brotherhoods in Peru's Indian parishes during colonial period and 19th century. Celestino and Meyers systematically examine multifaceted economic and social roles of *cofradías*, including those of communal defense and acculturation. Well documented.

2610 Cook, Noble David. The people of the Colca Valley: a population study. Boulder, Colo.: Westview Press, 1982. 101 p.: bibl., ill., index (Dellplain Latin American studies; no. 9)

Model history of the state and movement of a local population, the people of the Colca Valley in southern Peru, especially of the Indian component, from eve of Spanish conquest through most recent national census (1972). Includes analysis of colonial parish registers.

Costales, Alfredo and **Piedad Costales.** Amazonia: Ecuador-Perú-Bolivia. See item **1614.**

2611 Deler, Jean-Paul. Genèse de l'espace équatorien: essai sur le territoire et la formation de l'état national. Paris: Editions A.D.P.F., 1981. 279 p., 12 leaves of plates: bibl., chiefly maps, ill. (Recherches sur les grandes civilisations; synthèse no. 4. Travaux de l'Institut français d'études andines; t. 19)

Excellent essay on Ecuador's emergence as a nation state. Also, a valuable synthesis of what is known and presumed about the demographic and economic history of Ecuador from preconquest through present. Coverage is regionally balanced and author's approach is quasi-integral.

2612 Fellman Velarde, José. Historia de Bolivia. t. 1, Los antecedentes de la bolivianidad. t. 2, La bolivianidad semifeudal. t. 3, La bolivianidad semicolonial. 2a. ed., corr. y aumentada. La Paz: Editorial Los Amigos del Libro, 1978. 3 v.: bibl., ill.

Updated but not revised political history of Bolivia. Chapters on "cultural" history, however, have been revised as well as amplified and published separately as *Historia de la cultura de Bolivia* (La Paz: Editorial Los Amigos del Libro, 1978?). Vol. 1 on colonial period is anarchronistic in approach and coverage. Vols. 2–3 not available for review before press time. For first ed. of all three volumes, see *HLAS 34:2172a.*

2613 González, Nelly S. Ecclesiastical archives of the *parroquias de* [sic] Nuestra Señora de La Paz, Bolivia, 1548–1940: description and analysis (AAFH/TAM, 40:1, July 1983, p. 109–120, bibl., tables)

Solid introduction to and inventory of extant pre-Registro Civil holdings of La Paz's parish archives, particularly baptism, marriage, and burial registers.

2614 Hamerly, Michael T. Archives of Guayaquil (AAFH/TAM, 38:3, Jan. 1982, p. 379–391; 38:4, April 1982, p. 515–523; 39:1, July 1982, p. 107–116, tables)

Tripartite guide to and description of administrative and historical repositories of Guayaquil: 1) colonial and 19th-century institutions and administrative archives; 2) ecclesiastical entities and archives; and 3) historical archives and private collections. Examines their history and details organization and holdings. [Ed.]

2615 Historia general del ejército peruano. t. 1, Arqueología del antiguo Perú: los orígenes de la guerra y el ejército del Perú [by] Leonor Cisneros Velarde and Luis Guillermo Lumbreras. t. 2, El Imperio del Tahuantinsuyu: el ejército incaico; interpretación contemporánea [by] Edmundo Guillén Guillén and Víctor López Mendoza. t. 3, pt. 1, La dominación española del Perú [by] Juan José Vega. t. 3, pt. 2, Campañas militares durante la dominación española [by] Alejandro Seraylan Leiva. Prólogo, Eugenio Alarcón. Dirección general, Víctor López Mendoza. Lima: Comisión Permanente de la Historia del Ejército del Perú, 1980. 4 v.: bibl., indexes.

Official account of "the Peruvian Army" from pre-colonial times through the present. Vol. 1 covers pre-Inca period; vol. 2, Tahuantinsuyu and Spanish conquest; and vol. 3 (pts. 1–2), colonial period. Important because it illuminates how the military and their sympathizers perceive Peru's past and present and the armed forces' role therewithin.

2616 Kennedy Troya, Alexandra. Catálogo del Archivo General de la Orden Franciscana del Ecuador, AGOFE. Quito: Banco Central del Ecuador, Instituto Nacional de Patrimonio Cultural, 1980. 330 p.: index (Colección Archivos y bibliotecas; 1)

Detailed catalog of Quito's Franciscan archives. Well organized and indexed. A model research aid.

2617 Lombardi, John V. Venezuela: the search for order, the dream of progress. New York: Oxford University Press, 1982. 348 p.: bibl., maps, tables (Latin American histories)

Masterful survey of Venezuelan history. Gracefully written, carefully articulated, laden with insights. All periods and most themes are treated equitably. Complemented by chapter on Venezuelans' perceptions of themselves and their land, excellent bibliographic essay, and superior statistical supplement. For sociologist's comment, see *HLAS 45:8271.*

2618 Nineteenth-century South America in photographs. Compiled by H.L. Hoffenberg. New York: Dover Publica-

tions, 1982. 152 p.: ill. (Dover photograph collections)

Anthology of well chosen and reproduced late 19th-century photographs of people and places of South America. Captions, however, leave much to be desired.

2618a Pang, Eul-Soo. Buenos Aires and the Argentine economy in world perspective, 1776–1930 (Journal of Urban History [Sage Publications, Beverly Hills, Calif.] 9:3, May 1983, p. 365–382)

Review article of four books on Argentine economic development since late colonial period. Proposes extensive commercialization model be applied to Argentina. Finds that books under consideration—monographs by Socolow, Brown and Reber, and Platt's edited volume—present convincing material to support Wallerstein's idea of Atlantic capitalist world-system. [SMS]

2619 Pichincha: monografía histórica de la región nuclear ecuatoriana. Compilador, Segundo E. Moreno Yáñez. Quito: Consejo Provincial de Pichincha, 1981. 565 p.: bibl.

Anthology of original studies on history of corregimiento and city of Quito from paleolithic times through independence and on geography of modern Pichincha prov. Noteworthy are Moreno Yáñez's "La Epoca Aborigen," a solid synthesis of current state of knowledge, and Christiana Borchart de Moreno's "El Período Colonial" (see item 2673). Includes documentary appendix by Nadia Flores de Núñez on colonial period.

SPANISH SOUTH AMERICA: Colonial Period

MICHAEL T. HAMERLY, *Precolumbian Studies, Dumbarton Oaks Research Library and Collection, Washington, D.C.*
SUSAN M. SOCOLOW, *Associate Professor of History, Emory University*
KATHY WALDRON, *International Division, Chemical Bank, New York*

RETRENCHMENT AND SPECIALIZATION were the hallmarks of the 1982–83 biennium to an even greater extent than they had been in the preceding biennium. In *HLAS 44*, the number of items in the subsections entitled SPANISH SOUTH AMERICA: GENERAL and SPANISH SOUTH AMERICA: COLONIAL PERIOD was 219, or 10 percent less than it had been on the average. The mean of annotated citations in said subsections in *HLAS 36*, *HLAS 38*, *HLAS 40*, and *HLAS 42* was 243, with a standard deviation of four. In this volume, we annotated only 203 publications, or approximately 17 percent fewer than the 1972–79 average. In fact, the number of citations in this *Handbook* would have been even more reduced had Susan M. Socolow and Kathy Waldron—both of whom it was a privilege as well as a pleasure to welcome as fellow contributing editors—not included retrospective imprints of importance on colonial Venezuela, Colombia, Argentina, and Paraguay that had eluded this contributor and John Hoyt Williams. Also, although works by several new North American colonialists were annotated in *HLAS 44*, not one appeared in 1982–83. Moreoever, the number of books declined too. Almost all monographs were specialized. And the overwhelming majority of articles constitute what Socolow elsewhere characterizes as "microhistorical essays," not because of their brevity but on account of their limited focus.

The quality of virtually all books and articles annotated below, on the other hand, is high, regardless of whether the approach or theme is traditional or new. Furthermore, the reduction in production is not uniform. Peruvian historiography continues to be robust and to mature as exemplified by a new journal of high caliber, *Revista Andina*, published by the Centro de Estudios Rurales Andinos Bartolomé de las Casas in Cuzco (for articles appearing in vol. 1, nos. 1–2 reviewed in this section, see items **2701, 2705, 2711, 2735,** and **2736**). The Centro also inaugurated a monographic and source series of major importance, "Archivos de Historia Andina" (see *HLAS 44:2704*, and in this *Handbook*, item **2699**). Several new Peruvian historians made their debut in 1982–83, most notably Luis Miguel Glave and Efraín Trelles Aréstegui. Also, although many aspects of the colonial period in Ecuador, Bolivia, and Paraguay are yet to be researched, much has been added to our knowledge. Insofar as the Río de la Plata area is concerned, the most innovative as well as exciting work is being done on Paraguay.

GENERAL WORKS: Several syntheses grace this *Handbook*: John V. Lombardi's excellent essay on past and present Venezuela (item **2617**); Jean-Paul Deler's quasi-historical geography of Ecuador (item **2611**); and the vol. 1 of Sergio Villalobos' new approach history of Chile (item **2751**). However, there are no new digests of the colonial period for any Spanish South American country. Nonetheless, there are many thematically and/or geographically specialized new works which cover all or a substantial portion of the colonial period. The most readable of these is Luis Martín's *Daughters of the conquistadores*, an anecdotal yet scholarly account of Spanish women in Peru (item **2626**), which is eminently suitable for classroom use. Less appealing but far more important is Bernard Lavalle's doctoral dissertation on the emergence of criollismo among the regular clergy (item **2625**). Moreover, Lavelle's *Recherches sur l'apparition de la conscience créole* transcends modern boundaries: it takes in the whole of the former Viceroyalty of Peru.

Proceeding from north to south, the other chronologically comprehensive works which struck us as especially significant are: Nicolás de Castillo's masterful study of Cartagena as a port and slave entrepôt (item **2653**); Nicholas P. Cushner's monograph on "the Jesuits and the development of agrarian capitalism in colonial Quito," vol. 2 of his trilogy on Jesuit entrepreneurship in Spanish South America (item **2675**); Olinda Celestino's and Albert Meyers' major monograph on religious brotherhoods in Indian parishes of Peru (item **2609**); Luis Miguel Glave's article on traffic between Lower and Upper Peru (item **2705**); Glave's and María Isabel Remy's socioeconomic history of postconquest Ollantaytambo and its district (item **2706**); an anthology of previously published and new studies on *Hacienda, comercio, fiscalidad y luchas sociales: Perú colonial* by Javier Tord Nicolini, new director of Lima's Archivo General de la Nación, Carlos Lazo, and Jorge Polo y La Borda (item **2731**); Imelda

Cano Roldán's substantial and substantive history of women in Chile (item **2745**); Armando de Ramón and José Manuel Larraín's pioneering reconstruction and analysis of prices in Santiago de Chile and its district (item **2750**); the final volume in Cushner's tripartite study, *Jesuit ranches and the agrarian development of colonial Argentina* (item **2764**); and Juan Carlos Garavaglia's fundamental studies of yerba mate as the motor of Paraguay's economy (items **2774** and **2775**).

BIBLIOGRAPHY, HISTORIOGRAPHY, AND OTHER RESEARCH AIDS: Fewer reference works appeared than during the preceding biennium. All are specialized. Only two constitute bibliographic or historiographic studies: Joseph Barnadas' comprehensive review and list of recent literature on colonial Bolivia (item **2735**); and Susan M. Socolow's superior survey of "Recent Historiography of the Río de la Plata: Colonial and Early National Periods" in *Hispanic American Historical Review* (64:1, Feb. 1984, p. 105–120). Other items treat archives, their holdings, or paleography: Michael T. Hamerly's tripartite description of archives and manuscript collections in Guayaquil (item **2614**); J.B. Lassegue's and F. Letona's "Catálogo General del Archivo del Monasterio de Santa Catalina del Cusco . . ." (item **2711**); Nelly S. González's inventory of the parish archives of La Paz (item **2613**); Juan Heriberto Jáuregui's calendar of documents in the Archivo Nacional de Bolivia on the Túpac Amaru and Túpac Katari rebellions (item **2739**); Heloisia Liberalli Bellotto's description of Paraguayan mission documents at the University of São Paulo's Institute of Brazilian Studies (item **2759**); and José Ricardo Morales' reproduction and transliteration of common abbreviations in early colonial manuscripts (item **2627**).

CONQUEST AND EARLY COLONIAL PERIOD: There was an increase in significant scholarship on the discovery, exploration, and conquest of Spanish South America. At least nine scholars produced studies of importance. The most noteworthy of the new contributions are: Steve J. Stern's revised Ph.D. thesis on the conquest of Huamanga and its peoples' endeavours to accommodate their new overlords at least cost to themselves (item **2728**); Thomas Flickema's review of 1536 siege of Cuzco (item **2703**); Teodora M. Hampe's meaty biography of Bishop Valverde (item **2709**); and Rolando A. Laguarda's monograph on Vespucci's discovery of the River Plate (item **2781**).

The immediate postconquest or early colonial period continues to be popular, at least with South American and European scholars. Almost all 1982–83 contributions are specialized and relatively brief, constituting "microhistorical essays." Still, in addition to Cook's *Demographic collapse* (item **2695**) to be discussed below, and Stern's *Peru's Indian peoples* (item **2728**), there are two pioneering books: Sonia Pinto Vallejo's thesis on Cuzco's extraordinary contributions to the royal fisc (item **2719**), and Efraín Trelles Aréstegui's case study of a Peruvian encomendero and his encomienda (item **2732**). The microhistorical essays are numerous and disparate, the most significant being items **2645, 2646, 2663, 2678, 2681, 2691, 2707, 2720, 2774, 2782,** and **2799**).

INTERMEDIATE COLONIAL PERIOD: Although not entirely neglected, the intermediate colonial period, or the 17th and early 18th centuries, has yet to attract nearly as many scholars as the conquest/early colonial and late colonial periods. Only 15 contributions of importance came to our attention. Four, however, are books: Lucas Castillo Lara's exhaustive history of the Mercedarians in Caracas (item **2636**), latecomers to the future capital of Venezuela; vol. 2 of José María Vargas' modern chronicle of colonial Quito (item **2682**), the city, not the presidency (for vol. 1, see *HLAS 40:3188*); Carlos Antonio Moncaut's account of short-lived

Jesuit mission among Pampas Indians (item **2789**); and José María Mariluz Urquijo's valuable monograph on attempts to establish a trading monopoly in Buenos Aires (item **2787**). The quality of articles tends to compensate for their lack of quantity. Novel ones are those on Lower and Upper Peru by Antonio Acosta (item **2683**), Kenneth J. Andrien (item **2620**), Carmen Martín Rubio (item **2714**), René Millar Corbacho (item **2715**), Rafael Varón (item **2733**), and Jeffrey A. Cole (item **2737**).

LATE COLONIAL PERIOD: There was the customary abundance of publications on the late colonial period. All of those included in this *Handbook* are of high caliber. Well researched and written for the most part, all contribute new data and/or insights. At the same time, however, all these new contributions are specialized, many ultraspecialized. The most important books in our joint opinion are: Pablo Vila's digest of Bishop Martí's visita (item **2650**); Ann Twinam's socioeconomic history of 18th-century Antioquia (item **2669**); the new anthology of Tupac Amaru studies (item **2721**); Ernesto Maeder's economic history of viceregal Corrientes (item **2785**); and a multi-authored study of material culture in 18th-century Buenos Aires (item **2793**). Five articles are also outstanding: two documentary studies by Spanish historian Alfredo Moreno Cebrián on the finances of Lima's cabildo (item **2716**) and the city's morphology (item **2717**); Lyman L. Johnson's "The Impact of Racial Discrimination on Black Artisans in Colonial Buenos Aires" (item **2779**); and Socolow's "Buenos Aires at the time of Independence" in *Buenos Aires: 400 years* (item **3187**).

HISTORICAL DEMOGRAPHY: Only a handful of historical demographic studies appeared in 1982–83. And new population works treat only Ecuador, Peru, and Paraguay. Foremost is Noble David Cook's *Demographic collapse* (item **2695**), a superior reexamination of the probable size of the population of Peru proper on the eve of the conquest—which Cook now estimates to have been nine million—and of its subsequent decline through the early 17th century, its data base unfortunately being published separately (item **2696**). Cook also authored *The People of the Colca Valley* (item **2610**), a model history of a local population. Other recent historical demographic studies are: Javier Ortiz de la Tabla's solid review of known sources and studies of Audiencia de Quito's Indian population in the early and intermediate colonial periods (item **2679**); Ortiz de la Tabla's preliminary analysis of the conjointly published and heretofore unknown 1581–82 *visita* of the corregimiento of Riobamba (item **2680**); Rafael Eladio Velásquez's survey of the rise of the non-Indian population of Paraguay (item **2807**); and Pedro Vives Azancot's excellent essay on the population of Misiones as of the mid–1700s (itm **2813**).

SOURCES: Last but far from least, fewer primary sources were published than during preceding bienniums. As usual Venezuelanists and Peruvianists were the most active in this regard. Two works appeared which transcend boundaries and nationalities: John J. TePaske and Herbert S. Klein's compendium of treasury accounts of Lower and Upper Peru, Chile, and the Río de la Plata (item **2631**); and *Nineteenth-century South America in photographs* (item **2618**). The most monumental of the new Venezuelan sources are a set on the Capuchin missions in Guayana (item **2635**), compiled by the indefatigable Buenaventura de Carrocera; and the abstracts of *censos* or Church held mortages in the Archdiocesan Archives of Caracas (item **2637**), largely prepared by the equally prolific Ermila Troconis de Veracoechea. Most significant among new Peruvian materials are: a Franciscan chronicle of the order activities in the Upper Ucayali (item **2685**); Viceroy Chichón's confidential memoirs (item **2686**); an indexed edition of Calancha's *Coronica moralizada*, the standard ethnohistorical and historical source (item **2689**); a multi-volume collection on the Tupac Amaru rebellion (item **2693**); a heretofore unknown 1649 chronicle and description of Cuzco (item **2714**); the 1689 *relaciones geográficas* of the Cuzco diocese (item **2699**); and a critical edition of Viceroy Jáuregui's *relación de mando* (item **2686**). Hardly any sources appeared on the other colonies. The most noteworthy are: 1608 *relación geográfica* of Pacaje (item **2740**); a 1744 description of the Santiago diocese (item **2747**); the 1700–50 *actas* of San Luis' Cabildo (item **2800**); and writings by Manuel Genaro de Villota, late 18th-century Crown attorney of the Buenos Aires Audiencia (item **2811**).

GENERAL

2620 Adrien, Kenneth J. The sale of fiscal offices and the decline of royal authority in the Viceroyalty of Peru, 1633–1700 (HAHR, 62:1, Feb. 1982, p. 49–71, tables)
Examines effects of sale of treasury offices in 17th century. Although practice was not sole, let alone primary cause of concurrent decline in royal revenues, it did contribute to subsequent deterioration in royal authority. [MTH]

2621 Congreso Venezolano de Historia, *4th, Caracas, 1980. Memoria. v. 1/3.* Caracas: Academia Nacional de la Historia, 1983. 3 v. (552, 533, 474 p.): indexes.
Important reference work consists of 47 excellent papers on topics related to economic history of the *Real Hacienda*: accounting practices, local institutions, the Consulados, Intendancies, encomiendas, and *cajas reales* mostly related to Venezuelan and Latin American history. Among most significant articles (to be reviewed separately in next humanities volume HLAS 48) are: François Chevalier's and Ermila Troconis de Veracoechea's two analyses of royal fisc; Antoinette da Prato-Perelli's and Virgilio Tosta's works on encomiendas; Pedro Grases' review of sources on cacao; Manuel Lucena Salmoral's essay on last Venezuelan intendant; Ramón María Serena's contribution to Caracas' history; and an original study of Aroa's copper mines by Brito Figueroa's students. [KW]

2622 Cross, Harry E. South American bullion production and export: 1550–1750 (*in* Precious metals in the later medieval and early modern worlds. Edited by J.F. Richards. Carolina Academic Press, 1983, p. 397–424, ill., maps, tables)
Meticulous recalculation of New World's silver and gold output (1500–1800). Revises Earl Hamilton's figures and indicates that American production exceeded what is commonly believed and that Brazilian production (1700–60) exceeded in value Potosí's and Peru's (1580–1640). Challenges view that Peru's silver decline during later 17th century can be called catastrophic, contradicting accounts of John Parry, Charles Gibson, and John Elliott. [F.W. Knight]

2623 Durán, Juan Guillermo. El Catecismo del III Concilio Provincial de Lima y sus complementos pastorales: 1584–1585: estudio preliminar, textos, notas. Buenos Aires: Facultad de Teología de la Pontificia Universidad Católica Argentina Santa María de los Buenos Aires: Editorial El Derecho, 1982. 523 p.: bibl., ill., indexes (Teología; 5)
Solidly researched doctoral thesis on efforts of III Council of Lima to produce cathecism appropriate for proselytizing Indians of South America, especially Andean ethnic groups (p. 7–358). Includes text of 1584 *Doctrina cristiana y catecismo* and related sources (p. 359–513). [MTH]

2624 Jáuregui y Aldecoa, Agustín. Relación y documentos del gobierno del Virrey del Perú, Agustín de Jáuregui y Aldecoa, 1780–1784. Edición y estudio por Remedios Contreras. Madrid: Instituto Gonzalo Fernández de Oviedo, 1982. 320 p.: ill., index (Colección tierra nueva y cielo nuevo; 4)
Critical edition of Jáuregui's *relación de mando* and accompanying documents. Enhanced by notes and meaty biobibliographical introduction. Jáuregui was viceroy during Tupac Amaru and Tupac Katari rebellions. [MTH]

2625 Lavalle, Bernard. Recherches sur l'apparition de la conscience créole dans la Vice-Royauté du Pérou: l'antagonisme hispano-créole dans les ordres religieux: XVIème-XVIIème siècles. Lille, France: Atelier national de reproduction des thèses, Université de Lille III, 1982. 2 v. (1312 p.): bibl., index, tables.

Monumental doctoral thesis on emergence of *criollismo* in Peru's Viceroyalty as manifested by internecine quarrels and struggles for supremacy among Old and New World-born members of Augustinian, Dominican, Franciscan, and Mercedarian monasteries, especially in Bogotá, Quito, Lima, and Cuzco. Thoroughly researched in European and South American repositories. [MTH]

2626 Martín, Luis. Daughters of the conquistadores: women of the Viceroyalty of Peru. Albuquerque: University of New Mexico Press, 1983. 354 p.: bibl., ill., index.

Elegantly written, well researched, insightful albeit anecdotal history of Spanish women in the Viceroyalty of Peru, mostly in Peru proper. Nearly half the work is given over to convent life, which for the most part Martín demonstrates to have been loose. The chapter on "Beatas and tapadas" is a gem. [MTH]

2627 Morales, José Ricardo. Estilo y paleografía de los documentos chilenos: siglos XVI y XVII. Santiago: Departamento de Estudios Humanísticos, Facultad de Ciencias Físicas y Matemáticas, Universidad de Chile, 1981. 124 p., 9 leaves of plates: bibl., ill. (Ediciones del Departamento; 13)

Originally published in 1942, this introduction's value to Spanish American paleography lies in its reproduction and transliteration of 829 abbreviations commonly employed in early colonial texts. [MTH]

2628 Olaechea Labayén, Juan B. Un recurso al Rey de la primera generación mestiza del Perú (EEHA/AEA, 32, 1975, p. 155–186)

Abstracts and analyzes late 16th-century *expediente* on ordination of mestizos. Prohibited from receiving holy orders in 1578, various mestizo groups petitioned Crown and Church for redress. Crown revoked earlier stance 10 years later but only in dioceses of Cuzco, La Plata, Quito, and Tucumán. [MTH]

2629 Ronan, Charles E. Francisco Javier Iturri, S.J. and Alcedos's *Diccionario geográfico* (JGSWGL, 18, 1981, p. 164–186)

Publishes with introducion four letters by Argentine born Jesuit to Alcedo, praising and critiquing latter's *Diccionario geográfico*.

Of interest to historians of ideas as well as historical geographers. [MTH]

2630 Szászdi, Adám. Dos fuentes para la historia de la empresa de Pizarro y Almagro: la *Crónica rimada* y la *Relación Sámano* (EEHA/HBA, 25, 1981, p. 89–146, plates)

Returns to question of *Crónica rimada*'s authorship (see *HLAS 44:2641* and *2657*) and publishes new, more accurate transcription together with photographs of original text of *Relación Sámano*, critical source for ethnohistory of Ecuador's coast. [MTH]

2631 TePaske, John J. and Herbert S. Klein. The royal treasuries of the Spanish Empire in America. Durham: Duke University Press, 1982. 3 v.: bibl.

Publishes *cartas cuentas*—or periodic, usually annual, summaries of receipts and disbursements—of *cajas reales* (royal treasuries) of Peru proper (vol. 1), Upper Peru (vol. 2), Chile and Río de la Plata (vol. 3). Major data set provides answers to questions of imperial and colonial finances and their economic bases and mixes. [MTH]

VENEZUELA

2632 Arcila Farías, Eduardo. La historia cuantitativa y sus problemas (PUCP/H, 5:2, dic. 1981, p. 141–147, bibl.)

Explanation of purpose behind, and value of, project to analyze development and history of colonial treasury of Caracas prov. being conducted by Venezuela's Central University. Mostly a general defense of quantitative history. Says little about project itself. [J.D. Riley]

2633 Cal Martínez, María Consuelo. La defensa de la integridad territorial de Guayana en tiempos de Carlos III. Caracas: Academia Nacional de la Historia, 1979. 441 p.: ill., maps (Biblioteca de la Academia. Fuentes para la historia colonial de Venezuela; 142)

Carefully researched study of Spain's failure to populate Guayana (between Orinoco and Amazon rivers) in response to Portuguese and French incursions. Felipe de Inciarte led 1779 exploratory expedition after French attacked Spanish outposts but could not obtain support to settle Guayana, later becoming its governor. Reveals Spain's inability to react and protect its possessions, even under direct threat. Also presents Venezuela's historical claim to Esequibo territory, still under dispute. Useful maps. [KW]

2634 Carrocera, Buenaventura de. Expediciones de Capuchinos de la Provincia de Cataluña de la Misión de Guayana (ISTM/MH, 37:109/111, enero/dic. 1980, p. 211–262)

Additional material on Capuchinos sent to Guayana not covered in author's excellent three-volume study (see item **2635**). Documents, in Archivo de la Corona de Aragón, list departures and arrivals of missionaries and some information on their selection process. [KW]

2635 ———. Misión de los Capuchinos de Guayana. v. 1, Introducción y resumen histórico: documentos: 1682–1758. v. 2, Documentos: 1760–1785. v. 3, Documentos: 1785–1819. Caracas: Academia Nacional de la Historia, 1979. 3 v.: bibl., indexes (Biblioteca de la Academia. Fuentes para la historia colonial de Venezuela; 139–141)

Three-volume compendium of archival material on Catalan Capuchin missions in Guayana (1682 until independence wars). Documents from AGI and Cataluña's Archivo Provincial de Capuchinos. Missionaries established 52 towns (18 still exist), introduced cattle ranching as economic basis of Indian *reducciones*, and recorded native languages in bilingual dictionaries. Autonomy from religious and civil authorities was maintained until revolutionaries dominated region in 1817, after which most missionaries fled or died for loyalist sympathies. Useful, well organized source, with good introduction. [KW]

2636 Castillo Lara, Lucas G. Los mercedarios y la vida política y social de Caracas en los siglos XVII y XVIII. Caracas: Academia Nacional de la Historia, 1980. 2 v.: bibl., ill., indexes (Biblioteca de la Academia. Fuentes para la historia colonial de Venezuela; 143–144)

Exhaustively researched and highly detailed history of Mercedarios in Caracas. After troubled start, religious order finally established convent in 1637. Also examines city's political forces and social life through power struggles among bishops, governors, and ecclesiastic and civil cabildos. Clearly demonstrates harmful effects of often petty squabbles and clashing personalities on the community's harmonious development. [KW]

2637 Los Censos en la Iglesia colonial venezolana: sistema de préstamos a interés. Estudio preliminar y recopilación de Ermila Troconis de Veracoechea, Gladis Veracoechea, and Euclides Fuguett. Caracas: Academia Nacional de Historia, 1982. 3 v. (674, 434, 633 p.): indexes (Biblioteca de la Academia. Fuentes para la historia colonial de Venezuela; 153–155)

Three-volume catalogue of documents from 17th through 19th centuries in Archivo Arzobispal de Caracas' Censo section. Compilers thoroughly summarize each manuscript and provide useful geographic and onomastic indexes to 79 manuscript volumes dealing with establishment and litigation of *censos* throughout Venezuela. Vol. 1 includes material on convents, parishes, *cofradías*, hospitals, and *obras pías*, while vols. 2–3 are exclusively devoted to *capellanías*. *Censos* encumbered private property from sale or transfer while providing perpetual source of income to religious institutions. Veracoechea's introduction reviews Church's economic role and concludes that in Venezuela it was powerful but not wealthy. [KW]

2638 Cisneros, Joseph Luis de. Descripción exacta de la Provincia de Venezuela. Estudio preliminar por Pedro Grases. Caracas: Academia Nacional de la Historia, 1981. 184 p.: ill. (Biblioteca de la Academia. Fuentes para la historia colonial de Venezuela; 149)

Cisneros wrote fascinating, literary description of Venezuela in 18th century, recounting economic and cultural characteristics of cities and towns he visited during 25 years of travel as itinerant Creole merchant. Published 1764 in Spain, it is reproduced here in facsimile ed. with useful introduction by Pedro Grases. He believes that Cisneros may have worked for the Compañía Guipuzcoana because of his evident sympathy for the trading company. [KW]

2639 Gómez Parente, Odilo. Labor franciscana en Venezuela. t. 1, Promoción indígena. Caracas: Universidad Católica Andrés Bello, Instituto de Investigaciones Históricas, Centro de Lenguas Indígenas, 1979. 523 p.: bibl., index.

Carefully researched, well written history of Franciscan missions in eastern Venezuela. Through extensive use of archival material, author recounts how Franciscans established over 80 missions near Cumaná and along the Orinoco. Provides valuable population estimates and descriptions of each mission. Also notes linguistic work of Franciscans among Caribes and details their early bilingual publications. [KW]

2640 González F., Luis Enrique. La Guaira: conquista y colonia. Caracas: Editorial Grafarte, 1982. 200 p.: bibl., ill.

First history of La Guaira, port town founded 1589 to service Caracas and protect it from pirate attacks. Concentrates on its evolution from fortified town to thriving commercial center, noting port's dependency on capital city and inland economy. Also provides much information on other coastal towns and Caracas. Lack of footnotes detracts from an otherwise scholarly presentation. [KW]

2641 Izard, Miquel. Colonizadores y colonizados: Venezuela y la Guipuzcoana (Saoiak [San Sebastián, Spain] 4, 1980, p. 53–67, tables)

Repeats Ronald Hussey's thesis that contraband trade intensified as Compañía Guipuzcoana underpaid Venezuelan producers and overcharged for European manufactured goods. Importance of contraband and direct benefits achieved by Creole agriculturalists weakens argument that Basques monopolized economy to Creoles' detriment. [KW]

2642 ———. Ni cuatreros ni montoneros: llaneros (UB/BA, 23:31, 1981, p. 83–142, tables)

Good overview of *llanero*, Venezuela's equivalent of gaucho. Llanos' harshness made region fit only for those escaping Spanish domination (e.g., runaway slaves, Indians, mestizos, outcasts). Nomadic horseman dedicated to cattle and hide contraband, llanero developed unique culture. Llanos remained rebellious zone until 20th century, providing powerful caudillos and fierce armies for independence and Federal wars. [KW]

Lovera De-Sola, R.J. Catálogo de libros de historia colonial de Venezuela compilado en 1950–1978. See item **28**.

2643 Lucena Salmoral, Manuel. La sociedad de la Provincia de Caracas a comien-

zos del siglo XIX (EEHA/AEA, 37, 1980, p. 157–189)

Focuses on conflicts among social and racial groups and is based on published documents. Province was one-fourth white, one-third pardo, 16 percent black slave, 12 percent Indian, and seven percent free black at end of colonial period. Whites opposed Crown's *gracias al sacar cédulas* and local officials suspended slave trade for fear of slave revolts. Establishes racial background of Venezuela's independence movement, but offers no new insights. [KW]

2644 Miguel López, Isabel. Relaciones comerciales entre Santander y La Guaira en el período 1778–1785 (VANH/B, 65:260, oct./dic. 1982, p. 963–976, graphs)

Original essay, based on Simancas' ship documents. Shows existence of lively trade between La Guaira and Santander during supposed Guipuzcoana Co.'s monopoly. Santander's exports were mostly foreign, primarily textiles, and Spanish wines and food. More diversified than Guipuzcoana exports, goods provided significant revenues to Santander. [KW]

2645 Troconis de Veracoechea, Ermila. Contribución al estudio de la formación de algunos pueblos de Venezuela (VANH/B, 64:253, enero/marzo 1981, p. 61–73)

Good overview of town formation in colonial Venezuela. Encomiendas interrupted town foundations begun by conquistadores until 17th century when missionaries and Crown revitalized urban system. Makes legal distinction among doctrinas, parroquias, villas, encomiendas, misiones and ciudades, but does not clarify economic differences. [KW]

2646 ———. Venezuela: indígenas, siglo XVII (VANH/B, 64:255, julio/sept. 1981, p. 609–617, bibl.)

Interesting, but unproven, thesis that eastern and western Venezuela developed along distinct lines during 16th and early 17th centuries. Discusses evolution of encomiendas and repartimientos while briefly mentioning *apuntamiento* and *datas* as systems for allocating indigenous labor. General article outlines labor systems without details about specific Venezuelan Indians. [KW]

2647 Uslar Pietri, Arturo. Los libros de Miranda. Advertencia bibliográfica,

Pedro Grases. Caracas: La Casa de Bello, 1979. 156 p.: appendices, facsims.

When Francisco de Miranda's library was put up for sale in London (1828 and 1833), bookdealer prepared two catalogues, listing over 3000 volumes, reproduced here in facsimile. Two distinguished writers comment on library's merit. [KW]

2648 Vila, Marco Aurelio. Aportación a la geohistoria venezolana de 1777 (UB/BA, 23:31, 1981, p. 219–239, bibl.)

Discusses Jesuit Antonio Julián's *La perla de la América: Provincia de Santa María* (written 1777, published Madrid 1787). Notes Julián's interesting descriptions of agriculture and indigenous peoples as he traveled (1749–67) from Santa Marta to Maracaibo, and then along the Orinoco. [KW]

2649 ———. Síntesis geohistórica de la economía colonial de Venezuela. Caracas: Banco Central de Venezuela, 1980. 365 p.: bibl., indexes (Colección histórico-económica venezolana; v. 18)

Somewhat unsatisfactory review of Venezuela's colonial economy, arranged by activity and geographic location. Devotes chapters to labor, agriculture, minerals, manufacturing, and commerce. Arrangement makes for discontinuity although many interesting facts are provided. [KW]

2650 Vila, Pablo. El Obispo Martí: interpretación humana y geográfica de la larga marcha pastoral del Obispo Mariano Martí en la Diócesis de Caracas. Caracas: Universidad Central de Venezuela, Dirección de Cultura, 1980. 1 v.: ill. (Colección Humanismo y ciencia; 16)

Useful summary of Bishop Martí's pastoral visit to Caracas dioceses (1771–84), entire account of which was published by Venezuela's Academia Nacional de la Historia in seven volumes. Present work benefits from author's knowledge of Venezuelan geography and detailed maps. Short biography of Martí sheds light on this unusual bishop. [KW]

NUEVA GRANADA

2651 Camargo Pérez, Gabriel. Exploraciones históricas: sucesos, personajes y pueblos de Colombia. Tunja: Universidad Pedagógica y Tecnológica de Colombia, 1981.

639 p.: bibl., ill. (Ediciones La Rana y el águila)

Prosaic account of foundation of some of Colombia's earliest towns and cities. Also presents short biographies of leading historical figures. Useful only for occasional facts and interesting folklore. [KW]

2652 ———. El intelectual de las *Capitulaciones*: Don Agustín Justo de Medina (ACH/BHA, 48:733, abril/junio 1981, p. 444–460, bibl.)

Relying on Berbeo's testimony, concludes that Agustín Justo de Medina authored the famous *Capitulaciones*. Creole from Lima and owner of Santa Fé hacienda, Medina was selected by Tunja's cabildo abierto as city deputy during Comunero revolt. Medina's pro-American sentiments and sympathy for Indians' plight appear in *Capitulaciones*, making him independence precursor, argues author. [KW]

2653 Castillo Mathieu, Nicolás de. La llave de las Indias. Bogotá: Ediciones El Tiempo, 1981. 378 p.: bibl., ill., index, maps.

Masterful study of Cartagena's evolution as port and slave trade center, based on secondary sources. Spanish flotas contributed to city's greatness until contraband trade surge satisfied local demand for European products. Illegal trade was abetted by royal licenses granted to import slaves to foreigners, especially the English. Analyzes slave demographics, noting that over 4000 slaves a year, mostly from Angola, entered city during early 17th century. [KW]

2654 Chandler, David L. Health and slavery in colonial Colombia. New York: Arno Press, 1981. 307 p.: appendices, bibl., tables (Dissertations in European economic history; 1981)

Carefully researched dissertation on sanitary conditions of international slave trade to Nueva Granada and health of African slaves in Viceroyalty during colonial period. Uses sources from gold mines, sugar haciendas, and cattle ranches to record deplorable conditions under which slaves lived. Over half died enroute to America, 20 percent more succumbed to disease, malnutrition, overwork, climate, and altitude after arriving. New World diseases decimated slave populations which introduced African illnesses to Indians and Spaniards. Concludes slavery was more benign in Spanish America than elsewhere. [KW]

Ensayos sobre historia económica colombiana. See *HLAS 45:3275.*

2655 Galán Gómez, Mario. *La Carta de Guaduas atribuída a Galán es apócrifa* (ACH/BHA, 68:735, oct./dic. 1981, p. 1099–1135)
Impassioned defense that José Antonio Galán did not write controversial letter cited by historians showing he betrayed movement by advising Regente Visitador Gutiérrez de Piñerez to flee. Reproduces entire letter. Concludes postscripts were added by *Regente's* associate attempting to exonerate him for abandoning post. [KW]

2656 Galvis Noyes, Antonio J. Restablecimiento del orden colonial en la Provincia de Tunja después del movimiento comunero (ACH/BHA, 49:736, enero/marzo 1982, p. 146–165, tables)
Examines recovery of royal revenues in 1782 to prove order was quickly reestablished throughout Tunja following comunero revolt. Credits lenient policies of Viceroy, Audiencia, and Archbishop Caballero y Góngora's visita with restoring control. Some quantitative data is provided, but more comprehensive treatment of revenue figures is needed. [KW]

2657 Gómez, Tomás. Or, monnaie et prix en Nouvelle Grenade au XVIᵉ siècle (UTIEH/C, 39, 1982, p. 5–25, tables)
Interesting analysis of New Granada's economy emphasizes monetarization process and inflationary cycles. High prices during conquest were followed by decline in local commodity prices until 1575 when demographic growth and increased trade put pressure on cost of domestic goods. Article lacks quantitative data. [KW]

2658 Gómez Latorre, Armando. La Revolución de los comuneros en Pasto y en la Antigua Provincia de los Pastos (ACH/BHA, 68:735, oct./dic. 1981, p. 950–965, bibl.)
Regional study of comuneros in Pasto and surrounding province. Concludes general unrest over economic conditions prevailed throughout late colonial period. Cites murders of official and hacendados as manifestations of local opposition to new taxes. Killings, however, are not meaningfully related to larger comunero movement. [KW]

2659 González Luna, María Dolores. Los resguardos de Santa Marta y Cartagena en la segunda mitad del siglo XVIII (UB/BA, 23:31, 1981, p. 53–81, facsim., maps, tables)
Excellent article on Indian *resguardos* (reservations) explores little-studied interior of coastal regions and provides interesting comparison with Villamaríns' highland studies (see *HLAS 42:2784*). Indians engaged in litigation to preserve lands, succeeding in areas furthest removed from Spanish population. Santa Marta's resguardos were affected by Spaniards' reaction to unpacified Chimilas' raids. [KW]

2660 Lee López, Alberto. El Colegio Seminario de San Luis de Tolosa: cuarto centenario del Seminario Conciliar de Bogotá (ACH/BHA, 49:736, enero/marzo 1982, p. 11–71)
Detailed account of 1581 foundation by second Archbishop, Zapata de Cárdenas, of San Luis de Tolosa, Bogotá's first seminary. Closed later due to financial problems, school reopened in 1590 under Jesuits. Reproduces documents related to seminar's early years. [KW]

2661 Lucena Salmoral, Manuel. La noticia anónima de 1787 [sic] sobre la revolución neogranadina de los comuneros (EEHA/AEA, 36, 1979, p. 41–79, bibl.)
Reproduces little known source: *Noticia de la conmoción popular ocurrida en el Nuevo Reyno de Granada y capital de Santa Fee, año de 1781* (26 p. discourse written anonymously 1782, typo in title should read 1781). *Noticia's* author favors Spanish officials and blames Socorro and San Gil inhabitants for unreasonable reaction to taxes. Speculates author was Francisco Fernández de Córdoba. [KW]

2662 Meisel R., Adolfo. Esclavitud, mestizaje y haciendas en la Provincia de Cartagena: 1533–1851 (CEDE/DS, 4, julio 1980, p. 229–277, tables)
Carefully researched analysis of encomiendas' transition from slave to free wage labor. Uses censuses and hacienda records, demographic factors such as decline of Indians, importation of African slaves, miscegenation, and rise of free castas to explain labor system transformation. Argues haciendas were essentially feudal. [KW]

2663 Mesa, Carlos E. Primeras diócesis novogranadinas y sus prelados: pt. 1, La diócesis de Santa María del Darién; pt. 2, El Obispado de Santa Marta durante su primera centuria; pt. 3, El Obispado de Popayán durante el período hispánico (ISTM/MH, 32:95/96, mayo/dic. 1975, p. 113–164; 33:97/99, enero/dic. 1976, p. 93–164, bibl.)

Pts. 1–3 of four-part article not previously annotated in *HLAS* (for pt. 4, see *HLAS 44:2630*). Covers: 1) Santa María de Antigua del Darién's creation by Balboa in 1510; 2) Tenure of four Santa Marta bishops until 1562 move to Santa Fe; and 3) Popayán Bishopric and relevant activities. [KW]

2664 Molina García, María Paulina. La sede vacante en Cartagena de Indias, 1534–1700 (EEHA/AEA, 32, 1975, p. 1–23)

Biographical analysis of 12 men appointed by ecclesiastic cabildos to serve as provisional bishops during 70 years of vacancies in Bishopric of Cartagena. Temporary appointments could last 10 years. [KW]

2665 Pacheco, Juan Manuel. Dos curiosos manuscritos coloniales (ACH/BHA, 66:727, oct./dic. 1979, p. 507–519)

Interesting account of two Jesuit manuscripts in Biblioteca Nacional de Bogotá: 1) 1755 treatise by Antioquian Juan Antonio Ferraro demonstrates influence of natural sciences at Universidad Javeriana; and 2) 1762 whimsical dialogue on manners probably by Ignacio Julián, Spanish Jesuit teacher at Santa Fé's Colegio de San Bartolomé. [KW]

2666 Pérez Gómez, Carmen. Los extranjeros en la América colonial: su expulsión de Cartagena de Indias en 1750 (EEHA/AEA, 37, 1980, p. 279–311)

Cautious analysis of Crown's efforts to limit contraband through 1750 expulsion of foreigners from Cartagena. Padrón reports 55 foreigners, mostly married Italians, with over 10 years city residence, who entered illegally and worked as local merchants. Author does not follow outcome of expulsion decision, nor does she equate specific individuals with contraband trade. [KW]

2667 Santiago de Cali, 450 años de historia. Margarita Pacheco González *et al.* Edited by Ana María Alzate de Sanclemente. Cali: Alcaldía de Santiago de Cali, 1981.

320 p., 20 p. of plates: bibl., ill. (some col.)

Consists of 27 essays of varying quality on Cali's history, urban development, and culture from 1536 foundation until present. Pacheco González's most useful essay for colonial period concludes city's ejidos disappeared by 1630 due to demographic pressures and expanding estancias. [KW]

2668 Tovar Pinzón, Hermes. El estado colonial frente al poder local y regional (GEE/NA, 5, 1982, p. 39–77, graphs, map)

Excellent archival study of regional interests in conflict with Crown. Uses Cartagena and Santa Fé to demonstrate how local elites consolidated their power through intermarriage. Makes interesting observation about viceroys' tendency to mediate between hacendados and Crown when their interests clashed. [KW]

2669 Twinam, Ann. Miners, merchants, and farmers in colonial Colombia. Austin: Institute of Latin American Studies, University of Texas, 1982. 193 p.: bibl., ill., index (Latin American monographs; no. 57)

Exceptionally well written, researched, and organized economic and social history of 18th-century Antioquia and its capital Medellín. Twinam argues à-la-Parsons that antioqueños became entrepreneurs par excellence because region their ancestors settled left them no choice, if they were to survive and prosper. [MTH]

2670 Vidales, Carlos. Estrategias y tácticas en la rebelión de masas: los comuneros de la Nueva Granada, 1781–1782 (LI/IA, 8:1, 1983, p. 3–25, bibl.)

Important theoretical analysis of much studied comuneros. Suggests that two-stage rebellion succeeded at armed struggle, but turned conservative during process of institutionalization of rebels' goals. Movement contained two truly revolutionary currents: tupamarismo and independence from Spain, as evidenced by Galán's connection with Tupac Amaru and Berbeo's ties to British. [KW]

2671 Zamora, Alonso de *et al.* Universidad Santo Tomás: 400 años. Bogotá: Universidad Santo Tomás, Centro de Enseñanza Desescolarizada, Sección de Publicaciones, 1980. 314 p., 1 leaf of plates: bibl., ill., ports.

Collection of 11 essays written 1937–

71, many of which repeat story of foundation of Universidad Santo Tomás in Bogotá. Papal bull of 1580 authorized Dominicans to erect a university but they could not do so until 1639. Government suppressed university in 1861, and it was not reopened until 1965. [KW]

QUITO

2672 Andrade Reimers, Luis. La conquista española de Quito. Quito: Consejo Provincial de Pichincha: Editorial Epoca, 1981. 444 p.: bibl., ill.

Reviews published sources and studies on Benálcazar, his *entrada* into Ecuador's highlands and Quito's foundation. Offers revisionist "reconstrucción de los hechos." [MTH]

2673 Borchart de Moreno, Christiana. El período colonial (*in* Pinchincha: monografía histórica de la región nuclear ecuatoriana [see item **2619**] p. 193–274)

Study of economic exploitation of what is now Pichincha prov. and its Indian inhabitants by vecinos of Quito. Based on published sources and Borchart's ongoing research on emergence of great estates in north central highlands (see *HLAS 44:2638–2640*). [MTH]

2674 Bromley, Raymond J. Precolonial trade and the transition to a colonial market system in the Audiencia of Quito (GEE/NA, 1, 1978, p. 269–283)

Analyzes continuity and change in patterns of trade between precolonial and colonial periods. Significant contribution to little-known theme in Ecuadorian ethnohistory and history. [MTH]

2675 Cushner, Nicholas P. Farm and factory: the Jesuits and the development of agrarian capitalism in colonial Quito, 1600–1767. Albany: State University of New York Press, 1982. 231 p.: bibl., index, maps.

Case study of Jesuits as capitalists in what is now Pichincha prov. Rich in detail on ranches, farms, and textile mills developed by Jesuits in Chillos. Not as satisfactory as vol. 1 of three on Jesuit entrepreneurship in Peru (see *HLAS 44:2672* and item **2764**), partly because of the less developed state of Ecuadorian historiography, but also because

this volume seems to have been produced in haste. [MTH]

2676 Larraín Barros, Horacio. Demografía y asentamientos indígenas en la Sierra Norte del Ecuador en el siglo XVI: estudio etnohistórico de las fuentes tempranas, 1525–1600. Otavalo, Ecuador: Instituto Otavaleño de Antropología, 1980. 2 v.: ill. (Coleccción Pendoneros; 11–12. Serie Etnohistoria)

Careful analysis of published data regarding ethnic groups of highlands of northern Ecuador and southern Colombia on eve of Spanish conquest and of the population losses suffered following the conquest, especially by otavaleños. Considerably advances knowledge of period and area's ethnohistory and historical demography. See also Larraín Barros' *Cronistas de raigambre indígena* (Otavalo, Ecuador: Instituto Otavaleño de Antropología, 1980, 2 v.). [MTH]

2677 Laviana Cuetos, María Luisa. Organización y funcionamiento de las Cajas Reales de Guayaquil en la segunda mitad del siglo XVIII (EEHA/AEA, 37, 1980, p. 313–349)

Well documented monograph on Guayaquil's Royal Treasury from its reorganization in 1757 through 1804. Includes new data on Sarratea's and Pizarro's visitas and local resistance to establishment of tobacco and aguardiente monopolies in 1778. [MTH]

2678 Ortiz de la Tabla Ducasse, Javier. Extranjeros en la Audiencia de Quito: 1595–1603 (*in* América y la España en el siglo XVI. Madrid: Instituto Gonzalo Fernández de Oviedo, 1983, v. 2, p. 93–113, tables)

Novel analysis of foreign-born residents in early colonial period. Not surprisingly, majority were Portuguese and in Guayaquil. Illuminates little-known aspect of social history. [MTH]

2679 ———. La población ecuatoriana en la época colonial: cuestiones y cálculos (EEHA/AEA, 37, 1980, p. 235–277)

Reassesses known sources on Audiencia de Quito's native population movement in 16th and early 17th centuries. Demonstrates that whereas other provinces lost population, Quito's grew. Uncertain whether growth resulted from in migration, more accurate enumerations, or favorable fertility schedules.

Also criticizes Burgos Guevara's 1972 data manipulation (see *HLAS 38:2098*) and Tyrer's depopulation curve. [MTH]

2680 ———. La población indígena del corregimiento de Riobamba, Ecuador, 1581–1605: la visita y numeración de Pedro de León (EEHA/AEA, 25, 1981, p. 19–87)

Publishes newly discovered 1581–82 *visita* of central highlands, a major historical demographic and ethnohistorical source. Compares its population data to those in 1605 *relación geográfica* of Riobamba. Considerably advances knowledge of post-conquest movement of region's native population. [MTH]

2681 Szászdi, Adám and Dora León Borja.
Los recursos y el desarrollo económico de Guayaquil: 1535–1605 (RUC, 28:117, enero 1979, p. 475–488)

Excellent review of Guayaquil's early emergence as major port, commercial and manufacturing center. Emphasizes importance of port city's exploitation of local and regional resources,including human (e.g., *indios balseros*). [MTH]

2682 Vargas, José María. Historia del Ecuador, siglo XVII. Quito: J.M. Vargas, between 1977 and 1981. 296 p.: bibl.

Modern 17th-century chronicle. Primarily concerned with Audiencia presidents, Quito bishops, other authorities and dignitaries. Slights developments outside capital and its immediate district. [MTH]

PERU

2683 Acosta, Antonio. Religiosos, doctrinas y excedente económico indígena en el Perú a comienzos del siglo XVII (PUCP/H, 6:1, julio 1982, p. 1–34, bibl., tables)

Preliminary study of how much legally sanctioned income rural pastors could derive from their Indian charges. Takes into account the demographics as well as economics of rural communities. Data suggests that clergy constituted at least as much and probably more of a burden than tribute. [MTH]

2684 Anderle, Adám. Vihar a sierrába: indián függetlenségi küzdelmek a XVI–XVIII. században. Budapest: Gondolate, 1981. 290 p.: ill.

Surveys Indian revolts and black slave rebellions in Viceroyalty of Peru from 16th through 18th centuries, based on chronicles and published documents. Devotes long chapter to analysis of Túpac Amaru rebellion and its ramifications. [G.M. Dorn]

2685 Biedma, Miguel. La conquista franciscana del Alto Ucayali. Introducción y notas, Antonine Tibesar. Editor, Carlos Milla Batres. Lima: Editorial Milla Batres, 1981. 187 p., 8 p. of plates: facsims., ill., map, port.

First ed. of late 17th-century chronicle of Franciscan missionary activities in Upper Ucayali. Well edited with solid introduction by Antonine Tibesar. Important ethno-historical as well as ecclesiastical historical source. [MTH]

Brading, David A. The city in Bourbon Spanish America: elite and masses. See item **1960**.

2686 Bronner, Fred. Advertencia privada de un Virrey peruano del siglo XVII a su presunto sucesor (IGFO/RI, 41:163/164, enero/junio 1981, p. 55–77)

Publishes and analyzes Viceroy Chinchon's secret memoirs intended only for eyes of presumed successor, his relative, Marqués de Villena. Far more revealing of the man, his administration, and early 17th-century Lima than Chinchón's official *relación de mando.* [MTH]

2687 Busto Duthurburu, José Antonio del.
La Hueste perulera. Lima: Pontificia Universidad Católica del Perú, Fondo Editorial, 1981. 332 p.

Mini-biographies of 27 conquistadores, ranging from *maestre de campo* Rodrigo Núñez to black slave Alonso Prieto. Well researched. [MTH]

2688 ———. José Gabriel Túpac Amaru antes de su rebelión. Fotografías, Juan Ossio Acuña. Lima: Pontificia Universidad Católica del Perú, Fondo Editorial, 1981. 134 p., 24 leaves of plates: bibl., ill. (some col.)

Sketches infancy, childhood, and pre-revolutionary adulthood of Túpac Amaru and his wife, Micaela. Includes color photographs of their natal pueblos, houses, and other coeval buildings, its only novel feature. [MTH]

2689 Calancha, Antonio de. Corónica moralizada del Orden de San Agustín en el Perú, con sucesos egenplares en esta monarquía. Transcripción, estudio crítico, notas bibliográficas e índices de Ignacio Prado Pastor. Lima: Universidad Nacional Mayor de San Marcos, 1974–1982. 6 v.: bibl., index.

Republishes early 17th-century chronicle of Augustinians in Viceroyalty of Peru. Originally published Barcelona (1638–39) and never before reissued in its entirety. Prado Pastor has modernized orthography and punctuation, added a bibliography of identifiable sources used by Calancha, 1584–1654 (v. 1, p. xxix–lvi), and extraordinarily detailed index (v. 6). Invaluable ethnohistorical as well as historical source. Includes much data on history and religious beliefs and practices of Indians of Peru, especially coastal groups. [MTH]

2690 Cárdenas Ayaipoma, Mario. José Gabriel Tupa Amaro, a propósito de un documento (PUCP/H, 4:2, dic. 1980, p. 229–232, bibl., facsims.)

Recently found 1777 declaration of some of Túpac Amaru's personal effects exemplifies extent and ways in which he was Europeanized. [MTH]

2691 Castelli G., Amalia. La primera imagen del Hospital Real de San Andrés a través de la visita de 1563 (PMNH/HC, 13/14, 1981, p. 207–216, bibl., map)

Multidisciplinary analysis of early colonial description and review of accounts of one of the hospitals of Lima. [MTH]

2692 Catholic Church. Province of Peru. Concilio Provincial, 3rd, 1583. Actas del III Concilio Provincial Limense, 1582–1583. Edición facsimilar ofrecida por el Venerable Cabildo de la Catedral de San Juan Evangelista de Lima con motivo del cuarto centenario de dicho Concilio Provincial. Lima: El Cabildo, 1982. 6 leaves, 19 leaves of facsims.

Photofacsimile ed. of Acts of III Council of Lima. See also item **2716.** [MTH]

Cole, Jeffrey A. An abolitionism born of frustration: the Conde de Lemos and the Potosí mita, 1667–73. See item **2737.**

2693 Colección documental del bicentenario de la revolución emancipadora de Túpac Amaru. t. 1, Documentos varios del Archivo General de Indias. t. 2, Descargos del Obispo del Cuzco Juan Manuel Moscoso. t. 3–5, Los procesos a Túpac Amaru y sus

compañeros: pt. 1–3. Edición e introducción de Luis Durand Flórez. Lima: Comisión Nacional de Bicentenario de la Rebelión Emancipadora de Túpac Amaru, 1980–1982. 5 v.: indexes.

Well edited and indexed collection of major and minor archival sources—many published here for first time—on 1780–82 Indian rebellions. [MTH]

2694 Contreras y Valverde, Vasco. Relación de la ciudad del Cusco. Prólogo y transcripción de María del Carmen Martín Rubio. Cuzco: Imprenta Amauta, 1982. 197 p.: facsims., ill.,

Publishes mid-17th-century *relación* mentioned in item **2714.** Invaluable source which describes city, inhabitants and environs, including flora and fauna. Also chronicle, particularly of Cuzco's bishops. Contreras (1605–66) was dean of ecclesiastical chapter and hence privy to its and diocesan archives. [MTH]

2695 Cook, Noble David. Demographic collapse: Indian Peru, 1520–1620. Cambridge; New York; Cambridge University Press, 1981. 310 p.: bibl., ill., index (Cambridge Latin American studies)

In-depth, methodologically sophisticated analysis of probable size of precontact population of Peru proper (pt. 1) and of its preconquest decline through early 17th century (pt. 2). Cook estimates population of Peru itself to have been approximately nine million ca. 1520. Analysis of demographic impact of Spanish conquest is by regions. Model study. For author's data base, see item **2695.** [MTH]

2696 ———. Population data for Indian Peru: sixteenth and seventeenth centuries (HAHR, 62:1, Feb. 1982, p. 73–120, map, table)

Data base for item **2695.** Summarizes results of early colonial census of Indians and related sources by total population and/or number of tributaries, corregimiento by corregimiento, year by year. Published separately through no fault of author. [MTH]

2697 Cortés Alonso, Vicenta. El valor de las palabras y la lectura de documentos antiguos: el bando emancipador de Túpac Amaru (PUCP/H, 4:2, dic.1980, p. 233–236)

Reminds scholars that sources should be interpreted in accordance with mentality and conditions of the time, using as example Túpac Amaru's often cited but not necessarily understood *bando emancipador* of Nov. 16, 1780. [MTH]

2698 El Cristianismo colonial (IPA/A, 16:19, 1982, p. 1–291, bibl., maps)
Entire issue of this well established but as of yet inadequately known journal—it is not indexed in *HAPI*, for example—is devoted to Catholic Church's efforts to christianize, westernize, and control Indians of Peru, from Spanish conquest through Túpac Amaru rebellion. Original articles by leading ethnohistorians and historians will amply repay reading by generalists as well as specialists. *Allpanchis* belongs in every Latin American collection. [MTH]

2699 Cuzco 1689: informes de los párrocos al Obispo Mollinedo, economía y sociedad en el sur andino. Prólogo y transcripción, Horacio Villanueva Urteaga. Prefacio, Pablo Macera. Cuzco, Perú: Centro de Estudios Rurales Andinos Bartolomé de las Casas, 1982. 508 p.: bibl., indexes (Archivos de historia andina; 2)
Publishes late 17th-century *descripciones* of 135 parishes of Cuzco and its diocese. Invaluable historical demographic and geographic sources. On their utility, see *HLAS 42:2706*. Well indexed. [MTH]

2700 Durand, José. Trujillo en el XVII: un manuscrito ignorado (PEMN/R, 44, 1977–1980, p. 215–233)
Publishes with introduction first three chapters of unknown hagiography of 1708, in which city of Trujillo, its churches, convents, other institutions, and notable personages are described. Important local source. [MTH]

2701 Duviols, Pierre. Guamán Poma, historiador del Perú antiguo: una nueva pista (Revista Andina [Centro de Estudios Rurales Andinos Bartolomé de las Casas, Cuzco, Perú] 1:1, enero/junio 1983, p. 103–116)
Suggests that "historiography" which influenced Waman Puma was not Andean and hence authoctonus, but European, and primary sources on which *Nueva Coronica* were based, were writings of Francisco de Córdoba, a Creole, and/or of his father, Diego de Aguilar y Córdoba, a peninsular. Provocative but farfetched hypotheses. [MTH]

2702 Fisher, John. Regionalism and rebellion in late colonial Peru: the Aguilar-Ubalde conspiracy of 1805 (Bibliotheca Americana [Bibliotheca Americana, Inc., Coral Gables, Fla.] 1:1, Sept. 1982, p. 45–59)
Revisionist study of 1814–15 "revolution" as well as 1805 conspiracy. Stresses need to study regional developments and rivalries in order to understand politics of late colonial and independence periods. [MTH]

2703 Flickema, Thomas. The siege of Cuzco (PAIGH/H, 92, julio/dic. 1981, p. 17–47)
Review of 1536 siege of Cuzco. Flickema argues that Incas' failure to take city lay not in ineffective leadership on Manco's part but in Indian adherence to traditional tactics, inferior weaponry, and aid Spaniards received from native allies. [MTH]

2704 Flores-Galindo, Alberto. La pesca y los pescadores en la Costa Central: siglo XVIII (PUCP/H, 5:2, dic.1981, p. 159–165, bibl.)
Contends from archival sources that fishing allowed some ethnic groups not only to survive on coast, but more importantly to live in relative freedom and isolation from Spanish society. [MTH]

2705 Glave, Luis Miguel. Trajines: un capítulo en la formación del mercado interno colonial (Revista Andina [Centro de Estudios Rurales Andinos Bartolomé de las Casas, Cuzco] 1:1, enero/junio 1983, p. 9–76, bibl., maps, tables)
Fascinating article on intercolonial trade between Upper and Lower Peru, especially in cocoa and wine. Well written and documented. Includes documentary appendices and commentaries by Roberto Choque Canqui, Manuel Burga, Efraín Trelles A., and Olinda Celestino. [MTH]

2706 ———— and María Isabel Remy. Estructura agraria y vida rural en una región andina: Ollantaytambo entre los siglos XVI–XXIX. Cuzco, Perú: Centro de Estudios Rurales Andinos Bartolomé de las Casas, 1983. 554 p.: bibl., ill., indexes, maps.
Unusually well researched social and economic history of Ollantaytambo and its district—modern provinces of Calca, Urubamba, Anta, and Convención in Cuzco dept.—from mid 1500s through early 1900s.

Major contribution to altiplano's post-conquest history. [MTH]

2707 González de San Segundo, Miguel Angel. El Doctor Gregorio González, Oidor de la Audiencia de Lima y sus *Ordenanzas* sobre caciques e indios principales, 1566 (IGFO/RI, 42:169/170, julio/dic. 1982, p. 643–667)

Delineates and explicates 1566 regulation of ethnic lords as issued by high court judge of period. Includes sketch of González's life and career. [MTH]

2708 Guarda, Gabriel. Los planos de la ciudad de San Marcos de Arica: siglos XVII y XVIII (EEHA/AEA, 37, 1980, p. 741–752, plates)

Describes and publishes in b/w plates three 17th-century and six 18th-century plans of Arica. [MTH]

2709 Hampe M., Teodora. La actuación del Obispo Vicente de Valverde en el Perú (PMNH/HC, 13/14, 1981, p. 109–153, appendix, bibl., facsims.)

Solid monograph on Valverde's participation in conquest of Peru and in organization of early colonial society, particularly as first Bishop of Cuzco, in which role he had not heretofore been studied in depth. Enriched by many new details on Valverde's life and career, and supplemented by documentary appendix. [MTH]

2710 Huertas, Lorenzo. Diezmos en Huamanga (IPA/A, 17:20, 1982, p. 209–235, tables)

Working paper on agricultural tithes paid in diocese of Huamanga, especially but not exclusively in 18th-century, and what their varying amounts reveal about region's economy and its trends. [MTH]

Jáuregui y Alcedoa, Agustín. Relación y documentos del gobierno del Virrey del Perú, Agustín de Jáuregui y Aldecoa, 1780–1784. See item **2624.**

2711 Lassegue, J.B. and F. Letona. Catálogo general del Archivo del Monasterio de Santa Catalina del Cusco, Perú (Revista Andina [Centro de Estudios Rurales Andinos Bartolomé del as Casas, Cuzco, Perú] 1:1, enero/junio 1983, p. 127–133)

Inventories colonial and 19th-century records of major Cuzco convent. Unclear whether libros and legajos in question are

still in convent or have been transferred to Archbishop's Archives. [MTH]

2712 Lohmann Villena, Guillermo. El memorial del racionero Villarreal al Virrey Toledo (PUCP/H, 5:1, julio 1981, p. 21–43, bibl.)

Publishes one of many testimonies solicited by Toledo on state and customs of Peru's Indians. Of ideological rather than ethnohistorical interests as Villarreal was far more familiar with Mesoamerica than the Andes. [MTH]

2713 ———. Los regidores perpetuos del Cabildo de Lima, 1535–1821: cronología y estudio de un grupo de gestión. Sevilla: Diputación Provincial de Sevilla. 2 v.: ill. (V centenario del descubrimiento de América; no. 1)

Chronological review and prosopographic study (vol. 1), and biographical dictionary (vol. 2) of alderman appointed for life to Lima's municipal council. Weak analysis and interpretation, but strong in data and citations. [MTH]

2714 Martín Rubio, Carmen. Indios y mestizos en Cuzco según dos fuentes inéditas del siglo XVII (IGFO/RI, 43:171, enero/junio 1983, p. 59–75)

Examines variegated status and activities of Indians and mestizos in 17th-century Cuzco as depicted in two coeval sources, a 1650 relación and a 1690 memoria. Apparently both sources, neither of which has been published, are treasure troves of data. See also item **2694.** [MTH]

2715 Millar Carvacho, René. Las confiscaciones de la Inquisición de Lima a los comerciantes de origen judío-portugués de "La Gran Complicidad" de 1635 (IGFO/RI, 43:171, enero/junio 1983, p. 27–58, tables)

Quantitative study of Inquisition confiscations of 1630s and disposal of expropriated estates. Includes considerable new data on great complicity of 1635 as well as on financial aspects of Inquisition. Altogether a novel piece. [MTH]

2716 Moreno Cebrián, Alfredo. Un arqueo a la hacienda municipal limeña a fines del siglo XVIII (IGFO/RI, 41:165/166, julio/dic. 1981, p. 499–540, ill., tables)

Solid study of revenues and expenditures of Lima's Cabildo as of 1783. Includes lists of municipal debtors, creditors, and beneficiaries. In case of debtors, specifies original date of concession and grantor. Also compares finances of Lima with those of other Peruvian cities. [MTH]

2717 ———. Cuarteles, barrios y calles de Lima a fines del siglo XVIII (JGSWGL, 18, 1981, p. 97–161, plans, tables)

Extraordinarily detailed morphological study of late colonial Lima. Lists streets by district, ward, coeval enumeration of houses, and number of doors. Considerably enriches our knowledge of city's growth and organization. [MTH]

2718 O'Phelan Godoy, Scarlett. Elementos étnicos y de poder en el movimiento tupacamarista: 1780–1781 (GEE/NA, 5, 1982, p. 79–101)

Mostly novel analysis of several aspects of 1780s Indian uprisings. Compares and contrasts rebellion's two phases, second of which was characterized by alliance between Túpac Amaru and Túpac Catari. Sheds additional light on rebels' ethnic origins and above all, illuminates rebel leaders' utilization of their networks of relatives and clients. [MTH]

2719 Pinto Vallejos, Sonia. El financiamiento extraordinario de la Real Hacienda en el Virreinato Peruano: Cuzo, 1575–1650. Santiago: Centro de Estudios Humanísticos, Facultad de Ciencias Físicas y Matemáticas, Universidad de Chile, 1981. 83 p.: bibl., ill.

Detailed study of Cuzco's extraordinary contributions—servicios y préstamos—to royal fisc in late 16th century and first half of 17th. Includes data on amounts "lent" to Crown by Viceroyalty's cities and regions. [MTH]

2720 Ramos Gómez, Luis J. El primer gran secuestro de metales procedentes del Perú a cambio de juros para costear la empresa de Tunez (EEHA/AEA, 32, 1975, p. 217–278, tables)

Importance of this monograph to Peruvian history lies in lists of conquistadores and agents affected by 1535 impoundment and amounts in gold and/or silver seized. [MTH]

2721 La Revolución de los Túpac Amaru: antología. Edición y prólogo de Luis

Durand Flórez. Carlos Daniel Valcárcel *et al.* Lima: Comisión Nacional del Bicentenario de la Rebelión Emancipadora de Túpac Amaru, 1981. 486 p.: bibl.

Useful anthology of old and new, mostly scholarly studies on Túpac Amaru, Túpac Katari and/or the uprisings they led. Includes substantial documentary appendix. [MTH]

2722 Rowe, John H. Genealogía y rebelión en el siglo XVIII: algunos antecedentes de la sublevación de José Gabriel Thupa Amaro (PUCP/H, 6:1, julio 1982, p. 65–85, bibl.)

Abstracts 1776–80 *pleito* between Túpac Amaru and Betancur family over claim to more direct descent from first Túpac Amaru and hence right to royalty. Details ascent of both contenders. [MTH]

2723 Sáenz de Santa María, Carmelo. Hacia un pleno conocimiento de la personalidad de Pedro de Cieza de León (EEHA/AEA, 32, 1975, p. 329–373)

Good summary of what is known regarding life and work of foremost chronicler of conquest. Enhanced by new details from Seville's notarial archives. [MTH]

2724 ———. La hueste de don Pedro de Alvarado en la historia del Perú (IGFO/RI, 43:171, enero/junio 1983, p. 314–325)

Lists men who accompanied Alvarado from Central America to Ecuador, some of whom played major role in conquest and colonization of greater Peru. Based on newly found AGI source. [MTH]

2725 Schaedel, Richard P. Late Incaic and early Spanish changes in land use—their effect on dry land: the Peruvian coast (IAA, 7:3, 1981, p. 309–319, bibl., table)

Masterful summary of what is known and may be presumed about changes in land use on Peru's coast from ca. 1500 through early 1800s. Takes into account three variables: 1) demographic; 2) introduction of Old World cultigens and domestic animals; and 3) Spanish perception of environment. Includes analysis of Indian population decline on north coast through 1680, which Schaedel believes to have been on order of seven to one. [MTH]

2726 Schapers, Joachim. Francisco Pizarro Marsch von San Miguel nach Cajamarca (IAA, 9:2, 1983, p. 241–251, bibl., map)

Combines recent archaeological and traditional literary evidence to clarify Pizarro's route and itinerary from Tumbes to Cajamarca. Includes Spanish abstract. [MTH]

2727 Spalding, Karen. Exploitation as an economic system: the state and the extraction of surplus in colonial Peru (in The Inca and Aztec states, 1400–1800 [see item **1544**] p. 321–342)

Revisionist analysis of nature of colonial society. Although there may have been two societies—Spanish and Indian or more properly, European and Andean— Spalding argues that "the economy of colonial Peru was not a dual system but an integrated economic system." [MTH]

2728 Stern, Steve J. Peru's Indian peoples and the challenge of Spanish conquest: Huamanga to 1640. Madison: University of Wisconsin Press, 1982. 295 p.: bibl., ill., index.

Well documented case study of "how the Indian peoples of Huamanga met challenge of European conquest, and consequences for themselves, their colonizers, and the society that was created." Somewhat tendentious, but undoubtedly a major contribution to early history of postconquest Peru. [MTH]

Szászdi, Adám. Dos fuentes para la historia de la empresa de Pizarro y Almagro: la *Crónica rimada* y la *Relación Sámano*. See item **2630**.

2729 Szemiński, Jan. Acerca del significado de algunos de los términos empleados en los documentos relativos a la revolución tupacamarista: 1780–1783 (PAN/ES, 8, 1981, p. 65–102, tables)

Analyzes meaning of ethnic terminology employed in corpus of Túpac Amaru documentation. Szemiński makes transcendental point: language must be interpreted not only in terms of time and place but also of subcultures employing it. [MTH]

——. Los objectivos de los tupamaristas: las concepciones de los revolucionarios peruanos de los años 1780–1783. See item **1729**.

Tibesar, Antonine S. The suppression of the religious orders in Peru, 1826–1830, or the King versus the Peruvian friars: the King won. See item **3017**.

2731 Tord Nicolini, Javier; Carlos Lazo García; and Jorge Polo y La Borda. Hacienda, comercio, fiscalidad y luchas sociales: Perú colonial. Lima: Biblioteca Peruana de Historia, Economía y Sociedad, 1981. 320 p., 5 leaves of plates: bibl., ill. (Colección Colonia. Estudios de historia económica y social; 1)

Republishes, with revisions, Polo y La Borda's "La Hacienda Pachachuca" (see *HLAS 42:2711*), Tord's "Sociedad Colonial y Fiscalidad" (*HLAS 42:2718*), Lazo García and Tord's *El tumulto esclavo* (*HLAS 44:2683*) and *Del negro señorial al negro bandolero* (*HLAS 44:2682*), and two new studies by Tord and Lazo García on nature of the economy and on the corregidor as agent of control and exploitation. In terms of sources utilized, especially treasury accounts, quantitative approach, themes and findings, a highly significant anthology of recent and new contributions to the colonial history not just of Peru but of Spanish America in general. [MTH]

2732 Trelles Aréstegui, Efraín. Lucas Martínez Vegazo: funcionamiento de una encomienda peruana inicial. Lima: Pontificia Universidad Católica el Perú, 1982. 280 p.: map, bibl.

Two-part monograph which illuminates many aspects (e.g., demographic, economic, ethnic, social) of transitional period between Spanish conquest and ordered colony. Pt. 1 reconstructs life and times of Martínez Vegazo (ca. 1511–67), one of the Camajarca men, and pt. 2, history of his encomienda—largely comprised of tributaries of Tarapacá and Arica—its organization, amount and kinds of tribute authorized and actually rendered, and Martínez's varied utilization thereof. [MTH]

2733 Varon, Rafael. Cofradías de indios y poder local en el Perú colonial: Huaraz, siglo XVII (IPA/A, 17:20, 1982, p. 127–146, bibl.)

Argues that religious brotherhoods functioned as intermediaries of "brokers" between the Indian and Spanish worlds, using those of Huaraz as examples. Suggestive but somewhat myopic inasmuch as that was hardly the only and not necessarily the most important function of *cofradías*. [MTH]

2734 Vega, Juan José. Incas contra españoles: treinta batallas. Editor, Carlos Milla Batres. Lima: Editorial Milla Batres, 1980. 170 p.: bibl.

Scholarly, dispassionate account of Apo Quisquis' opposition to Spanish conquest after Atahualpa's execution, and of Manco's subsequent rebellion. [MTH])

ALTO PERU

2735 Barnabas, Josep. Panorama historiográfico de estudios recientes sobre Charcas colonial (Revista Andina [Centro de Estudios Rurales Andinos Bartolomé de las Casas, Cuzco] 1 : 2, julio/dic. 1983, p. 475–543, bibl.)

Comprehensive review of recent literature on colonial Bolivia. Includes contributions by North American and European as well as Bolivian and other Latin American scholars. [MTH]

2736 Cajías, Fernando. Los objetivos de la revolución indígena de 1781: el caso de Oruro (Revista Andina [Centro de Estudios Rurales Andinos Bartolomé de las Casas, Cuzco, Perú] 1 : 2, julio/dic. 1983, p. 407–428, bibl.)

Utilizing newly found archival evidence, author demonstrates that Oruro Indians participated in and supported 1780s rebellions, because they wanted back that which had been theirs, the land, in usufruct as well as in title. [MTH]

2737 Cole, Jeffrey A. An abolitionism born of frustration: the Conde de Lemos and the Potosí mita, 1667–73 (HAHR, 63 : 2, May 1983, p. 307–333)

Reviews abortive attempts by Peru's viceroys to reform and ultimately abolish draft labor system. Argues that Lemus advocated suppression of mita not out of any moral aversion to it but because of his inability to control the then corregidor of Potosí. [MTH]

2738 Diez de Medina, Francisco Tadeo. Diario del alzamiento de Indios conjurados contra la Ciudad de Nuestra Señora de La Paz, 1781. Transcripción, introducción,

notas y estudio, María Eugenia del Valle de Siles. Prólogo, Gunnar Mendoza L. La Paz: Banco Boliviano Americano, 1981. 275 p., 33 leaves of plates (2 folded): bibl., ill (some col.), indexes.

Excellent ed. of first half of heretofore unpublished diary by Charcas Audiencia *oidor* on Túpac Catari's seige of La Paz. Enhanced by Mendoza's bibliographic essay on related sources, Siles' detailed analysis of diary's importance, and coeval graphic materials. Whereabouts of second half of Diez de Medina's diary is known, but Siles was unable to obtain permission to include it. [MTH]

Glave, Luis Miguel. Trajines: un capítulo en la formación del mercado interno colonial. See item **2705.**

2739 Jáuregui Cordero, Juan Heriberto. Documentación existente en el Archivo Nacional de Bolivia sobre rebeliones indígenas, 1780–83. La Paz: Centro de Investigaciones Históricas, 1980. 38 p.: indexes (Serie Indices y catálogos; 2)

Calendar of documents in National Archives of Bolivia on Túpac Amaru and Túpac Katari 1780–83 rebellions. Includes onomastic and topographic indexes. [MTH]

La Revolución de los Túpac Amaru: antología. See item **2721.**

2740 Saignes, Thierry. Una provincia andina a comienzos del siglo XVII: Pacajes según una relación inédita (EEHA/AEA, 24, 1980, p. 3–21, map)

Publishes with pithy introduction Pacajes' 1608 *relación geográfica*, invaluable source on continuity and change in southern altiplano, especially when studied in conjunct with long since known 1586 relación. [MTH]

2741 Santamaría, Daniel J. Iglesia y economía campesina en el Alto Perú, siglo XVIII. Miami: Florida International University, Latin American and Caribbean Center, 1983. 21 p.: tables (Occasional papers series; no. 5)

Working paper on direct and indirect appropriation by rural clergy of peasant income, and how administrative and fiscal reforms of late 18th century affected economic relations between clergy and their parishioners. [MTH]

2742 Tandeter, Enrique. La producción como actividad popular: *ladrones de minas* en Potosí (GEE/NA, 4, 1981, p. 43–65)

Cogent review of socioeconomic importance of illicit mining (*kajcheo*) in Potosí, which took place on weekends when mines were abandoned by free and forced labor, a practice which Crown could not regulate, let alone prevent. [MTH]

2743 TePaske, John J. The fiscal structure of Upper Peru and the financing of the empire (*in* Essays in the political, economic and social history of colonial Latin America. Edited by Karen Spalding. Newark: University of Delaware, Latin American Studies Program, 1982, p. 69–94, tables)

Delineates and analyzes total receipts, amounts, and proportions corresponding to silver taxes, Indian tributes, sales taxes, and surpluses remitted to Lima and Buenos Aires per Caja Real per decade for 1561–1800. Primarily concerned with surpluses and their utilization for viceregal and Crown needs. For sources utilized, see item **2631**. [MTH]

2744 Triano, María Antonia. Cobija, salida a la Mar del Sur del Virreinato del Río de la Plata (IGFO/RI, 43 : 171, enero/junio 1983, p. 343–348)

Brief description based on single expediente and accompanying map in AGI about plan to found Pacific port for Potosí. Also includes transcription of original document. Minor historical episode. [SMS]

CHILE

2745 Cano Roldán, Imelda. La mujer en el Reyno de Chile. Santiago: Municipalidad de Santiago, 1981. 680 p.: bibl., ill.

Mine of information, mostly called from unpublished sources, on women in colonial Chile. Includes chapters on them as wives and mothers, their education and usual occupations, morality, before the law, and as nuns. [MTH]

2746 Cobos, María Teresa. La institución del Juez de Campo en el Reino de Chile durante el siglo XVIII (Revista de Estudios Histórico-Jurídicos [Universidad Católica de Valparaíso, Escuela de Derecho, Chile] 5, 1980, p. 85–165)

Pioneering study of rural judges and justice in 18th century. [MTH]

2747 Fernández Campino, José. Relación del Obispado de Santiago. Introducción de Patricio Estellé M. Santiago: Editorial Universitaria, 1981. 102 p.: facsims. (Escritores coloniales de Chile; no. 12)

First ed. of 1744 *relación geográfica* of Norte Chico, Central Chile, and what are now provinces of Mendoza, San Luis, and San Juan in Argentina. Major historical geographic and socioeconomic source. [MTH]

2748 Flusche, Della M. and Eugene H. Korth. Forgotten females: women of Africa and Indian descent in colonial Chile, 1535–1800. Detroit: B. Ethridge Books, 1983. 112 p.: bibl., index.

At best working paper on social and economic rules and treatment of black, Indian, and mestizo women in colonial Chile. Includes some archival data, but mostly based on published sources and secondary literature. See also item **2745**. [MTH]

2749 Méndez, Luz María. Instituciones y problemas de la minería en Chile, 1787–1826. Santiago: Universidad de Chile, 1979. 173 p.: bibl., ill.

Pioneering study of institutional aspects of mining in late colonial and early independent Chile, especially of Crown's attempts to regulate the industry through Real Administración de Minería, established in 1787, and to stimulate production through Banco de Avíos. Well researched and written. [MTH]

2750 Ramón, Armando de and José Manuel Larraín. Orígenes de la vida económica chilena, 1659–1808. Santiago: Centro de Estudios Públicos, 1982. 416 p.: bibl., maps.

Exceptionally well researched and articulated price history of Santiago and its district during second half of colonial period. Includes lengthy series of average annual prize of subsistence commodities, especially foodstuffs An historiographic first as well as model monograph. See also Larraín's thesis, prepared under Ramón's direction (*HLAS 44:2736*). [MTH]

2751 Villalobos R., Sergio. Historia del pueblo chileno. Julio Retamal Avila, investigador. Sol Serrano, ayudante de investigación. Santiago: Instituto Chileno de Estudios Humanísticos, 1980. 1 v.: bibl., ill.

Inaugural volume of new, general history of Chile from prehistoric times through present. Highly interpretative. Well balanced and quasi-integral in that Villalobos treats all social groups and most themes equitably. Reflects not only mastery of literature but also considerable original research. Vol. 1 (only one seen to date) covers precolumbian and conquest period, latter of which Villalobos extends to 1598, and includes lengthy introduction on strengths and weaknesses of traditional histories of Chile. [MTH]

2752 ———. Revisita de los indios del Corregimiento de Arica en 1753 (SCHG/R, 148, 1980, p. 68–84, appendix)

Publishes and analyzes the 1753 revisita of Arica. Important economic, ethno and historical demographic source. [MTH]

RIO DE LA PLATA

2753 Abadie-Aicardi, Aníbal. La Isla de Santa Catalina y el Atlántico Sur en la visión geopolítica del Virrey Cevallos (JGSWGL, 18, 1981, p. 45–72)

Within context of Spanish-Portuguese-English geopolitical rivalries in South Atlantic from middle of 18th-century, traces Pedro de Ceballos' strategic thinking in his two Brazilian campaigns (1762 and 1776–77). Central to Cevallos' plans was conquest of Santa Catalina island which Cevallos feared would be used by Portuguese and their English allies to conquer Maldonado, Buenos Aires, and eventually Upper Peru. [SMS]

2754 Acevedo, Edberto Oscar. El abastecimiento de Mendoza: 1561–1810 (UNC/RHAA, 10: 19/20, 1978/1980, p. 9–33, tables)

Based mainly on Cabildo records, discusses city's supply of bread, fish, poultry, and most of all meat. Reviews various methods used to insure meat supply, and includes some rudimentary price information. More detailed study would need more varied sources. [SMS]

2755 ———. La sisa para el mantenimiento de las poblaciones del Chaco: 1760-1776 (ANH/IE, 28, enero/junio 1980, p. 125–158)

Discusses changing tax on mules, cattle, and alcohol, used to pay soldiers along Indian frontier. Gives no idea of sums collected over long periods nor of tax's influence on local commerce. Instead, provides detailed essay on sisa's legal history. [SMS]

2756 Arenas Luque, Fermín Vicente. Don Gerónimo Luis de Cabrera y sus descendientes. Buenos Aires: Talleres Gráficas San Francisco, 1980. 115 p., 8 p. of plates: ports.

Traditional ascendant and descendant genealogy of Gerónimo Luis de Cabrera, late 16th-century conquistador and founder of Córdoba city. Includes as descendants: Sor María Paz de Figueroa, late 18th-century beata; Gen. Julio Roca, President of Argentina (1880–86); Hugo Wast, polemicist; and Victoria Ocampo, literary figure. [SMS]

2757 Avellá Cháfer, Francisco. La situación económica del clero secular de Buenos Aires durante los siglos XVII y XVIII: pt. 1 (ANA/IE, 29, julio/dic. 1980, p. 295–218)

Entirely based on AGI documentation. Concentrates on lengthy controversy over allocation of tithes in Buenos Aires, and income and expenses of porteño clergy, especially members of ecclesiastical Cabildo. Although somewhat uneven, presents interesting information on 18th-century material life. [SMS]

2758 Barba, Enrique M. Sobre el contrabando de la Colonia de Sacramento (ANH/IE, 28, enero/junio 1980, p. 57–76)

Based on a 1796 report found in Madrid's National Palace Library. Presents wealth of information on Buenos Aires contraband channeled through Colonia de Sacramento. Also details incidental expenses, host of payments and gifts, which Buenos Aires royal officials expected to receive for inspecting goods imported through legal channels. Most interesting. [SMS]

2759 Bellotto, Heloísa Liberalli. Documentação missioneira no Instituto de Estudos Brasileiros da Universidade de São Paulo, S.P. (in Simpósio Nacional de Estudos Missioneiros, 2nd, Santa Rosa, Brazil, 1977. Anais. Santa Rosa, Brazil: Faculdade de Filosofia, Ciências e Letras, 1978, p. 198–217, bibl.)

Description of 15 documents which cover not only religious and social life in 18th-century Jesuit missions of Paraguay, but also description of Corrientes and Montevideo at mid-century. Interesting information for specialist. [SMS]

2760 Bentancur, Arturo Ariel. Contrabando y contrabandistas: historias coloniales. Montevideo: Arca, 1982. 119 p.: bibl.

Study of Banda Oriental contraband trade from 1749 (date of gobernación's creation) to 1797 (when Spanish Crown authorized "trade with neutrals.") Finds that 1777 end of active Portuguese presence in Colonia da Sacramento made little difference in clandestine trade, which flourished often with covert government support. Argues that Montevideo and hinterland replaced Buenos Aires as illegal trade center. Although based on AGI and Simancas documents, work lacks footnotes. [SMS]

Biblioteca de Martín Ferreyra. Sección Historia, Genealogía y Heráldica. Catálogo. See *HLAS 45:29.*

2761 Bischoff, Efraín U. Cristóbal de Aguilar: su época, sus obras, su familia (ANH/IE, 28, enero/junio 1980, p. 165–212)

Biography of Aguilar, Spanish immigrant to Córdoba in 1750 decade, who in addition to serving as chief notary of city's Bishopric, and later secretary to Intendent Sobremonte, was local literary figure. Several pages are dedicated to career of son Bernabé Antonio, Catamarca priest. [SMS]

Buenos Aires: 400 years. See item **3187.**

2762 Cardozo, Efraim. Historiografía paraguaya: pt. 1, Paraguay indígena, español y jesuíta. 2a. ed. México: Instituto Panamericano de Geografía e Historia, Comisión de Historia, 1979. 610 p.: bibl. (Historiografía; 5)

Massive annotated bibliography-cum-historiography especially strong on 16th-century chroniclers of conquest, 17th and 18th-century Jesuit missionaries and their detractors, and various late 18th-century demarcation commissions set up to determine boundaries between Spanish and Portuguese dominions. Coverage ends with 1950s imprints as this is second printing rather than new ed. A must for serious students of colonial Paraguay. [SMS]

2763 Cooney, Jerry W. Foreigners in the intendencia of Paraguay (AAFH/TAM, 39:3, Jan. 1983, p. 333–357)

Based on series of 1804–05 declarations by foreigners, supplemented by 1809 list of French-born residents. Describes small (albeit growing), interesting foreign community. Argues that foreigners (all men) reflected microcosm of Paraguayan society at all social levels and occupations. Analyzes their declarations to give us representative sample of merchants, artisans, hacendados, *arrendatarios*, and day laborers. Another fine article by a preeminent American historian of colonial Paraguay. [SMS]

2764 Cushner, Nicholas P. Jesuit ranches and the agrarian development of colonial Argentina, 1650–1767. Albany: State University of New York Press, 1983. 206 p.: bibl., index.

Vol. 3 in series of path-breaking monographs (see *HLAS 44:2672* and item **2675**), study concentrates on Jesuit ranches of Córdoba region whose income supported several colleges throughout Río de la Plata. Excellent conclusion compares Jesuit rural activities in Peru, Quito and Argentina, and contrasts their ranches and farms with those owned by private estancieros and hacendados. [SMS]

2765 Destéfani, Laurio Hedelvio. El descubrimiento de las Islas Malvinas: aporte para un estudio crítico. 2a. ed. Buenos Aires: Comando de Jefe de la Armada, Secretaría General Naval, Departamento de Estudios Históricos Navales, 1981. 46 p.: bibl., ill. (Serie B, Historia naval argentina; no. 24)

Discusses historical evidence supporting 10 different possible discoverers of Malvinas (Falklands). Concludes islands were first sighted by so-called *Incógnita*, ship sailing in Bishop of Plasencia's 1540 Spanish expedition, and not by English sailor John Davis 52 years later. [SMS]

2766 Difrieri, Horacio A. El Virreinato del Río de la Plata: ensayo de geografía histórica. Buenos Aires: Universidad del Salvador, 1980. 61 p.: bibl., ill. (Colección Conferencias)

Interesting essay on geographical organization of La Plata Viceroyalty. Argues that Viceroyalty was given sound geopolitical dimensions based on goal of creating unit capable of maintaining and defending itself if cut off from metropolis (i.e. Lima). Notes demographic balance with Peru and Viceroyalty's regional economic equilibrium as proof of sound logic for area's independence. Major geopolitical weakness was rudimentary technology which made distances difficult to overcome. Also, Spain failed to concentrate adequate manpower in region. Controversial but noteworthy interpretation. [SMS]

2766a Fajardo Terán, Florencia. Los *ganchos* [sic] de la Villa de San Carlos. Montevideo: Imp. Editorial GOES de S.C. de Fontanillas, 1981. 52 p.

Brief historical notes about Maldonado region that mostly concern 18th century and origins of term *gaucho*. [R. Etchepareborda]

2767 Fanelli, Antonio María. Relación de un viaje a Chile a través de la Argentina, en 1698 (JEHM/R, 9:2, 2a. época, 1980, p. 318–357, plates)

Spanish version of two letters authored by Italian Jesuit Fanelli. Recounts his trans-Atlantic crossing and subsequent overland journey from Buenos Aires via Mendoza to Chile. Letters which originally appeared in 1710 in Italian, and 1929 in Spanish, present interesting first-hand picture of both life in southern South America and mentality of missionizing clergy. [SMS]

2768 Figuerola, Francisco José. Por que Hernandarias. Buenos Aires: Plus Ultra, 1981. 138 p.: bibl., indexes (Colección Esquemas históricos; v. 34)

Hagiographic biography of Hernandarias, Paraguayan-born co-founder of Buenos Aires in 1580 (with Juan de Garay), sometimes *teniente de gobernador*. Pictured as fervent Catholic, Hernandarias was dedicated to humanity's spiritual salvation and locked in struggle with "culture of money" represented by Buenos Aires merchants. [SMS]

2769 Flores, Moacyr. As vacarias e as estâncias missioneiras (*in* Simpósio Nacional de Estudos Missioneiros, 2nd, Santa Rosa, Brazil, 1977. Anais. Santa Rosa, Brazil: Faculdade de Filosofia, Ciências e Letras Dom Bosco, 1978, p. 107–112, bibl.)

Somewhat skimpy article about areas of wild cattle and ranches which, according to author, provided meat for inhabitants of Jesuit missions. Spanish and Portuguese incursions into area seem to have destroyed *vacarias* sometime during early 18th century. [SMS]

2770 Fulgencio Yegros: bicentenario de nacimiento. Asunción: Edición Estudios Históricos, 1982. 125 p., 2 folded leaves of plates: ill. (some col.)

Series of minor papers, delivered at symposium celebrating 100th anniversary of Yegros' birth, is rather typical example of "hero" history. Best essay by far is Rafael Eladio Velásquez's "Los Yegros en la Historia del Paraguay," which shows role of one of few "elite" Asunción families of 17th and 18th centuries. [SMS]

2771 Galmarini, Hugo R. Comercio y burocracia colonial: a propósito de Tomás Antonio Romero: pts. 1/2 (ANH/IE, 28, enero/junio 1980, p. 407–439; 29, julio/dic. 1980, p. 387–424)

Solidly researched two-part article deals with rather atypical *porteño* merchant and local and metropolitan bureaucracy. Pt. 1 describes his varied commercial enterprises (e.g., transport of government funds and mercury from Potosí to Buenos Aires, salted-meat production for royal troops, fishing industry in Patagonia, African slave trade, contraband). Pt. 2 focuses on his fall from local favor and declining role between independence and death in 1820. Fine job of understanding the man and his time. [SMS]

2772 Gammalsson, Hialmar Edmundo. Los pobladores de Buenos Aires y su descendencia. Buenos Aires: Municipalidad de la Ciudad de Buenos Aires, Secretaría de Cultura, 1980. 505 p.: bibl.

Sketchy genealogies of two groups of *porteños*: original settlers who accompanied Juan de Garay in 1580; and other assorted 17th and 18th-century residents. Surprisingly vague on dates, book fails to make use of any parish records. Major use for historians will no doubt be citations of wills and estate papers in Archivo General de la Nación. Unfortunately, Buenos Aires still lacks a work comparable to Juan Alejandro Apolant's *Génesis de la familia uruguaya* (see *HLAS 36:2617*). [SMS]

2773 Gandía, Enrique de. Roberto Levillier: su obra histórica (ANH/B, 52, 1979, p. 119–140)

Text of speech delivered on 10th anniversary of Levillier's death. Makes reference to Levillier's work on conquest period and succeeding century in northwest Argentina, but is vague on sources and ideas. Gandía more than agrees with Levillier's traditional justification of Spanish conquest of Peru (Incas' despotism) and his vision of colonial civilization based on highest idealism. [SMS]

2774 Garavaglia, Juan Carlos. Un capítulo del mercado interno colonial: el Paraguay y su región, 1537–1682 (GEE/NA, 1, 1978, p. 11–55, tables)

Excellent article draws on variety of sources to trace Paraguayan production of wine, cereals, sugar, animal products, and yerba mate during colony's first 150 years. Finds that originally diversified economy gave way to one increasingly dependent on production and export of yerba mate. A must for students of Río de la Plata region's colonial economy. See also item **2775.** [SMS]

2775 ——. El mercado interno colonial y la yerba mate: siglos XVI–XIX (GEE/NA, 4, 1981, p. 163–210)

Like item **2774,** another path-breaking work on Paraguay's colonial economy and internal markets. Garavaglia traces here gradual spread of yerba from Tupi-Guaraní religious use to product widely used by Indians, mestizos and Spaniards throughout much of South America. Also contains interesting information on mate's commercialization, including figures on exports from both Paraguay and Jesuit missions. [SMS]

2776 García Heras, Raúl. Aspectos económicos y sociales de Virreynato del Río de la Plata en 1776. Buenos Aires: Fundación para el Estudio de los Problemas Argentinos, 1978. 19 p.: bibl. (Documento de trabajo; no. 1)

Working paper attempts to generalize on entire course of colonial Argentine history, but is based entirely on secondary sources. [SMS]

2777 Granda, Germán de. Origen, función y estructura de un pueblo de negros y mulatos libres en el Paraguay del siglo XVIII: San Agustín de la Emboscada (IGFO/RI, 43:171, enero/junio 1983, p. 229–264)

Interesting account of 1718 creation of Arecutacuá fort and subsequent 1745 founding of Emboscada town, both established to prevent Chaco Indian raids. Although both settlements made use of free blacks as colonizers, Emboscada was noteworthy because it attempted to organize settlers along lines associated with Indian communities. Appendix contains Governor Melo's *Instrucción para el govierno del pueblo.* [SMS]

2778 Hoffmann, Werner. Vida y obra del P. Martín Schmid S.J., 1694–1772:

misionero suizo entre los chiquitanos: músico, artesano, arquitecto y escultor. Buenos Aires: Fundación para la Educación, la Ciencia y la Cultura, 1981. 158 p.: bibl.

Solid biography of Jesuit missionary who spent more than 30 years among Chiquitanos. Traces Schmid's life from birth in Switzerland, through education and years as missionary, to imprisonment, exile, and death. Also includes transcriptions of letters from Schmid to family, and demographic data for Chiquitos missions in 1743. Important addition to history of 18th-century Jesuit missions. [SMS]

2779 Johnson, Lyman L. The impact of racial discrimination on black artisans in colonial Buenos Aires (Social History [Methuen & Co., London] 6:3, Oct. 1981, p. 301–316, chart)

Excellent study tests commonly held idea that mulattoes were more successful than blacks in gaining access to urban economy's skilled and semi-skilled jobs. Argues that mulattoes who became skilled artisans were those who could be accepted as "white." Furthermore, city's rapid growth during late 18th century and immigration of European-born artisans institutionalized discrimination, forcing castas out of guild participation. By colonial period's end, porteño artisan trades evolved into two-tier racial stratification system which inhibited social and economic mobility for non-whites. A must for students of colonial society and race relations. [SMS]

2780 Krüger, Hildegard. Función y estructura social del Cabildo colonial de Asunción (JGSWGL, 18, 1981, p. 31–44)

Reviews social composition of Asunción's Town Council from 1541 creation to eve of comuneros revolt. Finds that cabildo was controlled by local mestizo elite but included prestigious Spaniards or Creoles from neighboring provinces. Underlines importance of kinship ties among cabildo members. Concludes comunero revolt was elite attempt to maintain power in face of slow social change. Interesting article. [SMS]

2781 Laguarda Trías, Rolando A. El hallazgo del Río de la Plata por Amerigo Vespucci en 1502. Montevideo: Academia Nacional de Letras, 1982. 252 p.: bibl., ill. (Biblioteca de la Academia Nacional de Letras. Serie III, Escritos)

Latest in series of monographs on Portuguese voyages into Río de la Plata during first decades of 16th century. Argues convincingly that Vespucci sailed into area as part of expedition to determine where Tordesillas line lay. Examines both letters and maps to argue that Vespucci and his men were first "discoverers" of River Plate. Solid research in published and archival sources. [SMS]

Lazzarotto, Danilo. Encomiendas e povos das missões. See item **1654.**

2782 Leiva, Alberto David. Supervivencia del régimen señorial y transición al derecho moderno en los inicios de la colonización del Río de la Plata (PAIGH/H, 93, enero/junio 1982, p. 59–71)

After lengthy discussion of *adelantados* in early conquest of Latin America, and *capitulaciones* signed between Crown and its agents, author discusses contract to conquer Río de la Plata, signed 1534 by Pedro de Mendoza. [SMS]

2783 Levaggi, Abelardo. La fundamentación de las sentencias en el derecho indiano (Revista de Historia del Derecho [Instituto de Investigaciones de Historia del Derecho, Buenos Aires] 6, 1978, p. 45–73)

Juridical study presents 21 examples of legal justifications in Viceroyalty of Río de la Plata's criminal courts. While author presents cases as proof that 1768 royal *cédula* instructing courts not to include legal justifications in sentences was less than universally adopted, examples are more interesting as insights into period's social realities. [SMS]

2784 Luque Colombres, Carlos. Análisis crítico del *Ensayo sobre la genealogía de los Tejedas* (UNC/R, 1979/1980, p. 49–99, facsims.)

In attempt to determine author of 1794 *Genealogía* of Córdoba's Tejeda family, resorts to textual analysis of manuscript's two versions. Believes author was Juan Luis de Aguirre y Tejeda, prominent family member, priest, and lawyer. Appendix reproduces genealogy's prologue. Unfortunately, there is no published copy of entire genealogy. [SMS]

2785 Maeder, Ernesto J.A. Historia económica de Corrientes en el período virreinal, 1776–1810. Advertencia de Enrique M. Barba. Buenos Aires: Academia Nacional de la Historia, 1981. 458 p., 14 leaves of plates: bibl., ill. (Colección de historia económica y social; 6)

Important study of Corrientes' economy from beginning of 18th century. Examines city's growth, expansion of rural frontier, population, agriculture, livestock, and commerce. Also includes interesting chapter on revenue production (tribute, *diezmos* and *estancos*). Fundamentally important, well documented, and well illustrated book on developing northeast region. [SMS]

2786 ———. Los jesuítas en el Río de la Plata: nacionalidad y composición de la Compañía entre 1585–1768 (CRIT, 55:1879, abril 1982, p. 158–161)

Interesting analysis of Río de la Plata Jesuits based on data published in Hugo Storni's *Catálogo de los jesuítas de la provincia del Paraguay.* Maeder finds that in addition to majority of Spaniards among 1559 men in Jesuit group, there were many from other areas of Europe and present-day Argentina. Although an international organization, Jesuits, perhaps prudently, seldom gave non-Spaniards positions of authority. [SMS]

2787 Mariluz Urquijo, José María. Bilbao y Buenos Aires: proyectos dieciochescos de compañías de comercio. Buenos Aires: Universidad de Buenos Aires, 1981. 157 p.: bibl., appendix, 1 facsim. (Colección del IV centenario de Buenos Aires; 3)

Interesting study of early 18th-century attempts to set up monopoly trading company in Buenos Aires like Caracas' Compañía Guipuzcoana. Outlines growth of Buenos Aires as trading center, points to rivalry between Bilbao and Andalucía for American trade, and concentrates on three projects to link Buenos Aires to Bilbao (1737–45). Although projects failed, suggests that discussion generated by them raised *porteño* merchants' awareness of such problems and possible solutions. Valuable work by leading traditional historian. [SMS]

2788 ———. El diputado del Consulado de Lima en Buenos Aires (*in* Congreso Venezolano de la Historia, 4th, Caracas, 1980. Memoria [see item **2621**] v. 2, p. 331–343)

Discussion of fruitless attempt (1753–57) to set up deputy representative of Lima's Consulado in Buenos Aires. Although Lima's Consulado wanted *porteño* merchants under its legal jurisdiction, their resistance to accept a hostile Peruvian jurisdiction led to Buenos Aires' eventual victory. Until 1794 founding of local Consulado, Buenos Aires merchant cases were tried by local Cabildo. Solid article which fails to address larger question of port city's mercantile policies. [SMS]

2789 Moncaut, Carlos Antonio. Reducción Jesuítica de Nuestra Señora de la Concepción de los Pampas, 1740–1753: historia de un pueblo desaparecido a orillas del Río Salado bonaerense. La Plata: Ministerio de Economía de la Provincia de Buenos Aires, 1981. 141 p., 25 leaves of plates (some folded): bibl., ill. (some col.)

History of short-lived Jesuit mission among Pampas Indians, based on traditional sources (Dobrizhoffer, Charlevoix, Falkner, Furlong) and archival material. Blames mission's failure on Spanish resentment of Jesuit success and hostility of neighboring Indian groups. Well illustrated with pictures taken from Florian Paucke. [SMS]

2790 Oddo, Vicente. Abogados de Santiago del Estero durante el primer siglo de existencia de la ciudad, 1553–1653. Santiago del Estero, Argentina: Editorial Herca, 1981. 253 p.: ill.

Biographical and professional sketches of 13 lawyers active in Santiago de Estero's legal life. Somewhat impressionistic biographical history includes several transcribed documents. [SMS]

2791 Olaso, Ezequiel de. Las ideas ilustradas de Manuel José de Lavarden en el *Discurso* de 1778: una contribución al estudio de la influencia del Padre Feijóo en el Río de la Plata (in Coloquio Ilustración Española e Independencia de América, Bellaterra, Spain, 1978. Homenaje a Noël Salomon: ilustración española e independencia de América. Edición preparada por Alberto Gil Novales. Barcelona: Universidad Autónoma de Barcelona, 1979, p. 367–371)

Discerns Feijóo's philosophical influences and moderate Spanish interpretation of Enlightenment in *Discurso*. Lavarden was *porteño* lawyer educated in Charcas, and possibly Peru and Spain. Like Feijóo, he found no incompatibility between new respect for reason and belief in God. Thus, knowledge of nature through experimentation could lead

to contemplation of God. Interesting example of 18th-century thought in Río de la Plata. [SMS]

2793 Porro, Nelly R.; Juana E. Astiz and María M. Rospide. Aspectos de la vida cotidiana en el Buenos Aires virreinal. Buenos Aires: Universidad de Buenos Aires, 1982. 2 v. (592 p.): bibl. (Colección del IV centenario de Buenos Aires; 8)

Attempt to study "material culture" especially kitchenware, clothing and bed-clothing, etc. found in colonial estate inventories. Includes especially useful dictionary on use, price, and variety of items. Cryptic citations seem to refer to *Sucesiones* in Archivo General de la Nación (Argentina). [SMS]

2794 Rabuske, Arthur. A *Carta-Magna* das reduções do Paraguai (in Simpósio Nacional de Estudos Missioneiros, Santa Rosa, Brazil, 1977. Anais. Santa Rosa, Brazil: Faculdade de Filosofia, Ciências e Letras Dom Bosco, 1978, p. 171–187)

Portuguese translation of 1609–10 instructions sent by Padre Diego de Torres Bollo, Rector of Peru's Jesuit *colegios*, to fellow Jesuits in Guairá and Paraná. Rabuske and several Argentine Jesuit historians believe instructions served as model used by all Jesuit missions in Paraguay. [SMS]

2795 ———. O modelo das reduções guaranis: brasileiro ou peruano? (in Simpósio Nacional de Estudos Missioneiros, 2nd, Santa Rosa, Brazil, 1977. Anais. Santa Rosa, Brazil: Faculdade de Filosofia, Ciências e Letras Dom Bosco, 1978, p. 87–98)

Superficial review of on-going controversy about model used by Jesuits to set up Paraguayan missions. Rabuske believes model was Spanish-American (e.g., Pablo Hernández, Guillermo Furlong) rather than Portuguese-American (e.g., Serafim Leite). Identifies model as Diego de Torres Bollo's (see item **2794**), arguing that Jesuits were extreme realists rather than utopians. [SMS]

2796 Ramos Pérez, Demetrio. Recomendaciones y súplicas como muestras del ambiente en el que se organizó la expedición de Cevallos al Plata (EEHA/AEA, 32, 1975, p. 279–301)

Detailed study of organization of 1776 Cevallos expedition. Concentrates on royal determination to sent only well organized batallions under trained and qualified officers.

While documenting officers who were not appointed to go, Ramos Pérez does not explain why so many were eager to be sent to Río de la Plata. Based largely on one source from Archivo General de Simancas. [SMS]

2797 Rípodas Ardanaz, Daisy. El Obispo Azamor y Ramírez: tradición cristiana y modernidad. Buenos Aires: Universidad de Buenos Aires, 1982. 278 p.: bibl., ports (Colección del IV centenario de Buenos Aires; 1)

Biography of Manuel de Azamor y Ramírez, Buenos Aires conservative bishop (1788–96). Also includes analysis of his library and writings. Concludes that while living at end of 18th century, Azamor was hardly a *philosophe.* [SMS]

2798 Rodríguez Molas, Ricardo. Esclavos indios y africanos en los primeros momentos de la conquista y colonización del Río de la Plata (IAA, 7:4, 1981, p. 325–366, bibl.)

Article says very little about Río de la Plata Africans but presents mass of evidence about perception and treatment of indigenous peoples. Finds that regardless of law, in Buenos Aires, Tucumán and Paraguay, so-called "free" Indians were brought and sold as late as first half of 17th century. [SMS]

2799 Romero, Luis A. Decadencia regional y declinación urbana en el interior argentino: 1776–1787 (CPES/RPS, 15:42/43, mayo/dic. 1978, p. 47–56)

Despite title, discussion covers regional economies of Tucumán, Córdoba, and Cuyo from beginning of 18th century to 1876. Although marred by scarcity of hard data and footnotes, argues that Northeast economies, originally tied to Potosí and Chile, were re-oriented toward Buenos Aires after 1776. Finds regional economies suffered with independence, but points to 1830–60 resurgence when Bolivian and Chilean markets regained importance. [SMS]

2800 San Luis, Argentina (*province*). Actas capitulares de San Luis. t. 1, Años 1700 a 1750. Introducción de José M. Mariluz Urquijo. Buenos Aires: Academia Nacional de la Historia, 1980 [i.e. 1982]. 1 v.

Literal transcription of Town Council minutes of northwestern city of San Luis (1700–50). Also includes transcriptions of

documents reflecting area's administrative organization. [SMS]

2801 Santos Martínez, Pedro. Administración y economía del agua de riego en la región cuyana del Virreinato Ríoplatense (*in* Congreso Venezolana de la Historia, 4th, Caracas, 1980. Memoria [see item **2621**] v. 2, p. 347–355)

Concentrates on Mendoza's Cabildo legislation to maintain local irrigation system. Concludes that while water rights policy was within *Recopilación*'s general outlines, by late 18th century Cabildo often adjusted legislation to local usage. [SMS]

2802 Segreti, Carlos S.A. En torno al traslado de la aduana seca de Córdoba (*in* Congreso Venezolano de la Historia, 4th, Caracas, 1980. Memoria [see item **2621**] v. 3, p. 123–153, bibl.)

Solid article discusses late 16th and 17th-century Spanish attempts to come to grips with trade through Buenos Aires, attempts which resulted in creation of Córdoba's Customs House (1623–1703). Stresses Córdoba's interest in continuation of strong Buenos Aires trade, both because of trade with Brazil and Upper Peru. Córdoba's *aduana seca*, created as trade barrier, proved unsuccessful in dealing with problem. [SMS]

2803 Soler, Amadeo P. Los 823 [i.e. ochocientos veintitrés] días del Fuerte Sancti Spiritus y la vigencia permanente de Puerto Gaboto. Rosario: Editorial Amalevi, 1981. 293 p.: bibl., maps.

Uses two cloying fictional characters to retell story of Sancti Spiritus, fort founded by explorer Sebastian Cabot along Coronda River, branch of Paraná. First Spanish settlement in the area, fort was set up June 1527 and destroyed by hostile Indians Sept. 1529. Among interesting details provided by Soler was inclusion of five or six women in Cabot's expedition, "needed to provide additional domestic services which could not be provided by the male sex." [SMS]

2804 Susnik, Branka. Las relaciones interétnicas en la época colonial: Paraguay (UCNSA/SA, 16:2, dic. 1981, p. 19–27, bibl.)

Interesting article reviews complex relations among multitude of ethno-tribal groups both in Chaco and near Asunción.

Susnik, an anthropologist, looks at relations among groups of differing cultural levels (planters, nomads, nomads on horseback), and between individual groups and Spaniards. Synthesis lacks footnotes but includes brief bibliography of Susnik's works on Paraguay's colonial Indians (see also item **1728**). [SMS]

2805 Velázquez, Rafael Eladio. Caracteres de la encomienda paraguaya en los siglos XVII y XVIII (*in* Congreso Venezolano de la Historia, 4th, Caracas, 1980. Memoria [see item **2621**] v. 3, p. 439–474)

Fine article traces Paraguay's encomienda from relatively late 1556 creation under Governor Martínez de Irala to its late 1803 demise. Sees encomienda as the preeminent institution for tapping Indian labor, especially for 17th-century cultivation of yerba mate. While declining in importance because of various reasons, encomienda continued in Paraguay long after it was supplanted throughout Spanish America. Although Velázquez fails to ask why, a solid piece of research. [SMS]

2806 ———. Indígenas y españoles en la formación social del pueblo paraguayo (UCNSA/SA, 6:2, dic. 1981, p. 29–67, appendix, maps, tables)

Summary, based on Velásquez' earlier monographs (see *HLAS 30:2354* and *HLAS 32:2382*), of Indian-Spanish relations from Asunción's founding to independence. Discusses early Guaraní acceptance of Spaniards and their amalgamation through kinship, encomienda system, Indian rebellions, local legislation on Indians, population patterns and mestizaje. Appendix includes 16th, 17th, and 18th-century population data. Fine overview. [SMS]

2807 ———. Poblamiento en el Paraguay en el siglo XVIII: fundación de villas y formación de los núcleos urbanos menores (CPES/RPS, 15:42/43, mayo/dic. 1978, p. 175–189, map)

Traces growth of Paraguay's non-Indian population from 16th to 18th centuries, underlining geographical restriction of 17th-century settlements and expansion of early 18th century. Especially interesting is growth of rural mestizo population which occupied much of Cordillera by end of colonial period. Solid article by solid historian. [SMS]

2808 ———. La sociedad paraguaya en la época de la Independencia (CPES/RPS, 13:35, enero/abril 1976, p. 157–169)

Stresses emergence of mestizo-Creole elite, noting it was allied with rising middle class until 1735 failure of comunero movement. Suggests that when sons of this elite were displaced by new group of peninsular merchants, they became leaders of Paraguay's early independence movement. Interesting and provocative article. [SMS]

2809 Viaje al Río de la Plata y Chile: 1752–1756 (JEHM/R, 9:2, 2a. época, 1980, p. 359–376, plates)

Spanish version of unpublished manuscript describes travels of unidentified Scottish doctor who arrived in Buenos Aires aboard British slaver, *George*. Physician, who eventually accompanied slaves to Chile, provides lively picture of Buenos Aires, road through Mendoza to Chile, and Englishmen met. Early example of visiting Englishman literature that became major source of information on Río de la Plata. [SMS]

2810 Villegas, D. Juan. La primera generación de jesuitas fundadores de reducciones en Paraguay (SGHS/A, 51:51, enero/dic. 1978, p. 217–219)

Misleading title for short article which reproduces two extracts from letter written early 16th century (no date given) by Roque González de Santa Cruz, S.J. What author interprets as Guaraní Indians fleeing from Christianity may have also been Guaraní Indians fleeing from some epidemic disease. [SMS]

2811 Villota, Manuel Genaro de. Los escritos del Fiscal de la Audiencia de Buenos Aires, Manuel Genaro de Villota. [Biografía y notas de] Abelardo Levaggi. Buenos Aires: Fundación para la Educación, Ciencia y la Cultura, 1981. 738 p.

Solid study of Villota, Buenos Aires Fiscal del Crimen (1799–1804) and Fiscal de lo Civil (1804–10), later Lima Oídor (1812–22). Includes Levaggi's short biography and all of Villota's written decisions. His writings on nature of justice to political theory to the local economy serve as excellent example of moderate Enlightenment thinking in colonial Spanish America. [SMS]

2812 Vives Azancot, Pedro A. Asunción, 1775–1800: persistencias rurales en la revitalización de su estructura urbana (IFGO/RI, 39:155/158, enero/dic. 1979, p. 209–234, ill.)

Most interesting, well argued, important article for students of Hispanic-American urbanization. Presents Asunción as model of Hispanic-American frontier city. Asunción's irregular series of blocks and buildings failed to conform to regular urban plan. Although originally military outpost, Asunción remained semi-rural throughout colonial period. [SMS]

2813 ———. Entre el esplendor y la decadencia: la población de Misiones, 1750–1759 (IFGO/RI, 42:169/170, julio/dic. 1982, p. 469–543, graphs, maps, tables)

Detailed demographic study based on 1759 report by Padre José Cardiel on Jesuit missions' population. Argues that it was in decline before Jesuits' expulsion due to epidemic diseases, military encounters with Portuguese, and inability of missions to ac-commodate growing Spanish population pressure. Excellent work. [SMS]

2814 Zylberberg, Michel. Négriers et Indiens dans le Río de la Plata au début du XIXème siècle (in Coloquio Ilustración Española e Independencia de América, Bellaterra, Spain, 1978. Homenaje a Noël Salomon: ilustración española e independencia de América. Edición preparada por Alberto Gil Novales. Barcelona: Universidad Autónoma de Barcelona, 1979, p. 251–258)

Brief article on Domingo Cabarrus' plan to colonize Maldonado by importing 2,400 African slaves. Cabarrus' quixotic ideas (based on supposed existence of area's gold, silver, copper, etc.) combined Spanish royal support, German colonists, stock company, and blacks supplied by English slavers. Curiously, Zylberberg perceives proposal—approved 1802 by Spanish government— as proof of intransigence in face of foreign competition. [SMS]

Independence Period

DAVID BUSHNELL, *Professor of History, University of Florida*

THE GREATEST NOVELTY in the section that follows is one of format: the inclusion of a separate subsection devoted to Bolivariana. Works relating to the Liberator Simón Bolívar have always formed a significant portion of the publications on Spanish South America's independence, but this time they loomed even larger because of the combined impetus derived from the sesquicentennial of his death (1980) and bicentennial of his birth (1983). Undoubtedly there are more sesquicentennial and bicentennial publications that deserve to be annotated and are not yet included in the *Handbook*. But enough have come to hand to warrant a new subdivision for at least the present volume, even though not many of them are of truly exceptional importance. Most noteworthy are new editions of three basic documentary collections on the life and times of the Liberator: Mendoza and Yanes (item **2826**), Blanco and Azpurúa (item **2828**), and O'Leary (item **2837**). Particularly as something new has been incorporated with each of the three, they more than make up for the bothersome flood of superfluous reeditions that the commemorations have spewed forth. Among recent works of original scholarship, that of Father Gutiérrez on Bolívar and the Church (item **2831**) is probably most important, with Kahle's on Bolívar and Germany (item **2832**), the runner-up; yet Leopoldo Zea's slim volume on Bolívar's thought (item **2842**) must also be singled out, and not purely because of the author's identity. Finally, there have been numerous Bolívar bicentennial issues of historical or other journals with articles or conference papers that vary widely in quality and topic but do give an idea of current directions of research and interpretation with respect to Bolívar. Some of the special issues are represented in this *Handbook* by, at most, a single article. Only the contents of the *Hispanic Ameri-*

can *Historical Review*'s bicentennial contribution are listed in full (items **2824**, **2825**, **2827**, and **2835**).

There has further been a decided increase in scholarly attention given to the losing side of the independence struggle. The works in question, since they normally deal with imperial policy or with Spanish reaction to the American rebellions generally, are for the most part annotated in the History: General section of the *Handbook*, but their importance for Spanish South America still requires that they be noted here. Timothy Anna's *Spain and the loss of America* (item **1880**) is the prime and most comprehensive example. The one other book-length treatment is Pérez Guilhou's on Spanish attitudes 1808–14 (item **1893**). However, these are complemented by the significant monographic articles of Cuenca Toribio on episcopal appointments (item **1883**) and Costeloe on Catalan trade (item **1882**).

For the rest, the literature specifically referring to the Gran Colombian theater has been enriched through the appearance of important subregional studies by Araúz on Panama (item **2844**) and Cubitt on Guayaquil (items **2846** and **2847**). A good biography of the pardo leader Manual Piar by Asdrúbal González has also appeared (item **2850**), while De Grummond's work on Renato Beluche (item **2848**) adds substantially to existing coverage of privateering warfare. D.A.G. Waddell has published a welcome overview of British policy toward the independence movement in northern South America (item **2860**). Elsewhere, Américo A. Tonda has contributed what will certainly be the definitive biography of the royalist bishop of Córdoba, Argentina (item **2893**), but on the whole, the publications about the Platine area have been less impressive than usual. Moreover, independence studies in or concerning Peru and Chile appear to have entered something of a lull, for which Bolivia has partly compensated with Arze Aguirre's impressive study of "popular participation" (item **2866**) and Gunnar Mendoza's masterly edition of the Santos Vargas diary (item **2869**).

GENERAL

2815 Avila Martel, Alamiro de. Andrés Bello y la primera biografía de O'Higgins. Santiago: Ediciones de la Universidad de Chile, 1978. 71 p.: plates.

Republishes what appears to be first biography of O'Higgins, written by Bello in London, 1819. What it says concerning O'Higgins is hardly new, but it is of interest for Bello's defense of autocratic Chilean constitution of 1818. Preceded by good dicussion of Bello and other Spanish and Spanish American expatriates or agents in London political-intellectual scene.

2816 Congreso Nacional de Historia Sanmartiniano-Moreniano: conmemorativo del bicentenario del nacimiento de los próceres Gral. José F. de San Martín y Dr. Mariano Moreno, 24 al 31 de julio de 1978. Con los auspicios de Academia Nacional de la Historia *et al.* Quilmes, Argentina: Municipalidad de Quilmes, 1978. 495 p.: bibl., ill.

These conference proceedings include ceremonial addresses, trivia, and serious contributions, all having to do with San Martín or Mariano Moreno but ranging widely in content and approach. Examples of the serious are Aníbal Jorge Luzuriaga's "Episodios de la Independencia del Perú a través de la Correspondencia entre el Libertador y el Marqués de Torre Tagle," treating San Martín's relations with the volatile Peruvian, on the basis of unpublished correspondence; and Antonio José Pérez Amuchástegui's "El Pensamiento Político de Moreno y su Incidencia en el Compromiso Libertador Sudamericano," an interpretative paper claiming Moreno as properly Americanist and antiliberal.

2817 Sucre, Antonio José de. De mi propia mano. Selección y prólogo, J.L. Salcedo-Bastardo. Cronología, Inés Mercedes Quintero Montiel, Andrés Eloy Romero. Caracas: Biblioteca Ayacucho, 1981. 479 p.: bibl. (Biblioteca Ayacucho; 90)

Selection of Sucre's writings, including personal letters and official papers; 225 out of "about 7,000" known items. Technically well done, with brief prologue and more extensive chronology of Sucre's career.

2817a Verna, Paul. Bolívar y los emigrados patriotas en el Caribe: Trinidad, Curazao, San Thomas, Jamaica, Haití. Caracas: INCE, 1983. 200 p.: bibl., ill.

Traces escape of Caribbean patriots fleeing Spanish forces from Venezuela and New Granada, and their subsequent exile. Includes capsule biographies of 336 patriots identified by author. [A. Pérotin-Dumon]

BOLIVARIANA

2818 Aljure Chalela, Simón. Bibliografía de Manuelita Sáenz (CBR/BCB, 18:2, 1981, p. 234–253)

Alongside a few scholarly items, includes many—hardly all—periodical articles that have appeared. Clearly reflects Manuela's place in Colombian popular history.

2819 Arze, José Roberto. Páginas sobre Bolívar. La Paz: Ediciones Roalva, 1981. 142 p.

Collected short pieces mostly dealing with: 1) Bolívar as seen by Marx and Russian writers; and 2) Bolívar's commitment to Spanish American solidarity. Based on rather wide familiarity with Bolivarian literature and generally reasonable in judgments, though overindulgent towards Soviet historiography.

2820 Bolívar, el libro del sesquicentenario, 1830–1980: compilación documental sobre los últimos momentos, la muerte, las exequias y el posterior traslado de los restos del Libertador. Realizada por Manuel Pérez Vila. Caracas: Comité Ejecutivo del Bicentenario de Simón Bolívar, Ediciones de la Presidencia de la República, 1980. 383 p.: ill. (Colección Bicentenario; no. 2)

Source collection on death and worldly afterlife of Bolívar, prepared with Pérez Vila's customary professional skill.

2821 Bolívar, Simón. Escritos del Libertador. t. 13, Documentos No. 2583-

2939, 1 enero–30 junio 1818. t. 14, Documentos Nos. 2940–3588, 1 julio 1818–14 febrero 1819. Caracas: Sociedad Bolivariana de Venezuela, 1980–1981. 2 v. (436, 742 p.): appendix, facsims., maps.

Two more installments of this excellently edited series. Vol. 13 contains detailed prologue by Héctor Bencomo Barrios, "Campaña del Centro: 1818," and vol. 14 an appendix of documents (1808–17) that failed to be included in earlier volumes. For preceding volumes, see *HLAS 42:2872.*

2822 ———. Escritos fundamentales. Selección, prólogo y reseña biográfica de Simón Bolívar, Germán Carrera Damas. Caracas: Monte Avila Editores, 1982. 274 p., 1 leaf of plates: col. port. (Colección Simón Bolívar)

Much more accessible reedition with new title of Bolívar anthology first published in Montevideo (see *HLAS 40:3312*). Its prologue is useful condensation of compiler's *El culto a Bolívar* (see *HLAS 32:2418*).

2823 ———. The hope of the universe. Introduction, selection, biographical notes, and chronology by J.L. Salcedo-Bastardo. Prologue by Arturo Uslar Pietri. Paris: UNESCO, 1983. 326 p.: index.

Best one-volume anthology of Bolívar's writings in English. Unfortunately lacks index even of names and places, but does contain useful chronology and extensive introduction by Salcedo-Bastardo, which is lucid statement of generally conventional themes.

2824 Bushnell, David. The last dictatorship: betrayal or consummation? (HAHR, 63:1, Feb. 1983, p. 65–105)

Treats historiographic image, policies, and structure of generally conservative dictatorship Bolívar imposed on Gran Colombia (1828–30).

2825 Carrera Damas, Germán. Simón Bolívar: el culto heroico y la nación (HAHR, 63:1, Feb. 1983, p. 107–145)

Not easy reading, but worth the effort. Develops themes that were mostly present in author's *El culto a Bolívar* (see *HLAS 32:2418*), with special attention to theoretical significance of hero cults.

2826 Colección de documentos relativos a la vida pública del Libertador de Co-

lombia y del Perú, Simón Bolívar. Recopilación hecha por Cristóbal Mendoza. Ed. facsimilar del original de la primera ed., 2a. ed. Caracas: Fundación Diana Mendoza Ayala, 1983. 22 v.: col. ports.

Reprint of first great Bolivarian documentary collection, originally published 1826–29. Had been rare, though its contents incorporated in other compilations. Vol. 22, *Appendix*, is new with this ed. Contains documents on Cristóbal Mendoza, who made original compilation with Francisco Javier Yanes and who played significant role in Venezuela from late colonial regime through Gran Colombia and was ephemeral "first president of Venezuela" during First Republic.

2827 Collier, Simon. Nationality, nationalism, and supranationalism in the writings of Simón Bolívar (HAHR, 63 : 1, Feb. 1983, p. 37–64)

Welcome ray of lucidity on often muddied topic, making needed distinctions between Bolívar's concept of nation, his "Americanist idealism," and such intermediate propositions as Gran Colombian experiment.

2828 Documentos para la historia de la vida pública del Libertador. [Reunidos por] José Félix Blanco y Ramón Azpurúa. Presentación, J.L. Salcedo-Bastardo. Vida y obra de José Félix Blanco, J.A. Calcaño y R. Azpurúa. Vida y obra de Ramón Azpurúa, Manuel Pérez Vila. Caracas: Comité Ejecutivo del Bicentenario de Simón Bolívar: Ediciones de la Presidencia de la República, 1977–1979. 15 v.: indexes.

Facsimile reproduction of one of basic documentary collections on independence movement in Bolivarian theater. Particularly welcome in that paper of original edition (1875–77) has long since begun to crumble. Vol. 1 of this ed. includes an older biographic sketch of José Félix Blanco and adds superb new study of Ramón Azpurúa by Manuel Pérez Vila, which fully describes circumstances surrounding appearance of first ed.

2829 Fainshtein, Mijail. Bolívar en la prensa rusa y soviética (URSS/AL, 9 : 33, 1980, p. 44–52, facsim.)

Useful short review of references in Russian press at time of Spanish-American independence as well as later treatment in reference works, biography, historical literature, up to present. Issue in which this article appears is another, not very impressive, example of same, featuring items by various Soviet authors in conventional praise of Bolívar as well as one on Simón Rodríguez which is somewhat better and listed separately (item **1897**).

2830 Filippi, Alberto. En torno a la visión bolivariana de Europa (RO, 30/31, dic. 1983, p. 114–132)

This essay repeats much that is familiar but offers perceptive brief treatment of Bolívar as "liberal" and caustic comments on Eurocentric distortions of his thought and action. Part of special issue containing wide range of Bolívar bicentennial papers.

2831 Gutiérrez, Alberto. La Iglesia que entendió el Libertador Simón Bolívar. Caracas: Universidad Católica Andrés Bello, 1981. 288 p.: bibl., index (Colección Manoa; 30)

Jesuit scholar analyzes Bolívar's attitude toward Church, as manifested chiefly in letters and addresses, seeing gradual evolution—under influence of American reality— from Enlightenment preconceptions to more orthodox position. Does not pretend to be comprehensive treatment of Bolívar's approach to religion but is probably best thing available on this topic. Perspective is explicitly post-Vatican II but not "liberation theology."

2832 Kahle, Günter. Simón Bolívar und die Deutschen. Berlin, FRG: Dietrich Reimer Verlag, 1980. 115 p.: bibl., ill.

Analyzes Bolívar's impact on Germans and German historiography. Believes Humboldt had most influence on Germany's view of Latin America. Interesting chapters cover Bolívar and his relationship to Humboldt, Johann von Uslar, and Otto Philip Braun. Excellent treatment of German legionnaires who fought in Bolívar's armies. Important contribution for specialists and laymen. [G.M. Dorn]

2833 Lavretski, I. Simón Bolívar. Moscow: Progress Publishers, 1982. 190 p.: bibl., plates.

It is good to have readily accessible Spanish translation of this work, not for its intrinsic merit but because of its stature as a basic Soviet manual on Bolívar and its rather wide acceptance in Latin America. For Russian editions, see *HLAS 24:4161* and *HLAS 34:2350*.

2834 Lima, Nestor Santos. A imagem do Brasil nas cartas de Bolívar (IBRI/R, 21:81/84, 1978, p. 29–50)
At least for Brazilians, a more accessible ed. of *HLAS 42:2878*.

2835 Lynch, John. Bolívar and the caudillos (HAHR, 63:1, Feb. 1983, p. 3–35)
Thoughtful essay, on basis of printed sources, concerning Bolívar's problematic relations with Venezuela's "regional chieftains," whom in the end "he failed to coopt."

2836 Miramón, Alberto. Bolívar en el pensamiento europeo de su época. Bogotá: Banco de la República, 1980. 115 p.: bibl. ill.
Four unpretentious but informative and well executed essays on Bolívar as seen by Byron, Balzac, and others. They also contain much on broader reflections in Europe of Latin American independence movement.

Naranjo de Castillo, Cira and **Elke Niesculz de Stockhausen.** El Libertador en su centenario: una bibliografía. See item **38a.**

2837 O'Leary, Daniel Florencio. Memorias del General O'Leary. t. 1–12, Correspondencia de hombres notables con el Libertador. t. 13–26, Documentos. t. 27–28, [Narración]. t. 29–31, Cartas del Libertador. t. 32, Apéndice. t. 33–34, Indice de los documentos contenidos en las Memorias del general Daniel Florencio O'Leary, elaborado por Manuel Pérez Vila. Ed. facsimilar del original de la primera ed., con motivo de la celebración del sesquicentenario de la muerte de Simón Bolívar, Padre de la Patria. Caracas: Ministerio de la Defensa, 1981. 34 v.: appendix, ill., ports. (some col.)
Another extremely useful reedition, in this case with Manuel Pérez Vila's index to entire printed series (first pub. 1956) added as vols. 33–34.

2838 Prieto F., Luis B. El magisterio americano de Bolívar. 2a. ed. Caracas: Academia Nacional de la Historia, 1982. 327 p.: bibl. (El Libro menor; 21)
Collected short pieces on Bolívar's educational ideas, capably bringing together much conventional wisdom.

Santa-Cruz, Andrés. Archivo histórico del Mariscal Andrés de Santa Cruz. See item **3049.**

2839 Stoetzer, O. Carlos. Bolívar y el poder moral (PAIGH/H, 95, enero/junio 1983, p. 139–158)
Mostly restates familiar themes in Bolívar's thought, but with some comments on European sources and parallels of "moral power" he proposed at Angostura and included in modified form in Bolivian constitution. This is one new item in Bolívar bicentennial issue of *Revista de Historia de América* otherwise devoted to anthology of writings by and on Bolívar (e.g., Unamuno, Martí, Rodó).

2840 Torrealba Lossi, Mario. Bolívar en diez vertientes: ensayo. Caracas: Colegio de Profesores de Venezuela, 1982. 202 p.: bibl.
Reviews treatment of Bolívar by leading Venezuelan writers of last century and this, by Madariaga, and in recent Venezuelan historiography. Makes valid contribution to study of Bolívar cult even though Germán Carrera Damas is conspicuously absent from bibliography.

2841 Verna, Paul. María Antonia Bolívar y las minas de Aroa. Caracas: Asociación de Escritores Venezolanos, 1977. 60 p. (Cuadernos literarios; 137)
Well researched minimonograph on Bolívar's most important property holding, Aroa copper mines, his effort to sell them to English investors and troubles with sister's management of his affairs.

2842 Zea, Leopoldo. Simón Bolívar: integración en la libertad. México: Editorial Edicol, 1980. 112 p.: bibl. (Temas filosofía y liberación latinoamericana; 10)
Series of essays, with some overlapping, on Bolívar's thought with special reference to problems of Latin American identity and integration. Material is familiar and interpretation is current orthodoxy, all masterfully presented.

GRAN COLOMBIA

2843 Aljure Chalela, Simón. Bibliografía relacionada con el 20 de julio de 1810 (CBR/BCB, 18:1, 1981, p. 132–151)

Lists poetic tributes and newspaper articles as well as pertinent scholarly studies. Certainly not exhaustive, but quite comprehensive.

2844 Araúz, Celestino Andrés. La independencia de Panamá en 1821: antecedentes, balance y proyecciones. Panamá: Academia Panameña de la Historia, 1980. 251 p.: bibl., ill., facsims., appendices.

Best treatment yet of movement for Panamanian independence from Spain and self-annexation to Gran Colombia. Drawing on Spanish, Colombian, Panamanian archives and printed sources, recreates Isthmian developments of independence era with much economic and financial data and identification of individual alignments. Impressive contribution, even if less than definitive.

2845 Bastidas Urresty, Edgar. Las guerras de Pasto. Pasto, Colombia: Ediciones Testimonio, 1979. 184 p.: bibl., map.

Expanded, revised edition of *HLAS 38:3248* and *HLAS 40:3360*. Despite author's solidarity with royalist Pasto in its sufferings at patriots' hands, this is good general account of independence in far southwestern New Granada, with some additional material on Pasto's role in subsequent events to 1863.

2846 Cubitt, David J. La composición de una elite hispanoamericana a la independencia: Guayaquil en 1820 (PAIGH/H, 94, julio/dic. 1982, p. 7–31)

Attempts to draw collective picture of political leadership of Guayaquil, with inclusion of both individual case studies and some modest quantitative analysis. Limited by available data and offers no startling findings—merchants and landowners loom large—but a solid contribution.

2847 ———. The government, the criollo elite and the revolution of 1820 in Guayaquil (IAA, 8:3, 1982, p. 283–295, bibl.)

Soundly researched discussion of Guayaquil in decade preceding its own independence revolution. Argues that colonial order was weakened by political controversy over Spanish constitution, problems in administration of Indian tribute, and growing financial difficulties of coastal merchants.

2848 De Grummond, Jane Lucas. Renato Beluche, smuggler, privateer, and patriot: 1780–1860. Baton Rouge: Louisiana State University Press, 1983. 300 p.: bibl., ill., index.

Unvarnished narrative history of Louisiana-born seaman who became privateer for Cartagena, served later as Gran Colombian naval officer, ultimately settled and died in Venezuela. Fills various gaps in maritime history of independence.

2849 Friede, Juan. La otra verdad: la independencia americana vista por los españoles. 3a. ed. Bogotá: C. Valencia Editores, 1979. 106 p.: bibl.

Very slightly rev. ed. of *HLAS 36:2702.*

2850 González, Asdrúbal. Manuel Piar. Valencia, Venezuela: Vadell, 1979. 213 p.: bibl.

Fine military biography of Curaçao-born pardo officer who played key role in liberation of Guayana only to be executed on charge of stirring race war against Bolívar. Treatment is sympathetic to Piar but accepts ultimate validity of verdict against him.

2851 Mora Mérida, José Luis. Comportamiento político del clero secular de Cartagena de Indias en la pre-independencia (EEHA/AEA, 35, 1978, p. 211–231)

Focusing mainly on Episcopate (two royalist bishops) and to lesser extent other higher clergy, reviews adjustments and maladjustments to changing political environment at different stages of revolution and reconquest.

2852 Nariño, Antonio. Escritos políticos. Selección y recopilación, Gabriel Fonnegra. Bogotá: El Ancora Editores, 1982. 156 p.

Valuable brief compilation, whose contents go from French Declaration of Rights of Man that Nariño translated to his 1823 self-defense before Gran Colombian Senate (in unexpurgated version). Good selection; unfortunately no prologue and only minimal annotations.

2853 *El Patriota de Guayaquil* y otros impresos. Recopilación, introducción y notas por Abel Romeo Castillo. v. 1, 1821. Guayaquil: Banco Central del Ecuador: Archivo Histórico del Guayas, 1981. 125 p.: facsims. (Colección histórica, reproducción de impresos antiguos; no. 1)

Reproduces a collection (not quite

complete) of Guayaquil's first newspaper in its first year of publication, which was also first for printing in Guayaquil. Plus number of printed broadsides or bulletins of same period.

2854 Pérez Jurado, Carlos. Los uniformes de la era emancipadora (VANH/B, 64:154, abril/junio 1981, p. 405–418)
Brings together some scattered information on military uniforms of Venezuela and Gran Colombia, including those of British legionnaires.

2855 Pérez O., Eduardo. La guerra irregular en la independencia de la Nueva Granada y Venezuela: 1810–1830. Tunja: Universidad Pedagógica y Tecnológica de Colombia, 1982. 467 p.: bibl., maps, plates.
Written originally as master's thesis, examines role of guerrilla formations and related tactics on both patriot and royalist sides. Incorporates original archival research on anti-republican Pasto insurgencies and offers useful synthesis elsewhere, though inevitably superficial at times.

2856 Ramos Guédez, José Marcial. Orígenes de la emancipación venezolana: aporte bibliográfico. Caracas: Instituto Panamericano de Geografía e Historia, Comisión de Historia, Comité Orígenes de la Emancipación, 1982. 334 p.: bibl., index (Publicación; no. 25)
As introduction explains, this bibliography really concerns "orígenes y años iniciales" of Venezuelan emancipation; and many of works listed cover also later independence period. Entries (1950 in all) are unfortunately arranged not topically but by "Fuentes," "Libros y Folletos" and "Hemerografía."

2857 La Revolución de Quito, 1809–1822: según los primeros relatos e historias por autores extranjeros. Selección, estudio introductorio y notas, Jorge Salvador Lara. Quito: Corporación Editora Nacional, 1982. 486 p.: bibl., map (Colección Ecuador, testimonios de autores extranjeros; 1)
Authors anthologized here—William B. Stevenson, Mariano Torrente, and Colombian classic historians—are all well known and accessible, but Salvador Lara's introduction makes net contribution. He gives useful overview of historiography of Ecuadorian independence, with more detailed comments on its treatment by Stevenson *et al.*

2858 Suceso de la invasión y toma del Puerto Real de la Vela de Coro y Ciudad de Coro, año de 1806: diario de un oficial realista (VANH/B, 64:255, julio/sept. 1981, p. 714–722)
Some new light on royalist response to Miranda's abortive 1806 liberation attempt.

2859 Vila, Marco Aurelio. Josep Sardá, un general català en le independéncia d'América. Barcelona: R. Dalmau, 1980. 125 p.: bibl. (Episodis de la história; 245)
Unpretentious short biography of Catalan who served Napoleon, joined Mina expedition to Mexico, later took part in liberation of Tierra Firme. Stayed on in Gran Colombia and met death in 1834 for conspiracy against Santander's presidency.

2860 Waddell, D.A.G. Gran Bretaña y la independencia de Venezuela y Colombia. Palabras preliminares por Pedro Grases. Caracas: Ministerio de Educación, Dirección de Información y Relaciones, División de Publicaciones, 1983. 278 p., 3 folded leaves of plates: ill.
Though focusing on role of British authorities in Caribbean area, this methodical overview also deals with policy of government in London and, to lesser extent, activities of British merchants and adventurers. Gives up-to-date synthesis of previously published materials and incorporates results of original research in London, Bogotá, Caracas.

PERU

2861 Chassin, Joëlle and **Martine Dauzier.** La participation des Indiens au mouvement d'indépendance: le soulèvement de Huánuco, Pérou, en 1812 (CDAL, 23:1, semestre 1981, p. 7–45)
Another look at debated significance of Indian participation in Huánuco uprising. Based largely on published documents, concludes that disaffected Creoles were instigators in this particular case and that Indians' aims and role, despite their obvious grievances, were ambiguous.

2862 Hünefeldt, Christine. Cimarrones, bandoleros y milicianos: 1821

(PUC/H, 3:2, dic. 1979, p. 71–88)
Looks at role of blacks and pardos in
military service and bands of runaways, in
year of San Martín's occupation of Lima.
Related to author's "Los Negros de Lima:
1800–1830" (see *HLAS 42:3085*).

2863 Pacheco Vélez, César. José Gregorio
Paredes y el primer patriotismo republicano (PMNH/HC, 13/14, 1981,
p. 171–194)
"Versión ampliada" of address honoring Peruvian prócer on 200th anniversary of
his birth (1778); based on author's extensive
research concerning him. Traces career of
limeño aristocrat Paredes as moderate autonomist in era of Abascal, patriot publicist and
collaborator with San Martín regime, ultimately diplomatic agent for Bolívar. Also
published in *Revista de la Academia Diplomática del Perú* (Lima, 21, enero/dic. 1980,
p. 139–164).

2864 Ratto Ciarlo, José. Choquehuanca y la
contrarrevolución. Caracas: Comité
Ejecutivo del Bicentenario de Simón Bolívar,
1980. 152 p.: bibl., ill. (Colección Contorno
bolivariano; 5)
This study of mestizo José Domingo
Choquehuanca, mainly known for his pane-
gyric to Bolívar, is often rambling and includes irrelevant material but has value for
study of *bolivarianismo* in Peru. Also follows
subsequent career of Choquehuanca as minor
political figure and reformist in Peruvian
highlands.

2865 Vergara Arias, Gustavo. Montoneras y
guerrillas en la etapa de la emancipación del Perú (EEHA/AEA, 32, 1975,
p. 509–540)
For those who do not have time to read
or access to *HLAS 40:3379*.

ALTO PERU

2866 Arze Aguirre, René Danilo. Participación popular en la independencia de
Bolivia. La Paz: Organización de los Estados
Americanos, 1979. 271 p.: appendices, bibl.,
ill., index.
Excellent, carefully researched examination—with useful tables and appendices,
and running commentary on sources—of

condition of Bolivian masses, Indians especially, on eve of independence and their participation in assorted protests and uprisings. Mainly covers period 1809–11 and
thus avoids dealing with popular participation or lack of it in final achievement of
independence.

2867 Bidondo, Emilio A. La Guerra de la Independencia en el Alto Perú. Buenos
Aires: Círculo Militar, 1979. 283 p., 1 folded
leaf of plates: bibl., ill. (Biblioteca del oficial;
v. 700. Colección histórico-militar)
Narrative military history, with numerous documentary and other "anexos."
Part of monographic series of Argentine military's "Biblioteca del Oficial," it naturally
emphasizes activities of Platine forces, but
covers entire story 1808–25. Nothing new,
but useful manual.

2868 Polisenský, Josef V. Tadeo Haenke y la
Guerra de la Independencia (PAN/ES,
8, 1981, p. 103–115)
Brief note, with some new details, on
Bohemian scientist who came to Alto Perú in
1790s under Spanish official auspices, eventually had dealings with revolutionary authorities as well, and died there 1816 under
slightly ambiguous circumstances.

2869 Santos Vargas, José. Diario de un
comandante de la independencia
americana, 1814–1825. Transcripción, introducción e índices de Gunnar Mendoza L.
México: Siglo Veintiuno, 1982. 513 p., 2 p.
of plates: ill., indexes (Colección América
nuestra; 34. Caminos de liberación)
Basic primary source on Bolivian independence, written in popular and realistic
style. Fine introduction by Gunnar Mendoza,
glossary, and full indexing further enhance its
value.

CHILE

2870 Cubitt, David J. ¿Cuándo se decidió
Lord Cochrane a atacar Valdivia?
(SCHG/R, 148, 1980, p. 177–190)
By exhaustive analysis of primary
sources, manuscript and printed, sets out to
revise accepted views on question posed in
title and relate it to larger strategic and political issues.

Méndez, Luz María. Instituciones y problemas de la minería en Chile, 1787–1826. See item **2749.**

2870a Moreno Martín, Armando. La misión del Coronel Parlamentario Clemente Lantaño en Chiloé (SCHG/R, 150, 1982, p. 66–95)

Detailed account of former royalist colonel's role in O'Higgins' attempt to negotiate 1821 surrender of royalist forces holding Chiloé. Useful footnote to independence history. [T.C. Wright]

2871 ———. Venturas y desventuras de Fray Almirall (SCHG/R, 148, 1980, p. 137–155)

Original research on second or third-rank figure whose historiographic image has been somewhat negative. But this Catalan Franciscan, adviser to successive royalist commanders, is seen as increasingly favorable to patriots.

RIO DE LA PLATA

2872 Assunção, Fernando O. and **Wilfredo Pérez.** Artigas. v. 1, El jefe de los orientales. Montevideo: Editorial Próceres, 1982. 1 v.: bibl., ill. (some col.)

First installment of popularly written but well documented and extensively illustrated life of Artigas. Volume covers family antecedents and early career up to start of independence struggle in Uruguay.

2873 Bidondo, Emilio A. Coronel Juan Guillermo de Marquiegui: un personaje americano al servicio de España, 1777–1840. Madrid: Servicio Histórico Militar, 1982. 245 p., 5 leaves of plates: appendices, bibl., ill., maps.

Biography of jujeño royalist who served in Alto Perú and on Argentine northern front. Extensively researched, with documentary appendices.

2874 Bose, Walter B.L. Las postas en las provincias del norte y Cuyo, en la época del Congreso de Tucumán (JEHM/R, 9:2, 1980, p. 453–483, bibl., ill., maps)

Describes system of post houses and traces communication routes in North and West of independence-era Argentina. By lifelong specialist in these matters.

2875 Cervera, Fernando Guillermo. Las baterías de Santa Fe: 1810–1814 (ANH/IE, 28, enero/junio 1980, p. 221–246, bibl., maps)

Rather specialized study of military and provincial urban history, on role of Santa Fe in struggle against river squadrons from Spanish-held Montevideo.

2876 Destéfani, Laurio Hedelvio. Belgrano y el mar. Prólogo por V. Mario Quartaruolo. Buenos Aires: Fundación Argentina de Estudios Marítimos, 1979. 203 p.: bibl., ill.

Dealing more with Belgrano's contributions as Secretary of Consulado before independence than with his role as patriot leader, reviews his thinking and actions on foreign trade, privateering, port development etc. Solidly documented positivist history.

2877 Documentos para la historia del General Don Manuel Belgrano. Buenos Aires: Instituto Belgraniano Central, 1982. 1 v.: bibl., ill., indexes.

Vol. 1 of planned new documentary collection that will substantially add to classic *Documentos del Archivo de Belgrano* (Buenos Aires: Museo Mitre, 1913). This volume covers personal and family background, Consulado service, involvement in Carlota intrigue. Technically leaves something to be desired, as numerous items are printed with unexplained deletions or simply as *extractos*.

Gallardo, Guillermo. Viaje a Buenos Aires del primer agente comercial de los Estados Unidos de Norteamérica. See item **1886.**

2878 Gandía, Enrique de. Artigas y la expedición de Cádiz (IHGB/R, 325, out./dez. 1979, p. 5–23)

In rather more words than necessary, argues plausibly that *porteños'* refusal to aid Artigas against Portuguese was less selfish than traditionally held; it reflected realistic understanding that Portugal's presence in Uruguay effectively prevented cooperation with Spain in Platine reconquest.

2879 García, Flavio A. El "ciudadano" Felipe Cardoso. Montevideo: Dirección General de Extensión Universitaria, 1980. 93 p.: facsims.

Original research on second-rank figure: Buenos Aires-born soldier who aligned himself with more radical wing of May Revolution and ultimately Artigas, whom he served in various civil capacities (d. 1818, Uruguay).

2880 ———. Vademecum uruguayo-sanmartiniano. Montevideo: Dirección General de Extensión Universitaria, División de Publicaciones y Ediciones, 1981. 125 p.: bibl., ill.

Contains two rather different parts: 1) San Martín's family antecedents, with special reference to father's military service connections with Montevideo; and 2) relationship between San Martín himself and Uruguayan affairs, including his abortive return to Río de la Plata in 1829 and Uruguayan honors since his death. Conventional but authoritative, with useful chronologies.

2881 García-Godoy, Christián. La educación de Tomás Godoy Cruz (PAIGH/H, 94, julio/dic. 1982, p. 115–131, bibl.)

Detailed look at intellectual formation, in Córdoba and Santiago de Chile, of *mendocino* who would become San Martín's close collaborator at regional level.

2882 Güemes documentado. v. 5, Untitled. v. 6, Epistolario. v. 7, Untitled. Edited by Luis Güemes. Buenos Aires: Plus Ultra, 1979–1982. 3 v. (473, 527, 447 p.): bibl., ill., indexes.

Continuation of *HLAS 44:2833a.* Vol. 5 (untitled) contains documents (1817–18); vol. 6, *Epistolario*, has letters to and from Güemes (1811–12); vol. 7 (untitled) is devoted to his genealogy, "Catolicidad," and miscellaneous special topics including *fuero gaucho.*

2883 Guerro, César H. José Ignacio de la Roza, un apóstol de la libertad. San Juan, Argentina: Comisión Pro Homenaje al Dr. José Ignacio de la Roza, 1981. 376 p.: bibl., ill.

Biography of San Juan civilian patriot who was overthrown as teniente gobernador in 1820 "anarchy" and died in exile. Narrative of events, based on documentary research, by competent local historian.

2883a Gutiérrez, Pedro Rafael. La bandera argentina: origen de las banderas centroamericanas. San José: Ediciones Lena, 1983. 48 p., 12 p. of plates: ill.

Elaborates on Carlos A. Ferro's assertion that when Bouchard's ships visited Central America's coast in 1819 Argentina's flag was adopted as model. [R. Etchepareborda]

2884 Levaggi, Abelardo. Espíritu del constitucionalismo argentino de la primera mitad del siglo XIX (Revista de Historia del Derecho [Instituto de Investigaciones de Historia del Derecho, Buenos Aires] 9, 1981, p. 239–301)

Original treatment of familiar topic, seeking to distinguish relative importance of North American, European, and traditional/autochthonous influence on Argentine constitutional theory and practice, at both national and provincial levels. Of methodological as well as substantive interest. Tends to revise downward supposed influence of US model. Covers 1810–52 but with most detailed treatment of revolutionary period.

2885 Martínez Valverde, Carlos. Santiago de Liniers en el Río de la Plata (SHM/RHM, 26:52, 1980, p. 7–46, bibl., maps, plates)

Clear, succinct, informative recounting by Spanish naval historian of Liniers' service in defense of Buenos Aires against British, then a viceroy, and as counter-revolutionary in 1810. Not original research, but well done and nicely illustrated.

2886 Moreno, Mariano. Artículos que *La Gazeta* no llegó a publicar. Recopilados y comentados por Eduardo Dürnhöfer. Buenos Aires: Casa Pardo, 1975. 126 p.: facsims.

Previously unpublished writings on religion, French Revolution, Voltaire and Rousseau, which further illuminate intellectual roots of Moreno's position as leader of radical wing of May Revolution. Dürnhöfer adds introduction and appendix, latter being additional evidence for Moreno's authorship of controversial 1810 *Plan de operaciones.*

2887 Peña, Roberto I. El doctor Manuel A. de Castro: gobernador de Córdoba, 1817–1820 (ANH/B, 51, 1978, p. 271–296)

Examines provincial administration—its dealings with Church, university, *montoneras*, etc.—of jurist who ruled Córdoba toward end of Directory period. Well researched in Córdoba archives, clearly organized and presented.

2888 ———. El Dr. Manuel Antonio de Castro y el Colegio Universitario de Montserrat (JPHC/R, 10, 1982, p. 57–84)

Mostly documents with connecting commentary, on problems of secondary education in Córdoba during Castro's governorship.

2889 Pérez, Joaquín. Artigas, San Martín y los proyectos monárquicos en el Río de la Plata y Chile, 1818–1820. Buenos Aires: Editorial y Librería Misión, 1979. 280 p.: bibl., facsims.

Important study (see *HLAS 26:1001*) now finally in book form.

2889a Ramallo, José María. Los grupos políticos en la revolución de Mayo. 3a. ed., corr. Buenos Aires: Ediciones Macchi, 1983. 115 p.: bibl.

Relevant essay illustrates emergence of emancipation movement. Disagrees with accepted views that three principal groups were led by Alzaga, Castelli, and Saavedra. [R. Etchepareborda]

2889b Rato de Sambuccetti, Susana. La revolución de Mayo: interpretaciones conflictivas. Buenos Aires: Ediciones Siglo Veinte, 1983. 254 p.: bibl. (La Nueva historia argentina)

Vol. 1 of ambitious project presents different and controversial interpretations of various issues. Each essay is accompanied by well selected set of documents. [R. Etchepareborda]

2890 Sanz, Luis Santiago. Proyección internacional de la *Declaración del 9 de julio de 1816* (ANH/B, 52, 1979, p. 79–89)

Based on published sources, reviews process of gaining diplomatic recognition of independence from 1816 declaration to final Spanish recognition in 1860.

2891 Tonda, Américo A. El Dr. Agüero en el Colegio de la Unión del Sud (JPHC/R, 10, 1982, p. 43–56)

Research note on secondary education at Buenos Aires 1818–20. Emphasizes personal role of Córdoba cleric José Eusebio Agüero somewhat less than storm stirred up by an Italian of Voltairean leanings on teaching staff.

2892 ———. Los frailes que conoció San Martín en San Lorenzo (ANH/IE, 29, julio/dic. 1980, p. 197–227)

Though title might suggest this is an item of solely antiquarian or filiopietistic interest, it is actually a well researched look at Franciscan Convent of San Lorenzo, on Paraná River, site of San Martín's first battle on home soil. Examines both origins of friars and their relations with revolutionary authorities.

2893 ———. El Obispo Orellana y la Revolución. Córdoba, Argentina: Junta Provincial de Historia de Córdoba, 1981. 540 p.: bibl. (Libros de la Junta; 7)

Detailed, authoritatively researched study of peninsular royalist caught by outbreak of revolution as Bishop of Córdoba and eventually sent to exile. Major contribution on ecclesiastical repercussions of independence movement.

19th and 20th Centuries Colombia, Venezuela and Ecuador

WINTHROP W. WRIGHT, *Associate Professor of History, University of Maryland, College Park*

COLOMBIA: AS IN THE PAST, the quantity of material on modern Colombia has fallen behind that of Venezuela, but the quality has remained high. As demonstrated by a series entitled "Pensadores Políticos Colombianos," Colombians still have a propensity to collect documents from collections of their great political leaders. This often uneven document series does provide a good cross section of Colombia's many political factions. It does not show any particular partisan position, and includes examples of the writings and speeches of men such as Gilberto Alzate Avendaño (item **2894**), Abel Cardonell (item **2896**), Jorge Eliécer Gaitán (item **2899**), Laureano Gómez (item **2900**), Alfonso López Pumarejo (item **2903**), Mariano Ospina Pérez (item **2904**), Eduardo Santos (item **2907**), and Hernán Toro Agudelo (item **2908**).

Taxation, credit, and regionalism have interested several scholars. One, Malcolm Deas (item **2897**), has reviewed the difficulties encountered by 19th-century governments as they attempted to raise revenue. According to Deas, who relied extensively on the *Memorias de Hacienda,* Colombia's poor exporting record made taxation an unsatisfactory means of raising public funds. Richard P. Hyland's excellent article (item **2901**) shows the mechanism by which Colombian elites maintained control over land, labor, capital, and political power. His essay also touches upon the regional nature of Colombia, and argues that nation building was not a unitary process, but rather resulted in part from a credit network created by regional banks which governments used to promote domestic integration. Marco Palacios also described regionalism in his article on localism and Colombian politics (item **2905**). Like Hyland, Palacios concluded that most Colombian policies through 1930 were incompatible with national unity. Loy's piece on the llaneros (item **2927**) complements this observation in that she, too, emphasizes the fragmentation of Colombia into separate states and regions.

VENEZUELA: Once again, Venezuelan historians have produced an unprecedented number of studies on 20th-century topics. Much credit for this increase should go to Ramón Velásquez. He has encouraged young Venezuelan historians to write contemporary history, and they have heeded his call. The Ediciones Centauro press has published a singularly large proportion of the new monographs.

International relations has joined the Gómez and Betancourt eras as an important historical topic. As Judith Ewell so clearly demonstrates in a recent article on Venezuelan geopolitical thinkers (item **2918**), Venezuelans have a deep-seated interest in their role in hemispheric and world affairs. Among the best diplomatic studies, Pablo Ojer has put together two carefully documented reviews of the disputes between Venezuela and Colombia for possession of the Golfo de Venezuela (items **2928** and **2929**). Like Ojer, Armando Rojas (item **2933**) and Freddy Vivas Gallardo (item **2938**) also made extensive use of Venezuelan and foreign diplomatic archives. As a result, they have written solid and innovative monographs on several aspects of Venezuela's foreign policies during the late 19th and early 20th centuries.

The post–1935 period has received a great deal of attention. Robert J. Alexander has written a biography of Rómulo Betancourt (item **2910**), which while neither definitive nor official is the best available in any language. Two works, one by Julio Godio (item **2922**) and another by Alberto J. Pla *et al.* (item **2937**) deal with Venezuelan labor following the death of Gómez. A seemingly endless stream of titles have treated aspects of the *trienio*, the administrations of Rómulo Gallegos and Marcos Pérez-Jiménez, as well as the post–1958 period. Not many merit notice in this short essay, but all portend a healthy future for the study of modern Venezuelan history. Among those worth mentioning, Steven Ellner continues to unravel the political threads of the Venezuelan left during the 1930s and 1940s (item **2917**), and Fred Jongking (item **2925**) and Jesús Caballero Ortiz (item **2914**) have offered provocative investigations of the Venezuelan industrialization process.

John Lombardi's general history of Venezuela (item **2617**) gives a clear overview of the formation of a modern nation, with emphasis upon the role of Caracas as a primatial city. That book and a short article by Robert Lavenda (see *HLAS 45: 8270*) stress the importance of Caracas in the development of Venezuela, especially during the 19th century. In sharp contrast, Jane Loy (item **2927**) describes the llaneros in somewhat romantic terms as individuals left behind by modernization. In another essay related to the theme of modernization, María Elena González Deluca (item **2923**) explains the failure of the British to establish the same type of economic empire in Venezuela as they did in other Latin American nations.

ECUADOR: In contrast with the other Gran Colombian nations, Ecuador's output seems meager. With so much history remaining to be written, the few works listed in this *Handbook* hardly serve to offer either an indication of the direction in which Ecuadorian historians are moving or give a clear picture of where they have been. At this juncture two points seem clear: 1) topics related to working class issues have appealed to a new generation of Marxist historians, who have eschewed the traditional great man approach to modern history; and 2) despite the shift in focus to socioeconomic issues, politics still remains a central theme for the great majority of those dealing with modern Ecuador.

A history of the Ecuadorian labor movement by Osvaldo Albornoz Peralta (item **2940**) offers an example of the trend. Essentially a chronological analysis of labor since the 1920s, this work attributes to workers a number of accomplishments which have transformed society. That thesis certainly fits into a developmental scheme spelled out by Oswaldo Hurtado (see *HLAS 44:2900*). In an older essay, Agustín Cueva (item **2941**) also focused upon Ecuador's class structure following the 1929 world Depression. John Martz also contributed a useful essay on the evolution of Ecuadorian Marxists since the mid-1920s, in which he chronicles the success that both socialists and communists have had (item **2942**).

COLOMBIA

2894 Alzate Avendaño, Gilberto. Obras selectas. Presentación y compilación, Jorge Mario Eastman. Bogotá: Cámara de Representantes, 1979. 619 p. (Colección Pensadores políticos colombianos; t. 7)

Historical writings, political articles, and speeches, selected from *La Patria* of Manizales, *Eco Nacional*, and *Diario de Colombia* of Bogotá. Covers period 1934–60. Good series of editorials written for *Diario de Colombia* during 1950s.

Arango, Mariano. El café en Colombia, 1930–1958: producción, circulación y política. See *HLAS 45:3264*.

Bustamante Roldán, Darío. Efectos económicos del papel moneda durante la Regeneración. See *HLAS 45:3268*.

2895 Calle, Benjamín de la. El comercio en Medellín, 1900–1930: fotografías. Medellín: Fenalco Antioquia, 1982. 10 p., 48 leaves of plates: bibl., chiefly ill.

Photographs of Medellín's business district by photographer Benjamín Calle (1869–1934). Not only shows businesses, but also street scenes, interiors of industries, important buildings, and family groups.

2896 Carbonell, Abel. Obras selectas. Presentación y compilación, Ramiro Carranza Coronado. Bogotá: Imprenta Nacional, 1981. 388 p. (Colección Pensadores políticos colombianos; t. 27)

Three works written 1928–37 by conservative politician from Barranquilla. They include lectures he gave at Universidad Atlántica (1934–37). Often critical of conservative governments, Carbonell presents clear thoughts of one who wanted neither to maintain status quo nor to bring about change in the distant future through revolutionary activities.

Coral Quintero, Laureano. Historia del movimiento sindical del magisterio. See *HLAS 45:4393*.

2897 Deas, Malcolm. The fiscal problem of nineteenth-century Colombia (JLAS, 14:2, Nov. 1982, p. 287–328, tables)

Based extensively on 19th-century *Memorias de hacienda*, which Deas says "contain a whole particular political economy of poverty" (p. 208). Reviews sources of revenue available to Colombian governments, especially through taxation. Sees exports as essential to government revenues. Yet, Colombia's poor exporting record made taxation an unsatisfactory means of raising public funds. Monopolies did not work, either.

Ensayos sobre historia económica colombiana. See *HLAS 45:3275.*

Fajardo, Darío et al. Campesinado y capitalismo en Colombia. See *HLAS 45:8245.*

Fierro, Marco F. The development of industrial capital in Colombia. See *HLAS 45:8248.*

2898 Forero Benavides, Abelardo. Grandes fechas. Bogotá: División de Edición DANE, 1979. 245 p.: bibl. (Colección Escritores paralamentarios; t. 1)

Selected writings of 20th-century liberal intellectual. Touches history, sociology, and nationalism.

2899 Gaitán, Jorge Eliécer. Obras selectas. Compilación y presentación, Jorge Mario Eastman. Bogotá: Imprenta Nacional, 1979. 2 v.: bibl. (Colección Pensadores políticos colombianos; t. 5–6)

Writings and speeches by Gaitán, mostly of his juridical positions, including his doctoral thesis on penal law (1927), essays on criminal sociology, and in appendix his debates in Congress on Las bananeras (1929). Last entries from 1940–43 cover education, and interview given to *El Siglo* (July 1943).

2900 Gómez, Laureano. Obras selectas. v. 1. Compilación y presentación, Alberto Bermúdez. Bogotá: Cámara de Representantes, 1981. 836 p. (Colección Pensadores políticos colombianos; t. 15)

Collection of newspaper articles and speeches by Gómez (1909–38). Excellent source for following the political evolution of leading Colombian conservative. Presents Gómez's opposition to liberal policies before World War II.

2901 Hyland, Richard P. A fragile prosperity: credit and agrarian structure in the Cauca Valley, Colombia, 1851–87 (HAHR, 62:3, Aug. 1982, p. 369–406, tables)

Studies mechanisms by which elites maintained control over labor, land, capital, and political power in changing regional society. Credit was central element as labor moved from bondage to free labor; agriculture from subsistence to commercial; and credit from Church to modern banking. Argues that nation building was not a unitary process in Colombia. But credit network created by regional banks could be used to promote domestic integration and give meaning to abstract concept of nation. "Paper money was, therefore, at one and the same time a symbol of trust and a symbol of tyranny" (p. 406).

2902 Kline, Harvey F. Colombia: portrait of unity and diversity. Boulder, Colo.: Westview Press, 1983. 169 p.: bibl., ill. (Westview profiles. Nations of contemporary Latin America)

Overly simple and popularized view of Colombia for non-specialists. Chapters deal with land, people, history, economy, and foreign affairs. Well illustrated, highly readable but often subjective and brief.

2903 López Pumarejo, Alfonso. Obras selectas. Presentación y compilación, Jorge Mario Eastman. Bogotá: Cámara de Representantes, 1979–1980. 2 v.: bibl. (Colección Pensadores políticos colombianos; t. 10–11)

Vol. 1 includes articles and political statements from first presidential campaign and messages from first presidency (1934–38). Gives López's philosophy of governing and presents his attitudes toward military. Vol. 2 treats later period and includes political speeches between presidencies (1943–45) as well as important speeches from second administration and late speeches given 1959. Appendix has texts of important laws (Regimen de Tierras of 1936 and Reform of Constitution of 1936). Both volumes, taken from newspapers and speeches to National Assembly, give López's basic philosophy and national ideals. For political scientist's comment, see *HLAS 43:6354.*

Loy, Jane M. Horsemen of the tropics: a comparative view of the *llaneros* in the history of Venezuela and Colombia. See item **2927.**

Ojer, Pablo. La década fundamental en la controversia de límites entre Venezuela y Colombia: 1881–1891. See item **2928.**

———. El Golfo de Venezuela: una síntesis histórica. See item **2929**.

2904 Ospina Pérez, Mariano. Obras selectas. Compilación, Francisco Plata Bermúdez. Bogotá: Cámara de Representantes, 1982. 1 v.: bibl. (Colección Pensadores políticos colombianos; t. 14)

Consists of 85 selections by Ospina (written 1925–48) as selected by his son to present breadth and direction of Ospina's thought on national problems.

2905 Palacios, Marco. La fragmentación regional de las clases dominantes en Colombia: una perspectiva histórica (*in* State and region in Latin America: a workshop. Editors, G.A. Banck, R. Buve, and L. Van Vroonhoven. Amsterdam: Centrum voor Studie en Documentatie van Latijns-Amerika, 1981, p. 41–75, bibl.)

Responds to basic observation that localism has characterized Colombian politics. By 1930, average Colombian still identified more with region than nation. One reason, Colombian elites never felt threatened by popular pressures, either during or after independence movement. Absence of authentic hegemonic class encouraged regional fragmentation of political power. Free trade advocated by 19th-century liberals also led to type of economic development incompatible with national unity.

2906 Restrepo Uribe, Jorge and **Luz Posada de Greiff.** Medellín, su origen progreso y desarrollo. Medellín: Servigráficas, 1981. 655 p.: bibl., ill. (some col.)

Useful but not interpretive source of photos, maps, pamphlets, guidebooks, and other documents.

2907 Santos, Eduardo. Obras selectas: editoriales del diario *El Tiempo*, 1913–1930. Compilación y presentación, Jorge Mario Eastman. Bogotá: Cámara de Representantes, 1981. 702 p.: bibl. (Colección Pensadores políticos colombianos; t. 13)

Consists of *El Tiempo* editorials (1913–30). Santos, part of generation of young nationalistic intellectuals/politicians who began strong anti-imperialist campaign in post–1910 period, wrote on international relations, politics, patriotism, and socioeconomic problems such as educational reform, social conflict, and taxation.

2908 Toro Agudelo, Hernán. Obras selectas. Compilación, Jaime Sierra García, Ramiro Carranza Coronado. Prólogo, Jorge Mario Eastman. Bogotá: Cámara de Representantes, 1982. 478 p. (Colección Pensadoares políticos colombianos; t. 28)

Writings and lectures by leading 20th-century Liberal thinker who helped formulate the party's views on social reform. Wrote extensively on land reform. Served as Minister of Agriculture under Alberto Lleras Camargo, and briefly as Supreme Court magistrate.

2909 Torres Londoño, Fernando. *El Tiempo, El Siglo* y la reforma constitucional de 1936 (Cuadernos de Filosofía y Letras [Facultad de Filosofía y Letras de la Universidad de Los Andes, Bogotá] 4 : 3 / 4, julio/dic. 1981, p. 209–245)

Compares Liberal and Conservative positions on central issues in the constitutional reform of 1936 as respectively presented in *El Tiempo* and *El Siglo*. Whereas Conservatives saw end of personal freedom and property through increased state intervention, Liberals predicted reforms would usher in era of intelligent and socially responsible government. Debates carried seeds of violence that ultimately broke out between the two factions.

Zapata Cuéncar, Heriberto. Antioquia, periódicos de provincia. See *HLAS 45 : 60*.

VENEZUELA

2910 Alexander, Robert Jackson. Rómulo Betancourt and the transformation of Venezuela. New Brunswick: Transaction Books, 1982. 737 p.: bibl., index.

Although not definitive or official, best biography to date in any language. Betancourt was stricken while reading the proofs. Praises him but also points out his weaknesses and errors. Based largely on interviews with some 125 individuals, including over 40 with Betancourt. His personal archives were not open to Alexander. For political scientist's comment, see *HLAS 45:6251*.

2911 Anzola, Juvenal. De Caracas a San Cristóbal. 2a. ed. (facsimilar). Caracas:

Biblioteca de Autores y Temas Tachirenses, 1981. 226 p.: ill. (Biblioteca de autores y temas tachirenses; 79)

First published 1913, facsimile makes available classic statement of Tachiran attitudes. Good descriptions of Táchira at beginning of century. Excellent source of local color.

2912 Avendaño Lugo, José Ramón. El militarismo en Venezuela: la dictadura de Pérez Jiménez. Caracas: Ediciones Centauro, 1982. 393 p. (Colección XXV aniversario del 23 de enero de 1958)

Concludes that 1948 military coup marked armed forces' coming to power in institutional form. Coup gave way to dictatorship that let US penetrate Venezuelan economy in order to establish neocolonialism. Claims that Pérez Jiménez tried to form his new nationalism in order to accommodate military hegemony. Relies mostly on secondary sources.

Blanco Muñoz, Agustín. Oposición ciudad-campo en Venezuela. See *HLAS 45:8267.*

2913 Caballero, Manuel. La sección venezolana de la Internacional Comunista: un tema para el estudio de las ideas en el siglo XX venezolano (*in* Encuentro de Historiadores Latinoamericanos y del Caribe, 2nd, Caracas, 1977. Los estudios históricos en América Latina. Caracas: Universidad Central de Venezuela, Facultad de Humanidades y Educación, Escuela de Historia, 1979, v. 1, t. 2, p. 798–807)

Very generalized discussion of Venezuelan leftists' connections with Third International (1935–43).

2914 Caballero Ortiz, Jesús. Antecedentes históricos de las empresas públicas en Venezuela (ACPS/B, 38:84, abril/junio 1981, p. 79–89)

Points out that both before and after 1928 founding of first public companies, Venezuela's tradition of economic liberalism worked against State's participation in economy. Decisions in Gómez era allowed for evolution of policy that let government participate in diverse sectors of national economy, including public services, airlines, petroleum, maritime transport, and credit activities.

2915 Cipriano Castro en la caricatura mundial. Recopilador de las caricaturas, y fotografías, William Sullivan. Prólogo, Jesús Sanoja Hernández. Caracas: Instituto Autónomo Biblioteca Nacional: Fundación para el Rescate del Acervo Documental Venezolano, 1981. 243 p.: bibl., ill.

Caricatures of Cipriano Castro collected by William Sullivan from US and French newspapers, magazines, and journals (1902–09). Prologue by Jesús Sanoja Hernández. Excellent period photographs. Most caricatures cover Anglo-German debt blockage and related subjects.

2916 Documentos para la historia de Acción Democrática. v. 1, 1936–1941. Compilación, José Agustín Catalá. Caracas: Ediciones Centauro, 1981. 409 p.: bibl. (Los Partidos políticos en Venezuela)

Documents cover clandestine activities of Partido Democrático Nacional (precursor of Acción Democrática) and abortive 1941 candidacy of Rómulo Gallegos. Includes early platforms, manifestos, and statements by party leaders, campaign speeches as well as documents related to A.D.'s organization in 1941.

2917 Ellner, Steve. Factionalism in the Venezuelan Communist Movement: 1937–1948 (SS, 45:1, Spring 1981, p. 52–70)

Analysis of Venezuelan Communist movement's division into two factions. First viewed bourgeoisie as unreliable ally, second considered them as positive force. Shows split had regional as well as ideological origins. Good discussion of Browderism and dilemma posed by Acción Democrática's populist movement which some communists saw as having similar goals. For political scientist's comment, see *HLAS 45:6258.*

2918 Ewell, Judith. The development of Venezuelan geopolitical analysis since World War II (SAGE/JIAS, 24:3, Aug. 1982, p. 295–320)

Venezuelans have complex problem in defining their nation's role since it is a Caribbean, Andean, and Amazonian state. Writers agree that Venezuela's own objectives must be defined in terms of limited autonomy within US zone of influence. Frontier questions divide hard-liners from moderates. Former want to regain 1810 boundaries, latter emphasize security gains. Venezuelan geo-political writers agree their country can integrate South America and Caribbean. For political scientist's comment, see *HLAS 45:7433.*

2919 Flórez, Carlos M. Gómez: patriarca del crimen, el terror y el trabajo forzado en Venezuela. Prólogo, Gustavo Machado. Caracas: Editorial Ateneo de Caracas, 1980. 159 p. (Colección Testimonios)

Account of life as political prisoner under Gómez, written by Salvadoran journalist/revolutionary. First published 1933 in Bogotá as clandestine *folleto* and republished 1938 in Managua. Anti-imperialist critic of US, Flórez took part in 1929 invasion of Venezuela from Curaçao. Describes conditions and prisoner treatment in Gómez's jails. First hand account of forced labor.

2920 Franceschi González, Napoleón. Caudillos y caudillismo en la historia de Venezuela: ensayos históricos, Venezuela, 1830–1930. Caracas: EXIMCO, 1979. 165 p.: bibl.

Argues that political parties shared common liberal ideology at outset of Venezuela's national history. Sees caudillo or personal leadership as product of civil wars that persisted until Venezuela's conversion from agricultural to oil exporter. Emphasizes Guzmán Blanco period. Concluding chapter reviews various interpretations of Venezuelan caudillismo.

2921 García Ponce, Antonio. Panorámica de un período crucial en la historia venezolana: estudio de los años 1840–1847. Caracas: Academia Nacional de la Historia, 1982. 135 p.: bibl. (El Libro menor; 29)

Treats 1840–47 as pivotal political period. Stresses contributions of free press, liberal constitutional opposition, popular violence, and new generation of political thinkers. Páez forced to let Monagas come to power. By 1846 oligarchs held power by military force after liberal rebellion, but could not maintain their political position. As result, liberalism emerged as source of hegemonistic political currents during latter half of 19th century.

2922 Godio, Julio. Venezuela: la gran huelga petrolera de 1936 y la lucha por la democracia (Desarrollo Indoamericano

[Barranquilla, Colombia] 15:64, nov. 1980, p. 39–50, table]

Provocative review of political, social, and economic implications of petroleum workers general strike begun Dec. 1936 at Zulia and Falcón. Argues that despite government and company repression, strike facilitated shift towards broadly based democratic political environment. Working class solidarity and widespread support for strikes was part of anti-gomecista reaction. Written by Argentine scholar as part of larger study of Venezuelan working class movements.

2923 González Deluca, María Elena. Los intereses británicos y la política en Venezuela en las últimas décadas del siglo XIX (UB/BA, 22:30, 1980, p. 89–123)

Industrial revolution led British to expand to Latin America, but 19th-century internal situation in Venezuela and its limited role in world market led to results different from Southern Cone's and Brazil's. German merchant houses and strong anti-British sentiments exacerbated problem. Typical pattern of late 19th-century European immigrants, capital, and railways did not work in Venezuela because right conditions did not exist. Entirely based on British sources. For political scientist's comment, see *HLAS 45:7434.*

2924 Irazábal, Carlos. Hacia la democracia: contribución al estudio de la historia económica, política, social de Venezuela. 4a. ed. Caracas: Editorial Ateneo de Caracas, 1979. 279 p.: bibl. (Colección Historia)

Fourth ed. of 1939 classic.

2925 Jongkind, Fred. Venezuelan industrialization, dependent or autonomous?: a survey of national and foreign participation in the industrial development of a Latin American OPEC country. Amsterdam: CEDLA, 1981. 229 p.: bibl. (CEDLA incidentele publicaties; 21)

Modest empirical study based on data gathered while author worked at Caracas Instituto de Estudios Superiores de Administración. Centers on questionnaire sent to business executives. Evidence leads author to reject dependency theory and to show how Venezuelan nationals and government control complex industrialization process. Examination of export possibilities shows no indication of foreign dominance.

Lombardi, John V. Venezuela: the search for order, the dream of progress. See item **2617**.

2926 Lavenda, Robert H. Social urbanization and Caracas: a historical anthropological analysis (Urban Anthropology [State University of New York, Brockport] 8 : 3 / 4, Winter 1979, p. 365–381, table)

Historical study of 1870–1908 period by anthropologist who sees era as beginning of modernization in Venezuela. Concentrates on increasing primacy of Caracas. Studies urban patterns, movement of elite to new suburban sections, rise of middle class, etc. For sociologist's comment, see *HLAS 45:8270*.

2927 Loy, Jane M. Horsemen of the tropics: a comparative view of the *llaneros* in the history of Venezuela and Colombia (UB/BA, 23 : 31, 1981, p. 159–171)

Somewhat romantic treatment of subject traces *llaneros* from colonial times through 20th century, as ranch hands, soldiers in wars of independence, and as permanent mid-20th-century frontiersmen. Unlike Argentine gauchos, Venezuelan and Colombian llaneros were never outlaws, but rather horsemen living under permanent frontier conditions as modernization left them behind.

Mommer, Bernard and **Ramón A. Rivas A.** El petróleo en la transformación burguesa de Venezuela. See *HLAS 45:3344*.

2928 Ojer, Pablo. La década fundamental en la controversia de límites entre Venezuela y Colombia: 1881–1891. Caracas: Instituto de Derecho Público, Universidad Central de Venezuela, 1982. 618 p.: bibl., index, map.

Trata de probar—y lo hace con erudición y argumentos formidables—que el laudo de 1891 está lleno de errores e injusticias graves en perjuicio de Venezuela. Esto se debió, según el autor, a la poca habilidad de los negociadores venezolanos y la ignorancia de los expertos españoles. Demuestra que su autor conoce profundamente el tema. [L. Gómez-Canedo]

2929 ———. El Golfo de Venezuela: una síntesis histórica. Caracas: Instituto de Derecho Público, Universidad Central de Venezuela, 1983. 624 p.: bibl., index, maps.

Estudio de límites con Colombia en La Guajira. Analiza el laudo español de 1891,

demarcación de 1900, laudo suizo de 1922, Tratado de 1941 entre Venezuela y Colombia, y dedica extenso capítulo (p. 397–481) a "circunstancias espaciales históricas de la soberanía de Venezuela en el Golfo." Similar a item **2928** en cuanto a método, documentación y argumentación. [L. Gómez-Canedo]

2930 Pensamiento político venezolano del siglo XIX. No. 1– . Caracas: Congreso de la República, 1983– .

Monographic series consists of re-edition (see *HLAS 28:1058a*) of excellent collection of writings by 19th-century political philosophers. Important contribution to Venezuelan historiography. Vols. 1–15 are devoted to following individuals and topics: Fermín Toro; Juan Vicente González; Tomás Lander; Antonio Leocadio Guzmán; Pedro José Rojas; Cecilio Acosta; Liberales y Conservadores; Textos Doctrinales; Conservadores y Liberales; Los Grandes Temas Políticos; La Doctrina Positivista; and Indices y Guía de la Colección.

2931 Perazzo, Nicolás. Historia de la inmigración en Venezuela. t. 2, 1850–1900 y documentos anexos. Caracas: Congreso de la República, 1982. 1 v.: bibl.

For vol. 1 (1973) on 1830–50 period, see *HLAS 38:3402*. Vol. 2 devoted to Guzmán Blanco period covers immigration 1851–90 with little data analysis. Third of book comprises documents including decrees and legislation.

Pollak-Eltz, Angelina. Regards sur les cultures d'origine africaine au Vénézuela. See *HLAS 45:1118*.

Rangel, Domingo Alberto. Capital y desarrollo. See *HLAS 45:8276*.

2932 Rodríguez, Adolfo. Trama y ámbito del comercio de cueros en Venezuela (UB/BA, 23 : 31, 1981, p. 187–218)

Useful but not definitive study tries to show influence of cattle-producing llanos on formation of modern Venezuela. Based on secondary accounts, travellers' descriptions, and newspapers. Treats social and political development as well as economic changes.

2933 Rojas, Armando. Historia de las relaciones diplomáticas entre Venezuela y los Estados Unidos. v. 1, 1810–1899. Caracas: Ediciones de la Presidencia de la República, 1979. 1 v.: indexes, ports.

First of two volumes on Guzmán Blanco's diplomacy. Chronological narrative argues US claims against Venezuela shaped their relations. Because of need to respond to aggressive US and European policies, Venezuelans could not initiate their own. Until Guzmán Blanco, neither US nor Venezuela had clearcut policies and relations depended on individuals. Shows excellent grasp of Venezuelan and US diplomatic archives. Concludes that despite Venezuela's weakness, its policies had limited success. For political scientist's comment, see *HLAS 43:7478*.

Sonntag, Heinz R. and **Rafael de la Cruz.** Estado e industrialización. See *HLAS 45:3368.*

2934 Soublette, Carlos. Carlos Soublette, correspondencia. Recopilación, introducciones y notas de Ligia Degaldo y Magaly Burguera. Caracas: Academia Nacional de la Historia, 1981. 3 v.: bibl., indexes, ports (Biblioteca de la Academia Nacional de la Historia; 24–26. Fuentes para la historia republicana de Venezuela)

Extensive compilation of Soublette's correspondence (1830–70) drawn from Venezuelan and Colombian archives. Limited and without any historical editing that would have made collection more useful to readers.

2935 Stockhausen, Elke de. Periodismo y política en Venezuela: cincuenta años de historia. Caracas: Universidad Católica Andrés Bello, Instituto de Investigaciones Históricas, 1981. 203 p.: bibl., ill.

Catalogue of Venezuelan press (1808–58). Good introduction treats laws and attitudes that affected press. Lists each newspaper, identifies directors, place of publication, and current location.

2936 Suzzarini Baloa, Manuel A. Rómulo Betancourt: proyecto de modernización. Caracas: Editorial Ateneo de Caracas, 1981. 148 p.: bibl.

Depicts Betancourt as capitalistic modernizer who established the State as the engine of change. State helped bourgeoisie accumulate wealth, yet guaranteed that the masses would not be entirely excluded.

Tarre Murzi, Alfredo. López Contreras, de la tiranía a la libertad. See *HLAS 45:6274.*

2937 Universidad Central de Venezuela, Caracas. Taller de Historia del Movi-

miento Obrero en Venezuela. Clase obrera: partidos y sindicatos en Venezuela, 1936–1950. Alberto J. Pla *et al.* Caracas: Ediciones Centauro, 1982. 456 p.: bibl.

Attempts to survey politics of Venezuelan labor movement immediately following Gómez's death. Somewhat uneven treatment of topic results from fact different authors dealt with short chronological periods. Some continuity results from authors' emphasis on basic theme of communist failure to lead labor movement and A.D.'s success in controlling labor.

Valery S., Rafael. Las comunidades petroleras. See *HLAS 45:3370.*

2938 Vivas Gallardo, Freddy. Venezuela en la Sociedad de las Naciones, 1920–1939: descripción análisis de una actuación diplomática. Caracas: Universidad Central de Venezuela, Facultad de Ciencias Jurídicas y Políticas, Escuela de Estudios Políticos y Administrativos, 1981. 350 p.: bibl. (Monografías; no. 2)

Well written traditional narrative, based on wide use of archives of Miraflores and Venezuelan Ministry of Foreign Relations. Argues that Venezuela joined League of Nations at urging of *gomecista* factions who favored drawing Venezuela away from US orbit and closer to Europe. Participation in League brought Venezuela out of isolation in world affairs but to play minor role. Venezuela finally withdrew in favor of tighter Western hemisphere relations and growing feeling in post-Gómez era that Venezuela gained little from solidarity with European nations.

2939 Walter, Rolf. Venezuela und Deutschland, 1815–1870. Wiesbaden, FRG: Franz Steiner Verlag, 1983. 406 p.: ill., tables.

Thorough study of German trade with and immigration to Venezuela during 1815–70 period. Presents succinct history of economic and demographic development and national growth, based on consular documents and manuscript sources. Enhanced by numerous tables documenting economic and fiscal trends. [G.M. Dorn]

ECUADOR

2940 Albornoz Peralta, Osvaldo. Historia del movimiento obrero ecuatoriano:

breve síntesis. Quito?: Editorial Letranueva, 1983. 187 p.: bibl.

Partisan narrative which gives chronological analysis of labor movement since 1920s. Attributes small labor movement to lack of industries. Emphasizes strikes and political actions. Argues that working class emerged slowly but clearly, and worked to transform society. Along with leftist parties, working class has been major force in resolving fundamental problems in Ecuador. Especially praises the Confederación de Trabajadores del Ecuador for its anti-imperialism, defense of democratic liberties, and support of agrarian reform. Accuses CIA of infiltrating labor movement in order to divide workers.

2941 Cueva Dávila, Agustín. El Ecuador en los años treinta (*in* América Latina en los años treinta. Luis Antezana E. *et al.* Coordinador, Pablo González Casanova. México: Instituto de Investigaciones Sociales, Universidad National Autónoma de México, 1977, p. 214–238, tables)

Focuses on political, social, and economic repercussions of Depression upon Ecuador's class structure. Crisis gave birth to populism and campesino involvement, among other changes.

————. The process of political domination in Ecuador. See *HLAS 45:6277.*

Deler, Jean-Paul. Genèse de l'espace équatorien: essai su le territoire et la formation de l'état national. See item **2611.**

Hamerly, Michael T. Archives of Guayaquil. See item **2614.**

Hurtado, Oswaldo. El poder político en el Ecuador. See *HLAS 45:6281.*

Kennedy Troya, Alexandra. Catálogo del Archivo General de la Orden Franciscana del Ecuador, AGOFE. See item **2616.**

2942 Martz, John D. El marxismo en el Ecuador (UNCR/R, 4:8, enero/julio 1979, p. 31–57)

Introduction gives description of splits in Marxist groups since founding of Ecuadorian Socialist Party in 1926. Socialists generally have not included workers, and have worked with various non-Marxist administration. In contrast, the Ecuadorian Communist Party, which formed in 1931, has created workers' base. Ideological conflicts have also split both socialists and communists, especially since Chinese and Cuban revolutions. Bulk of article deals with 1970s and party posturing. Shows that communist have used electoral fight effectively. Despite successes, party faces delicate situation, especially due to divisions. As yet, Ecuador still dominated by conservative oligarchical thought.

Quintero, Rafael. El mito del populismo en el Ecuador: análisis de los fundamentos del estado ecuatoriano moderno, 1895–1934. See *HLAS 45:6284.*

2943 Salvador Lara, Jorge. La República del Ecuador y el General Juan José Flóres. Caracas: Academia Nacional de la Historia, 1980. 206 p.: bibl. (El Libro menor; 13)

Attempt to study complex and often contradictory image of Venezuelan general who led Ecuador out of Gran Colombia and who played a seminal role in nation's formation after 1830.

2944 Uzcátegui, Emilio. La educación ecuatoriana en el siglo del liberalismo. Quito: Editorial Voluntad, 1981. 346 p.: bibl.

Frank critique of education in Ecuador since late 19th century. Attributes much improvement to liberalism, especially introduction of lay institutions, but points out that liberals did not accomplish all they set out to do. Certainly Ecuador's economic and political accomplishments prove nation's improved educational system. Since 1979, efforts to end illiteracy among 25 percent of the population have had considerable success.

2945 Vargas, José María. Historia de la Provincia Dominicana del Ecuador en el siglo XIX. Quito: Editora Royal, 1982. 300 p., 8 leaves of plates: bibl., ports.

Chronological narrative of the Dominican's 19th-century experiences. Treats simple and complex topics equally, with very little interpretation. Good for understanding internal workings of order as well as reviewing changing Church/State relations.

Peru

VINCENT C. PELOSO,*Associate Professor of History, Howard University*

A HIGH PROPORTION of the works reviewed for this issue focus on the social history of Peru. For the most part, they fall within a tendency noted by this contributor in earlier volumes of the *Handbook*. Specifically, recent studies by and large give attention to themes derived from a strong need to weave together a historical tapestry from the many dangling threads of the country's multifaceted culture.

Many of these works are grounded in questions raised by José Carlos Mariátegui in his brief lifetime of writings. If nothing else, they pay tribute to the broad character of his concerns and their durability in 20th-century Peruvian history and culture. It might even be fair to say that his ideas have given recent Peruvian historical inquiry its most recognizable form.

Prominent among the works on Peruvian culture annotated below is a multi-authored volume entitled *Perú: identidad nacional* (items **2947** and **3026**) that notes the absence of an agreed upon condition of nationality in the country, but tries nevertheless to point the way toward future studies and further debate on this fundamental multidisciplinary theme. Of more profound merit is the publication of the memoirs of the venerable archaeologist, Luis Valcárcel (item **3019**). His recollections underscore the close relationship between field work and ideas in the definition of Peruvian culture. Valcárcel vividly recalls his association with the central issues of Peruvian politics and his friendships with both Haya and Mariátegui. Along the same lines, a two-volume set of essays edited by Franklin Pease G.Y., the new director of the Biblioteca Nacional, and others, evokes the spirit of Jorge Basadre in its title, *Historia: problema y promesa* (item **2980**). The diversity of topics that appear in this work is bound together by Basadre's favorite theme, the evolution of Peru's culture.

Studies of the internal structure of classes and of class conflict in the history of republican Peru draw attention to the lack of well defined boundaries between different groups within the culture. A notable work by Antonine Tibesar (item **3017**) suggests that the Bourbon reforms may have set the stage for the demise of the Church as a culture leader in the early republic, while Paul Gootenberg (item **2976**) does an outstanding job of documenting the similarities in the outlook of Lima artisans and early republican industrialists. In both cases, group ambivalence on the issue of protectionism inadvertently delayed and hurt industrialization. Rory Miller (item **2995**) and Gonzalo Portocarrero (item **3010**) find that this ambivalence similarly characterized the leaders of the "aristocratic republic" at the turn of the 20th century. Their internal bickering prompted deceitful policies that in turn incited widespread popular rebellions. Some of the studies of such uprisings that bear mention include those of Patrick Husson (item **2982**) on Huanta, and Jorge A. Flores Ochoa and Félix Palacios R. on Chucuito (item **2972**), while significant studies of the pro-Indian movement emphasize the social divisions that fired up popular politics well into the 20th century. Notable among the latter are the works of Wilfredo Kapsoli (item **2984**) on the debates within the movement, and that of David Wise (item **3024**) which concludes that the movement itself, though perhaps united against the landlords, was deeply divided on how to best achieve cultural harmony in Peru.

The divisions within those sectors of the political spectrum may serve as an appropriate context for understanding the split that occurred with seeming finality between Mariátegui and Haya, and that has survived the two imposing figures. Each of them draws attention from perceptive scholars. Frederick B. Pike (item **3007**) eloquently reinterprets the meaning of Haya's ideas and existence for Peru and Latin America in general by applying Jungian and Freudian personality theory to his life to argue that the spiritualist content of his outlook ultimately shaped his populism. Meanwhile, students of Mariátegui will welcome the appearance of a handful of articles that probe specific facets of the youthful thinker's life and ideas. Noteworthy among them are the formidable efforts of Fernando Mires (item **2997**) to focus on Mariátegui's use of *gamonalismo, latifundio,* and *servidumbre* as analytical tools, and the thoughtful essay by José Aricó (item **2948**) that persuasively explores the influence of the Italian thinkers Gobetti and Gramsci on his perspective. An essay by Carlos Franco (item **2973**) admirably represents many others like it that explored the problems of ideology and party-building in search of a "national" movement through discussion of the relationship between the two men. A little known ideological angle of another sort received treatment in the César Arrospide de la Flor recollection (item **2949**) of his involvement in the Peruvian Catholic Action movement of the 1920s.

Outstanding works among those annotated below bring critical themes of Peruvian culture to bear on historical problems of wide interest and profound importance. In alphabetical order they include the study by Julian Laite (item **2986**) of the proletarianization of the miners, the examination of peasant struggle in the central highlands by Florencia Mallon (item **2989**) and the detailed examination of the famed La Breña campaign by Nelson Manrique (item **2990**). These works significantly advance our understanding of patterns of human behavior that result when economic processes and their accompanying political and social undulations evolve not in harmony but in utter discord. Because of its particular evolution, the history of Peru may effectively be compared with that of other countries. There is every reason to expect that despite wretchedly inadequate and inconsistent funding, this history will continue to be unearthed to the benefit of us all.

2946 Albert, Bill. Yanaconaje and cotton production on the Peruvian coast: sharecropping in the Cañete Valley during World War I (Bulletin of Latin American Research [Oxford Microform Publishers, England] 2:2, May 1983, p. 107–115)

Evaluation of use of sharecropping in coastal region, using Hacienda Santa Bárbara in Cañete Valley as case to stress how switch from sugar to cotton agriculture required less capital investment by owners than would be supposed. Argues that savings came from passing on burden of costs to renters of small plots within hacienda. Ends by making a comparative theoretical critique on role of sharecropping in development of capitalist agriculture.

2947 Althaus, Miguel de. Identidad nacional y Estado en el Perú (*in* Perú: identidad nacional. Lima: Ediciones CEDEP, 1979, p. 209–234, bibl.)

In search for the State's role and configuration of society in Peruvian nationhood, mixes Deutsch, Weber, and 19th-century Peruvian legislation to analyze bureaucracy, political parties and Leguía. Concludes that Peru is a nation in formation. Suggests that the State has not yet taken clear form.

2948 Aricó, José. Mariátegui y los orígenes del marxismo latinoamericano (Socialismo y Participación [Centro de Estudios para el Desarrollo y la Participación, Lima] 5, dic. 1978, p. 13–42)

Examines Mariátegui's ideological links with Aprismo, his so-called "populism," and his so-called "immature Sorelianism." Believes Mariátegui's Italian experience was decisive influence in his thinking—particularly his familiarity with Gramsci and Gobetti. Discusses him in context of APRA thinkers, Peru's CP, and Peruvian intellectual atmosphere. Points out Mariátegui tried to prevent Haya from transforming mass movement into political party, a fatal move for Peru's left. Highly expressive, persuasive study that fails to take into account Chavarría's biography.

2949 Arróspide de la Flor, César. El movimiento católico seglar en los años 20 (Revista de la Universidad Católica [Pontificia Universidad Católica del Perú, Lima] 5, agosto 1979, p. 5–24)

Traces origins of Peru's Catholic Action movement, influenced by European literati (Maritain, Rouault, Messaiaen and Claudel) and L'Action Française, monarchist and pre-fascist movements. When it broadened into Acción Social de la Juventud (ASJ), it did not develop cohesive political ideas. Fascinating document about little-known movement.

2950 Arroyo, Eduardo. La hacienda costeña en el Perú: Mala-Cañete, 1532–1968. Prólogo, Pablo Macera. Fotos, María Burela. Lima: Centro de Proyección Cristiana, 1981. 202 p., 1 folded leaf of plates: bibl., ill.

Concerns land use and labor utilization problems on 20th-century Cañete Valley estates. Employs documentation from Lima's AGN, Biblioteca Nacional, Cañete's municipal archive, CENCIRA's, etc. Analyzes cotton, especially in Mala region. Argues that area's capitalist agriculture must be considered peculiar and carries with it "transitional" labor forms such as "*compañero*" sharecropping. Useful data and analysis for comparative purposes.

2951 Asociación Trabajo y Cultura (ATC). Manual de prensa obrera y popular. Lima: TAREA, 1981. 125, 3 p.: bibl., ill.

Preliminary survey of Peru's non-establishment communications media. Examines needs, aims, history, successes, and failures of underfunded popular communications media, in their struggle against wealth and purposes of established press, TV, etc. Exploratory, useful effort to outline Peru's communications problems in historical perspective.

Barba Caballero, José. Defensa del aprismo: homenaje póstumo a Haya de la Torre. See *HLAS 45:6331.*

2952 ———. Historia del movimiento obrero peruano. Lima: Ediciones Signo, 1981. 298 p., 12 leaves of plates: bibl., ill.

Self-admitted defense of APRA's labor activities. Bases evaluations on theoretical works of European Marxists, Peruvian intellectuals, periodical literature, oral testimony of Aprista leaders, and archives of CGTP (APRA arm of labor movement). Revealing argument posed by young APRA lawyer and leader.

2953 Basadre, Jorge. Peruanos del siglo XIX. Lima: Ediciones Rikchay Perú, 1981. 235 p. (Serie popular; 4)

Somewhat patriotically chosen figures are subject to brief, unsupported biographical treatments (e.g., Cáceres, 8 p.; Bolívar and San Martín, 4 p. each; Castilla, 12 p.; Grau, 8 p.; Matto de Turner and Ricardo Palmer, 6 p. each; González Vigil, 10 p.; Herrera, 8 p.).

2954 ———. Peruanos del siglo XX. Lima: Ediciones Rikchay Perú, 1981. 171 p. (Serie popular; 3)

Brief, biographical characterizations of 20th-century Peruvians chosen at random from all walks of life.

2955 ———. Sultanismo, corrupción y dependencia en el Perú republicano. Editor, Carlos Milla Batres. Lima: Editorial Milla Batres, 1981. 160 p., 64 p. of plates: bibl., ill. (Biblioteca peruana del siglo XX; 5)

Consists of essays on character of classes in 19th century, liberalism, the State, and dependent economy. Much has appeared elsewhere, print is overly large, and accompanying photo and prints, though attractive and illustrative, appear to capitalize on late historian's name in bookseller's market.

2956 Bedoya Garland, Eduardo. Ocupaciones de tierras en el fundo Saipai: antecedentes e historia del movimiento (PUCP/DA, 8, mayo 1982, p. 77–106, bibl., tables)

Detailed description of land seizure in Huallaga prov., north of highland Tingo María, before recent agrarian reform. Based on estate's archives, reviews land tenantry

politics of 1945–64 period, especially usu-
fructual sources of peasant claims. Details
legal efforts to consolidate seizures and
APRA's limited role. Peasants fought to control only land that gave best access to
markets.

2957 Béjar, Héctor. APRA-PC, 1930-1940:
itinerario de un conflicto (Socialismo y
Participación [Centro de Estudios para el
Desarrollo y la Participación, Lima] 9, 1980,
p. 13–40)

Primarily concerned with why Communists lost their competition with APRA.
Reviews recent studies, works by CP and
APRA leaders, contemporary periodicals, etc.
Ascribes inability of left to produce common
campaign for social change in 1920s to hard-
ening of internal divisions within each
movement.

2958 Benavides de Peña, Paquita *et al.* El
Mariscal Benavides: su vida y su obra.
v. 2. Lima: s.n., 1981. 1 v.: ill.

Vol. 2 focuses on subject's public, political life. Presents information on 1911–50
presidential politics, concentrating particularly on 1930s presidency. Apparently based
solely on public documentation, this somewhat useful biography is overly laudatory,
prone to highlight the trivial and to obscure
uglier aspects of the man's career.

2959 Blanchard, Peter. The origins of the
Peruvian labor movement, 1883–1919.
Pittsburgh: University of Pittsburgh Press,
1982. 214 p.: bibl., index (Pitt Latin American series)

Surveys myriad labor organizations
that emerged in period. Discusses wage and
price problems, political repression, internal
divisions and labor's faulty leadership on way
to securing eight-hour day under government
sponsorship in 1919. Stresses economic goals
and related politics, especially labor's symbiotic relationship with the State. Well written narrative that raises more questions than
it answers.

2960 Bonilla, Heraclio. Comunidades de indígenas y Estado Nación en el Perú
(PUCP/H, 6:1, julio 1982, p. 35–51, bibl.)

Suggests that polarization between
State and rural community was major long-
term consequence of Spanish colonial reduction policy, especially because it left

rural power in hands of local groups and
individuals.

2961 ——— . La dimensión internacional de
la Guerra del Pacífio (IDES/DE, 19:73,
abril/junio 1979, p. 79–93)

Seeks to correct both traditional denial
of international dimension of war and conspiracy theory against Great Britain. Emphasizes economic and financial interest in war's
conduct and aftermath that resulted in British hegemony over Peru and Chile. Extensive
use of US Senate documents and bondholder
reports.

2962 ——— . Etnia, región y la cuestión nacional en el área andina: proposiciones
para una discusión (*in* Indianité, ethnocide,
indigénisme en Amérique latina. Paris: Centre national de la recherche scientifique;
Toulouse, France: Centre interdisciplinaire
d'études latino-américaines, Groupe de recherches sur l'Amérique latine [GRAL],
1982, p. 59-77, tables)

Uses Peruvian case to illustrate persistence of ethnicity and regionalism in Andes.
A re-statement of dependency perspective
applied to Andean history down to the
1969–80 military government period.

2963 Brass, Tom. Class formation and class
struggle in La Convención, Perú (JPS,
7:4, July 1980, p. 427–457, graphs, maps,
tables)

Applies class analysis to single estate
in valley affected by 1969 agrarian reform.
Analyzes continuity of earlier struggles as
they emerged in CP Pintobamba Grande in
1970s, and notes that poorest peasants were
re-feudalized at expense of the wealthier
sectors.

2964 Bustamante, Cecilia. Intelectuales peruanas de la generación de José Carlos
Mariátegui (Socialismo y participación
[Centro de Estudios para el Desarrollo y
la Participación, Lima] 14, junio 1981,
p. 107–119)

Highlights difficult social context in
which notable early 20th-century women
carried on their work, a discriminatory atmosphere that likened their condition to Flora
Tristán's. Reviews efforts of Clorinda Matto
de Turner, Dora Mayer, Magda Portal, and
María Wiesse de Sabogal, etc. Unfocused and
overly ambitious study which nevertheless

calls attention to important women in Peruvian political and intellectual life.

2965 Caballero Martín, Víctor. Imperialismo y campesinado en la Sierra Central. Huancayo, Peru: Instituto de Estudios Andinos, 1981. 170 p.: bibl., ill. (Serie Historia agraria peruana; 1)

Studies rise of vast estate in central Andes that became CERRO corporation's cattle operations. Explores problems of lands and mines, village's and working population's relationship to the enterprise. Emphasizes crises that arose up to 1960. Solidly based upon materials in Archivo del Fuero Agrario, Cerro de Pasco Corp. reports, etc. Constant reference to impact of national economy. Concentrates on Mantaro valley estates to illustrate argument.

2966 Castro Vásquez, Aquilino. Los guerrilleros de Chupaca en la Guerra con Chile. Lima: Editorial Universo, 1982. 116 p.: bibl., ill.

Strong on Huancayo's heroic feats during Chilean invasion but weak on context and analysis of local military events. Use of oral sources not clearly indicated. Of value merely as introduction.

2967 Dammert Bellido, José. Cajamarca durante la Guerra del Pacífico. Cajamarca: Imp. MACS, 1983. 178 p.: bibl. (Publicaciones del Obispado de Cajamarca; 3)

Anecdotal narrative about contributions of northern Andean dept. to major encounters of highland campaign. Based upon some parish archival sources and few standard works, and limited to military aspects of war in region. Concentrates on activities of Miguel Iglesias, and strains to point up the Church's role. Too sketchy.

2968 Demelas, Marie-Danielle. Une réponse du berger à la bergère: les Créoles andins entre l'Amérique et l'Europe au XIXᵉ siècle (in Etudes sur l'impact culturel du Nouveau Monde. Seminaire interuniversitaire sur l'Amérique espagnole coloniale. Jean-Pierre Clément et al. Paris: Editions L'Harmattan, 1982, v. 2, p. 111–130, plate)

Surveys ambivalence of self-questioning and identity in 19th-century writings of Bolivian and Peruvian thinkers (e,g., Avelino Aramayo, Manuel Prado, Jaime Mendoza, Federico More). Such 19th-century figures as Carlos Lissón and Bartolomé Herrera portend early 20th-century thinkers such as González Prada, Valcárcel, and Arguedas. Suggestive addition to Herrera Tamayo's work.

2969 Dore, Elizabeth. Social relations and the barriers to economic growth: the case of the Peruvian mining industry (GEE/NA, 1, 1978, p. 245–267, tables)

Rejects dependency theory as framework for historical analysis of Latin American underdevelopment. Favors analysis of social relations of production. Illustrates approach by examining metal mining in Peru (1900–45), when it was most dynamic sector in pre-capitalist economy. Provides statistical and analytical details in mining stages (e.g., Cerro de Pasco Corp.). Attributes variations in development to backward technological and social policies of mineowners. Based on government sources.

2970 Favre, Henri. Capitalisme et ethnicité: la politique indigeniste du Pérou (in Indianité, ethnocide, indigénisme en Amérique latine. Paris: Centre national de la recherche scientifique; Toulouse, France: Centre interdisciplinaire d'études latinoaméricaines, Groupe de recherches sur l'Amérique latine [GRAL], 1982, p. 79–91.)

Surveys Peruvian state policies on Indian populations from 19th century through 1970s. Finds needs of capitalist state have reinforced present structure of society to Indians' hopeless disadvantage. Makes comparisons with Mexico.

2971 Flores Galindo, Alberto. Juan Croniqeuer, 1914–1918 (UP/A, 5:10, 1980, p. 91–98)

Ponders continuity and contradiction in works of Juan Croniqueur (Mariátegui's pseudonym). Argues that ignorance of his early romantic writings has distorted interpretations of his work and obscured its value. Concludes that Mariátegui's religiosity marks important step along the road to his Marxism. Provocative suggestions.

2972 Flores Ochoa, Jorge A. and Félix Palacios Ríos. La protesta de 1909: un movimiento de pastores de la Puna Alta a comienzos del siglo XX (PUCP/DA, 2, mayo 1978, p. 75-88, bibl.)

Analyzes turn-of-the-century shepherd uprising in barren *puna* motivated by alpacas' need to shift pasturage to lower levels during winter. Forms part of background of Rumi Maqui movement that arose during World War I. For ethnologist's comment, see *HLAS 45:1453*.

2973 Franco, Carlos. Mariátegui Haya: surgimiento de la izquierda nacional (*in* Socialismo y Participación [Centro de Estudios para el Desarrollo y la Participación, Lima] sept. 1979, p. 11–44)

Sees both Haya and Mariátegui as having formed the national left movement in Peru, its point of departure being heretical Marxism. Explores their ideological similarities and critical differences, and examines their handling of the Indian question. Challenging, provocative analysis.

Geng T., Luis. Consumo histórico de derivados del petróleo: alternativas futuras. See *HLAS 45:3451*.

2975 Gilbert, Dennis. Cognatic descent groups in upper-class Lima, Peru (AES/AE, 8:4, Nov. 1981, p. 739–757, tables)

Anthropological study of two ruling families of 20th-century Peru: Prados and Miró Quesadas. Demonstrates that descent is as important in technologically advanced world as in traditional societies. Shows family ties are critical in determining fortune, identity, leadership, and authority. Important for historians because author secured extensive oral testimony from family members as well as others.

González Vigil, Fernando; Carlos Parodi Zevallos; and Fabián Tume Torres. Alimentos y transnacionales: los complejos sectoriales del trigo y avícola en el Perú. See *HLAS 45:1809*.

2976 Gootenberg, Paul. The social origins of protectionism and free trade in nineteenth-century Lima (JLAS, 14:2, Nov. 1982, p. 329–358)

Demonstrates convincingly that protectionist interests fought vigorously at mid-century to hold down cost of imports and of labor. Incipient Lima industrialists and artisans demanded protection while they pushed for elimination of tariffs on such essentials as textiles and food.

2977 Guice, C. Norman. Giving Peru a voice: Federico Larrañaga and *El Canal de Panamá* (AAFH/TAM, 39:1, July 1982, p. 85–106)

During War of Pacific, Panama's Peruvian consul edited a government-funded newspaper that rivaled English-language *Star and Herald*. Details periodical's financial support coverage, rivalries and eventual demise. Extensive use of Archivo Piérola in Lima's Biblioteca Nacional.

2978 Guzmán, Virginia and **Virginia Vargas.** Cronología de los movimientos campesinos, 1956–1964. Colaboradores, Cecilia Blondet; Jaime Joseph; Sinesio López. Lima: Investigación, Documentación, Educación, Asesoría, Servicios, 1981. 208 p.: bibl., ill., tables.

Attempts list of major movements linked to mid-1950s and early 1960s political organizations, culled from periodical literature. Lists seven categories of information per movement, including forms of struggle, organization and leadership, stages and results. Uses no government records or local testimony. Nevertheless, a handy guide for students of period.

Henderson, Donald C. and **Grace R. Pérez.** Literature and politics in Latin America: an annotated calendar of the Luis Alberto Sánchez correspondence, 1919–1980. See *HLAS 45:31*.

2979 Los Héroes de La Breña. Lima: Comisión Permanente de la Historia del Ejército del Perú, 1982. 353 p., 12 p. of plates: bibl., ill. (some col.), index, ports. (Serie biográfica; t. 1)

Biographical sketches of leading participants of La Breña campaign, regular military as well as guerrillas, based upon sources in military archives. Of potential reference value to regional studies of war.

Historia general del ejército peruano. See item **2615**.

2980 Historia, problema y promesa. Homenaje a Jorge Basadre. Edición a cargo de Francisco Miró Quesada C., Franklin Pease G.Y., David Sobrevilla A. Lima: Pontificia Universidad Católica del Perú, Fondo Editorial, 1978. 2 v.: bibl. ill.

Two-volume multilingual compilation dedicated to Jorge Basadre. Consists of eclectic essays, each including notes or bibliography. Overriding theme appears to be the culture of Peru in historical perspective.

Hunt, Shane. Evolución de los salarios reales en el Perú: 1900–1940. See *HLAS 45:3457.*

2982 Husson, Patrick. Changement social et insurrections indiennes: la "révolte du sel" à Huanta, Pérou, en 1896 (CDAL, 23:1, 1981, p. 102–149, map)

Huanta rebellion was not a spontaneous response to inflation and salt tax but a consequence of 1850s highland struggle between traditional landlords and new bourgeoisie. Examines interpretations of rebellion by political factions and the military. Based on judicial and administrative archives and periodicals.

2983 Jorge Basadre: la política y la historia. Noé Jave, compilador. Lima: Lluvia Editores, 1981. 225 p.: bibl., ill.

Richly insightful interview (1980) in which Basadre discusses Peruvian culture, Tello, Mariátegui, and 1980 presidential election. Also includes essays on Basadre's influence on historiography by Kapsoli; Basadre and Andean culture by Waldemar Espinoza; and on Basadre and the War of the Pacific by Nelson Manrique.

2984 Kapsoli Escudero, Wilfredo. El pensamiento de la Asociación Pro Indígena. Cuzco: Centro de Estudios Rurales Andinos Bartolomé de las Casas, 1980. 151 p.: bibl., ill. (Debates rurales; 3)

Concerns intellectuals who formed and headed pre-World War I nativist movement. Notes magnitude of sources available to make fuller study of organization and character of its leadership. Includes papers by representative figures.

2985 Kuhl, Paul E. The bans of marriage: Thomas Bond Wood and the Civil Marriage Bill in Peru (Secolas Annals [Journal of the Southeastern Council on Latin American Studies, Macon, Ga.] 14, March 1983, p. 85–100)

Details efforts to gain legal and social recognition of non-Catholic marriages in Peru through lobbying Parliament and Executive in Piérola era. Study of turn-of-the-century ideological clash between resident foreigners and the Church. Based on private papers and US National Archives materials.

2986 Laite, Julian. Industrial development and migrant labor in Latin America. Austin: University of Texas Press, 1981. 229 p.: bibl., ill., indexes (The Texas Pan American series)

Concerned with historical pattern of proletarianization, focuses on growth of mining in Peru. Believes the political economy of industrial growth can be understood only as an aspect of economic development. By studying a multi national-controlled industry and the Peruvian State's role in process of proletarianization, illustrates processes found throughout underdeveloped world. Covers rise of Peru's mining industry to and since 1900, efforts at centralization of mine ownership, organization of labor to 1972, rural origins of migrant labor, etc. Author's use of Cerro de Pasco Corp. documents, company officials memoirs, and wide reading in published literature make comparisons possible and strengthens a work more sociological than historical in its perspective.

2987 Luna Vegas, Emilio. Perú y Chile en 5 siglos: revisión histórica. Lima: Librería Editorial Minerva, 1982. 646 p.: bibl.

Supported by little documentation, alarmist essays rummage in colonial and conquest periods, then heavily rework Chilean relations with Peru after independence, concentrating on "abuses" and "deceits." Hardly a "revisionist" essay, it presents a handy summary of War of Pacific and its aftermath from standpoint of intense Peruvian patriotism.

2988 Madueño, Víctor A. La Primera Guerra Mundial y el desarrollo industrial del Perú (UP/EA, 8:17/18, 1981, p. 41–53, tables)

Attacks "generally acknowledged idea" that during World War I manufactured goods replaced food as imports, stimulating development of national industry. Analysis of Lima cotton and woolen goods supports contrary view that internal production system was not sufficiently developed. Relies on Thorp and Bertram and other published data sources.

2989 Mallon, Florencia E. The defense of community in Peru's central highlands: peasant struggle and capitalist transition, 1860–1940. Princeton: Princeton University Press, 1983. 384 p.: appendices, bibl., index, maps.

Three sections highlight fundamental antagonism between landlords and peasants: 1) events in 1780–1900, culminating in vengeful reprisals and new antagonisms following War of Pacific; 2) entry of foreign capital and social consequences of manufacturing investment and industrialization; and 3) migration problem and reformation of rural society. Concludes that despite appearances, a peasantry no longer exists in Mantaro region. Carefully researched, powerfully written portrait of the social impact of industrialization in highland Peru. Based on local archives, oral testimony and much documentation collected over two years in Mantaro valley.

2990 Manrique, Nelson. Campesinado y Nación: las guerrillas indígenas en la guerra con Chile. Lima: Centro de Investigación y Capacitación: Editora Ital Perú, 1981. 418 p., 1 fold. leaf of plates: appendices, bibl., maps.

Makes highly effective use of many archives (e.g., Jauja, Huancayo, Junín, Lima). Places La Breña military campaign in social and political context, offering provocative solution to puzzle of popular, rural participation in war against Chile. Details economic and social conditions in Junín, Chilean occupation, Peruvian counter-offensive, collaboration with the enemy by landlords, and actions of Peruvian guerrillas against both Chilean and Peruvian enemies. Points out Cáceres' admiration for Indian guerrillas. Suggests they fought to maintain and extend their interests, which they perceived as national. Well-researched study takes strong exception to conclusions drawn by Bonilla and Flores Galindo, among others, on national consciousness of Junín villagers.

2991 Melgar Bao, Ricardo. La Revolución Mexicana en el movimiento popular-nacional de la región andina (Boletín de Antropología Americana [Instituto Panamericano de Geografía e Historia, México] 6, dic. 1982, p. 85–104)

Points out immediate impact of Mexican Revolution on Peru and examines many aspects of Mexican Revolution (e.g., agrarian and anti-imperialist character, State's role in economy, laicism, education, Indian countryside, Mexico as center of revolutionary conspiracy). Draws on Haya, Mariátegui, etc.

2992 Melis, Antonio. José Carlos Mariátegui y la reforma universitaria (UP/A, 5:10, 1980, p. 73–80)

Uses contemporary journals to discuss Mariátegui's "counter-culture" point of view as addendum to university reform debate in Peru. Concludes that Mariátegui rejected Euro-North American scholasticism but did not come up with an alternative model.

2993 Mendoza Meléndez, Eduardo. Historia de la Campaña de La Breña. Lima: Editorial Milla Batres, 1981. 299 p., 8 p. of plates: ill.

Based on materials from military archives and Biblioteca Nacional, this extended essay surveys strategies and battles that occupied Cáceres and his guerrillas from Lima to end of campaign in Arequipa. Concentrates exclusively on military affairs.

2994 Miller, Robert Ryal. James Orton: a Yankee naturalist in South America, 1867–1877 (APS/P, 126:1, Feb. 1982, p. 11–25, bibl., plates)

Details South American travels and discoveries of scientist, explorer and theologian (d. 1877), including his observations on Peruvian society. Emphasizes his career.

2995 Miller, Rory. The coastal elite and Peruvian politics: 1895–1919 (JLAS, 14:1, May 1982, p. 97–120)

Challenges assumption that oligarchy's rule in that era was either coherent or cohesive, especially given intra-class divisions between coastal and highland sectors. Deftly surveys historiography, notes relative homogeneity of coastal elite (industrial and agrarian sectors), and suggests how divisions were reflected in congressional politics. Solid, thoughtful survey.

2996 ———. The wool trade of southern Peru: 1850–1915 (IAA, 8:3, 1982, p. 297–311, tables)

Compares production figures of late 19th century and discusses implications. Uses earlier studies, parliamentary papers, and Anthony J. Gibbs archive to discuss trade's internal structure in aftermath of railway construction and expansion of estates toward end of 19th century.

2997 Mires, Fernando. Los indios y la tierra: o como concibió Mariátegui la revolución en el Perú (NOSALF/IA, 8/9[2]:1/2, 1980, p. 68–99)

Analyzes sources of Mariátegui's ideas on land and Indians, especially meaning of his attack upon *gamonalismio, latifundio, servidumbre.* Emphasizes notion of historic antagonism between feudalism and capitalism in Peru. Attempts to clarify political meaning of Mariátegui's ideas, emphasizing those not yet fully appreciated. Extended, formidable analysis.

2998 Ortiz Sotelo, Jorge. Ex-cadetes navales del Perú. Lima: Asociación de Ex-Cadetes Navales del Perú, 1982. 461 p.: bibl., ill. (some col.).

Celebrates 25th anniversary of naval cadet veterans organization, occasion which produces reflections on organization and development of Peru's Naval War College and biographical sketches of four naval figures, two of which founded the College.

2999 Pacheco Vélez, César. Jorge Basadre, 1903–1980: o la pasión por la historia (PAIGH/H, 92, julio/dic. 1981, p. 195–213)

Comments on irreparable loss of Basadre's death for Hispanic American culture and historiography. Extended, heartfelt necrology with evaluations of the man's career and writings.

3000 Paris, Robert. Los italianos en el Perú (UP/A, 7:12, 1982, p. 33–45, bibl.)

In contrast to Argentina and Brazil, Italian immigration to Peru— shrunk by Chinese indenture—was small and little noticed. Mostly farmers and merchants, some acquired wine, oil and sugar estates, or mines, but majority were in "tertiary" sector— coastal shipping and export-import banking. Suggests Italians made substantial contributions to Peru's intellectual life.

3001 Paulo Netto, José. O contexto histórico-social de Mariátegui (ECB, 21[3]: 3, março 1980, p. 32–52, tables)

Finds that Mariátegui's evolution from rebellious enthusiast to revolutionary activist corresponded dialectically with evolution of Peru's labor movement.

3002 Pereda Torres, Rolando. Historia de las luchas sociales del movimiento obrero en el Perú republicano, 1858–1917. v. 1. La Victoria, Perú: EDIMSSA, 1982. 1 v.: bibl., ill.

Surveys organized labor's mid 19th-century origins, focusing on artisan, mutualist and bakers' struggles. Covers State's response to labor expansion, noting significance of first national workers' congress of 1900. Examines ties between Lima and provincial labor movements, and ends with discussion of strikes at Vitarte, Huacho, and day laborers' strike of 1916–17. No bibliography but notes reveal extensive use of contemporary periodical literature, recent studies, unpublished documents, oral testimony, broadsides, and the working class press. Vol. 1 of several.

3003 Pérez-Mallaína Bueno, Pablo Emilio. Profesiones y oficios en la Lima de 1850 (EEHA/AEA, 37, 1980, p. 191–233)

Analysis of French Consul's manuscript memoir (1850) written to encourage emigration to Peru. Influenced by 1848 upheavals, Félix Letellier viewed Lima as city moving towards modernization. Report is based on his own experiences. Analysis considers document's advantages and limitations. Includes memoir's Spanish translation.

3004 The Peruvian experiment reconsidered. Edited by Cynthia McClintock and Abraham F. Lowenthal. Princeton: Princeton University Press, 1983. 442 p.: appendices, bibl., index, tables.

Reviews earlier judgments on military-led *docenio* in chapters that provide historical perspective on problems of democracy, social cohesion, and economy's evolution (Julio Cotler and Rosemary Thorp); observations on the economy (E.V.K. Fitzgerald, Daniel Schydlowsky, Juan Wicht, Barbara Stallings, and Laura Gausti); discussion of policy alternatives (Peter Cleaves, Henry Pease G.Y., Liisa North, Cynthia McClintock, and Luis Pásara); examination of income redistribution (Susan Edelstein); comparisons of Peru to Cuba, Bolivia, and Mexico (John Sheahan); and review of entire era in a comparative framework (Abraham Lowenthal). Includes valuable tables.

3005 Piel, Jean. Crise agraire et conscience créole au Pérou. Paris: Editions du Centre national de la recherche scientifique, 1982. 119 p.: bibl., ill. (Amérique latine: pays ibériques)

Surveys Peru's 19th-century agrarian

movements. Concentrates on two aspects of tension between landlord and communities: uprisings of Indian villages (1900–20) and the State's response to agrarian problems. Argues that agrarian reformism diverted the problem away from its most effective solution—communalism led by Indian communities.

3006 Pike, Frederick B. Peru's Haya de la Torre and archetypal regeneration mythology (IAMEA, 34:2, Autumn 1980, p. 25–65)

Focuses on use of myth in 1920s' APRA politics. Considers applicability of "frontier" mythology to explain Latin American history. Argues that Haya's quest to free men from repressive rational categories was essentially a frontier-like reaction designed to free the Indians while finding accommodation between reason and impulse. Employs Freudian and Jungian ideas to explore *négritude* and *indigenismo* regeneration myths in Africa and Latin America, and use of regeneration myth by its charismatic leaders.

3007 ——. Visions of rebirth: the spiritualist facet of Peru's Haya de la Torre (HAHR, 63:3, Aug. 1983, p. 479–516)

Analyzes Haya's so-called "complete works" in terms of Jungian ideas. Argues that Haya of twilight years had abandoned confrontational politics in favor of a search for harmonies. Wide-ranging analysis and provocative interpretation.

3008 Podestá, Bruno. Estudios latinoamericanos en Italia: el caso peruano, 1960–1979 (UP/A, 6:11, 1981, p. 79–91, bibl.)

Surveys weak institutional support for the field in the country, ranking Italian scholarship on Peru below that on Chile, Cuba, and Argentina. Ends with helpful summary of Italian publications on Peru.

3009 Portal, Magda. Flora Tristán, precursora. Lima: Editorial La Equidad, 1983. 156 p.: bibl.

Peruvian novelist draws attention to precursorial activities of this 19th-century Franco-Peruvian socialist and links her with 1975 International Women's Year celebrations. Biographical study largely based on published works on Tristán's writings.

3010 Portocarrero, Gonzalo. La oligarquía frente a la reivindicación democrática

(UP/A, 7:12, 1982, p. 61–73)

After emergence of mass parties in 1930s, oligarchy could only offer weak candidates. Analyzes ideological and institutional underpinnings of such candidates and concludes that suspending vote count signified APRA's popularity. Thereafter, the country returned to false democracy. Well written analysis of politics and society in 1895–1919.

3011 Puente, José Agustín de la. Imagen de la emancipación en el centenario de 1921 (Revista de la Universidad Católica [Pontificia Universidad Católica del Perú, Lima] 5, agosto 1979, p. 43–61)

Attempts to recapture Peru's general intellectual atmosphere at independence centennial. Suggests largely traditional outlook, affirmation of founding father ideas, and preoccupation with meaning of war with Chile.

Ratto Ciarlo, José. Choquehuanca y la contrarrevolución. See item **2864.**

3012 Reflexiones sobre la resistencia de La Breña: significado y proyección histórica. Lima: Comisión Permanente de la Historia del Ejército del Perú, 1982. 266 p., 4 p. of plates: ill. (some col.), ports.

Some of Peru's best known scholars in history, philosophy, and letters (along with a few military men and politicians) give their views on social and political aspects of Peru's highland guerrilla campaign. Led by Andrés Cáceres, campaign was social and political highlight of war for Peru. Includes photos and valuable biographical data on contributors, several post-Basadre historians.

3013 La Resistencia de La Breña. t. 1, De los reductos a Julcamarca, 16 enero 1881–22 febrero 1882. t. 2, La contraofensiva de 1822, 23 febrero 1882–5 mayo 1883. Lima: Ministerio de Guerra, Comisión Permanente de la Historia del Ejército del Perú, 1981–1982. 2 v.: bibl., ill. (some col.), indexes, maps.

Vol. 1 is summary of economic and political life in Lima during Chilean occupation, including some testimony from La Breña campaign participants. Written sources unspecified. Vol. 2 reviews early actions of highland campaign against Chile with narrative supplemented by oral testimony, offering various versions of events. Includes detailed battle maps. Questions asked to elicit testimony lacked specificity and interviewers were mostly military.

3014 Revilla, Julio. Industrialización temprana y lucha ideológica en el Perú: 1890–1910 (UP/EA, 9:17/18, 1981, p. 3–28, tables)

Describes social impact of industrialization of Lima consumer goods and ensuing debate at turn of century. Details representative industries, looks at patterns and rates of growth and stimulation by the banks, and examines the State's role. Useful summary of subject.

3015 Salisbury, Robert V. The Middle American exile of Víctor Raúl Haya de la Torre (AAFH/TAM, 40:1, July 1983, p. 1–15)

Rests upon State Dept. materials and published Haya writings to examine Central American reception given the Peruvian anti-imperialist in 1920s. Argues that vivid evidence of foreign influence in area awakened Haya to realities of imperialism.

3015a Stephens, Evelyne Huber. The Peruvian military government, labor mobilization, and the political strength of the left (LARR, 18:2, 1983, p. 57–93, bibl., tables)

Examines legacy of military regime for labor and left-wing parties by focusing on Comunidad Industrial, institution that helped spread labor consciousness. Notes that labor was weak, fragmented, barely organized and poorly funded in a country in economic crisis. Attributes labor's electoral strengh to ties with political parties and APRA's decline. Ends by speculating on why the army did not install a "bureaucratic-authoritarian" regime. Based on interviews, government labor figures, and electoral data.

3016 Szlaifer, Henryk. Los enclaves de exportación y la agricultura alimenticia en el Perú de los años 1890–1920: a propósito de las tesis de R. Thorp y G. Bertram (PAN/ES, 8, 1981, p. 181–199, tables)

Takes exception to Thorp-Bertram conclusion that export agriculture expansion before 1920 did not displace food crops but rather food price hikes due to rising food imports and expansion of demand. Uses 1901–05 data to argue that boom cycle occurred in sugar in year they cite decline. Argument differs but data do not.

3017 Tibesar, Antonine S. The suppression of the religious order in Peru, 1826–1830 or the King versus the Peruvian friars:

the King won (AAFH/TAM, 49:2, Oct. 1982, p. 205–239, appendices, tables)

Explains demise of Church influence in republic's early years by tracing it to heritage of royal (especially Bourbon) interference in activities of religious orders, especially after Napoleonic invasion and post–1820 pressures exerted by Spanish Parliament for orders' suppression. These policies were duplicated in early Peruvian Congress and Andrés Santa Cruz's decree "secularizing" orders. Appendices.

3018 Ulloa y Sotomayor, Alberto. Don Nicolás de Piérola, una época de la historia del Perú. Prólogo, Enrique Chirinos Soto. 2a. y difinitiva ed. Lima: Imprenta-Editorial Minerva, 1981. 495 p., 12 leaves of plates: ill., index.

Reprint of 1949 well known biography. Definitive full-blown biographical account of late 19th-century figure, although Enrique Chirinos Soto's prologue indicates it is a "public" biography. Points out lasting quality of Piérola's influence in Peruvian politics.

3019 Valcárcel, Luis E. Memorias. Editadas por José Matos Mar, José Deustua, José Luis Rénique. Lima: Instituto de Estudios Peruanos, 1981. 478 p., 16 p. of plates: ill.

Recollections of profoundly influential octogenarian archaeologist and anthropologist whose remembrances constitute a valuable historical 20th-century document. Three themes predominate: Cuzco at turn of century (his youth); politics of nationalism and rise of Haya and Mariátegui; and effort to sharpen Peruvian cultural consciousness since 1930. Of great value to many disciplines.

3020 Valderrama, Mariano. Haya de la Torre y la APRA de los años veinte (Revista de la Universidad Católica [Pontificia Universidad Católica del Perú, Lima] 5, agosto 1979, p. 121–145)

Distinguishes between "movement" and "party" and analyzes exiled student activities in 1920s. Discusses confrontation of Haya and Mariátegui over proper solution for Peru's problems. Relies on Haya's *Obras escogidas* and other publications.

3021 Vásquez, Emilio. El maestro Raúl Porras Barrenechea. Lima: Taller Gráfico P.L. Villanueva, 1981. 71 p.

Brief, largely anecdotal, biographical

essay was completed after exposition in Lima's Biblioteca Nacional of works of the subject, former National Librarian and pre-eminent historian of colonial Peru. Originally published in *La Prensa* (Lima, 1977).

3022 Vayssiere, Pierre. Le fait de le droit dans la politique indigéniste du Pérou indépendent (*in* Indianité, ethnocide, indigénisme en Amérique latine. Paris: Centre national de la recherche scientifique; Toulouse, France: Centre interdisciplinaire d'études latino-américaines, Groupe de recherches sur l'Amérique latine [GRAL], 1982, p. 53–57)

Reinterpretation of Thomas M. Davies Jr.'s ideas in *Indian integration in Peru.* Posits thesis that Indians' integration rests on good will of Lima's bucreaucratized political class, their assimilation consisting of a homogeneous identity conceived by coastal Creoles. Suggestive rather than empirical.

3023 Wilson, Fiona. Property and ideology: a regional oligarchy in the Central Andes in the nineteenth century (*in* Ecology and exchange in the Andes. Edited by David Lehmann. Cambridge: Cambridge University Press, 1982, p. 191–210, bibl. [Cambridge studies in social anthropology; 41])

Notes that Tarma's oligarchy found it impossible to control or survive transition from localized economy to expansion and production for export at end of 19th century. European investor demand for alcohol and coca, plus state limitations on real estate expansion when War of Pacific began, damaged the oligarchs' economic flexibiity. Based on

extensive use of regional records, provincial council minutes and local newspapers.

3024 Wise, David. Indigenismo de izquierda y de derecha: dos planteamientos de los años 1920 (IILI/RI, 49:122, enero/marzo 1983, p. 159–169)

In order to examine decade's nativism, points out disjunctive features between, on the one hand, Indian uprisings of 1910s and their provincial intellectual support and, on the other, petty-bourgeois awakening to Indian social plight in 1920s.

3025 Worrall, Janet E. Immigrant losses in wartime: Peru, 1879–1886 (IAMEA, 34:4, Spring 1981, p. 3–16)

Uses Peruvian diplomatic archive correspondence to study consequences of War of Pacific for Italians and British immigrants. Finds claims of neutrality were brushed aside by xenophobic, violent mob rampages against Chileans, sweeping Italian and British merchants along with others in their path.

3026 Zamalloa Armejo, Raúl. El proceso de la nacionalidad (*in* Perú, identidad nacional. César Arróspide de la Flor *et al.* Lima: Centro de Estudios para la Desarrollo y la Participación, 1979, p. 17–36 [Serie Realidad nacional])

Explores national identity and argues that a collective Peruvian will exists, even if not adequately expressed. Reviews stages of Peru's cultural history, and varied meanings given to notions like "*patria*" and "*nación*," etc.

Bolivia and Chile

THOMAS C. WRIGHT, *Professor of History, University of Nevada, Las Vegas*

BOLIVIA: LITTLE NEW GROUND has been broken in scholarship on Bolivia's national period history during this biennium. Indeed, production in Bolivia and abroad has fallen off, quantitatively and qualitatively. As usual, politics, biography, and the Chaco War have engaged historians of Bolivia more than other themes. Scholarly interest in the War of the Pacific, whose centennial has been observed over the past four years, has been surprisingly slight in Bolivia.

Those studies deserving special mention do not fit any thematic or methodological pattern. Among the noteworthy studies are vol. 2 of Antezana Villagrán's military history of the Chaco War (item **3030**) and vols. 1–2 of the Santa Cruz papers (item **3049**). Other important contributions include Lara's study of Che Guevara's companion Inti Peredo (item **3043**), Alexander's survey of Bolivian politics and history (item **3028**), Klein's article on Indian communities (item **3040**), and Kohl's study of peasant violence and national politics (item **3042**).

CHILE: A large amount of good scholarship has appeared since *HLAS 44* on Chilean national period history. Historical scholarship in Chile shows encouraging signs of renewed vigor after a long period of relative quiescence. Chileans in Britain have continued to express themselves, especially through the pages of *Nueva Historia*. University presses in the US have also made important contributions to the current flow of scholarship.

The War of the Pacific has continued as an important theme in Chilean historiography. The main thrusts are uncritical biography and unabashed flag-waving, but within the mass of publication, the reedition of Ahumada's compendium of original reports (item **3095**) and a comparative historiographical study (item **3071**) stand out. Another large theme is Andrés Bello, the bicentennial of whose birth stimualted a mild but undistinguished outpouring of articles.

Historians of Chile have turned increasingly to the 50 years between the War of the Pacific and the Great Depression to locate the roots of the dilemma and the promise of contemporary Chile. Several important studies examine and reinterpret the economy and politics of the nitrate era. Some attempt broad syntheses such as Castedo (item **3068**), Vial (item **3147**), and Monteón (item **3116**), while Góngora (item **3092**) and Heise González (item **3097**) trace narrower political themes through the period. DeShazo's study of the early labor movement (item **3073**), O'Brien's work on the nitrate economy (item **3120**), and Millar's book on the 1920 presidential election (item **3115**) are outstanding contributions to our understanding of specific aspects of the period, and García de la Huerta (item **3087**) and Bowman and Wallerstein add a noteworthy study of the 1891 civil war (item **3065**). Overall, the historiography of the nitrate era has been substantially enhanced during this biennium.

The remaining works that deserve special mention fit no particular pattern. The early years of the republic are treated in Salinas Campos' study of the Sociedad Chilena de Agricultura (item **3135**), Torres Marín's biography of Maroto (item **3144**), and Collier's study of conservative thought (item **3070**). Vols. 1–6 of *Historia del Ejército de Chile* (item **3099**) are a valuable factual and reference source. Vaysierre's study of mining (item **3146**) is an important contribution, and McCaa's demographic work on Petorca (item **3107**) breaks new ground. Two excellent studies of the Church in politics have appeared: Krebs *et al* cover the 1875–85 secularization issue (item **3104**), and Smith examines the recent and contemporary scene (item **3142**). Palma continues the debate over the timing of industrialization (item **3121**), while Barnard (item **3060**), and Ruiz (item **3132**) offer insights into politics and political thought of the 1930s. Finally, Paul Drake has done a major service by assembling a bibliography of historical works on Chile published 1977–83 in the US, Britain, and Canada (item **3075**).

BOLIVIA

3027 Academia Boliviana de la Historia.
Anales de la Academia Boliviana de la Historia: 1973–1979. Publicación hecha con el auspicio de la Comisión Nacional de Conmemoración de la Guerra del Pacífico. La Paz: La Academia, 1980. 319 p., 11 p. of plates: bibl., ill.

Contains minutes of academy meetings, records of special events, and most important, inaugural essays presented by 13 new members incorporated 1973–80. Essays range widely through Bolivian political, social, and intellectual history of all periods. Useful addition.

Albó, Xavier. Achacachi, media siglo de lucha campesina. See *HLAS 45:6376*.

3028 Alexander, Robert Jackson. Bolivia: past, present, and future of its politics. New York: Praeger; Stanford, Calif.: Hoover Institute Press, 1982. 157 p.: bibl., index (Politics in Latin America)

Analytical political history of Bolivia pays considerable attention to economy and society. Emphasizes period since Chaco War. Although undocumented, offers convenient summary of topic and reflects author's long interest in Bolivia. Good introduction and reference source.

3029 Antezana Ergueta, Luis. Daza no ocultó la noticia de la invasión chilena: definitiva dilucidación histórica. La Paz: Empresa Editora Offset Millán, 1982. 70, 5 p.: bibl., ill.

Title reflects author's thesis for his defense of President Hilarión Daza, long condemned by Bolivian writers as a traitor in War of Pacific. In this undocumented but passionate study, Antezana adds to the revisionist trend of raising Daza from infamy (see *HLAS 44:3046*, *HLAS 44:3054*, and in this volume, item **3046**).

3030 Antezana Villagrán, Jorge. La Guerra del Chaco: análisis y crítica sobre la conducción militar. 2a. ed. La Paz: Editorial CALAMA, 1981-1982. 2 v.: bibl., ill.

Vol. 1 is second ed. of excellent study noted in *HLAS 44:3013*. Vol. 2 continues story from March 1933 to war's end in June 1935, with same attention to detail and careful analysis. Especially interesting for military historians.

3031 ———. Memorias de un minero. La Paz: Litografías e Imprentas Unidas, 1980. 269 p.

Basically author's memoirs, focusing on his youthful experience in the mines and participation in Chaco War. Also contains biographical sketches of all of Bolivia's military presidents. Useful primarily for observations of working conditions in the mines.

3032 Aranzaes, Nicanor. Las revoluciones en Bolivia. La Paz: Librería Editorial

Juventud, 1980. 305 p.: bibl.

Second ed. (first 1918) of exhaustive chronological study of "revolution" in Bolivia from republic's establishment in 1825 through 1923. Identifies and describes 184 conspiracies, rebellions, and successful and failed coups in this catalog of Bolivia's thwarted attempt at governmental stability (a record of 20 "revolutions" occurred in 1849, 15 in 1841).

3033 Arguedas, Alcides. Historia de Bolivia. v. 1, La fundación de la República. v. 2, Los caudillos letrados. v. 3, La plebe en acción. v. 4, La dictadura y la anarquía. v. 5, Los caudillos bárbaros. La Paz: Librería-Editorial Juventud, 1981. 5 v.: bibl.

New ed. of classic five-volume narrative political history of Bolivia from independence to 1870s (originally published 1920–29). Still valuable for detail it provides.

3034 Canelas L., René. Teoría del motín y las sediciones en Bolivia. La Paz: Editorial Los Amigos del Libro, 1983. 361 p.: bibl.

Departing from Aranzaes' study of "revolutions" in Bolivia (item **3032**), author defines most such movements as "motines" or "sediciones" and analyzes them in context of Bolivia's economic and institutional development. Somewhat sophisticated analysis that falls short of offering a theory, extends from independence to 1981.

3035 Cárdenas Paravicini, Elvira and **Daniel Mamani.** Documentos para la historia de Oruro. La Paz: Museo Nacional de Etnografía y Folklore, Centro de Investigaciones Históricas, 1982. 24 p. (Documentos de divulgación; 1)

Collection of documents dealing with diverse aspects of 19th-century history of Oruro, with brief annotations.

Demelas, Marie-Danielle. Une réponse du berger à la bergère: les Créoles andins entre l'Amérique et l'Europe au XIXᵉ siècle. See item **2968**.

Fellman Velarde, José. Historia de Bolivia. See item **2612**.

3036 González, F. William. Historia del petróleo boliviano y su defensa en la Guerra del Chaco. La Paz: Asociación de Oficiales Beneméritos de la Guerra del Chaco, 1981. 109 p., 1 folded leaf of plates: ill.

Superficial overview of Chaco War and oil's role in its origin, designed to vindicate Bolivian army.

González, Nelly S. Ecclesiastical archives of the *parroquias de* Nuestra Señora de La Paz, Bolivia, 1548–1940: description and analysis. See item **2613.**

3037 González Torres, René and **Luis Iriarte Ontiveros.** Villarroel: mártir de sus ideales y el atisbo de la revolución. La Paz: Talleres-Escuela de Artes Gráficas del Colegio Don Bosco, 1983. 280 p.: port.

Analytical narrative of the brief (1943–46) presidential regime of Gualberto Villarroel, precursor of MNR Revolution. Although undocumented and partisan, book brings out important background to 1952 Revolution.

3038 Guzmán, Augusto. Historia de Bolivia. 5a. ed. rev. y actualizada. Cochabamba: Editorial Los Amigos del Libro, 1981. 454 p.: bibl., ill.

New, slightly updated, ed. of standard history (for last ed., see *HLAS 38:3537*).

3039 Ichazo Urquidi, Armando. Acciones y hombres olvidados: Bolivia heroica. Tarija: Universidad Boliviana Juan Misael Saracho, 1981. 300 p.: bibl., ill.

Personal account of author's role in Chaco War. Useful for detail and participant's views on strategy and morale.

3040 Klein, Herbert S. Peasant response to the market and the land: question in 18th and 19th-century Bolivia (GEE/NA, 5, 1982, p. 103–133, map, tables)

Reinforcing revisionist studies of Bolivian rural history, argues that Indian communities retained strong presence until 1880s. Using tribute census records from La Paz dept., finds that growth of marginal *forastero* class within ayllus allowed communities to produce more while maintaining their essential integrity until government destroyed them in 1880s–90s.

3041 Knudson, Jerry. Shock of recognition: the Bolivian press views the Mexican and Cuban revolutions (PCCLAS/P, 9, 1982, p. 83–89)

Brief comparative sketch of Bolivian reaction to Cárdenas administration and the first four years of Cuban Revolution, through MNR press organs. Argues that the MNR identification with revolution was tempered by Castro's turn to Marxism.

3042 Kohl, James V. The Cliza and Ucureña war: syndical violence and national revolution in Bolivia (HAHR, 62:4, Nov. 1982, p. 607–628, map)

Detailed analysis of strugggle between rival peasant sindicatos in Cochabamba Valley (1959–60), set against backdrop of national politics. Contends that sindicatos' power demonstrated in Cliza-Ucureña war turned urban MNR leadership against sindicatos and paved way for 1964 military resurgence.

3043 Lara, Jesús. Guerrillero Inti Peredo. 3a. ed. Cochabamba, Bolivia: J. Lara, 1980. 183 p., 12 p. of plates: ill.

New ed. (earlier ones not annotated in *HLAS*) of interesting and significant work about important member of Che Guevara's guerrilla band who survived campaign but was killed by Bolivian police in 1969. Gives excellent insight into Bolivian Communist Party's policy on guerrilla activity, development of Ñancahuazú war, Inti's role and his guerrilla memoirs. Important book.

3044 Maida Rojas, Segundo T. Bolivia. Santa Cruz, Bolivia: Editorial América, 1980. 375 p.: bibl., ill. (some col.).

Consists of short biographies of precursors and leaders of independence and all presidents through 1980, with portraits of each. Useful reference.

3045 Morales Guillén, Carlos. La nacionalización de las minas: la verdad en la historia. Sucre: División de Extensión Universitaria, 1977. 220 p.: bibl.

Interpretation of and excerpts from unpublished official 1952 study of projected nationalization of major mines, by member of Commission which wrote report. Argues that report was never made public because it advised against compensation for companies, which MNR government ignored.

3046 Oblitas Fernández, Edgar. ¿Quién mató al ex-Presidente Hilarión Daza? Sucre: Librería-Editorial Tupac Katari, 1982. 26 p.

Brief exposé of Daza's 1894 murder blamed by author on same oligarchy that covered its own complicity by labeling him traitor in War of Pacific.

3047 Ovando-Sanz, Jorge Alejandro. Historia económica de Bolivia. La Paz: Librería Editorial Juventud, 1981. 261 p.

Interesting interpretation of Bolivia's development from paleolithic times to 1900, based on class struggle. Examines land, taxation, and labor system that "enslaved" common Indian since Tiahuanaco period, emphasizing legalistic aspects. Lacks clear documentation.

3048 ———. La invasión brasileña a Bolivia en 1825: una de las causas del Congreso de Panamá. La Paz: Ediciones Isla, 1977. 182 p.: bibl., index.

Competent study of little known episode in Bolivian international relations. Encouraged by Holy Alliance, Brazil attempted to annex Chiquitos prov. as part of its expansionist policy, but failed when confronted with unexpected resistance by government and populace.

3049 Santa-Cruz, Andrés de. Archivo histórico del Mariscal Andrés de Santa-Cruz. t. 1, 1820–1829. t. 2, 1829–1831. Compilador, Andrés de Santa-Cruz Schuhkrafft. La Paz: Universidad Mayor de San Andrés, Instituto de Investigaciones Históricos, 1976–1981. 2 v.: index, ports.

Two volumes bring to light unpublished correspondence (1820–31) from Santa Cruz Archive in La Paz, of independence hero and president. Written to leading figures of his period, letters include many to Bolívar and are valuable source for independence and early republican periods.

3050 Saracho Calderón, Julio C. Una ráfaga en la historia de la Guerra del Chaco. Potosí, Bolivia: Empresa Editora Urquizo, 1980. 315 p., 4 leaves of plates: forms, ill., maps, ports.

Chronicle of war combines personal experience of front-line soldier with general military history. Based on campaign diary and other unnamed sources. Contains numerous photographs and frequent patriotic exhortations.

3051 Valencia Vega, Alipio. Manuel Isidoro Belzú: soñó con la "Utopía" de la liberación de indios y mestizos. La Paz: Librería Editorial Juventud, 1981. 134 p.: bibl. (Colección Tradición historia)

Narrative biography of popular mid-

19th-century caudillo, lacking scholarly apparatus but quite readable.

3052 Zavaleta, René. El proletariado minero boliviano entre 1940–1980 (CEDLA/B, 32, junio 1982, p. 29–37, bibl.)

Brief study of political organization and role of Bolivia's miners in background and execution of MNR Revolution and later military governments. Underscores importance of miners' radicalism in disproportionate power they have wielded since Catavi massacre (1941).

CHILE

3053 Acuña Peña, Manuel. Chile en la historia. Santiago: Editorial Salesiana, 1980. 331 p.: bibl., ill.

Illustrated survey of Chilean history through 1970, useful as basic text or introduction to subject.

3054 Alvarez Gómez, Oriel. Atacama de plata. Santiago: Ediciones Toda América, 1980–1983. 266 p.: bibl., ill.

Consists of varied short essays on 19th-century Atacama prov., featuring discoveries and workings of mines (especially Chañarcillo), vignettes of local and regional history, and biographies of several "hijos ilustres." Potentially useful as reference work for regional history.

3055 Antología de Rancagua. Selección y prólogo, Carlos Ruiz-Tagle. Santiago: Root Impresores, 1982. 151 p.: bibl., ill.

Well chosen selections of works by nine modern authors on history of Rancagua and its region. Includes pieces on city's founding, Battle of Rancagua, historic names, local journalism, etc.

3056 Araneda Bravo, Fidel. Arturo Alessandri Palma. Santiago: Editorial Nascimento, 1979. 266 p.: bibl.

Undocumented but informative narrative biography of Alessandri by admirer.

3057 ———. Más antecedentes sobre la intervención de los eclesiásticos en la caída del Presidente Balmaceda. Santiago: Editorial Nascimento, 1982. 42 p.: bibl.

Brief polemic designed to establish active participation of Church hierarchy against Balmaceda, despite official statements of clerical neutrality.

3058 ———. Oscar Larson, el clero y la política chilena. Santiago: Imprenta San José, 1981. 176 p.: ill.

Solid biography of influential priest, writer, academic, and early proponent of Christian democracy (1893–1974). Written by friend and based largely on Larson's unedited memoirs, this is laudatory but informative.

3059 Así lo vió Zig-Zag. Redacción edición, Claudia Adriasola *et al.* Santiago: Empresa Editora Zig Zag, 1980. 324, 26 p.: ill. (some col).

History of popular news and society weekly *Zig-Zag* from its founding to its demise in 1968 through selected reproduction of pictures and stories. Has nostalgic value.

Avila Martel, Alamiro de. Reseña histórica de la Universidad de Chile, 1622–1979. See *HLAS 45:4373.*

3060 Barnard, Andrew. El Partido Comunista de Chile y las políticas del Tercer Período, 1931–1934 (Nueva Historia [Revista de historia de Chile, London] 2:8, abril/dic. 1983, p. 211–250)

Thorough examination of Chilean Communist Party's tactics and development (1931–34) set against backdrop of interaction between Comintern policy and Chilean reality. Comintern policy for "third period" of capitalist development was militant and aggressive, and Depression-era conditions in Chile seemed to create prerevolutionary situation. However, Barnard argues, for several reasons, no-compromise, no-alliance policy worked against Chilean CP, opening way for its Socialist rival. Important article.

3061 Barriga Kreft, Sergio. Historia de LAN-Chile. v. 1, 1929–1964. Santiago: Lan-Chile, 1983. 1 v.: ill.

Narrative history of national airline from first bi-plane mail service in 1929 to incorporation of jet aircraft in 1964. Offers great deal on personnel, materiel, and expansion of LAN's routes over 35 years.

3062 Bermúdez, Oscar. San Andrés de Pica: perfiles históricos (SCHG/R, 148, 1980, p. 191–199)

Sketches history of San Andrés de Pica oasis, Tarapacá prov., from colonial inception to 1930. Describes area's changing economic base and crucial role of water resources.

3063 Blancpain, Jean-Pierre. Intelligentsia nationale et immigration européenne au Chili de l'indépendance à 1914 (JGSWGL, 18, 1981, p. 249–289)

Heavily documented article traces evolution of Chilean thought on European immigration over a century. Enthusiasm for immigration throughout 19th century was gradually replaced by nationalistic, even xenophobic reaction by 1900s.

3064 Bouvier, Virginia Marie. Alliance or compliance: implications of the Chilean experience for the Catholic Church in Latin America. Syracuse, N.Y.: Maxwell School of Citizenship and Public Affairs, Syracuse University, 1983. 105 p.: bibl. (Foreign and comparative studies. Latin American series; no. 3)

Brief examination of the Chilean Church under military regime, with background on Church-State relations and projections of Chilean experience for Latin America. Draws heavily on Brian Smith's work (item **3142**).

3065 Bowman, John R. and **Michael Wallerstein.** The fall of Balmaceda and public finance in Chile: new data for an old debate (SAGE/JIAS, 24:4, Nov. 1982, p. 421–460, tables)

Well reasoned inquiry into meaning of 1891 civil war, assessed by impact on fiscal policy. After overview of evolution of civil war historiography, article endorses recent theory that 1891 was not important watershed. Concludes that parliamentary period governments (1891–1924), after three-year deviation, resumed Balmaceda's fiscal policies demonstrating continuity over supposed watershed.

Bravo, Juan Alfonso. Inversiones norteamericanas en Chile: 1904–1907. See *HLAS 45:3378.*

3066 Campos Harriet, Fernando. Andrés Bello y la enseñanza de la historia (UC/AT, 443/444, 1981, p. 309–316)

Examination of Bello's influence in establishment of Chilean national historiography. Argues that Bello's requirement of annual *memoria* on national history, to be presented by outstanding University of Chile student, stimulated study of history in which 19th-century Chileans excelled.

3067 Carrasco Delgado, Sergio. El Arzobispo Crescente Errázuriz (UC/AT, 446, 1982, p. 119–125)
Brief overview of career of Archbishop Errázuriz (1839–1931) emphasizing his longstanding campaign to keep clerics out of politics.

3068 Castedo, Leopoldo. Chile en tiempos de Bello: la organización de la libertad (UC/AT, 443/444, 1981, p. 135–144)
Useful sketch of Bello's intellectual and practical role in shaping Chile's legal system, including 1833 Constitution and 1855 civil code which became a model for much of Latin America.

3069 Chile, sociedad y política: del Acta de la Independencia a nuestros días. A cargo de Alejandro Witker. México: Universidad Nacional Autónoma de México, 1978. 710 p.: bibl., ill. (Lecturas universitarias; 30)
Selection of essays by well-known Chilean writers on all aspects of national history from independence to 1977, with emphasis on politics. Half of book covering Allende years and military regime also contains key political party and government statements. Worthwhile anthology.

3070 Collier, Simon. Conservatismo chileno, 1830–1860: temas e imágenes (Nueva Historia [Revista de historia de Chile, London] 2 : 7, enero/marzo 1983, p. 143–163)
Informative analysis of Conservative ideology in period of *pelucón* dominance, derived from a close reading of themes emphasized by Conservative leadership in official documents, private papers, and especially the press. Finds that two dominant themes, reflecting prevailing values, were *order* (contrasting with scenario of chaos and revolution) and *material progress*, suggesting parallel with contemporary English Conservatives.

3071 Cruz, Nicolás and Ascanio Cavallo. Las guerras de la guerra: Perú, Bolivia y Chile frente al conflicto de 1879. Santiago: Instituto Chileno de Estudios Humanísticos, 198?. 108 p.
Analysis of predominant Peruvian,

Bolivian, and Chilean interpretations of causes and conduct of War of Pacific, based on early and later histories that have had greatest influence on each country. Each of eight topical chapters (e.g., remote causes, Peru at war) treats each country's view and ends with summary of Peruvian, Bolivian, and Chilean version of causes or events. Despite brevity and selectivity, a useful tool for understanding century-long historiographical war over the war.

3072 Cuadra Gormaz, Guillermo de la. Familias chilenas: origen y desarrollo de las familias chilenas. 3a ed. Santiago: Editorial Zamorano y Caperán, 1982. 2 v. (713 p., 1 leaf of plates): indexes, ports.
Third ed. of standard genealogical reference work on leading Chilean families.

3072a Cumplido, Francisco *et al.* Visión de Chile, 1920–1970. Presentación, Carlos Martínez Sotomayor. Santiago: Ediciones CINDE, 1980. 99 p.: index (Biblioteca Ediciones CINDE; 1)
Eight brief interpretive essays by prominent academics on historical, political, social, and economic aspects of 1920–70 period and its background. Useful as expression of current interpretations of modern history.

3073 DeShazo, Peter. Urban workers and labor unions in Chile, 1902–1927. Madison: University of Wisconsin Press, 1983. 351 p.: bibl., ill., index.
Detailed examination of formative period of Chilean labor movement. Offers four important revisionist propositions: 1) that urban rather than nitrate workers were labor movement's driving force; 2) that anarcho-syndicalists were most successful organizing agents during 1902–27 period; 3) that FOCH was regional rather than national organization; and 4) that politics and politicians were less influential on labor than normally assumed. These arguments, supported by extensive research and documentation, make this solid book indispensible for Chilean specialists and labor historians.

3074 Doursther, Juan Francisco. Aventuras y desventuras de un mercader de perlas de Valparaíso: diario. Con un estudio preliminar de Regina Claro Tocornal. Santiago: Editorial Universitaria, 1982. 82 p.: bibl., ill. (Colección Fuera de serie)
Diary recounts Valparaíso Dutch Con-

sul's 1831 pearling expedition to South Pacific islands. Introductory study sheds some light on Consul's activities and contemporary Valparaíso society.

3075 Drake, Paul. El impacto académico de los terremotos políticos: investigaciones de la historia chilena en inglés, 1977–1983 (Alternativas [Centro de Estudios de la Realidad Contemporánea, Academia de Humanismo Santiago, Santiago] 2, enero/ abril 1984, p. 56–78)

Comprehensive analysis of work on Chilean history produced in the US, Canada, and Britain (1977–83). Drake organizes 247 books and articles into chronological and thematic categories and explores impact of recent Chilean politics on Anglophone historiography. This piece dovetails nicely with Sater's 1979 summary of Chilean historiography between 1965 and 1976. Very useful and welcome tool.

3076 Encina, Francisco Antonio. Resumen de la historia de Chile. Redacción, iconografía y apéndices de Leopoldo Castedo. Santiago: Zig-Zag, 1954–1982. 4 v.: diagrams., fascims., fold. plates, ill., maps, plans, ports.

Lavishly illustrated narrative and analysis of 1891–1925 period by editor of Encina's abridged *Historia de Chile* (first published 1954). Straightforward account of period's main political, economic, social, and cultural developments. Very readable and informative. Welcome as reliable introduction to period.

3077 Escala Escobar, Manuel. Un capítulo olvidado de nuestra historia patria (SCHG/R, 149, 1981, p. 179–191)

Carabinero Colonel offers sketchy history of Chilean police from late colonial period to Ibáñez's 1927 creation of Carabineros de Chile. Potentially useful as first step toward full-scale history of Chilean police.

3078 Escobar, Roberto. Teoría del chileno. Santiago: Corporación de Estudios Contemporáneos, 1981. 245 p.: bibl., ill., index.

Offers thoughts of prominent academic, philosopher, and musical composer on *lo chileno*, in all its dimensions. Drawing on history, geography, anthropology, literature, attempting equilibrium between "myth and utopia," author presents his visions of

Chile in loosely connected chapters. Of interest to those concerned with national characater and contemporary intellectual history.

3079 Espinosa, Januario. Don Manuel Montt, uno de los más grandes estadistas de América. Prólogo de Ricardo A. Latcham. 2a. ed. Santiago: Editorial Universitaria, 1981. 286 p.: ill.

New ed. (for 1944 original, see *HLAS 10:3039*) of novelist's narrative biography of Montt. Undocumented and laudatory but readable.

3080 Espinosa Moraga, Oscar. Latorre y la vocación marítima de Chile. 2a. ed. Santiago: Eire, 1980. 109 p.: appendices, ill.

Substantive biography of Admiral Juan José Latorre (1846–1912), career naval officer, hero of War of Pacific, and Liberal Democratic politician and Senator (1894–1906). Based partly on family archives. Includes documentary appendixes.

3081 Estrada, Baldomero. Tesis sobre historia de Chile realizadas en Gran Bretaña, Estados Unidos y Francia (Nueva Historia [Revista de historia de Chile, London] 2 : 8, abril/dic. 1983, p. 251–275)

Useful compilation of British, French, and US graduate theses from earliest through 1980.

3082 Eyzaguirre, Jaime. Historia de las instituciones políticas y sociales de Chile. 4a. ed. Santiago: Editorial Universitaria, 1979. 215 p.: bibl. (Cormorán. Colección Manuales y monografías)

Fourth ed. of Eyzaguirre's conservative interpretation of Chilean history through 1938.

3083 Flores F., Sergio and **Juan Saavedra A.** Bello y la ciencia histórica: una tradición vigente (SCHG/R, 149, 1981, p. 7–20)

Brief derivative essay asserts that Chilean national historiography began with Andrés Bello's establishment of Faculty of Humanities of University of Chile which produced, by Bello's dictum, a long and distinguished series of *memorias históricas*.

3084 ——— and ———. Los caminos Santiago-Valparaíso en la observación del viajero John Miers (SCHG/R, 148, 1980, p. 115–136, maps)

History of two principal roads with

their variants, that linked capital and port in colonial period. Focus is on sections of John Miers' *Travels in Chile and La Plata* dealing with these roads as he found them in 1819. Some interesting descriptions.

3085 Fuenzalida Contreras, Abraham. Memorias de un proscrito: pt. 4 (SCHG/R, 148, 1980, p. 85–114)

Concluding installment of memoirs of Balmacedista Abraham Fuenzalida Contreras dealing with 1891 civil war (for pts. 1–3, see *HLAS 42:3221*). Memoirs detail end of author's ill-fated participation, culminating in exile.

3086 Galdames Rosas, Luis Alberto *et al.* Historia de Arica. Santiago: Editorial Renacimiento, 1981. 155 p.

Collectively-authored historical synthesis of Arica and its region, emphasizes Spanish and Chilean periods. Useful as introduction to regional history.

3087 García de la Huerta I., Marcos. Chile 1891, la gran crisis y su historiografía: los lugares comunes de nuestra conciencia histórica. Santiago: Centro de Estudios Humanísticos, Universidad de Chile, 1981. 214 p., 10 p. of plates: bibl., ill., tables.

Study of 1891 civil war historiography focuses on major schools. Examines prevalent interpretations in detail, rejects traditional constitutional and economic arguments, and delineates thesis based on relation between changing mode of nitrate production and conflict with political elite. Thoughtful piece, very useful for understanding important conjuncture. Includes tables.

3088 Gariazzo, Alicia. Orígenes ideológicas de los movimientos obreros chileno y argentino (CPES/RPS, 18:51, junio/sept. 1981, p. 59–96)

Well researched study of differing ideological and political circumstances of early (1880–1930) phases of Chilean and Argentine labor movements. Argues that differences in degree of capitalist development, demand for labor, and proletariat's cultural levels were responsible for greater influence of socialism in Chile and anarchism (combined with economic action) in Argentina.

3089 Gazmuri Riveros, Cristián. Notas sobre la influencia del racismo en la obra de Nicolás Palacios, Francisco A. Encina

y Alberto Cabero (UCCIH/H, 16, 1981, p. 225–247)

Compares and contrasts racial views of three influential 20th-century writers, and examines their use of racism in interpreting Chilean history and society. Using racial explanations exclusively (Palacios) or in conjunction with other factors (Encina and especially Cabero), these writers pronounced Chileans different from and, in the case of Palacios and Cabero, superior to their neighbors.

3090 ———. Testimonios de una crisis: Chile, 1900–1925. Santiago: Editorial Universitaria, 1979. 90 p.: bibl. (Fascículos para la comprensión de la ciencia, las humanidades y la tecnología; 31)

Analysis of writings of 10 contemporary critics of 1900–25 period with lengthy quotations from their works. Useful synthesis covers critiques of Chile's latent crisis offered by Enrique Mac-Iver, Nicolás Palacios, Tancredo Pinochet, Alejandro Venegas, Francisco Encina, Luis E. Recabarren, Agustín Ross, Víctor Celis, Guillermo Subercaseaux, and Alberto Cabero.

3091 Godoy Urzúa, Hernán. El carácter chileno: estudio preliminar y selección de ensayos. 2a. ed., aum. Santiago: Editorial Universitaria, 1981. 530 p.: bibl., ill.

Consists of 2nd ed. (for first, 1976, see *HLAS 52:3223*) of extensive anthology of 16th through 20th-century writings that illuminate the Chilean "national character."

3092 Góngora, Mario. Ensayo histórico sobre la noción de Estado en Chile en los siglos XIX y XX. Santiago: Ediciones La Ciudad, 1981. 149 p.: bibl.

Based on contention that "Chilean nationality has been formed by a State that preceded it," book consists of incisive interpretive essays on changing idea and form of the State. Focusing on 1891–1932 period of transition from aristocratic to popular politics, Góngora offers both intellectual history of a notion and selective history of important political developments. Major contribution.

3093 González P., José Antonio. Luis Silva Lezaeta y la historia regional norteña (SCHG/R, 148, 1980, p. 201–209)

Bio-bibliography of Monseñor Silva Lezaeta (1860–1929), first Bishop of Antofagasta, historian, and educator. Silva Lezaeta wrote major biography of conquistador Francisco de Aguirre and made numerous contributions to northern history.

3094 ———. Un soldado de la Guerra del Pacífico: apuntes y episodios de José Ramón Lira (SCHG/R, 150, 1982, p. 14–28, ill.)

Excerpts from soldier's diary and vignettes of his participation in War of Pacific.

3095 Guerra del Pacífico: documentos oficiales, correspondencias y demás publicaciones referentes a la guerra, que ha dado a luz la prensa de Chile, Perú y Bolivia. Recopiladas por Pascual Ahumada. Santiago: Editorial Andrés Bello, 1982. 8 v. in 4: bibl.

Facsimile reproduction of vols. 1–2 of eight (originally published 1883–91), consisting of government documents, correspondents' dispatches, editorials, and other press information on war from Peruvian and Bolivian as well as Chilean sources. Vols. 1–2 cover from 1874 Chilean-Bolivian Treaty through Battle of Tacna (May 1880). This extremely valuable resource for war's history is organized chronologically, with variety of sources and viewpoints elucidating major events. Important reedition.

3096 Heise González, Julio. 150 [i.e. Cientocincuenta] años de evolución institucional. 4a. ed. Santiago: Editorial Andrés Bello, 1979. 157 p.: bibl.

Enduring synthesis (4th ed.) of Chile's institutional and constitutional history from independence through 1950s (for first ed., 1960, see *HLAS 26:1147*).

3097 ———. El período parlamentario, 1861–1925. t. 2, Democracia y gobierno representativo en el período parlamentario. Santiago: Editorial Universitaria, 1982. 1v.: bibl., ill.

Revisionist treatment of extended Parliamentary Period questions prevailing assumptions about era's politics. Rather than sterility and corruption, author sees organic process of "democratization" as period's hallmark: steady extension of electoral participation, strengthening of electoral and party systems, and parties' attempts to deal with "social question" paved way for post-1925 period of more competitive politics. This important volume by respected historian is

required reading for Chilean specialists and political historians. Vol. 1 was unavailable to reviewer before press time.

3098 Heredia M., Luis. El anarquismo en Chile: 1897–1931. México: Ediciones Antorcha, 1981. 57 p.

Anarchist interpretation of Chilean labor and political history (1897–1930) devoid of documentation and new information.

3099 Historia del Ejército de Chile. t. 1, El Ejército del Reyno de Chile, 1603–1810. t. 2, De la Patria Vieja a la Batalla de Maipo, 1810–1818. t. 3, El Ejército y la organización de la República, 1817–1840. t. 5, El Ejército en la Guerra del Pacífico. Santiago: Estado Mayor General del Ejército, 1980–1981. 4 v.: appendices, bibl., ill. (some col.), ports.

Vols. 1–3 and 5 are result of military-civilian collaboration, under army's direction, designed to produce comprehensive history of Chilean army from 1603 formal creation to present. Covers organization, personnel, armament, warfare, and related matters in a professional way and includes notes, bibliography, illustrations, and documentary appendices. Very useful for ascertaining basic facts about army through its history.

Huerta de Pacheco, María Antonieta. Reforma agraria chilena, 1938–1978: evaluación histórica. See *HLAS 45:3402.*

3100 Izquierdo Araya, Guillermo *et al.* Diego Portales, bosquejos de su vida y de su obra. Santiago: Círculo Portaliano, 1979. 151 p.: bibl., ill. (Boletín anual del Círculo Portaliano)

Collection of essays by little known writers on diverse aspects of Portales' career and legacy.

3101 Jaksić, Iván. Philosophy and university reform at the University of Chile: 1842–1973 (LARR, 19:1, 1984, p. 57–86)

Studies evolution of philosophical thought at University of Chile. Finds that philosophy evolved from practical guide for educational policy in university's early years into esoteric and detached discipline. Debate over philosophy's role in social concerns sparked 1968 university reform.

3102 Kay, Cristóbal. Transformaciones de las relaciones de dominación y dependencia entre terratenientes y campesinos en el período post-colonial en Chile (Nueva Historia [Revista de historia de Chile, London] 2:6, oct./dic. 1982, p. 74–110)

Analytical study of patron-client relationship in Chilean countryside (1850–present) covers: 1) traditional landlord-campesino patronage (1850–1930); 2) transition (1930–64); and 3) fully developed clientelism (1964–73) in which political groups and the State replaced landlords as dominant force. Sees post-1973 as reversion to landlord patronage. Sound schematic analysis. For sociologist's comment, see *HLAS 45:8340*.

3103 Krebs, Ricardo. Proyecciones del pensamiento histórico de Andrés Bello (CONAC/RNC, 43:249, abril/dic. 1982, p. 267–296)

Useful synthesis of Bello's ideas about historical meaning and method, extracted from his publications. Bello sided with empiricists in lively debate that engaged early Chilean historians.

3104 ——— et al. Catolicismo y laicismo: las bases doctrinarias del conflicto entre la Iglesia y el Estado en Chile, 1875–1885: seis estudios. Santiago: Ediciones Nueva Universidad, Vicerrectoría de Comunicaciones, Pontificia Universidad Católica de Chile, 1981. 255 p.: bibl.

Latest collective effort by research team continues high quality of earlier publications (see *HLAS 42:3222* and *HLAS 44:3120*). Each essay analyzes debate over secularization of marriage, cemeteries, and patronage from viewpoint of major ideological positions: the Church's; Conservative Party's; Conservative leader Abdón Cifuentes'; Liberal Party's; Radical Party's; and positivists'. Thoroughly researched and documented, a first-rate study in Chilean intellectual and political history.

3105 Larenas Q., Víctor H. Patricio Lynch, almirante, general, gobernante y diplomático. Santiago: Editorial Universitaria, 1981. 161 p.: appendices, ill.

Narrative biography of War of Pacific naval hero and Lima's wartime governor. Lengthy appendices produce documents on military operations in Peru and reports on Lynch's administration in Lima. Worthwhile addition to war's centennial literature.

3106 Larraín de Castro, Carlos. La familia Larraín: sus orígenes en España e historia de la rama mayor en Chile. Santiago: Academia Chilena de la Historia, 1982. 399 p.: bibl., ill., index.

Posthumous genealogical study of major branch of influential Larraín family by noted historian and man of letters (1899–1973). Profusely illustrated work meticulously traces Larraín clan from Navarrese origins through 19th century. Includes large appendix. Very useful contribution to Chilean family and social history.

3107 McCaa, Robert. Marriage and fertility in Chile: demographic turning points in the Petorca Valley, 1840–1976. Boulder: Westview Press, 1983. 207 p.: bibl., ill., index (Dellplain Latin American studies; no. 14)

Detailed, complex study of population of Petorca valley (200 km north of Santiago), using family reconstitution methods. Finds that Chile has made the transition from traditional demographic regime to modern one and that this change, originating in urban areas, has spread to rural population as well. Ground-breaking study with far-reaching implications for Chilean and Latin American demography.

3108 Martínez Lemoine, René. Desarrollo urbano de Santiago: 1541–1941 (CPES/RPS, 15:42/43, mayo/dic. 1978, p. 57–90, ill.)

Interpretive overview of geographical factors governing Santiago's physical growth over four centuries. Interesting for urban historians.

3109 Martinic Beros, Mateo. Centenario de la expedición de La Romanche (SCHG/R, 150, 1982, p. 185–190)

Brief account of French scientific expedition that explored Tierra del Fuego in 1881–83, and assessment of importance.

3110 ———. La tierra de los fuegos: historia, geografía, sociedad, economía. Tierra del Fuego: Municipalidad de Porvenir, 1982. 221 p.: bibl., ill.

Social, economic, and political history of Tierra del Fuego commemorates century of Chilean occupation. Solid study by prolific historian of Chile's south includes chronology and bibliography.

3111 Matte Varas, Joaquín. Correspondencia del Capellán Mayor Presbítero Don Florencio Fontecilla Sánchez durante la

Guerra del Pacífico (SCHG/R, 150, 1982, p. 193–231)

Collection of 23 letters from chief military chaplain of War of Pacific, selected from archive of Archbishopric of Santiago, with brief introduction. Letters, written from front, offer useful commentary on military operations and personalities.

3112 ———. Monseñor Crescente Errázuriz, historiador, en el cincuentenario de su fallecimiento (SCHG/R, 149, 1981, p. 192–203)

Commemorative biographical sketch of Monseñor Crescente Errázuriz (1839–1931) and chronological analysis of his main works on colonial history. Useful as overview of life and works of conservative Catholic historian.

3113 Mayorga Santana, Ramiro. La colonización de Aysén y la guerra de Chile Chico (SCHG/R, 150, 1982, p. 283–300)

Examines 1918 incident called "la guerra de Chile Chico" as example of conflict between powerful land speculators and poor squatters in haphazard settlement of Aysén.

3114 ———. El proceso a Los Rabudos (SCHG/R, 150, 1982, p. 251–282, tables)

Study of 1916 lawsuit between Deputy Agustín Gómez García and the State involving southern channel area. Protracted conflict, pitting private versus fiscal claims to land, stimulated establishment of legislation and tribunals dealing with thorny question of *propiedad austral*.

3115 Millar Carvacho, René. La elección presidencial de 1920: tendencias y prácticas políticas en el Chile parlamentario. Santiago: Editorial Universitaria, 1982. 293 p.: bibl., maps.

Sophisticated, detailed study of 1920 election focuses on 1918–20 period, examines factors in Alessandri victory and Chilean electoral behaviour. Analyzes changes in Radical and Liberal positions and rise of anti-party groups to explain new reformist tendency. Presents demographic analysis of election results, including extensive appendices. Indispensable for students of modern Chilean history and model for future election studies.

3116 Monteón, Michael. Chile in the nitrate era: the evolution of economic dependence, 1880–1930. Madison: University of Wisconsin Press, 1982. 256 p.: bibl., ill., index.

Ambitious study of Chilean economics and politics (1880–1930) focuses on dependent nature of nitrate economy. Provides good insights into its working and rise of nitrate proletariat, and offers useful interpretive framework for entire period. Important study for historians of Chile and students of economic development.

3117 Montt, Manuel S. Carta del Comandante Holley sobre la Batalla de Tacna (SCHG/R, 148, 1980, p. 251–254)

Brief letter describing Battle of Tacna (26 May 1880) from a private archive. Contains interesting observations.

3118 Morales Ocaranza, Luis Joaquín. Historia del Huasco. Edición crítica moderada de Mario Ferreccio Podestá. La Serena: Universidad de Chile, 1981. 345 p., 8 leaves of plates: bibl., ill. (Biblioteca Chilena Regional; 2)

New ed. (original 1896–97) of narrative political, social, and economic history of Huasco Valley. Includes preliminary study of author-physician and intellectual influences on his work. First half covers colonial period, second republic to 1860. Useful for detail and as example of 19th-century historiography.

3119 Muniziga Vigil, Gustavo. Notas para un estudio comparativo de la trama urbana Santiago de Chile (CPES/RPS, 15: 42/43, mayo/dic. 1978, p. 171–251, maps, tables)

Useful essay on theories of urban history and sources for Santiago's urban development. Appendices (36 p.) offer chronology of Santiago history and sample maps.

3120 O'Brien, Thomas F. The nitrate industry and Chile's crucial transition, 1870–1891. New York: New York University Press, 1982. 211 p.: bibl., index.

Solid work focuses on dependent relationship between center and periphery and on "crucial transition" from foreign dominance of international trade before 1880 to direct control of Chile's primary economic resource. Well researched book provides wealth of detail on nitrate economy and its impact on Chilean society and politics. Required reading for students of Chile and as first-rate case study in dependency, valuable to students of economic development. For economist's comment, see *HLAS 45:3412.*

3121 Palma, J. Gabriel. Chile, 1914–1935: de economía exportadora a sustitutiva de importaciones (Nueva Historia [Revista de historia de Chile, London] 2:7, enero/marzo 1983, p. 165–192)

Detailed analysis of transition from export economy to import substitution. Convincingly argues against traditional view that Depression caused import-substitution industrialization. Believes World War I collapse of nitrate exports led to a transition accelerated by Depression. Valuable addition to literature on Chilean development.

3122 Peri Fagerstrom, René. Los batallones Bulnes y Valparaíso en la Guerra del Pacífico. Santiago: Imprenta de Carabineros, 1981. 205 p.: bibl., ill. (some col.).

Chronicles participation of two batallions of Santiago and Valparaíso policemen in War of Pacific. Reproduces relevant photos, documents, and memorabilia.

3123 Philipps, David Atlee. My not-so-golden newspapering days in wildest Chile (Smithsonian [Smithsonian Institution, Washington] 14:3, June 1983, p. 104–121)

Popularized reminiscences of US national who took over venerable *South Pacific Mail* in 1949, with sketchy but useful information on history of English-language journalism in Chile.

Pino Zapata, Ricardo. Pacificación y colonización de la frontera y la Araucania. See item **1693.**

3124 Porteous, J. Douglas. The annexation of Easter Island: geopolitics and environmental perception (NS, 6:11, 1981, p. 67–80, maps)

Interesting article examines Chilean motives for annexing Easter Island in 1888 during heyday of Big Power island-grabbing in Pacific. Analyzes contrast between Chilean perceptions of island's value and its actual economic and strategic worth. Concludes Chile overestimated island's value.

3125 Przeworski, Joanne Fox. Mines and smelters: the role of the coal oligopoly in the decline of the Chilean copper industry (GEE/NA, 1, 1978, p. 169–213, tables)

Detailed examination of decline of Chilean copper production between 1880s and 20th-century revival under US ownership. Concludes that companies' restricting amount of coal reaching smelting plants contributed to decline. Interesting chapter in Chile's frustrated economic development.

3126 Ramírez Rivera, Hugo R. La Batalla de Huamachuco y su polémica: 1885–1914, publicación de inéditos (SCHG/R, 150, 1982, p. 301–320, bibl.)

Surveys early Chilean historiography of Battle of Huamachuco (9–10 July 1883) in Peruvian Sierra, Chilean victory in which led to signing of Treaty of Ancón. Includes unpublished letters from participant Luis Dell'Orto.

3127 Ramón, Armando de. Santiago de Chile, 1850–1900: límites urbanos y segregación espacial según estratos (CPES/RPS, 15:42/43, mayo/dic. 1978, p. 253–276, maps, tables)

Using census data, ministerial memoranda, maps, and other contemporary sources, examines Santiago's spatial growth (1850–1900). Also analyzes segregation by examining administrative policy, location of factories, property values, degree of literacy, and availability of potable water. Good insights into urbanization process.

3128 Ravest Mora, Manuel. Juan Martínez, comandante de los mineros del Atacama. Santiago: Mutual de Seguridad, C.Ch.C., 1979. 102 p., 6 leaves of plates: bibl., facsims., port.

One of more serious and successful attempts to resurrect unknown heroes of War of Pacific. Chronicles life and wartime activities of commander of Atacama Batallion, celebrated Chilean unit. Based on extensive collection of Martínez's papers.

3129 ———. Narración del Combate de Concepción escrita por el soldado Marcos Ibarra Díaz del Segundo de Línea (SCHG/R, 150, 1982, p. 7–13)

Brief unpublished account of Battle of Concepción (July 1882) in the sierra where Peruvian montoneros defeated Chilean detachment.

3130 Retamal Avila, Julio. Monseñor Manuel Vicuña Larraín, 1841–1843: primer Arzobispo de Santiago. Santiago: Editorial Salesiana, 1981. 44 p. (Serie Arzobispo de Santiago)

Part of series on Santiago archbishops, this booklet, oriented to pious readers, offers biographical data on first office holder.

Riz, Liliana de. Sociedad y política en Chile: de Portales a Pinochet. See *HLAS 45 : 8344.*

3131 Rogers Figueroa, Patricio. La astronomía en Chile durante la segunda mitad del siglo XIX (SCHG/R, 150, 1982, p. 29–48, bibl.)

Outlines history of Chilean astronomy, practitioners, and contributions to scientific knowledge. Established by US' Gillis Mission (1849–52), South America's first astronomical observatory was later turned over to Chile.

3132 Ruiz, Carlos. Notes on authoritarian ideologies in Chile (NS, 6:11, 1981, p. 17–36)

Sound analysis of role of Jaime Eyzaguirre's early works (1930s) in promoting authoritarian ideologies embraced by Chile's current rulers. Interprets Catholicism, politics, Hispanism, arguing that his political model was "oligarchic corporatism." Study links intellectual and political history, offering important insights into rise of vigorous and enduring ideological movement.

3133 Salas Silva, Irma; Carlos Andrade Geywitz; and René Rojas Galdames. Homenaje a Don Luis Galdames en el centenario de su nacimiento, 8 de octubre de 1981. Santiago: Instituto de Chile, 1982. 77 p. (Documentos; no. 5)

Texts of three speeches offered in homage to the late historian and educator on his birth's centennial. Useful primarily for biographical information.

3134 Salinas, Francisco. Catálogo de marcas prefilatélicas, sellos y enteros postales de Chile. Santiago: Ediciones SELCHI, 1981. 92 p.: ill.

Catalog consists of b/w reproductions of late colonial and early republican postal marks and 1853–1970s stamps. Of interest to historians and philatelists.

3135 Salinas Campos, Maximiliano A. El laicado católogo de la Sociedad Chilena de Agricultura y Beneficiencia, 1838–1849: la evolución del catolicismo y la Ilustración en Chile durante la primera mitad del siglo XIX. Santiago: Universidad Católica de Chile, 1980. 174 p.: bibl., index, ports (*Anales de la Facultad de Teología; v. 29. Cuaderno 1, 1978*)

Well researched and documented study of Chile's first agricultural society as expression of Catholic Enlightenment extending beyond independence era. Examines society's personalities and activities, demonstrating Catholic inspiration of its charitable and educational endeavours. Good intellectual and institutional history that should be consulted with Izquierdo (see *HLAS 32 : 2675*).

3136 Salvat Monguillot, Manuel. Abogados y poetas en 1842: influencia de Andrés Bello (UC/AT, 443/444, 1981, p. 291–307)

Useful contribution to polemic over relative influence of Bello and Lastarria in 1842 literary and philosophical movement. Examining careers and testimonies of "generation of 1842" and Lastarria's writings, rejects attempts to discount Bello's pervasive influence.

3137 Santiago, nueva antología. Realización y prólogo de Carlos Ruiz-Tagle. Selección y notas biográficas de Victoria Roepke. Santiago: Ilustre Municipalidad de Santiago, Fundación Pacífico: Editorial Mar del Sur, 1981. 226 p.

Anthology of descriptive, historical, and literary writings on Santiago, from Pedro de Valdivia to contemporary commentaries. Well chosen to convey city's ambience throughout its evolution.

3138 Sater, William F. La agricultura chilena y la Guerra del Pacífico (UCCIH/H, 16, 1981, p. 125–149)

Examination of war's impact on Chilean agriculture, based on contemporary observations and statistics. Finds that agricultural sector prospered during wartime and that dislocations, such as labor shortages and commercial disruptions, were minimal and transitory.

3139 Schmutzer Susaeta, Karin. Aventuras de un inglés en Chile: Guillermo

Watkins, 1838–1880 (UCCIH/H, 16, 1981, p. 67–124)

Observations of English teacher/ miner, who lived in Chile 1838 to his 1880 death, on trip to center and south (1852–53). Useful information on vegetation, climate, and customs (including those of Indians).

3140 Schnepf, Ryszard. Ideas de Ignacy Domeyko (PAN/ES, 8, 1981, p. 143–168)
Analysis of thought of Polish refugee scientist whose 19th-century observations of Chilean natural history still attract interest. Presents Domeyko's ideas on religion, society, politics, Indians, and public instruction.

3141 Silva Bijit, Roberto. Viajeros en Quillota durante el siglo XIX. Quillota, Chile: Editorial *El Observador*, 1980. 70 p.: ill. (Colección Pelicano; no. 1)
Interesting anthology, with editor's introduction, of observations of nine foreign travelers who visited Aconcagua Valley town of Quillota (1814–63). Includes Maria Graham, Charles Darwin, and lesser-known travelers. Useful for local history.

3142 Smith, Brian H. The Church and politics in Chile: challenges to modern Catholicism. Princeton, N.J.: Princeton University Press, 1982. 383 p.: bibl., index.
Incisive study of religio-political relations in Chile from breakdown of traditional alliances (1920–35) to 1980, with focus on post-1958 period. Based on historical documentation, opinion surveys, interviews with Chilean religious elites, and author's personal experiences as participant-observer. Work offers valuable insights into Church's interaction with variety of political regimes. Indispensable for both modern Church history and Chilean politics, and a useful model for studies in other countries.

3143 Sosa, Ignacio. Conciencia y proyecto nacional en Chile, 1891–1973. México: Universidad Nacional Autónoma de México, Facultad de Filosofía y Letras, Centro de Estudios Latinoamericanos, 1981. 269 p.: bibl., ill. (Colección Seminarios)
Interpretive political history of Chile (1891–1973) focuses on frustrated goal of nationalist development. Tracing failures of economic nationalists from Balmaceda to Allende, sees anti-national bourgeoisie as insuperable obstacle to autonomous development. Selectively documented study offers a few new insights but no convincing interpretation of modern Chile.

3144 Torres Marín, Manuel. Chacabuco y Vergara, sino y camino del Teniente General Rafael Maroto Yserns. Santiago: Editorial Andrés Bello, 1981. 483 p., 4 leaves of plates: bibl., ill., index.
Thorough biography of "champion of lost causes" on both sides of Atlantic. Maroto (1783–1853) led losing royalist forces at Chacabuco (1817) and signed Convention of Vergara (1839) for defeated Carlists. Biography, solidly researched and engagingly written, raises protagonist from obscurity and contributes to our knowledge of both Chile and Spain.

3145 Vamos Szabo, Emmerich. The traveling post offices of Chile. Omaha, Neb.: Mobile Post Office Society, 1983. 32 p.: ill. (International T.P.O. markings series; no. 3)
Interesting sketch of development and functioning of railway postal service (i.e., ambulancias) from 1860s to present. Contains many of the marks and delineates routes. Of interest to antiquarians and philatelists.

3146 Vayssière, Pierre. Un siècle de capitalisme minier au Chile, 1830–1930. Paris: Editions du Centre national de recherches scientifiques (C.N.R.S.), 1980. 333 p.: bibl., ill., index, maps (Amérique latine—pays ibériques)
Thorough, incisive study of Chilean mining (1830–1930) divided into artisanal (1830–80) and industrial (1880–1930) periods. Based on extensive archival and secondary research, study traces rise of mining, labor practices, mining finance, role of mining in national economy, and denationalization of mining sector after 1880. Thoroughly-documented, well-argued work is important addition to Chilean and Latin American mining history.

3147 Vial Correa, Gonzalo. Historia de Chile, 1891–1973. v. 2, Triunfo y decadencia de la oligarquía, 1891–1920. Santiago: Editorial Santillana del Pacífio, 1981–1983. 1 v.: bibl., ill., indexes.
Vol. 2 of Vial's ambitious history complements and builds upon vol. 1's social analysis (see *HLAS 44:3125*). Organized along lines of political chronology, this lucidly written work covers politics and government, economics, and international

relations, drawing on broad range of sources. Organizing focus is the oligarchy which, author argues, ruled without challenge in every realm of public life during 1891–1920 period. Important work.

3148 Vial Solar, Javier. Tapices viejos. Prólogo, semblanza y notas de Patricio Tupper León. 2a. ed. Santiago: Editorial F. de Aguirre, 1982. 262p.: bibl., ill., index, ports. (Biblioteca Francisco de Aguirre. Colección Memorialistas; 69)

Second ed. (first 1924) of collected writings of Javier Vial Solar (1854–1935), prominent lawyer, diplomat, and man of letters. Vignettes, reminiscences, and short stories reflect ambience of aristocratic Santiago in 1850–1900. Includes author's brief biography.

3149 Villalobos R., Sergio. Los comienzos de la historiografía económica de Chile, 1862-1940. Santiago: Editorial Universitaria, 1981. 108 p. (Fascículos para la com-
(Fascículos para la comprensión de la

prensión de la ciencia, las humanidades y la tecnología; 37. Humanidades: historia)

Overview of development of Chile's economic history from Claudio Gay to Encina's *Historia de Chile*. Reviews work and influence of Courcelle-Seneuil, Agustín Ross, Benjamín Vicuña MacKenna, Jaime Barros Arana, Daniel Martner, etc., categorizing them as Liberals or state interventionists. Lacking documentation and bibliography, brief work skims lightly over vast subject.

3150 Yeager, Gertrude M. Women's role in nineteenth-century Chile: public education records, 1843–1883 (LARR, 18:3, 1983, p. 149–156)

Interesting research note discusses potential use of extensive 19th-century Chilean public education records as source for women's history. Examines documentation available, its relevance to women, and value for social and women's history. Offers good insights for research.

Argentina, Paraguay and Uruguay

ROBERTO ETCHEPAREBORDA, *Visiting Lecturer, School of Advanced International Studies, The Johns Hopkins University*

ARGENTINA: RECENT HISTORICAL WRITINGS continue to reflect previous trends both in quality and quantity as is evident in a considerable number of commendable if not entirely significant works. The prevalence of 19th-century topics notwithstanding, one detects a rising interest in contemporary affairs. Publications on the 1900s–30s and post-1930 era are in the lead, with 117 as compared to 130 on the 19th century. Works by foreign authors continue to stand out, constituting more than 30 percent of works annotated below or 48 out of 172. For contributions by American authors during the 1976–83 period, please see the survey noted below (item **3236**). An unusual number of reference aids such as bibliographic studies have appeared as have various *festchriften*.

Political upheavals of the last years have affected the selection of themes and influenced present trends in Argentina. The long-standing preoccupation with peronism continues as does interest in the history of the labor movement, but a neglected topic, the study of recent military regimes, received an important boost. Another new development is interest in the Radical Party which, for the time being, seems to have displaced Rosas and rosismo as a leading topic. On the other hand, well established social history themes such as immigration continue to command interest.

The most important contributions of the last biennium are varied in genre and topic. One should mention Ezequiel Gallo's *Pampa gringa* (item **3250**), as an outstanding work of research on a theme crucial for understanding present-day Argentina. Horacio Videla's *Historia de San Juan* (item **3370**) offers a balanced picture of both regional and national history; Norma L. Pavoni's study (item **3321**) introduces an entirely new interpretation of the Argentine Interior in the 1830s; Armando R. Bazán's work (item **3169**) skillfully blends local history with a scholarly vision of historiography; Carlos Escudé's provocative effort (item **3233**) offers a lively polemic on a crucial subject; Alberto Ciria's colorful study, *Política y cultura política: la Argentina peronista* (item **3205**) illuminates with great skill many unknown facets of the era; Richard Gillespie's rigorous research (item **3255**) brings back the most relevant aspects of the guerrilla and terrorist period; Hiroshi Matsushita's mature analysis of the working class (item **3299**) sets forth important data; Guillermo O'Donnell completes his interpretation of the Revolución Argentina years in *1966–1973: estado burocrático autoritario* (item **3314**); Joseph Page's biography of Perón (item **3317**) opens the way for a better understanding of the period he dominated. Other studies worthy of mention are Eugene R. Sofer's contribution (item **3356**) to a better understanding of the process of social mobilization; and Horacio A. Difrieri's work on Buenos Aires (item **3227**). More than 150 essays presented at the Sexto Congreso Internacional de Historia de América, organized by the Argentine Academy of History, provide important information on the most diverse topics (item **3214**).

The Argentine labor movement has been thoroughly reexamined from various angles in attempts to seek a more encompassing interpretation of the phenomenon of peronism. Much light has been shed on the 1930–40 period by the already cited Matsushita (item **3299**), as well as Cherensky (item **3202**) and Joel Horowitz (item **3269**) essays. In addition to Page, Navarro, and Ciria, Juan José Sebreli (item **3346**) also examines the period of peronist dominance in a formidable critique that seeks to demolish peronism's political and ideological claims. Finally, the 1973–76 peronist administrations are canvassed in the collective effort *Juan Perón and the reshaping of Argentina* (item **3276**), and in Guido Di Tella's economic study (item **3226**).

Diverse studies evoke the era of Radical Party dominance as, for example, Roberto Etchepareborda's (item **3237**) and Hebe Clementi's (item **3208**). Radical dissensions and schisms that have deeply affected Argentine political development are reviewed by both Ricardo Gallo in his excellent work (item **3251**), and by Julio E. Nosiglia (item **3310**). Nicolás Babini's controversial but well documented contribution clarifies an important issue in the party's history (item **3163**).

The process of continuous military intervention into Argentina's institutional process accounts for numerous entries. The origins of the process are traced by Ricardo Rodríguez Molas in *Servicio militar obligatorio* (item **3335**), and by Alain Rouquié in his by now classic interpretation of the topic (item **3338**).

The celebration of the Fourth Centennial of Buenos Aires' second foundation together with the centennial of its federalization in 1980 continue to yield many worthwhile publications. Among them are *Buenos Aires: historia de cuatro siglos* (item **3188**), the last great editorial achievement of José Luis Romero. The publication of the third installment of César A. García Belzunce's original effort, *Buenos Aires: 1800–1830* (item **3231**), opens the way for a renewed vision of the city's past. We should also mention the collective effort that is represented in the outstanding *Buenos Aires: 400 years* (item **3187**), edited by the deceased Thomas F. McGann and Stanley R. Ross. Finally, the city's traditional history is evoked in a new edition of Manuel Bilbao's *Tradiciones y recuerdos* (item **3175**), as is its iconography in *Buenos Aires, anteayer* (item **3322**).

Several biographies should be mentioned: the Spanish translation of Marysa Navarro's *Evita* (item **3308**); Néstor Tomás Auza's *Garmendia* (item **3162**); the already noted Page's *Perón* (item **3317**); and Roberto Etchepareborda's *Yrigoyen* (item **3237**).

Economic history is represented by a number of valuable revisionist contributions that break new ground by challenging traditional interpretations. Examples worthy of mention are: Ferrari's perceptive study of the *Pacto Roca-Runciman* (item **3241**); Llach's work on the 1940 *Plan Pinedo* (item **3285**); and Arturo O'Connell's examination of Argentine behavior during the Depression (item **3313**). Roberto Cortés-Conde opens new perspectives on landownership (item **3217**); and Tim Duncan (item **3230**) vindicates the much maligned economic policies of Juárez Celman that preceded the crisis of 1890. Other economic subjects are explored by Hilda Sábato (item **3341**) in her examination of the wool industry and trade, and by Marcello Carmagnani in his study of the role played by Argentine capital in the emergence of British railway companies (item **3196**), a topic also discussed by Eduardo Miguez (item **3304**). Eu-Soo-Pang sheds light on the growth and diversification of the Argentine economy (item **2792**), as does the productive Donna J. Guy on the industrialization process (item **3262**).

Interest in social history is evident in the timely reissue of Rodríguez Molas' *Historia social del gaucho* (item **3334**) which makes an admirable combination with Richard W. Slatta's book on the pampas' inhabitants (item **3354**). New aspects of the immigration process are thoroughly explored by Juan Carlos Korol and Hilda Sábato in their study of the Irish (item **3278**), and by Herbert S. Klein and his commentators (item **3277**), as well as by Samuel L. Bailey (item **3165**) in scholarly studies that provide a wealth of new ideas.

The field of international relations will benefit from the issue of Joaquín Nabuco's classic (item **3307**). Gustavo Ferrari's untimely death enhances our appreciation of his essays as well as of his *Esquema de la política exterior argentina* (item **3242**), which broadened our perspectives of the topic. Carlos Escudé's major work cited above and its retort by Mario Rapoport, break new ground (item **3330**); Isidoro J. Ruiz Moreno further clarifies Argentine foreign relations in *Orígenes de la diplomacia ítalo-argentina* (item **3339**).

Worthwhile contributions to religious history are Father Cayetano Bruno's continued efforts (item **3184**) and Américo A. Tonda's exploration of a neglected ideological debate (item **3363**).

The proliferation of local histories seems to have abated. Current examples are Efraín Bischoff's *Historia de Córdoba* (item **3176**), an updated reedition, and Oscar F. Urquiza Almandoz's promising vol. 1 on the history of the river port, Concepción del Uruguay (item **3366**).

Armando R. Bazán has two excellent historiographical studies in *La Rioja y sus historiadores* (item **3169**) and in his concise essay "La Historiografía Regional Argentina" (item **3168**). Tulio Halperin Donghi has written a carefully, thought out analysis of the historical contributions of José Luis Romero (item **3263**), and various authors examine Julio Irazusta's historiographical endeavors (item **3376**).

General histories have been scarce. There is a new and, as usual, controversial volume of *Historia argentina* by the recently deceased Vincent D. Sierra (item **3352**), as well as Leonardo Paso's *Compendio* (item **3320**). Antonio E. Brailovsky (item **3183**) also covers a lengthy period in his examination of the origins and development of the Argentine crisis as does Oscar Oszlak (item **3315**) in his study of the growth of the nation-state.

Other periods of the Argentine past subject to historical scrutiny are exemplified by Carlos S.A. Segreti's solid study *El país disuelto* (item **3248**), and Marta Sáenz Quesada's work on the 1850s secession of Buenos Aires (item **3342**). Two additional essays that marshall interesting new data and use novel approaches to illuminate the 19th century are Bonifacio del Carril's on the 1868 presidential elections (item **3197**) and F.J. McLynn's on Urquiza's dual political behavior (item **3295**). The 1966–76 period is examined in the cited contribution of Guillermo O'Donnell and in Rubén Perina's excellent study (item **3323**). A number of compilations of essays address more recent periods as does the one edited by Peter Waldmann and Ernesto Garzón Valdez (item **3326**), Rouquié's *Argentina hoy* (item **3158**), and articles published in *Crítica y Utopía* (items **3220** and **3321**). Richard Gillespie, in turn, carefully examines recent guerrilla activities (item **3254**).

New historical journals worthy of note are: *Boletín Histórico de la Ciudad de Buenos Aires*, *Revista Histórica* del Instituto de la Organización Nacional, and *Nuestra Historia* which has become more influential. With regard to the publishing sector, one is pleased to note that Centro Editor de la América Latina has returned to center stage with renewed vigor and some notably good titles.

Bibliographies are well represented in the worthwhile compilations of Nicolás Matijevich (item **3298**), Norma Girbal de Blacha (item **3256**), Raúl Rey Balmaceda (item **3331**), and Alberto Ciria (item **3203**), as well as in those on Rosas published in *Crítica e Utopía* (item **3220**) and on the 1943–82 period in *Criterio* (item **3219**).

Among historical sources of interest are the *Archivo de Juan María Gutiérrez* (item **3259**), the *Acuerdos de la H. Legislatura de Buenos Aires* (item **3154**), and *Mensajes de los Gobernadores de Córdoba* (item **3303**).

Memoirs, an uncommon genre in Argentine historiography, are well represented below in Esteves Sagui's *Apuntes* (item **3234**), Angel Gallardo's reminiscences (item **3249**), and Joaquín Castellano's *Páginas evocativas*, all of which provide a wealth of information on the political and intellectual history of the latter 19th century. Finally, Bonifacio del Carril's memoirs (item **3198**) are of interest to students of the 1943 revolutionary process.

To conclude, we can state that in contrast to *HLAS 44*, contemporary topics and socioeconomic history command a great deal more attention among publications annotated below. Nevertheless, there are still regrettable gaps in our knowledge of Argentine history exemplified by the lack of rigorous scrutiny of the 1930s or the 1958–66 civilian administrations.

PARAGUAY: Unfortunately, few contributions of value appeared during this period. Among the most significant is the diplomatic correspondence exchanged during the Chaco War between Paraguay's President Ayala and his Minister in Buenos Aires (item **3381**). A fresh approach can be detected in some works by Juan Carlos Herken Krauer, particularly his *Gran Bretaña y la Guerra de la Triple Alianza* (item **3389**). Two excellent studies that offer valuable reconstructions of the past are Josefina Plá's "La Cultura Paraguaya y el Libro" (item **3398**) and Alicia Vidaurreta's "El Paraguay a través de los Viajeros, 1843–1917" (item **3403**).

That progress has been made in the publication of primary sources and reference tools is exemplified by the contributions of Thomas Lyle Whigham and Jerry W. Cooney (item **3409**), and of Alfredo M. Seiferheld (item **3402**).

Works on the Chaco War continue to dominate in numbers if not in quality, a trend represented by Arturo Bray's (item **3379**) and Amancio Pampliega's memoirs (item **3395**), as well as by Margarita Kalssen's bibliography (item **3390**).

An additional topic explored was the 1931 crisis by M. Agustín Avila (item **3377**). The reign of *El Supremo* is forcefully dealt with in "El Paraguay del Doctor Francia" (item **3386**). Two valuable reprints are Harris Gaylord Warren's classic *Paraguay: an informal history* (item **3408**) and Sánchez Quell's *Política internacional del Paraguay* (item **3400**).

URUGUAY: Positive advances in the writing of Uruguayan history are evident in Barrán's and Nahum's two-volume *Batlle, los estancieros y el Imperio Británico* (item **3413**), a study which lives up to the interpretative breadth and depth of the authors' previous achievement. The same topic is examined by Germán d'Elía in *El Uruguay neo-batllista: 1946–1958* (item **3418**) and by Raúl Jacob in *Benito Nardone, el ruralismo hacia el poder* (item **3424**).

The productive Raúl Jacob also contributes several articles on Uruguay's economic crisis of 1929 (items **3425, 3426,**and **3427**). Socioeconomic studies related to urbanization are exemplified by Jaime Klaczko's "El Uruguay de 1908: su Contexto Urbano-Rural" (item **3429**), Lombardi's "El Proceso de Urbanización en el Uruguay en los Siglos XVIII y XIX" (item **3431**), and by Germán W. Rama's study (item **3438**).

There are also some important contributions on the 19th century such as Alicia Vidaurreta's (item **3444**), Iwan Morgan's on French interventionist policies (item **3433**), and Freitas' examination of the 1827 *Acta Oriental* (item **3421**), one of the country's first military interventions.

Juan Rial and Jaime Klaczko (item **3439**) have greatly facilitated our access to sources; Luis Alberto Musso continues his valuable bibliographic work (item **3434**); and the physical makeup and urban beauty of Montevideo are set forth in an excellent pictorial work, *100 años de Montevideo en imágenes* (item **3417**).

ARGENTINA

3151 A Piedra Buena en el centenario de su muerte: 1883–1983. Buenos Aires: Comisión Nacional de Homenaje al Tte. Coronel de Marina Don Luis Piedra Buena en el Centenario de Su Fallecimiento, 1983. 182 p.: appendix.

Several authors describe life and exploits of celebrated naval officer. Appendix reproduces G.H. Gardiner's *Diary* about their sojourn in Isla de las Estados (Feb. 1869–Jan. 1870).

3151a Acevedo, Edberto Oscar. El comercio de carne de Mendoza (Historiografía Rioplatense [Instituto Bibliográfico Antonio Zinny, Buenos Aires] 2, 1982, p. 7–42, tables)

Rigorous research focuses on aspects of region's meat market, such as supply and its significance as direct tax and financial resource in time of crisis. Tables show prices, supply, and principal taxpayers.

3152 ———. Los empréstitos en Mendoza: 1820–1833 (UNC/RHAA, 11:21/22, 1981–1982, p. 11–67)

Continuation of author's research on Cuyo's economy. Uses much data to examine what he defines as "politically enforced loans" in money and kind. Information on both amount and number of Argentine loans of this period is very rare.

3153 Acuña, Hugo. Diario del estafeta Hugo Acuña: pionero de la soberanía argentina en la Antártica. Bahía Blanca, Argentina: Centro de Documentación Patagónica, Departamento de Humanidades, Universidad Nacional del Sur, 1982. 245 p.: ill., maps.

Acuña was member of 1904 first expedition to South Orkneys which established an Argentine presence in the islands. Diary provides interesting factual information on year he served as islands' postmaster.

3154 Allende, Andrés R. Acuerdos de la Honorable Junta de Representantes, 1822. Con una introducción sobre "El Período Legislativo de 1822 en la Provincia de Buenos Aires." La Plata, Argentina: Archivo Histórico de la Provincia de Buenos Aires Ricardo Levene, Ministerio de Educación y Cultura, Subsecretaría de Cultura,1981. 311 p.

Reproduces legislative sessions during this active period of Rivadavia's extraordinary influence.

3155 Alonso, Beatriz. La presidencia de Alvear. Buenos Aires: Centro Editor de América Latina, 1983. 139 p.: bibl. (Biblioteca política argentina; 33. Las Presidencias radicales)

Informative account accurately recreates the prosperous world of the period.

3156 Amaral, Samuel. El empréstito de Londres de 1824 (IDES/DE, 27:92, enero/marzo 1984, p. 557–588)

Objective discussion of controversial topic concludes that previous studies lacked an accurate analysis of financial problems prevalent at the time. Concludes loan was "Neither a gloomy affair nor the prescience of warmongers; the loan was designed to take advantage of differential rates of interest between the Buenos Aires and London markets."

3157 Ansaldi, Waldo. La forja de una dictadura: el caso de Juan Manuel de Rosas (Crítica y Utopía [Editorial Latinoamericana de Ciencias Sociales, Buenos Aires] 5, 1982, p. 213–224, bibl.)

States: "interrogarse o reflexionar sobre Rosas . . . tiene vigencia en la medida en que se pueda responder a cuestiones tales como la formación de la estructura agraria, . . . la inserción de la economía del país en el sistema capitalista mundial y el aporte al triple proceso sincrónico de constitución del mercado nacional, el Estado nacional y la propia nación." More important than sterile debates between liberals and revisionists. Excellent bibliography.

3158 Argentina hoy. Compiled by Alain Rouquié. Buenos Aires: Siglo Veintiuno Editores, 1982. 279 p.: bibl. (Historia inmediata)

Seven essays depict the state of Argentina in early 1980s. Very critical compilation provides balanced, if hetereogenous view, of policies implemented by the military, as seen through the last half century of Argentine decadence: A. Rouquié's "Hegemonía Militar: Estado y Dominación Social;" R. Sidicaro's "Poder y Crisis de la Gran Burguesía Agraria Argentina;" A. Ferrer's "La Economía Argentina Bajo una Estrategia Preindustrial: 1976–1980;" F. Delich's "Después del Di-

luvio, la Clase Obrera;" S. Sigal and E. Verón's "Perón: Discurso Político e Ideológico;" Peter Waldmann's "Anomía Social y Violencia;" and A. Rama's "La Narrativa en el Conflicto de las Culturas."

3159 Armendariz de Fava, María del Carmen. Gobierno de Don Francisco S. Alvarez: 1914–1917 (JEHM/R, 9:2, 1980, p. 137–148, plate)

Describes short-lived experience in power of Conservative Party's reformist industrialist wing swept away by populist Radical tide. Interesting chapter also examines failure of modernizing conservative movement led by Lisandro de la Torre.

3160 Arni, Haim. La agricultura judía en la Argentina: ¿éxito o fracaso? (IDES/DE, 22:88, p. 535–548)

Brief survey of colonization experience initiated by Baron Maurice de Hirsch and continued through Asociación de Colonización Judía until World War I.

3161 Arturo Frondizi: historia y problemática de un estadista. v. 1, El hombre. Directores de la obra: Roberto Gustavo Pisarello Virasoro y Emilia Edda Menotti. Prólogo de Enrique de Gandía. Buenos Aires: Ediciones Depalma, 1983. 1 v.: ill.

Vol. 1 of joint venture designed to present the political and human sides of the former President. Written sympathetically, somewhat uncritically. Includes excerpts from his memoirs.

3162 Auza, Nestor Tomás. José Ignacio Garmendia, militar y escritor. Buenos Aires: Círculo Militar, 1982. 152 p., 8 leaves of plates: bibl., ill., ports. (Biblioteca del oficial; vol. 703)

Personality of one of the nation's best military historians is effectively recreated in this interesting book.

3163 Babini, Nicolás. Frondizi: de la oposición al gobierno. Buenos Aires: Editorial Celtia, 320 p.: ill., index, tables.

First class account and severe critical appraisal by close collaborator of former President. Describes and assesses with rigor and objectivity Radical Party's political history (1945–59) and Frondizi's ideological evolution after his 1959 meeting with Rogelio Frigerio.

3164 Bagú, Sergio *et al.* De historia e historiadores: homenaje a José Luis Romero. México: Siglo Veintiuno Editores, 1982. 436 p.

Festschrift in honor of founder of Argentine social history covers several fields. Especially valuable contributions are: Sergio Bagú "José Luis Romero: Evocación y Evaluación;" John Lynch "Rosas y las Clases Populares;" Roberto Cortés Conde "Aspectos Económicos en la Formación de las Ciudades Argentinas;" James R. Scobie "Consideraciones acerca de la Atracción de la Plaza en las Ciudades Provinciales Argentinas: 1850–1900;": Ezequiel Gallo "Notas sobre el Surgimiento de Villas y Centros Urbanos en la Campaña de Santa Fe, Argentina: 1870–1895;" Alberto Ciria "Buenos Aires, entre el Congreso y la Plaza de Mayo: 1945–1955;" Leandro H. Gutiérrez "Condiciones Materiales de Vida de los Sectores Populares en el Buenos Aires Finisecular."

3165 Bailey, Samuel L. The adjustment of Italian immigrants in Buenos Aires and New York, 1870–1914 (AHA/R, 88:2, April 1983, p. 281–305, maps, tables)

Comparative study demonstrates how "the occupational structure of Buenos Aires provided the basis for the growth of a multiclass society, moving into higher status economic positions," whereas in New York most immigrants remained in the lower strata. According to author, this disparity was due to immigrant skills and attitudes, cultural characteristics of receiving societies and changing nature of immigrant communities.

3166 Barbero, María Inés and **Fernando Devoto.** Los nacionalistas: 1910–1932. Buenos Aires: Centro Editor de América Latina, 1983. 188 p. (Biblioteca Política argentina)

Thoughtful analysis of topic, from origins through works of forerunners (e.g., Ricardo Rojas, Manuel Gálvez) to 1930 revolution, its moment of glory. Supported by much documentation.

3167 Barco, Ricardo del *et al.* 1943–1982 [i.e. Mil novecientos cuarenta y tres-mil novecientos ochenta y dos]: historia política argentina. Buenos Aires: Editorial Belgrano, 1983. 376 p.: bibl. (Colección estudios políticos)

Del Barco, Roberto Etchepareborda, Carlos A. Floria, Félix Luna, Guido di Tella, Luis González Esteves, Marcelo Monserrat, and Roberto Russell sum up and analyze political events in Argentina throughout the last 20 years. Papers illuminate instability of fragile political systems and present-day Argentine dilemmas. Includes exhaustive bibliography on 1930–82. [G.M. Dorn]

3168 Bazán, Armando Raúl. La historiografía regional argentina (PAIGH/H, 96, julio/dic. 1983, p. 121–152)

Seminal review of principal authors and their contributions, presented in chronological order. Examines first attempts, salvage of sources, revisionist manifestations, following institutionalization of the field and current status of Argentine history.

3169 ———. La Rioja y sus historiadores. Prólogo de A.J. Pérez Amuchástegui. Buenos Aires: Platero S.R.L., 1982. 227 p.

Distinguished revisionist and regional historian recreates his province's past through rigorous study of historical texts.

3170 Beaujón, Oscar. Buenos Aires en la prensa venezolana del siglo XIX (VANH/B, 64:253, enero/marzo 1981, p. p. 29–60)

Quick review of Venezuelan periodicals records important events (1808–1900).

3171 Becquer Casaballe, Amado and **Miguel Angel Cuarterolo.** Imágenes del Río de la Plata: crónica de la fotografía rioplatense, 1840–1940. Buenos Aires: Editorial del Fotográfo, 1983. 94 p.

Worthwhile contribution on neglected topic. Informative text is enhanced by excellent photographs.

3172 Béjar, María Dolores. Uriburu y Justo: el auge conservador, 1930–1935. Buenos Aires: Centro Editor de América Latina, 1983. 177 p.: bibl. (Biblioteca política argentina; 32)

Careful examination of both administrations focuses on performance of Buenos Aires prov.'s Conservatives and exposes key features of period (e.g., extension of central government controls, chronic political instability, intra-party feuds).

3173 Benítez, Norma; Violeta Díaz; and **Milna M. de Díaz Zorita.** La Pampa total: desde la prehistoria pampeana hasta la incorporación definitiva de este territorio a la nación. Santa Rosa, Argentina: Centro de Dcumentación Educativa, 1983. 107 p.: ill., maps.

Contains useful information about local history, particularly Indian customs and first military campaigns to occupy the area.

3174 Bidondo, Emilio A. Los tenientes de gobernador de Jujuy. Buenos Aires: Ediciones Culturales Argentina, Secretaría de Cultura de la Presidencia de la Nación, 1983. 372 p.

Precise study of 33 who governed region (1810–34) when it was part of Salta prov. Includes detailed description of institutional development of intendencia de Salta de Tucumán.

3175 Bilbao, Manuel. Tradiciones y recuerdos de Buenos Aires. 2a. ed. Buenos Aires: Ediciones Dictio, 1981. 356 p.: ill.

Reprint of first 1934 ed. of this vivid chronicle, rich in local events and customs.

3176 Bischoff, Efraín U. Historia de Córdoba: cuatro siglos. 2a. ed., corr. e actualizada. Buenos Aires: Plus Ultra, 1979. 726 p.: bibl., ill. (Colección Historia de nuestras provincias; 2)

Revised ed. of outstanding contribution by leading regional historian. Extends his historical narrative of Córdoba province and city to 1973.

3177 Bisio, Carlos A. Nuestros primeros pasos. Buenos Aires: Fundación Cristiana de Evangelización, Librería Editorial Cristiana, 1982. 273 p., 24 p. of plates: bibl., ill., ports.

Brief account of Evangelical Church's first centennial. Book's first half contains brief biographical sketches of founders and principal members and propagation of faith in the Interior. Includes lengthy bibliography.

3178 Blackwelder, Julia Kirk and **Lyman L. Johnson.** Changing criminal patterns in Buenos Aires: 1890 to 1914 (JLAS, 14:2, Nov. 1982, p. 359–379, tables)

Provides new perspective for evaluating social impact of urbanization. Describes human costs that large numbers of marginal, mainly foreign workers, can have for a developing society.

3179 Blasi Brambilla, Alberto. Crónicas del extraño Buenos Aires. Buenos Aires:

Ediciones Tres Tiempos, 1981. 119 p. (Colección Buenos Aires; 2)

Trifling, but instructive local history. Uses agreeable, anecdotical approach to discuss many topics from colonial times to 20th century.

3180 Boletín del Instituto de Historia Argentina y Americana Dr. Emilio Ravignani. Año 17, No. 27, 1982- . Buenos Aires.

Issue includes interesting articles: Olga Gracia de D'Agostino's "Visión Francesa de la Argentina: 1800–1880" and Elena Rebok's "La Vida Cotidiana en la Argentina Vista por los Viajeros de Lengua Alemana: 1849–1879" (sociocultural environment through foreign eyes); Miguel Angel Rosal's "Artesanos de Color en Buenos Aires: 1750–1810" (new statistical data); and Juan Severino López's "Augusto Brougnes y la Colonia San Juan de Corrientes: 1851–1858" (sheds new light on early colonization).

3181 Bose, Walter Björn Ludovico and **Julio C. Sáenz.** Sellos postales argentinos con historia = Argentine postage stamps and history. Fotografía, Jorge Salatino. Notas especializadas, Jorge Bossio. Versión Inglesa, Harold Sinnott. Buenos Aires: M. Zago, 1981. 192 p.: bibl., ill. (some col.)

Well crafted, bilingual art book. Draws parallel between country's historical evolution and development of its postal service. Beautifully illustrated.

3182 Bourdé, Guy. L'état-patron et les luttes des cheminots en Argentine, 1947–1967 (Le Mouvement Social [Centre national de la recherche scientifique, Centre de recherches d'histoire des mouvements sociaux, Université Paris I] 121, oct./déc. 1982, p. 7–43, graphs, tables)

Informed account of railway workers' long struggle against several different regimes, from Perón to Onganía.

3183 Brailovsky, Antonio Elio. 1880–1982 [i.e. Mil ochocientos ochenta a mil novecientos ochenta y dos], historia de las crisis argentinas: un sacrificio inútil. Buenos Aires: Editorial de Belgrano, 1982. 228 p.: bibl., ill. (Colección Testimonios contemporáneos)

Sharp interpretative analysis of several important crisis undergone by Argentina since 1876, and of the different liberal and "developmentalist" responses they evoked. Concludes that previous experiences seem not to have registered: "¿Es que la historia gira en redondo y el último siglo ha trascurrido inútilmente?"

3184 Bruno, Cayetano. Los Salesianos y las Hijas de María Auxiliadora en la Argentina. v. 1, 1875–1894. Buenos Aires: Instituto Salesiano de Artes Gráficas, 1981. 1 v.: bibl., ill., index.

Another contribution to the history of religion provides important information on Patagonia and missions in southern Argentina. Well documented and illustrated.

3185 Buenos Aires, *Argentina* **(city). Municipalidad. Instituto Histórico de la Ciudad de Buenos Aires. Sección Archivo Histórico.** Indice temático general, 1880–1887: Gestión Torcuato de Alvear. Dirección del trabajo: Estela Pagani. Ejecución: Marta Celis G. de Molina and Estela Pagani. Buenos Aires: El Instituto, 1981. 58 p.

Accurate guide to city's historical holdings covers wide variety of topics on its administration, during city's notable growth period. For bibliographer's comment, see item **64.**

3186 ——. ——. ——. ——. Indice temático general, 1880–1887: Gestión Torcuato de Alvear. Dirección de trabajo: Estela Pagani. Ejecución: Marta Celis de Molina and Estela Pagani. Colaboración: Luis A. Alvarez. Buenos Aires: El Instituto, 1983. 205 p.

Well prepared guide will facilitate research into Alvear's outstanding administration, one that transformed the "Gran Aldea" into modern metropolis. Excellent reference aid for a better understanding of 1880s. For bibliographer's comment, see item **65.**

3187 Buenos Aires, 400 years. Edited by Stanley R. Ross and Thomas F. McGann. Austin: University of Texas Press, 1982. 192 p.: bibl., ill., index, maps.

Several authors commemorate the city's fourth centennial by examining different aspects of its past: Jonathan C. Brown's "Outpost to Entrepôt: Trade and Commerce in Colonial Buenos Aires;" Susan M. Socolow's "Buenos Aires at the Time of Independence;" Richard J. Walter's "The Socioeconomic Growth of Buenos Aires in the Twentieth Century;" and James R.

Scobie's "The Argentine Capital in the Nineteenth Century."

3188 Buenos Aires: historia de cuatro siglos. Edited by José Luis Romero and Luis Alberto Romero. Buenos Aires: Editorial Abril, 1983. 2 v. (438, 639 p.): bibl., ill.

Important compilation edited by distinguished historian José Luis Romero, including several introductions by him as well as notable contributions by James Scobie, John Lynch, Halperin-Donghi, Natalio Botana, Enrique Barba, Cortés Conde, Alberto Ciria, Mora y Araujo, and Juan Carlos Tedesco. Vol. 1 covers 1580–1880 and is divided into: "Las Fundaciones, 1536–1580;" "La Ciudad Indiana, 1580–1806;" "La Ciudad Jacobina: 1806–1820;" "La Ciudad Criolla, 1820–1852" and "La Ciudad Patricia; 1852–1880." Vol. 2 consists of "La Ciudad Burguesa, 1880–1930." Romero's book is woven around a theory of urban history or that: "La ciudad es, tanto el habitat de un grupo como una cultura, objetivada, materializada y trasmisible; es un legado que imprime su sello a las generaciones sucesivas, que la asuman y la modifican."

3189 Buenos Aires criolla, 1820–1850. Selección y prólogo, Luis Alberto Romero. Buenos Aires: Centro Editor de América Latina, 1984. 94 p. (Historia testimonial argentina: documentos vivos de nuestro pasado; 7)

Excellent introduction precedes representative selection of travelers' impressions of city governed by Rivadavia and Rosas.

3190 Burns, E. Bradford. Bartolomé Mitre: the historian as a novelist; the novel as history (RIB, 32:2, 1982, p. 155–167)

Speculates on connections between novel and history in 19th-century Latin American authors. According to Burns, Mitre's early novel, *Soledad*, predates his interpretation of South American emancipation in his major works: "the literary and historical ideas of Mitre were identical in his conception of the meaning, purpose and, directions of the new nations of South America."

3191 Buroni, José Raúl and Alberto Juan Gancedo. Reseña histórica del Hospital Militar Central. Buenos Aires: Círculo Militar, 1979 [i.e. 1980]. 160 p., 1 leaf of plates: bibl., ill. (Biblioteca del oficial; v. 699. Colección histórico-militar)

Summary of historical precedents to Military Hospital created in last quarter of 19th century.

3192 Busala, Amalía and **Analía Gross.** La realidad histórica argentina desde 1880 hasta al centenario de la Revolución de Mayo: un sector de la opinión pública liderado por el Dr. Estanislao S. Zeballos y su posición frente a la comunidad de naciones, 1898–1909 (UNL/U, 95, enero/abril 1980, p. 61–104)

Emphasizes Zeballos' ideas on foreign policy and Argentine relations with other South American countries. Follows Roberto Etchepareborda's thesis that Zeballos led a public opinion sector that was expansionist and influenced by geopolitical notions.

3193 Campo, Hugo de. Sindicalismo y peronismo: los comienzos de un vínculo perdurable. Buenos Aires: Consejo Latinoamericano de Ciencias Sociales (CLASCO), 1983. 273 p.: bibl., ill. (Biblioteca de ciencias sociales; 5)

Based on wide-ranging research. Examines two crucial periods in evolution of labor movement: 1) 1930–43; and 2) during peronist regime. Shows there was no sudden breakdown in continuity and notes presence of common features: bureaucratization, pragmatic reformism and their linkages with political power, traits already typical of syndicalist trade unions.

3194 Capie, Forrest. Invisible barrier to trade: Britain and Argentina in the 1920s (IAMEA, 35:3, Winter 1981, p. 91–96, tables)

Shows how imposition of British regulations on meat imports followed by fixing of quotas led to dramatic fall of Argentine exports, damaging both Argentina's trade balance and economic development. For economist's comment, see *HLAS 45:3548.*

3195 Caputo, Sara de Astelarra. La Argentina y la rivalidad comercial entre los Estados Unidos e Inglaterra: 1899–1929 (IDES/DE, 23:92, enero/marzo 1984, p. 589–608)

Examines competition between both countries' attempts to sell manufactured goods to Argentina, in order to identify their effects upon the nation's economic development.

3196 Carmagnani, Marcello and **Chiara Vangelista.** Mercati monetari e ferrovie inglesi in Argentina: 1880–1914 (GEE/NA, 1, 1978, p. 135–166, tables)

Careful reconstruction of development of financial resources of British entreprises. Shows that a great proportion originated outside the UK, particularly from the savings of Argentine investors.

3197 Carril, Bonifacio del. La combinación Urquiza-Alsina en las elecciones de 1868. Buenos Aires: Emecé Editores, 1982. 199 p.: 8 p. of plates: ill.

Revised, lengthier version of 1961 study. Consists of excellent presentation of presidential campaign won by Sarmiento, after the failure of the Urquiza-Adolfo Alsina ticket. Based on numerous documents.

3198 ———. Memorias dispersas: el Coronel Perón. Buenos Aires: Emecé Editores, 1984. 212 p.

Former member of the nationalist political establishment that participated in 1943 revolution recalls his early relationship with Perón. Highly critical of his opportunism.

Carroll, Glenn R. and **Jacques Delacroix.** Organizational mortality in the newspaper industries of Argentina and Ireland: an ecological approach. See *HLAS 45:8310.*

3199 Castellanos, Joaquín. Páginas evocativas. Selección y prólogo de Bernardo González Arrili. Buenos Aires: Academia Argentina de Letras, 1981. 206 p.: port. (Biblioteca. Serie Clásicos argentinos; v. 14)

Fascinating selection of articles and notes—culled from *Caras y Caretas* (1923–29)—by renowned politician and poet. Of particular interest are his recollections of important events in which he participated actively (e.g., 1880 and 1890 rebellions, Pellegrini's tough 1892 repression of Radical followers). Includes colorful personal notes on José Hernández and Lucio Mansilla.

3200 Cavarozzi, Marcelo. Autoritarismo y democracia: 1955–1983. Buenos Aires: Centro Editor de América Latina, 1983. 142 p.: bibl. (Biblioteca política argentina; 21)

Encompassing appraisal of unstable period of predominant military involvement. Selected documents support the narrative.

3201 Centenario de la Campaña del Desierto: homenaje de la Universidad Nacional de Cuyo, Mendoza, 23 de agosto–18 de octubre de 1979. Mendoza, Argentina: Universidad Nacional de Cuyo, 1980. 188 p.: bibl.

Consists of several lectures of which one merits attention for its insights: Patricio Randle's "La Conquista del Desierto y la Maduración de la Conciencia Territorial" (p. 95–124).

3202 Cheresky, Isidoro. Sindicatos y fuerzas políticas en la Argentina pre-peronista: 1930–1943 (CEDLA/B, 31, dic. 1981, p. 5–42, tables)

Another assessment that attests to growing interest in peronism. Perceives development of its coalition as resulting from a particular process of social struggle engaging bourgeoisie and working class.

3203 Ciria, Alberto. La década del treinta en la historiografía argentina: una introducción (RIB, 32:3/4, 1982, p. 322–329)

After outlining period's chief characteristics, comments on state of the art and its principal manifestations. Concludes by suggesting new lines of research. For bibliographer's comment, see *HLAS 45:12.*

3204 ———. Flesh and fantasy: the many faces of Evita and Juan Perón (LARR, 18:2, 1983, p. 150–165)

Timely, masterful review essay submits recently published interpretations of personalities and political roles of both Peróns to strict critical analysis. Concludes that much research remains to be done.

3205 ———. Política y cultura popular: la Argentina peronista, 1946–1955. Buenos Aires: Ediciones de la Flor, 1983. 357 p.: bibl. ill.

Pioneer contribution by distinguished political scientist. Presents colorful overview of period, recreating diverse aspects of those crucial times. Carefully describes party system, symbols, myth, peronism's effects on education and on cultural life as a whole. Also examines congressional debates and political attitudes of both peronism and its political opposition.

3206 Clementi, Hebe. Juventud y política en la Argentina. Buenos Aires: Editorial Siglo Veinte, 1982. 155 p.

Political opening of 1983 and impact of new generation of voters enhances this book's relevance. Examines several crucial historical events in which youth played an important role (e.g., reaction to Saénz Peña's electoral law, university reform movement, nationalism, and 1930 crisis)

3207 ———. Puntos de partida para una historia de la historiografía argentina (Boletín del Instituto Histórico de la Ciudad de Buenos Aires [Municipalidad de la Ciudad de Buenos Aires] 4:7, 1982, p. 49–58)

Brief but substantive analysis. Author considers that since this sort of intellectual history is essentially political, new approaches are required as well as good understanding of ideological currents, especially their American manifestations.

3208 ———. El radicalismo: nudos gordianos de su economía. Buenos Aires: Ediciones Siglo Veinte, 1982. 201 p.

Continues author's examination of Radical Party by pondering attitudes towards three basic aspects of Argentina's economy: railways, oil, and meat. Well documented work.

3209 ———. El Radicalismo: trayectoria política. 2a. ed. Buenos Aires: Ediciones Siglo Veinte, 1982. 219 p.

Valuable non-partisan examination of Radical activities from party's origins until 1930s. Reflects on several important aspects such as its conduct while in the opposition and in power and consequences of 1930 crisis on its development.

3210 Coghlan, Eduardo A. Andanzas de un irlandés en el campo porteño. Buenos Aires: Ediciones Culturales Argentinas, Secretaría de Cultura de la Presidencia de la Nación, 1982. 207 p.

John Brabazon's memoirs (1846–64) translated and annotated by author, discuss the Irishman's experiences in the Argentine countryside and political developments he witnessed (e.g., Caseros, Buenos Aires' secession, Pavón).

3211 Colautti, Carlos E. Proyectos constitucionales patrios: 1811–1826. Buenos Aires: Ediciones Culturales Argentinas, Secretaría de Cultura de la Presidencia de la Nación, 1983. 143 p.

Brief comments on nation's first institutional experience. Describes outside influences and principal features.

3212 La Colonización del Chaco: regiones y sociedades. Selección y prólogo, Nicolás Iñigo Carrera. Buenos Aires: Centro Editor de América Latina, 1983. 96 p.: bibl. (Biblioteca Historia testimonial argentina; 3)

Well documented and combative essay examines region's absorption into dominant economic system as cotton-producing area and its sequel of sorrow and plunder.

3213 Comadrán Ruiz, Jorge. Julio Irazusta y la Confederación Argentina (UNC/RHAA, 10:19/20, 1978/1980, p. 53–59)

Brief interpretation of the influence on contemporary Argentine historiography of the distinguished, nationalist, revisionist historian.

3214 Congreso Internacional de Historia de América, 6th, Buenos Aires, 1980. Sexto Congreso Internacional de Historia de América. Celebrado del 13 al 18 de octubre 1980 con el patrocinio de la Municipalidad de la Ciudad de Buenos Aires. Buenos Aires: Academia Nacional de la Historia, 1982–1983. 6 v. (486, 484, 522, 526, 522 p.): bibl., ill. (some col.), index.

Held in commemoration of fourth centennial of Buenos Aires' foundation which coincided with first 100 years of district's federalization. Papers delivered at Congress were devoted to foundation of Latin American urban centers and history of city itself. Includes 159 contributions.

3215 Córdoba, Alberto Octavio Buenos Aires, cronología del barrio de Belgrano y sus alrededores, 1855–1910. Buenos Aires: Asociación Amigos del Museo Histórico Sarmiento, 1981. 158 p.: ill., index.

Useful survey recreates neighborhood events and its social evolution from 1855 *pueblo* to city and finally to *barrio* incorporated 1887 to Federal District.

3216 Correas, Edmundo. Sarmiento y las maestras norteamericanas (JEHM/R, 9:2, 1980, p. 43–69, plate)

Narrative (with pictures) of activities of 65 US teachers who taught in different Argentine regions (1870–1900).

3217 Cortés Conde, Roberto. El mercado de tierras en Argentina: 1880–1912 (GEE/NA, 1, 1978, p. 105–134, tables)

Thorough research presents quite accurate picture of topic. Based on new data tabulated by author. Ably demonstrates what new factors influenced increase of land value, not merely concentrated ownership and speculative ventures.

3218 Crespo, Alfonso. Evita viva o muerta. Barcelona, Spain: Fontalba, D.L., 1980. 422 p., 1 leaf, 4 p. of plates: bibl., ill., index.

New ed. of novelistic interpretation of her life (see *HLAS 44:3189*).

3219 *Criterio.* Vol. 55, Nos. 1894/1895, 24 dic. 1982– . Buenos Aires.

Several authors examine last 40 years of Argentine political and institutional life: Ricardo del Barco "Del Gobierno Militar al Régimen Peronista: 1943–1955;" Roberto Etchepareborda "Crónica de Años Difíciles: 1955–1966;" Carlos A. Floria "El Régimen Militar y la Argentina Corporativa: 1966–1973;" Editorial Board "El Peronismo Gobernante: 1973–1976;" Félix Luna "El Proceso: 1976–1982;" Guido Di Tella "La Argentina Económica: 1943–1982;" Luis González Esteves "La Argentina Electoral: 1946–1973;" Roberto Etchepareborda "Elementos Bibliográficos para una Historia Argentina: 1943–1982." These articles also available in book form (see item **3167**).

3220 *Crítica y Utopía.* Editorial Latinoamericana de Ciencias Sociales. No. 5, 1982– . Buenos Aires.

Special issue devoted to "Dictaduras y Dictadores: una Reflexión Teórica sobre sus Peculiaridades en América Latina." For articles of relevance, see items **3157** and **3386**).

3221 ———. ———. Nos. 10/11, 1983/1984– . Buenos Aires.

Special double issue dedicated to Argentina's sociopolitical situation in 1970s and 1980s. Articles: Francisco Delich "La Metáfora de la Sociedad Enferma;" Oscar Landi "Cultura y Política en la Transición a la Democracia;" Roque Carranza "La Política Económica en una Sociedad Democrática: La Argentina Futura;" Oscar Oszlak "Privatización Autoritaria y Recreación de la Escena Pública;" Gustavo Druetta "Guerra, Política y Sociedad en la Ideología de la Corporación Militar Argentina;" Torcuato Di Tella "Argentina: ¿una Australia Italiana?". Also includes important bibliographic essay that will continue in next issue.

3222 Dalton, Laura. Juan Perón and the reshaping of Argentina: an annotated bibliography. Storrs: Center for Latin American Studies, University of Connecticut, 1982? 30 p. (mimeo) (Occasional papers; no. 1)

Useful research tool lists books, articles, doctoral dissertations. Despite title, it is *not* annotated.

3223 Delacroix, Jacques and **Glenn R. Carroll.** Organizational foundings: an ecological study of the newspaper industries of Argentina and Ireland (CU/ASQ, 28:2, June 1983, p. 274–291, bibl.)

Comparative study uses historical data to explore thesis that an environmental model accounts for emergence of certain organizations. Suggests other ecological influences for changes in membership. Posits that political turbulence accounts for launching of most press ventures.

3224 Destéfani, Laurio H. Marcos A. Zar, 1891–1955: fundador de la aviación naval. Buenos Aires: Instituto Argentino de Historia Aeronáutica Jorge Newbery, 1980. 30 p.

Summary of life-and-works of distinguished aviation and naval pioneer.

3225 Di Ció, Miguel Angel. La intervención anglo-francesa en el Río de la Plata (Revista Nacional de Cultura [Secretaría de Estado de Cultura, Buenos Aires] 5:13, 1983, p. 3–26)

Brief presentation of background, causes and main events in 1845–50 foreign intervention.

3226 Di Tella, Guido. Perón-Perón: 1973–1976. Buenos Aires: Editorial Sudamericana, 1983. 369 p.: appendix, bibl., ill.

Unconventional interpretation examines, from economic perspective, peronism's crucial 1973–76 years in power. Attributes regime's demise to party's rebellion against leadership's rightward drift.

3227 Difrieri, Horacio A. Buenos Aires: geohistoria de una metrópoli. Buenos Aires: Universidad de Buenos Aires, 1981. 215 p., 1 folded leaf of plates: bibl., ill.

(Colección del IV centenario de Buenos Aires; 1)

Intelligent reconstruction of capital city's evolution emphasizes geographical aspects.

3229 Domingo, Hugo Luis. Poderes constitucionales de guerra del Presidente de la Nación: su ejercicio durante la Guerra del Paraguay (Revista de Historia del Derecho [Instituto de Investigaciones de Historia del Derecho, Buenos Aires] 10, 1982, p. 433–456)

Well researched illustration of a generally forgotten aspect of the war.

3230 Duncan, Tim. La política fiscal durante el gobierno de Juárez Celman, 1886–1890: una audaz estrategia financiera internacional (IDES/DE, 23:89, abril/junio 1983, p. 11–34, tables)

Revisionist appraisal reveals shortcomings of conventional wisdom regarding Juarista liberal period (i.e., favorable to laissez-faire economics, inept, corrupt). Uses good arguments to present different picture: consolidation of the State by using foreign loans, budget, and fiscal policies.

3231 Equipos de Investigación Histórica, *Buenos Aires, Argentina.* Buenos Aires, 1800–1830. t. 1, Su gente. t. 2, Salud y delito. t. 3, Educación y asistencia social. César A. García Belsunce, director. Investigadores, Susana R. Frías *et al.* Buenos Aires: Emecé Distribuidora, 1976–1979. 3 v.: bibl.; ill.

Social history of city and *campaña.* Consists of four volumes of which only vol. 3 was available for review at press time. Concerned with day-to-day developments. Offers vague observations lacking data (e.g., "la educación se convirtió en un valor trascendente . . ." ". . . alcanzando un aspecto social cada vez más amplio . . .").

3232 Escudé, Carlos. Cuando el mundo dependía de nuestros alimentos . . . Argentina, Gran Bretaña y el hambre (Todo es Historia [Buenos Aires] 192, mayo 1983, p. 76–93)

Documented article, based mainly on British sources, demonstrates Argentina's strong negotiating position vis-à-vis the British during Perón's first years.

3233 ———. Gran Bretaña, Estados Unidos y la declinación argentina: 1942–1949.

Dirigida por Félix Luna. Buenos Aires: Editorial de Belgrano, 1983. 399 p.: bibl. (Colección Conflictos y armonías en la historia argentina)

Highly provocative and controversial interpretation of triangular relationship based on extensive research and new documentation. Attributes Argentina's economic decline to combination of US attempts to impose "moral imperialism" (e.g., Argentina's refusal to adopt US political patterns being punished by economic boycott) together with Perón's erroneous economic policies. Uses comparative quantitative data to show damage to Argentine economy. For political scientist's comment, see *HLAS 45:6420*.

3234 Esteves Saguí, Miguel. Apuntes históricos: recuerdos para mis hijos al correr de la pluma. Introducción de Roberto Etchepareborda. Buenos Aires: Academia Nacional de la Historia, 1980. 292 p.: bibl. (Biblioteca de publicaciones documentales; t. 15)

Memoirs of important public figure, particularly useful for period of Buenos Aires' secession in which he participated. Also brings to light neglected aspects of both conspiracies against Rosas and period of widespread terror (1840–42).

Etchepareborda, Roberto. La bibliografía reciente sobre la cuestión Malvinas: pts. 1/2. See item 72.

3235 ———. La cuestión Malvinas en perspectiva histórica: historia de la controversia desde al siglo XVI hasta nuestros días (PAIGH/H, 96, julio/dic. 1983, p. 27–67)

Well documented study examines Malvinas controversy by reviewing island's history. Summarizes discovery, international law, British objectives in South Atlantic, Spanish and Argentine occupation (1774–1829), and analyzes negotiations begun 1965. Author's findings support the Argentine case. [T.C.Wright]

3236 ———. Interpretaciones recientes del pasado argentino (UNS/CS, 16, enero/dic. 1983, p. 99–116)

Major contribution that succinctly synthesizes most important works on Argentine history, including important doctoral dissertations since 1980. Notes that contributions to 20th-century Argentina, far exceed works on earlier periods. Of great interest to students of Southern Cone countries. For

bibliographer's comment, see item 20. [G.M. Dorn]

3237 ———. Yrigoyen: biografía. Buenos Aires: Centro Editor de América Latina, 1983. 2 v.: ill.

One of Argentina's leading historians presents keen, insightful, and factual assessment of Yrigoyen and his times. [G.M. Dorn]

3238 ———; **Ricardo M. Ortiz;** and **Juan Orona.** La crisis de 1930: ensayos. Buenos Aires: Centro Editor de América Latina, 1983. 163 p. (Biblioteca Política argentina; 15–16)

New ed. of special issue of *La Revista de Historia* (Buenos Aires, 3, 1958). Etchepareborda deals with political aspects of 1930 crisis, presents excellent chronology of period, and adds complete bibliography of 1930 events. Ortiz analyzes economic and social implications of Yrigoyen's overthrow, and Orona describes secret military society that played crucial role in 1930 revolution. Considering fact that above journal is rare item, this new ed. is of utmost importance for students of Argentina. [G.M. Dorn]

3239 Falcoff, Mark. Argentina (*in* The Spanish Civil War, 1936–1939: American hemispheric perspectives [see item **1913**], p. 291–348)

Novel approach uses international perspective to explain region's and countries' domestic politics. Examines internal confrontations in Argentina (e.g., the Church, the intellectuals) that were caused by the Spanish struggle.

3240 La Federalización de Buenos Aires: debates y documentos. Isidoro J. Ruiz Moreno, compilador. Buenos Aires: Emecé Editores, 1980. 337 p.: bibl.

Compilaton of principal parliamentary debates, laws, and documents that reflect prolonged confrontation between Buenos Aires and remaining provinces. Author examines all aspects of issue in introductory essay.

3241 Ferrari, Gustavo. La Convención Roca-Runciman (CRIT, 56:1905, 14 julio 1983, p. 331–338)

Brief objective summary of controversial trade treaty and its background on its 50th anniversary. Explains previous agreements such as Lord D'Abernon's (1929).

3242 ———. Esquema de la política exterior argentina. Buenos Aires: Editorial Universitaria de Buenos Aires, 1981. 137 p.: bibl., index (Colección Temas)

Collects previously published essays by recently deceased historian. Relevant are: "Constantes en la Política Exterior Argentina," "La Política Exterior Argentina en la Bibliografía General," and "Esquema de la Política Exterior Argentina," an excellent condensed review.

3243 ———. Esquema del nacionalismo liberal en la Argentina (CRIT, 54 : 1856, marzo 1981, p. 126–134)

Provocative essay examines works of leading Liberal thinkers (e.g., Sarmiento, Mitre, Alberdi, Ingenieros) in order to show that they held strongly nationalistic views, predating more vocal revisionist attitudes.

3244 Ferro, Emilio E.J. La Patagonia inconclusa: relatos de un viejo poblador patagónico. Buenos Aires: Ediciones Marymar, 1981. 275 p., 1 leaf of plates: ill. (Colección Patagonia)

Vivid narrative based on varied personal recollections of old settler. Covers region's pioneer history, including episodes of banditry such as the 1909 one involving Butch Cassidy and his cohorts.

3245 Folino, Norberto. Barceló, Ruggierito y el populismo oligárquico. Buenos Aires: Ediciones de la Flor, 1983. 200 p.: bibl., ill. (Cuadernos de la nostalgia; 6)

Worthwhile reprint of pioneer study of neglected fact: strong populist support commanded by Conservatives until peronism's emergence. Chronicle of activities of Avellaneda's caudillo and his political machine sheds much light on period.

Fontanella de Weinberg, María Beatriz. La asimilación lingüística de los inmigrantes: mantenimiento y cambio de lengua en el sudoeste bonaerense. See *HLAS 45 : 8317*.

3246 Fornos Peñalba, José Alfredo. Draft dodgers, war resisters and turbulent gauchos: the War of the Triple Alliance against Paraguay (AAFH/TAM, 38 : 4, April 1982, p. 463–479, tables)

Revisionist approach insists on Great Britain's crucial role and responsibility in war. Unfortunately, fails to document main point.

3247 Framini, Andrés *et al.* Sindicalismo: el poder y la crisis; reportajes. Buenos Aires: Editorial de Belgrano, 1982. 116 p. (Colección Diálogos. Colección Testimonios contemporáneos)

Important eyewitness accounts: three peronist labor and political leaders relive crucial episodes (e.g., March 1962 elections in Buenos Aires prov., President Illia's 1966 overthrow, March 1976 coup).

3248 Frondizi, Arturo. Mensajes Presidenciales: 1958–1962. Buenos Aires: Ediciones Centro de Estudios Nacionales, 1978–1982. 2 v. (347, 363 p.): indexes.

New installments of useful collection. Vol. 3 covers 1 Jan 1960–4 Nov. 1960; vol. 4, 13 Nov. 1960–7 Dec. 1961.

3249 Gallardo, Angel. Memorias para mis hijos y nietos. Prólogo de Guillermo Gallardo. Buenos Aires: Academia Nacional de la Historia, 1982. 510 p., 2 leaves of plates: ill. (Biblioteca de publicaciones documentales; v. 17)

Useful recollections by distinguished scientist, diplomat, and Minister of Foreign Affairs during President Alvear's administration. Includes valuable information on crisis in relations with the Vatican.

3250 Gallo, Ezequiel. La pampa gringa: la colonización agrícola en Santa Fe, 1870–1895. Buenos Aires: Editorial Sudamericana, 1983. 457 p.: bibl., ill., maps (Colección Historia y sociedad)

Scholarly study of grain "boom" and careful analysis of landownership and immigrants. Shows how and why most of them went into business and the social mobility they enjoyed as result. Also examines involvement of immigrants in local politics.

3251 Gallo, Ricardo. Balbín, Frondizi y la división del radicalismo: 1956–1958. Buenos Aires: Editorial de Belgrano, 1983. 188 p.: bibl. (Colección Conflictos y armonías en la historia argentina)

Study of important recent episode based on careful eyewitness accounts. Considers Radical split was chiefly caused by combination of ideological conflict, political strategies, and factionalism. Concludes by noting that Radical Party lost opportunity to become balancing force in equation peronism-antiperonism, its split opening the way for peronism's effective return as the popular mass movement.

3252 García, César Reinaldo. Historia de los grupos y partidos políticos de la República Argentina desde 1810 a 1983. Buenos Aires: Sainte- Claire Editora, 1983. 196 p.: appendix, index, maps, tables.

Unpretentious but very informative handbook. Lists principal parties, their ideologies and platforms. Outlines electoral returns, cabinet members, etc. Special tables show evolution of political system.

3253 García Costa, Víctor. Los primeros diez años del movimiento feminista y la primera sufragista sudamericana (Boletín del Instituto Histórico de la Ciudad de Buenos Aires [Municipalidad de la Ciudad de Buenos Aires] 4:6, 1982, p. 65–75)

Important contribution to unexplored topic. Describes first steps of long struggle towards political equality of women, first political organization, and leading roles played by first outstanding feminists.

Gariazzo, Alicia. Orígenes ideológicos de los movimientos obreros chileno y argentino. See item **3088.**

3254 Gillespie, Richard. Armed struggle in Argentina (UCSD/NS, 8, 1982, p. 387–427)

Intelligent and informed essay reports on almost a decade of Argentina's guerrilla war. Explores its origin, sociopolitical conditions and causes, and ideologies of principal organizations. Concludes that their emergence constituted response to political stalemate and a middle-class challenge to the system, given leading role played in guerrilla movement by petty bourgeoisie, especially students, contrary to what terrorist leaders claimed or that theirs was a class-struggle enacted by labor.

3255 ———. Soldiers of Perón: Argentina's Montoneros. Oxford, UK: Clarendon Press; New York: Oxford University, 1982. 310 p.: bibl., index, maps.

Outstanding critical history of Latin America's largest urban guerrilla force. Examines it from its emergence in late 1960s to its demise in 1981. Reconstructs bloody urban warfare of 1970s. Excellent use of untapped sources and oral history. For political scientist's comment, see *HLAS 45:6424.*

3256 Girbal de Blacha, Norma M. Aportes bibliográficos para el estudio del Gran Chaco argentino y la explotación forestal, 1880–1914 (RIB, 33:3, 1983, p. 331–354)

Pioneer attempt to report economic facts about usually neglected forest region. Consists of valuable selection of materials published on topic.

Goldar, Ernesto. Buenos Aires, vida cotidiana en la década del 50. See *HLAS 45:8318.*

3257 González, Rubén. Los dominicos en Argentina: biografías. v. 1, Isidoro Celestino Guerra, Justo de Santa María de Oro, Juan Grande, Olegario Correa, Moisés Vicente Burela, Angel María Boisdron, Reginaldo Saldaña Retamar. Tucumán, Argentina: Universidad del Norte Santo Tomás de Aquino Católica de Tucumán, 1980. 1 v.: bibl.

Records life and works of several relevant Dominican friars from colonial times to 20th century. Important contribution to religious history of country and order.

3258 Guglielmino, Osvaldo. Rafael Hernández, el hermano de Martín Fierro. 2a. ed., corr y con apéndice documental. Buenos Aires: Centro Editor Argentino, 1981. 158 p.: bibl., ill.

Revised ed. of 1954 book describes life of active *porteño* politician who introduced bill creating University of La Plata and was driving force in many projects.

3259 Gutiérrez, Juan María. Colección Doctor Juan María Gutiérrez: archivo-epistolario. Buenos Aires: Biblioteca del Congreso de la Nación, 1979. 1 v.: index.

Excellent compilation of papers belonging to eminent scholar and public figure. Includes both personal correspondence (1830–45) and documents on Argentine history. Very useful for the study of Argentine cultural history and Liberal emigration during Rosas dictatorship.

3260 Gutiérrez, Leandro. Condiciones de la vida material de los sectores populares en Buenos Aires: 1880–1914 (IGFO/RI, 41:163/164, enero/junio 1981, p. 167–202, tables)

Follow-up to previous contribution (see *HLAS 44:3265*) that enhances our knowledge of period's social structure. For another assessment, see item **3264.**

3262 Guy, Donna J. La industria argentina, 1870–1940: legislación comercial, mercado de acciones y capitalización extranjera (IDES/DE, 22:87, oct./dic. 1982, p. 351–374)

Argues that industrialization as well as its control by foreign capital are closely linked to pecularities of legal system and stock market behavior, factors that allowed established elites to control credit and stay in power.

3263 Halperin-Donghi, Tulio. José Luis Romero y su lugar en la historiografía argentina (IDES/DE, 20:78, julio/sept. 1980, p. 249–274)

Combines brilliant, thoughtful evocation of the personality and main contributions of an eminent social historian with an excellent essay on a half-century of Argentine cultural history.

3264 Hardoy, Jorge Enrique; Diego Armus; María Elena Làngdon; and Juan Rial. Desigualdades regionales en Chile, Uruguay y Argentina, vistas a través de sus redes urbanas: 1865–1920 (IGFO/RI, 42:169/170, julio/dic. 1982, p. 317–369, maps, tables)

Excellent comparative research based on census data. Describes different effects of modernization process on each region with resulting differences.

3266 Herz, Enrique Germán. Villa Devoto, un barrio de quietud patriarcal. Buenos Aires: Municipalidad de la Ciudad de Buenos Aires, 1978. 114 p.: bibl., ill. (Cuadernos de Buenos Aires; 49)

Part of series devoted to recreating the colorful parts of different *barrios*.

3267 *Historia.* Revista libro trimestral. Año 2, No. 7, sept./nov. 1982 [through] Año 4, No. 13, marzo/mayo 1984– . Buenos Aires.

New journal, directed by Armando Alonso Piñeiro, publishes many worthwhile articles. No. 7, sept./nov. 1982: Néstor Ortiz Oderigo "Orígenes Etnoculturales de los Negros Argentinos;" Eduardo Durhofer "Las Nuevas Pruebas sobre la Legitimidad del Plan de Operaciones de Mariano Moreno." No. 9, marzo/mayo 1983: Isaías J. García Encisco "Una Curiosa Logia Política de 1890." No. 11, sept./nov. 1983: Néstor Ortiz Oderigo "Influencias Sudanesas en el Río de la Plata;"

Roberto Etchepareborda "Diálogo entre Libertadores." No. 12, dic. 1983: Alonso Piñeiro "Torcuato de Alvear: el Primer Intendente de Buenos Aires." No. 13, marzo/mayo 1984: Alberto Allende García "El Ideario Político del General Iriarte;" Roberto Etchepareborda "La Cuestión Malvinas en la Perspectiva Histórica."

3268 Historia del peronismo. v. 1. Buenos Aires: Editorial Oriente, 1982? 355 p.: ill. (some col.).

First installment of popular history (1945–50) provides useful background material in the form of eyewitness accounts and biographical sketches. Vol. 2–3 were not available before press time.

3269 Horowitz, Joel. The impact of the pre–1943 labor union traditions on peronism (JLAS, 15:1, May 1983, p. 101–116)

Shows continuity in union leadership's goals (i.e., willingness to cooperate with authorities, social welfare concerns).

3270 La Huelga de inquilinos de 1907: movimientos sociales. Selección y prólogo de Juan Soriano. Buenos Aires: Centro de América Latina, 1983. 94 p. (Historia testimonial argentina. Documentos vivos de nuestro pasado; 2)

Based on rich contemporary sources, rescues instructive episode of social history: *conventillos* protest movement involving slum tenants protesting against inhuman living conditions.

3271 Ibáñez, Francisco Maximiliano. Historia de Salto Grande. Entre Ríos, Argentina: s.n., 1980. 106 p.: ill.

Local history of area where binational project has been built.

3272 Inmigración e integración nacional en la época del centenario: Programa 64 del Consejo de Investigaciones de la U.N.T.: documentos de trabajo. Responsable, Lucía Piossek de Zucchi. San Miguel de Tucumán, Argentina: Universidad Nacional de Tucumán, Facultad de Filosofía y Letras, Centro de Historia y Pensamiento Argentinos, 1981. 2 v.: bibl.

Essays examine aspects of Tucumán's region (1900–20) from different perspectives and disciplines. Draws interesting observations from Juan B. Terán's work.

3273 La Inmigración europea en la Argentina. v. 1, Su organización. v. 2, La radicación de extranjeros en la Provincia de Santa Fé. v. 3, Memorias de los agentes oficiales. v. 4, Informes y estadísticas. v. 5, Comisiones de Inmigración en el Interior. v. 6, Comisiones de Inmigración en el Interior, Córdoba y San Luis. v. 10, Crónicas sobre inmigrantes y colonistas. Alberto Kleiner, compilador. Buenos Aires: Libreros y Editores del Polígono, 1983. 7 v.: bibl.

Reproduces in facsimile reports and documents on immigration issued by government agencies as of 1875, covering their activities in Europe and settlement of immigrants in Argentina's provinces. Useful compilation for understanding both settlement policies and economic development.

3274 *Investigaciones y Ensayos*. Academia Nacional de la Historia. No. 29, julio/dic. 1980 [through] No. 30, enero/junio 1981– . Buenos Aires.

Important contributions are in: No. 29: Carlos Paéz de la Torre Jr. "Aportes para el Estudio de los Propósitos y Acciones Conspirativas de los Emigrados Argentinos en Bolivia entre 1841 y 1852." No. 30: Néstor Tomás Auza "Un Desconocido Documento de la Revolución de 1930."

James, Daniel. Rationalisation and working class response: the context and limits of factory floor activity in Argentina. See *HLAS 45:8323*.

3275 Jauretche, Arturo. La colonización pedagógica y otros ensayos: antología. Selección y estudio preliminar por Aníbal Ford. Buenos Aires: Centro Editor de América Latina, 1982. 188 p. (Capítulo. Biblioteca argentina fundamental; 138)

Selection of writings by influential nationalist populist author.

3276 Juan Perón and the reshaping of Argentina. Frederick C. Turner *et al.* Edited by Frederick C. Turner and José Enrique Miguens. Pittsburgh: University of Pittsburgh Press, 1983. 264 p.: bibl., ill., index (Pitt Latin American series)

Collection of essays depicts diverse aspects of Justicialista movement from a balanced perspective: Frederick C. Turner "The Cycle of Peronism" and "Entrepreneurs and Estancieros in Perón's Argentina;" Marysa Navarro "Evita and Peronism;" Gary W.

Wynia "Workers and Wages: Argentine Labor and the Incomes Policy Problems;" Wayne S. Smith "The Return of Peronism;" José Enrique Miguens "The Presidential Elections of 1973 and the End of an Ideology;" and Manuel Mora y Araujo and Peter H. Smith "Peronism and Economic Development: the 1973 Elections."

3277 Klein, Herbert S. The integration of Italian immigrants into the United States and Argentina: a comparative analysis; [and] Comments by Jorge Balán, J.D. Gould, Tulio Halperin-Donghi; [and] Reply by Herbert S. Klein (AHA/R, 88:2, April 1983, p. 306–346, tables)

Seminal work seeks to explain differences in social integration of Italians in both countries. Finds that opportunities in Argentina: "were such that many immigrants were attracted to invest their savings in the local economy" and consequently played greater role than in US. Points out that process of assimilation took much longer in US. Includes valuable critical comments by Balán, Gould, and Halperin-Donghi. For Spanish version, see *Desarrollo Económico* (21:81, abril/junio 1981, p. 3–28).

Kloberdanz, Timothy J. Plainsmen of three continents: Volga German adaptation to steppe, prairie, and pampa. See *HLAS 45:8325*.

3278 Korol, Juan Carlos and **Hilda Sábato.** Cómo fue la inmigración irlandesa en la Argentina. Buenos Aires: Plus Ultra, 1981. 213 p.: bibl., ill. (Colección Esquemas históricos; 33)

Scholarly case-study of one of earliest immigrant groups. Analyzes development and pecularities of Buenos Aires' "sheep farm" economy. Records relative success of this enterprise.

3279 La Plata: ciudad milagro. Dirección, Catalina Lerange. Fotografías, Celia Freyre *et al.* Buenos Aires: Corregidor, 1982. 679 p.: bibl., ill.

Encyclopedic treatment consists of short notes on multitude of city topics.

3280 La Plata vista por los viajeros, 1882–1912. Edición, Pedro Luis Barcia. Fotografía, Armando J. Lértora. Traducciones, Amelia Aguado de Costa. La Plata, Argentina: Ediciones del 80 y Librerías

Juvenilia, 1982. 273 p., 1 leaf of plates: bibl., ill.

Compilation of 32 travelers' accounts (1822–1912) provides vivid picture of city's development.

3281 Larra, Raúl. El General Baldrich y la defensa del petróleo argentino. Buenos Aires: Editorial Mariano Moreno, 1981. 112 p.: bibl., ports.

Popular biography of individual who with Mosconi was driving force in nationalization of Argentine oil.

3282 Lascano, Julio Raúl. Los estudios superiores en la historia de Buenos Aires: homenaje al IV Centenario de la Fundación de la Ciudad de Buenos Aires. Buenos Aires: Municipalidad de la Ciudad de Buenos Aires, 1981. 347 p.: bibl., plan.

Survey from colonial times to present provides wealth of statistics on different professions and university degrees. Good summary of conditions at University of Buenos Aires in Rosas' times. Also includes data on post 1959–private universities.

3283 Liehr, Reinhard. El Fondo Quesada en el Instituto Ibero-Americano de Berlín (LARR, 18:2, 1983, p. 125–133)

Outlines principal holdings and includes biographical sketches of Vicente and Ernesto Quesada.

3284 Little, Walter. A note on political incorporation: the Argentine Plan Político of 1955 (JLAS, 14:2, Nov. 1982, p. 455–464)

Discusses peronist's preparations for 1957 elections which stressed need to broaden popular appeal and mobilization. Author quotes voting projections that offer fascinating inside picture of peronist appraisal of political equation with Peronist Party accounting for 30 percent plurality. For political scientist's comment, see *HLAS 45:6429.*

3285 Llach, Juan José. El Plan Pinedo de 1940: su significación histórica y los orígenes de la economía política del peronismo (IDES/DE, 23:92, enero/marzo 1984, p. 516–558)

Intelligent presentation of two economic strategies. Attributes their failure chiefly to political causes in first instance, to economic ones in second.

3286 Llorca, Carmen. Llamadme Evita. Barcelona: Planeta, 1980. 302 p., 1 leaf; bibl., ill., index.

Semi-fictional popular history exemplifies trend in hagiographies of certain individuals. To be used with caution.

3287 López Alonso, Gerardo. 1930–1980 [i.e. Mil novecientos treinta-mil novecientos ochenta]: cincuenta años de historia argentina, una cronología básica. 3a. ed. Buenos Aires: Editorial de Belgrano, 1982. 414 p., 8 p. of plates: bibl., ill.

Quick overview of difficult five decades. Each well selected entry provides precise abstract of topic. Excellent reference tool.

3288 López Seghesso, María Cristina de. El acceso del Lencinismo al poder, 1918–1926: una visión a través de las elecciones de Gobernador (UNC/RHAA, 11:21/22, 1981/1982, p. 103–145)

Saenz Peña's Electoral Law led to the emergence of certain Radical Party populist movements that split from Yrigoyen's national leadership (e.g., San Juan, Mendoza). Article records relevant electoral results, depicts party contenders, and describes characteristics of so-called *lencinista chusmocracia.*

3289 Luna, Félix. Buenos Aires y el país. 2a. ed. Buenos Aires: Editorial Sudamericana, 1982. 225 p.: bibl.

Traditional historical rivalry noted in title provides basis for popular historian's musings. Suggests solution to confrontational relationship: great port city must cease to be nation's capital and it must be moved to Interior.

3290 ———. Golpes militares y salidas electorales. Buenos Aires: Editorial Sudamericana, 1983. 175 p.

Based on newspaper articles. Represents serious attempt to understand tragic evolution of Argentine political democracy since 1930. Largely attributes its failure to military attitudes: lack of common ideology and program, narrow focus on technical functions, propensity to see issues in black-and-white terms. Emphasizes long-range consequences of past strongly influenced by arbitrary and totalitarian tendencies. Notes need to develop confidence in politicians.

3291 Luqui Lagleyze, Julio A. and **José Ré.** Una epopeya porteña. v. 1, Sitios de volación en Buenos Aires. v. 2, La conquista del cielo patrio. Buenos Aires: Instituto Argentino de Historia Aeronáutica Jorge Newberry, 1982. 38 p.

Basic reference work reports initial stages of Argentine aviation.

3292 Maceyra, Horacio. Cámpora, Perón, Isabel. Buenos Aires: Centro Editor de América Latina, 1983. 167 p. (Las Presidencias peronistas. Biblioteca política argentina; 25)

Thoughtful, informative reconstruction of tumultuous three years (1973–76). Includes close examination of principal issues, protagonists, political parties, armed forces, entrepreneurs, intellectuals and students. Also examines economic issues, terrorism, and foreign relations.

3293 McGee, Sandra. The visible and invisible Liga Patriótica Argentina, 1919–28: gender roles and the right wing (HAHR, 64:2, 1984, p. 233–258)

Continues exploration of relevant topic. Shows importance of female participation, offering new insights into nature of organization, and interplay of gender role, class, and political activity.

3294 McLynn, F.J. The political thought of Juan Domingo Perón (CEDLA/B, 32, junio 1982, p. 15–23)

Honest but naive interpretation based on famous ca. 1949 speech authored by Carlos Astrada. Believes Perón's ideology is based on an eclectic positivism that merits attention.

3295 ———. Urquiza and the Montoneros: an ambiguous chapter in Argentine history (IAA, 8:3, 1982, p. 283–295)

Ably examines caudillo's lack of response to both Peñaloza and Varela's rebellions (1863, 1866–67). Shows Urquiza's self-serving attitude exemplified by his battles for his own "objective interests."

3296 Marcin Kowaleski, Zbigniew. La formación del Partido Revolucionario de los Trabajadores de Argentina: 1963–1972 (PAN/ES, 8, 1981, p. 37–63)

Sympathetic, partisan chronicle of emergence of leftist party, its internal doctrinal disputes and activities of its military arm, Ejército Revolucionario del Pueblo or ERP.

Martínez Paz, Fernando. El sistema educativo nacional: formación, desarrollo, crisis. See *HLAS 45:4361.*

Martini de Vatausky, Yoli Angélica. Los franciscanos de Río IV, los indios ranqueles y otros temas de la vida en la frontera. See item **1663.**

3297 Matamoro, Blas. La emigración cultural española en Argentina durante la posguerra de 1939 (CH, 384, junio 1982, p. 576–590, bibl.)

Brief examination of influx of Spanish exiles that enriched Argentine culture in most varied disciplines. Alphabetic list records their life and deeds.

3298 Matijevic, Nicolás. Bibliografía sobre la Conquista del Desierto. Bahía Blanca, Argentina: Departamento de Ciencias Sociales–UNS, Centro de Documentación Patagónica, 1979 or 1980. 30 leaves.

Bibliographical guide of 415 entries commemorates event's centennial.

3299 Matsushita, Hiroshi. Movimiento obrero argentino, 1930–1945: sus proyecciones en los orígenes del peronismo. Prólogo de Rubén H. Zorrilla. Buenos Aires: Ediciones Siglo Veinte, 1983. 347 p.: bibl.

Masterful research seeks explanation for massive support workers gave Perón (1943–45). Eschewing conventional explanations (e.g., replacement of traditional labor leaders, emergence of "new worker"), author explores ideological changes undergone in previous decade (e.g., "politization" of labor leaders, their active challenge to traditional institutions and economic system). Finally, believes profound change took place in 1944 and rejects notion of a continuity between 1930s and peronism.

3300 Mayo, Carlos; Osvaldo Mayo; and **Fernando García Molina.** La diplomacia del petróleo: 1916–1930. 2a. ed. Buenos Aires: Centro Editor de América Latina, 1983. 200 p.: tables (Biblioteca Política argentina; 24)

First published 1976. Describes US reaction to oil nationalization by Radical administrations (1916–30) and Gen. Mosconi's struggle with Standard Oil. Based on US diplomatic archives.

3301 Mazo, Gabriel del and **Roberto Etchepareborda.** La segunda presidencia de Yrigoyen: antecedentes de la crisis de 1930. Buenos Aires: Centro Editor de América Latina, 1984. 158 p. (Biblioteca Política argentina; 52)

Important analysis of Yrigoyen's second presidential term. Partly based on oral histories (e.g., Ratto, Vice-President Martínez, González, Oyhanarte, Gen. Toranzo, Luzuriaga). Provides intriguing picture of fateful two years that changed course of Argentine history for next half century. [G.M. Dorn]

3302 Mendelson, José. Génesis de la colonia judía de la Argentina: 1889–1902.` Buenos Aires: Libreros y Editores del Polígono, 1982. 77 p.: bibl. ill.

Reprint of 1939 book published to commemorate 50th anniversary of Jewish colonization. Includes important data.

3303 Mensajes de los Gobernadores de Córdoba a la Legislatura. t. 1, 1828–1847. Advertencia, Carlos S.A. Segreti. Recopilación e introducción, Ana Inés Ferreyra. Córdoba, Argentina: Centro de Estudios Históricos, 1980. 1 v.

Excellent compilation fills important gap in province's history. Provides wealth of political, military, and socioeconomic information that will be very useful for future interpretations of 1828–47 period. Designed to continue coverage up to 1900.

3304 Miguez, Eduardo. Inversiones familiares británicas en tierras argentinas: 1850–1914 (IGFO/RI, 41 : 165 / 166, julio/ dic. 1981, p. 637–674)

Part of major research underway. Demonstrates importance of neglected feature of Argentine 1850–1914 indebtness (i.e., invisible transfer of Argentine capital to UK, insignificant transfer of British financial resources). Underscores significance of such aspects of British investment.

3305 Mirelman, Victor A. Early Zionist activities among Sephardim in Argentina (AJA, 34 : 2, Nov. 1982, p. 190–205)

Describes successive attempts and failures to win Argentine Sephardim allegiance to cause.

3306 Musso Ambrosio, Luis Alberto. Anotaciones de bibliografía uruguaya sobre historia argentina en el período 1831–1852:

época de Rosas (EEHA/HBA, 23, 1979, p. 121–138, bibl.)

Useful but unnannotated list of rare works.

3307 Nabuco, Joaquim. La Guerra del Paraguay. Versión castellana de Gonzalo Reparaz. Buenos Aires: Editorial de Belgrano, 1977. 412 p.: bibl. (Colección La Argentina histórica)

Reprint of Brazilian classic written by statesman / diplomat. Presents relevant documents on Brazilian / Argentine relations concerning division of Paraguayan territory, according to Treaty of Triple Alliance and 1876 peace negotiations. Includes illuminating transcripts of Imperial Council of State.

3308 Navarro, Marysa. Evita. Buenos Aires: Corregidor, 1981. 371 p.: bibl., ill., ports.

Translation of biography by acknowledged expert originally published in English with Nicholas Frazer (see *HLAS 44:3240*). More encompassing, this new version presents balanced and objective overview of subject's life and influence. Concludes: "Nunca olvidó a quien debía el llegar a ser *Evita* y nunca se desvió de su meta."

3309 Newton, Ronald C. Indifferent sanctuary: German-speaking refugees and exiles in Argentina, 1933–1945 (SAGE/JIAS, 24 : 4, Nov. 1982, p. 395–420)

Well documented contribution by known specialist chronicles vicissitudes of European immigrants, Jews, and political exiles and their struggle against Nazism. Also explores World War II propaganda.

3310 Nosiglia, Julio E. El desarrollismo. Buenos Aires: Centro Editor de América Latina, 1983. 193 p. (Biblioteca Política argentina; 3)

Describes origins, emergence, and activities of political movement led by Arturo Frondizi after 1957 Radical Party split. Provides objective overview of its accomplishments and failures.

3311 Nuestra Historia. Revista del Centro de Estudios de Historia Argentina. No. 31/32, dic. 1983– . Buenos Aires.

Special issue devoted to 1981 *Segundo Congreso de Historia de la Confederación, 1831–52*. Principal contributions are: Jorge Comadrán Ruiz "Mendoza y las Relaciones con Chile durante la Epoca de Rosas;" Mario Guillermo Saraví "Pascual Echagüe y el Bloqueo Francés;" and Oscar Abadie-Aicardi and Raúl Abadie-Aicardi "La Política Río-platense entre 1829 y 1843 Vista por dos Comerciantes."

3312 Nunn, Frederick M. Yesterday's soldiers: European military professionalism in South America, 1890–1940. Lincoln: University of Nebraska Press, 1983. 365 p.: bibl., index.

Scholarly contribution solidly based on comprehensive examination of military literature. Adds to our knowledge of contemporary attitudes and behavior of Argentina's officer corps. Stresses continuous influence of "ideologized" past when German and French professional military thinking was the standard. Emphasizes this is why Argentina's military "confronted what they perceived to be major problems of their modernizing nation by professing solutions derived from their European orientations."

Oberti, Federico. Historia y folklore del mate. See item **974.**

3313 O'Connell, Arturo. La Argentina en la Depresión: los problemas de una economía abierta (IDES/DE, 23:92, enero/marzo 1984, p. 479–514)

Examines Argentina's inter-war economy (1919–39) to show that slumps were not exceptional and that 1930 Depression was merely one more instance of established pattern. Attributes Argentine crisis to early Wall Street boom accompanied by fall in grain prices rather than to 1929 crash.

3314 O'Donnell, Guillermo. 1966–1973 [i.e. Mil novecientos sesenta y seis-mil novecientos setenta y tres], el estado burocrático autoritario: triunfos, derrotas y crisis. Buenos Aires: Editorial de Belgrano 1982. 499 p.: bibl., ill., index, tables (Colección Testimonios contemporáneos)

Outstanding contribution by distinguished scholar, of great interest to historians. Uses wealth of primary sources and data to determine new features of the authoritarian State in a study of breadth and depth. For political scientist's comment, see *HLAS 45:6432.*

3315 Oszlak, Oscar. La formación del Estado argentino. Con la colaboración de

Andrés Fontana y Leandro Gutiérrez. Buenos Aires: Editorial de Belgrano, 1982. 270 p.: ill. (Colección Conflictos y armonías en la historia argentina)

Very interesting compilation of essays that examine different but complementary aspects of the State's formative process in several well balanced analyses of economic and political factors. Notes tragic fate of Argentina's political process: "La unidad nacional fue siempre el precio de la derrota de unos y la consagración de privilegios de otros."

3316 Pagano, Mabel. Eterna. Buenos Aires: Nuevo Sol Editores, 1982. 284 p.: (Narrativa Argentina)

Another biography of Eva Perón's that exemplifies prevailing mythical interpretations.

3317 Page, Joseph A. Perón: a biography. New York: Random House, 1983, 594 p., 8 p. of plates: bibl., ill., index.

First full-length biography of Justicialismo's founder that is documented and highly informative. Well structured narrative runs smoothly. Despite its objectivity vis-à-vis Perón himself, book is somewhat lacking in knowledge of the country in 1940s and 1950s. Pt. 1 is available in Spanish as *Perón: una biografía. v. 1, 1895–1952* (Buenos Aires: Javier Vergara, 1984).

3318 Panettieri, José. Devaluaciones de la moneda, 1822–1835: debate nacional. Buenos Aires: Centro Editor de América Latina, 1983. 158 p.: appendix, ill. (Biblioteca Política argentina; 22)

Specialist discusses 1864 and 1899 currency conversion laws that established paper money/gold equivalence as well as origins and social and economic consequences of such legislation. Peruses public debates that preceded it.

Pang, Eul-Soo. Buenos Aires and the Argentine economy in world perspective, 1776–1930. See item **2792.**

3319 Paso, Leonardo. Historia de los partidos políticos en la Argentina, 1900–1930. Buenos Aires: Ediciones Directa, 1983. 574 p.: bibl.

Marxist interpetation of Argentine political development is informative if sometimes biased and mistaken. For vol. 1 on 1810–1918, see *HLAS 36:3252.*

3320 ———; **Enrique Palomba; María Litter;** and **Pedro Calderón.** Compendio de historia argentina: desde la colonia hasta 1943. Buenos Aires: Ediciones Directa, 1982. 380 p.: bibl., ill., maps.

Interesting presentation by Argentina's Communist Party consists of its official interpretation of the nation's past.

3321 **Pavoni, Norma L.** El noroeste argentino en la época de Alejandro Heredia. v. 1, La política. v. 2, Economía y·sociedad. Tucumán, Argentina: Ediciones Fundación Banco Comercial del Norte, 1981. 2 v.: bibl. (Colección Historia; 8)

Outstanding study, thoroughly researched and written from regional perspective. Describes 1832–39 period when Tucuman's Governor held a sort of "protectorate" over neighboring provinces. Attributes outbreak of war with Bolivia to his hegemonic plans to turn Bolivia into a market for produces of Argentine Northeast, a return to the colonial economy.

3322 **Peña, José María.** Buenos Aires anteayer: testimonios gráficos de una ciudad, 1854–1910. Textos y selección de las imágenes, José María Peña. Colaboración técnico-fotográfica en la selección, Eduardo Vázquez. Fotografía de archivo y laboratorio, Enrique Shore. Diagramación, Anteo del Mastro. Coordinación editorial, Claudio Jodzinsky. Conducción y realización general, Manrique Zago. Buenos Aires: M. Zago Ediciones, 1981. 191 p.: chiefly ill.

Beautifully crafted book consists of magnificent collection of photographs that record different aspects of Buenos Aires' life as it grew from "Gran Aldea" into huge metropolis.

Pérez Lindo, Augusto. Etat oligarchique, désintégration sociale et violence politique en l'Argentine. See *HLAS 45:8327.*

3323 **Perina, Rubén M.** Onganía, Levingston, Lanusse: los militares en la política argentina. Traducción, Antonio Bonanno. Buenos Aires: Editorial de Belgrano, 1983. 267 p.: bibl. (Colección Conflictos y armonías en la historia argentina)

Thoroughly researched examination of performance of military governments of the "Revolución Argentina." Concludes that they failed in their goals to modernize and develop.

3324 **Perón, Juan Domingo.** Correspondencia. v. 1, 1936–1974. v. 2, 1944–1973. Edited by Enrique Pavón Pereyra. Buenos Aires: Corregidor, 1983. 2 v.: index.

Collection of 14,000 uneven and unannotated letters that contain wealth of information but are organized chronologically rather than topically, an arrangement that hinders access. Vol. 1 consists of 1936–74 correspondence including particularly interesting letters of instruction to Perón's followers during crucial exile years. Vol. 2 covers 1944–73 and consists of 41 items.

3325 **Platt, D.C.M.** Foreign finance in Argentina for the first half-century of independence (JLAS, 15:1, May 1983, p. 23–47)

Documented study underscores important role of domestic finance in nation's development and disproves some well known conspiratorial interpretations of 1824 Baring Brothers loan.

3326 **El Poder militar en la Argentina, 1976–1981:** aspectos históricos y socio-políticos. Editors: Peter Waldmann and Ernesto Garzón Valdez. Frankfurt, FRG: Vervuert Verlag, 1982. 220 p.: bibl. (Editionen der Iberoamericana; Reihe 3)

Critical evaluations of 1976–81 military regime by foreign and Argentine scholars are divided into three parts: 1) *Analysis of Historical Processes in the 20th Century*: Natalio R. Botana "¿Habitantes o Ciudadanos?: La Argentina del Ochenta y el Problema de la Identidad Política;" David Rock "Las Dos Primeras Décadas del Siglo XX: la Influencia de la Inmigración;" Ryszard Stamplowski "Las Concepciones Nacionalistas y sus Contextos Políticos en la Argentina: de Lugones a Perón;" Peter Waldmann "La Argentina en la II Guerra Mundial y el Surgimiento del Peronismo: una Interpretación desde la Perspectiva de la Dependencia;" 2) *Study of the Armed Forces in Power*: Alain Rouquié "El Poder Militar en la Argentina de Hoy: Cambio y Continuidad;" Arnold Spitta "El Proceso de Reorganización Nacional de 1976 a 1981: los Objetivos Básicos y su Realización Práctica;" Francisco J. Delich "Desmovilización Social: Reestructuración Obrera y Cambio Sindical;" León E. Bieber "El Movimiento Obrero Argentino a Partir de 1976;" Dante Caputo "Balance Provisorio;" 3) *Analysis of Argentina's Position in the World*: Félix Peña "La Argentina en el Mundo que Cambia: Prioridades de la Política Exterior a Partir de los Años 70;" Wolf Grabendorff "¿De País Aislado a Aliado Preferido: las Relaciones entre la Argentina y los Estados Unidos, 1976–1981;" Dieter Noblen "Consideraciones Acerca de la Cuenca del Plata como Sistema de Relaciones Internacionales: el Papel de la Argentina en el Proceso de Cooperación y Conflicto;" Ernesto Garzón Valdez "La Emigración Argentina: acerca de sus Causas Eticopolíticas." Most provocative and innovative contribution, a selected bibliography, closes volume.

3327 Quentin-Mauroy, Dominique. J.B. Alberdi, 1810–1884, et la formation de la conscience nationale argentine (UTIEH/C, 38, 1982, p. 71–88)

Painstaking analysis of the great *pensador's* writings. Sees him as authentic nation-builder.

3328 Rafael, Juan. El federalismo y las intervenciones nacionales. Buenos Aires: Plus Ultra, 1982. 215 p.: bibl. (Colección Política e historia)

Summarizes interventions suffered by Santiago del Estero prov. (1852–1953). Each instance is preceded by informative captions.

3329 Rama, Carlos M. Nacionalismo e historiografiá en América Latina. Madrid: Tecnos, 1981. 175 p.: bibl. (Colección Ventana abierta)

Leftist critique includes several errors of fact. Examines Argentine revisionist historical writings to establish their links with militant nationalist ideology. Two final chapters cover similar trends in other Latin American countries.

3330 Rapoport, Mario. El factor político en las relaciones internacionales: política internacional vs. teoría de la dependencia, un comentario (IDES/DE, 23:92, enero/marzo 1984, p. 627–636)

Strong argument challenges Carlos Escudé's conclusions in item **3233**. For Escudé's response, see above issue of *Desarrollo Económico* (p. 631–636).

3331 Rey Balmaceda, Raúl. Comunidades extranjeras en la Argentina: contribución a una bibliografía. Buenos Aires: Oikos Asociación para la Promoción de los Estudios Territoriales y Ambientales, 1980. 73 p.: bibl., index (Documento de referencia, 0325–4240; 1–02)

First full-fledged effort to compile scattered bibliographical information on topic. Consists of 1,000 entries.

3332 Rivanera Carlés, Raúl. Nuestros próceres: biografías sintéticas, contribución a la verdad histórica. Buenos Aires: Liding, 1979. 1 v.: bibl. (Serie Historia argentina)

Vol. 1 of four consists of brief revisionist biographies (written 1943, published 1979). They convey flavor of early confrontation between liberal and revisionist schools of thought.

3333 ———. Rosas, ensayo biográfico y crítico del Brigadier General de la Confederación Argentina y fundador del federalismo. Buenos Aires: Liding, 1979. 321 p.: bibl., ill. (Serie Historia argentina)

First ed. of eulogistic, revisionist biography of Rosas written 1940s, at peak of revisionist, nationalist sentiment. Final chapters are devoted to criticizing Sarmiento.

3334 Rodríguez Molas, Ricardo E. Historia social del gaucho. Buenos Aires: Centro Editor de América Latina, 1982. 302 p.: bibl. (Capítulo. Biblioteca argentina fundamental; 159. Serie complementaria, sociedad y cultura; 11)

New revised version of 1968 book. Strongly criticizes prevailing social conditions endured by inhabitants of the plains and harassment they suffered.

3335 ———. El servicio militar obligatorio: debate nacional. Buenos Aires: Centro Editor de América Latina, 1983. 189 p. (Biblioteca Política argentina; 18)

Reproduces parliamentary debates that led to approval of military draft, including discussions of alternatives such as National Citizen Militia, etc. Short introduction provides historical background, analyzing the law itself, the frontier, Indian threats, etc.

3336 Romero, José Luis. El drama de la democracia argentina. Buenos Aires: Centro Editor de América Latina, 1983. 142 p. (Biblioteca Política argentina; 35)

Compilation of essays by distinguished historian covers political themes. Of special interest are those concerning last peronist administration in 1970s.

3337 Romero, Luis Alberto. Buenos Aires: la sociedad criolla, 1810–1850 (IGFO/RI, 41:163/164, enero/junio 1981, p. 143–165)

Brisk account of transition from colonial times to Rosas period ably describes new elites and tensions and violence permeating society.

3338 Rouquié, Alain. Poder militar y sociedad política en la Argentina. v. 2, 1943–1973. Buenos Aires: Emecé Editores, 1982. 461 p.: bibl., index.

Vol. 2 of seminal sociological analysis of successive "intervenciones estabilizadoras" and institutional role of armed forces. "Ante una sociedad fragmentada por las rivalidades sectoriales y las divisiones provocadas por la dependencia externa y la homogeneidad institucional justifica su intervención . . . El golpe de Estado, como proceso de redistribución política, fortalece su legitimidad . . . favoreciendo alternativamente a cada gran sector social . . . e impone un empate social, que de ninguna manera permite superar la crisis hegemónica." For French original, see *HLAS 43:8328.*

3339 Ruiz Moreno, Isidoro Jorge. Orígenes de la diplomacia ítalo-argentina. Buenos Aires: Instituto Histórico de la Organización Nacional, 1983. 101 p.

Pioneer essay on relatively forgotten topic based on Italian and Argentine sources. Explores initial relations between Kingdom of Sardinia and Argentine Confederation in 1852–58, during difficult period of Buenos Aires' secession.

3340 Sábato, Hilda. Trabajar para vivir o vivir para trabajar: empleo ocasional y escasez de mano de obra en Buenos Aires, ciudad y campaña, 1850–1880. Buenos Aires: Centro de Investigaciones Sociales sobre el Estado y la Administración, Programa de Estudios de Historia Económica y Social (PEHESA), 1982. 1 v. (Documento de trabajo)

Part of ongoing research on Buenos Aires prov. labor force. Describes its main features in 1850–80 as being: increasing demand for manual labor, lack of elasticity in global supply, over-representation of certain workers because of their cultural and social background.

3341 ———. Wool trade and commercial networks in Buenos Aires: 1840's to 1880's (JLAS, 15:1, May 1983, p. 49–81, tables)

Close examination of wool trade as engine that drove national economy by mid 19th century. Eloquently describes its various mechanisms, commercial networks, principal exporters, and product's destination.

3342 Sáenz Quesada, María. El estado rebelde: Buenos Aires entre 1850–1860. Buenos Aires: Editorial de Belgrano, 1982. 434 p.: bibl. (Colección Conflicto y armonías en la historia argentina)

Comprehensive, detailed portrait of proud *porteño* city at time of secession. Customs, daily life, prevailing attitudes are evoked in pleasing style.

3343 Sánchez, Pedro. La presidencia de Illia. Buenos Aires: Centro Editor de América Latina, 1983. 167 p. (Biblioteca Política argentina; 26. Las Presidencias radicales)

Intelligent, detailed chronicle of 1963–66 period.

3344 Sanz, Luis Santiago. Personalidad de Zeballos: internacionalista y fundador de la Sociedad Científica Argentina. Buenos Aires: Sociedad Científica Argentina, 1981. 51 p.

New summary of life and multiple activities of prominent public figure. Includes chronology within context of principal national and international events.

———. Proyección internacional de la *Declaración del 9 de julio de 1816*. See item **2890.**

3345 Scenna, Miguel Angel. FORJA: una aventura argentina, de Yrigoyen a Perón. 2a. ed. Buenos Aires: Editorial de Belgrano, 1983. 400 p. (Colección Testimonios contemporáneos)

Reprint of detailed reconstruction of Forjismo. For first ed., see *HLAS 36:3304.*

3346 Sebreli, Juan José. Los deseos imaginarios del peronismo: ensayo crítico. 3a. ed. Buenos Aires: Editorial Legasa, 1983. 281 p.

Important, ideological exercise consists of severe and witty criticism of peronist movement by celebrated free-thinking intellectual. Also includes self-criticism, given author's own early romantic views of peronism.

3347 Segreti, Carlos S.A. Límites con Chile bajo Austrias y Borbones. Córdoba, Argentina: ERA Editorial Raíces Argentinas, n.d. 16 p.: maps.

Brief, informative study illustrates Argentine claims in boundary controversy with Chile. Provides useful background information on years preceding colonial times, a period usually overlooked.

3348 ———. El país disuelto: el estallido de 1820 y los esfuerzos organizativos. Buenos Aires: Editorial de Belgrano, 1982. 396 p.: bibl. (Colección Conflictos y armonías en la historia argentina)

Updates information on chaotic period and stresses Córdoba's Governor Bustos' efforts and eventual failure to establish a federal institutional order.

3349 Seguí, Juan Francisco and **Bartolomé Mitre.** Polémica sobre la Constitución. Estudio preliminar de Néstor Tomás Auza. Buenos Aires: Instituto Histórico de la Organización Nacional, 1982. 253 p.: bibl. (Documento; no. 3)

Compilation recreates first (1860) debate on topic, one that went unnoticed by historians. Valuable contribution to constitutional history and to history of ideas.

3350 Sempat Assadourian, Carlos. El sector exportador de una economía regional del interior argentino, Córdoba, 1800–1860: esquema quantitativo y formas de producción (GEE/NA, 1, 1978, p. 57–104, tables)

New archival sources allows author to determine economic and trade patterns of this central province, particularly after colonial period when Buenos Aires and international markets became crucial for its economy.

3351 Sidicaro, Ricardo. Estado intervencionista, grandes propietarios rurales y producción agropecuaria en Argentina: 1946–1976 (GEE/NA, 5, 1982, p. 399–432, tables)

Worthwhile effort includes instructive data that shows main provisions adopted by administrations of most varied political tendencies as they grappled with the nation's powerful landowners and farming sector.

3352 Sierra, Vicente D. Historia de la Argentina. v. 10, Vida, pasión y muerte de la Confederación Argentina: 1852–1862.

Buenos Aires: Unión de Escritores Latinos, 1980. 1 v.: bibl., ill.

Another volume of handbook written by deceased revisionist historian. Informative but controversial because of his historical approach and lack of attribution in use of sources. For previous volumes, see *HLAS 28:1019a, HLAS 30:2277, HLAS 34:2801a,* and *HLAS 36:3316.*

3353 Síntesis histórica de la Policía de la Provincia de Buenos Aires, 1580– 1980. Realizado por la Comisión Permanente de Investigaciones Históricas de la Policía de la Provincia de Buenos Aires. Buenos Aires: La Policía, 1981. 304 p.: bibl., ill.

Brief commemorative chronicle of historical evolution of Buenos Aires police force from colonial times to present.

3354 Slatta, Richard W. Gauchos and the vanishing frontier. Lincoln: University of Nebraska Press, 1983. 1 v.: bibl., index.

Well documented, thoughtful analysis of pampas dweller and his environment is best scholarly study of topic to date in English. Covers gaucho's losing battle against modernization and capitalist way. Examines predominant social conditions in plains, different servitudes gauchos were subject to, their xenophobic attitudes towards foreigners, and development of popular myth.

3355 Soares, María Regina de Lima and **Gerson Moura.** Brasil-Argentina: fontes bibliográficas (RIB, 32:3/4, 1982, p. 295–321)

Annotated selection of 123 entries on bilateral relations, divided by topics: 1) General Historical Interpretations; 2) Specific Historical Questions; 3) Contemporary Issues; 4) International Politics; 5) Geopolitical Matters; 6) River Plate Basin Resources; and 7) Atomic Energy.

3356 Sofer, Eugene F. From pale to pampa: a social history of the Jews of Buenos Aires. New York: Holmes & Meier, 1982. 165 p.: bibl., index.

Perceptive book concentrates on establishing links among occupational mobility, existing patterns of Argentine social and economic history, and Argentine politics. Provides intelligent analysis of Jewish community's experience in Buenos Aires. For comment on author's previous contribution, see *HLAS 44:3384.*

3357 Solberg, Carl E. Peopling the prairies and the pampas: the impact of immigration on Argentina and Canadian agrarian development, 1870–1930 (SAGE/JIAS, 24:2, May 1982, p. 131–161, bibl., tables)

Well researched article by serious scholar ponders striking similarities of economic development in both countries. Concludes by stressing that in both cases, whether as tenants in Argentina or as small prairie farmers in Canada, immigrants were peripheral.

3358 Sulé, Jorge Oscar. Los heterodoxos del 80. Buenos Aires: Ediciones Macchi, 1982. 63 p.: bibl.

Liberal creed adhered to by so-called Generation of 1880s undergoes severe criticism by revisionist author. Opinions of Liberal opponents such as Fragueiro, V.F. López, Zeballos, Estrada, Magnasco are used to make author's point.

3359 Taravella, Ambrosio L.V. Setenta años de servicios aeronáuticos: historia ilustrada. Buenos Aires: Presidencia de la Nación, Secretaría de Cultura, Ediciones Culturales Argentinas, 1982. 173 p.: ill.

Aviation pioneer's memoirs record main events, types of aircraft used, creation of Fábrica Militar de Aviones in Córdoba prov., and first Argentine-built airplanes.

3360 Taylor, Julie M. Eva Perón, los mitos de una mujer. Buenos Aires: Editorial de Belgrano, 1981. 260 p.: bibl. (Colección Testimonios contemporáneos)

Spanish ed. of outstanding contribution (see *HLAS 45:3393*).

Teijeiro, Mario O. Inversión británica en Argentina: causas y consecuencias del pánico Baring. See *HLAS 45:3577*.

3361 Tesler, Mario. Aportes de Diego Luis Molinari a la cultura hispanoamericana: ensayo bibliográfico (RA/H, 2:7, sept./nov. 1982, p. 132–138)

Pt. 2 of *HLAS 44:3396*.

3362 Todo es Historia. Revista mensual de divulgación histórica. Honneger S.A. No. 194, julio 1983 [and] No. 197, dic. 1983– . Buenos Aires.

Popular magazine devoted to Argentine and Latin American history includes several articles of interest: No. 194: Alfredo Galetti "Ambigüedades e Incongruencias de la Revolución de los Coroneles;" Alberto Blasi Brambilla "Los Primeros Pasos del Gobierno Militar;" Leonardo Senkman "El 4 de Junio y los Judíos." No. 197: Cristián Buchmacker "Las Corrientes Ideológicas en la Década del 40;" Rubén H. Zorilla "Líder, Elite y Masa en el Peronismo;" Robert A. Potash "Las Fuerzas Armadas en la Década del 40;" and Teodoro Blanco "Atlas, la Proyección Sindical Peronista en América Latina."

3363 Tonda, Américo A. La eclesiología de los Doctores Gorriti, Zavaleta y Agüero. Buenos Aires: Universidad Católica Argentina, Facultad de Derecho y Ciencias Sociales del Rosario, Instituto de Historia, 1981. 64 p.: ill. (Monografías y ensayos; no. 19)

Theological history and unusual contributions on the subject. Peruses attitudes of three distinguished prelates regarding problems that afflicted the new nations (e.g., relations between Church and State, the Pope and his Bishops). Considers that all three men were influenced by Jansenism and the Enlightment.

3364 Torre, Juan Carlos. El movimiento obrero y el último gobierno peronista, 1973–1976 (Crítica y Utopía [Editorial Latinoamericana de Ciencias Sociales, Buenos Aires] 6, 1982, p. 99–136)

Examines changing role of labor during peronist restoration noting it was marginal. Concludes: "El retorno de Perón al gobierno y la puesta en marcha de la política concertada de ingresos indicaron limitaciones severas para los sindicalistas en sus funciones de articuladores de las demandas obreras, entre sus bases y los poderes públicos y los empresarios."

3365 Trask, Roger R. Spruille Braden versus George Messersmith: World War II, the Cold War, and Argentine policy, 1945–1947 (UM/JIAS, 26:1, Feb. 1984, p. 66–95)

Illustrates bitter personality conflict that impaired the US' ability to formulate coherent policy towards Argentina until new developments such as the Cold War changed the world situation.

3366 Urquiza Almandoz, Oscar F. Historia de Concepción del Uruguay. v. 1, 1783–1826. Concepción del Uruguay, Argentina: Municipalidad de Concepción del Uruguay, 1983. 609 p.: indexes.

Solid local history, full of information about this *villa*. Provides information on background of original settlers, *hijos de la tierra*, López Jordán, Urquiza, Ramírez, and aspects of social history such as population, culture, education, religion, etc.

3367 Vanni, José Miguel. Evita, la razón de su vida. Guadalajara, Spain: OPE, 1981? 223 p.: col. port.

Another contribution to the myth. Of little historical value.

3368 Vera de Flaches, María C. El ferrocarril andino y el desarrollo socioeconómico del sur de Córdoba, 1870–1880. Buenos Aires: Fundación para la Educación, la Ciencia y la Cultura, 1982. 237 p.: bibl., ill., maps (folded).

Excellent monograph demonstrates crucial role played by railways that linked Littoral and Cuyo regions, opening Córdoba to colonization and industrial progress in 1880s.

3369 Vicens, Luis. El lopezreguismo. Buenos Aires: El Cid Editor, 1978? 202 p. (Colección Testigo directo)

Informative chronicle of 1973–75 period. Severely criticizes Perón's advisor, the "wizard" José López Rega, whose leadership led to bureaucratization and loss of revolutionary spirit in Isabel Perón's administration.

3370 Videla, Horacio. Historia de San Juan. t. 1, Epoca colonial: 1551–1810. t. 2, Epoca patria: momento año X. t. 3, Epoca patria: 1810–1836. t. 4, Epoca patria: 1836–1862. t. 5, Epoca patria: 1862–1875. Buenos Aires: Academia del Plata, 1981. 5 v.: bibl., ill.

Local history at its best, this is a monumental effort that encompasses the nation's evolution, as well as Cuyo's historical development. Moreover, the narrative includes numerous essays on specific subjects (e.g., the Independence movement, Rosas' dictatorship, Mitre and Sarmiento administrations). Mildly revisionist interpretation.

3371 Villegas, Juan. La Iglesia en la Argentina y en el Uruguay: un paralelo histórico (CRIT, 52:1808, 22 marzo 1979, p. 127–134)

Comparative outline stresses special aspects of the Church in each national framework. Concludes that Argentina's Church was stronger and more influential.

3372 Vogliano, Oscar R.C. Hospital de Niños: estampas y apuntes para su historia. 3a. ed. Buenos Aires: Cini Hnos., 1982. 130 p.: bibl., ill.

Intimate evocation of activities of celebrated hospital established in 1875.

Whiteford, Scott. Workers from the North: plantations, Bolivian labor, and the city in northwest Argentina. See *HLAS 45:8335.*

3373 Williams Alzaga, Enrique. Cinco retratos. Buenos Aires: Emecé Editores, 1980. 66 p.

Consists of useful, short biographical sketches of eminent Argentines. Of particular interest are the ones of Ricardo Rojas and Amancio Alcorta.

3374 Winston, Colin M. Between Rosas and Sarmiento: notes on nationalism in peronist thought (AAFH/TAM, 39:3, Jan. 1983, p. 305–332)

Preliminary findings of attempt to analyze peronism from within. Regards it as unique Argentine product. After examining country's past, concludes that peronism addressed its message to a wide constituency and was not splintered by ideological rhetoric.

3375 Ygobone, Aquiles D. Figuras señeras de la Patagonia y Tierra del Fuego. Buenos Aires: Ediciones Depalma, 1981. 187 p.: bibl.

Knowledgeable and instructive biographical sketches about pioneers who settled and developed Argentina's South.

3376 Zuleta Alvarez, Enrique; Mario Guillermo Saravi; and Enrique Díaz-Araujo. Homenaje a Julio Irazusta. Mendoza, Argentina: s.n., 1984. 118 p.

Three lectures examine the distinguished historian's contribution to the study of Argentina's past, especially the Rosas' period and political ideas.

PARAGUAY

3377 Avila, Manuel Agustín. 23 [i.e. Veintitrés] de octubre de 1931: una página enlutada y gloriosa del estudiantado paraguayo y algunas notas sobre la Guerra del Chaco. Asunción: Editorial El Foro, 1981. 221 p.: ill.

Lively personal accounts of main events of 1930s, in which author was active participant. Important primary source for 1931 episode and Febrerista regime. Includes relevant documentation.

3378 Bejarano, Ramón César. Síntesis de la Guerra del Chaco: homenaje al cincuentenario de la defensa del Chaco Paraguayo. Asunción: Editorial Toledo, 1982. 95 p.: ill. (some col.) (Serie Guerra del Chaco; no. 8)

Another by-product of war's half-centennial, but one which includes important data and cartographic information.

3379 Bray, Arturo. Armas y letras: memorias. Asunción: Ediciones NAPA, 1981. 3 v.: ill. (Libro paraguayo del mes; año 1, no. 8, 10, 12)

Distinguished military officer and historian's posthumous memoirs are important and relevant to 1930s political history. Highly critical of Liberal Party squabbles, Estigarribia's ambitions, and Franco's Febrerista conspiracies.

3380 Caballero Irala, Basiliano. Acción de nuestros zapadores durante la Guerra del Chaco, 1932–1935. Asunción: Ediciones Comuneros R. Rolón, 1981. 54 p.: ill.

Interesting contribution to military history. Reproduces 1939 lecture.

3381 Cartas diplomáticas: Eusebio Ayala, Vicente Rivarola; Guerra del Chaco. Compilador, Vicente Rivarola Coelho. Asunción: Industria Gráfica del Libro, 1982. 421 p.: ill., index, ports.

Documentary collection that is basic for knowledge of the Chaco War and domestic infighting. Reproduces until now secret correspondence between President Ayala and his Minister in Buenos Aires (1932–36). Confirms other sources that attest to Argentina's effective financial and military aid. Complements Rivarola's own *Memorias diplomáticas* published decades ago.

3382 Céspedes Ruffinelli, Roberto. El febrerismo: del movimiento al partido, 1936–1951. Asunción: s.n., 1983. 168 p.: bibl.

Despite theoretical approach, offers important data for historians about development of febrerismo.

3385 Franco Vera, Optaciano. General José Elizardo Aquino, héroe de Boquerón del Sauce e hijo dilecto de Luque: su vida y sus obras a través de su correspondencia y otros documentos. Asunción: s.n., 1981. 1 v.: bibl., ill.

Biographical sketch of manager of Ybycui's pioneer ironworks. Very useful if overburdened by lengthy reproductions of secondary sources.

3386 Guerra Vilaboy, Sergio. El Paraguay del Doctor Francia (Crítica y Utopía [Editorial Latinoamericana de Ciencias Sociales, Buenos Aires] 5, 1982, p. 250–270)

Justifies Francia's regime as "especie de república campesina . . . una dictadura nacional revolucionaria que contaba con la ayuda del pueblo . . . realizando profundas transformaciones económicas y sociales."

3386a Herken Krauer, Juan Carlos. Diplomacia británica en el Río de la Plata: el caso Rafael Barrett, 1908–1910 (UTIEH/C, 41, 1983, p. 39–61)

Case-study built around conflict between Great Britain and Paraguay provoked by detention of influential anarchist intellectual, arrested for his mordant criticism of Partido Liberal oligarchy. Important contribution illustrates mechanisms articulating British diplomacy in region.

3387 ———. La inmigración en el Paraguay de posguerra: el caso de los *Lincolnshire farmers*: 1870–1873 (CPES/RPS, 18:52, set./dic. 1981, p. 33–107, tables)

Outstanding case-study of failed colonization effort which together with other factors gave rise to "black legend" in European financial markets about Paraguay's development opportunities. Includes much background material.

3388 ———. Proceso económico en el Paraguay de Carlos Antonio López: la visión del Cónsul Británico Henderson, 1851–1860 (CPES/RPS, 19:54, mayo/agosto 1982, p. 83–116, bibl., tables)

Uses consular reports to determine specific features of period's state-run economy. Includes wealth of statistics.

3389 ——— and María Isabel Giménez de Herken. Gran Bretaña y la Guerra de la

Triple Alianza. Asunción: Editorial Arte Nuevo, 1983. 167 p., 16 leaves of plates (some folded): ill. (some col.) (Serie Historia)

Important contribution designed to show reactions of European powers to war and to recreate contemporary ambience. Scrutinizes British attitudes at the time and rejects recent conspiratorial interpretations of British involvement. Final portion analyzes coverage of conflict in *The Times*, including index to all its entries on topic.

3390 Kallsen, Margarita. Referencias bibliográficas de la Guerra del Chaco. 2a. ed. actualizada. Asunción: Centro de Publicaciones de la Universidad Católica Ntra. Sra. de la Asunción, 1982. 68 p.: indexes (Serie Bibliografía paraguaya; 1)

Important collection of bibliographical data consists of more tha 450 entries. For bibliographer's comment, see item **26.**

3391 ———. Referencias bibliográficas de la historia paraguaya (UCNSA/EP, 10:1, junio 1982, p. 265–316)

Revised, enlarged ed. of 1972 work. Lists more than 600 books and brochure titles, unfortunately not annotated.

3392 Machuca, Vicente. La Guerra del Chaco: desde la terminación del armisticio hasta el fin de la guerra. Asunción: s.n, 1981. 234 p., 16 p. of plates: ill.

Chiefly concerned with operations of II Army Corps since early 1934.

3393 Melid, Bartomeu. El fusilamiento del Obispo Palacios: documentos vaticanos (UCNSA/EP, 11:1, junio 1983, p. 25–50)

Depicts details of death of victim of 1868 conspiracy and repercussion bishop's death had on the Church's situation in Paraguay. Based on untapped sources.

3394 Mondain, Pierre. La Guerre du Chaco: Paraguay contre Bolivie, 1932–1935 (PUF/RH, 247[106]: 541, jan./mars 1982, p. 43–64)

Accurate, updated overview of background and diplomatic/military aspects of the conflict.

3395 Pampliega, Amancio. Fusil al hombro. Asunción: Ediciones NAPA, 1982. 208 p., 7 p. of plates: ill. (Libro paraguayo del mes; no. 22)

Pt. 1 of distinguished officer's memoirs. Covers war until 1940.

3396 Pastore, Carlos. Participación de los criptógrafos en la Guerra del Chaco (UNCSA/EP, 7:2, dic. 1979, p. 41–64)

Pioneer effort assesses crucial impact that breaking Bolivia's secret code had for Paraguay's success in its military and diplomatic strategies.

3397 Peters, Heinz. Das Paraguayische Erziehungswesen von 1811 bis 1865: Schule und Staat in einem Modell autozentrierter Entwicklung. Frankfurt Am Main, FRG: Verlag Peter Lang, 1984. 397 p.: appendices, bibl. (Eruditio. Studien zur Erziehungs-und Bildungswissenschaft; 16)

Thorough examination of Paraguay's educational system from independence to Carlos Antonio López's administration, based on Archivo Nacional primary sources (e.g., Actas del Cabildo, Sección Propiedades y Testamentos, etc.). Appendix lists Paraguayan school districts and levels of education offered therein. Important contribution of interest to the historian, anthropologist, and education specialist. [G.M. Dorn]

3398 Plá, Josefina. La cultura paraguaya y el libro (UCNSA/EP, 9:1, junio 1981, p. 257–378, bibl.)

Pt. 2 of informative contribution on cultural history. Examines 1810–51 period and book collections of El Supremo and other personalities. Shows profound change that took place under first López administration and lists what Imprenta Nacional published.

3399 Recalde A., Sergio. 1932–1935 [i.e. Mil novecientos treinta y dos-mil novecientos treinta y cinco], la sanidad militar en la Guerra del Chaco y el Dr. Juan Francisco Recalde V. Asunción: ORBIS, 1981. 454 p.: ill.

Informative chronicle discusses health and medical aspects of war. Includes some biographical data.

3399a Rengger, Johann Rudolph; Thomas Carlyle; and Alfred Demersay. El Doctor Francia. Asunción: Lector, 1982. 318 p.: bibl. (Colección Historia; 1)

Consists of three important 19th-century European essays that follow a traditional approach in their evaluations of El Supremo.

3400 Sánchez Quell, Hipólito. La diplomacia paraguaya de Mayo a Cerro-Corá. 6a. ed., con nuevas aportaciones docu-

mentales y bibliográficas. Asunción: Casa
América: Librería Comuneros, 1981. 288 p.:
bibl., ill.
> Sixth ed. of 1935 Paraguayan diplo-
matic history is enhanced by numerous documents and additional bibliography.

3401 Seiferheld, Alfredo M. Las comunicaciones postales y telegráficas en
el Paraguay de postguerra, 1870–1900
(UCNSA/EP, 8:2, dic. 1980, p. 217–240)
> Well structured chronicle of develop-
ment of postal and telegraph services, and
significant role they played in war's aftermath
and reconstruction.

3402 ———. El Paraguay visto a través del
idioma alemán: un intento de bibliografía en alemán sobre el Paraguay. Asunción:
Talleres Gráficos de Editorial Universo, 1981.
95 p.: ill.
> Interesting bibliography on most var-
ied topics includes Spanish translation of
each German entry.

3403 Vidaurreta, Alicia. El Paraguay a través
de los viajeros, 1843–1917
(UCNSA/EP, 11:1, junio 1983, p. 51–102)
> Scholarly, critical evaluation of valu-
able sources is organized according to decades. Offers significant contributions on
most varied topics.

3404 Viola, Alfredo. El Fuerte Olimpo: su
origen e importancia geopolítica
(Anuario del Instituto de Investigaciones Históricas Dr. José Gaspar Rodríguez de Francia
[Asunción?] 4:4, sept. 1982, p. 65–105)
> Chronicles deprivations suffered by
the Spanish in their takeover of Portuguese
fort. Built in 1792 as Fuerte Borbón, Francia
changed its name to Olimpo in 1823.

3405 ———. La medicina durante la dictadura del Dr. Francia (UCNSA/EP,
10:1, junio 1982, p. 195–218)
> Disorganized but informative account
provides interesting data on topic.

3406 Volta Gaona, Enrique. La revolución
del 47. Asunción: Editora Litocolor,
1982. 285 p.
> Highly partisan and controversial but
informative chronicle of 1947 bloody revolution, written by Colorado participant from
victors' point of view.

3407 Warren, Harris Gaylord. Journalism in
Asunción under the allies and the
Colorados: 1869–1904 (AAFH/TAM, 39:4,
April 1983, p. 483–498)
> Distinguished specialist explores for-
gotten topic. Lists period's major newspapers,
etc., and discusses issue of press freedom.

3408 ———. Paraguay, an informal history.
Westport, Conn.: Greenwood Press,
1982. 393 p., 15 leaves of plates: bibl., ill.,
index.
> Reprint of still outstanding historical
synthesis, based on wealth of bibliographical
sources.

3409 Whigham, Thomas Lyle and **Jerry W.
Cooney.** Paraguayan history: manuscript sources in the United States (LARR,
18:1, 1983, p. 104–117)
> Useful report describes provenance,
content, and value of important primary
sources. Also available in Spanish in *Revista
Paraguaya de Sociología* (19:53, enero/abril
1982, p. 145–157).

URUGUAY

3410 Abadie-Aicardi, Raúl. La revolución
brasileña de 1930 en la prensa uruguaya
(EIA, 7:1/2, julho/dez. 1981, p. 31–55)
> Interesting footnote to 1930 revolu-
tion. Author might have found richer material in Uruguayan responses to Liberal
Alliance program of early 1930, however.
[M.L. Conniff]

Alonso, José María. Proceso histórico de la
agricultura uruguaya. See *HLAS 45:3516.*

3411 Armúa Larraud, Pedro. Historia de
Paso de los Toros, 1790–1930. Montevideo: Impresos Multicolor, 1981. 293 p.,
12 p. of plates: bibl., ill.
> Documented local history of this
township in Tacuarembó. Describes social
improvements and its principal settlers.

**3412 Arteaga Sáenz, Juan José; Silvia Reyes;
and Sergio Silva.** Constitución de
1830: bibliografía. Montevideo: Instituto de
Filosofía, Ciencias y Letras, Departamento de
Investigación y Estudios Superiores de Historia Americana, 1981. 82 p. (Cuadernos; 10.
Historia)
> Selection of 299 texts that concern

1830–1919, when the Constitution was in force.

3413 Barrán, José Pedro and **Benjamín Nahum.** Batlle, los estancieros y el Imperio Británico. t. 2, Historia rural. t. 3, El nacimiento del batllismo. Montevideo: Ediciones de la Banda Oriental, 1982. 2 v.: bibl.
Intelligent and important historical interpretation. Vol. 2 examines "reformist" movement, characteristics, political platform, conservative reactions. Vol. 3 describes emergence of batllismo as modern political movement, analyzing its rise to power and origin of followers. Believes movement was end product of State's consolidation and of professionalization of politics as a career. For vol. 1, see *HLAS 44:3448*.

3414 Barrios Pintos, Aníbal. Canelones, su proyección en la historia nacional. Canelones, Uruguay: Intendencia Municipal de Canelones, 1981. 2 v. (682 p., 40 p. of plates): bibl., ill.
Colorful local history of progressive dept., full of useful data.

3415 La "Belle époque" montevideana. v. 1, Vida social y paisaje urbano. Alfredo Castellanos, compilador. Montevideo: Arca, 1981. 1 v.
Recreates what life was like for upper echelons of Uruguayan society via pleasing selection of excerpts from contemporary sources.

3416 Benvenuto, Luis Carlos. Breve historia del Uruguay: economía y sociedad. Montevideo: Arca, 1981. 101 p., 8 p. of plates: bibl., ill.
Rev. ed. of 1967 brief historical survey that emphasizes economic and social developments.

3417 100 [i.e. Cien] años de Montevideo en imágenes. Montevideo: Intendencia Municipal de Montevideo, 1981. 210 p.: ill., indexes, ports.
Photographs from city's municipal archive illustrate each decade of city's history, emphasizing important events.

3418 D'Elía, Germán. El Uruguay neobatllista, 1946–1958. Montevideo: Ediciones de la Banda Oriental, 1982. 113 p.: bibl. (Temas del siglo XX; 8)
Scholarly, interpretative survey of pe-

riod of great change. Explores sociopolitical origins of batllismo's demise in Oct. 1958 election. Attributes it to structural dependency that limited the movement's evolution and possibilities for development.

3419 El Día, 1886–1981: 95 años al servicio de la libertad. Montevideo: Imprenta Artegraf, 1981. 299 p.: ill.
Publication designed to commemorate well known newspaper. Notes world and local events as well as life and deeds of *El Día*'s founder, José Batlle y Ordóñez, as recorded in the pages of this daily.

3420 Fernández Labeque, Alicia *et al.* La fotografía en la perspectiva histórica nacional (UBN/R, 19, junio 1979, p. 131–147, facsim., photos)
Useful report on historical photographs as documents since photography begun in 1840s. Describes holdings and resources of Biblioteca Nacional's Archivo Iconográfico.

3421 Freitas, Antonio M. de. El Acta Oriental. Montevideo: República Oriental del Uruguay, Palacio Legislativo, Biblioteca, 1978. 126 p., 9 p. of plates: bibl., ill. (Serie de temas nacionales; 3)
Revisionist interpretation of Oct. 1827 historical episode when military commanders took over rejecting centralizing tendencies of Junta de Representantes.

3422 Galmes, Héctor. Los últimos años de Eduardo Acevedo Díaz: correspondencia familiar, 1917–1918 (UBN/R, 20, 1980, p. 7–41, appendix)
Examines neglected period in life of distinguished politican, when he served on diplomatic mission. Appendix includes much correspondence.

3423 Hanson, Simon Gabriel. Utopia in Uruguay: chapters in the economic history of Uruguay. Westport, Conn.: Hyperion Press, 1979. 1 v.: index.
Reprint of 1938 classic which describes the "miracle" of Batlle's Uruguay and its "social" State.

3424 Jacob, Raúl. Benito Nardone: el ruralismo hacia el poder, 1945–1958. Montevideo: Ediciones de la Banda Oriental, 1981. 187 p. (Temas del siglo XX: 1)
Pioneer study of fairly unknown move-

ment and leader. Covers period of expansion and consolidation, before 1958 elections. Includes good analysis of political issues.

3425 ———. La crisis de 1929 en el Uruguay: las inversiones extranjeras (CDAL, 3:21/22, 1980, p. 81–191)

Examines consequences of 1929 crash on foreign investments. Research concerns British and North American involvement in banks, land, construction, railroads, etc. Shows there was a general withdrawal of investment with few exceptions.

3426 ———. El Frigorífico Nacional en el mercado de carnes: la crisis de 1919 en el Uruguay. Montevideo: Fundación de Cultura Universitaria, 1979. 162 p.: bibl. (Cuadernos de historia; 14)

Another contribution by active researcher on crucial topic. Examines different aspects of 1929 crisis' effects on Uruguay.

3427 ———. Inversiones extranjeras y petróleo: la crisis de 1919 en el Uruguay. Montevideo: Fundación de Cultura Universitaria, 1979. 186 p.: bibl.

Deals with foreign investments in key areas (e.g., oil refineries, alcohol, Portland cement). For economist's comment, see *HLAS 45:3527*.

———. Uruguay, 1929–1938: depresión ganadera y desarrollo fabril. See *HLAS 45:3528*.

Jellinek, Sergio and **Luis Ledesma.** Uruguay: del consenso democrático a la militarización estatal. See *HLAS 45:6456*.

3428 Klaczko, Jaime. El Uruguay de 1908: obstáculos y estímulos en el mercado de trabajo, la población económicamente activa (IGFO/RI, 41:165/166, julio/dic. 1981, p. 675–720, tables)

Important research, based on data reassessment, restates previous interpretations of Uruguay's socioeconomic structure. Contends that in 1908, nation was not yet "modern," nor were its middle sectors as important as assumed.

3429 ———. El Uruguay de 1908: su contexto urbano-rural: antecedentes y perspectivas. Montevideo: Centro de Informaciones y Estudios del Uruguay, 1981. 216 p.: bibl., ill. (Cuaderno; no. 42)

Preliminary findings, based on census

data, confirm that population distribution led to rapid modernization and strongly contributed to the country's early emergence as a modern state.

3430 Lago, Julio. José Batlle y Ordóñez: ensayos sobre el período crítico de la República Oriental, 1903–1916. La Paz, Uruguay: Taller Gráfico Vanguardia, 1982. 141 p.: bibl.

Revisionist study of period of batllismo predominance. Criticizes its development, pro-urban policies as having deformed the country's social and economic structure. Regards July 1916 elections—that ended experiment—as democratic triumph.

3431 Lombardi, M. El proceso de urbanización en el Uruguay en los siglos XVIII y XIX: la estructuración del espacio en una economía de producto principal (CPES/RPS, 15:42/43, mayo/dic. 1978, p. 9–45, bibl., graphs, maps, tables)

Another contribution to much discussed topic. Hypothesizes that structuring of national space was response to nation's dependency on international market. Disagrees that national structure was substantially changed by modernization.

3432 Martínez Rovira, Eduardo. Entre el olvido y la memoria. Ilustraciones de Enrique Castells Capurro. Montevideo: Universidad de la República, Dirección General de Extensión Universitaria, División Publicaciones y Ediciones, 1982. 239 p.: appendix, ill., maps.

Compilation of short articles and notes on Rocha and Maldonado depts.' local history. Includes important documentary appendix and maps.

3433 Morgan, Iwan. Orleanist diplomacy and the French colony in Uruguay (The International History Review [Simon Fraser University, Ontario, Canada] 5:2, May 1983, p. 201–228)

Describes French involvement in River Plate and its failures in face of Argentine resistance and British diplomacy. According to author: "It did not achieve either its principal objectives, having failed to ensure the growth of the French colony, or to secure the foundations of Uruguay's independence against Rosas ambitions."

3434 Musso, Luis Alberto. Bibliografía básica de la historia de la República Oriental del Uruguay hasta 1973: pt. 2 (EEHA/HBA, 24, 1980, p. 103–125, bibl.)

Pt. 2 of four consists of 179 entries on most varied topics.

3435 Pastorino, Enrique. A batalha do Uruguai: C.N.T., unidade solidariedade e luta. Tradução, José Prudêncio. Lisbon: Plataforma Editor, 1981. 95 p. (Os Trabalhadores no mundo; 1)

Militant narrative of struggle of Uruguayan working class, particularly since 1973, against military regime and oligarchic forces.

3436 Puentes de Oyenard, Sylvia. Tacuarembó, historia de su gente. Tacuarembó, Uruguay: Intendencia Municipal de Tacuarembó, 1981. 231 p.: bibl., ill., indexes, ports.

Short biographical sketches about Tacuarembó individuals. Organized according to activities and professions.

3437 Rama, Carlos M. Historia del movimiento obrero y social uruguayo. Stockholm: Institute of Latin American Studies, 1978. 22 p.: bibl. (Occasional papers)

Short lecture offers leftist, condensed history of Uruguay's labor movement.

3438 Rama, Germán W. Dependencia y segmentación en Uruguay en el siglo XIX (CPES/RPS, 16:44, enero/abril 1979, p. 31–70)

Interesting essay explores nature of country's socioeconomic structure in second half of 19th century. Finds co-existence of three different social structures, each related to different economic markets.

Rial Roade, Juan. Estadísticas históricas de Uruguay, 1850–1930: población, producción agropecuaria, comercio, industria, urbanización, comunicaciones, calidad de vida. See *HLAS 45:3532.*

3439 ———— and Jaime Klaczko. Historiography and historical studies in Uruguay (LARR, 17:3, 1982, p. 229–250)

Able review essay discusses recent historical works of significance. Also surveys research institutions and their methodologies.

3440 ————; Angel Mario Cocchi; and Jaime Klaczko. Proceso de asentamientos urbanos en el Uruguay: siglos XVIII y XIX (CPES/RPS, 15:42/43, mayo/dic. 1978, p. 91–114, tables)

Provisional results of major study on causes underlying extension of urban networks. Divides process into three phases: 1) colonial; 2) 1810–75; and 3) 1875–1914.

3441 Rodríguez Navarro, Waldemar. Villa Ceballos: historia de Rivera. Rivera, Uruguay: Impresora Atlántida, 1981. 1 v.

Lively, local history stresses continuous Luso-Brazilian expansionism.

3442 Rodríguez Villamil, Silvia. La participación femenina en el mercado de trabajo uruguayo: 1880–1914 (Servicio de Documentación Social [Instituto de Estudios, Centro de Documentación, Montevideo] 4, 1982, p. 211–218, tables)

Concentrates on Montevideo and outlying area. Describes characteristics of female working force and notes decline since 1889.

3443 Souza, Susana Bleil de. La construction du port de Montevideo de 1890 a 1913 (Travaux & Memoires de l'Institut des Hautes Etudes de l'Amérique Latine [Université de Paris III] 33, 1980, p. 33–45, map, table)

Describes Montevideo's historical rivalry with Buenos Aires, political difficulties in early years, misfortunes while it was being built.

3444 Vidaurreta, Alicia. La emigración uruguaya en Argentina: 1862–1863. Buenos Aires: Instituto Histórico de la Organización Nacional, 1980. 205 p. (Separata de la *Revista Histórica*; no. 6)

Studies political unrest (e.g., Flores uprising and other episodes that spread in Pavón's aftermath) sowing seeds of discord that led to unleashing of Paraguayan War.

3445 Zubillaga, Carlos. Deuda externa y desarrollo en el Uruguay batllista, 1903–1915. Montevideo: Centro Latinoamericano de Economía Humana, 1979. 216 p.: bibl. (Serie Investigaciones; no. 8)

Examines role of foreign capital in financing development (1903–15) and prevailing attitudes towards it.

BRAZIL

RODERICK J. BARMAN, *Associate Professor of History, University of British Columbia, Vancouver, Canada*
JEAN A. BARMAN, *University of British Columbia, Vancouver, Canada*
MICHAEL L. CONNIFF, *Associate Professor of History, University of New Mexico, Albuquerque*

WHILE THE SLUMP IN HIGH QUALITY publications noted in *HLAS 44* has not abated, some grounds for optimism exist. New levels of sophistication are evident in the study of slavery, as in Saunders' work on 15th and 16th century Portugal (item **3512**) and Mattoso's long-awaited overview of conditions in Brazil (item **3466**). A wide range of source materials are being utilized, including legal records (items **3541** and **3641**), estate inventories (item **3674**), and notarial archives (item **3573**). Perhaps most exciting is the growing willingness of the broader historical community in North America to take an interest in Brazilian slavery and social structure: Schwartz has recently published in *The American Historical Review* (item **3513**) and Graham in *Comparative Studies in Society and History* (item **3583**). The article by Martins and Martins appearing in *Hispanic American Historical Review* (item **3620**) was considered of sufficient significance to merit comment not only from fellow Brazilianists (items **3559** and **3681**) but from two leading writers on North American slavery (item **3567**).

Another field showing special promise is economic history. Weinstein's study of the Amazon rubber boom (item **3694**) is a model for other historians, and Leff's two-volume general analysis (item **3601**) is one of the best additions to the literature since Stein's and Furtado's studies (see *HLAS 21:3342*, *HLAS 22:3889*, and *HLAS 19:1718* and *HLAS 25:1721–1722*, respectively) of the late 1950s. Lago's revisionist essay on external trade during the mid–19th century (item **3599**) shows what can be done by reworking published data. Of particular interest is the growing attention being given by Brazilian historians to the economy of the far south. Twentieth-century Rio Grande do Sul has been analyzed by Pesavento (item **3652**) and Reichel (item **3657**), landowning in colonial Paraná by Ritter (item **3506**), 19th–century Florianópolis by Hübener (item **3592**), and Santa Catarina as a whole by the Centro de Assistência Gerencial (item **3457**).

Other contributions stand out. Pt. 1 of Carvalho's excellent Stanford dissertation on the governing system of the Empire has finally been published in Brazil (item **3547**), as well as appearing in summary form in the US (item **3548**). Bauss' and Peterson's essays on the colonial period (items **3485** and **3502**) deserve mention as do Colson's and Riding's on the Empire (items **3554** and **3663**). The studies of Araújo (item **3522**), Bak (item **3527**), and Schwartzman (item **3568**) maintain the high quality of work on the Vargas period. Hilton's essay on the arms industry (item **3587**), Dutra's memoir (item **3615**), and two oral histories (items **3570** and **3610**) provide essential material on the military in the 20th century. The flow of publications on immigration, often of indifferent quality, continues. The best works focus on the German rather than the Italian communities (items **3617, 3626,** and **3639**). Rural society and unrest in the countryside are examined in four new works (items **3579, 3595, 3627,** and **3645**). Several researchers, perhaps inspired by the politics of the *abertura*, have written about the press (item **3635**), leftist movements (items

3564 and 3677), and labor relations (items 3534 and 3597). A number of mediocre accounts of the 1932 revolt in São Paulo have appeared.

The national parliament of Brazil continues to be a topic for original scholarship, in part because it has both the intelligence and the funds to support the writing of special studies such as items 3551 and 3665. Its support has also underwritten: 1) documentary series such as *HLAS 44:3556*; 2) collections of major speeches by leading politicians such as Mangabeira (item 3672); 3) the *Perfís Parlamentares* series including Alencar Jr. (item 3519), Castro Pinto (item 3549), and Salgado (item 3667); and 4) the *Bernardo Pereira de Vasconcelos* series, reprinting important earlier works, for example item 3546.

The appearance of Hallewell's history of publishing in Brazil (item 3461) draws attention to the fundamental change undergone by the book industry since 1964, a change masked by continuing adverse economic conditions. Indicative is the production by Brasiliense of its *Tudo é História* series. Written by established historians, these tiny booklets present the latest research on key subjects (with baby bibliographies) to a general public. Some 40 titles had appeared by 1982, several already in second edition, with as many titles *a sair*. Impressive in a different way is the ability of *Itatiaia* and other publishers to produce high quality reprints of classics (such as item 3629) which they clearly expect will sell. Most of these reprints were noted in *HLAS* at first publication and so are not annotated again. They include Luis da Câmara Cascudo, *História da cidade do Natal* (*HLAS 13:1687*), Alfredo Ellis Jr., *Feijó e a primeira metade do século XIX* (*HLAS 6:3629*), Gilberto Freyra, *O Escravo nos anúncios de jornais brasileiros do século XIX* (*HLAS 26: 1200*), Walter Spalding, *A Revolução farroupilha* (*HLAS 5:3240*), and João Camilo de Oliveira Tôrres, *História de Minas Gerais* (*HLAS 25:3802*). Gone, indeed, are the days of the pocket-sized, individually numbered editions, printed on newsprint, which were issued by the Companhia Editora Nacional in the 1930s.

A similar transformation of the Brazilian historical community from a collection of amateur authors, often specialists in traditional fields like law and medicine, to a full-fledged profession is symbolized by the publication of the proceedings of the *II Semana de História* (item 3478) and of the *Simpósio Nacional de estudios Missionários* (item 3514). The growing sophistication which marks the analysis of slavery and the economy aptly reflects this professionalization.

GENERAL

3446 Almeida, Aluísio. Vida e morte do tropeiro. São Paulo: Livraria Martins Editora: Editora da Universidade de São Paulo, 1981. 228 p., 4 p. of plates: bibl., ill.

Subject of considerable import for the history of Brazil. Not only mule trains but breeding and trade in mules were crucial to country's economy. Centers on town of Sorocaba (São Paulo), with its annual market for mules. While quoting from town's archives, work is less well-developed study than summary of author's lifetime knowledge on topic.

3447 Amaral, Antônio Barreto do. Dicionário de história de São Paulo. Prefácio de Brasil Bandecchi. São Paulo: Governo do Estado de São Paulo, 1981. 480 p. (Coleção paulística; v. 19)

Compendium of common knowledge about individuals, institutions, and events important in São Paulo history to 1932. Traditional in scope and focus.

3448 Araújo, María Walda de Aragão. Os dois ciclos do ouro (MAN, 12:144, dez. 1981, p. 10–27, bibl.)

Inspired by recent mining boom in Carajás region, overview laments in vivid language unending repetition of "rush" cycle in Brazil's development since first colonization.

3449 Baldin, Nelma. A Intendência da Marinha de Santa Catarina e a questão da Cisplatina. Florianópolis: Fundação Catarinense de Cultura, 1980. 127 p.: bibl., ill. (Coleção Cultura catarinense.

Série História)
Despite unimaginative title, useful case study, largely based on archival materials, of administrative office introduced into Brazil in Enlightenment period to enhance royal control over navy's fiscal and logistical affairs. Intendency at Santa Catarina played, as work shows, central role in Portuguese conquest of Uruguay (1815–27).

3450 Beltrão, Romeu. Cronologia histórica de Santa Maria e do extinto município de São Martinho: 1787–1930. 2a. ed. Canoas: Tipografia Editora La Salle, 1979. 582 p.: bibl., index.
Day-by-day chronology (15 April 1787–30 Dec. 1930) of every happening in a Rio Grande do Sul market town. More detailed than most local histories and includes extensive bibliography and index.

3451 Berger, Paulo. Bibliografia do Rio de Janeiro de viajantes e autores estrangeiros, 1531–1900. 2a. ed., aum. e rev. Rio de Janeiro: SEEC–RJ, 1980. 478 p.: bibl., facsims.
New and expanded ed. of 1965 work reprints title pages of 690 foreigners' travel accounts which included visit to Rio. Entries indicate date of visit, full bibliographical detail, and location. Organized only by author.

3452 Bittencourt, Gabriel Augusto de Mello. Agricultura: base económica capixaba (MAN, 12:5, 1981, p. 8–14)
Short overview of main crops of Espírito Santo state, which author terms a "preeminently agricultural region." Emphasizes importance of coffee boom for creation of state's basic infrastructure.

3453 Cartas baianas, 1821–1824: subsídios para o estudo dos problemas da opção na independência brasileira. Organizador, Antônio d'Oliveira Pinto de França. São Paulo: Cia. Editora Nacional, 1980. 184 p.: bibl., ill., index (Brasiliana; v. 372)
Letters of Oliveira Pinto da França family reveal, in all their cruel starkness, dilemma faced in 1821–23 by "Luso-Brazilians," those who felt equally loyal to Brazil and Portugal and were forced to choose between them. Unfortunately, poorly edited.

3454 Catálogo da exposição de história do Brasil. Introdução de José Honório Rodrigues. Apresentação pelo B.F. Ramiz Galvão. Ed. fac-similada. Brasília: Editora Universidade de Brasília, 1981. 3 v. (1758, 98 p.): indexes (Coleção Temas brasileiros; v. 10)
Facsimile reprint of what is still most complete bibliography of works on Brazilian life and history published up to 1881. Also contains information on important manuscript sources. Includes introduction by José Honório Rodrigues, setting original publication in context.

3455 Costa, Francisco Augusto Pereira da. Dicionário biográfico de pernambucanos célebres. Prefácio de José Antonio Gonsalves de Mello. Fac-similar da 1a. ed. de 1882. Recife: Prefeitura da Cidade do Recife, Secretaria de Educação e Cultura, Fundação de Cultura Cidade do Recife, 1982. 804 p., 1 leaf of plates: port. (Coleção Recife; vol. 16)
Welcome facsimile reprint of 1882 biographical dictionary, length and specificity of entries making it an indispensable source for historians of Northeast during colony and Empire.

3456 Cruz, Avertano. D. Pedro I e o Brasil: revisão da história: o Príncipe Regente e primeiro Imperador do Brasil não é a figura representativa da Independência. Rio de Janeiro: Pallas, 1981. 142 p.: bibl.
Book's gaudy cover (noble Tiradentes and scraggly Pedro I divided by noose) is good indication of its polemical contents. Significant only as updating of historical tradition which seeks to deny Pedro I any central role in achievement of independence, a tradition particularly popular among Northeast writers.

3457 Evolução histórico-econômica do Santa Catarina. Florianópolis: Centro de Assistência Gerencial (CEAG)/SC, 1980. 214 p.: bibl., ill., maps.
Notwithstanding format and short text, work is notable attempt to provide strong, well conceived, well structured analysis of dynamics of Santa Catarina's development from 1640. Extremely intelligent and informative (excellent maps). A model of what can be done with limited resources. Recommended.

3458 Fabricio, José de Araújo. Os Vargas: um estirpe faialense no Rio Grande do Sul (Revista do Instituto Histórico e Geográfico do Rio Grande do Sul [Porto Alegre] 123, 192, p. 63–122)

Traditional family tree of Rio Grande do Sul clan founded by Azores immigrant in mid 18th century and made prominent by founder's great-great-great grandson, Getúlio. Only for experts.

3459 Ferreira, Tito Lívio. A Ordem de Cristo e o Brasil. São Paulo: Instituição Brasileira de Difusão Cultural, 1980. 235 p.: bibl., ill. (Biblioteca História; 29)

Far from being study of the Order of Christ in Brazil, this is no more than a simplistic repetition, written by a very old man, of conservative, Lusophile, pro-Catholic myths about Brazil's settlement and development.

3460 Freitas, Maria Aparecida Rezende Gouveia de. Bananal: cidade histórica, berço do café. São Paulo: M. Onho/Roswitha Kempf, 1981. 300 p.: bibl., ill., ports.

Assorted historical facts about São Paulo town which was leading producer of coffee before 1860. Mostly devoted to life and times of local pioneer, Luciano José de Almeida (1761–1806), and his 2,235 descendants.

3461 Hallewell, Lawrence. Books in Brazil: a history of the publishing trade. Metuchen: Scarecrow Press, 1982. 485 p., 25 p. of plates: bibl., ill., index.

Account of publishing and printing in Brazil (1747–1980), organized around major publishers and so packed with detail, it is not easy to read. Best as reference encyclopedia for cultural historians.

3462 Laytano, Dante de. Manual de fontes bibliográficas para o estudo da história geral do Rio Grande do Sul: levantamento crítico. Prefácio de Arthur Ferreira Filho. Porto Alegre: Gabinete de Pesquisa de História do Rio Grande do Sul, Instituto de Filosofia e Ciências Humanas, Universidade Federal do Rio Grande do Sul, 1979. 293 p.: bibl.

Guide to principal printed histories, descriptions, biographical, and other dictionaries on Rio Grande do Sul. Each entry includes author's biography with full description and evaluation of work.

3463 Linhares, Maria Yedda Leite. História do abastecimento: uma problemática em questão, 1530–1918. Brasília: BINAGRI Edições, 1979. 246 p.: ill. (Coleção estudos sobre o desenvolvimento agrícola; 5)

Overview of development of Brazil's internal food market is both too short and too descriptive to be a satisfactory analysis. Strongest sections are on Rio's food supply during Empire, a subject researched by author. Written as part of deliberate campaign by government agency to draw attention to serious bottleneck in Brazilian economy.

3464 Maciel, José de Almeida. Obras completas. v. 1, Pesqueira e o antigo termo de Cimbres. Recife: Centro de Estudos de História Municipal, 1980. 404 p.: bibl., ill. (Biblioteca pernambucana de história municipal; 9)

Articles from newspapers written by local historian on native region in Pernambuco state. Masses of random information, mainly genealogical. For experts.

3465 Matos, Raimundo José da Cunha. Corografia histórica da Província de Minas Gerais. Colaboração com o I.H.G.B. Introdução e notas de Tarquínio J.B. de Oliveira. Belo Horizonte: Arquivo Público Mineiro, 1979–1981. 2 v.: bibl., index (Publicações do Arquivo; no. 3–3A)

Publication of 1837 manuscript survey of Minas Gerais prov.: population, resources, and administration written by government bureaucrat who drew on official sources. Useful source for study of region in 1750–1830. Original manuscript in Rio's Instituto Histórico.

3466 Mattoso, Kátia M. de Queirós. Ser escravo no Brasil. São Paulo: Brasiliense, 1982. 267 p.: bibl., ill.

Consummation of long years of research in Bahia archives. Interesting as study is, it suffers from considerable weakness. Within 240 small p., attempts to present all aspects of slave experience in Brazil from capture in Africa. Treatment is summary without footnoting, style dry and academic. Nonetheless, important new source for students of slavery.

3467 Medeiros, Manoel da Costa. História do Herval: descrição física e histórica. Caxias do Sul: Universidade de Caxias do Sul, 1980. 402 p. (Coleção Temas gaúchos; 11)

Detailed geographical and historical account, written 1927, of Rio Grande do Sul cattle town, includes biographies and genealogies of local notables.

3468 Meireles, Mario Martins. História do Maranhão. 2a. ed. São Luís-Maranhão: Fundação Cultural do Maranhão, 1980. 426 p.: bibl.

Solid, traditional history, unfortunately lacking footnotes but including bibliography of printed sources upon which it is apparently based.

3469 Mello, Frederico Pernambucano de. O ciclo do gado no Nordeste do Brasil: uma cultura da violência? (Ciência & Trópico [Instituto Joaquim Nabuco de Pesquisas Sociais, Recife] 7:2, julho/dez. 1979, p. 263–306)

Presents "ideal type" of man in Northeast interior, milieu which emphasized toughness and force. Consequence, as illustrated by numerous folk songs, was culture of violence. Discusses evolution from this general culture of violence to organized criminal social groups epitomized by *cangaceiros*.

3470 Memória de Ilhéus: edição comemorativa do centenário de sua elevação a cidade. Estudo introductório e compilação da coletânea de Fernando Sales. São Paulo: Edições GRD; Ilhéus: *em convênio com a* Prefeitura Municipal de Ilhéus, 1981. 187 p.: bibl. (Coleção Grapiuna; 1)

Summary of impressions of 30 visitors from 16th to 20th centuries of the Bahian town, now center of cocoa region (see also item **3531**).

3471 Piazza, Walter Fernando. Santa Catarina: sua história. Florianópolis: Editorial da Universidade Federal de Santa Catarina, 1983. 750 p.: ill., maps.

Though hardly polished, book brings together material gathered during Piazza's long career as state's historian. Encyclopedic format includes maps, statistics, diagrams, photos, drawings, names. Especially good on 19th-century immigrant colonies, as is chapter on Contestado. Thin on present. Still, welcomed by specialist.

3472 Pinheiro, Fernandes. Estudos históricos: acrescidos de estudos avulsos, brasileiros ilustres. 2a. ed. Rio de Janeiro: Livraria Editora Cátedra; Brasília: *em con-*

vênio com o Instituto Nacional do Livro, Ministério da Educação e Cultura, 1980. 569 p.: bibl., ill.

Collected works on history by leading Empire intellectual, whose writings still merit consultation, particularly those which drew on author's personal knowledge.

3473 Pombo, José Francisco da Rocha. O Paraná no centenário, 1500–1900. 2a. ed. Rio de Janeiro: Livraria J. Olympio Editora, 1980. 147 p., 1 leaf of plates: bibl., port.

Reprint of short, fairly general account of Paraná's development written in 1900 by historian born therein.

3474 Queiroz, Suely Robles Reis de. Aspectos ideológicos da escravidão (IPE/EE, 13:1, 1983, p. 65–101)

Short think-piece uses limited range of sources to discuss changing ideological justifications for slavery in New World.

3475 Rossi, Pompeu. História de Ouro Fino: seus registros, sua gente e suas lendas. Belo Horizonte: Imprensa Oficial, 1981. 238 p.: bibl.

Unimaginative account of typical mid-18th-century Minas Gerais mining town.

3476 Rotermund, Harry. História de Bagé do século passado. Bagé: Academia Bageense de Letras, 1981. 82 p.

Disjointed miscellany of facts about Rio Grande do Sul cattle town, including biographies of local notables.

3477 São Paulo: onde está sua história? Patrocínio, Secretaria de Estado de Cultura, Secretaria Municipal de Cultura. São Paulo: Museu de Arte de São Paulo Assis Chateaubriand, 1981. 190 p.: chiefly col. ill.

Handsome colored reproductions of documents, drawings, maps, and plans relating to the political, economic, and social history of São Paulo state. Perhaps most useful for making slides for the classroom, otherwise a coffee table work.

3478 Semana da História, 2nd, França, Brazil, 1980. Memória da II Semana da História: 24 a 28–XI–1980 Universidade Estadual Paulista Júlio de Mesquita Filho, Instituto de História e Serviço Social. França: O Instituto, 1981 or 1982. 662 p.: bibl., ill.

Very diverse collection of essays by São Paulo and other southern Brazilian scholars, delineating new sources and methodologies for researching Brazil's history. Could probably be perused with profit by every historian of Brazil.

3479 Tapajós, Vicente Costa Santos. História administrativa do Brasil. Brasília: Universidade de Brasília: Fundação Centro de Formação do Serviço Pública, 1981. 1 v.

Begun 1955 to educate public employees, project was suspended in 1960s. Now being resurrected to include 40 volumes. Pitched at civil servant mentality, written by high school teachers. Of no scholarly interest.

3480 Thaumaturgo, Newton. História de Panelas: terra dos cabanos, 1783–1978. Panelas: N. Thaumaturgo, 1980. 195 p., 2 leaves of plates: ill.

Hodge-podge of facts and documents on Pernambucan town at geographical heart of early 1930s Cabanos revolt.

3481 Vargas, Alvaro Rocha. Do Caapi ao Carazinho: notas sobre trezentos anos de história, 1631–1931. Porto Alegre: Empresa Gráfica Carazinhense, 1980. 121 p.: ill.

Short history of Carazinho is, because of maps and photographs, an illuminating case study of process of settlement in hill country of northeastern Rio Grande do Sul.

COLONIAL

3482 Abreu, João Capistrano de. Capítulos de história colonial, 1500–1800 [and] Os caminhos antigos e o povoamento do Brasil. Brasília: Universidade de Brasília, 1982. 337 p.: bibl. (Biblioteca básica brasileira)

Welcome reprint of principal works of historian distinguished for originality and perceptiveness of his insights into social and geographical formation of Brazil.

3483 Andrade, Gilberto Osório de and Rachel Caldas Lins. João Pais do Cabo: o patriarca, seus filhos, seus engenhos. Com estudo genealógico por Sílvio Pais Barreto. Recife: Editora Massangana-Fundação Joaquim Nabuco, 1982. 143 p.: ill. (Serie Estudos e pesquisas; 19)

Well written micro-study, based on published sources, of prominent Pernambucan sugar family and their land holdings

up to 1650. Compare with item **3502**, on the same topic.

3484 Bandecchi, Brasil. Narrativa da perseguição que sofreu Hipólito José da Costa (APL/R, 39:101, out. 1982, p. 109–125)

Recounting, based on sources and accounts generally available, of arrest, imprisonment, and ultimate escape of freemason who, after his flight to England, established *Correio Brasiliense*.

3485 Bauss, Rudy. Rio Grande do Sul in the Portuguese Empire: the formative years, 1777–1808 (AAFH/TAM, 39:4, April 1983, p. 519–535, tables)

Useful survey, drawing on printed works and archival sources in Rio de Janeiro, on development of Rio Grande do Sul as supplier of foodstuffs for booming economy of central Brazil (1777–1808). Commended.

3486 Cardoso, Geraldo. Negro slavery in the sugar plantations of Veracruz and Pernambuco, 1550–1680: a comparative study. Washington: University Press of America, 1983. 211 p.: bibl., index.

Less a comparative analysis of two slave systems within their larger socioeconomic settings than juxtaposition of two descriptions of slavery in two regions of New World. Largely based on secondary and general sources.

3487 Carneiro, Edison. A cidade do Salvador, 1549: uma reconstituição histórica [and] A conquista da Amazónia. 2a. ed. Rio de Janeiro: Civilização Brasileira; Brasília: em convênio com o Instituto Nacional do Libro, Ministério da Educação e Cultura, 1980. 264 p.: bibl. (Coleção Retratos do Brasil; v. 146)

While second work is reedition (see *HLAS 21:1409*), first was never published. Drawing on secondary sources, analyzes planning, construction, and first population (including at least five blacks) of Salvador da Bahia.

3488 Costa, Iraci del Nero da. Algumas características dos proprietários de escravos de Vila Rica (IPE/EE, 11:3, sep./dez. 1981, p. 151–157, tables)

Addition to existing work (*HLAS 42:3570, HLAS 44:3484, HLAS 44:3508,* and *HLAS 44:3522*), uses information in entries on slave deaths in Ouro Preto parochial registers to analyze slave percentages by age and sex, and owners by sex and status—freed or free: 1743–45, 1760–62, 1799–1801, and 1809–11. In early period freed persons were seven percent of male slaveowners and 58 percent of female slaveowners. Latter were more likely to hold female slaves than were freedmen.

3489 Couto, Domingos Loreto. Desagravos do Brasil e glórias de Pernambuco. Apresentação e índice de José Antônio Gonsalves de Mello. Recife: Prefeitura da Cidade do Recife, Secretaria de Educação e Cultura, Fundação de Cultura Cidade do Recife, 1981. 611 p.: index (Coleção Recife; v. 11)

Facsimile reprint of first ed. (1909) of work, written 1759, lauding loyalty and feats of author's *pátria*, captaincy of Pernambuco. Illustrative of sense of identity and self-confidence that emerged in late colonial period.

Cross, Harry E. South American bullion production and export: 1550–1750. See item **2622.**

3490 Dutra, Francis A. Blacks and the search for rewards and status in seventeenth-century Brazil (PCCLAS/P, 6, 1977/1979, p. 25–35)

Demonstrates how difficult it was even for such reputable blacks as Henrique Dias, hero in expulsion of Dutch from Northeast, to achieve social status in colonial Brazil. Suggests that social mobility was a little easier for mulattoes.

3491 Fontes para a história do Brasil holandês. Textos editados por José Antônio Gonsalves de Mello. Recife: Parque Histórico Nacional dos Guararapes; Brasília: MEC/SPHAN/Fundação Pro-Memória, 1981. 1 v.: bibl.

Although basically composed of text of seven documents on socioeconomic structure of Northeast (1623–55), work is enriched by its commentaries written by leading expert on region in period. Useful both for research and as source for illustrative documents in classroom use.

3492 Freyre, Gilberto. Nassau numa perspectiva brasileira: seu imperialismo confrontado com o da Companhia das Indias (Ciência & Trópico [Instituto Joaquim Nabuco de Pesquisas Sociais, Recife] 7:2, julho/dez. 1979, p. 185–200)

In true Freyrean tradition, uses figure of Nassau, most successful governor during Dutch conquest, as anchor for series of observations on nature of Brazil, imperialism and other favorite topics.

3493 Grinberg, Isaac. Mogi das Cruzes de 1601 a 1640. São Paulo: I. Grinberg, 1981. 175 p.: bibl.; ill.

Description of town life and personalities in early São Paulo settlement. Includes transcription of 55 sessions of câmara municipal (1612–27).

3494 Lockhart, James and **Stuart B. Schwartz.** Early Latin America: a history of colonial Spanish America and Brazil. New York: Cambridge University Press, 1983. 480 p.: bibl., ill., index (Cambridge Latin American series; no. 46)

Colonial Brazil is assigned such limited space in this study that the second author, leading expert on period, can be no more than summary in his analysis. As textbook for students, work suffers from its layout: narrow margins and short indents with overlong paragraphs.

3495 Luís, Washington. Na Capitania de São Vicente. Belo Horizonte: Editora Itaiaia; São Paulo: Editora da Universidade de São Paulo, 1980. 357 p.: bibl., ill. (Coleção Reconquista do Brasil; nova série, v. 28)

In addition to his political career, Washington Luís showed strong interest in history of his native São Paulo. Written in his old age, work is, as author notes, series of studies on São Paulo settlement (1530–1650) rather than integrated history.

3496 Luna, Francisco Vidal and **Iraci del Nero da Costa.** Posse de escravos em São Paulo no início do século XIX (IPE/EE, 13:1, 1983, p. 211–221, tables)

Based on data for 1804, examines extent and nature of slavery in São Paulo's sugar economy. Only few households included slaves, two-thirds owning just one to five. Not unexpectedly, largest slaveholders were plantation owners.

3497 Martin de Nantes, *père.* Relação de uma missão no Rio São Francisco. Tradução e comentários de Barbosa Lima

Sobrinho. São Paulo: Companhia Editora Nacional; Brasília: *em convênio com o* Instituto Nacional do Livro, Ministério da Educacão e Cultura, 1979. 123 p.: bibl. (Brasiliana; v. 368)

Translation of account, published 1706 in French, of missionary work among Indians of São Francisco Valley. Important original source.

3498 Moreau, Pierre and **Roulox Baro.** História das últimas lutas no Brasil entre holandeses e portugueses [and] *Relação da viagem ao país dos tapuias.* Tradução e notas, Lêda Boechat Rodrigues. Nota introductória, José Honório Rodrigues. São Paulo: Editora da Universidade de São Paulo; Belo Horizonte: Livraria Itatiaia Editora, 1979. 128 p.: bibl. (Coleção Reconquista do Brasil; vol. 54)

Translation of two works first published together 1651 in French. Both authors were employed by Dutch West India Company and their accounts are useful sources for study of Brazil's Northeast under Dutch rule.

3499 Nobre, Maria do Socorro Silva. História da medicina no Ceará: período colonial. Fortaleza: Secretaria de Cultura, Desporto e Promoção Social, 1978. 142 p.

Miscellany of information on medical practices and health conditions in colonial Ceará.

3500 Novinsky, Anita Waingort. Inquisicão: inventários de bens confiscados a cristãos novos: fontes para a história de Portugal e do Brasil. Lisbon: Imprensa Nacional, Casa de Moeda: Livraria Camões, 1976? 1 v.: bibl., indexes.

Abstracts inventories taken by Lisbon Inquisition in cases of 130 residents of Brazil condemned by it (1704–61, but most pre–1730). Rich source of social and economic information for researchers.

3501 Palacín, Luís. Limites de posibilidades de um administrador colonial: o governo do Conde dos Arcos em Goiás, 1749–1755 (Estudos Goianienses [Revista da Universidade Católica de Goiás, Goiânia, Brasil] 4:5, 1977, p. 119–128)

Short and slight discussion of first governor of Captaincy of Goiás, who, despite adverse conditions, "placed the government on solid bases of order, honesty, justice and development."

3502 Petersen, Dwight E. Sweet success: some notes on the founding of a Brazilian sugar dynasty, the Pais Barreto family of Pernambuco (AAFH/TAM, 39:3, Jan. 1983, p. 325–348)

Studies founder and son of prominent clan of sugar plantation owners in Pernambuco in late 16th century. Crisply written and intelligently constructed. Compare with item **3483** on the same family.

3503 Pombal e a cultura brasileira. Antônio Paim, organizador. Rio de Janeiro: Fundação Cultural Brasil-Portugal: Tempo Brasileiro, 1982. 137 p.

Articles consider Pombaline period to be from 1761 (creation of Colégio dos Nobres) until 1810 (creation of Rio's military academy). Tone is neutral, chapters examine figures influenced by Pombal (e.g., Melo Freire, Azeredo Coutinho, Rodrigo Sousa Coutinho). Focus is unquestionably Pombal's impact on Brazil.

3504 Pompeu Sobrinho, Thomaz. Protohistória cearense. 2a. ed. Fortaleza: Edições Universidade Federal do Ceará, 1980. 314 p.: ill., port.

Reedition of 1946 work. Composed of separate studies of voyages of discovery, cartography of discovery, original *donatários,* and Ceará's settlement. Of interest to researchers on that state.

3505 Randazzo, Vera. Catálogo de documentos históricos de Mato Grosso. Cuiabá: Fundação Cultural Mato Grosso, 1977. 80 p.: facsims.

Calendar of documents, laws, and decrees in Mato Grosso state archives, relating to first half of 1700s.

3506 Ritter, Marina Lourdes. As sesmarias do Paraná no século XVIII. Curitiba: Instituto Histórico, Geográfico e Etnográfico Paranaense, 1980. 248 p., 1 folded leaf of plates: bibl.,map (Estante paranista; 9)

Much broader than title indicates, since analysis covers all *sesmaria* grants in Paraná (1614–1788). Outlines land grant policies in Portugal and Brazil in book's first half, but analysis, while useful, is not as profound as could be. Study's core is second half, including map of 161 *sesmarias,* where analysis could have been deeper too. Rarity of case studies on evolution of land holding in Brazil makes work extremely valuable for colonial experts. Master's thesis at University of São Paulo.

3507 Rosário, Adalgisa Maria Vieira do. O Brasil filipino no período holandês. São Paulo: Editora Moderna; Brasília: em convênio com o Instituto Nacional do Livro, Ministério da Educação e Cultura, 1980. 146 p.: bibl.

Originally written as doctoral thesis (Madrid, 1970), work suffers, as author terms it, from *lacunas*. Argues, against accepted interpretation, that Spanish Crown did not neglect Brazil after 1618, but work is too short and documentation too slight to make this case.

3508 Russell-Wood, A.J.R. The Black man in slavery and freedom in colonial Brazil. New York: St. Martin's Press, 1982. 295 p., 8 p. of plates: bibl., ill., index.

Although essentially compilation of previously published articles, book is of considerable value, presenting within single cover and in revised form writer's extensive knowledge on slavery in Portuguese world. Especially useful for researchers on slavery in New World and for students when writing papers.

3509 ———. A Brazilian student at the University of Coimbra in the seventeenth century (*in* Medieval Renaissance studies on Spain and Portugal in honour of P.E. Russell. Frederick William Hodcroft *et al.* Oxford, England: Society for the Study of Medieval Language and Literature, 1981, p. 129–209)

Based on virtually unique material, letters from Bahian-born student to his father when at Coimbra (1695–97) provide pioneering study of group psychology and sense of identity in Brazilian-born of period. Pity article was published where no one will find it. Commended.

3510 Salvador, José Gonçalves. Os magnatas do tráfico negreiro: séculos XVI e XVII. São Paulo: Livraria Pioneira Editora: Editora da Universidade de São Paulo, 1981. 212 p.: bibl., index (Biblioteca Pioneira de estudos brasileiros)

Author's further contribution to study of *cristãos novos* in Portuguese colonial world (see *HLAS 34:2693a* and *HLAS 42:3607*). Argues that Sephardic traders, as vanguard of capitalism, were natural organizers of international slave trade centered upon Portugal. While the study's scope is comprehensive, treatment of specific topics tends to be superficial and rhetorical.

3511 Santos, Luiz Gonçalves dos. Memórias para servir à história do Reino do Brasil. Belo Horizonte: Editora Itatiaia; São Paulo: Editora da Universidade de São Paulo, 1981. 2 v.: facsims., ill., indexes, ports (Coleção Reconquista do Brasil; nova série, vol. 36–37)

Reprint of second ed. (1943) with notes by Noronha Santos of detailed narrative written 1821 about Dom João VI's residence in Rio (1808–21). Contemporary account of great utility to historians.

3512 Saunders, A.C. de C.M. A social history of black slaves and freedmen in Portugal, 1441–1555. New York: Cambridge University Press, 1982. 283 p., 4 p. of plates: bibl., ill., index (Cambridge Iberian and Latin American studies)

Although limited to Portugal, findings of this model study on growth and extent of slavery, on its legal, economic and social characteristics, and on attitudes of Portuguese to race and color are indispensable for any study of slavery, not just in Brazil but in all of New World. Highly commended to both experts and students.

3513 Schwartz, Stuart B. Patterns of slaveholdings in the Americas: new evidence from Brazil (AHA/R, 87:1, Feb. 1982, p. 55–86, map, plate, tables)

Richly textured article, rewarding at several levels. Through sophisticated statistical measurements of concentration of slavery in colonial Bahia, relates distribution of slavery to land use patterns. Lowest concentrations found in urban areas, but institution more general than usually acknowledged. Compares Brazilian experience with other countries. For Portuguese version, see *Estudos Econômicos* (13:1, 1983, p. 259–287).

3514 Simpósio Nacional de Estudos Missioneiros, *3rd, Santa Rosa, Brazil, 1979.* As reduções na época dos sete povos: anais. Santa Rosa: Faculdade de Filosofia,

Ciências e Letras Dom Bosco, 1980? 286 p.: bibl., ill.

Collection of short papers, mainly drawing on published materials, on Jesuit missions in River Uruguay basin in colonial period.

3515 Tavares, Luís Henrique Dias. Documentos para o estado do comércio de escravos para o Brasil: 1808–1814 (MAN, 12:4, abril 1981, p. 3–6)

Succinct bibliographical overview of materials existing in Arquivo Nacional on Brazilian slave trade in early 19th century.

3516 Thomaz, Joaquim. Anchieta. Rio de Janeiro: Biblioteca do Exército Editora, 1981. 231 p.: bibl. (Publicação; 512. Coleção General Benício; v. 191)

Hagiographic biography based entirely on secondary sources of leading Jesuit missionary in early colonial Brazil. Historiographically interesting as attempt to correlate Catholicism with Brazilian identity.

3517 Westphalen, Cecília Maria. Urumbebas e cochonilhas do Brasil meridional (UFP/EB, 4:8, 1979, p. 223–235, tables)

Short but instructive article on failure of Portuguese colonial authorities to implant cochineal-bearing cactus in Santa Catarina and Rio Grande do Sul in late 18th century.

3518 Wiederspahn, Henrique Oscar. A colonização açoriana no Rio Grande do Sul. Porto Alegre: Escola Superior de Teologia São Lourenço de Brindes: Instituto Cultural Português, 1979. 140 p.: bibl. (Coleção Caravela; 2. Coleção Temas gaúchos; no. 22)

Straightforward and clearly written account, based on secondary sources, of settlement by Portuguese Crown of Azores families in Santa Catarina in middle of 18th century.

NATIONAL

3519 Alencar, José Martiniano de. José de Alencar, discursos parlamentares: obra comemorativa do centenário de morte de José de Alencar. Brasília: Câmara dos Deputados, 1977. 670 p.: ill., index (Perfís parlamentares; 1)

Part of continuing series of extracts from speeches by famous men, volume

covers less known political side of famous writer, during 1869–74. For more on this series, see *HLAS 42:3732*.

3520 Andrade, Manuel Correia de. Transição do trabalho escravo para o trabalho livre no Nordeste açucareiro: 1850–1888 (IPE/EE, 13:1, 1983, p. 71–83, bibl.)

Useful overview of role of slavery in sugar economy of Pernambuco. Argues that in practice abolition did little to change status of blacks who, when freed, simply remained at bottom of socioeconomic order.

3521 Antônio Netto, José. Memórias do General Zeca Netto. Porto Alegre: Martins Livreiro, 1983. 168 p.

Straightforward memoir, account provides intimate view of military life and times in Rio Grande do Sul in most troubled period (1889–1936). Zeca Netto's name came to have frightening connotations because of his reputation for bloodshed.

3522 Araújo, Maria Celina Soares d'. O segundo governo Vargas, 1951–1954: democracia, partidos e crise política. Rio de Janeiro: Zahar Editores, 1982. 181 p.: bibl., ill. (Política e sociedade)

Early fruit of CPDOC holdings for 1950s and of interviews conducted there, book reinterprets Vargas' second presidency in important ways and is a must for students of 20th century. Documentation mostly from Vargas' later files.

3523 Araújo, Rosa Maria Barboza de. O batismo do trabalho: a experiência de Lindolfo Collor. Prefácio de Evaristo de Moraes Filho. Rio de Janeiro: Civilização Brasileira, 1981. 193 p.: ill., ports., tables (Coleção Retratos do Brasil; v. 156)

Lindolfo Collor, first Minister of Labor under Vargas, left deep if often overlooked imprint on social policy in Brazil. Book provides account of Collor's 1.5 years in office. Based on Centro de Pesquisa e Documentação (CPDOC) archives and newspapers, fully documented and balanced in its conclusions.

3524 Assis Brasil, Joaquim Francisco de. História da República Rio-Grandense. Porto Alegre: Estante Rio-Grandense União de Seguros, 1982. 211 p.: bibl., facsim., port. (Publicações do Club Vinte de Septembro; 3)

Facsimile reprint of 1882 work, written while future ideologue of Republicanism in Rio Grande do Sul was student at São Paulo. More propaganda than history, shows heavy influence of positivism on movement.

3525 Aufderheide, Patricia. Upright citizens in criminal records: investigations in Cachoeira and Geremoabo, Brazil, 1780–1836 (AAFH/TAM, 38:2, Oct. 1981, p. 173–184, tables)

Based on physical and cultural attributes of 996 free and freed male witnesses in 37 criminal investigations held in two Bahian towns (1780–1836), studies groups of mixed bloods, mostly small farmers, sellers and artisans, caught between free (white) and slave (black) worlds. Nothing of great significance transpires from analysis.

3526 Azevedo, Ferdinand. Ensino, jornalismo e missões jesuíticas em Pernambuco, 1866–1874. Recife: Fundação Antônio dos Santos Abranches, 1981. 291 p.: bibl., ill.

Carefully researched study of Jesuits' mission in Pernambuco which ended in their expulsion in 1874. Focusing on their educational work, shows that they clashed with Catholic status quo. Poor format makes reading difficult.

3527 Bak, Joan L. Cartels, cooperatives, and corporatism: Getúlio Vargas in Rio Grande do Sul on the eve of Brazil's 1930 revolution (HAHR, 63:2, May 1983, p. 255–275)

Demonstrates that in two years prior to 1930, Vargas carried out corporatist policies in Rio Grande that foreshadowed his actions later. Concludes that Vargas deserved his reputation as nation-builder due to these accomplishments.

3528 Bakos, Margaret Marchiori. RS, escravismo & abolição. Porto Alegre: Mercado Aberto, 1982. 165 p.: bibl. (Série Documents; 13)

While not profound, study employs wide range of sources, mainly printed, to give vivid impression of texture of slavery and of process of its demise in far south of Brazil. Chapters on "Abolition and the Positivist Republicans" and on "Abolition and the Press" are particularly useful.

3529 Bandecchi, Pedro Brasil. Liga Nacionalista. Prefácio de Vinício Stein Campos. São Paulo: Parma, 1980. 94 p.: bibl., ill. (Cadernos de história; 14)

Thin but welcome account of civic organization that promoted progressive reforms (1917–24) and that had its greatest influence in subsequent Partido Democrático of São Paulo.

3530 ———. Notas e perfis. São Paulo: Fundo de Pesquisas do Museu Paulista da Universidade de São Paulo 1980. 191 p. (Coleção Museu Paulista. História; vol. 9)

Collected essays of well-known São Paulo historian cover: slavery; 1824 Constitution; late 19th-century São Paulo; immigration; plus short biographies of Couto de Magalhães, Tobias Barreto, Capistrano de Abreu, Antônio de Padua Sales, and Juscelino Kubitschek.

3531 Barbosa, Carlos Roberto Arléo. Notícia histórica de Ilhéus: edição comemorativa do centenário de sua elevação a cidade. Rio de Janeiro: Livraria Editora Cátedra; Ilhéus: *com o patrocínio da* Prefeitura Municipal de Ilhéus, 1981. 190 p.: bibl.

Brief compilation of information, mainly from present century, on Bahian town which is center of cocoa region.

3532 Barreto, Antônio Emílio Muniz *et al.* História econômica: ensaios. São Paulo: Instituto de Pesquisas Econômicas, 1983. 181 p.: bibl., ill., tables (Série Relátorios de pesquisa; no. 13)

Seven essays focus on Minas in late 18th and São Paulo in 19th and early 20th centuries. They are high grade, based on archival and quantitative material. One essay estimates silver drain from Buenos Aires in 18th century; two examine social structure in Minas; one looks at slave holdings in São Paulo; one examines taxes in São Paulo; and two look at credit and 1929 Depression in São Paulo.

3533 Barroso, Véra Lúcia Maciel. A expressão de ideologia liberal no RS através da revolução farroupilha (PUC/V, 27:108, dez. 1982, p. 543–552, bibl.)

Brief analysis, based on handful of primary materials, that sees farroupilha revolt of 1835 as protest of rising socioeconomic group, local cattle raisers, against control of local economy from Rio. Emphasizes that revolt was liberal but not democratic.

3534 Barsted, Dennis Linhares. Medição de forças: o movimento grevista de 1953 e a época dos operários navais. Rio de Janeiro: Zahar Editores, 1982. 204 p. (Biblioteca de ciências sociais. Sociologia)

Originally MA thesis in political anthropology, study will interest historians of modern Brazil because of its solidly researched text. Strike in Rio, following larger one in São Paulo, was ultimately crushed by government. Episode was important for fostering militancy among maritime workers and fits into growing literature on labor in post–1945 period.

3535 Brandão, Antonio José Costa. Almanach da Província de Goyaz, para o anno de 1886. Prefácio de José Cruciano de Araújo. Foto, Joaquim Craveiro de Sá. Reedição. Goiânia: Editora da Universidade Federal de Goiás, 1978. 1567 p. (Coleção Documentos goianos; no. 1)

Reprint useful because of detailed information to researchers on provincial society and administration of Imperial Brazil.

3536 Brasil, 1900–1910. Apresentação, Plinio Doyle. Rio de Janeiro: Biblioteca Nacional, 1980. 3 v.: ports. (Coleção Rodolfo Garcia. Série A., Textos)

These 22 essays were commissioned to celebrate 70th anniversary of Biblioteca Nacional. Lightly written, virtually without footnotes, they provide sketches of Rio and life-and-times in *belle époque*.

3537 Brazil. Congresso Nacional. Câmara dos Deputados. Diretoria Legislativa. Deputados brasileiros: repertório biográfico dos Senhores Deputados, abrangendo o período de 1946–1967. Pesquisa e introdução de David V. Fleischer. Brasília: Centro de Documentação e Informação, Coordenação de Publicações, 1981. 858 p.: indexes.

Hefty tome should become standard reference for researchers, because it contains biographical data on virtually all federal deputies during period.

3538 ———. ———. Senado Federal. Dados biográficos dos ex-Presidentes do Senado, 1826 a 1979. Projeto de Biografias dos Senadores do Império e da República. Versão preliminar. Brasília: O projeto, 1981. 80 p.: bibl.

Very brief facts on 46 notables, taken from printed sources.

3539 ———. Ministério das Relações Exteriores. Arquivo Histórico. Catálogo do arquivo particular do Visconde do Rio Branco. Nadir Duarte Ferreira, organizador. Brasília: Editora Universidade de Brasília, 1981. 201 p. (Coleção Temas brasileiros; v. 9)

Calendar of papers of leading Empire politician, held at Itamaratí. Unfortunately, organized only by broad subject category and without annotations.

3540 ———. Serviço de Documentação Geral da Marinha. História naval brasileira. v. 2, t. 2. Rio de Janeiro: O Serviço, 1979. 1 v.: bibl., ill.

Vol. 2, pt. 2 consists of glossy, lavishly illustrated collection of studies on 18th and early 19th-century naval history, with much on diplomatic, political, and strategic developments. Traditional approach, based on published and ms. documents, attempts to create view of Brazil as maritime country. Worth consulting for military history and Cisplatine rivalry.

3541 Bresciani, Maria Stella. Condições de vida do escravo na província de São Paulo, no século XIX (AM/R, 42:192, jan./dez. 1979, p. 7–95)

Uses Campinas municipal records to draw data on cases against slaves (1871–86) in order to shed light on their living conditions and criminal acts deemed heinous enough for them to be brought to court. Offenses were chiefly murder or attempted murder against fazendeiro or overseer.

Bruneau, Thomas C. The Church in Brazil: the politics of religion. See *HLAS 45:6494.*

3542 Cabral, Oswaldo R. Nossa Senhora do Desterro. Florianópolis: Editora Lunardelli, 1979. 2 v.: bibl., ill.

While it might be worthwhile for dedicated researcher on 19th-century Santa Catarina's capital to spend much effort combing through these two volumes for spasmodic data, others should avoid this work which exemplifies worst aspects of Brazilian amateur history.

3543 Calmon, Pedro. Miguel Calmon: uma grande vida. Prefácio de Afonso Arinos de Melo Franco. Rio de Janeiro: José Olympio; Brasília: Instituto Nacional do Livro, 1983. 173 p., 8 p. of plates: ill. (Coleção Documentos brasileiros; 192)

Admiring, solidly documented study of Bahia's leading statesman in Old Republic. Author, who needs no introduction, was subject's godson. Good glimpse of turn-of-the-century elite at work in Rio.

3544 Campello, Netto. História parlamentar de Pernambuco. Reprodução facsimilar da ed. de 1923. Recife: Assembléia Legislativa do Estado de Pernambuco, 1979. 192, 162, 42 p.: appendix, bibl.

Reprint of 1923 work lists names and terms of all parliamentarians and governors of Pernambuco up to 1925, with supplement (giving party affiliation) to 1982.

3545 Campos, Eduardo. As irmandades religiosas do Ceará provincial: apontamentos para sua história. Fortaleza: Secretaria de Cultura e Desporto, 1980. 128 p., 5 leaves of plates: ill.

Basically compilation of information from legal texts and travel accounts of institutional structure and authorized activities of key social institution during Empire: the Church's lay brotherhoods. Despite its superficiality and limitation to Ceará, of utility because there is so little on subject.

3546 Carreira, Liberato de Castro. História financeira e orçamentária do Império do Brasil. v. 1, Até a guerra do Paraguai. v. 2, Após a guerra do Paraguai. Introdução, Washington Luís Neto. Brasília: Senado Federal; Rio de Janeiro: Fundação Casa de Rui Barbosa, MEC, 1980. 2 v.: index (Coleção Bernardo Pereira de Vasconcelos; 26–26A)

Most welcome reedition of 1889 work which remains indispensable for study of Empire's financial and fiscal history.

3547 Carvalho, José Murilo de. A construção da ordem: a elite política imperial. Rio de Janeiro: Editora Campus, 1980. 202 p.: bibl., ill. (Contribuições em ciências sociais; 8)

Revision of first (and stronger) part of author's 1974 Stanford doctoral thesis. Most coherent and well documented explanation of governing system of Brazilian Empire, based on prosopographical analysis of those who held power, yet produced. Highly recommended. For overview in English, see item **3548.**

3548 ———. Political elites and state building: the case of nineteenth-century

Brazil (CSSH, 24:3, July 1982, p. 378–399, tables)

Basically English summary of author's main arguments in Portuguese book (see item **3547**).

3549 Castro Pinto, João Pereira de. Discursos parlamentares. Seleção e introdução, Pedro Paulo de Elysséa. Brasília: Câmara dos Deputados, 1982. 400 p.: bibl., indexes (Perfis parlamentares; 17)

Continues series first annotated in *HLAS 42:3742*. Abolitionist and republican from Paraíba, Castro Pinto spent good part of his life in Rio. Excerpts his congressional speeches (1906–12).

3550 Cerqueira, Dionísio. Reminiscências da Campanha do Paraguai, 1865–1870. Rio de Janeiro: Biblioteca do Exército Editora, 1980. 341 p., 8 p. of plates: ill. (some col.), ports. (Publicação; 499. Coleção General Benício; v. 179)

Reprint of graphic account of Paraguayan War by soldier who participated in conflict from start to finish.

3551 Cervo, Amado Luiz. O Parlamento Brasileiro e as relações exteriores, 1826–1889. Brasília: Editora Universidade de Brasília, 1981. 254 p.: bibl. (Coleção Temas brasileiros; v. 21)

Analysis of role of Brazilian Parliament in formulation of directives and in conduct of foreign affairs during Empire, shows that parliament played only limited part, important for its ability to block treaties and to bring pressure. Wishing to make sense of mass of debates, author perhaps overemphasizes continuity and rationality. Good introduction to subject.

3552 Chacon, Vamireh. História das idéias socialistas no Brasil. 2a. ed., rev. e aum. Fortaleza: Edições Universidade Federal de Ceará; Rio de Janeiro: Civilização Brasileira, 1981. 344 p.: bibl., index.

Second ed. of work which concentrates on development of socialist ideas in Brazil, includes new chapter on social democracy and updates its dicussion of socialist thought in modern Brazil. Probably best survey available.

3553 Cláudio, Affonso. Insurreição do queimado: episódio da história da Província do Espírito Santo. Apresentação e notas de Luiz Guilherme Santos Neves. Com uma relação de documentos existentes no Arquivo Público Estadual. Elaborada por Fernando Achiamé. Vitória: Editora da Fundação Ceciliano Abel de Almeida, 1979. 157 p.: bibl. (Coleção Estudos capixabas; v. 2)

Reprint of 1977 study on 1849 slave rising which sought to force granting of freedom and involved Italian missionary priests. Supplement of documents on rising located in state archives has been added.

3554 Colson, Frank. The failed reform: society and the fiscal crisis in late nineteenth century Brazil (GEE/NA, 5, 1982, p. 270–294)

Pioneering article draws attention to shortfalls in revenues which were important cause for both Empire's collapse and instability of early Republic. Study worth pursuing further. Commended.

Correia, Serzedello. O problema econômico no Brasil: 1903. See *HLAS 45:3613*.

3555 Costa, Renato. Os três institutos históricos do Rio Grande do Sul (Revista do Instituto Histórico e Geográfico do Rio Grande do Sul [Porto Alegre] 123, 1982, p. 43–51)

Reviews three historical institutes of Rio Grande do Sul, that of 1855 which was abortive, that of 1861–62, and existing one founded in 1920. Perhaps of interest to cultural and intellectual historians.

3556 Cunha, Cenilde Loch Vieira da. Joaquim Pinto Júnior e a política de imigração e colonização no Brasil (MAN, 13:4, 1982, p. 118–130, graphs)

Short study of promoter of immigration into southern Brazil. His contract of 1874 to bring in 100,000 colonists failed, while his 1881 contract to create Grão Pará settlement in Santa Catarina was of limited success.

Cunha, Luiz Antônio. A organização do campo educacional: as conferências de educação. See *HLAS 45:4537*.

3557 Dantas, Antônio Arruda. Luciana Maria Machado, pioneira e matriarca. São Paulo: Editora Pannartz, 1981. 75, 39 p., 4 leaves of plates: bibl., ill.

Despite idiotic format and amateur presentation, work has value as case study of life of family which moved in mid 19th century from southern Minas Gerais to "oeste" of São Paulo as participants in expansion of agricultural frontier.

3558 Dantas, Orlando Vieira. Vida patriarcal de Sergipe. Rio de Janeiro: Paz e Terra, 1980. 190 p.: bibl., ill. (Coleção Estudos brasileiros; v. 47)

No more than ramshackle compilation of memories and facts about author's family and native state, with extraneous material. Some value in genealogical information and transcribed documents on 19th-century Sergipe.

3559 Dean, Warren. Comments on "Slavery in a Nonexport Economy" (HAHR, 63:3, Aug. 1983, p. 582–585)

Among other objections to Martins and Martins (item **3620**), contests their claim that coffee export economy in 19th-century Minas Gerais was not important cause for slavery's survival in area.

3560 Debes, Célio. Relações de trabalho no Brasil: aspectos de sua evolução histórica, 1822–1917 (IHGSP/R, 76, 1980, p. 241–260)

Tracing labor legislation up to early 20th century, concludes that workers received little protection under the law. No indication of extent to which these laws were enforced.

3561 ———. O surto ferroviário paulista: a importância de Rio Claro (AM/R, 194:44, jan/dez. 1981, p. 33–49)

Short sketch of origins of first railroad to be financed entirely in Brazil, one which played important role in promoting rapid advance of coffee frontier in São Paulo state.

3562 Denys, Odylio. Ciclo revolucionário brasileiro: memórias, 5 de julho de 1922 a 31 de março de 1964. Rio de Janeiro: Editora Nova Fronteira, 1980. 191 p., 16 p. of plates: ill. (Coleção Brasil século 20)

Offered as partial memoir, account stresses author's growing role in civil-military politics (1922–64). He was principal in 1964 coup, and his portrayal is valuable contribution.

3563 Duarte, Paulo de Queiroz. Os Voluntários da Pátria na Guerra do Paraguai. v. 1, O imperador: os chefes militares, a mobilização e o quadro militar da época. Rio de Janeiro: Biblioteca do Exército Editora, 1981.

1 v.: bibl., ill. (Publicação; 513. Coleção General Benício; v. 192)

Despite weaknesses, such as inevitable paeon to Caixas, this work has merit as first systematic study drawing on wide range of materials of logistical and manpower aspects of Paraguayan War (1865–70). To be followed by five volumes.

3564 Dulles, John W.F. Brazilian communism, 1935–1945: repression during world upheaval. Austin: University of Texas Press, 1983. 1 v.: bibl., ill.

Detailed, neutral chronicle of Brazil's PC during worst period of its existence continues account begun in *HLAS 38:238*. More documentary than history, book eschews analysis, interpretation, comparisons with other periods, and even character development. Still, raw facts provide a chilling portrait of danger of leftist politics in Estado Novo.

3565 Eisenberg, Peter L. Escravo e proletário na história do Brasil (IPE/EE, 13:1, 1983, p. 55–69, bibl.)

Some reflections, within Marxist context, on resemblances between slave and proletarian labor and on transition from slave to free labor in Brazil. Slight.

3566 Enciclopédia de estudos euclidianos. Organizador e coordenador, Adelino Brandão. Ilustrações, Elvio Sántiago, Geraldo Tmanik. Fotos, A. Adelino Louzada Brandão *et al.* Jundiaí: Gráfica-Editora Jundiaí, 1982. 1 v.: bibl., ill.

Critical studies, uneven in quality, of da Cunha's writings.

3567 Engerman, Stanley L. and **Eugene D. Genovese.** Comments on "Slavery in a Nonexport Economy" (HAHR, 63:3, Aug. 1983, p. 585–590)

Indicates similarities between slaveholdings in Minas Gerais's non-export economy as postulated by Martins and Martins (item **3620**) and case of Virginia where slavery persisted under comparable economic conditions. However, vigorously rejects Martinses' main contention by arguing that continuance of slavery in Minas was dependent on existence of larger Brazilian export-oriented plantation economy and could not "have long survived the absence of a world market for plantation staples."

3568 Estado Novo: um auto-retrato. Simon Schwartzman, organizador. Brasília: Editora Universidade de Brasília: *com o apoio* Fundação Roberto Marinho, 1982. 623 p. (Coleção Temas Brasileiros; v. 24)

In early 1940s, Minister of Education Capanema set out to compile book about Vargas era, based upon reports submitted by anonymous functionaries in government. Publication of this official history was prevented by Vargas's ouster. Schwartzman reconstructs project from many proofs. Amazing document shows Estado Novo in best light. Modern historians should consult.

3569 A Expedição científica de G.I. Langsdorff ao Brasil, 1821–1829: catálogo completo do material existente nos arquivos da União Soviética. Edição organizada por D.E. Bertels, B.N. Komissarov, T.I. Licenko. Coordenação de L.A. Chur. Brasília: Ministério da Educação e Cultura, Secretaria do Patrimônio Histórico e Artístico Nacional, Fundação Nacional Pró-Memória, 1981. 230 p.: bibl., ill., index (Publicações da Secretaria; no. 32)

Annotated catalogue of 800 documents on the Russian Langsdorff scientific expedition to Brazil (1821–29). Indicates which materials have been published and includes useful introduction, subject index, and maps.

3570 Farias, Cordeiro de. Meio século de combate: diálogo com Cordeiro de Farias. Editors: Aspásia Camargo e Walder de Góes. Rio de Janeiro: Editora Nova Fronteira, 1981. 575 p.: appendices, ill., index (Coleção Brasil século 20)

First-rate oral history from leading military figure in 20th-century Brazil, with rich and engaging materials on *tenentes*, 1930 revolution, Estado Novo, Força Expedicionária Brasileira, Escola Superior de Guerra, 1950s politics, and 1964 revolution. Professional organization provides easy access for students of any topic.

3571 Ferreira, Joaquim Carvalho. Presidentes e governadores de Goiás. Ed. póstuma. Goiânia: Editora da Universidade Federal de Goiás, 1980. 188 p. (Coleção Documentos goianos: no. 5. Publicação; no. 13)

Contrary to implication of title, an eclectic miscellany of events that occurred during tenure of Goiás' different chief executives (1824–1946).

3572 Franco, Sérgio da Costa. As causas da Revolução Farroupilha (Revista do Instituto Histórico e Geográfico do Rio Grande do Sul [Porto Alegre] 123, 1982, p. 53–61)

Short overview of causes of 1835 rebellion which, after discussing historiography on subject, opts for three main causes: existence of independent military base, sense of economic and political exploitation, and conjunction of political intrigues.

3573 Galliza, Diana Soares de. O declínio da escravidão na Paraíba, 1850–1888. João Pessoa: Editora Universitária, Universidade Federal de Paraíba, 1979. 229 p.: bibl. (Coleção Documentos paraibanos; 9)

Federal University of Paraíba master's thesis, notable for its use of surviving notarial archives to produce study set firmly within North American scholarship on slavery. Shows that after 1850, slavery flourished only in areas of prosperous agriculture while elsewhere owners sold their slaves to realize capital assets. Abolitionist movement had little impact. Recommended as case study which does not claim to be complete.

3574 Galvão, João Batista. Subsídios para a história da abolição do cativeiro no Rio Grande do Norte. Mossoró: Fundação Guimarães Duque, 1982. 96 p. (Coleção mossoroense; v. 211)

Yet another confused collection of facts and documents about native son's home state, this time Rio Grande do Norte. Contains enough original materials on ideas and activities of abolitionist movement to justify use by researchers.

3575 Gama, Arthur Oscar Saldanha da. A Marinha do Brasil na Segunda Guerra Mundial. Rio de Janeiro: CAPEMI Editora e Gráfica, 1982. 291 p.: bibl., index (Publicação; 5)

Former naval officer, now historian, provides superficial account of navy's role in World War II. Of interest to military historians, but style and lack of scholarly apparatus limit its value.

3576 Gambeta, Wilson Roberto. Ciência e indústria farmacêutica: São Paulo, Primeira República (IPE/EE, 12:3, dez./março 1982, p. 87–98, bibl.)

Uses history of São Paulo's Instituto Pasteur founded 1904, to supply state with anti-rabies vaccine, to show how state government failed both to initiate such institutes for scientific research and to promote their evolution into viable Brazilian pharmaceutical industry.

3577 Garcez, Angelina Nobre Rolim and **Antonio Fernando G. de Freitas.** Bahia cacaueira: um estudo de história recente. Salvador: Universidade Federal da Bahia, Núcleo de Publicações do Centro Editorial e Didático, 1979. 108 p.: bibl. (Coleção de estudos baianos; no. 11)

Based on author's MA thesis, study examines government policy toward cacao production and marketing after 1930. While highly technical, it contributes to growing literature on commodity controls and marketing schemes in contemporary Brazil.

3578 Gay, João Pedro. Invasão paraguaia na fronteira brasileira do Uruguai. Comentada e editada pelo Major Sousa Docca. Porto Alegre: Escola Superior de Teologia São Lourenço de Brindes, 1980. 381 p.: bibl.

Graphic, detailed account written by eyewitness of 1865 Paraguayan invasion of Rio Grande do Sul.

3579 Gomes, Eduardo Rodrigues. Campo contra cidade: o ruralismo e a crise oligárquica no pensamento político brasileiro, 1910–1935 (UMG/RBEP, 56, jan. 1983, p. 49–96)

Synthesizes author's MA thesis which found that ideal of small agrarian property as solution to Brazil's problems failed to win acceptance, much less implementation. Intellectual history.

Gordon-Ashworth, Fiona. Agricultural commodity control under Vargas in Brazil, 1930–1945. See HLAS 45:3636.

3580 Graf, Márcia Elisa de Campos. Imprensa periódica e escravidão no Paraná. Curitiba: Grafipar: co-edição com a Secretaria de Estado da Cultura e do Esporte do Paraná, 1981. 167 p.: bibl., ill. (Estudos paranaenses; 1)

Close analysis of references to slavery and slaves (1871–88) in 60 Paraná newspapers and journals of every political and cultural persuasion. Emphasizes types of emancipation granted and abolitionists' activities. Reproduces many quotations and statistical tables.

3581 Graham, Richard. Obstacles to re-democratization in Brazil: a historical pespective. Bundora, Australia: La Trobe University, Institute of American Studies, 1982? 15 p. (Occasional paper series; 6)

Contends that, since Brazil's economy and its political system have always been controlled by small elite which is resolved not to lose its position (see item **3582**), current prospects for successful "democratization" (that is, rule of country by majority of Brazilians) are highly doubtful.

3582 ———. A reforma eleitoral há 100 anos, como agora (MAN, 13:145, jan. 1982, p. 11–16)

Brief discussion of campaign to reform electoral system which culminated in 1881 law. Emphasizes that governing elite's fears of the masses, particularly of artisan and industrial classes in town, produced sharp restriction of existing franchise by the new law.

3583 ———. Slavery and economic development: Brazil and the United States South in the nineteenth century (CSSH, 23:4, Oct. 1981, p. 620–665, tables)

Provocative and challenging analysis argues that "Brazil's developmental sluggishness" in 19th century cannot be attributed to slavery since US South, also dominated by slavery, surged ahead. Points to importance of other factors in creating economic growth, including South's entrepreneurial spirit due to greater social mobility. Despite acknowledgement of very great differences between both areas, study may not adequately appreciate that, while in Brazil, slave areas were heart of national economy, US South was part of much larger industrial economic base using free labour. For Portuguese version, see *Estudos Econômicos* (13:1, 1983, p. 223–257).

3584 Greenfield, Sidney M. Barbadians in the Brazilian Amazon (UW/LBR, 20:1, Summer 1983, p. 44–64a, ill.)

Fascinating story of settlement built for Madeira-Mamoré railroad (1907–12), which evolved into special English-speaking community and was eventually absorbed by host society.

3585 Guia de pesquisa, Joaquim Nabuco em Washington. Brasília: Editora Universidade de Brasília, 1981. 170 p.: bibl., indexes (Coleção Temas brasileios; v. 11)

Nabuco's ambassadorship to Washington (1905–10) was crucial to Baron Rio Branco's diplomatic plans. This guide to Rio-Washington correspondence is fully indexed and professionally organized.

3586 Haberly, David T. Three sad races: racial identity and national consciousness in Brazilian literature. Cambridge, England: Cambridge University Press, 1983. 198 p.: bibl., index, ports.

Much narrower in scope than subtitle suggests, work is basically study of six "non-white" writers and their writings. Probably useful as supplementary reading for students on history of race in Brazil.

3587 Hilton, Stanley E. The armed forces and industrialists in modern Brazil: the drive for military autonomy, 1889–1954 (HAHR, 62:4, Nov. 1982, p. 629–673)

Detailed account of attempts to develop Brazilian suppliers for military materiel requirements. Argues that period up to 1930 saw emergence of consensus that such suppliers were essential to national security, and that after 1930, under Vargas' tutelage, goal was largely achieved.

3588 ———. Guerra secreta de Hitler no Brasil: a espionagem alemã e a contra-espionagem aliada no Brasil. Rio de Janeiro: Nova Fronteira, 1983 (Coleção Brasil século 20)

Expanded version of author's controversial *Suastica sobre Brasil*, work is exhaustively documented from US, Brazilian, German, and other sources. For all the posturing and attempted spying, little actually happened. Potboiler style, milktoast content.

3589 História da polícia civil da Bahia. Salvador: Empresa Gráfica da Bahia: Governo do Estado da Bahia, 1979. 363 p.: bibl., ill. (some col.)

In-house administrative history covers entire span since Salvador's founding. Neither writing nor coverage are adequate, but compilations of laws and reports will be of use to students of the police.

3590 A História vivida. Lourenço Dantas Mota, coordenador. São Paulo: O *Es-*

tado de São Paulo, 1981. 1 v. (Documentos abertos)

Consists of 16 interviews (1978) commissioned by *Estado de São Paulo.* Most are with writers, intellectuals, and politicians. Neither well researched nor thorough, they nonetheless contain tantalizing insights and tidbits of information. Lack of index undermines usefulness.

3591 Hofmeister Filho, Carlos Bento. O pote de geléia. Porto Alegre: Escola Superior de Teologia São Lourenço de Brindes, 1980. 143 p.: bibl. (Coleção Imigração alemã; no. 8)

Recounting, in popularized style, of episodes in lives of 19th-century German settlers in Rio Grande do Sul. No sources given and of limited value.

Horta, José Silvério Baia. Liberalismo, tecnocracia e planejamento educacional no Brasil: uma contribuição à história da educação brasileira no período 1930–1970. See *HLAS 45:4554.*

3592 Hübener, Laura Machado. O comércio da cidade do Desterro no século XIX. Apresentação de Walter Fernando Piazza. Florianópolis: Editora da Universidade Federal de Santa Catarina, 1981. 120 p.: bibl.

Useful case study, based on surviving original sources, of internal dynamic and external linkages of Santa Catarina's capital during Empire. Value of work is restricted by fragmentary nature of sources and author's failure to provide strong analytical framework.

3593 A Igreja na República. Seleção e introdução, Anna Maria Moog Rodrigues. Brasília: Câmara dos Deputados: Editora Universidade de Brasília, 1981. 185 p.: bibl. (Biblioteca do pensamento político republicano; v. 4)

Selection of articles, pastoral letters, and other Catholic writings is a fine place to begin to understand 1889 disestablishment and Church accommodation in Republican Brazil. Well researched introduction.

3594 Impasse na democracia brasileira, 1951–1955: coletânea de documentos. Organizadores, Adelina Maria Alves Novaes e Cruz *et al.* Prefácio de Hélio Jaguaribe. Rio de Janeiro: Fundação Getúlio Vargas: Centro de Pesquisa e Documentação de História

Contemporânea do Brasil, 1983. 477 p.: ill.

Given newness of second Vargas presidency, researchers on period will welcome this collection of documents from CPDOC. Wisely selected and profesionally organized, they cover era's main episodes. Vargas' last letters are especially poignant.

3595 Inojosa, Joaquim. República de Princesa: José Pereira x João Pessoa, 1930. Rio de Janeiro: Civilização Brasileira; Brasília: *em convênio com o* Instituto Nacional do Livro, Ministério da Educação e Cultura, 1980. 329 p., 8 p. of plates: bibl., ill., index (Coleção Retratos do Brasil; v. 144)

Well written account of Princesa revolt that helped trigger 1930 revolution, with fine attention to backland politics. Much local color and personal experience enhance the narrative.

José, Oiliam. Racismo em Minas Gerais. See *HLAS 45:8394.*

3596 Keith, Henry Hunt. The symbiosis of love and hate in Luso-Brazilian relations: 1822–1922 (CEHU/S, 43/44, Jan./Dec. 1980, p. 325–342, tables)

While useful as review of understudied area, adds nothing new to subject. Mostly based on Antonio da Silva Rego's *Relações luso-brasileiras, 1822–1953.*

3597 Koval, Boris Iosifovich. História do proletariado brasileiro: 1857 a 1967. Traduzido do russo por Clarice Lima Avierina. São Paulo: Editora Alfa-Omega, 1982. 568 p.: bibl., index (Biblioteca Alfa-Omega de cultura univeral. Série. la.; v. 15. Coleção Esta América)

Specialists in intellectual and labor history will consult this book for its frankly Marxist interpretation. Based on 1968 Russian ed., study uses secondary sources and newspapers, plus strong dose of Leninist analysis. Contains few surprises but is exhaustive and consistent in viewpoint.

3598 Lacerda, Carlos. Discursos parlamentares: seleta. Rio de Janeiro: Editora Nova Fronteira, 1982. 808 p., 10 p. of plates: ill., indexes, ports. (Coleção Brasil século 20)

Mastermind or spoiler, Lacerda left strong imprint on Brazilian politics in 1950s and 1960s. These extracts from his congressional speeches in 1950s continue series begun in *HLAS 42:3681.*

3599 Lago, Luiz Aranha Correo do. Balança comercial, balanço de pagamentos e meio circulante no Brasil no Segundo Império: uma nota para uma revisão (IBE/RBE, 36:4, out./dez. 1982, p. 489–508, graphs, tables)

Significant, revisionist work demonstrates weaknesses for 1846/47–1867/68 period of import/export tables published in *Anuario Estatístico do Brasil: 1939–40,* long used by historians. Includes good discussion of flow of specie in period. Researchers should take note of this article.

3600 Lazzari, Beatriz Maria. Imigração e ideologia: reação do Parlamento Brasileiro à política de colonização e imigração, 1850–1875. Porto Alegre: Escola Superior de Teologia São Lourenço de Brindes; Caxias do Sul: Universidade de Caxias do Sul, 1980. 134 p.: bibl. (Coleção Imigração italiana; 20)

Soundly written, intelligent study of debates in Brazilian Parliament on immigration and colonization (1850–75). Argues that large landowners' interests were always upheld in resulting policy decisions.

3601 Leff, Nathaniel H. Underdevelopment and development in Brazil. London: Allen & Unwin, 1982. 2 v.: bibl., index.

Sweeping and original synthesis of Brazilian ecomic history (1822–1947) based upon much new data recently available. Vol. 1 charts relatively slow growth in 19th century, followed by increased pace of 20th, based on industry. Vol. 2 analyzes major reasons for retardation in 19th, including surplus labor, slavery, backward domestic agriculture, and poor transportation. Essential for all students of Brazil.

3602 Leite, Miriam Lifchitz Moreira; Maria Lúcia de Barros Mott; and Bertha Kauffmann Appenzeller. A mulher no Rio de Janeiro no século XIX: um índice de referências em livros de viajantes estrangeiros. São Paulo: Fundação Carlos Chagas, 1982. 167 p.: bibl.

List of references, with brief annotations, to women in some 150 foreign travel accounts during 19th century. Organized by subject and then by date of visit.

3603 Lewis, Márcia. A presença dos industriais na política riograndense durante a República Velha (EIA, 7:1/2, julho/dez 1981, p. 73–80, bibl.)

Concludes that industrialists were weak and ineffectual in promoting their interests in politics. Sketchy but useful.

3604 Lima, Lana Lage da Gama. Rebeldia negra e abolicionismo. Rio de Janeiro: Achiamé, 1981. 165 p.: bibl. (Série Universidade; vol. 19)

Combines fairly standard discussion of slaves' lack of passivity with short study of abolitionist movement in city of Campos, Rio de Janeiro, in which slaves and blacks took active part. Minor work.

3605 Lima Júnior, Olavo Brasil de. Electoral participation in Brazil, 1945–1978 (UN/LBR, 20:1, 1983, p. 65–92)

Demonstrates that electoral participation has continued to rise even after 1964, and that rising dissatisfaction with regime in 1970s caused high participation rates. Excellent survey of legislation and party structures also.

3606 Lobo, Eulália Maria Lahmeyer. Condições de vida dos artesãos e do operariado no Rio de Janeiro da década de 1880 a 1920 (GEE/NA, 4, 1981, p. 299–333, tables)

Research report suggests how Rio industrialized despite decadent hinterland; union movement achieved significant strengh early in century; industrialists displayed progressive ideas in response. Presents new data from Rio archives.

3607 ———. La revolución industrial y la vivienda popular en Río de Janeiro: 1880–1920 (IGFO/RI, 40:159/162, enero/dic. 1980, p. 301–335)

Using fresh data from official and business archives, shows how factories replaced coffee in Rio and how early industrial relations became unusually complex, including attempt to provide workers' housing. Essential economic history.

3608 Lyra, Heitor. Minha vida diplomática. Brasília: Editora Universidade de Brasília: *com o apoio da* Fundação Roberto Marinho, 1981. 2 v.: ill., ports. (Coleção Temas brasileiros; v. 17)

Long-winded and gossipy memoir, covering 1916–55, reveals more by what it fails to say. A persevering reader will form an idea of how Itamarati operated on the inside, even though author is uncritical.

3609 Macedo, F. Riopardense de. O *Diário de Porto Alegre* na história da cidade (Revista do Instituto Histórico e Geográfico do Rio Grande do Sul [Porto Alegre] 123, 1982, p. 33–42)

Analysis of first newspaper printed in Porto Alegre (1827–28). Uses handful of surviving issues to show utility of newspaper in history.

3610 Magalhães, Juracy Montenegro. Minhas memórias provisórias: depoimento prestado ao CPDOC. Alzira Alves de Abreu, coordenadora. Rio de Janeiro: Civilização Brasileira, 1982. 337 p., 30 p. of plates: ill., ports (Coleção Retratos do Brasil; v. 157)

Another fine oral history from CPDOC, covering career of 1930 *tenente* and later politician until his retirement in 1967. First rate political material, well indexed. For political scientist's comment, see *HLAS* 45:6553.

3611 Magnani, Sílvia Ingrid Lang. O movimento anarquista em São Paulo, 1906–1917. São Paulo: Brasiliense, 1982. 189 p.: bibl.

Straightforward account of anarchist principles in São Paulo (1906–13) concludes that movement was not an exotic flower but rather a response to government labor policies and to time's socioeconomic conditions.

3612 Mangabeira, João. Idéais políticas de João Mangabeira. v. 1, Atuação política e parlamentar na Primeira República. v. 2, A ordem constitucional e a luta contra o Estado Novo. v. 3, Da esquerda democrática ao Ministério da Justiça. Organizador, Francisco de Assis Barbosa. Cronologia e textos selecionados, introdução de Hermes Lima. Brasília: Senado Federal; Rio de Janeiro: Fundação Casa de Rui Barbosa, MEC, 1980. 3 v.: ill., indexes (Ação e pensamento da República; 3, 3–A, 3–B)

João Mangabeira (Bahiano, 1880–1964) became protegé of Rui Barbosa and carried on his tradition for half-century. Life-long socialist, he defended civil liberties and social programs in Congress and after World War II, led Socialist Party. Finely organized volumes are eminently useful for student of political and intellectual history.

3613 Manor, Paul. Higher studies and cultural regionalism in Brazil at the turn of the century: a survey. Amherst, N.Y.: Council on International Studies; Buffalo: State University of New York at Buffalo, 1979. 57 p. (Special studies; no. 127)

Value of survey of higher education and culture at state level would be enhanced by greater depth of research and precision in discussion.

3614 Marcílio, Maria Luiza. Sistemas demográficos no Brasil do século XIX (VOZES, 74:1, jan./fev. 1980, p. 39–48, tables)

Overview suggests four demographic systems or models for 19th-century Brazil: subsistence economy, plantation economy, slave populations, and urban populations. Sketches likely characteristics of each.

3615 Marechal Eurico Gaspar Dutra: o dever da verdade. Edição organizada por Mauro Renault Leite e Novelli Júnior e Luiz Gonzaga. Rio de Janeiro: Nova Fronteira, 1983. 768 p. (Coleção Brasil século 20)

Dutra began working on memoir covering 1935–45, and had arranged his papers for purpose. Editors provide light introductions to chapters and reprint documentation from Dutra's files. Material on army is especially useful. Volume ends with Dutra's presidential inauguration. Good raw material.

3616 Marinho, Joaquim Saldanha. O Rei e o Partido Liberal. São Paulo: Editora Semente, 1981. 85 p.: bibl. (Coleção Revelações)

Reprint of two pamphlets (1869) by disappointed Liberal politician, which epitomize Liberal outlook and ideas of emerging Republican movement. Significant for Empire's political history.

3617 Martin, Hardy Elmiro. Santa Cruz do Sul de colônia a freguesia, 1849–1859. Santa Cruz do Sul: Associação Pró-Ensino em Santa Cruz, 1979. 139 p.: bibl., ill. (Coleção História de Santa Cruz do Sul; 2)

Micro-study, based on extensive archival research, of German group immigration into eastern Rio Grande do Sul in mid 19th century. Numerous documents are transcribed and detailed biographies given on individual settlers.

3618 Martins, Roberto Borges. Minas Gerais, século XIX: tráfico e apego à escra-

vidão numa economia não-exportadora
(IPE/EE, 13:1, 1983, p. 181–209, tables)

Challenges dominant view that decline of mining economy in 19th-century
Minas Gerais led to outflow of slaves to work
on new areas of coffee production. Shows
that number of slaves used in mining was already small before coffee boom. Sophisticated
exercise in analysis, employing sources ranging from census data and contemporary
travel literature to recent English-language
works analyzing slavery in Brazil and
elsewhere.

3619 ——— and **Amilcar Martins Filho.**
"Slavery in a Nonexport Economy:" a
reply (HAHR, 64:1, Jan. 1984, p. 135–146)

As well as replying to comments on
their article (see items **3559, 3567,** and **3681**),
authors include documented discussion of
external linkages of Minas Gerais coffee
plantations.

3620 ——— and ———. Slavery in a non-
export economy: nineteenth-century
Minas Gerais revisited (HAHR, 63:3, Aug.
1983, p. 537–568, tables)

Refutes existing historiography that
Minas Gerais exported slaves during 19th
century to work on coffee frontier elsewhere
by demonstrating that number of Minas
slaves actually grew from 170,000 (1819) to
380,000 (1873), despite its being non-export
economy. Suggests that crucial condition for
survival of slavery was not, as generally argued, existence of export economy but rather
availability of free land permitting independent peasant subsistence economy, which resulted in paucity of wage labor. For related
article, see item **3618;** for critiques of this
essay, see Dean (item **3559**), Engerman (item
3567), and Slenes (item **3681**). For authors'
response to these criticisms, see item **3619.**

3621 Maurício, Augusto. Algumas palavras
sobre Augusto Frederico Colin (MAN,
11:9, set. 1980, p. 10–15, ill.)

Brief biographical account of bureaucrat in Ministry of Finance during Pedro II's
reign.

3622 Mauro, Frédéric. Vers une ethnologie
économique: le rôle des nationalités
dans le développement du sud du Brésil,
1850–1950 (Travaux & Memoires de l'Institut des Hautes Etudes de l'Amérique Latine

[Universiité de Paris III] 33, 1980, p. 103–119,
tables)

Without breaking new ground, discusses ethnic and economic effects of European immigration. Ethnically, it whitened
the country. Economically, it provided labor
but not technology nor enterprise received
by US.

3623 ———. La vie quotidienne au Brésil au
temps de Pedro Segundo, 1831–1889.
Paris: Hachette littérature, 1980. 316 p.:
bibl., map.

Slight and disappointing work by leading French historian. Based on long quotes
from French travel accounts, mainly of Rio
de Janeiro, and garnished with facetious comments. Not recommended.

3624 Mello, Pedro Carvalho de. Estimativa
da longevidade de escravos no Brasil na
segunda metade do século XIX (IPE/EE, 13:1,
1983, p. 151–179, tables)

Uses local accounts, census data, and
statistical analysis to construct life expectancy tables for slave population by color and
sex for 1872. Mean life expectancy of male
slave is calculated at 18 to 23 years.

**3625 Melo, Jerônimo Martiniano Figueira
de.** Autos do inquérito da Revolução
Praieira. Introdução de Vamireh Chacon.
Brasília: Senado Federal, 1979. 465 p.: bibl.
(Coleção Bernardo Pereira de Vasconcelos; v.
no. 15: Série Estudos políticos)

Prints text of judicial proceedings
against those accused of complicity in
1848–49 rebellion in Pernambuco, including
original documents, depositions and newspaper articles. Useful source for period's political and social historian. Editor is not
Figueira de Melo (Chefe de polícia of Pernambuco in 1850) but Vamireh Chacon, who
provides 100–p. introduction on rising.

Mendes Júnior, Antônio. Movimento estu-
dantil no Brasil. See *HLAS 45:4563.*

3626 Miranda, Beatriz F. de Melo. A importancia da imigração na sociedade curitibana (UFP/EB, 5:10, nov. 1980,
p. 131–142)

Using printed sources, primary and
secondary, argues that foreign immigration
into Paraná was distinctive from start, since
it involved homesteading settlement rather
than labor for export agriculture and that

colonists supplied important element in "modernization" of state, by promoting both urbanization and industrialization.

3627 Monteiro, Hamilton de Mattos. Crise agrária e luta de classes: o Nordeste brasileiro entre 1850 a 1889. Brasília: Horizonte Editora, 1980. 203 p. (Movimento cultural brasileiro)

General study of condition of violence, group and personal, that was chronic during 19th century, particularly in Northeast. While containing useful insights and information, does not really come to grips with specific conditions in region.

3628 Monteiro, Norma de Góes. A revolução de 30: Vargas e sua luta pela hegemonia política em Minas (*in* Seminário sobre a Cultura Mineira, 2nd, Belo Horizonte, Brazil, 1979. II Seminário sobre a Cultura Mineira: período contemporâneo. Belo Horizonte: Conselho Estadual de Cultura de Minas Gerais, 1980, p. 13–37)

Political account of Vargas' gradual hegemony in Minas contains little that is new.

3629 Monteiro, Tobias. História do Império. [t. 1–2?], A elaboração da Independência. [t. 3–4?], O primeiro reinado. [t. 5?], Pesquisas e depoimentos para a história. Belo Horizonte: Editora Itatiaia; São Paulo: Editora da Universidade de São Paulo, 1981–1982. 5 v.: bibl. (Coleção Reconquista do Brasil; nova série, vols. 39–40, 41–42, 60)

Reprint of three substantial contributions (in five vols.) to history of independence period and Empire, by writer whose independent wealth allowed him to undertake systematic research in a wide range of archives and to compose at leisure.

3630 Montenegro, João Alfredo de Souza. O liberalismo conservador de Cairu (TEMBRAS, 65/66, abril/set. 1981, p. 82–91)

Short but powerful overview argues that Cairu, early and influential exponent in Brazil of Adam Smith's doctrines, depended for his political philosophy upon William Burke's and ultimately Locke's ideas, emphasizing importance of property as basis for the polity.

3631 Moraes, Alexandre José de Mello. História do Brasil-Reino e do Brasil-Império. Belo Horizonte: Editora Itatiaia; São Paulo: Editora da Universidade de São Paulo, 1982. 2 v.: bibl. (Coleção Reconquista do Brasil; nova série, vols. 63–64)

Weaknesses of this melange of narrative, comment and transcribed documents (not always reliably so) are manifest, but this 1871 work is still a most useful source for any historian working on Brazil's Independence period. A reprint has long been needed.

3632 Moraes, Evaristo de. As idéias fundamentais de Tavares Bastos. Rio de Janeiro: DIFEL; Brasília: em convênio com o Instituto Nacional do Livro, Ministério da Educação e Cultura, 1978. 215 p.

Consists of the thought of one of most influential ideologues of Liberalism during 1860s extracted from his writings and organized by subject. Includes brief chronology of his life and works and introduction discussing his thought.

3633 Moral Ruiz, Joaquín del. La independencia brasileña y su repercusión en el Portugal contemporáneo: 1810–1834 (*in* Coloquio Ilustración Española e Independencia de América, Bellaterra, Spain, 1978. Ilustración española e independencia de América: Homenaje a Noël Salomon. Edición preparada por Alberto Gil Novales. Barcelona: Universidad Autónoma de Barcelona, 1979, p. 315–332, tables)

Brief analysis, based on foreign trade balances of Portugal, showing how devastating to Portuguese economy was Brazilian independence.

3634 Moreira, Earle Diniz Macarthy. A Banda Oriental e o reconhecimento da independência do Brasil pela Espanha (Revista do Instituto Histórico e Geográfico do Rio Grande do Sul [Porto Alegre] 123, 1982, p. 25–31)

Brief discussion of how Spain's dreams of regaining the Banda Oriental (Uruguay), conquered by Portuguese in 1815 and held by Brazil after 1822, prevented recognition of the new Empire until 1834.

3635 Mota, Carlos Guilherme and Maria Helena Capelato. História da *Folha de São Paulo*: 1921–1981. São Paulo: Impres, 1980. 416 p., 66 p. of plates: ill.

Excellent study traces rise of small newspaper to premier status it enjoys today. Text quotes heavily from articles and editorials, yet keeps story moving. Selection of articles and photos complement text. Vir-

tually first professional history of a newspaper, this work will benefit researchers in
many fields.

3636 Moure, Telmo. A lavoura tritícola
gaúcha: 1930–1937 (EIA, 7:1/2,
julho/dez. 1981, p. 171–178, bibl.)
Competent discussion of wheat-
growers and their responses to Depression
and 1930s government changes.

3637 Nabuco, Joaquim. Joaquim Nabuco:
política. Organizadora, Paula Beiguelman. São Paulo: Editora Atica, 1982. 192 p.:
bibl., ill. (Coleção Grandes cientistas sociais; 23)
Thoughts of leader of Brazilian abolitionist movement. Lengthy introduction by
Paula Beiguelman is followed by short extracts from Nabuco's principal writings.
Useful if brief overview.

3638 Nabuco de Araújo, José Thomaz. O
Centro Liberal. Introdução de Vamireh
Chacon. Brasília: Senado Federal, 1979.
162 p.: bibl. (Coleção Bernardo Pereira de Vasconcelos; v. no. 21. Série Estudos políticos)
Welcome reedition of 1869 *Manifesto*
of Centro Liberal. Important source for study
of political ideas of Liberal Party in later
part of Empire.

3639 Nadalin, Sergio Odilon. Os alemães no
Paraná e a comunidade evangélica
luterana de Curitiba (UFP/EB, 7:12, dez.
1981, p. 5–36, graphs)
Drawing on registers of German Evangelical Lutheran Church in Curitiba, analyzes demographic data associated with
marriage, origin, birth. Compares findings
with data for Germanic world. Preliminary
study is interesting but narrower than title
suggests.

3640 Needell, Jeffery D. Rio de Janeiro at the
turn of the century: modernization
and the Parisian ideal (SAGE/JIAS, 25:1, Feb.
1983, p. 83–103, bibl.)
Restates obvious about dominance of
France as model for life among Rio de Janeiro
governing circles in 1900.

3641 Nequete, Lenine. As relações entre
senhor e escravo no século 19: o caso
da escrava Honorata (UMG/RBEP, 53, junho
1981, p. 223–248)
Uses case (Olinda, 1882) of master accused of having sexual relations with pre-

pubescent slave girl to examine general legal
relationship existing between slaves and
owners.

3642 Neves, Décio Vignoli das. Vultos do
Rio Grande, da cidade e do município.
Santa Maria: Livraria Editora Pallotti, 1981.
1 v.: bibl.
Contains some but not much biographical information of interest to researchers on Rio Grande do Sul during Imperial
period.

3643 Nogueira, Arlinda Rocha. Como São
Paulo hospedava seus imigrantes no
início da república (USP/RIEB, 23, 1981,
p. 27–49, bibl., tables)
This "snapshot" of Immigration Service in 1890s São Paulo, shows how immigrants were cared for while awaiting
contracts on plantations.

3644 Oliveira, João Pacheco de. O caboclo e
o brabo: notas sobre duas modalidades
de força-de-trabalho na expansão da fronteira
amazônica no século XIX (Encontros com a
Civilização Brasileira [Rio de Janeiro] 11,
maio 1979, p. 101–140, bibl., tables)
Postulates, within anthropological
model, two modes of labor during Amazon
rubber boom, linking them to region's later
social and economic conditions. Sees first, or
peasant mode, as replaced historically by second, or exploitative, mode. Compare with
Weinstein (item **3694**).

3645 Pang, Eul-Soo. Banditry and Mes-
sianism in Brazil, 1870–1940: an
agrarian crisis hypothesis (PCCLAS/P, 8,
1981/1982, p. 1–23)
Argues that both phenomena resulted
from modernization of agriculture and sociopolitical structures in South, with consequent worsening of rural life in Northeast.
Coronéis and rebels shook off central
authority.

3646 Pedreira, Pedro Tomás. O 1° [i.e. pri-
meiro] barco à vapor da América do Sul
e o *Marqués de Barbacena* (MAN, 11:9, set.
1980, p. 3–9)
Description of brief life of first Bahia
steamboat (1819–23), illustrates how difficult it is to maintain a new invention
imported without its technological
infrastructure.

3647 Pellizzetti, Beatriz. Os intelectuais imigrantes italianos na história do Brasil (UFP/EB, 6:1, junho 1982, p. 5–62)

Short study, in florid language, of Italian settlement in Santa Catarina's old German region and of role of Italians' leader, Ermembergo Pellizzetti.

3648 ——. Pioneirismo italiano no Brasil meridional: estudo de caso. Curitiba: Instituto Histórico, Geográfico e Etnográfico Paranaense, 1981. 330 p., 2 folded leaves: bibl., ill., index (Estante paranista; 13)

Study of Italian settlers in Santa Catarina's interior is one of more serious efforts to understand South's social evolution. Rises above local and family history to provide flavor of life for Europeans in early 20th-century Brazil.

3649 Pereira, Antônio Carlos. Folha dobrada: documento e história do povo paulista em 1932. Pesquisa, Flávio Galvão et al. São Paulo: Estado de São Paulo, 1982. 559 p.: bibl.

Most serious of many volumes commemorating 50th anniversary of 1932 revolution, this documentary collection covers same ground as Hélio Silva's early Ciclo de Vargas, but is organized to highlight São Paulo's viewpoint. Most materials reprinted from Estado de São Paulo and Vargas papers.

3650 Pereira, Astrojildo. Construindo o PCB: 1922–1924. Organização e apresentação de Michel Zaidan. São Paulo: Livraria Editora Ciência Humanas, 1980. 151 p.: bibl. (A Questão social no Brasil; 2)

Lively articles by one of founders of Brazil's CP, largely from Movimento Comunista, comments on wide variety of national and international issues.

3651 Pereira, Rubem Carneiro de Almeida. Conselheiro João de Almeida Pereira Filho (MAN, 12:6, 1981, p. 8–12)

Brief biography of politician during Empire who, despite rapid rise (appointed Minister at 33), failed to fulfill early promise.

3652 Pesavento, Sandra Jatahy. A República Nova Gaúcha: o estado e os pecuaristas, 1930–1937 (IFCH/R, 8, 1979/1980, p. 157–172, bibl.)

Continues author's long-term project of tracing relationship between politics and beef industry in Rio Grande. This article demonstrates how federal government, with aid of beef interests, gained control over state in 1932 and 1937.

3653 ——. República Velha Gaúcha: charqueadas, frigoríficos, criadores. Porto Alegre: Editora Movimento: em convênio com o Instituto Estadual do Livro, Departamento de Cultura, Secretaria de Cultura, Desporto e Turismo, 1980. 304 p.: bibl. (Coleção Documentos; v. 18)

Good study, based on primary sources and statistics, which concludes that continual crises of ranching and processing groups forced them into politics and to experiment with state-sponsored schemes to secure markets.

3654 Piccolo, Helga Iracema Landgraf. Contribuição para a interpretação do processo político-partidário Sul-Riograndense no Império (IFCH/R, 8, 1979/1980, p. 119–139, bibl.)

Combines analysis, with copious quotes from relevant laws, of respective power of provincial president and local assembly (1823–35), with short overview, based on secondary sources, of party development in Rio Grande do Sul (1845–89). Does not deliver what title implicitly promises, since it has no social content.

3655 Pinheiro, Paulo Sérgio and Michael M. Hall. A classe operária no Brasil, 1889 a 1930: documentos. v. 2, Condições de vida e de trabalho, relações com os empresários e o Estado. São Paulo: Brasiliense: FUNAMP, 1981. 1 v.: bibl., ill., index.

Vol. 2 contains sampling of writings on urban working class and industrial relations in São Paulo. Ample introductions place each piece and character in appropriate setting. For vol. 1, see HLAS 42:3734.

Porto Alegre, Aquiles. Homens ilustres do Rio Grande do Sul. See item **90.**

3656 Rassi, Sarah Taleb and Maria Cristina Teixeira Machado. Aspectos culturais da província de Goiás através da imprensa, 1873–1877 (Estudos Goianienses [Revista da Universidade Católica de Goiás, Goiânia] 4:5, 1977, p. 79–102, bibl., tables)

Admirably illustrates weaknesses of quantification unintelligently applied. Over 17 tables break down contents of Correio Official of Goiás for 1877. Everything you did not want to know.

3657 Reichel, Heloísa Jochims. A indústria téxtil do Rio Grande do Sul: 1910–1930. Porto Alegre: Mercado Aberto: *coedição com o* Instituto Estadual do Livro, 1980. 102 p.: bibl., ill., tables.

Competent analysis of problems facing Rio Grande's textile industry prior to 1930, with statistical tables.

3658 Reis, Arthur Cezar Ferreira. O início da experiência republicana (EEHA/AEA, 34, 1977, p. 173–185)

Brief reiteration of traditional view that in 1889, Empire had fulfilled its historic task for Brazil and that, with Republic's founding, Brazil "came to be, with limitations, member of the American family."

Reis Filho, Casemiro dos. A educação e a ilusão liberal. See *HLAS 45:4573.*

3659 Renault, Delso. O dia-a-dia no Rio de Janeiro segundo os jornais, 1870–1889. Rio de Janeiro: Civilização Brasileira; Brasília: *em convênio com o* Instituto Nacional do Livro, Ministério da Educação e Cultura, 1982. 238 p., 4 p. of plates: bibl., ill.

Chronology of social life in Rio during Empire's last two decades based on city's newspapers. As expected of this author, entertaining but not profound.

3660 ———. Raul Soares de Moura, o professor, o homem de letras, o estadista. Belo Horizonte: Imprensa Oficial, 1979. 202 p., 1 leaf of plates: bibl., facsims., ports.

Thin and flattering biography contains some original material on life of a Minas governor who served 1922–24. Should be used in conjunction with *HLAS 40:4187.*

3661 A Revolução de 30: textos e documentos. Organizadores, Manoel Luz Lima Salgado Guimarães *et al.* Brasília: Editora Universidade de Brasília, 1982. 1 v.: bibl., ill., index, ports. (Coleção Temas brasileiros; v. 14)

Collection of documents from 1920s and early 1930s, focuses on background to and execution of 1930 revolution. Though intelligently selected, they add little to collections produced by Hélio Silva and should have contained more introductory and interpretative apparatus.

3662 Ridings, Eugene W. Business interest groups and communications: the Brazilian experience in the nineteenth century (UW/LBR, 20:2, Winter 1983, p. 241–257)

Studies attempts to create modern infrastructure in Brazil as seen through eyes of commercial associations. More a discussion of declared goals and ambitions of associations than analysis of their actual impact on growth of infrastructure.

3663 ———. Business, nationality and dependency in late nineteenth century Brazil (JLAS, 14:1, May 1982, p. 55–96, tables)

Uses previously unexamined printed data concerning tax on professions and businesses imposed in 1871, to study levels of wealth and nationality of business community in Rio de Janeiro. Substantial contribution which could be taken farther.

3664 Rodrigues, José Honório. História combatente. Rio de Janeiro: Editora Nova Fronteira, 1982. 407 p.: bibl., index (Coleção Logos)

Useful compilation of articles by country's leading historiographer, comments on profession, leading figures in 20th-century letters, and governmental traditions.

3665 ———. O Parlamento e a consolidação do Império, 1840–1861: contribuição à história do Congreso Nacional do Brasil, no período da monarquia. Brasília: Câmara dos Deputados, Diretoria Legislativa, Centro de Documentação e Informação, Coordenação de Publicações, 1982. 213 p.: bibl., index, port.

Good introduction to political development of Brazil (1840–61) through spectrum of Imperial Parliament but not, despite title, a close analysis of Assembléia Geral's role in Empire's consolidation.

3666 Saes, Flávio A.M. O término do escravismo: uma nota sobre a historiografia (IPE/EE, 12:3, dez./março 1982, p. 29–40)

Compares explanations given in recent historical works for abolition of slavery, and suggests need for further reflection on subject.

3667 Salgado, Plínio. Discursos parlamentares. Seleção e introdução, Gumercindo Rocha Dorea. Brasília: Câmara dos Deputados, 1982. 982 p.: bibl., ill., indexes, ports. (Perfis parlamentares; 18)

Continues series first annotated in

HLAS 42:3742. Speeches excerpted here were made in 1959–73, when former leader of Integralist Party became elder statesman of the right.

3668 Sampaio, Consuelo Novais. Os partidos políticos da Bahia na Primeira República: uma política de acomodação. Salvador: Universidade Federal da Bahia, Núcleo de Publicações do Centro Editorial e Didático, 1978. 196 p.: bibl. (Estudos baianos; no. 10)

Complete, albeit wholly political, account of succession of parties in Bahia during Old Republic. Originally MA thesis, work is based on considerable research in newspapers and private papers. Supplements *HLAS 42:3727.*

3669 Santos, Corsino Medeiros dos. Mauá e o desenvolvimento brasileiro (IHGB/R, 325, out./dez. 1979, p. 32–60, bibl.)

Curious piece, more propaganda than history, which uses Mauá's prestige as railroad construction pioneer to justify and promote upgrading and extension of railroad network in contemporary Brazil.

3670 Santos, Mario Augusto da Silva. Uma fonte para a história social de Salvador: as teses de doutoramento da Faculdade de Medicina da Bahia (Universitas [Revista de cultura da Universidade Federal da Bahia] 29, jan./abril 1983, p. 41–57)

Discusses "social" content (e.g., health aspects of housing and nutrition) of 29 theses at Bahia's Medical Faculty (1889–1930). More indicative than profound. Most detailed on tuberculosis.

3671 Santos, Paulo Ricardo da Silveira. Contribuição para a história da imprensa em São Paulo (AM/R, 42:192, jan./dez. 1979, p. 143–236, bibl., ill.)

First winner of Carlos Rizzini Prize established by Order of Retired Journalists, this chronological recounting of journalism in São Paulo state from 1827 epitomizes weaknesses of prize essays.

3672 ———. História da Associação Paulista de Imprensa: 1933–1978 (AM/R, 194:44, jan./dez. 1981, p. 116–295, bibl., plates)

Organization's chronicle that does little more than trace various administrations and their efforts to provide social bene-

fits to members. Virtually no sense of politics or larger role in society.

Santos, Roberto. História econômica da Amazônia: 1800–1920. See *HLAS 45:3675.*

3673 Santos Filho, Lycurgo de Castro. As cartas de Ricardo Gumbleton Daunt: os padres do Patrocínio de Itu e outros assuntos (IHGSP/R, 76, 1980, p. 170–198, plates)

Details contents of five unpublished letters written by amateur historian of São Paulo. Difficult to understand why he did not use space to transcribe the letters.

3674 Scarano, Julita. Familia extensa e escravaria (AM/R, 193:43, jan./dez. 1980, p. 105–122)

Fairly short discussion of geographical origins, life styles, and relationships of fazendeiros and slaves in Paraíba Valley coffee zone of São Paulo during 19th century. Based on information taken from printed sources and from censuses and estate inventories but not systematically investigated.

3675 Schimmelpfeng, Gisela Paschen. Maria Thomazia: o amor à liberdade. Fortaleza: Editora H. Galeno, 1980. 82 p.: port.

Short, emotional biography of fiery advocate of abolition in Ceará. Shows how interlinked were feminist and anti-slavery causes in late Empire.

3676 Schneider, Regina Portella. Flores da Cunha, o último gaúcho legendário. Porto Alegre: Escola Superior de Teologia São Lourenço de Brindes: Martins Livreiro-Editor, 1981. 389 p.: bibl.,ill., ports. (Coleção Temas gaúchos; 27)

Flores da Cunha is best known as flamboyant caudilho from Rio Grande, who tried to prevent Vargas' Estado Novo coup. His career is sketched in this disappointing work, but his impact on history is barely plumbed. Text is larded with quotes from correspondence canvassed by author. Only for specialists.

3677 Segatto, José Antônio. Breve história do PCB. São Paulo: Livraria Editora Ciências Humanas, 1981. 115 p.: bibl. (A Questão social no Brasil; 8)

This primer, while not heavily documented, provides brief introduction to Brazil's Communist Party up to the present.

3678 Semana de Estudos de História Agrária. Anais. Assis: Universidade Estadual Paulista, Instituto de Letras, História e Psicologia, 1982. 355 p.

Most papers contained here concern research underway and even personal experiences. This young but growing field will be helped by serious though uneven volumes like this. Major themes are land tenure, labor, and colonization.

3679 Silva, Florêncio de Abreu e. O Senador do Império Florêncio de Abreu e a política do seu tempo. Caxias do Sul: Universidade de Caxias do Sul: Escola Superior de Teologia São Lourenço de Brindes: co-edição com o Instituto Estadual do Livro, Departamento de Cultura, Secretaria de Cultura, Desporto e Turismo, 1979. 109 p.: bibl.

Brief study, based on handful of sources, of political career and philosophy of one of most colorful leaders of younger, crypto-Republican wing of Liberal Party during Empire's last years.

Simão, Azis. Sindicato e estado: suas relações na formação do proletariado de São Paulo. See *HLAS 45:8428.*

3680 Skidmore, Thomas E. Race and class in Brazil: historical perspectives (UW/LBR, 20:1, Summer 1983, p. 104–118)

Timely review of the literature calls attention to recent studies documenting race discrimination. Essential for students of race relations.

3681 Slenes, Robert W. Comments on "Slavery in a Nonexport Economy" (HAHR, 63:3, Aug. 1983, p. 569–581)

Valuable critique of Martins and Martins' revisionist essay (item **3620**), suggests existence of greater links between slaveholding in Minas Gerais and export economy than Martins acknowledge.

3682 ———. O que Rui Barbosa não queimou: novas fontes para o estudo da escravidão no século XIX (IPE/EE, 13:1, 1983, p. 117–149, tables)

Analyzes in great detail historical utility of surviving records on slavery in form of matriculation of slaves taken in 1872 and 1886, which have, despite Rui Barbosa's orders to burn, survived at local level and which author used for Campinas and Vassouras.

3683 Smith, Joseph. American diplomacy and the Naval Mission to Brazil: 1917–1930 (IAMEA, 35:1, Summer 1981, p. 73–91)

Earliest permanent US military influence in Brazil, the Naval Mission of 1922–30, signaled rising American prestige. However, it was not the occasion for promoting strategic or commercial interests.

3684 Stolcke, Verena and Michael M. Hall. The introduction of free labour on São Paulo coffee plantations (JPS, 10:2/3, Jan./April 1983, p. 170–200)

Well argued, nicely documented study of planters' approach to supply of labor in coffee province of São Paulo (1850–1914). Concludes that planters always took sufficient action, either directly or indirectly through government, to maintain minimum supply of labour, whether slave or free.

3685 Tavares, Aurélio de Lyra. Vilagran Cabrita e a Engenharia de seu tempo. Rio de Janeiro: Biblioteca do Exército Editora, 1981. 306 p.: bibl., facsims., ill., music, ports. (Publicação; 514. Coleção General Benício; v. 193)

This biography of official "patron" of Brazilian Corps of Engineers is important not for its subject but for what it reveals about mentality and psychological imperatives of Brazil's military since 1930. Written in his old age by one of most influential generals who served as Minister of War, work is in fact a deification and justification of the corps in which he made his career.

3686 Tavares, Luis Henrique Dias. A economia da província da Bahia na segunda metade do século XIX (Universitas [Revista de cultura da Universidade Federal da Bahia] 29, jan./abril 1982, p. 31–39, bibl., tables)

Brief discussion, mainly using data from 1860s presidential reports, of Bahia state's economy which is seen as similar to national economy, both being a combination of traditional export crops.

3687 Teschauer, Carlos. O escravo dos escravos ou São Pedro Claver, o Apóstolo dos Negros (FFCL/EL, 16[15]:55, 1980, p. 43–88)

Essay written by Jesuit priest of Rio Grande do Sul in immediate aftermath of abolition in 1888. Although basically laudatory biography of St. Peter Clavier and his work, introduction discusses future of freed slaves and role of Catholic Church in reconciling different races. Interesting mainly for its outlook on race.

3688 Torres, Acrísio. Sergipe no processo da independência do Brasil (MAN, 12:5, 1981, p. 14–19, bibl.)

Succinct account of how creation of Sergipe as political unit independent of Bahia was delayed by 1820–23 events. Useful for experts.

Uricoechea, Fernando. The patrimonial foundations of the Brazilian Bureaucratic State. See *HLAS 45:8347.*

3689 Vangelista, Chiara. Per una ricerca sul mercato del lavoro: la mobilitá della manodopera in una filatura paulista (GEE/NA, 1, 1978, p. 215–230, tables)

Look at labor conditions in one São Paulo factory in 1920s and 1930s, showing, among other things, great turnover in the force.

3690 Verger, Pierre. Notícias da Bahia, 1850. Salvador: Corrupio: Fundação Cultural do Estado da Bahia, 1981? 237 p.: bibl. (Baianada; 1)

Collation of information, mainly from 18th- and 19th-century travel accounts, on social groups and life in Bahia. Mostly a work of superficial popularization with few original sources. Disappointing.

3691 Viana, Francisco. Daniel Krieger: um liberal na República. Brasília: Senado Nacional: Editora Dom Quixote, 1982. 225 p., 1 leaf of plates: ports. (Brasil, memória política; v. 1)

Uneven but valuable supplement to Krieger's memoirs, volume covers 1960s.

3692 Viana Filho, Luís. Três estadistas: Rui, Nabuco, Rio Branco. Notas de Eduardo Portella *et al.* Rio de Janeiro: Livraria J. Olympio Editora; Brasília: *em convênio com o* Instituto Nacional do Livro, Ministério da Educação e Cultura, 1981. 1218 p., 35 p. of plates: bibl., facsims., index, ports. (Coleção Alma do tempo; v. no. 2)

Reedition of three biographies of political notables of which two have already been annotated (see *HLAS 15:1826* and *HLAS 19:4031*), but not the one on younger Rio Branco. Study is sound analysis, based on Baron's own papers, of character and career of

Brazil's most successful diplomat and Foreign Minister (1902–12). While respectful, does discuss less attractive traits in Rio Branco's personality.

3693 Vieira, José. A cadeia velha: memória da Câmara dos Deputados, 1909. Introdução de Francisco de Assis Barbosa. Brasília: Senado Federal; Rio de Janeiro: Fundação Casa de Rui Barbosa-MEC, 1980. 239 p.: bibl., ill., index (Coleção Bernardo Pereira de Vasconcelos; 27)

Vieira covered Congress for various Rio and São Paulo newspapers in 1900s, and chose to chronicle 1909 session in this 1912 book. Insightful, humorous, full of caricatures of leading figures, story covers Hermes' twisted rise to presidency.

3694 Weinstein, Barbara. The Amazon rubber boom: 1850–1920. Stanford, Calif.: Stanford University Press, 1983. 356 p.: bibl., ill., index, tables.

Excellent analysis of Amazon rubber economy from origins through dreary decline, covers all aspects of subject, sections on lives of tappers and traders being particularly vivid. Emphasizes sickeningly exploitative nature of boom in both ecological and human terms. Model study on long neglected subject. Recommended to expert and student alike.

3695 Wiederspahn, Henrique Oscar. O convênio de Ponche Verde: o que sabemos sobre a marcha das negociações de paz tentadas desde 1839 e de como se conseguiu a pacificação do Rio Grande do Sul em 1845, graças à atuação pessoal do então Barão de Caxias. Porto Alegre: Escola Superior de Teologia São Lourenço de Brindes, 1980. 137 p., 1 leaf of plates: bibl., ports. (Coleção Farroupilha; 1)

Intelligent study, based on published sources, of conjunction of events which led to ending of farroupilha revolt in Rio Grande do Sul in March 1845 by Convention of Poncho Verde. Good introduction to subject.

3696 Wolff, Egon. Judeus nos primórdios do Brasil-República: visto especialmente pela documentação no Rio de Janeiro. Rio de Janeiro: Biblioteca Israelita H.N. Bialik, Centro de Documentação, 1981?. 384 p.: bibl., facsims., ill., index.

Because so little has been written on Jews in modern Brazil, this study fills a gap in social and business history. It is so poorly written that it only qualifies as raw material—basically clippings from newspapers and gleanings from archives (1889–1904).

JOURNAL ABBREVIATIONS
HISTORY

AAA/AA American Anthropologist. American Anthropological Association. Washington.

AAFH/TAM The Americas. A quarterly publication of inter-American cultural history. Academy of American Franciscan History. Washington.

ACH/BHA Boletín de Historia y Antigüedades. Organo de la Academia Colombiana de Historia. Bogotá.

ACPS/B Boletín de la Academia de Ciencias Políticas y Sociales. Caracas.

AES/AE American Ethnologist. American Ethnological Society. Washington.

AESC Annales: Economies, Sociétés, Civilisations. Centre national de la recherche scientifique *avec le concours de la* VIe Section de l'Ecole pratique des hautes études. Paris.

AGS/GR The Geographical Review. American Geographical Society. New York.

AHA/R American Historical Review. American Historical Association. Washington.

AHS/AH Agricultural History. The quarterly journal of the Agricultural History Society. Washington.

AISA/TA Terra Ameriga. Associazione Italiana Studi Americanistici. Genova, Italy.

AJA American Jewish Archives. The American Jewish Archives. Cincinnati, Ohio.

AM/R Revista do Arquivo Municipal. Prefeitura do Município de São Paulo, Departamento Municipal de Cultura. São Paulo.

ANH/B Boletín de la Academia Nacional de Historia. Buenos Aires.

ANH/IE Investigaciones y Ensayos. Academia Nacional de la Historia. Buenos Aires.

APL/B Boletín de la Academia Panameña de la Lengua. Panamá.

APS/P Proceedings of the American Philosophical Society. Philadelphia, Pa.

ASE/E Ethnohistory. Journal of the American Society for Ethnohistory. Buffalo, N.Y.

AU/P Phylon. Atlanta University. Atlanta, Ga.

BCE/C Cultura. Revista del Banco Central del Ecuador. Quito.

BISRA/BS Belizean Studies. Belizean Institute of Social Research and Action [and] St. John's College. Belize City.

BMHS/J Journal of the Barbados Museum and Historical Society. Barbados.

BYU/S Brigham Young University Studies. Provo, Utah.

CAAAP/AP Amazonía Peruana. Centro Amazónico de Antropología y Aplicación Práctica, Departamento de Documentación y Publicaciones. Lima.

CAM Cuadernos Americanos. México.

CBR/BCB Boletín Cultural y Bibliográfico. Banco de la República, Biblioteca Luis-Angel Arango. Bogotá.

CDAL Cahiers des Amériques Latines. Paris.

CEDE/DS Desarrollo y Sociedad. Universidad de Los Andes, Facultad de Economía, Centro de Estudios sobre el Desarrollo Económico (CEDE). Bogotá.

CEDLA/B Boletín de Estudios Latinoamericanos. Centro de Estudios y Documentación Latinoamericanos. Amsterdam.

CEHSMO Historia Obrera. Centro de Estudios Históricos del Movimiento Obrero Mexicano. México.

CEHU/S Studia. Revista semestral. Centro de Estudos Históricos Ultramarinos. Lisboa.

CEM/ECM Estudios de Cultura Maya. Universidad Nacional Autónoma de México, Centro de Estudios Mayas. México.

CH Cuadernos Hispanoamericanos. Instituto de Cultura Hispánica. Madrid.

CM/HM Historia Mexicana. El Colegio de México. México.

CM/RE   Relaciones. Estudios de historia y sociedad. El Colegio de Michoacán. Zamora, México.

CONAC/RNC   Revista Nacional de Cultura. Consejo Nacional de Cultura. Caracas.

CP   Cuadernos Políticos. Revista trimestral. Ediciones Era. México.

CPES/RPS   Revista Paraguaya de Sociología. Centro Paraguayo de Estudios Sociológicos. Asunción.

CPU/ES   Estudios Sociales. Corporación de Promoción Universitaria. Santiago.

CRIT   Criterio. Editorial Criterio. Buenos Aires.

CSSH   Comparative Studies in Society and History. An international quarterly. Society for the Comparative Study of Society and History. The Hague.

CSUCA/ESC   Estudios Sociales Centroamericanos. Consejo Superior de Universidades Centroamericanas, Confederación Universitaria Centroamericana, Programa Centroamericano de Ciencias Sociales. San José.

CU/ASQ   Administrative Science Quarterly. Cornell University, Graduate School of Business and Public Administration. Ithaca, N.Y.

DGV/ZE   Zeitschrift für Ethnologie. Deutschen Gesellschaft für Völkerkunde. Braunschweig, FRG.

ECB   Encontros com a Civilização Brasileira. Editora Civilização Brasileira. Rio de Janeiro.

ECO   Eco. Librería Bucholz. Bogotá.

EEHA/AEA   Anuario de Estudios Americanos. Consejo Superior de Investigaciones Científicas [and] Universidad de Sevilla, Escuela de Estudios Hispano-Americanos. Sevilla.

EEHA/HBA   Historiografía y Bibliografía Americanista. Escuela de Estudios Hispano-Americanos de Sevilla. Sevilla.

EHA/J   Journal of Economic History. New York University, Graduate School of Business Administration *for the* Economic History Association. Rensselaer, N.Y.

EIA   Estudos Ibero-Americanos. Pontifícia Universidade Católica do Rio Grande do Sul, Departamento de História. Pôrto Alegre, Brazil.

ESME/C   Cultura. Revista del Ministerio de Educación. San Salvador.

FFCL/EL   Estudos Leopoldenses. Faculdade de Filosofia, Ciências e Letras. São Leopoldo, Brazil.

FIU/CR   Caribbean Review. Florida International University, Office of Academic Affairs. Miami.

GEE/NA   Nova Americana. Giulio Einaudi Editore. Torino, Italy.

GIIN/GI   Guatemala Indígena. Instituto Indigenista Nacional. Guatemala.

HAHR   Hispanic American Historical Review. Duke University Press *for the* Conference on Latin American History of the American Historical Association. Durham, N.C.

HSSC/SCQ   Southern California Quarterly. Historical Society of Southern California. Los Angeles.

IAA   Ibero-Amerikanisches Archiv. Ibero-Amerikanisches Institut. Berlin, FRG.

IAHG/AHG   Antropología e Historia de Guatemala. Instituto de Antropología e Historia de Guatemala. Guatemala.

IAI/I   Indiana. Beiträge zur Volker-und Sprachenkunde, Archäologie und Anthropologie des Indianischen Amerika. Ibero-Amerikanisches Institut. Berlin, FRG.

IAMEA   Inter-American Economic Affairs. Washington.

IBE/RBE   Revista Brasileira de Economia. Fundação Getúlio Vargas, Instituto Brasileiro de Economia. Rio de Janeiro.

IBRI/R   Revista Brasileira de Política Internacional. Instituto Brasileiro de Relações Internacionais. Rio de Janeiro.

IDES/DE   Desarrollo Económico. Instituto de Desarrollo Económico y Social. Buenos Aires.

IEAS/R   Revista de Estudios Agro-Sociales. Instituto de Estudios Agro-Sociales. Madrid.

IFCH/R   Revista do Instituto de Filosofia e Ciências Humanas. Universidade Federal do Rio Grande do Sul. Pôrto Alegre, Brazil.

IFEA/B   Bulletin de l'Institut Français d'Etudes Andines. Lima.

IGFO/RI   Revista de Indias. Instituto Gonzalo Fernández de Oviedo [and] Consejo Superior de Investigaciones Científicas. Madrid.

IGME/RG   Revista Geográfica. Instituto Geográfico Militar del Ecuador, Departamento Geográfico. Quito.

IHGB/R   Revista do Instituto Histórico e Geográfico Brasileiro. Rio de Janeiro.

IHGSP/R   Revisto do Instituto Histórico e Geográfico de São Paulo. São Paulo.

III/AI   América Indígena. Instituto Indigenista Interamericano. México.

IILI/RI   Revista Iberoamericana. Instituto Internacional de Literatura Iberoamericana. Patrocinada por la Universidad de Pittsburgh. Pittsburgh, Pa.

IJZ/H   Hispania. Revista española de historia. Instituto Jerónimo Zurita, Consejo Superior de Investigaciones Científicas. Madrid.

IPA/A   Allpanchis. Instituto de Pastoral Andina. Cuzco, Peru.

IPE/EE   Estudos Econômicos. Universidade de São Paulo, Instituto de Pesquisas Econômicas. São Paulo.

IPGH/RHI   Revista de Historia de las Ideas. Instituto Panamericano de Geografía e Historia. Editorial Casa de la Cultura Ecuatoriana. Quito.

ISA/CUR   Comparative Urban Research. International Sociological Association, Committe for Community Research. College Park, Md.

ISTM/MH   Missionalia Hispánica. Instituto Santo Toribio de Mogrovejo [and] Consejo Superior de Investigaciones Científicas. Madrid.

JDA   Journal of Developing Areas. Western Illinois University Press. Macomb.

JEHM/R   Revista de la Junta de Estudios Históricos de Mendoza. Mendoza, Argentina.

JGSWGL   Jahrbuch für Geschichte von Staat, Wirtschaft und Gesellschaft Lateinamerikas. Köln, FRG.

JHI   Journal of the History of Ideas. City College. New York.

JHS/R   Jamaican Historical Review. Jamaican Historical Society. Kingston.

JIH   Journal of Interdisciplinary History. MIT Press. Cambridge.

JLAS   Journal of Latin American Studies. Centers or institutes of Latin American studies at the universities of Cambridge, Glasgow, Liverpool, London, and Oxford. Cambridge University Press. London.

JPHC/R   Revista de la Junta Provincial de Historia de Córdoba. Archivo Histórico Monseñor P. Cabrera. Córdoba, Argentina.

JPS   Journal of Peasant Studies. Frank Cass & Co. London.

LAP   Latin American Perspectives. University of California. Riverside.

LARR   Latin American Research Review. University of North Carolina Press *for the* Latin American Studies Association. Chapel Hill.

LI/IA   *See* NOSALF/IA.

LNB/L   Lotería. Lotería Nacional de Beneficencia. Panamá.

MAGN/B   Boletín del Archivo General de la Nación. Secretaría de Gobernación. México.

MAN   Mensário do Arquivo Nacional. Ministério da Justiça, Arquivo Nacional, Editoração e Expediente, Divisão de Publicações. Rio de Janeiro.

NMC/N   Nicaráuac. Revista bimestral del Ministerio de Cultura. Managua.

NOSALF/IA   Ibero Americana. Scandinavian Association for Research on Latin America (NOSALF). Stockholm.

NS   NS NorthSouth NordSud NorteSur NorteSul. Canadian journal of Latin American studies. Canadian Association of Latin American Studies, University of Ottawa. Ottawa.

PAIGH/H   Revista de Historia de América. Instituto Panamericano de Geografía e Historia, Comisión de Historia. México.

PAN/ES Estudios Latinoamericanos. Polska Akademia Nauk [Academia de Ciencias de Polonia], Instytut Historii [Instituto de Historia]. Warszawa.

PCCLAS/P Proceedings of the Pacific Coast Council on Latin American Studies. University of California. Los Angeles.

PEMN/R Revista del Museo Nacional. Casa de la Cultura del Perú, Museo Nacional de la Cultura Peruana. Lima.

PF/AIA Archivo Ibero-Americano. Los Padres Franciscanos. Madrid.

PMNH/HC Historia y Cultura. Museo Nacional de Historia. Lima.

PP Past and Present. London.

PUC/H Humanidades. Pontificia Universidad Católica del Perú, Facultad de Letras. Lima.

PUC/V Veritas. Revista. Pontifícia Universidade Católica do Rio Grande do Sul. Pôrto Alegre.

PUCP/DA Debates en Antropología. Pontificia Universidad Católica del Perú, Departamento de Ciencias Sociales. Lima.

PUCP/H Histórica. Pontificia Universidad Católica del Perú, Departamento de Humanidades. Lima.

PUF/RH Revue Historique. Presses Universitaires de France. Paris.

QS Quaderni Storici. Istituzioni agrarie nel decollo industriale. Facoltà di Economia e Commercio, Istituto di Storia e Sociologia. Ancona, Italy.

RCLL Revista de Crítica Literaria Latinoamericana. Latinoamericana Editores. Lima.

RCPC Revista del Pensamiento Centroamericano. Centro de Investigaciones y Actividades Culturales. Managua.

RIB Revista Interamericana de Bibliografía [Inter-American Review of Bibliography]. Organization of American States. Washington.

RO Revista de Occidente. Madrid.

RUC Revista de la Universidad Complutense. Madrid.

SAGE/JIAS Journal of Inter-American Studies and World Affairs. Sage Publications *for*

the Center for Advanced International Studies, University of Miami. Coral Gables, Fla.

SCHG/R Revista Chilena de Historia y Geografía. Sociedad Chilena de Historia y Geografía. Santiago.

SGHG/A Anales de la Sociedad de Geografía e Historia de Guatemala. Guatemala.

SHG/B Bulletin de la Société d'Histoire de la Guadeloupe. Archives départamentales *avec le concours du* Conseil général de la Guadeloupe. Basse-Terre, West Indies.

SHM/RHM Revista de Historia Militar. Servicio Histórico Militar. Madrid.

SJUG Saeculum. Jahrbuch für Universalgeschichte. München, FRG.

SMHN/R Revista de la Sociedad Mexicana de Historia Natural. México.

SS Science and Society. New York.

TEMBRAS Tempo Brasileiro. Revista de cultura. Rio de Janeiro.

UA Urban Anthropology. State University of New York, Department of Anthropology. Brockport.

UA/AW Arizona and the West. University of Arizona. Tucson.

UB/BA Boletín Americanista. Universidad de Barcelona, Facultad de Geografía e Historia, Departamento de Historia de América. Barcelona.

UBN/R Revista de la Biblioteca Nacional. Ministerio de Educación y Cultura. Montevideo.

UC/AT Atenea. Revista de ciencias, letras y artes. Universidad de Concepción. Concepción, Chile.

UC/PHR The Pacific Historical Review. University of California Press. Los Angeles.

UCCIH/H Historia. Universidad Católica de Chile, Instituto de Historia. Santiago.

UCLA/JLAL Journal of Latin American Lore. University of California, Latin American Center. Los Angeles.

UCLV/I Islas. Universidad Central de las Villas. Santa Clara, Cuba.

UCNSA/EP Estudios Paraguayos. Universidad Católica de Nuestra Señora de la Asunción. Asunción.

UCNSA/SA Suplemento Antropológico. Universidad Católica de Nuestra Señora de la Asunción, Centro de Estudios Antropológicos. Asunción.

UCPR/H Horizontes. Revista de la Universidad Católica de Puerto Rico. Ponce.

UCSD/NS The New Scholar. University of California, Center for Iberian and Latin American Studies [and] Institute of Chicano Urbano Affairs. San Diego.

UFB/EB Estudos Baianos. Universidade Federal da Bahia, Centro Editorial e Didático, Núcleo de Publicações. Bahia, Brazil.

UFSI/R UFSI Reports. Universities Field Staff International, Inc. Hanover, N.H.

UJSC/ECA ECA: Estudios Centroamericanos. Revista de extensión cultural. Universidad Centroamericana José Simeón Cañas. San Salvador.

UM/JIAS Journal of Inter-American Studies and World Affairs. University of Miami Press *for the* Center for Advanced International Studies. Coral Cables.

UM/REAA Revista Española de Antropología Americana: Trabajos y Conferencias. Universidad de Madrid, Facultad de Filosofía y Letras, Departamento de Antropología y Etnología de América. Madrid.

UMG/RBEP Revista Brasileira de Estudos Políticos. Universidade de Minas Gerais. Belo Horizonte.

UNAM/AA Anales de Antropología. Universidad Nacional Autónoma de México, Instituto de Investigaciones Históricas. México.

UNAM/ECN Estudios de Cultura Náhuatl. Universidad Nacional Autónoma de México, Instituto de Historia, Seminario de Cultura Náhuatl. México.

UNAM/L Latinoamérica. Anuario de estudios latinoamericanos. Universidad Nacional Autónoma de México, Facultad de Filosofía y Letras, Centro de Estudios Latinoamericanos. México.

UNAM/RMS Revista Mexicana de Sociología. Universidad Nacional Autónoma de México, Instituto de Investigaciones Sociales. México.

UNC/RHAA Revista de Historia Americana y Argentina. Universidad Nacional de Cuyo, Facultad de Filosofía y Letras, Instituto de Historia. Mendoza, Argentina.

UNC/R Revista de la Universidad Nacional de Córdoba. Córdoba, Argentina.

UNCR/R Revista de Historia. Universidad Nacional de Costa Rica, Escuela de Historia. Heredia.

UND/RP The Review of Politics. University of Notre Dame. Notre Dame, Ind.

UNESCO/CU Cultures. UNESCO. Paris.

UNL/H Humanitas. Universidad de Nuevo León, Centro de Estudios Humanísticos. Monterrey, México.

UNL/U Universidad. Universidad Nacional del Litoral. Santa Fe, Argentina.

UNM/NMHR New Mexico Historical Review. University of New Mexico [and] Historical Society of New Mexico. Albuquerque.

UNS/CS Cuadernos del Sur. Universidad Nacional del Sur. Instituto de Humanidades. Bahía Blanca, Argentina.

UO/R Revista de la Universidad de Oriente. Santiago, Cuba.

UP/A Apuntes. Universidad del Pacífico, Centro de Investigación. Lima.

UP/CSEC Cuban Studies/Estudios Cubanos. University of Pittsburgh, University Center for International Studies, Center for Latin American Studies. Pittsburgh, Pa.

UP/EA Estudios Andinos. University of Pittsburgh, Latin American Studies Center. Pittsburgh, Pa.

UP/LAIL Latin American Indian Literatures. A new review of American Indian texts and studies. University of Pittsburgh, Department of Hispanic Languages and Literatures. Pittsburgh, Pa.

UP/PSN Peasant Studies Newsletter. University of Pittsburgh, Center for International Studies [and] Department of History. Pittsburgh, Pa.

UPR/CS Caribbean Studies. University of Puerto Rico, Institute of Caribbean Studies. Río Piedras.

UPR/RCS Revista de Ciencias Sociales. Universidad de Puerto Rico, Colegio de Ciencias Sociales. Río Piedras.

UR/L Lateinamerika. Universität Rostock. Rostock, FRG.

URSS/AL América Latina. Academia de Ciencias de la Unión de Repúblicas Soviéticas Socialistas. Moscú.

USP/RA Revista de Antropología. Universidade de São Paulo, Faculdade de Filosofia, Letras e Ciências Humanas [and] Associação Brasileira de Antropologia. São Paulo.

USP/RIEB Revista do Instituto de Estudos Brasileiros. Universidad de São Paulo, Instituto de Estudos Brasileiros. São Paulo.

UTIEH/C Caravelle. Cahiers du monde hispanique et luso-brésilien. Université de Toulouse, Institute d'études hispaniques, hispano-américaines et luso-brésiliennes. Toulouse, France.

UV/PH La Palabra y el Hombre. Universidad Veracruzana. Xalapa, México.

UW/LBR Luso-Brazilian Review. University of Wisconsin Press. Madison.

UWI/JCH The Journal of Caribbean History. University of the West Indies, Department of History [and] Caribbean Universities Press. St. Lawrence, Barbados.

UY/R Revista de la Universidad de Yucatán. Mérida, México.

VANH/B Boletín de la Academia Nacional de la Historia. Caracas.

VOZES Vozes. Revista de cultura. Editora Vozes. Petrópolis, Brazil.

WHQ The Western Historical Quarterly. Western History Association, Utah State University. Logan.

ZRP Zeitschrift für Romanische Philologie. Tübingen, FRG.

LANGUAGE

D. LINCOLN CANFIELD, *Professor Emeritus of Spanish, Southern Illinois University*

SEVERAL NAMES FIGURE PROMINENTLY and often in the literature on language phenomena in Latin America. The outstanding of these designations is the Instituto Caro y Cuervo (ICC), Bogotá, Colombia, another is that of the Mexican linguist, editor and organizer, Juan M. Lope Blanch, and the third is María Beatriz Fontanella de Weinberg of Argentina.

The completion of the six-volume *Atlas lingüístico-etnográfico de Colombia* (ALEC), has elicited several articles, some of them by people who took part in the planning, field work, and writing of this task of nearly 30 years (items **4530, 4533, 4542, 4550,** and **4551**). Also, one should note that vol. 1 of what promises to be an excellent tool for Americanists came off the presses of the Imprenta Patriótica of the Instituto Caro y Cuervo (item **4504**). Moreover, a former ICC student has given us a good study of the Spanish of Tucumán, Argentina (item **4554**).

The name of Juan M. Lope Blanch is associated with the *Proyecto de estudio coordinado de la norma lingüística culta de las principales ciudades de Iberoamérica y de la Península Ibérica* (items **4538** and **4543**), which he initiated in 1964 (see *HLAS 34:3099* and *HLAS 42:4537*), and several parts of which have been done. He contributes, too, as a writer (items **4514, 4540,** and **4585**).

Fontanella continues apace her valuable work in the sociolinguistic aspects of *porteño* Spanish (items **4531** and **4532**), and Eugenio Chang-Rodríquez (item **4555**) and Gary Scavnicky (item **4527**) have been able to bring together the efforts of several dialectologists.

Several Spanish glossaries of a special lexicon have appeared: highway vocabulary, communication terms, the terminology of centers of human habitation, demographic and juridical vocabularies.

In the Portuguese of Brazil the interest in the production of technical vocabularies continues (items **4609, 4610,** and **4612**), but Brazilian scholars are now also doing very good work in linguistic geography (items **4603a** and **4605**).

There are studies on Creole of Haiti and on the English of Jamaica which examine the intriguing relation between pidgins and code-switching.

Two Ph.D. dissertations should be mentioned: Rosa María Sanou de los Ríos' *Variación sociolingüística en el español de la ciudad de San Juan, Argentina* (University of New Mexico, Garland Bills); Pedro Escamilla's *A sociolinguistic study of modal selection among Mexican American college students in Texas* (University of Texas, Carlos A. Solé).

SPANISH
GENERAL AND BIBLIOGRAPHY

4501 Alvarez Nazario, Manuel. El castellano
de los conquistadores y primitivos
vecinos españoles de Puerto Rico (ICP/R,
21:81, oct./dic. 1978, p. 13–19)
Once-over of the development of
Island's Spanish in terms of indigenous substratum, Peninsular origins of settlers, military and maritime lexicon and *arcaísmos*.

4502 ———. Visión en el tiempo de los trabajos de enseñanza e investigación del
español en Puerto Rico (UPR/LT, 24:93/94,
julio/dic. 1976 [i.e. 1981] p. 39–65)
Traces origins of Island's Spanish, educators' perception of it in 19th and early 20th
centuries, and how it fares in judicial system
under US aegis. Nineteenth- and 20th-
century educators promoted pronunciation
that emulated Northern Spain. This reviewer
recalls 1920s Puerto Rican students who read
Spanish with a distinction between /θ/ and
/s/ as well as between *ll* and *y*.

4503 Delgado Cintrón, Carmelo. Pensamiento jurídico e idioma en Puerto
Rico: un problema ético, jurídico y lingüístico (UPR/LT, 24:91/92, enero/junio
1976 [i.e. 1981] p. 103–124)
Writer describes results of imposition
of American judicial system in Puerto Rico:
"un ordenamiento jurídico híbrido," and US
district Court for District of Puerto Rico that
carries on in English!

4504 El Español de América. v. 1, pts. 1–2.
Coordinador, Marius Sala. Bogotá: Instituto Caro y Cuervo, 1982. 2 v. (Publicaciones; 60)
Publication destined to be one of the
best tools for researchers in Latin American
studies. Vol. 1 (lexicon) in two tomes to be
followed by vol. 2 (phonology and morphosyntactic phenomena). Lexical information is
much more detailed than in previous dictionaries of American Spanish or regional vocabularies. Compilers use system of symbols
to indicate entries that are not in Academy's
Dictionary, to head list of derivatives, to
separate DRAE definitions from others not
listed by Academy. With each entry, reference
is made to other sources (e.g., Santamaría,
Diccionario de americanismos); geographical
distribution previously recognized and also

newly discovered; productivity in terms of
derivatives; semantic wealth. Perhaps dictionary's most unusual feature is long series
of analyses of elements of non-Spanish origin: Indigenous, English, French, Italian, African, Portuguese, and German. Hundreds of
pages are devoted to these in terms of *di-
astrático, etimológico, onomasiológico*. It
will be interesting to see how writers handle
phonology and morphology.

4505 Filgueira Alvarado, Alejandro. Capacidad intelectual y actitud del indio
ante el castellano (IGFO/RI, 39:155/158,
enero/dic. 1979, p. 163–185)
Although there are bits of information
on interrelations of Spaniard (later *criollo*)
and Indian in realms of economics, law, political life, etc., our knowledge of colonial society has not advanced much, nor has our
understanding of circumstances of acculturation and *castellanización* of Indian. Suggests
that perhaps serious study of this acculturation will incidentally reveal Indian's capacity
and attitude toward this.

4506 Fontanella de Weinberg, María Beatriz.
La asimilación lingüística de los inmigrantes: mantenimiento y cambio de
lengua en el sudoeste boanerense. Bahía
Blanca, Argentina: Universidad Nacional del
Sur, Departamento de Ciencias Sociales,
1979. 93 p.: bibl., tables.
Uses language choice after period of
residence in order to measure assimilation
into the community. Examines matter both
diachronically and synchronically. Apparently at turn of century there was much
multilingüismo, now very little. Among
many non-Hispanics who entered Argentina,
Italians were fastest to assimilate, Russians
and Germans slowest. For sociologist's comment, see *HLAS 45:8317*.

4507 Kubarth, Hugo. Probleme und perspektiven der dialektologie Lateinamerika
(Iberoromania [Max Niemeyer, Verlag, Tübingen, FRG] 16, 1982, p. 23–37)
German review of literature on development of American Spanish. Sources not
quite up-to-date.

4508 León Rivera, Jorge de. Obra poética en
Náhuatl de Santos Acevedo López
(UNAM/ECN, 15, 1982, p. 237–245)
Shows how quickly after conquest
nahuatlatos (speakers of Aztec and Spanish)

were developed and appreciated. "Defenders" of the Indian sent back to Spain samples of their work as proof of their skill and intelligence.

4509 Lingüística. Medellín: Centro de Documentación, Departamento de Bibliotecas de la Universidad de Antioquia, 1979. 29 p. (Serie Bibliografías especializadas; no. 13)

No. 13 of monographic series, *Bibliografía especializada*. Contains 58 entries under categories such as "Americanismos," "Semántica," "Inglés-Español."

4510 López Iñiguez, Iraida. Bibliografía comentada de estudios lingüísticos en Cuba; 1959–1979 (UP/CSEC, 13:1, Winter 1983, p. 41–68, bibl.)

Considers only linguistic studies published in Cuba during 21-year period, 207 items in all, 132 of which were written by nationals. Maintains that Cuban linguistic research is in embryonic state, that not until 1977–80, was much done in phonology and morphosyntactics. Shows, incidentally, strong influence of Eastern European scholars. Reviews books and articles by linguistic categories (e.g., fonología) and within divisions: "General," "Hispanic," "Non-Hispanic," "Applied," and "Spanish of Cuba."

4511 Menéndez Díaz, Conrado. Origen y evolución del idioma español (UY/R, 24:141/142, mayo/agosto 1982, p. 112–121)

Very good once-over of history of Spanish language. Although somewhat weak on phonological development, history of lexical origins is well done: Latin, Arabic, Náhuatl, especially.

4512 Obregón, Hugo and **Annerys Pérez.** Algunas observaciones metodológicas sobre el análisis científico del habla televisiva (Letras [Instituto Universitario Pedagógico de Caracas] 38/39, 1982, p. 5–13, bibl.)

Admitting TV's responsibility in Venezuela's educational development, writers examine linguistically different approaches to standards of language use according to type of program. Conclusion: there is room for criticism, especially in *telenovelas*.

4513 Osborne, F. and **S. Rojas.** Glosario poético. S.l.: s.n., 1980. 53, 5, 4 p.: appendix.

One of the best combinations of terminology for Spanish syllable-based system of classification and the Latin "foot" system. Appendix has good examples of each in separate sections.

4514 Perspectivas de la investigación lingüística en Hispanoamérica: memoria. Papers presented at a colloquium held 6/18–22/79, organized by the Centro de Lingüística Hispánica. Editor, Juan M. Lope Blanch. Antonio Quilis *et al.* México: Centro de Lingüística Hispánica, Instituto de Investigaciones Filológicas, Universidad Nacional Autónoma de México, 1980. 140 p.: bibl., ill. (Publicaciones del Centro; 12)

UNAM's 50th anniversary colloquium was attended by Mexican and foreign linguists who answered: "¿Cuáles son las directrices de las investigaciones?" Contributions edited by Lope Blanch, Director of Centro de Lingüística Hispánica, were: Antonio Quilis on perspectives in phonological research; Yolanda Lastra and Jorge Suárez on interference in contact of Amerindian languages and Spanish; Edward L. Bansitt on perspectives on research in syntactic phenomena in Spanish and Indian languages; Humberto López Morales on future of sociolinguistic research in Spanish, with good discussion of beliefs and attitudes; Manuel Alvar on future of linguistic geography; Tomás Buesa Oliver and Guillermo L. Guitarte on diachronic works. Conclusion: that *Estudio coordinado de la norma lingüística culta de las principales ciudades de Hispanoamérica y de la Península Ibérica* (See *HLAS 34:3099* and *HLAS 42:4537*) should be expedited, and that studies on intonation and sociolinguistic variants should be encouraged.

4515 Teachers of English to Speakers of Other Languages (TESOL). The acquisition and use of Spanish and English as first and second languages: selected papers from the twelfth annual convention of Teachers of English to Speakers of Other Languages, Mexico City, April 4–9, 1978. Edited by Roger W. Anderson. Washington: TESOL, 1979. 181 p.: bibl.

Selected papers from this convention (e.g., acquisition and use of English by speakers of Spanish; acquisition and use of Spanish by speakers of English; Spanish and English in bilingual communities). Contains several good suggestions on "immersion" devices, code-switching, pidginization.

SPANISH
PHONOLOGY AND GRAMMAR

4516 Godínez, Manuel, Jr. An acoustic study of Mexican and Brazilian Portuguese vowels (AATSP/H, 64, 1981, p. 594–600)

Further evidence that traditional tongue-arching model of vowel production, although neat on paper, may not be entirely accurate. Researcher uses spectrographic analysis of informants from Tijuana (México) and São Paulo and Rio (Brazil) to depict plotted frequencies in drawings. Portuguese system seems to overlap more than the Spanish.

4517 Perissinotto, Giorgio. Spanish *hombre*: generic or specific? (AATSP/H, 66, 1983, p. 581–586)

Using sentence, "Adulterers are treated with leniency by the law," author describes scarcity of research on language by and about women, and uses 140 UNAM informants to test semantics of utterance such as *todo hombre tiene derecho* . . . Finds case for generic masculine rather weak in Mexican Spanish; "specific" interpretation, very common.

SPANISH
DIALECTOLOGY

4518 Academia Nacional de Letras. Selección de paremias. Montevideo: La Academia, 1981. 199 p.: bibl., index (Biblioteca. Serie II, Vocabularios)

Carefully documented study of some 300 *dichos criollos* of 3000 that were originally collected. The documention of each saying includes area of usage, its origin, whether it is still heard or not, whether it is urban or *campesino*. All idioms that figure in the Academy Dictionary were discarded. Index is topical.

4519 Amaro Gamboa, Jesús. El uayeísmo en la cultura de Yucatán (UY/R, 140:24, marzo/abril 1982, p. 123–144)

Defines task of establishing Yucatecan identity (see *HLAS 44:4524*) as *uayeísmo*. Also says that indígenas of Mexico must "untribe" themselves, becoming free of leaders, anthropologists, Indian bureaucrats, and without ceasing to be Indians, enter category of Mexican citizens.

4520 ———. Vocabulario del uayeísmo en la cultura de Yucatán: continuación (UY/R, 24:140, marzo/abril 1982, p. 145–161; 24:141, mayo/agosto 1982, p. 129–150; 24:144, nov./dic. 1982, p. 125–152)

Three additional contributions to author's continuing study of Yucatecan expressions (see item **4519** and *HLAS 44:4524*).

4521 Arrom, José Juan. Estudios de lexicología antillana. La Habana: Casa de las Américas, 1980. 167 p.: bibl., index (Colección Investigaciones)

Little volume traces origins of several non-Hispanic Caribbean terms (e.g., *Cuba*, from Arawakan *Kuba-annaken* meaning "in the middle of the island;" *chévere* from elegant Flemish member of Charles V's court). Believes African influence in Antilles' vocabulary has been exaggerated.

4522 Barreto Peña, Samuel. Modismos y barbarismos trujillanos. Caracas: Santino Distribuidora Escolar, 1980. 160 p.: port.

Deals with idiomatic usage of conservative mountain region of western Venezuela. As in many works of this type, classifies as *venezolanismos* terms that are heard in several parts of Spanish America.

4523 Capparelli, Vicente Alberto. Recopilación de voces del lunfardo: de lo sórdido, de lo popular y del reo. Buenos Aires: Corregidor, 1980. 152 p.: bibl. (Serie mayor)

Often discussed jargon of *antisociales* of Buenos Aires area is described by one who had many contacts with them—a former policeman. Favorite device used by lunfardo speakers is extended semantic permutation, *abanicarse* (to flee), for instance. Another is transposition of syllables, *vesre* (revés). Among foreign words used, Italianisms rank first.

4524 Cárdenas A., Renato and **Carlos Alberto Trujillo A.** Apuntes para un diccionario de Chiloé. Castro, Chile: Ediciones Aumen, 1978. 95 p.: bibl.

Vocabulary first appeared 1976 (mimeo), "para dotar a Chiloé de un verdadero manual lingüístico," and to record obsolete words, *toponimia, flora y fauna*. Includes discussion of island's Spanish dialect and, like many books of this type, attributes to Indian influence (i.e., Mapuche) phonological traits that are found elsewhere in Spanish America. Still, vocabulary does have many Indian influences.

4525 Costa Sánchez, Manuel and **Susana Carrera Gómez.** Realización de la *n* velar en el español de Cuba (UCLV/I, 71, enero/abril 1982, p. 179–189, ill.)

Part of series on *consonantismo* of Cuban Spanish. Uses three informants and spectrographic analysis of their speech. Finds that /n/ tends to be velar not only final word before pause or vowel in following word, but before /c, r, t, f, d, m/. Approach to problem appears sound, but background reading is lacking.

4526 Cuestionario para delimitar las áreas dilectales de Venezuela. Caracas: Centro de Investigaciones Lingüísticas y Literarias Andrés Bello, 1979. 63 p., 6 p. of plates: ill.

Rather "neat" instrument for notation of dialectal variants in phonology and lexicon. Authors recommend giving up morphosyntaxis because informants tend to respond positively to all questions, something that seems quite typical of Spanish-speaking people to this writer. The *Material de apoyo para la aplicación del cuestionario* is a set of drawings designed to elicit lexical and phonological responses. One interesting set of lexical variants is: *trepar un árbol; montar un palo; monear una mata*.

4527 Dialectología hispanoamericana: estudios actuales. Gary E. Scavnicky, editor. R.M. Hammond *et al.* Washington: Georgetown University Press, 1980. 127 p.

Fine collection of investigation into trends in Spanish American dialectology: Editor reviews contemporary work; R.M. Hammond describes allophonic manifestations of /s/ in Miami's rapid Cuban Spanish; B. Saciuk writes of phonetic manifstations of /y/ in Caribbean, and finds that *puertorriqueño* has more variants than Cuban; J. M. Guitart examines aspects of Havana's *consonantismo*, and reexamines misconceptions; K.H. Kvavik describes melodic units of Mexican Spanish (probably first inventory of

Mexican *formas intonativas*, illustrating how complex matter is); N. Gutiérrez writes on Quechua influence on Cochabamba, Bolivia Spanish); J. J. Staczek examines Bogotá *gamín* street-urchin jargon (same devices of *Caló*, underworld argot such as syllable inversion, i.e., *fercho* [chofer]; *feje* [jefe]); S.T. Becerra writes of implosive consonants in Cartagena's urban dialect, and finds dialect close to *andaluz*; L.A. Grace draws from Mexican 16th-century sources, to show how many *indigenismos* were used by mestizo speakers of both languages (*naguatlatos*).

4528 Estudios sobre el español del Uruguay. Adolfo Elizaincín, compilador. María Cristina Azqueta *et al.* Montevideo: Universidad de la República, Facultad de Humanidades y Ciencias, Dirección General de Extensión Universitaria, División de Publicaciones y Ediciones, 1981. 1 v.: bibl., ill.

Compilation of articles on sociolinguistic phenomena in Uruguay's Spanish. Includes seven articles that fill void on: *voseo* (*voceo* in index) in gaucho literature; use of preposition *a* with complement; verb forms used with second-person subject in Montevideo; middle-class treatment of clitic and object; duplicity of objects, *tuteo* and *voseo* (*voceo* in index) in Montevideo Spanish: *tú cantas, tú cantás, vos cantás*; and interesting study in semantics: *color de los caballos* in rural southeast Uruguay.

4529 Fernández, Roberto G. English loanwords in Miami Cuban Spanish (MS, 58:1, Spring 1983, p. 13–19)

In 20 years plus since major Cuban exodus, Miami Spanish has become Spanglish lexically and syntactically among many speakers, especially the young. Uses books, papers, recordings, conversations, radio, and TV to study languages in contact. Finds that there are loan shifts, hybrid creations, hybrid compounds, and loan translations, called by Kany (*American Spanish Semantics*) correlative analogy (e.g., *mandar pa tra*: send back; *afordear; cortar clases; no hay escuela, fuera de orden*: out of order; *algo foni*).

4530 Figueroa Lorza, Jennie. Léxico de la vivienda y el vestido en algunas regiones de Colombia (ICC/NC, 2:6, mayo/junio 1983, ill.)

Summarizes and reviews ALEC's vol. 4's lexical variation of country in realms of clothing and home and its equipment. Accompanied by fine testimony by Luis Flórez of his valuable work during years of *encuestas*. Headings: "Prendas para Abrigarse," "Vivienda desde Fuera para Adentro," etc.

4531 Fontanella de Weinberg, María Beatriz. Adquisición fonológica en español bonaerense. Bahía Blanca, Argentina: Universidad Nacional del Sur, Departamento de Humanidades, 1981. 441 p.: bibl., tables.

Using language behavior of her own son, tracing his sound acquisition from 23 March 1979 until late March 1980, to produce good research. Describes evolution of his consonantal system, vowels, structure of words and strategies of learning. Charts show sequences of learning: /a/ is first vowel and /m/ and /n/ are first consonants. Child develops what she calls a *sonido-comidín* (joker for cards that he doesn't have!). Useful contribution to investigation of universals.

————. La asimilación lingüística de los inmigrantes: mantenimiento y cambio de lengua en el sudoeste bonaerense. See *HLAS 45:8317*.

4532 ————. Habla aniñada en el español bonaerense: Bahía Blanca, Argentina (UC/BF, 1980/1981, 31, p. 647–665, bibl.)

Based on Charles Ferguson's "Baby Talk in Six Languages" (1964), writer produces very good study of speech of adults who speak to her own son from birth until 15 months. Finds that people have two guiding principles when addressing her son: 1) endearment; and 2) saying something child can imitate better than adult talk. Notes how men and women differ in this. Common traits seem to be lack of copulative verbs, palatalization [edmóšo] instead of *hermoso*, simplification of diphthongs (*tienes* becomes *tenes*), use of many diminutives, and avoidance of /r/.

4533 Gómez Latorre, Armando. Galardones culturales: *Atlas lingüístico-etnográfico de Colombia* (ICC/NC, 2:10, enero/feb. 1984, p. 23)

Describes ca. 30-year effort to bring forth first *Atlas* of this type in Spanish America. Final vol. 6 completed in 1983. *Atlas* describes speech and customs of 262 Colombian localities, providing authentic picture of country's speech with hundreds of maps, drawings, photographs, designs. De-

picts regional idioms, sayings, dialectal lexicon of what writer calls Colombia's *atormentada geografía*. Credit: Project Director Luis Flórez and dedicated crew of researchers; Directors José Manuel Rivas Sacconi and Rafael Torres Quintero.

4534 Granda, Germán de. Condicionamientos históricos de un fenómeno lingüístico: léxico de origen militar en el español del Paraguay (IGFO/RI, 39:155/158, enero/dic. 1979, p. 297–325)

Finds proof in Paraguay of many cases of military terminology that entered American Spanish lexicon: *campaña* (rural area); *retreta* (open-air concert); *desertor* (a peon); *ranchero* (food preparer); *rancho* (food). One often hears in southern Mexico *disparar* meaning "to dish out." Maritime influence on American Spanish is now common knowledge: *amarrar, virar*, etc.

4535 Guitart, Jorge M. En torno a la sílaba como entidad fonemática en los dialectos del Caribe hispánico (ICC/T, 36:3, sept./dic. 1981, p. 457–463)

Believes that typical Caribbean aspiration of -/s/, velarization of /n/, lambdecism of syllable-final /r/ do not occur because they are at end of syllable, but because they are in contact with other segments or are on word border, as author says. His examples of consonantal simplification, however, are clusters (*palabras cultas*) that are really not "native" to Spanish: *obstáculo, extraño, instituto*.

4536 Gutiérrez Eskildsen, Rosario María. Cómo hablamos en Tabasco y otros trabajos. México: Consejo Editorial del Gobierno del Estado de Tabasco, 1981. 192 p. (Cuadernos del Consejo Editorial; 6)

Although author's investigations go back to 1930s and 1940s, early material is not available. This little volume includes many efforts before and after she received her 1944 UNAM doctorate. Interesting to see how certain misconceptions have been cleared up by work of North American scholars, especially with relation to origins of American Spanish.

4537 ————. Sustrato y superestrato del español de Tabasco. México: Consejo Editorial del Estado de Tabasco, 1978. 126 p.: bibl., ill., maps (Serie Lingüísica; 3)

First ed. of 1944 doctoral thesis of well known Tabasco linguist. Deals with substratum influence on Spanish, chiefly Chontal. Methods she used in 1930s were ahead of her time, especially in described relation between language traits and area's demographic conditions. However, her assignment of Tabasco *voseo* (now practically gone) to Chontal influence, indicates little reading in history of Spanish from Latin.

4538 El Habla culta de Santiago de Chile: materiales para su estudio. Ambrosio Rabanales y Lidia Contreras, editors. Santiago: Universidad de Chile, Facultad de Filosofía y Letras, Departamento de Lingüística y Filología, 1979. 1 v. (*Boletín de Filología*; 0067–9674. Anexo; no. 2)

Another contribution to *Proyecto de estudio coordinado de la norma lingüística culta del español hablado en las principales ciudades de Iberoamérica y de la Península Ibérica* (see *HLAS 34:3099*; *HLAS 36:3847*; *HLAS 42:4537* and *4562*; and item **4543** in this volume). Study's informants range in age from 25 to 74, and there are 30 *muestras*. Recordings were made in four situations: 1) secret; 2) not secret; 3) directed dialogue; 4) free dialogue. Recorded lectures in next volume.

4539 Henríquez Ureña, Pedro. El español en Santo Domingo. 3a. ed. Santo Domingo: Editora Taller, 1978. 301 p.: bibl., indexes (Biblioteca Taller)

Landmark of early Spanish American dialectology (1940). Very rich in details, but modern works show more accuracy in notation, especially phonology (see *HLAS 42:4551–4552*).

4540 Lope Blanch, Juan M. Sobre la influencia fonética maya en el español de Yucatán (ICC/T, 36:3, sept./dic. 1981, p. 413–428)

Evidence resulting from *encuestas* made in Chetumal, Valladolid, Tizimín, Mérida, Ticul, and Campeche. Aside from previously reported glottalization, article reports considerable occurrence of occlusive articulation of /b,d,g/ and final /n/ as m, and a retroflex /r/ (see *HLAS 44:4567*).

4541 López Morales, Humberto. Estudio de la competencia sociolingüística: los probabilísticos (Revista Española de Lingüística [Editorial Gredos, Madrid] 11:2, julio/dic. 1981, p. 247–268)

Shows almost infinite variation in distribution of -/r/, and although phonetic context may be a factor, Cuban author says most are extralinguistic: age, sex, social level.

4542 Lozano Ramírez, Máximo. Del español hablado en Casanare (ICC/NC, 2:8, sept./oct. 1983, p. 6–8)

Survey, made in 1976 in Trinidad, Orocué and Maní (Colombia), shows many surnames of Indian origin, and pronunciation very similar to that of coastal areas: an /s/ that tends to be "ceceosa" and aspirated at end of a syllable, and the use of *mirar* for *ver* (*No lo he mirao*).

4543 Luna Traill, Elizabeth. Sintaxis de los verboides en el habla culta de la Ciudad de México. México: Instituto de Investigaciones Filológicas, Universidad Nacional Autónoma de México, 1980. 246 p.: bibl., ill. (Estudio coordinado de la norma lingüística culta de la Ciudad de México. Segunda parte, tomo V, El Verbo. Publicaciones del Centro de Lingüística Hispánica; 8)

Part of ambitious project initiated 1964 by Juan M. Lope Blanch: *Proyecto de estudio coordinado de la norma lingüística culta de las principales ciudades de Iberoamérica y de la Península Ibérica* (see *HLAS 34:3099*; *HLAS 36:3847*; *HLAS 42:4537* and *4562*; and item **4538** in this volume). Syntactic study based on 46 surveys, with 61 informants of university level or better, all over 25. Four types of *encuesta* were made: 1) spontaneous dialogues; 2) arranged dialogues; 3) dialogue with researcher; and 4) formal lectures. Analysis of corpus made on basis of parts of speech.

4544 Mántica, Carlos. Diccionario de nahualismos nicaragüenses (RCPC, 37:174, enero/marzo 1982, p. 47–86)

Extensive and useful vocabulary of terms brought to Central America after Spanish conquest for most part, although Indians of Uto-Aztecan family did occupy part of what is now Nicaragua and El Salvador. Surprising number of words listed by Mántica are identical to those used in El Salvador under same circumstances.

4545 ———. Introducción a la obra *Lengua Madre* de César A. Ramírez Fajardo (RCPC, 37:174, enero/marzo 1982, p. 126–129)

Considers Ramírez's "Frases que se Escuchan en la Consulta Externa de Pediatría," richest contemporary document of Nicaraguan speech. Evaluates Hispanic expression generally: "Lo primero que salta a la vista es que el nicaragüense no se expresa mediante conceptos, sino mediante imágenes. No define, sino que ilustra." Speaker has five *pinceles*: simile, metaphor, onomatopeya, invention, and gesture. Examples: "El cansancio se le destierra por un día y luego le vuelve;" "Es una tos que hasta que parece carrizo cuando suena."

4546 ———. Morfología del habla nicaragüense (RCPC, 37 : 174, enero/marzo 1982, p. 25–46)

Good list of common nicknames is part of good study of suffixes and popular expressions. Most interesting is description of habit that Mántica calls *comosellamear*: use of nonsense terms to fill lapses in memory of terminology (e.g. "El turulo que se le cayó a la carambada del planchador;" to indicate relative distance, "Ay nomasito" as opposed to, "Por el culo del mundo").

4547 ———. Orígenes y desarrollo del habla nicaragüense (RCPC, 37 : 174, enero/marzo 1982, p. 14–24)

Makes two important points: 1) that conquistador had also been conquered, and that he brought many cultural vestiges of coexistence with Semitic peoples; and 2) that several area Indian languages were replaced by Náhuatl, when in early 16th century Spaniards came with Aztec army.

4548 ———. Toponimias nahuatl de Nicaragua (RCPC, 37 : 174, enero/marzo 1982, p. 87–125, ill.)

Very well documented explanation of origins of Nicaragua's place names. Notes many go back only to 16th century, when Spaniards moved in with Náhuatl army. Same phenomenon is evident in southern Mexico, where Aztec was never spoken by residents. Oaxaca, an Aztec word, is in midst of Zapoteca territory!

4549 Mellado de Hunter, Elena. Anglicismos profesionales en Puerto Rico. Río Piedras: Editorial Universitaria, Universidad de Puerto Rico, 1981. 204 p.: bibl. (Colección Mente y palabra)

Up-date of 1961 work, with much more 1978 data. Interviews with 50 subjects (10 each from medicine, odontology, engineering, law, and education) reveals extent of

English penetration which is very objectively discussed. Combining occasional and frequent use of English terms, profession that uses them most: engineering; least: teaching. Excellent bibliography.

4550 Montes Giraldo, José Joaquín. El español de Colombia: propuesta de clasificación dialectal (ICC/T, 37 : 1, enero/abril 1982, p. 23–92)

Eternal question of dialect demarcation within geographical or political unit is always difficult, as is actual distinction between language and dialect. Colombia with three *cordilleras* has many manifestations of Spanish. Easiest division is *cachaco* and *costeño* (interior and coast). Now that *Atlas lingüístico-etnográfico de Colombia* has been completed (for related material, see items **4530, 4533, 4542, 4550,** and **4551**), bases for classification will be clearer. One of most involved in ALEC's 20-year project, author makes zones and sub-zones based on phonological and morphological traits. Good bibliography and 36 maps from ALEC.

4551 ———. Sobre el sintagma "haber + sustantivo" (ICC/T, 37 : 2, mayo/agosto 1982, p. 383–385)

Based on data from new *Atlas lingüística-etnográfico de Colombia* (ALEC). One of its leading researchers finds that of 227 cases of some form of *haber* (impersonal) plus plural noun, only 19 informants used singular of verb, in spite of traditional grammatical rule (in Bogotá: three out of eight).

4552 Ortiz Mayans, Antonio. Nuevo diccionario español-guaraní, guaraní-español: nombres de la toponimia, de la flora y de la fauna, voces de la mitología, de la leyenda y del folklore: apéndice de voces regionales, un compendio gramatical. Buenos Aires: Editorial Universitaria de Buenos Aires, 1980. 576 p.: appendix, map.

Very extensive vocabulary of Paraguay's second language once spoken as far as 1,000 miles to north and over vast areas. Author's statement that *letras* of Guaraní alphabet are same as those of Castilian would be disputed by many linguists who worked in region. But since Guaraní has been nurtured since *misiones*, language has many *híbridas populares*. Author's claim that after Latin, Guaraní gave greatest number of terms to natural sciences, might also be disputed by Náhuatl and Arawak scholars. Appendix has excellent synthesis of Guaraní's syntactic structure.

4553 Ramírez F., César A. *Lengua Madre* (RCPC, 37 : 174, enero/marzo 1982, p. 130–165)

See above comments on this article (item **4545**).

4554 Rojas, Elena M. Aspectos del habla en San Miguel de Tucumán. Tucumán, Argentina: Facultad de Filosofía y Letras, Universidad Nacional de Tucumán, 180. 280 p.: bibl., ill., maps, ports.

Valuable study modeled on Colombia's ALEC. Rojas studied under Montes Giraldo at Instituto Caro y Cuervo, and her work has Luis Flórez's thoroughness. Within structural linguistics framework, book treats phonological and morphosyntactic features of Tucumán speech on three cultural levels and involves informants ages 18 to 70. More objective contribution than David Lagmanovich's (see *HLAS 42:4555*), since latter was based on written data. Some dialectal features are similar to those of porteño speech: /y/ is [ž]; -/s/ tends to be [h]; but like most of western Argentina, /rr/ is generally [ṛ̌]. Final /m/ is often like that of Cali, Colombia, [m]. Author writes of morphosyntactic phenomena such as *Ya me parece que me voy; se vamos ya* (nivel bajo), and change of gender: *macheta, ceba, bromisto.*

4555 Spanish in the Western Hemisphere in contact with English, Portuguese, and the Amerindian languages. Edited by Eugenio Chang-Rodríguez (Word [Journal of the International Linguistic Association, New York] 33 : 1/2, April/Aug. 1982, p. 5–198, bibl., tables)

As member of Joint Committee on Latin American Studies of the Social Science Research Council and Council of Learned Societies, Chang-Rodríguez promoted idea of study of Spanish as a research priority, and especially in contact with other languages. Contributions: S. Beardsley on Spanish in US; D.N. Cárdenas on morphosyntactic preferences in southern California Spanish; A.C. Zentella on Puerto Rican Spanish and English in contact in US; J.M. Guitart on use of subjunctive among Spanish-English bilinguals; R.C. Troike on US language planning for Spanish; R. Nash on Puerto Rican Spanish law in jobs, gender, and civil rights;

Alvarado de Ricord on impact of English on Panama's Spanish; D. Lincoln Canfield on diachronic factor in American Spanish in contact; F.G. Hensey on *castellanización* in Oaxaca, Mexico; P.V. Cassano on language influence theory as exemplified by Quechua and Maya; M.J. Hardman-de-Bautista on mutual influence of Spanish and Andean languages; J.C. Zamora on Amerindian words in American Spanish; F.G. Hensey on Uruguayan *fronterizo* as linguistic sampler; and Editor on language-planning problems in Peru.

4556 Stevens, Paul. The possibility of French influence on velar /r/ and other phonemes in Puerto Rican Spanish (Anales [Universidad Interamericana de Puerto Rico, Departamento de Ciencias Sociales, San Germán] 1 : 1, 1980, p. 2–14, bibl.)

Discounts theory of French influence proposed by Theodore Beardsley (*HLAS 38:6067*) and believes that it raises more questions than it answers. Points out, as does Megenney (*HLAS 42:4560*) that the French velar vibrant is voiced; that of Puerto Rico is voiceless. Perhaps principle of least effort should be considered.

4557 Usandizaga y Mendoza, Pedro María de. El chingolés: primer diccionario del lenguaje popular mexicano. 6a. ed. México: Costa-Amic Editores, 1979. 250 p., 1 leaf of plates: ill.

Sixth ed. of 1972 book. Entirely dedicated to phrases and derivatives of word *chingado*, which author claims is most Mexican of all words: *nacionalista y revolucionaria*, and basis of exclamations for any occasion. Like chile, he says, you add to everything. Includes hundreds of entries with illustrations on use (e.g., Hijo de la *chingada* has 34). Statement that word is of Germanic origin and came from Chile may be questioned.

4558 Vance, Birgitta. Idioma argentino: sí o no (Revista de Artes y Letras de la Universidad de Costa Rica [San José] 5 : 1, enero/junio 1981, p. 137–144, bibl.)

Referring to Capdevila's *Babel y el castellano* (1940) and Américo Castro's *La peculiaridad lingüística ríoplatense* (1940), author reinforces popular misconceptions of type, "He don't speak American," and apparently believes that Argentines deliberately try to create a new language. Although Vance consulted several works on Spanish American dialects, more reading on language's history, especially in *voseo*, would have been beneficial.

4559 Vocabulario del *caló* en Guatemala
(IPGH/FA, 30, 1980, p. 102–108, bibl.)
Although *caló* is usually thought of as speech of *antisociales*, created in atmosphere of incarceration, it is also good example of creative dynamics of popular expression and another case of Hispanic preference for image over concept.

Article has several samples of trend, among youth especially, to embellish even word *sí* (e.g., *circo, ciriaco, simón*) or *igual* (e.g., *iguanas*). *Orégano* stands for anything made of gold.

SPANISH LEXICON

4560 Alvarado de Ricord, Elsie. Nueva edición del *Diccionario de anglicismos* del Dr. Ricardo J. Alfaro (LNB/L, 317, agosto 1982, p. 172–177)
Fairly brief account of Gredos ed. of Alfaro's well known 1950 work. Although Alvarado agrees that certain *neologismos* are necessary, she thinks that many are *hijos de la ignorancia* (see item **4569**).

4561 Arrom, José Juan. Aportes antillanos al español de América (AR, 7:25, 1981, p. 10–13)
One of the favorite *temas* of this popular Yale professor. Such common terms as *enaguas, tabaco, canoa, bohío, güira, maíz, iguana, cacique* were introduced to Spanish, and thence into many other languages early in the settlement of America.

4562 Boyd-Bowman, Peter. El léxico hispanoamericano del siglo XVI (*in* International Congress of Hispanists, 4th, Salamanca, Spain, 1971. Actas. Dirección, Eugenio de Bustos Tovar. Salamanca, Spain: Asociación Internacional de Hispanistas, 1982, v. 1, p. 191–198)
Since 1950, Boyd-Bowman has been amassing data on Peninsular origins of Spanish settlers in America, and in 1964, vol. 1 of much-consulted *Indice geobiográfico de 40,000 pobladores españoles de América*

was published by Bogotá's Instituto Caro y Cuervo; vol. 2 in Mexico, 1968. Since then his attention has turned to collection of other data, mainly lexical from same documents used to determine origins of first settlers. Finds sources (i.e., non-literary documents of transactions, court records) rich in information on semantic changes, forms of address, indigenisms, and even 16th-century pronunciation.

4563 Bradomín, José María. Toponimia de Oaxaca. 2a. ed. México: Imprenta Arana, 1980. 377 p.: bibl., index.
Effort to give "real" meaning of náhuatl place names in Oaxaca state, or terms' etimological authenticity, "adulterated" with time. Chief source of definitions is Fray Alonso de Molina's famous *Vocabulario en lengua mexicana* (1555). Oaxaca itself is náhuatl, in spite of fact that language was never natively spoken there.

4564 Cicalese, Vicente O. Las semanas y los días. Montevideo: Libros del Astillero, 1982. 200 p.: bibl.
In belief that language encloses in words and phrases all stages of a people's cultural history, takes us through five "books" of Hispanic heritage: *ferias y feriados*; Pagan names of week days; origins of *semana ferial* (Portuguese); New Year's and Christmas; propaganda and the Roman daily; and Latin sayings still extant in Spanish.

4565 Congreso Panamericano de Carreteras, *13th, Caracas, 1979.* Vocabulario vial. Washington: Organización de los Estados Americanos, 1981. 368 p. (OEA/Ser.K/1.13.1 COPACA/42–79)
Result of resolution passed at 12th Congreso Panamericano de Carreteras (San José, Costa Rica, 1975), book represents report of Commission charged with making study: *vocabulario vial* in Spanish, English, French, Portuguese. Very extensive lexicon of roads, road conditions, construction, control systems, bridges, and vehicles, consists of entries followed by explanations and dialectal variants (e.g., *Acabado áspero*: Terminado áspero de la capa superfical de una calzada).

Fajardo Terán, Florencia. Los *ganchos* de la Villa de San Carlos. See item **2766a.**

4566 Glosario de términos demográficos. La Habana: Editorial de Ciencias Sociales,

1977. 118 p.: bibl., ill., index (Demografía)

Vocabulary that not only defines but explains with limitations and qualifications for case at hand. Such matters as births, fecundity, mortality, migrations, age pyramids are further broken down into sub-divisions, such as identification of illness that caused death of individual. Definitions are followed by indexes, rates of change, and demographic coefficients.

4567 Glosario de términos sobre asentamientos humanos. México: Secretaría de Asentamientos Humanos y Obras Públicas, 1978. 175 p.: bibl. (Colección de documentos básicos; 1)

Very useful book, not only for vocabulary pertaining to centers for human habitation, but for account of how Mexico dealt with urban development. Categorizes inhabited localities as: *ciudades, villas, pueblos, congregaciones, rancherías, haciendas, ranchos, colonias, agrícolas*. Introduction gives account of work's planning.

4568 Herrera, Guillermina and Linda Blackburn. Terminología lingüística inglés-español. Guatemala: Instituto Lingüístico de Verano, 1980. 24 leaves.

Glossary of 1,258 terms includes some that might be called poetic. Up-to-date vocabulary on generative terminology.

4569 Isaza Calderón, Baltazar. *El diccionario de anglicismos* de Ricardo J. Alfaro (LNB/L, 317, agosto 1982, p. 163–171)

Critique and defense of Panamanian Ex-President and jurist's dictionary, a very useful tool for 30 years. Alfaro writes of flood of Anglicisms into Spanish as natural trend, given US-Spanish American situation, similar to that which existed between France and Spain in 18th century. While so many Hispanic scholars speak out against *barbarismos* and *en defensa del idioma*, Alfaro reminds us that human speech is not a lagoon but a river.

4570 Landívar U., Manuel A. Refranes y aforismos (CCE/RA, 7, nov. 1981, p. 58–113)

Although Landívar died before revising work, his efforts in science he calls "paremiología" will be appreciated in two ways: 1) ability to define neatly often confused terms: *refrán, proverbio, adagio, aforismo, máxima, sentencia*, and *dicho*; and 2) his

collection of nearly 1,000 also neatly packaged topically. Wisdom of common people expressed more often by image than concept.

4571 Megenney, William W. Common words of African origin used in Latin America (AATSP/H, 66:1, March 1983, p. 1–10)

Characteristically well documented article on language contacts during Atlantic slave trade with resulting appearance of African terms in superstrate languages (e.g., Portuguese, Spanish, English, Dutch). Author's list of several of fairly high frequency is followed in each entry by definition, his information on origins, other scholars' information. Common Spanish adoptions are: *chango, congo, banana, guineo, mandinga, marimba, merengue, sandunga*. Good bibliography.

4572 Mejías, Hugo A. Préstamos de lenguas indígenas en el español americano del siglo XVII. México: UNAM, Instituto de Investigaciones Filológicas, Centro de Lingüística Hispánica, 1980. 182 p.: bibl., index, maps (Publicaciones del Centro; 11)

Uses data from Boyd-Bowman's *Léxico hispanoamericano del siglo XVI* (*HLAS 40: 6070*) and from dissertations he directed at SUNY-Buffalo, as well as from Juan Lope Blanch's *El léxico indígena en el español de México* (Mexico, 1969), in order to give us neat pictures of variety and quantity of loans from about 12 languages.

4573 Pacheco Guzmán, Gerardo. Diccionario del quechua al castellano. Cuenca: Publicaciones y Papeles, 1981. 131 p.

Three-part book: 1) Old Quechua; 2) Quechua introduced into languages of the North; and 3) *el quichua castellanizado*. Correspondence of symbol and sound would seem to be rather casual, and there are many spelling and printing errors.

4574 Palomar de Miguel, Juan. Diccionario para juristas. Colaboraron en esta edición, María del Carmen Coll de Palomar, Arturo López Hernández. México: Mayo Ediciones, 1981. 1439 p.

Combination of extensive legal lexicon and etymological dictionary of such terms. Dialectal variants are given for many words, with emphasis on Mexican variant.

4575 Peláez Bazán, Mario. Diccionario razonado de palabras y definiciones parlamentarias: catálago de términos, conceptos, principios, locuciones, síntesis biográficas, secuela de procedimientos, instituciones y usos parlamentarios: concordado con *La Nueva Constitución*, la *Declaración universal de los derechos del hombre* y otros textos legales. Lima: Editorial Universo, 1980. 240 p.: bibl.

From *abogado* to *zafarrancho*, indicates wide coverage of this volume which seems quite Peru-centered. Vocabulary includes names of several prominent Peruvian politicians and lists labor unions. Publication apparently coincides with installation of Congress after "doce años de oprobio."

4576 Prieto, Raúl. Madre academia. Nueva ed. aum. y corr. México: Editorial Grijalbo, 1981. 759 p.: ill.

Pornographically-oriented series of gibes directed at Spain's Royal Academy. Says *Mamá Academia* has provincial and antiquated point of view and supports contention with hundreds of examples. Main objective is to entertain.

4577 Santamaría, Francisco Javier. Americanismos y barbarismo. 2a. ed., facsimilar. México: Consejo Editorial del Gobierno del Estado de Tabasco, 1980. 268 p. (Serie Lingüística; 9)

Second ed. of 1921 vocabulary, forerunner to author's well known *Diccionario de americanismos* (1942). Written in charming conversational manner: "Oh, I just thought of another case!"

4578 Suárez Molina, Víctor M. *Acicalar con cosméticos y perfumes* (UY/R, 24:144, nov./dic. 1982, p. 41–43)

Interesting piece, a *curiosidad filológica*. Shows changes in meanings of Arabic *as-sigal*, now *acicalar*, originally meant to polish swords and knives, then to put on makeup, and of *alcohol*, originally *polvo de antimonio*, used to blacken. Also, Greek *kosmos* (i.e., order, harmony) gives us *cosmético*, while Latin *fumar* becomes eventually *perfumar* and its derivative *perfume*.

4579 Terminología del comercio internacional. Compilador, Jorge A. Velásquez P. Medellín?: Corporación Educativa ESUMER, 1980? 135 p.

Compiled by Corporación Educativa ESUMER, under Jorge Velásquez's leadership. Alphabetically arranged vocabulary of international trade terms is designed for students and teachers of economics, customs, services, importers and exporters. Much English is included, especially in acronyms, which are spelled out in appendix. Many terms turn out to be mixed Spanish/English: *Ronda Kennedy, buque tramp*, and latter entry refers one to *buque trampa*, which might be misunderstood by Spanish-speaker.

4580 Vázquez-Presedo, Vicente. Vocabulario avanzado de la economía. Buenos Aires: Ediciones Macchi, 1891. 143 p.

Rather detailed definitions and explanations with British rather than American orientation, of hundreds of English terms. Spanish index refers back to items of English-Spanish section.

Williams, Barbara J. and **Carlos A. Ortiz-Solorio.** Middle American folk soil taxonomy. See *HLAS 45:5122.*

SPANISH
SYNTAX

4581 Avila, Elvio Aroldo. Santiago del Estero, Indo-Hispania lingüística: cómo habla el santiagueño; ensayo histórico, sociológico y de investigación lingüística. Santiago del Estero, Argentina: Impresiones Arte, 1980. 260 p.: bibl.

Perhaps best linguistic-ethnographic study of region which has several speech habits much more conservative than those of nearby Tucumán: syllable final /s/ still pronounced as [s]; distinction between /ll/ and /y/, the latter as [ž]. Author supplies long list of typical idioms and sayings, description of several children's games and interesting local vocabulary (e.g., *apanar*: ocultar; *abigarrado*: apretada multitud; *chapar*: robar; *chango*: muchacho).

4582 Cuervo, Rufino José. Notas a la *Gramática de la lengua castellana* de Don Andrés Bello. Edición, variantes y estudio preliminar por Ignacio Ahumada Lara. Bogotá: Instituto Caro y Cuervo, 1981. 438 p.: bibl., facsims.

Although this is, in essence, a reproduction of 1911 ed., it is a very good one to work with because of extensive notes that align chronologically Rufino José Cuervo's prolific and sound criticisms.

4583 Franco, Fabiola and **Donald Steinmetz.** Ser y estar + adjetivo calificativo en español (AATSP/H, 66, 1983, p. 176–184)

Clever answer to old problem for teachers and students ever since Nebrija: real difference between *ser* and *estar* with an adjective. Authors say that test is whether person or thing is compared with others or with himself/itself (e.g., *la playa es bonita*: compared to others, *la playa está bonita*: compared to same playa). Would it work with, *El profesor es distraído?* Present reviewer prefers distinction "innate" versus "due to environmental influence."

4584 Jiménez Borja, José. La *Gramática* de Bello: antes, entonces y ahora (CONAC/RNC, 43:249, abril/dic. 1982, p. 113–143)

Points out that altough Bello's work was solid contribution, Rufino José Cuervo's copious notes have been even more useful.

4585 Lope Blanch, Juan M. Análisis gramatical del discurso. México: UNAM, Instituto de Investigaciones Filológicas, Centro de Lingüística Hispánica, 1983. 181 p. (Publicaciones del Centro; 17)

Collection of essays on methodology, syntax, and terminology for Spanish utterances (e.g., *cláusula, oración, frase, período*). Pt. 2 examines structure of five Mexican writers.

4586 Ozete, Oscar. On the so-called Spanish gerund-participle (AATSP/H, 66, 1983, p. 75–83)

After describing functional features of *-ndo* word forms, indicates that Bello and Caro disagreed on part of speech involved. Former thought of it as adverb, latter as adjective participle. In the belief that normative grammars fall short of describing present-day usage, votes for adjective participle.

4587 Pávez, María Mercedes. Decodificación de tres tipos de estructuras sintácticas en efásicos (ICC/T, 37:2, mayo/agosto 1982, p. 268–289)

Drawing heavily on writings of American specialists, especially Sheila Blumstein, discusses types of aphasia. Sentence *amanece pronto* is taken as model for pho-

nemic analysis and order and sum of lexemes to be decoded.

4588 Resnick, Melvyn C. Spanish verb sentences: their names and meanings (AATSP/H, 67, 1984, p. 92–99)

Inadequacy of nomenclature of Spanish verb tenses has been recognized for over 100 years—from Bello to Bull, so to speak. Points out difficulties with current terminology, and says teaching of Spanish as foreign language is affected, and recommends that set of names be devised based on objective considerations of notions of time, order, and aspect.

4589 Solé, Yolanda R. On *más/menos...que* versus *más/menos de* comparatives (AATSP/H, 65, 1982, p. 614–619)

Writer finds that *más/menos...que* has many more situational applications than does *más/menos...de*. Latter, however, occurs not only with overt or covert numerical estimate, but also in nominalized clauses: *ha dicho más de lo que esperaba*.

4590 Teschner, Richard V. and **Frank Muñoz.** Statistics on morphological irregularity in Spanish verb tenses (AATSP/H, 67, 1984, p. 99–104)

Examination of 4,862 verbs and rank-ordering depiction of irregularity on bases of separate morphological processes, average per group, percentage of irregular forms of total verb count. Very useful set of charts is produced, showing this rank of irregularity: present tense, preterite, gerund, past participle, future-conditional, and the least is the imperfect.

PORTUGUESE
GENERAL

4591 Campos, Apio. O verbo e o texto: estudos lingüísticos e literários. Belém: Falangola Editora, 1982. 226 p.

Compilation of essays, for the most part, done as member of faculty of Universidad Federal do Pará. Includes both literary and linguistic studies.

4592 Guérios, Rosario Farani Mansur. Tabus lingüísticos. Capa, lay-out, Haniel. Arte, Silva Maria Mesquita. 2a. ed. aum. São Paulo: Companhia Editora Nacional;

Curitiba: Editora da Universidad Federal do Paraná, 1979. 184 p.: bibl., indexes (Biblioteca universitária. Série 5a., Letras e lingüística; v. 15)

Very cleverly ordered discussion of taboos (sagrado-proibido or proibido-sagrado, according to Guérios), with categories such as names of people, relatives, authorities, religious, bad spirits, deceased, animals, physical defects, etc. Good study of euphemisms as well as superstition.

PORTUGUESE
GRAMMAR

4593 Ayres, Vera Marina Monjardim. Relações de lugar: um tratamento semântico. Apresentação de Mônica Rector. Rio de Janeiro: Editora Rio: em convênio com as Faculdades Integradas Estácio de Sá, 1980. 141 p.: bibl. (Série universitária; 4)

Applying Geoffrey Leech's theory in *Towards a semantic description of English*, attempts to describe semantically some so-called prepositional and adverbial phrases in order to add a semantic dimension to the traditional lexical-grammatical. After several chapters on terminology, examines situations involving relation to place, and illustrates function of semantics in clarifying or avoiding ambiguity.

4594 Barbosa, Maria Aparecida. Léxico, produção e critividade: processos do neologismo. São Paulo: Global Editora, 1981. 323 p.: ill.

Diagramatic representation of dynamics of production, of interest to both formalists and functionalists. Apparently seeks solution to problems through cybernetic model.

4595 Camacho, Roberto Gomes. Norma, ideologia e a teoria da linguagem (FFCLM/A, 25, 1981, p. 19–30, bibl.)

Having in mind *grupos desfavorecidos* of population, recommends more "democratic" instruction through less normative prescription and tolerance of regional differences and variations according to circumstances.

4596 Comrie, Bernard. Remarks on clitic-climbing in Brazilian Portuguese (LINGUA, 58:3/4, Nov./Dec. 1982, p. 243–265)

Discovers wide range of stylistically correlated variation in position of object pronoun, and climbing refers to moving pronoun to "higher" auxiliary verb (e.g., *O médico queria examinar-nos* moves to *O médico nos queira examinar*). Refers to Chomsky's specified subject condition, and to Carlos A. Quicoli "Conditions in Clitic-Movement in Portuguese" (1976).

4597 Cunha, Antônio Geraldo da. Dicionário etimológico Nova Fronteira da língua portuguesa. Assistentes, Cláudio Mello Sobrinho et al. Rio de Janeiro: Editora Nova Fronteira, 1982. 839 p.: bibl.

Good dictionary of origins and development of Portuguese, although it is not quite up-to-date in lexicon of recent discoveries and inventions.

4598 Rocco, Maria Thereza Fraga. Crise na linguagem: a redação no vestibular. São Paulo: Editora Mestre Jou, 1981. 276 p.: bibl., ill.

Using entrance examinations taken by students who are candidates for *vestibulares*, Rocco is apparently shocked by poor writing ability of Brazilian youth. Examines some 1500 texts, but finds only about 40 that are "creative." One of greatest sins is use of cliché.

4599 Silva, Myrian Barbosa da. Leitura, ortografia e fonologia. São Paulo: Editora Atica, 1981. 110 p.: bibl. (Coleção Ensaios; 75)

Book is extension of 1972 Master's thesis and deals with sound-symbol correspondence of Portuguese orthographic system. Referring to Charles Fries' *Linguistics and reading*, discusses consequences of this correspondence or lack of it to teaching of reading.

PORTUGUESE
DIALECTOLOGY

4600 Cabral, Tomé. Novo dicionário de termos e expressões populares. Fortaleza: Edições Universidade de Ceará, 1982. 786 p.: bibl.

Revised ed. of 1972 dictionary, based on model of Amadeu Amaral, founder of scientific dialectological investigation in Brazil, especially regional lexicon. Deals with popular language of Brazil's interior. Very extensive vocabulary, and each entry is documented as to source of information.

4601 Cunha, Celso Ferreira da. Língua, nação, alienação. Rio de Janeiro: Editora Nova Fronteira, 1981. 110 p.: bibl., index (Coleção Logos)

Author, student of "mestre" Antenor Nascentes, is now working on rather ambitious project, *História da língua portuguesa no Brasil*. This little volume brings together studies that will be of interest to those who study Portuguese. Some material is actually political because Cunha is concerned about Portuguese's future in the world, a language that now ranks, he says, fifth in terms of number of speakers.

4602 Laytano, Dante de. O linguajar do gaúcho brasileiro. Porto Alegre: Escola Superior de Teologia São Lourenço de Brindes, 1981. 255 p.: bibl. (Coleção Temas gaúchos; 23)

Review of gaucho literature and examination of typical grammar, is followed by references to *cancioneiros*, Spanish influences, Africanisms, and Indian sources of vocabulary. Chap. 2 of pt. 1 describes typical grammar, including phonology and morphology, and next chapter categorizes lexicon. Pt. 2 of book is glossary of *pescadores* of Northeast of Rio Grande do Sul.

4603 Melo, Gladstone Chaves de. A língua do Brasil. 4a. ed. melhorada e aum. Rio de Janeiro: Padrão, 1981. 209 p.: bibl.

Good survey of early works on Brazilian Portuguese, on problems of analysis, doctrines that have prevailed. Discusses Tupi and African lexical contributions, pronunciation of American Portuguese compared to that of Peninsula, and present lexical differences between both manifestations.

4603a Ribeiro, José *et al.* Esboço de um atlas lingüístico de Minas Gerais. Rio de Janeiro: Ministério da Educação e Cultura, Fundação Casa de Rui Barbosa, 1977. 1 v.?: bibl., maps (some col.)

Valuable Latin American companion to six-volume *Atlas lingüístico-etnográfico de Colombia* (completed 1983). As in its case, this Minas Gerais document consists mostly of large maps that show results of field work over time. Each map indicates by colored dots, phonetic or lexical variants of terms. At map's bottom are phonetic transcriptions of these variants (e.g., *arco-iris*, also called in some sections, *arco-da-velha*). Atlas surveyed 116 localities in a state of 11 million people. Lists and describes all localities and procedures of *pesquisas*.

4604 Rodrigues, Ermínio. Português do Brasil e português de Portugal: diferenças (FFCLM/A, 25, 1981, p. 69–96, bibl.)

Uses Collins *Portuguese-English, English-Portuguese dictionary* (1978) as source for lexical comparison of two main dialects of language. There are, of course, hundreds of differences, but finds that often Brazilian speakers will know both Peninsular word and Brazilian, and will pick one that fits situation.

4605 Vieira, Maria de Nazaré da Cruz. Aspectos do falar paraense: fonética, fonologia, semântica. Belém: Universidade Federal do ará, Pró-Reitoria de Planejamento e Desenvolvimento, 1980. 208 p.: bibl., ill. (Série Pesquisa; no. 11)

Very good description of phonology and some important lexical items of municipalities of Santarém, Alenquer, Obidos, Oriximiná, and Itaituba of Pará state, Brazil. List of informants is presented, with age and education level.

PORTUGUESE
LEXICON

4606 Almeida, Napoleão Mendes de. Dicionário de questões vernáculas. São Paulo: Editora Caminho Suave, 1981. 351 p.

Very extensive compilation of *questões* is actually dictionary of idiomatic sayings, for most part, although there are many choice recommendations among synonymous expressions (e.g., long discussion of *espanhol* and *castelhano*).

4607 Basílio, Margarida. Estruturas lexicais do português: uma abordagem gerativa. Petrópolis: Editora Vozes, 1980. 128 p.: bibl. (Coleção Perspectivas lingüísticas; 18)

Study of derivational morphology and notion of lexical competency of native

speaker. Phenomenon of nominalization in
Portuguese is considered with historical
perspective.

4608 Bastos, Clidenor Ribeiro. Introdução à
metodologia da linguagem. Rio de
Janeiro: Livraria F. Bastos, 1981. 191 p.: ill.

Examination of theories of language:
referential, intentional, and law of great ex-
pressional extension, with respect to form,
content, and meaning of terms. Suggests
good example of latter is: *a pessoa de Sua
Santidade* instead of *o Papa.*

4609 Branco, Périco de Moraes. Dicionário
de mineralogia. 2a. ed. rev. e ampliada.
Porto Alegre: Editora da Universidade, Universidade Federal do Rio Grande do Sul, 1982.
264 p.: appendices, bibl.

Author holds degree in geology (Universidade Federal do Rio Grande do Sul). Provides definitions for 4,500 entries, and much
additional information (e.g., chemical composition, physical properties, principal uses,
mode of occurrence, varieties). Three appendices deal with chemical elements, obsolete
minerals, popular terminology, and jargon of
miners.

**4610 Carvalho, Mario Bezerra de; Eneide
Carvalho de Arruda; and Geraldo
Pereira de Arruda.** Glossário de entomologia.
Ed. rev. e ampliada do *Glossário de termos
tecnicos de entomología.* Recife: Universidade Federal Rural de Pernambuco, Departamento de Biologia, 1977. 342 p.: bibl.

Enlarged edition of glossary published
earlier in *Boletim Técnico* (24) by Instituto
de Pesquisas Agronômicas, Pernambuco. Extensive list of scientific designations of insects is followed by vocabulary of popular
names.

Cascudo, Luís da Câmara. Dicionário de
folclore brasileiro. See item **991.**

4611 Chiesa, Dirceu Antônio. Mini-
vocabulário econômico-financeiro e de
abrangências afins: bolsa de volares, câmbio,
economia, finanças internas e internacionais,
moedas e bancos, mercado de capitais, mercado financeiro, mercado interno e internacional, mercado monetário: produção,
indústria, comércio, serviços. Porto Alegre:
Editora Sulina, 1981. 175 p.: bibl. (Coleção
universitária)

Useful glossary of economic, trade and
financial terminology, including great many
English terms that have been made international, so to speak.

4612 Dicionário das profissões. 3a. ed. rev.
atualizada e ampliada. São Paulo: Centro de Integração Empresa-Escola, Divisão
Técnica, 1981. 2 v. (1032 p.): bibl., form,
indexes.

Designed as guide for those who may
enter professions or who may train for voca-
tional career. Describes some 200 situations
in terms of what goes on, where one finds
this type of activity, personal requisites,
necessary basic courses, minimum curriculum or course of study, specializations, references for further information. While book
would seem to be quite helpful, it could be
brought more up-to-date in computer science, environmental engineering, and urban
administration.

**4613 Katz, Chaim Samuel; Francisco An-
tonio Doria; and Luiz Costa Lima.**
Diccionario básico de comunicación. Traduc-
ción, Eva Grosser Lerner. México: Editorial
Nueva Imagen, 1980. 513 p.: bibl. (Serie
Comunicación)

This 1980 ed. is translation of 1975
Portuguese ed. Entries are classified by *temas*
(e.g., anthropology, philosophy, linguistics,
psychology, sociology, information theory,
cybernetics). Each entry has summary of following discussion). Latter is often pages long
and generally gives historical background.
Some 220 terms are explained and fairly
lengthy bibliography seems to favor European sources.

4614 Leitão, Elaine Vasconcellos. A mulher
na língua do povo. Rio de Janeiro:
Achiamé, 1981. 86 p.: bibl. (Série Universidade; v. 17)

Rather humorous account that originally had title, *Sexo e linguagem.* Believes
that language is not spoken by us, it is the
one who speaks to us, in that it tells us what
attitudes prevail. Maintains that "A pátria
jamais será mátria," and while *João está ba-
rrigudo, Maria está barriguda* is an insult.
Clever compilation of words and expressions
applied to women, with certain connotations
and implications. In a restaurant, she explains, male cook is *mestre,* while woman is
still just *cozinheira.*

4615 Mello, William Agel de. Dicionário
português-romeno. Goiânia: Oriente,
1979. 153 p. (Publicação Editora Oriente;
289a)

Another useful contribution to collection of reference books on Romance linguistics by diplomat and scholar. Helpful addition to Romanian definitions would be Vulgar Latin or Slavic term from which it came.

4616 Nascentes, Antenor. Dicionário de sinónimos. 3a. ed. rev. Rio de Janeiro: Editora Nova Fronteira, 1981. 485, 4 p.: bibl., index.

Third ed. of very useful tool includes new material, index of all terms, and additional explanations of fine distinctions in definition. Fine distinctions among synonyms are further defined in nearly all entries.

4617 Pereira, Valdemar Alves. Entre excelências e majestades: da linguagem erudita à popular. Fortaleza: Editora H. Galeno, 1981. 73 p.

Pt. 1 of little volume describes certain aspects of *erudita* speech in Brazil's apparent dichotomy of expression; pt. 2, *linguagem popular*. Much attention is given to forms of address, even *excelencias e majestades*, but one also learns of linguistic importations, especially from France.

4618 Pugliesi, Márcio. Dicionário de expressões idiomáticas: locuções usuais da língua portuguesa. São Paulo: Parma, 1981. 205 p.

Rather useful collection of idiomatic expressions organized alphabetically, *verbetes* entered on following bases: phrases with noun are entered under noun; phrases with verb are entered under verb; those with adjective, under adjective; those with pronoun, under pronoun; those with adverb, under adverb. As author suggests: if these aren't sufficient, try to find what you want word by word.

4619 Rosa, Ubiratan; Angelina Cardoso Câmera; and Edith C. da Costa. Dicionário inglês/português, português/inglês. Supervisão, Maxim Behar e quipe Hemus. São Paulo: Hemus, 1982. 865 p.

In spite of British flag on cover of this neatly packaged dictionary, there are many basic terms that refer to things that the Anglo community has developed in recent years that are not included among entries (e.g., atomic, nuclear, computer, linguistic terminology).

4620 Seraine, Florival. Contribuição metodológica aos estudos lexicais (IC/R, 100, jan./dez. p. 15–43)

Taking off from Dell Hymes *Foundations in sociolinguistics* (1974), attempts to chart methodological orientation for study of *fatos de comunicação*, basic function of language. Concludes with Hymes: lexical "event" of human speech can be analyzed and described satisfactorily on synchronic plane, according to principles which conform to "ethnography of communication." Many linguists would insist that diachronic considerations are very important.

4621 Torres, Júlio di Paravicini. Vocábulos aplicados à classificação comercial dos produtos vegetais. São Paulo: Livraria Nobel, 1979. 145, 5 p.: bibl.

Author spent 32 years in critical post of Brazil's Ministry of Agriculture. Much more than title indicates, book is actually Portuguese-English export-import-trade vocabulary. When there is no Portuguese word, offers only English: *dumping, warrant, drawback*, etc.

4622 Zlochevsky, Huzeff. Pequeno dicionário português-hebraico. São Paulo: Sociedade Cemitério Israelita de São Paulo, 1980. 150 p.: bibl.

Fairly basic vocabulary of about 14,000 entries. Hebrew definitions are given in traditional Yiddish-English spelling and in Hebrew characters.

PORTUGUESE
SYNTAX

4623 Rehfeldt, Gládis Knak. Polissemia e campo semântico: estudo aplicado aos verbos de movimento. Porto Alegre: Editora da Universidade Federal do Rio Grande do Sul, 1980. 172 p.: bibl., ill.

One of several works recently published by Universidade Federal do Rio Grande do Sul. Examines five Brazilian newspapers published over 12-day period, to study occurrence of 57 verbs of motion in politics, police, and football (soccer). Concludes that research in synonyms on purely lexical plan is insufficient to explain variations in meaning. By employing 3,950 total occurrences, makes very good argument for semantic consideration.

CREOLE

4624 Amstae, Jon. Agentless constructions in Dominican Creole (LINGUA, 59 : 1, Jan. 1983, p. 47–75, bibl., ill.)

Argues that dependency grammar is most economical way to describe impersonal constructions and other aspects of Dominican French Creole (DFC). General approach of embedding passive predicate to semantic static BE and external source of *by*-agent phrases allows explanations of several other problems in description of DFC as well as Indian Ocean French Creole.

4625 Fayó, Néstor A. 3333 [i.e., Three thousand three hundred and thirty three] proverbs in Haitian Creole, the 11th Romance language. Port-au-Prince: Editions Fardin, 197? 428 p.: ill.

Good collection of 3333 native proverbs in eleventh "romance language." English translations are clever and idiomatic.

4626 A Festival of Guyanese words. Edited by John R. Rickford. 2d ed. Georgetown: University of Guyana, 1978. 272 p.: bibl., ill., index.

Information for second ed. emanates from "festival" rather than conference at University of Guyana (1975), in connection with course in descriptive linguistics. Out of this all-day discussion in which many students participated, came large vocabulary of words and expressions that are not standard English. "Creole" lexicon consists of 411 terms having to do with body, sex, kinship, appearance, home, food, clothing, superstition, etc., some from Africa, some from India, some from Caribbean Spanish. Book is not only good stock of source materials, but suggests devices for eliciting information.

Fontaine, Pierre-Michel. Language, society and development: dialectic of French and Creole use in Haiti. See *HLAS 45 : 1075.*

4627 Historicity and variation in Creole studies. Edited by Arnold Highfield

and Albert Valdman. Ann Arbor, Mich.: Karoma Publishers, Inc., 1981. 126 p.: bibl.

While cross-regional in scope, collection contains several articles pertaining to Caribbean Creoles: Genevieve Escure (Belize), John Holm (Miskito coast Creole, Nicaragua), Raleigh Morgan, Jr. (Guadeloupe), and Martha M. Baudet (general Caribbean). [L. Comitas]

4628 Lawton, David. Code-shifting in Jamaican Creole: a Caribbean context (CIDG/O, 29 : 1/2, 1980, p. 234–250, bibl., graphs)

Much has been written lately about code-shifting among Mexican-Americans (e.g., *HLAS 44 : 4595*). Raises question of relation of this phenomenon to Creolization in Caribbean, where one finds a prestige language in contact with less prestige dialect. Having grown up in Jamaica, author understands code-switching between Jamaican Creole and Jamaican English (i.e., understands Jamaican culture and society). Creole has been gaining respectability in recent times.

4629 Romain, Jean Baptiste. Africanismes haïtiens: compilations et notes. Port-au-Prince: Impr. M. Rodríguez, 1978. 102 p.: bibl., ill. (*Revue* de la Faculté d'éthnologie, Université d'Etat d'Haïti; no. 31. *Bulletin de l'Académie des sciences humaines et sociales d'Haïti;* no. 6)

Rather thorough study of surviving Africanisms, most of them from Ivory Coast, in realms of religion, magic, art, music, folklore, economy. Text includes several photographs of drums, dolls, pottery.

4630 Taylor, Douglas R. and Brerend J. Hoff. The linguistic repertory of the island-Carib in the seventeenth century: the men's language—a Carib pidgin? (IU/IJAL, 46 : 4, Oct. 1980, p. 301–312, tables)

Interesting suggestion that in a society that is known to have political and ritual cleavages, there may have been a men's language, and that this mode of speech may have survived as pidgin when Carib became extinct by mid-17th century to be replaced by Arawakan, already spoken by many women who had been captured elsewhere.

4631 Vernet, Pierre. L'écriture du Créole et ses réalités de fonctionnement. Port-au-Prince: Université d'Etat d'Haïti, Centre de linguistique appliquée, 1981. 19 leaves (Cahiers du CLAP; no. 1)

Recommendations for common depiction of sound-symbol correspondence in Creole of Haiti, where there have always been questions because of lack of correspondence in mother tongue, French.

4632 William, Germain. Aurélien à paré le saut: petit traité des créolismes en usage à la Guadeloupe: chronique du temps de bonne-maman suivie d'un glossaire des mots et locutions employés. Basse-Terre, C.C.I., 1980. 68 p., 7 leaves of plates: ill.

Collection of words and expressions with meanings quite different from those given in French-language dictionary. Seems that some retain meanings that were those of French 200–500 years ago, others may reflect Spanish applications of early colonial period.

JOURNAL ABBREVIATIONS
LANGUAGE

AATSP/H Hispania. American Association of Teachers of Spanish and Portuguese. University of Cincinnati. Cincinnati, Ohio.

AR Areíto. Areíto, Inc. New York.

CCE/RA Revista de Antropología. Casa de la Cultura Ecuatoriana, Núcleo del Azuay. Cuenca, Ecuador.

CIDG/O Orbis. Bulletin international de documentation linguistique. Centre international de dialectologie générale. Louvain, Belgium.

CONAC/RNC Revista Nacional de Cultura. Consejo Nacional de Cultura. Caracas.

FFCLM/A Alfa. Universidade de São Paulo, Faculdade de Filosofia, Ciências e Letras. Marília, Brazil.

IC/R Revista do Instituto do Ceará. Fortaleza, Brazil.

ICC/NC Noticias Culturales. Instituto Caro y Cuervo. Bogotá.

ICC/T Thesaurus. Boletín del Instituto Caro y Cuervo. Bogotá.

ICP/R Revista del Instituto de Cultura Puertorriqueña. San Juan.

IGFO/RI Revista de Indias. Instituto Gonzalo Fernández de Oviedo [and] Consejo Superior de Investigaciones Científicas. Madrid.

IPGH/FA Folklore Americano. Instituto Panamericano de Geografía e Historia, Comisión de Historia, Comité de Folklore. México.

IU/IJAL International Journal of American Linguistics. Published by Indiana University *under the auspices of the* Linguistic Society of America, American Anthropological Association, *with the cooperation of the* Joint Committee on Native Languages. Bloomington.

LINGUA Lingua. North-Holland Publishing Co. Amsterdam.

LNB/L Lotería. Lotería Nacional de Beneficiencia. Panamá.

MS Música Sacra. Editôra Vozes. Petrópolis, Brazil.

RCPC Revista del Pensamiento Centroamericano. Centro de Investigaciones y Actividades Culturales. Managua.

UC/BF Boletín de Filología. Universidad de Chile, Instituto de Filología, Santiago.

UCLV/I Islas. Universidad Central de las Villas. Santa Clara, Cuba.

UNAM/ECN Estudios de Cultura Náhuatl. Universidad Nacional Autónoma de México, Instituto de Historia, Seminario de Cultura Náhuatl. México.

UP/CSEC Cuban Studies/Estudios Cubanos. University of Pittsburgh, University Center for International Studies, Center for Latin American Studies. Pittsburgh, Pa.

UPR/LT La Torre. Universidad de Puerto Rico. Río Piedras.

UY/R Revista de la Universidad de Yucatán. Mérida, México.

LITERATURE

SPANISH AMERICA: General

ROBERTO GONZÁLEZ ECHEVARRÍA, *Professor of Spanish, Yale University*

THE DISMAL ECONOMIC SITUATION in Latin America has affected the production of criticism. I have not received as many anthologies of literature or criticism as in previous years, and the publication of books of criticism seems to have diminished. Journals continue to publish, but the time elapsed between issues seems to be growing. Unfortunately, this decrease does not mean that only the very best finds its way into print. It is easy to pick the major work on criticism published in the past two or three years: Octavio Paz's *Sor Juana Inés de la Cruz o las trampas de la fe*, annotated in the LITERATURE: COLONIAL section (item **5057**). The book would be ranked just as high in a more auspicious moment.

Paz's book on Sor Juana is also a good indication of one of the major trends in Latin American criticism of late: interest in the colonial period. This is exemplified by the publication of Spain of a projected *Historia de la literatura hispanoamericana* (Madrid: Ediciones Cátedra, 1982) which attests to the sustained interest in Latin American literature in the *madre patria*. Vol. 1 of the *Historia* is dedicated to *Epoca colonial* (item **5085**) and consists of a collection of essays on various topics, some of which (e.g., Mignolo, Sabat, Roggiano) are excellent. Furthermore, Ediciones Cátedra, publishers of *Historia*, have also issued a very good series of modestly-priced critical editions of Latin American classics.

Interest in the colonial period also means that Latin American criticism is becoming more scholarly and specialized. The times are not ripe for journalism or for the old-fashioned general introductions to Latin American literature, written for the most part with the intention of proving that there was a Latin American literature. The few reprints or translations of "classics" mentioned in this section pale before the efforts by more recent critics. Enrique Pupo-Walker's study of historical prose in the colonial period (item **5066**) is the best example of the new trend. The book, by the way, was also published in Spain by Gredos.

That criticism of Latin American literature is flourishing in the US is exemplified by the appearance of major works such as Cornell's Enrico Mario Santí's study of Neruda (item **5854**); Tittler's examination of irony in the contemporary novel, also from Cornell, (item **5025**); Cathy L. Jrade's *Rubén Darío and the romantic search for unity* (Austin: University of Texas Press, 1983); and finally, Julie Greer Johnson's *Women in colonial Latin America: literary images* (item **5086**). The publication of these works is proof both of the interest of US presses in Latin American literature and of the expansion of colonial studies.

Johnson's book also attests to another trend: the continued interest in writings by and about women. Beth Miller's study (item **5027**), following in the wake of Ivette Miller's special issue of *The Latin American Literary Review* devoted to "Latin

American Women Writers Yesterday and Today" (Pittsburgh, Pa., 1977), provides further evidence that research in this area is beginning to yield important insights.

National Public Radio has taken an interest in Latin American literature and produced a set of 13 programs *in English* entitled "Faces, Mirrors, Masks: 20th-Century Latin American Writers," all of them prose-writers such as Borges, Carpentier, Lispector, Asturias, Cabrera Infante, and others. The programs were broadcast nationally from June through Aug. 1984. For further information on cassettes available for purchase, call toll free (800) 253–0808 or write National Public Radio, Customer Service, P.O. Box 55417, Madison, Wisconsin 53705.

This biennium saw the passing of Julio Cortázar (1914–84), one of the major writers of our time and a man of sincere convictions. And on Nov. 22, 1984, a single accident in Madrid took the lives of Angel Rama, Marta Traba, Eduardo Ibargüengoitia, and Manuel Scorza.

5001 Araujo, Helena. Narrativa femenina latinoamericana (HISPA, 11 : 32, 1982, p. 23–34)

Eloquent appeal in favor of the study of Latin American women writers includes survey of their production from 19th century to present. Covers Latin America from Mexico to Argentina, but virtually leaves out the Caribbean.

5002 Bareiro Saguier, Rubén *et al.* Cultura y sociedad en América Latina y el Caribe. Paris: UNESCO, 1981. 183 p.: bibl.

Otherwise negligible collection of speeches includes three important essays: Rubén Bareiro Saguier "El Mundo Indígena y la Literatura Latinoamericana Contemporánea;" René Depestre "Aventuras del Negrismo en América Latina"; and Arturo Uslar Pietri "Cultura y Política."

Bellini, Giuseppe. Bibliografia dell ispanoamericanismo italiano. See item **10.**

5003 Benedetti, Mario. El ejercicio del criterio: crítica literaria, 1950–1970. México: Editorial Nueva Imagen, 1981. 306 p.: bibl.

Title of book taken from a phrase by Martí. Benedetti is not up to the task, his criticism being journalistic and dispersed. Nevertheless, book should be of interest to readers of his fiction, for it gives a good account of the writer's preferences and influences.

5004 Campra, Rosalba. America latina, l'identità e la maschera. Con interviste a Borges *et al.* Roma: Riuniti, 1982. 226 p.: bibl., index (Universale; 63. Scienze sociali)

Interest in Latin American literature in Europe is obvious, and books such as this

are the best proof. There are no revelations in the interviews with Borges and Carpentier.

5005 Candido, Antonio. Los brasileños y la literatura latinoamericana (CDLA, 23 : 136, enero/feb. 1983, p. 82–92)

Lucid essay by one of Latin America's best critics. Candido gives us a critical overview of modern Brazilian literature, in relation to Spanish American writing. Important contribution.

5006 Casas Dupuy, Rosario. Algunas reflexiones sobre la teoría literaria en Latinoamérica (Cuadernos de Filosofía y Letras [Facultad de Filosofía y Letras de la Universidad de los Andes, Bogotá] 4 : 3/4, julio/dic. 1981, p. 157–167)

Somewhat hasty overview of current critical theory, with a plea in form of Gadamer's phenomenological approach.

Chatman, James R. Dissertations in the Hispanic and Luso-Brazilian languages and literatures: 1982. See item **67.**

5007 Cortázar, Julio. Reality and literature in Latin America: our literature remains faithful to its destiny (INDEX, 10 : 6, Dec. 1981, p. 89–91, bibl.)

Light essay by recently deceased author of *Rayuela*, decries lack of freedom to write in many Latin American countries, yet celebrates Latin American literature's ability both to provide beauty and to reveal negative aspects of Latin American reality. Of interest to Cortázar experts.

5008 Corvalán, Octavio. La letra en el espejo Salta, Argentina: Universidad Nacional de Salta, 1982. 1 v.

Consists of 10 elegant and insightful essays on Borges, Vallejo, Asturias, and others.

Strong on relationship between Latin American and US literatures.

5009 Durán Luzio, Juan. Creación y utopía: letras de Hispanoamérica. Heredia, Costa Rica: Editoria de la Universidad Nacional, 1979. 199 p.: bibl. (Colección Barva. Serie Pensamiento. Subserie Literatura)

Based on Cornell dissertation, book makes significant contribution to study of important topic in Latin American literature. Contains chapters on Columbus, Ericilla, Valbuena, Garcilaso de la Vega, Sarmiento, Martí, Rodó, Darío, Vasconcelos, Carpentier, Cortázar, and García Márquez. Most original material concerns colonial period.

5010 Gnutzmann, Rita. La novela hispanoamericana en segunda persona (Iberoromania [Max Niemeyer Verlag, Tübingen, FRG] 17, 1983, p. 100–120)

Very competent analysis of special kind of novel, with reference to Spanish examples and using sound theoretical bases.

5011 Gutiérrez-Vega, Zenaida. Max Henríquez Ureña: cartas de un maestro a José María Chacón y Calvo; 1915–1935, 1956–1965 (CH, 380, feb. 1982, p. 298–343)

Extremely important correspondence between two major Latin American literary scholars. Excellent introduction and notes. Important for students of Latin American literary history. A must for students of Dominican and Cuban letters. A model of scholarship.

5012 Jitrik, Noé. La lectura como actividad. México: Premiá Editora, 1982. 48 p. (La Red de Jonas)

Jitrik's turgid style masks the banality of his analyses, or is this a parody of some contemporary criticism? This ambiguity is sustained throughout. Entire last page is one sentence.

5013 Jozef, Bella. História da literatura hispano-americana. 2a. ed. Rio de Janeiro: F. Alves; Brasília: *em convênio com o Instituto Nacional do Livro, Fundação Nacional Pró-Memória*, 1982. 421 p.: bibl., index.

Traditional and reliable reference work by noted Brazilian critic and scholar.

5014 Langowski, Gerald J. El surrealismo en la ficción hispanoamericana. Madrid: Gredos, 1982. 228 p.: appendices, bibl. (Biblioteca románica hispánica. II, Estudios y ensayos: 320)

Appendices contain useful information, but most of text consists of very superficial and scantily informed survey of topic.

5015 The Latin American short story: a critical history. Margaret Sayers Peden, editor. Boston: Twayne Publishers, 1983. 160 p.: bibl., index (Twayne's critical history of the short story)

Useful general introduction for English-speaking reader, with some bibliographical aids. Generally reliable information, but numerous typographical errors.

Morse, Richard M. La cultura política iberoamericana de Sarmiento a Mariátegui. See item **1775.**

5016 La narrativa latinoamericana y la literatura soviética multinacional: pts. 1/3 (URSS/AL, 12:62, dic. 1982, p. 58–88, ill.; 1:61, enero 1983, p. 58–92, ill.; 2:62, feb. 1983, p. 47–86, ill.)

Wide-ranging discussion about possible similarities between the novel in marginal Soviet republics (e.g., Georgia, Ukraine, Armenia) and the new Latin American novel. Influence of Latin American writers, particularly García Márquez, appears indisputable, in spite of dissenting views. Many critics and writers welcome such influence as antidote to crass realism and stylistic preciousness. Very interesting and compelling exchanges include critics and writers from various Soviet republics as well as Latin Americanists (e.g., Ter Ospovat, Vera Kuteischikova).

5017 Olivares, Jorge. La recepción del decadentismo en Hispanoamérica (HR, 48:1, Winter 1980, p. 57–76)

Wide-ranging and well-researched piece, strong on sources, weak in analyses. Good source of information for future studies on subject.

5018 Oviedo, José Miguel. Escrito al margen. Bogotá: Procultura: Instituto Colombiano de Cultura, 1982. 383 p.: bibl. (Temas latinoamericanos; 2)

Elegant collection of essays by Peruvian critic. Oviedo combines a sober, journalistic style, with some of the caution of academic criticism. His close reading of Paz's *Pasado en claro* shows Oviedo at his best, which is very good indeed.

5019 Paz, Octavio. Literatura y crítica
(UY/R, 24:139, enero/feb. 1982,
p. 44–54)
Compelling essay about the lack of
original literary criticism in Latin America
which Paz ascribes to lack of a real Romanticism. Brilliant if at times hasty
generalizations.

5020 Rama, Angel. La novela en América
Latina: panoramas 1920–1980. Bogotá:
Instituto Colombiano de Cultura, 1982. 519
p.: bibl. (Temas latinoamericanos; 1)
Collection of essays by deceased Uruguayan critic is good sample of his work in
past 15 years. Rama's old-fashioned, rhetorical style clashes with modernity of his subjects. Among Latin American critics of his
generation, Rama distinguished himself by
approaching literature as part of larger, complex entity. Although results were often disappointing, because he could not shed the
journalist's hastiness and superficiality,
Rama's philosophical and political preoccupations serve as valuable guide for further
study.

5021 Robb, James Willis. Variedades de en-
sayismo en Alfonso Reyes y Germán
Arciniegas (ICC/T, 36:1, enero/abril 1981,
p. 109–122)
Brief but informative overview of
Reyes' and Arciniegas' work by leading
scholar on the Latin American essay. Because
of superior quality of Reyes' work, Robb's observations on him are of greater interest.

5022 Román-Lagunas, Jorge. La literatura
hispanoamericana en *La Nouvelle Revue Française* (UC/RCL, 19, abril 1982,
p. 115–121)
Useful bibliographical article discusses
influential journal that has devoted space to
Latin American literature. One is surprised
to note lack of any reference to seminal work
of this type (e.g., Franco-Latin American literary relations) carried out by Silvia Molloy.

5023 Sánchez, Luis Alberto. Nueva historia
de la literatura americana. 6a. ed. Valparaíso: Ediciones Universitarias de Valparaíso, Universidad Católica de Valparaíso,
1982. 615 p.: bibl., index.
New ed. of classic that retains all its
virtues and vices: good panorama, many er-

rors of fact (e.g., p. 478: Carpenteir lived in
Haiti for several years, Lezama was editor of
magazine *Ciclón, El Recurso del método*
cited as *El Método del recurso*; p. 479: *El
Libro de Manuel* cited as *El Libro de
Emmanuel*). One wonders if historian had
time to read books he writes about.

5024 Shaw, Donald Leslie. Nueva narrativa
hispanoamericana. Madrid: Ediciones
Cátedra, 1981. 247 p.: bibl., index (Crítica y
estudios literarios)
Intelligent and well-informed overview
of history of the Latin American novel, with
insightful readings and up-to-date bibliography. Good introduction for students.

5025 Tittler, Jonathan. Narrative irony in
the contemporary Spanish-American
novel. Ithaca: Cornell University Press, 1984.
210 p.: bibl., index.
First and most successful analysis of
irony in the contemporary Spanish-American
novel, aspect that is often mentioned but seldom studied. Detects two kinds of irony:
static and kinetic. Analyzes works of Fuentes,
Rulfo, Puig, Cabrera-Infante, Vargas Llosa,
Cortázar, and Goldemberg. Important book
that ought to be translated into Spanish.

5026 Torres-Rioseco, Arturo. New World literature: tradition and revolt in Latin
America. Westport, Conn.: Greenwood Press,
1983. 250 p.: bibl., index.
Reprint of dated classic of Latin
American criticism. One wonders what English readers it will attract today, and how
many uninformed ones will rely on its opinions and information.

5027 Women in Hispanic literature: icons
and fallen idols. Edited by Beth Miller.
Berkeley: University of California Press,
1983. 373 p.: bibl., index.
Excellent collection of essays on very
important topic, covering from Middle Ages
to present. Includes very important pieces by
Deyermont, Arenal, and Philips.

5028 Zeitz, Eileen M. and **Richard A.
Seybolt.** Hacia una bibliografía sobre el
realismo mágico (IUP/HJ, 3:1, Fall 1981,
p. 159–167)
Fairly compendious bibliography includes separate sections on Carpentier,
Rulfo, Roa Bastos, Arguedas, and Uslar Pietri.

Colonial Period

DANIEL R. REEDY, *Professor of Spanish, University of Kentucky*

THE FLOWERING OF INTEREST IN COLONIAL Spanish American letters and culture of which we spoke a few years ago has come to full bloom. Books and essays on major literary figures, and studies which move across generic and disciplinary lines, have ceased to be a rarity and are increasing annually in quantity and quality. There is also a positive orientation, in this writer's view, toward a renewed emphasis on the sociocultural and historical context of writers and their works. These changes are the result, it would appear, of the greater availability of primary source materials and of the broader dissemination of contextual information growing out of the research efforts of scholars on several continents, both in the field of literature and in sister disciplines.

Seldom has a single work stood out so prominently, at least in my 20 years of experience at preparing this bibliography, as does the monumental study which Octavio Paz has written: *Sor Juana Inés de la Cruz, o, Las trampas de la fe* (item **5057**). Without fear of contradiction, I believe that I can assert that it is the best and most complete study ever done of Sor Juana, her life, her writings, and her times. Unlike many of his predecessors, Paz does not ignore the social, cultural, and historical circumstances which surrounded Sor Juana; rather, he brings to life the history of viceregal New Spain, giving the reader a feeling for its society and vibrant intellectual environment in which Sor Juana interacted, and from which she was also isolated. Unlike many historical biographies, the central figure here is not obscured by a ponderous mass of historical information. On the contrary, the figure of Sor Juana is visible to the reader at all times, her works becoming the focal point of biographical interaction through which Paz draws yet another portrait of the Monja. His is not an "engaño colorido" but a clearer depiction than we have yet seen. Paz does not ignore past scholarship on Sor Juana and her works, but he does discard what has not stood the test of time and skillfully incorporates that which is long enduring. This is a work of one great literary figure about another, of one poet on another, of one Mexican who keenly perceives the enduring worth of a fellow Mexican. In some respects, this study may well be one of the most important books Octavio Paz has written. Its significance is found in what it says about Sor Juana and her times and in the model which it offers for future studies of colonial Spanish American letters.

Several other important studies which offer evidence of the ongoing high level of interest in Sor Juana and her works are included among items annotated below. Scholars, students, and the general readership will applaud the first complete English translation of the *Respuesta a Sor Filotea de la Cruz* by Margaret Sayers Peden (item **5048**). Several other articles are the product of a Symposium on Sor Juana and Viceregal Culture organized by Georgina Sabat-Rivers and held at the State University of New York, Stony Brook, in 1983 (item **5073**).

We would also like to draw attention to two masterful studies by Enrique Pupo-Walker, one in which he deals with creative and imaginative aspects of Spanish American historiography (item **5066**), and another which examines the works of the Inca Garcilaso de la Vega (item **5064**), one of the important contributions to scholarship on the Inca in recent years.

Finally, the publication of a facsimile edition of 66 issues of the *Gaceta de Lima* (item **5084**) by José Durand represents a noteworthy contribution as a source of important historical and cultural materials on viceregal Peru. We look forward to subsequent volumes that are being prepared and which will extend the availability of the *Gaceta* from 1765 through 1794.

INDIVIDUAL FIGURES

5029 Adorno, Rolena. Bartolomé de las Casas y Domingo de Santo Tomás en la obra de Felipe Waman Puma (IILI/RI, 48 : 120/121, julio/dic. 1982, p. 673–679)

Delineates clearly Felipe Waman Puma's ability to put into practice in his *Primer nueva corónica . . .* theories of two Spanish defenders of legal rights of Indians: B. de las Casas (*Tratado de las doce dudas*) and D. de Santo Tomás (*Grammática o arte de la lengua . . .*). Of cultural and historical interest.

5030 Alatorre, Antonio. Para leer la *Fama y obras pósthumas* de Sor Juana Inés de la Cruz (CM/NRFH, 29 : 2, 1980, p. 428–508)

Detailed examination of the Castorena 1700 Madrid ed. of Sor Juana's *Fama y obras pósthumas.* Valuable study which leaves few aspects of the ed. without comment. Well annotated, for the Sor Juana scholar.

5031 Arrom, José Juan. Bartolomé de las Casas, iniciador de la narrativa protesta (RCLL, 7 : 16, 1982, p. 27–38)

Examines various aspects of the Las Casas' works with emphasis on his *Apologética historia de las Indias* and the condemnation of Spanish atrocities against the Indians. Of historical/cultural interest.

5032 Bastos, María Luisa. El viaje atípico y autopico de Alonso Carrió de la Vandera (PUC/L, 5 : 2, dic. 1981, p. 51–57)

Sees purpose of Carrió de la Vandera's *Lazarillo* as being essentially pragmatic. More descriptive than analytical article.

5033 Bernal, Alfredo Alejandro. *La Araucana* de Alonso de Ercilla y Zúñiga y *Comentarios reales* del Inca Garcilaso de la Vega (IILI/RI, 48 : 120/121, julio/dic. 1982, p. 549–562)

Details use of the *Araucana* as source of information for Book VII of *Comentarios reales* in which Inca Garcilaso treats Conquest of Chile (i.e., use of literary creation as

historical source). Worthwhile comparative study of sources.

5034 Caeiro, Oscar. El espíritu de Santa Teresa en la obra de Tejeda (CRIT, 54 : 1868, 24 de sept. 1981, p. 562–567)

Treats instrumental role played by poet Luis de Tejeda in founding of first Carmelite Convent in South America (Córdoba, 1628). Examines Tejeda's *Libro de various tratados y noticias* and the *Coronas líricas.* Of interest to specialist.

5035 ———. Hacia una valoración literaria de la obra de Tejeda (UNC/R, 1979/1980, p. 19–33)

Primarily laudatory essay deals with various aspects of life and works of Argentine poet Luis de Tejeda. Four sonnets are appended.

5036 Chang-Rodríguez, Raquel. Armonía y disyunción en *La Florida del Inca* (CAM, 247 : 2, marzo/abril 1983, p. 148–156)

In Inca Garcilaso's *La Florida* (1605), author finds underlying tension between idealization of New World and of reality of the Conquest—between concepts of harmony and disharmony, ideas which are more clearly developed subsequently in *Comentarios reales.* Valuable perspective and contribution.

5037 ———. Coloniaje y conciencia nacional: Garcilaso de la Vega Inca y Felipe Guamán Poma de Ayala (UTIEH/C, 38, 1982, p. 29–43)

Essays contribute to our cultural, historical, and political awareness of colonial Peru. Deals with process of self identity leading to national conscience in works of Inca Garcilaso and Felipe Guamán Poma de Ayala.

5038 ———. Sobre los cronistas indígenas del Perú y los comienzos de una escritura hispanoamericana (IILI/RI, 48 : 120/121, julio/dic. 1982, p. 533–548, ill.)

Recounts particular contributions and historical viewpoints of three indigenous chroniclers of Viceroyalty of Peru in whose works writing and act of writing are a form of struggle and resistance against colonalism (e.g., Titu Cusi Yupanqui, Joan de Santacruz Pachacuti, Guamán Poma de Ayala). Excellent study.

5039 Colombí-Monguió, Alicia de. Las visiones de Petrarca en la América virreinal (IILI/RI, 120/121, julio/dic. 1982, p. 563–586)

Petrarch's "Canzone delle Visioni," first translated about 1580 by Enrique Garcés (Spain-Peru), influenced other New World writers: D. Dávalos y Figueroa (*Miscelánea austral*, 1602) and Sor Juana and J. de Guevara (*Amor es más laberinto*, 1689). Includes text of Garcés' translation. Of interest to specialist.

5040 IV [i.e. Cuarta] Jornadas Nacionales de Filosofía: homenaje a Fray Luis de Tejeda; conferencia del Doctor Gaspar Pío del Corro (UNC/R, 1979/1980, p. 35–47, bibl.)

Essay lauds aspects of Luis de Tejeda's major works (i.e., *Libro de varios tratados y noticias* and *Coronas líricas*). Includes worthwhile biographical and bibliographical notes.

5041 Echavarren, Roberto. Transposiciones: un roman epistolar de Sor Juana (IILI/RI, 48:120/121, julio/dic. 1982, p. 621–646)

Analysis of Sor Juana's poetic art through her *romances epistolares*, treating specifically characteristics of her *romance* to Don Diego de Valverde, Oidor de Indias ("Señor Don Diego Valverde . . ."); valuable insights into little studied aspect of Sor Juana's poetry.

5042 Emilfork, Leónidas. La doble escritura americana de Oviedo (UC/RCL, 19, abril 1982, p. 21–38)

Lengthy analysis of aspects of Fernández de Oviedo's *Historia general y natural* and the *Sumario*, focusing on two concepts of writing (*escritura de la hazaña* and *escritura del reconocimiento*). Presents valuable concepts.

5043 Gimbernat de González, Ester. En el espacio de la subversión barroca: el *Poema heroico* de H. Domínguez Camargo (ICC/T, 37:3, sept./dic. 1982, p. 523–543)

Interesting treatment of Domínguez Camargo's heroic life of St. Ignatius of Loyola.

Deals with complexity of concepts related to textual tensions growing out of the poem's bellicose aspects which go beyond the obviously bellicose stages in the saint's life.

5044 González, Aníbal. Los infortunios de Alonso Ramírez (AR, 51:2, Spring 1983, p. 189–204)

Analyzes in detail significant historical and picaresque aspects of Sigüenza y Góngora's Los infortunios . . ., growing out of chronicles of the Conquest (e.g., Cabeza de Vaca, Díaz del Castillo) and picaresque novel (e.g., M. Alemán). Presents cogent and convincing arguments.

5045 Hernández, Max and Fernando Saba. Garcilaso Inca de la Vega: historia de un patronímico (*in* Perú: identidad nacional. Lima: Centro de Estudios para el Desarrollo y la Participación [CEDEP], 1979, p. 109–121 [Serie Realidad nacional])

Points out psychological stages in life and works of Inca Garcilaso de la Vega in relationship to his *mestizaje*. Interesting approach to topic.

5046 Infante, Víctor Manuel. Bibliografía e iconografía de Luis José de Tejeda: 1604–1680 (Revista Nacional de Cultura [Ediciones Culturales Argentinas, Buenos Aires] 2:7, 1980, p. 39–64, ill.)

The 300th anniversary of Luis José de Tejeda's death (1680), prompts this article. Lists significant bibliographical sources on Tejeda published during preceding 30 years, as addendum to J.M. Furt's 1947 ed. of *Libro de varios tratados y noticias*. Valuable bibliographical source.

5047 Jornadas de Teatro Clásico Español, 5th, Almagro, Spain, 1982. V [i.e. Cinco] Jornadas de Teatro Clásico Español: el trabajo con los clásicos en el teatro contemporáneo. Dirección y revisión de materiales, Juan Antonio Hormigón. Madrid: Dirección General de Música y Teatro, Ministerio de Cultura, 1982/1983. 2 v.: bibl., ill.

Contains two essays: Carlos Miguel Suárez Radillo, "Visión Panorámica del Teatro Barroco Virreinal del Mestizaje Hispanoamericano" (p. 249–270); and Hugo Gutiérrez Vega "Sor Juana y el Barroco Mexicano" (p. 273–293). Both works contain general comments on major Spanish American Baroque dramatists.

5048 Juana Inés de la Cruz, *Sor.* A woman of genius: the intellectual autobiography of Sor Juana Inés de la Cruz. Translated and introduction by Margaret Sayers Peden. Photographs by Gabriel North Seymour. Salisbury, Conn.: Lime Rock Press, 1982. 181 p.: bibl., ill.

First complete translation published in English of Sor Juana's famous *Respuesta a Sor Filotea de la Cruz.* Translation and text are on facing pages. Notes provide Latin citations which appear in English in translated version. Translation is excellent and edition well done. Welcome addition to bibliography on Sor Juana and of great utility to student, scholar, and reading public.

5048a Lastra, Pedro. Sobre Juan Rodríguez Freyle: notas de lectura (ECO, 6:252, 1982, p. 625–637)

Treats interrelationship of intercalated *historielas* (*relatos, cuentos*) in Rodríguez Freyle's *El carnero* to concept of the chronicle (e.g., Díaz del Castillo, Núñez Cabeza de Vaca, Inca Garcilaso). Also published in *University of Dayton Review* (item **5073**).

Lavrin, Asunción. Unlike Sor Juana?: the model nun in the religious literature of colonial Mexico. See item **1995.**

5049 Lerner, Isías. Pero Mexía en Alonso de Ercilla (Bulletin of Hispanic Studies [Institute of Hispanic Studies, Liverpool, England] 60:2, April 1983, p. 129–134)

Points out direct relationship between Pero Mexía's *Silva de varia lección* (1540) and Ercilla's *Araucana,* primarily in Cantos II, XXI, and XXIX. Of interest primarily to specialist.

5050 Lewis, Robert E. Los Naufragios de Alvar Núñez: historia y ficción (IILI/RI, 48:120/121, julio/dic. 1982, p. 681–694)

Insightful examination of fictional/historical tensions in *Naufragios* based on text and prologue addressing Carlos V. Alvar Núñez's work, contains personal recollections, autobiographical information, and intercalated tales which project work beyond strict confines of historiography.

5051 López Baralt, Mercedes. La crónica de Indias como texto cultural: articulación de los códigos icónico y lingüístico en los dibujos de la *Nueva corónica* de Guamán Poma (IILI/RI, 48:120/121, julio/dic. 1982, p. 462–531, ill.)

Treats linguistic and iconographic aspects of Guamán Poma's *Primer nueva corónica . . .* in light of semiotic premise that most important signs of human society are based on sight and sound. Includes 46 illustrations from the chronicle. Valuable contribution to our knowledge of this *cronista.* For historian's comment, see item **1658.**

5052 Luis de Tejeda: homenaje en el tercer centenario de su muerte, 1680–1980. Córdoba, Argentina: Universidad Nacional de Córdoba, Facultad de Filosofía y Humanidades, 1981. 84 p.: facsim., plates.

Three essays presented as *homage* to Argentina's first poet, Luis de Tejeda, at Córdoba's National University on 300th anniversary of poet's death. Of interest only to specialist.

5053 Luzuriaga, Gerardo. Sigüenza y Góngora y Sor Juana: disidentes de la cultura oficial (CAM, 243:3, mayo/junio 1982, p. 140–162)

Finds in writings of Sor Juana and Sigüenza y Góngora dawn of Enlightenment as well as prelude of intellectual and political independence in Mexico and the New World. Comments center on Sigüenza's *Libra astronómica* and Sor Juana's *Respuesta a Sor Filotea* and the *Primero sueño* with remarks on Johannes Kepler's influences.

5054 Martínez, José Luis. Una muestra de la elaboración de la *Historia verdadera,* de Bernal Díaz del Castillo (IGFO/RI, 41:165/166, julio/dic. 1981, p. 723–731)

Compares aspects of Ch. 152 of Díaz del Castillo's *Historia verdadera* to comparable accounts by Cortés and Gómara. Finds Díaz del Castillo's version to be more truthful as well as more imaginative, and written with greater narrative style than those of his contemporaries.

5055 Martínez Chacón, Elena. *Arauco domado*: Lope de Vega y Ercilla; motivación de venganza y panegírico (UC/RCL, 16/17, oct. 1980/abril 1981, p. 229–256)

Article traces influence of Ercilla's *La Araucana* and Oña's *El Arauco domado* on Lope de Vega, principally in Lope's *comedia, Arauco domado.* Includes comparative analysis.

5056 Montross, Constance M. Virtue or vice: Sor Juana's use of Thomistic thought. Washington: University Press of America, 1981. 91 p.: appendix, bibl.

Analyzes combination of belief and questioning in Sor Juana's two letters, *Carta atenagórica* and *Respuesta a Sor Filotea* and in the *Sueño*. Also examines her use of scholastic doctrine and methodology in light of St. Thomas Aquinas' and Aristotle's writings. Valuable contribution.

5057 Paz, Octavio. Sor Juana Inés de la Cruz, o, Las trampas de la fe. Barcelona: Seix Barral, 1982. 658 p., 32 p. of plates: ill., index (Biblioteca breve; 608)

History, biography and literary criticism are skillfully interwoven into this volume on Sor Juana. Pt. 1 examines Viceroyalty of New Spain; pts. 2–6, different stages of Sor Juana's life and works. History, society, and literary creativity are thoroughly integrated into a monumental study of the Tenth Muse. Possibly the finest contribution to Sor Juana studies ever published. For historian's comment, see item **2011.**

5058 ———. Sor Juana: testigo de cargo (Vuelta [México] 8:78, mayo 1983, p. 46–49)

Comments on importance of *Carta de la Madre Juana Inés de la Cruz escrita al R.P.M. Antonio Núñez de la Compañía de Jesús*, discovered in Monterrey and published in 1981 by Padre Aureliano Tapia Méndez. Letter appears to be an early draft (ca. 1682) of ideas contained subsequently in the *Respuesta*. Contains valuable information.

5059 Perelmuter Pérez, Rosa. Los cultismos herrerianos en el *Primero sueño* de Sor Juana Inés de la Cruz (UB/BH, 83:3/4, juillet/déc. 1981, p. 439–446)

Catalog of *cultismos* in Sor Juana's *Primero sueño* which come directly from Fernando de Herrera's work and not through Góngora as intermediary. Valuable study of linguistic sources for Sor Juana specialist.

5060 ———. La estructura retórica de la *Respuesta a Sor Filotea* (HR, 51:2, Spring 1983, p. 147–158)

Focuses on function of rhetoric in organization and content of *Respuesta a Sor Filotea*, according to precepts of classical models of argumentative discourse. Excellent article.

5061 ———. La hipérbasis en el *Primero sueño* (IILI/RI, 48:120/121, julio/dic. 1982, p. 715–725)

Detailed examination of stylistic features of Sor Juana's *Primero sueño*, notably poem's syntactical complexity owing to frequent syntactical dislocations occasioned by use of hyperbaton. Adds clarity to our understanding of this important work.

5062 Pérez Gutiérrez, Leticia. Presencia de Calderón de la Barca en México (UNL/H, 22, 1981, p. 1331–43, bibl.)

Focuses on Calderón de la Barca's influence on Matías de Bocanegra, Sor Juana Inés de la Cruz, Eusebio Vela, and Cayetano de Cabrera y Quintero. Also recounts Mexican stagings of Calderón's works from 1655 through 19th century.

5063 Piras, Pina Rosa. I simboli trasparenti di Sor Juana Inés de la Cruz, in *Este que ves, engaño colorido* (QIA, 7:53/54, 1979/1980, p. 271–282)

Exegetical study of Sor Juana's famous sonnet to her portrait (145) which deals primarily with poem's linguistic and structural aspects. Contains interesting observations.

5064 Pupo-Walker, Enrique. Historia, creación y profecía en los textos del Inca Garcilaso de la Vega. Madrid: José Porrúa Turranzas, 1982. 205 p., 2 leaves of plates: ill. (Ensayos)

Critical evaluation of historical concepts in the Inca's works. Examines relationship of biographical elements to texts, narrative structure and creative elaboration of historical discourse in *Comentarios*, and intercalation of fictional accounts in *La Florida* and *Comentarios*. Important contribution to scholarship on the Inca in recent years.

5065 ———. Notas para una caracterización de *El Lazarillo de ciegos caminantes* (IILI/RI, 120/121, julio/dic. 1982, p. 647–670)

Well-documented study of multifaceted organization of Carrió de la Vandera's work whose importance is both historical and literary. Examines text in cultural and historiographic context. Compares importance of work to that of other 17th-18th-century New World texts of similar characteristics.

5066 ———. La vocación literaria del pensamiento histórico en América: desarrollo de la prosa de ficción; siglos XVI, XVII, XVIII y XIX. Madrid: Editorial Gredos, 1982. 220 p.: bibl., index (Biblioteca románica hispánica; 2. Estudios y ensayos; 318)

Important essays on imaginative elements in Inca Garcilaso's *Comentarios reales*, Rodríguez Freyle's *El carnero*, Carrió de la Vandera's *Lazarillo de ciegos caminantes*, and early 19th-century *cuadro de costumbres* and short story. Of special note, Ch. 1 on creative aspects of Spanish-American historiography.

Rieu-Millan, Marie-Laure. Une lettre inédite de Fray Servando de Mier, 1810. See item **1944.**

5067 Rodríguez-Vecchini, Hugo. Don Quijote y *La Florida del Inca* (IILI/RI, 48:120/121, julio/dic. 1982, p. 587–620)

Significant article which compares major works by Cervantes and the Inca Garcilaso. Examines *Don Quijote* as history of writing a novel and *La Florida* as history of writing America's true history. Analyzes historical discourse in light of theories by Della Volpe and H. White.

5068 Sabat de Rivers, Georgina. Sor Juana: diálogo de retratos (IILI/RI, 48:120/121, julio/dic. 1982, p. 703–713)

Analyzes Sor Juana's special fondness for poems related to feminine portraiture in connection with two poems: "Copia Divina, en Quien Veo . . ." and "A Tus Manos Me Traslada . . .". Author's comments contribute significantly to our knowledge of the Monja's poetic art.

5069 Sáenz de Santa María, Carmelo. Un manuscrito de Cieza localizado en la Biblioteca Apostólica Vaticana (IFGO/RI, 41:163/164, enero/junio 1981, p. 31–42)

Extensive comments on Vatican manuscript of pts. 2–3 of Cieza de León's *Crónica del Perú* with additional remarks on ed. by Francesca Cantu (Rome, 1979). Of value to specialist.

5070 Sáinz, Enrique. Silvestre de Balboa y la literatura cubana. La Habana: Editorial Letras Cubanas, 1982. 151 p.: bibl. (Colección Espiral)

Volume of essays on 16th- and 17th-century Cuban literature covers aspects of *Espejo de Paciencia*, and includes biographi-

cal sketch of Silvestre de Balboa (1563?–1644?). Worthwhile but not exhaustive study.

5071 Sor Juana Inés de la Cruz ante la historia: biografías antiguas; *La Fama* de 1700, *Noticias* de 1667 a 1892. Recopilación de Francisco de la Maza. Revisión de Elía Trabulse. México: Universidad Nacional Autónoma de México, 1980. 612 p., 17 p. of plates: bibl., ill. (some col.) (Estudios de literatura; 4)

Prodigious collection of comments about Sor Juana gathered from multiple sources (1667–1892). Reproduces numerous illustrations and contains extensive bibliography. Of prime importance to Sorjuanistas.

5072 Turner, E. Daymond, Jr. Gonzalo Fernández de Oviedo y Valdés: prosista (IGFO/RI, 43:717, enero/junio 1983, p. 327–334)

Reviews various critics' comments made over several decades about Oviedo's prose works (e.g., *Quincuagenas, Historia general . . ., Sumario, Claribalte.*)

5073 *The University of Dayton Review.* Vol. 16, No. 2, Spring 1983– . Dayton, Ohio.

Issue contains essays on Balbuena, Rodríguez Freyle, Sor Juana, and viceregal culture and language by several distinguished scholars in the field. Reproduces proceedings of symposium on Sor Juana Inés de la Cruz and viceregal culture held at SUNY (Stony Brook, 1982). Significant contributions to colonial scholarship.

TEXTS

5074 Acosta, José de. Peregrinación de Bartolomé Lorenzo. Edición y prólogo de José Juan Arrom. Lima: PetroPerú: Ediciones Copé, 1982. 66 p.

Edition of novelesque, fictionalized biography of Portuguese Jesuit, Bartolomé Lorenzo, recorded by Jesuit historian and naturalist José de Acosta (1540–1600). The *Peregrinación* seems intended as brief travel and adventure novel. Prologue provides historical and critical comments on Acosta and his work. Valuable addition to our knowledge of early fictionalized narrative.

5075 Cancionero peruano del siglo XVII. Estudio preliminar, edición y bibliografía: Raquel Chang-Rodríguez. Lima:

Pontíficia Universidad Católica del Perú, 1983. 168 p.: bibl.

Valuable collection of 21 poems, composed 1607–16, of which 10 are by known poets who resided in 17th-century Peru. Preliminary remarks provide valuable historical, textual, and critical comments.

5076 Ercilla, Alonso de. La araucana. Selección y notas intermedias de Roque Esteban Scarpa. Santiago: Editorial A. Bello, 1982. 253 p.

Anthologized selection of various cantos of Ercilla's *Araucana* in modernized version intended for students and popular readership. Without benefit of explanatory notes. Primarily of value as inexpensive classroom text.

5077 Flores de baria poesía. Prólogo, edición, crítica e índices de Margarita Peña. México: Universidad Nacional Autónoma de México, Facultad de Filosofía y Letras, 1980. 549 p.: bibl., facsim., indexes (Seminarios)

Annotated ed. of manuscript no. 2973 (Biblioteca Nacional, Madrid), a *Cancionero* containing works by several peninsular poets as well as others such as Creoles and poets who traveled to the New World (e.g., Francisco de Terrazas, Martín Cortés, Carlos de Sámano, Hernán González de Eslava). Poems are from 1543–77. Valuable collection of 16th-century authors.

5078 Juana Inés de la Cruz, Sor. Inundación Castálida. Edición, introducción y notas de Georgina Sabat de Rivers. Madrid: Editorial Castalia, 1982. 502 p.: bibl., indexes (Clásicos Castalia; 117)

Excellent ed. based on princeps of Sor Juana's *Inundación Castálida* (Madrid, 1689). Contains extensive selection of poetic and prose texts edited with scholarly criteria. Introduction, notes, bibliography, and onomastic index add to value for student and scholar.

5079 Poemas en alabanza de los defensores de Cartagena de Indias en 1741. Recogidos y publicados por Guillermo Hernández de Alba. Edición y anotaciones de Guillermo Hernández Peñalosa. Bogotá: Instituto Caro y Cuervo, 1982. 283 p., 14 leaves of plates: bibl., ill. (Publicaciones; 50)

Contains two sections: one of poems, the other of historical materials related to Cartagena's 1741 siege in Nuevo Reino de Granada. Poems and historical documents were written and/or published before end of 18th century. Of greater historical than esthetic interest.

MISCELLANEOUS

5080 Beverly, J. El gongorismo, discurso colonial post-épico (UR/L, Spring 1980, p. 57–65)

Brief but interesting examination of Gongorism in New World, post-Conquest period, which argues that it represents essentially a new form of colonialization by letters and not by arms.

5081 Carilla, Emilio. La lírica rococó en Hispanoamérica (IILI/RI, 48:120/121, julio/dic. 1982, p. 727–738)

Rococó in Hispanic America is seen primarily as derivative of Baroque. Author examines theoretical concepts of *rococó*, details general characteristics, and lists major writers associated with style (e.g., Peralta Barnuevo, Vélez Ladrón de Guevara, Aguirre, Martínez de Navarrete). Valuable historical and theoretical insights.

5082 Durán Pombo, Jaime. El idioma del descubrimiento (ACH/BHA, 66:725, abril/junio 1979, p. 199–215, bibl.)

Traces employment by Columbus of New World vocabulary and toponyms in *Diario* and *Cartas*. Places this American enrichment of language in the linguistic context of 15th-16th-century Spain.

5083 Escobedo Mansilla, Ronald. El tributo de los zambaigos, negros y mulatos libres en el Virreinato peruano (IGFO/RI, 41:163/164, enero/junio 1981, p. 43–54)

Essay of value for its sociological perspective on important racial and cultural components of colonial Spanish American society. Well documented study.

5084 Gaceta de Lima. v. 1, 1756 a 1762: de Superunda a Amat. v. 2, 1762 a 1765: Apogeo de Amat. Compilación y prólogo de José Durand. Lima: Corporación Financiera de Desarrollo (COFIDE), 1982. 2 v. (409, 319 p.): appendices, indexes.

Facsimile ed. of 66 issues of *Gaceta de Lima* (20 April 1756 through 28 Dec. 1765). Noteworthy collection, handsomely edited, with ample introductory study by Durand. Extremely valuable contribution of great historical and cultural interest. Subsequent volumes will present extant numbers for 1765–94.

5085 Historia de la literatura hispano-americana. t. 1, Epoca colonial. Coordinador: Iñigo Madrigal. M. Alvar *et al.* Madrid: Ediciones Cátedra, 1982. 434 p.: bibl., ill., tables.

Projected vol. 1 of several on topic. Divided into: 1) La América Colonial; 2) Cartas, Crónicas y Relaciones; 3) Epoca Hispanoamericana Colonial; 4) Lírica Hispanoamericana Colonial; 5) Teatro Hispanoamericano Colonial; and 6) Novela Hispanoamericana Colonial. Contributors: M. Alvar, R.A. Borello, E. Camacho Guizado, E. Carilla, J. Concha, M. Díaz Roig, J. Franco, C. Goíc, B. Lavalle, M. Lucena Salmoral, G. Meo-Zilio, W. Mignolo, F. Pierce, P. Piñero Ramírez, D.R. Reedy, A.A. Roggiano, G. Rojo, G. Sabat de Rivers, A. Saint Lu, and K. Shelly. [Ed.]

5086 Johnson, Julio Greer. Women in colonial Spanish American literature: literary images. Westport, Conn: Greenwood Press, 1983. 212 p.: bibl., index (Contributions in women's studies; 43)

Studies literary image of females in several Spanish American colonial sources, principally works of Inca Garcilaso, Díaz del Castillo, Las Casas, Ercilla, Oña, Núñez de Pineda, Terrazas, Balbuena, Rosas de Oquendo, Caviedes, Carrió de la Vandera, González de Eslava, Sor Juana, Madre Castillo, and others. Well-researched and documented contribution on important and timely aspect of colonial culture.

5087 Leinhard, Martin. La crónica mestiza en México y el Perú hasta 1620: apun-

tes para su estudio histórico-literario (RCLL, 9:17, 1983, p. 103–115)

Preliminary examination of historical and literary characteristics of several *mestizo* chronicles by Peruvian and Mexican authors. Contains valuable observations.

5088 Phillips, Rachel. Marina/Malinche: masks and shadows (*in* Women in Hispanic literature: icons and fallen idols. Edited by Beth Miller. Berkeley: University of California Press, 1983, p. 97–114)

Excellent, imaginative article which traces evolution from historical reality to myth of Cortes' companion, Marina (Malinche).

5089 Shelly, Kathleen. El teatro en la América Hispana durante el siglo XVI (UT/RCEH, 7:1, otoño 1982, p. 89–101)

Studies 16th-century theatre written in Spanish and indigenous languages—religious and didactic pieces growing out of religious and civil sources whose purpose was ideological. Treats works by unknown dramatists as well as pieces by Pérez Ramírez, González de Eslava, de Llerena, and others.

5090 TePaske, John J. An interview with Irving A. Leonard (HABR, 63:2, May 1983, p. 233–253)

Delightful conversation with eminent historian of Spanish American literature, first contributor to prepare the colonial literature section of *HLAS* (see *HLAS 1*, p. 190–195), and author of two classics on colonial Latin America: *Books of the brave* and *Baroque times in old Mexico*. Interesting background on the composition of these books and development of studies in colonial Latin America in 1930s and 1940s. [R. González-Echevarría]

19th Century: Prose Fiction, Other Prose Writings and Poetry (1800–1900)

NICOLAS SHUMWAY, *Associate Professor of Spanish, Yale University*

WITH THE BICENTENNIAL COMMEMORATION of Andrés Bello's birth in 1781, it is not surprising that much of this biennium's scholarly effort deals with Venezuela's most illustrious man of letters. Most significant in this connection is the last in three sets of two-volume works regarding different stages in Bello's life, published by La Fundación Casa de Bello. In *HLAS 44* (p. 417), I commented on the two earlier sets in this series, *Bello y Caracas* and *Bello y Londres* (*HLAS 44:5121–5122*). In a sense, these two titles may be more significant than the third one, discussed below, because they concern preparatory periods in Bello's life which are generally less known. Nonetheless, the two volumes discussed below, entitled *Bello y Chile* (item **5103**) contain several excellent pieces on Bello's most productive, and thereby more familiar, years in Chile. Particularly interesting in *Bello y Chile* are several articles devoted to Bello's work in jurisprudence. Also highly significant in Bello scholarship is a collection from Seix Barral of Pedro Grases's essays on Bello (item **5117**). For nearly three decades, Grases has published on virtually every aspect of Bello's career. This edition of his best essays stands as a monument, both to Bello's memory and to Grases' careful scholarship. For Bello studies in English-speaking countries, special thanks is also in order to the Organization of American States which, in *Anthology of Andrés Bello* (item **5101**), has given us the best English-language collection of Bello's works yet to appear. Also noteworthy but not discussed below for reasons of space are Salvador Tenreiro's "Epistolario de Bello en Chile," Pedro Grases' "Bello, Humanista y Universitario," and Arturo Uslar Pietri's "Bello, el Venezolano" which appeared in the two 1982 issues of *Revista Nacional de la Cultura* (Consejo Nacional de Cultura, Caracas).

Also in the centennial spirit is a proliferation of essays and books on Argentina's pivotal "Generación del 80," a watershed generation of writers and intellectuals caught up in debates about liberal elitism, populist resentment, the Radical movement towards real democracy, Buenos Aires vs. the provinces, the materialism brought on by unprecedented prosperity, the abandonment of Hispanic values, and the ethnic transitions, particularly in Buenos Aires, forced on the country by the urban migrations of the rural poor and the crushing numbers of immigrants arriving daily from southern Europe. Particularly useful in this regard are the published papers of a Symposium held in Bahía Blanca at the Universidad del Sur in Argentina. Again for reasons of space, only a few of these papers are mentioned below (items **5095, 5107,** and **5109**); the entire volume of the proceedings, however, would be worth acquiring. Special reference must also be made to Evelyn Fishburn's excellent *Portrayal of immigration in nineteenth century Argentine fiction: 1845–1902* (item **5112**) which discusses with careful intelligence writers like Cané, Cambeceres, and Martel. Also worthy of mention with regards to the 1880s generation is Alejandro Losada's *La literatura en la sociedad de América Latina* (item **5120**).

PROSE FICTION AND POETRY

Almafuerte. Poesías completas. See item **5656**.

5091 Echeverría, Esteban. Antología de prosa y verso. Antología, cronología, edición, bibliografía, prólogo y notas de Osvaldo Pellettieri. Buenos Aires: Editorial de Belgrano, 1981. 580 p.: bibl. (Colección Clásicos argentinos)

Another successful anthology from monographic series "Clásicos Argentinos," this collection of Echeverría's representative works also contains biographical essay and critical notes which Juan María Gutiérrez wrote for *Obras completas de Esteban Echeverría* (1870–72). Well represented in this lengthy anthology are main areas of Echeverría's work, including poetry, political writings, literary criticism, letters, and autobiographical notes. Recommended.

5092 Hudson, William Henry. La tierra purpúrea [and] Allá lejos y hace tiempo. Prólogo y cronología, Jean Franco. Traducción, Idea Vilariño. Caracas: Biblioteca Ayacucho, 1980. 615 p.: bibl. (Biblioteca Ayacucho; 63)

Volume combines two of Hudson's best known works in readable Spanish translation: *La tierra purpúrea* is a novel that in Kipling-like fashion defends notion of British empire, while providing fine portrait of Argentine life prior to large immigrations that began in 1880s; *Allá lejos y hace tiempo* recalls fondly Hudson's childhood and youth in the pampas. Franco's foreword supplies useful and cogently presented information about Hudson, his works and times; same cannot be said for "Cronología" (200 p.) inserted by editors listing historical events whose relationship to Hudson's life is left to readers' imagination. Is Biblioteca Ayacucho staff so hard up for things to publish that they have to devote fully a third of this expensive volume to virtually useless lists of undifferentiated and arbitrarily selected historical data?

5092a Jiménez, José Olivio. Dos símbolos existenciales en la obra de José Martí (UY/R, 24:139, enero/feb. 1982, p. 99–119)

Aguda exploración de la máscara como emblema del dolor de la inautenticidad en Martí, vista en el contexto filosófico de su época, particularmente el Nietzsche de *Más allá del bien y del mal* y de *Ecce homo*. [R. Ríos Avila]

5093 Meza y Suárez Inclán, Ramón. Carmela. Prólogo de Salvador Bueno. La Habana: Editorial Arte y Literatura, 1978. 161 p. (Biblioteca básica de literatura cubana)

Overshadowed by Meza's best novel, *Mi tío, el empleado*, and overlooked as "hermana menor de *Cecilia Valdés*," *Carmela* is finally available in popular edition. Since *Cecilia Valdés* and *Carmela* both tell tragic stories of two beautiful mulatto women, comparisons are inevitable. Each however, should be studied in its own right, since both are cast against different historical backgrounds and narrated in distinct novelistic traditions. Unlike other editions from "Biblioteca Básica" series, contains weak introduction and no notes. Not useful outside classroom.

Poetas parnasianos de Venezuela. See item 5653.

5094 Riva Palacio, Vicente. Antología de Vicente Riva Palacio. Introducción y selección, Clementina Díaz y de Ovando. México: Universidad Nacional Autónoma de México, 1976. 135 p. (Biblioteca del estudiante universitario; 79)

Best suited for classroom use, short anthology nonetheless includes lengthy and informative introduction to Riva Palacio's writings. Selections, however, are successful, partly because one longs for more short stories, a genre in which Riva Palacio did his best work.

LITERARY CRITICISM AND HISTORY

5095 Anderson Imbert, Enrique. Alejandro Korn y la generación del 80 (*in* Simposio Internacional de Lengua y Literaturas Hispánicas, Bahía Blanca, Argentina, 1980. Simposio Internacional de Lengua y Literaturas Hispánicas. Dinko Cvitanovic and María Beatriz Fontanella de Weinberg, compiladores. Bahía Blanca: Departamento de Humanidades, Universidad Nacional del Sur, 1981, p. 23–30)

Partly documentary, partly personal, article outlines briefly Korn's careful self-distancing from positivism of contemporaries. Particularly interesting for literary scholars is Anderson Imbert's analysis of Korn's early novel, *Juan Pérez*, where Korn anticipates themes developed in later discursive writings.

5096 Antología del bellismo en Venezuela. Selección y prólogo de Pedro Grases. 2a. ed. aum. Caracas: Monte Avila Editores, 1981. 478 p.: bibl., index (Colección El Dorado)

Although Bello's intellectual life transpired mostly outside of his native Venezuela, this collection of essays on him demonstrates that Venezuelans have led the way in documenting his monumental contribution to Hispanic letters. Since Grases' selection required deceased contributors, many texts were written in the last century. Result: the collection serves dual purpose of illuminating different aspects of Bello's life while giving us glimpse of how he was viewed by past generations of Venezuelan intellectuals.

5097 Araya, Guillermo. Historia y sociedad en la obra de Alberto Blest Gana (RCLL, 7:14, 1981, p. 29–64)

Superbly documented introduction to Blest Gana, this careful article not only outlines his life and works, but convincingly locates his novels within sociopolitical fabric of their time. Highly recommended.

5098 Ardao, Arturo. Del mito Ariel al mito anti-Ariel (CNC/A, 2, 1977, p. 7–27)

Rather than study of *Ariel, arielismo,* and their detractors as suggested by title, article is lengthy refutation of statements concerning *Ariel* in Carlos Rangel's *Del buen salvaje al buen revolucionario* (see *HLAS* 41:7065, p. 94–97). Rangel accuses Rodó of being anti-democratic, elitist, and befogged on subject of US. With mixed success Ardao seeks to refute Rangel using extensive quotations from Rodó. Interested readers would be well served to look at Rodríguez Monegal's superb introduction to Rodó's *Obras completas.*

5099 Bareiro Saguier, Rubén. La poesía de Andrés Bello: lectura actualizada del significado (CONAC/RNC, 43:249, abril/dic. 1983, p. 144–160)

Sensitive article with misleading title, this reading of several of Bello's best known poems finds that, underlying his *americanismo* and hopes for the future is the nostalgia of an exile. Bareiro Saguier makes his point particularly poignant with his own testimony as exile from Paraguay.

5100 Barrenechea, Ana María. Sobre la modalidad autobiográfica en Sarmiento (CN/NRFH, 29:2, 1980, p. 509–519)

Exceptionally fine article looks at Sarmiento's work through the glass of the most recent theories on autobiography, both from North America and Europe. Article has additional merit of concentrating on two of Sarmiento's lesser known autobiographical works, namely *Campaña en el Ejército Grande* and *Mi defensa.* Highly recommended.

5101 Bello, Andrés. Anthology. Compiled by Pedro Grases. Foreword by Rafael Caldera. Translated by Barbara D. Huntley and Pilar Liria. Washington: General Secretariat, Organization of America States, 1981. 259 p., 1 leaf of plates: bibl., ill.

Excellent anthology makes available for first time in English, Bello's most representative texts. Grases has done a superb job of choosing selections that reflect vast range of Bello's genius, including essays on language, literary criticism, law, education, philosophy, and journalism. Anthology also contains several of Bello's lesser known poems, translated for first time, some better than others. Highly recommended.

5102 Bello en Colombia: homenaje a Don Andrés Bello en el segundo centenario de su nacimiento. Estudio y selección de Rafael Torres Quintero. 2a. ed. Bogotá: Instituto Caro y Cuervo, 1981. 260 p., 1 leaf of plates: ill.

Collection of essays by writers of several generations. Covers some new and much old ground. Contrary to what title suggests, only connection with Colombia stems from fact that most contributors are Colombian. Most useful essays are by Marco Fidel Suárez, Lucio Pabón Nuñéz, and Manuel Antonio Bonilla, who comment on Bello's continuing importance as grammarian.

5103 Bello y Chile: Tercer Congreso del Bicentenario. Caracas: Fundación la Casa de Bello, 1981. 2 v.: bibl., ill., index

Two-volume set contains proceedings of splendid congreso. Papers all worthwhile, by: Pedro Grases, Paul Verdevoye, Colin Smith, Leopoldo Zea, Germán Arciniegas, and Fernando Murillo Rubiera. Although some discuss more than Chile, most concern Bello's writings and activities during his extended residence there. Particularly interesting are nine fine pieces on Bello as legal philosopher. Highly recommended.

5104 Brushwood, John Stubbs. Genteel barbarism: experiments in analysis of nineteenth-century Spanish-American novels. Lincoln: University of Nebraska Press, 1981. 241 p.: bibl., index.

No North American critic has contributed to our understanding of the 19th-century Spanish American novel more than Brushwood. Readers used to his solid, historicist approach, will be surprised at this experimental, inconclusive book. Applies contemporary theories of reading ranging from New Criticism to semiotics, to seven novelists including Mármol, Blest, Gana, Isaacs, and Matto de Turner. Concludes by evaluating aptness of each theory and his success in applying it. Although novelists studied are among last century's best, one regrets arbitrariness with which theorists were chosen (e.g., excluding Derrida, Ecco, Bakhtin, de Man, Foucault, Miller). Still, among the most important books of the biennium and certainly deserving of attention.

5105 Burns, E. Bradford. Bartolomé Mitre: the historian as novelist, the novel as history (RIB, 32:2, 1982, p. 155–167)

Major Latin American historian examines self-serving intentions of Mitre's novel, *Soledad* and his biographies of San Martín and Belgrano. Without mentioning Foucault and Haydn White, argues that historian Mitre and novelist Mitre used similar premises, prejudices and procedures, creating for the Argentine upper classes a "formidable ideology" that justified their privileges. For historian's comment, see item **3190.**

5106 Caillet-Bois, Julio. Naturaleza, historia y providencia en *Facundo* (*in* International Congress of Hispanists, 4th, Salamanca, Spain, 1971. Actas. Dirección, Eugenio Bustos Tovar. Salamanca: Asociación Internacional de Hispanists, 1982, v. 1, p. 817–832)

Maintains that underlying much of Sarmiento's selection and presentation of materials in *Facundo* is a profound, perhaps unconscious, belief in divine destiny, hope, and retribution. Even detractors from Caillet-Bois' position cannot but be impressed with his lucid and well documented argumentation.

5107 ———. Sobre *Facundo*: notas al Cap. II, Pte. 1 (*in* Simposio Internacional de Lengua y Literaturas Hispánicas, Bahía Blanca, Argentina, 1980. Simposio Internacional e Lengua y Literatura Hispánicas. Dinko Cvitanovic and María Beatriz Fontanella de Weinberg, compiladores. Bahía Blanca: Departamento de Humanidades, Universidad Nacional del Sur, 1981, p. 37–48)

As title suggests, less an article than series of notes regarding themes, sources, development, authorial motives, style, etc., in much anthologized second chapter of *Facundo*. At same time, Caillet-Bois' insightful and well supported "notes" deserve attention.

5108 Campo, Estanislao del. *Fausto*: impresiones del gaucho Anastasio el Pollo en la representación de esta ópera. Prólogo y notas de Enrique Anderson Imbert. Buenos Aires: Editorial de Belgrano, 1981. 130 p.: bibl. (Colección Clásicos argentinos)

Monographic series "Clásicos Argentinos" has mixed record, so that I have excluded several of their publications from this bibliography. Others, like this edition of Estanislao del Campo's *Fausto*, comprise significant contribution to study of Latin American letters and are worth seeking out. Particularly useful is Anderson Imbert's introduction (half the book).

5109 Carilla, Emilio. La lírica del 80 (*in* Simposio Internacional de Lengua y Literaturas Hispánicas, Bahía Blanca, Argentina, 1980. Simposio Internacional de Lengua y Literaturas Hispánicas. Dinko Cvitanovic and María Beatriz Fontanella de Weinberg, compiladores. Bahia Blanca: Departamento de Humanidades, Universidad Nacional del Sur, 1981, p. 49–69, bibl.)

Concise, useful overview of poets and poetry of Argentine "Generación del 80." Also provides ample bibliographical information on both original works and criticism.

5110 Caro, Miguel Antonio. Obras completas. t. 2. Bogotá: Instituto Caro y Cuervo, 1979? 1 v.: bibl., ill., index (Biblioteca colombiana; 20?)

Vol. 2 of Caro's *Obras completas* consists entirely of material written about Bello. Although one must thank Caro for being among first Latin American critics to write extensively on Bello, his biobibliographical information (bulk of book) has been superseded by more recent works. Other essays provide interesting guide to Caro's own values, particularly his tedious insistence that Bello was as devout a Catholic as Caro himself.

Cerutti, Franco. Una fuente olvidada de la historia nicaragüense del siglo XIX: Pedro Ortiz. See item **2387.**

5111 Díaz de Fortier, Matilde. La crítica literaria en Puerto Rico: 1843–1915. San Juan: Instituto de Cultura Puertorriqueña, 1980. 430 p.: bibl.

Massive study, impressive in both detail and documentation, demonstrates how much Puerto Rico was attuned to critical doctrines both in and beyond Spanish-speaking world. Organized primarily around specific critics rather than movements, devotes considerable space to Eugenio María de Hostos, as well as to several lesser known figures and definitively demonstrates liveliness and wealth of Puerto Rican critical writing. Necessary addition to study of Puerto Rican literature.

5112 Fishburn, Evelyn. The portrayal of immigration in nineteenth-century

Argentine fiction: 1845–1902. Berlin: Colloquium Verlag, 1981. 259 p.: bibl., index (Bibliotheca Ibero-Americana; Bd. 29)

Enormously helpful study of both immigration phenomenon in Argentina and attitudes it engendered, from Creoles' xenophobia to hopeful industriousness of immigrants. Includes especially thorough, traditional analysis of several nearly forgotten novels written by immigrants (e.g., Francisco Grandmontagne's *Teodoro Foronda*; Francisco Sicardi's serial novels *Libro extraño, Genar, Don Manuel Paloche, Méndez,* and *Hacia la justicia*). Only objection is author's arbitrary cut-off point: 1902. Immigration to Argentina did not peak until well into this century and continued as important fiction theme long after 1902. Highly recommended.

5113 Fontanella, Lee. Mystical diction and imagery in Gómez de Avellaneda and Carolina Coronado (LALR, 9:19, Fall/Winter 1981, p. 47–55)

Argues that both Avellaneda and Coronado derived much of their religious imagery from San Juan de la Cruz. Maintains that while Coronado's portrayal of God, the *Amado,* is unfailingly orthodox, Avellaneda's suggests fascinating merger of divine and idealized human lovers which imbues her poetry with vague eroticism, numinous yet sensual.

5114 Franco, Jean. La heterogeneidad peligrosa: escritura y control social en vísperas de la independencia mexicana (HISPA, 34/35, 1983, p. 3–34)

Despite somewhat misleading title, insightful article deals with Lizardi's role as transition author working to supplant aristocratic art with genuinely popular literature. With customary incisiveness, Franco argues that Lizardi, although never a real revolutionary, rebelled against colonial notions of "good literature" while seeking to impose values of rising middle class on "dangerous peoples" (i.e., disinherited, inherently unstable poor).

5115 Gallardo Ballacay, Andrés. Andrés Bello y la conciencia del idioma (UC/AT, 445, 1982, p. 123–136)

Compares Bello's grammar with Noah Webster's work, who sought to describe English away from its received cultural center, England itself. Both did their work on the American continent, and both sought libera-

tion from weight of linguistic tradition tied to mother countries. Good article, but ideas deserve lengthier treatment.

5116 García Barragán, María Guadalupe. El naturalismo en México: reseña y notas biobibliográficas. México: Universidad Nacional Autónoma de México, Instituto de Investigaciones Filológicas, 1979. 110 p.: bibl., index (Cuaderno del Centro de Estudios Literarios)

Noting that naturalism never took root in Mexico, proceeds to demonstrate and document that Mexican naturalism led lively existence among writers yet to be recognized. Despite solid presentation on European naturalism, one quibbles with some readings of Amado Nervo and José Portillo y Rojas. Nevertheless, a most important book of the biennium and essential for our understanding of Mexican 19th-century literature.

5116a Gotschlich Reyes, Guillermo. La aritmética en al amor de Alberto Blest Gana (UC/RCL, 18, nov. 1981, p. 95–119)

Excelente y completo análisis de la novela que inicia el ciclo mayor de la obra de Blest Gana, publicada originalmente en 1860. Considera la estructura del narrador y diversos aspectos del mundo narrado con gran detenimiento y competencia. [C. Goić]

5117 Grases, Pedro. Obras. v. 1–2, Estudios sobre Andrés Bello. Barcelona: Seix Barral, 1981. 2 v.: bibl., ill., indexes, ports.

Ever since appearance of his *Andrés Bello: el primer humanista de América* (Buenos Aires: Ediciones del Tridente, 1946) and of his multi-volume edition of Bello's *Obras completas* (Caracas: Ministerio de Educación, 1951), author has figured as leading *bellista* scholar. Here he republished several monographs, articles, and forewords on Bello that cover Bello's life and writings (criticism, poetry, grammar, legal theory, personal letters, etc.) and on criticism about Bello. Lucid, exhaustively documented, both volumes are major scholarly contribution. Highly recommended.

5118 Hernández, Luis Guillermo and **Jorge Rodríguez Cabrera.** José Ramón Yepes, 1822–1881: homenaje en el centenario de su muerte. Maracaibo: s.n., 1981. 73 p.: bibl., ill.

Minor romantic novelist and poet, José Ramón Yepes of Venezuela was one of first nativistic Spanish American writers. Written with more patriotism than insight, short biographical essay offers beginner's bibliography and outline of Yepes' life.

5119 Lagmanovich, David. Paul Groussac, ensayista del 80 (RIB, 32:1, 1982, p. 28–46)

Groussac remains a man of uncertain stature in Argentine letters who, nonetheless, left a much imitated style known for its stark vigor. Article, unfortunately, belabors theoretical questions (e.g., essay as literary form) and neglects aspects of Groussac's intellectual development. Useful article but more promising than enlightening.

5120 Losada, Alejandro. La literatura en la sociedad de América Latina: Perú y el Río de la Plata, 1837–1880. Berlin: Verlag Klaus Dieter Vervuert, 1983. 243 p.: bibl. (Editionen der Iberoamericana Reihe; 3. Monographien und Aufsätze; 9)

Certainly one of the most capable critics working in Latin American literature, Losada again demonstrates his ample grasp of Marxist historiography, theories of production and class development, and their relationship to Latin American literature. Notwithstanding its ambitious (and misleading) title, book deals specifically with 19th-century literature of Argentina and Peru. Highly recommended.

5121 Marinello, Juan. Dieciocho ensayos martianos. La Habana: Editora Política, 1981. 364 p.: bibl. (Colección de estudios martianos)

Book reflects breadth of Marinello's interest and includes commentary on Martí's literary criticism, as well as on his role as pre-Revolution nationalist. Particularly recommended is his "¿Qué Cosa fue el Modernismo?" in which Marinello uses Martí to refute modernist scholars such as Max Henríquez Ureña and Manuel Pedro González.

5122 Miller, Beth. Gertrude the Great: Avellaneda, nineteenth-century feminist (*in* Women in Hispanic literature: icons and fallon idols. Edited by Beth Miller. Berkeley: University of California Press, 1983, p. 201–214)

Short but well documented article discusses Avellaneda's feminist ideas in terms of feminist developments beyond Cuba and

Spain, where she lived. Finds Avellaneda anticipates feminist themes in early novel *Sab* (1841) and later develops activist feminist awareness which distinguishes her as a particularly prescient woman.

5123 Morejón, Nancy. Cecilia Valdés: mito y relidad (UH/U, 212, enero/dic. 1980, p. 52–61, ill.)

Analyzes the protagonist as focal point of three major themes: racial tension, economic class, and gender conflict. A fine poet, Morejón is also a sensitive and lucid reader.

Morse, Richard M. La cultura política iberoamericana de Sarmiento a Mariátegui. See item **1775.**

5124 Ocón Murillo, Armando. Rubén Darío, desde el punto de vista de la prosa: ensayo. Managua: Editorial Atenas, 1976. 93 p.: bibl. ill.

Short book focuses on several of Darío's less familiar prose works and devotes considerable attention to his correspondence, with writers as diverse as Blanco Fombona and Unamuno. Worthwhile.

Perdomo, Omar. Bibliografía martiana de Angel Augier. See item **39.**

5125 Pérez Huggins, Argenins. El positivismo en la narrativa del Gil Fortoul (Letras [Instituto Universitario Pedagógico de Caracas] 38/39, 1982, p. 15–25, bibl.)

Little known outside of Venezuela, Fortoul should nonetheless be studied in connection with other novelists of positivist-naturalism orientation (e.g., Eugenio Cambeceres, Julián Martel, Baldomero Lillo). Short article is adequate beginning towards such a project.

5126 Rama, Angel. Los gauchipolíticos rioplantenses. Buenos Aires: Centro Editor de América Latina, 1982. 222 p.: bibl. (Serie complementaria sociedad y cultura; 4. Biblioteca argentina fundamental; 152)

Odd compilation of essays, published separately over the years, not intended as book. It discusses, in surprisingly traditional terms, not 19th-century gaucho-caudillos but development and social significance of gauchesque literature. Book's decidedly non-controversial stance will compromise its long-term value.

5127 Reyes de Viana, Celia and **Celia I. Viana Reyes.** José Enrique Rodó, "genio" educador iberoamericano. Montevideo: Dirección General de Extensión Universitaria, División Publicaciones y Ediciones, 1980. 120 p.: bibl.

Largely remembered as ideologue of *arielismo*, Rodó's work covered vast intellectual terrain. Short work brings to light Rodó's insightful observations on education generally and in Latin America specifically. Written in oddly aphoristic style, reminiscent of Rodó's, book outlines his philosophy of education and portrays him as the embodiment of his own ideas.

5128 Rivas D., Rafael Angel. Andrés Bello en publicaciones periódicas del exterior: una bibliografía (Letras [Instituto Universitario Pedagógico de Caracas] 37, 1982, p. 103–171)

Updates previous bibliographical studies on Bello and documents his importance throughout Spanish-speaking world during last century. Important, useful work.

5128a Roca Martínez, José Luis. Contribución a la bibliografía literaria del dictador Juan Manuel Rosas (IGFO/RI, 41: 163/164, enero/junio 1981, p. 203–262, tables)

Clasifica la bibliografía "rosista" en tres partes: 1) hasta la batalla de Caseros, que marca el fin de Rosas; 2) hasta la aparición de las ideas "nacionalistas;" 3) desde 1916 hasta ahora. Organización confusa del material pero valioso rastreo de fuentes y textos sobre la figura que produjera un ciclo importante de la literatura argentina. [S. Sosnowski]

5129 Rodríguez, Ileana. Romanticismo literario y liberalismo reformista: el grupo de Domingo Delmonte (UPR/CS, 20:1, March 1980, p. 35–56)

Questions usefulness of European concepts like "romanticism" and "liberalism" when applied to colonial country, such as 19th-century Cuba. Outlines conditions of literary production under Delmonte's protectorate and concludes concepts may be useful if tempered by sophisticated understanding of period.

5130 Sava, Walter. Literary criticism of *Martín Fierro* from 1873 to 1915 (HISP, 25:75, mayo 1982, p. 51–68)

Useful overview of period's critical writing about *Martín Fierro* that ignores important political considerations that inspired

poem and determined critics' reactions. Without broader context, statements by Mitre, Bunge, Lugones, Gálvez, Ugarte, Borges, etc., are easily misunderstood.

5131 Scari, Robert M. Las ideas estéticas de Echeverría y el romanticismo de *El matadero* (Iberoromania [Max Niemeyer Verlag, Tübingen, FDR] 16, 1982, p. 38–53)

Carefully links Echeverría's aesthetic theories, Romanticism, and *El matadero*. One wishes author had taken broader theoretical approach and discussed Echeverría's representing more general romantic sensibility rather than focusing on his theories.

5132 Skirius, John. The interpenetration of some ideas and images in González Prada's prose (UCLA/M, 8:2, Fall 1979, p. 4–17)

Uses imagery in *Horas de lucha* and *Anarquía* to trace development of several key ideas as they evolved from rational optimism to moralistic anarchy. Informative article on two levels: as overview of González Prada's thinking and as analysis of his style.

5133 Sommer, Doris. El otro *Enriquillo* (RCLL, 9:17, 1983, p. 117–145)

Exceptional article, one of this biennium's best. With insight and originality, Sommer affirms that in *Enriquillo*, Galván successfully created populist myth, or guiding fiction, to inspire viable sense of nationhood in a fragmented people. Questioning novel's historical accuracy overlooks work's intention and principal success. Highly recommended.

5134 Suárez, Marco Fidel. Ensayo sobre la *Gramática castellana* de D. Andrés Bello (ACO/B, 31:134, oct./dic. 1981, p. 255–271)

Article's two purposes: to examine Bello's *Gramática* in context of philological practice of his time and to consider his ideas on language in terms of more recent linguistic theory. Despite dearth of documentation, meets first goal much better than second.

Uslar Pietri, Arturo. Los libros de Miranda. See item **2647.**

5134a Vitier, Cintio and **Fina García Marruz.** Temas martianos. 2a. ed. Río Piedras, Puerto Rico: Ediciones Huracán, 1981. 352 p.: bibl. (Colección La Nave y el puerto)

Reedition of important 1969 study of Martí, divided into essays by Cintio Vitier and Fina García Marruz. Required text for understanding the multiple facets of this great writer, including Martí, The Prophet. [W. Luis]

5134b Watson-Espener, Maida Isabel. El cuadro de costumbres en el Perú decimónico. Lima: Pontificia Universidad Católica del Perú, Fondo Editorial, 1979. 161 p.: bibl., index.

Aunque las primeras 50 p. estudian el costumbrismo en el siglo XIX, el trabajo se centra en la obra de cuatro cultores del género en el Perú entre 1830–70: Felipe Pardo y Aliaga, Manuel Ascencio Segura, Ramón Rojas y Cañas y Manuel Atanasio Fuentes. Estudio bien documentado peca de cierta monotonía en su estructura y método. [J.M. Oviedo]

5135 Zorrilla de San Martín, Juan. La leyenda patria. Introducción de Arturo Sergio Visca. Estudio crítico de Eustaquio Tomé. Montevideo: Ministerio de Educación y Cultura, Biblioteca Artigas, 1979. 106 p.: bibl. (Biblioteca Artigas. Colección de clásicos uruguayos; vol. 164)

Like others in this series, book is intended primarily for classroom use. Scholars, however, may find it useful since it contains little known first version of Zorilla's *La leyenda patria* with interesting comparisons to later version now considered definitive.

MISCELLANEOUS (ESSAYS, MEMOIRS, CORRESPONDENCE, ETC.)

5136 Acosta, Cecilio. Epistolario de Cecilio Acosta con Miguel Antonio Caro, Rufino José Cuervo y otras colombianos. Edición, introducción y notas de Mario Germán Romero. Bogotá: Instituto Caro y Cuervo, 1981. 289 p., 18 leaves of plates: bibl., ill., index (Publicaciones. Archivo epistolar colombiano; 15)

Journalist and diplomat, Venezuelan Cecilio Acosta (1818–81) corresponded regularly with several Colombian writers of note. Letters collected here provide running commentary on period's political, social, and literary preoccupations along with some highly forgettable occasional verse.

5137 Ayala, José de la Cruz. Desde el infierno. Asunción: Ediciones NAPA, 1982. 209 p., 4 leaves of plates: ill. (Libro paraguayo del mes; no. 19 [Mayo de 1982])

Ediciones NAPA provides another book in praiseworthy project of making available works by Paraguayans. Hardly known outside of Paraguay, de la Cruz Ayala (pseud.: Alón), lived short, impassioned life during which he contributed frequently to Paraguayan newspapers, writing mostly on morality in politics. These articles and letters also include short biographical essay written by four contemporaries shortly after his death in 1892.

5138 García Mérou, Martín. Recuerdos literarios: antología. Selección, prólogo y notas por Omar Borré. Buenos Aires: Centro Editor de América Latina, 1982. 145 p.: bibl. (Capítulo. Biblioteca argentina fundamental; 137)

Abridged edition puts within popular reach a most valuable personal testimony of Argentina's 1880 Generation. A so-so poet and derivative novelist, García Mérou was first-class chronicler of his age. Sarmiento, Miguel Cané, Bartolomé Mitre, José C. Paz, and Rafael Obligado are just a few of important literary figures populating his *Recuerdos*. Of limited scholarly value, book refocuses our attention on important witness of important time.

5139 Letras hispanoamericanas en la época de la Independencia: una antología general. Prólogo, selección y notas de Jaime Erasto Cortés. México: Secretaría de Educación Pública; Universidad Nacional Autónoma de México, 1982. 274 p.: bibl. (Clásicos americanos; 9)

Continuing tradition begun by José Vasconcelos in famous series "Pensamiento de América," series "Clásicos Americanos" has issued some of our best anthologies of Anglo and Latin American literature. In that tradition of excellence, this anthology contains good selection of carefully annotated texts dating from independence period (1808–24). Some like Bolívar's "Carta a un Caballero de Jamaica" and Olmedo's "La Victoria de Junín" are standard fare for such anthologies; others are less accessible works by active revolutionaries (e.g., Miguel Hidalgo, Francisco de Miranda, José de San Martín) and essayists (e.g., José María Luis Mora, Lucas Alamán, Juan Cruz Varela).

5140 Magariños Cervantes, Alejandro. Crónicas y correspondencia desde Europa: 1851–1853 (UBN/R, 21, dic. 1981, p. 203–255)

Magariños Cervantes of Uruguay travelled extensively in Spain, France, Italy, and England (1851–53). His political and cultural articles relating his experiences and observations are collected in this anthology. Not celebrated for his fiction, drama and poetry, Magariños was an astute observer whose overblown romantic rhetoric can occasionally charm.

20th Century: Prose Fiction: Mexico

FERNANDO GARCIA NUÑEZ, *Associate Professor of Spanish, The University of Texas at El Paso*

EL PANORAMA DE LA NARRATIVA MEXICANA en curso ofrece abundancia, variedad, ingenio, experimentación y calidad. Esta perspectiva optimista contrasta con la crisis económica tan profunda por la que pasa el país, extendida ya al cuestionamiento moral del régimen de gobierno y a la inconformidad de las clases populares y la media, las más afectadas. La crisis se encuentra ya reflejada en la narrativa en diversas formas, pero todas se compendian en un símbolo vicario recurrente: la Ciudad de México. Esta es vista como el centro del poder arbitrario, corrupto y violento en la narrativa urbana, la predominante. En ella y en el resto de la escritura de ficción se notan algunas constantes ahora más intensas y matizadas que antes. Las podemos resumir así: tendencia a textos breves, inclusión de todos los géneros, versatilidad discursiva, influencia de las formas y técnicas de los medios masivos de comunicación, contrapunto y, finalmente, conscientización escritural.

La narrativa tiende a ser breve en cuanto es más cuidadosa de la economía verbal, o sea, de utilizar sólo las palabras necesarias para el texto. Pero la parquedad verbal llega casi al virtuosismo en la obra de Carlos Monsiváis, *Nuevo catecismo para indios remisos* (item **5166**). Mas no se trata, claro está, de pobreza léxica, sino de trabajar el texto hasta podarlo de lo innecesario. En cuanto a la inclusión libre de los géneros en la narrativa, todos sabemos que no es algo nuevo en México. Pero sí lo es el mayor número de escritores que acuden a ella y, además, ahora se da fusión y no simple agregado de los géneros. Los más recurrentes son la crónica, la poesía, el teatro y la crítica literaria. Un ejemplo, entre muchos, sería el de José Joaquín Blanco, *Las púberes canéforas* (item **5147**). En lo concerniente a la versatilidad discursiva hay que anotar que implica la convicción de la variedad de los registros discursivos en las diversas clases sociales, los sexos, los barrios, las profesiones, las generaciones, los estados emotivos, etc. En consecuencia se procura utilizar los registros adecuados al texto. Un concierto discursivo, casi enciclopédico, es el excelente libro de José Rafael Calva, *Variaciones y fuga sobre la clase media* (item **5148**).

La influencia de los medios masivos de comunicación es intensa y extensa. En la narrativa se hace uso de las técnicas fílmicas desde hace tiempo, mas no es sino hasta hace poco que la técnica periodística de la crónica invade casi todo libro; a veces en la forma misma, en otras en el espíritu de percepción profunda de lo cotidiano que ella implica. Así Alejandro Rossi generó *Sueños de Occam* (item **5175**) de la observación minuciosa de las trivialidades diarias; o las publicitadas declaraciones testimoniales sirven de estructura a libros tan magníficos como el de

Elena Garro, *Testimonios sobre Mariana* (item **5160**); o se acude a formas masivas y populares en tiempo de la colonia, como lo ha hecho Carlos Monsiváis en *Nuevo catecismo para indios remisos* (item **5166**). La otra constante de la narrativa en México, el contrapunto, a veces se manifiesta culturalmente, como en la contraposición de la cultura Occidental y la cultura Gofa, metáfora de la Oriental, de Hugo Hiriart en *Cuadernos de Gofa* (item **5161**). Otras el contrapunto es verbal, como el creado por Luis Zapata entre una sirvienta y una matrona en *De pétalos perennes* (item **5181**). También se da en la contraposición de la versión oficial de la historia de México y la del narrador de *Los pasos de López* de Jorge Ibargüengoitia (item **5162**); o en la confrontación creativa entre el texto del autor y el del lector en *Textos extraños* de Guillermo Samperio (item **5178**). La última constante es la permanente reflexión que el escritor hace de la escritura en el mismo acto de escribir. Así José Joaquín Blanco permite que el narrador de *Las púberes canéforas* (item **5147**) utilice, comente, lea, critique y corrija la proyectada novela de un escritor fracasado.

Si pasamos ahora a la crítica de la narrativa como se hace en México, notaremos que ésta es publicada de ordinario en periódicos, suplementos y revistas en forma de reseñas, anotaciones y entrevistas; pero son escasos los artículos de fondo. Tres excepciones a lo anterior serían los semanarios *Proceso*, *Siempre* y *Sábado*, este último suplemento del periódico *Uno Másuno*. Tambien cubren la narrativa, sobre todo en el ámbito de las reseñas, las revistas *Vuelta*, *Cuadernos Americanos*, *Plural*, *Diálogos* y *Revista de la Universidad*; pero hasta ahora ninguna de ellas ha suplido la diseminación crítica generada por la ya desaparecida revista *La Semana de Bellas Artes*, bajo la dirección de Gustavo Sainz. Tampoco es muy rica en este campo la producción de libros en México. Las instituciones más interesadas en ello se reducen a la Universidad Nacional Autónoma de México, la Universidad Veracruzana, el Instituto Nacional de Bellas Artes y El Colegio de México. Además son contadas las veces en que una editorial comercial se aventura en este campo. En cambio éstas, tanto como las institucionales, son muy diligentes en la publicación de textos de creación narrativa. Aparte de las editoriales ya establecidas, han surgido algunas nuevas, tan agresivas como las primeras, como Oasis, Katún y Martín Casillas. Pero la crítica se hace sobre todo en los Estados Unidos, a través de revistas como *Hispania*, *Revista Iberoamericana*, *Mester* y *World Literature Today*; las más consuetudinarias de crítica de textos mexicanos. Esa reflexión crítica, independientemente de su procedencia geográfica, se manifiesta en general como una crítica complaciente que hace uso de una gran variedad metodológica, pero que se concentra principalmente en unos cuantos autores.

La complacencia de la crítica nada tiene que ver con la validez de sus aproximaciones, sino con la dificultad para encontrar en ella cuestionamientos de la obra narrativa, así como la tendencia a aplaudir lo que se lee. De los artículos y libros estudiados sólo he encontrado dos que cuestionan con argumentos sólidos las obras que analizan: el artículo de Roberto González-Echevarría, "*Terra Nostra*: Teoría y Práctica" (item **5205**) y el de Jorge Ruffinelli, "*Compadre Lobo* de Gustavo Sainz: un Ejercicio de Autobiografía" (item **5228**). Por los demás la variedad metodológica ofrece riqueza de perspectiva en los textos estudiados. Se encuentran los estudios basados en riguroso análisis de texto y los fundamentados en la historia de las ideas. También se publican los que utilizan el modelo estructuralista, el semiótico y el mítico. Además se encuentra la crítica sociológica, así como la ideológica. Pero esa crítica tan variada se concentra principalmente en cuatro autores, por orden de preferencia: Carlos Fuentes, Juan Rulfo, Mariano Azuela y Alfonso Reyes. Los estudios consagrados a Fuentes doblan los dedicados a Rulfo; así como los de este último doblan a su vez los de Reyes y Azuela. Entre los demás autores, está dándose alguna atención a Gustavo Sainz; pero hay un buen número de autores de valía, cuya obra es poco estudiada. Tal es el caso, entre otros, de José Emilio Pacheco, Carlos Monsiváis y Elena Garro, de los ya establecidos. De los más nuevos es probable que, por la calidad de sus creaciones, pronto sean estudiados José Joaquín Blanco, Luis Zapata, Hugo Hiriart y Jesús Gardea. Una ausencia notable dentro de la actividad crítica es la de una antología de la narrativa mexicana en curso. En cambio sí se publicó ya la magnífica bibliografía de William D. Foster, *Mexican literature: a bibliography of secondary sources* (item **5201**).

PROSE FICTION

5141 Agustín, José. Ciudades desiertas. México: Edivisión, Compañía Editorial, 1982. 200 p.: ill.

Conocido escritor surgido del grupo de "La Onda," novelista básicamente urbano. Esta novela conserva la viveza del lenguaje de la "Onda," sin sus excesos, pero la encamina a enjuiciar el sistema de vida norteamericano con énfasis en el universitario. Se cuestiona la relación machista de una pareja mexicana en viaje por Estados Unidos. Regresan a México con críticas estereotipadas a la cultura norteamericana pero con una relación menos machista.

5142 Aridjis, Homero. Espectáculo del año dos mil. México: J. Mortiz, 1981. 106 p. (Serie del volador)

Dominan elementos teatrales, principalmente del absurdo, sobre todo en el primer texto, casi un "happening" a fin de siglo (31 dic. 1999) cuando hay esperanza simulada, ritual y teatral de un cambio para bien en el mundo. Pero acabado el "happening" el mundo sigue igual. El texto "Moctezuma" presenta el fin de la hegemonía azteca y el principio de la española. Finalmente, "El Ultimo Adán" presenta el fin del hombre y del mundo, aunque un tanto dulcificado por el amor.

5143 Avilés Fabila, René. La canción de Odette. México: Premiá Editora, 1982. 113 p. (La Red de Jonás)

Este libro es una canción a la vida de escritores y artistas del México de Diego Rivera, Frida Kahlo, Tina Modotti, etc. de los años 1930 y 1940. La canción reiterativa los evoca y reencarna a todos ellos en un ser maravilloso y trágico, Odette, consciente de su anacronismo y senectud acelerada ante los

jóvenes, pero contenta de continuar de alguna manera viviendo en la pareja de sus más fieles y jóvenes amigos. Avilés Fabila logra recrear magníficamente ese mundo del pasado mexicano.

5144 ———. Los oficios perdidos. México: Universidad Nacional Autónoma de México, 1983. 110 p. (Cuento y relato)

Libro de composiciones brevísimas pero bien trabajadas. Al ingenio de su organización hay que agregar la reflexión, acompañada de ironía y humorismo, acerca de los valores imputados a la Civilización Occidental. Quizás se les podría calificar de reflexiones fantásticas y críticas, más que de cuentos, algunas geniales. La mitad del libro es sobre ocupaciones ya desaparecidas, la otra mitad incluye composiciones muy variadas en su temática. Excelente libro de ejercicios de composición literaria en cápsulas.

5145 Bestard Vásquez, Joaquín. La calle que todos olvidan. México: J. Mortiz, 1982. 292 p. (Nueva narrativa hispánica)

Novela de la vida en las barriadas en la Ciudad de México. Se propone hacernos ver a los ajenos al barrio, lugares donde es imposible el desarrollo de la persona humana, así como cuestionar en qué medida somos responsables del modo de vida de esa gente. Lenguaje de narración realista fuertemente entremezclado con jerga del barrio. Tono de cierta concientización a nivel individual, más que social.

5146 Blanco, José Joaquín. Función de medianoche: ensayos de literatura cotidiana. México: Ediciones Era, 1981. 190 p. (Crónicas)

Reúne prosa periodística del autor (1978–80) en *Uno Másuno* (México), prosa no sometida a las exigencias de los medios masivos de comunicación, sino detallada, ágil, conversacional y democrática que proporciona una voz a los lectores. Todo esto y más logra Blanco en el desfile de tipos y actitudes de la clase media mexicana, envidiosa de los poderosos pero atenta a imitarlos en su desprecio por campesinos y trabajadores. Proporciona un panorama complejo del México actual. Excelente libro que, por su complejidad y variedad, convendría leer a trancos, como los lectores del periódico del cual surgió.

5147 ———. Las púberes canéforas. México: Ediciones Océano, 1983. 148 p.: ill.

Toma como punto de partida una escena policíaca cotidiana en el mundo nocturno de la Ciudad de México: el autor ficticio, homosexual, intenta escribir una novela, su sueño fallido, partiendo de la escena de brutalidad policíaca. Presenta el mundo nocturno, violento y sediento de pasiones, de la Ciudad de México, principalmente en el ámbito homosexual, como una urgencia también fallida de escapar al horroso mundo diurno, controlado por un sistema político y económico también corrupto. Excelente novela, intencionalmente fuerte en su temática y lenguaje.

5148 Calva, José Rafael. Variaciones y fuga sobre la clase media. Xalapa, México: Universidad Veracruzana Editorial, 1980. 187 p. (Ficción Universidad Veracruzana)

Excelente libro de cuentos sobre la clase media mexicana, organizado a manera de concierto ligero. El tema y cambio de ritmo en cada cuento da unidad y variedad, utilizando para cada relato un tinglado verbal específico (e.g., el discurso de la aristocracia decadente, la burocracia jubilada, la familia tradicional, el mundo femenil en la intimidad del juego de canasta). Los tres cuentos más sobresalientes son: "Tarde al Cesto," "Allegro ma non Troppo" y "Fuga."

5149 Campos, Marco Antonio. Que la carne es hierba. México: J. Mortiz, 1982. 108 p. (Serie del volador)

Novela sobre la adolescencia del narrador a 10 años de distancia, acabando de regresar del exilio voluntario, acompañada de relato paralelo de la que fue novia de juventud. El fracaso amoroso sirve para analizar somera y profundamente la significación del Movimiento estudiantil de 1968 en la Ciudad de México, en que participaron.

5150 Corazón de palabras: una antología de los mejores cuentos eróticos. Gustavo Sainz, compilador. México: Editorial Grijalbo, 1981. 310 p.: bibl., ill.

Subtítulo, *Una antología de los mejores cuentos eróticos*, seguramente con propósitos comerciales. Varios versan sobre el amor pero no son *eróticos* en la connotación contemporánea del adjetivo. Lo de "mejores" es también técnica mercantil porque algunos son incipientes. Creo que Sainz, lector cuidadosísimo, no avaló ese subtítulo. Los cuentos son de escritores de diversas partes del mundo, especialmente estadounidenses y mexicanos. Sainz hace asequibles a un público más vasto excelentes cuentos de Elena Garro "La Culpa es de los Tlaxcaltecas;" de Juan García Ponce "La Gaviota;" de Francisco Tario "Entre tus Dedos Helados;" y de René Avilés Fabila "La Lluvia no Mata las Flores." Un acierto es presentar a Francisco Tario, escritor de cuentos fantásticos, poco conocido por el gran público.

5151 Curiel, Fernando. Manuscrito hallado en un portafolios. México: Editorial Oasis, 1981. 205 p. (Colección Lecturas del milenio; 5)

La violenta vida política de México, principalmente al final de los sexenios de los presidentes Echeverría y López Portillo, ha hecho surgir algunos libros importantes por su valor testimonial más que por su valor estético. En éste se planea un golpe de estado, semejante al rumorado al terminar el gobierno de Echeverría. Para no comprometerse, se utiliza el truco del manuscrito encontrado.

5152 Domecq, Brianda. Bestiario doméstico. México: Fondo de Cultura Económica, 1982. 126 p. (Letras mexicanas)

Este ingenioso y bien escrito libro reúne con ironía y humorismo pequeñas composiciones, algunas semejantes a las tradicionales fábulas de animales, para abordar, bajo diversas formas, insistentemente el mito de las relaciones entre las dos bestias primordiales: el hombre y la mujer. Esto se evidencia más en la segunda parte del libro, "Trilogía," dedicado exclusivamente al mito del hombre y de la mujer pimigenios y sus concomitantes Dios y Diablo.

5153 Fernández, Sergio. Los desfiguros de mi corazón. México: Editorial Nueva Imagen, 1983. 222 p.

Anecdotario de acontecimientos relacionados con la vida y el mundo del novelista: ". . . tal cual escribir lo vivido." Utiliza lenguaje lúdico pero bien trabajado y recursos del cuento, novela, cine, teatro y ensayo. No es necesariamente autobiográfico, sino que intenta enmarcar mitos circundantes a acontecimientos vividos. Al autor le interesa rescatar la Ciudad de México vieja, de los años 50 y 60. Mas el libro se concentra en anécdotas del extranjero y la provincia mexicana, algunas memorables con fuerza generadora del mito evocado.

5154 García Bergua, Jordi. Karpus Minthej. México: Fondo de Cultura Económica, 1981. 150 p. (Letras mexicanas)

Novela cuya temática y estilo procede de la bella época del siglo XIX europeo. El texto sería la defensa de los actos aparentemente criminales del personaje contradictorio Karpus Minthej, hecha por un prominente médico muerto en 1904. El manuscrito logra recrear el esplendor y la decadencia de la Europa aristocrática del siglo pasado, así como el carácter voluble del protagonista en un estilo casi jesuítico; pero no logra establecerse como verdadera defensa de Karpus.

5155 Gardea, Jesús. La canción de las mulas muertas. México: Editorial Oasis, 1981. 107 p. (Lecturas del milenio; 3)

Novela motivada probablemente en una rivalidad pueblerina ocasionadora de tragedias. Prosa parca y medida desarrolla el proceso de la rivalidad como quien cuenta un corrido. Gardea cuida de mantener un aura mítica, folklórica y legendaria en sus personajes, así como en Placeres, espacio lleno de odio, envidia, sol quemante y soledad. Novela valiosa por el modo en que maneja los elementos de la leyenda.

5156 ———. Septiembre y los otros días. México: J. Mortiz, 1980. 152 p. (Serie del volador)

Colección de cuentos, ganadora del Premio Villaurrutia en 1980. En ellos Gardea crea un mundo dominado por la soledad y violencia gratuita, surgida quizás de la abundancia de sol. Utiliza imágenes breves para dibujar personajes de ordinario a grandes rasgos y definiéndolos desde un principio, pero dejando algunos matices de misterio que luego conducen a la sorpresa esperada. Cuentos breves, construidos con precisión verbal y organización.

5157 ———. El sol que estás mirando. México: Fondo de Cultura Económica, 1981. 97 p. (Serie letras mexicanas)

Recuerdos de la infancia en Placeres desde una perspectiva todavía infantil pero signada ya por la muerte del padre. El discurso narrativo tiene la sencillez de la imaginería pueril, así como rapidez y concreción. La narración rondea alrededor del padre recordado, pero acompañada de recuerdos insistentes del resto de la familia. El tono de intimidad logrado por la utilización del "yo," no llega, intencionalmente, a los escollos de la nostalgia. Se limita simplemente a recordar en medio del sol omnipresente.

5158 ———. El tornavoz. México: J. Mortiz, 1983. 145 p. (Serie del volador)

Novela donde la trama principal es de diversos matices de voces y su persistencia a través de tres generaciones en medio del sol alucinador de Placeres, el pueblo creado poco a poco por la prosa de Gardea. Las voces condensadas en la novela, tornavoz metafórico, hacen a los personajes en sus repeticiones y metamorfosis. El ambiente generado es de ensueño y fantasmagoría. Gardea es fiel a la síntesis y a la precisión en el lenguaje.

5159 Garro, Elena. La casa junto al río. Barcelona: Editorial Grijalbo, 1983. 103 p. (Colección Autores mexicanos)

Garro ha mostrado en varios ocasiones facultades para hacer surgir fantasmagóricamente en la escritura a los muertos o el pasado. La protagonista, ya sin nadie en México, decide intentar encontrarse a sí misma regresando al pueblo de sus padres en España, donde vive de nuevo las luchas de la Guerra Civil española cuyas pasiones persisten. Al final será asesinada. El final se anuncia desde el principio, pero la prosa de Garro roba la atención del lector transformando lentamente la realidad real en fantasmagórica.

5160 ———. Testimonios sobre Mariana. México: Editorial Grijalbo, 1981. 353 p.

En tres testimonios Garro sondea a un personaje insondeable y misterioso, Mariana, así como al hombre que dice tener dominio absoluto sobre ella, su marido Augusto. Los testimonios son puestos en boca de dos amantes y una amiga de Mariana. Utiliza sabiamente la ambigüedad, la sugerencia y diversas tonalidades para crear al personaje contradictorio e inolvidable de Mariana. El último testimonio es problamente una de las piezas más bellas de la prosa amorosa en México.

5161 Hiriart, Hugo. Cuadernos de Gofa. México: J. Mortiz, 1981. 359 p.: ill. (Nueva narrativa hispánica)

Libro denso por su estructura, su contenido y su extensión; pero valioso por su capacidad para crear, tomando como puntos de reflejo recíproco la civilización Occidental y una ficticia civilización Gofa parecida a la Oriental, un universo total y propio. Su autor ficticio es uno de los protagonistas, quien reconoce su filiación con *Las mil y una noches* y el continuar hasta el infinito. El lector, inconscientemente pero manejado por el autor, va haciendo una reflexión sobre la validez de los principales valores de la cultura Occidental. Hiriart es un filósofo socrático, platicador, profundo y ameno.

5162 Ibargüengoitia, Jorge. Los pasos de López. México: Ediciones Océano, 1982. 154 p.: ill.

De acuerdo con la familiaridad del lector con la historia oficial del inicio de la independencia de México, este libro puede tener varias lecturas básicas. Si se conoce bien esa historia, se harán constantes comparaciones entre ésa y la versión desmitificadora y sencilla de la novela. Pero si el lector está al margen de la versión oficial de la independencia, leerá la novela simplemente como la desmitificación de los protagonistas de una conspiración que a la larga fue victoriosa y cuyos héroes fueron sacralizados. Quizás por ello la edición española, simultánea a la mexicana, se tituló simplemente *Los Conspiradores*.

5163 Isla, Carlos. Chucho el Roto. México: Ediciones ELA, 1980. 196 p.: ill. (Colección Paladines mexicanos; 1)

Chucho el Roto, legendario personaje prerrevolucionario, sigue viviendo en la literatura mexicana probablamente a causa de la situación económica tan estrecha para la mayoría, después del gobierno de Echeverría. Redentor de los pobres y látigo de los poderosos, Chucho el Roto, es personaje añorado por el pueblo de hoy. Carlos Isla lo presenta en una versión populachera y sentimental, cercana al género de telenovelas.

5164 Jacobs, Bárbara. Doce cuentos en contra. México: Martín Casillas Editores, 1982. 155 p. (Serie La invención)

Cuentos desiguales en sus logros. La mayoría de ellos toman como voz narrativa la situada en el paso de la niñez a la adolescencia. El que más certeramente la utiliza es el titulado "Carol Dice." En él la autora crea un ambiente entre niñas de tres lenguas distintas (francés, inglés y español), visibles en la verbalización del relato.

5165 Manero, Mercedes. Río revuelto. México: Editorial Grijalbo, 1982. 209 p. (Colección Autores mexicanos)

Novela sobre la lucha por el poder y la corrupción aneja al mismo en el México contemporáneo. La autora no menciona nombres, pero el conocedor podría encontrar a algunos políticos importantes en los personajes presentados.

5166 Monsiváis, Carlos. Nuevo catecismo para indios remisos. México: Siglo Veintiuno Editores, 1982. 119 p. (La Creación literaria)

Monsiváis es desde hace tiempo maestro en la crónica citadina de México. Basta recordar sus libros *Días de guardar*, *Amor perdido* y *A ustedes les consta*, para confirmalo. El presente libro consta de breves textos catequéticos o hagiográficos que proporcionan una relación irónica de la práctica cristiana en el México colonial. La prosa se acomoda a la intención didáctica de un catecismo pero salpicada de sutil ironía y humorismo: porque Monsiváis se propone escribir un catecismo al revés, un discurso fiel a la tradición catequética pero organizado de tal forma que la cuestiona. Cuidadosamente trabajado, el estilo extremadamente pulcro se aparta de la prosa acostumbrada del autor. Algunas composiciones no rebasan las dos páginas, también inusitado en Monsiváis. Joyas de la prosa mexicana.

5167 Ojeda, Jorge Arturo. Octavio. México: Premiá Editora, 1982. 77 p. (La Red de Jonás)

Novela desigual en sus logros. En la primera mitad presenta la aventuras amorosas, reales o imaginarias, de un narrador homosexual contrapunteándolas con anécdotas y reflexiones pertinentes. Después la novela se pierde en párrafos inconexos.

5168 Pacheco, Cristina. Para vivir aquí. México: Editorial Grijalbo, 1983. 168 p. (Colección Autores mexicanos)

Cristina Pacheco es una periodista reconocida en México por su profesionalismo e inventiva. Recopilación fiel de crónicas publicadas en *El Día* (México, 1977–80), sobre la vida citadina. Presenta breves narraciones, organizadas a modo de pequeños cuentos o dramas. La nota predominante es la tristeza aunada a la violencia e indiferencia imperantes en la capital hacia los desheredados. A ellos quiere darles voz Pacheco, sin asumir en ningún momento un papel paternalista o redentor. Desea simplemente perpetuar y hacer audible la voz de los pobres con una prosa bien trabajada.

5169 Pitol, Sergio. Cementerio de tordos. México: Ediciones Océano, 1982. 297 p.: ill.

Pitol, por su carrera diplomática, ha escrito y vivido gran parte de su vida adulta fuera de México. Esta colección de cuentos presenta las actitudes del mexicano en el extranjero, principalmente en Europa. En el caso de Pitol no se presencia en su escritura la nostalgia sentimental o patriotera, sino el deseo permanente de examinar lo mexicano desde la diversas perspectivas ofrecidas por sus frecuentes desplazamientos diplomáticos.

5170 ———. Juegos florales. México: Siglo Veintiuno Editores, 1982. 195 p. (La Creación literaria)

Ingenioso intento de recuperar el pasado propio y ajeno del autor ficticio, así como de llevar a cabo el intermitente proyecto de escribir una novela que termina cuando el autor ficticio termina la suya. La escritura de la novela podría considerarse como el rito exorcista para liberarse de los propios fantasmas.

5171 Puga, María Luisa. Accidentes. Cuernavaca, México: Martín Casillas Editores, 1981. 166 p. (Serie La Invención)

Libro que se propone atrapar la naturaleza ordinaria de los accidentes más que el sobresalto que ocasionan. Probablemente por esto Puga apenas si le da un lugar al accidente que se menciona en los cuentos, mas resguardando cuidadosamente la naturalidad de su acontecer y evitando toda reiteración. Se logra principalmente en: "Difícil Situación," "Helmut y Florián" y "Ramiro.:

5172 Rábago Palafox, Gabriela. Todo ángel es terrible: novela. México: Martín

Casillas Editores, 1981. 139 p. (Serie La Invención)

Novela acerca de la infancia del narrador, quien se sitúa ya en la edad adulta. Desde allí analiza los traumas y los gozos de su niñez, presentes todavía en su vida adulta. Es ingenioso el discurso del mundo infantil, utilizado por la autora, profesional en la escritura de cuentos para niños, pero incursionando por primera vez en novelas para adultos.

5173 Ramírez, Armando. Tepito. México: Terra Nova, 1983. 111 p. (Colección Letra risueña)

Armando Ramírez es ya conocido dentro de la novela popular suburbana de la Ciudad de México por sus novelas *Chin Chin el teporocho* y *Violación en Polanco*. Pero en el presente libro, sin cambiar el tema de su querido barrio de Tepito, supera los anteriores en organización y en el manejo del lenguaje. Aquí persiste la protesta por la situación social y económica en el barrio, mas sin los gritos excesivos de libros anteriores. El conjunto de personajes, presentado en forma conversacional, proporciona una imagen profunda de la vida y filosofía del barrio.

5174 Reyes, Alfonso. Antología personal. Edición, palinodia y notas de Ernesto Mejía Sánchez. México: Martín Casillas Editores, 1983. 86 p. (Serie La Invención)

El libro tiene tres valores fundamentales: 1) introducción crítica de Ernesto Mejía Sánchez que documenta cada selección y hace ver como forma parte de un proyecto antologizador de Reyes, llevado a cabo sólo en parte, lo aquí presentado; 2) hacer asequible al gran público publicaciones de Reyes solo al alcance de eruditos; y 3) el más importante: la rigurosa y hermosa selección hecha por Reyes.

5175 Rossi, Alejandro. Sueños de Occam. México: Universidad Nacional Autónoma de México, 1983. 70 p.

Todos estos breves cuentos poseen el ingenio de mostrarnos algo aparentemente trival, pero la composición parte de allí para introducirse a profundidades filosóficas y de agudeza mental. Una hermosa disquisición sobre el libro albedrío se encuentra en "En Plena Fuga." Una demostración casera y cotidiana de la filosofía de Guillermo de Occam (i.e., *entia non multiplicantur sine necessitate*) en "Sueños de Occam." Este libro muestra el arte del bien contar.

5176 Ruiz, Bernardo. Olvidar, tu nombre. México: Premiá Editora, 1982. 77 p. (La Red de Jonás)

Ruiz es un escritor joven. En *La otra orilla* (ver *HLAS 44:5195*) se veían sus primicias. La presente novela corta muestra un dominio más acertado ante la problemática de narrar algo tan manoseado como el tema del primer amor. El autor se libra de caer en la cursilería, aunque a veces, sobre todo al medio de la novela, la prosa se hace pesada.

5177 Sainz, Gustavo. Fantasmas aztecas. México: Editorial Grijalbo, 1982. 209 p. (Colección Autores mexicanos)

A Sainz le gusta experimentar nuevas formas de narrar en cada novela. Esta nos presenta diversos proyectos que podrían incorporarse a la misma y que giran alrededor de los dioses aztecas y del antropólogo descubridor de las ruinas del Templo Mayor en el Centro de la Ciudad de México. Todos los proyectos son formulados por el narrador, inmiscuido narrativamente en ellos, desde el interior de un minitaxi en las calles de la capital.

5178 Samperio, Guillermo. Textos extraños: cuentos. México?: Folios Ediciones, 1981. 121 p.: ill. (Colección Narrativa latinoamericana: NL2)

Cuentos fantásticos breves, familiares a la fábula y signados fuertemente por la simbología cromática. Composiciones organizadas en forma de cuento pero explicadoras y surgidas de las lecturas más obsesivas del autor. Asumen algo del ensayo o artículo crítico, en que predomina la lectura como generadora de textos paralelos en el lector Samperio. "Manifiesto de Amor," el cuento más extenso, es una verdadera disquisición, envuelta en ironía y humorismo, de la epistemología de la lectura.

5179 Turrent, Jaime. Los encantados. México: Editorial Oasis, 1982. 72 p.: ill. (Lecturas del milenio; 6)

Novela corta, cuyo interés principal radica en el proceso de interiorización personal de la repulsa social sufrida por el protagonista. El narrador relata el último día de vida del suicida, el protagonista. Sus problemas sociales, surgidos de la desmitifica-

ción de los héroes patrios, le acarrean tortura y represión brutal por parte de la policía. La novela es la derrota personal ocasionada por un régimen político represivo.

5180 Vicens, Josefina. Los años falso: novela. México: Martín Casillas Editores, 1982. 101 p. (Serie La Invención)

Vicens no publicaba una novela desde 1958. Esta es corta, escrita en la intimidad del monólogo poético y sencillo del hijo que recuerda la muerte de su padre. El hijo resiente y agradece al mismo tiempo la semejanza total con el padre, pero el conflicto no tiene solución. Tal vez el hijo nunca pueda ser otra cosa que su padre. Este fue, como lo es ahora su hijo, el producto de un sistema político corrompido, generador por antonomasia de la falsedad. De esta forma la novela, muy sutilmente, se convierte en crítica social y política.

5181 Zapata, Luis. De pétalos perennes. Ilustraciones, Carlos Herrera. México: Editorial Katún, 1981. 97 p.: ill. (Colección Libro de bolsillo. Serie Arte-literatura; 3)

Zapata se siente atraído por la cultura popular: la correspondencia amorosa iniciada a través de un anuncio en revistas. Organiza el libro en parlamentos exclusivos e intermitentes entre una señora otoñal de la clase media alta y su sirvienta, cebo para los amoríos a hurtadillas de aquélla, resultando casi una obra de teatro a dúo. Lo más logrado del libro es la confrontación de los lenguajes totalmente distintos: la sirvienta hablando en su mundo cotidiano y la matrona intentando penetrar al modo de hablar de la sirvienta. El resultado es una crítica sutil a la alta clase media mexicana.

5182 ———. Melodrama. México: El Enjambre, 1983. 102 p.

El libro utiliza las técnicas del cine mexicano tradicional y de la televisión comercial actual para plantear en suspenso una historia de amor al gran público. La diferencia está en que Zapata hace uso irónico de tales técnicas y las aplica a los amores homosexuales. En el melodrama común hay tragedia, mucho enredo y abundancia de lágrimas; pero el final es feliz. Así sucede aquí: al final la pareja homosexual cena alegremente con la familia en la noche de Navidad. Un libro con lenguaje e imaginería dinámicos y bien escrito.

5183 Zepeda, Eraclio. Andando el tiempo. México: Martín Casillas Editores: FONAPAS, 1982. 132 p.: ill.

Colección de cuentos del escritor más calificado para escribir sobre el mundo indígena del México de ahora. Zepeda sabe conservar en su prosa la primitividad de las leyendas, mitos y personajes indígenas al interiorizarse de ellos. Sus cuentos son una recreación estética del mundo indígena del sureste de México, pero se encuentran muy lejos del realismo indigenista de protesta social, sin que ésta esté del todo ausente. El mito vibra en la prosa mágica de Zepeda.

LITERARY CRITICISM AND HISTORY

5184 Adelstein, Miriam. La vida y la obra de Juan Rulfo (in International Congress of Hispanists, 4th, Salamanca, Spain, 1971. Actas. Dirección, Eugenio de Bustos Tovar. Salamanca, Spain: Asociación Internacional de Hispanistas, 1982, v. 1, p. 91–94)

Artículo de pretensiones enclopédicas que empiezan por el enunciado de su título. A través de unos cuantos rasgos de la vida de Rulfo se pretende mostrar como ésta se encuentra presente en su obra. Se reduce a hacer juicios generales sobre los cuentos de Rulfo.

5185 Anadón, José. Arturo Azuela: entrevista (HISPA, 33, 1982, p. 61–78)

Entrevista sobre las novelas de Arturo Azuela, en especial sobre Manifestación de silencios, El tamaño del infierno y Un tal José Salomé. Discute la escritura y organización de las mismas, sus relaciones con los acontecimientos del México contemporáneo a su escritura, sobre todo, el papel que en ellas juega la Ciudad de México.

5186 ———. Entrevista a Carlos Fuentes, 1980 (IILI/RI, 123/124, abril/sept. 1983, p. 622–630)

Entrevista donde el entrevistado conduce totalmente el hilo de la conversación a causa de las preguntas tan generales y ambiguas del entrevistador. Sin embargo se encuentran aquí aspectos no reiterados en las múltiples entrevistas hechas a Fuentes, como su admiración por el novelista cubano Reinaldo Arenas y por los escritores mexi-

canos Gustavo Sainz, José Agustín y David Huerta.

5187 Barrientos, Juan José. El grito de Ajetreo: anotaciones a la novela de Ibargüengoitia sobre Hidalgo (UNAM/RUM, 39:28, agosto 1983, p. 15–23)

Documentado e interesante ensayo que presenta la novela como una reelaboración de tres relatos anteriores sobre Hidalgo: Hidalgo: la vida del héroe de Luis Castillo Ledón; Sacerdote y caudillo de Juan A. Mateos; y el relato de Pedro García, acompañante de Hidalgo. Según Barrientos, Ibargüengoitia se propone en la novela bajar al héroe del pedestal de la demagogia oficial para devolverlo al pueblo.

5187a Benítez, Fernando et al. Juan Rulfo: homenaje nacional. México: Instituto Nacional de Bellas Artes/SEP, 1980. 60 p., 100 p. of plates: ill. (some col.)

Contiene uno de los mejores ensayos sobre la obra de Rulfo, el de Carlos Monsiváis: "Sí, Tampoco los Muertos Retoñan, Desgraciadamente." Según Monsiváis la obra de Rulfo logra presentarnos la voz de los marginados de México, objetivo nunca antes logrado. Fuentes presenta aspectos interesantes del desarrollo mitológico en Rulfo. Fernando Benítez y Poniatowska presentan entrevistas comentadas a Rulfo; García Márquez ofrece testimonio de la importancia de Rulfo en su propia obra, mientras que José Emilio Pacheco, utilizando frases textuales de Rulfo, hace un poema que retrata al México de hoy. El libro se cierra con 100 fotografías de Rulfo, ilustradoras también de su mundo.

5188 Brushwood, John S. Sobre el referente y la transformación narrativa en las novelas de Carlos Fuentes y Gustavo Sainz (IILI/RI, 116/117, julio/dic. 1981, p. 49–54)

Brushwood hace uso de la semiótica para analizar la evolución del "referente" en las novelas de Fuentes y Sainz, pero termina por extender sus conclusiones a toda la narrativa mexicana de hoy. Según Brushwood la realidad extratextual es de dos clases: de tendencia representacional y de tendencia conceptista.

5189 Carlos Fuentes: a critical view. Edited by Robert Brody and Charles Rossman. Austin: University of Texas, 1982. 221 p.: bibl. (Texas Pan American series)

Los editores han escogido entre los

más conocedores eruditos de la obra de Fuentes a aquéllos que tuvieran algo nuevo que decir en la ya vasta bibliografía del autor. Presentan estudios que abarcan su obra desde muy distintas perspectivas metodológicas y enfoques, sin descuidar la producción dramática, ensayística y crítica del autor, así como la crítica sobre él. Este es, sin duda, el libro colectivo más ambicioso en el estudio de la obra de Fuentes.

5190 Cluff, Russell M. Alegoría e intuiciones arquetípicas en *El hombre de los hongos* de Sergio Galindo (AATSP/H, 65:4, Dec. 1982, p. 544–553)

Análisis minucioso e inteligente de la novela de Galindo, en la que se plantean intuiciones arquetípicas en el marco de la "alegoría vacilante." No existiendo ningún intento moralizador por parte del narrador, el lector es obligado traductor de la simbología implícita en el nivel literal de la narración.

5191 ———. Immutable humanity within the hands of time: two short stories by José Emilio Pacheco (LALR, 10:20, Spring/Summer, 1982, p. 41–56, tables)

Excelente artículo donde Cluff analiza minuciosamente las estructuras narrativas y temporales de dos cuentos: "La Noche del Inmortal," su primer cuento publicado y "Civlización y Barbarie," en relación a *Morirás lejos*, la famosa novela de Pacheco, y el resto de su obra. Cluff muestra la persistencia en ésta de estructuras narrativas y temporales experimentadas ya en el primer cuento.

5192 Cobo Borda, J.G. El *Taller* de Paz (ECO, 41[3]:249, julio 1982, p. 319–335)

Artículo donde se comenta la obra de Octavio Paz en la revista *Taller* con ocasión de su reproducción facsimilar en 1982 por el Fondo de Cultura Económica de México. La perspectiva de Cobo Borda es totalizadora en el sentido de que examina la obra de Paz en *Taller*, en relación a lo hecho por él en las revistas *Plural* y *Vuelta*, pero sin olividar el marco de sus demás obras.

5193 Corominas, Juan M. Juan José Arreola y Juan Rulfo: visión trágica (ICC/T, 35:1, enero/abril 1980, p. 110–121)

Artículo con pretensiones mayores a las apuntadas en el título, pues quiere hacer ver tres etapas fundamentales, semejantes a las de la literatura clásica, en el desarrollo de la novela en México (e.g., etapa épica: novela

de la Revolución; trágica: Arreola y Rulfo; comedia: autores posteriores a Arreola y Rulfo). Aunque las ideas son atractivas, pecan de esquematismo y generalidades en su análisis de la novelas que las sustentan.

5194 Cuervo, Mariela. Juan Villoro (UNAM/PP, 71, 1981?, p. 88–94)

Entrevista pobremente conducida con preguntas triviales. Pero lo apuntado por Villoro sirve como aproximación inicial al sentir de la más nueva narrativa mexicana que incluye, entre otros, a Bernardo Ruiz, David Ojeda, Luis Zapata e Ignacio Betancourt.

5195 Davis, Mary E. The twins in the looking glass: Carlos Fuentes' *Cabeza de la hidra* (AATSP/H, 65:3, Sept. 1982, p. 371–376)

Analiza la utilización de la parodia del cine y de la novela detectivesca hecha por Fuentes para esconder el enigma de la novela. Este se cifraría en la imposibilidad de delimitar la identidad personal. La autora cree que Félix Maldonado es el doble de Trevor y viceversa, aunque reconoce el papel dominante del segundo.

5196 Durán, Manuel. "Contemporáneos:" ¿grupo, promoción, generación, conspiración? (IILI/RI, 48:118/119, enero/junio 1982, p. 37–46)

Excelente artículo que, de modo claro y suscinto, da un panorama de este grupo, sus pretensiones, sus exponentes más representativos, sus obras mejor logradas y su influencia actual en la literatura mexicana. Aunque enfoca sobre todo a poetas, en él se hace ver la importancia de la obra de este grupo en tres autores fundamentales de México: Octavio Paz, Juan Rulfo y Carlos Fuentes.

5197 Faris, Wendy B. Carlos Fuentes. New York: Ungar Pub. Co., 1983. 241 p.: bibl., index (Literature and life series)

Analiza toda la obra de Fuentes con énfasis especial en *La región más transparente* y en *La muerte de Artemio Cruz*, bajo la perspectiva de la relación entre imagen y estructura narrativa proporcionada a muchas voces. La voz múltiple la logra Fuentes con frecuentes cambios en la voz del narrador, con voces múltiples implícitas en el doblar, triplicar y hasta multiplicar indefinidamente los personajes; y, finalmente, por medio de la resonancia de textos míticos, literarios, fílmicos, pictóricos, etc. Los análisis de Faris pueden leerse como ensayos autónomos de obras individuales de Fuentes. Incluye interesante biografía, excelentes notas y bibliografía. Este es uno de los proyectos individuales más ambiciosos de abordar la vasta obra de Fuentes.

5198 ———. *Desyoización*: Joyce/Cixous/Fuentes and the multi-vocal text (LALR, 9:19, Fall/Winter 1981, p. 31–39)
Faris reflexiona sobre el libro de Carlos Fuentes *Cervantes o la crítica de la lectura* y sobre sus relaciones con la obra de Joyce, Cixous, Borges y Octavio Paz. El artículo no parece ir más allá de lo establecido por Fuentes en el libro mencionado y en otros de sus ensayos.

5199 Fiddian, Robin W. Beyond the unquiet grave and the cemetery of words: myth and archetype in *Palinuro de México* (IAA, 8:3, 1982, p. 243–255)
Examina las alusiones mitológicas, principalmente las homéricas y virgilianas, en la novela para hacer ver su relación con una escondida estructura figurativa y arquetípica que le proporciona unidad verbal y temática. Esa estructura se identificaría con Palinuro insepulto en búsqueda, en medio de la novela: cementerio de palabras, vida, expresión y resurrección.

5200 Fiscal, María Rosa. La imagen de la mujer en la narrativa de Rosario Castellanos. México: Universidad Nacional Autónoma de Méxco, 1980. 123 p.: bibl. (Cuadernos del Centro de Estudios Literarios)
Intenta hacer ver, con una aproximación sociológica a las obras de Castellanos, que el propósito fundamental de ésta era verificar un cambio en la imagen de la mujer de clase media en México. Fiscal estudia esa imagen en los personajes creados por Castellanos y llega a la conclusión de que su falta de identidad responde a circunstancias socioeconómicas dominantes secularmente en México. Castellanos, partiendo del cardenismo experimentado por ella, se habría propuesto encontrar una identidad para la mujer mexicana. Estudio bien documentado, claro en sus propósitos e iluminador de un aspecto descuidado por la crítica de Castellanos.

5201 Foster, David William. Mexican literature: a bibliography of secondary sources. Metuchen, N.J.: Scarecrow Press, 1981. 386 p.: index
Compilación selectiva de crítica sobre la literatura mexicana, desde Sor Juana hasta José Agustín y Gustavo Sainz, aparecida en revistas de cierto prestigio o en monografías. La intención del compilador no es registrar todo lo habido sobre un autor, sino sólo lo mejor, incluyendo lo accesible en América Latina y en Estados Unidos. Ha excluido la literatura indigenista, así como a Alfonso Reyes y José Vasconcelos, por razones de espacio. Pero eso no obsta para que éste sea un libro de consulta muy útil y necesario en toda biblioteca, sobre todo si se considera la escasez de índices cumulativos en revistas hispanoamericanas.

5202 Fuentes, Carlos. *La Ilíada* descalza (Vuelta [México] 7:80, julio 1983, p. 5–10)
Fuentes toma como ejemplo del espacio donde circula la novela hispanoamericana al México revolucionario de Mariano Azuela en *Los de abajo*. La permanencia de ese espacio hace imposible la epopeya en Hispanoamérica porque no ha habido un cambio profundo en ella: "La historia revolucionaria despoja a la épica de su sostén mítico: *Los de abajo* es un viaje del origen al origen, pero sin mito. Ya la novela, en seguida, despoja a la historia revolucionaria de su sostén épico."

5203 Gertel, Zunilda. Semiótica, historia y ficción en *Terra Nostra* (IILI/RI, 116/117, julio/dic. 1981, p. 63–72)
Interesante lectura de *Terra Nostra* con el fin de mostrar la forma en que el espacio histórico puede hacerse presente en la escritura y la lectura de lo hispánico. Sin embargo la lectura de *Terra Nostra* como posibilidad de acabar rupturas y fragmentaciones en la historia hispánica, así como una vuelta a los orígenes, fue desacreditada por González Echevarría (ver item **5205**).

5204 González, Juan E. Entrevista con Juan Rulfo (RO, 9, 1981, p. 105–114)
Inteligente y alumbradora entrevista hecha a Rulfo: que a *Pedro Páramo* lo tuvo en su mente por 10 años antes de poderlo plasmar en la escritura; que el cuento "Luvina" fue clave importante para ubicar el ambiente de la novela; habla también de su planeada, pero ya descartada, novela *La cor-*

dillera; y de proyectos de escribir cuentos parecidos a los de *El llano en llamas.*

5205 González Echevarría, Roberto. *Terra Nostra:* teoría y práctica (IILI/RI, 116/117, julio/dic. 1981, p. 289–298)

El mejor artículo que se ha escrito sobre *Terra Nostra.* Aborda la novela bajo la doble perspectiva de la teoría (el ensayo de Fuentes "Cervantes o la Crítica de la Lectura") y de la práctica (el texto de la novela). Según la teoría, Fuentes se propone proporcionar un conocimiento total de la cultura hispánica llegando hasta los orígenes para, desde allí, ir recreando esa cultura dividida por la lucha de clases (Américo Castro) y por ello fragmentada (Foucault) en su régimen social (Lukács) y generadora de la novela moderna (Cervantes). Afirma González Echeverría: "Pocas obras como ésta hacen de su lectura un acontecimiento notable en la vida real de sus lectores y críticos."

5206 Gyurko, Lanin A. Sátira social y los antiguos dioses mexicanos en la narrativa de Fuentes (UNAM/RMCPS, 26, oct./dic. 1980, p. 65–102)

Extenso ensayo sobre la utilización de Fuentes de la voz y de la personalidad de los dioses aztecas para hacer una sátira social del México contemporáneo en su primera novela, *La region más transparente,* y en sus antecedentes, los cuentos "Chac Mool" y "Por Boca de los Dioses." Concluye diciendo que la venganza de los dioses se logra sangrientamente en los cuentos, pero es menos efectiva en la novela.

5207 Hancock, Joel. Elena Poniatowska's *Hasta no verte Jesús mío:* the remaking of the image of woman (AATSP/H, 66:3, 1983, p. 353–359, bibl., ill.)

Analiza al personaje Jesusa Palancares como no sujeto al común estereotipo femenino, sino que reúne entre sus características las propias tanto a hombres como a mujeres. Pero Jesusa critica a los primeros por sus abusos en las segundas. Según Hancock la protagonista participa de elementos encontrados en la picaresca. Un artículo bien escrito, documentado y analítico de la novela toda, aunque centrádose en el papel de Jesusa Palancares.

5208 Holdsworth, Carole A. A modernist Maecenas: J.E. Valenzuela (UCSB/NS, 8, 1982, p. 211–222)

Incisivo artículo sobre uno de los hombres más importantes en la promoción de la literatura en Hispanoamérica a través de *La Revista Moderna,* si bien fue escritor de pocas capacidades. En esa revista publicó solamente tres cuentos. El más interesante sería "Oremus," por su insistencia en compaginar la ciencia y la religión. Analiza además los artículos críticos y la poesía de Valenzuela. Artículo certero aunque panorámico.

5209 Koldewyn, Philip Mediation and regeneration in the sacred zones of fiction: Carlos Fuentes and the nature of myth (UCLA/JLAL, 7:2, Winter 1981, p. 147–169)

Excelente ensayo donde se analiza *Zona sagrada* de Fuentes, haciendo uso inteligente e iluminador de las diversas teorías acerca de los mitos, pero principalmente de tres conceptos fundamentados en Mircea Eliade y en Lévi-Strauss: *Mater* (la naturaleza), *Materia* (la cultura) y los símbolos mediadores entre ambas. Según el articulista la actitud del protagonista sería representativa del fracaso del mexicano en dar fuerza verdaderamente mítica a realidades tan importantes como la Revolución Mexicana.

5210 Krauze, Enrique. Pasión y contemplación en Vasconcelos (Vuelta [México] 8:78, mayo 1983, p. 12–19)

Interesante artículo que invita a una lectura platónica de las *Memorias* de Vasconcelos (Fondo de Cultura Económica, 1983). Según Krauze fueron escritas teniendo como motivo principal el amor de Vasconcelos por una mujer y, después, por la necesidad de recurrir a la mística plotiniana para resarcirse de la pérdida de ella. Amor y misticismo serían los motores del escribir de Vasconcelos, más que los acontecimientos de la Revolución Mexicana.

5211 Larson, Ross. Archetypal patterns in Carlos Fuentes "La Muñeca Reina" (UCLA/M, 11:1, 1982, p. 41–46)

Aplica las teorías de C.G. Jung a la lectura del cuento de Fuentes. Utiliza principalmente los conceptos de *anima, animus* y *umbra,* los cuales le sirven para sostener que el cuento es una readaptación moderna del motivo arquetípico de la búsqueda del héroe.

5212 Leal, Luis. Agustín Yáñez y la novela mexicana: rescate de una teoría (IILI/RI, 48:118/119, enero/junio 1982, p. 121–129)

Se aventura con destreza en la difícil tarea de sopesar las características generales de la novela mexicana de acuerdo a una teoría inconclusa de Yáñez. Pretende concluirla y ejemplificarla con la obra de Yáñez y autores más representativos de la novela en México. Está de acuerdo con características apuntadas por Yáñez (enfoque nacionalista, sentido realista, estilo caracterizado por la sintaxis y el retrato crítico), pero descarta el profetismo como algo exclusivo a la novela mexicana.

5213 ———. Arquetipos femeninos en la literatura mexicana (PCCLAS/P, 7, 1980/1981, p. 75–82)

Panorama esquemático de los arquetipos femeninos en la literatura mexicana: la mujer violada, proveniente de la leyenda de la Malinche; y la mujer virgen, generada de la creencia en la Virgen de Guadalupe. De esta última surgen los arquetipos de madre, beata, novia y mujer santa. De la Malinche se desprende el de concubina, novia asequible y prostituta. Versión inglesa de este artículo en item **5027.**

5214 Lipski, John M. Vincente Leñero: narrative evolution as religious search (IUP/HJ, 3:2, Spring 1982, p. 41–59)

Analiza novelas de Leñero bajo el enfoque de la estructura narrativa como paralela a la búsqueda de un destino o identidad en la religión. Las estructuras narrativas utilizadas por Leñero impedirían el desarrollo de una trama, así como la solución de los enredos planteados en correspondencia a la dificultad para encontrar la verdad y el conocimiento en la búsqueda religiosa.

5215 Martínez, Eliud. The art of Mariano Azuela: modernism in *La malhora, El desquite, La luciérnaga.* Introduction by Luis Leal. Pittsburgh: Latin American Literary Review Press, 1980. 101 p.: bibl. (Exploration)

Presenta un aspecto descuidado por la crítica de Azuela: su producción novelística experimental al modo de lo que entonces se hacía en la vanguardia norteamericana y francesa. Martínez hace ver que Azuela, antes que cualquier otro mexicano, escribió tres novelas utilizando el fluir de la consciencia y las técnicas anejas a ello. Esto lo hace precursor de la nueva novela hispanoamericana.

5216 Ortega, Julio. Tres notas mexicanas (CH, 381, marzo 1982, p. 667–676)

Interesantes reflexiones sobre la segunda versión de *Morirás lejos,* novela de José Emilio Pacheco y *Compadre Lobo* de Gustavo Sainz. Las analiza en función de la lectura como proceso narrativo y de decodificación a que el lector es obligado por las técnicas utilizadas. Según Ortega *Compadre Lobo,* una novela sobre la lectura, no ha sido suficientemente estudiada por la crítica.

5217 Pacheco, Carlos. Algunas consideraciones metodológicas sobre la narrativa de la dictadura: el caso de *La sombra del caudillo* de Martín Luiz Guzmán (Fragmentos [Centro de Estudios Latinoamericanos Rómulo Gallegos, Departamento de Investigaciones, Caracas] 8, sept./dic. 1980, p. 49–62)

Sistematiza el estudio de la narrativa de la dictadura, tomando como ejemplo de verificación la novela de Guzmán. Las características básicas de la narrativa de dictadura son: la soledad y la desconfianza, la represión, la corrupción y el simulacro de la legitimidad del poder del dictador.

5218 Puga, María Luisa. Literatura y sociedad (UNAM/RMCPS, 26, oct./dic. 1980, p. 103–108)

Reflexiones sobre su condición de escritora y mujer en México y la sorpresa que este exotismo genera en los demás. Más que ensayo, las reflexiones constituyen una composición poética íntima y lírica sobre el inicio, el esfuerzo, el temor, la alegría y el vivir de la escritura en un país machista, donde la mayoría de la población es analfabeta.

5219 Ramírez, Arthur. Juan Rulfo: dialectics and the despairing optimist (AATSP/H, 65:4, Dec. 1982, p. 580–585)

Intenta hacernos ver la presencia del optimismo, la vida y la esperanza en la obra de Rulfo, considerada como pesimista. No procede a analizarla en sí misma para llegar a su tesis, sino que utiliza como válidos *a priori* los principios dialécticos de Hegel y otros pensadores. Si se procediera así, absolutamente ninguna obra podría ser pesimista.

5220 Reeve, Richard. Fuentes' "Chac Mool:" its ancestors and progeny (UCLA/M, 11:1, 1982, p. 67–74)

Rastrea la historia del cuento de Fuentes más que analizarlo. Según Reeve el cuento tiene su antecedente en otros.

Muestra asimismo como "Chac Mool" juega un papel importante en cuentos logrados de Julio Cortázar, Elena Garro y José Emilio Pacheco.

5221 Roa Bastos, Augusto. Los trasterrados de Comala (UTIEH/C, 37, 1981, p. 105–115)

Interesantísmo artículo sobre lecturas críticas que se han hecho sobre *Pedro Páramo* relacionándolo preferentemente con mitologías y textos de culturas dominantes, como la griega y latina, más que con la azteca, cultura periférica pero cercana a Rulfo. Roa Bastos quisiera que la lectura se liberara del colonialismo cultural. El artículo es un capítulo del libro, *El texto cautivo: apuntes de un narrador sobre la producción y la lectura de textos bajo el signo del poder cultural.*

5222 Robb, James Willis. Alfonso Reyes y Cecília Meireles: una amistad mexicano-brasileña (AATSP/H, 66, 1983, p. 164–230, bibl.)

Robb conoce más que nadie la obra y la vida de Alfonso Reyes, así como el ambiente que le tocó vivir y su relación con la obra que produjo. El artículo muestra uno de los muchos ejemplos de comunicación humana que siempre acompañó a Reyes por el mundo y dejó plasmada en su obra. En este caso, sobre todo, en la escrita durante su estancia en Brasil.

5224 ———. "La Cena" de Alfonso Reyes, cuento onírico: /surrealismo o realismo mágico? (ICC/T, 36:2, mayo/agosto 1981, p. 272–283)

Detallado e interesante análisis del cuento de Reyes al cual se le enmarca en la obra total de su autor. Menciona someramente las asociaciones literarias y pictóricas del cuento, para conjeturar luego que éste manifiesta oníricamente la huella de la trágica muerte del Gen. Bernardo Reyes, padre de Alfonso. Según Robb, Reyes es precursor tanto del surrealismo como del realismo mágico.

5225 Rosser, Harry L. Conflict and transition in rural Mexico: the fiction of social realism. Waltham, Mass.: Crossroads Press, 1980. 173 p.: bibl., index.

Analiza 15 novelas mexicanas en función de su relación con la sociedad, sin descuidar el peculiar modo de escribir de cada autor. Proporciona un interesante cuadro de la sociedad mexicana rural, de sus problemas e inquietudes bajo la mira narrativa de los autores. El libro ganaría en precisión si proporcionara una descripción más definida de lo que se entiende aquí por "realismo social," término aplicado por el autor a escritores tan disímiles como Rulfo y Mauricio Magdaleno.

5226 ———. Oposiciones estructurales en "El Hombre" en Juan Rulfo (UA/REH, 16:3, oct. 1982, p. 411–418)

No usa, como sugiere el título, un modelo estructuralista, sino que centra su intento de comprensión del caos fragmentario y semántico del relato en la unidad escondida que le proporcionan los sistemas de oposiciones (e.g., perseguido vs. perseguidor; enfoque interior vs. exterior; lo que ocurrió vs. lo que relata el borreguero al final).

5227 Ruffinelli, Jorge. *Compadre Lobo* de Gustavo Sainz: un ejercicio de autobiografía (HISPA, 10:29, 1981, p. 4–13)

Según Ruffinelli esta novela es una continuación ambigua y simultánea de *Gazapo* (novela) y *Gustavo Sainz* (autobiografía). La diferencia con la primera estaría en el lenguaje. Es más difícil diferenciarla de la autobiografía, de la cual se incorporan a la novela muchos datos. Dice Ruffinelli que hay intento de presentar una metáfora de autobiografía, pero precisa de más análisis para lograrlo.

5228 ———. Literatura e ideología: el primer Mariano Azuela, 1896–1918. México: Premiá Editora, 1981. 116 p.: bibl. (La Red de Jonas)

Ruffinelli se propone analizar la producción narrativa de Azuela (1896–1918) en contrapunto a la ideología manifestada en ella. Esta, según el autor, siempre fue la ideología de la pequeña burguesía liberal, de la cual procedía Azuela, a pesar de las críticas que de ella hace en sus obras. A través de ese lente Azuela leyó diariamente el cambio que se daba en la Revolución, aunque su inconformidad inicial con la realidad mexicana fue encontrando poco a poco objetivos políticos y sociales. Sin embargo, Azuela nunca formuló una visión global de esa realidad, sino observaciones aisladas.

5229 ———. El lugar de Rulfo y otros ensayos. Xalapa, México: Biblioteca, Universidad Veracruzana, 1980. 217 p.: bibl.

Tres artículos dedicados a Rulfo y entrevistas con Salvador Elizondo, Juan García Ponce y Fernando del Paso. El resto versa sobre otros escritores hispanoamericanos. La aproximación de Ruffinelli a la obra de Rulfo no descuida los aspectos formales, pero da especial énfasis al contexto social en que ésta surgió, sin excluir el mundo cultural. En este marco cabe la comparación entre Rulfo y el novelista suizo C.F. Ramuz. Las entrevistas son verdaderos cuestionamientos de un lector entendido a la obra de los entrevistados.

5230 Salcedo, Fernando F. Los "monjes:" personajes claves en *Cambio de piel* de Carlos Fuentes (HISP, 25:75, mayo 1982, p. 69–82)

Analiza "los monjes," personajes secundarios en la novela pero importantísimos como clave para entender la parodia de juicio. En su función explicativa los "monjes" son deliberadamente delineados como títeres o marionetas manejadas al capricho del narrador. Este no se ocupa de darles profundidad sino de especificar el papel que representan como "narradores auxiliares que cumplen una función explicativa."

5231 Schaffer, Susan C. Entrevista a José Agustín (UCLA/M, 8:2, Fall 1979, p. 27–33)

José Agustín afirma que lo común en la llamada Generación de la Onda consistía en ser sus integrantes escritores jóvenes, interesados en el mundo que les tocó vivir. Dentro de ese mundo estaría la música del roc y su influencia en sus obras. También habla de su interés por hacer cine profesional basado en sus novelas.

5232 Siemens, William L. Celestina as *Terra Nostra* (UCLA/M, 11:1, 1982, p. 57–66)

Interesante artículo que parte de la Celestina de Fernando de Rojas. Fuentes le ofrecería a esa Celestina la oportunidad de rejuvenecerse y de mantener perpetuamente unidos a hombre y mujer en el andrógino. Para ello la Celestina de Fuentes toma rasgos arquetípicos relacionados con la madre tierra y tejidos sutilmente por dos milenios en diversas figuras de Celestina, hasta que sea posible la *terra nostra* en el andrógino.

5233 Solotorevsky, Myrna. Una aproximación estructural a "El Hombre" de Juan Rulfo (CH, 383, mayo 1982, p. 35–364)

Minucioso e iluminador análisis del cuento de Rulfo utilizando como modelo un método estructuralista fundamentado principalmente en Genette y Barthes. Acude a la terminología estructualista, pero con claridad, orden y sentido. Al final de equemas analíticos múltiples, el lector conoce mejor la organización del relato y el porqué de ella, así como la significación desprendida del cuento.

5234 Sosnowski, Saúl. Entrevista a Carlos Fuentes (ECO, 44[6]:240, oct. 1981, p. 615–649)

Perspicaz e inteligente entrevista. Habla de su vida de viajero cosmopolita, la relación de sus viajes con su obra y su amor al trabajo, Balzac como modelo a seguir en el mundo narrativo de México, la función del lenguaje y la novela, la imposibilidad de la épica en Hispanoamérica y, finalmente, la función de la novela en esta región en las circunstancias actuales.

5235 Steele, Cynthia. Literature and national formation: indigenista fiction in the United States, 1820–1860, and in Mexico, 1920–1960 (PCCLAS/P, 9, 1982, p. 91–99)

Compara la narrativa indigenista en los Estados Unidos del siglo pasado y en el México postrevolucionario. La semejanza estaría en que en los dos países se vio simultáneamente al indio como el "buen salvaje" y "salvaje cruel." La falla del artículo es no concretar sus afirmaciones con bibliografía de la narrativa indigenista, casi ausente.

5236 Williams, Raymond L. The reader and the recent novels of Gustavo Sainz (AATSP/H, 65:3, Sept. 1982, p. 383–387)

Analiza la función del lector, principalmente el encontrado en el texto, en dos novelas de Sainz: *La princesa del Palacio de Hierro* y *Compadre Lobo*. Muestra como Sainz crea tensiones entre el "reader of fiction," el "fictionalized reader" y el lector implícito. Según Williams esas tensiones hacen más diversificada, atractiva y enigmática la lectura del lector actual.

20th Century: Prose Fiction: Central America

LISA E. DAVIS, Centro de Estudios Puertorriqueños, Hunter College

THE LAST TWO YEARS HAVE CERTAINLY brought Central America to the forefront in international affairs and politics while those who report the news through commentary, film, and video have found themselves again and again traveling to one or more of the region's small countries. This new interest in Central America on the part of the public has its complement in several innovative cultural phenomena whose purpose is the wider diffusion of the best and most informed attitudes toward the area. In that sense, we can cite the recent establishment in Nicaragua of a national publishing apparatus—Editorial Nueva Nicaragua— together with various subsidiaries which provide both for the reedition of works by well known local authors and also for the issue of a variety of new items in poetry, prose, criticism and history. These are publications of a quality in design, materials and format far above anything previously accomplished by smaller presses in Nicaragua, and should be better known outside the region. While we cannot give an exhaustive list of the items printed so far, we offer some idea of the trajectory of Editorial Nueva Nicaragua in new editions of Sergio Ramírez's *Charles Atlas también muere* (item **5253**), Lizandro Chávez Alfaro's *Los monos de San Telmo* (item **5246**), and Fernando Silva's *El comandante* (item **5255**), and in the publication of Julio Cortázar's personal tribute in *Nicaragua: tan violentamente dulce* (item **5263**). Younger writers like Alejandro Bravo, *El mambo es universal y otros relatos* (item **5244**), may find a publisher in "Ediciones Primavera Popular," as does Fernando Silva's new collection of short stories *Más cuentos* (item **5256**). Likewise, Editorial Nueva Nicaragua contributes to the growth and diffusion of that important genre in new Latin American literature, the testimonial, with their edition of Omar Cabeza Lacayo's *La montaña es algo más que una inmensa estepa verde* (item **5245**).

Recently such first-person narratives have opened up unexplored vistas on the contemporary history of Central America, and more such accounts by figures outside the traditional power structures in those countries will document for the future this century's progress. In that regard, the late Roque Dalton's recopilation of the life of the labor leader Miguel Mármol, *Miguel Mármol: los sucesos de 1932 en El Salvador* (item **5264**), stands as the popular history of those tragic events and beyond. By the same token, Dalton's own *Pobrecito poeta que era yo . . .* (item **5248**) is obviously a slightly more fictionalized version of his own early experiences as a politicized writer in El Salvador, an account which ends significantly in a lengthy and harrowing imprisonment and his escape. Dalton's genius and geniality are reflected once again in his third major work in prose, *Las historias prohibidas del Pulgarcito* (item **5247**), an original mixture of story and poetry, reality and fiction, which demonstrates his overriding concern with the bloody history of El Salvador. Another internationally known poet, Claribel Alegría, has often turned her hand to prose showing a similar preoccupation with a terrible past and faith in a better future. El Salvador in 1932 is the stage for *Cenizas de Izalco* (item **5238**), while the recent *Album familiar* (item **5237**) takes the Sandinista campaigns against Somoza as its theme. Also, happily for the English-speaking reader, the international notoriety achieved by El Salvador and alluded to above has given rise to the publication in the distinguished new series "Aventura: The Library of Contemporary Literature" of one of Manlio Argueta'a novels almost impossible to get in Spanish, *One day of life* or *Un día en la vida* (item **5239**). We see its appearance as a recognition by North American publishers of the contemporary importance of Central America and the quality of its literature, which is little known in the US. The availability of this inexpensive paper edition could be a windfall for literature classes in translation and for others interested in the region.

Finally, the literary attempts to chronicle the true reality of Central America in the 20th century range far and wide. The Honduran writers Julio Escoto, *Días de ventisca, noches de huracán* (item **5249**), and Eduardo Bähr, *El cuento de la guerra* (item **5243**), coincide in their desire to confront the circumstances that led up to and, accompanied the disastrous "football" war between Honduras and El Salvador. The Costa Rican Samuel Rovinski's *Cuentos judíos de mi tierra* (item **5254**), which gives a voice and a literary shape to the fortunes of Jewish immigrants in Central America. Likewise, in the realm of scholarship and criticism, it would be impossible to forego references to a new and essential volume of the critical edition of Miguel Angel Asturias' *Obras completas: Hombres de maíz* (item **5142**); and to Ramón Luis Acevedo's informative and ambitious history of *La novela centro-americana: desde el Popul-Vuh hasta los umbrales de la novela actual* (item **5259**), published in Puerto Rico.

PROSE FICTION

5237 Alegría, Claribel. Album familiar. San José: Editorial Universitaria Centroamericana, 1982. 61 p. (Colección Séptimo día)

New book by Salvadoran poet and novelist describes life of young Nicaraguan woman married to Frenchman and living in Paris, and how, through members of her family who enter Sandinista rebel ranks against Somoza, she becomes involved with the movement.

5238 ——— and **Darwin J. Flakoll.** Cenizas de Izalco. 3a. ed. San José: Editorial Universitaria Centroamericana, 1982. 209 p. (Colección Séptimo día)

First published Seix Barral 1966, this novel traces tragic events of 1932 in El Salvador through lives of one family. Daughter reconstructs her mother's past, and changes her attitude toward the older woman. Dual authorship of Alegría and her husband gives authenticity to many episodes.

5239 Argueta, Manlio. One day of life. Translated from the Spanish by Bill Brow. New York: Vintage Books, 1983. 215 p. (Aventura: the Vintage library of contemporary world literature)

Novel, banned for last few years in El Salvador and happily made available in translation, defines tragedy in the life of Lupe, the grandmother. Author focuses on terror in Salvadoran countryside through deaths, threats and savage beatings of members of her family and others.

5240 Arroyo, Justo. Geografía de mujer. Panamá: Grupo Editorial Encuentro, 1982. 161 p.: ill.

Latest work by the Panamanian novelist shows very different but not contradictory face of Central American reality. World of the protagonist— Panamanian writer who supports himself by translating while living in Mexico City (probable autobiographical elements)—is highly cosmopolitan but vacuous.

5241 Asturias, Miguel Angel. Leyendas de Guatemala. Madrid: Alianza Editorial, 1981. 157 p., 1 leaf (Sección Literatura. El Libro de bolsillo; 847)

Attractive reedition of Asturias' popular volume introduced by Paul Valery's letter celebrating magical world created by author. Drawn mostly from rich Guatemalan Indian heritage of folklore and myth, volume also has tales relating to country's colonial history.

5242 ———. Obras completas. v. 4, Hombres de maíz: edición crítica. Prefacio, Jean Cassou. Estudios, Mario Vargas Llosa, Gerald Martin, Giovanni Meo Zilio. Texto establecido por Gerald Martin. Paris: Klincksieck;

Madrid: Fondo de Cultura Económica, 1981. 474 p.: bibl.

Another critical volume in series of the *Complete Works* published by international team of scholars. This ed. contains lengthy preliminary study (p. xxv–ccxliv), by Gerald Martin, with shorter essays on various facets of the work by Jean Cassou, Mario Vargas Llosa, and Giovanni Meo Zilio.

5243 Bähr, Eduardo. El cuento de la guerra. 2a. ed. Tegucigalpa: Editorial Universitaria de la Universidad Nacional Autónoma de Honduras, 1977. 77 p.

Collection of six short stories by noted Honduran writer, mostly dealing directly or indirectly with "football" war between Honduras and El Salvador (1969). Emphasizes ridiculous essence of that war while better stories relate dehumanization of common soldiers through a senseless conflict.

5244 Bravo, Alejandro. El mambo es universal y otros relatos. Managua: Conjunta de la Unión de Escritores de Nicaragua e IMELSA, 1982. 59 p.: ill. (Ediciones primavera popular; 7)

Also poet and Director of the National University Press, Bravo represents new generation (b. 1953) of writers, and these nine stories reveal some of their concerns (e.g., torture and murder under Somoza, recollections of Sandino and Farabundo Martí of El Salvador).

5245 Cabezas Lacayo, Omar. La montaña es algo más que una inmensa estepa verde. 2a. ed. Managua: Editorial Nueva Nicaragua, 1982. 259 p. (Biblioteca popular Sandinista)

First-person narrative about early years of Sandinista movement in cities of Nicaragua, and guerrilla in the mountains: physical hardships, training period, and contacts with peasant communities who immediately saw those young men as continuation of the liberation struggle under Sandino.

5246 Chávez Alfaro, Lizandro. Los monos de San Telmo. 5a. ed. Managua: Editorial Nueva Nicaragua, 1982. 177 p. (Biblioteca popular Sandinista; 13)

Originally published by Casa de las Américas as 1963 prize for short story, this new Nicaraguan ed. contains 13 stories, generally violent or subtle denunciations of the state of the country under Somoza's dic-tatorship. Several stories deal with Sandino's campaigns against the US Marines.

5247 Dalton, Roque. Las historias prohibidas del Pulgarcito. 5a. ed. México: Siglo Veintiuno Editores, 1980. 232 p. (La Creación literaria)

Regarding Gabriela Mistral's definition of El Salvador as "el Pulgarcito de América," here Dalton gives his version of Salvadoran history, from Spanish conquest to "football" war between El Salvador and Honduras. Some texts are copied from other sources; others are original with author.

5248 ———. Pobrecito poeta que era yo: novela. 2a. ed. Ciudad Universitaria Rodrigo Facio, Costa Rica: Editorial Universitaria Centroamericana, 1981. 476 p. (Colección Séptimo día)

Novel by Salvadoran author is in many ways autobiographical. Recreates literary forays of young Salvadoran of upper middle class, his contacts within the country's intellectual circles, and his coming to terms with the misery of the great majority of the people.

5249 Escoto, Julio. Días de ventisca, noches de huracán. San José: Editorial Nueva Década, 1980. 139 p.

New original novel by talented Honduran author of *El árbol de los pañuelos*, traces progress of several characters in isolation, whose stories come together at end in atmosphere of corruption, war, and chaos. Recalls again "football" war (Honduras-El Salvador) in remarkable prose.

5250 Gutiérrez, Joaquín. Manglar: novela. 3a. ed. San José: Editorial Costa Rica, 1982. 140 p.

One of the Costa Rican novelist's classics (for 1st ed. 1947, see *HLAS 14:2759*) based on experiences of young woman from the capital who goes as rural schoolteacher to Guanacaste. In a prose often lyrical in its descriptive force, narrates social, political, and emotional episodes from that remote region.

5251 Monterroso, Augusto. Mr. Taylor & Co. La Habana: Casa de las Américas, 1982. 130 p. (Colección La honda)

Collection of 25 short pieces by the Guatemalan author, contains some of his best previous work taken from other volumes. Story that gives collection its title relates the rise and fall of a business in shrunken heads set up by an American ne'er-do-well in Brazil.

5252 Pitty, Dimas Lidio. Los caballos estornudan en la lluvia. Panamá: Ediciones Instituto Nacional de Cultura, 1979. 73 p. (Colección Premio Ricardo Miró. Sección cuento; 1978)

Awarded the Ricardo Miró Prize for Short Story, collection recalls Panama's rural world where life presents itself in very basic terms. Themes are birth, death, isolation, and violence in the countryside, and prose complements subject matter in its purity and sensitivity.

5253 Ramírez, Sergio. Charles Atlas también muere. 2a. ed. Managua: Editorial Nueva Nicaragua, 1982. 118 p. (Biblioteca popular Sandinista)

Collection, originally published by Joaquín Mortiz (México, 1976), includes six stories ranging from title story—which narrates death of farsical Charles Atlas—to several stories chronicling the people's terror and absurd fantasies of the upper classes, including Somoza himself, during the latter's reign.

5254 Rovinski, Samuel. Cuentos judíos de mi tierra. San José: Editorial Costa Rica, 1982. 91 p.

In eight short stories, Rovinski provides insight into the unique experience of Jewish emigrants (*los polacos*) to Costa Rica. All episodes have stamp of truth, with particular sensitivity regarding the survivors of Holocaust. Valuable book for those studying the Jewish experience in Latin America.

5255 Silva, Fernando. El comandante. 6a. ed. Managua: Editorial Nueva Nicaragua, 1983. 200 p. (Colección Letras de Nicaragua; 4)

New ed. (first 1969) of novel whose simplicty and directness have proved persistently attractive to Nicaraguan public. Set in tropical jungle region that borders San Juan River, it relates extraordinary histories of several individuals as told by the local *comandante.*

5256 ———. Más cuentos. Managua: Ediciones Primavera Popular, 1982. 126 p. (Ediciones Primavera Popular; 4)

Author's simple poignant style of story-telling is considered classic in Nicaragua, and these latest stories recapture flavor of country life, particularly on the banks of country's lakes and rivers. Portraits of the poor people of city and village, toward the end against a background of National Guard terror.

5257 Sinán, Rogelio. El candelabro de los malos oficios y otros cuentos. México: Editorial Signos, 1982. 114 p. (Colección Portobelo; 10. Serie Autores panameños)

Small volume, edited by Panamanian author well known in his own right, satisfies need for more of Sinán's work in print. On Sinán's 80th birthday (1982), some of his principal short works appear here in reverse chronological order, beginning with recent stories and going back to 1925 (see also item **5258**).

5258 ———. Homenaje a Rogelio Sinán: poesía y cuento. Selección y prólogo de Enrique Jaramillo Levi. México: Editorial Signos, 1982. 121 p.: bibl. (Colección Portobelo; 1. Serie Autores panameños)

Collection is companion piece to item **5257,** by same author and editor, with prologue by latter and interview with Sinán by Jorge Ruffinelli. Volume recalls classic stories like "La Boina Roja" and "A la Orilla de las Estatuas Maduras."

Skármeta, Antonio. La insurreción. See item **5492.**

LITERARY CRITICISM AND HISTORY

5259 Acevedo, Ramón L. La novela centroamericana: desde el *Popul-Vuh* hasta los umbrales de la novela actual. Río Piedras: Editorial Universitaria, Universidad de Puerto Rico, 1982. 503 p.: bibl. (Colección Mente y palabra)

This recent critical publication, including lengthy and useful bibliography, fills near vacuum in history and analysis of Central American literature. Acevedo begins with precolumbian literature, and takes his history up to 1940, when Central American novel initiates new stage in its development.

5260 Albizúrez Palma, Francisco. Rafael Arevalo Martínez (Cultura de Guatemala [Universidad Rafael Landívar, Guatemala] 3:1, enero/abril 1982, p. 95–111)

Life and times of famous Guatemalan literary figure (1884–1975), best known for his zoomorphic short stories. [M. MacLeod]

5261 —— and **Catalina Barrios y Barrios.** Historia de la literatura guatemalteca. Bibliografía de Lourdes Bendfeldt Rojas. Guatemala: Editorial Universitaria de Guatemala, 1981. 1 v.: bibl. (Colección Historia nuestra; v. no. 2)

Helpful tool in analysis of Guatemalan literature from its indigenous roots to end of 19th century, including periodical publications and extensive bibliography by Lourdes Bendfeldt Rojas. Projected vols. 2–3 will cover 1900–30 and 1930–80 period, respectively.

5262 Bogantes, Claudio and **Ursula Kuhlmann.** El surgimiento del realismo social en Centroamérica: 1930–1970 (RCLL, 9:17, 1983, p. 39–64)

Detailed attempt to explain relation of social processes in the area to cultural production ranges widely, from an analysis of Central America's peculiar situation within Latin America, to Costa Rica's historical and political development, to the works of Carlos Luis Fallas and Fabián Dobles, taken as exemplary.

5263 Cortázar, Julio. Nicaragua tan violentamente dulce. Managua: Editorial Nueva Nicaragua: Ediciones Monimbó, 1983. 108 p.: port (Palabra de nuestra América)

Collection of 16 items includes one poem, short story "Apocalipsis de Solentiname," and Cortázar's essays and speeches on Nicaragua. They trace his profound admiration and affection for the Nicaraguan people and their government after 1979. A moving and historic declaration by one of Latin America's greatest writers.

5264 Dalton, Roque. Miguel Mármol: los sucesos de 1932 en El Salvador. La Habana: Casa de las Américas, 1983. 267 p. (Colección nuestros países. Serie Estudios)

First-person narrative was taken down by the youthful Roque Dalton, from the oral testimony of Miguel Mármol, one of the earliest participants in the country's organized labor movement, who was actually executed by government forces in 1932, but survived to be an old man and relate many remarkable experiences.

5265 Echeverría C., Evelio. Indice general del *Repertorio Americano.* v. 1, A-B. San José: Editorial Universidad Estatal a Distancia. 1 v.: bibl., ports.

Vol. 1 (A-B), of what will be a lengthy series, containing succinct bibliographical notes on all articles published in this extraordinary journal edited by Costa Rican Joaquín García Monge, (1919–59). Invaluable guide to one of Latin America's most important literary reviews.

Stansifer, Charles L. Cultural policy in the old and the new Nicaragua. See item **2444.**

5266 Turcios, Froylán. Memorias. Tegucigalpa: Universidad Nacional Autónoma de Honduras, Editorial Universitaria, 1980. 419 p.: bibl. (Colección Letras hondureñas; no. 5)

Important autobiography by one of Honduras' leading literary figures goes beyond his comments on the arts to recreate a whole cultural context for Latin American modernistas, their aristocratic background, political involvements, wide travels (particularly Paris and Madrid), and their nationalism. Very illuminating for students of that era.

20th Century: Prose Fiction: Hispanic Caribbean

WILLIAM LUIS, *Associate Professor of Spanish, Dartmouth College*
CARLOS R. HORTAS, *Professor of Spanish, Hunter College*

THE PUBLICATION OF FIVE MAGAZINES characterizes this biennium. *Mariel* (item **5290**), *Término* (item **5303**), *Unveiling Cuba* (item **5305**), *La Oveja Negra* (no issue available for review at press time), and *Revista de Literatura Cubana* (item

5344), with *Linden Lane Magazine* (see *HLAS 44:5325*), are welcome additions to the field of Cuban literature. The first four are published in the US by emigrés who left Cuba as late as 1982. These magazines provide an outlet for artistic creation and a dissenting voice for those who, for one reason or another, were not able to publish in Cuba. In most cases, political affiliation determines publication. In this sense, these periodicals fall into the same traps as those in Cuba by excluding positions ideologically different from their own. Of the new exile magazines, *Linden Lane Magazine*, first, and *Mariel*, second, are the most important.

Unlike the others, *Revista de Literatura Cubana* (item 5344) is published twice a year in Cuba and may offer a new and more objective perspective into the island's literature. It is also important to note that since 1982, *La Gaceta de Cuba*, of the Union de Escritores y Artistas de Cuba, has been renamed *La Nueva Gaceta* (item 5294) to accommodate works of broader interest.

The fleeing of both young and established writers has added to the quantity and enhanced the quality of Cuban literature outside of the island. Of these, Reinaldo Arenas has been very active with numerous articles, his latest novel *Otra vez el mar* (item 5271) and his announced *Que trine Eva* (item 5269). The increased activity has contributed to a continuing tense dialogue between those for and against the Cuban Revolution. This is certainly the case with the comments expressed in the four new exile magazines and those published in others such as *Areito* (item 5339).

During this two-year period we have witnessed the death of a great writer, Lino Novás Calvo (d. March 24, 1983). Homage was paid to him at the AATSP meeting in August of the same year and published in *Linden Lane Magazine* (item 5327). We should also mention the death of another great writer, Virgilio Piñera. Best known as a writer of short stories and plays, his *Cuentos* were recently reedited by Alfaguara (item 5297). For political reasons, their deaths were downplayed in Cuba. Regarding writers both living and deceased, in and out of Cuba, Carpentier continues to be the most recognized, followed by Lezama Lima.

Of notable importance is *Alejo Carpentier: bibliographic guide/guía bibliográfica* compiled by Roberto González Echevarría and Klaus Müller-Bergh (item 5326). By far this is the most up-to-date bibliography of and about Carpentier's work. It is an indispensable tool for the study of Carpentier, in particular, and Cuban literature, in general. With this important reference available to scholars, we expect to see more definitive studies on Carpentier.

We have received a number of detective novels published in Cuba, a genre which first appeared in 1971. Although they are many in number, we, for the moment, have decided not to review them individually because they lack literary value. All seem to follow the same pattern and theme: they are written from the same ideological perspective and narrate, for the most part, the peoples' action against counter-intelligence, delinquency, etc., in defense of socialist justice and the State. Many are sponsored by the Concurso Aniversario del Triunfo de la Revolución of the Ministerio del Interior. Others are gaining acceptance through traditional circles and participation in literary contests. For example, Luis Rogelio Noguera's popular *Y si muero mañana* received the UNEAC's Cirilo Villaverde Prize in 1977, and was reprinted in 1982.

In Puerto Rico, two young writers have published works that mark them as new voices to be considered alongside Luis Rafael Sánchez as important prose innovators. These new voices belong to Ana Lydia Vega and Edgardo Rodríguez Juliá. Vega, together with Carmen Lugo Filippi, has coauthored, *Vírgenes y mártires* (item 5289), a collection of short stories with a stunning literary and feminist perspective. These stories are exceptionally well written and offer fine insights into Puerto Rican life and mores. Ana Lydia Vega has also published *Encancaranublado* (item 5306), another extraordinary collection of short stories.

Edgardo Rodríguez Juliá is the author of two works of prose which elude normal generic classification: *Las tribulaciones de Jonás* (item 5299a) and *El entierro de Cortijo* (item 5299). Each chronicles the death of a very important figure in Puerto Rican life, and offers a retrospective and selective look at these personages' lives in Puerto Rican society. The narratives are accompanied by photographs and may be best defined as "chronicles" or perhaps examples of creative photo-journalism. Whatever the classification, both books are exceptional. The protagonists are finely and subtly drawn and Juliá's talent for capturing telling details of their lives is absolutely uncanny. Both Juliá's books as well as Ana Lydia Vega's short stories are required reading for any student of Puerto Rican literature.

Although Dominican literature continues to lag behind Cuban and Puerto Rican literatures, we are encouraged by the number of works we have received on this country's literature. Many of them pertain to the US invasion of the Dominican Republic in 1965, a theme of much concern to young and up-and-coming writers (e.g., see *Cambio*, item 5301). We are also happy to report that articles on Dominican narrative are increasing in both number and quality.

PROSE FICTION

5267 Angel Buesa, José. Año bisiesto: autobiografía informal. Santo Domingo: Universidad Nacional Pedro Henríquez Ureña, 1981. 420 p.: ill.

Novelistic autobiography written in diary form. Divided into daily entries during 12 months of 1976 leap year. In this *Ulysses*-type novel, protagonist is aware of act of writing and his reader.

5268 Antología literaria dominicana. v. 1, Poesía. v. 2, Cuento. v. 3, Teatro. v. 4, Discursos, semblanzas, ensayos. v. 5, Folklore, índice acumulativo. Editado por Margarita Vallejo de Paredes. Colaboradores, Lilia Portalatín Sosa, Pedro Pablo Paredes V., Jorge Max Fernández. Santo Domingo: Instituto Tecnológico de Santo Domingo, 1981. 5 v.: bibl., indexes.

Of these five volumes comprising an anthology of Dominican literature, two are relevant: v. 2, *Cuento* and v. 4, *Discursos, semblanzas, ensayos*. Juan Bosch's previously known "Apuntes sobre el Arte de Escribir Cuentos" opens short story collection. Unfortunately, the two volumes reviewed lacked bio and bibliographic data and contained some errors.

5269 Arenas, Reinaldo. Final de un cuento (Mariel [Revista de literatura y arte, New York] 1 : 1, 1983, p. 3–5)

Chapter of Arenas' next novel, *Que trine Eva*. Novelized autobiography in which narrator refuses, under any circumstances, to return to Cuba and prefers living in New York City.

5270 ———. El mundo alucinante. Barcelona: Montesinos, 1981. 249 p.

Reedition of Arenas' excellent 1969 novel which narrates life of Fray Servando Teresa de Mier.

5271 ———. Otra vez el mar. Barcelona: Argos Vergara, 1982. 420 p. (Biblioteca del fenice; 7)

Clever novel with poetic moments in which protagonist Héctor assumes all voices in narration. Story takes place in 1960s Cuba. Protagonist's tragic ending represents an unwillingness to continue his present life and his desire to gain freedom.

5272 Barnet, Miguel. Gallego. Madrid: Editorial Alfaguara, 1981. 224 p. (Literatura Alfaguara; 76)

Testimonial of Manuel Ruiz, a Galician, who, like many others, went to Cuba at a young age to find work. His travels to and from Cuba provide an understanding of

Cuban and Spanish history. Although well written and researched, *Biografía de un cimarrón* (see *HLAS 32:1944*) continues to be Barnet's most important work.

5273 Bosch, Juan. Cuentos escritos antes del exilio. 2a. ed. Santo Domingo: Editora Alfa y Omega, 1980. 284 p.

Reedition of Bosch's 1974 collection of short stories comprises fiction published in newspapers and magazines before his 1936 exile.

5274 Cardoso, Onelio Jorge. Cuentos completos. Prólogo de Raúl Aparicio. Madrid: Ediciones de la Torre, 1981. 230 p. (Libro compacto; no. 40. Serie Literatura)

Collection of narrations by one of Cuba's best-known short story writers, with brief prologue by Raúl Aparicio. Selections are from Cardoso's *Cuentos completos* (1962) and *La otra muerte del gato* (1964).

5275 ———. Cuentos escogidos. La Habana: Editorial Letras Cubanas, 1981. 279 p.

Another anthology of Cardoso's short stories drawn from previous collection, except his latest *Caballito blanco* (1974).

5276 ———. Gente de un nuevo pueblo. La Habana?: Girón, 1981. 149 p.

Collection of previously published journalistic articles (1960–72). Cardoso's recording of local Cuban history reads almost like his short stories. Lacks introduction and entries do not follow any particular order.

5277 Carpentier, Alejo. El camino de Santiago. Montevideo: Editorial Arca; Buenos Aires: Editorial Galerna, 1981. 91 p. (Aves del Arca; 11)

Reedition of Carpentier's well known short story. Originally published in 1954 and later included in his *Guerra del tiempo* (1958), Galerna published story in its present form in 1967, 1968, and again in 1981.

5278 ———. Los pasos perdidos. Madrid: Alfaguara, 1981. 333 p. (Literatura Alfaguara; 83)

Reedition of Carpentier's 1953 novel which contrasts origin of Latin America with contemporary society and denies possibility of returning to that past.

5279 ———. Razón de ser: conferencias. La Habana: Editorial Letras Cubana, 1980. 91 p.

Series of four conferences delivered by Carpentier during his stay in Caracas in May 1975. His talks, Rafael José Neri's "Noticia sobre Este Libro," and Alexis Márquez Rodríguez's introduction were originally published 1976 by Universidad Central de Venezuela.

5280 Cofiño López, Manuel. Amor a sombra y sol. La Habana: Editorial Letras Cubanas, 1981. 360 p. (Colección Saeta)

In Cofiño's latest novel, the love relationship of both protagonists, Magdalena and Marcos, parallels struggle for a betterment of their society and a just life. Prevalent elements in the narration are the CIA and espionage.

5281 Cuza Malé, Belkis. Páginas de un diario salvado (Linden Lane Magazine [Princeton, N.J.] 3:1, 1984, p. 18–19)

Fragment of diary written 1970 which captures Heberto Padilla's and Belkis Cuza Malé's participation in 1970 sugar harvest. Entries are preceded by introduction which provides context for events narrated.

5282 Encarnación, Angel M. Noches ciegas. 2a. ed. Río Piedras, P.R.: Editorial Antillana, 1982. 133 p.: ill.

Although this novel shows flashes of insight into the human condition with reference to Puerto Rico and otherwise, it is stylistically flawed and tiring. Its ceaseless preoccupation with the tedium of life becomes the tedium of style.

5283 García Vega, Lorenzo. Los años de Orígenes. Caracas: Monte Avila Editores, 1979. 338 p., 4 leaves of plates (Colección Continentes)

Autobiographical and almost psychopathic novel in which a member of Grupo de Orígenes recalls his life both in US and Cuba. Narration revolves around obsession over years of Orígenes and how to come to terms with them. Tragic past is exorcised and fiction is mixed with reality. Characters mentioned in novel retain their true identities.

5284 Garrastegui, Luis. Ya mato, tu matas, nosotros amamos. Santurce, P.R.: Editorial Lares, 1981. 193 p.

Interesting novelistic account of political violence and political revolutionaries. Plot and style manage to keep reader interested, but novel fails to create convincing literary characters. Stereotypes eventually grow tiresome.

5285 Jusino Campos, Edgardo. El más azul de todos los príncipes. Río Piedras: Editorial Edil, 1981. 281 p.

Although in 1978 this novel was awarded Premio Manuel Zeno Gandía, it is a failed attempt to fuse myths and realities of Puerto Rican society à-la-García Márquez. Some stylistic touches at times reveal narrative talent but book is ultimately too self-conscious and pretentious.

5286 Leante, César. A propósito de la noche (Linden Lane Magazine [Princeton, N.J.] 3 : 1, 1984, p. 22–23)

Chapter of unpublished novel entitled *Calembour* which recapitulates culture in first years of Revolution, specifically events surrounding censorship of controversial film "P.M." Names of people involved have been changed but can be easily deciphered.

5287 ———. Capitán de cimarrones. Barcelona: Argos Vergara, 1982. 230 p.

Should not be mistaken for a new novel. With different title, it is another re-edition of his *Los guerrilleros negros* (La Habana, 1976). Erroneously, book's cover shows cotton, not sugar plantation.

5288 Lezama Lima, José. Juego de las decapitaciones. Prólogo de José Angel Valente. Barcelona: Montesinos, 1982. 93 p. (Colección Edda Menor)

Collection of five important short stories published 1936–46. Includes brief prologue by José Angel Valente.

5289 Lugo Filippi, Carmen and **Ana Lydia Vega.** Vírgenes y mártires: cuentos. Río Piedras, P.R.: Editorial Antillana, 1981. 139 p.

One of the distinguished books of recent years, this collaboration by writers Vega and Filippi exposes the fragile underpinnings of Puerto Rican bourgeois society and punctures the Puerto Rican male ego along the way. Presenting a veritable tragicomedy of contemporary Puerto Rican life, Vega and Filippi's satire is masterful. Their voices are strong, clear and impossible to ignore. Major advance for the voice of women and their role in Puerto Rican literature.

5290 Mariel. Revista de literatura y arte. Vol. 1, No. 1, Primavera 1983– . New York.

New literary magazine issued three times a year by Reinaldo Arenas, Juan Abreu and Reinaldo García Ramos. It publishes fiction, poetry, theatre, criticism and aggressive commentary. Magazine is mainly for Cuban writers in exile but also for sympathizers. Issue includes selections from works by Severo Sarduy, Lezama Lima, Lydia Cabrera, and the editors.

5291 Maunez-Vizcarrondo, Santiago. Transparencias: cuentos y divagares. San Juan?: Publigraph de Puerto Rico, 1981. 115 p.

Collection of short stories totally undistinguished in spite of author's good intentions. Anecdotal and familiar in style, author makes mistake of trying to win over his readers by being "chummy," rather than by creating a world that the reader wishes to enter.

5292 Mir, Pedro. Buen viaje, Pancho Valentín!: memorias de un marinero. Santo Domingo: Taller, 1981. 144 p., 2 leaves of plates: col. ill. (Biblioteca Taller; 130)

In this *Familia de Pascual Duarte*-type novel, Mir questions concept of fiction and history in a document written by Pancho Valentín about himself.

5293 Noticias de Arte. Año 6, No. 11, nov. 1981– . New York.

Special issue which presents selections from narrators, poets, and painters of the "Mariel generation" (e.g., Reinaldo Arenas, Miguel Correa, Roberto Valero). Most of the writings denounce injustices in present-day Cuba. Some were written before the May 1980 Mariel boat-lift.

5294 La Nueva Gaceta. Unión de Escritores y Artistas de Cuba. Epoca 2, No. 2, 1981– . La Habana.

Originally known as *La Gaceta de Cuba*, *La Nueva Gaceta* continues with same editorial board and is published by Unión de Escritores y Artistas de Cuba. Name was changed to include "interesantes trabajos periodísticos en torno a los más diversos temas del mundo cultural cubano y extranjero." Issue includes interviews with actress Rosita Fornés and Polish film director Jerzy Kawalerowicz.

5295 Padilla, Heberto. Algunos visitantes (Linden Lane Magazine [Princeton, N.J.] 3 : 1, 1984, p. 32)

Selection of Padilla's next novel *Autorretrato del otro* in which he narrates humorous encounter between agronomist André Voisin and Fidel Castro.

5296 Pietri, Pedro. Perdido en el Museo de Historia Natural = Lost in the Museum of Natural History. Río Piedras, P.R.: Ediciones Huracán, 1980? 1 v. (De orilla a orilla)

Short bilingual narrative of life in New York City, which calls into question concept of narrative distance. Author's hand is evident as he moves in and out of the narrative, tongue in cheek. Some surrealist techniques and touches of serious humor offer insights into dehumanization of life in the big city.

5297 Piñera, Virgilio. Cuentos. Madrid: Ediciones Alfaguara, 1983. 317 p.

Reedition of Piñera's short stories previously published 1970, Editorial Sudamericana. Stories (1944–67) are not arranged in any order. Unfortunately, collection lacks an introduction.

5298 Rivero, Ramón. Por qué se ríe la gente. 2a. ed. San Juan: Biblioteca de Autores Puertorriqueños, 1981. 70 p.

One might refer to this small volume as "remarks" on what makes people laugh. Of interest because of the importance of "Diplo," perhaps best known of Puerto Rican comedians.

5299 Rodríguez Juliá, Edgardo. El entierro de Cortijo. Río Piedras, P.R.: Ediciones Huracán, 1983. 96 p.: ill. (Colección La nave y el puerto; 1)

Chronicle of events surrounding wake and burial of Puerto Rican salsero, Rafael Cortijo. Author manages to capture the crowd, grief, confusion, and sense in which farewell to Cortijo by his family, friends, and admirers becomes a "happening" which can barely be contained within the limits of the funeral cortege. Rodríguez Juliá's fine, carefully wrought style enriched by vital, contemporary Puerto Rican idiom, marks him as one of the island's finest young writers today.

5299a ——. Las tribulaciones de Jonás. Río Piedras, P.R.: Ediciones Huracán, 1981. 105 p. (Colección La nave y el puerto)

Wonderfully evocative and sensitive portrayal of Luis Muñoz Marín. The contradictions in his political and personal lives and his undeniable popular appeal are brought into sharp profile. One gains an understanding of Muñoz Marín's central role in the

shaping of Puerto Rican history and politics. An exceptionally well written and carefully crafted chronicle with important insights about the political legacy of Muñoz Marín.

5300 Sarduy, Severo. Guerra de escrituras (Linden Lane Magazine [Princeton, N.J.] 1984, p. 3–5)

Fragment of Sarduy's latest novel Colibrí. As he stops in his travels, protagonist Colibrí is depicted, among other things, as coloring trained fleas and tearing off his clothes.

5301 Soriano, Claudio. Cambio, please: tres cuentos y un relámpago. Santo Domingo: Editora Taller, 1981. 104 p. (Colección Antología de la sangre; no. 2)

Interesting three or four short stories or possibly a four-part novel in which Trujillo, the 1965 US invasion, and communism constitute related themes.

5302 ——. Ciclos de nuestros orígenes. Santo Domingo: Editora Taller, 1980. 138 p. (Colección Literatura; no. 3)

Loose but fair interpretation of Taíno mythology from creation to Indians' genocide, after arrival of Spaniards. Mainly based on José Juan Arróm's and Fray Ramón Pané's studies. Book contains a useful glossary.

5303 Término. Vol. 1, No. 1, Fall 1982– Cincinnati, Ohio.

New bilingual literary magazine published quarterly and edited by Roberto Madrigal Ecay and Manuel F. Ballagas, divided into: "Fiction," "Poetry," "Ideas" (including politico-cultural commentary), and "Books and Movie Reviews." Mainly but not exclusively for Cuban writers, magazine attempts to provide pluralistic view without political biases. Of 14 contributors, only Allen Ginsberg, Richard Hague, and Steve Grossman are non-Cubans, so issue does not exemplify the desired pluralism. Contributors include Rogelio Llopis, Jorge Posada, Reinaldo Arenas, Manuel Ballagas and others.

5304 Torriente Brau, Pablo de la. Cartas cruzadas. Selección, prólogo y notas de Víctor Casaus. La Habana: Editorial Letras Cubanas, 1981. 602 p. (Testimonio)

More than 230 letters from and to Cuban activist and writer (April 1935–Aug. 1936). About 160 from Brau offers insight into post-Machado years. Víctor Casaus' prologue divides correspondence into sections and provides narrative context for period. Useful footnotes clarify letters.

5305 *Unveiling Cuba*. Boletín de información literaria. No. 1, 1982– . New York.

New magazine about Cuban literature and commentary in exile. Published quarterly and edited by Ismael Lorenzo in New York. First issue is brief and consists of Giulio V. Blanc's "Introduction," a commentary on Cuban culture; a fragment from Reinaldo Arenas' *El central*; a selection from Carlos Alberto Montaner's *Informe secreto*; Jaime Bellechasse's "Mira, Justo;" and Ismael Lorenzo's "Antología Literaria o Panfleto Político," a review of Desnoes' *Los dispositivos en la flor*. Magazine provides outlet for literature in exile and forum for those who disagree with Cuba's official policy.

5306 Vega, Ana Lydia. Encancaranublado y otros cuentos de naufragio. Río Piedras, P.R.: Editorial Antillana, 1983. 141 p. (Cuadernos de Jacinto Colón: colección de joven narrativa puertorriqueña; no. 1)

Excellent collection of Ana Lydia Vega's short fiction demonstrates why she must be considered a leader among Puerto Rican writers of her generation. Well-crafted and psychologically insightful, stories constitute real contribution to Puerto Rican literature.

5307 Villaverde, Fernando. El ingeniero (Linden Lane Magazine [Princeton, N.J.] 3 : 1, 1984, p. 8–9)

Almost surrealistic story in which protagonist is allowed to leave Cuba only after being covered in workers' spit.

LITERARY CRITICISM AND HISTORY

5308 Acosta, Leonardo. Música y épica en la novela de Alejo Carpentier. La Habana: Editorial Letras Cubanas, 1981. 130 p.: bibl. (Colección Crítica)

Promising study undermined by limited intent to show Carpentier's interest in music and epic themes. Does little more than single out their presence in his works. Moreover, Acosta ignores important body of criticism about Carpentier's texts.

5309 Arrabal, Fernando. 1984 [i.e. Mil novecientos ochenta y cuatro]: carta a Fidel Castro. Madrid: Editorial Playor, 1983. 116 p.

Similar to his *Carta a Franco*. In this pamphlet, Arrabal denounces backward slide of Castro's government and includes demystification of widely acclaimed educational and medical systems. Arrabal's information is based on undocumented conversations.

5310 Bejel, Emilio. Miguel Barnet (HISPA, 10:29, 1981, p. 41–52)

Candid interview regarding Barnet's life and works, up to his *Akeké y la jutiá*.

5311 Benítez Rojo, Antonio. El camino de Santiago de Alejo Carpentier y el Canon perpetuus de Juan Sebastián Bach: paralelismo estructural (IILI/RI, 123/124, abril/sept. 1983, p. 293–322)

Insightful study relates music to fiction. Musical structure of theme and copy of Bach's *Canon perpetuus a 2* is present in *El camino de Santiago*. This is explicitly demonstrated in chaps. 4 and 10, latter chapter(s) also contains both elements.

5312 ———. La cultura caribeña en Cuba: continuidad versus ruptura (UP/CESC, 14:1, 1984, p. 1–15)

Uses special issue of *Latin American Literary Review* devoted to Spanish Caribbean in order to discuss ideas about Afro-Cuban culture. Polemicizes, mainly with Miguel Barnet, origins of such a culture, noting how Cuban official policy towards Afro-Cubans will stagnate their culture and alter its composition.

5313 ———. "Semejante a la Noche" de Alejo Carpentier y el Canon per tonos de Juan Sebastián Bach: su paralelismo estructural (ECO, 43:6, abril 1983, p. 645–662)

Excellent and imaginative study convincingly traces intertextuality between music and literature, between modulating themes of Bach's *Canon per tonos* and six thematic stages of Carpentier's "Semejante a la Noche."

5314 Bosch, Juan. Hostos, el sembrador. 3a. ed. Santo Domingo: Editora Alfa y Omega, 1979. 207 p.: ill.

Third printing of Bosch's book of Hostos. Dominican ed. combines elements of 1939 Cuban and 1976 Argentine editions.

5315 Bueno, Salvador. México en la literatura cubana (BNJM/R, 72[23]:1, enero/abril 1981, p. 175–191)

Informative but not analytical essay traces ties between Cuba and Mexico, within context of Cuban intellectuals living in Mexico from 18th century to pre-Revolutionary Cuba. Examines question of Mexico as theme in their writings.

5316 Carpentier, Alejo. Ese músico que llevo dentro. Selección de Zoila Gómez. La Habana: Editorial Letras Cubanas, 1980. 3 v.

Posthumous three-volume collection underscores importance of Carpentier, the musicologist. Consists of 196 articles (1923–27) divided into: "Los Hombres que Hacen la Música," "Musicología," "Música en la Escena," "Reflexiones en Torno a la Música," and "Ensayos." Collection, however, does not include Carpentier's writings in *Letra y Solfa* and *El Nacional* and omits important *Tristán e Isolda en tierra firme* (1949). Highly recommended. For musicologist's comment, see *HLAS 44:7002*.

5317 Contín Aybar, Néstor. Historia de la literatura dominicana. San Pedro de Macorís, República Dominicana: Universidad Central del Este, 1982–1983. 2 v.: bibl., indexes.

Two-volume history of Dominican literature from discovery to Second Republic divided into politico-historical periods and each author's date of birth. Vol. 2 emphasizes literary history and biographical information, but entries are uneven.

Díaz de Fortier, Matilde. La crítica literaria en Puerto Rico: 1843–1915. See item **5111.**

5318 Dorfman, Ariel. Entre Proust y la momia americana: siete notas y un epílogo sobre *El recurso de método* (IILI/RI, 47:ll4/115, enero/junio 1981, p. 95–128)

Shows that Proust's absence in *El recurso del método* is not unintentional. His friends and imaginary characters, scenes and narrative structure of *A la recherche du temps perdu* are present in Carpentier's novel.

5318a Dossier Calvert Casey (Quimera [Barcelona] 26, dic. 1982, p. 39–62)

Memorial articles on this important Cuban writer who committed suicide in Rome (May 16, 1969). Contributions include: Vicente Molina Foix's "Los Papeles de Calvert

Casey;" Guillermo Cabrera Infante's "¿Quién Mató a Calvert Casey?;" Italo Calvino's "Las Piedras de La Habana;" María Zambrano's "Entre el Ser y la Vida;" and Severo Sarduy's "El Libro Tibetano de los Muertos." As a whole, they narrate Casey's life and works.

5319 Feijóo, Samuel. La crítica del mediocre (Signos [Biblioteca Martí, Santa Clara, Cuba] 26, sept./dic. 1980, p. 33–63, ill.)

At times humorous essay traces the mediocre critic in literary history and criticism. Implicitly and explicitly, criticizes such mediocrity in Cuba. For Feijóo, a critic must be brave and write the truth.

5320 Fernández Retamar, Roberto. Para el perfil definitivo del hombre. La Habana: Editorial Letras Cubanas, 1981. 538 p.: bibl.

Anthology consisting of Retamar's published works, includes his well known "Calibán." Some essays have been modified, others have new titles, but most remain in their original form. Also contains prologue by Abel Enríquez Prieto, underscoring Retamar's revolutionary background.

Figueres, Myriam. Catálogo de la colección de la literatura cubana en la Biblioteca Colón. See item **50.**

5321 Flores, Juan. The insular vision: Pedreira's interpretation of Puerto Rican culture. New York: CUNY, Centro de Estudios Puertorriqueños, 1978. 104 leaves: bibl. (Centro working papers; 1)

Key work offers critical revision of political ideology in Puerto Rico and calls into question both Antonio Pedreira's perspective in *Insularismo* as well as his conclusions in that celebrated essay.

5322 Fuentes, Norberto. Finca vigía: Hemingway en su santuario cubano (Texto Crítico [Universidad Veracruzana, Centro de Investigaciones Lingüístico-Literarias, Xalapa, México] 6:16/17, 1980, p. 3–36, ill.)

Chapter of important work on Hemingway's life in Cuba. Fuentes' research, which includes recollections from Hemingway's Cuban friends, contributes little known information about his life and corrects other established notions. Appendix contains 16 photographs.

5323 González Echevarría, Roberto. Isla a su vuelo fugitiva: ensayos críticos sobre literatura hispanoamericana. Madrid: José Porrúa Turanzas, 1983. 264 p.: bibl.

Excellent essays on important authors and themes in Hispanic American literature including Carpentier, Sarduy, Lezama, and Luis Rafael Sánchez. Of equal academic rigor is a section on "Notas Críticas" which incorporates book reviews. Most selections have been published. As a unit, the compilation makes an important statement on Hispanic American criticism.

5324 ———. El primer relato de Severo Sarduy (IILI/RI, 48:118/119, enero/junio 1982, p. 73-90)

Sarduy's first short story (1957) is significantly different from his mature work. González Echevarría attempts to find a relationship between early and late Sarduy.

5325 ———. El reino de este mundo alucinante: era imaginaria de Fray Servando (ECO, 43:6, abril 1983, p. 663-667)

Short but incisive article underscores Carpentier's and Lezama's influence on Reinaldo Arenas and places his *El mundo alucinante* within the historiography of America.

5326 ——— and Klaus Müller-Bergh. Alejo Carpentier: bibliographical guide/guía bibliográfica. Westport, Conn.: Greenwood Press, 1983. 217 p.: index.

Most impressive piece of scholarship which undoubtedly is the most complete bibliography of works by and about Carpentier published in and out of Cuba. *Guide* is composed of 3,191 entries divided into two main categories: Active and Passive Bibliography. Brief but useful comments accompany more than 1,900 entries from his weekly column *Letra y Solfa*. Invaluable reference work will be a must for students of Carpentier. For bibliographer's comment, see item **38.**

Gutiérrez-Vega, Zenaida. Max Henríquez Ureña: cartas de un maestro a José María Chacón y Calvo, 1915-1935, 1956-1965. See item **5011.**

5327 Homenaje a Lino Novás Calvo (Linden Lane Magazine [Princeton, N.J.] 3:1, 1984, p. 24-28)

Posthumous homage to Lino Novás Calvo, organized by Fina Wuppermann and Lorraine Elena Roses, consists of following papers: Raymond Souza on Novás Calvo and Labrador Ruiz; Ignacio Galbis on Novás

Calvo and the Boom; and Antonio Benítez Rojo and William Luis on *El negrero,* respectively.

5328 Juan Marinello (*in* Cuba, les étapes d'une libération: hommage à Juan Marinello et Noël Salomon; actes du colloque international des 22, 23 et 24 novembre 1978. Toulouse, France: Centre d'études cubaines, Université de Toulouse-Le Mirail, 1979, v. 2, p. 1-59)

Informative essays in honor of poet, essayist, leader, and teacher Juan Marinello (d. March 27, 1977). Texts include: José Antonio Portuondo's "Juan Marinello y Noël Salomon: Dos Modos Diversos de Crítica Marxista;" Julio Le Riverend's "Aproximación a la Biografía de Juan Marinello;" and Alfred Melon's "Sur les Discours de Juan Marinello."

5329 Laguna-Díaz, Elpidio. *Cuando amaban las tierras comuneras*: visión mitopoética de una historia (HISPA, 11:31, 1982, p. 15-32)

Comprehensive article on this important novel. Among other factors, it takes into account Pedro Mir's essays, Vico's ideas, and mythopoetics.

5330 Lezama Lima, José. Imagen y posibilidad. La Habana: Editorial Letras Cubanas, 1981. 203 p. (Colección crítica)

Posthumous collection of political and literary articles drawn from newspapers, magazines, prologues, and introductions to books. Except for "Un Día del Ceremonial," all have been previously published. They were written as early as 1936 and range in theme from Ernesto Guevara to Juan Ramón Jiménez to José Clemente Orozco. As a unit, they reveal Lezama's broad interest and his poetic talent. Ciro Bianchi Ross' introduction highlights Lezama's life during publication of *Grafos.*

5331 ———. El reino de la imagen. Caracas: Biblioteca Ayacucho, 1983. 609 p.: bibl. (Biblioteca Ayacucho; 83)

Broad but incomplete and at times fragmented selection of Lezama's published works drawn from his fiction, poetry, and essays, including his posthumous *Oppiano Licario* and *Fragmentos a su imán.* Also contains useful chronology of his life in relation to activities in Cuba and Latin America and the world. Although Julio Ortega's prologue underscores important aspects of Lezama's works, it is general and contributes little to an understanding of his texts.

5332 Luis, William. America revisited: an interview with Edmundo Desnoes (LALR, 11:21, 1982, p. 7–20)

Interview in which Desnoes talks about his recent visit to the US. Although, he discusses his novels and essays, emphasis is on *Memorias del subdesarrollo* and a comparison between different editions and the film.

5333 ———. La novelística de César Leante (CAM, 24:5, 1982 p. 226–236)

Essay on this important writer who developed in the Cuban Revolution. His works, *El perseguido, Padres e hijos, Muelle de Caballería*, and *Los guerrilleros negros* are analyzed within context of history, culture, and politics.

5334 ———. Re-writing history: César Leante's *Los guerrilleros negros* (Journal of Caribbean Studies [Association of Caribbean Studies, Miami, Fla.] 2:2/3, Autumn/Winter 1981, p. 250–265)

Thorough and convincing study of Leante's compelling novel, in context of evolution of the antislavery novel in Cuba. Luis successfully links Leante to a tradition that reaches back to 19th century, both underlining differences and noting similarities. [R. González Echevarría]

5335 Matas, Julio. Revolución: literatura y religión afrocubana (UP/CSEC, 13:1, Winter 1983, p. 17–23)

Analyzes Benítez Rojo's "El Cielo y la Tierra" within Afro-Cuban context. Story questions ideological reason for abandoning religious values.

5336 Méndez Rodenas, Adriana. Severo Sarduy: el neobarroco de la transgresión. México: Universidad Nacional Autónoma de México, Facultad de Filosofía y Letras, 1983. 165 p. (Colección Opúsculos)

Chiefly analyzes Sarduy's early works, *Gestos* and *De donde son los cantantes*, as a movement away from literary currents present at the outset of the Revolution and towards the neo-Baroque.

5337 Merrim, Stephanie. *La Habana para un Infante difunto* y su teoría topográfica de las formas (IILI/RI, 48:118/119, enero/junio 1982, p. 403–413)

Believes narrator presents events not as real but as memory. Narrative techniques (re)order memory or the image of memory. In memory, the metaphysical, physical, erotic, and eroticism are present.

5338 Pérez Rivera, Francisco. Budismo y barroco en Severo Sarduy (Linden Lane Magazine [Princeton, N.J.] 2:1, enero/marzo 1983, p. 6)

Brief interview in which Sarduy reveals that his Buddhist concern for emptiness is related to his interest in the Baroque, that is, a desire to fill a void and saturate the page. Also talks about his most recent work, *La simulación*.

5339 Pérez-Stable, Marifeli. El CILC y la "generación del Mariel (AR, 8:29, 1982, p. 19–22, plate)

Polemical article traces history and questions ideological position and credibility of Comité de Intelectuales por la Libertad de Cuba (CILC) and Mariel generation of Cuban writers.

Pérotin-Dumon, Anne. Témoignages sur la Guadeloupe en 1794. See item **2505**.

5340 Piña Contreras, Guillermo. Doce en la literatura dominicana. Corrección e índice, José Alcántara Almánzar. Santiago, República Dominicana: Universidad Católica Madre y Maestra, Departamento de Publicaciones, 1982. 292 p. (Colección Estudios)

Consists of 12 informative interviews with contemporary Dominican narrators and poets. However, some interviews are outdated and thus incomplete (e.g., Mir's, conducted in 1974, describes him as poet and not as important novelist he is today). Also includes essay on Dominican politics and literature, brief biography of authors and passive bibliography.

5341 Portuondo, José Antonio. Capítulos de literatura cubana. La Habana: Editorial Letras Cubanas, 1981. 584 p.: bibl.

Collection of Portuondo's published essays and articles (1937–77) and others appearing for first time. They explore topics such as the *Papel Periódico* and figures such as Guillén and Carpentier. Salvador Arias' prologue divides Portuondo's literary production into four stages.

5342 Prats Sariol, José. Nuevos críticos literarios cubanos (BNJM/R, 72[23]:1, enero/abril 1981, p. 119–142)

Directory of mostly young, up-and-coming Cuban critics living on the island.

5343 Pujals, Enrique J. La obra narrativa de Carlos Montenegro. Miami, Fla.: Ediciones Universal, 1980. 153 p.: bibl. (Colección Polymita)

Introductory study on a fine Cuban writer. Provides plot summaries of Montenegro's novel and short stories and relies on biographical information for analysis of texts.

5344 *Revista de Literatura Cubana*. Crítica, historia, bibliografía. Año 1, No. 0, julio 1982– . La Habana.

New literary magazine published by Ediciones Unión, of Unión de Escritores y Artistas de Cuba, scheduled to appear twice a year. Purpose: to study "crítica e investigación sobre autores, obras, temas, personajes, tendencias, etapas y características de la literatura cubana desde sus orígenes hasta nuestros días." First issue is in honor of Nicolás Guillén's 80th birthday and includes some previously published essays by Regino E. Boti, Juan Marinello, Mirta Aguirre, etc. Magazine may provide open forum for criticism in Cuba.

5345 Rincón, Carlos. Sobre capítulo de novela y Luis Garrafita: textos desconocidos de Alejo Carpentier y Miguel Angel Asturias (CNC/A, 2, 1977, p. 95–105)

Discusses chapter of Carpentier's *El reino de este mundo* not included in novel, originally published in *Gaceta del Caribe* (May 1944).

5346 Rodríguez, Emilio Jorge. Pluralidad e integración en la literatura caribeña (UH/U, 212, enero/dic. 1980, p. 4–14)

Interesting article on cultural identity in the Caribbean based on plurality and syncretism. However, it sacrifices depth for breadth.

5347 Rodríguez Monegal, Emir. Cabrera Infante: la novela como autobiografía total (IILI/RI, 116/117, julio/dic. 1981, p. 265–271)

Investigation into Cabrera Infante's family and his *La Habana para un Infante difunto*. Devotes special attention to relationship between Cabrera's mother and act of writing.

5348 Rozencvaig, Perla. Reinaldo Arenas: entrevista (HISPA, 10:28, abril 1981, p. 41–48)

Insightful interview in which Arenas talks mostly about his novels up to *El palacio de las blanquísimas mofetas*.

5349 Santí, Enrico Mario. Hacia *Oppiano Licario* (IILI/RI, 116/117, julio/dic. 1981, p. 273–279)

Brief but important study compares Lezama's sketch of *Oppiano Licario*, which Santí consulted in 1979 while in Havana, to the novel.

5350 Sarduy, Severo. La simulación. Caracas: Monte Avila Editores, 1982, 134 p.: bibl. (Colección Estudios)

Collection of essays in which literature is seen as simulation. Relationship between copy and model is further studied in painting and sculpture and in works of Lezama Lima, Botero, Rubens, etc.

5351 Sklodowska, Elzbieta. La cuentística de Antonio Benítez Rojo: la experiencia revolucionaria desde la marginalidad (CAM, 14:1, 1984, p. 7–16)

Good article on Benítez Rojo's short stories *Tute de reyes* (1967) and *El escudo de hojas secas* (1969). Focuses on writer's treatment of marginal characters, including blacks, in pre- and post-revolutionary Cuba.

5352 Souza, Raymond D. Lino Novás Calvo. Boston: Twayne Publishers, 1981. 146 p.: bibl., index (Twayne's world author series; TWAS 598. Cuba)

Good introduction to Novás Calvo's life and works. Covers periods before and after Cuban Revolution and contains summaries of all his works.

5353 ———. The poetic fiction of José Lezama Lima. Columbia: University of Missouri Press, 1983. 149 p.: bibl., index.

First major study in English on Lezama offers sound introduction to his works. Souza concentrates mainly on *Paradiso* and *Oppiano Licario*.

5354 Speratti-Piñero, Emma Susana. Pasos hallados en *El reino de este mundo*. México: El Colegio de México, 1981. 212 p.: bibl., ill.

Well researched study uncovers Carpentier's detailed investigation when writing his second novel and presents other information not used by him. Divided into "La Gran Historia," "El Mosaico Increíble," and "Vudú y . . ." Also separates novel's fictitious elements from historical ones.

5355 Tornés, Emanuel. Acercamiento a *El pan dormido* (UH/U, 213, enero/abril 1981, p. 62–72)

Thematic study of works by writer who developed in the Cuban Revolution. Uncritical essay concentrates on José Soler Puig's latest novel which narrates life of a petit-bourgeois family during Machado's dictatorship.

5356 Valero, Roberto. La generación del Mariel (Término [Cincinnati, Ohio] 2 : 5, Fall 1983, p. 14–16)

Attempts to define a new generation of intellectuals with a common historical bond: the take-over of the Peruvian Embassy and, most importantly, the Mariel boatlift. Many were unknown in and outside of Cuba. In US, they are actively pursuing their artistic and intellectual goals. Although sincere, article suffers from generalizations and misinformation.

5357 Weber, Frances Wyers. Los contextos de *El recurso del método* de Carpentier (IILI/RI, 123/124, abril/sept. 1983, p. 323–334)

Uses mainly Descartes' and Bahtin's ideas to explore contexts of this novel, which include binary oppositions as reason/nonreason, country/city, myth/revolution, and telluric/historical.

20th Century: Prose Fiction: Andean Countries (Bolivia, Colombia, Ecuador, Peru and Venezuela)

JOSE MIGUEL OVIEDO, *Professor of Spanish, University of California, Los Angeles*
DJELAL KADIR, *Professor of Spanish and Comparative Literature, Purdue University*

EL VOLUMEN DE LA CRITICA DEDICADA el género en esta área cultural ha sido notoriamente superior a otros años, y posiblemente mayor que nunca, lo que es un índice tanto del número de temas estimulantes que ha descubierto la investigación literaria, como de la presencia de nuevas generaciones de críticos que intentan revisiones o enfoques nuevos en asuntos clásicos.

El hecho más significativo que puede señalarse en este período es que, al lado de las dos figuras máximas del área (Gabriel García Márquez y Mario Vargas Llosa), la de José María Arguedas ha emergido con una fuerza inesperada, veintitantos años después de que el novelista empezara a producir sus obras mayores. No sólo es hoy el escritor más estudiado en la región, mediante libros, monografías y artículos, superando incluso a los dos famosos autores citados; también por su calidad, los aportes críticos al conocimiento de la obra arguediana superan a los que aquéllos han merecido en este bienio, por lo menos teniendo en cuenta el material revisado para la presente sección. (La excepción, para García Márquez, debe ser el importante trabajo que Eduardo González dedica a un cuento suyo; ver item **5378**).

La crítica, sobre todo la que tiene una orientación sociológica, ha encontrado en Arguedas, el dramático ejemplo de un autor violentamente escindido entre los reclamos de lenguas, culturas, valores y hasta ideologías dispares, que parecen resumir todos los dilemas de un creador instalado en el contexto de un país dependiente, al mismo tiempo arcaico y moderno, indígena y occidental. Aunque muchos métodos y modelos críticos se han probado para desentrañar la riqueza de esta obra, puede decirse que el enfoque antropológico y sociolingüístico han sido, por razones obvias, los privilegiados (items **5403, 5404, 5405, 5409, 5410, 5417, 5418, 5420, 5421, 5422, 5424, 5426,** and **5428**). En el fondo, este renovado interés por Arguedas debe ser visto como parte de un proceso mayor, que ya se insinuaba en el período inmediatamente anterior a éste: el de la revaluación de los indigenismos de los países andinos, que bien necesitados estaban de estudios más modernos y de exámenes a la luz de obras más recientes que, dentro o fuera de la región (J.M. Arguedas, Scorza, Roa Bastos), tienen diversos grados de relación con las tendencias indigenistas clásicas.

Por su parte, los trabajos críticos sobre Vargas Llosa, un poco menos numerosos que en otros años, se concentran en *Pantaleón y las visitadoras* (item **5396**) y sobre todo en su última y monumental novela *La guerra del fin del mundo* que, por lo menos en un par de casos (items **5402, 5423, and 5427**) ha sido comentada en artículos que exceden los límites de una simple reseña. En Colombia, el predominio de artículos y trabajos sobre García Márquez es casi total. Incluso los consagrados a la narrativa colombiana contemporánea (items **5372 y 5384**), están en cierta medida vinculados a la figura del gran autor, Premio Nobel de Literatura 1982. De todos esos trabajos que se le han dedicado, el libro "conversado" con Plinio Apuleyo Mendoza (item **5376**), la recopilación de textos periodísticos bogotanos del autor (item **5382**) y el mencionado artículo de Eduardo González son los más valiosos e ilustrativos.

Como siempre, hay una marcada diferencia en volumen y nivel crítico entre la producción crítica relativa al Perú y Colombia, y los restantes de la zona. El caso de Venezuela es más visible, precisamente porque el interés intrínseco de su narrativa contemporánea (de Gallegos a Salvador Garmendia y Luis Britto), su dinamismo cultural y sus organizaciones editoriales no están acompañados, todavía hoy y salvo contadísimas excepciones, por un movimiento crítico comparable. Curiosamente, tanto para este país como para Bolivia, algunos de los mejores aportes son de críticos provenientes de otras áreas geográficas; los trabajos del argentino Horacio Jorge Becco sobre Gallegos (item **5433**) y del chileno Pedro Lastra sobre Alcides Arguedas (item **5369a**) son un par de ejemplos. Los ecos del centenario del nacimiento de Gallegos (1879) todavía se han dejado sentir en varios de los artículos, recopilaciones y bibliografías que se le han dedicado. Otro autor venezolano que ha sido favorecido por la crítica es Julio Garmendia, menos conocido continentalmente pero decisivo en su país.

En Ecuador, la figura de Jorge Icaza ha seguido siendo central, como lo demuestran dos libros sobre su obra narrativa (items **5390 and 5393**) y una revaloración de *Huasipungo* por el escritor Jorge Eduardo Adoum (item **5385**). Por cierto, ésta es otra manifestación del interés general por el fenómeno indigenista. La insólita obra de Pablo Palacio, redescubierto en el bienio anterior, ha seguido atrayendo a los críticos (items **5391 and 5392**) y haciendo verosímil que pronto sea reconocido como el gran escritor que es en el resto de América Latina. Poco hay de interés en la producción crítica sobre la literatura de Bolivia, salvo el ya citado aporte de Lastra a la bibliografía de Alcides Arguedas y, en grado menor, la investigación sobre los temas agrarios en Jesús Lara (item **5370**).

Seguramente el artículo más polémico de toda esta sección es el de Gerald Martin (item **5362**), escrito en repuesta a otro sobre la novelística de la dictadura, que es una ocasión para ventilar teorías, conceptos y métodos que están hoy en el centro de la activad crítica de este continente. Puede decirse que la brecha estre quienes siguen fieles a una concepción inmanentista del texto literario y los que lo ven como mero producto de factores socioculturales, se ha hecho más amplia y que eso promete nuevos debates y planteamientos teóricos en los años inmediatos. [JMO]

The highlight of this biennium for the region and, indeed, for the whole American hemisphere is the Nobel Prize for Literature awarded to Gabriel García Márquez in 1982 (see item **5733**). The fourth Nobel Prize for Latin America, and the second awarded to a novelist, has renewed world-wide interest in Latin American letters, particularly in the areas of literary criticism and translations. Not surprisingly, prose fiction continues to occupy the limelight of world attention. The repercussions, aside from critical studies and translations, are yet to be manifested in the form of intensified literary production by younger writers.

The Nobel Prize comes at a dire time. The biennium covered by this volume of *HLAS* has seen the scantiest publication of fiction in the region in years. No doubt socioeconomic and political hardships are taking their toll. But we should take heart. Things are looking up already as evidenced by the high quality of works by the young writers reviewed here. First I should like to refer to a couple of other newsworthy occurrences dealing with the region. Recently the Association of North-American Colombianists was founded (Raymond Williams, Washington University, St. Louis, Mo., President). On Sunday, Nov. 27, 1983, a number of Latin American writers and intellectuals bound from Paris to Colombia for an international congress on Hispanic culture perished in an air disaster on the periphery of Madrid's Barajas Airport. Among them were the Peruvian poet and novelist Manuel Scorza, the Uruguayan critic Angel Rama, and the Argentine novelist and art critic Marta Traba.

Mario Vargas Llosa, one of the better known Andean writers, has given us a blockbuster during this period: *La guerra del fin del mundo* (item **5473**). Dedicated to the Brazilian novelist Euclides da Cunha, Vargas Llosa's work narrates in apocalyptic/eschatological terms the story of the Canudos uprising, an event central to the Brazilian master's classic *Os sertões*. Vargas Llosa's may well be the most significant work to have appeared in the last two years. It is certainly the most notable given the author's past accomplishment and international stature. Generally, however, Vargas Llosa is the exception on the Peruvian scene. The only other notable but lesser Peruvian achievement in the genre is Carlos Thorne's political novel *Viva la república* (item **5472**). The acerbic, satirical tone of Thorne's novel epitomizes a number of works that deal with social and political realities in Latin America (e.g., the Colombian Helena Araujo's *Fiesta en Teusaquillo*, item **5452**, the Ecuadorian Javier Vasconez's *Ciudad lejana*, item **5465**, and the Venezuelan Earl Herrera's *Sábado que nunca llega*, item **5476**). Two other noteworthy but drastically divergent works of institutional criticism are by the Ecuadorians Francisco Tobar García (item **5464**), a traditional social vignette, and Fernando Artieda (item **5460**), a revealing portrait of a more contemporary phenomenon.

The most accomplished meditation on social and moral foundations, however, is a devastating novel by the Colombian Fernando Soto Aparicio, *Hermano hombre* (item **5459**). While ponderous and weighty in parts, Soto Aparicio's work reinforces his position among the most distinguished novelists writing today.

The baneful socioeconomic and political realities of the hemisphere have engendered a less doleful, though by no means less acerbic, incisive, and earnest figuration of literary portrayal. I refer to certain works that effectively exploit humor as a damning weapon. The most outstanding works in this vein are by the Colombians Carlos Perrozo, *Juegos de mentes* (item **5455**) and Enrique Cabezas Rher, *Miro tu lindo cielo y quedo aliviado* (item **5454**), and by the Venezuelan Otrova Gomas, *El terrorista* (item **5475**). This is Perrozo's second novel and Cabezas Rher's first. We can anticipate great things from the potential demonstrated by these young authors in these works.

In technical terms, the most impressive writer to emerge is the Ecuadorian Carlos Carrión whose award-winning short story collection *El más hermoso animal nocturno* (item **5463**) is a compelling narrative achievement. Carrión's command of the language is truly outstanding. Furthermore, two authors stand out in terms of technical experimentation. David Sánchez Juliao of Colombia, *Abraham al humor* (item **5457**), already an established narrator, experiments with "unexpurgated" orality by giving us "cassette stories," posing as mere transcriber of his protagonists' palaver. The procedure is not novel but Sánchez Juliao renders it extremely effective. The other experimental work of note already has a history and is authored by the Ecuadorian Béjar Portilla, *Tribu si* (item **5462**). Portilla's novel was runner-up in the 1973 Seix Barral prize and is finally published for the first time in 1981. Although somewhat dated, it remains a significant and telling period piece. [DjK]

LITERARY CRITICISM AND HISTORY
GENERAL

5359 Colloque de l'Association Française pour l'Etude e la Recherche sur les Pays Andins, 4th, Grenoble, France, 1979. L'indigenisme andin: approches, tendances et perspectives; actes. Grenoble, France: Université de langues et lettres de Grenoble, Centre d'études et de recherches sur le Pérou et les pays andins, 1980. 288 p.: bibl.

Recoge 11 ponencias sobre este tema de estudiosos franceses e hispanoamericanos. Aunque, como en otras recopilaciones, el material es de valor desigual, siendo refundiciones de trabajos ya conocidos, su publicación en un solo volumen les agrega interés, como aporte colectivo al mejor conocimiento de la literatura indigenista. [JMO]

5360 Earle, Peter G. Utopía, Universópolis, Macondo (HR, 50:2, Spring 1982, p. 143–157).

Reflexión general sobre la utopía en autores hispanoamericanos (e.g., Martí, Rodó, Vasconcelos, Cortázar, García Márquez). Pero lo que el autor afirma es que en ellos, y en la literatura hispanoamericana en general, la Utopía "has . . . succumbed to counter-utopianism" (p. 152). Según él, la mentalidad de este continente está más inclinada a la visión mágica que a la utópica. [JMO]

Henderson, Donald C. and **Grace R. Pérez.** Literature and politics in Latin America: an annotated calendar of the Luis Alberto Sánchez correspondence, 1919–1980. See item *HLAS 45:31.*

5362 Martin, Gerald M. On dictatorship and rhetoric in Latin American writing: a counter-proposal (LARR, 17:3, 1982, p. 207–227).

Polémica refutación de ideas sobre historia y novela expuestas por Roberto González Echeverría en un artículo sobre novelas de la dictadura (ver *HLAS 44:5371*). Las discrepancias son, al comienzo, espléndidas y prometen mucho; luego, el ardor polémico lo lleva a extremar sus puntos de vista, ideológicamente fundados en conceptos como "lucha de clases" o "causas populares" que no son necesariamente más convincentes que los de RGE. [JMO]

5363 Rivera, Francisco. Inscripciones. Caracas: FUNDARTE, 1981. 199 p.: bibl. (Colección Ensayo; 1)

Notas y artículos críticos (1979–80) dedicados a poetas y narradores hispanoamericanos (e.g., Roberto Juarroz, José Emilio Pacheco, J. G. Cobo-Borda, Guillermo Meneses, José Donoso, Juan Calzadilla, Alejo Carpentier), y algunos escritores de otras lenguas (e.g., Cavafy, Pessoa, Henry Miller) o sobre arte. Prueba la fina percepción crítica del autor venezolano, y su frecuentación de las más modernas teorías de análisis poético. [JMO]

5364 Rodríguez-Luis, Julio. Hermenéutica y praxis del indigenismo: la novela indigenista, de Clorinda Matto a José María Arguedas. México: Fondo de Cultura Económica, 1980. 279 p.: bibl., index. (Colección Tierra firme)

Aparte de los novelistas mencionados en el título, estudia a Alcides Arguedas, Jorge Icaza y Ciro Alegría, o sea el sector propiamente andino-quechua de esta tendencia narrativa. Acierta más en su parte descriptiva de esos autores, que en su valoración, que tiende a ser vagamente concesiva. Título desorientador: se trata más bien de una breve historia del indigenismo. [JMO]

BOLIVIA

5365 Alcázar V., Reinaldo M. El cuento social boliviano. La Paz: Editorial e Imprenta Alenkar, 1981. 378 p.: bibl.
Useful critical study of the genre. Takes Chaco War (1935) and National Revolution (1952) as pivotal dates around which author weaves his historical survey of the genre and its social themes. US doctoral dissertation (University of Colorado) that fares well in the transposition to historical survey. [DjK]

5366 Antología de la revista *Gesta Bárbara*, 1918–1926. Compilación Aurora Valda Cortés de Viaña. Potosí, Bolivia: Club del Libro *Gesta Bárbara 1918*, 1981. 124 p., 1 leaf of plates.
Breve antología de revista potosina que difundió la obra de la "Generación del 18" y otros autores bolivianos, aparte del peruano Arturo Peralta (seudónimo "Juan Cajal") y europeos como Unamuno y Pirandello. Humilde edición con fallas de impresión; no da fechas de publicación original de los textos. [JMO]

5367 Araujo Subieta, Mario. Temas literarios. La Paz: Editorial Popular, 1977. 232 p.: bibl.
Semblanzas, notas y comentarios sobre temas literarios y culturales bolivianos, con una parte final dedicada a entrevistas. Material misceláneo y desigual en calidad. El trabajo titulado "Escritores Bolivianos Suicidas" es posiblemente el mejor. [JMO]

5368 Díez de Medina, Fernando. Literatura boliviana: introducción al estudio de las letras nacionales del tiempo mítico a la producción contemporánea. Prólogo de Hugo Bohórquez R. 4a. ed. La Paz: Editorial Los Amigos del Libro, 1982. 425 p.: bibl., index (Enciclopedia boliviana)
Cuarta edición, actualizada hasta 1980, de esta historia literaria, obra clásica del escritor boliviano. Recuento de su proceso desde la época precolombina, escrito con criterio de catalogar todo lo posible y de afirmar lo nacional. El tono solemne característico del autor se vuelve admonitorio especialmente en capítulos dedicados a fenómenos recientes, que no pasan de ser una sucesión lineal de fichas de autor. [JMO]

5369 Fernández Naranjo, Nicolás *et al.* Oficio de coraje: Néstor Taboada Terán, 30 años de literatura. La Paz: Editorial Los Amigos del Libro, 1981. 113 p.
Homenaje a Taboada Terán, bastante conocido en su país por los cuentos *Indios en rebelión*, pero completamente ignorado fuera. Recopila numerosos artículos y reseñas periodísticos de autores nacionales y extranjeros dedicados al escritor. De valor meramente documental, sólo puede interesar al estudioso de la obra de Taboada Terán. [JMO]

Guzmán, Augusto. Biografías de la literatura boliviana: biografía, evaluación, bibliografía. See *HLAS 45:43.*

5369a Lastra, Pedro. Sobre Alcides Arguedas (RCLL, 6:12, 1980, p. 213–223)
Relectura del autor boliviano que rectifica el error habitual de considerar que hay un divorcio entre sus opiniones como ensayista y las que expresó como narrador, sobre todo respecto de la condición indígena. Sostiene que hay una correspondencia general y que su obra es "un caso notable de intertextualidad refleja" (p. 214). Sugiere que esta visión de Arguedas implicaría la corrección del término "indigenismo," como forma englobadora. [JMO]

5370 Sánchez Parga, José. La tierra ocupada: estudio sobre la novelística de Jesús Lara. La Paz: Editorial Los Amigos del Libro, 1980. 125 p.
Estudio de la problemática agraria del novelista boliviano. Aunque el enfoque no es muy profundo, hace oportunas críticas a la visión social y la calidad literaria de Lara. [JMO]

COLOMBIA

5371 Ayala Poveda, Fernando. Novelistas colombianos contemporáneos. Bogotá: Universidad Central, 1983. 209 p.: bibl., ill.
Un poco a la manera de *Los nuestros* de Luis Harss, presenta retrato de la nueva novela colombiana, escogiendo a un grupo de

escritores representativos (Pedro Gómez Valderrama, Plinio Apuleyo Mendoza, Fernando Cruz Kronfly, Jorge Eliécer Pardo, etc.), los entrevista, hace una síntesis intelectual y comentario crítico de su obra. Ejemplo de periodiosmo literario que vale al llamar la atención sobre un conjunto de narradores casi completamente desconocidos fuera de su país. Es notoria la ausencia de Gustavo Alvarez Gardeazábal. [JMO]

5371a Canfield, Martha L. *El otoño del patriarca* (ECO, 6 : 252, 1982, p. 567–602)

Inspirada en ciertas ideas de Barthes, Todorov y de la crítica psicoanalítica, análisis bastante completo y detallado de la novela que cubre, entre otros, cuestiones del zoomorfismo, presunción de divinidad del protagonista, motivo excremental, polivalencia semántica del discurso, etc. Análisis riguroso y bien fundado. [JMO]

5372 Fuenmayor, Alfonso. Crónicas sobre el Grupo de Barranquilla. Bogotá: Instituto Colombiano de Cultura, Subdirección de Comunicaciones, División de Publicaciones, 1978. 208, 20 leaves of plates (some col.): ill. (Colecciones regionales. Atlántico; 3. Colección popular)

A pesar del tono anecdótico e informal, hay aquí algún material documental interesantes para quien desee conocer la historia íntima de este grupo de escritores colombianos, hoy famoso por la asociación con el joven García Márquez. [JMO]

5373 Gabriel García Márquez. Edición de Peter G. Earle. Madrid: Taurus, 1981. 294 p.: bibl. (Persiles; 129. Serie El Escritor y la crítica)

Reúne 20 trabajos de críticos (y algunos narradores) de Hispanoamérica, Estados Unidos, España y Francia que ofrecen un examen plural de diversos aspectos de su obra. El *editor* ha hecho de *Cien años* el eje alrededor del cual distribuye el material, agregando al final tres trabajos que se refieren a la persona del autor. Incluye bibliografía. [JMO]

5374 Gallo, Marta. El tiempo de *Cien años de soledad* de Gabriel García Márquez (*in* International Congress of Hispanists, 4th, Salamanca, Spain, 1971. Actas. Dirección, Eugenio de Bustos Tovar. Salamanca, Spain: Asociación Internacional de Hispanistas, 1982, v. 1, p. 561–572)

Basándose en una observación de Lévi-Strauss sobre la estructura histórica y ahistórica del mito, estudia el problema del tiempo en la novela, discutiendo tres puntos principales: la polivalencia de los ciclos temporales, su finitud y la abolición del futuro. El trabajo es válido, pero un tanto arduo de leer. [JMO]

5375 García Márquez, Gabriel. Obra periodística. v. 2–3, Entre cachacos. Recopilación y prólogo de Jacques Gilard. Barcelona: Bruguera, 1982. 2 v.: bibl. (Narradores de hoy; 65)

Estos dos tomos continúan la exhaustiva recopilación de la obra periodística del autor en que se ha empeñado el crítico Jacques Gilard (ver *HLAS 40:6811*). Precedidos por su extenso prólogo, los volúmenes recogen la producción periodística en *El espectador* (1954–55), durante su primera residencia bogotana. La abundancia del material es asombrosa: casi mil páginas en ese breve lapso, algunas de gran importancia para su obra literaria. [JMO]

5376 ———. El olor de la guayaba: conversaciones con Plinio Apuleyo Mendoza. Bogotá: Editorial La Oveja Negra, 1982. 133 p., 1 leaf of plates: ill.

Esta debe ser la más animada, sincera y detallada conversación que García Márquez haya sostenido (aquí, con un escritor amigo), y los más cercano que exista a una autobiografía oral. El novelista habla, con el brillo y humor de costumbre, de sus orígenes, formación intelectual, lecturas, la política, el amor, sus gustos, la fama, etc. [JMO]

5377 ———. La soledad de la América Latina (CDLA, 137, marzo/abril 1983, p. 3–5)

Texto del discurso pronunciado por el autor ante la Academia Sueca al recibir el Premio Nobel de Literatura 1982, que es sobre todo una declaración de fe en el destino de América Latina. [JMO]

5378 González, Eduardo. Beware of gift-bearing tales: reading García Márquez according to Mauss (MLN, 97:2, March 1982, p. 347–364)

Excelente trabajo que propone una lectura completamente diferente de "La Prodigiosa Tarde de Baltazar," examinando el texto a la luz del ensayo *The Gift* de Mauss, que estudia la función etno-social del intercambio de regalos en las sociedades arcaicas.

Artículo de considerable riqueza inter-
pretativa (e.g., funciones simbólicas del re-
galo), pero el cuento es un pretexto para
plantear un polémico punto de vista sobre estudios estructuralistas y semiológicos. [JMO]

5379 Grossman, Edith. Truth is stranger
than fact (REVIEW, 30, Sept./Dec.
1981, p. 71–73, plates)

Nota que destaca las relaciones entre
Crónica de una muerte anunciada y los
acontecimientos reales registrados por el periodismo local, en los que García Márquez se
inspiró. ¿Ficción, crónica, periodismo? Para
la autora "the important question is not
whether García Márquez has engaged in a
facile confusion of genres, but rather how
he has reshaped the reality of historical
events and people and altered them with
his uniquely comic and mythic touch"
(p. 72–73).

5380 Higgins, James. The political symbolism of the letter and the cock in *El
coronel no tiene quién lo escriba* (ATSP/VH,
31:3, Autumn 1982, p. 19–24)

Análisis de dos *leitmotiven:* 1) el de la
carta que nunca llega permite al protagonista
"to endure and survive" (p. 20) sin caer en la
desesperación; y 2) el del gallo de pelea ofrece
"the hope of good times just around the corner," y lo impulsa "seek other means of rem-
edying his predicament" (p. 21). Los
principales aportes del trabajo son esta interpretación del segundo motivo y el paralelo
entre política y juego. [JMO]

5381 Peña Gutiérrez, Isaías. La narrativa del
Frente Nacional: génesis y contratiem-
pos. Bogotá: Fundación Universidad Central,
1982. 460 p.: bibl.

Recopilación de artículos del autor
sobre el grupo de narradores— más conocidos
como generación de la revista *Mito* y "la violencia"—que surge en la década del 50 y
madura al comienzo de la siguiente. Material
básicamente periodístico; de mayor valor los
dos primeros textos ("Génesis y Contra-
tiempo de una Narrativa," "La Nuestra, ¿Otra
Generación Frustrada?"), aunque el tono be-
ligerante y reivindicatorio reducen su objetividad a la de una crónica inmediata del
período. [JMO]

5382 Rodríguez Núñez, Víctor. "La peregrinación de la Jirafa:" García Márquez, su periodismo costeño (CDLA, 137,
marzo/abril 1983, p. 27–39)

Revisión general de la obra periodística
temprana de García Márquez (1948–52), publicada en *El Universal* y *El Heraldo* y recientemente recopilada por Jacques Gilard bajo el
título *Textos costeños* (1981). Rodríguez
Núñez insiste en los valores políticos y de
observación realista de esas crónicas. Al
final, polemiza sobre la valoración que de
ellas hace Gilard, pero sus razones (y su tono)
no parecen del todo justificados. [JMO]

5383 Ruffinelli, Jorge. Las memorias de
García Márquez (ECO, 6:252, 1982,
p. 613–623)

Nota en la que el autor mezcla recuerdos personales de García Márquez con
sus impresiones de lector de *El olor de la
guayaba*, en el que Plinio Apuleyo Mendoza
entrevista al novelista (ver item **5376**). [JMO]

5384 Zuluaga, Conrado. Puerta abierta a
García Márquez y otras puertas. Oleos
de Cecilia Delgado. Bogotá: La Editora, 1982.
198 p.: bibl., ill.

De este volumen misceláneo y con-
fusamente editado, sólo tienen algún interés
los cuatro primeros textos. Bajo títulos deso-
rientadores, contienen una reseña, casi siempre anecdótica, de los comienzos literarios
de García Márquez y de su actividad como
periodista. [JMO]

ECUADOR

5385 Adoum, Jorge Enrique. *Huasipungo*: el
indio, ¿persona o personaje? (CDLA,
22:127, julio/agosto 1981, p. 22–29)

Claramente polémico, hace una eficaz
revisión de la crítica adversa sobre *Huasipungo*. Sostiene que el error está en considerar que Icaza trató de crear personajes,
cuando quiso plantear problemas y hechos.
La verdadera cuestión— si esa intención crea
una verosimilitud narrativa—queda en pie a
pesar del tono un poco agresivo del crítico. [JMO]

5386 Barriga López, Franklin and **Leonardo
Barriga López.** Diccionario de la litera-
tura ecuatoriana. 2a. ed., corr. y aumn.
Guayaquil: Casa de la Cultura Ecuatoriana,
Núcleo del Guayas, 1980. 5 v.: bibl., indexes
(Colección Letras del Ecuador; no. 103–104,
106–108)

Este diccionario es tan amplio y gene
roso que afecta su propia utilidad: incluye

centenares de autores en cinco tomos, además de instituciones culturales y periodísticas, lo que es a todas luces excesivo. Las fichas mismas son convencionales. [JMO]

5387 Carrión, Benjamín. Obras. v. 1. Quito: Editorial Casa de la Cultura Ecuatoriana, 1981. 1 v.: facsims.

Demorado hace muchos años, es el vol. 1 de lo que serán las *Obras completas* del autor. El proyecto original suponía papel biblia y tomos encuadernados. El presente tomo sólo conserva lo primero, pero la encuadernación, los tipos y el cuidado editorial son lamentables. El volumen incluye cuatro libros: *Los creadores de la Nueva América*, *Mapa de América*, *Indice de la poesía ecuatoriana* y *El nuevo relato ecuatoriano*, pero ni siquiera indica la fecha de su publicación original. [JMO]

5388 Diez, Luis A. The apocalyptic tropics of Aguilera Malta (LALR, 10:20, Spring/Summer 1982, p. 31–40)

Revisión crítica de la obra novelística de Aguilera Malta, con particular atención a *Siete lunas y siete serpientes*. Esta obra es considerada como "a highly complex and profound piece of fiction" (p. 39), que recuerda los mundos míticos de. *Cien años de soledad* y otras novelas recientes. [JMO]

5389 Febres Cordero, Francisco. Retratos con jalalengua. Quito: Editorial El Conejo, 1983. 244 p.: bibl., ports (Colección Ecuador/testimonio; 3)

Recopilación de breves entrevistas a escritores ecuatorianos y algunos otros hispanoamericanos (e.g., Eduardo Galeano, Miguel Otero Silva, Augusto Monterroso). Su interés informativo está limitado por la intención con que fueron hechos (como parte de la actualidad periodística); los subtítulos de los textos son francamente absurdos. [JMO]

5390 Lorente Medina, Antonio. La narrativa menor de Jorge Icaza. Valladolid, Spain: Universidad de Valladolid, Departamento de Literatura Española, 1980. 325 p.: bibl., ill.

El origen—tesis universitaria—de este libro se nota demasiado en su estructura, enfoque y lenguaje: el análisis de los textos se divide en "argumento," "temática," "estructura," "composición narrativa," etc.; los temas y los personajes se clasifican toscamente en: los celos, la opresión, la muerte, el

indio, el blanco, el cholo, etc. El libro se concentra en la narrativa breve del autor, poco estudiada; en ese sentido, es un trabajo complementario del de Manuel Corrales Pascual (ver item **5393**). [JMO]

5391 Pareja Diezcanseco, Alfredo. El reino de la libertad en Pablo Palacio (CDLA, 22:127, julio/agosto 1981, p. 3–20)

Revisión general de la obra narrativa de Palacio, con algunos apuntes biográficos y anecdóticos. Aunque no penetra mucho en la naturaleza específica de sus relatos, vale como presentación de un escritor singular. Insiste en que Palacio fue, pese a todo, un realista, pero por completo ajeno a las premisas del realismo socialista que luego se difundirían por toda América Latina. [JMO]

5392 Prada Oropeza, Renato. La metaliteratura de Pablo Palacio (HISPA, 10:28, abril 1981, p. 3–17)

Intento de descripción de un "elemento constructivo" o metaliterario (la reflexión que la estructura narrativa hace de sí misma) en la obra del insólito autor ecuatoriano. Aunque el trabajo quiere ser preciso y científico, resulta un poco confuso: al comienzo parece desconfiar de las interpretaciones psicológicas, pero al final afirma que son indispensables en el análisis literario. [JMO]

5393 Situación del relato ecuatoriano: nueve estudios. Edición e introducción de Manuel Corales Pascual. S. Aguinaga Z. *et al*. Quito: Centro de Publicaciones, Pontificia Universidad Católica del Ecuador, 1977. 380 p.: bibl., ill.

Nueve estudios críticos sobre otros tantos cuentistas, bien conocidos como Icaza, Adalberto Ortiz y Pedro Jorge Vera, o nuevos como León Vieira, Raúl Pérez y Alicia Yáñez. Como en tantos otros repertorios, la calidad de éste es muy desigual. Predominio de enfoques estructuralistas y formalistas, con abundancia de gráficos; el trabajo de Gonzalo Pérez Terán sobre Estupiñán Bass, debe ser el punto más bajo del volumen. [JMO]

PERU

5394 Alcibíades, Mirla. Mariátegui, *Amauta* y la vanguardia literaria; pts. 1/2 (RCLL, 8:15, 1982, p. 123–139)

Sólo pt. 2 de este trabajo corresponde al título: pt. 1 está dedicada a comentar la posición ideológica y política de la revista *Amauta* : "Encontramos que en el autor de los 7 *ensayos* su aproximación crítica (sic) al fenómeno de la vanguardia literaria en Perú se inscribe en el interior (*sic*) de un proceso más vasto, caracterizado en el plano político en función de la dicotomía campesino-indígena/gamonal, y en el plano ideológico por el enfrentamiento Inkario/Colonia" (p. 138). [JMO]

5395 Ballón, Enrique. La semiótica en el Perú (UP/A, 6:11, 1981, p. 39–59)

Completo recuento del nacimiento, desarrollo y actividades presentes de la semiótica en el Perú, con detenidos comentarios sobre sus avances en las más diversas áreas: literatura, lingüística, film, artes plásticas, antropología, derecho, etc. La utilidad del trabajo se acrecienta con la exhaustiva bibliografía que agrega al final; sólo habría sido deseable que el autor emplease un tono menos militante y airado para defender su disciplina. [JMO]

5396 Boland, R.C. *Pantaleón y las visitadoras*: a novelistic theory put into practice (UA/REH, 16:1, enero 1982, p. 15–33)

Descubre en la novela una aplicación rigurosa de bien conocidos conceptos y técnicas de Vargas Llosa: su afán de reducir "his obtrusive role as narrator," el uso de "parallel plots" y niveles narrativos (p. 19) que ofrecen visiones psicológicas, sociales y mágicas de la realidad peruana, etc. Aunque no es el primero en estudiar esos aspectos, los presenta en un conjunto ordenado y detallado. [JMO]

5397 Bonneville, Henry. Ricardo Palma au présent (UTIEH/C, 39, 1982, p. 27–47)

Extenso artículo, por un lado, un recuento de lo que falta por hacer en los estudios sobre Palma para mejor conocimiento de su obra y persona, con la idea de preparar sus *Obras completas*, proyecto hasta ahora no intentado; por otro, comentario del valor documental e histórico de sus *Cartas a Piérola*, publicadas recientemente. [JMO]

5398 Castro-Klarén, Sara. Crimen y castigo: sexualidad en J.M. Arguedas (IILI/RI, 49:122, enero/marzo 1983, p. 55–65)

Aunque otros trabajos hayan hecho referencia al tema, éste es el primero que lo

trata específicamente y con amplitud. Afirma que la sexualidad arguediana es casi sin excepción una forma de la alienación, porque el sexo es un encuentro o choque "entre dos seres marcados por la disparidad más intensa y obvia" (p. 57). Por eso, es una realidad infernal, degradante y culpable, observada además desde un punto de vista estrictamente masculino. [JMO]

5399 Christian, Chester. Alrededor de este nudo de la vida: entrevista con José María Arguedas, 3 de agosto de 1966, Lima, Perú (IILI/RI, 49:122, enero/marzo 1983, p. 221–234)

Esta entrevista, realizada en Lima tres años antes de su muerte, ofrece algunos datos interesantes sobre la personalidad y las ideas del novelista. [JMO]

5400 Chrzanowski, Joseph. Consideraciones estructurales y temáticas en torno a la *Tía Julia* (UV/PH, 45, enero/marzo 1982, p. 22–26, ill.)

Sólo la segunda parte ofrece interés y novedad donde el autor discute las formas cómo el protagonista Pedro Camacho se desdobla en sus personajes atribuyéndoles rasgos que pertenecen a su *yo real* o su *yo ideal*. [JMO]

5401 *Colónida.* Ediciones Copé. Año 1, No. 1, 15 enero 1916 [through] Año 1, No. 4, 1 mayo 1916– . Lima.

Edición facsimilar de revista literaria limeña de comienzos de siglo, que representa un momento interesante aunque fugaz en la literatura peruana, cuya mayor figura es Abraham Valdelomar. El prólogo de Luis Alberto Sánchez, escrito de prisa, es más anecdótico que crítico. La parte crítica de la edición, por desgracia, es muy descuidada y abunda en enojosas erratas. [JMO]

5402 Cornejo Polar, Antonio. *La guerra del fin del mundo*: sentido—y sin sentido—de la historia (HISPA, 11:31, 1982, p. 3–14)

Lectura crítica de la novela de Vargas Llosa que destaca la estructura de oposición en que se sustenta, la función de ciertos acontecimientos regidos por el azar, la visión de la historia como una realidad inconexa e incomprensible, el extremo rigor formal de su composición, etc. Esos aspectos están observados con claridad, pero sobre todo al final el análisis formal que había planteado el trabajo es suplantado por un enfoque de preceptiva ideológica. [JMO]

5403 Febres, Eleodoro J. *Los ríos profundos* de Arguedas: estructura e intención (UPR/LT, 24:93/94, julio/dic. 1976 [i.e. 1981] p. 161–178)

Aunque escrita sin mayores pretensiones, ésta es una relectura razonada, comprensiva y útil de dos aspectos (más algunos otros) de la novela. Destaca la función de la memoria, los episodios menores, visión del paisaje y hombre andino como un ser complejo y a veces contradictorio, para destacar la distancia a la que se coloca Arguedas respecto de la tradición indigenista. [JMO]

5404 Harrison, Regina. José María Arguedas: el substrato quechua (IILI/RI, 49:122, enero/marzo 1983, p. 111–132)

Valiosa e informada exposición de la relación de Arguedas con la lengua y la literatura quechuas, como traductor y como novelista. Relación conflictiva, tanto por la dificultad inherente de verter el mundo verbal quechua al español, como por el desajuste cultural y emocional que nunca subsanó el autor. [JMO]

5405 Harss, Luis. *Los ríos profundos* como retrato del artista (IILI/RI, 49:122, enero/marzo 1983, p. 133–141)

Parte de dos premisas: *Los ríos profundos* es el retrato autobiográfico de un aprendizaje artístico; y es una "ontología poética" (p. 133). Quiere mostrar que la obra responde "menos a una dialéctica social que a una metafísica de la poesía" (p. 135). Enfoque poco frecuente al considerar el trazado de los personajes arguedianos; hay que destacar que el lenguaje crítico de Harss, sin dejar de ser riguroso, tiene, él tambien, un impulso lírico, adecuado a la búsqueda de los fundamentos de la poética del novelista. [JMO]

5406 Jones, Julie. The search for paradise in *Captain Pantoja and the special service* (LALR, 9:19, Fall/Winter 1981, p. 41–46)

Estudia un aspecto de la novela no considerado por la crítica: "the search for paradise," implícita en la naturaleza erótica de la misión del personaje y sugerida por el exuberante paisaje tropical en que tiene lugar. Lo que le ocurre a Pantaleón es frecuente en las novelas de Vargas Llosa: "Instead of accepting the absurdity of their situation, they either cling blindly to worn-out codes or erect new forms which are parodies of the old ones" (p. 45).

5408 Lewis, Marvin A. From Lima to Leticia: the Peruvian novels of Mario Vargas Llosa. Lanham, Md.: University Press of America, 1983. 157 p.: bibl., index.

Estudia en cuatro principales novelas de Vargas Llosa, cuatro asuntos que constituyen "the central thematic matrix" de su obra: el heroísmo, la ironía, la relación entre el determinismo y el influjo existencialista, su visión de la historia peruana. El comprehensivo estudio concluye con un interesante capítulo dedicado a *La tía Julia y el escribidor*. [JMO]

5409 Lienhard, Martin. Cultura popular andina y forma novelesca: zorros y danzantes en la última novela de Arguedas. Lima: Latinoamericana Editores, 1981. 212 p., 1 leaf of plates: bibl., ill.

Primer libro dedicado íntegramente al estudio de la compleja novela póstuma de Arguedas, *EL zorro de arriba y el zorro de abajo*. El autor, de origen suizo, enfrenta la cultura indígena con algún candor y el texto arguediano con algún desorden. Pero su esfuerzo alcanza a destacar, siguiendo la tesis de Bakhtin sobre la "carnavalización de la literatura," que la novela incorpora formas literarias, estéticas e ideológicas provenientes del mundo andino popular, que implican una ruptura del modelo "occidental" llamado *novela*. [JMO]

5410 Lindstrom, Naomi. *El zorro de arriba y el zorro de abajo*: una marginación al nivel del discurso (IILI/RI, 49:122, enero/marzo 1983, p. 211–218)

Quiere aplicar "un modelo ecléctico de análisis de discurso" para estudiar principalmente tres fenómenos: organización del texto, pluralidad conflictiva de *standards* lingüísticos y los comentarios que hace Arguedas sobre "el discurso desgarrado entre sistemas irresolublemente opuestos" (p. 213). Trabajo que promete más de lo que ofrece, tal vez porque es parte de un estudio mayor; sus observaciones son, sin embargo, acertadas en general. [JMO]

5411 Literatura y sociedad en el Perú. v. 1, Cuestionamiento de la crítica. v. 2, Narración y poesía: un debate. Debaten, Antonio Cornejo Polar *et al.* Mario Montalbetti, moderador. Lima: Hueso Húmero Ediciones, 1981–1982. 2 v.

Cinco escritores peruanos, críticos profesionales y ocasionales, debaten cuestiones de sociología literaria, como crítica e ideología, literatura y clases sociales, literatura y política, y luego temas más específicamente vinculados al desarrollo de la narrativa y poesía contemporáneas. Aunque el debate es extenso, no es muy variado porque los participantes discuten desde posiciones que son básicamente similares. Más que por lo que dicen sobre literatura, sus declaraciones son interesantes por lo que dicen sobre ellos y sobre un "estado de crisis" que se advierte en los medios intelectuales peruanos a fines de la década del 70. [JMO]

5412 Luchting, Wolfgang A. Los mecanismos de la ambigüedad: *La juventud en la otra ribera* de Julio Ramón Ribeyro (Iberoromania [Max Niemeyer, Tübingen, FRG] 17, 1983, p. 131–150)

El extenso análisis de ciertos motivos que se prestan a diversas interpretaciones del cuento de Ribeyro, revela a un lector atento y devoto. Pero buena parte de sus méritos están disminuidos por un lenguaje crítico poco ortodoxo y poblado de neologismos, observaciones triviales y construcciones sintácticas anómalas. [JMO]

5413 Machen, Stephen M. "Pornoviolence" and point of view in Mario Vargas Llosa's *La tía Julia y el escribidor* (LALR, 9:17, Fall/Winter 1980, p. 9–16)

Interesante trabajo que estudia, aprovechando unas precisiones sobre la "pornoviolence" y la "mass-culture" hechas por Tom Wolfe, la presentación del material pornográfico en *La tía Julia y el escribidor*, con referencias a *La ciudad y los perros*. Demuestra que es la falta de elaboración del material presentado y el uso de punto de vista que se confunde con el del lector mismo, lo que genera la violencia grotesca en los "radioteatros" del personaje Camacho y lo que convierte al lector en un "agressor." [JMO]

5414 Meneses, Carlos. Vargas Llosa y los dos periodistas convertidos en personajes (ESME/C, 66/67, julio/dic. 1979, p. 74–82)

El autor identifica los modelos reales de dos personajes de ese oficio (Carlitos y Norwin) que aparecen en *Conversación en la catedral*, ofreciendo información sobre ellos y sobre la actitud de Vargas Llosa frente al periodismo. La ausencia de notas que indiquen sus fuentes de información es notoria. [JMO]

5415 Merrell, Floyd. Antropología y *La casa verde*: Vargas Llosa dialoga con un mundo en degeneración (VA/REH, 16:1, enero 1982, p. 103–113)

Usando un concepto proveniente de la física como el de la *entropía* y siguiendo sus aplicaciones al campo del arte según Rudolf Arnheim, estudia el juego de tensiones entre caos y orden en *La casa verde*. Analiza los niveles de organización, las permutaciones temáticas y transformaciones de personaje; y la "base axiológica," que transforma el dinamismo en atemporalidad. Pese a ciertas imprecisiones, el estudio tiene el mérito de usar un enfoque totalmente nuevo para examinar la novela. [JMO]

5416 Moraña, Mabel. Función ideológica de la fantasía en las novelas de Manuel Scorza (RCLL, 9:17, 1983, p. 171–192)

Análisis marxista que sostiene que el autor falla porque "los elementos fantásticos aparecen . . . como una emanación directa del nivel material, y la clase oprimida como productora de un sistema de representaciones que la vinculan en (sic) la realidad, aunque no la insertan acativamente en ella," reflejando así una concepción "idealista" de la historia (p. 191). [JMO]

5417 Mróz, Marcin. José María Arguedas como representante de la cultura quechua: análisis de la novela *El zorro de arriba y el zorro de abajo* (PAN/ES, 8, 1981, p. 11–36, tables)

Traducción al español de tediosa lectura, pero tiene el innegable valor de estudiar la lengua literaria de Arguedas basado en un conocimiento etnológico de la cultura quechua (ver *HLAS 45:1465*). Cubre el influjo autóctono en la estructura de su lengua, su modo de percibir el mundo y su visión social de la cultura. Todo eso, permite justificar la afirmación de que más que un escritor "indigenista," Arguedas es un escritor "indígena," cuyos valores son los de la realidad quechua.

5418 Muñoz, Silverio. José María Arguedas y el mito de la salvación por la cultura. Minneapolis: Instituto para el Estudio de Ideologías y Literatura, 1980. 152 p.: bibl. (Serie Hacia una historia social de las literaturas hispánicas y luso-brasileira)

Análisis de las primeras obras narrativas (*Agua* y *Yawar Fiesta*) para tratar de explicar el "zigzagueo ideológico" entre el realismo de ese período, inspirado por el pensamiento de Mariátegui, y el "culturalismo," de origen etnológico o antropológico, visible en su obra posterior. El trabajo parte de conceptos propios del análisis marxista, pero hace un uso dogmático e ingenuo de ellos, agravado por el tono propagandístico de la exposición. Esto no le impide al autor calificar su propia obra como "un contribución valiosa" (p. 1144). [JMO]

5419 Ortega, Julio. Crisis, identidad y cultura en el Perú (*in* Perú: identidad nacional. Lima: Ediciones Centro de Estudios para el Desarrollo y Participación [CEDEP] 1979, p. 191–208, tables)

Reflexión muy personal sobre "el discurso político" peruano y sobre modelos culturales que ha desarrollado a lo largo de la historia. Aunque hace referencias a cronistas y autores coloniales, se concentra en la actualidad y esboza una especie de proyecto político para el país, teniendo en cuenta la identidad plural del pueblo peruano, las demandas de su masa indígena y la necesidad de cambiar los sistemas de información cultural. [JMO]

5420 ———. Texto, comunicación y cultura: *Los ríos profundos* de José María Arguedas. Lima: Centro de Estudios para el Desarrollo y la Participación, 1982. 131 p.: bibl., ill.

Aplicando ideas y métodos de análisis provenientes de la semiótica cultural, se propone un examen de la estructura textual y organización semántica de la comunicación, tal como se presentan en la famosa novela de Arguedas. Demuestra así que el texto "genera un sistema de comunicación peculiar" y que "este sistema dramático y desgarrado reformula el sentido del texto" (p. 10). El estudio de voces y funciones narrativas es particularmente interesante. [JMO]

5421 Pantigoso, Edgardo J. La rebelión contra el indigenismo y la afirmación del pueblo en el mundo de José María Arguedas. Lima: Editorial Juan Mejía Baca, 1981. 301, 2 p.: bibl., ill.

Revisión general, algo superficial, de la obra narrativa del escritor peruano, a quien presenta, un poco discutiblemente, como exponente de la estética de lo "real-

maravilloso" en una etapa de su producción. La edición es muy descuidada (e.g., p. 177–192 están invertidas). [JMO]

5422 Paoli, Roberto. *Los ríos profundos*: la memoria y lo imaginario (IILI/RI, 48:118/119, enero/junio 1982, p. 177–190)

Lo más interesante de este extenso análisis de las funciones que la emoción y la memoria tienen en el personaje Ernesto, son las precisiones que el crítico hace al comienzo de su trabajo: más que narrador, Arguedas es *escritor*, capaz de superar las torpezas de su prosa y estructura narrativa, para ofrecernos una admirable visión lírica y elegíaca de un pasado irrecuperable. La utopía de Ernesto está puesta en "la edad del pensamiento mágico" (p. 185). [JMO]

5423 Rama, Angel. *La guerra del fin del mundo*: una obra maestra del fanatismo artístico (ECO, 40[6]:246, abril 1982, p. 600–640)

Muy completa e ilustrativa nota crítica sobre la novela de Vargas Llosa, que destaca sus conexiones con *Os sertões* y el *Facundo*, su maestría técnica, su visión social, etc. Al final, Rama discrepa de las "conclusiones" de carácter histórico e ideológico que propone la obra. [JMO]

5424 ———. *Los ríos profundos*, ópera de pobres (IILI/RI, 49:122, enero/marzo 1983, p. 11–41)

Copioso ensayo que estudia la novela de Arguedas, como forma artística original y como resultado de componentes ideológicos. Se concentra en el problema de la lengua quechua, la función de la música y canto, y finalmente en su carácter singular de "ópera de pobres," vinculándola con la opera china y la renacentista. Este último punto de vista es verdaderamente nuevo y está defendido con gran despliegue dialéctico, aunque con un lenguaje crítico a veces trabajoso. [JMO]

5425 Rodríguez-Peralta, Phyllis. Narrative access to a feminine childhood world: a new Peruvian novel (LALR, 9:17, Fall/Winter 1980, p. 1–8)

Bien razonado estudio de *El truco de los ojos* de Laura Riesco, uno de los poquísimos ejemplos valiosos de novela escrita por una mujer recientemente en el Perú. Compara las innovaciones técnicas y la función que la memoria cumple en este relato, con las que se observan en Vargas Llosa y Bryce Echenique. Por su hábil creación de "a female tone" (p. 6), que se revela sobre todo en su relación con temas sexuales, y por el sesgo experimental adoptado para presentar la infancia, la novela ofrece un caso bastante singular en la literatura peruana. [JMO]

5426 Rowe, William. Arguedas: el narrador y el antropólogo frente al lenguaje (IILI/RI, 49 : 122, enero/marzo 1983, p. 97–109)

Título no muy preciso: antes que el lenguaje, discute las ideas que sobre Arguedas han expresado algunos antropólogos (e.g., Rodrigo Montoya, Juan Ossio) y traza las líneas de oposición que él mismo encuentra entre las formas de cultura que pugnan en la obra arguediana. Los conceptos de "discurso mítico" frente a "discurso político" tienen dentro de ésta una relación ambigua. [JMO]

5427 Ruffinelli, Jorge. Vargas Llosa: Dios y el diablo en la tierra del sol (UV/PH, 42, abril/junio 1982, p. 10–18, plates)

Detenido análisis crítico, lleno de agudas observaciones, sobre *La guerra del fin del mundo*, su relación con *Os sertões* de Da Cunha, su diseño narrativo y su visión histórica. Sobre este último aspecto, Ruffinelli hace unos reparos a la presentación novelística de lo que es un "movimiento liberador en busca de su propia libertad y autonomía" (p. 17). [JMO]

5428 Unruh, Vicky Wolff. El mundo disputado al nivel del lenguaje (IILI/RI, 49 : 122, enero/marzo 1983, p. 193–202)

Análisis del "sistema comunicativo" de *Los ríos profundos*, que trata de demostrar que el conflicto básico de la novela es una lucha por la información cultural entre dos mundos separados por la lengua y códigos sociales. Enfoque básicamente lingüístico del texto apoyado en tesis provenientes de la semiótica cultural. [JMO]

5429 Vargas Llosa, Mario. El elefante y la cultura (Vuelta [México] 70 : 6, sept. 1982, p. 13–16)

Breve reflexión del novelista peruano sobre temas muy polémicos: el nacionalismo cultural, la dependencia respecto de modelos extranjeros y el libre acceso a las fuentes de cultura e información. [JMO]

5430 ———. Historia de una matanza (Vuelta [México] 7 : 81, agosto 1983, p. 4–15)

Minuciosa y dramática crónica de un grave incidente de violencia política ocurrido en el Perú: el asesinato de periodistas a manos de campesinos que los tomaron por terroristas del grupo "Sendero Luminoso." Recoge testimonios y documentación abundantes. Puede leerse como un aporte de esclarecimiento de un hecho cuya crueldad conmovió la conciencia de un país, pero también como un texto cuya epicidad y detallismo puede examinarse en cotejo con *La guerra del fin del mundo*. [JMO]

5431 Wise, David O. Writing for fewer and fewer: Peruvian fiction, 1979–1980 (LARR, 18 : 1, 1983, p. 189–200)

Reseña de cinco obras narrativas de Fernando Ampuero, Angel Avendaño, Jorge Díaz Herrera, Manuel Scorza y Guillermo Thorndike. Tan interesante como su comentario, es la visión de conjunto que ofrece, al comienzo y al final, sobre el contexto en que esa narrativa se produce y sobre "the comatose Peruvian book industry" que limita drásticamente el público lector de estos autores. [JMO]

VENEZUELA

5432 Almoina de Carrera, Pilar. Cronistas e historiadores: ¿antecedentes de la literatura venezolana? Caracas: Universidad Central de Venezuela, Facultad de Humanidades y Educación, Instituto de Investigaciones Literarias, 1982. 51 leaves (Prepublicaciones)

Breve trabajo sobre la relación que los escritores coloniales pueden tener sobre la literatura venezolana moderna, sobre todo en cuanto a la conformación de arquetipos mentales, visión de la naturaleza y relaciones entre el poblador indígena y el forastero. Somera aproximación al tema. [JMO]

5433 Becco, Horacio Jorge. *Doña Bárbara* de Rómulo Gallegos: bibliografía en su cincuentenario, 1919–1979 (Actualidades [Centro de Estudios Latinoamericanos Rómulo Gallegos, Caracas] 5, agosto 1979, p. 49–87)

Muy valioso trabajo bibliográfico, complementario del de Efraín Subero (ver *HLAS 44 : 5422*). Contiene, con breves anotaciones: obras de referencia; ediciones de *Obras completas*, traducciones, estudios galleguianos y trabajos críticos sobre la clásica novela. [JMO]

5434 Belrose, Maurice. Présence du Noir dans la roman vénézuélien. Paris: Editions caribéenes; Pointe-à-Pitre, Guadeloupe: Centre universitaire Antilles-Guyane, 1981. 217 p., 4 p. of plates: bibl., ill. (Textes, études, documents; no. 3)

Detallado estudio del tema del negro en la novela venezolana (1890–1950) es decir desde *Peonía* de Romero García a *Cumboto* de Díaz Sánchez, con breve referencia a antecedentes históricos. Es el primer trabajo extenso sobre el tema, con la particularidad de que está hecho desde la perspectiva de un crítico de las Antillas francesas. Incluye bibliografía y anexos. [JMO]

5435 García Riera, Gladys. Guillermo Meneses: una bibliografía. Caracas: Centro de Investigaciones Lingüísticas y Literarias Andrés Bello, Departamento de Castellano, Literatura y Latín, Instituto Universitario Pedagógico de Caracas, 1981. 169 p.

Recopila más de 1,600 *items* de y sobre el narrador venezolano. Aporte documental importante para el conocimiento de su obra. Las fichas no están anotadas y aparecen ordenadas por orden alfabético en cada sección, criterio que en el caso de los prólogos escritos por Meneses no resulta el más claro. [JMO]

5436 Lerner, Elisa. Yo amo a Colombo, o, La pasión dispersa: ensayos, 1958–1978. Caracas: Monte Avila Editores, 1979. 395 p. (Colección Documentos)

Colección de crónicas, de muy variado valor, cuyos temas cubren la literatura, impresiones de viaje, cine, arte, televisión y otras formas de cultura popular. [JMO]

5437 Liscano, Juan. Rómulo Gallegos y su tiempo: ensayo. 2a. ed. Caracas: Monte Avila Editores, 1980. 316 p.: bibl. (Colección Estudios)

Biografía del mayor novelista venezolano, que incluye además referencias críticas a su obra literaria. Propone una imagen ejemplar de Gallegos, más como personalidad moral e intelectual, que como escritor (e.g., "constructor antes que inventor, maestro antes que artista, educador antes que inspirado"). El autor ha limitado al mínimo el aparato crítico y las referencias bibliográficas, lo que resta utilidad a la biografía. [JMO]

5438 Llebot Cazalis, Amaya. El tiempo interior en los personajes garmendianos. Caracas: Ediciones de la Facultad de Humanidades y Educación, Universidad Central de Venezuela, 1980. 120 p.: bibl.

Lectura, demasiado literal, del tema del tiempo en las novelas del autor de *Días de ceniza*. Quizá debido a que los fundamentos conceptuales de la autora no son firmes, el trabajo da la impresión de que pasa sobre el tema, sin realmente tocarlo. [JMO]

5439 Medina, José Ramón. Ochenta años de literatura venezolana: 1900–1980. Cronología y bibliografía por Horacio Jorge Becco. Caracas: Monte Avila Editores, 1980. 473 p.

Reedición y puesta al día de un trabajo anterior, que cubre ahora los géneros y tendencias más recientes del presente siglo en la literatura venezolana. El enfoque es claramente histórico-literario y la intención, la divulgación general. Incluye cronología y bibliografía preparadas por Horacio Jorge Becco que le agrega interés documental. [JMO]

5440 Niño de Rivas, María Lya. Julio Garmendia: una bibliografía (CNC/A, 3/4, 1977/1978, p. 141–155)

Más de 300 fichas de y sobre el narrador, incluyendo referencias a libros, publicaciones en revistas y periódicos, y cuentos en antologías y otros libros. [JMO]

5441 Osorio T., Nelson. La tienda de muñecos de Julio Garmendia en la narrativa de la vanguardia hispanoamericana (CNC/A, 3/4, 1977/1978, p. 11–36)

Sólo una breve sección trata directamente de Garmendia. En su mayor parte, es un examen del contexto de la literatura de vanguardia hispanoamericana, no para sumarlo a esa tendencia, sino para examinar sus contactos y semejanzas. [JMO]

5442 Rivas D., Rafael Angel. Rómulo Gallegos en publicaciones periódicas del exterior: una hemerografía (Actualidades [Centro de Estudios Latinoamericanos Rómulo Gallegos, Caracas] 5, agosto 1979, p. 89–130)

Casi 600 fichas de y sobre Gallegos exclusivamente recogidas de publicaciones no venezolanas. Han sido ordenadas alfabéticamente y agrupadas en dos grandes categorías. Incluye índice temático para facilitar la consulta. [JMO]

5443 **Santos Urriola, José.** Rómulo Gallegos y la primera versión de *El forastero.* Caracas: Ediciones Centauro, 1981. 215 p.: bibl.

Para los estudiosos de la obra de Gallegos, este detallado estudio de una olvidada novela inédita del autor tendrá sin duda interés documental e histórico, más por sus comentarios sobre las relaciones del texto con el período "gomecista" de la política venezolana, que por el análisis de sus aspectos estrictamente literarios. La monotonía de su estilo expositivo hace parecer el estudio más largo de lo que es. [JMO]

5444 **Shaw, Donald.** La revisión de *Doña Bárbara* por Gallegos: 1929–1930 (Actualidades [Centro de Estudios Latinoamericanos Rómulo Gallegos, Caracas] 5, agosto 1979, p. 17–29)

Compara las ediciones primera (1929) y segunda (1930) de la novela, y descubre una serie de interesantes cambios estructurales y materiales entre ambas. Esto prueba que hubo un intenso proceso de revisión, que llega a afectar el trazado de los personajes y aún la presentación del tema mismo de la obra. [JMO]

5445 **Uslar Pietri, Arturo.** Fachas, fechas y fichas. 2a. ed. Caracas: Editorial Ateneo de Caracas, 1982. 223 p. (Colección Literatura)

Miscelánea de textos recientes, que tratan prácticamente de todo (e.g., Carlos III, OPEP, Simón Bolívar, Joan Miró). La mayoría de origen periodístico, no lucen bien incluidos en un libro. [JMO]

5446 **Zemskov, Valeri.** Héroes, historia, ironía (URSS/AL, 1/2:37/38, 1981, p. 241–256, ill.)

Presentación general de la obra narrativa de Miguel Otero Silva, con particular atención a *Cuando quiero llorar no lloro* y *Lope de Aguirre, príncipe de la libertad.* [JMO]

PROSE FICTION
BOLIVIA

5447 **El Cuento en el Oriente boliviano.** Compilación de Edgar Oblitas Fernández. La Paz: Ediciones Populares Camarlinghi, 1980? 258 p. (Ediciones Populares Camarlinghi; ser. 22, v. 62)

Regional anthology attempts to show up the other Bolivia, other than the altiplano which only forms one third of the country. Consists of 32 writers from eastern lowlands. Unfortunately, quality is often lacking and production of book less than satisfactory—number of blank pages. Printer's errors not helpful to a less than convincing effort. [DjK]

5448 **Lema Vargas, Gonzalo.** Nos conocimos amando: cuentos. Cochabamba, Bolivia: Gráfica Nacional, 1981. 62 p.

Seven short stories of uneven quality with central theme of adolescence and coming of age. Most convincing is first story "Desolado en Dos Estrellas." A young writer with straightforward narrative style, touching on universal theme of sentimental education. [DjK]

5449 **Olmos Saavedra, Raúl.** Cuentos de la tierra, de sangre, oro y vegetación. La Paz: Talleres de Editorial Calama, 1981. 190 p.

Uniform collection, thematically tied to nationalistic portrayal of Bolivia. Technically a bit of an anachronism. Straight Romanticism for most part. Tales interesting for what they divulge of Bolivian history and regionalisms. [DjK]

5450 **Pinedo Antezana, Alvaro.** Selva, oro y sangre: cuentos. Cochabama, Bolivia: Editorial Universo, 1981. 197 p.

Collection of 14 short stories set in eastern jungle region of Bolivia. Intense, well-wrought, crime tales written by lawman. Author is police official with knack for tale telling. Realistic, convincing, and captivating crime fiction. Psychologically well developed characters but mostly stock, outlaw types. [DjK]

5451 **Santillán, Carlos Condarco.** Arteaga, el inmortal. La Paz: Ediciones Casa Municipal de la Cultura Franz Tamayo, 1981. 63 p. (Biblioteca Paceña. Nueva serie)

Slim collection of four well done stories that won Bolivia's 14th Franz Tamayo Prize. Intense, suspenseful narration with interesting psychological studies of character and narrative development. Stories vary from detective genre to Indianist theme, but all equally accomplished. [DjK]

COLOMBIA

5452 Araújo, Helena. Fiesta en Teusaquillo. Bogotá: Plaza & Janes, 1981. 151 p. (Narrativa colombiana. Novelistas del día)
Telling indictment of modern Colombia's uppercrust. Novel with clear message and scathing portrait of official corruption, cronyism, and political prostitution. Traces a night in the life of Bogota's elite. The party turned into a ship of fools, where all characters from all segments of society—politics, Church, university, industry—prey on each other with exquisite scavenging instincts. [DjK]

5453 Arévalo, Milcíades. Ciudad sin fábulas: cuentos. Bogotá: Ediciones Puesto de Combate, 1981. 71 p. (Colección Linea de fuego)
Uneven collection of seven stories with widely ranging focus. Somewhat ill-integrated, stories range from Paris' Latin quarter to rural Colombia. Mixed bag of testimonial narrative and social commitment with poetic intensity. Undercurrent of violence—political and psychological—is only discernible thread that holds collection together. [DjK]

5454 Cabezas Rher, Enrique. Miro tu lindo cielo y quedo aliviado. Bogotá: Tiempo Americano Editores, 1981. 266 p. (Textos populares)
Delightful novel of social satire, eroticism, and linguistic artistry. Author's first novel, juxtaposes love story with political violence so famous in Colombia's recent past. Exciting first novel with great promise for its author who manifests a keen eye for social situations and human folly. Social criticism at its best. [DjK]

5455 Perozzo, Carlos. Juegos de mentes. Bogotá: Plaza & Janes Editores, 1981. 241 p. (Narrativa colombiana. Novelistas del día)
Demented mental games implied by title are those of a group of university intellectuals caught in the web of their ideologies, ambitions, fantasies, and hallucinations. Well-narrated, richly textured, linguistically accomplished. Revealing portrait of intellectual self-involvement and an involved tale of crime and perplexity. Perrozo is a talented writer with solid accomplishment— four books of fiction—and great promise. [DjK]

5456 Rubiano Vargas, Roberto. Gentecita del montón. Bogotá: Carlos Valencia Editores, 1981. 137 p.
Collection of 10 stories with common theme of human alienation and involution. Lyrical, intense, straightforward language. Offers cross section of human situations from 1970s. Volume won 1981 Guberek National Prize for short fiction. A first book with good potential for its author. [DjK]

5457 Sánchez Juliao, David. Abraham al humor; El pachanga; El flecha. Comentarios, Jacques Gilard. Diseño y artes, Nelson Beltrán. Fotografías, Vicente Stamato. Bogotá: Tiempo Americano Editores, 1981. 72 p.: ill. (Textos populares)
Poetic realism at its best. Tryptich of vocal portraits in which author allows characters to speak for themselves through their own dialect and lingo. Captivating experiment in cassette literature where orality stretches written language to its limits. Sánchez Juliao is a consummate artist of the short story and this collection reconfirms his powers. [DjK]

5458 Selección del cuento colombiano. Dibujos, Carlos Posso. Cali, Colombia: Taller Gráfico, 1981. 167 p.: bibl., ill.
Somewhat lame anthology of 19 Colombian authors from end of last century to present. Idiosyncratic selections and choices. Bio-bibliographical notes on authors not always accurate. Editors' brief introduction not particularly helpful. [DjK]

5459 Soto Aparicio, Fernando. Hermano hombre. Medellín, Colombia: Bedout, 1982. 310 p. (Bolsilibros Bedout; v. 224)
Tortured novel about tortured human beings in modern Colombian society. Traces itinerary of embattled intellectual caught in inextricable web of faith, disbelief, unmovable God, and unmoving, stagnant Church. As counterpoint, novel traces tragic life of abused and exploited prostitute. Allegorical juxtaposition with intense and dramatic force. Significant work from one of Colombia's most important contemporary novelists. [DjK]

ECUADOR

5460 Artieda, Fernando. Cuentos de guerrilleros y otras historias. Guayaquil:

Casa de la Cultura Ecuatoriana, Núcleo del Guayas, 1981. 174 p. (Colección Letras del Ecuador; 114)

Includes long short story and 25 others with common theme of armed struggle in contemporary Latin America. Fascinating document of ideological commitment and insurgency. Dedicated to the urban guerrilla group Tupamaru as an act of solidarity. Suspenseful, well narrated, and tragic. Revealing social statement and indictment of official terror. [DjK]

5461 Bajo la carpa: una antología temática. Varios autores. Guayaquil: Casa de la Cultura Ecuatoriana, Núcleo del Guayas, 1981. 125 p. (Colección Letras del Ecuador; 117)

Thematic anthology centered on theme of the circus. Interesting concept, it includes 11 contemporary Ecuadorian authors, some of whom are well known. Stories are uneven. Each author is introduced with a brief bio-bibliographical note. [DjK]

5462 Béja Portilla, Carlos. Tribu si: novela. Guauyaquil: Casa de la Cultura Ecuatoriana, Núcleo del Guayas, 1981. 153 p. (Colección Libros para el pueblo)

Fascinating period piece from late 1960s, early 1970s. Finalist in the 1973 Seix Barral Prize but has gone unpublished until now. Interesting sojourn through cool, groovy, and flower-child epoch with technical accomplishment and engaging narrative style. Cultural infra-history of an era and its cultural highlights, from A. Ginsberg to J.L. Borges to the Beatles and T.M. A *Rayuela* in miniature. [DjK]

5463 Carrión, Carlos. El más hermoso animal nocturno: cuentos. Quito: Editorial El Conejo, 1982. 193 p.: ill.

Winner of the 1981 José de la Cuadra Prize of Ecuador. The 12 short stories are uniformly good though very diverse. Author can best be characterized as a combination of García Márquez and Guillermo Cabrera Infante. He has tremendous range, an acute ear for orality in his writing, and an insightful capacity for depicting human situations of incomprehensible character. One of the best collections to come out of Ecuador in a long time. An irreverent celebration of the human condition. [DjK]

5464 Tobar García, Francisco. Los quiteños: nueva narrativa. Quito?: LetraNueva, 1981. 183 p. (Serie Narrativa)

Fascinating portrayal of a city's human types and idiosyncracies. Biting, ironic, incisive, lyrical at times, but mostly unforgiving in its ambivalent depiction of author's beloved native city. The 15 pieces collected here are well written, exquisite at times, and in a traditional narrative mode. Author is accomplished man of letters. [DjK]

5465 Vásconez, Javier. Ciudad lejana: cuentos. Quito: Editorial El Conejo, 1982. 141 p.: ill. (Colección Ecuador/letras)

Good specimen of socially committed literature. Collection consists of 11 short stories. It was a finalist in prestigious Casa de las Américas Literary Prize of 1982. The stories are uneven technically. Most accomplished entitled "Angelote, Amor Mio . . ." Stylistically interesting. Author achieves some interesting results through syntactical distortion and extenuations. [DjK]

5466 Vera, Alfredo. Un héroe de doce años y otros cuentos. Guayaquil: Casa de la Cultura Ecuatoriana, Núcleo del Guayas, 1981. 176 p. (Colección Letras del Ecuador; 115)

Eighteen short stories of varied quality. Author primarily preoccupied with social themes of family structure and interpersonal relations. Very traditional technically, psychological probing, though at times unnecessarily too revealing, telling instead of showing. Generally a good selection of an older writer's accomplishment. Feminists might find it of interest as a specimen of "masculine superiority." [DjK]

5467 Zavala Cataño, Víctor. Color de la ceniza y otros relatos. Quito?: Ediciones Nueva Crónica, 1981. 113 p. (Serie El tungsteno)

Collection of eight short stories by young, socially-committed playwright turned narrator. Brief introduction by the author on his literary development and importance of literature to his native region. Stories based on childhood recollections for the most part. Predominant theme: loss of rural innocence and values at the hands of urban contamination and modernization. [DjK]

PERU

5468 Calderón Fajardo, Carlos. El que pestañea muere y otros cuentos. Ilustraciones interiores, Max Ernst. Lima: Ediciones La Vieja Morsa, 1981. 152 p.: ill. (Serie Literatura)

Collection of eight short stories. Explores psychological states and fantasies of socially marginal characters. Most accomplished stories are title story and initial one of collection. Young author with number of literary prizes and considerable promise. [DjK]

5469 El Cuento Huanuqueño. Ambrosio Malpartida Besada, compilador. Samuel Armando Cárdich et al. Huánuco, Perú: Instituto Nacional de Cultura, Filial en Huánuco, 1982.

Collection of regional tales from Huánuco, Peru, by area natives or residents. Includes 11 authors, each introduced with brief bio-bibliographical sketch. Collection carries general introduction on the region's short story. While thematically tight, there is great variety in narrative technique. Valuable collection. [DjK]

5470 Huamán Cabrera, Félix. Río de Arena, Agomayo. Lima: Amaru Editores, 1981. 108 p.

Consists of 15 very short stories with regionalist themes of modern campesino caught in time warp. Intense and lyrical at times. Author captures quality of rural Peruvian dialogue and permutations of traditional speech infused with modern lingo. Collection of valuable sociological snapshots. [DjK]

5471 Sánchez Aizcorbe, Alejandro. Maní con sangre. Lima: Arte Reda, 1981. 118 p.

Collection of 19 short pieces of varied quality. Decidedly a first book by young author exploring possibilities in his own voice. For most part, stories are irreverent and iconoclastic portrayals of staunch institutions and middle class values. Author shows good potential as narrator and social critic. A matter of time and finding his own voice. [DjK]

5472 Thorne, Carlos. Viva la república. Lima: Editorial Milla Batres, 1981. 257 p.

Scathing novel on military governments and despotism in contemporary Latin America. In the vein of *Autumn of the patriarch* by García Márquez and *Yo, El Supremo* of Roa Bastos. Well narrated, intense, devastating, and insightful. An accomplished novel. [DjK]

5473 Vargas Llosa, Mario. La guerra de fin del mundo. Barcelona: Seix Barral, 1981. 531 p.: ill. (Biblioteca breve)

Significant addition to corpus of Peru's foremost contemporary novelist. Apocalyptic novel centered on millennarian uprising of the poor in Canudos, Brazil, at end of last century. Vargas Llosa consciously harks back to Euclides da Cunha's Brazilian classic *Os sertões* in retelling the eschatological tale of this remote region for which medieval apocalypticism of the Joachite tradition became so central. A blockbuster that could have benefitted from some editorial trimming, particularly in the last 200 p. [DjK]

VENEZUELA

5474 Gallegos, Rómulo. Cuentos completos. Prólogo de Gustavo Luis Carrera. Caracas: Monte Avila Editores, 1981. 432 p.

Welcome volume that collects all of Gallegos' short stories from earliest part of his career. Valuable collection preceded by very useful introduction by Gustavo Luis Carrera who traces historical and cultural background of the author's oeuvre and offers bibliographical chronology of Gallegos' short story collections. [DjK]

5475 Gomas, Otrova. El terrorista. Caracas: Ediciones OOX, 1982. 245 p.: ill.

Sociohistorical satire at its best. Author hilariously terrorizes modern terrorism. Ironic, biting, incisive novel-documentary that spares no ideology at its terroristic phase. Its scope is global and traces intrigues of its characters through major capitals of the world. Very valuable book for our times. [DjK]

5476 Herrera, Earle. Sábado que nunca llega. Caracas: Monte Avila Editores, 1981. 135 p. (Colección Donaire)

Uneven collection of a dozen stories of a testimonial nature. Author most effective when he narrates from his own experiences. Most accomplished story: "Detrás de Cada Puerta el Silencio"—a fine tale. This is author's second work to be published. A talented narrator with a sharp eye for social realities of contemporary life in Venezuela. [DjK]

5477 Meneses, Guillermo. Espejos y disfraces. Selección y prólogo, José Balza. Cronología, Salvador Tenreiro. Caracas: Biblioteca Ayacucho, 1981. 652 p.: bibl. (Biblioteca Ayacucho; 81)

Indispensable volume in Biblioteca Ayacucho's monumental project aimed at collecting complete works of most significant national authors in Venezuela's literary history. Meneses is such a figure, and volume is fitting tribute. As usual, the editors present a thorough edition with complete bibliographical, biographical, and historico-chronological apparatus. Highly recommended for library collections. [DjK]

5478 Otero Silva, Miguel. Un morrocoy en el infierno: humor—humor—humor. Prólogo de Adriano González León. Ilustraciones de Zapata. 2a. ed. Caracas: Editorial Ateneo de Caracas, 1982. 377 p.: bibl., ill.

Collected humorous pieces of one of Venezuela's foremost novelists. Irreverent, iconoclastic, book spoofs various literary genres and sacred cows of literature, politics, Church, and State. The 27 pen-and-ink illustrations by Zapata capture book's spirit.

Valuable glimpse at yet another face of this significant literary figure. Should not be ignored by his biographers and critics. [DjK]

5479 Palacios, Antonia. Una plaza ocupando un espacio desconcertante: relatos, 1974–1977. Caracas: Monte Avila Editores, 1981. 122 p. (Colección Continentes)

Confessional, poetic, and allusive tales where nothing happens other than the record and recording of mental states, psychological associations, and subjecive perceptions of narrating voice. Lyrical realism after the French new wave of the 1950s and 1960s. [DjK]

5480 Quicios y desquicios: antología de jóvenes narradores, Aragua-Carabobo-Miranda. Selección, José Napoleón Oropeza. Jesús Alberto León et al. Caracas: Fundación para la Cultura y las Artes del Distrito Federal, 1978. 92 p. (Cuadernos de difusión; 1. Presencia cultural de los estados)

Useful collection of Venezuelan regional literature of recent writers includes 10 young authors, preceded by a short editor's introduction. Each writer presented with brief bio-bibliographical note. Vol. 1 of series intended to survey contemporary production in various regions of Venezuela. [DjK]

20th Century: Prose Fiction: Chile

CEDOMIL GOIC, *Domingo Faustino Sarmiento Professor of Spanish American Literature, The University of Michigan, Ann Arbor*

LA PRODUCCION LITERARIA de los años 1981 y 1982, como la de los años anteriores, muestra la constante actividad literaria de José Donoso, la figura dominante de la década, que retorna a las formas de la novela corta, aparte de incursionar por primera vez en el teatro con la escenificación de una de sus cuentos, *Sueños de mala muerte* y en la poesía con sus *Poemas de un novelista.* Hernán Valdés publica su tercera novela (item **5494**), importante por su visión del proceso chileno y la crítica que realiza de la actuación política de la izquierda. Entre los escritores de la generación siguiente Cristián Hunneus prosigue el juego de la neoescritura con una breve narración de humor y erotismo (item **5487**). Antonio Skármeta, el más activo creador de su grupo, publica una novela corta (item **5493**) y su segunda novela larga (item **5492**) ésta sobre los antecedentes de la revolución sandinista de Nicaragua. Francisco Coloane, narrador regionalista y representativo del viejo neorrealismo publica una novela fiel a sus antecedentes que le dan un lugar en la narrativa chilena (item **5482**). Entre los escritores de la generación joven destaca Antonio Ostornol autor de dos novelas bien acogidas por la crítica, que lo ponen a la cabeza de la joven generación (items **5488** and **5489**). Entre los autores reeditados debe destacarse la reedición de *Un juez rural* de Pedro Prado (item **5490**), una de sus obras más estimables. Jorge Edwards reedita con un extenso prólogo autobiográfico su primer libro de cuentos (item **5485**). La crítica continúa prestando atención preferente a la obra de José Donoso con especial interés en *Casa de campo* (items **5501** and **5503**) y *El obsceno pájaro de la noche* (items **5498, 5502,** and **5506**), *Este Domingo* (item **5497**) y la *Historia personal del boom* (items **5499** and **5504**). María Luisa Bombal (item **5495**), fallecida en 1980, y Carlos Droguett (item **5496**) son otros autores estudiados con particular detenimiento. Con relación a las ediciones de autores nacionales del pasado es de lamentar la pobre preparación de ellas. Los prólogos son de escasa o ninguna importancia; están desprovistos de todo aparato crítico, y se presentan carentes de estudios, información bibliográfica y notas que contribuyan a consolidar los valores y la comprensión de la literatura nacional. El fenómeno de mayor interés de estos años es la aparición de los jóvenes escritores nacidos después de 1950 cuya producción se acumula en estos años en el período inicial de una nueva generación aspirante.

PROSE FICTION

5481 Amunátegui Jordán, Gregorio. La decisión: novela. Santiago: Editorial Universitaria, 1979.

Sexta novela del autor. Aborda una historia de amor en el contexto de los antecedentes y elección de Allende. El título apunta a la voluntad de un banquero de no abandonar el país cuando muchos de su grupo socioeconómico y edad emigran ante la agresiva política del gobierno. Convencional en su estilo, narra desapasionadamente las tensiones de aquel proceso.

5482 Coloane, Francisco. Rastros del guanaco blanco. Santiago: Zig-Zag, 1980. 234 p.

Novela regionalista sobre el exterminio de los indígenas de Tierra del Fuego por la acción dominante de los colonos extranjeros.

5483 Cuentos chilenos contemporáneos. Santiago: Editorial Andrés Bello, 1981. 206 p. (Colección Biblioteca Andrés Bello)

Selección de cuentos presentada sin información ni talento. Tiene la novedad de recoger algunos nombres nuevos de la narrativa chilena.

5484 Donoso, José. Cuatro para Delfina. Barcelona: Seix Barral, 1982. 268 p. (Biblioteca breve; 612)

Donoso vuelve a cultivar el cuento o novela corta por primera vez después de *Tres novelitas burguesa* (ver *HLAS 36:4430*). Los cuatro relatos oscilan entre la crónica veraniega llena de resonancias locales y el cuento en que lo insólito postula la liberación de lo convencional y esclerosado. Una nueva expresión de la maestría del gran narrador chileno.

5485 Edwards, Jorge. El patio. 2a. ed. Santiago: Ediciones Ganymedes, 1980. 113 p. (Colección Ganymedes de poesia; 5)

Segunda edición del primer libro del autor (1952) seguida de un extenso prólogo de carácter autobiográfico.

5486 Edwards Bello, Joaquín. Cuentos y narraciones. Selección de Alfonso Calderón. Santiago: Editorial Nascimiento, 1980. 210 p.

Primera recolección de los cuentos y narraciones del gran cronista. Deja afuera el único cuento que había merecido antes un lugar en las antologías: "El Bandido."

5487 Hunneus, Cristián. Gaspar Ruiz: *El verano del ganadero.* Prólogo de Cristián Hunneus. Edición, diseño gráfico e ilustraciones, Oscar Gacitúa. Santiago: Ediciones del Camaleón, 1983. 69 p.: ill.

La novela propone una humorada en la línea de la "neoescritura." Gaspar Ruiz el presunto autor, es un personaje de la novela *El rincón de los niños* (ver *HLAS 44:5477*). El autor real, Hunneus, se reduce a presentar el relato con un prólogo en que fija su participación, reducida a eliminar la dedicatoria y a poner una distancia moral entre el narrador y el prologuista. Hunneus caracteriza el libro como obsceno y a su autor honesto en el espíritu de Henry Miller, por su llaneza de estilo, su fantasía para desinhibir toda represión moral y para dar expresión a una larga experiencia de la vida. La obra de Hunneus cumple con estos rasgos. Es su novela más espontánea y natural y la expresión de un libre y desinhibido erotismo. La narración adopta una modalidad autobiográfica que envuelve un breve lapso de tiempo y un escenario campesino y ganadero.

5488 Ostornol A., Antonio. El obsesivo mundo de Benjamín. Barcelona: Editorial Pomaire, 1982. 168 p. (Nueva Narrativa)

Segunda obra del autor. Benjamín Cruz rememora en forma autobiográfica obsesiones fundamentales de sus 42 años. Mudo y paralítico, una libreta es el medio de sus comunicaciones escritas, pero no contiene referencias sobre el acto de escritura misma. Erotismo, una herencia familiar violenta y funesta, crisis política, madre posesiva, distanciamiento del padre, son obsesiones recurrentes y progresivas de esta narración. Un discurso narrativo fluido elimina convenciones que delimitan los dichos de los personajes. El estilo es desigual pero fuerte y seguro. En esta obra se confirma el talento del joven novelista.

5489 ———. Los recodos del silencio. Santiago: Editorial Aconcagua, 1981. 257 p. (Colección Mistral)

Primera novela del joven escritor (n. Santiago, 1954). Confrontación de tiempos y destinos diferentes en los cuales los motivos de la dignidad y de la indignidad, de la comunicación y de la incomunicación predominan. Entre los elementos de información entran en juego los derivados del golpe militar y la decepción de las consignas políticas. Novela de nostalgia, de clima generacional y decepciones. Muestra a un nuevo autor aparentemente destinado a un lugar importante en la narrativa chilena.

5490 Prado, Pedro. Un juez rural: texto original completo. 2a. ed. Santiago: Editorial Andrés Bello, 1980. 137 p. (Colección Club de lectores; 14)

Segunda edición de la última novela del autor de Alsino (1920) y La reina de Rapa-Nui (1914). Se publicó por primera vez en 1924. Merecía una edición precedida de un estudio cuidadoso.

5491 Ruiz-Tagle, Carlos. El jardín de Gonzalo. Santiago: Editorial Acon-

cagua, 1982. 110 p. (Colección Mistral)

Cuentos que refieren y se destinan a la imaginación infantil, escritos con sencillez y humor.

5492 Skármeta, Antonio. La insurreción. Hanover, N.H.: Ediciones del Norte, 1982. 240 p.

El joven narrador chileno escribe sobre la etapa que precede a la revolución sandinista en Nicaragua. Los rasgos salientes del arte narrativo de Skármeta no parecen convenir al género largo y abigarrado que es la novela.

5493 ———. No pasó nada. Ilustraciones, Federico Aymá. Barcelona: Editorial Pomaire, 1980. 88 p.: ill.

Novela corta que narra desde el punto de vista autobiográfico una pequeña anécdota de agresividad adolescente, marcada con notas derivadas del exilio político y la existencia en mundo ajeno. Las peculiaridades lingüísticas y psicológicas son las notas salientes de la narración.

5494 Valdés, Hernán. A partir del fin. México: Ediciones Era, 1981. 252 p. (Biblioteca Era. Serie Claves)

Hernán Valdés (n. Santiago, 1934), poeta y novelista, tiene en ésta su tercera novela. Las anteriores Cuerpo creciente (1966) y Zoom (1971) le daban un lugar entre los novelistas de su generación. Sin embargo es su testimonio de Tejas verdes (1974) el que le brinda mayor atención y reconocimiento. La presente novela representa el mundo que comienza a partir del golpe militar. Envuelve principalmente a un personaje llamado Hache, simbólico del nombre del autor, de Hombre y de la sinécdoque usual que asocia una cualidad viril con la torpeza o la candidez. El protagonista denuncia la inautenticidad del proceso revolucionario de la Unidad Popular. Es la primera autocrítica de la izquierda al hueco retoricismo político de las actuaciones que se confrontan con el golpe: el discurso de Allende, el llamado a las armas y a la resistencia, el fracaso político. La narración se hace parcialmente en primera persona y en parte en tercera teniendo siempre como personaje a Hache, por lo general con omnisciencia selectiva fija en su interior. El capítulo inicial—retorno a un mundo matriarcal—y el capítulo XIII—elevación del volantín—tienen claras resonancias simbólicas, pero de dudosa eficacia. De entre las novelas de los acontecimientos políticos relacionados con el proceso chileno ésta es una de las más destacadas.

LITERARY CRITICISM AND HISTORY

5495 Concha, Jaime. En los aledaños de *El compadre*: sufrimiento e historia en Carlos Droguett (RCLL, 7:16, 1982, p. 77–99)

Excelente análisis interpretativo del sufrimiento como motivo y visión del mundo en la obra de Droguett, con una cuidadosa elaboración de los antecedentes literarios y filosóficos del mismo como categoría fundamental de la comprensión de la existencia humana.

5496 Guerra Cunningham, Lucía. Entrevista a María Luisa Bombal (IUP/HJ, 3:2, Spring 1982, p. 119–127)

Interesante entrevista que recoge datos biográficos y puntos de vista literarios de María Luisa Bombal. Algunos de ellos, contradicen ciertas interpretaciones excesivas de la crítica de su obra narrativa.

5497 Gutiérrez Mouat, Ricardo. La figura infantil en *Este domingo* y *Chattanooga Choochoo* (UA/REH, 16:2, mayo 1982, p. 223–239)

Detenido análisis de la "figura infantil" como papel desempeñado igualmente por personajes infantiles y adultos en la obra de José Donoso.

5498 Holt, Candace Kay. Voz narradora y estructura vertebrada en *El obsceno pájaro de la noche* (UCLA/M, 10:1/2, 1981, p. 33–42)

Análisis de la estructura contradictoria y flotante del narrador protagonista de la novela. Toma en consideración parte de la crítica previa sobre el tema.

5499 Joset, Jacques. El imposible boom de José Donoso (IILI/RI, 48:118/119, enero/junio 1982, p. 91–101)

Penetrante y acertado análisis de *Historia personal del boom*, de Donoso, que más allá de las reticiencias del novelista revela una visión histórico-literaria del *boom* y de sus compenentes. Discute la unidad, el proceso de cierre/apertura que describe, la

visión histórica y la comprensión de la institución literaria.

5500 Lastra, Pedro. Concepto y función de la literatura en Chile: 1920–1970 (Atenea [Revista de ciencia, arte y literatura, Universidad de Concepción, Chile] 446, 1982, p. 137–149)

Reseña histórica del concepto y función de la literatura del neoclasicismo al mundonovismo; y de la manera cómo su tradición afecta la literatura chilena e hispanoamericana de los años 20 a 70 del siglo XX.

5501 Mac Adam, Alfred J. José Donoso: *Casa de campo* (IILI/RI, 116/117, julio/dic. 1981, p. 257–263)

Proposición de varias lecturas contradictorias de la novela—entre ellas la más importante es la que ilustra la idea marxista de la propiedad privada y de la interdependencia de la riqueza y el proletariado. Las lecturas son alegóricas y desconfiadas de una interpretación ceñida del texto, aparentement, por inadvertencia de algunas citas y de ciertos contextos.

5502 Magnarelli, Sharon. The Baroque, the picaresque, and *El obsceno pájaro de la noche* by José Donoso (IUP/HJ, 2:2, Spring 1981, p. 81–93)

Excelente artículo que establece relaciones entre el barroco y el neobarroco y las ilustra con la novela picaresca y la obra de Donoso, respectivamente. El análisis considera varios niveles, pero principalmente el lenguaje figurativo y la elipsis en particular, entre las figuras.

5503 Martínez, Z. Nelly. *Casa de campo* de José Donoso: afán de descentralización y nostalgia de centro (HR, 50:4, Autumn 1982, p. 439–448)

Interesante artículo que aborda la novela desde el punto de vista de la producción textual como quehacer novelístico que se resuelve en el juego de un significar buscado y nunca cristalizado y de un texto que quiere ser todos los textos.

5504 Montero, Oscar. *El jardín de al lado*: la escritura y el fracaso del éxito (IILI/RI, 123/124, abril/sept. 1983, p. 449–467)

Excelente y bien meditado artículo que relaciona la *Historia personal del boom* y *El jardín de al lado*, como comentarios variados sobre el mito del éxito literario.

5505 Moreno, Fernando. Notas sobre la novela chilena actual (CH, 386, agosto 1982, p. 381–395)

Reseña de la producción novelística de los últimos diez años presentada en forma incompleta, superficial y no falta de contradicciones.

5506 Solotorevsky, Myrna. Fluidez y estatismo en *El obsceno pájaro de la noche* (Texto Crítico [Centro de Investigaciones Lingüístico-Literarias, Universidad Veracruzana, Veracruz, México] 5 : 15, oct./ dic. 1979, p. 193–208)

Excelente artículo que se concentra especialmente en la configuración del doble en la novela y en el modo cómo se regula por la tensión entre fluidez y estatismo en la representación del espacio social. Las tentativas de fluidificación de los límites de espacios estáticos se ven frustradas: no consiguen traspasarlos y quedan sólo en aspiración.

5507 Williams, Lorna V. *The shrouded woman*: marriage and its constraints in the fiction of María Luisa Bombal (LALR, 10 : 20, Spring/Summer 1982, p. 21–30)

Considera a la mujer en la narrativa de la Bombal como perteneciente al tipo general de una "amortajada," es decir, alguien sometido socialmente a los límites de su condición y en busca de una significación social y humana propia. Referencias principales a "La Amortajada," "La Ultima Niebla" y "El Arbol."

20th Century: Prose Fiction: River Plate Countries (Argentina, Paraguay and Uruguay)

EARL M. ALDRICH, JR., *Professor of Spanish, University of Wisconsin, Madison*
SAUL SOSNOWSKI, *Professor and Chairman, Department of Spanish and Portuguese, University of Maryland*

WITH FEW EXCEPTIONS the items of prose fiction reviewed here were published between 1980 and 1983. Every effort has been made to include those works which best represent the esthetic trends of the years in question. It is apparent that these novels and short narratives are much like those produced during the decade of the 1970s. Complex narrative strategies and a high level of abstraction continue to characterize a significant number of the works. Although conventional fiction with its underlying preconception of a common sense world is again represented, many of the novels and short stories are designed to confront the reader with exceptional orders of reality, sealing him off from familiar reference points.

The quality of the fiction is not consistently high but several novels and short story collections by Argentine writers are worthy of special note. Manuel Puig again demonstrates his unique mastery of narrative techniques in two novels: *Maldición eterna a quien lea estas páginas* (item **5543**) and *Sangre de amor correspondido* (item **5544**). Hugo Corra and Enrique Medina continue their relentless but arresting novelistic exploration of personal and societal degradation in *Contramarcha* (item **5517**) and *Las muecas del miedo* (item **5535**), respectively. Other meritorious novels are: *Escándalo bancario* (item **5515**) and *Después del escándalo* (item **5514**) by Silvina Bullrich and *¡Somos!* (item **5528**) by Eduardo Gudiño Kieffer. The short story genre is well represented by Marta Lynch's *Los años de fuego* (item **5533**) and Martha Mercader's *De mil amores* (item **5536**).

The quantity of Uruguayan fiction is up a bit but the quality remains generally low. Mario Benedetti's latest novel, *Primavera con una esquina rota* (item **5552**), is mentioned here only for bibliographical reasons. Unfortunately, it does not compare well to his previous works. Antonio Larreta's first novel, *Volavérunt* (item **5562**), is a provocative piece of historical fiction. Devotees of Felisberto Hernández will welcome *Nadie encendía las lámparas y otros cuentos* (item **5559**), a representative collection of his short fiction. [EMA]

The absence of readings of Borges is unimaginable in any review of Argentine literary criticism. In addition to the proliferation of footnotes and endless interviews (Macedonio would have appreciated this new "arte de la conversación"), the analysis offered by Arturo Echevarría (item **5580**) is a valuable addition, as is the growing presence of Mauthner as an influence on Borges' philosophical projections (María Rosa Lida de Malkiel's dictum on the subject must be recalled). A broader look at Borges' circle includes memories of Victoria Ocampo by the exquisite José Bianco (item **5571**) and Mujica Lánez's revealing sketches (item **5599**). The latter's death will certainly lead to a thorough review of his vast novels and the historical cycles he traced through Western civilization. While Borges' luminous presence may have cast a shadow on his contemporaries, it may lead to greater recognition of those who are not his precursors.

Latin America suffered irreplaceable losses with the deaths of Argentine writer Julio Cortázar—whose most recent publications include important contributions to the debate on the writer and society and to the issue of exile (item **5579**)—and Uruguayan critic Angel Rama. Each, within clearly defined spheres and discourses, contributed to the elucidation of literature's presence and its importance for an understanding of the hemisphere's history and traditions. Future studies will surely incorporate areas where their paths intersected, leading to diverse literary *and* political responses to current developments. In contrast to the state-imposed order and silent acquiescence of the past, there is now a wide divergence of opinion in Argentina, as exemplified by the following works: Gregorich's articles (item **5586**); Kovadloff's piece (item **5591**); Agosti's opinions (item **5569**); as well as readings of Arlt (item **5598**), Kordon (item **5606**), and Sábato (item **5608**); Viñas' continuing interest in the military (item **5613**); and texts on the polemic between Boedo and Florida (item **5572** and **5623a**). Anthologies published by Centro Editor de América Latina (items **5518, 5581, 5608,** and **5611**), and interest in "Boedo y Florida," already cited, attest to the persisting rivalry as well as to the continuing dialogue between opposites, in this case between *vanguardias* and traditional realist modes. In this respect, the literary pages of Groussac (item **5587**), Kamenszain's brief and probing insights, César Tiempo's recollections (item **5612**), and Martínez Estrada's presence also provide a wider perspective of literary developments, while scrutinizing recent intellectual legacies.

In Uruguay, Onetti is as major a figure for critics as Borges has proven to be in Argentina (items **5620** and **5622**). Benedetti's collection of critical essays (item **5003**) provides valuable ideological views of literature and a further understanding of his own fiction. The increasing attention that Cristina Peri Rossi earns is a justified recognition of her merits (items **5624** and **5625**). Felisberto Hernández, much like Macedonio Fernández, continues to elicit attention and to interest readers in realities that challenge preconceptions about established norms (item **5621**). A forthcoming issue of *Escritura* dedicated in its entirety to Felisberto, should prove to be as important as the Poitiers publication.

In spite of Roa Bastos' recognition as a paramount figure in contemporary Latin American letters, attention has not spread to other Paraguayan writers who deserve to be studied. Perhaps his own analysis (item **5617**) of Paraguay's position in the general literary context of Latin America, offers some answers to this situation.

Finally, one detects these trends in the last biennium: the prevailing attention to established writers, a growing concern with broad and complex literary issues, the examination of intellectual traditions, and the limited analysis of heretofore neglected or unknown authors. [SS]

PROSE FICTION
ARGENTINA

5508 Absatz, Cecilia. Té con canela. Buenos Aires: Editorial Sudamericana, 1982. 142 p. (Colección El espejo)

Narrator reveals her most intimate responses to people and life: obsessions, attitudes, and sensations are presented with irony and outrageous humor. In the end the reader is left with a caricature. [EMA]

5509 Aguinis, Marcos. El combate perpetuo. Buenos Aires: Editorial Planeta Argentina, 1981. 185 p.

Excellent historical novel which recreates the fascinating and significant role of naval warfare in the Wars of Independence with Spain and turbulent years which followed that struggle. Guillermo Brown, an English corsair, is work's protagonist. [EMA]

5510 Antología de cuentistas argentinos. La Plata, Argentina: Fondo Editorial Bonaerense, 1979. 613 p. (Colecciones antológicas del Fondo Editorial Bonaerense)

Anthology's avowed purpose is to present 67 representative selections from works of short story writers who are talented but have not yet achieved prominence. [EMA]

5511 Arlt, Roberto. Antología. Selección y prólogo de Noé Jitrik. México: Siglo Veintiuno Editores, 1980. 262 p.: bibl. (La Creación literaria)

Includes 12 selections chosen to illustrate points made by Jitrik in his concise and provocative introductory study. Useful for students of Arlt's work. [EMA]

5512 Asís, Jorge. El Buenos Aires de Oberdán Rocamora. Buenos Aires: Editorial Losada, 1981. 302 p. (Colección Prisma)

Collection of Asís' newspaper columns—in the tradition of Arlt's *Aguafuertes* (published in *Clarín*, 1976–80). Fascinating as social-cultural commentary of the times. [EMA]

5513 Borges, Jorge Luis. Páginas de Jorge Luis Borges. Seleccionadas por el autor. Estudio preliminar de Alicia Jurado. Buenos Aires: Editorial Celtia, 1982. 269 p.: bibl. (Colección Escritores argentinos de hoy)

Collection of representative short narratives, poetry, and essays selected by author. Prefatory essay by Jurado provides interesting commentary on selections. Especially useful for those with little or no previous knowledge of Borges' works. [EMA]

5514 Bullrich, Silvina. Después del escándalo. Buenos Aires: Emecé Editores, 1981. 285 p.

Logical continuation of *Escándalo bancario* (item **5515**). The reader is reintroduced to some characters from preceding novel as well as meeting new ones. Most effective is the study of the children who must cope with the moral and economic morass left by their parents. [EMA]

5515 ——. Escándalo bancario. Buenos Aires: Emecé Editores, 1980. 263 p. (Escritores argentinos)

This novel is a fascinating depiction of Mafia activity in Argentina. The murky, sometimes frantic machinations of the characters who seek desperately to legitimize themselves and to climb the social ladder are examined with acute psychological insight. Action culminates in 1980 crisis in Buenos Aires. [EMA]

5516 Carón, Carlos María. La majareta, o los 107 locos. Buenos Aires: Editorial Galerna, 1981. 201 p.

Outrageous humor characterizes this novel which is reminiscent of Filloy's works. [EMA]

5517 Corra, Hugo. Contramarcha. Buenos Aires: Corregidor, 1983. 274 p.

This novel provides an unusual insight into the alienated state of an exile who has returned to the fragmented society from which he had previously escaped. He remains an essentially tormented character incapable of defining his motivations or goals. [EMA]

5518 El Cuento argentino, 1930–1959: antología. v. 1, L. Gudiño Kramer, J.P. Sáenz y otros. v. 2, M. Booz, P. Rojas Paz y otros. v. 3, R. Arlt, J.L. Borges y otros. Editado por Marta Bustos y Eduardo Romano. Buenos Aires: Centro Editora de América Latina, 1981. 3 v.: bibl. (Capítulo. Biblioteca argentina fundamental; 77–78, 83)

Three-volume anthology presents helpful panorama of the rich and varied short story production during 1930–59. Brief introduction orients reader well to fictional trends during years in question. [EMA]

5519 Dal Masetto, Antonio. El ojo de la perdiz. Hanover, N.H.: Ediciones del Norte; New York: Ediciones Vitral, 1980. 214 p.

Trip to Bariloche provides setting for this novel of initiation in which young protagonist-narrator responds to series of life-shaping experiences. [EMA]

5520 Della Valle, Eric. El bache. Buenos Aires: Emecé Editores, 1981. 297 p. (Escritores argentinos)

Novel of raucous humor, mordant satire, and subtle irony in which foibles of the upper middle class and alienating character of bureaucracy are mercilessly examined. Winner of Premio Emecé 1980–81. [EMA]

5521 Diaconu, Alina. Enamorada del muro. Buenos Aires: Corregidor, 1981. 231 p. (Serie Mayor)

Conflicting emotions, rebellions, fears, frustrations, and initiatory experiences of an adolescent girl are the subject of this novel. [EMA]

5522 Estrázulas, Enrique. Lucifer ha llorado. Buenos Aires: Editorial Sudamericana, 1980. 245 p. (Colección El espejo)

Ambiguity, mystery, irrationality are relentlessly cultivated in this novel which is concerned basically with man's alienation. [EMA]

5523 Ghiano, Juan Carlos. Noticias más o menos sociales. Buenos Aires: Editorial Sudamericana, 1981. 180 p. (Colección El espejo)

Collection of 24 short stories in which author moves skillfully from world of immediate or common-sense reality into realm of mystery, unanswered questions, effects without causes. [EMA]

5524 Giacosa, Ana María. Viaje alrededor de mí misma. Buenos Aires: Editorial del Mar Dulce, 1982. 184 p. (Colección feminista)

Collection of ironic reflections and anecdotes about the experience of being a woman in a male-dominated society. [EMA]

5525 Giardinelli, Mempo. Vidas ejemplares. Hanover, N.H.: Ediciones del Norte; New York: Ediciones Vitral, 1982. 141 p.

Collection of 13 short stories which are rich in existential irony: the heroic act that leads to unnecessary and tragic consequences, the noble gesture which terminates in ignominy, etc. Plot is a prime element in these works which capture reader interest. [EMA]

5526 Gómez Bas, Joaquín. Suburbio. Dibujos del autor. Buenos Aires: Editorial Fraterna, 1982. 237 p.: ill.

After establishing the *suburbio*'s squalid setting, author presents 19 short narratives in which inhabitants' dreary, deprived, and sometimes tragic lives are depicted. [EMA]

5527 Gudiño Kieffer, Eduardo. Jaque a pa y ma. Buenos Aires: Emecé Editores, 1982. 107 p. (Escritores argentinos)

The questions and logic of children which confound adult wisdom provide material for this collection of delightfully humorous parent-child dialogues. [EMA]

5528 ———. ¿Somos? Buenos Aires: Emecé Editores, 1982. 221 p. (Escritores argentinos)

Skillfully varied narrative point-of-view depicts initiation process of adolescent boy who visits Buenos Aires with his father. The complex, intense, frequently painful relationship between the boy and his father and his father's girl friend is captured with extraordinary effectiveness. [EMA]

5529 Guido, Beatriz. Apasionados. Buenos Aires: Editorial Losada, 1982. 186 p.: ill. (Novelistas de nuestra época)

The two novelettes in this collection—the first one about a young woman in 1970s Buenos Aires and the second about Facundo Quiroga at the time of his Barranca Yaco journey—have as unifying element the skillful unfolding of powerful and irrational forces which possess and drive the protagonists to their destinies. [EMA]

5530 Jurado, Alicia. Los hechiceros de la tribu. Buenos Aires: Emecé Editores, 1981. 260 p. (Escritores argentinos)

Novel which describes the world of intellectuals, or more accurately, the world of pseudo-intellectuals. Ironic examination of the pretensions and faddishness of aspiring writers. [EMA]

5531 Kordon, Bernardo. El misterioso cocinero volador y otros relatos. Selección, presentación y noticia bibliográfica por Jorge B. Rivera. Buenos Aires: Centro Editor de América Latina, 1982. 129 p.: bibl. (Biblioteca argentina fundamental; 133)

Representative collection of short narratives by author whose contributions to Argentine fiction—especially his innovative works of the late 1930s and 1940s— have not been fully appreciated. Helpful introduction and bibliography. [EMA]

5532 Lugones, Leopoldo. Cuentos desconocidos. Compilación, estudio preliminar y notas de Pedro Luis Barcia. Buenos Aires: Ediciones del 80, 1982. 218 p.: bibl.

Previously uncollected 38 short stories which originally appeared in newspapers and magazines (1927–1938). Carefully done introduction will be helpful to those interested in Lugones' fiction. [EMA]

5533 Lynch, Marta. Los años de fuego. Buenos Aires: Editorial Sudamericana, 1980. 251 p. (Colección El espejo)

Collection of 14 short stories effectively continues Lynch's scrutiny of the interplay between the individual and unique forces of Argentine society. A few selections come perilously close to popularized fiction, but most reveal the author's special ability to develop character subtly and succinctly. [EMA]

5534 Masciángioli, Jorge. Atmósfera terrestre. Buenos Aires: Emecé Editores, 1982. 191 p. (Escritores argentinos)

Of 15 short stories, some are subtly ironic; others, notable for their wry humor, but all contain disturbing questions about the meaning of life. Uniformly excellent, provocative work by gifted writer. [EMA]

5535 Medina, Enrique. Las muecas del miedo. Buenos Aires: Editorial Galerna, 1981. 365 p.

Medina's seventh novel uses dialogue, stream of consciousness narrative, and snippets from newspapers, advertisements, and television programs to rivet the reader's attention on evils of present-day Argentine society. It is presented graphically, relentlessly as a decaying society caught between chaos and oppression. [EMA]

5536 Mercader, Martha. De mil amores. 2a. ed. Buenos Aires: Editorial Sudamericana, 1982. 284 p. (Colección El espejo)

Unusually varied collection of short stories which range from the humorous to mysterious. Stories are richly textured, resolving conflicts, reaching conclusions, and at same time provoking additional questions. Diversity and unity go hand in hand in selections, which are both independent and complementary of one another. [EMA]

5537 ———. Juanamanuela, mucha mujer. 2a. ed. Buenos Aires: Editorial Sudamericana, 1980. 449 p. (Colección El espejo)

Fascinating historical novel in which the author not only sheds light on her main character but on significant events of 19th-century Argentina. [EMA]

5538 Mujica Láinez, Manuel. Obras completas. v. 4, Los ídolos. La casa. Discurso en la Academia. Buenos Aires: Editorial Sudamericana, 1981. 1 v.: bibl.

Vol. 4 of Mujica Láinez's complete works contains Los ídolos and La casa, plus the text of an address given on the occasion of his entrance into the Academia Argentina de Letras. [EMA]

5539 ———. Páginas de Manuel Mujica Láinez. Seleccionadas por el autor. Estudio preliminar de Oscar Hermes Villordo. Buenos Aires: Editorial Celtia, 1982. 233 p.: bibl. (Colección Escritores argentinos de hoy)

Excerpts from author's journalistic and poetic works. Useful introductory study. [EMA]

5540 Olivera, Miguel Alfredo. Las décadas del Dr. Savignac. Buenos Aires: Emecé Editores, 1982. 218 p.: ill. (Escritores argentinos)

Narrator of this novel traces evolution of prominent Argentine family to which he belongs through series of significant episodes which cover 1898–1970. In so doing, he offers particular vantage point from which the historical era of Argentina could be interpreted. [EMA]

5541 Peralta, Renato. Cadena de la felicidad. Buenos Aires: Emecé Editores, 1982. 237 p.: ill. (Escritores argentinos: novelas, cuentos, relatos)

Life in 1930s tenement house as interpreted through eyes of a nine-year-old boy is subject of this novel. Sensitive psychological insights. Winner of Premio Emecé 1980–81. [EMA]

5542 Plager, Sylvia. Amigas. Buenos Aires: Editorial Galerna, 1982. 183 p.

In this novel fascinating psychological insights are given into personalities of four female protagonists. Their fears, frustrated aspirations, hopes, and pretenses are effectively presented through skillful manipulation of changing narrative point of view. [EMA]

5543 Puig, Manuel. Maldición eterna a quien lea estas páginas. Barcelona: Seix Barral, 1980. 278 p. (Nueva narrativa hispánica)

Warning conveyed in title of this novel is, to be sure, exaggerated. Nonetheless, work does advance devastating message of despair: the essential inability of man to communicate authentically with others or even to know himself. The theme is orchestrated by an ironic, brilliantly conceived series of character monologues and dialogues. [EMA]

5544 ——. Sangre de amor correspondido. Barcelona: Seix Barral, 1982. 208 p. (Nueva narrativa hispánica)

This novel is an extraordinary and sordid evocation of adolescent love in which Puig again demonstrates his unusual mastery of narrative strategies. As the evocation unfolds, the reader is given stark, often brutal insights into the human psyche. Fascinating questions regarding man's problematical relationship with his past are raised. [EMA]

5545 Sánchez Sorondo, Fernando. El corte. Buenos Aires: Editorial Sudamericana, 1981. 105 p. (Colección El espejo)

In the 10 stories, author captures with extraordinary sensitivity the torment of the loneliness, pressure of guilt, mixed emotions that accompany initiatory experiences of life. [EMA]

5546 ——. Risas y aplausos. Buenos Aires: Editorial Sudamericana, 1980. 188 p. (Colección El espejo)

First-person narrative of this novel plunges the reader into the emotionally-charged world of the adolescent who has discovered "love." A theme which has captured the imagination of many Latin American writers. [EMA]

5547 Svanascini, Osvaldo. Breves cuentos fantásticos. Buenos Aires: Emecé Editores, 1982. 241 p. (Escritores argentinos)

Collection of 30 short narratives which fit the classification of fantastic fiction. In each story creatures, characters, and other narrative elements are totally isolated from the world of common-sense reality. [EMA]

5548 Szichman, Mario. A las 20:25, la señora entró en la inmortalidad. Hanover, N.H.: Ediciones del Norte; New York: Ediciones Vitral, 1981. 292 p.

Extraordinary novel details in picaresque fashion attempts of a family of Jewish immigrants to blend into *porteño* society. The humor is at times black and at other times altogether delightful. Winner of Premio Norte 1981. [EMA]

5549 Torres, Ana María. ¿Qué le hicieron? Buenos Aires: Ediciones Agon, 1981. 135 p. (Colección Cuentos)

Persistent irony runs through these 24 short stories. Their characters— particularly the female protagonists—are opposed by rigid routines and oppressive expectations of a society which ultimately causes alienation. [EMA]

5550 Traba, Marta. Conversación al sur. México: Siglo Veintiuno Editores, 1981. 175 p. (La Creación literaria)

In this novel, Traba skillfully alternates the narrative point of a view in order to record the dialogue and interior monologue of two women of different generations. The psychological interplay of the women and their differing responses to a common political reality are effectively captured. [EMA]

5551 Weil, Clara. Una cruz para el judío y otros cuentos. Buenos Aires: Mantícora, 1982. 171 p. (Colección La Mirada en el tiempo)

Alienation is the dominating theme of these 17 short stories in which the author examines responses of immigrants to life's experiences. [EMA]

PROSE FICTION
URUGUAY

5552 Benedetti, Mario. Primavera con una esquina rota. México: Editorial Nueva Imagen, 1982. 239 p.

As a social realist with concern for narrative technique, Benedetti has produced fiction with both popular appeal and literary merit. Unfortunately, his latest novel, which details a political prisoner's life, does not enhance his reputation. His characters— either good revolutionaries or despicable non-revolutionaries—lack credibility as does the overly simplified presentation of ideas. [EMA]

5553 Blengio Brito, Raúl. El último hombre: novela. Montevideo: Ediciones de la Banda Oriental, 1982. 98 p.

In this narrative, which does not quite fall within either the category of novel or story, author comments ironically on man's inability to deal with life's basic questions. [EMA]

5554 Butazzoni, Fernando. La noche abierta. San José: Editorial Universitaria Centroamericana, 1982. 244 p. (Colección Séptimo día)

This novel—winner of Certamen Educa 1981—is a tedious examination of the loneliness and frustration of economically deprived people and the search for values and political activities of university students. The shifting narrative point of view is not effective. [EMA]

5555 Canobra, Amado. Gente de piedras y vientos. Montevideo: Acali Editorial, 1981. 157 p. (Colección Los premios novela: 1)

This novel, winner of the Concurso El Día-Acali, is an evocation of life in rural Uruguay. [EMA]

5556 Dabezies, Antonio M. El mudo Benítez. Montevideo: Acali Editorial, 1980. 104 p. (Colección Los premios Acali)

These 12 short narratives are remarkable for their outrageous humor. While each story is complete in itself, there is a thread which links them together. [EMA]

5557 Figueredo, Ricardo Leonel. Boca de barra: cuentos. Montevideo: Ediciones de la Banda Oriental, 1982. 86 p. (Los Libros del caballito. Segunda serie; 9).

Collection of 20 short narratives which depict effectively the starkness and deprivation associated with rural life. [EMA]

5558 Gerona, Magdalena. Las muertes repetidas. Montevideo: s.n., 1981. 81 p.

Death is the main concern of eight short narratives in this collection. Plot is secondary to the evocation of highly personal impressions and ambiguous concepts. [EMA]

5559 Hernández, Felisberto. Nadie encendía las lámparas y otros cuentos. Barcelona: Lumen, 1982. 164 p.

Welcome collection of Hernández's most representative short stories. They are prime examples of his highly imagistic style and his extraordinary attempts to challenge common-sense reality. [EMA]

5560 ———. Obras completas. v. 1–2. Introducción, ordenación y notas de José Pedro Díaz. Montevideo: Arca-Calicanto, 1981–1982. 2 v.

Annotated collection that includes some previously unpublished works. Brief but useful introduction. [EMA]

5561 Ipuche Riva, Rolina. El transeúnte. Montevideo: Paréntesis, 1982. 91 p.

Novelette provides interesting character study of protagonists whose attempts to escape loneliness, failure, and boredom are ultimately thwarted. Winner of Premio de la Intendencia Municipal de Montevideo 1982. [EMA]

5562 Larreta, Antonio. Volavérunt. Barcelona: Planeta, 1980. 261 p. (Colección Autores españoles e hispanoamericanos)

First novel by Larreta, Uruguayan dramatist of some note who lives in Spain, is a provocative piece of historical fiction. Author describes in well documented detail the political intrigue rampant in Spain just prior to the Napoleonic invasion, and at the same time subtly undercuts the very reliability of the historical accounts. [EMA]

5563 Mendive, Carlos L. Los rincones. Montevideo: Acali Editorial, 1982. 173 p. (Colección ABC del lector; 34)

In this collection of 60 short narratives, the author skillfully develops the poignant, sometimes mysterious implications of commonplace human experiences. [EMA]

5564 Núñez, Sandino A. Diverso y universo. Montevideo: Acali Editorial, 1980. 75 p.

Collection of eight narratives awarded first prize in short fiction category for 1980 by Acali Editorial. Young author of considerable promise writes in a manner reminiscent of Onetti, studiously limiting readers to the non-referential world of the text. [EMA]

5565 Paternain, Alejandro. Crónica del descubrimiento: novela. Prólogo, Alcides Abella. Montevideo: Ediciones de la Banda Oriental, 1980. 114 p. (Lectores de Banda Oriental; 30. Literatura uruguaya)

This novel is about "discovery"—the discovery of the New World. Only in this case, the discoverers are Indians from America and the discovered culture in Europe. Essentially an allegorical novel in which irony abounds. [EMA]

5566 Puppo, Julio César. Crónicas. Prólogo de Heber Raviolo. Montevideo: Ediciones de la Banda Oriental, 1982. 95 p. (Lectores de Banda Oriental. Segunda serie; 9)

Representative selection of *costumbrista* sketches by one of Uruguay's best chroniclers of Montevideo life. [EMA]

5567 Stefanovics, Tomás. El divorcio: cuentos. Montevideo: Ediciones Geminis, 1980. 242 p.

These 16 stories examine crises, misunderstandings, doubts, and pressures which cause the distintegration of human relationships. [EMA]

5568 Trece narradores uruguayos contemporáneos. Montevideo?: Cámara Uruguaya del Libro, 1981. 116 p.

Anthology consists of 13 prominent Uruguayan writers. Selections have not previously appeared in book form. [EMA]

LITERARY CRITICISM AND HISTORY
ARGENTINA

5569 Agosti, Héctor Pablo. Cantar opinando. Buenos Aires: Editorial Boedo, 1982. 134 p.

Más que lectura obligatoria y esclarecedora sobre autores tan diversos como Puig, Gerchunoff, Beatriz Guido, Torre Nilsson o Viñas, estos apuntes sirven para comprender rápidamente las posturas fijadas

(¿fijas?) de este estudioso de Ingenieros, Aníbal Ponce, Echevarría, Zola y de conocidas prosas políticas. [SS]

5570 Avellaneda, Andrés. El habla de la ideología: modos de réplica literaria en la Argentina contemporánea. Buenos Aires: Editorial Sudamericana, 1983. 207 p.: bibl.

En "Tiempo de Vivir y Tiempo de Escribir" estudia el significado e impacto del surgimiento del peronismo y el consiguiente debate cultural. En "El Uso de los Códigos" analiza textos de Borges y Bioy Casares y del temprano Cortázar articulando modos de réplica tendidos a lo largo de las formas policial y fantástica. Bajo "El Uso de la Alusión" estudia relatos de Martínez Estrada y Anderson Imbert. [SS]

5571 Bianco, José. Victoria (Vuelta [México] 5:53, abril 1981, p. 4–6, facsim., ill)

Homenaje del amigo y Secretario de Redacción de *Sur*, que recorre con admiración los recuerdos de esa mujer dueña de "tal poder de sugestión" que sin hacer gala de sus conocimientos era notable por su cultura y el buen gusto de su inteligencia. Ese "genio tutelar" de la Argentina sigue quedando bien con el sincero afecto de su círculo. [SS]

5572 Boedo y Florida. Selección, prólogo y notas por María Raquel Llagostera. Jorge Luis Borges et al. Buenos Aires: Centro Editora de América Latina, 1980. 175 p.: bibl. (Biblioteca argentina fundamental; 64)

Materiales y textos de autores que participaron en memorables polémicas literarias de la década del 20 bonaerense. Notables por el humor y diálogo con contrincantes reales y ficticios. Sus manifiestos harían coherentes muchas de esas declaraciones. Edición de divulgación general. [SS]

5573 Boldori, Rosa et al. Narrativa argentina del litoral: Greca, Castellani, Pisarello, Riestra, Saer, Gorodischer. Rosario: Grupo de Estudios Semáticos, 1981. 226 p. (Cuadernos Aletheia)

A pesar del regionalismo que marca el título, varios de los autores estudiados—especialmente Saer—ya han adquirido reconocimiento internacional. Estudios parciales que siguen lineamientos teóricos. Una sólida introducción general al territorio literario que comparten estos autores hubiera contribuido a su difusión y a una ubicación más precisa en la geografía de las letras. [SS]

5574 Borges, Jorge Luis. Borges at eighty: conversations. Edited and with photographs by Willis Barnstone. Bloomington: Indiana University Press, 1982. 176 p.

Incluye conversaciones grabadas en Indiana University, etc. (e.g., memorable charla con Dick Cavett). Borges a los 80 sigue aportando las curiosidades de la memoria y variantes de los recuerdos. Ante la sensación de la compañía grata y el desvanecimiento de las palabras, queda su comentario: "Remember that Swedenbog wrote that God gave us a brain so that we would have the capacity to forget." [SS]

5575 ———. Borges, el memorioso: conversaciones de Jorge Luis Borges con Antonio Carrizo. México: Fondo de Cultura Económica, 1982. 313 p. (Colección Tierra firme)

Diez entrevistas realizadas en 1979 (item **5574**) transmitidas por Radio Rivadavia, Buenos Aires, en el programa del locutor Antonio Carrizo. Borges vuelve a manejar sus temas, calles, personajes y pasajes favoritos. [SS]

5576 Cantraine, Philippe. Borges filósofo y la filosofía de la existencia: la conciencia, la existencia y el tiempo (Iberoromania [Max Niemeyer, Verlag, Tübingen, FDR] 16, 1982, p. 110–128)

Notando las ausencias filosóficas contemporáneas y la certidumbre única de Schopenhauer, "que admite el error porque el error es precioso," considera a Borges "uno de los últimos filósofos de la desesperación romántica y del pensamiento humanista adolecido por la enfermedad del absurdo," quien sigue jugando con la filosofía de su infancia, parte de las ocupaciones *gratuitas* del arte. [SS]

5577 Cavallari, Héctor M. Leopoldo Marechal: el espacio de los signos. Xalapa, México: Universidad Veracruzana, Centro de Investigaciones Lingüístico-Literarias, 1981. 165 p.

"El contorno de la obra marechaliana" sirve como conclusión para delinear etapas ideológicas que atravesara Marechal desde su "cristianismo metafísico" (ineludible en su poesía y en *Adán Buenosayres*) hasta la apertura a un humanismo más progresista. Resulta especialmente útil el muestrario de las fisuras por las que se insertarían algunos de los experimentos narrativos posteriores, tanto de Marechal (limitado ya en *Megafón*) como de sus seguidores. [SS]

5578 Cortázar, Julio. Discurso en la constitución del Jurado del Premio Literario Casa de las Américas 1980 (CDLA, 20:119, marzo/abril 1980, p. 2–8)

Texto central para una comprensión de la posición ideológica de Cortázar. Elabora, desde adentro, una postura *crítica* frente al desarrollo de la Revolución cubana a la vez que defiende los logros alcanzados. Amplia visión del abanico político latinoamericano y del lugar que la cultura y la educación deben ocupar en los caminos de la renovación social e individual. [SS]

5579 ———. The fellowship of exile (REVIEW, 30, Sept./Dec. 1981, p. 14–16)

Apuesta a las posibilidades de transformar la "cruel beca" de las dictaduras en experiencias enriquecedoras que inaugurarán nuevos horizontes de comprensión individual y continental para el día del retorno al país propio. Documento importante dentro de la polémica en torno a los exilados y su relación con los países de origen y la producción cultural nacional. [SS]

5580 Echavarría, Arturo. Lengua y literatura de Borges. Barcelona: Ariel, 1983. 238 p.: bibl. (Letras e ideas. Minor; 15)

Posiblemente el mejor texto sobre la fundamentación de la teoría literaria que surge de la obra de Borges y que la sustenta, luego de los estudios de Jaime Rest y Sylvia Molloy. Traza los nexos con la filosofía del lenguaje de Fritz Mauthner. Sólida coordinación de las múltiples referencias de Borges sobre este problema y dos excelentes capítulos "ilustrativos." [SS]

5581 El Ensayo argentino, 1930–1970: antología. Selección por Rodolfo A. Borello. Prólogo y notas por Juan Carlos Gentile. Aníbal Ponce *et al.* Buenos Aires: Centro Editor de América Latina, 1981. 126 p.: bibl. (Biblioteca argentina fundamental; 110)

Con un criterio muy amplio, recoge textos del "moderno ensayo de interpretación" de Aníbal Ponce, Héctor P. Agosti, H.A. Murena, Arturo Jauretche, Carlos Mastronardi, Juan José Sebreli y Julio y Rodolfo Irazusta. Fragmentos que marcan etapas de desencuentros ideológicos no siempre mantenidos dentro de los límites de la página escrita. Texto de divulgación general. [SS]

5582 Filer, Malva E. La novela y el diálogo de los textos: *Zama* de Antonio di Benedetto. México: Editorial Oasis, 1982. 113 p.: bibl. (Colección Alfonso Reyes; no. 1)

Suma de consideraciones teóricas y de los sub-textos que organizan *Zama*. Un aporte significativo a la escasa bibliografía de un autor que aun antes de *Zama* marcaba una tónica singular en la literatura del interior argentino. Inevitablemente el Asesor Letrado de di Benedetto iniciará un diálogo con los personajes de *Yo el Supremo*. [SS]

5583 Gai, Adam. Lo fantástico y su sombra: doble lectura de un texto de José Bianco (HISPA, 12 : 34/35, abril/agosto 1983, p. 35–50)

Lectura doble de *Sombras suele vestir*: apuesta a una definición de lo fantástico y a su cuestionamiento. Reflexión, a partir de Bianco, sobre la capacidad mimética de la ficción y de todo "ejercio crítico" que busca asir *un* sentido. [SS]

5584 García, Erica C. Marta Riquelme: ¿cargada criolla? (UH/RJ, 31, 1980, p. 364–382, bibl.)

Radiografía de un texto que cuestiona su propia escritura y que sabotea sistemáticamente toda "inferencia." Al quebrar el pacto tácito entre narrador y receptor sobre la coherencia interna del mundo narrado, inaugura los interrogantes sobre la coherencia misma de la referentes y sobre la fe posible en realidades verosímiles y creíbles. [SS]

5585 Garganigo, John F. Historia y fantasía en *El viaje de los siete demonios* de Mujica Láinez (EEHA/AEA, 36, 1979, p. 467–502)

Se estudia esta novela como continuación de un vasto proyecto paródico y satírico de los subtextos históricos sobre los que monta su andamiaje. Al relativizar la historia como versión ficticia se pasa a una ficcionalización de la realidad inmediata que resiste visiones subjetivas: análisis que queda por hacer con la obra de Mujica Láinez. [SS]

5586 Gregorich, Luis. Tierra de nadie: notas sobre literatura y política argentinas. Buenos Aires: Editorial Mariano Moreno, 1981. 169 p.: bibl.

Recoge trabajos publicados en diarios y revistas (1974–80). Ofrece un panorama fundamental para la comprensión de múltiples líneas desarrolladas durante el reciente embate militarista. Las tres partes del libro (artículos y notas sobre literatura; tres entrevistas; y notas sobre política, historia y vida social) documentan las múltiples actividades de Gregorich e inauguran un sano espacio polémico. Para los lectores no especializados en literatura argentina, la nota "Dos Décadas de Narrativa Argentina" (1978) será particularmente útil. [SS]

5587 Groussac, Paul. Jorge Luis Borges selecciona lo mejor de Paul Groussac. Buenos Aires: Editorial Fraterna, 1981. 1 v.: bibl.

No resulta ajeno decir que Borges haya creado a Groussac como precursor y que la "economía verbal" y la "probidad" que éste ansiaba hallaran su morada en su fundador. A pesar de su legendario "¿Qué puedo hacer yo en un país donde Lugones es un helenista?," las selecciones de *Del Plata al Niágara*, de *El viaje intelectual* y de su *Crítica literaria*, claramente demuestran su comercio con las palabras occidentales, aún con el mero español. [SS]

5588 Hahn, Oscar. Borges: de los meros simulacros a los coincidentes puntuales (UC/RCL, 18, nov. 1981, p. 121–129)

De las concepciones sobre el lenguaje que figuran en la obra de Borges, Hahn "intenta mostrar y describir aquellos aspectos de lo concepción mimética que redundan en la invención de esos artefactos borgianos que denomino 'coincidentes puntuales'." "Del Rigor de la Ciencia," "Funes el Memorioso" y "Pierre Menard, Autor del Quijote," contribuyen a formular una metáfora moderna de la obra literaria que quiere imponerse al mundo como entidad autónoma gracias al arte de la palabra. [SS]

5589 Huerga, Feliciano. Genio y figura de Jorge W. Abalos. Buenos Aires: Editorial Universitaria de Buenos Aires, 1981. 214 p.: bibl., ill. (Colección Genio y figura; 33)

Merecida presentación del autor de *Shunko* que hasta la fecha sólo sigue gozando de un reducido núcleo de lectores críticos locales. Teñida de amistad, la presentación es informativa. [SS]

5590 Isaacson, José. Macedonio Fernández, sus ideas políticas y estéticas. Buenos

Aires: Editorial de Belgrano, 1981. 125 p. (Colección Figuras contemporáneas)

Glosas de las "muchas lecciones" de Macedonio que con fluidez periodística y tonos de admiración servirán para una primera aproximación. La foto de la tapa—Macedonio pulsando una guitarra—no deja de ser un comentario feliz sobre páginas superfluas. [SS]

5591 Kovadloff, Santiago. Una cultura de catacumbas y otros ensayos. Buenos Aires: Botella al Mar, 1982. 102 p.

Reúne 15 ensayos publicados desde fines de la década pasada y un trabajo inédito, "Un Concepto Decisivo: el de Cultura Nacional." Las casi intemporales notas sobre filosofía, la precisión de sus lecturas poéticas y la bien calibrada organización de la mesura crítica, reflejan el conocimiento de este poeta, traductor y ensayista durante el reciente vértigo argentino. [SS]

5592 Latorre, Guillermo. Elementos de ciencia-ficción en los cuentos de Jorge Luis Borges (UCC/TL, 9, 1981, p. 95–107, bibl.)

Aunque Latorre restringe erróneamente el campo de la ciencia ficción en habla hispana a incursiones de Borges y Cortázar, soslayando múltiples contribuciones de otros autores, la relación de motivos "maravillosos o sobrenaturales" en Borges con los primeros cuentos de Wells y su posible camino paralelo a la evolución de la ciencia ficción, es válida al ampliar el radio de acción de lo especulativo, y al verlo como posible correlato con los nexos entre lo metafísico y teológico y lo ficticio. [SS]

5594 Levine, Suzanne Jill. Parody islands: two novels by Adolfo Bioy Casares (IUP/HJ, 4:2, 1983, p. 43–49)

Las novelas *La invención de Morel* (1940) y *Plan de evasión* (1945) son vistas como obras pioneras del renacimiento del barroco en la ficción latinoamericana y como síntesis de la tradición de obras utópicas. Discute filiaciones con *The Island of Doctor Moreau* (1896) de H.G. Wells y su sentido carnavalesco, que sigue las nociones de Bakhtine sobre la canibalización de todas las literaturas, su parodia y revitalización. Fragmento de *Guia de Bioy Casares* (Madrid: Fundamentos, 1982). [SS]

5595 McCraken, Ellen. Manuel Puig's *Heartbreak tango*: women and mass culture (LALR, 9:18, Spring/Summer 1981, p. 27–35)

Entre los múltiples aportes asignados a esta novela de Puig se encuentra la utilización de la cultura de masas como barómetro de una época y "unmasking the workings of mass culture of women." [SS]

5596 Masiello, Francine. Grotesques in Cortázar's fiction: toward a mode of signification (UK/KRQ, 29:1, 1982, p. 61–73)

Demuestra que el grotesco no sólo tiene como fin la incomodidad o el temor del lector, ni resulta de la incomprensión ante un mundo que desafía órdenes racionales, sino que cumple una función literaria que tiende a subvertir la coherencia temática y a centrarse en los artificios de la producción literaria. [SS]

5597 Medeiros, Paulina. Prefacio a "Felisberto Hernández y Yo" (CH, 374, agosto 1981, p. 322–343)

Testimonio por el que transitan la amistad, literatura, poetas y tristezas de nostalgias que recomponen figuras humanas y armazones de libros capitales para la narrativa latinoamericana. Recompone un nutrido epistolario (1943–48). [SS]

5598 Melis, Antonio. La deformación social y su reflejo en el cuerpo en un cuento de Roberto Artl (CH, 390, dic. 1982, p. 683–689)

Análisis de "Pequeños Propietarios," incluido en *El jorobadito* (1933). Melis analiza la obsesión de Arlt por la temática económica, degradación y sufrimiento que inflige al cuerpo individual y social de ciertos segmentos de las capas medias. Propone que la obsesión por lo económico se manifiesta a través de lacras físicas que dan cabida al triunfo de la "antinaturaleza" en la presencia frecuente de seres deformados. [SS]

5599 Mujica Láinez, Manuel. Los porteños. Buenos Aires: Ediciones Librería la Ciudad, 1980. 254 p.

Notas, esbozos, conferencias, prólogos, necrológicas, reflexiones (1939–79) que representan múltiples inquietudes del recientemente fallecido "porteño." Páginas selectas merecen ser ubicadas junto a lecturas memoriosas de Victoria Ocampo y recuerdos de Borges. [SS]

5600 Petit de Murat , Ulises. Borges, Buenos Aires. Buenos Aires: Municipalidad de la Ciudad de Buenos Aires, Secretaría de Cultura, 1980. 220 p.: ill.

Sería inútil exigirle a Ulyses Petit de Murat una presentación crítica analítica de Borges. Este es otro paseo, en este caso literal, por los rincones geográficos y culturales que Borges ha frecuentado a través de las décadas. El libro en sí es otra muestra de homenaje y de la transformación de Borges en producto de consumo público. [SS]

5601 Porras Collantes, Ernesto. Texto y subtexto de "Tlön, Uqbar, Orbis Tertius" de Jorge Luis Borges (ICC/T, 36:3, sept./dic. 1981, p. 464–526)

Expone "cómo la *narración* y la *descripción*, como categorías del Texto, son expresión de un contenido subtextual connotado en Tlön, Uqbar, Orbis Tertius." Lo hace meticulosa, agotadoramente, mostrando una lectura sistemática de la que se ausentan las propuestas mismas de Tlön. [SS]

5602 Prada Oropeza, Renato. El túnel: sentido y proyección (Texto Crítico [Centro de Investigaciones Lingüístico-Literarias, Universidad Veracruzana, Veracruz, México] 5:15, oct./dic. 1979, p. 7–22)

Analiza la "configuración discursiva" de El túnel y "la relación (valor) del texto en el contexto del sistema literario del narrador Sábato." Incorpora al estudio de la correlación semiótica de las relaciones sémicas, un nivel interpretativo que relaciona esta primera novela con *Sobre héroes y tumbas* y con *Abaddón el exterminador*. [SS]

5603 Puig, Manuel. Síntesis y análisis, cine y literatura (ECO, 42:5, marzo 1983, p. 483–488)

Testimonio de la realidad apetecible que saltaba desde la pantalla pampeana; del salto a Roma y a la vigencia del neorrealismo y de la transición a la novela: territorio que propone el encuentro del autor con el lector. [SS]

5604 Quiénes son los escritores argentinos. Buenos Aires: Ediciones Crisol, 1980. 206 p.: bibl.

La pregunta debió responder a los intereses personales y a los avatares del correo. Unos 600 escritores (de 4000 identificados) respondieron a un escueto cuestionario que los identifica a través de sus publicaciones. Util guía de direcciones y bibliografías mínimas; dudoso como panorama cultural. [SS]

5605 Rest, Jaime. El cuarto en el recoveco. Buenos Aires: Centro Editor de América Latina, 1982. 82 p. (Biblioteca argentina fundamental; 158. Serie complementaria Sociedad y cultura)

Homenaje póstumo (Rest m. 1979). Contiene ensayos sobre Sarmiento, Martínez Estrada, Arlt y Borges, que documentan su interés central por el ensayo como espacio discursivo de la literatura argentina. Si bien sus estudios sobre Borges perdurarán como máximos aportes, este libro, al igual que *Mundos de la imaginación* (Buenos Aires: Monte Avila, 1978), refleja sus capacidades plurales. [SS]

5606 Rivera, Jorge B. Bernardo Kordon: escorzo de un narrador argentino (CH, 398, agosto 1983, p. 372–385)

Panorama general de la obra de Kordon (n. Buenos Aires, 1915) que traza algunos de los motivos básicos del autor de *Vagabundo de Tombuctú* (1956), *Hacele bien a la gente* (1961) y *A punto de reventar* (1971). Uno de los mejores exponentes de la tradición realista que mantiene opciones abiertas a múltiples exploraciones. [SS]

5608 Sábato, Ernesto R. La robotización del hombre y otras páginas de ficción y reflexión. Selección y prólogo por Graciela Maturo. Buenos Aires: Centro Editor de América Latina, 1981. 162 p. (Capítulo; 91)

Este panorama antológico de Sábato cubre sus énfasis filosóficos, literarios, políticos y sociales. De la fina ironía de las páginas escritas "a la manera de . . ." a las obsesiones que publicara ya en *Uno y el universo* y *El túnel*, su imagen se perfila ante sus días conflictivos, vaivén incesante entre las superficies planas de la página y la calle. [SS]

5609 Shumway, Nicolás and Thomas Sant. The hedonic reader: literary theory in Jorge Luis Borges (LALR, 9:17, Fall/Winter 1980, p. 37–55)

Tras los comentarios de Borges negando una teoría literaria subyacente a sus comentarios críticos, estos autores reconocen "dos principios anárquicos: a relativistic notion of taste, and, what is even more radical, a relativistic theory of meaning." Registran la influencia de Mauthner. [SS]

5610 Siebenmann, Gustav. Ernesto Sábato y su postulado de una novela metafísica (IILI/RI, 48:118/119, enero/junio 1982, p. 289–302)

Consigna las dificultades a las que se enfrenta el lector de las novelas de Sábato—por "el modo de narrar complicado y deliberadamente enajenante que Sábato considera ineludible para su escritura." Son particularmente útiles las reflexiones sobre el acto de la lectura y la modelización de un nuevo pacto narrativo que surgiría de las novelas de Sábato. [SS]

5611 Sur: selección. Selección, prólogo y notas por Eduardo Paz Leston. Buenos Aires: Centro Editor de América Latina, 1981. 137 p.: bibl. (Biblioteca argentina fundamental; 106)

Muestrario breve de cuentos, poemas, ensayos, reseñas, crónicas teatrales y cinematográficas de la revista fundada en 1931 por Victoria Ocampo. Aun esta mínima selección alcanza a explicar la trascendencia y el impacto de Sur sobre la cultura argentina y sus alcances continentales. [SS]

5612 Tiempo, César. Manos de obra. Buenos Aires: Corregidor, 1980. 325 p. (Serie Mayor)

César Tiempo (n. Israel Zeitlin) partícipe de las múltiples polémicas literarias porteñas aporta estas notas periodísticas y recuerdos de figuras literarias que no siempre acapararon la atención de un público amplio ni el detenido escrutinio de los cronistas y críticos. Del primer sainetero a Sholem Aleijem, de Arlt a García Lorca, de Gerchunoff a Vallejo a Storni, Tiempo aceptaría la denominación de Guilherme Figuereido, "universal y porteño." [SS]

5613 Viñas, David. Indios, ejército y frontera. México: Siglo Veintiuno Editores, 1982. 326 p.: bibl. (Historia)

Como continuación de los intereses que desplegara en su obra narrativa, Viñas ha escrito una introducción a la campaña del desierto que dirigiera el Gen. Roca y a sus correlatos políticos e ideológicos. Etapa de la gran ilusión nacional que culminaría con los hombres del 80, tiene sus momentos previos en proyectos de conquista que van hacia la Patagonia y el Chaco. [SS]

PARAGUAY

5613a Barrett, Rafael. Barrett en Montevideo. Compilador, Vladimiro Muñoz. Montevideo: Imprenta García, 1982. 128 p.: ill.

Quizá el rigor bibliográfico atenuado por la devoción a la obra y la personalidad de Barrett, han llevado a V. Muñoz a omitir semblanzas bio-bibliográficas generales. Ofrece en cambio documentos personales, cartas a Peyrot, bibliografía de y sobre Barrett, y breve sección iconográfica del autor de El dolor paraguayo (editado por la Biblioteca Ayacucho con prólogo de Augusto Roa Bastos). Referencias indispensables para todo estudioso de la trayectoria de este intelectual paraguayo. [SS]

5614 Ferrer Agüero, Luis María. El universo narrativo de Augusto Roa Bastos (UCNSA/EP, 10:1, junio 1982, p. 21–104)

Sintetiza de la tesis doctoral homónima el apartado sobre el sustrato guaraní en Yo el supremo. Material esencialmente descriptivo de la obra más reciente de Roa Bastos. [SS]

Galbis, Ignacio R.M. Hugo Rodríguez-Alcalá: a bibliography, 1937–1981. See item **37.**

5615 Ospovat, Lev. El Supremo ante el juicio del lector (URSS/AL, 1[49], 1982, p. 87–107, ill.)

Insightful piece, in which the critic realizes that there is an identification between author and dictator that is at the core of Roa Bastos' masterful novel. [R. González Echevarría]

5616 Roa Bastos, Augusto. The exiles of the Paraguayan writer (REVIEW, 30, Sept./Dec. 1981, p. 17–20, plates)

Apuntes de Nueva sociedad (1978, número dedicado al exilio) en que Roa Bastos traza las múltiples tragedias a las que fue sometida la nación paraguaya desde la colonia (e.g., fragmentación geográfica y cultural, exilio "interno" y "externo," etc.). [SS]

5617 ——. La narrativa paraguaya en el contexto de la narrativa hispanoamericana actual (CPES/RPS, 19:54, mayo/agosto 1982, p. 7–20)

Polemiza con las proclamas de Carlos Fuentes sobre el alcance de la nueva literatura latinoamericana y rechaza el excesivo entusiasmo liberal que cifraba la liberación de Latinoamérica en sus letras. Rescata el nivel de la oralidad y la semantización de mitos persistentes para fundar una literatura anc101da en la realidad social e histórica. Ensayo que se perfila como parte de la reflexión que organiza una "poética" traducida fictivamente en los apuntes de Yo el Supremo. [SS]

URUGUAY

5618 Baccino Ponce de León, N. Brenda en el mundo narrativo de Eduardo Acevedo Díaz (UBN/R, 21, dic. 1981, p. 37–120, bibl.)
Intenta rescatar una obra aceptada como "débil" frente a la notoriedad de las novelas de su ciclo histórico, subrayando "los valores extraliterarios de la novela," y afianzándose en las intenciones didácticas que expusiera Acevedo Díaz. Lectura tradicional de ediciones y fuentes literarias e históricas. [SS]

Benedetti, Mario. El ejercicio del criterio: crítica literaria, 1950–1970. See item **5003.**

5620 Curiel, Fernando. Onetti: obra y calculado infortunio. México: Universidad Nacional Autónoma de México, Instituto de Investigaciones Filológicas, 1980. 252 p.: bibl.
Guía para lectores semi-iniciados. Integra apuntes bibliográficos de otros críticos y reflexiones no exentas del toque novelesco de Curiel. Los fragmentos que componen capítulos varios están animados por una "visión de conjunto," "absolutista," que a través del reportaje crítico lee la producción más reciente de Onetti en su temprana literatura. [SS]

5621 Felisberto Hernández, valoración crítica. Introducción, selección y bibliografía de Walter Rela. Textos de Elisa Rey et al. Montevideo: Editorial Ciencias, 1982. 137 p.: bibl.
En los textos reunidos aquí se pueden rastrear variantes de la glosa fácil al análisis pormenorizado al dato incisivo que justifica una página. No sorprende que se recuerden los pasajes de Italo Calvino, Cortázar y Onetti. Es útil la cronología de Felisberto (1902–64); la bibliografía merecerá revisiones con las próximas publicaciones en torno al autor de Las hortensias. [SS]

5621a Leante, César. Horacio Quiroga: el juicio del futuro (CH, 383, mayo 1982, p. 367–380)

Resalta las influencias de Poe, Kipling, Dostoievski y otros sobre quien, según Leante, diera origen al movimiento que se designa como "nativismo, narrativa de la tierra, indigenismo" y que tuviera como continuadores a Payró, Rivera, Amorim, Gallegos. Se ratifica el lugar de Quiroga como precursor de las letras contemporáneas y su triunfo sobre los contemporáneos que le habían vaticinado el silencio. [SS]

5622 Prego, Omar and **María Angélica Petit.** Juan Carlos Onetti o la salvación por la escritura. Alcobendas, Madrid: Sociedad General Española de Librería, 1981. 246 p.: bibl. (Colección Clásicos y modernos; no. 6)
Investigación realizada en París (1978–79) que contiene además un esbozo de datos biográficos, una entrevista a Onetti y una bibliografía sumaria. Vasto panorama que recorre la casi totalidad de la producción de Onetti analizando recursos narrativos y lanzando puntos de contacto con sus contemporáneos. Sólida introducción que rebasa lo sugerido por el título. [SS]

5623 Rama, Angel. Bibliografía sumaria: 1926–1983. Coordinador, Alvaro Barros-Lémez. College Park: University of Maryland, Department of Spanish and Portuguese, 1984. 31 p.: ill.
Edición de homenaje coordinada por su discípulo, con motivo de la trágica muerte del crítico uruguayo Angel Rama, profesor titular de literatura hispanoamericana de la Universidad de Maryland y Director Literario de la Biblioteca Ayacucho. Contiene secciones dedicadas a: "Ensayos, Artículos, Notas;" "Prólogos, Ediciones Críticas, Antologías;" "Participación en Volúmenes Colectivos" y "Libros y Colecciones de Ensayos." [SS]

5623a Rojas, Santiago. Enrique Amorim y el grupo de Boedo (RIB, 31:3, 1981, p. 378–384)
Amorim se acercaba más al grupo de Boedo en sus relatos rurales y a Florida en los urbanos. Su caso podría ser especialmente útil para estudios adicionales de los polemistas de Boedo y Florida. [SS]

5624 Sosnowski, Saúl. Los museos abandonados (SUR, 349, julio/dic. 1981, p. 147–155)
Los cuatro relatos publicados por Cristina Peri Rossi (n. 1941) en 1974 re-

cuperan motivos de la mitología clásica que son encuadrados en un sistema alegórico sobre el museo uruguayo que se desenmascara ante y con la violencia. [SS]

5625 Verani, Hugo J. Una experiencia de límites: la narrativa de Cristina Peri Rossi (IILI/RI, 48:118/119, enero/junio 1982, p. 303–316)

Ensayo de presentación de una de las figuras literarias más importantes de su generación. Tanto en su obra poética como en su narrativa, Peri Rossi ha marcado un lugar singular. [SS]

5626 Zum Felde, Alberto. Zum Felde, crítico militante. Editor, Uruguay Cor-

tazzo. Montevideo: Arca, 1981. 132 p.: bibl. (Documentos literarios)

Cubre el período 1919–29 que el propio Zum Felde, a partir de la práctica de la seria crítica periodística, "popular" y sistemática que ejerciera en el vespertino *El Día*, denominara "militante." Esos diez años significaron 843 artículos notables que incluyeron un panorama de la literatura uruguaya y una meticulosa atención a problemas de actualidad cultural que no rehuían la polémica ni la reflexión sobre el contexto amplio del cual surgía la actividad cultural. Valiosa publicación. [SS]

Poetry

RENE DE COSTA, *Professor of Spanish, University of Chicago*
MAGDALENA GARCIA PINTO, *Associate Professor of Spanish, University of Missouri*
JAIME GIORDANO, *Associate Professor of Spanish, State University of New York at Stony Brook*
OSCAR HAHN, *Professor of Spanish, University of Iowa*
NORMA KLAHN, *Assistant Professor of Spanish, Columbia University*
PEDRO LASTRA, *Professor of Spanish, State University of New York at Stony Brook*
JULIO ORTEGA, *Professor of Spanish, University of Texas, Austin*
RUBEN RIOS AVILA, *Assistant Professor of Spanish, University of Puerto Rico, Río Piedras*
GEORGE YUDICE, *Assistant Professor of Spanish, Emory University*

ANTHOLOGIES ARE A STAPLE of the genre. This period registers some novel thematic approaches including poems on motherhood (item **5627**), on revolution (item **5642**), poems by ill-fated revolutionaries (item **5652**), and by those who do not normally write poetry: the newly literate. Poetry workshops ("talleres de poesía") in Nicaragua have produced several interesting collections of verse by farmworkers and soldiers (items **5646** and **5647**) as well as a journal, *Poesía Libre* (item **5881**) which diffuses the art and ideas of these new poets. New and younger writers everywhere seem to be having greater access to print these days thanks to the proliferation of publicly sponsored series such as the Fundación Argentina para la Poesía (items **5644, 5657, 5703, 5710,** and **5774**) and Fundarte in Venezuela, which has brought out individual volumes and regional anthologies, mostly of new poets (items **5628, 5635,** and **5650**). Comprehensive anthologies of younger poets in Cuba (item **5649**) and Mexico (item **5640**) were complemented by an International Festival of Poetry in Morelia (item **5633**) which brought together new and established figures from North and South America. What is now called "poesía nueva" was consecrated by Manuel Ruano in an ambitious anthology (item **5638**) bringing together some 150 contemporaries of various tendencies. The traditional has also witnessed innovations, notably in Panama and Paraguay, with historically oriented anthologies revealing these countries' hitherto ignored women writers (items **5639** and **5655**).

Indeed, throughout the continent, one notes the appearance of significant new works by established women poets, most of which go beyond the usual themes of love and loss. Noteworthy in this sense are volumes by Bustamente (item **5679**), Ferré (item **5705**), Murillo (item **5743**), Orozco (item **5749**), Ramos (item **5762**), and Vitale (item **5782**).

The Caribbean area has been the focus of several major congresses devoted to Puerto Rican and Cuban literature (e.g., Lezama Lima, Poitiers, May 1982; Puerto Rico, Rutgers, April 1983; Caribbean Congress, Universidad Interamericana, May 1983). In Cuba, Martí continues to draw the most scholarly attention (see the LITERATURE: 19th CENTURY section of this volume), while there is a growing interest in Lezama and the poets of *Orígenes*, with continued attention to established figures such as Guillén.

Central America, in the midst of its political turmoil and social change, is witnessing a cultural explosion of considerable magnitude. New poets, new publications, and increasing critical attention to the literary tradition of the area are apparent. Despite the fact that there are no major publishing houses in the region, new books and journals are appearing, most being sponsored by governments and universities. Notable in this vein are the activities of the Ministry of Culture in Nicaragua, with its journals (items **5650, 5866,** and **5881**) and poetry workshops.

Despite the financial crisis in Mexico, publishing there seems unabated with new houses like Katún, Oasis, and Premiá bringing out younger authors, while the established presses continue to republish or reedit items with a more assured market. Fondo de Cultura Económica continues its valuable reprint series of important literary reviews of the past, such as *Taller* and *Taller Poético* (items **5884** and **5885**), while contemporary journals such as *Casa del Tiempo, Diálogos, Plural,* and *Vuelta* continue to devote considerable space to poetry and poetics. In 1982 and 1983, the prestigious Premio Nacional went to Elías Nandino and Jaime Sabines, recognizing the importance of these figures in the post-vanguard period. Another major poet of this generation, Rubén Bonifaz Nuño, was also the object of homage on the occasion of the appearance of his *Antología personal* (item **5674**). New works by somewhat younger established figures like Pacheco and Aridjis (items **5662** and **5752**) show a continuing evolution and development. Of major importance now, and probably for years to come, is Sandro Cohen's anthology of "new poets," *Palabra nueva* (item **5640**) which picks up where *Poesía en movimiento* left off some 20 years ago, with poets born after 1940.

In Venezuela and Colombia, there are important collections of scattered prose and new studies of major poets like León de Greiff (item **5713**) Ramos Sucre (items **5849** and **5881a**), and Andrés Eloy Blanco (item **5846**). Of significant importance in the region is the journal *Eco* which continues to exercise a leadership role in criticism and the diffusion of new literary values. Pioneering studies of the avant-garde movement in Venezuela and Colombia (items **5805, 5806,** and **5810**) seem to be part of a general trend of discovery and reassessment of the phenomenon in the less metropolitan areas of the continent, including Paraguay, Uruguay, and Nicaragua (items **5808, 5809** and **5866**).

In Ecuador, an important round-table discussion devoted to the current situation of literature there (item **5813**) was sponsored by El Conejo, a new publisher with plans to bring out attractive editions of contemporary writers. Also noteworthy is a carefully documented edition of the complete poetry of Jorge Carrera Andrade, which is supplemented by bibliographic information regarding other writings by and about this important writer-diplomat (item **5682**).

In Bolivia, special mention should be made of an unusually comprehensive tri-lingual anthology including poetry in Quechua and Aymara (item **5641**). Peru's economic crisis has seriously curtailed publishing activities there, yet Mosca Azul continues to bring out the best of the country's new writing, although in extremely limited editions of some 500 copies. *Hueso Húmero*, a journal of the same house, devotes considerable attention to poetry, criticism, and articles on the current cul-tural situation. The *Revista de Crítica Literaria Latinoamericana*, ably directed by Antonio Cornejo Polar, is based in Lima and contains several thought-provoking articles on the concept and character of the avant-garde in the Americas (items **5799** and **5806**). These articles are really part of a much larger and as yet unannounced debate seeking to formulate a new concept of the movement which is less Euro-centric, giving more importance to local and indigenous elements (items **5804, 5810** and **5811**).

In Chile, the lifting of indirect censorship has made possible the circulation of books and magazines which were previously suppressed, such as Hahn's *Mal de amor* (see *HLAS 44:5692*) and, more importantly, has loosened up self-censorship. One consequence was Enrique Lihn's outspoken *El Paseo Ahumada* (item **5725**) whose public presentation in the mall of its title resulted in the poet's arrest. A series of poetry recitals sponsored by the Instituto Chileno-Norteamericano was similarly aborted. Nevertheless, publishing activity is picking up and several neo-vanguard periodicals have appeared of which *Hojo X Ojo* and *La Castaña* are most directly concerned with novel trends in poetry. One interesting new direction seems to derive from the cross-fertilization of video arts and poetry, with Raúl Zurita as its leading figure (see *HLAS 44:5759*). His latest book, *Anteparaíso* (item **5787**), pro-voked a lively debate after *El Mercurio's* officious critic (Ignacio Valente) classed him among the giants of Chilean literature along with Mistral, Huidobro, and Neruda.

Argentina is witnessing something of a publishing boom, with new editions of previously suppressed works and considerable promotion of younger authors. Sev-eral important anthologies have appeared (items **5643, 5644,** and **5648**), along with the revival and expansion of Centro Editor's *Capítulo* (item **5865**) devoted to the mass promotion of basic books at a modest price. Collected works of major fig-ures like Almafuerte and Mastronardi (items **5656** and **5731**) are complemented by scholarly compilations of the diverse prose writings of Pizarnik (item **5880**). Out-standing among the new critical works are a sensitive study of Ultraism and several reassessments of poets by poets: Borges on Lugones (item **5728**), and Girri on William Carlos Williams (item **5871**). New volumes and important collections of the work of Argentina's best women poets have appeared: Nira Etchenique (item **5698**), Ruth Fernández (item **5703**), and Olga Orozco (items **5749** and **5750**). Interestingly enough, this trends seems to coincide with the more limited publishing activities in Uru-guay and Paraguay where collections of Ibarbarourou (item **5718**) and Plá (items **5759** and **5760**) are complemented by new volumes of Idea Vilariño (item **5781**) and Ida Vitale (item **5782**).

In conclusion, poetry during this period seems to show a healthy rostrum; criti-cism reveals a balance of interests throughout the continent with reassessments of Modernism (item **5802**) as well as the avant-garde, along with attention to new voices and new directions. [RdC]

ANTHOLOGIES

5627 A la madre: poemas. Elegidos por María Elena Walsh. Ilustraciones de María Cristina Brusca. Buenos Aires: Editorial Sudamericana, 1981. 185 p.: ill.

M.E. Walsh (n. 1930), entre los mejores representantes de la generación del 50, ha encontrado rico material sobre un tema que prejuicios devenidos de la mala literatura pueden haber desprestigiado. El hecho es que los mejores poetas argentinos de todos los tiempos han abordado el tema con sinceridad y buena poesía. El resultado es una "canción de gesta:" 88 poemas que consuman una auténtica reivindicación. [JG]

5628 Aldaba en vivo: antología de jóvenes poetas—Aragua, Carabobo, Miranda. Selección, José Napoleón Oropeza. Caracas: Dirección General de Cultura: FUNDARTE, 1978. 111 p. (Cuadernos de difusión. Presencia cultural de los estados)

Una de las mejores muestras regionales de la serie iniciada por FUNDARTE. En su prólogo (p. 9–23), Oropeza explica la inclusión de poetas establecidos (Montejo, Tortolero, Ovalles) como "inmediata referencia frente a los nombres de las generaciones más recientes:" Luis Alberto Angulo, Luiz Azócar Granadillo, Elí Galindo, Jaime López Sanz, Francisco Martínez Liccioni, Enrique Mujica, Carlos Ochoa, Alejandro Oliveros, Reynaldo Pérez Só y Rafael Humberto Ramos Giugni. [PL]

5629 Antología de la poesía modernista. Selección, Antonio Fernández Molina. Madrid: Júcar, 1981. 269 p.: ill., ports (Los Poetas; 35)

Abanico de textos mayores y menores de unos 50 poetas con un orientador estudio preliminar sobre el movimiento como fenómeno epocal prendido en América y extendido a España. La escueta documentación bibliográfica es suplementada en parte por la iconografía (fotos de escritores y portadas de ediciones). Se destaca por su amplitud de criterio que coloca a Ricardo Gil y a Carlos Pezoa Véliz al lado de los grandes como Darío y J.R. Jiménez. [RdC]

5630 Antología de poesía puertorriqueña 1982. Selección y prólogo de Manuel de la Puebla y Marcos Reyes Dávila. Río Piedras, P.R.: Editorial Cultural, 1983. 156 p.: ill.

Muestra, más generosa que selectiva, de algunos poemas sacados de los 51 libros de poesía publicados en Puerto Rico en 1982. Testimonio del auge extraordinario del género en la isla, y algunas selecciones (e.g., Francisco Matos Paoli, Rosario Ferré, Angela María Dávila) sobresalen claramente. [RRA]

5631 Cinco poetas hondureños. Selección y prólogo de Hernán Antonio Bermúdez. Tegucigalpa: Editorial Guaymuras, 1981. 102 p. (Colección Salamandra)

Antología indispensable para conocer las direcciones estéticas de una nueva generación poética. En la introducción se explica que surge al impacto de la nueva situación política centroamericana y que se procura elaborar un riguroso trabajo con el lenguaje que "se aparta de la expresión . . . panfletaria que está de moda." Predominan dos tendencias: 1) la expresión despojada de Rigoberto Paredes (n. 1948) y Horacio Castellanos Moya (n. 1957); y 2) la palabra órfica de José Luis Quesada (n. 1948) y Ricardo Maldonado (n. 1949), con Alexis Ramírez a caballo entre ambos extremos. [GY]

5632 Fajardo, Miguel and Miguel Alvarado. Estación del asedio [de] Miguel Fajardo. Insurrección de las cosas [de] Miguel Alvarado. San José: Editorial Costa Rica, 1981. 165 p. (Colección Joven creación; no. 8)

Fajardo: Su poesía surge como transgresión al "silencio cómplice" y búsqueda de la paz. Se compromete con la revolución, pero la de la palabra. Alvarado: En contraste, su poesía se funda en la lucha revolucionaria. Es sobre todo poeta irónico que resalta las contradicciones del oficio mismo de ser poeta. [GY]

5633 Festival Internacional de Poesía, 1st, Morelia, México, 1981. Antología. Edición, selección y notas de Homero Aridjis. México: J. Mortiz, 1982. 469 p.: ill.

Selección de poemas leídos por poetas que concurrieron al Primer Festival Internacional de Poesía, que se llevó a cabo en Morelia. Participaron 37 poetas mexicanos (e.g., Aridjis, Bañuelos, Chumacero, Labastida, Montemayor, Montes de Oca, E. Nandino, Alberto Blanco, Coral Bracho, S. Cohen, V. Volkow) y 28 poetas de distintas nacionalidades (e.g., Borges, E. de Andrade, Cuadra, Ida Vitale, Allen Ginsberg, Cintio Vitier, Günter Grass, W.S. Merwin). Interesantes fotografías (72 p.) tomadas durante el festival completan el libro. [NK]

5634 Indice antológico de la poesía sal-vadoreña. Selección, prólogo y notas de David Escobar Galindo. San Salvador: UCA Editores, 1982. 767 p. (Colección Gavidia. Serie mayor; v. 2)

El texto más importante para conocer la poesía salvadoreña. Valiosa "nota preliminar" puntualiza: 1) que los poetas no suelen agruparse en escuelas ni tendencias; 2) prevalecen individuos; y 3) se cultiva una escritura multifacética, asimilando tendencias varias. No obstante, hay dos propensiones que originan en Gavidia: la metafísica/existencialista y la marcadamente ideológica. El rasgo más destacado, según Escobar, es la marginalidad, no sólo a escala global sino en Latinoamérica misma. [GY]

5635 Jóvenes poetas de Lara y Yaracuy: "raza común de adoloridos." Introducción, selección de poemas y notas bio-bibliográficas, Ramón Querales. Caracas: FUNDARTE, 1980. 142 p. (Serie Presencia cultural de los estados; no. 6)

Textos de 25 poetas pertenecientes a las últimas promociones, nacidos en la región o vinculados a ella (ver item **5650**). La muestra es meritoria, aunque no aporta mayores revelaciones. Los poemas de Luis Alberto Crespo (n. 1941) y de Alvaro Montero (n. 1946) sobresalen en el conjunto de manera notoria. [PL]

5636 Lírica ecuatoriana contemporánea. Compilación de Hernán Rodríguez Castelo. Quito: Círculo de Lectores, 1979. 2 v. (731 p.): indexes.

Uno de los críticos más conocidos de Ecuador, Rodríguez Castelo emprende la dilatada tarea de antologar la poesía contemporánea de su país a partir de César Dávila Andrade (n. 1918) hasta Mariana Cristina García (n. 1951), alrededor de 80 poetas. Presenta a cada uno con información bibliográfica y opinión crítica. Más que antología es una muestra ecléctica. Aunque hubiese sido preferible una selección más estricta, y más poemas por poeta seleccionado, tiene la virtud del panorama necesario para el juicio posterior. [JO]

5637 El Modernismo poético en el Paraguay, 1901–1916: antología. Edición, introducción, bibliografía, cronología y notas de

Raúl Amaral. Asunción: Alcándara, 1982. 188 p.: ill. (Colección Poesía; 5)

Edición corregida y aumentada (1a., 1973). Incluye ensayo importante, aunque breve, para la historiografía del modernismo latinoamericano. Propone una periodización y da información acerca de revistas difusoras del movimiento. Incluye varios documentos inéditos, muestra antológica representativa de cada período, poemas en inglés y francés (Poe y Casabianca) más valiosa bibliografía. [MGP]

5638 Muestra de la poesía nueva latino-americana. Selección, Manuel Ruano. Lima: Ediciones El Gallinazo, 1981. 268 p.

Muestrario breve, ambicioso y útil de más de 150 poetas "nuevos" en selecciones representativas abarcando los intentos más diversos de los últimos años (exteriorismo, concretismo, nadaísmo, anti-poesía, poesía en movimiento, poesía crítica, poesía social, etc.). Apéndice ("Datos para un Fichero Personal") ofrece relevantes datos biográficos y juicios cándidos de Ruano sobre los autores antologizados. [RdC]

5639 La Mujer y la poesía en Panamá. Panamá: Ediciones INAC, 1977. 196 p.: bibl. (Colección Dabiabe)

Primera muestra de la poesía femenina panameña, representa 18 poetas e incluye breves notas biobibliográficas. [GY]

5640 Palabra nueva: dos décadas de poesía en México. Compilación, prólogo y notas de Sandro Cohen. México: Premiá Editora, 1981. 355 p. (Libros del bicho; 20)

Valiosa antología que recoge lo más representativo de esta generación de poetas mexicanos (n. 1940–58). Incluye a la "generación perdida," quienes por sus fechas de nacimiento no aparecieron ni en *Poesía en movimiento* que termina con Aridjis (n. 1940), ni en *Asamblea de poetas* que reúne poetas n. 1950 en adelante. Prólogo y notas que preceden las selecciones son informativos y orientadores. [NK]

5641 Panorama de la poesía boliviana: reseña y antología. Selección y notas, Luis Ramiro Beltrán S. Bogotá: Secretaría Ejecutiva Permanente del Convenio Andrés Bello, 1982. 708 p.: bibl., ill. (*Cuadernos Culturales Andinos*; 3:4)

Amplia visión de la poesía boliviana. Incluye épocas precolombina, colonial y republicana; en aymara, quechua y español. Las complementa con nota de referencia a la evolución de las culturas originadoras de la poesía, y con útil bibliografía tanto de obras literarias y poéticas como de obras de referencia al contexto político, económico y cultural. [A.R. Prada]

5642 Para el combate y la esperanza: poesía política en El Salvador. Introducción y selección de Esther María Osses. Santo Domingo: Editora Taller, 1982. 188 p.: bibl., ill.

Selección de poesía política salvadoreña contextualizada por testimonios, artículos periodísticos, comunicados, boletines, informes sobre violaciones de derechos humanos, etc. La aqueja un desequilibrio que otorga a Dalton la tercera parte del espacio mientras que a otros se les permite uno o dos poemas. La introducción, en contraste, es de gran valor. [GY]

5643 Poesía argentina contemporánea. Buenos Aires: Fundación Argentina para la Poesía, 1978–1980. 6 v.: bibl.

Una de las selecciones más comprehensivas de poesía argentina contemporánea. Aunque consta de seis gruesos tomos y 49 poetas representados, los volúmenes se hacen atractivos por la claridad de la diagramación y la abundancia y representatividad de los textos con que se representa a cada poeta. La palabra "contemporáneo" se usa aquí en un sentido más estricto, pues se excluye a la generación del 22. Las generaciones del 40 y del 60 están adecuadamente representadas. [JG]

5644 Poesía argentina del siglo XX: antología. Selección introducción, notas y propuestas de trabajo, Delfina Muschietti. Buenos Aires: Ediciones Colihue, 1981. 166 p.: bibl., ill. (Colección Literaria LYC [Leer y Crear])

Excelente manual para estudiantes. Contiene cronología que, aunque inevitablemente incompleta, resultará informativa para el lector no argentino. Introducción, dividida en "Evolución Histórica" y "Estructuras," posee claridad didáctica y adecuado ordenamiento de corrientes y tendencias. La selección (desde Lugones hasta Pizarnik) es funcional y de eficacia pedagógica. [JG]

5645 Poesía boliviana, siglos XIX y XX. De acuerdo con el Programa de Lenguaje y Literatura del Ciclo Medio, autorizado por el Departamento Nacional de Curriculum del Ministerio de Educación. Selección, Armando Soriano Badani y Julio de la Vega. La Paz: Ultima Hora, 1982. 246 p.: bibl., ports (Biblioteca popular boliviana de Ultima Hora)

Antología y reseña de intención didáctica que reune tanto a poetas incluidos en los programas de enseñanza escolar como a algunos novísimos creadores. Obra concisa y útil para básica referencia. [A.R. Prada]

5646 Poesía campesina de Solentiname. Selección y prólogo de Mayra Jiménez. Managua: Ministerio de Cultura, 1980. 187 p. (Colección popular de literatura nicaragüense; no. 4)

En 1976–77 Jiménez condujo un taller de poesía en Solentiname. Se trata de hacer disponible la palabra poética a las inmensas mayorías excluidas en el sistema poético culto. A pesar de que se dice que la poesía surgió "natural" y "espontáneamente" no deja de reconocerse la estética-ética exteriorista cultivada por Cardenal. Hasta tal extremo que los 23 poetas parecen confundirse en una misma voz. Predominan los temas amorosos, nostálgicos, cotidianos y guerrilleros. [GY]

5647 Poesía de las fuerzas armadas: de los talleres de poesía. Managua: Ministerio de Cultura, 1981. 24 p.

Se oye una voz colectiva que encarna un estilo llano que comenta las aspiraciones, los sentimientos y los quehaceres cotidianos. Desde un *hic et nunc* casi obligatorio estos poetas-soldados cantan—"prosan"—la pérdida de amantes y compañeros/as; el estudio; la alfabetización. Los mejores poemas recuerdan los sucintos epigramas de Catulo. [GY]

5648 Poesía de un tiempo indigente. Compilación y coordinación, Luis Alberto Ballester, Rogelio Bazán y Carlos Velazco. Introducción, Guillermo Ara. Buenos Aires: Plus Ultra, 1981. 196 p.

Incluye poetas de las tres últimas décadas. Un libro estéticamente coherente, actual y sugestivo, dirigido a un lector comprometido con los valores existenciales de la poesía. El hermoso prólogo de Guillermo Ara apunta hacia la interpretación de los textos como expresión de la indigencia: "la propia y la ajena." [JG]

5649 Poesía joven. La Habana: Editorial Letras Cubanas, 1980. 237 p. (Pluma en ristre)

Valiosa recopilación de una muestra de la obra de 33 poetas jóvenes entregados a la poesía y a la Revolución. Sorprenden más el entusiasmo y el optimismo que la depuración o perfección formal de los poemas. [RRA]

5650 La Poesía larense. Selección de Guillermo Morón y Hermann Garmendia. Selección de los poetas más nuevos por Pascual Venegas Filardo. Prólogo de Hermann Garmendia. Nota a la segunda edición de Pascual Venegas Filardo. 2a. ed. Caracas: Ediciones de la Presidencia de la República, 1982. 448 p.: bibl. (Biblioteca de autores larenses; 4)

Se reedita el vasto e irregular panorama de la producción poética del Estado Lara publicado en 1951: muestras de 62 poetas, desde el romántico Simón Escovar (1840–88) a Francisco José Escalona Romero (n. 1910). La adición de 17 poetas aparecidos con posterioridad sigue de cerca el trabajo antológico de Ramón Querales (ver item **5635**). Interés estrictamente local. [PL]

5651 Poesía panameña contemporánea, 1929–1979. Selección, prólogo y notas de Enrique Jaramillo Levi. México: Liberta-Sumaria, 1980. 339 p.: bibl. (Colección Continente; no. 4)

Compilación panorámica de 69 poetas desde la vanguardia hasta el presente. La introducción señala direcciones de la poesía panameña haciendo hincapié en el tema del enclave canalero, de repercusiones literarias. Incluye breves notas biobibliográficas y buenas bibliografía y hemerografía. [GY]

5652 Poesía trunca. Selección y prólogo de Mario Benedetti. 2a. ed. Madrid: Visor, 1980. 462 p. (Colección Visor de poesía; 97)

Antología/homenaje a 27 poetas muertos en diferentes momentos de la lucha revolucionaria en Latinoamérica. Selección y prólogo de Mario Benedetti incluye tres grupos: poetas de obra madura (Dalton, Castillo, Viau, Urondo y Jara); poetas más jóvenes, menos conocidos en el ámbito literario (Heraud, Obregón, Rugama, Morales, Gutiérrez, Lescouflair, Tello); y una muestra de poemas sueltos de jóvenes cuya actuación política excede en importacia a la literaria (Pais, Carlos Marighella, Gabaldón, López

Pérez, Valdivia, Ertl, Gómez-Lubián, Gómez García, Sá Brito, Salerno). Excelente muestra y contribución al género de poesía política. [MGP]

5653 Poetas parnasianos de Venezuela. Compilación, selección, prólogo y notas de Pedro Antonio Vásquez. Caracas: Presidencia de la República, 1982. 189 p.: bibl., ill. (Biblioteca de autores y temas yaracuyanos; 4)

Aunque la mayor parte de los poemas no es memorable, este libro documenta un fenómeno interesante: las repercusiones de un movimiento cuyos "postulados de equilibrio, de disciplina, de austeridad formal [contrarrestaban] la incuria de la expresión," según resume Jorge Schmidke (p. 12). Incluye biobibliografía y textos de J. Gutiérrez Coll (1835–1901); M. Sánchez Pesquera (1851–1920); M. Pimentel Coronel (1863–1905); Gabriel E. Muñoz (1863–1908); L. Churión (1869–1945); A. Mata (1870–1931); J.E. Arcia (1872–1931); A. Méndez Loynaz (1879–1914); E. Carreño (1881–1954); J.T. Arreaza Calatrava (1885–1970); A. Carías (1883–1918); L. Correa (1884–1940); J. Schmidke (1890–1981). [PL]

5654 El Regreso de Sandino. Selección e introducción, Juvenal Herrera Torres. Medellín, Colombia: Editorial Aurora, 1980. 195 p. (Antología universal de la poesía revolucionaria; v. 5)

Agrupamiento de poetas nicaragüenses y latinoamericanos con el propósito de facturar una solidaria crónica poética del proceso revolucionario desde el levantamiento de Sandino hasta el triunfo en 1979. Se yuxtaponen todos los estilos de la modernidad, desde Darío a Dalton y los poetas talleristas, todos cantando el mismo fin: libertad e identidad propia. [GY]

5655 Voces femeninas en la poesía paraguaya. Edición, introducción, bibliografía y notas de Josefina Plá. Asunción: Alcándara, 1982. 162 p.: bibl., indexes (Colección Poesía; 7)

La selección, de criterio histórico, va precedida de una valiosa introducción sobre la literatura femenina como vehículo de liberación de la mujer. Incluye una panorámica de la poesía femenina hasta el momento actual más bibliografía. [MGP]

BOOKS OF VERSE

5656 Almafuerte. Poesías completas. Buenos Aires: Ediciones del 80, 1980. 199 p.

Una pulcra edición de toda la poesía de Almafuerte que incluye las "milongas clásicas." El prólogo de Ernesto Morales ubica al poeta en su tiempo y discute el valor de su obra a la luz de su extraordinaria personalidad. [JG]

5657 Alonso, Rodolfo. Cien poemas escogidos: 1952–1977. Buenos Aires: Fundación Argentina para la Poesía, 1980. 79 p.: bibl. (Colección Poetas argentinos contemporáneos)

Permite conocer la obra poética de R. Alonso (n. 1934) que ya tiene más de 12 libros publicados. Es una poesía escueta, precisa, capaz de gran eficacia expresiva. La combinación de sencillez y sorpresa genera un discurso lírico rápido, elípticamente emotivo. [JG]

5658 Alvarado Tenorio, Harold. Recuerda cuerpo. Bogotá: Papagayo de Cristal, 1983. 135 p.

Reune la poesía de Alvarado Tenorio (n. 1945), publicada desde 1972. Incluye comentarios de Fernando Cruz Kronfly, Jorge Rodríguez Padrón, Helena Araujo y Hernán Toro (p. 115–130). Característica de esta escritura es la exploración de la sensualidad. [PL]

5659 Alvarez Tuñón, Eduardo. El amor, la muerte y lo que llega a las ciudades: poemas, 1974–1976. Buenos Aires: s.n., 1980. 92 p.

"La niñez es una hermosa puerta para una horrible casa" es el primer verso de un libro nutrido de poemas de larga respiración y sostenida intensidad. La elocuencia del lenguaje lírico da salida a una dolorida reflexividad. Alvarez Tuñón (n. 1957) maneja las tonalidades dramáticas con agudeza e inteligencia. [JG]

5660 Antezana, René. Imaginario. Portada e ilustraciones de René Antezana. Cochabamba, Bolivia: Universidad Mayor de San Simón, Editorial Universitaria, 1979. 38 p.: ill. (Cuadernos de poesía; 2)

En un lenguaje que hace uso de la sorpresa de la imagen, Antezana funde sensualidad y búsqueda existencial en poemas de nostalgia y sensibilidad. No faltan en el con-junto la presencia certera del humor crítico, de la ciudad subjetivizada, de una mirada atemporal a un Cuzco—aún—herido. [A.R. Prada]

5661 Arellano, Jorge Eduardo. La entrega de los dones. Managua: Ediciones Americanas, 1978. 97 p.: ill.

El poeta, individuo solitario, se entrega a los otros por medio del trabajo con las palabras, lucha contra la dispersión y el olvido. Poesía varia: vanguardista al estilo de Coronel; amorosa a la manera epigramática y tallerista; recreación indigenista; crónica del proceso revolucionario; epitafios; ironización de la burguesía a la manera daltoniana. El volumen carece de coherencia estructural. [GY]

5662 Aridjis, Homero. Construir la muerte. México: J. Mortiz, 1982. 101 p. (Las Dos orillas)

Este libro de uno de los principales poetas mexicanos de hoy parte de la frase de Montaigne "Construir la muerte es la obra continua de vuestras vidas." El poeta ambulante se pasea por espacios y tiempos definidos y reflexiona sobre el pasado inalterable, el presente problemático y el futuro inminente. Los poemas cortos y concisos configuran un espacio poético en un lenguaje directo que crea impresiones y reflexiones por medio de una imaginería sensorial y sensual en que las sombras, luces y colores dibujan un mundo en el que el poeta "llora la gracia dudosa de haber nacido." [NK]

5663 Armijo, Roberto. Homenajes y otros poemas. Tegucigalpa: Universidad Nacional Autónoma de Honduras, 1979. 88 p.

Sobresale la solidaridad con los grandes poetas y artistas latinoamericanos y de la cultura universal, incluyendo a Marx, el Che, Ho Chi Minh y Allende entre los homenajeados. De tono conversacional que busca sus palabras en el diálogo con los otros. [GY]

5664 Azofeifa, Isaac Felipe. Cruce de vía. San José: Editorial Costa Rica, 1982. 156 p. (Libros de poesía; 10)

Cuidadosamente estructurado en cuatro partes: 1) nombrar y poblar el vacío; 2) impugnación del mundo tecnificado que lleva al silencio de la muerte; 3) irónica desconstrucción de valores vigentes; y 4) incorporación del hombre a la "ronda infinita," el cambio perpetuo donde se salvan las distin-

ciones de clase. Expresión tersa y directa.
[GY]

5665 Bartolomé, Hernán Efraín. Ciudad bajo relámpago. México: Editorial Katún, 1983. 1 v.

Segundo libro de este joven poeta ganador del Premio Plural de Poesía, 1983. Poemas de tema citadino en los que se elabora un mundo sensual y sensorial de original intensidad lírica. [NK]

5666 Batres y Montúfar, José. Obras completas. Recopilación y clasificación, Mario Alberto Carrera. 2a. ed. Guatemala: Editorial Piedra Santa, 1981. 170 p.

Precedida de un valioso estudio estilístico se nos presenta la obra de Batres en seis secciones: *Las tradiciones de Guatemala;* tres relatos en octava real; poesías líricas; poemas satírico-humorísticos; ejercicios poéticos; traducciones. Resalta la visión crítica en las "tradiciones" y un pleno romanticismo en la fantasía evocadora de "Yo pienso en ti." [GY]

5667 Bayard Lerma, José Manuel. Los días del incendio: poesía. México: Editorial Signos, 1982. 54 p. (Colección Portobelo; 7. Serie autores panameños, Poesía)

Poesía de temática heterogénea, recorriendo anécdotas del mundo negro panameño, incluyendo ritmos jitanjafóricos, oscuras indagaciones de la interioridad y crítica social. [GY]

5668 Belli, Gioconda. Truenos y arco iris. Managua: Editorial Nueva Nicaragua, 1982. 99 p.: ill. (Letras de Nicaragua; 2)

Pasión desbordante por el otro, que le viene "armando de truenos y arco iris" para plantársele como "astro deslumbrante en las entrañas." Canta "nuevas formas de amar" ubicando su voz en la colectividad. Reformulación femenina del logos romántico si bien siempre está a flor del ripio y de la convencionalidad sexual. [GY]

5669 Benarós, León. El bello mundo. Buenos Aires: Emecé Editores, 1981. 95 p.: ill.

Hermoso libro que combina una profunda sensibilidad ontológica con una inteligente observación lírica del mundo. Dividido en seis partes: "El Bello Mundo;" "La Tierra Fecunda;" "Ceremonias y Conjuros;" "Precauciones;" "Las Artes;" y "Los Otros Mundos," conforma un universo coherente, y una escritura trabajada con habi-

lidad y concierto. Benarós (n. 1915) es una figura importante de la generación del 40. [JG]

5670 Benedetti, Mario. Poemas de la oficina. Ilustrado por Antonio Martorell. México: Editorial Nueva Imagen, 1981. 41 p.: ill.

En la modalidad conversacional de Benedetti, se exploran acontecimientos sin importancia en la rutina mecánica de la oficina. La protesta se origina en el juego inesperado de la imaginación disparada y liberadora. [MGP]

5671 Berenguer, Carmen. Bobby Sands desfallece en el muro. Santiago: EIC Producciones Gráficas, s.d. 1 v.

Monólogo lírico en el que se escucha la voz de Bobby Sands (el poeta y miembro del Ejército Republicano irlandés), jornada a jornada, mientras realiza la huelga de hambre que lo conduciría a la muerte. En el fondo el verdadero centro del poema es el hambre misma y su efecto devastador. [OH]

5672 Bermúdez, Ricardo J. Poesía selecta de Ricardo J. Bermúdez. Prólogo de Rodrigo Miró. México: Editorial Signos, 1982. 88 p. (Colección Portobelo; 9. Serie Autores panameños, Poesía)

Poeta de temple surrealista, rehuyendo lo cotidiano crea un mundo autónomo, con propia fauna y flora y propio paisaje compuesto de sangre y mar. De rigor formal y hondo subjetivismo. [GY]

5673 Bernard, Eulalia. Ritmohéroe. San José: Editorial Costa Rica, 1982. 92 p. (Libros de poesía; 11)

Poesía rica y variada, con ecos del movimiento negrista y sus ritmos jitanjafóricos, representa la lucha por la "construcción del templo," denunciando con ironía la explotación del pueblo. Un rico aporte (negro) a la cultura costarricense. [GY]

5674 Bonifaz Nuño, Rubén. Antología personal. México: Universidad Autónoma Metropolitana, 1983. 201 p.

Bonifaz Nuño hace entrega, en orden personal, de su obra poética escrita entre 1953–81. Recopilación valiosa para el conocimiento de este importante poeta mexicano. [NK]

5675 ———. As de oros. Mexico: UNAM, 1981. 84 p.

Naipe fijo y cambiante, símbolo de la

letra cuya significación varía según su configuración en el juego/escritura. Clasicismo y modernidad, hermetismo y transparencia, lo cotidiano y lo mitológico marcan estos poemas en que el hombre moderno se reconoce en los mitos antiguos y reflexiona sobre la soledad, la ciudad, la mujer y los cambios inevitables que trae el tiempo. Libro importante de uno de los poetas de más estatura en la poesía mexicana actual. [NK]

5676 ———. El corazón de la espiral. México: Miguel Angel Porrúa, 1983. 44 p.
Catorce poemas en arte mayor con unidad temática de inusual belleza sensorial. Principio femenino armoniza el mundo en constante "desorden." [NK]

5677 Borges, Jorge Luis. Antología poética, 1923–1977. Madrid: Alianza Editorial, 1981. 147 p. (Sección Literatura. El Libro de bolsillo; 805)
La selección es del propio autor y resulta una excelente introducción para el estudiante que desee familiarizarse con la poesía de Borges. La edición es bien presentada, y constituye una manera expedita de conocer aspectos fundamentales de Borges. [JG]

5678 ———. La cifra. Madrid: Alianza, 1981. 107 p. (Alianza tres; 72)
Borges (n. 1899), cuyas poesías completas ya se han publicado, agrega aquí una cincuentena de textos que complementan su trabajo anterior. Casi todos ellos podrían encontrar cabida en libros anteriores. Bajo la heterogeneidad, hay una poderosa coherencia imaginaria e intelectual. [JG]

5679 Bustamante, Cecilia. Discernimiento, 1971–1979. México: Premiá Editora, 1982. 123 p. (Libros del bicho; 27)
Su primer libro desde El Nombre de las cosas (1970), con un lenguaje todavía más despojado y a la vez incisivo, C. Bustamante explora dimensiones de la nostalgia, los viajes, el país natal, la memoria familiar. "Cultora rigurosa y honda de la palabra, ha ido trazando un proceso creador de maduración continua, en el que cada nuevo poemario ha aportado mayor destreza verbal y riqueza significativa," opina el crítico Ricardo González Vigil. [RdC]

5680 Campos, Marco Antonio. Hojas de los años: 1970–1979. México: Premiá Editora, 1981. 108 p. (Libros del bicho; 15)

Poemario que recoge la obra de este joven poeta desde 1969–79: Los Naipes del perro, Muertos y disfraces, Una Seña en la sepultura y Monólogos. Poemas en verso y prosa que configuran un sujeto poético confesional. Interioriza su existencia en un tono coloquial en que la desilusión es la nota primordial. [NK]

5681 Carías Lindo, Erasmo. Segrario. 2a. ed. Tegucigalpa: Publicaciones Sagitario-Acuario, 1981. 50 p.
Poesía de amor al estilo vanguardista, inclusive con disposición gráfica a manera del ultraísmo. [GY]

5682 Carrera Andrade, Jorge. Jorge Carrera Andrade, los caminos de un poeta: obra poética completa. Biografía, iconografía, bibliografía: Jorge Aravena, editor. Quito: Música, Palabra e Imagen del Ecuador, 1980. 476 p., 1 leaf of plates: ill. (Colección Música, palabra e imagen del Ecuador)
Aunque este volumen tiene un carácter de homenaje, el editor no deja de incluir información bibliográfica útil y algunos artículos sobre una de las figuras literarias más conocidas del Ecuador. En ese sentido, este volumen permite un mejor acceso a esta vasta poesía para posibilitar su mejor evaluación. [JO]

5683 Casal, Lourdes. Palabras juntan revolución: poesía. La Habana: Casa de las Américas, 1981. 112 p.
Hermoso recuento poético de las experiencias del exilio de la autora y de su visión del mundo desde ese exilio. Son poemas de sencillez, conmovedores sobre todo por su ingenuidad. [RRA]

5684 Castillo, Otto René. Informe de una injusticia: antología poética. Introducción de Roque Dalton y Huberto Alvarado. 2a. ed. San José: Editorial Universitaria Centroamericana, 1982. 419 p. (Colección Séptimo día)
El poeta más venerado en la historia reciente de su país, su obra sigue dos direcciones: la amorosa y la político-ideológica, fundidas en algunas composiciones. Ama sobre todo la vida, "la poesía más alta," por la cual estaría dispuesto a matar. [GY]

5685 Cervantes, Francisco. Cantado para nadie. México: J. Mortiz, 1982. 109 p. (Las Dos orillas)
Recuperación del verso medieval

galaico-portugués. Ecos de Gil Vicente, Rosalía de Castro, Fernando Pessoa, y Alvaro Cunqueiro en esta vuelta insólita impulsada por la nostalgia de "un tiempo heroico" irrecuperable. Cantigas, cantares de amigo y de amor, serranillas, canciones dialogadas y barcarolas de originalidad y belleza en que los motivos del mar, de la "morriña," y del amor cortés logran darle presencia a lo ausente. Explícito en el bilinguismo (español/galaico-portugués) la búsqueda de una lengua poética innovadora. [NK]

5686 Chanove, Oswaldo. El héroe y su relación con la heroína. Arequipa, Perú: Macho Cabrío, 1983. 53 p. (Libros de Macho Cabrío; 2. Omnibus. Libro de Poesía)
Chanove se ha beneficiado de las exploraciones coloquialistas de los poetas del 70 y plantea su coloquio con desenfado, ya sin conflicto, sin énfasis vitalista y con un ritmo controlado y eficaz. Entre tentativas, preguntas, circunloquios y reafirmaciones el poema logra comunicarnos una intimidad abierta y alerta. [JO]

5687 Chase, Alfonso. Obra en marcha: poesía, 1965–1980. San José: Editorial Costa Rica, 1982.
Recopilación de cinco poemarios en los cuales se atestigua la transformación de sus figuraciones—giros—sobre sí mismo a la manera de Rilke en *Los reinos de mi mundo*, en dueto amoroso en *Arbol del tiempo* y *Cuerpos* y luego en solidaridad con la patria y los desvalidos en *El libro de mi patria* y *Los pies sobre la tierra*. Una de las voces mayores de la poesía centroamericana. [GY]

5688 Chumacero, Alí. Poesía completa. Prólogo de Marco Antonio Campos. México: Premiá, 1981. 161 p. (Libros del bicho; 10)
Valiosa edición, ganadora del Premio Xavier Villaurrutia 1980, con prólogo de Marco Antonio Campos. Comprende la obra poética del poeta más conocido del grupo "Tierra Nueva:" *Páramo de sueños* (1944), *Imágenes desterradas* (1948), *Palabras en reposo* (1956) y una sección de *Poemas no coleccionados*. [NK]

5689 Cisneros, Antonio. Crónica del Niño Jesús de Chilca. México: Premiá Editora, 1981. 76 p. (Libros del bicho; 31)
Con su habitual control expresivo y capacidad para reavivar las palabras, Antonio

Cisneros ensaya aquí recobrar también la escena colectiva de una comunidad costeña. Esa búsqueda de un hablante colectivo, hecha con agudeza poética y sabiduría económica, lo lleva de una persona a otra, dramatizando así una voz popular que declara los signos vitales de afirmación como denuncia los de explotación. [JO]

5690 Cohen, Sandro. Los cuerpos de la furia. México: Katún, 1983. 102 p. (Poesía contemporánea; 3)
Este tercer libro de Cohen, oriundo de N.J., demuestra su extraordinario dominio sobre una lengua distinta a la natal. El motivo del claroscuro establece una estructura binaria: noches de insomnio en espera de mañanas claras, soledad y comunión amorosa y sobre todo búsqueda, lucha y encuentro de un espacio y de una lengua poética. [NK]

5691 Coronel Urtecho, José. Papeles de infierno. Ilustraciones, Leoncio Sáenz. s.l.: J. Coronel Urtecho, 1981. 14 leaves: ill.
Inspirado por el triunfo de la revolución nicaragüense, Coronel vuelve a su labor poética ya no como experimentalista de vanguardia sino para denunciar al "marrano octogenario . . . que primero se robó Nicaragua" y a todos los filibusteros e imperialistas que le siguieron. [GY]

5692 Cross, Elsa. Tres poemas. México: Universidad Nacional Autónoma de México, 1981. 110 p. (Colección Cuadernos de poesía)
Volumen dividido en tres secciones que la autora anuncia como tres libros independientes: *Espejo al sol*, serie de estampas con un hilo narrativo; *Las edades perdidas*, 20 poemas con cierta unidad temática; y *Pasaje de fuego*, poema largo de fundación. Versos libres de imaginería sensual y relumbrante. [NK]

5693 Droz, Vanessa. La cicatriz a medias. Río Piedras, P.R.: Editorial Cultural, 1982. 80 p. (Colección El trabajo gustoso)
De un erotismo depurado, casi abstracto, donde formas arquetípicas—el bosque, el anillo, la orilla del mar, la cuchara—adquieren la autoridad emblemática que metaforiza la crisis del deseo. Muchos poemas son reescrituras de poemas, o más bien, poéticas, de otros: Palés, Paz, Villaurrutia, Gorostiza. Es precisamente en la reescritura donde se dramatiza la infructuosa aprehensión erótica de la forma. [RRA]

5694 Escobar, Francisco Andrés. Petición y ofrenda. Ilustraciones de Eduardo Stein. San Salvador: UCA Editores, 1979. 65 p.: ill. (Colección Gavidia; v. 21. Serie Poesía)

Visión constructiva de la revolución sin desdeñar las exigencias de la poesía: forma, métrica, estilo y un elaborado universo simbólico, predominantemente cristiano. El poeta, como Cristo, se compromete a ser *mediador* de la solidaridad y de la identidad común. [GY]

5695 Escobar Galindo, David. Campo minado, 1968. 2a. ed. San Salvador: Editorial Ahora, 1981. 104 p.

Poesía, "milagro profundo," elaborada en variadas y ricas imágenes, se ofrece como antídoto a los males de nuestro tiempo que "rabia/sin qué ni para qué." Se plantea la problemática de la existencia estrictamente dentro del orden poético o según un humanismo difuso. [GY]

5696 ——. Sonetos penitenciales. 5a. ed. aum. San Salvador: Editorial Ahora, 1892. 72 p.

Se emplea el soneto para dirigirse a la acuciante situación del país por su "forma abrásica y extraña de irrenunciable libertad." Frente al abismo la deslumbrante autonomía poética, identificada con la trascendencia divina. Los poemas más interesantes denuncian el papel que ha venido a desempeñar El Salvador para el mundo avanzado: espectáculo/simulacro que satisface su cuota de terror. [GY]

5697 Estrada, Hugo. Ya somos una gran ciudad. Guatemala: RIN 78, 1981. 97 p. (Colección Literatura; 13)

Poesía de observación irónica que impugna la modernidad enajenante de la tecnificación. Guatemala se convierte en una "gran ciudad" donde "hay que comprar hasta el aire, el agua y el horizonte." El poeta sabe modular registros: se habla en voz de niño, cura o reportero. [GY]

5698 Etchenique, Nira. Diez y punto. Ultimo oficio. Buenos Aires: Adiaz, 1980. 88 p.: ill.

Se combinan aquí dos libros anteriormente publicados: *Diez y punto* (1965) y *Ultimo oficio* (1967), creándose así un nuevo volumen donde cada unidad se enriquece. Un bello conjunto: la musicalidad y sensibilidad de N. Etchenique (n. 1930) le confieren fuerza y personalidad al tema amoroso. [JG]

5699 Fajardo, Miguel. Urgente búsqueda. San José: Editorial Costa Rica, 1981. 136 p. (Libros de poesía; 7)

"Urgente búsqueda" en el silencio— "escribo a la verdad del silencio"— que se puebla de voces solidarias: "He venido/porque necesito/tu existencia/en mi poema." Un nuevo registro en la tradición vallejiananerudiana. [GY]

5700 Fernández, Francisco de Asís. En el cambio de estaciones. México: Editorial Universitaria de la UNAM, 1981. 136 p.: ill. (Colección Poesía; no. 13)

Volumen multívoco: metáforas en base de la naturaleza tropical; solidaridad con el pueblo; poesía "guerrillera;" retratos y autorretratos; juegos intertextuales como los antisalmos. Todo unido por una constante energía imaginística. Ni retórico del compromiso social ni individuo encerrado en su autonomía poética, Fernández enuncia la dialéctica entre la diversidad del mundo y la individualidad del yo. [GY]

5701 Fernández, Guillermo. Bajo llave: poemas. México: Katún, 1983. 100 p. (Poesía Contemporánea; 4)

Destacado como el divulgador y traductor más importante de poesía y narrativa italiana en México, este poeta jalisciense demuestra, con éste su sexto poemario, su virtuosismo como poeta y traductor. Las primeras tres secciones comprenden sus propias composiciones: visión de un mundo real e inhóspito que encuentra en el espacio irreal de la memoria y de la fantasía una apertura. La última sección presenta sus traducciones al español de Dino Campana, Umberto Saba, Giuseppe Ungaretti, Eugenio Montale, Salvatore Quasimodo y Mario Luzi. [NK]

5702 Fernández, Janina. Certeza. San José: Editorial Universitaria Centroamericana, 1982. 86 p.: ill. (Colección Séptimo día)

Poesía de amor y de solidaridad con las revoluciones latinoamericanas. No obstante, rehuye la denuncia demagógica para realizar los aspectos creativos de la liberación: "en lugar de llorar por Chile/sonr(eír) por Nicaragua." [GY]

5703 Fernández, Ruth. El sol y la rebelión. Buenos Aires: Fundación Argentina para la Poesía, 1981. 71 p.

Bella poesía que fluye con dulzura, como manifestación "de una curiosa y triste inteligencia" (epígrafe de su *Amor sobre la piel del tiempo*, 1978). Consta de dos series poemáticas: "Las Extrañas Criaturas" y "Los Constructores de la Sangre," más otros tres poemas. [JG]

5704 Fernández Moreno, César. Sentimientos completos. Buenos Aires: Ediciones de la Flor, 1981. 397 p.

C.F. Moreno (n. 1919) reúne aquí toda su producción poética con la advertencia de que ha revisado todo lo publicado, de modo que ésta debiera considerarse la edición definitiva de su poesía (definitiva, por lo menos, hasta 1981). En el prólogo nos advierte que "tengo todo en permanente corrección." Es un libro necesario en todo sentido. [JG]

5705 Ferré, Rosario. Fábulas de la garza desangrada. México: J. Mortiz, 1982. 75 p. (Las Dos orillas)

Ambiciosa arqueología literaria y sentimental de lo femenino, donde se abandona la estereotípica agresividad feminista y se prefiere un tono triunfal "a favor del gozo y de la gloria." Es un viaje por los nombres, las labores y los espacios de la femineidad donde se ejerce dominio de ese amplio ámbito cultural a medida que se *deshace* la madeja, el texto masculino que lo oficializó. [RRA]

5706 Fierro, Enrique. Las oscuras versiones: poesía, 1966–1973. México: Universidad Nacional Autónoma de México, Coordinación de Humanidades, Dirección General de Publicaciones, 1980. 221 p. (Colección Poemas y ensayos)

Esta colección reúne selecciones de volúmenes escritos entre 1966–79. Excelente muestra de la poesía de este poco conocido poeta uruguayo, cuyos rasgos prominentes son el carácter experimental y la expresión tensa y desnuda, casi hermética. Poemas breves, casi todos centrados en inquirir en el significado de la palabra poética. [MGP]

5707 Flores, Miguel Angel. Contrasuberna. México: J. Mortiz, 1981. 104 p.

Importante primer libro que mereció el Premio de Poesía Aguascalientes. Expresión concisa y depurada, intensa y provocativa. Llama la atención la disciplina rigurosa, y la madurez del tono de estos poemas que abren un espacio intertextual en que se distinguen las voces de Pound y Pacheco. [NK]

5708 Franco, Luis Leopoldo. Insurrección del poema. Buenos Aires: Colihue/Hachette, 1979. 201 p. (Colección Letras de hoy)

Franco (n. 1898) es uno de los más grandes ensayistas de Hispanoamérica. Maestro y hombre de sabiduría, merece ser conocido también en su poesía que ha sido generosa y profunda. Este libro representa su producción madura y debiera recomendarse como la mejor manera de ingresar a su inteligencia poética. [JG]

5709 Gandolfo, Ricardo Ezequiel. Diario de Babel. Buenos Aires: Editorial Sudamericana, 1980. 113 p.

Poesía sencilla, atractivamente editada, de fácil ritmo y lectura. Consta de cinco partes que mantienen igual fuerza seductora hasta culminar en un excelente poema final: "El Ciego en el Laberinto." Un gran ejemplo de las inclinaciones objetalistas y confesionales de la poesía hispanoamericana actual. [JG]

5710 García Saraví, Gustavo. De uniones y separatas. Buenos Aires: Fundación Argentina para la Poesía, 1980. 81 p. (Colección Poetas argentinos contemporáneos)

García Saraví (n. 1920) distribuye su libro en tres secciones de sonetos, y cuatro de poemas en verso libre. En ambas formas despliega su intensidad discursiva, su agudeza e ingenio, su sensibilidad lírica. De amplio registro temático (histórico, erótico, cotidiano, etc.), impone siempre su sello de riqueza formal y musical. [JG]

5711 ———. Ensayo general. Buenos Aires: Plus Ultra, 1980. 101 p.

Colección de 88 sonetos dividida en dos secciones: "Serie de las Intimidades: Confesiones y Rogativas" y "Amigos Inolvidables y Olvidados Enemigos." García Saraví (n. 1920) es un reconocido maestro del género. [JG]

5712 Gardea, Jesús. Canciones para una sola cuerda. Toluca, México: Universidad Autónoma del Estado de México, 1982. 84 p. (Colección La abeja en la colmena; 11)

Primer libro de poesía del reconocido cuentista chihuahuense consta de 74 composiciones cuyos versos en su mayoría alternan entre bisílabos y trisílabos en poemas de hasta 18 líneas. Poesía de imágenes visuales cargadas de sugerencias, variaciones reminiscentes de los *hai-kais*. [NK]

5713 Greiff, León de. Libro de relatos. Ilustraciones de Antonio Roda. Bogotá: Carlos Valencia Editores, 1979. 123 p., 4 leaves of plates: ill.

Hermosa reimpresión de los 18 relatos publicados por primera vez en *Variaciones alrededor de nada* (1936). Libro importante, que evidencia la originalidad y audacia de una propuesta poética temprana. El recurso a la narratividad y la configuración de personajes o máscaras, que mani festaban sendas mitologías, anticipan algunas notas de la poesía actual (ver item **5810**, *HLAS 38:6952*, *HLAS 40:7081–7082 y 7206, y HLAS 42:5757 y 5922*). [PL]

5714 Guillén, Nicolás. Obra poética, 1920–1972. v. 1, 1920–1957. v. 2, 1958–1972. Ilustraciones del autor. Prólogo de Guillermo García Oropeza. Guadalajara, México: Universidad de Guadalajara, 1978. 2 v.: bibl., ill., index.

Reedición de la obra poética de Guillén publicada en 1972 en La Habana con un prólogo de Angel Augier, y reimpresa 1980. Versión ilustrada por el mismo Guillén con prólogo de García Oropeza. Incluye una detallada y valiosa cronología. [RRA]

5715 Hahn, Oscar. Imágenes nucleares. Santiago: Ediciones América del Sur, 1983. 17 p.

La guerra nuclear es uno de los temas centrales en la obra de Hahn, resumido en esta oportuna antología. "La proliferación de las armas nucleares debe terminar ahora o terminará con nosotros," advierte Hahn en un "Prólogo para Sobrevivientes" no menos inquietante que los seis poemas seleccionados, entre los cuales aparece "Reencarnación de los Carniceros," datado 1955 (ver item **5837**, *HLAS 40:7088, HLAS 42:5763 y HLAS 44:5692*). [PL]

5716 Henderson, Carlos. Identidad. Lima: Mosca Azul Editores, 1982. 54 p.

Desde *Los días hostiles* (1965) hasta *Ahora mismo hablaba contigo, Vallejo* (1976), la voz poética de este destacado miembro de la poesía peruana del 60 ha ido afirmando su calidad personal. Es una poesía de exploración interior, cargada de vibraciones psicológicas, dramatizada por las preguntas de un sujeto inquieto, insumiso. Con una sintaxis elaborada y un fragmentarismo de verso breve y cortado, estos poemas plantean su indagación con autoridad y sin respuestas comunes. [JO]

5717 Huidobro, Vicente. Altazor. Temblor de ciclo. Edición de René de Costa. Madrid: Cátedra, 1981. 190 p. (Letras hispánicas; 133)

Excelente reedición de dos libros fundamentales de Huidobro, precedida por un estudio preliminar en el cual de Costa sigue sorprendiéndonos con nuevos aportes documentales sobre el poeta chileno, que revelan la importancia de *Temblor de cielo* y, por ejemplo, su relación con la ópera de Wagner *Tristán e Isolda*. La edición se completa con un interesante apéndice que recoge versiones primitivas de algunos textos que después pasarían a formar parte de *Altazor*. [OH]

5718 Ibarbourou, Juana de. Antología de poemas y prosas. Selección y notas de Arturo Sergio Visca y Julio C. da Rosa. Montevideo: Ministerio de Educación y Cultura del Uruguay: Organización de los Estados Americanos, 1980. 199 p.

Selección que incluye una muestra representativa de toda la obra poética y ciertos escritos en prosa tomados de *El cántaro fresco* (1920), *Estampas de la Biblia* (1934), *Chico Carlo* (1944), *Destino* (1953) y *Angeles pintados* (1968). Dividida en secciones correspondientes a cada título antologado, cada sección va precedida de una introducción. Edición panorámica valiosa. [MGP]

5719 Illescas Hernández, Carlos. Usted es la culpable. México: Editorial Katún, 1983. 66 p. (Poesía; 6)

Illescas, en este séptimo libro, Premio Villaurrutia 1983, establece un diálogo con la poesía de Garcilaso de la Vega. El libro, compuesto de octavas reales, sonetos y epigramas, nos remite por su versificación, ritmos y diestro uso del encabalgamiento a la poesía española clásica. [NK]

5720 Incháustegui Cabral, Héctor. Poemas de una sola angustia: obra poética completa, 1940–1976. Santiago, República Dominicana: Universidad Católica Madre y Maestra, 1978. 572 p. (Colección Contemporáneos; 36)

Este volumen recoge la extensa obra poética de este escritor que se destaca por su voz rebelde y por sus preocupaciones sociohistóricas. [RRA]

5721 Isla, Carlos. La hora quieta. México: Universidad Nacional Autónoma de México, 1982. 80 p. (Colección Cuadernos de poesía)

Las composiciones breves insertas en la tradición del *hai-kai*, unas líricas de fina imaginería sensorial y otras de tono irónico y lúdico representan lo mejor del libro de este joven poeta de la última promoción de escritores mexicanos. [NK]

5722 Juarroz, Roberto. Séptima poesía vertical. Caracas: Monte Avila Editores, 1982. 149 p.

Desde 1958, Juarroz (n. 1925) ha venido creando una magna obra poética: la Poesía Vertical. El cuerpo de su producción ha mantenido este título general; este libro es el séptimo de la serie. Consta de 114 poemas donde se cultiva lo que todavía habría que llamar "el sentido ontológico y existencial de la poesía." [JG]

5723 Láinez, Daniel. Manicomio. Tegucigalpa: Universidad Nacional Autónoma de Honduras, Editorial Universitaria, 1980. 200 p., 1 leaf of plates (Colección Letras hondureñas; no. 2)

Libro perdido por más de 25 años en que el conocido poeta de la generación del 35 lanza una crítica satírica—graciosa si bien superficial—a las poetas de entonces. Es un libro cómico que daría con los poetas en el manicomio por exceso de ripios y otras construcciones poéticas fallidas. [GY]

5724 Lastra, Pedro. Noticias del extranjero. 2a. ed. México: Premiá Editora, 1982. 66 p. (Libros del bicho; 1)

Reedición del excelente libro publicado en 1979, pero con cambios considerables: suprime el prólogo de Lastra y algunos textos, y agrega 12 poemas nuevos. Además, el poema "Posdata," de Enrique Lihn, es reemplazado por un extenso texto del mismo autor, titulado "Noticias del Extranjero: Pedro Lastra Cumple Cincuenta Años." [OH]

5725 Lihn, Enrique. El Paseo Ahumada: poema. Fotografías de Paz Errázuriz y Marcelo Montecino. Dibujos de Germán Arestizábal. Santiago: Ediciones Minga, 1983. 27 p.: ill.

Impreso en papel de diario, e imitando el formato de algunos tabloides, este libro quiere concordar físicamente con su contenido. El Paseo Ahumada es para Enrique Lihn un microcosmos de Chile entero, en el que se exhiben el desempleo, la mendicidad y la represión. Configurado con la fuerza y el despliegue verbal característicos de Lihn, el volumen es sin duda el mejor alegato ético y poético contra la dictadura de Pinochet publicado hasta ahora. [OH]

5726 Lima, José María. La sílaba en la piel: obra poética, 1952–1982. Río Piedras, P.R.: Ediciones qeAse, 1982. (Colexión Ilo [sic] de Ariadna)

Cubriendo una extensa, y en su mayoría inédita, producción que abarca 30 años, este libro constituye una extraordinaria revelación de un singular poeta. De ritmo ligero, verso corto, fluido, cada poema se destaca por su claridad que encadena le repetida historia de la injusticia y la voluntad de la palabra, sílaba encarnada, encarnizada, en busca de la creación regeneradora. Claros ecos de la voz profética nerudiana y del Vallejo de *Poemas humanos*. [RRA]

5727 Lizalde, Eduardo. Memoria del tigre. México: Editorial Katún, 1983. 256 p. (Poesía contemporánea; 2)

Antología que recoge el bestiario poético de este excelente poeta: *Cada cosa es Babel* (1966); *El tigre en la casa*, Premio Villaurrutia 1970; *La zorra enferma* (1974); *Casa mayor* (1979) y una selección de textos inéditos de los últimos cinco años. Su obra desarrolla una poética del tigre, poética de la desesperanza y el terror. [NK]

5728 Lugones, Leopoldo. Antología poética. Selección e introducción de Jorge Luis Borges. Madrid: Alianza, 1982. 152 p. (Sección Literatura. El Libro de bolsillo; 885)

Esta antología permite una lectura diferente de Lugones (1874–1938). Borges es el autor de la selección y el prólogo. Lugones queda increíblemente "desmodernizado:" se nos ofrecen de él 39 bellos poemas (breves y extensos) que harán revisar positivamente el juicio sobre Lugones de más de un especialista, a la vez que servirán de privilegiada introducción a quienes aún no lo conozcan. [JG]

5729 ———. El payador y antología de poesía y prosa. Prólogo, Jorge Luis Borges. Selección, notas y cronología, Guillermo Ara. Caracas: Biblioteca Ayacucho,

1979. 469 p.: music (Biblioteca Ayacucho; 54)

Guillermo Ara ha realizado un excelente y utilísimo trabajo de edición (con prólogo extenso de Borges) de una selección de textos de Lugones (1874–1938). Incluye *El payador*, una apreciable selección de poesía, y prosas de variado interés (narrativo, político, histórico, etc.). La cronología al final (que precede a una completa bibliografía) ha sido ampliada por los editores y constituye un instrumento eficaz para la enseñanza. [JG]

5730 Macías, Elva. Imagen y semejanza. México: Universidad Nacional Autónoma de México, Difusión Cultural, 1982. 73 p. (Cuadernos de humanidades; no. 20)

Poemas, mayormente breves, de reminiscencias orientales en que el sujeto poético teje tapices verbales en un intento de "restaurar la imagen extraviada." Contemplación desmitificadora que culmina con "Imagen y Semblanza," notable poema sobre la mujer contemporánea. [NK]

5731 Mastronardi, Carlos. Poesías completas. Prólogo de Juan Carlos Ghiano. Buenos Aires: Academia Argentina de Letras, 1982. 171 p.: ill.

Edición de Mastronardi (1900–78), dirigida por J. Calvetti con prólogo de J.C. Ghiano, es el texto definitivo de este extraordinario poeta en el que la tensión existencial se une a un acendrado tono clásico y un heroico perfeccionismo. Se incluyen cuatro libros de Mastronardi, pero se omite uno que el autor retiró de circulación y algunos poemas sueltos que pidió que fueran olvidados. [JG]

5732 Matos Paoli, Francisco. Cancionero VIII. Río Piedras, P.R.: Ediciones Mairena, 1982. 1 v.

Forma parte de un ciclo de 10 libros de 150 sonetos cada uno. Dan muestra, una vez más, del control diestro del poeta sobre esta difícil forma. De corte neo-barroco, su estilo exhibe una predilección por lo místico y metafísico en un contexto criollo que lo acercan a su desaparecido contemporáneo cubano José Lezama Lima, aunque sin el exuberante horizonte cultural del poeta de *Orígenes*. [RRA]

5733 Mazzotti, José A. Poemas no recogidos en libro. Lima?: EMAPI, 1981. 66 p.

Con este poemario Mazzotti obtuvo en 1980 el primer premio de los Juegos florales

Universitarios en Lima, convocado por la Universidad de San Marcos, y la decisión del jurado está refrendada por la buena calidad de estos poemas desenfadados, juveniles y sensibles. La vida cotidiana irrumpe en este libro con su crudeza y su alegría, y lo hace en un lenguaje crítico y emotivo. [JO]

5734 Mejía Vallejo, Manuel. El viento lo dijo: décimas. Medellín: Universidad de Antioquia, 1981. 140 p.: col. ill. (Ediciones Literatura, arte y ciencia; 2)

Cien décimas de notable factura constituyen este libro. Los títulos de sus partes: "Al Nacer Vino la Muerte," "Intermedio para el Amor" y "Recordará el Olvido," resumen una característica reflexiva del conjunto, fiel al sentir y a la expresividad populares manifestados en una tradición de vieja estirpe, asumida aquí con singular eficacia. [PL]

5735 Melendes, Joserramón. Desimos désimas [sic]. Prólogo de Luis Rafael Sánchez. 2a. ed. rev. Río Piedras, P.R.: Editorial qeAse, 1983. 123 p. (Colexión [sic] Libre)

Segunda edición de este singular poemario que añade poemas nuevos y presenta un formato más unitario. Meléndes rescata la décima jíbara del neocriollismo pintoresquista y le imparte energía, actualidad, y un lirismo fresco y contundente. Su temario se mueve de lo metafísico a lo cotidiano con comodidad y sin altibajos. El elogioso prólogo de Sánchez es una importante contribución crítica. [RRA]

5736 Méndez de la Vega, Luz. Tríptico: Tiempo de amor, Tiempo de llanto, y Desamor. Guatemala: Editorial Marroquín Hermanas, 1980. 158 p.: ill.

Crónica lírica del amor, su muerte y el desamor. En el primer poemario predominan los temas eróticos, elaborados con sensualidad sobre todo táctil. El segundo lamenta la muralla infranqueable de la muerte del amante. En el tercero se articula la incapacidad de conjugar "yo" y "tú" en un nosotros estable. [GY]

5737 Mizón, Luis. Poème du Sud et autres poèmes. Edition bilingue. Traduit de l'espagnol par Roger Caillois et Claude Couffon. Introduction de Claude Couffon. Paris: Gallimard, 1982. 155 p.

Libro filiable en la línea de poesía trabajada por Neruda en las *Residencias*. Estructuración de un hablante, que a la vez que pronuncia el mundo del poema, lo recorre como un viajero maravillado y atónito, contemplador de imágenes de cuño surrealista, en medio de una atmósfera densa y fantasmal. [OH]

5738 Modern, Rodolfo. En blanco y negro. s.l.: Editorial Rodolfo Alonso, 1981. 44 p.

R. Modern (n. 1922), conocido por sus estudios de literatura alemana y sus excelentes traducciones al español, ha desarrollado una escritura poética diáfana e inteligente, de hondura metafísica y pureza clásica. Aires de Hölderlin y música ideal se desprenden de estos versos. [JG]

5739 Montemayor, Carlos. Finisterra. México: Premiá Editora, 1982. 60 p. (Libros del bicho; 42)

Este tercer libro del poeta chihuahuense establece un diálogo con la poesía de Ledo Ivo, Whitman y Neruda. La confianza en la palabra y el afán de decir o "cantar" el mundo en su totalidad, lo esencial y lo nimio, queda implícito en su preferencia por los poemas largos que integran el libro y son lo más logrado del poemario. [NK]

5740 Montes de Oca, Marco Antonio. Cuentas nuevas y otros poemas. México: Casillas Editores, 1983. 118 p. (Serie La poesía)

Libro más reciente del destacado poeta mexicano que anuncia desde el título una nueva dirección. Poesía más escueta que mantiene la riqueza imaginista que asociamos con el poeta. Las metáforas e imágenes parten del mundo concreto y buscan captar lo inefable detrás de lo visible. El poemario comprende dos partes: "Los Vitrales de la Mariposa," 39 poemas de temple reflexivo sobre la existencia, el tiempo, el amor, la muerte y "El Cielo Errante," 13 poemas de tema urbano. [NK]

5741 Morales Avilés, Ricardo. Prosa política y poemas. Recopilación de textos del Instituto de Estudio del Sandinismo. Managua: Editorial Nueva Nicaragua, 1981. 158 p. (Colección Pensamiento vivo; 2)

Visión nacionalista de la liberación con base marxista-leninista pero en la que "ni Fidel ni Lenin (son) palabra de Dios." Menos lúcido en su análisis de la cultura pues casi exige un realismo socialista (ver su

crítica de Cardenal por plantear trascendencias "idealistas"). Cultor de un socialismo cientificista, ve la cultura como epifenómeno de lo económico-político. Su poesía de amor—dirigida a su compañera—, por otra parte, expresa una solidaridad tanto poética como social. [GY]

5742 Muñoz, Alberto. Almagrosa, poemas del arroyo Felipe-Tigre. Fotografía, Federico Chuhurra. Buenos Aires: Ediciones Ciclo 3, 1981. 74 p., 4 leaves of plates: ill. (Serie de draga)

"Cerrojo. / Duermo," es uno de los 63 poemas, casi todos breves, que forman este fresquísimo poemario "escrito íntegramente en una isla del Tigre durante 1980." Es el tercer libro de A. Muñoz (n. 1951). Ingenio, precisión, emoción limpia, son sus virtudes más notorias. [JG]

5743 Murillo, Rosario. Un deber de cantar. Managua: Ministerio de Cultura, 1981. 63 p. (Colección Premio Nacional de Poesía Joven Leonel Rugama)

Lejos de ser abiertamente política—como sugiere el título, esta poesía ofrece el mundo del sueño, el amor y la imaginación como poetización de lo cotidiano, contribuyendo así a la constitución de un imaginario nacional. La ideología popular no se riñe con la expresión subjetiva e individual. [GY]

5744 Mutis, Alvaro. Caravansary. México: Fondo de Cultura Económica, 1981. 61 p. (Colección Tierra firme)

Los ocho extensos y fascinantes poemas en prosa de Caravansary son otra vez los desplazamientos y avatares del inquietante personaje Maqroll el Gaviero, figura central de la vasta mitología creada por Mutis en sus libros anteriores. En el último poema ocurre la muerte del personaje, cuyo destino parecen resumir y proyectar simbólicamente estas palabras de la secuencia inicial: "Se habla de navegaciones, de azares en los puertos clandestinos, de cargamentos preciosos, de muertes infames y de grandes hambrunas. Lo de siempre" (ver items **5859** and **5867**). [PL]

5745 Nandino, Elías. Eco. Río de sombra. México: Editorial Katún, 1982. 60 p.: ill.

Bella edición facsimilar que recoge dos poemarios de Nandino: Eco (1934), con prólogo de Xavier Villaurrutia y Río de sombra (1935). Contemporáneo de Gorostiza, Torres

Bodet, Novo y Villaurrutia, gana el Premio Nacional de Literatura en 1982. [NK]

5746 Nogueras, Luis Rogelio. Imitación de la vida. La Habana: Casa de las Américas, 1981. 108 p.

Como ya lo sugiere el título, se trata aquí de realismo social inadulterado: la poesía puesta al servicio de la "vida" o de la "realidad." No hay variaciones interesantes, aunque los poemas están en su mayoría acertadamente concebidos. [RRA]

5747 Oquendo de Amat, Carlos. 5 [i.e. Cinco] metros de poemas. Lima: Editorial Ausonia Talleres Gráficos, 1980. 25 p.

Primera Edición facsimilar del libro más importante, después de *Trilce* (1922), de la vanguardia en el Perú. Esta edición incluye además los otros cuatro poemas que se conocen del autor. Perseguido y encarcelado en sus país, Oquendo de Amat terminó sus días, muy enfermo, en un hospital de la sierra de Guadarrama. Su poesía ha sido recuperada por las nuevas promociones como un emblema de experimentación y calidad. Preserva toda su frescura, su fino juego y su capacidad de fundir una imaginería rural dentro de un discurso cosmopolita. [JO]

5748 Orihuela Ascarrunz, Juan Carlos. De amor, piedras y destierro: poemas. La Paz: Ediciones Altiplano, 1983. 202 p.: ill.

Estrofas de Hernández, Martí y Vallejo encabezan las tres partes de este logrado intento de un lenguaje particular que expresa la posibilidad del amor como salvación, el apego a la tierra en el amor a la ciudad, la actitud política y crítica evitando el estilo testimonial directo. Una voz renovadora y lúcida en la nueva generación de poetas bolivianos. [A.R. Prada]

5749 Orozco, Olga. Mutaciones de la realidad. Buenos Aires: Editorial Sudamericana, 1979. 97 p.

Continuación de la extraordinaria obra poética de Orozco (n. 1920). Un gran libro de 19 piezas magistrales en que la fibra sensitiva del neorromanticismo se reapropia los filones expresivos abiertos por el surrealismo. [JG]

5750 ———. Obra poética. Buenos Aires: Ediciones Corregidor, 1979. 196 p. (Biblioteca de poesía; 1274)

Quizá no se encuentre en su generación otra voz que alcance la intensidad emotiva de Orozco (n. 1920). Verso y respiración largos, fuerza sostenida en unidades extensas que nunca decaen. Este volumen reúne toda su producción poética (1946–78). [JG]

5751 Ossa, Carlos de la. Imprimatur I–II–III–IV. San José: Ministerio de Cultura, Juventud y Deportes, Dirección de Publicaciones, 1981. 313 p.

Poeta trascendental ("blanco" y "celeste") cuya modalidad dilecta es la elegía. El ansia, lo terrenal, la abyección, la explotación—todo—, asciende hacia lo "puro" y "cristalino." Invirtiendo la negatividad mallarmeana su "Azul" tropical transpira "rocío . . . puro . . . cristalino . . . la faz de Dios." [GY]

5752 Pacheco, José Emilio. Los trabajos del mar. México: Ediciones Era, 1983. 83 p. (Biblioteca Era. Poesía)

Más reciente poemario de uno de los poetas más importantes de Hispanoamérica hoy día. La visión apocalíptica que el poeta presenta altera de manera significativa su presentación del fluir temporal, tema reiterativo en sus libros anteriores. El tiempo/presente y el espacio/tierra se convierten en espacios desiderativos ante su posible aniquilación. [NK]

5753 Parra, Nicanor. Chistes para desorientar a la poesía-policía. Santiago: Ediciones de la Galería Epoca, 1983. 1 v.

En su afán por alejarse más y más de lo literario, Nicanor Parra experimenta ahora con estos "poemas" breves, presentados según la forma simple del chiste. Textos inscritos en tarjetas llevan ilustraciones de artistas plásticos y poetas chilenos. Físicamente el "libro" es una caja—diseñada por Oscar Gacitúa— que contiene 200 tarjetas de tamaño postal. El blanco de estos chistes desacralizadores e irreverentes son el problema ecológico y el Chile de Pinochet. Dado que la gran mayoría de estos textos no funcionan ni como chistes ni como pequeños antipoemas, el experimento resulta más interesante que logrado. Incluye un corrosivo y divertido prólogo de Enrique Lihn. [OH]

5754 ———. Coplas de Navidad. Santiago: Ediciones del Camaleón, 1983. 10 p.: ill.

Retorno de Parra a uno de sus predilecciones más antiguas: la poesía popular chilena. En versos octosílabos con rima consonante, llenos de gracia e ingenio, el poeta se dirige a la Virgen María para pedirle que libere a Chile de la dictadura que lo atormenta. Mención especial merece la original y hermosa edición de este libro, diseñado por el pintor Oscar Gacitúa. [OH]

5755 Paz Castillo, Fernando. Antología poética. Caracas: Monte Avila Editores, 1979. 185 p. (Colección Altazor)

Dispuesta como recorrido totalizador—desde *La voz de los cuatro vientos* (1931) hasta un poema inédito fechado 1977—ofrece un adecuado panorama de la obra de Paz Castillo (1893–1981, ver item **5847**). El prólogo de Eugenio Montejo (p. 7–25) diseña, con finura, características reflexivas y coloquiales de esta poesía. Omite informaciones bibliográficas, indispensables para lectores no venezolanos (ver *HLAS 40:7223, HLAS 42:5917* y *HLAS 44:5727*). [PL]

5756 Pellicer, Carlos. Obras: poesía. México: Fondo de Cultura Económica, 1981. 981 p. (Letras mexicanas)

Edición de la poesía completa de un miembro de la generación de los "Contemporáneos." La primera sección del libro empieza con *Colores en el mar* (1921) y termina con *Reincidencias*, libro póstumo de 1978; la segunda la constituyen los "Poemas no Coleccionados" (1912–21); y la tercera la componen los "Primeros Poemas" de su época adolescente (1912–21). Termina con una bibliografía extensa de y sobre su obra. [NK]

5757 Perlongher, Néstor. Austria-Hungría. Buenos Aires: Ediciones Tierra Baldía, 1980. 48 p. (Serie Poesía; 4)

Poesía de "hybris" trágica, imprecatoria, audaz, carnavalesca. Consta de dos secciones: "Escenas de la Guerra" y "Por qué Seremos tan Hermosas," construidas alrededor de las experiencias de la violencia histórica contemporánea y la rebeldía homosexual. [JG]

5758 Picado, Mario. Absurdo asombro. San José: Editorial Costa Rica, 1982. 80 p. (Libros de poesía; 12)

Fiel a su título los absurdos iconoclastas asombran, producen en el lector los cortocircuitos que Macedonio buscaba en sus chistes conceptuales. [GY]

5759 Plá, Josefina. Follaje del tiempo. Asunción: Ediciones NAPA, 1981. 51 p. (Serie Poesía; año 1, no. 2)

Breve colección de poemas escritos 1965–70. Dividido en tres secciones cuyo tema central es la confrontación con el tiempo. Tono que va de la resignación a la desesperanza. [MGP]

5760 ———. Tiempo y tiniebla. Asunción?: Alcándara, 1982. 110 p. (Colección Poesía; 9)

Poemario de diferentes períodos de la poesía de Plá, precedido de una entrevista informativa acerca de su poesía y la poesía del Paraguay. Los temas que informan la colección son el tiempo interno, la sociedad y el ingreso a la edad madura. [MGP]

5761 Portogalo, José. Los pájaros ciegos y otros poemas. Selección de José Portogalo. Prólogo de Josefina Mercado Longhi. Buenos Aires: Centro Editor de América Latina, 1982. 89 p. (Capítulo. Biblioteca argentina fundamental; 132)

Portogalo (n. 1904) representa con distinción la poesía social, imbuida del sentir del inmigrante italiano. Reúne textos seleccionados por el propio autor, desde *Tregua* (1933) hasta *Letra para Juan Tango* (1958). [JG]

5762 Ramos Collado, Lilliana. Proemas para despabilar cándidos. San Juan: Taller Reintegro, 1981. 68 p.: ill.

Lilliana Ramos abandona elementos tradicionales de la poesía femenina en Puerto Rico (e.g., el sentimentalismo lírico, el resentimiento herido de Julia de Burgos), para moverse a una poesía calculadamente fría, hasta cínica, desmitificadora de su propio impulso lírico, que el libro sabotea estructuralmente con la noción estridente y equívoca de "proema." [RRA]

5763 Rivas, José Luis. Tierra nativa. México: Fondo de Cultura Económica, 1982. 69 p. (Letras mexicanas)

Poema largo dividido en seis partes que capta las vivencias del trópico y cuya primera línea "También enero es un mes cruel" nos remite de inmediato a *The wasteland*. Configuración de un hablante que narra poéticamente sus recuerdos, ensoñaciones, y vivencias al Gran Capitán, su interlocutor, en un tono conversacional altamente simbólico e imaginista. [NK]

5764 Rodas, Ana María. Cuatro esquinas del juego de una muñeca. Guatemala: Litografías Modernas, 198? 73 p.

Poesía gráfica, de una ironía icono-
clasta. Sabe modular la voz para que en ella
se produzca el choque de varias conciencias.
[GY]

5765 Rodríguez Alcalá, Guido. Leviatán. Et
cétera. Asunción: Ediciones NAPA,
1981. 64 p. (Serie Poesía; v. 1, no. 1)

Buena muestra de poesía política en el
Paraguay en dos partes: 1) *Leviatán*: contiene
15 poemas de alta calidad centrados en denuncia de la situación política del Paraguay y
de América Latina, con tono personal y exas-
perado en algunos de ellos; 2) *Et cétera*:
poemas sueltos de tono personal. Es el quinto
libro de Rodríguez Alcalá (n. 1946). [MGP]

5766 Rojas, Gonzalo. Del relámpago. México: Fondo de Cultura Económica,
1981. 276 p. (Colección Tierra firme)

Entre el poema tradicional y el anti-
poema, la voz poética de Gonzalo Rojas ha
creado su propio espacio: elevado y coloquial,
íntimo y altisonante. *Del relámpago* recoge y
reordena casi toda su poesía desde *La miseria
del hombre* (1948) hasta *Trastierro* (1980). El
sugerente prólogo, "No al Lector, al Oyente,"
nos recuerda que la suya es poesía para ser
leída y releída, un discurso lírico para el oído.
[C. Grau]

5767 Romero, Armando. El poeta de vidrio.
Caracas: Fundarte, 1979. 90 p. (Cuadernos de difusión; no. 32)

"Como agua que una noria febril de-
volviera a su cauce primero," dice Alvaro
Mutis de estos poemas en un prólogo breve y
cordial (p. 9–10). Esa nota describe bien una
desmesura verbal muy cercana al tremen-
dismo, no siempre a salvo de la dilución gratuita de la intensidad. [PL]

5768 Rosas, Patrick. Las claves ocultas y
otros poemas. Lima: Mosca Azul Editores, 1981. 67 p.

Poemas del exilio, el amor, la muerte y
otros agonías lo consagran como un poeta
serio, que hace de la persona poética un
emblema de la marginalidad y del poema un
espacio de contestación. También se trata
aquí de una reflexión diferida sobre la locura
del destino artístico en la sociedad negadora,
y, a la vez, del diálogo afirmado en un lenguaje de las precisiones. [JO]

5769 Rubio, Armando. Ciudadano. Selección y prólogo de Alberto Rubio. Santiago: Ediciones Minga, 1983. 112 p.

Libro póstumo del poeta fallecido a los
25 años. Ordenado por su padre, es en realidad la publicación del borrador que el poeta
estaba corrigiendo antes de morir. A pesar de
ello, ya se vislumbra la configuración de una
poesía a la vez desacralizadora y melancólica,
escrita en un lenguaje coloquial, que revela
un sentimiento de soledad y una especie de
tedium vitae provocado por la ciudad capi-
talina. [OH]

5770 Rugama, Leonel. Poemas. Managua:
s.n., 1981. 79 p. (Colección Juan de
Dios Muñoz. Serie Hombre nuevo; 1)

Buena muestra de la obra del talentoso
poeta joven muerto en 1970. Los poemas
fluctúan entre la ironización de los símbolos
del poder, la solidaridad con el pueblo y el
elogio de los héroes de la historia latinoamericana y la revolución nicaragüense. [GY]

5771 Sabines, Jaime. Poemas sueltos. México: Papeles Privados, 1981. 31 p.

Libro más reciente del poeta coloquial
mexicano actual más importante, contiene
20 composiciones en verso y prosa que parten
de las vivencias contidianas. Poemas directos,
reflexivos, lúdicos e irónicos. Este poemario
se incluye como última sección de la tercera
edición aumentada de *Nuevo recuento de
poesía* (J. Mortiz, 1983) que comprende su
obra desde 1950. [NK]

5772 Silva, Fernando. Poesía, 1957–1981.
Managua: Ministerio de Cultura,
1982. 177 p.

Poeta popular, casi por antonomasia,
habla con la voz del pueblo en imágenes
vivas si bien sencillas. Puede profundizar en
lo cotidiano a la vez que elaborar una poesía
aparentemente utilitaria como en "Cuido de
la Criatura," pero siempre con imágenes
vivas, palpables. [GY]

5773 Silva Bélinzon, Concepción. Antología
poética. Selección de textos, Marosa
Di Giorgio, Claudio Ross. Prólogo de Arturo
Sergio Visca. Montevideo: Imprenta Vinaak,
1981. 177 p.

Selección de 14 poemarios (1943–79)
ofrece una muestra representativa de esta importante voz poética femenina del Uruguay.
Su poesía diseña un mundo lírico que revela
los estados de conciencia de una genuina vi-
vencia poética, elaborando un lenguaje transparente, sin artificio retórico. [MGP]

5774 Sola González, Alfonso. El soñador y otros poemas. Buenos Aires: Fundación Argentina para la Poesía, 1980. 57 p.: bibl. (Colección Poetas argentinos contemporáneos)

Sola González (1917–75) fue uno de los animadores de la generación del 40. Esta selección le hace justicia a su mundo onírico desplegado desde *La casa muerta* (1940) hasta *Cantos a la noche* (1963). [JG]

5775 Sotomayor, Aurea María. Sitios de la memoria. Ilustraciones de José A. Peláez. San Juan: Taller Huracán, 1983. 72 p.: ill.

Ceñida exploración de la memoria del deseo, una memoria nietzscheana, más del olvido que del recuerdo. La densa articulación metafórica de este proceso delata un sub-texto menos intelectual: se trata de un libro de amor, del dolor del amor perdido y de la familia como imagen de la permanencia. Los bellísimos grabados de Peláez ilustran los signos recurrentes del deseo: el pulpo, el abánico, la rosa. [RRA]

5776 Succar, Habib. Agua fértil: poesía, 1975–1978. San José: Editorial Costa Rica, 1980. 60 p.

Miembro fundador del "Grupo sin Nombre," todavía en formación. Sobresale en la expresión de aproximación al otro. [GY]

5777 Szinetar, Miguel. Sol quinto. Caracas: FUNDARTE, 1980. 63 p. (Cuadernos de difusión; no. 48)

Intensidad y diafanidad son notas adecuadas para definir el libro de M. Szinetar. Sus brevísimos textos condensan a menudo imágenes o reflexiones de rara armonía y precisión. Una voz poética muy promisoria en la literatura venezolana más reciente. [PL]

5778 Ulacia, Manuel. La materia como ofrenda. México: Universidad Nacional Autónoma de México, 1890. 56 p. (Colección Cuadernos de poesía)

Poesía reflexiva, de tono sobrio y templado, llena de preocupaciones y sentires de un sujeto en particular ante las múltiples facetas que componen su mundo. Formas tradicionales que recuerdan a Borges y Cernuda en el uso de la imagen y la metáfora. [NK]

5779 Vallarino, Roberto. Exilio interior: poemas, 1979–1981. México: Fondo de Cultura Económica, 1982. 110 p. (Letras mexicanas)

Cuarto poemario en siete secciones que recoge poemas escritos entre 1979–81. Recuperación angustiada de las vivencias diarias en la gran urbe en un intento logrado del hablante de definirse y transfigurarse en un espacio que lo contiene y lo distancia a la vez. [NK]

5780 Vélez, Jaime Alberto. Reflejos. Medellín, Colombia: Universidad de Antioquia Ediciones, 1980. 111 p.

La escritura de Vélez (n. 1950) se ciñe al modelo del epigrama clásico. Los subtítulos de las partes del volumen reafirman su propósito: "Palimpsesto de Marcial" y "Voces: Poemas Apócrifos." El acercamiento parece ser extremo, pero un sútil trabajo de actualizaciones posibles del paradigma confiere interés al experimento. [PL]

5781 Vilariño, Idea. Segunda antología. Prólogo, Luis Gregorich. Buenos Aires: Calicanto Editorial, 1980. 89 p.

Idea Vilariño es figura central en la poesía uruguaya contemporánea. Esta segunda antología preparada por la autora incluye poemas de volúmenes anteriores sin dejar constancia de ello. Como toda su poesía anterior, los poemas son muy breves, en apariencia sencillos, pero configurando un diálogo entre un yo angustiado, obsesionado por el dolor, y un tú que es la representación lírica de la imposibilidad de realización del deseo. [MGP]

5782 Vitale, Ida. Jardín de sílice. Caracas: Monte Avila Editores, 1980. 91 p. (Colección Altazor)

A partir de sus primeros poemarios, todos breves, *La luz de esta memoria* (1949), *Palabra dada* (1953) hasta *Oidor andante* (1970), se mantiene una continuidad en la depuración y el rigor del lenguaje lírico. Este nuevo poemario es la colección más importante de esta poeta uruguaya. Temas recurrentes son el pasaje de pasado a presente-futuro, el sentido de la vida, el amor, y un diseño "Magrittiano" del paraíso. [MGP]

5783 Volkow, Verónica. El inicio. Oaxaca, México: Ayuntamiento Popular de Juchitán, 1983. 1 v. (Colección Guchiochi Coyuiunda)

Tercer libro de la joven poeta que comprende 12 poemas con unidad temática. Poética del cuerpo en que la imagen y la metáfora configuran el tiempo sin tiempo del deseo y el amor. [NK]

5784 Wiethüchter, Blanca. Madera viva y árbol difunto. Dibujos interior y tapa, Luis Zilveti. La Paz: Ediciones Altiplano, 1982. 49 p., 4 leaves of plates: ill.

La Paz es la ciudad proyectada en su presencia física de círculo y pendiente y en su realidad de entidad en espera y en potencialidad de cambio. El presente, urgencia de la crisis y contacto con la muerte impuesta, es situado en diálogo poético con el pasado a través de textos recogidos de la tradición indígena. Obra de primera importancia. [A.R. Prada]

5785 Wong, Oscar. He brotado raíces. México: Editorial Katún, 1982. 84 p. (Poesía; 3)

Tercer libro del joven poeta y crítico chiapaneco. Coloquialismo y lirismo que conceden un tono encantatorio a estos poemas mayormente amorosos en verso libre. [NK]

5786 Yurkievich, Saúl. Acaso acoso. Valencia: Pre-Textos, 1982. 165 p. (Poesía; 44)

La vena lúdica de S. Yurkievich (n. 1931) puede atrapar a un lector que acepte este juego. Una imaginación inagotable. Su riqueza lingüística puede, sin embargo, disipar toda inocencia y abrir un abismo para el vértigo del que lee. Crítico agudo y audaz, su pensamiento literario no presenta fronteras con su creación poética. [JG]

5787 Zurita, Raúl. Anteparaíso de Raúl Zurita. Santiago: Editores Asociados, 1982. 169 p.: col. ill.

Obra magna de neovanguardismo chileno. El hablante adopta una postura "profética," en cuanto busca el conocimiento de lo absoluto mediante la revelación; pero en este caso, lo absoluto tiene su sede en Chile, considerado a la vez como categoría del espíritu y Tierra Prometida. El hablante—que frecuentemente recurre a un correlato bíblico y dantesco—acepta al dolor de ser chileno, como una fuerza cognoscitiva que lo conduce a una suerte de epifanía de la Patria. En contraste con los antipoemas de Parra, Zurita intenta una re-sacralización del mundo mediante la poesía, en una verdadera fiesta del intelecto, que dentro de su tono de cántico elevado no excluye el uso de formulaciones coloquiales, dialógicas y narrativas. Gráficamente, Anteparaíso se aparta de la poesía vigente en Chile y ofrece nuevas posibilidades de visualización del texto en la página. [OH]

GENERAL STUDIES

5788 Arbeláez, Fernando. Poesía venezolana: pasado y presente (CONAC/ RNC, 41:247, abril/nov. 1981, p. 54–78)

Visión panorámica muy útil, que fija el inicio de la actividad poética en la obra de Juan de Castellanos y avanza hasta al período contemporáneo. La síntesis introduce a "una muestra de poesía venezolana en diferentes épocas," y cumple con eficacia el propósito de informar sobre momentos y personalidades claves del proceso. [PL]

5789 Bolaños Ugalde, Luis. Raíces indígenas de la literatura costarricense: la poesía lírica (Revista de Artes y Letras de la Universidad de Costa Rica [San José] 4:1, 1980, p. 3–18, bibl.)

Sigue dos propósitos: rescatar el pasado (literario) indígena, negado en Costa Rica y comprobar la literariedad del "folklor" (canciones preliterarias con valor poético). Con sofisticación teórica y crítica, Bolaños destaca las funciones poética (según Jakobson) y mágica-hipnótica de las canciones de guatusos, bribris, cabécares y borucas. [GY]

5790 Carrasco M., Iván. Notas sobre la poesía apocalíptica hispanoamericana (UC/RCL, 18, nov. 1981, p. 139–148)

Esboza la presencia de lo apocalíptico en figuras como Cardenal, Neruda y Arteche para abordar un estudio más pormenorizado del tema en *Futurologías*, utópico discurso poético del reverendo José Miguel Ibáñez que oficia de crítico literario en *El Mercurio*. [RdC]

5791 Castagnino, Raúl Héctor. Fenomenología de lo poético. Buenos Aires: Plus Ultra, 1980. 187 p.: bibl.

Minuciosa información, amplia ilustración, inteligente discusión sobre la poesía. El libro está orientado hacia un público estudiantil, pero puede ser disfrutado por cualquier neófito y, desde, luego, por los fieles seguidores de los varios esfuerzos ensayísticos de Castagnino por comprender la literatura en general. [JG]

5792 Cerutti, Franco. *El Güegüence* y otros ensayos de literatura nicaragüense. Roma: Bulzoni, 1983. 184 p. (Letterature iberiche e latino-americane)

En su análisis del *Güegüence* donde puntualiza el impacto de lo popular; en su recorrido de la cultura literaria de León en tiempos de Darío cuando la escuela poética de Occidente (1850–1900) escamotea la realidad nicaragüense en pro de la universalidad (i.e., afrancesamiento); Cerutti sienta las bases para una comprensión ampliamente cultural de la literatura nicaragüense. Su ensayo sobre Salomón de la Selva y su concepción del liderazgo es clave en el nuevo clima político. [GY]

5793 Coddou, Marcelo. Poesía chilena en el exilio a la luz de ciertos conceptos literarios fundamentales (HISPA, 10:29, 1981, p. 29–39)

Una propuesta metodológica para el estudio de textos publicados en el exilio. Según Coddou habría que distinguir en ellos los siguientes niveles: 1) concepción de la naturaleza de la poesía y su función; 2) imágenes del yo lírico; 3) niveles de realidad poetizados; 4) lenguaje poético. Después de abocarse a los aspectos mencionados, proporciona un repertorio de los motivos recurrentes en la poesía chilena en el exilio. Loable esfuerzo que representa una primera tentativa de ordenamiento y sistematización de ese campo, caótico en apariencia, constituido por una poesía que se fragmenta y reparte por todos los rincones del planeta. [OH]

5794 Concha, Jaime. Mapa de la nueva poesía chilena (ECO, 44[6]:240, oct. 1981, p. 661–671)

Siguiendo el plan anunciado en el título de su nota, Jaime Concha realiza un viaje de norte a sur por la "nueva poesía chilena," según el lugar de residencia de los poetas, antes del golpe militar de 1973. Concha se demora brevemente en algunas estaciones: Oscar Hahn (Arica), Waldo Rojas (Santiago), el grupo "Trilce" (Valdivia) y llega a su destino que es la poesía de Gonzalo Millán, la cual es analizada con mayor detención. Trabajo más bien informativo sobre los poetas que surgen alrededor de 1965, pero que tiene el mérito de llamar la atención sobre un sector de la poesía chilena descuidado por la crítica. [RdC]

5795 Díaz Quiñones, Arcadio. El almuerzo en la hierba: Lloréns Torres, Palés Matos, René Marqués. Río Piedras, P.R.: Ediciones Huracán, 1982. 168 p.: bibl. (Colección La nave y el puerto)

Recopilación de ensayos que no llegan a superar su carácter fragmentario pero que se destacan por la mesura y objetividad de la óptica crítica. Díaz Quiñones encuadra la obra de estos tres autores en sus tres generaciones, reconstruyendo sus espacios ideológicos y estilísticos. [RRA]

Durán, Manuel. "Contemporáneos:" ¿grupo, promoción, generación, conspiración? See item **5196.**

5796 García Marruz, Fina. Introducción a un debate sobre la poesía joven cubana (AR, 7:27, 1981, p. 14–23)

La gran escritora cubana señala que el estado de concurrencia poética por el que abogaba Lezama, aunque aparente ser ahistórico no lo es; de hecho, es lo más definitorio de la nueva hornada de poetas, más comprometidos con la raíz popular que con la metafísica insular de los poetas de *Orígenes*, pero igualmente cubanos en su intención fundacional y en su optimismo regenerador. [RRA]

5797 Hernández Rueda, Lupo. La generación del 48 en la literatura dominicana. Santiago de los Caballeros, República Dominicana: Universidad Católica Madre y Maestra, 1981. 537 p.: appendix, index (Colección Estudios; 58)

Recuento histórico y temático de las características fundamentales de los poetas que sucedieron al movimiento esteticista y cosmopolita de los poetas de "la poesía sorprendida" con una poesía más arraigada en la búsqueda de lo autóctono. El autor junto con Abelardo Vicioso, Freddy Gatón Arce y otros, fue miembro de dicha generación. Curiosamente Pedro Mir, único poeta dominicano de visibilidad internacional, queda relegado a unos breves comentarios donde se describe su obra como fundamentalmente pesimista. [RRA]

5798 Higgins, James. The poet in Peru: alienation and the quest for a superreality. Liverpool, England: Cairns, 1982. 166 p.: bibl. (Liverpool monographs in Hispanic studies; 0261–1538, 1)

Higgins es un reconocido peruanista cuyo trabajo ha girado especialmente sobre la poesía de César Vallejo. En este libro desarrolla un intrigante esquema de análisis: estudia a un grupo de poetas bajo el rubro de una "poetry of alienation" y a otro grupo bajo el de "visionary poetry." Sin embargo, el esquema no es meramente dualista: poetas como Eguren y Vallejo caen dentro de ambos rubros. Higgins presenta su hipótesis con buenos argumentos, y, además sus lecturas de la obra de Belli, Moro y Cisneros añaden interpretaciones válidas más allá del mismo esquema. Una buena introducción a la poesía peruana contemporánea. [JO]

5799 Jitrik, Noé. Papeles de trabajo: notas sobre vanguardismo latinoamericano (RCLL, 8:15, 1982, p. 13–24)

Sugestiva constelación de críticas, notas e ideas sobre varios postulados del vanguardismo. Una tentativa por desligar el análisis del fenómeno de sus tradicionales esquemas cronológicos y eurocéntricos. [RdC]

5800 Laguerre, Enrique A. Encuentro de Luis Palés Matos con Jorge de Lima (ICP/R, 21:81, oct./dic. 1978, p. 21–26, ill., plate)

Valioso acercamiento de las nunca transitadas concurrencias entre la poesía puertorriqueña y la del Brasil, partiendo de los mitos femeninos (Fili-Melé y Mira-Celi) de Palés y Lima, donde Laguerre encuentra significativos paralelos. [RRA]

5801 Lewis, Marvin A. Afro-Hispanic poetry, 1940–1980: from slavery to Negritude in South American verse. Columbia: University of Missouri Press, 1983. 190 p.: bibl., index.

Analiza detalladamente la producción artística de temática negra en la poesía reciente del Uruguay, Perú, Colombia y Ecuador. Exposición equilibrada de formas y contenido de la poesía de Virginia Brindis de Salas y Pilar Barrios (uruguayas), de Nicomedes Santa Cruz (peruano), de Nelsón Estupiñan Bass y Adalberto Ortiz (ecuatorianos) y de Antonio Preciado, Jorge Artel, Hugo Salazar Valdés y Juan Zapata Olivella (colombianos). [RdC]

5802 Marfany, Joan-Luis. Algunas consideraciones sobre el modernismo hispanoamericano (CH, 382, abril 1982, p. 82–124)

Meditado repaso del estado actual de la crítica sobre el modernismo hispanoamericano. Basándose en su propio análisis del modernismo en Cataluña y ayudado por estudios de otras disciplinas sobre el período, el autor señala deficiencias en la crítica. Sugiere otras sendas de investigación interdisciplinar para llegar a una mejor comprensión del movimiento. [RdC]

5803 Mignolo, Walter D. La figura del poeta en la lírica de vanguardia (IILI/RI, 48:118/119, enero/junio 1982, p. 131–148)

Confrontando procedimientos de textos modernistas y vanguardistas, descubre una característica "volatilización" de la figura del hablante en la poesía de vanguardia. [RdC]

5804 Müller-Bergh, Klaus. El hombre y la técnica: contribución al conocimiento de corrientes vanguardistas hispanoamericanas (IILI/RI, 48:118/119, enero/junio 1982, p. 149–176)

Importante enfoque de la estética vanguardista, sus varias y variadas manifestaciones en las más representativas revistas de la época. Destaca con acierto los registros locales e indigenistas en el encuadre cosmopolita e internacional del fenómeno analizando sus variantes en las distintas regiones de América. [RdC]

5805 Osorio Tejeda, Nelson. Antecedentes de la vanguardia literaria en Venezuela: 1909–1925 (HISPA, 33, 182, p. 3–30)

Documenta la recepción de las nuevas tendencias artísticas, desde el futurismo, a través de un examen de la polémica crítica y de la producción literaria del período. De particular interés el apartado sobre la influyente presencia de José Juan Tablada en Caracas en 1919. Estudio valioso por las informaciones que proporciona y por las relaciones contextuales que establece. [PL]

5806 ———. La recepción del *Manifiesto futurista* de Marinetti en América Latina (RCLL, 8:15, 1982, p. 25–37)

Documentado estudio de la cautelosa recepción del futurismo en América en 1909. Argumenta contra un enfoque deductivo de la vanguardia latinoamericana tomando como modelo la europea. Queda por demostrar la tesis implícita: una fisonomía particular (y diferente) del vanguardismo literario latinoamericano. [RdC]

5807 Paz, Octavio. Antivíspera Taller (Vuelta [México] 76, marzo 1983, p. 6–12)

Esclarecedora historia de Paz sobre el grupo de "Taller," la nueva generación literaria de la que él formó parte, y que apareció en México entre 1935–38. Discute la formación del grupo, su poética e ideología y las publicaciones que los definieron, *Taller Poético* y *Taller* (ver items **5884** and **5885**). [NK]

5808 Rodríguez-Alcalá, Hugo. El vanguardismo en el Paraguay (IILI/RI, 48:118/119, enero/junio 1982, p. 241–255)

Examen de la situación histórica del Paraguay con respecto al desarrollo de la literatura vanguardista. Énfasis en la recepción de la nueva poesía por parte de Josefina Plá, quien contribuyó a su divulgación entre los jóvenes poetas. Especial atención al surrealista Campos Cervera. [MGP]

5809 Rodríguez Monegal, Emir. El olvidado ultraísmo uruguayo (IILI/RI, 48:118/119, enero/junio 1982, p. 257–274)

El crítico uruguayo propone un estudio del ultraísmo en Uruguay (olvidado por la crítica) a partir de la compilación de Ildefonso Pereda Valdés, *Antología de la nueva poesía uruguaya* (1927), que incluye un iluminador texto de Borges. Es imprescindible, además, un estudio de las revistas vanguardistas *Alfar, La Pluma* (ver item **5816**), *La Cruz del Sur, Los Nuevos*, junto a varios ensayos de Borges sobre poesía uruguaya de esos años. Estas fuentes permitirán una revaluación del vanguardismo uruguayo. [MGP]

5810 Romero, Armando. Ausencia y presencia de las vanguardias en Colombia (IILI/RI, 48:118/119, enero/junio 1982, p. 275–287)

Revisión polémica del proceso. Considera la significación de Silva para la poesía colombiana moderna; anota atisbos y limitaciones de las instancias de transición (Barba Jacob, Luis C. López), y enfatiza los escasos hitos establecidos desde la aparición de León de Greiff (ver item **5713**, *HLAS 38:6952, HLAS 40:7081–7082 y 7206, y HLAS 42:5757 y 5922*) hasta la importante tarea de la revista *Mito* en la década del 50. [PL]

5811 Schwartz, Jorge. La vanguardia en América Latina: una estética comparada (UNAM/RUM, 38:21, enero 1983, p. 12–16, plates)

Sucinto esbozo de puntos en común entre la literatura de la vanguardia en Brasil y en Hispanoamérica para fundamentar un análisis dentro de la línea de la literatura comparada. [RdC]

5812 ———. Vanguardias enfrentadas: Oliverio Girondo y la poesía concreta (Maldoror [Arca Editorial, Montevideo] 16, nov. 1981, p. 22–35, ill.)

Interesante yuxtaposición en el tiempo y el espacio de los encuentros y desencuentros del vanguardista argentino con los brasileños, desde Mario de Andrade a Oswald y los poetas concretistas. Valioso rescate y confrontación de textos olvidados. Sugerente relectura de *En la masmédula* a la luz del concretismo. [RdC]

5813 Seminario-Simposio de la Literatura Ecuatoriana en los Ultimos 30 Años, *1st, Quito, Ecuador, 1983.* La literatura ecuatoriana en los últimos 30 años, 1950–1980. Hernán Rodríguez Castelo *et al.* Quito: Editorial El Conejo, 1983. 132 p.: bibl. (Colección Ecuador/letras)

A pesar de su brevedad, esta transcripción de una mesa redonda sobre la situación de la literatura ecuatoriana (efectuada en junio de 1983) es un valioso testimonio crítico de las preocupaciones, temas y valoraciones tanto de los distintos géneros, como de las figuras principales de la renovación del escenario literario de ese país. La lírica, el cuento, la novela y el escritor y su medio son los tópicos que cada uno de los panelistas desarrolla con bastante información y capacidad analítica. [JO]

5814 Vargas, Vilma. El devenir de la palabra poética: Venezuela, siglo XX. Caracas: Universidad Central de Venezuela, Ediciones de la Biblioteca, 1980. 199 p.: bibl. (Colección Arte y literatura; 8)

La propuesta metodológica persigue conjugar comentario textual y examen de las condiciones histórico-culturales, pero el resultado es muy pobre: el instrumental analítico, extraído principalmente del libro de Jean Cohen, se aplica con vaguedad y ligereza; las relaciones extratextuales son obvias o previsibles. El anexo final constituye una válida antología de los 27 autores considerados, desde Enrique Planchart hasta Manuel Hernández. [PL]

5815 Vegas García, Irene. Nueva conciencia, nueva expresión: seis poetas en la Revolución cubana (RCLL, 9:17, 1983, p. 213–229)

Presentación general de seis poetas (Miguel Barnet, Guillermo Rodríguez Rivera, Nancy Morejón, Víctor Casaus, Luis Rogelio Nogueras y Raúl Rivero), y su desarrollo poético en el seno de la Revolución cubana. El criterio aquí es demasiado generacional y tiende a aislar a estos poetas de otros (Lezama, Vitier, Marruz) quizás no tan obviamente insertables en el esquema sociohistórico de la autora. [RRA]

5816 Videla de Rivero, Gloria. Poesía de vanguardia en Iberoamérica a través de la revista *La Pluma*, de Montevideo: 1927–1931 (IILI/RI, 48:118/119, enero/junio 1982, p. 331–349)

Otra valiosa contribución de esta destacada investigadora a la historiografía de la vanguardia latinoamericana, teniendo en cuenta el doble caracter de movimiento americano e internacional. Examen de la influencia que ejerció la revista *La Pluma* en la difusión del vanguardismo europeo, norteamericano y uruguayo. [MGP]

5817 ———. El runrunismo chileno, 1927–1934: el contexto literario (UC/RCL, 18, nov. 1981, p. 73–87)

Según Gloria Videla, el "runrunismo" fue un movimiento de adolescentes surgido en Chile hacia 1927, que creyendo estar en la vanguardia, repitieron rigurosamente lo que ya habían hecho los primeros vanguardistas, incluyendo ciertos "escándalos" de obvio origen dadaísta. Programáticamente, se manifestaron en favor de una poesía que sintetizara lo mejor del mundonovismo y la vanguardia, pero en la práctica terminaron por prescindir de los ingredientes mundonovistas. Su "teórico" y cabeza visible fue el poeta Benjamín Morgado. [OH]

5818 Yurkievich, Saúl. *Vanguardia*, the Latin American avant-garde movement: rupture and permanence (UNESCO/CU, 8:2, 1982, p. 83–100)

Sugerente repaso del fenómeno del modernismo y la vanguardia, viéndolo como un proceso dinámico de contrastes cuyas conecciones causales reverberan en despliegues posteriores—como la nueva novela y el concretismo. [RdC]

5819 Zulueta, Ignacio M. *El Nuevo Mercurio*: 1907 (RIB, 31:3, 1981, p. 385–403) Indice analítico y comentario crítico del contenido de *El Nuevo Mercurio*, importante revista difusora del modernismo dirigida por Enrique Gómez Carrillo.

Destaca la presencia del modernismo en las páginas de la revista como tema de debate en la famosa "encuesta" de 1907 y como práctica literaria de sus colaboradores. [RdC]

SPECIAL STUDIES

5820 Aguirre Lavayen, Joaquín. Adela Zamudio: guerrilla del Parnaso. Cochabamba, Bolivia: Editorial Los Amigos del Libro, 1980. 69 p.: ill.

Breve apreciación de la vida y obra de la "poetisa y pensadora de América." Intento de provocar una lectura más profunda de sus escritos exponiendo lo ideológicamente revolucionario en ellos. Una selecta colección de poemas acompaña el ensayo. [A.R. Prada]

5821 Andueza, María. La flama en el espejo, Rubén Bonifaz Nuño: análisis y comentarios del texto. México: Universidad Nacional Autónoma de México, 1981. 197 p.: bibl., ill. (Colección Poemas y ensayos)

Util análisis semiológico que estudia el nivel morfosintáctico, semántico, retórico y pragmático de este excelente poemario de · Rubén Bonifaz Nuño cuya complejidad lo hace difícil al lector no iniciado. [NK]

5822 Arellano, Jorge Eduardo and **José Jirón Terán.** Contribuciones al estudio de Rubén Darío [de] Jorge Eduardo Arellano. Investigacones en torno a Rubén Darío [de] José Jirón Terán. Managua: Dirección General de Bibliotecas y Archivos, 1981. 150 p.: bibl.

Arellano presenta a un Darío ecléctico, heteróclito. La mayoría de los estudios enfocan los *marginalia* en torno a la figura y obra dariana. Jirón también indaga los *marginalia*—pero de mayor interés son los poemas inéditos reproducidos aquí. [GY]

5823 Armas, Emilio de. Julián del Casal, crítico de la sociedad colonial habanera (*in* Cuba, les étapes d'une libération: hommage à Juan Marinello et Noël Salomon: actes du colloque international des 22, 23 et 24 novembre 1978. Toulouse, France: Centre d'études cubaines, Université de Toulouse-Le Mirail, v. 1, p. 31–43)

Partiendo de la distinción entre la poesía *verbal*, de un exilio combativo, de Martí, y la poesía de la *escritura*, triste y aislada, de Casal, De Armas elabora un interesante examen de la dimensión social en la poesía y la obra periodística de Casal. Es una interpretación parecida a la que hace Benjamin sobre Baudelaire, y muy apropiada en el caso de este, el más importante poeta simbolista cubano. [RRA]

5824 Barradas, Efraín. La negritud hoy: nota sobre la poesía de Nancy Morejón (AR, 6:24, abril 1980, p. 33–39)

Barradas examina la poesía de Morejón en el contexto de un renacimiento de la negritud, liberada del exotismo etnocéntrico que caracterizó el afroantillanismo. La dimensión histórica y el tono fundacional de su poesía la distingue también significativamente del urgente tono sociológico de protesta del "black movement" norteamericano. [RRA]

5825 ———. Premonición y esperanza: un momento de transición en la poesía de Cintio Vitier (UNION, 4, 1981, p. 52–63)

Recuento del desarrollo poético de Vitier con la intención de demostrar que el Vitier de la poética metafísica de *Orígenes* y el más reciente de su obra comprometida con la Revolución no son mutuamente excluyentes, sino todo lo contrario: su poesía es un largo proceso de depuración y objetivización del lenguaje poético que progresivamente va asumiendo un contacto definitorio con el mundo material. [RRA]

5826 ———. Sobre el origen de unos versos palesianos (HISPA, 34/35, 1983, p. 69–79, bibl.)

Encomiable labor investigativa sobre el posible modelo para "El Pozo:" un poema de una escritora menor norteamericana que usa el seudónimo de Richard Stranger. A pesar de una intención quizas demasiado genealógica y pendiente de influencias, el artículo arroja luz sobre el proceso de formación de la conciencia poética palesiana y es una aportación imprescindible a su bibliografía. [RRA]

5827 Benítez, Angel Ernesto. Luisa Luisi: el ensueño dolorido. Montevideo: Barreiro y Ramos, 1981. 71 p.

Luisi, poeta y educadora uruguaya, cumplió una labor fundamental en su país. En este brevísimo y efusivo ensayo se incluye una muestra mínima de su poesía junto a algunos textos sobre educación. Esta obra poética queda todavía por estudiarse. [MGP]

5828 Berge, Walter Bruno. Ernesto Cardenal: dichtung und/als revolution (Iberoromania [Max Niemeyer Verlag, Tübingen FRG] 15, 1982, p. 97–125)

Se estudia el sincretismo de elementos marxistas, cristianos, críticos e indios, el cual anula el enajenamiento al restituir un lenguaje propio y a la vez trascendente como en las *Coplas a la muerte de Merton.* [GY]

5829 Biermann, Karlheinrich. Die Theologie der Befreiuyng unds Ansätze einer neuen Volkskultur in Lateinamerika: ein Vergleich mit Tendenzen in der literarisch-poloitischen Offentlichkerit Frankreichs um 1848 (IAA, 9/2, 1983, p. 131–154, bibl.)

Análisis de los *Salmos* y *El Evangelio en Solentiname* de Cardenal a la luz de la "teología de liberación," avatar, según Biermann, del "socialismo utópico religioso" que afloró en Francia en 1830–51. El primer texto todavía pertenece a la vanguardia occidental mientras el segundo expresa la nueva cultura democrática. [GY]

5830 Calvo Fajardo, Yadira. Poesía en Jorge Debravo. San José: Ministerio de Cultura, Juventud y Deportes, División de Publicaciones y Divulgación, 1980. 287 p.: bibl., index (Serie D. El Creador analizado; título no. 8)

Valioso análisis estilístico influenciado por D. Alonso y C. Bousoño. Demuestra cómo lo incorpóreo—en las cuatro temáticas básicas: amor, muerte, religión y compromiso social—deviene material por medio de la metáfora antitética, "reflejando lo contradictorio de su propia actitud ante las cosas." [GY]

5831 Cardenal, Ernesto. La poesía nicaragüense de Pablo Antonio Cuadra (BNBD, 50, nov./dic. 1982, p. 74–76)

Primer libro vanguardista centroamericano y primera poesía verdaderamente nicaragüense, los *Poemas nicaragüenses* (1934) transforman en símbolos poéticos la cotidianidad nicaragüense: *albarda, comal, aites, rancho,* etc. Se trata de "crear" a Nicaragua, preocupación del mismo comentarista. [GY]

5832 Carrillo-Herrera, Gastón. Tradición, popularismo e innovación lingüística en la poesía de Neruda y en la lírica hispanoamericana (UH/RJ, 31, 1980, p. 301–311)

El lingüista chileno Gastón Carrillo escoge la poesía de Neruda para mostrar: a) la pervivencia en ella de formas lingüísticas peninsulares por tradición retórica; b) la presencia de formas lingüísticas americanas; y c) ciertas innovaciones del propio Neruda. Publicación póstuma de gran interés para los lingüistas, y llamado de alerta para evitar confusiones en el análisis literario de textos. [OH]

5833 Carter, Shiela. Superstitution in the poetry of Manuel de Cabral (*in* Conference of Hispanists, 5th, Mona, Jamaica, 1982. Myth and superstitution in Spanish-Caribbean literature: conference papers. Mona, Jamaica: University of the West Indies, Department of Spanish, 1982, p. 22–44, bibl.)

Este artículo (temático e introductorio) es valioso por constituir una de las pocas aportaciones bibliográficas sobre la poesía de uno de los poetas más admirados actualmente en la República Dominicana. [RRA]

Cobo Borda, J.G. El *Taller* de Paz. See item **5192.**

5834 Díaz-Casanueva, Humberto *et al.* Gabriela Mistral. Introducción de Mirella Servodidio y Marcelo Coddou. Xalapa, México: Centro de Investigaciones Lingüístico-Literarias, Instituto de Investigaciones Humanísticas, Universidad Veracruzana, 1980. 153 p.: bibl. (Cuadernos de texto crítico; 9)

Reúne los trabajos leídos en el simposio "Una reevaluación de Gabriela Mistral después de su muerte," realizado en Barnard College, en abril de 1978. Incluye ensayos de Humberto Díaz-Casanueva, Eliana Rivero, Gastón von dem Bussche, Marie-Lise Gazarian, Fernando Alegría, Jaime Concha, Jaime Giordano, Martin Taylor, Margaret T. Rudd, Pedro Lastra, Emir Rodríguez Monegal, Cedomil Goić, Gonzalo Rojas, y una presentación a cargo de Mirella Servodidio y Marcelo Coddou, organizadores del simposio. [OH]

5835 Feliciano Mendoza, Ester. Juana de Ibarbourou, oficio de poesía. Río Piedras, P.R.: Editorial Universitaria, Universidad de Puerto Rico, 1981. 284 p.: bibl. (Mente y palabra)

Estudio de la vida y obra de la poeta uruguaya y su ubicación en el espacio de la literatura femenina. Sigue la estructura tradicional de temas, mundo poético e ideas estéticas que caracterizan su obra. Incluye también un capítulo sobre la literatura infantil de Ibarbourou. [MGP]

5836 Goić, Cedomil. "Cima" de Gabriela Mistral (IILI/RI, 48:118/119, enero/junio 1982, p. 59–72)

Después de establecer la relación de Gabriel Mistral con la poesía de vanguardia, a ratos comprensiva y a ratos polémica, Goić realiza un análisis minucioso del poema "Cima," síntesis de tradición e innovación, que se acerca y aleja al mismo tiempo de la primera vanguardia, y que se caracteriza por el empleo de imágenes de cuño creacionista, en contraste con la producción mistraliana mundonovista. [OH]

5837 Hill, W. Nick. Oscar Hahn o el arte de mirar (UC/RCL, 20, nov. 1982, p. 99–112)

Excelente lectura de la poesía de Hahn (ver item **5715**) y *HLAS 40:7088, HLAS 42:5763* y *HLAS 44:5692*) centrada en el análisis de las transformaciones de un motivo: "la mirada que enciende" es a menudo en este poeta "la mirada que incendia," lo que ilustra de manera notable el poema "Visión de Hiroshima." Penetrante y renovadora propuesta crítica que favorece la intelección de un corpus poético fundamental, signado por la dimensión visionaria. [PL]

5838 Mansour, Mónica. Análisis textual e intertextual, "Elegía a Jesús Menéndez" de Nicolás Guillén. Reportaje fotográfico del entierro de Jesús Menéndez, Raúl Corral. México: Facultad de Filosofía y Letras, Colegio de Letras, Universidad Nacional Autónoma de México, 1980. 93 p., 6 p. of plates: bibl., ill. (Colección Cuadernos)

Sugestivo análisis lingüístico de los siete poemas que componen esta elegía para esclarecer la relación entre el nivel ideológico y la función poética. Se trata de un esfuerzo útil, y más aún en el caso de Guillén, un autor cuya obra tiende a ser vista más temática que estructuralmente. [RRA]

5839 ———. Tuya, mía, de otros: la poesía coloquial de Mario Benedetti. México: Instituto de Investigaciones Filológicas, Universidad Nacional Autónoma de México, 1979. 102 p.: bibl., ill. (Cuadernos del Seminario de Poética; 4)

Utilizando el aparato teórico estructuralista desarrollado por Jakobson y Hjemslev en particular, Mansour se propone un análisis del lenguaje de la poesía coloquial de Mario Benedetti, específicamente en *Poemas de otros* (1973–74). [MGP]

5840 Márquez, Roberto. Racism, culture and revolution: ideology and politics in the prose of Nicolás Guillén (LARR, 17:1, 1982, p. 43–68)

Márquez considera la prosa de Guillén como complemento de su poesía, algunas veces anticipándola, y otras proveyendo un marco conceptual paralelo al que se desarrolla en la visión poética. Su propósito es demostrar que existe un sistema de pensamiento unitario que une a la poesía con la prosa. [RRA]

5841 Medina Vidal, Jorge et al. Delmira Agustini: seis ensayos críticos. Montevideo: Editorial Ciencias, 1982. 83 p.: bibl., ill.

Seis ensayos que enfocan la poesía de Agustini desde diferentes posturas críticas. Predomina el psicocrítico y el estructural. Se examinan los grados de conversión, lo poético como producto de cultura, la poesía como producto del hombre e independiente del autor, y el poema, la actualización lingüística. El más original es el sexto ensayo, "El Cuerpo como Signo Poético en la Poesía de Agustini." [MGP]

5842 Mendieta y Núñez, Lucio and **María Elena de Anda.** Vida y obra de Amado Nervo. 2a. ed. México: Instituto Mexicano de Cultura, 1979. 58 p., 13 leaves of plates: bibl., ill.

Ofrece algunos datos biográficos, fotografías, descripciones de objetos y pertenencias que se encuentran en el Museo de Amado Nervo en la Ciudad de México, y presenta algunas anécdotas que podrían ser de interés al estudioso de su obra. [NK]

5843 Ortega, Julio. Vallejo: la poética de la subversión (HR, 50:3, Summer 1982, p. 267–296)

Relectura de España, aparta de mí este cáliz como "exteriorización de la poesía como pensamiento radical." Hace resaltar la coherencia ideológica y poética del utopismo que conforma el texto. [RdC]

5844 Oviedo, José Miguel. Los pasos de la memoria: lectura de un poema de Octavio Paz (CM/D, 17:3[99], mayo/junio 1981, p. 20–29)

Explicación de texto de Pasado en Claro desde las teorías poéticas de Paz para demostrar el lugar que ocupa el texto dentro

de su obra y confirmar "la profunda unidad y consistencia de su visión." [NK]

5845 La Poesía de Carlos Pellicer: interpretaciones críticas. Editor, Edward J. Mullen. Benjamín Carrión et al. México: Universidad Nacional Autónoma de México, Coordinación de Humanidades, Dirección General de Publicaciones, 1979. 239 p.: bibl. (Textos contemporáneos)

Colección de ensayos sobre la obra de Pellicer, miembro de Los Contemporáneos (1927–74). El libro, dividido en cuatro secciones, ofrece: 1) una introducción del compilador; 2) estudios de Benjamín Carrión, Merlin H. Foster, Andrew Debicki, Frank Dauster, Octavio Paz, Frank Reiss, y E.J. Mullen; 3) una sección de "Documentos" sobre distintas facetas de su vida y obra de Porfirio Martínez Peñaloza, Gabriela Mistral, J.M. González de Mendoza y otros; y 4) una bibliohemerografía de y sobre su obra. [NK]

5846 Prieto F., Luis B. Homenaje a Andrés Eloy Blanco. Caracas: La Casa de Bello, 1981. 72 p.: bibl.

Discurso de Luis Beltrán Prieto en el homenaje realizado en La Casa de Bello (1980), al cumplirse 25 años de la muerte del poeta. Nota sugestiva del comentario temático de Prieto es el registro de ciertos motivos—hilo, aguja, tejer y destejer—que revelan modos de construcción del mundo poético de Blanco (ver HLAS 40:7045–7046 y 7224, y HLAS 44:5807). [PL]

5847 ———. Persistencia y trascendencia en la poesía de Fernando Paz Castillo. Caracas: Editorial Arte, 1981. 87 p.: bibl., ill.

Formulaciones especulativas algo generales, no siempre corroborada de manera convincente por los textos atraídos como pruebas. Menos sugeridor que el ceñido prólogo de E. Montejo (ver item **5755**), vale como homenaje a la noble tarea poética de Paz Castillo (1893–1981), figura destacada de la generación del 18 (ver HLAS 40:7223 y HLAS 44:5727). [PL]

5848 Rama, Angel. La poesía en el tiempo de los asesinos (ECO, 40[2]:236, junio 1981, p. 219–225)

Reseña analítica de Hechos y relaciones de Juan Gelman, libro que reune varias colecciones de poemas de la década anterior y que abarca el período de la represión en la

Argentina y su eventual exilio. Rama analiza con perspicacia los mecanismos estilísticos de esta "poesía de la adversidad." [RdC]

5849 Ramos Sucre ante la crítica. Selección y prólogo de José Ramón Medina. Caracas: Monte Avila Editores, 1980. 254 p.: bibl. (Colección Ante la crítica)

Excelente y muy necesaria antología de notas y estudios sobre una figura principal de las letras venezolanas del siglo XX, reconocida como maestro de la contemporaneidad poética. El editor dispone, con criterio cronológico, una muestra de trabajos en "los cuales puede apreciarse una progresiva comprensión del poeta." Util bibliografía de y sobre J.A. Ramos Sucre, preparada por Sonia García (véase item **5881a** y *HLAS 44: 5466*). [PL]

5850 Ríos-Avila, Rubén. The origin and the island: Lezama and Mallarmé (LALR, 8 : 16, Spring/Summer 1980, p. 242–255)

Exploración de la sensibilidad insular y la vocación metafísica de la poética lezamiana a la luz de su parentesco con Mallarmé. Ríos-Avila acentúa las filiaciones americanistas de la relectura lezamiana de Mallarmé. [RdC]

5851 Rivera, Francisco. La poesía de Eugenio Montejo (ECO, 38[4]:232, feb. 1981, p. 415–432)

La notable poesía de Montejo (n. 1938) tiene en Rivera a un condigno estudioso, capaz de explicar con rigor y finura su dimensión simbólica y la vastedad de sus relaciones temáticas (ver *HLAS 44:5708*). [PL]

5852 Román Riefköhl, Raúl. Una aproximación lingüística a la "Danza Negra" de Luis Palés Matos (IUP/HJ, 3 : 1, Fall 1981, p. 137–146)

Examen de la correspondencia entre lo fonético y lo léxico sintáctico en "Danza Negra" para demostrar como todo el poema actualiza la presencia motivadora del tambor. [RRA]

5853 Running, Thorpe. Borges' Ultraist movement and its poets. Lathrup Village, Mich.: International Book Publishers, 1981. 194 p. (Studies in language and literature)

Un estudio de alto nivel profesional y necesario para el estudio del ultraísmo. Empieza desde el manifiesto madrileño de 1919

y su aparición en Buenos Aires (1921): la revista *Prisma* y la gestión de Borges. Continúa con lo que llama "pure ultraism;" Eduardo González Lanuza y Nora Lange; un "ultraist middle course:" Bernárdez y Marechal, y "the outer edges of ultra:" Molinari y Girondo. Termina examinando algunos precursores, como Güiraldes. [JG]

5854 Santí, Enrico Mario. Pablo Neruda: the poetics of prophecy. Ithaca, N.Y.: Cornell University Press, 1982. 256 p.: bibl., index.

Basándose en los conceptos de M.H. Abrams sobre la imaginación romántica, Santí muestra los diferentes modos en que la fe en un apocalipsis por revelación es reemplazada en la poesía de Neruda por la fe en un apocalipsis mediante la revolución, lo que a su vez abre un camino para la fe en un apocalipsis mediante la imaginación y el conocimiento. La tesis de E.M. Santí es convincente e iluminadora, y su constatación en los textos, rigurosa y lúcida, y brilla con fulgor propio dentro de la copiosa bibliografía sobre Neruda. [OH]

5855 Sucre, Guillermo. Ramos Sucre: anacronismo y/o renovación (Tiempo Real [Universidad Simón Bolívar, Caracas] 8, nov. 1978, p. 9–15)

Breve y fina imagen crítica de Ramos Sucre y su anómala poesía. El crítico señala que su obra poética ha sido quizá mal leída, quizá porque una de su claves recónditas es "el equívoco mismo." Anacrónico y paradójico, Ramos Sucre usa símbolos que no contienen solución al enigma del mundo. [J.M. Oviedo]

5856 Taborga de Villaroel, Gabriela. La verdadera Adela Zamudio. Cochabamba, Bolivia: Editorial Canelas, 1981. 344 p.: bibl., ill.

Sobrina nieta de la poetisa, polemista y educadora boliviana (1854–1928), la biógrafa desarrolla su tarea a partir de datos y anécdotas familiares, y de una lectura personal de diversos documentos públicos y privados. La interpretación del trabajo literario de la poetisa se lleva a cabo relacionándolo con el ambiente político e intelectual de la época. Constituye importante fuente de información e interpretación de la vida y obra de la biografada. [A.R. Prada]

5857 Torres, Edelberto. La dramática vida de Rubén Darío. San José: Editorial Universitaria Centroamericana, 1980. 966 p.: bibl., ill. (Colección Rueda del tiempo) Indispensable biografía de Darío. Cada capítulo lleva notas sustanciosas y una bibliografía puesta al día. De lectura casi novelesca, también es de interés para el lector general. [GY]

5858 Valdivieso, Jaime. Bajo el signo de Orfeo: Lezama Lima y Proust. Madrid: Orígenes, 1980. 126 p.: bibl. (Colección Tratados de crítica literaria)

Lectura del mito de Orfeo en *Paradiso* y de la presencia de la poética de Lezama en *Paradiso*. El título es confuso porque la parte dedicada a Proust y la parte dedicada a Lezama tienen poco que ver entre sí. [RRA]

5859 Volkening, Ernesto. El mundo ancho y ajeno de Alvaro Mutis (ECO, 41[3]:2137, julio 1981, p. 259–265)

Nota sobre *Caravansary* (ver item 5744), que contiene observaciones pasibles de buen desarrollo crítico: entre ellas, la función del elementos épico en la obra de Mutis como contrapeso del sustrato eminentemente lírico. [PL]

5860 Williams, Lorna V. Self and society in the poetry of Nicolás Guillén. Baltimore, Md.: Johns Hopkins University Press, 1982. 177 p.: bibl., index (Johns Hopkins studies in Atlantic history of culture)

Notable visión de conjunto de la obra de Guillén con un interés especial en el aspecto referencial (el negro y su contexto cultural, social y económico) y una crítica implícita al formalismo crítico de Vitier y Rodríguez Monegal que tienden a neutralizar la idiosincracia del poeta al inscribirlo automáticamente en un marco de referencia hispánico o al fijarse en el aspecto musical de su voz poética y no en la dimensión social de su negritud. [RRA]

5861 *World Literature Today.* A literary quarterly of the University of Oklahoma. Vol. 56, No. 4, Autumn 1982– . Norman.

Número dedicado a Octavio Paz en ocasión de haber ganado el Premio Internacional Neustadt de Literatura 1982. Incluye presentaciones de Ivar Ivask, Jorge Guillén, y Manuel Durán; palabras de aceptación de Paz, un texto de Paz, "The Liberal Tradition;" una bibliografía seleccionada y una serie de artículos que discuten varios y distintos aspectos de su obra. [NK]

MISCELLANEOUS

5862 Adán, Martín. Obras en prosa. Edición, prólogo y notas de Ricardo Silva-Santisteban. Lima: Fundación del Banco Continental para el Fomento de la Educación y la Cultura, Ediciones EDUBANCO, 1982. 689 p., 22 leaves of plates: ill.

Poeta y prosista excéntrico y brillante, Martín Adán es autor de *La casa de cartón* (1928), la primera novela experimental peruana, de tendencia urbana y resonancias vanguardistas, considerada como uno de los instantes más logrados de la prosa en el Perú. Su otro libro en prosa es *De lo barroco en el Perú* (1968), una tesis universitaria que es ella misma un ejemplar barroco. Estos textos, y otros dispersos, se reúnen en este volumen, que completa la obra reunida de Martín Adán junto al tomo de su poesía, publicado en 1980 también por EDUBANCO. [JO]

5863 *Boletín Nicaragüense de Bibliografía y Documentación.* Banco Central de Nicaragua. No. 46, marzo/abril 1982– . Managua.

Número dedicado a Santiago Argüello, centro del modernismo nicaragüense en ausencia de Darío. Se recoge una muestra varia y sustancial de sus escritos, así como ensayos bio y bibliográficos. Documento indispensable para el conocimiento del modernismo nicaragüense. [GY]

5864 Borge, Tomás. El arte como herejía (NMC/N, 2:4, enero/marzo 1981, p. 111–120, ill.)

Se asimila el concepto romántico-moderno del "artista" como renovador y visionario (antiburgués) a la lucha hegemónica de los sandinistas, con la diferencia que ahora "artista" es el pueblo y no el individuo enajenado. [GY]

5865 *Capítulo.* Biblioteca argentina fundamental. 1– . Buenos Aires: Centro Editor de América Latina, 1970?– .

Serie monográfica, de gran tirada, destinada al lector medio, reúne textos básicos del proceso literario argentino con informativos estudios preliminares. Merecen destacarse aquí las antologías de las entregas No. 69 (*Generación de 1920*), No. 105 (*La poesía del cuarenta*), No. 123 (*La poesía del cincuenta*), y los Nos. 33, 108, 129, 139, 141, 144 dedicados a la obra de Almafuerte, Barbieri, Girri, Fernández Moreno, Orozco, y Pizarnik. [RdC]

5866 50 [i.e. Cincuenta] aniversario del Movimiento de Vanguardia de Nicaragua: 1928–29, 1978–79. Managua: El Pez y la Serpiente, 197? 182 p.: ill. (*Revista de Cultura; no. extraordinario 22/23*)

Importante número de *El Pez y la Serpiente* que deja ver cómo la construcción de una cultura nacional parte de la labor de los vanguardistas. Se rechaza el antifaz preciosista dariano, la intervención norteamericana, lo burgués. Se procura recuperar la herencia indohispana y católica y solidarizar con Sandino. Selección de poesía popular, "chinfónica," lúdica y experimental, caligráfica. [GY]

5867 Cobo Borda, J.G. "Soy gibelino, monárquico y legitimista:" Alvaro Mutis (ECO, 41[3]:237, julio 1981, p. 250–258)

Diálogo incisivo, en el que Mutis expone sus rechazos y preferencias en política y literatura. Reflexiones importantes para la comprensión de su obra: los imperios del pasado "vividos" como instancias poéticas. Destaca también su interés por la narrativa brasileña, cuyo desconocimiento "es gravísimo para América" (ver item **5744**). [PL]

5868 Conference of Latin-Americanists, *3rd, Mona, Jamaica, 1980.* Poetry of the Spanish-speaking Caribbean. María Cristina Rodríguez *et al.* Mona: Department of Spanish, University of West Indies, 1981. 166 p.: bibl.

Los trabajos presentados en este simposio son todos de carácter temático e introductorio. Constituyen una variada presentación de algunos autores del Caribe hispano, pero no se distinguen por su novedad o profundidad. [RRA]

5869 Cuadra, Pablo Antonio. Fronteras y rasgo de mi comarca literaria (BNBD, 50, nov./dic. 1982, p. 1–8, ill.)

Según Cuadra la poesía nicaragüense nace respondiendo a la adversidad ("terremotos" naturales y políticos) y al silencio (de ahí la necesidad de inventar un idioma litera-

rio propio). Por comarca se entiende la dualidad geográfica e ideológica (clasista) que se trasciende en la ética cristiana y el rescate del pueblo. [GY]

5870 Ghiano, Juan Carlos. Vividuras, ó, Libro de muchas advertencias y algunas incertidumbres. Buenos Aires: Editorial CREA, 1981. 230 p.

Extensa selección de fragmentos (lírica, narrativa, ensayo, etc.) que el autor considera "inolvidables," donde "me había reconocido con felicidad." Desea compartirlos con los lectores, propósito cumplido con éxito: las citas, desprendidas de sus contextos, provocan reacciones diversas, desde el sacudón emotivo o intelectual hasta la risotada. [JG]

5871 Girri, Alberto. Homenaje a W.C. Williams. Buenos Aires: Editorial Sudamericana, 1981. 158 p.

Admirable ejercicio de intertextualidad. El poeta dialoga con la poesía de W.C. Williams; el producto oscila entre textos en los que se reconoce la escritura de A. Girri (1918) y "versiones." Un diálogo con Enrique Pezzoni, "El Hacedor en su Crítico," se agrega como tercera parte. [JG]

5872 Juarroz, Roberto. Poesía y creación: diálogos con Guillermo Boido. Buenos Aires: Ediciones Carlos Lohlé, 1980. 173 p.

Apasionante diálogo entre Juarroz (n. 1925) y Boido sobre la poesía. El lector se sentirá contagiado por la ejemplaridad y altura de estas reflexiones que, además, ilustran convincentemente el lugar prominente de Juarroz dentro de su generación, al lado de "grandes" de Hispanoamérica como Paz o Lezama. [JG]

5873 *Latin American Literary Review*. Carnegie Mellon University, Department of Modern Languages. Vol. 8, No. 16, Spring/Summer 1980– . Pittsburgh, Pa.

Número especial, dedicado al Caribe, y dirigido por Roberto González-Echevarría. Su introducción general es una valiosa aproximación a la cultura del Caribe, explorando las dimensiones de una ontología poética caribeña. Hay, además, útiles traducciones de Nancy Morejón por Andrew Bush y de varios poetas puertorriqueños por Frederick Luciani. También hay un estudio comparativo de Lezama con Mallarmé (ver item **5850**). [RRA]

5874 León, Carlos Augusto. Los círculos concéntricos. Caracas: Facultad de Humanidades y Educación, Universidad Central de Venezuela, 1980. 298 p.: bibl., ill.

El texto participa muy libremente de la autobiografía y la memoria, e informa sobre algunos aspectos interesantes del acontecer cultural y político venezolano (1920–39). Los últimos años se refieren al exilio del autor en México. Las 211 ilustraciones constituyen un animado comentario gráfico del relato. [PL]

5875 *Linden Lane Magazine*. Publisher: Heberto Padilla. Vol. 1, No. 1, enero/marzo 1982– . Princeton, N.J.

Revista de crítica y creación dirigida por Belkis Cuza Malé con una prestigiosa lista de colaboradores que incluye, entre otros, a Severo Sarduy, Roberto González, Guillermo Cabrera Infante y Alastair Reid. La revista adopta muchas veces un tono polémico, agresivo, que tiende a convertirse en postura de un sector de la intelligentsia cubana en el exilio. A veces aparecen fragmentos inéditos de obras de algunos de estos autores, lo que constituye el mayor atractivo de la revista. [RRA]

5876 Ortega, Julio. Adiós a Lacan y vuelta a Mallarmé: entrevista a Rodolfo Hinostroza (ECO, 4[3]:237, julio 1981, p. 301–312)

Amena entrevista en que el poeta habla de su trabajo sobre Mallarmé en función de su propia poética y de la articulación de su libro *Aprendizaje de la limpieza* (1978). [RdC]

5877 Pérez Silva, Vicente. Atahualpa Pizarro, Américo Mármol y José Eustasio Rivera (CBR/BCB, 18:2, 1981, p. 145–233)

Una de las polémicas sobre *Tierra de promisión* (periódico *Gil Blas*, Bogotá, 1921–22). Se reproducen los ingeniosos textos de Manuel Antonio Bonilla publicados con los seudónimos Atahualpa Pizarro y Américo Mármol. Estas piezas son interesantes, pero su presentación es muy informal y descuidada, e ignora las exigencias bibliográficas de este tipo de trabajo (ver *HLAS 44:5372*). [PL]

5878 ———. La bardolatría, el caracol y los cangrejos: una polémica sobre la poesía de Guillermo Valencia (CBR/BCB, 17, 1980, p. 134–204)

Transcribe numerosos textos de la po-

lémica iniciada por Eduardo Carranza en 1941: B. Sanín Cano, Daniel Arango, Antonio García, etc. Gran parte del material procede del libro de Gloria Serpa de De Francisco sobre Carranza (ver *HLAS 42:5913*), pero este módico empeño agrega algunas páginas de interés, como las ponderadas intervenciones de Alfonso Reyes, E. González Martínez y Octavio Paz publicadas en México. [PL]

5879 Perron-Moisés, Leyla and **Emir Rodríguez Monegal.** Lautréamont español: pt. 1 (Vuelta [México] 7:79, junio 1983, p. 4–14)

Se defiende la legitimidad de considerar a Lautréamonte uruguayo con nueva evidencia que indica que Ducasse conocía bien el español, idioma en que leyó con cuidado a Homero en la traducción de Hermosilla. También conocía el *Arte de hablar* del mismo autor, manual de retórica que puede verse como generador de los procedimientos retóricos desarrollados en *Chants/Poésies*. [MGP]

5880 Pizarnik, Alejandra. Textos de sombra y últimos poemas. Buenos Aires: Editorial Sudamericana, 1982. 217 p.

Admirable esfuerzo de Olga Orozco y Ana Becciú por reunir y ordenar textos de Pizarnik (1936–72) publicados en periódicos o encontrados entre sus papeles. El material está a la altura de lo mejor que ella escribió y justifica este decoroso y extenso volumen. [JG]

5881 *Poesía Libre*. Ministerio de Cultura. Año 1, No. 1, julio 1981– . Managua.

Según el editorial el propósito de la revista es "divulgar poesía . . . para que el pueblo nicaragüense pueda encontrarse y confrontarse con la poesía." Se representa una multiplicidad de formas: verso, prosa, diálogo, carta, testimonio; poesía primitiva, extranjera, tallerista, etc. [GY]

5881a Ramos Sucre, José Antonio. Los aires del presagio. Caracas: Monte Avila Editores, 1976. 128 p. (Colección El dorado)

Recopilación de artículos y cartas de Ramos Sucre (1890–1930), dispuesta por Rafael Angel Insausti y publicada por primera vez en 1960. Se añaden ocho cartas que, como las anteriores, informan sobre las dramáticas circunstancias de los últimos años del poeta. Insausti describe el conjunto como "un itinerario mental y emotivo" de Ramos Sucre (véase item **5849** y *HLAS 44:5466*). [PL]

5882 Reintegro. Revista de las artes y la cultura. Año 3, No. 1, 1983– . San Juan.

Revista de divulgación cultural más importante de Puerto Rico con especial interés en poesía y narrativa joven. Dirigida por Marya Axtman, Dwight García y Lilliana Ramos. Es de especial interés el No. 1 (Año 3, 1983) dedicado a la joven poesía puertorriqueña, donde Joserramón Meléndez, Vanessa Droz, Lilliana Ramos, Aurea Sotomayor, etc., se interpretan entre sí. Contienen una valiosa bibliografía. El No. 2 (Año 3, 1983), está dedicado a Juan Antonio Corretjer, el máximo poeta marxista de Puerto Rico, con entrevista y selección de poemas nuevos. Dirección: Taller Reintegro, Caleta de las Monjas No. 5, Apto. No. 2, Viejo San Juan, P.R, 00901. [RRA]

5883 Stanisfer, Charles L. Cultural policy in the old and the new Nicaragua (UFSI/R, 41, 1981 [South America, OLS-2-1981] p. 1–17, ill., maps)

Aporta un valioso caudal de información sobre la política cultural de la nueva Nicaragua. Se cuestiona la contradicción de que los Sandinistas conviertan al apolítico Darío en héroe del pueblo y la aparente falta de crítica independiente en los órganos literarios oficiales y extraoficiales. No obstante, se valora los grandes avances en la incorporación de las masas en la construcción de la cultura nacional. [GY]

5884 Taller. México: Fondo de Cultura Económica, 1982. 2 v. (Revistas literarias mexicanas modernas)

Edición facsimilar en dos volúmenes de los 12 números de Taller que aparecieron en 1938–41. Reune al grupo de Taller Poético, O. Paz, E. Huerta, A. Quintero Alvarez y N. Beltrán. En Taller amplían su proyecto original e incluyen cuentos, notas críticas y traducciones, además de poesía. Los volúmenes incluyen textos del grupo mencionado y también de Juan Ramón Jiménez, A. Reyes, Neruda, Vallejo, Pellicer, y R. Alberti, entre otros. A partir del número cinco colaboran exiliados españoles (e.g., Juan Gil Alberto, Ramón Gaya, Antonio Sánchez Barbudo). De interés: el primer capítulo de una novela

corta inédita de Revueltas; la traducción de The wasteland de Angel Flores; ensayos de Paz sobre Bergamín y Vasconcelos. [NK]

5885 Taller Poético. México: Fondo de Cultura Económica, 1981. 4 v. (Revistas literarias mexicanas modernas)

Edición facsimilar que comprende cuatro números de la revista Taller Poético (1936–38) y tres números de Poesía (1938). Taller Poético agrupa a una nueva generación literaria en México que si bien era heredera de los "Contemporáneos" mostraba otra visión más comprometida ante su circunstancia. En sus páginas aparecieron todos los poetas de valía de esos años: González Martínez, Paz, Huerta, Novo, Pellicer, Villaurrutia, Nandino, Torres Bodet, y Efren Hernández. Cada número incluye una interesante sección de reseñas sobre poemarios de la época. Poesía reúne a los poetas nacionales más representativos del momento, entre otros a Novo, Nandino, Reyes Pellicer, Paz, y Villaurrutia. Cada número contribuye a la divulgación de autores extranjeros. Los primeros dos se dedican a un solo poeta: Walt Whitman y T.S. Eliot, respectivamente. El tercero incluye una antología notable de la poesía surrealista, compilada por César Moro. [NK]

5886 Torres Fierro, Danubio. Entrevista con Marco Antonio Montes de Oca (Vuelta [México] 4:46, sept. 1980, p. 22–28)

En un habla lúcida y provocativa Montes de Oca conversa y reflexiona sobre sus comienzos como poeta, sus influencias, sus libros, la imagen y la metáfora en el discurso poético, el surrealismo, la poesía prehispánica, la poesía actual y sus proyectos próximos. [NK]

Turcios, Froylán. Memorias. See item **5266.**

5887 Vitier, Cintio. De las cartas que me escribió Lezama (CDLA, 137, marzo/abril 1983, p. 106–113)

Fascinante introspección en el mundo de la poética de Lezama por medio de su correspondencia con Vitier, y un elocuente testimonio de una de las amistades literarias más fructíferas e importantes de la modernidad hispanoamericana. [RRA]

Drama

GEORGE WOODYARD, *Professor of Spanish, University of Kansas*

THE VOLUME OF MATERIAL in Spanish American drama continues to be supris-ing. Argentina is reprinting in its *Capítulo* monographic series (item **5865**), and there are new plays by Mauricio and Pavlovsky (items **5893, 5924, 5929,** and **5933**), plus various anthologies. Venezuela's major promotion includes new plays by Chal-baud and Lerner (items **5901** and **5922**). In Mexico, Carballido and Hernández are not yet surpassed by the young generation of playwrights (items **5928** and **5945**). A handsome volume commemorates the efforts of Social Security and the Teatro de la Nación (item **6019**). The occasional publications from Chile (items **5930** and **5955**), Costa Rica (items **5897, 5898** and **5910**), and Cuba (items **5932** and **5934**) indicate sustained activity; the accumulation of materials from the Dominican Republic is surprising (items **5888, 5890, 5906,** and **5914**). Themes of the new plays include the now time-honored issues of sociopolitical misery and abuse, but the turn to psychological problems, sometimes with a nostalgic touch, is, if not refresh-ing, perhaps an admission that there are limits. The rate of innovation and experi-mentation with new techniques may be less noticeable, since no major trend has developed, after absurdism, Brechtian theater and the "creación colectiva," to cap-ture world attention.

Several new bibliographies are available: Argentina (item **6024**); Ecuador (item **5996**); and Venezuela (item **6013**). The major new critical books include insightful studies on Chile (item **5968**) and Venezuela (item **5969**). Current semiotic theory is in vogue (item **5981**) and the application of theories of tragedy to Spanish American drama wears well (item **5975**). One critic has revised his thinking on generational theory in the drama (item **6014**), and one study delves into the deeper human mean-ing at work beyond social forces (item **5999**). Political theater from a German perspective provides a fresh approach (item **5956**), as does the political framework of the plays of Galich (item **5967**). The range of dramatic criticism continues to be broad, but still lacking, too often, in the application of recent critical theory.

Festivals and symposia continue to be a major source of inspiration in the devel-opment of Spanish American drama, and the magnitude of the Caracas world the-ater festival in May 1983 was impressive, as was the assembly of writers now work-ing the theater whose reputations were established in prose fiction (e.g., Vargas Llosa, José Donoso, Vicente Leñero, Antonio Skármeta).

PLAYS

5888 Acevedo, Carlos. Teatro. Santo Do-mingo?: Ediciones Siboney, 1981. 306 p. (Colección Contemporáneos; no. 3)
In *Los calvos,* the objective of a child's game hovers between the tragic and absurd. Acevedo's other three plays focus on man and gods of ancient civilizations: *Gilgames* ques-tions distinction between myth and history: *Momo* offers poignant analysis of human character in search of the perfect disguise; the exalted defiance of the gods in *Sísifo* ad-monishes and affirms the continuous con-flict between multiple facets of the human existence.

5889 Adoum, Enrique. *El sol bajo las patas de los caballos* (UCLA/M, 6:1, oct. 1976, p. 39–63)
What might pass for exhilarating po-etry fails as theater through lack of defined characters, abrupt jumps in time and heavy hand in dealing with time-worn subject of oppression.

5890 Antología literaria dominicana. v. 3, Teatro. Edición de Margarita Vallejo de Paredes. Colaboradores, Lilia Portalatín Sosa, Pedro Pablo Paredes V., Jorge Max Fernández. Santo Domingo: Instituto Tecnológico de Santo Domingo, 1981. 1 v.: bibl., index.

Anthology of 11 Dominican plays stretching from Cristóbal de Llerena's 16th-century *Entremés* to present. Two useful introductions on authors, plays, and productions; most known works are Avilés Blonda's *La otra estrella en el cielo* and Franklin Domínguez's *La espera* (both 1960s).

5891 Arango, Alfredo Alberto and **Edgar Soberón Torchia.** Pepita de Marañón: es más, el día de la lata. Panamá: Ediciones Instituto Nacional de Cultura, 1979. 33 p. (Colección Premio Ricardo Miró. Sección teatro; 1978)

In a Panamanian show-club style, play exemplifies problems of society. Simplistic theme but language and culture rich in popular elements.

5892 Arrau, Sergio. *El rey de la Araucanía* (UTIEH/C, 40, 1983, p. 111–133)

Avoiding heavy historical framework, Arrau dramatizes unlikely episode of Orllie-Antoine de Tounens who established himself as a king in Chilean territory. Facile dialogue energizes the mid-19th-century historical atmosphere.

5893 Betti, Atilio and **Julio Mauricio.** Fundación del desengaño [by] Atilio Betti. La valija [by] Julio Mauricio. Selección y prólogo de Luis Ordaz. Buenos Aires: Centro Editor de América Latina, 1982. 115 p. (Capítulo. Biblioteca argentina fundamental; 140)

Strange combination of two recent plays: one by Betti set in the period of Carlos V focuses on bigger-than-life figures involved in power struggles; the other by Mauricio attracted public attention for its penetrating look at the problems of a compassionate contemporary couple.

5894 Boletín Nicaragüense de Bibliografía y Documentación. Banco Central de Nicaragua, Biblioteca. No. 41, mayo/junio 1981– . Managua.

Entire issue is devoted to Nicaraguan theater, from early colonial period to most recent, including plays by Pablo Antonio Cuadra (*Pastorela*), Rolando Steiner (*Antígona en el infierno, La pasión de Helena*),

and Octavio Robleto (*Doña Ana no está aquí*). Thematically, plays range from religious and folkloric to political issues. *Corte de chaleco* offers mordant view of original Sandinistas and US Marines.

5895 Botelho Gosálvez, Raúl. La lanza capitana. La Paz: Librería-Editorial Juventud, 1980. 111 p.: ill. (Colección Ayer y hoy)

Bolivian version of struggle of Tupaj Katari, Tupac Amaru's follower in struggle for Indian liberation from Spanish colonial rule. Existentialist currents in this prize-winning (1961) play are reminiscent of Dragún's *Tupac Amaru*.

5896 Campesino, Pilar. *Superocho* (Tramoya [Cuaderno de Teatro, Universidad Veracruzana, Xalapa, México] 20, julio/sept. 1980, p. 71–104, ill.)

Campesino continues in tradition of Tlatelolco with young Mexican film crew that imposes an external reality of political terrorism on internal reality of film-making.

5897 Cañas, Alberto F. Tarantela: farsa en dos actos. San José: Editorial Costa Rica, 1978. 106 p., 2 leaves of plates: ill.

Humorous, satirical family situation with threats and promises of marriage, divorce and even homicide. Light entertainment.

5898 ———. San José: Editorial Costa Rica, 1980. 206 p.: bibl., ill. (Libros de teatro; 1)

Interaction of protagonist Uvieta with friends and acquaintances in neighborhood bar; murder, mystery, and intrigue provide sprightly dramatic action.

5899 Cantón, Wilberto. Retrato de mi padre: obra de teatro en dos estampas. México: Editorial Popular de los Trabajadores, 1978. 48 p.

Two-act play spanning 37 years (1913–50) in which protagonist maintains his commitment to ideals of Revolution in spite of changing times, marital problems, and insubordinate children. Eloquent testimony to principles of justice, even though play suffers from shallow characterization, sudden changes, and some inconsistencies. First prize in Obras de Teatro Social national contest.

5900 Carballido, Emilio. Te juro, Juana, que tengo ganas; Yo también hablo de la rosa; Fotografía en la playa. 2a. ed. México: Editores Mexicanos Unidos, 1980. 240 p. (Colección literaria universal; 123. Teatro)

Reprint of two enduring plays by Mexico's leading playwright plus *Fotografía en la playa*, curious reunion that reveals neuroses and secrets of an extended family.

5901 Chalbaud, Román. El viejo grupo: pieza en dos actos. Caracas: FUNDARTE, 1981. 86 p. (Colección Cuadernos de difusión; no. 66)

Two women protagonists engaged in production of internal play (*El águila de dos cabezas*) reveal their own background and intimate relationship. Jealousy, pride, love, and sex are principal motifs in compassionate revelation of intertwined lives.

5902 Coronado, Martín. Obras dramáticas. Selección y prólogo de Raúl H. Castagnino. Buenos Aires: Academia Argentina de Letras, 1981. 391 p. (Biblioteca de la Academia Argentina de Letras. Serie Clásicos argentinos; v. 13)

Handsome, annotated new edition of three major successful plays by one of Argentina's principal playwrights of early 1900s, contemporary of Florencio Sánchez.

5903 —— and Nicolás Granada. La piedra de escándalo [by] Martín Coronado. ¡Al campo! [by] Nicolás Granada. Selección, prólogo y notas de Luis Ordaz. Buenos Aires: Centro Editor de América Latina, 1980. 209 p. (El Teatro argentino; 3. Capítulo. Biblioteca argentina fundamental; 35)

Reprint of two classic plays, both performed in 1902, that sustain the legitimate value of rural life as opposed to urban pleasures.

5904 Cossa, Roberto M. and Ricardo Monti. El viejo criado [by] Roberto M. Cossa. Marathon [by] Ricardo Monti. Selección, prólogo y notas de Luis Ordaz. Buenos Aires: Centro Editor de América Latina, 1981. 134 p. (El Teatro argentino. Cierre de un ciclo; 16. Capítulo. Biblioteca argentina fundamental; 111)

Two plays from 1980 represent the best of recent Argentine theater. *El viejo criado* is inspired by tangos and illusions of Paris in a timeless past; *Marathon* is a metaphorical statement about consequences of 1930s.

5905 Debesa, Fernando. *Ca-ta-ion* (EC/M, 27, 1979, p. 35–58) Chilean Debesa's one-act play about the miserable human condition, in which themes of solitude, anguish, stress, and lack of communication focus on a three-time divorcée and her defective son, who babbles the enigmatic "ca-ta-ión."

5906 Domínguez, Franklin. Lisístrata odia la política: obra teatral en tres actos inspirada en un tema de Aristófanes. Santo Domingo: Secretaría de Estado de Educación, Bellas Artes y Cultos, 1981. 127 p. (Colección Premios nacionales)

When Lisistrata declares war on politics, women "strike" against their husbands with the same felicitous ending as the classic play. Facile but entertaining. Premio Nacional de Teatro Cristóbal de Llerena, 1980.

5907 Dragún, Osvaldo. *Violador* (Tramoya [Cuaderno de teatro, Universidad Veracruzana, Xalapa, México] 21/22, sept./ dic. 1981, p. 144–173)

Vitriolic play related to self-censorship in oppressive society, and the way effects are reflected in basic human emotions. Another Dragún classic.

5908 Espinoza, Tomás. *Santísima la Nauyaca* (Tramayo [Cuaderno de teatro, Universidad Veracruzana, Xalapa, México] 20, julio/sept. 1980, p. 5–33)

One of the best of the young Mexican playwrights, Espinoza uses character change, folk tales, and fantasy to create a mythic, sometimes surrealistic, venture into Mexican life, but with overriding philosophical concerns.

5909 Frisch, Uwe. Alcestes. México: J. Mortiz, 1980. 139 p. (Serie del volador)

An Orwellian treatment of Alcestes' legend of conjugal sacrifice. Dramatic tension is sacrificed to philosophical disquisitions.

5910 Gallegos, Daniel. En el séptimo círculo. San José: Editorial Costa Rica, 1982. 234 p., 6 p. of plates: ill. (some col.) (Libros de teatro; 2)

Threat of violence rages inside house invaded by sadists who abuse two elderly couples for enigmatic reasons. Powerful drama. Premio Editorial Costa Rica 1981.

5911 Galván, Felipe. *La historia de Miguel* (Tramoya [Cuaderno de teatro, Univer-

sidad Veracruzana, Xalapa, México] 20, julio/
sept. 1980, p. 37–56)

Strong political theater about compassionate, hard-working family whose members, many accused unjustly of robbery, are taken prisoner by the military and disappear.

5912 Gambaro, Griselda. *El despojamiento*
(Tramoya [Cuaderno de teatro, Universidad Vercruzana, Xalapa, México] 21/22, sept./dic. 1981, p. 119–127)

Pathetic monologue of faded actress, waiting for screen test, as she clings desperately to a withered illusion of beauty and recognition. Poignant and powerful.

5913 ———. Teatro: Nada que ver; Sucede lo que pasa. Edición y entrevistas por Miguel Angel Giella, Peter Roster y Leandro Urbina. Ottawa: GIROL Books, 1983. 178 p. (Colección Telón. Obras inéditas; 2)

Nada que ver is a dramatic verson of Gambaro's à-la-Frankenstein novel; *Sucede lo que pasa* is rite of passage of young woman searching for happiness and fulfillment. Not Gambaro's best, but worthy additions to the repertoire.

5914 García Guerra, Iván. Teatro, 1963–1981. Santiago, República Dominicana: Universidad Católica Madre y Maestra, Departamento de Publicaciones, 1982. 344 p. (Colección Contemporáneos; 78)

Eight plays by major Dominican playwright, with themes ranging from solitude and despair to current political issues, and techniques characteristic of absurdism and Brechtian mode.

5915 Garro, Elena. *El rastro* (Tramoya [Cuaderno de teatro, Universidad Veracruzana, Xalapa, México] 2l/22, sept./dic. 1981, p. 55–67)

Highly stylized (à la García Lorca) Mexican peasant intrigue of basic human emotions and passions—love, jealousy, fear—leading to murder. Garro at her best.

5916 González, Lydia Milagros. Textos para teatro de El Tajo del Alacrán. San Juan: Instituto de Cultura Puertorriqueña, 1980. 234 p.: ill. (Serie Literatura hoy)

Texts written 1966–71 for Puerto Rican group, El Tajo del Alacrán, some already performed, all first published here. A militant group that addressed social issues and survived three phases although plagued

by economic difficulties. Introduction by author/director.

5917 Gorostiza, Manuel Eduardo de. *Tal para cual, o las mujeres y los hombres* (Tramoya [Cuaderno de teatro, Universidad Veracruzana, Xalapa, México] 21/22, sept./dic. 1981, p. 5–44)

This recently uncovered Don Juan play by Mexican/Spaniard Gorostiza shows wit and grace that characterize his later classic *Contigo pan y cebolla*.

5918 Halac, Ricardo and **Carlos Somigliana.** Soledad para cuatro [by] Ricardo Halac. El ex-alumno [by] Carlos Somigliana. Selección y prólogo de Luis Ordaz. Buenos Aires: Centro Editor de América Latina, 1982. 137 p. (Capítulo. Biblioteca argentina fundamental; 135)

Two Argentine plays that capture frustrations and obsessions of youth, by two authors who have established their credentials in the field.

5919 Hernández, Efrén. *Casi sin rozar el mundo* (Tramoya [Cuaderno de teatro, Universidad Veracruzana, Xalapa, México] 23, enero/marzo 1982, p. 13–99)

Very long, poetic work of separation by death and reunion by mystery.

5920 Hernández, Luisa Josefina. *La calle de la gran ocasión* (Tramoya [Cuaderno de teatro, Universidad Veracruzana, Xalapa, México] 21/22, sept./dic. 1981, p. 73–87)

Seven fascinating, ultra-brief dialogues with full range of enigmatic topics (e.g., alcohol, sex, love, prostitution, madness, frustrations, trust), many of them in family-style relationships.

5921 Leñero, Vicente. La mudanza. Fotografías de Rogelio Cuéllar. México: J. Mortiz, 1980. 123 p., 8 p. of plates: ill. (Teatro del volador)

Leñero's play about a couple bickering while moving to a different location takes a chilling, sociopolitical, and surprising turn when the *miserables* invade. First-class suspense.

5922 Lerner, Elisa. Vida con mamá. 2a. ed. Caracas: FUNDATE, 1981. 68 p. (Cuadernos de difusión; no. 52)

Successful game-play in which mother and daughter play detectives in a revelaton of their own life history; some political implications. Includes three short plays written earlier.

5923 Liera, Oscar. La piña y la manzana: viejos juegos en la dramática; obras en un acto. México: Universidad Nacional Autónoma de México, 1982. 171 p.

Twelve one-act plays in Liera's typical irreverent style, in which he parodies Mexican customs, bureaucracies and systems. Among the best are the scandalous *Cúcara y Mácara* about the miracle of the Virgin of Siquitibum; *La fuerza del hombre*, a parody of modern medical techniques; and the title play, a ludicrous and fatal encounter of a carnivore with a group of hostile vegetarians. Clever material.

5924 Lizarraga, Andrés and **Eduardo Pavlovsky.** Tres jueces para un largo silencio [by] Andrés Lizarraga. El señor Galíndez [by] Eduardo Pavlovsky. Selección y prólogo de Luis Ordaz. Buenos Aires: Centro Editor de América Latina, 1982. 92 p. (Capítulo. Biblioteca argentina fundamental; 47)

Two Argentine plays that deal with social injustice, oppression and terrorism, Lizarraga's from 1960 and Pavlovsky's from 1973.

5925 Magdaleno, Vicente. Sacramento. México: Costa-Amic Editores, 1979. 142 p. (Colección Xochipilli)

Another in the corpus of Maximilian-in-Mexico plays, this one, written in 1956, focuses on the Maximilian-Juárez conflict and attempts to elevate Max to the level of Hamlet.

5926 Marqués, René. Purificación en la Calle de Cristo: cuento. Los soles truncos: comedia dramática en dos actos. Río Piedras, P.R.: Editorial Cultural, 1978. 84 p.

The first ed. of Marqués' now classic *Los soles truncos* to be published in a single volume, with the short story "Purificación en la Calle del Cristo" from which it was derived. Unfortunately, no critical commentary.

5927 Martí, José. Teatro. La Habana: Editorial Letras Cubanas, 1981. 434 p.: bibl. (Colección Textos martianos)

New ed. with original, unaltered versions of Martí texts, with numerous reviews, critical writings, and notes by Martí on his own theater. Includes *Abdala*, a dramatic poem with political overtones; *Adúltera*,

realistic theater based on Kant; *Amor con amor se paga*, verse drama with metatheatrical dimensions; and *Patria y libertad*, Martí's best, advocating Guatemalan independence and expressing Martí's desire to free American culture from foreign influence.

5928 Más teatro joven de México. Edición de Emilio Carballido. México: Editores Mexicanos Unidos, 1982. 431 p.

Sequel to earlier collection which included some of the same authors, this volume contains 19 plays, most of which reflect the writers' concern both with language as a dramatic resource and with problems of youth. *Bill* by Sabina Berman and *La pira* by Oscar Villegas are outstanding.

5929 Mauricio, Julio. Elvira: tres conversaciones en dos actos. Buenos Aires: Galerna, 1982. 97 p.

The frustration of unrequited love puts on 20th-century dress in a play where the failure to communicate is a major theme.

5930 Mayorga, Wilfredo. Teatro. Prólogo de Juan Uribe Echevarría. Santiago: Editorial Nascimento, 1982. 307 p. (Biblioteca Popular Nascimento)

Three of Mayorga's best: his masterpiece, *La bruja* (1941), reflects through folklore the domination of superstition in the lives of peasant women; *Por el camino del alba* (1970–76), in the same *criollista* vein but with poetic and epic overtones, examines the interior conflicts of the coastal peasantry; and *Un señor de clase media* (1964) is a sociopsychological study of a street vendor's transformation into a corporate executive and his subsequent derangement.

5931 Mejía Sánchez, Ernesto and **Ernesto Durand.** Los doce pares de Francia de Niquinohomo: estudio y notas (BNBD, 49, sept./oct. 1982, p. 11–33)

An ancient text, presumably lost, is recovered and examined as part of Nicaraguan lore in the tradition of Charlemagne.

5932 Orihuela, Roberto. La emboscada. La Habana: Unión de Escritores y Artistas de Cuba, 1981. 101 p.: ill.

Cuban play about the reality of civil strife when two brothers have divided political loyalties. Set in pre-Revolutionary days, initial scene "previews" a better ending.

5933 Pavlovsky, Eduardo A. El señor Laforgue. Buenos Aires: Ediciones Búsqueda, 1982. 63 p. (Colección Literatura de hoy)

Pavlovsky uses techique of his earlier play, *El señor Galíndez*, to expose scandalous repression and brutality of Papa Doc Duvalier's regime in Haiti during late 1950s. Another chilling representation of political savagery in Latin America.

5934 Paz Hernández, Albio. Huelga. La Habana: Casa de las Américas, 1981. 91 p.

Dramatic reconstruction of 1930s workers' strike against the American Steel Company of Cuba, protesting miserable working conditions and salaries. Prize-winning semi-documentary with good human interest.

5935 Los Poetas en el teatro. Selección y prólogo de Luis Ordaz. Buenos Aires: Centro Editor de América Latina, 1981. 158 p., 3 p. of plates: music (El Teatro argentino; 13. Capítulo. Biblioteca argentina fundamental, 90)

The first play, *Donde la muerte clava sus banderas* by Omar del Carlo, is a semi-religious portrayal of a provincial caudillo on the Uruguayan border; the second, *El carnaval del diablo* by Juan Oscar Ponferrada, is a tragicomedy rich in regional folklore set during Carnival (La Chaya) of the Calchaquíes valleys; both are steeped in poetic language or written in verse.

5936 ¿Qué hacemos con la vieja? (Tiempo Real [Universidad Simón Bolívar, Caracas] 7, marzo 1978, p. 34–65)

The ubiquitous search for identity gains little from this clichéd text. Even flashbacks to explain the characters cannot overcome the superficiality of a text presumably written collectively.

5937 Quiroga, Horacio. *Las sacrificadas* (UBN/R, 19, junio 1979, p. 75–130)

This four-act play by Quiroga is of greater historical than dramatic interest, since it is one of only three extant plays by him.

5938 Quiroga Pérez, Héctor. *Muerte excepcional* (UNAM/PP, 71, p. 60–87)

Bizarre play, apparently based on a bizarre occurrence, involving a cadaver retained with hopes of later resuscitation. Some lyric qualities.

5939 Randall, Margaret and **Angel Antonio Moreno.** Sueños y realidades de Guajiricantor. México: Siglo Veintiuno Editores, 1979. 163 p., 4 leaves of plates: ill.

Two short plays, *El guajiricantor* and *Callejón*, are embedded in this sociopolitical documentary of Che Carballo, poet *extraordinaire*, master of *décima*, and descendant of the medieval troubador, within the context of Revolution in Cuba.

5940 Rascón Banda, Víctor Hugo. Los ilegales, nueva dramaturgia mexicana. México: Dirección de Difusión Cultural, Departamento Editorial, 1980. 83 p. (Molinos de viento; 4)

Another in long series of plays that describe plight of the Mexican laborer who flees from a miserable situation in Mexico only to encounter persecution and prejudice on the American side. Better than most, with intercalated documentary material.

5941 Rengifo, César. Un Fausto anda por la avenida. Caracas: FUNDARTE, 1979. 47 p. (Cuadernos de difusión; 38)

Latin-style political coup catapults elderly bureaucrat, Faust, into a crisis of conscience (Guardian Angel vs. the Devil); the allegory wears well in a modern-day setting.

5942 Ribeyro, Julio Ramón. Atusparia. Prólogo de Washington Delgado. Lima: Ediciones Rikchay Perú, 1981. 139 p. (Serie Popular; no. 5)

Set high in Peruvian mountains in late 1800s, Ribeyro's work eulogizes struggle of Atusparia to achieve agrarian reform. Excessive wordiness detracts from the dramatic impact, but play is interesting for its historical content in the tradition of Tupac Amaru and other Peruvian rebels.

5943 Riera, Pedro. El sueño de las tortugas. Caracas: FUNDARTE, 1980. 30 p. (Cuaderno de difusión; 54)

Illusion of happiness animates two old folks who die of exposure in the park, but not before achieving their dream.

5944 Rovinski, Samuel. Las fisgonas de paso ancho. 6a. ed. San José: Editorial Costa Rica, 1981. 59 p.: ill.

A 1971 play based on hyperactive imagination of neighborhood ladies who witness a crime-to-be leading to series of sight gags à la Keystone Cops, to the probable delight of a public wanting easy entertainment.

5945 Schmidhuber de la Mora, Guillermo. Fuegos truncos (*in* Antología del fuego. México: Nuevos Valores, 1983, p. 22–23)

Included in an anthology on "fire," this short play set in a rural Mexican village exemplifies the superstition, religiosity and paranoia that surface when values are challenged, with disastrous results for the outsider. Interesting dramatic experiment.

5946 Shand, William. Las andanzas de Rubino. Buenos Aires: Ediciones Centro Cultural Corregidor, 1983. 163 p.

Man besieged by his wife's complaints of insufficient resources turns in desperation to deceit and crime.

5947 Steiner, Rolando. *La noche de Wiwilí* (BNBD, 49, sept./oct. 1982, p. 64–72)

Brief Sandinista play that expresses outrage about gratuitous violence and dramatizes the commitment to the Revolutionary struggle.

5948 Teatro breve contemporáneo argentino: antología. Introducción, notas y propuestas de trabajo, Elvira Burlando de Meyer y Patricio Esteve. Buenos Aires: Ediciones Colihue, 1981. 140 p.: ill. (Colección literaria)

Collection of six one-act plays in the vein of intimate realism, some from Teatro Abierto cycle, all selected for student reading and exercises. Bortnik's *Papá querido* and Gorostiza's *El acompañante* center on shattered dreams; Cossa's *Gris de ausencia* is an example of pathetic solipsism in an exiled family; also includes Halac's *Tentempié*, Mauricio's *Los datos personales*, and Viale's *Convivencia*.

5949 Teatro breve del Paraguay. Selección de Antonio Pecci. Asunción: Ediciones NAPA, 1981. 138 p., 6 leaves of plates: ill. (Libro paraguayo del mes; 1:6)

Anthology of eight short plays (two of them also in Guaraní versions). Mostly nationalistic (or regionalistic), two deserve special mention: Josefina Plá's *Historia de un número*, about man lost in the modern bureaucratic world; and Alcibiades González Delvalle's *Los casos de Perú Rima*, which

presents the essence of Paraguayan peasant life through prototypical characters.

5950 Teatro peruano. v. 3, Cuento del hombre que vendía globos [by] Gregor Díaz. El gran giro [by] L. Gómez Sánchez. Lima: Ediciones Homero Teatro de Grillos, 1982. 1 v.

Vol. 3 includes two plays. The humiliation of the aristocracy, forced to face reality in the Díaz play, is surpassed by Gómez Sánchez in *El gran giro*, in which the parody of *The taming of the shrew* takes on bizarre and violent tones (for vols. 2–4, see *HLAS 44:5901a*).

5951 Tessier, Domingo. *Por Joel* (EC/M, 28, 1980, p. 53–95)

Moving documentary about the pointless killing of an underprivileged 17-year-old. Artistic technique enhances the socioeconomic conflict.

5952 Torres, Adolfo. ¡*Todas queremos ser reinas!* (Tramoya [Cuaderno de teatro, Univesidad Veracruzana, Xalapa, México] 16, julio/sept. 1979, p. 65–94)

Deadly accurate dialogue and undercurrent of repressed hostility make this slow-moving farce both comical and satirical. Promising playwright.

5953 Tres sainetes criollos: Justo S. López de Gomara, Ezequiel Soria y Enrique García Velloso. Estudio preliminar, Luis Ordaz. Buenos Aires: Centro Editor de América Latina, 1981. 166 p. (Biblioteca básica universal; 163)

Ordaz's excellent introduction puts these three late 19th-century plays into perspective as representative works of "zarzuelismo criollo." While the Soria and García Velloso plays are reasonably available, volume rescues the poetic *De paseo en Buenos Aires* from oblivion.

5954 Villasis Endara, Carlos. Los caminos oscuros de la gloria y otras piezas de teatro. Quito: Editorial Casa de la Cultura Ecuatoriana, 1978. 157 p.: ill.

Of the five plays in this volume, title play is weakest. With emphasis on man's struggle against the absurdity and the inequity of life, all have some merit; among the best are *Las ratas huyen del sol* and the metatheatrical *Anatomía del disparate*.

5955 Wolff, Egon. *El sobre azul* (UTIEH/C, 40, 1983, p. 89–109)

A blue envelope becomes a mysterious symbol of power in an industrial enterprise where management has lost its control of labor. Resonances of earlier Wolff plays abound in what he terms the "useless act of writing farce."

CRITICISM

5956 Adler, Heidrun. Politisches Theater in Latein amerika: von der Mythologie über die Mission zur kollektiven Identität. Berlin: Dietrich Reimer Verlag, 1982. 171 p. (Beiträge zur Kulturanthropologie)

Valuable study of political theater in Latin America from earliest times to present, with special emphasis on Cuba, Chile, Colombia, and Brazil.

5957 Agramonte, Roberto D. Dos dramas de Montalvo (UPR/LT, 24:93/94, julio/dic. 1976 [i.e. 1981] p. 199–159)

Serious discussion of two plays by the Ecuadorian Juan Montalvo, *La leprosa* (1872) and *Jara* (1872), both of which author finds to be of considerable merit.

5958 Bancroft, Roberto L. Jodorowsky y Vilalta en el teatro mexicano actual (*in* International Congress of Hispanists, 4th, Salamanca, Spain, 1971. Actas. Dirección de Eugenio de Bustos Tovar. Salamanca, Spain: Asociación Internacional de Hispanistas, 1982, v. 1, p. 143–150)

Bancroft concludes that Jodorowsky and Vilalta have made similarly valuable contributions to contemporary Mexican theater with their "anti-theatrical" pieces, but both the value and the points of similarity are left unsubstantiated.

5959 Bejel, Emilio. Abelardo Estorino habla sobre su teatro (Tramoya [Cuaderno de teatro, Universidad Veracruzana, Xalapa, México] 23, enero/marzo 1982, p. 103–107)

Estorino comments on his theater, especially on the structure and success of *El robo del cochino.*

5960 Bonilla Castellón, Socorro. Reseña histórica de la Comedia Nacional de Nicaragua (BNBD, 49, sept./oct. 1982, p. 119–138, ill.)

Traces the development of the Comedia Nacional de Nicaragua from its formation in 1965 until 1982. Complete with photos, reviews, and programs.

5961 Borges Pérez, Fernando. Teatros de Costa Rica. San José: Editorial Costa Rica, 1980. 116 p., 18 p. of plates: ill.

Interesting documentary material, theater by physical theater, of artists, groups, and plays that make up Costa Rican theater (1837–1941).

5962 Bravo Elizondo, Pedro. Sobre el teatro aficionado en Chile: 1973–1979 (CDLA/CO, 49, julio/sept. 1981, p. 88–94)

Brief overview of amateur theater in a country with a long tradition (since 1872). Bravo Elizondo justifies sociopolitical intention as valid in this society.

5963 Burgess, Ronald D. Gerardo Velásquez: pieces of the puzzle (LALR, 9:19, Fall/Winter 1981, p.17–30, ill.)

Comprehensive view of this young Mexican writer's 12 plays, in which dynamism as a cubist characteristic is integral to themes of solitude and sadness.

5964 ———. Social criticism from the stage: the concerns of current Mexican dramatists (SECOLAS/A, 13, March 1982, p. 48–56)

Overview of social preoccupations in the works of several young Mexican playwrights, especially Oscar Villegas, Willebaldo López, and José Agustín.

Campo, Estanislao del. *Fausto*: impresiones del gaucho Anastasio el Pollo en la representación de esta ópera. See item **5108.**

5965 Candeau, Alberto. Cada noche es un estreno. Con la colaboración de Carlos Mendive. Montevideo: Acali Editorial, 1980. 2 v.: ill. (Colección ABC del lector; 6, 30)

Memories—via tape-recorder—of the famous Uruguayan actor and director, reliving his experiences in theater and film in River Plate area.

5966 Carballido, Emilio. Sobre creación colectiva (Tramoya [Cuaderno de teatro, Universidad Veracruzana, Xalapa, México] 20, julio/sept. 1980, p. 34–36)

Thoughtful, creative, and humorous definition of "creación colectiva," with analysis and comparisons of the *modus operandi* of Ictus, Escambray, La Candelaria, TEC, Living and Experanza. Very helpful.

5967 Carrera, Mario Alberto. Las ideas políticas en el teatro de Manuel Galich. Guatemala: Impresos Industriales, 1982. 98 p.: bibl.

Brief but useful study by a Guatemalan of Galich's political theater, which explains and justifies his popularity in spite of years of exile.

5968 Castedo-Ellerman, Elena. El teatro chileno de mediados del siglo XX. Santiago: Editorial Andrés Bello, 1982. 240 p.: bibl., index.

Author justifies this particular period of Chilean theater history (1955–70) as a confluence of authors and activity not equalled before or since. Structured around five types of theater (social realism, folklorism, absurdism, Brechtianism, and "taller"), book discusses works of 17 playwrights in these categories, admittedly forced in some cases. Extremely valuable overview of Chilean theater during these productive years.

5969 Castillo, Susana D. El "desarraigo" en el teatro venezolano: marco histórico y manifestaciones modernas. Caracas: Editorial Ateneo de Caracas, 1980. 189 p.

First serious book-length study of the contemporary Venezuelan theater, tracing its roots from the conquest but focusing on today's important writers: Rengifo, Cabrujas, Chalbaud, Chocrón, Schön, Lerner, Santana, and Núñez.

5970 ———. El Juego: un deseperado recurso de supervivencia (Tramayo [Cuaderno de teatro, Universidad Veracruzana, Xalapa, México] 20, julio/sept. 1980, p. 61–70, ill.)

Insightful analysis of important and tough-hitting psycho-sociological play by Venezuelan Mariela Romero, together with available comments about conventional and non-conventional stagings.

5971 ———. Un friso histórico: la obra de César Rengifo (CDLA/CO, 49, julio/sept. 1981, p. 26–38, plates)

Study of Las torres y el viento, the late Rengifo's bitter play about economic and moral disintegration after the Venezuelan oil boom.

5972 Castro, Oscar. Informe sobre el Teatro Aleph (CDLA/CO, 49, julio/sept. 1981, p. 7–13, plates)

Brief summation of Teatro Aleph's experiences in exile in Paris and the development of their successful play, La increíble y triste historia del General Peñaloza y del exiliado Mateluna.

5973 Collins, J.A. Contemporary theater in Puerto Rico: the decade of the seventies. Río Piedras, P.R.: Editorial Universitaria, Universidad de Puerto Rico, 1982. 261 p.: bibl., ill.

Collins, critic for the San Juan Star, has pulled reviews written in the 1970s into a cohesive text. With slick paper and abundant photos, book portrays Puerto Rican theater activity in four sectors: Puerto Rican plays, Puerto Rican productions of international theater, international theater festivals, and plays in English. Useful overview.

5974 Dauster, Frank. Concierto para tres: Kindergarten y el teatro ritual (UTIEH/C, 40, 1983, p. 9–15)

Solid study that relates Los invasores and Flores del papel to Wolff's Kindergarten, points out essential ritualistic ingredients that make the latter play effective, and assesses the basic human qualities of the characters.

5975 ———. Toward a definition of tragedy (UT/RCEH, 7:1, Otoño 1982, p. 3–17)

Dauster discards reductionist theories of tragedy, turns to Francis Fergusson for interpretaton of Aristotle, and tests his hypothesis on a wide range of Spanish American plays. Valuable study.

5976 Descalzi, Ricardo. El teatro en la vida republicana: 1830–1980 (in Arte y cultura: Ecuador, 1830–1980. Fernando Tinajero Villamar et al. Quito: Corporación Editora Nacional, 1980, p. 345–358 [Libro del sesquicentenario; 2])

Brief synthesis of Ecuadorian theater (1830–1980) by theater historian who wrote the definitive book in six volumes.

5977 Driskell, Charles B. Power, myths, and aggression in Eduardo Pavlosky's theater (AATSP/H, 65:4, Dec. 1982, p. 570–579)

Driskell establishes Pavlosky's place within the context of Argentine theater, and then points up major techniques in his plays, through Telarañas (1975).

5978 Entretiens: [avec] Jorge Lavelli, Norman Briski, Edmundo Guibourg,

Cipe Lincovsky, Griselda Gambaro, Carlos Gorostiza, Oscar Castro (UTIEH/C, 40, 1983, p. 137–177)

Series of interviews with six of Argentina's most dynamic directors, actors and playwrights, plus one Chilean. Interesting personal observations about their experiences, accomplishments and objectives in the contemporary theater.

5979 Ezquerro, Milagros. Le fonctionnement sémiologique des personnages dans *Bajo un manto de estrellas* de Manuel Puig (UTIEH/C, 40, 1983, p. 47–58)

This penetrating study of Puig's first play analyzes the function of character duplication, archetypes, and structural interrelationships, utilizing Patrice Pavis' semiotic theories.

5980 Feo Calcaño, Guillermo. Teatro Municipal, 1881–1981. Caracas: FUNDARTE, 1981. 67 p., 17 p. of plates: bibl., ill.

Brief history of Teatro Guzmán Blanco—later Teatro Municipal— during 100 years of Venezuelan development. Illustrations and useful listings.

5981 Foster, David William. Carlos Gorostiza's *Los prójimos* as a metatheatrical drama (SU/V, 2:1, Spring 1978, p. 66–77)

Foster points out that the balcony in this play, modeled on the Kitty Genovese story, functions as a metatheatrical duplication of the proscenium arch, and as such involves the reader/spectator as an implied participant in the anguish of frustrated solidarity.

5982 Garavito, C. Lucía. *La señorita de Tacna* o la escritura de una lectura (UK/LATR, 16:1, Fall 1982, p. 3–14)

Garavito provides penetrating structural analysis of Vargas Llosa's clever metatheatrical play about the art of story-telling, by building on theories of Culler and Iser.

5983 García, Angel Cristóbal *et al.* Apuntes sobre el léxico del teatro bufo en el siglo XIX (UCLV/I, 69, mayo/agosto 1981, p. 171–209, bibl., table)

Interesting annotations to the Cuban lexicon on *bufo* theater, with ample illustrations.

5984 Golluscio de Montoya, Eva. Innovación dentro de la tradición escé-

nica rioplatense: el caso de Nemesio Trejo (UTIEH/C, 37, 1981, p. 85–103)

Interprets Trejo's *Los óleos del chico* to be an important link (not so much as a by-product of the Spanish *género chico*) between the local tradition (à la *Juan Moreira*) and the modernization of popular River Plate theater.

5985 González, Aníbal. *La cuarterona* and slave society in Cuba and Puerto Rico (LALR, 8:16, Spring/Summer 1980, p. 47–54)

Interesting speculation into sociological reasons Tapia y Rivera's play was set in Cuba rather than in his native Puerto Rico.

5986 Graupera Arango, Elena. Bibliografía sobre teatro cubano: libros y folletos. La Habana: Biblioteca Nacional José Martí, 1981. 27 leaves.

Useful compilation of Cuban theater items listing 124 plays and/or anthologies and 36 works of criticism. Mimeographed with some brief annotations.

5987 Gyurko, Lanin A. Cinematic image and national identity in Fuentes' *Orquídeas a la luz de la luna* (UK/LATR, 17:2, Spring 1984, p. 3–24)

Thorough examination of the cosmic vision in Fuentes' latest play, based on the glories and defeats of two Mexican film stars.

5988 Hernández, Gleider. La búsqueda de lo popular (CONAC/RNC, 41:247, abril/dic. 1981, p. 117–132)

Penetrating analysis of José Ignacio Cabrujas' *Profundo*, showing the desacralization (à la Mircea Eliade) and degradation of contemporary society.

5989 Historias de artistas contadas por ellos mismos. Recogidas por Julio Ardiles Gray. Buenos Aires: Editorial de Belgrano, 1981. 328 p. (Colección Testimonios contemporáneos. Colección Figuras contemporáneas)

Compilation of 23 taped interviews of Argentine stage and screen artists, actors, directors, musicians. Of particular interest are the interviews with Roberto Cossa, Ricardo Monti and Jaime Kogan.

5990 Justa López, Dora. El teatro de Conrado Nalé Roxlo: presencia y función del mito en *La cola de la sirena* (UTIEH/C, 40, 1983, p. 59–65)

In this interesting character analysis,

author concludes that the lyric element helps sustain the credibility of the fantastic in this mythical play (1941) of Alga, the mermaid, and her lover Patricio.

5991 Lasarte, Francisco Javier V. Significación de los Talleres de Textos Teatrales del CELARG en la actual dramaturgia venezolana (CNC/A, 6, 1980/1982, p. 91–98)
Brief overview of activities of CELARGE and its Taller de Textos Teatrales which in its brief life (since 1976) has involved senior Venezuelan playwrights (e.g., Rengifo, Schön, Chocrón, Santana) in training a younger and so far successful generation (e.g., José Gabriel Núñez, Mariela Romero, Larry Herrera, Edilio Peña).

5992 *Latin American Theatre Review.* University of Kansas, Center for Latin American Studies. Vol. 16, No. 1, Fall 1982 [through] Vol. 7, No. 2, Spring 1984– . Lawrence.
In addition to articles annotated elsewhere in this section, these issues (vols. 16:1, 16:2, 17:1, and 17:2) contain reports on theater festivals in Argentina, Berlin, Bogotá, Caracas, Chile, Cuba, Kansas, Mexico, and Nicaragua. Major articles deal with plays of such authors as Tomás Espinosa, Elena Garro, Osvaldo Dragún, José Triana, Alonso Alegría, and Isadora Aguirre, as well as interviews with Manuel Galich, Sergio Corrieri, Juan Radrigán, Sergio Vodanović, and Ilonka Vargas.

5993 Layera, Ramón. La revista *Conjunto* y el nuevo teatro latinoamericano (LARR, 18:2, 1983, p. 35–55)
As the oldest Spanish American theater review in continuous publication (since 1964), *Conjunto* has promoted theater and theater criticism throughout the Americas. Layera criticizes the editorial policies for excluding major playwrights, but concludes that the journal has performed an invaluable service in revitalizing theater in Latin America.

5994 Lindstrom, Naomi. Anomalous eloquence in a drama by Samuel Eichelbaum (Chasqui [Revista de literatura latinoamericana, College of William & Mary, Williamsburg, Va.] 11:1, Nov. 1981, p. 3–12)
Observes that Eichelbaum's characters shift linguistic registers in plays such as *Rostro perdido* and *Un tal Servando Gó-*

mez, and therefore, lose credibility and effectiveness.

5995 López-Iñiguez, Iraida and **Albor Ruiz.** Un teatro hecho por el pueblo: entrevista a Sergio Correiri, director del Grupo Esbambray (AR, 8:30, 1982, p. 37–41, plates)
Interview with the director of one of Cuba's most important theater groups on the occasion of the first visit since the Revolution, by a touring company (Grupo Esbambray) with *Ramona*, a play dealing with women in contemporary Cuban society.

5996 Luzuriaga, Gerardo. Bibliografía del teatro ecuatoriano: 1900–1980. Quito: Editorial Casa de la Cultura Ecuatoriana, 1984. 131 p.
Valuable national theater bibliography in three parts: reference works, plays, and criticism.

5997 Lyday, Leon F. Whence Wolff's canary: a conjecture on commonality (UK/LATR, 16:2, Spring 1983, p. 23–29)
Lyday compares Wolff's *Los invasores* with Strindberg's *Miss Julie* and concludes that, although there is no direct influence, there are many similarities in the process of artistic creation.

5998 Mayorga, Wilfredo. Andrés Bello, analista de la literatura dramática y fundador de la crítica teatral en Chile (UC/AT, 443/444, 1981, p. 197–228, facsims.)
Traces Bello's impact on the cultural development of Chile, and especially his contributions to an improved sense of theater criticism.

5999 Moretta, Eugene. Sergio Magaña and Vicente Leñero: prophets of an unredeemed society (IUP/HJ, 2:2, Spring 1981, p. 51–70)
Moretta uses *Los signos del Zodíaco* and *Los albañiles* to penetrate incisively not only the social characteristics of the two plays, but also the profound forces that spring from the human character in a societal framework.

6000 Natella, Arthur A., Jr. Bibliography of the Peruvian theatre, 1946–1970 (IUP/HJ, 2:2, Spring 1981, p. 141–147)
Listing of Peruvian plays (1946–70), regardless of publication or performance.

6001 ———. The new theatre of Peru. New York: Senda Nueva de Ediciones, 1982.

130 p.: bibl. (Senda de estudios y ensayos)

Natella's study highlights the theater of Salazar Bondy, Solari Swayne, and Juan Ríos, but does not give the panoramic view its title suggests. Useful critique but limited to three playwrights.

6002 Neglia, Erminio G. El tema de la tortura en el teatro hispánico (NS, 8 : 16, 1983, p. 91–102)

Neglia studies three plays with torture as the central theme: *Pedro y el capitán* (Mario Benedetti), *El señor Galíndez* (Eduardo Pavlovsky), and *La doble historia del doctor Valmy* (Antonio Buero Vallejo). From different countries and different decades, plays share a common objective of analyzing human aspects of repressive systems.

6003 Novoa, Bruce. Drama to fiction and back: Juan García Ponce's intratext (UK/LATR, 16 : 2, Spring 1983, p. 5–13)

Bruce Novoa examines the complexities of *Catálogo razonado* (1979) and concludes that García Ponce's work is a commentary on the interrelationships of identity and art.

6004 Obra teatral soviética puesta en escena en México: conversación con Evgueni Lázarev y Selma Ancira (URSS/AL, 11 : 59, nov. 1982, p. 90–104, ill.)

Interview with Russian director Lazarev who staged the first contemporary Soviet play in Mexico: Volodin's *Lagartija*. Fascinating commentary about Mexican and Russian theatrical relations and impressions, greatly assisted by translator Selma Ancira.

6005 Obregón, Osvaldo. Apuntes sobre el teatro latinoamericano en Francia (UTIEH/C, 40, 1983, p. 17–42, bibl.)

Documents interesting reversal of activity that brings Latin American influence to France: plays, directors, groups, and festivals.

6006 Østergaard, Ane-Grethe. El realismo de los signos escénicos en el teatro de Elena Garro (UK/LATR, 16 : 1, Fall 1982, p. 53–65)

Refutation of the traditional realist/fantasy distinction in Garro's work in favor of a semiological analysis that offers broader interpretive possibilities of ideals.

6007 Pailler, Claire. Hablan cinco teatristas hondureños: variété (UTIEH/C, 40, 1983, p. 83–85)

Deceptive title for very brief article that reviews efforts to develop a theater movement in Honduras, especially in light of the objectives announced at a first Congress in July 1982.

6008 Peña, Edilio. Apuntes sobre el texto teatral. Caracas: FUNDARTE, 1979. 57 p. (Cuadernos de difusión; no. 37)

Schematic collection of thoughts about the history, originality, value, and perception of the theatrical text, calling on examples from Shakespeare to Chocrón. Provocative reminiscences.

6009 Pereira, Joe R. Theatre as demythification: the Jehovah's Witnesses in Cuba (*in* Conference of Hispanists, 5th, University of the West Indies, Mona, Jamaica, 1982. Myth and superstition in Spanish-Caribbean literature: conference papers, 6–9 July 1982. Mona, Jamaica: University of the West Indies, Department of Spanish, 1982, p. 112–134)

Intriguing study that shows, by means of five examples, how theater in Cuba was used to expose the negative influence of Jehovah's Witnesses in carrying out economic socialization and other revolutionary goals.

6010 Ramírez de Espinoza, Gladys. Reseña historia del Teatro Experimental Managua (BNBD, 49, sept./oct. 1982, p. 92–118, ill.)

Valuable historical overview of the Teatro Experimental Managua (TEM) from its inception in the late 1950s until its dissolution into two new groups at the time of the Revolution: with intercalated reviews, programs, and photos.

6011 Rela, Walter. El teatro de Ernesto Herrera: El león ciego. Montevideo: Editorial Ciencias, 1981. 81 p.: bibl.

With his typical carefulness, Rela documents Herrera's biography and provides a succinct introduction to all his plays, with special emphasis on *El león ciego*, Herrera's best. Text and bibliography follow.

6012 Reynolds, Bonnie H. Coetaniety: a sign of crisis in *Un niño azul para esa sombra* (UK/LATR, 17 : 1, Fall 1983, p. 37–45)

Reynolds contends that the signals within Marques' play portend the same disastrous consequences for Puerto Rico as are found in the life cycle of the young protagonist.

6013 Rojas Uzcátegui, José de la Cruz and **Lubio Cardozo.** Bibliografía del teatro venezolano. Mérida, Venezuela: Universidad de Los Andes, Facultad de Humanidades y Educación, Instituto de Investigaciones Literarias Gonzalo Picón Febres, Consejo de Publicaciones, 1980. 199 p.: bibl., index.

Invaluable bibliography of 949 Venezuelan plays written 1801–1978, plus additional references to translations, operas, and other plays not fully documented. Cross-indexed by date and title, with a final compilation of theater criticism.

6014 Rojo, Grinor. En torno a la llamada generación de dramaturgos hispano-americanos de 1927 más unas pocas observaciones sobre el teatro argentino moderno: elementos de autocrítica (RCLL, 7:16, 1982, p. 67–76)

With the attitude of a revisionist historian, author compares his 1972 book with perceptions 10 years later, and suggests that the great variety of conditions and styles in the modern theater makes generational theory designations potentially dishonest.

6015 ———. Muerte y resurrección del teatro chileno: observaciones preliminares (UTIEH/C, 40, 1983, p. 67–81)

Valuable analysis of Chilean theater in three phases: 1) 1943–73, from its modern inception with TEUCH and TEUC to end of Allende regime; 2) overview of residual theater which soon sought exile, given difficult conditions in Chile under Pinochet; and 3) "new theater" which has developed since 1975 and which characterizes what is now possible in Chile.

6016 Rosell, Avenir. Biorama de Ernesto Herrera (UBN/R, 20, 1980, p. 79–118, photos)

Interesting biographical treatment, by day and year, of Ernesto Herrera, famous Uruguayan playwright (1889–1917), together with marginalia of concomitant events.

6017 Sánchez V., Jorge. A cuarenta y un años del Teatro Experimental (UC/AT, 446, 1982, p. 151–159, ill.)

Interesting reflections, 41 years later, about the creation of experimental theater in Chile, through an interview with one of the original participants, Hilda Larrondo.

6018 Singerman, Berta. Mis dos vidas. Buenos Aires: Ediciones Tres Tiempos,

1981. 334 p., 36 p. of plates: ill.

Autobiographical account by internationally famous star of stage and screen, in which the Argentine Singerman discusses her experiences as a woman/artist traveling the world. With her own company she starred in *El pacto de Cristina*, written especially for her by Nalé Roxlo.

6019 Teatro de la Nación del Instituto Mexicano del Seguro Social. México: Instituto Mexicano del Seguro Social (IMSS), 1982. 227 p.: ill.

With an introduction by Carlos Solórzano, executive director of Teatro de la Nación, volume chronicles the five theater cycles promulgated by Social Security during the López Portillo presidency: classical, Mexican, American, experimental and lyric. Excellent documentation, profusely and handsomely illustrated.

6020 Umpierre, Luz María. Inversiones, niveles y participación en *Absurdos en soledad* de Myrna Casas (UK/LATR, 17:1, Fall 1983, p. 3–13)

Umpierre departs from previous existentialist-absurdist criticism of Casas' plays and insists on a new view grounded in semiotics and radical feminism.

6021 Veinte años del Teatro Municipal General San Martín, 1960–1980. Buenos Aires: El Teatro, 1980. 206 p.

Documentation on all productions scheduled in Teatro Municipal General San Martín (1960–80), with indexing of authors, directors, scenographers, choreographers, etc. Unfortunately, no photos.

6022 Waldman, Gloria F. Myrna Casas: dramaturga y directora (ICP/R, 21:78, enero/marzo 1978, p. 1–9, ill., plates)

Good overview of principal works of important Puerto Rican writer and director, with special emphasis on absurdist tendencies.

6023 Zayas, Dean M. La formación del actor en Puerto Rico (Tramoya [Cuaderno de teatro, Universidad Veracruzana, Xalapa, México] 20, julio/sept. 1980, p. 57–60)

Brief but informative picture of theater companies and training in Puerto Rico.

6024 Zayas de Lima, Perla. Diccionario de autores teatrales argentinos, 1950–1980. Buenos Aires: Editorial R. Alonso, 1981. 188 p.

Indispensable research tool for Latin American theater scholars, this dictionary includes essential bio-bibliographical data on more than 300 contemporary Argentine playwrights.

BRAZIL: Novels

REGINA IGEL, Associate Professor, Department of Spanish and Portuguese, University of Maryland, College Park

A READING OF RECENT BRAZILIAN prose fiction encourages optimism about the country's literary scene in the remaining two decades of the century. Established writers continue to work in styles already accepted and recognized by the general public but have turned toward themes more attuned to the social realities of the last decade such as the anguish of political exile, oppression and repression, and personal fears engendered by these experiences. There is much variety in the exploration of these subjects as exemplified by Trabajara Ruas in *O amor de Pedro por João* (item **6067**), Carmen Fisher in *Travessia* (item **6041**), Antônio Callado in *Sempreviva* (item **6035**), and Heloneida Studart in *O estandarte da agonia* (item **6072**). Other novelists have chosen to focus on crimes of passion, the type largely exploited by the press in the past, transmuting their fictions into denunciations of the social order. This is the case of the semi-fictional account *Sinais de vida no planeta Marte* (item **6044**) by the controversial Fernando Gabeira. Although equally concerned with the question of crime in Brazilian society, Ricardo Gontijo uses compassion and introversion to deal with it in *Prisioneiro do círculo* (item **6047**). Emerging new authors that have maintained a sensitive balance between traditional values and the need to experiment are exemplified by the following: Amílcar D. Matos in *Os doze caminhos* (item **6059**); Wilson Lins in *Militão sem remorso* (item **6052**); Cláudio Aguiar in *Caldeirao* (item **6026**); Hério Saboga in *Paniedro* (item **6068**), Oswaldo França Júnior in *Aqui e outros lugares* (item **6042**); and Sônia Coutinho in *O jogo de Ifá* (item **6037**).

Literary contests, a traditional Brazilian way of stimulating established as well as new talents, have singled out the following novels with prizes: Maranhão's *O tetraneto do rei* (item **6057**), awarded the 1980 Guimarães Rosa Prize, is a clever combination of several well known passages from Brazilian and Portuguese literature that satirizes aspects of the history of both countries; Gema Benedikt's *Curral dos mortos* (item **6031**), awarded the 1980 Brazilian Academy of Letters' Coelho Neto Prize, is a *Bildungsroman* that encompasses four generations of landowners, ranging from the medieval mentality of the first generation to the anti-establishment activities of the youngest one in contemporary times; Gilvan Lemos' *O anjo do quarto dia* (item **6049**), awarded the 1981 Erico Veríssimo Prize, deals with the time honored theme of oppressors and oppressed unfolding in an atmosphere of mystic suspense; Walmir Ayala's *Partilha de sombra* (item **6028**), awarded the 1981 Second Erico Veríssimo Prize, is a sophisticated and delicate narrative about the secrets and needs of a handful of misanthropic people.

Other novels that also merit attention are *Manhã transfigurada*, by Luís Antônio de Assis Brasil (item **6027**), noted by its innovative organization of episodes and lofty language, and Oswaldo França Júnior's *Aqui e outros lugares* (item **6042**), a combination of multifarious tiny plots, that resemble the minuscule dots of an impressionistic canvas that can be viewed from several different angles.

A recent development worthy of note is the emergence of prose fiction about the immigrant, a theme with great artistic potential. One such example is Eliezer Levin's *Sessão corrida* (item **6051**), memoirs without literary pretensions that are nevertheless worthwhile as a valuable record of immigrant reminiscences and their cultural legacies.

The proliferation of sociological novels, which tend to elucidate social problems in terms of abuse of power and the effects of poverty or corruption, are exemplified by works such as Wilson Lins' *Militão sem remorsos* (item **6052**), Alaor Barbosa's *O exílio e a glória* (item **6029**), and Ricardo G. Dicke's *Madona dos páramos* (item **6039**).

Relaxation in official censorship has led to an increase in novels of questionable literary value that denounce a variety of social ills brought about by economic hardship, lack of government support, and weak leadership. Former journalists, for example, have produced fiction, especially stories, based on their observations as investigative reporters. Only time will tell who among them attains literary posterity. The same applies to a handful of novels that experiment with the public's interest in works "dictated" by spirits "beyond the material world," such as the historical account based on the "Inconfidência Mineira" (item **6075**).

To conclude, one could say that most Brazilian novelists of the 1980s are well grounded in the social realities of their country. As conscious participants of a society undergoing development, these individuals are deeply aware of its problems, and as such have made a varied and prolific contribution to Brazilian fiction writing. Judging from their works—the diversification of themes, the wealth of techniques, the commitment to artistic values, the concern with sociopolitical phenomena—one cannot be but optimistic about the future.

6025 Aguiar, Adonias. O Largo da Palma. Rio de Janeiro: Civilização Brasileira, 1981. 102 p. (Coleção Civilização Brasileira; v. 325)

Collection of short novels consisting of distinct plots that unfold in a popular Bahia plaza and told mostly by characters who are physically handicapped. Infused by a mystical atmosphere, novels share a tragic perception of life.

6026 Aguiar, Cláudio. Caldeirão: romance. Rio de Janeiro: Livraria J. Olympio Editora, 1982. 282 p., 1 leaf of plates: ill.

In the style of Guimarães Rosa's *The devil to pay in the backlands*, Mestre Bernardino recounts an epic episode to a cultivated listener, an abstract embodiment of author and readers. Episode tells of tragic end suffered by inhabitants of a collective farm managed by Beato José Lourenço, a religious leader. The farm, located in Vale do Cariri, in southern tip of Ceará state, was destroyed by police in 1937.

6027 Assis Brasil, Luiz Antônio de. Manhã transfigurada. Porto Alegre: L&PM Editores, 1982. 124 p.

Possibly one of the most rewarding novels of recent years, this work attests to the maturity of Brazilian prose fiction. The banal story of a young woman who seduces two priests becomes a novelty because of its rich style and organization. The same episodes are told with skillful and direct language by the same narrator but more than once and from different perspectives. In the tradition of Eça de Queiroz and Machado de Assis, the young author reveals his own talents as an innovative novelist.

6028 Ayala, Walmir. Partilha de sombra: romance. Porto Alegre: Editora Globo, 1981. 111 p. (Coleção Sagitário)

This short novel presents five people who share a house belonging to one of them. Absorbed in their individual estrangement from the world, some of them are unconscious of their mutual needs. The lyrical narrative enhances solitude as a universal human predicament.

6029 Barbosa, Alaor. O exílio e a glória: romance. Goiânia: Oriente, 1980. 209 p.

As in Lima Barreto's *Recordações do escrivão Isaías Caminha* (1909), a young man leaves his hometown in search of an opportunity to develop his talents as a journalist. In both cases, a newspaper's newsroom serves a microcosm of the world, where young journalists learn to cope with the realities of a large urban center. Alaor Barbosa's character witnesses and participates against the Revolution of March 31, 1964.

6030 Barroso, Maria Alice. O globo da morte: Divino das Flores; romance. 2a. ed. Rio de Janeiro: Editora Record, 1981. 262 p.

Goyaesque account of the effects of a circus in a small town in Minas Gerais: family feuds are resumed, marriages collapse, and high-strung passions explode, culminating with assassination of one of the circus artists. An experimental graphic approach was used in the layout of the book, including different print types and unusual spacing between paragraphs.

6031 Benedikt, Gema. Curral dos mortos. Rio de Janeiro: Edições Antares, 1981. 364 p. (Coleção Diadorim)

Novel depicts four generations of rich, influential, rural bourgeois Brazilian family, from patriarch Miranda, landowner in Minas Gerais, to his grandson Fabio, black sheep of the family. Novel includes regional elements, with emphasis on local setting, speech and customs, as well as protest elements, with emphasis on turbulent 1970s. Excessively verbose.

6032 Borges, Alves. O método cronos. Petrópolis, Vozes, 1981. 1 v.

Science fiction, with mystical and religious overtones. May appeal to readers interested in the world as it may be 1,000 years from now.

6033 Brandão, Ignácio de Loyola. Não veras país nenhum: memorial descritivo. Rio de Janeiro: Codecri, 1981. 356 p. (Coleção Edições do Pasquim; v. 111)

Like a prophet of doom, Loyola presents the city of São Paulo as a hypothetical prototype of Brazil's future. Sousa, a history professor forced by military rulers to resign

from his university position, sees changes and rebellions taking places in his country. Despite its graphically realistic imagery, novel fails as a literary creation.

6034 Callado, Antônio. A Expedição Montaigne. Rio de Janeiro: Editora Nova Fronteira, 1982. 129 p.

Indians escaped from a prison are led through Brazilian jungle by a quixotic journalist, inspired by French philosopher Montaigne, who wants to reestablish a lost ethnic balance between Indians and whites. Satirical novel which depicts habits, aspirations, and languages of the Amazon forest.

6035 ———. Sempreviva. Rio de Janeiro: Editora Nova Fronteira, 1981. 288 p.

Allegorical novel about the return of young exiled Brazilian to his native country. Obsessed by his desire to avenge the death of his girlfriend kidnapped and tortured by the political police, narrator denounces the political situation in his country, but leaves to reader the task of interpretating his many metaphors and symbols.

6036 Castelo Branco, Renato. Rio da liberdade, a Guerra do Fidié: romance histórico. São Paulo: LR Editores, 1982. 173 p.: ill.

Historical narrative about struggle between Monarchy of Portugal and newly independent Brazil over northern provinces of Maranhão, Pará and Piauí. Of some interest as a fictional recreation of history.

6037 Coutinho, Sônia. O jogo de Ifá: romance. São Paulo: Editora Atica, 1980. 107 p. (Coleção de autores brasileiros; 61)

Well developed protagonist is an aspiring fictional author, as well as a real and an imaginary character for a novel-to-be. Each of these three facets highlights different aspects of the protagonist's feelings of confusion, oppression, and mental mutilation.

6038 Denser, Márcia M. O animal dos motéis: novela em episódios. Rio de Janeiro: Civilização Brasileira: Massao Ohno, 1981. 94 p. (Ficção hoje; v. 1)

Collection of short novels that describe sexual involvements and stages of depression undergone by the characters. Stories describe a big city's depraved life in foul language, a typical theme of Denser's antiestablishment fiction.

6039 Dicke, Ricardo Guilherme. Madona dos páramos. Rio de Janeiro: Edições

Antares *em convênio com o* Instituto Nacional do Livro, Fundação Nacional Pró-Memória, 1982. 423 p. (Coleção Diadorim)

Written in the epic tradition of Euclides da Cunha and Guimarães Rosa, novel depicts journey of a few outlaws or *jagunços* to the Brazilian backlands or *sertão*. A medieval search for the Holy Grail serves as the narrative's archetype.

6040 Faria, Alvaro Alves de. A faca no ventre: romance. São Paulo: Editora Atica, 1979. 95 p.: ill. (Coleção de autores brasileiros; 48)

Novel of scant literary merit but with powerful descriptions of tragedies common to big cities (e.g., hunger, unemployment, ignorance, police terrorism, alcohol, marihuana trade, prostitution). Some episodes dealing with the agony of a young factory worker in love with a prostitute and trapped by a corrupt police, are very explicit.

6041 Fischer, Carmen. Travessia. Rio de Janeiro: Editora Record, 1982. 221 p.

First person narrative by Lisa, young victim of Brazil's repressive rightist regime (1964), who first seeks asylum in Allende's Chile, then in Sweden. May be autobiographical, as author herself lived in Sweden for six years as a political exile.

6042 França Júnior, Oswaldo. Aqui e em outros lugares: romance. Rio de Janeiro: Codecri, 1980. 104 p. (Coleção Edições do Pasquim; v. 83)

Features of this novel are extreme economy in verbal communication and an abundance of small plots. Thus, words reduced to their barest are used to convey a profusion of daily minor episodes. Unpretentious work of fiction reveals surprising intellectual and emotional depth.

6043 Gabeira, Fernando. Hóspede da utopia. Rio de Janeiro: Editora Nova Fronteira, 1981. 216 p.

First person narrative of struggle of young man facing several stressful situations, metaphorically related to travels within and outside Brazil.

6044 ———. Sinais de vida no Planeta Minas. Rio de Janeiro: Editora Nova Fronteira, 1982. 185 p.

Novel based on the life and death of Angela Diniz, a well known, rich, young, Brazilian woman murdered by her lover in the

1970s. The trial and the public's reaction reflect life in the conservative state of Minas Gerais (here dubbed "planet Minas") where Diniz spent her youth.

6045 Gattai, Zélia. Um chapéu para viagem. Rio de Janeiro: Editora Record, 1982. 251 p.

Jorge Amado's wife recounts 40 years with the prominent author, including their political activities before they were sent to exile. Candid and witty narrative combines fiction and reality and gives some insight into her husband's creative process.

6046 Gomes, Carlos de Oliveira. A soldidão segundo Solano López: romance. Rio de Janeiro: Civilização Brasileira, 1980. 247 p. (Coleção Vera Cruz. Literatura brasileira; v. 307)

Historical novel about the long Paraguayan War (1865–70) between Brazil, Argentina, and Uruguay on the one side and Paraguay on the other. In spite of author's statement in the "Foreword," novel is strongly sympathetic to the Paraguayans.

6047 Gontijo, Ricardo. Prisioneiro do círculo. Rio de Janeiro: Civilização Brasileira, 1981. 265 p. (Coleção Retratos do Brasil; v. 149)

Narration, in the first person, of life of young man born in Minas Gerais, who was 20 when the 1964 rightist regime was established in Brazil. People's ideas, hopes, and frustrations are depicted clearly, objectively, and sensitively.

6048 Guimarães, Josué. Enquanto a noite não chega. 2a. ed. Porto Alegre: L&PM Editores, 1979. 115 p.

An elderly couple who, along with local cemetery grave-digger are the only survivors in a ghost town, discovers the beauty of reliving their past through their imagination, recalling their memories tenderly and lyrically.

6049 Lemos, Gilvan. O anjo do quarto dia: romance. Porto Alegre: Editora Globo, 1981. 168 p. (Coleção Sagitário)

Novel set in Brazil's Northeast deals with themes of corruption and abuse of power by a close-knit, extended family. Messianic redemption is all that the much sacrificed and suffering Northeastern people can expect while at the mercy of such a clan.

6050 Lessa, Orígenes. A desintegração da morte: novela. 5a. ed. São Paulo: Editora Moderna, 1981. 67 p.: ill.

Novel uses fantasy to explore the theme of eternal life and the absence of death. How would mankind react to such an eventuality, asks author of this satirical and finely crafted novel? First published 1948, work has been in print for almost 40 years.

6051 Levin, Eliezer. Sessão corrida: que me dizes, avozinho? São Paulo: Editora Perspectiva, 1982. 140 p.

Memoirs about 1940s life among São Paulo's Jewish immigrants. Author's raw description of experiences typical of new arrivals (men, women, and children) is clearly devoid of artistic ambition. Neverthless, book constitutes valid attempt to portray aspects of Jewish life in Brazil only recently available in fiction.

6052 Lins, Wilson. Militão sem remorso: romance. Rio de Janeiro: Editora Record, 1980. 145 p.

Author known for his social studies and novels about the San Francisco River region in Northeastern Brazil, has written a subtle study of the people of the region (mainly *jagunços*) and their corrupt and blood-thirsty tendencies.

6053 Lobato, Manoel. Somos todos algarismos. São Paulo: Editora Moderna, 1979. 75 p.

Short novel about the thoughts and attitudes of an old man absorbed by physical, religious, and mythical problems. Though brief, the narrative is outstanding because of its literary craft, depth, and sensitive portrayal of life's predicaments.

6054 Luft, Lya Fett. A asa esquerda do anjo. Rio de Janeiro: Editora Nova Fronteira, 1981. 141 p.

Author returns to favorite theme explored in previous works: problems confronting a German clan and their descendants who settle in southern Brazil. Realistic, analytical, and somewhat morbid narrative uncovers tensions, hopes, and frustrations of one such Teutonic-Brazilian family.

6055 Machado, Dyonelio. Fada. São Paulo: Editora Moderna, 1982. 112 p.

Novel revolves around banal theme of triumphant love of two young people and their enemies' defeat. Story, set in contempo-

rary southern Brazil, abounds in Latin and French quotations. Weaknesses include author's outmoded show of erudition and his bigoted approach to one of two ethnic groups depicted.

6056 ———. Sol subterrâneo. São Paulo: Editora Moderna, 1981. 328 p.

Last of a triology of novels—including *Deuses econômicos* (1976) and *Prodígios* (1980)—all dealing with the terror and repression imposed by Emperor Nero of Rome. Detailed descriptions of life in Imperial Rome among patricians and plebeians, oppressors and oppressed, makes triology intriguing if somewhat boring. Author is clearly drawing a contemporary parallel.

6057 Maranhão, Haroldo. O tetraneto del-Rei, o Torto, suas ideas e venidas. Rio de Janeiro: F. Alves, 1982. 210 p. (A Prosa do mundo)

Intelligent, amusing, and satirical tale of 16th-century Portuguese settlers and their native cannibal captors. Intriguing, faithful replica of *quinhentista* Portuguese language, interspersed with well known passages of Brazilian and Portuguese literature. Elegant, well wrought novel.

6058 Martins, Cyro. Obra completa. v. 9, Ficção: Sombras na correnteza; romance. 2a. ed. Porto Alegre: Editora Movimento, 1979. 244 p. (Coleção Rio Grande; v. 41)

Epic novel about the 1923 Revolution in Rio Grande do Sul. Novel resembles a *roman à clef* with soldiers like Flores da Cunha and Borges de Medeiros; its plot recalls several of Erico Veríssimo's novels.

6059 Matos, Amílcar Dória. Os doze caminhos: romance. São Paulo: Clube do Livro, 1982. 139 p.

Retired bachelor keeps postponing plans to organize an orphanage as a way of honoring his deceased parents and sister. Well written novel that reveals the underlying psychology of a somewhat misanthropic and procrastinating man.

6060 Menotti del Picchia, Paulo. A filha do inca. 4a. ed. São Paulo: Martins, 1980. 254 p.

Novel first published as *República 3000* in 1930 is a forerunner of much of today's science fiction. Two men, survivors of a scientific expedition, meet with citizens of an extra-terrestrial civilization in the heart of the Brazilian jungle.

6061 Montello, Josué. Aleluia: romance. Rio de Janeiro: Editora Nova Fronteira, 1982. 188 p.

Fictional recreation of passages of the New Testament, mainly those of Christ's times.

6062 ———. Largo do desterro: romance. Rio de Janeiro: Editora Nova Fronteira, 1981. 330 p.

A "macrobiotic" man and member of Maranhão's land oligarchy amazes everybody by celebrating his 100th birthday in perfect health. He further astonishes them when his 150th comes along and he marries a young unwed mother abandoned by her lover, a final act of chivalry that crowns a long life.

6063 ———. A luz da estrela morta: romance. Rio de Janeiro: Editora Nova Fronteira, 1981. 213 p.

First published 1948, novel has been revised and shortened twice by the author who regards this as the definite edition. Describes series of tragedies that strike a playwright's family as observed by an old grandfather clock and with time as one of the characters.

6064 Paiva, Manoel de Oliveira. Dona Guidinha do Poço: texto integral. São Paulo: Editora Atica, 1981. 139 p. (Série Bom livro)

Reprint of 19th-century novel about a love story and crime of passion in rural Ceará state, around 1850. Unnoticed at the time of publication, it was revived by critic Lúcia Miguel Pereira in 1952, who introduced it as a faithful representation of the popular language and habits of the period portrayed.

6065 Rodrigues, Nelson. Meu destino é pecar. Sob o pseudônimo de Suzana Flag. Rio de Janeiro: Editora Nova Fronteira, 1982. 587 p.

Published 1944 under pseudonym Susana Flag, this was the famous playwright's first novel. Its reissue together with his earlier novels is more of a literary curiosity than literary rediscovery.

6066 Rosenblatt, Sultana Levy. Reviravolta. Belém: Grafisa, 1978. 214 p.

Depicts changes in the lifes of a few people who share a Rio de Janeiro office, im-

mediately preceding World War II. Light *exposé* of a bureaucracy.

6067 Ruas, Tabajara. O amor de Pedro por João. Porto Alegre: L&PM Editores, 1982. 217 p.

Excessively detailed account of life among Brazilian political exiles in Chile at the time of Allende's fall, and their subsequent search for asylum in another country.

6068 Saboga, Hério. Paniedro. São Paulo: M. Ohno: P. Wrobel, 1981. 92 p.

Exaggerated attempt at experimenting with language and fiction. Any resemblance to Portuguese must be an optical illusion; any attempt to detect an organizational structure, a fruitless search. As an experiment, it is inconclusive; as literature, an erratic foray into typing.

6069 Sales, Antônio. Aves de arribação. Organização, atualização ortográfica, introdução crítica, e notas por Otacílio Colares. Rio de Janeiro: Livraria José Olympio Editora, 1979. 206 p., 4 p. of plates: ill. (Coleção Dolor Barreira; no. 4)

Reedition of novel originally serialized in Rio de Janeiro newspaper in 1902. Deals with problems faced by young judge who gets emotionally involved with two different women. Story unfolds in an unusually green and humid landscape in Ceará state rather than the frequently depicted drought, and concerns characters who symbolize certain psychological types in terms of personal ambitions, political intrigues, and sexual complexity.

6070 Scliar, Moacyr. Cavalos e obeliscos. Porto Alegre: Mercado Aberto, 1981. 60 p. (Série Novelas; 4)

Teenager, fascinated by the heroic adventures of his gaucho grandfather, writes about the old man's involvement with fame and his ensuing confusion. Family relations are a repetitive theme in Scliar's novels.

6071 Souza, Márcio. Mad Maria: romance. Rio de Janeiro: Civilização Brasileira, 1980. 346 p. (Coleção Vera Cruz; v. 301)

Confusing tale of construction of an endless railroad in Brazilian jungle. Though interesting, allegorical theme is overwhelmed by a tedious description of national and international forces in early 20th-century Brazilian politics. Poor dialogue; phony and unconvincing characters.

6072 **Studart, Heloneida.** O estandarte da agonia: romance. Rio de Janeiro: Editora Nova Fronteira, 1981. 223 p.

Tells of living agony suffered by a Brazilian "madre loca" for her "desaparecido" son. The crudely realistic portrayal of the sadistic and blood-thirsty military chieftains posing as public servants, is relieved by the novels telluric poetry.

6073 **Teófilo, Rodolfo.** A fome; Violação. Organização, atualização ortográfica, introdução crítica e notas por Otacílio Colares. Rio de Janeiro: Livraria J. Olympio Editora; Fortaleza: Academia Cearense de Letras, 1979. 256 p.: ill. (Coleção Dolor Barreira; v. no. 2)

Reedition of important novel of the "cycle of drought," followed by short story, "Violação." The Northeast is potrayed as a singular place, where both heroic and mean acts are the results of special circumstances. Author was part of Naturalist literary group "Padaria Espiritual," which included Manoel de Oliveira Paiva (item **6064**) and Antônio Sales (item **6069**).

6074 **Torres, Antônio.** Adeus, velho: romance. São Paulo: Editora Atica, 1981. 159 p.: ill. (Coleção de autores brasileiros; 73)

Several story lines about the lives of members of a Northeast rural family are interwoven to create this novel. Well written although episodes lack cohesion. Fiction that is almost a style in search of a theme.

6075 **Vasconcellos, Marilus Moreira.** Confidências de um inconfidente: romance mediúnico. Ditado por Tomás Antônio Gonzaga (spirit). São Paulo: EDICEL, 1981. 380 p.

Author claims book was "dictated" to her by the "spirit" of Tomás Antônio Gonzaga, poet and political activist (b. Minas Gerais 1744). Novel can also be seen as historical fiction portraying unsuccessful plot of young Brazilian laywers, landowners, and poets against the Portuguese Crown in second half of 18th century (i.e., "Inconfidência Mineira").

6076 **Veiga, José J.** Aquele mundo de Vasabarros. São Paulo: Difel, 1982. 144 p.

Allegorical satire of regime in 1960s and 1970s, that could take place anywhere. Lively description of people and their power games. Similar to Veiga's novels, *A Hora dos ruminantes* (1966) and *Sombras de reis barbudos* (1972).

Short Stories

MARIA ANGELICA GUIMARAES LOPES, *Assistant Professor, Department of Foreign Languages and Literatures, University of South Carolina, Columbia*

ALTHOUGH ONLY APPROXIMATELY 70 OF THE 200 collections annotated below can be considered outstanding, others range from adequate to very good. Undoubtedly the writing and publishing spurt that overcame Brazil in the last 15 years has subsided. The sometimes touching but pedestrian country childhood accounts that were published in great numbers in the late 1960s and 1970s are no longer as common.

Increasingly, the short story is being used as a didactic tool in high schools and universities, and knowledge of stories is also required for university entrance exams. There is thus a proliferation not only of reprinted short fiction, but also of critical anthologies of well-known authors, from Artur Azevedo to João Antônio (item **6107**). Proof of the genre's popularity are the many anthologies featuring authors from individual states (e.g., Piauí, Espírito Santo, Ceará, Paraíba, and Santa Catarina). Influenced by Brasília's and Goiás' lively literary activity, the Brazilian Congress, both Senate and House, published its own two-volume anthology, *Horas vagas* (*Leisure time*). The work of many new writers is now available in anthologies such as the one devoted to winners of the Osman Lins Contest (item **6090**).

Since most collections selected below deal with Brazilian reality, they are, in Machado de Assis' words in 1865, imbued with an "instinto de nacionalidade," or possessed of an "inner feeling that makes [a writer] a man of his time and his country, even when he deals with topics distant both in time and space." Indeed, even authors who have lived and studied abroad, adopting and adapting to foreign literatures, continue to maintain an "instinto de nacionalidade." By such adherence, these writers follow the 1922 Modernistas' injunction to assert, as Mario de Andrade wrote, "the permanent right to aesthetic research, and updating of the Brazilian artistic intelligence."

More and more authors are writing about the 1964 coup and its ugly ramifications of political oppression, torture, and murder. Although not all short stories are directly concerned with such incidents, the majority reflect them to some extent.

Regional emphasis is still significant and several stories include accounts of the urban *marginais* as in João Antônio's (item **6107**) and Moreira da Costa's (item **6089**). Their lexical and syntactical innovations can be directly attributed to Guimarães Rosa and are further evidence of the high quality of such fiction.

Predominantly socio-political themes are presented in carefully crafted narratives. The better authors are aware of recent Brazilian and Spanish American literary practices, as well as of North American and French literary theories. Such familiarity is a gratifying consequence of the numerous university departments of literature established throughout the country in the last 20 years. Some authors annotated below are professors, others are critics (e.g., Bruno), journalists (e.g., the two Drummonds, Emediato, Tavola), playwrights (e.g., Monteiro Martins) or novelists (e.g., Ribeiro). Thus, there is a healthy exchange underway not only between academia and the press, but among literary genres as well.

The tendency to experiment that marks the bolder writer, often influenced by foreign literature, is exemplified by Sergio Sant'Anna (an Iowa Writers' Conference alumnus) and his own brand of "non-fiction fiction" and by Roberto Drummond's brilliant use of recent factual matter. A major technical accomplishment of many of these books is the almost verbatim transposition of oral discourse or common speech into literature as exemplified by Ribeiro (item **6128**), Távola (item **6139**), R. Drummond (item **6092**), Sant'Anna (item **6130**), Antônio (item **6107**), and Moreira da Costa (item **6089**). The feat accomplished by these writers is indeed admirable in a language such as Brazilian Portuguese which, as Macunaima pointed out, ought to have two separate dictionaries, one for the written and another for the spoken language. The attempt to capture the latter, a process underway since Modernismo, is as major a literary achievement as was the introduction of stream of consciousness, including tabooed sexual words and other such expressions. Thus, by introducing the spoken into the written language, another barrier has been brought down, opening new possibilities for Brazilian literature.

Psychological tales annotated below are more persuasive and effective by the use of varied technical devices, including the ones mentioned above. The "intimista" type of story written by authors obsessed with their own *Angst* in an absurd universe (e.g., Ramos in *HLAS 38: 4398* and *HLAS 40: 1977*; and Nader in *HLAS 40: 7445*), have shifted direction and changed their emphasis. The tragic consequences of the 1964 coup raised public awareness of social and political issues and this in turn is reflected in Brazilian short story writers' concern with the ills and afflictions of their nation and its people. Major collections noted below are those by Ramos (item **6125**), Antônio (item **6107**), R. Drummond (item **6092**), Sant'Anna (item **6130**), Trevisan (items **6140–6141**), Tavares (item **6138**), Tutikian (item **6142**),

Monteiro Martins (item **6115**), and the anthologies *Muito prazer* (item **6122**), and *Histórias para um novo tempo* (item **6103**). The latter collection has a keen social focus and includes a moving tale about torture, "Além da Terra."

Muito prazer was organized by the able and combative Márcia Denser (see *HLAS 40: 7435*) and offers a superb selection of stories by women about female eroticism. For those who ask "Is the collective voice specifically female?" one could respond that although Virginia Woolf is right in that the writer's mind is androgynous, there is such a thing as a female viewpoint and that such is the case in *Muito prazer*. The collection, however, is not geographically representative since most authors are women from the Rio/São Paulo area.

In conclusion: Brazilian stories of the last biennium show that the genre is thriving and suggest that its higher standards can be attributed to more systematic university training. The above mentioned "instinto de nacionalidade" is apparent as writers grapple painfully with the numerous incidents of the 1960s and 1970s that destroyed the Brazilian illusion that we are a people incapable of habitual cruelty. Writers have not only become more socially committed, but have also achieved greater depth in and command of their art. This literary genre, then, gains an important dimension, as it reveals Brazilians to themselves and others.

6077 Almeida, Márcia de. Fios y navios. s.l.: Preto No Branco-Ficção, 197? 78 p., 2 leaves of plates: ill.

Intense and urgent narrator connects most of these stories, which are effective in spite of occasional lack of control. Almeida's narrator is almost as angry here as in her previous collection (see *HLAS 44:6008*), due to the deaths of most of the people she loved.

6078 Andrade, Carlos Drummond de. Contos plausíveis. Rio de Janeiro: Livraria J. Olympio Editora: Editora JB, 1981. 160 p.: ill.

Marvelous collection, culled from daily *Jornal do Brasil*, which includes prose poems, allegories, aphorisms, tales, jokes, etc. Notwithstanding author's disclaimer that these writings are just "plausible" and not "to be applauded," collection deserves enthusiastic hand.

6079 Báril, Fischel. Vida provisória: contos. Porto Alegre: Edições Porto Alegre: Prefeitura Municipal de Porto Alegre, Secretaria Municipal de Educação e Cultura, Divisão de Cultura, Plano Editorial, 1981. 94 p.

Stories cleverly emphasize sameness of things and flowing of time through long paragraphs consisting of compound sentences couched as interior monologues. Theme is misunderstanding among family members seen by sensitive narrator/character impotent to change situation despite their mutual affection. Author controls material well as he creates suspense.

6080 Bastos, Orlando. Confidências do viúvo: contos. Rio de Janeiro: Civilização Brasileira, 1981. 185 p. (Coleção Vera Cruz; v. 322)

Humane, poetical, and humorous, these stories sustain reader's interest to the end. Bastos understand the *sertão* and its inhabitants. A late beginner much acclaimed by critics.

6081 Borges, Durval Rosa Sarmento. Nove histórias fantásticas e uma verdadeira. Prefácio de Gilberto Freyre. Fotografias espaciais, criação de Sergio Christovão. São Paulo: Laboratório de Patologia e Diagnóstico, 1981. 261 p.: col. ill.

Excellent collection blends scientific data with imaginative story-telling in a manner reminiscent of Jules Verne and Asimov. Virtues include careful scientific descriptions, well developed plot, psychological acumen, and exotic settings (Tanzania, Mato Grosso's Pantanal, and Nepal). Engrossing reading; enthusiastic foreword by Gilberto Freyre.

6082 Borges, José Carlos Cavalcanti. O assassino: contos. Rio de Janeiro: J. Olympio, 1980. 85 p.

Distinguished collection includes old stories (e.g., "Coração de Dona Iaiá," 1934, translated into English) and recent ones (e., "Lobisomem," 1975), both recipients of important literary prizes. Title story constitutes amusing rendering of legal suit told in pompous legalese by uneducated character recounting how another let his birds die. Skillful handling of daily speech and minutiae of life.

6083 Bruno, Haroldo. O corpo no rio: contos. Recife: Edições Pirata, 1982. 80 p.
Symbolic and impressionistic collection that is admirably written in a dense, intricate style by critic, novelist, and children's author. Extraordinary mood is created in title story "Nenê" and "Começa a Cavalgada." Superb psychological probing in a lunar world of madness.

6084 Cavalcanti, Zaida. A pastora Mangarosa e outras estórias. Recife: Edições Pirata, 1980. 93 p.: ill.
Although style is at times pedestrian, regional tales exude life and present valid characters. Strong local color does not detract from psychological studies. Stories set in lovely, historic Olinda include folkloric elements (shepherdess festivals). Dila and J. Borges' illustrations resemble those of the "literatura de cordel" and enhance the narrative's mood.

6085 Cicarelli, João Marcos. Rebelião das prostitutas. São Paulo: Milesi Editores, s.d. 79 p.
Inventive tales include literary allusions, drama, ribald-and-gentle humor, social criticism, and above all, a feeling for humanity. Author's style flows with ease. Many stories are skillfully developed from jokes and contain numerous puns. "Quinta Feira 22 de Agosto" is one of the best of the genre of political oppression and torture.

6086 Coimbra, Maria de Lourdes. Tremor de mão. Rio de Janeiro: Editora Nova Fronteira, 1982. 155 p.: ill.
Intelligent and admirable collection by poet with astounding ear for dialogue and wealth of ironic clichés. Unusual stories range from evanescence ("A Queda de um Corpo que Cai") to pathos ("Proveitos . . .") to amusing, trite dialogue ("Yamaha") and cliché-ridden narrative ("Ilmo. Sr.").

6087 Comitti, Leopoldo. Jornada. Curitiba: Coo Editora, 1980. 88 p.
Dramatic short tales focus on specific incidents: man fleeing jungle, shipwrecked character among decaying companions, battling lovers, 15-year-old girl on birthday eve, and druken poet at party. Comitti has firm

narrative grasp; his language is muscular with incisive dialogue and descriptions.

6088 Costa, Dias da. Dias da Costa conta estórias do Mirante dos aflitos.
Artigos introductórios de Gumercindo Rocha Dorea e E. d'Almeida Vitor. São Paulo: Edições GRD em convênio com o Instituto Nacional do Livro, Ministério da Educação e Cultura, 180. 163 p. (Grande antologia brasileira. Série Literatura; 2, Contos)
Reissue of book published in 1960s by Bahian journalist who lived in Rio for 40 years. Well written, honest, lively, and witty narratives tell of average women and men in Bahia.

6089 Costa, Flávio Moreirada. Malvadeza Durão mais Nélson Barbante, Neizinho Copacabana, Coisa Ruim, Bezerro Bill, Drácula e outras contos malandros. Rio de Janeiro: Editora Record, 1981. 177 p.
Collection of stories, some previously published, by prize-winning author. Subtitled "Picaresque Tales" and "Shameless Street Humor," book is dedicated to samba dancers and *partideiros*. A tour de force, it conveys dramatic episodes in lives of big-city *marginais* in a style remarkable for its oral quality, in the style of João Antônio.

6090 10 [i.e. Dez] contistas cearenses: antologia. Fortaleza: Secretaria de Cultura e Desporto, 1981. 109 p.
Uniformly good collection has local color.

6091 Dourado, Waldomiro Autran. As imaginações pecaminosas. Rio de Janeiro: Editora Record, 1981. 143 p.
Like previous works, Mestre Autran's *Imaginações* can be read as short stories or chapters of a novel. Anonymous characters who think of or gossip about the most powerful and wealthiest in small town have "sinful imaginations." Majestic tales with multiple viewpoints. Possibly the best collection of the biennium.

6092 Drummond, Roberto. Quando fui morto em Cuba: contos. São Paulo: Editora Atica, 1982. 156 p.: ill., port (Coleção de autores brasileiros; 79)
With customary expertise, passion, and boldness, Drummond uses 1920s-1980s journalistic matter as the basis for stories (e.g., "Angela D.," "Carta ao Santo Padre,"

"Por Falar em Caça ás Mulheres," and "Heleno de Freitas"). This is vibrant fiction in which a moralist denounces the evil and madness of his time. A most Latin American book in its blend of scathing social satire and surrealism. Splendidly controlled exuberance. Major collection.

6093 Duarte, Otávio. Alice. Curitiba: Edições Zé Blue, 1982. 54 p.: ill.

Handsomely illustrated collection for Paraná Public Library includes poems, prose poems, *crônicas*, and stories. Title refers to Lewis Carroll's character. Talented, with wry humor, Duarte writes well and should be watched for future work of greater breadth.

6094 Engrácio, Arthur. Contos do mato. Manaus: Editora Metro Cúbico *co-edição com a* Fundação Cultural do Amazonas, 1981. 89 p.

In limpid, classical style, Engracio expertly tells of Amazonian mysteries (the "mato" of human actions and passions, and the supernatural). Stories are psychologically sound with keen social criticism. Important book preceded by Marcos Sousa's angry denunciation of 1964 regime selling Amazonia to multinationals.

6095 Fonseca, Elias Fajardo da. Cabeça quebrada. s.l.: Preto No Branco-Ficção, 197?. 71 p.: ill.

Versatile collection includes stories about anguished men and women, adventures of Rio secret agent/femme fatale, and fantasy about a bedroom in the clouds. Many deal with madness, often caused by political oppression and torture.

6096 Franco, Pedro Diniz de Araujo. Elas. Rio de Janeiro: Gráfica MEC Editora, 1981. 55 p.

Professor at Rio medical school presents his collection modestly as "leap year stories." *Elas* is a slender collection representing 20 years work. Crystalline, pared down style presents mostly female characters (*elas*). Emotion without pathos. "Anna Maria, Quase" is notable for its delicacy.

6097 Fróes, Leonardo. Sibilitz. Rio de Janeiro: Editoral Alhambra, 1981. 95 p.: ill.

Capable author handles language with authority and panache in poems and stories. The latter, mostly surrealistic in their free association, explore metaphors: schyzo-phrenic woman giving Jove-like birth to flesh and blood dolls, and mysterious wandering Russian.

6098 Frota, José Alcebíades de Rezende. Em vermelho. Belo Horizonte: Editora Vega, 1982. 58 p.

Competent stories deal with sentimental affairs (e.g., ex-spouses meeting) as well as with political ones. Title story is diary of a domestic interspersed with account of her trial and condemnation as a "subversive." Interesting document of proletarian struggles in feudal; and imperialistic society.

6099 Fuhr Júnior, Artur. Os protegidos da noite. Caxias do Sul: Gráfica da Universidade de Caxias do Sul, 1980. 116 p.

Although occasionally uneven and abrupt, stories offer variety, perspicacity, and humor. Author, like surrealists, deplores as "infantile" most people's fear of imagination. Varied fare in which dreams ("O Bucólico como Alvo") and neuroses (jealous wife, character unable to look at other faces) are imaginatively presented.

6100 Gomes, Duílio. Janeiro digestivo: contos. Belo Horizonte: Editora Comunicação, 1981. 78 p. (Coleção Estória brasileira; v. 17)

Distinguished collection shows author's command of medium and inventive powers. Eerie atmosphere but realistic characters and plots. Influences include "mineiros" Aníbal Machado, João Alphonsus, and Gumimarães Rosa, whose words serve as epigraphs, as well as Murilo Rubião's.

6101 Gomide, Júlio Borges. Liberdade para os pirilampos: contos. Rio de Janeiro: CODECRI, 1980. 86 p.: ill. (Coleção Edições do Pasquim; vol. 75)

Collection examines pretension and lack of love in light though unmistakably satirical style. Described by board that awarded it the Guimarães Rosa Prize as "cynical, excellent, uncomfortable, lyrical, anthological, frightening, pathetic, poignant, morbid, crystalline, burlesque, allegoric, and finally admirable." Fine pen-and-ink illustrations.

6102 Guerra, Guido. As aparições do Dr. Salu e outras histórias: novela e contos. 4a. ed., ampliada. Rio de Janeiro: Civilização Brasileira, 1981. 131 p. (Coleção Vera Cruz; v. 318)

Strong stories deal with Salvador characters (beggar, celebrated actress, young girls, and criminal) from a broad perspective which includes family and society around them. Emphatic, detailed style. A distinguished collection for its scope and breadth.

6103 Histórias de um novo tempo. Ilustrações de Benhamin. Editor, Jaguar. Revisão, Alfredo Gonçalves. Rio de Janeiro: Editora CODECRI, 1977. 112 p.: ill. (Coleção Edições do Pasquim; v. 11)

Includes stories by poet and painter Antônio Barreto and five well known short story writers: Monteiro Martins (see *HLAS 42:6147–6148*), Pellegrini Jr. (see *HLAS 42:6154* and *HLAS 44:7446*), Ribeiro de Andrade (see *HLAS 44:6004*), Abreu (see *HLAS 42:6111*), and Emediato. Superior collection is indeed representative of "o novíssimo conto brasileiro"—its subtitle—in its technical innovations and social focus on 1960s and 1970s political repression and its effects.

6104 Inda, Ieda. O cavalo persa: contos. Porto Alegre: Editora Movimento, 1979. 61 p. (Coleção Rio Grande; v. 40)

Fables written in fluid, classical language examine major philosophical questions: essence and appearance, life and death, family responsibilities vs. art, and alchemy. Gentle though wry humor is equally notable. For another distinguished work by Inda, see *HLAS 38:7366*.

6105 Jardim, Luís. Maria Perigosa: contos. Desenhos do autor. Poesia de Manuel Bandeira. Estudos e depoimentos de Afonso Arinos de Melo Franco *et al.* 6a. ed., ilustrada. Rio de Janeiro: Livraria J. Olympio Editora, 1981. 212 p.: ill.

Published 45 years ago, Maria Perigosa's stories still read well. Sensitive, imaginative author creates poetical world based on his own Pernambuco. Jardim also wrote novels, memoirs, a play, and children's stories, and won many prizes.

6106 Jardim, Rachel. A cristaleira invisível. Rio de Janeiro: Editora Nova Fronteira, 1982. 142 p.

Collection of memoirs and admirable portraits of eccentric, intellectual female characters in today's Brazil (e.g., Eduarda, Luísa, circus owner's wife), as well as other times and places (e.g., Cornish nun, Celtic

queen). Splendid portraits are delicately but firmly etched. Humor excels.

6107 João Antônio. Dedo-duro. Rio de Janeiro: Editora Record, 1982. 180 p.: ill.

In major collection, João Antônio again depicts a variety of *marginados* including burnt-out TV idol. Dwelling on the suffering (and rare joys) of the downtrodden, stories "erupt with elemental, unbridled force" (P. Ronai). Superb collection by a master.

6108 Leão, Ursulino. Rodovia preferencial: contos. Rio de Janeiro: Livraria Editora Cátedra, 1981. 119 p.

Perceptive Goiás author of fiction and political crônicas creates successful characters and moods in diverse, incisive stories that take place on highways. Topics include snake bite ("Té da Vicença"), ghost ("Curva"), and adolescent love ("Se Essa Rua Fosse Minha").

6109 Lispector, Clarice. A bela e a fera. Rio de Janeiro: Editora Nova Fronteira, 1979. 146 p.

At age 14, Lispector's enormous talent was already apparent in her authoritative choice of words, focus, and plot handling. These stories also reflect her later capacity to develop character through interior monologue and psychological inner time. Two superb tales, the title one and "Um Dia Menos" were written a few months before her 1977 death.

6110 Lopes, Harry Vieira. Os porões da utopia. São Paulo: Edições Populares, 1980. 83 p.: ill.

Author shows psychological acumen in these well written, dramatic stories that focus on despaire (e.g., young wife's existential anguish, estranged husband's restlessness, transvestite's suicide, young man who murdered his family). Some tales are Borgeslike such as "O Círculo dos Amigos de Edissa" and "A Outra Torre de Babel."

6111 Lyra, Bernadette. As contas no canto: contos. Vitória: Fundação Ceciliano Abel de Almeida, 1981. 58 p. (Coleção Letras capixabas; v. 2)

Pts. 1 and 3 consist of excellent, surrealistic, short narratives. In an oneiric atmosphere metaphors become literal: golden tresses are snakes, alligators live under a terrified woman's bed, etc. Pt. 2 deals with pangs of love. Winner of the prestigious Paraná Short Story Contest.

6112 Machado, Dalila. Prima prima primavera. Salvador: Fundação Cultural do Estado da Bahia, 1981. 62 p. (Coleção dos novos. Série Ficção; v. 5)

Author creates unusual universes—children's, women's madmen's—and impossible loves. Fluid, otherwordly atmosphere. Characters are presented by multiple narrators. An auspicious first book, notwithstanding its occasionally hermetic quality and abrupt passages.

6113 Machado, Mariette Telles. Narrativas do quotidiano. Goiânia: Oriente, 1978. 121 p.

Winner of 1977 Hugo de Carvalho Ramos Prize, these "everyday stories" present real, dramatic situations, often dealing with clashes between the traditional and the new in both city and country. Very fine book.

6114 Malta, Clóvis. Paixão roxa dos gato no escuro: contos. Rio de Janeiro: CODECRI, 1980. 91 p. (Coleção Ediçoes do Pasquim; v. 76)

Well-executed grotesquerie. Death prevails in stories which focus on obsession. They feature ghosts, crimes, libidinous sex, madness, and murder. Echoes of Poe, Tennessee Williams, and Nelson Rodrigues.

6115 Martins, Júlio Cesar Monteiro. O oeste de nada: contos. Rio de Janeiro: Civilização Brasileira, 1981. 145 p. (Coleção Vera Cruz: v. 317)

Collection exhibits inventiveness characteristic of Martins' previous work, as well as added technical skill, compassion, and breadth. Stories depict diverse characters' plights (e.g., woman's unrequited love; surfer abandoned by lover; sick young prostitute; courageous priest murdered by Indian-hating police). Impressive.

6116 Matos, Marco Aurélio. As magnólias do paraíso. Rio de Janeiro: CODECRI, 1982. 120 p. (Coleção Edições do Pasquim; v. 71)

Erudite, wry, metaphysical, and subtly ironic stories could have been written by one of Matos' characters, the versatile Migliorini, a *subito ingegno* of the Renaissance. Stories portray monkeys affected by erotic toxin, abyssal fish swimming to surface and tailor/monk vanishing through mirror. An added virtue is author's Machadian style. Not to be missed.

6117 Mello, Antônio Carlos de. A metáfora de Drácula: contos. Rio de Janeiro: Livraria J. Olympio Editora, 1982. 79 p.

Collection with varied themes, approaches and styles that is poetical, inventive, and very well written. Excellent title story recreates blood donor's fantastic world. "O Poeta da Noite" is obsessed dragster whose car is his poem, and "Concerto para Gaita e Tráfego" tells of adolescent couple wandering in Copacabana after abortion.

6118 Mello, Melilo Moreira de. Contos, recontos, satiricontos. Rio de Janeiro: Achiamé, 1981. 188 p.: bibl.

Sustained humor in uneven stories, the best of which show skillful plot development and enviable knowledge of literary history both of Brazil and abroad. Witty narratives skillfully develop absurd situations.

6119 Montenegro, Joaquim Braga. Uma chama ao vento: contos. 2a. ed. Fortaleza: Edições UFC, 1980. 167 p.

First published in 1946, stories show well developed plots and characters, as well as limpid style. States of mind and actions of introspective, taciturn characters are conveyed through interior monologues. Style reminiscent of Machado de Assis, Ciro dos Anjos, and early Osman Lins. Deserves to be read.

6120 Moraes, José do Nascimento. Vencidos e degenerados & Contos de Valério Santiago. 2a. ed. São Luís: Secretaria de Cultura do Estado do Maranhão, 1982. 331 p.

Reedition of novel *Vencidos e Degenerados* (1915) and short stories by Moraes (1882–1958). According to Neiva Moreira, Moraes "though black and poor, humble and without protection, opened his path by strokes of talent and by his moral courage." Sensitive, colorful, well written stories pleasantly recall Maranhão's (and Brazil's) mores of 70 years ago.

6121 Moreira, Ronaldo. O primeiro tiro: contos. Introdução de Cícero Sandroni. São Paulo: Edições GRD, 1980. 115 p.

Although not static, stories deal more with moods than with actions. Excellent handling of language in the examination of characters' solitude.

6122 Muito prazer: contos. Cecília Prada *et al.* Organização, Márcia Denser. Rio de Janeiro: Editora Record, 1982? 98 p.

Important collection compiled by Márcia Denser is uniformly excellent and includes her own scathing "O Vampiro da Alameda" and "Casablanca." Stories run the gamut of erotic experiences (e.g., heterosexuality, homosexuality, pedophilia, a woman attracted by a goat's beautiful eyes). All contributions are distinguished women writers. Only story not up to par is Christina Queiroz's disappointing "As Sensações Totais" (for a good collection by her, see *HLAS 38:7396*).

6123 O de casa!: contos. Teresina-Piauí: Editora Nossa, 1977. 56 p. (Coleção Ciranda)

Unpretentious volume by Piauí authors. Uniformly vibrant, witty, and sensitive storytelling.

6124 Proença, Manoel Cavalcanti. O alferes e outras estórias. Rio de Janeiro: Livraria J. Olympio Editora, 1982. 223 p.

Collection includes "Outras Estórias," "Uniforme de Gala," and posthumous "O Alferes." While the latter, a novella, is weak, some stories (e.g., title one, "Papagaio de Papel," "Dina Morreu . . .") show Proença's strength as a chronicler of the lower middle class, in the style of Lima Barreto and Marques Rebelo.

6125 Ramos, Ricardo. Os inventores estão vivos: contos. Rio de Janeiro: Editora Nova Fronteira, 1980. 137 p.: bibl.

Superb stories excel those of Ramos' two previous collections (see *HLAS 38:7398* and *HLAS 42:6157*). Equally polished and profound, these tales deal with anguish, fantasy, and social justice, demonstrating the author's empathy for others. Graciliano's son has attained his father's stature.

6126 Rawet, Samuel. Que os mortos enterrem seus mortos: contos. São Paulo: Vertente Editora, 1981. 83 p. (Coleção Prosa viva)

Exemplary collection. Somber short narratives focus on hatred (title story, "O Rato e o Pombo"), suffering ("Um Homem Morto, um Cavalo Morto . . ."), deception ("As Palavras"), meaningless modern urban life, and ineradicable memories.

6127 Reipert, Hermann José. Os cupins; Utopia; Paraíso comprometido. São Paulo: Editora do Escritor, 1982. 103 p. (Coleção do escritor; v. 52)

Novella *Os cupins* (first published 1972) exposes narrator's existential anguish as his house crumbles. Two shorter narrations show author's versatility: "Utopia" establishes telepathic conversation between earthling and extra-terrestrial, and "Paraíso Comprometido" is a brilliant erudite world "history," beginning with Adam and Eve.

6128 Ribeiro, João Ubaldo. Livro de histórias. Rio de Janeiro: Editora Nova Fronteira, 1981. 199 p.

Masterful novelist (e.g., *Sargento Getúlio*, see *HLAS 42:6670*) and short-story writer (see *HLAS 44:6007*) has produced another admirable collection. It features humor, social criticism and, above all, excels at rendering the spoken language. "Alandelão de la Patrie" is priceless.

6129 Rosa, Vilma Guimarães. Clique!: estórias. Rio de Janeiro: J. Olympio, 1981. 119 p.

Psychologically sound and well written stories focus on sudden discovery or awareness through intuition (i.e., *Clique* of title meaning to *click*, the stories' *leitmotif*). Some stories resemble travelogues (e.g., Germany, Alps), others concern spiritualism, urbanity, and author's optimism about mankind's progress, a trait she shares with her remarkable father.

6130 Sant'Anna, Sérgio. O concerto de João Gilberto no Rio de Janeiro: contos. São Paulo: Editora Atica, 1982. 237 p.: ill. (Coleção de autores brasileiros; 77)

Major collection by acclaimed author offers rich, complex narratives about family and love, social justice and politics, literature and life. Title story boldly experiments with techniques—the combination non-fiction and fiction, use of intellectual asides, trivia, and tropes—as it wittily introduces John Cage's gift to João Gilberto, the bird of perfection's empty cage. Few authors can handle love as well as Sant'Anna. "Dueto" exemplifies his powerful grappling with aspects of the erotic.

6131 Santos, Deoscoredes Maximiliano dos. Contos de Mestre Didi. Rio de Janeiro:

CODECRI, 1981. 87 p.: ill. (Coleção Alternativa; v. 03)

Unpretentious Afro-Brazilian fables by the well known Mestre Didi preserve African traditions and are both didactic and entertaining. Author is Bahiano descendant of ancient priestly lineage of Ketu-Nagô.

6132 Scliar, Moacyr. Max e os felinos. Porto Alegre: L&PM Editors, 1981. 78 p. (Coleção Nova leitura; v. 2)

Novella combines impressionistic ambiance and social analysis as it conveys vicissitudes of German intellectual and anti-Nazi in Brazil. Max hunts Nazis, eventually killing one, and accepts Brazil both figuratively and literally by marrying a "bruga" (Indian girl). Uneven but worth reading.

6133 Silvério, Bento. Entropia & [i.e. e] evasão: contos. Florianópolis: Universidade Federal de Santa Catarina (UFSC), 1980. 97 p. (Coleção Discente. Série Literatura; 1)

Solidly constructed stories examine major ethical questions (e.g., selling one's soul for money in a job) and the exploitation of the proletariat. Perceptive author is technically competent, ironic, and versatile.

6134 Sobreira, Francisco. Não enterrarei os meus mortos. Natal: Fundação José Augusto, 1980. 63 p.

Psychologically probing stories by Rio Grande do Norte author (see also *HLAS 42:6116*) are set in small country towns. Mysterious and suspenseful.

6135 Sousa, Aida Félix de. Filão extinto: contos. Rio de Janeiro: Civilização Brasileira; Goiânia: Oriente, 1981? 98 p.

Poetical and dramatic regional stories convey varied characters' daily lives. Psychologically sound, perceptive, and well written collection.

6136 Souza, Silveira de. O cavalo em chama: relatos. São Paulo: Editora Atica, 1981. 76 p., 1 leaf of plates (Coleção de autores brasileiros; 72)

Souza handles the short story in a classic manner, as "aprofundamento psicológico" (A. Hohfeld). Admirable "Psicocinésia" unites inner and outer turmoil. A very fine book.

6137 Tatagiba, Fernando. O sol no céu da boca: contos. Vitória: Fundação Cultural do Espírito Santo: Fundação Ceciliano Abel de Almeida, 1980. 91 p.: ill. (Coleção Letras capixabas; v. 1)

Fascinating mixture of social protest, surrealism, and literary expertise.

6138 Tavares, Zulmira Ribeiro. O japonês dos olhos redondos: ficções. Rio de Janeiro: Paz e Terra, 1982. 123 p. (Coleção Literatura e teoria literária; v. 45)

Admirable tales exhibit urbanity, serenity, intelligence, and wit as author examines life's vagaries and pitfalls. Tavares gently mocks excessive intellectualizing (title story and "O Homem do Relógio da Luz") and psychiatry ("Cai Fora"). Classic language and flowing narrative. One of the best collections of the biennium.

6139 Távola, Artur da. Leilão do mim: contos. Rio de Janeiro: Editora Nova Fronteira, 1981. 128 p.

Classic "desconcerto do mundo" in metropolis shown through conformists' and radicals' lives. Only a "silent and weak youth" who disregards appearances to concentrate on others' feelings understands life. Rich in philosophical inquiry, stories have breadth and fluidity. Should be read.

6140 Trevisan, Dalton. Chorinho brejeiro. Rio de Janeiro: Editora Record, 1981. 114 p.

Variations by expert on woes of love. Characters, many of them old and sick, reminisce. Trevisan is lucid, and his comic sense's shrewd, but *Chorinho* has less bite than its predecessors.

6141 !————. Essas malditas mulheres. Rio de Janeiro: Editora Record, 1982. 128 p.

Characters João and Maria, though ill and senile, still fight violently. Inimitable Trevisan again succeeds in presenting the prosaic and sordid with immense irony and compassion.

6142 Tutikian, Jane. Batalha naval: contos. Rio de Janeiro: Civilização Brasileira, 1981. 113 p. (Coleção Vera Cruz; v. 321)

Exciting collection creates subtle moods and focuses on the wonder that so often escapes us (e.g., "Fábula da Noite"). Excellent tale "No 7° Dia, Talves" depicts housewife's daily activities. A must.

6143 Valle, Alúsio P. O segredos de Cenira. Brasília: Horizonte Editora, 1979.

151 p. (Coleção Machado de Assis; v. 18)

Stories about Brasília examine new capital thoroughly and affectionately. Large and varied cast of characters presented with humor, compassion, and enthusiasm in well made, traditionally told narratives.

6144 Veríssimo, Luís Fernando. O analista de Bagé. Porto Alegre: L&PM Editores, 1981. 132 p.

With keen sense of the absurd, Veríssimo presents a self-styled, "orthodox," Freudian analyst who cures his clients by spanking them like naughty brats. Craftsmanship, variety, and plays on words prevail in this witty collection.

6145 ———. Outras do analista de Bagé. 7a. ed. Porto Alegre: L&PM Editores, 1982. 139 p.

Veríssimo's incisive satire again features his comical gaúcho analyst, criticizing bourgeois and flower children alike. Skillfully developed anecdotes. For a Veríssimo best-seller on topic, see item **6185.**

6146 Viana, Antônio Carlos. Em pleno castigo. São Paulo: Editora HUCITEC, 1981. 81 p. (Momento)

Most stories are interior monologues focussing on life's sorrows: fleeting youth, lack of children, and old age. Major virtues here are good grasp of character and classic, strong language. Includes admirably controlled "Aos Domingos" and fine fantasy "No Deserto." By young writer who deserves watching.

6147 Werneck, Armond. A sombra das personagens: contos. Belo Horizonte: Imprensa Oficial de Minas Gerais, 1981. 109 p.

Uneven collection offers many excellent stories, including "A Arvore de Zambro" and "O Juízo de Deus," stark tales of explosive passions in *sertão.* Amusing Biblical takeoffs (e.g., unchaste Susannah, lecherous prophet Daniel, cunning virgins). Basically classical style. Keen social commentary denounces indifference of the rich and powerful.

Crônicas

RICHARD A. PRETO-RODAS, *Director, Division of Language, University of South Florida*

THERE IS CONSIDERABLE EVIDENCE of the *crônica's* enduring popularity in Brazil. The last two years have seen the publication of a prodigious number of collections including Luis Fernando Veríssimo's *O Analista de Bagé* (item **6185**) which has become the all-time bestseller in Brazilian literary history. To be sure, there has been much chaff among the grain, which is not surprising given the *crônica's* elusive character as a genre which only *appears* to be artless, inconsequential, and journalistically objective. In truth, however, considerable talent is needed to avoid the twin pitfalls of plodding prose and excessive virtuosity, and it takes unusual insight to detect a spark of transcendental value in a simple occurrence. Perhaps the most difficult achievement for a *crônista* is attaining a personal tone and a critical stance without converting the *crônica* into an essay of subjective musing or didactic sermonizing. Most of the collections which are not annotated below failed to achieve one or more of the *crônica's* characteristics; others were omitted less for intrinsic deficiencies than for their subtle metamorphosis into full-fledged short stories. The distinction between a *crônica* and a *conto* or *historinha* is admittedly a difficult one to establish, and at least one example of an *historinha* by Carlos Drummond de Andrade ("Glória") has been included among the *crônicas* assembled in a volume of the collection *Para gostar de ler* (item **6149**). Generally, however, editors and readers alike usually discern between the two genres.

As observed in *HLAS 40* (p. 480) and *HLAS 42* (p. 634), the *crônica*'s increasing literary sophistication and prestige as a model of proper language usage is exemplified by the appearance of anthologies designed for student use in language and literature classes, both in Brazil and abroad. Multivolume editions comprising the best of several authors and annotated editions of *crônicas* by a single writer such as Rubem Braga (item **6153**), Fernando Sabino (item **6179**), and others figure among those noted below. Another note-worthy development pertains to *crônicas* devoted to a single theme or perspective. Examples include Almeida Reis' pieces on farming (item **6172**) and Wilson Roveri's selections relating soccer to sundry aspects of Brazilian life (item **6178**). Equally significant is the trend away from the light and humorous vein of the past and a concomitant tendency towards a critical perspective characterized by biting satire, angry denunciacion, and melancholic foreboding. The worrisome state of international affairs in general and the economic and social woes of Brazil in particular are persistent themes especially in the *crônicas* of Bandeira de Mello (item **6168**), Dilson Ribeiro (item **6174**), Flávio Rangel (item **6170**), Hélcio Carvalho de Castro (item **6156**), and Fausto von Wolffenbütell (item **6187**), all of whom have obviously benefitted from the relaxed censorship of recent years.

The genre's appeal, then, is multifaceted, since it affords literary appreciation and linguistic wealth as well as social insight and political analysis. The future of such an extraordinarily diversified genre continues to be a promising one. The numbers of writers and readers of *crônicas* will in all likelihood continue to increase. Once a minor genre cultivated by big-city journalists, the *crônica* is appreciated everywhere in contemporary Brazil. Recent collections by men and women of every age and professional background, have appeared from Mato Grosso and Maranhão to Santa Catarina and Rio Grande do Sul. One might safely assert that the genre is modern Brazil's favorite vehicle for literary expression.

6148 Alvim, Clóvis de Faria. Escritos bissextos. Apresentação, Carlos Drummond de Andrade. Belo Horizonte: Editora Vega, 1980. 175 p.

A departure from the doctor/author's usual activities as a scientist, these *crônicas* are charming evocations of early 20th-century life in the small interior town of Itabira: major figures, schools, cultural life, and the simple pleasures of a rural gentry that included the family of Carlos Drummond de Andrade.

6149 Andrade, Carlos Drummond de *et al.* Para gostar de ler. São Paulo: Editora Atica, 1977–1980. 6 v.: ill.

Delightful collection of 20 *crônicas* by four of Brazil's best practitioners of the genre: Rubem Braga, Carlos Drummond de Andrade, Fernando Sabino, and Paulo Mendes Campos. Only two have appeared in other anthologies. Each is a jewel, as are the opening statements wherein each author relates how he first began to write.

6150 Andrade, Maria Julieta Drummond de. O valor da vida. Rio de Janeiro: Editora Nova Fronteira, 1982. 296 p.

No need to worry about this daughter of a famous father. Her *crônicas* are captivating as she reflects and comments on life in Argentina, return trips to Brazil, and encounters with the famous. The two on Borges and his views of Camões are priceless.

6151 Arrigo, Renato d'. Nostalgia: crônicas. Rio de Janeiro: Salamandra, 1980. 170 p.

Yet another *gaúcho* who writes with verve on a remarkable range of topics, from politics and women's lib to Frank Sinatra and Spanish American prose. The point of departure is, in proper *crônica* fashion, the odd occurrence that makes the routine memorable.

6152 Bororó *[pseud. for* Alberto de Castro Simoens da Silva]. Gente da Madrugada: flagrantes da vida noturna. Rio de Janeiro: Guavira Editores, 1982. 238 p.

Author relives 1000 nights in Rio's old Lapa area with its *bas-fond* of seedy dandies, ladies of easy virtue, Portuguese saloon-keepers, and sidewalk troubadours. Despite some excessive enumeration and an occasional infelicitous attempt to produce dialect, these accounts read well and succeed in evoking a naughty past that seems impossibly innocent by current standards.

6153 Braga, Rubem. Rubem Braga. Seleção de textos, notas, estudo biográfico, histórico e crítico e exercícios por Paulo Elias Allane Franchetti, Antônio Alcir Bernardez Pecora. São Paulo: Abril Educação, 1980. 95 p. (Literatura comentada; 16)

Fine selection of a master *crônista's* work from the 1930s through 1960s. The collection, designed for students, includes supplementary documentation (e.g., an interview with Braga and short critical evaluations).

6154 Campos, Paulo Mendes. Crônicas escolhidas. São Paulo: Editora Atica, 1981. 192 p.: ill. (Coleção de autores brasileiros; 70)

Anthology of the best *crônicas* by an undisputed master of the genre. Despite years in Rio, his ingenious observations clearly reflect the wry humor of the outsider from Minas Gerais, whether writing about Ipanema or commenting on sojourns in Sweden and Siberia.

6155 Cardozo, Flávio José. Agua do pote: crónicas. Florianópolis: Editora da UFSC, 1982. 150 p.: ill.

More than 40 *crônicas* by a talented journalist who often derives inspiration from scenes, characters, and events peculiar to his state of Santa Catarina, written in a wide variety of tones and styles, from introspective to conversational. Cardozo's keen sense of social awareness accounts for his themes with a distinct point of view, such as the plight of endangered species and the suffering of Brazilian aborigenes. Humorous comments on such matters as popular malapropisms and spunky widows who resolve to go topless to the beach.

6156 Castro, Hélcio Carvalho de. Andanças de Macunaíma: crônicas. São Paulo: Editora Soma, 1980. 154 p.

These pieces by a first-rate journalist

situated in São Paulo are short, well written, and varied in style and theme. Politics, slang, Brazil's loss of cultural autonomy, and literary criticism are but a few of the many subjects which elicit this writer's perceptive comments.

6157 Cheuiche, Alcy José de Vargas. O planeta azul: crônicas. Porto Alegre: Editora Sulina, 1981. 94 p.

Author's highly successful, first attempt with *crônicas*. Lucid reflections on a wide range of topics, from international events to such local issues as the precarious state of rail travel in Brazil.

6158 Congílio, Mariazinha. Amanhã ser á hoje: crônicas. São Paulo: Escala 7 Editora Gráfica, 1982. 223 p.

Author is already justly famous for her ability to transform the slimmest topic into a lively and, usually comical event. Most of these *crônicas* deal with her travels in England, Canada, Spain, Portugal, Marocco, and US. Her comments on Disney World and Orlando's malls synthesize the Brazilian infatuation with such places.

6159 Franco, Sérgio da Costa. Achados e perdidos: crônicas, 1977–1981. Porto Alegre: Martins Livreiro-Editor, 1981. 122 p.

Third collection by one of the best practitioners of the genre. Colorful, varied, and consistently engaging album of *vignettes* of Porto Alegre. Franco succeeds especially well in depicting social types as symbols of classes, ethnic groups, and eras.

6160 Lima, Oswaldo. Bairro do Caju. Rio de Janeiro: Livraria Editora Cátedra; Brasília: *em convênio com o* Instituto Nacional do Livro, Ministério da Educação e Cultura, 1980. 356 p.

Published posthumously, this volume of *crônicas* by a journalist from Campos provides a detailed album of a typical lower-middle-class neighborhood in a small provincial city during the second quarter of this century. Even allowing for the rosy hue of nostalgia and an occasional lapse of memory, Oswaldo Lima charmingly recreates more stable times (and people).

6161 Maciel, Luiz Carlos. Negócio seguinte. Rio de Janeiro: CODECRI, 1981. 247 p. (Coleção Edições do Pasquim; v. 101)

Retrospective selection of author's essays, chronicles, and mini-dramas from the satirical magazine *Pasquim*, which he helped found in late 1960s. Even in the dour 1980s, one can still appreciate Maciel's talent and his gusto as he champions innovation and liberty as antidotes for creeping conformity.

6162 Maia, Carlos Vasconcelos. O leque do Oxum e algumas crônicas de Candomblé. Bahia: s.n., s.d. 100 p. (Coleção do autor; 1)

Most of this volume is devoted to author's account of a return to his native Bahia. However, he also includes nine *crônicas* on diverse aspects of *candomblé* and provides novel insights into the world of Eguns, Orixás, and other dignitaries from Afro-Brazilian spiritism.

6163 Martins, Luís. Ciranda dos ventos: crônicas. São Paulo: Editora Moderna, 1981. 51 p.: ill.

Twenty-five pieces which span 30 years of this gifted writer's best work. Whether presenting the Brazilian's cavalier attitude towards social and epistolary obligations or a parable of humanity as a chronically ill individual facing a final relapse, the author enhances variety of tone and theme with a fascinating interplay of irony and sincerity.

6164 Meireles, Cecília. Ilusões do mundo: crônicas. 2a. ed. Rio de Janeiro: Editora Nova Fronteira, 1982. 128 p. (Coleção Poiesis)

These elegantly written pieces, compiled by author's heirs, were originally presented in the early 1960s on the radio for the Ministry of Education and Culture. Like her poetry, they represent this remarkable woman's *Weltanschauung* of gently melancholic, incisive—if kindly—irony, and appreciation for all beings, from trees to people.

6165 ———. Janela mágica: crônicas. São Paulo: Editora Moderna, 1981. 46 p.: bibl.

Reissue of 21 titles culled from five previously published collections of *crônicas*. As always, the author provides her reader with a worthwhile experience thanks to her spare but elegant prose, charming insights, and bitter-sweet outlook on life which appears as something simply too complex (oxymoron intended) to be adequately comprehended.

6166 Meireles, José Dilermando. Deste Planalto central—o histórico e o pitoresco: crônicas. Capa e ilustrações, Aires. Luziânia: Jorluz Editora, 1978. 131 p.: ill.

Although a bit anecdotal and somewhat narrowly conceived, these *crônicas* present a novel view of the small town life in mid-century peculiar to the highlands region that was soon to become Brasília. The perspective is consistently comic and the characters are all drawn from real life.

6167 Mello, Gustavo Bandeira de. Do outro lado do rio. Brasília: Thesaurus, s.d. 202 p.

The author is clearly fascinated by the other (e.g., the co-passenger on a plane, the self-anointed pillar of conservative society at a party, the single woman who lives alone, the shanty dweller in the shadow of Brasília's new neighborhoods, the believer waiting to catch a glimpse of the Pope). Generally sad portraits of his long-suffering Northeast.

6168 ———. Todos os campos dão flores. Brasília: Thesaurus, 1981. 190 p.

Crônicas characterized by talent, insight, and a lively curiosity. They are, however, not likely to afford much escapism. Typical themes include inflation, alienation, unemployment, crime, and the suffocating weight of outmoded traditions.

6169 Nogueira, Armando *et al.* O melhor da crônica brasileira. Rio de Janeiro: Livraria J. Olympio Editora, 1980–1981. 2 v.

Vol. 1: *Crônicas* by Armando Nogueira, José Lins do Rego, Rachel Queiroz, and Sérgio Porto, about diverse topics including soccer, travel impressions, childhood reminiscences, and the drawbacks of modern life. Like vol. 1, vol. 2 is designed for the Brazilian classroom and provides a fairly extensive sampling from Manuel Bandeira and three less known but significant writers, Aldir Blanc, Doc Comparato, and João Saldanha. Perhaps the best are Blanc's *vignettes* of timid Dilma who finally gives her philandering husband a lesson, and Doc Comparato's medical odyssey sparked by efforts to remove a corn ("O Calo").

6170 Rangel, Flávio. A praça dos sem poderes: crônicas. Rio de Janeiro: Civilização Brasileira, 1980. 190 p. (Coleção Vera Cruz; v. 316)

In *A praça dos sem poderes*, the author returns to his favorite themes: inflation, declining expectations of the middle class, chicanery in high places, multinationals, and terrorism from both the left and the right. Lively colloquial style.

6171 ———. Os prezados leitores. São Paulo: Global Editora, 1981. 151 p. (Singular & plural; 12)

Rangel, one of Brazil's best-known stage directors, is also a regular contributor to *Folha de São Paulo*, the source of these satirical selections. The title refers to his custom of occasionally composing chronicles in reply to letters from his "dear readers." With acerbic wit, the author focuses on national problems such as inflation, ineptitude in high places, and sexism.

6172 Reis, Eduardo Almeida. Mulher, eleição e eucalipto. Porto Alegre: Editora Centaurus, 1981. 123 p.

Crônicas with a novel perspective, given the preference of the genre for an urban setting: short pieces about farming and cattle raising written by successful farmer-rancher in the state of Rio de Janeiro. He succeeds in interesting the reader in such topics as range fires and the plight of Dutch cows in a tropical climate.

6173 Reis, Elpídio. Eu por aí: crônicas. Rio de Janeiro: Folha Carioca Editora, 1978. 155 p.

This is a mixed bag which tends towards the didactic. But the breezy colloquial style is effective as the author bewails topics like the lack of municipal planning and the constant excavations it occasions, from his border town in Mato Grosso to the streets of Rio.

6174 Ribeiro, Dilson. No reino dos tecnocratas. Brasília: Horizonte, 1980. 164 p.: ill.

Thirteen *crônicas*, a parable, and several articles by an outspoken journalist. Author provides an unsettling view of contemporary Brazil in his caustic presentation of ecological depredation, tecnocratic mythmaking, and political bundling.

6175 Rio, João do. Histórias da gente alegre: contos, crônicas e reportagens da "Belle Epoque" carioca. Seleção, introdução e notas, João Carlos Rodrigues. Rio de Janeiro: Livraria J. Olympio Editora, 1981. 113 p., 1 leaf of plates.

To commemorate the centenary of this ignored but important writer, the editor has compiled some of his most remarkable *crônicas*. João do Rio, Rio's most Bohemian chronicler, captured the seamy side of Brazil's *Belle Epoque*, complete with Black Masses, criminal minors, prostitutes, etc.

6176 Rodrigues, Gonzaga. Notas do meu lugar: crônicas. João Pessoa: Editora Acauã, 1978. 259 p.

"Meu lugar" is the author's João Pessoa with rural Paraíba in the background, a novel locale for the *crônica*. Though uneven, selections subtly capture a sense of modern alienation and social dysfunction.

6177 Rodrigues, Moacir Danilo. Ainda há flores no meu caminho. Porto Alegre: Rígel Editora, 1981? 80 p.

The somber voice of a Catholic concerned with the social inequalities of his country pervades these selections. These sad, well written pieces strike a responsive chord in the reader, despite the author's penchant for heavy-handed satire.

6178 Roveri, Wilson. De Sócrates a Sócrates. São Paulo: Editora Soma, 1981. 140 p.: ill.

Collection almost entirely inspired by the Brazilian national sport (e.g., soccer and race, soccer and music, soccer and politics). Author's role as a radio commentator is apparent in his conversational style and lively dialogue.

6179 Sabino, Fernando Tavares. Fernando Sabino. Seleção de textos, notas, estudo biográfico histórico e crítico e exercícios por Flora Christina Bender. São Paulo: Abril Educação, 1980. 106 p. (Literatura comentada; 24)

While this school text encompasses more than *crônicas*, it provides a fairly good sampling of Sabino's work in the genre. Includes useful secondary material.

6180 Souza, José Hélder de. Coisas & [i.e. e] bichos. Brasília: Senado Federal, 1977. 82 p. (Coleção Machado de Assis; v. 2)

These pieces, gathered from Souza's column in *Correio Braziliense*, waver between true chronicles and short stories. Most are decidedly literary in flavor and are tinged with a traditional realism inappropriate for true *crônicas*.

6181 Tavares, Aurélio de Lyra. Crônicas ecléticas. Rio de Janeiro: A. de Lyra Tavares, 1981. 191 p.

Carefully crafted selections, compiled from Tavares' weekly column in *Jornal do Comércio*, cover wide range of issues, from news items to questions of cultural standards and religious practices. Written from a consistently conservative Catholic viewpoint.

6182 Turcato, Teresinha. Amo-te Hélade. Porto Alegre: Editora Metrópole, 1981. 70 p.: ill.

Predominantly meditative *crônicas* and short stories that often assume the structure of a soliloquy directed to author's son or daughter. Themes are traditional and piously conservative in their concern for small blessings, resignation to the inevitable, and acceptance of grown children's autonomy. Occasional lyrical moments of undeniable sincerity.

6183 Vasconcellos, Marcos de. Tragédias ligeiras. Rio de Janeiro: CODECRI, 1981. 126 p. (Coleção Edições do Pasquim; v. 108)

Author maintains intimate conversational tone throughout as he oscillates between bitter-sweet evocation (whatever happened to godmothers?) and tragic-comic portrayals of a bizzare present (a mugging seems almost preferable to the ordeal of an ensuing legal deposition).

6184 Vasconcellos, Sylvio de. Crônicas do exílio. Belo Horizonte: Editora Líttera Maciel, 1979? 115 p.

Exile in title refers to late author's long residence in US. His views reveal as much about Brazilian sensibilities as about his preferred subject: US white middle-class contemporary culture in Washington, D.C., New York City, and San Francisco.

6185 Veríssimo, Luís Fernando and **Edgar Vasques.** O analista de Bagé: em quadrinhos. Porto Alegre: L&PM Editores, 1983. 48 p. (Coleção Quadrinhos)

Record-breaking bestseller (73 editions since first printing), collection contains *crônicas* which lampoon the contemporary scene, from rock-and-roll weddings and self-help sexual manuals to middle-class paranoia and string-quartet recitals. Often zany and always humorous, the *crônicas* provide lively dialogue and ingenious word play. Includes seven hilarious visits to earthy gaucho psychiatrist of the title (see also items **6144–6145**).

6186 Wainberg, Paulo. Conversa de verão: crônicas. Porto Alegre: Editora Movimiento, 1981. 93 p. (Coleção Rio Grande; v. 49)

Decidedly humorous *crônicas* with a bite, written from an oddly European perspective. Topics include a vestigial belief in an (inept) Creator, Franz Kafka's ambiguous inspiration, and caricatures of the middle class.

6187 Wolffenbüttel, Faustin von. O dia em que comeram o ministro. Rio de Janeiro: Editora CODECRI, 1982. 231 p. (Coleção Edições do Pasquim; v. 135)

Title indicates the devastatingly irreverent tone and substance of this generous collection of author's contributions to the satirical journal *Pasquim*. Racism, sex, the bomb, and aggressive nationalism are only a few of the many polemical subjects which author subjects to his caustic wit. His biting satire ranges widely from Brazilian sacred cows such as soccer to US religious hucksters.

Poetry

RALPH E. DIMMICK, *General Secretariat, Organization of American States*

POETIC PRODUCTION IN BRAZIL operates at the level of industry: some 800 volumes were inspected in preparing the corresponding section for this volume of the *Handbook.*

The scene is dominated by figures of established reputation, whose bibliographies grow by the year. One notes new works by Walmir Ayala (item **6197**); Raúl Bopp (item **6200**); Geir Campos (items **6205–6206**); Paulo Mendes Campos (item **6208**); Hilda Hilst (item **6224**); Lêdo Ivo (items **6227–6228**); Waldemar Lopes (item **6238**);

Thiago de Mello (item **6241**); João Cabral de Melo Neto (items **6243–6244**); Mauro Mota (items **6250–6251**); Moacyr Félix (item **6254**); Telmo Padilha (item **6255**); Dirceu Quintanilha (items **6262–6264**); Afonso Félix de Sousa (item **6272**); and Gilberto Mendonça Teles (item **6274**). Anthologies, collected editions, and reissues attest continuing interest in the previous work of Ferreira Gullar (item **6223**); Homero Homem (item **6226**); Nauro Machado (item **6239**); Carlos Nejar (item **6252**); Domingos Carvalho da Silva (item **6269**); and a figure better known as a prose writer, Gilberto Freyre (item **6220**). The collected works of three notable poets of the past, Augusto dos Anjos (item **6191**), Ascenso Ferreira (item **6216**), and João da Cruz e Sousa (item **6273**), appeared in important new editions. Of interest to students of Cecília Meireles is the manuscript facsimile of *Cânticos* (item **6240**), which shows changes introduced by the poet in the course of composition.

One notes with pleasure the appearance of several new figures of promise: Antônio Morais de Carvalho (item **6211**); Ciro Figueiredo (item **6217**); Lúcia Garcia da Fonseca (item **6219**); Robert Kenard (item **6233**); Ivan Miziara (item **6246**); Diógenes da Cunha Lima (item **6236**); and Péricles Prade (item **6260**); also the reappearance of Ivan Junqueira (item **6231**). Highly unusual are João Manuel Simões' "translations into poetry" of paintings by Pablo Picasso (item **6271**).

Political and social protest is an increasingly frequent theme, but the product is distinguished for little other than sincerity. Gay love finds open expression (item **6268**), and rising black consciousness is reflected in an anthology of poets of *négritude* (item **6196**). Concern for the environment is another recurring issue; one may cite for example the work of Luiz F. Papi (item **6256**).

It is to be noted that poetic production is not confined solely to Rio and São Paulo: Recife, São Luís, and Florianópolis are also important centers of publication.

6188 Accioly, Marcus. O(de) Itabira. Ilustrações, Fernando de Araújo Jr. Rio de Janeiro: Livraria J. Olympio Editora; Brasília: *em convênio com o* Instituto Nacional do Livro, Ministério da Educação e Cultura, 1980. 111 p.: bibl., ill.

With its plays on words and graphic tricks, this tribute to the birthplace of Carlos Drummond de Andrade might be termed an example of Concrete regionalism.

6189 Aizim, Lucia. Exercício efêmero. São Paulo: Roswitha Kempf Editores, 1982. 75 p.

Of "fumo, ar e solidão," Aizim weaves the gossamer of her melancholic meditations on the fleeting nature of human existence.

6190 Almeida, Miguel de. Dobrando esquinas. Capa e ilustrações de Tomoshige Kusuno. São Paulo: M. Ohno: R. Kempf Editores, 1981. 52 p.: ill.

Nocturnal moods and street atmosphere of a great city, well captured in verse of erotic intent.

6191 Anjos, Augusto dos. Eu & outras poesias. Rio de Janeiro: Civilização Brasileira; Belo Horizonte: Itatiaia, 1982. 2 v. (143, 150 p.): indexes (Poetas de sempre; v. 2)

Contains 67 poems, collected from periodicals, not included in previous editions of Anjos' work, plus biographical and critical articles by Antônio Houaiss, Orris Soares, and Francisco de Assis Barbosa.

6192 Arruda, Eunice. Os momentos. São Paulo: Livraria Nobel: Secretaria de Estado da Cultura de São Paulo, 1981? 61 p.

In verse of great delicacy, Arruda communes with her soul as if peering into a well whose unbroken solitude reflects only the sight of her own face and the sound of her own voice.

6193 Assunção, Paulinho. Cantigas de amor & [i.e. e] outras geografias: poemas. Belo Horizonte: Governo do Estado de Minas Gerais, 1980. 61 p.

The sad realities of prostitution in a harsh frontier setting, gracefully and poignantly suggested in symbolic language.

6194 ———. A sagrada blasfêmia dos bares: poemas. Rio de Janeiro: Civilização Brasileira, 1981. 65 p. (Coleção Poesia hoje; v. 47)

Assunção sees the bar as a "retiro das almas penadas," in which the poet gives vent to "a bílis da impotência" in an "antielegia aos tempos modernos."

6195 Augusto, Eudoro. Carnaval, variações sobre 13 poemas. Ilustrações, Luiz Aquila. Rio de Janeiro: Aluísio Leite; São Paulo: M. Ohno-R. Kempf; Brasília: Jorge de Souza, 1981. 42 leaves: ill.

Carnival as the essence of Brazilian political wit, sensuality, and desire to escape from reality is well captured in Eudoro Augusto's verse. Illustrations entirely abstract.

6196 Axé: antologia contemporânea da poesia negra brasileira. Organização, Paulo Colina. São Paulo: Global, 1981. 103 p.

Rising black consciousness is evidenced by this anthology of poets (chiefly Paulistas, b. ca. 1950). The most significant appear to be Abelardo Rodrigues and Adão Ventura.

6197 Ayala, Walmir. Estado de choque. Desenhos de May Shuravel. São Paulo: Parnaso: Massao Ohno, 1980. 41 p.: ill.

Preoccupied by pollution, man's inhumanity to man, and other problems of the day, Ayala declares: "Não quero mais fazer poemas que não sejam tributo do instante. / . . . Os poemas eternos eu deixo para a vida eterna."

6198 Bell, Lindolf. As vivências elementares. São Paulo: Massao Ohno / Roswitha Kempf Editores, 1980. 147 p.: ill.

"Seja o poema . . . / o exercício / corpo a corpo do poeta / entre uma dúvida e outra dúvida / . . . a deflagração do homem / . . . e a vida passada a sujo."

6199 Blower, Patricia. Moinhas ao vento. Rio de Janeiro: Editora Fontana, 1981. 57 p.

A "have" in a land of "have-nots," Blower treats privilege with gentle irony and deprivation with feeling void of sentimentality.

6200 Bopp, Raúl. Mironga e outras poemas. Rio de Janeiro: Civilização Brasileira; Brasília: em convênio com o Instituto Nacional do Livro, Ministério da Educação e Cultura, 1978. 144 p.: bibl. (Coleção Poesia hoje; v. 22)

Previously uncollected poems from years as early as 1919 and as late as 1978, by

a writer best known for his association with the *Revista de Antropofagia* Modernists of 1920s. Bibliography; extensive selection of critical comment.

6201 Braga, Fernando. O exílio do viandante: em dois discursos. Brasília: Thesaurus Editora, 1982. 64 p.

In the urban nightmare "a carne é verdade / no longe tão perto / de um fosso infinito."

6202 Braga, Rubem. Livro de versos. Recife: Edições Pirata, 1980. 39 p., 5 leaves of plates: ill.

The rare poetic excursions of a distinguished *cronista*, notable for effectiveness of their simple language and candid view they give of author's soul.

6203 Cabral, Astrid. Torna-viagem: poesia. Recife: Edições Pirata, 1981. 85 p.

Past glories and present tragedies inspire these reflections on the Middle East, in which Cabral once again manifests her keen poetic sensitivity and her gift for striking imagery.

6204 Campos, Francisco Moura. O sorriso do drama. São Paulo: Massao Ohno; Roswitha Kempf, 1980. 67 p.: plate.

Good idea of this spiritual descendant of Carlos Drummond de Andrade is conveyed by verses of "Valsinha:" "A vida / Tão próxima, tão ingênua, / Que um gesto não seja mais que / O movimento de um sentir / Profundamente."

6205 Campos, Geir. Cantar de amigo: ao outro homem da mulher amada. Vitória: Fundação Ceciliano Abel de Almeida, Universidade Federal do Espírito Santo, 1982. 39 p. (Coleção Letras capixabas; v. 6)

Sonnet sequence, altogether traditional in form, dealing with sensuous but platonic attraction of one man for the female companion of another.

6206 ———. Tarefa. Rio de Janeiro: Civilização Brasileira; Brasília: em convênio com o Instituto Nacional do Livro, Ministério da Educação e Cultura; São Paulo: Massao Ohno, 1981. 127 p. (Coleção Poesia sempre; v. 5)

Selected verse by splendid craftsman of the Generation of 1945, whose inspiration shifts "entre a ilha que sou e o continente / de uma fraternidade que procuro."

6207 Campos, Maria Consuelo Cunha. Mineiridade. Rio de Janeiro: Achiamé, 1980. 62 p. (Coleção Anfion; no. 3)

Minas lives in a time world of its own, here suggested in terms of personal, political, and literary history.

6208 Campos, Paulo Mendes. Poemas. Rio de Janeiro: Civilização Brasileira, 1979. 205 p. (Coleção Poesia hoje; v. 30)

Reprints *O domingo azul do mar* and *Testamento do Brasil* and adds two new collections, *Balada de amor perfeito* and *Arquitetura*. Campos' long lines tend to lapse into prose; his parallelistic verse in the end becomes monotonous.

6209 Carlos Magno, Paschoal. Cantigas do cavaleiro. Rio de Janeiro: Editora Cátedra; Brasília: *em convênio com o* Instituto Nacional do Livro, Ministério da Educação e Cultura, 1980. 85 p.: ill.

At the end of life, poet writes "Serenamente emocionado/ pela fragilidade/ das coisas humanas,/ pelo amortalhamento . . . das idéias,/ pela rapidez como passam os homens."

6210 Carvalho, Age de. Arquitetura dos ossos. Belém: Gráfica Falangola Editora, 1980. 73 p.

Striving to convey a maximum of meaning with a minimum of words, Carvalho is more than successful in compositions such as "A Cadela" and "A Língua Insólita."

6211 Carvalho, Antônio Morais de. Persona. João Pessoa: A União Cia. Editora, 1982. 81 p.

Writing in forms ranging from folk rhyme through classical sonnet to concrete verse, on topics as varied as Jimi Hendrix and the threat of world war, Carvalho displays abundant talent but no clearly defined personality as yet.

6212 Cruz, Geraldo Dias da. Proclama aos incautos. São Paulo: Editora do Escritor, 1981. 67 p.: col. ill. (Coleção do poeta; v. 26)

"A vida/ é risco/ rasto/ rosto/ que no tempo dilui:" it should be appreciated for what it has to offer, while it exists.

6213 Espinheira Filho, Ruy. As sombras luminosas. Florianópolis: FCC Edições, 1981. 56 p.

Essentially an urban poet, Espinheira declares "Uma cidade me habita," evoking nostalgically its moods, atmosphere, and rhythms. Winner of 1981 Cruz e Sousa Prize.

6214 Fehlauer, Márcia. Nas entranhas. Rio de Janeiro: Achiamé, 1981. 64 p.

While her compositions are almost entirely self-centered, Fehlauer is singularly successful in conveying to reader a sense of participation in her reactions to love, motherhood, and, in rare instances, social issues.

6215 Ferreira, Antônio do Carmo. Mundolinda e outros mundos: poemas. Olinda: Companhia Editora de Pernambuco, 1981. 68 p.

A touch of whimsical humor characterizes the best of these poems evoking city of Olinda, slumbering in its colonial past.

6216 Ferreira, Ascenso. Poemas: Catimbó, Cana caiana, Xenhenhém. Recife: Nordestal, 1981. 214 p., 8 p. of plates: ill.

Collected poems, distinguished for their oral qualities, of a Northeastern representative of Paulista Modernism, accompanied by musical settings and useful biographical material and critical appreciations.

6217 Figueiredo, Ciro. Como se fôssemos os primeiros. São Paulo: M. Ohno Editor, 1981. 60 p.

"O poeta é/ delirante./ Tanto amante/ quanto só./ Vez de outras./ Vez ninguém./ Vez de alguém./ Vez mulher./ Sempre lavra a palavra/ do seu amor, da sua dor" writes Figueiredo in lines which sum up both manner and substance of this promising collection.

6218 Flores, Liane. O grande ausente: poesia. Porto Alegre: Editora Movimento, 1980. 101 p. (Coleção Poesia sul; v. 28)

Varying aspects of love—expectation, fulfillment, enthusiasm, separation, regret, reconciliation—treated without sentimentality or sensuality, in sincerity, simplicity, and truth.

6219 Fonseca, Lúcia Garcia da. Invenções do silêncio. Rio de Janeiro: Livraria J. Olympio Editora, 1980. 105 p.

Simple creatures of nature and objects of everyday existence inspire Fonseca to lyrical expansions and philosophical reflections which she seasons with an occasional dash of down-to-earth reality. Outstanding debut.

6220 Freyre, Gilberto. Poesia reunida. Ilustrações de Marcos Cordeiro. Recife: Edições Pirata, 1980. 107 p., 9 leaves of plates: ill.

Largely descriptive, these "leap-year" poems of a celebrated sociologist capture, at times rhapsodically, at times incisively, traditional aspects of Brazilian Northeast and their Portuguese counterparts.

6221 Giglio, Maria José. Elementares. São Paulo: Editora Soma, 1979. 77 p. Fairies, the golem, city of Samarkand, and the death instinct provide motifs for poetic plays on words.

6222 Guimarães, Luís Carlos. Ponto de fuga. Natal: Clima, 1979. 64 p., 8 leaves of plates: ill.

In his portraits and still-lives Guimarães exhibits a keen eye for telling detail and an unusual gift for expressive imagery.

6223 Gullar, Ferreira. Toda poesia: 1950–1980. Rio de Janeiro: Civilização Brasileira, 1980. 444 p. (Coleção Vera Cruz; v. 300)

Extensive anthology showing how from conventional beginnings Gullar advanced through concretist and neoconcretist experiments in form to verse of social protest.

6224 Hilst, Hilda. Da morte: odes mínimas: 50 poemas. São Paulo: Massao Ohno: Roswitha Kempf, 1980. 56 p., 6 leaves of plates: col. ill.

The curious courtship between the poet and Death is well exemplified by the lines "Te sei. Em vida/ Provei teu gosto./ Perda, partidas/ Memória, pó/ Com a boca viva provei/ Teu gosto, teu sumo grosso./ Em vida, te sei."

6225 Holanda, Gastão de. O jornal: poema. Rio de Janeiro: Achiamé, 1981. 117 p. Stream-of-consciousness meditations of all suggested to the poet by the various sections of a newspaper, from headlines and social column to sports page and literary supplement.

6226 Homem, Homero. O agrimensor da aurora: 11 livros de poesia. Rio de Janeiro: Forense-Universitária, 1981. 367 p.: ill.

Remarkable for far-ranging repertory, as a "national poet" Homen hails Brasília and the Trans-Amazon Highway, celebrates Brazilian scientists and writers, and expresses broad social concerns. He sings of the sea and space flight, and can write deeply personal compositions, such as those on the death of his second wife.

6227 Ivo, Lêdo. A noite misteriosa: poesia. Com un estudo de Carlos Montemayor. Rio de Janeiro: Editora Record, 1982? 147 p.

Ivo treats mysteries of life, death, and God in verse of classic simplicity, sobriety, and expressiveness. Excellent.

6228 ———. O soldado raso. Ilustrações de Genésio Fernandes. Recife: Edições Pirata, 1980. 63 leaves, 5 leaves of plates: ill.

Random reflections ("Somos todos espelhos/ que se multiplicam/ dentro de miragens") and *boutades* ("Aqui jaz a vanguarda/ rumor e celeuma/ convertidos em pó./ Mas antes de morrer deu/ muito trabalho aos tipógrafos.") of a major poet of the Generation of 1945.

6229 Jasiello, Franco Maria. Itinerário do imprevisto. Rio de Janeiro: Achiamé: *em co-edição com a* Fundação José Augusto, 1983. 77 p.: ill.

The eloquence of silence constitutes the substance of these poems— "Depois da intimidade da estórias/ a presença dos intervalos," as Jasiello says. Winner of Othoniel Menezes Prize.

6230 Jehovah, Carlos and **Esechias Araújo Lima.** Auto da gamela. Rio de Janeiro: Livraria J. Olympio Editora, 1980. 102 p.: ill.

Tragedy of the poor in drought-stricken Northeast, recounted in popular language; verse suggests, but does not reproduce, the forms of folk poetry.

6231 Junqueira, Ivan. A rainha arcaica. Rio de Janeiro: Editora Nova Fronteira, 1980. 119 p. (Coleção Poiesis)

Junqueira's grave, erudite lyrics, in which mystery's the dominant note, attain full flower in a splendid cycle of sonnets on the story of Inês de Castro.

6232 Juvenal, Amaro [*pseud. for* Ramiro Fortes de Barcellos]. Antônio Chimango: poemeto campestre. Prefácio, Carlos Reverbel. Ilustrações, Mário Mattos. Coordenação e posfácio, Rodrigues Till. Porto Alegre: Martins Livreiro-Editor, 1978. 78 p.: ill. (Coleção Obras redivivas; 2)

This satire of Borges de Medeiros,

originally published 1915 as political pamphlet, continues to enjoy public favor, thanks to its biting humor and clever use of the rustic literary style of Rio Grande do Sul.

6233 Kenard, Roberto. No meio da vida: poemas. São Luís: Edições FUNC/SIOGE, 1980. 71 p.

Slices of life are transfigured by inspiration and intelligence into compositions distinguished for insight and lyrical grace. Excellent debut.

6234 Lara, Ubirajara. Quedo livre: poesias. São Paulo: Editora Soma, 1980. 90 p.

Though thoroughly modern as regards the handling of language, these graceful lyrics are infused with the spirit of 19th-century *modinha*.

6235 Lemos, Lara de. Adaga lavrada. Rio de Janeiro: Civilização Brasileira, 1981. 72 p. (Coleção Poesia hoje; v. 51)

Nostalgic recollections of childhood and indelible memories of experiences undergone during politically motivated incarceration are principal themes of Lemos' simple but telling verse.

6236 Lima, Diógenes da Cunha. Corpo breve: poesia. Natal: Fundação Josę Augusto, 1980. 82 p.: ill.

Lima's spare compositions read like X-rays, so well do they capture the inner nature of people, animals, plants, and relationships of love. Work of unusual merit.

6237 Lopes, Hélio. Agua emendada. São Paulo: Vertente Editora, 1981. 66 p.

Classic in form, language, and themes, Lopes' graceful sonnets are distinguished by perfect naturalness, without trace of archaism or artifice.

6238 Lopes, Waldemar. O jogo inocente: alexandrinos com dedicatórias. Capa e ilustrações de Fernando de Castro Lopes. Rio de Janeiro: Edições Cadernos da Serra, 1979. 56 p.: ill.

Oscar Mendes well describes Lopes as "raro pela perfeição da forma . . . pela riqueza do conteúdo . . . pela adequação surpreendente das metáforas e . . . pela musicalidade admirável de seus versos," in which one finds "classicismo de forma, romantismo de temas, lavor parnasiano, imagética simbolista e sensibilidade modernista."

6239 Machado, Nauro. Antologia poética: 1958–1979. São Paulo: Edições Quirón; Brasília: *em convênio com o* Instituto Nacional do Livro, Ministério de Educação e Cultura, 1980. 484 p. (Coleção Selesis; 20)

One of the most prolific (18 collections in 23 years) of contemporary Brazilian poets, Machado is also one of the most serious, singular in his eschatological concerns and strong in his conviction of the redeeming power of language. Useful critical essay by Nelly Novaes Coelho.

6240 Meireles, Cecília. Cânticos. 2a. ed. São Paulo: Editora Moderna, 1982. 53 p.: facs.

Facsimile of manuscript, interesting for evidence of degree and manner in which poet reworked her texts.

6241 Mello, Thiago de. Mormaço na floresta. Rio de Janeiro: Civilização Brasileira; São Paulo: Massao Ohno, 1981. 117 p. (Coleção Poesia sempre; v. 2)

The humanitarian rhapsodist of the Amazon seeks "de servir de caminho/ para a esperança./ E de lavar do límpido/ a mágoa da mancha,/ como o rio que leva,/ e lava."

6242 Melo, Maria do Carmo Barreto Campello de. Ser em trânsito. Recife: Edições Pirata, 1979. 43 leaves.

Poems of uncertainty: one cannot definitely fix one's true nature, since life is a process of constant evolution.

6243 Melo Neto, João Cabral de. A escola das facas: poesia, 1975–1980. Rio de Janeiro: Livraria J. Olympio, 1980. 94 p.

Visions of people, places, and pecularities of Pernambuco, heightened and diffracted by the prism of João Cabral's surrealist poetry. Excellent.

6244 ———. Poesia crítica: antologia. Rio de Janeiro: Livraria J. Olympio Editora, 1982. 125 p.

Penetrating and suggestive reflections on artistic creation as practiced by painters, sculptors, architects, singers, and other writers, in addition to the poet himself.

6245 Miranda, José Tavares de. Tampa de canastra: poesia reunida. Apresentação, Oswald de Andrade e Nogueira Moutinho. Rio de Janeiro: Livraria J. Olympio Editora; São Paulo: *em co-edição com a*

Secretaria da Cultura do Estado de São Paulo, 1981. 182 p.

Lack of understanding, lost love, remorse, despair, renunciation, solitude, and death are recurring themes in these poems from 1937–52.

6246 Miziara, Ivan. Cotidiário. Fotos, Bruno Caramelli. São Paulo: Massao Ohno: Roswitha Kempf, 1981. 65 p.: ill.

Declaring "A poesia busca a vida, mesmo que por um só momento," Miziara reveals perceptions as acute as his expression is felicitous. Unusually good.

6247 Moisés, Carlos Felipe. Círculo imperfeito: poemas. Salvador: Fundação Cultural do Estado da Bahia, 1978. 75 p. (Coleção Ilha de Maré; v. 2)

Autumnal melancholy pervading these graceful lyrics, written for most part far from Brazil, is offset by wry humor of concluding composition, an expanded variation on Gonçalves Dias' celebrated "Canção do Exílio."

6248 Moraes, Vinícius de. A mulher e o signo. Desenhos de Otávio F. de Araújo. Rio de Janeiro: Rocco, 1980. 30 p.: ill.

Witty definitions of women's attributes as determined by signs of the zodiac.

6249 Moreira, Virgílio Moretzsohn. O síndico da noite. Rio de Janeiro: Forense Universitária; Brasília: em convênio com o Instituto Nacional do Livro, Ministério da Educação e Cultura, 1981. 114 p.

Moreira seeks refuge from anxieties of modern world in verse characterized by "o fino verbo/ o pensado termo/ certo e composto."

6250 Mota, Mauro. Pernambucânia dois. Ilustrações de Danilo S'Acre. Recife: Edições Pirata, 1980. 67 p., 11 leaves of plates: ill.

Anthology of poems by Mota relating to Pernambuco. Drawn chiefly from early works but in part from item 6251, whose qualities it shares.

6251 ———. Pernambucânia, ou, Cantos da comarca e da memória. Introdução de Haroldo Bruno. Rio de Janeiro: Livraria J. Olympio Editora; Brasília: em convênio com o Instituto Nacional do Livro, Ministério da Educação e Cultura, 1979. 68 p.: bibl.

Mota reaffirms his magic touch, transmuting the most commonplace objects into hauntingly poetic symbols. Extensive bibliography of works by and about author. Excellent.

6252 Nejar, Carlos. Obra poética. v. 1. Rio de Janeiro: Editora Nova Fronteira, 1980. 1 v.: bibl. (Coleção Poiesis)

"O passado é grão/ no pensamento./ Um homem se faz/ com o que vê/ e o que consente" declares Nejar in most recent of compositions included in vol. 1 of his collected verse. Highly cerebral poet, austere both in language and in thought. Extensive bibliography of works by and about him.

6253 Oliveira, Marly de. Invocação de Orpheu. São Paulo: Massao Ohno, 1979. 60 leaves: bibl., ill.

"Quem valoriza a solidão de um deus/ ou de um poeta? Ambos intuem/ —em secreta harmonia/ com o que não entendem—/ apenas o que existe, não o criam" writes Oliveira in this lament of Orpheus on his empty-handed return from Hades.

6254 Oliveira, Moacyr Félix de. Em nome da vida. Rio de Janeiro: Civilização Brasileira: São Paulo: Massao Ohno, 1981. 140 p. (Coleção Poesia sempre; v. 3)

Private lyricist who indulges in brief erotic rhapsodies is all but overwhelmed by the public prophet who gives vent to sweeping harangues against man's inhumanity to man.

6255 Padilha, Telmo. O punhal no escuro. Rio de Janeiro: Antares, 1980. 38 p.: bibl., ill.

It would be difficult to imagine a more intellectual description of the acts of love than that provided in these solemn, aseptic compositions. Includes bio-bibliographical information (p. 24–38).

6256 Papi, Luiz F. Desarvorávore: poluemas. Rio de Janeiro: Livraria Editora Cátedra; Brasília: Instituto Nacional do Livro, Ministério da Educação e Cultura, 1982. 82 p.: ill.

Skillful use of metaphor elevates protest at the destruction of environment to level of poetry.

6257 Pinheiro Neto, Liberato Manoel. Minha Senhora do Desterro. São Paulo: Orleans Gráfica, 1981. 68 p.

Author's affection for his native Florianópolis is vividly set forth in terms of carnal love.

6258 Pinto, Thereza Magalhães. Torre de marfim. Desenhos de Emeric Marcier. Rio de Janeiro: Editora Nova Fronteira, 1981. 167, 8 p.: ill.

"Entendo-me . . . na medida exata/ de meu egoismo honesto/ na incerteza própia/ que nega/ todo um resto inoperante" writes in all sincerity this "ensimismada" poet.

6259 Pisani, Osmar. As paredes do mundo. Florianópolis: Fundação Catarinense de Cultura Edições, 1981. 74 p.

"A beleza e a ordem/ paralizam o tempo/ na experiência órfica," declares Pisani, hoping mankind may have wisdom to avoid their destruction. A Cruz e Sousa Prize winner.

6260 Prade, Péricles. Os faróis invisíveis. Posfácio de Cláudio Willer. São Paulo: Massao Ohno, 1980. 53 p.

Surrealistic compositions, suggestive of vegetable and shell portraits of Giuseppe Arcimboldo. Thoughtful analysis of poet's work by Willer.

6261 Py, Fernando. Vozes do corpo. Rio de Janeiro: Fontana; Brasília: em convênio com o Instituto Nacional do Livro, Ministério da Educação e Cultura, 1981. 111 p.

Poems of mood ("Crepuscular") and reflection ("Quarenta e Cinco") are more effective than explicitly erotic verse that makes up bulk of this collection.

6262 Quintanilha, Dirceu. Arquiteto do siléncio. Rio de Janeiro: Editora Fontana, 1981. 49 p.

Stillness, absence, emptiness, and death are watchwords of this collection. "Arquiteto do silêncio/ e desta insônia/ do jamais alcançado/ . . . me liberto/ na ampla solidão."

6263 ———. Cais vazio. 2a. ed. Recife: Edições Pirata, 1980. 31 p.

Gracefully turned sentimental epigrams, some banal, others the product of true inspiration.

6264 ———. Pá de cal. Rio de Janeiro: Editora Fontana, 1980. 53 p.

Quintanilha counsels acceptance of life as it is: "Habite-se/ . . . Deixar/ que pequenas coisas/ nos abracem:/—Abraçá-las./ . . . Proprietários, enfim,/ daquilo que ninguém/ pode sonhar por nós."

6265 Ramos, Ricardo G. Sopa de sapato. Prefácio, Heloísa Buarque de Hollanda. Rio de Janeiro: Achiamé, 1981. 39 leaves: ill.

Tragic view of the modern world, heightened at times by sardonic humor.

6266 Reis, Geraldo. Pastoral de Minas: poemas. Belo Horizonte: Editora Comunicações: em convênio com a Secretaria de Cultura, Turismo e Esportes da Prefeitura de Belo Horizonte, 1981. 77 p.

Past and present, romance and reality, nostalgia and cynicism mingle in these highly effective evocations of the spirit of Minas Gerais. Winner of 1981 City of Belo Horizonte Literature Prize.

6267 Rillo, Apparicio Silva. Pago vago: poesia gauchesca. Porto Alegre: Martins Livreiro, 1981. 80 p. (Coleção Tarca; 12)

Spirit of the vanishing frontier of Rio Grande do Sul is nostalgically evoked in verse that skillfully avoid banalities of gaúcho folklore.

6268 Ruddy. Sabor do cio: poesia. Rio de Janeiro: Edições Trote, 1981. 74 p.: ill.

Poet's enjoyment of his bisexual adventures is recounted with simplicity and refreshing candor.

6269 Silva, Domingos Carvalho da. Rosa extinta: poemas. 2a. ed. São Paulo: Clube de Poesia, 1980. 57, 3 p.

Slightly modified second ed. of early work by leading member of Generation of 1945. Main themes: death of son, human solidarity, carnal love. Delightful preface by Péricles Eugênio da Silva Ramos.

6270 Silveira, Lucia Rios Peixoto da. Verso e vida. Goiânia: Gráfica Editora Lider, 1981. 153 p.: ill.

As units, these poems come to less than the sum of their individual verses, in which serendipitous combinations of words produce images of striking beauty.

6271 Simões, João Manuel. "Guernica" e outros quadros escolhidos de Picasso. Capa e ilustrações de Alvaro Borges. Curitiba: Editora Lítero-Técnica, 1982. 53 p.: ill. (Coleção Academia Paranaense de Letras)

Simões' poetic interpretations of pictures by Picasso are extraordinarily successful translations of one art form into another. Critical essay by Miguelina Soifer (p. 45–53).

6272 **Sousa, Afonso Félix de.** As engrenagens do belo. Recife: Edições Pirata, 1981. 17 leaves.

Beauty is in the memory of beholder according to Sousa, who shows brilliant mastery of technique in this cycle of interlocking sonnets, composed in 1950s but previously unpublished.

6273 **Sousa, João da Cruz e.** Poesia completa. Florianópolis: Fundação Catarinense de Cultura, 1981. 303 p., 5 leaves of plates: ill.

Complete poetic works of one of Brazil's two principal Symbolists. Useful introductory study by Maria Helena Camargo Régis.

6274 **Teles, Gilberto Mendonça.** Saciologia goiana. Rio de Janeiro: Civilização Brasileira; Brasília: em convênio com o Instituto Nacional do Livro, Ministério da Educação e Cultura, 1982. 153 p. (Coleção Poesia hoje; v. 53)

In sophisticated and humorous reworking of folkloric material, Teles updates pau brasil aspect of Modernism by concretist and poesia-práxis devices, with highly felicitous results.

6275 **Valladares, Luiz Fernando.** Ver de novo. Goiânia: Oriente, 1978. 97 p.: port.

Poet's revolt against mechanization of life and increasing triumph of synthetic over natural is conveyed in ironically expressive imagery.

6276 **Valle, Gerson.** Confetes de muitos carnavais. s.l.: s.n., 1982. 75 p.: ill.

Witty, intentionally "Brazilian" verse, reminiscent of lighter side of Manuel Bandeira and Mário de Andrade.

6277 **Vanzolini, Paulo Emílio.** Tempos de cabo. São Paulo: Palavra e Imagem Editora, 1981. 61 p., 1 p. of plates: ill. (Coleção Caros amigos; v. 1)

Realistic view of the love life of urban poor, humorously conveyed in corresponding dialect.

6278 **Venâncio, Nirton.** Roteiro dos pássaros: poemas. Fortaleza: Editora e Gráfica Lourenço Filho, 1981. 111 p.

Winner of the Filgueiras Lima Prize is still hesitant beginner, but shows promise in his handling of symbols in "Galope" and "Gato."

6279 **Ventura, Adão.** A cor da pele. Belo Horizonte: Edições do Autor, 1980. 30 leaves.

Poet's reflection on his origins and what it means to be black recall the early Langston Hughes.

6280 **Vieira, Antônio.** Cantares d'Africa = Songs of Africa. Rio de Janeiro: Gráfica Riex Editora, 1980. 101 p.: ill.

Black Brazilian identifies with black Africans in their struggle for freedom and dignity. English translations lamentable.

Drama

JUDITH ISHMAEL BISSETT, *Assistant Professor of Spanish and Portuguese, Miami University, Oxford, Ohio*

THE MAJORITY OF THE PLAYS reviewed in this section can be classified as political, social, or psychological drama. Many have won prizes or are the work of established playwrights like Alfredo Dias Gomes or Plínio Marcos. The most successful plays are those which achieve an effective balance between theme and structure. In the category of political drama, Alfredo Dias Gomes (item **6291**) has again used national history to investigate the way in which what he believes to be a necessary struggle against repression, affects the lives of the participants. In contrast to Dias Gomes' serious examination of one revolutionary act and its consequences, is the satirical, very humorous look at tyranny by Ricardo Meireles Viera, *O Palácio dos Urubús* (item **6306**). Here, consistently well executed humor serves as an alienation effect focusing the audience's attention on the message. Millôr

Fernandes (item **6289**) also utilized humor to protest repressive authority, and not history, but a recognizable literary landmark to frame his criticism. Plínio Marcos (item **6294**) and Otaviano Pereira (item **6296**) both structure their critical views of the Brazilian worker's problems through an alternative version of the life of Christ.

Carlos Carvalho's excellent portrayal of the destruction of a family by unrelenting social conditions (item **6285**) is particularly successful because of his use of characters who, although representative of the poor, are not only types or symbols. Maria Adelaide Santos do Amaral's psychological study of her characters (item **6282**) allows her to examine effectively the social pressures which cause their reactions. José Antônio de Souza (item **6303**), Aguinaldo Silva (item **6301**), and Sérgio Sant'Ana (item **6300**) all construct psychological dramas by depicting abnormal behavior in sometimes violent situations. However, unlike Santos do Amaral, these playwrights do not indicate a second level in structure or theme which protests social conditions.

Of particular interest to the student of Brazilian drama is the collection of national drama sponsored by Movimento Zero Hora. Many of the playwrights included have won prizes and one, Marlei Cunha (item **6286**) is annotated below. Although the quality of the plays is uneven and many tend toard hyperrealism—the faithful recreation of frequently repulsive and violent reality—it is useful to those working in Brazilian theater to review the plays presented and published by a group dedicated to the promotion of a national theater.

In the area of criticism, Mariam Garcia Mendes' study of the black character in Brazilian drama (item **6313**) offers the reader insight into the relationship between society and theatrical expression from the early 19th century to the present. Selma Suely Teixeira's article on Chico Buarque de Holanda (item **6315**) is a competent survey of the playwright's works.

For the most part, the plays selected reflect a continuing interest in political and social problems. Although direct confrontation with these problems is evident in, for example, Carlos Carvalho's study of life in a favela, some playwrights use history or literature as a format for the criticism of contemporary social or political injustice. This structure has been used over the years by playwrights like Augusto Boal, Jorge Andrade, and Alfredo Dias Gomes. It still characterizes the work by Millôr Fernandes mentioned above and that of other writers listed below. Marcos Vinícius employs this technique in both plays reviewed here (items **6308–6309**).

ORIGINAL PLAYS

6281 Aguiar, Adonias. Auto dos Ilhéus. Rio de Janeiro: Civilização Brasileira, 1981. 48 p.

In short scenes, author reviews history of Ilheus from 1500s to present. Characters including representatives of the first arrivals, Indians, missionaries, later immigrants portray events like Indian expeditions, the struggle against the French, and religious miracles.

6282 Amaral, Maria Adelaide Santos do. A resistência. Rio de Janeiro: Ministério da Educação e Cultura, DAC, FUNARTE, Serviço Nacional de Teatro, Departamento de Documentação e Divulgação, 1978. 120 p. (Coleção Prêmios; v. 15)

Writers for a magazine react to the news that personnel cuts may occur later in the day. Characters' interaction reveals their inability as workers to influence management's control over their personal and professional lives. In this world, there is no real personal victory.

6283 Assunção, Leilah et al. Vejo um vuelto na Janela, me acudam que eu sou Donzela (SBAT/RT, 438, abril/junho 1981, p. 26–63)

Action takes place in a boarding house for girls. Fragmented scenes portray tenants' activities inside as political and social climate changes outside the house. All the girls are either involved in or affected by the revolution. Author's first play.

6284 Brasini, Mario Farias. Nadim Nadinha contra o Rei de Fuleiró. Rio de Janeiro: Ministério da Educação e Cultura, SEAC, FUNARTE, Serviço Nacional de Teatro, 1980? 57 p. (Coleção Prêmios; v. 24)

In this fable, character Nadim represents man desirous of freedom from oppressive forces dedicated to eradicating him as a "subversive" element while others in society suffer. Here it is hungry children. Nadim is executed but he always returns in a different social slot. Action accompanied by music and chorus.

6285 Carvalho, Carlos. Berço esplêndido. Curitiba: Criar Edições, 1982. 60 p.

Well structured story of a family struggling to survive in a favela. Characters, rather than types, are individuals who are compelled by degrading pressures of poverty to destroy each other. Social criticism is achieved by placing characters with strengths and weaknesses in oppressive, inherently destructive environment.

6285a Corrêa Neto, Alarico et al. Teatro paraibano, hoje. João Pessoa: A União Cia. Editora, 1980. 486 p.: music.

Includes eight plays representing regional effort attempting freedom from influence of Rio or São Paulo. Several plays are collective works (e.g., *BR-230* by Alarico Corrêa Neto et al). Concerns corruption in industry and politics in an interior town.

6286 Cunha, Marlei. Suarentos. Fotos, Antônio Guerra, Sérgio Neves e Mauro Di Deus. Nova Granada: Editora Horizonte, 1979. 50 p.: ill.

Written after author had spent time with workers portrayed. Play illustrates how lives of workers do not change although landowners might. Incorporates folk music and dance. Dialogue in dialect.

6287 Dias, Antônio Gonçalves. Teatro completo. Rio de Janeiro: Ministério da Educação e Cultura, FUNARTE, Serviço Nacional de Teatro, 1979. 469 p., 5 leaves of plates: bibl., ill. (Clássicos do teatro brasileiro; v. 2)

Critical introduction. Contains chronology of Gonçalves Dias' life and works based in part on *Panteon maranhense* by Antônio Henriques Leal. No critical bibliography.

6288 Dramaturgia, 1978. Transaminases [by] Carlos Vereza. O acontecimento [by] Carlos Henrique Escobar. Trilogia de Treblinka: pt. 1, konzentrazion [by] Luís Henrique Cardim. Rio de Janeiro: Ministério da Educação e Cultura, Secretaria da Cultura, Serviço Nacional de Teatro, 197? 138 p. (Coleção Premios; v. 27)

All three plays take place in enclosed, prison-like setting or in prison. In each, outside artistic influences are unable to alter characters' circumstances. In fact, these influences can destroy the character involved in either the performance or preservation of some art form.

6289 Fernandes, Millôr. Vidigal: memórias de um sargento de milícias: inspirado no romance de Manuel Antônio de Almeida. Músicas de Carlos Lyra. Porto Alegre: L&PM Editores, 1981. 149, 18 p.: music (Coleção Teatro Millôr Fernandes; v. 10)

Based on Manuel Antônio de Almeida's novel, story follows Leandro's adventures from childhood until he blackmails Vidigal into promoting him. Vidigal represents repressive moral authority and Leandro the opposite. Action presented in fast-paced scenes with music and dance. Music by Carlos Lyra.

6290 França Júnior. Teatro de França Júnior. v. 1–2. Texto estabelecido e introdução por Edwaldo Cafezeiro, com a colaboração de Carmem Gadelha e Maria de Fátima Saadi. Rio de Janeiro: Ministério da Educação e Cultura, FUNARTE, Serviço Nacional de Teatro, 1980. 2 v.: bibl., facsims., ill. (Clássicos do teatro brasileiro; v. 5)

Biographical information by Arthur Azevedo dated 1906. Critical comments, but no bibliography of critical works.

6291 Gomes, Dias. Campeões do mundo: mural dramático em dois painéis. Rio de Janeiro: Civilização Brasileira, 1980. 146 p. (Coleção Teatro de Dias Gomes; v. 5)

Framed by 1970 World Cup soccer championship won by Brazil, play examines kidnapping of an American ambassador. Lives and motives of participants are portrayed in the past: incidents surrounding event and the present: return of one of the kidnappers after amnesty.

6292 Khüner, Maria Helena and **Celso Antônio da Fonseca.** A represa [by] Maria Helena Khüner. Suburbana [by] Celso Antônio da Fonseca. Rio de Janeiro: Ministério da Educação e Cultura, SEAC, FUNARTE, Serviço Nacional de Teatro, 1980? 105 p. (Coleção Prêmios, v. 26)

A Represa is the story of a family involved in politics and destroyed by pressures from social and political forces. Suburbana is structured so that three episodes from characters' lives seem to occur on stage simultaneously. Characters represent working class.

6293 Machado de Assis, Joaquim Maria. Teatro completo. Texto estabelecido por Teresinha Marinho, com a colaboração de Carmem Gadelha e Maria de Fátima Saadi. Rio de Janeiro: Ministério da Educação e Cultura, Serviço Nacional de Teatro, 1982. 376 p., 1 leaf of plates (Clássico do teatro brasileiro; v. 6)

Consists of 15 plays published 1860–1906. Publisher's note indentifies editions used in collection. No critical bibliography.

6294 Marcos, Plínio. Jesus homem: peça e debate. São Paulo: Editora do Grêmio Politécnico, 1981. 77 p.: ill.

Play about Christ's crucifixion. Underscores His humble beginnings. Christ is black thus emphasizing, according to Marcos, Brazil's racial heritage and need for racial unity. Volume contains interview with Marcos and description of Bando Theatre group in São Paulo.

6296 Pereira, Otaviano. Paixão segundo o operário: drama em dois atos. São Paulo: Cortez Editora, 1980. 55 p.

Written to commemorate death of a worker killed by São Paulo police in 1979. Story of Christ played by a mulatto. Other characters represent Brazil's racial make-up. Christ as revolutionary figure translates new religious order He represented into new social order for workers. Brechtian structures used.

6297 Qorpo-Santo. Teatro completo. Fixação do texto, estudo crítico e notas por Guilhermino César. Rio de Janeiro: Ministério da Educação e Cultura, FUNARTE, Serviço Nacional de Teatro, 1980. 404 p.: bibl., port (Clássicos do teatro brasileiro; v. 4)

Introduction includes biographical information, chronology of works and critical study. Notes on text of each play and bibliography of works by and about Qorpo-Santo.

6298 Quinto [a] Sétimo Movimento Zero Hora. Antologia do teatro. São Paulo: O Movimiento, 1981–1982. 3 v. (237, 293, 174 p.): ill.

Movimiento Zero Hora was founded in 1976 to provide national theater with stage. Goal was to present unpublished works in Rio and São Paulo as well as interior. In 1981, production stopped due to problems. Later collections of plays, like these three volumes, ranging in type from absurdist to traditional were published.

6299 Rodrigues, Nelson. Teatro completo. v. 1, Peças psicológicas. v. 2, Peças míticos. Organização e introdução de Sábato Magaldi. Rio de Janeiro: Editora Nova Fronteira, 1981. 2 v.

Vol. 1 contains psychological works and vol. 2, mythical works. Vols. 3–4 will be composed of plays under the theme: Carioca tragedies. Introduction discusses organization and examines theme and structure of plays in collection. No bibliography.

6300 Sant'Anna, Sérgio. Um romance de geração: comédia dramática em um ato. Rio de Janeiro: Civilização Brasileira, 1981. 93 p. (Coleção Vera Cruz; v. 315)

Play consists of "interview" of alcoholic writer by a woman journalist. Dialogue reveals his philosophy, politics, and role as a writer in society. Play is to be considered play-within-a-play sponsored by writer's mother after he attempts suicide.

6301 Silva, Aguinaldo. As tias: tragicomédia em dois atos. Rio de Janeiro: Achiamé, 1981. 108 p., 2 p. of plates.

Concerns yearly reunion of four aging homosexuals and woman who supports them. Scenes depicting past events explain their hold over her. This is maintained through the murder of her young, handsome driver. The evidence binds them together for another year. Several comic moments.

6302 Silva, Hélcio Pereira da. Maldito de todos os santos, Lima Barreto: peça. Edição, 1881–1981. Rio de Janeiro: Editora Divulgadora Nacional, 1981. 63 p.

Examines life and work of Lima Barreto through scenes depicting his relationship with self, family, and society. Using a juxtaposition of characters from his novels, Lima Barreto and his family, play shows failures he experienced due to racial discrimination.

6303 Souza, José Antônio de. Mal secreto. São Paulo: Semente, 1981. 63 p.

Takes place in one afternoon. Disturbed man kills woman visitor, his psychiatrist, and his own wife. Play's structure allows possibility that murders are hallucinations of a disturbed mind. Whether reality or fantasy, the character ultimately crosses line between sanity and criminal violence.

6304 Souza, Naum Alves de. A aurora de minha vida. São Paulo: MG Editores Associados, 1982. 127 p.

Amusing scenes recall experiences in school. They include characters like class bully, tattletales presented in scenes constructed like sketches. Scenes depict, for example, Mother's Day celebrations, student mischief, English class, up to graduation. Presents usual student-teacher, student-student confrontations.

6305 Teatro de bonecos, 1978. Rio de Janeiro: MEC, SEC, Serviço Nacional de Teatro, 1981? 171 p. (Coleção Prêmios; v. 33)

Collection of five plays for puppets and masked actors. Three prize-winning plays: *Paixão, amor e castigo* (characters play scenes containing religious and folk motifs); *Fábula de Automópolis* (a town is controlled by the automobile); and *Noite viro dia-e-noite* (characters in allegorical search for the sun).

6306 Vieira, Ricardo Meireles. O palácio dos urubus. Rio de Janeiro: Ministério da Educação e Cultura, DAC, FUNARTE, Serviço Nacional de Teatro, 1978. 108 p. (Coleção Prêmios; v. 12)

Takes place in fictitious country consisting of "bananas, sun and sea." Includes "special participation of Henry Kissinger." Satirical portrait of tyranny supported by outside elements characterized by the Company . . . of Candied Fruit Tropical. Cartoon-like characters in events illustrate oppression, revolution, and return to oppression under another name.

6307 ———. Os sobreviventes. Rio de Janeiro: Ministério da Educação e Cultura, DAC, FUNARTE, Serviço Nacional de Teatro, 1978. 51 p. (Coleção Prêmios; v. 16)

Three days in the engagement of a woman lasts three decades. Action takes place in 1954, 1964, 1974, and finally, 1977. National events cause young woman's fiancée to disappear each time. Theme of suicide—characters' involvement or country's—frames action. Final dream sequence weakens structure.

6308 Vinícius, Marcus. Boca do inferno. Rio de Janeiro: Ministério da Educação e Cultura, SEAC, FUNARTE, Serviço Nacional de Teatro, 1980? 119 p. (Coleção Prêmios; v. 25)

Traces life of poet Gregório de Matos through various clashes with authorities that lead to his exile in Angola. One theme focuses on conflict between freedom of artistic expression and government censorship. Another explores artist in a structured society.

6309 ———. Domingo, Zeppelin. Brasília: Ministério da Educação e Cultura, Departamento de Documentação e Divulgação, 1978. 132 p. (Coleção Prêmios; v. 11)

Family is caught up in activities of Liberal Alliance among Rio Grande do Sul, Minas Gerais, and Paraíba states. Characters symbolize types of people in resistance movement against repression by federal government. Illustrates different kinds of political commitment. Each act framed by songs commenting on action.

HISTORY AND CRITICISM

6310 Bibliografia de dramaturgia brasileira. v. 1, A-M. São Paulo: Escola de Comunicações e Artes da Universidade de São Paulo: Associação Museu Lasar Segall, 1981. 1 v.: indexes.

Bibliography of works in libraries of São Paulo. Bibliographic information in alphabetical order. Locates each library holding a play. Includes title index and index showing number of characters in plays, by author. Eight libraries or collections listed. Vol. 1 of set covers letters A-M.

6311 Costa, Marcelo Farias. Roteiro da dramaturgia cearense. Fortaleza: Edições Universidade Federal do Ceará, 1980. 110 p.: bibl. (Coleção Brincante; 1)

Contains history of theater in Ceará, and bibliography organized by title of play and author. Features chronology of presentations and bibliography of references consulted. Includes authors from Ceará and those who worked or were presented in the state.

6312 Lacerda, Maria Thereza B. Subsídios para a história do teatro no Paraná: as associações literárias e dramáticas e o teatro do Paraná, 1870–1892: Associações Literária Lapeana e o Teatro São João, 1873–1976. 2a. ed., rev. e ampl. Curitiba: Instituto Histórico Geográfico e Etnográfico Paranaense; Lapa: Prefeitura Municipal, 1980. 135 p. (Estante paranista; 10)

History of artistic activity in Paraná including theater during 19th and 20th centuries. First period: 1870–92; second period: literary associations and Teatro São João in Lapa. Provides information on theaters, audiences, playwrights as well as circuses, musical reviews.

6313 Mendes, Mariam Garcia. A personagem negra no teatro brasileiro: entre 1838 e 1888. São Paulo: Editora Atica, 1982. 205 p.: bibl. (Ensaios; 84)

Study of black characters in 19th-century drama. Illustrates how theatre reacted to society by creating stereotypes or using black characters to protest slavery. Introduces development of Brazilian theater to 1943, studies slave in literature and society and, analyzes three plays presented between 1838–88. Bibliography.

6314 Paranhos, Luiz Tosta. Orfeu da Coneição: tragédia carioca. Rio de Janeiro: Livraria J. Olympio Editora, 1980. 76 p.

Structuralist approach to *Orfeu da conceição* by Vinícius de Moraes. Conclusion: uses a combination of tragic form and Brazilian motifs in search of national expression.

6315 Teixeira, Selma Suely. Análise da dramaturgia de Chico Buarque de Holanda (UFP/EB, 7:12, dez. 1981, p. 37–68, bibl.)

Locates Buarque de Holanda in history of Brazilian theater. Includes biographical chronology of author's artistic production and studies theme and structure of plays. Plays analyzed: *Roda-viva, Calabar, Gota d'agua,* and *Opera do malandro.*

Literary Criticism and History

WILSON MARTINS, *Professor of Portuguese, New York University*

THIS WRITER FEELS somewhat embarrassed for singling out his own *A crítica litéraria no Brasil* (item **6336**) as the principal work in literary criticism published in 1983. However, all consideration of merit aside, this is the only complete, systematic and comprehensive history of Brazilian literary criticism, from its inception in the middle of the 18th century to the present (1981). A first and very rudimentary version of this work was published in 1952 (see *HLAS 18: 2751*); the book has been entirely rewritten and considerably expanded.

It is perhaps more than a coincidence that this new edition concurs with the resurgence of literary history as opposed to the glut of literary theory and analytic studies that have proliferated over the last 20 years. In general, the tendency towards ultra-theorizing is receding, and there is an increasingly skeptical reassessment of such theorizing for the understanding and evaluation of literature. The reedition of a number of well known textbooks of literary criticism attests to this trend. The following are annotated below in the General subsection: Bosi's (item **6319**); Cláudio's (item **6322**); and Sodré's (item **6347**); and a literary history of Mato Grosso do Sul, newly established state, by Pontes (item **6341**).

Several compilations of obvious historical interest are also worth mentioning: Teles' *Vanguarda européia e Modernismo brasileiro* (item **6350**), Tristão de Athayde's anthology of critical texts (item **6351**), Flávio Loureiro Chaves' collection of literary essays from Rio Grande do Sul (item **6326**). In the poetry section, one should note Cassiana Lacerda Carollo's (item **6382**) compilation of texts of critical significance to Symbolism. Both Chaves' and Carollo's anthologies were published as part of a series annotated in *HLAS 42* (see items 6412, 6445, and 6455). Since in this period the only three volumes of theory worthy of mention are by Grossmann (item **6327**), Costa Lima (item **6332**), and Moisés (item **6338**), it is easy to perceive recent differences in emphasis. Of course, all the biographies and critical studies about specific authors in the prose fiction and poetry sections must also be taken into consideration.

The year 1983 was saddened by the deaths of Alceu Amoroso Lima (1893–1983), the Tristão de Athayde of critical fame of the 1920s and 1930s (see items **6317** and **6351**), and Roberto Alvim Corrêa (1901–83), well-known as the founder of the respected Corrêa publishing house in Paris between the two world wars. [WM]

Among miscellaneous works of this biennium worthy of note, one should single out Mario de Andrade's letters to Murilo Miranda (item **6393**), the facsimile edition of the important Modernist review *Arco & Flexa* (item **6394**), and above all Pedro Nava's memoirs (item **6396**), an ongoing masterpiece. [R.E. Dimmick]

GENERAL

6316 Araripe Júnior, Tristão de Alencar.
Luizinha. Perfil literário de José de Alencar. Organização, atualização ortográfica e notas por Otacílio Colares. Introdução crítica, Pedro Paulo Montenegro. Rio de Janeiro: Livraria José Olympio Editora, 1980. 237 p.: bibl., ill. (Coleção Dolor Barreira; v. 5)
Still the best biography of José de Alencar, and clearly a source for all others. Strangely, it is reprinted here in same volume with one of Araripe Júnior's novels.

6317 Athayde, Tristão de [*pseud. for* Alceu Amoroso Lima]. Afonso Arinos. Prefácio de Bernardo Elis. 2a. ed., aum. São Paulo: LISA São Paulo: LISA; Brasília: *em convênio com o* Instituto Nacional do Livro, Ministério da Educação e Cultura, 1981. 172 p.: bibl., ill. (Coleção Brasil/Portugal;)
Reissue of classic, first comprehensive biography of Afonso Arinos and Lima's first book (see also item **6370**).

6318 Azevedo, Sânzio de. Aspectos da literatura cearense. Prefácio de Cláudio Martins. Fortaleza: Edições Universidade do Ceará: Academia Cearense de Letras, 1982. 359 p., 1 leaf of plates: bibl., index.
Contains some of the best essays ever written about Cearense authors, including Antônio Sales, Braga Montenegro, Oliveira Paiva, José de Alencar, Lívio Barreto and others.

6319 Bosi, Alfredo. História concisa da literatura brasileira. 3a. ed. São Paulo: Editora Cultrix, 1981. 582 p.: bibl., index.
Updated edition of one of the best histories of Brazilian literature.

6320 Bruno, Haroldo. Novos estudos de literatura brasileira. Rio de Janeiro: Livraria J. Olympio Editora; Brasília: *em convênio com o* Instituto Nacional do Livro, Ministério da Educação e Cultura, 1980. 294 p.: bibl., index.
Essays by minor critic, but worth noting because of his careful readings.

Candido, Antônio. Los brasileños y la literatura latinoamericana. See item **5005**.

6321 Carelli, Mario. L'identité brésilienne de Mário de Andrade face aux Italiens de São Paulo (UTIEH/C, 38, 1982, p. 119–134)
Mário de Andrade's latent prejudice against foreigners, as represented by Italian component of São Paulo population, is studied with acumen and competence. Nationalism as a source of mild xenophobia.

6322 Cláudio, Affonso. Historia da litteratura espirito-santente. Ed. facsimilar. Rio de Janeiro: Xerox, 1981. 556 p.: bibl., ill. (Biblioteca reprográfica Xerox)
Book was originally printed in 100 copies (1912) and rapidly became an antiquarian item. It is still a "rarity," useful for its data and for being only one on subject by a disciple of Sílvio Romero.

6323 Colares, Otacílio. Lembrados e esquecidos V: ensaios sobre literatura cearense. Fortaleza: Secretaria de Cultura, Desporto e Promoção Social, 1981. 189 p.: bibl.

Collected essays about literature of Ceará (for vols. 1–4, see *HLAS 40:7673* and *HLAS 42:6400*).

6324 Corrêa, Nereu. O canto do cisne negro e outros estudos. 2a. ed., rev. e aum. Florianópolis: FCC Edições, 1981. 136 p.: ill.

Collected literary essays about Cruz e Souza, Luís Delfino, Virgílio Várzea and others from Santa Catarina. Interesting in spite of being approximately 20 years old (see also item **6331**).

6325 Dines, Alberto. Morte no paraíso: a tragédia de Stefan Zweig. Rio de Janeiro: Editora Nova Fronteira, 1981. 475 p.: bibl., index

Account of Zweig's residence in Brazil up to his suicide in Petrópolis. Interesting but somewhat bombastic and unscholarly.

6326 O Ensaio literário no Rio Grande do Sul: 1868–1960. Seleção e apresentação, Flávio Loureiro Chaves. Rio de Janeiro: Livros Técnicos e Científicos Editora; Brasília: *em convênio com o* Instituto Nacional do Livro, Ministério de Educação e Cultura, 1979. 193 p.: bibl., index. (Biblioteca universitária de literatura brasileira. Série A., Ensaio, crítica, história literária; v. 9)

Excellent anthology of literary essays by authors from Rio Grande do Sul.

6327 Grossmann, Judith. Temas de teoria da literatura. São Paulo: Editora Ática, 1981. 119 p. (Ensaios; 79)

Themes include nature of literature, its functions, reality and irreality, and imagination (see also items **6337–6338**).

6328 Haberly, David T. Three sad races: racial identity and national consciousness in Brazilian literature. Cambridge, England: Cambridge University Press, 1983. 198 p.: bibl., index.

Scholarly and well researched study which nevertheless reflects American obsession with racial differences that do not have same impact in Brazil. End result is distorted picture. For historian's comment, see item **3586**.

6329 Hohlfeldt, Antônio. O gaúcho: ficção e realidade. Rio de Janeiro: Edições Antares; Brasília: *em convênio com o* Instituto Nacional do Livro, Fundação Nacional Pró-Memoria, 1982. 113 p.: bibl. (Antares universitária)

The *gaúcho*, native to Rio Grande do Sul, is above all a literary myth, studied here in relation to reality. Competent analysis (see also item **6360**).

6330 Inojosa, Joaquim. Sursum corda!: desfaz-se o "equívoco" do *Manifesto regionalista* de 1926: foi redigido em 1952, escreve Gilberto Freyre. Rio de Janeiro: s.n., 1981. 192 p., 1 leaf of plates: facsims., index.

Study of Gilberto Freyre's ultimate admission that his famous *Manifesto regionalista* of 1926 was written in 1952. Joaquim Inojosa's last salvo on the subject.

6331 Junkes, Lauro. Aníbal Nunes Pires e o Grupo Sul: um estudo sobre o Grupo Sul e uma antologia dos poemas e contos de Aníbal Nunes Pires. Florianópolis: Editora da Universidade Federal da Santa Catarina, 1982. 237 p.

Useful contribution to recent literary history of Santa Catarina (see also item **6324**).

6332 Lima, Luiz Costa. Dispersa demanda: ensaios sobre literatura e teoria. Rio de Janeiro: Livraria F. Alves Editora, 1981. 248 p.: bibl., index.

Essays by leading young critic, of uneven quality, but worth reading.

6333 Lowe, Elizabeth. The city in Brazilian literature. Rutherford, N.J.: Fairleigh Dickinson University Press; London: Associated University Presses, 1982. 229 p.: bibl., index.

Deserves reading as first study of this subject, but somewhat lacking in critical acumen.

6334 MacNicoll, Murray Graeme. Silvio Romero and Machado de Assis: a one-sided rivalry, 1870–1914 (RIB, 31:3, 1981, p. 366–377)

Good study of *cause célèbre*, although author misses the retaliatory aspect of Romero's enmity towards Machado de Assis because of his negative criticism of *Cantos do fim do século*.

6335 Martins, Maria Helena. Agonia do heroísmo: contexto e trajetória de

Antônio Chimango. Porto Alegre: Universidade Federal do Rio Grande do Sul: L&PM Editores, 1980. 182 p.: bibl.

Best and most comprehensive study to date about a classic political satire.

6336 Martins, Wilson. A crítica literária no Brasil. 2a. ed. Rio de Janeiro: Francisco Alves, 1983. 2 v. (1176 p.): bibl., index.

Comprehensive history of literary criticism in Brazil from 18th-century academies to 1981.

6337 Moisés, Massaud. A criação literária: prosa: formas em prosa, o conto, a novela, o romance, o ensaio, a crônica, o teatro, outras expressões híbridas, a crítica literária. São Paulo: Editora Cultrix, 1982. 367 p.: bibl., indexes.

Useful for didactic purposes (see also item **6338**).

6338 ———. Literatura, mundo e forma. São Paulo: Editora Cultrix: Editora da Universidade de São Paulo, 1982. 368 p.: bibl., index.

Study of literature's relation to outside world through form and style (see also item **6337**).

6339 No limiar de um século: 1887–1977, 90° aniversário de José Américo de Almeida: depoimentos. João Pessoa: Editora Universitária, Universidade Federal de Pernambuco, 1979. 210 p.: bibl., ill.

Articles, speeches, and documents related to José Américo de Almeida's 80th birthday (see *HLAS 42:6415*).

6340 Pinto, Rolando Morel. A língua literária do século XX (USP/RIEB, 22, 1980, p. 97–109)

Balanced and competent reevaluation of the nature of literary language, in this case the Portuguese of Brazil.

6341 Pontes, José Couto Vieira. História da literatura sul-mato-grossense. São Paulo: Editora do Escritor, 1981. 203 p.: bibl. (Coleção Ensaio; v. 12)

First literary history of newest state of Brazil, arranged as a catalog. Informative and useful.

6342 Portella, Eduardo. Raízes da literatura brasileira (TEMBRAS, 67, set./dez. 1981, p. 58–74)

Chapter of forthcoming book, *Literatura brasileira em processo* (vol. 1). Deals

with ideological elements that contributed to formation of Brazilian literature.

6343 Roth, Wolfgang. Zum Verhältnis von Kulturideologie und Literaturwissenschaft in Brasilien (Iberoromania [Max Niemeyer Verlag, Tübingen, FRG] 12, 1980, p. 130–144)

Examines ideology and culture in Brazilian literature and literary criticism, starting from guidelines established by Carlos Guilherme Mota in *Ideologia da cultura brasileira* (1978). Synthesizes for German scholars cultural and ideological underpinnings of contemporary Brazilian letters. [G.M. Dorn]

6344 Schwartz, Jorge. Vanguarda e cosmopolitismo na década de 20: Oliverio Girondo e Oswald de Andrade. Tradução, Mary Amazonas Leite de Barros e Jorge Schwartz. Revisão, Jorge Schwartz e Plínio Martins Filho. São Paulo: Editora Perspectiva, 1983. 253 p.: bibl., facsim., ill., plates (Coleção Estudos; 82. Literatura)

Similarities and differences between Brazilian and Argentine *avant-garde* of the 1920s, as seen through two representative authors. Excellent study, thorough and scholarly, although it still disseminates a few distorted historical facts.

6345 Schwarz, Roberto. Sereia e o desconfiado: ensaios críticos. 2a. ed. Rio de Janeiro: Paz e Terra, 1981. 204 p.: bibl. (Coleção Literatura e teoria literária; v. 37)

Reprint of collected essays by prestigious young critic whose potential seems greater than his accomplishments to date.

6346 Slater, Candace. Stories on a string: the Brazilian *literatura de cordel*. Berkeley: University of California Press, 1981. 313 p., 14 leaves of plates: bibl., ill., index.

It is only recently, says author, that *cordel* literature has become an acceptable subject for academic studies, which augurs for the loss of its innocence and spontaneity. Slater's book is the best to date in its systematic and scholarly approach; it is not far from being the definitive one. For folklorist comment, see item **1031**.

6347 Sodré, Nelson Werneck. História da literatura brasileira. 7a. ed. atualizada. São Paulo: DIFEL, 1982. 677 p.: bibl., index.

Reedition of study originally published

more than 40 years ago, no longer presented as a Marxist history of Brazilian literature; there is no specific mention of its "economic foundations." Text is unchanged; new footnotes acknowledge some of the more recent critical bibliography.

6348 Spina, Segismundo. A língua literária no período colonial: o padrão português; Gregório de Matos (USP/RIEB, 22, 1980, p. 61–75)

Indispensable study of the subject.

6349 ———. Na madrugada das formas poéticas. São Paulo: Editora Atica, 1982. 86 p.: bibl. (Ensaios; 86)

Author proposes comprehensive study of poetic techniques as they began appearing in ancient literatures.

6350 Teles, Gilberto Mendonça. Vanguarda européia e modernismo brasileiro: apresentação dos principais poemas, manifestos, prefácios e conferências vanguardistas de 1857 a 1972. 6a. ed., rev. e ampliada com documentos da vanguarda portuguesa. Petrópolis: Editora Vozes, 1982. 446 p.: bibl., index (Coleção Vozes do mundo moderno; 6)

Useful and convenient.

6351 Tristão de Athayde: teoria, crítica e história literária. Seleção e apresentação, Gilberto Mendonça Teles. Rio de Janeiro: LTC, 1980. 594 p. (Biblioteca universitária de literatura brasileira)

Convenient and comprehensive anthology of Tristão de Athayde's literary criticism (pseud. for Alceu Amoroso Lima, 1893–1983).

6352 Veiga, Cláudio. Aproximações, estudos de literatura comparada. Salvador: Universidade Federal da Bahia, Centro Editorial Didático, 1979. 177 p.

Excellent comparative studies between French literature and Portuguese and Brazilian authors. Among the best are: essays about Huysmans and Eça de Queiroz; Graciliano Ramos as a (faulty) translator of Camus; and Castro Alves and his French connections.

6353 Viver & [i.e. e] escrever. Edla van Steen, entrevistadora. Porto Alegre: L&PM Editores, 1981–1982. 2 v.

Writers discuss themselves and their work. Good contribution to their respective biographies.

PROSE FICTION

6354 Abdala Júnior, Benjamin. A escrita neo-realista: análise sócio-estilística dos romances de Carlos de Oliveira e Graciliano Ramos. São Paulo: Editora Atica, 1981. 127 p.: bibl. (Ensaios; 73)

Far-fetched parallel between Portuguese Carlos de Oliveira and Brazilian Graciliano Ramos under aegis of *neo-realismo*. Better read as two independent essays.

6355 Almeida, José Maurício Gomes de. A tradição regionalista no romance brasileiro, 1857–1945. Rio de Janeiro: Achiamé, 1981. 279 p.: bibl. (Série Universidade; 15)

Regionalism as a constant in Brazilian literature, from 19th-century Romanticism to the Northeastern novel. Among the best books on the subject.

6356 Arrigucci Júnior, Davi. El baile de las tinieblas y de las aguas (ECO, 38[1]:229, nov. 1980, p. 47–65)

Some think that Callado's *Reflexos do baile* is a failure as a novel; author disagrees and considers it his best.

6357 Barretto Filho. Introdução a Machado de Assis. 2a. ed. Rio de Janeiro: Livraria AGIR Editora, 1980. 177 p.: bibl.

Reissue of classic that is still indispensable in any machadian bibliography (see also item **6373**).

6358 Borelli, Olga. Clarice Lispector, esboço para um possível retrato. Rio de Janeiro: Editora Nova Fronteira, 1981. 147 p.

Contribution to psychological biography of Clarice Lispector (see also item **6372**).

6359 Brasil, Assis. A técnica da ficção moderna. Rio de Janeiro: Nórdica; Brasília: *em convênio com o* Instituto Nacional do Livro, Fundação Nacional Pró-Memória, 1982. 383 p.: bibl., indexes.

Contrary to what title may suggest, this is simply a collection of articles first published in periodicals. Covers number of Brazilian authors (e.g., Raul Pompéia, Olavo Bilac, Judith Grossmann) and many foreigners (e.g., Camus, García Márquez).

6360 Chaves, Flávio Loureiro. Simões Lopes Neto: regionalismo & literatura. Porto Alegre: Mercado Aberto, 1982. 239 p.: bibl. (Série Documenta; 12)

Best study to date, and perhaps definitive one, about classic of *gaúcho* regionalism (see also item **6365**).

6361 Curran, Mark J. Jorge Amado e a *literatura de cordel*. Salvador: Fundação Cultural da Bahia; Rio de Janeiro: Fundação Casa de Rui Barbosa, 1981. 89 p.: bibl.

First systematic survey of the essential part played by *literatura de cordel* in the development of Jorge Amado's literary technique (see also item **6374**).

6362 Dantas, Luiz. O segredo dos pinheiros (USP/RIEB, 23, 1981, p. 51–71)

Minor fictional narrative by J.-T. Lacordaire, published in *Revue des Deux Mondes*, lost author's name when transcribed by Portuguese periodical and thus became known as a historical document. Very interesting study for comparative literature and history of ideas, as well as questions of 19th-century authorship.

6363 Os Dois mundos de Cornélio Penna. Coordenação e pesquisa, Marco Paulo Alvim. Catálogo e montagem, Beatriz Folly e Silva *et al*. Reproduções fotográficas, Pedro Oswaldo Cruz. Rio de Janeiro: Fundação Casa de Rui Barbosa, Arquivo-Museu de Literatura, 1979. 57 p.: ill. (Memória literária; 5)

Cornélio Pena was perhaps artist first and writer second. Alexandre Eulálio's preface to catalog of his paintings and drawings is a sensitive introduction to his work (see also item **6385**).

6364 Fitz, Earl E. The problem of the unreliable narrator in Jorge Amado's *Tenda dos milagres* (UK/KRQ, 30:3, 1983, p. 311–321)

Excellent study on generally neglected aspect of Amado's work, his command of narrative technique.

Gattai, Zélia. Um chapéu para viagem. See item **6045**.

6365 Hohlfeldt, Antônio. Conto brasileiro contemporâneo. Porto Alegre: Mercado Aberto, 1981. 229 p.: ill. (Série Revisão; 6)

Good panorama, in spite of a number of small factual and analytical flaws.

6366 José Lins do Rêgo, o homem e a obra. Eduardo Martins, compilador. João Pessoa: Estado da Paraíba, Secretaria da Educação e Cultura, Diretoria Geral de Cultura, 1980. 425 p.: bibl., ill.

Convenient, if heterogeneous, compilation of material related to José Lins do Rego. Useful source of information.

6367 Knowlton, Edgar C., Jr. Mickiewicz and Brazil's Machado de Assis (Polish Review [The Polish Institute of Arts and Sciences of America, Inc., N.Y.] 26:1, 1981, p. 46–57)

Good comparative study of a little explored subject.

6368 Lindstrom, Naomi. A feminist discourse analysis of Clarice Lispector's *Daydreams of a drunken housewife* (LALR, 9:19, Fall/Winter 1981, p. 7–16)

Reading of Clarice Lispector through the eyes of Simone de Beauvoir.

6369 Magalhães Júnior, Raimundo. Vida e obra de Machado de Assis. v. 1, Aprendizado. v. 2, Ascensão. v. 3, Maturidade. v. 4, Apogeu. Rio de Janeiro: Civilização Brasileira; Brasília: em convênio com o Instituto Nacional do Livro, Ministério da Educação e Cultura, 1981. 4 v.: bibl. (Coleção Vera Cruz; v. 320, 320a-c)

Not scholarly, but still the definitive biography of Machado de Assis.

6370 Mello, Oliveira. De volta ao sertão: Afonso Arinos e o regionalismo brasileiro. 2a. ed., rev. e ampliada. Rio de Janeiro: Livraria Editora Cátedra; Brasília: em convênio com o Instituto Nacional do Livro, Ministério da Educação e Cultura, 1981. 219 p.: bibl., ill.

Unscholarly, but valuable informative biography by ardent admirer of Afonso Arinos (see also item **6317**).

6371 Monteiro, José Lemos. O discurso literário de Moreira Campos. Fortaleza: Edições Universidade Federal do Ceará, 1980. 128 p.: bibl.

Notable as only comprehensive study of Moreira Campos to date.

6372 Nunes, Benedito. Clarice Lispector ou o naufrágio da introspecção (COLOQ, 70, nov. 1982, p. 13–22, ill.)

Analysis of three of Lispector's works by one of her most competent critics (see also item **6358**).

6373 Nunes, Maria Luisa. The craft of an absolute winner: characterization and narratology in the novels of Machado de Assis. Westport, Conn.: Greenwood Press,

1982. 158 p.: bibl., index (Contributions in Afro-American and African studies, 0069–9624; no. 71)

Superb analysis of Machado de Assis's work through esthetic apparatus of narratology: a first in any language. Critically enriching and indispensable.

6374 Patai, Daphne. Jorge Amado's heroines and the ideological double standard (UCSD/NS, 8, 1982, p. 257–266)

Reading of Jorge Amado from a feminist point of view. Brilliant criticism, not to be ignored (see also item **6361**).

6375 Roig, Adrien. *O Ateneu* de Raul Pompéia ou le huis clos dans le roman (UTIEH/C, 37, 1981, p. 117–138)

Excellent new approach to a classic.

6376 Schwaderer, Richard. Tradition und Innovation in João Giumarães Rosas (Iberoromania [Max Niemeyer Verlag, Tübingen, FRG] 12, 1980, p. 155–174)

Insightful examination of *Grande sertão: veredas*. Addresses dual nature of its fictional universe: a world divided into two spaces, the *jagunços'* familiar territory and the legendary mythic universe beyond the river. Points out need for further probings of novel's epic and mythic qualities. [G.M. Dorn]

6377 Schwartz, Jorge. Murilo Rubião, a poética do uroboro. São Paulo: Editora Atica, 1981. 113 p.: bibl., ill. (Ensaios; 74)

First comprehensive analysis of Murilo Rubião, recently rediscovered realist of 1940s, praised in Brazil and abroad.

6378 Vozes do tempo de Lobato: depoimento. Paulo Dantas, organizador. São Paulo: Traço Editora, 1982. 251 p.

Commemorative books of marginal interest. Compilation of texts about Monteiro Lobato.

POETRY

6379 Buss, Alcides. *Cobra norato* e a especificidade da linguagem poética. Florianópolis: FCC Edições, 1982. 86, 3 p.: bibl.

Generally unrewarding formalist reading of Raul Bopp's work.

6380 Castro, Renato Berbert de. Em torno da vida de Junqueira Freire. Salvador:

Fundação Cultural do Estado da Bahia, 1980. 153 p.: bibl., facsims. (Coleção Cabrália; v. 9)

Important, if marginal, contribution to the biography of Junqueira Freire, particularly valuable for its meticulous listing of all editions of the poet's work.

6381 Coelho, Joaquim-Francisco. Manuel Bandeira, pré-modernista. Prefácio de Gilberto Freyre. Rio de Janeiro: Livraria J. Olympio; Brasília: *em convênio com o* Instituto Nacional do Livro, Ministério da Educação e Cultura, 1982. 74 p., 1 leaf of plates: bibl.

Excellent study, opening up new vistas about Bandeira's first phase as a poet.

6382 Decadismo e simbolismo no Brasil: crítica e poética. Seleção e apresentação, Cassiana Lacerda Carollo. Rio de Janeiro: Livro Técnicos e Científicos; Brasília: *em convênio com o* Instituto Nacional do Livro, Ministério da Educação e Cultura, 1980. 2 v.: bibl., ill., indexes (Biblioteca universitária de literatura brasileira. Série A, Ensaio, crítica, história literária; v. 11)

Comprehensive and complete collection of critical texts related to Symbolism in Brazil. Indispensable.

6383 Gledson, John. Poesia e poética de Carlos Drummond de Andrade. São Paulo: Livraria Duas Cidades, 1981. 316 p.: bibl.

Yet another item about Drummond. Scholarly, but contains little that is new.

6384 González Cruz, Domingo. No meio do caminho tinha Itabira: a presença de Itabira na obra de Carlos Drummond de Andrade. Fotos de Francisco Arraes. Rio de Janeiro: Achiamé: Calunga, 198? 113 p.: ill.

Subsidiary and marginal information for future biography of Carlos Drummond de Andrade.

6385 Lôbo, Danilo. O poema e o quadro: o picturalismo na obra de João Cabral de Melo Neto. Brasília: Thesaurus, 1981. 157 p.: bibl., ill.

Painting, particularly since Cubism, was well known source of inspiration for João Cabral. Danilo Lobo is first to propose systematic and comprehensive study of this inter-relationship (see also item **6363**).

6386 Manuel Bandeira: coletânea. Organizada por Sônia Brayner. Rio de Ja-

neiro: Civilização Brasileira; Brasília: *em
convênio com o* Instituto Nacional do Livro,
Ministério da Educação e Cultura, 1980. 345
p.: bibl. (Coleção Fortuna crítica; v. 5)

Another convenient and useful volume
issued by the Fortuna Crítica monographic
series (see *HLAS 42:6410*).

6387 Pace, Tácito. Biografia onomástica de
Castro Alves. Belo Horizonte: Editora
Comunicação; Brasília: *em convênio com o*
Instituto Nacional do Livro, Ministério da
Educação e Cultura, 1980. 555 p.: bibl.

Unique, complete biographical dictionary of all people related in any way with
poet. Invaluable reference aid.

6388 Pereira, Carlos Alberto M. Retrato de
época: poesia marginal, anos 70. Rio
de Janeiro: Edição FUNARTE, 1981. 363 p.: ill.

Pereira finds that the leading characteristics of "marginal" (offbeat) poetry produced
during 1970s, were "antitecnicismo, politi-
zação do cotidiano e antiintelectualismo," a
central issue in the activity being the question of the creation of a "cultura popular-
revolucionária." [R.E. Dimmick]

6389 Proença, Ivan Cavalcanti. O poeta do
Eu: um estudo sobre Augusto dos
Anjos. 3a. ed., acrescida de uma antologia de
Augusto dos Anjos. Rio de Janeiro: Livraria J.
Olympio Editora, 1980. 94 p.

Perceptive study of Anjos's "insane
pathological fancie" and harsh, angular verse,
which have both attracted and repelled readers for 70 years. [R.E. Dimmick]

6390 Senna, Marta de. João Cabral, tempo
e memória. Rio de Janeiro: Edições
Antares; Brasília: *em convênio com o* Instituto Nacional do Livro, Ministério da Educação e Cultura, 1980. 209 p.: bibl. (Antares
universitária)

Noting that "Permeando toda a obra de
João Cabral de Melo Neto, há a concepção do
tempo como un fluxo inexoravelmente
linear, que conduz á morte ou, quando pouco,
opera uma transformação essencial nos seres
e nas coisas," Senna declares that she finds in
the act of poetic creation the solution to his
obsession. [R.E. Dimmick]

6391 Tonczak, Maria Joanna. Lindolf Bell
e a catequese poética. Florianópolis:
Governo do Estado de Santa Catarina, 1978.
135 p.: bibl. (Coleção Cultura catarinense.
Série Literatura)

It is difficult to tell right now what
place Lindolf Bell and his *catequese poética*
will have in Brazilian poetry's history. This
title is the best source of information on the
topic.

MISCELLANEOUS

6392 Andrade, Mário de. Cartas a Murilo
Miranda, 1934–1945. Rio de Janeiro:
Editora Nova Fronteira, 1981. 182 p., 28 p. of
plates: bibl., index.

Correspondence of the "Pope of Modernism" throws fascinating light both on literary developments in Brazil and on his own
personality, the spontaneity of its style making for delightful reading. [R.E. Dimmick]

6393 ———. Cartas a um joven escritor: de
Mário de Andrade a Fernando Sabino.
Rio de Janeiro: Editora Record, 1981. 143 p.

One more volume in ever increasing
publication of Mário de Andrade's correspondence. Particularly interesting for what he
says about Lúcio Cardoso. Otávio de Faria,
and, of course, Sabino himself.

6394 *Arco & Flexa*: edição facsimilar,
1928–1929. Salvador: Fundação Cultural do Estado da Bahia, 1978. 66, 70, 77 p.

Reprints the three issues of the most
significant journal of Modernism in Bahia in
late 1920s. [R.E. Dimmick]

6395 Menezes, Emílio de. Obra reunida.
Organização, Cassiana Lacerda Car-
rollo. Apresentação, Ivan Cavalcanti Proença.
Introdução, Josué Montello. Rio de Janeiro:
J. Olympio; Curitiba: Secretaria da Cultura e
do Esporte do Estado de Paraná, 1980. 474 p.,
16 p. of plates: ill.

Excellent edition of the collected
works—best of which consist in satirical
verse—of Brazil's most celebrated turn-of-
the-century Bohemian. [R.E. Dimmick]

6396 Nava, Pedro. Memórias. v. 5, Galo-das-
trevas: as doze velas imperfeitas.
Poesia de Gastão Castro Neto e Olavo Drummond. Rio de Janeiro: J. Olympio, 1981. 48 p.

After lengthy melancholy reflections
on advancing old age, Nava breaks off his own
story to tell that of a cousin and fellow doctor, giving, in his inimitable Proustian/
Rabelaisian style, a lively and vastly divert-
ing account of young professional's activities

in provincial Minas just before the 1930 Revolution. [R.E. Dimmick]

6397 Ramos, Graciliano. Carts. 2a. ed. Rio de Janeiro: Record, 1981. 208 p.: ill.

In addition to its biographical interest, valuable for understanding of Ramos' psychology. First collection of his intimate papers published.

6398 Reverbel, Carlos. Um capitão da Guarda Nacional: vida e obra de J. Simões Lopes Neto. Caxias do Sul: Universidade de Caxias do Sul; Porto Alegre: Martins Livreiro-Editor, 1981. 298 p.: bibl.

Professional biography traces life and works of leading regionalist writer from Rio Grande do Sul. Based on family correspondence and clipping files, account covers not only his lifetime (1865–1916) but also editorial history of his books. Fascinating look at struggles facing writers outside capital. [M.L. Conniff]

6399 Sette, Mário. Memórias íntimas: caminhos de um coração. Prefácio de Hilton Sette. Recife: Prefeitura da Cidade do Recife, Secretaria de Educação e Cultura, Fundação de Cultura Cidade do Recife, 1980. 213 p., 16 leaves of plates: ill.

These sentimental memoirs of a novelist of second rank give a good idea of provincial Brazilian family life in first half of century. [R.E. Dimmick]

FRENCH AND ENGLISH WEST INDIES AND THE GUIANAS

ETHEL O. DAVIE, *Professor, West Virginia State College*
NAOMI M. GARRETT, *Professor Emeritus, West Virginia State College*

IF THERE IS A SPECIAL TREND discernible among the works appearing in this section, it is the continued growth in critical articles on the area's writers and their productions. The majority of items reviewed fall into this category. Three critics of French literature wrote studies of Aimé Césaire (items **6422, 6428,** and **6430**), and he is mentioned by several others. Haitian literature provides subjects for four essays (items **6419–6421** and **64243**). Critical articles on English language writers include studies of Edward Brathwaite items **6440** and **6448**), George Lamming (item **6445**); V.S. Naipaul (items **6441** and **6450**), and Claude McKay (item **6442**).

There are fewer entries in poetry than usual, with Haitian writers contributing most of the verse. Only a few of the offerings are by well established writers; moreover, two volumes are new editions of earlier out-of-print works.

Much new fiction was published during this biennium but few volumes reached the reviewers for inclusion in this *HLAS*.

Two works in progress are worthy of mention: Edward Brathwaite of the University of the West Indies, Mona, is preparing a bibliography of Caribbean poetry and Wilfred Cartey, City University of New York, is completing a study of 80 Caribbean novels. Brathwaite's work is intended to give recognition to original and relatively unknown publications of the region, while Cartey's study will feature internationally known writers, as well as those who have achieved only local recognition.

Important additions to the list of serial publications should help disseminate information about the region's writers and works. *Bim*, a highly rated Barbadian literary review, has reappeared after an absence of four years. A new publication, *La Torche* (items **6431–6432**) dedicated to Léon Damas, has appeared in French Guiana. It encourages writers across national and linguistic boundaries. *Carib* (item **6441**), an innovative magazine published in Jamaica by the West Indian Association for

Commonwealth Literature and Language Studies, invites contributions by English language writers from all the islands.

Talented new writers and critical studies of greater depth than in the past encourage optimism about the future of literature in the French and English-speaking Caribbean and The Guianas.

FRENCH WEST INDIES
PROSE FICTION

6400 Bennett, Ernest. Du rire aux larmes. Port-au-Prince: Editions Fardin, 1981. 392 p.

Collection of well written essays, anecdotes and artices by Haitian journalist. Author reveals keen sense of humor yet becomes serious when the subject requires. Topics include personal experiences, daily happenings, travel, world events, Haitian customs and history. Intriguing style.

6401 Christopher X [pseud. for Christophe Charles]. L'itinéraire du soleil: chants pour Gasner. s.l.: Editions Choucoune, 1981. 58 p.: ill. (Poésie; no. 14)

Collection of essays and poems paying homage to Gasnar Raymond, a young journalist, on the fifth anniversary of his death. Moving preface by Christophe Charles.

6402 Corbin, Jean-Claude. Majolé: contes et poèmes antillais. s.l.: Imprimerie Copyrapid Carbet, 197? 55 p.

Collection of five tales of animals with human characteristics and nine poems. One is paean to Martinique.

6403 Courtois, Félix. Profils de brume. Port-au-Prince: Imprimerie Le Natal, 1981. 220 p.

Consists of 16 tales of wasted, unhappy lives proscribed by rigid social attitudes in bourgeois Haitian atmosphere of faded, genteel melancholy.

6404 Innocent, Antoine. Mimola, ou, L'histoire d'une cassette: petit tableau de moeurs locales. Port-au-Prince: Editions Fardin, 1981. 169 p.

New edition of early 20th-century novel depicting religious and social customs among Haitian masses. Young woman suffering from mysterious and seemingly incurable ailment is healed when the spirit of her dead grandmother, a former slave, leads her to become an adherent of vodun.

6405 Marcelin, Emile. La Reine Anacaona. Port-au-Prince: Editions A. Damour, 1980. 110 p.: ill.

New edition of popular story about the tragic fate of Haiti's first inhabitants and their beloved queen.

6406 Victor, Gary. Symphonie pour demain. Port-au-Prince: Editions Fardin, 1981. 245 p.: ill.

Consists of 13 short stories of diverse interests. Several describe life and action in Haiti; majority depict adventures in space. All portray events in a fantastic future made to seem real and acceptable. Talented writer with fertile creative ability and style.

POETRY

6407 Césaire, Michel. Poignard au coeur: poèmes. Port-au-Prince: Ateliers Fardin, 1978. 112 p.: port.

Consists of 19 nostalgic poems inspired by love, memories of happier days, and concern for the less fortunate. Some reveal poetic talent.

6408 Christopher X [pseud. for Christophe Charles]. Love and liberty: poèmes. Port-au-Prince: Editions Choucoune, 1979. 22 p.

Ten poems of light, personal sentiment by prolific author. French version of each is followed by English translation.

6409 Dépestre, Etzer. L'amour au présent. Port-au-Prince: Editions populaires, 1981. 44 p. (Poésie)

Collection of 15 poems, first work of a young writer. Majority express memories of adolescence in a small Haitian town and experiences in US. Several are above ordinary.

6410 Doret, Michel R. Topologie: poème. Port-au-Prince: Imprimerie La Phalange, 1982. 28 p.

Nostalgic poems written in cold, dreary New York idealize Pétionville, poet's native city. Interesting, well constructed images of small-town Haitian life.

6411 Hall, Louis D. A l'ombre du mapou: poèmes. s.l.: Imprimerie H. Deschamps, 198? 52 p.: ill.

Reedition of 1931 volume of poetry exemplifying "indigéniste" movement of the era. New preface by poet Marie-Thérèse Hall, author's widow.

6412 Lizaire, Margareth. Nuit d'assaut: poèmes. Dessins, Jean Marie Derenoncourt. Port-au-Prince: Editions Choucoune, 1981. 35 p.: ill. (Poésie; no. 13)

Collection of 19 poems, four in Haitian Creole. Young author protests strongly against conditions of underprivileged: reminiscent of the young René Depestre. Preface by Christophe Charles.

6413 Monchoachi. Dissidans. Poèmes présentés et annotés par la Ligue d'Union antillaise. Illustration de Mama. s.l.: Germinal, 198? 56 p.: ill.

Small volume of protest poems in Martinican Creole designed to bring literature closer to the masses. Justification for use of common language is given in French.

6414 Romain, Rose-Marie. Au seuil de l'adolescence. s.l.: Imprimerie Le Natal, s.d. 63 p.

Collection of 49 poems of varied inspiration, many recall thoughts of poet's youth. Considerable artistic ability is demonstrated.

6415 Sylvain, Georges. Confidences et mélancolies: poésies, 1885–1898: précédées d'une notice sur la poésie haïtienne par l'auteur. Port-au-Prince: Imprimerie H. Deschamps, 1979. 136 p.: bibl., ill. (Bibliothèque haïtienne)

Always serious and sincere poet confides personal sentiments and concern for underprivileged in this reedition. Includes useful sketch of Haitian poetry.

DRAMA

6416 Numa, St. Arnaud. Anacaona, reine martyre: tragédie en 3 actes. Port-au-Prince: Editions Fardin, 1981. 134 p., 1 leaf of plates: ill.

Original 1960 play by then amateur playwright Numa, restaged 13 years later, re-

lates romanticized history of the legendary Arawak queen whose blind faith in unarmed peace and goodness of man ends in the destruction of the aboriginal Haitian people.

SPECIAL STUDIES

6417 Blérald, Alain Ph. Négritude et politique aux Antilles. Paris: Editions caribéenes, 1981. 91 p.: bibl. (Collection Partipris)

Writer asserts that Négritude began as a literary movement, but its ideology of decolonization soon expressed a political vision of the world. The poet must enlighten masses by interpreting their past and charting a better future.

6418 Bostick, Herman F. and **Maurice Lubin.** Poetic encounters: an interview with Jean F. Brierre (CLA/J, 26:3, March 1983, p. 277–287)

In interview with Herman Bostick and Maurice Lubin of Howard University, Haitian poet Jean Brierre speaks of influences on his verse and his ideas on younger poets. Exiled from Haiti and living in Senegal, he sees the continuing importance of Négritude and offers words of counsel for aspiring young writers.

6419 Chassagne, Raymond. Seuils de rupture en littérature antillaise (IFH/C, 155, déc. 1982, p. 57–68)

Criticism from two perspectives: traditional history of literary thought and structural analysis of texts. Notes that ideas in early Haitian literary journals were influenced by Du Bois and Price Mars. Other seminal events in Antillean literature were the Congress of Rome and works by Césaire, Fanon, and Glissant.

6420 Christopher X [*pseud. for* Christophe Charles]. Magloire Saint-Aude, griot et surréaliste: essai critique. Port-au-Prince: Editions Choucoune, 1982. 114 p.: bibl. (Essai; no. 4)

Homage to Magloire Saint-Aude presents selections from his works and literary history. Of particular importance to students of Haiti's best known surrealist poet. Includes helpful bibliography.

6421 Dash, J. Michael. Literature and ideology in Haiti, 1915–1961. Totowa,

N.J.: Barnes & Noble, 1981. 213 p.: bibl., index.

Scholarly study of Haitian literature and forces which have influenced it. Stresses developments since American occupation of Haiti. Author gives critical analysis of selected contemporary works and foresees a bright future for literature despite obstacles. Chronology of internal and external events helps keep Haitian and world developments in focus.

6422 Dayan, Joan. The figure of negation: some thoughts on a landscape by Césaire (The French Review [American Association of Teachers of French, Baltimore] 56:3, Feb. 1983, p. 411–423)

Critic views Césaire's poetic language as an attempt to construct new linguistic reality as his words take on the power of creation. Violent figures of extinction and obliteration of the universe are metamorphosed into the movement of an awakening, transformed earth.

6423 Doret, Michel R. Frédéric Doret et le Créole (IFH/C, 152, jan. 1982, p. 28–41)

Writer asserts that articles by Frédéric Doret, his father, represent first attempts at codification of Haitian Creole orthography, employing a system close to French. He advocated using Creole in primary instruction but rejected its adoption as the national language.

6424 Hoffmann, Léon-François. The originality of the Haitian novel (FIU/CR, 8:1, Jan./March 1979, p. 44–50, ill.)

In attempt to depict realities of their society, Haitian novelists have often been misunderstood by compatriots or by French readers abroad. Nevertheless, many writers suceed in producing a humorous portrayal of Haitian life while protesting the nation's unhappy experiences.

6425 ———. Pour une bibliographie des études littéraires haitiennes (IFH/C 152, jan. 1982, p. 44–57)

Supplement to author's well-researched 1977 bibliography (see HLAS 42:6566). Invaluable aid to Haitian literature scholars.

6426 ———. Slavery and race in Haitian letters (FIU/CR, 9:2, Spring 1980, p. 28–32, ill.)

Slavery and race are predominant themes in Haitian literature because of the country's distinctive history and traditions. Writers have always boasted of their slave ancestors' heroic action in emancipating the island from French domination. Color and class differences based on historical influences continue to permeate the country's life and to serve as favorite subjects for writers.

6427 Howlett, Jacques. Mythes et réalités dans la littérature antillaise d'expression française (La Torche [Revue culturelle guyanaise, Association des amis de Léon Damas, Cayenne] 3, jan./mars 1981, p. 23–35)

Products of literary imagination are linked to sociocultural factors. The unique quality of Antillean texts is the effect of subjection and dependence, resulting in a literature of alienation. Counterreaction, a stimulating myth of liberty, culminates in dynamic integration and emerges as marvelous realism. Negritude incorporates the myth, operating as a dimension of lived reality.

6428 Scharfman, Ronnie. Repetition and absence: the discourse of deracination in Aimé Césaire's "Nocturne d'une nostalgie" (The French Review [American Association of Teachers of French, Baltimore] March 1983, p. 572–578)

Author offers thought-provoking interpretations of Césaire's "Nocturne d'une nostalgie." Through repetition and other poetic devices, deracination of blacks from their African homeland becomes an almost present phenomenon in the Martinican's verse.

6429 Smith, Robert, Jr. Racial imperialism as satire and humor: Bertène Juminer's "La Revanche de Bozambo: (CLA/J, 26:1, Sept. 1982, p. 23–33)

Discussion of Bertène Juminer's satirical attack on injustices of colonization and imperialism. Reversing roles, traits, attitudes and actions of the European colonizer and non-white colonized, French Guyanese writer shows that racial oppression and tyranny are undeniably evil regardless of victim's race.

6430 Songolo, Aliko. Surrealism and black literature in French (The French Review [American Association of Teachers of French, Baltimore] May 1982, p. 724–732)

Two selections from Aimé Césaire provide partial basis for author's discussion of whether black writers identified as "surrealists" are inappropriately labeled (if the movement is being defined in the European context).

6431 La Torche. Revue culturelle guyanaise. Association des amis de León Damas. No. 2, oct./déc. 1980?–. Cayenne.

Promising journal dedicated to the memory of Léon Damas whose international renown serves as inspiration to indigenous creative writers. In its pages fledgling versifiers take their place beside more famous poets. Accomplished novelists and respected university critics compare English and French language works, encouraging closer Caribbean artistic collaboration (see also item **6432**).

6432 ——. ——. ——. No. 3, jan./mars 1981?–. Cayenne.

Damas' poem furnishes journal's title and preface reiterates praise for the African oral tradition. This issue includes several essays, a short story, other poems by Damas and original verse dedicated to the late poet. Critical article comments on inseparability of myth and reality in Antillean literature (see also item **6431**).

6433 Wiener, Wanda. Une heure avec Paul Laraque (SU/V, 2:2/2, Summer 1979, p. 108–110)

Paul Laraque discusses his literary intentions on the occasion of receipt of 1979 Franco-Caribbean prize awarded by Casa de las Américas. Originally dedicated to Hispanic American works, award was extended to French-speaking writers for the first time in recognition of Laraque's *Les armes quotidiennes/poésie quotidienne.*

ENGLISH WEST INDIES
PROSE FICTION

6434 Edgell, Zee. Beka Lamb. London: Heinemann, 1982. 171 p. (Caribbean writers series; 26)

Entertaining story of black family's struggles for social advancement in a changing society brings into focus Belize's problems of integrating diverse cultural heritages.

POETRY

6435 Bennett, Louise. Selected poems. Edited, with an introduction, notes and teaching questions by Mervyn Morris. Kingston: Sangster's Book Stores, 1982. 175 p.

Collection of Louise Bennett's dialect poems contains examples of her most popular verse. Introduction reviews her literary career and examines aspects of poetic techniques and characteristic attitudes. Spelling system designed to facilitate reading, extensive notes and glossary make this a useful edition.

6436 Mutabaruka. Mutabaruka: the first poems, 1970–1979. With an introduction by Mervyn Morris. Kingston: P. Issa, 1980. 64 p.

Consists of 40 poems on rebellion, black pride, and Rastifarian ideology. Many were published in earlier volumes. Young poet speaks with emotional intensity but insecure technical skills.

6437 Rebirth in words: poetry and prose from Suriname. Edited by Shrinivâsi and Thea Doelwijt. Translations in cooperation with the Language Institute of the Ministry of Education, Suriname. Paramaribo: Ministry of Culture, Youth, and Sports, 1981. 85 p.

Anthology of 23 poets and fiction writers from Suriname who contributed to the 1981 Barbados Carifesta. A few poems are printed in both Surinamese and English. Selections reflect multi-ethnic society.

6438 Smith, Obediah Michael. 43 [i.e., Forty three] poems. Nassau: O.M. Smith, 1979. 56 p.

First published efforts of young Bahamian writer give evidence of considerable poetic ability. One can hope that he will continue to write and to mature.

SPECIAL STUDIES

6439 Barloewen, Constantin von. Auf der Suche nach Metropolis: Zur Kulturphilosophie V.S. Naipauls (NR, 93:4, 1982, p. 124–144)

Well written analysis of Naipaul's world vision and his struggle against the commonplace. Sees the quest for a civilized metropolis as a distinct feature of Naipaul's oeuvre. Also examines his skill as a cultural critic. [G.M. Dorn]

6440 Brathwaite, Edward Kamau. Afternoon of the status crow: lecture at the University of Bremen, June 1980, Caribbean culture. s.l.: s.n.: 1980. 39 leaves.

Reiteration of Brathwaite's poetic themes that social, geographic, and psychic fragmentation has inflicted psychological damage on Caribbean people. One remedy resides in cultivating a supportive psychocultural/spiritual system. Article is linguistic tour de force ranging over invented words, puns, juxtapositions, several European and African languages, and variety of Caribbean tongues.

6441 Carib. West Indian Association for Commonwealth Literature and Language Studies. No. 1, 1979– . Kingston.

Journal dedicated to linguistic research contains three articles on aspects of works by Naipaul, de Lisser, and Dennis Scott. Three other essays concern language studies of Creole in Jamaica, Trinidad, and Belize.

6442 Eliminian, Isaac I. Theme and technique in Claude McKay's poetry (CLA/J, 25:2, Dec. 1981, p. 203–211)

Study of Claude McKay's poetic devices and major themes which render his verse as pertinent today as when it first appeared.

6443 Kitchen, Arthur. Allan Mutabaruka: rasta poet (The Sunday Gleaner Magazine [Kingston?] March 27, 1981, p. 8)

Mutabaruka, Rastifarian poet who frequently expresses general concerns of Jamaican society in dialect poems, has begun recording his verse as songs without music.

6444 Lawrence, Leota S. Women in Caribbean literature: the African presence (AU/P, 44:1, March 1983, p. 1–11)

In author's view, women are generally portrayed in Caribbean literature as self-assertive, self-sufficient persons of great strength, compassion, and determination. As with their African counterparts, their success is determined largely by their roles in a family situation.

6445 Mateo Palmer, Margarita. En el castillo de mi piel: lenguaje y estructura (UH/U, 212, enero/dic. 1980, p. 25–38)

Analysis of George Lamming's novel in terms of language and structure comments on author's dexterity in using two languages, dialect and standard English, with poetic force. Complicated structure has much variation in narrative technique, point of view, and temporal relationships. Lamming's stylistic contributions mark the beginning of a new esthetic in English-Caribbean literature.

6446 Morris, Mervyn. Trevor Rhone (IJ/JJ, 16:1, Feb. 1983, p. 2–13, photos)

In two interviews, 1980 and 1982, Rhone, Jamaican playwright, director and producer of successful plays and films, discusses his artistic concern with presenting local situations and language. Published and dramatic presentations have gained an international audience for his work.

6447 Rahming, Melvin B. Complacency and community: psychocultural patterns in the West Indian novel (CLA/J, 26:3, March 1983, p. 288–302)

Social concerns are more of an issue than racial identity in the West Indian novel. Citing six major authors, Rahming concludes that preoccupation with racial tension is not a prominent literary theme. Instead, there is emphasis on a sense of community and the nature of individual relationships in a multiethnic setting.

6448 Rohlehr, Gordon. "This past I borrowed:" time, history, and art in Brathwaite's Masks (UPR/CS, 17:3/4, Oct. 1977/Jan. 1978, p. 5–82)

Carefully researched article takes issue with critics' statements that African elements in Brathwaite's Masks were purely ornamental. Particularly skeptical criticism was voiced by poet Derek Walcott in an article declaring his ideological differences. Rohlehr contends that the symbolism, cultural, and historical references of Masks grew out of Brathwaite's on-site study of Akan language and folklore which shapes the thought, language, and intricate structure of the work.

Thompson, L. O'Brien. How cricket is West Indian cricket?: class, racial, and color conflict. See HLAS 45:8208.

6449 Warner, Keith Q. Kaiso!, the Trinidad calypso: a study of the calypso as oral literature. Washington: Three Continents Press, 1982. 155 p.: bibl., ill.

Study, in dissertation format, provides review of scholarly research on origin of calypso, definition of terms, bibliography, and useful discography. Analysis of language, major themes, and popular calypsonians illuminates roles of contemporary musical form as a mirror of society.

6450 Wilson-Tagoe, Nana. No place: V.S. Naipaul's vision of home in the Caribbean (FIU/CR, 9:2, Spring 1980, p. 37–41, plates)

Author examines V.S. Naipaul's increasingly pessimistic vision and acute disillusionment with the world in general.

TRANSLATIONS INTO ENGLISH

MARGARET SAYERS PEDEN, *Professor of Spanish, University of Missouri, Columbia*

AN ERA THAT SURELY must be considered a golden age of Latin American literature in English translations ended with the death of Julio Cortázar in 1984. Though there had been translations of the works of other Latin American authors (e.g., Cortázar's own *The winners,* 1965; Fuentes' *Where the air is clear,* 1960 and *The death of Artemio Cruz,* 1964; Vargas Llosa's *The time of the heroes,* 1966), Gregory Rabassa's translation of *Hopscotch,* published in 1966, stands as a landmark. *Hopscotch* burst onto the scene on the front page of the *New York Times Book Review.* It was Rabassa's first translation and it won the American Book Award for the figure who almost single-handedly introduced Latin American literature to the North American reading public. The publication in 1984 of Rabassa's translation of Cortázar's *We love Glenda so much, and others tales* (item **6467**) closes the parenthesis around a 20-some year period characterized by the enthusiastic reception of a literature that until the 1960s was virtually invisible to North American readers.

Within that period, the most recent phenomenon is the very visible presence of political prose and poetry in translation. The strongly political coloration of Latin American literature is a historical fact, but a fact known only to Spanish-language readers. The average North American was happily blind to the fact that political oppression existed in countries within his own hemisphere. Recently, however, television brought news of the "dirty war" in Argentina into North American living rooms. Breakfast and dinner hours were darkened by daily accounts of the violence and barbarity of conflicts in Central America. Reality was followed into American homes by works of political poetry and prose in translation. Not since the poetry of Neruda swept across university campuses in the 1960s was there the kind of reaction occasioned by Carolyn Forché's readings of Claribel Alegría's poetry in English (item **6457**) and her own writing on El Salvador. Argueta's *One day of life* (item **5239**) explores those tragedies in novel form. Jacobo Timerman's accounts of torture and oppression in Argentina elicited innumerable print features and television interviews (item **6491**). Constantini's *The gods, the little guys, and the police* (item **6473**) is a novelistic probing into Argentina's pain. Chile's agonies, perhaps receding in the minds of those who never wished the information in the first place, are revived in Fernando Alegría's *Chilean spring* (item **6471**) and *Chilean writers in exile,* and in Dorfman's *Widows* (item **6476**).

Latin American literature's influence becomes ever more pervasive in our culture. In 1983, the first Latin American Book Fair was held in Washington, D.C., and in 1985, the second one in New York City. They both featured works in Spanish, Portuguese, and English-language versions. It is expected that these events will become annual celebrations. Writing about *Hopscotch* in 1966, Donald Keen said,

"Cortázar transcends our immense ignorance of his country to move us and make us his companions." We still have much to learn, but in 20 years the literature of Latin America in English translation has at least modified our ignorance.

TRANSLATIONS INTO ENGLISH FROM SPANISH AND PORTUGUESE ANTHOLOGIES

Bello, Andrés. Anthology. See item **5101.**

6451 Contemporary women authors of Latin America. Edited by Doris Meyer and Margarite Fernández Olmos. Brooklyn, N.Y.: Brooklyn College Press, 1983. 2 v.: bibl. (Brooklyn College Humanities Institute series)

Admirable venture. Editors' selection criteria may have been based more on availability of translations than on what authors should be translated, but anthology includes excellent variety of genre, geography, style, and established/new writers. Poetry originals are reproduced in back of book. Quality of translations varies but is generally higher than average.

6453 Poets of Nicaragua: a bilingual anthology, 1918–1979. Edited and translated from the Spanish by Steven F. White. Introduction by Grace Schulman. Greensboro, N.C.: Unicorn Press, 1982. 209 p.: bibl.

Consists of 13 poets—only one woman?—following Rubén Darío. Not comprehensive, but interesting selection. The known are, not surprisingly, strongest: Pablo Antonio Cuadra, Ernesto Cardenal. White knows country and people. Good, accurate and sensitive translations; occasionally, too literal. *En face.*

6454 Spanish-American poetry: a bilingual selection. Edited by Seymour Resnick. Illustrated by Anne Marie Jauss. Irvington-on-Hudson, N.Y.: Harvey House, 1979. 96 p.: ill.

Brief selections range from Alonso de Ercilla to Neruda, attractive in their variety. Most appropriate for pre-college classroom use, as they are often truncated versions. Translations vary radically. *En face.*

6455 Toward an image of Latin American poetry. Edited, with an introduction, by Octavio Armand. Durango, Colo.: Logbridge-Rhodes, 1982. 173 p.

Armand claims, with justice, that boundaries of Latin American poetry in US are defined by limited number of poets in translation and thus too narrow. This vol. aims to address that deficiency and expand the boundaries. Includes 11 lesser known—in US—poets. Excellent translations. *En face.*

POETRY

6456 Albán, Laureano. Autumn's legacy. Translated from the Spanish by Frederick H. Fornoff. Athens: Ohio University Press, 1982. 77 p.

These poems won the 1979 Spanish Premio Adonais. Even with this distinction, one wishes for a more contemporary, more original voice in these lines by a Costa Rican who has often shown preference for traditional forms. Translations vary considerably, ranging from overly-literal to interpretative. *En face.*

6457 Alegría, Claribel. Flowers from the volcano. Translated from the Spanish by Carolyn Forché. Pittsburgh, Pa.: University of Pittsburgh Press, 1982. 87 p. (Pitt poetry series)

These "poems of passionate witness and confrontation" (Forché) have received more attention since their publication than any translation since *Cien años de soledad.* With them, Forché focuses the attention of North American intellectuals on Central America. They begin "In Salvador, death still patrols," and end with farewells. Excellent translations, with the exception of strange rearrangement of lines.

6458 Fraire, Isabel. Poems in the lap of death. Translated from the Spanish by Thomas Hoeksema. Pittsburgh, Pa.: Latin American Literary Review Press, 1981. 99 p.: index.

Winner of 1978 Villaurrutia Prize. Expatriate poems filled with sounds and scenes of England and Europe. As in *Only this light,* very personal poems with good sense of image, although overly dependent on typographical effects. Allusions to Stevens and Cummings more frequent than, for example, Juan García Ponce. Second collection of fine translations by Hoeksema. *En face.*

6459 Gama, José Basílio da. The Uruguay: a historical romance of South America. The Sir Richard F. Burton translation from the Portuguese, Huntington Library manuscript HM 27954. Edited, with introduction, notes, and bibliography, by Frederick C.H. García and Edward F. Stanton. Berkeley: University of California Press, 1982. 1 v.: bibl.

Excellent introduction to Burton's "scrupulously honest, yet bold, personal and vigorous" translation, pointing out its strengths (sympathy to the culture, experience as poet) and weaknesses (overfidelity to line and overuse of cognates). Extensive notes, including Burton's. Facsimile of 1769 edition of this famous narrative poem.

6459a Goldemberg, Isaac. Hombre de paso = Just passing through. Translated from the Spanish by David Unger and Isaac Goldemberg. s.l.: Point of Contact; Hanover, N.H.: Ediciones del Norte, 1981. 81 p.

Excellent collection. Fresh and striking new voice: "the 'broken echo' of Quechua alongside the 'twisted silence' of Yiddish" (Richard Elman). Poems of family, race, place, exile, and memory. Sensitively translated by David Unger. *En face.*

6460 Huidobro, Vicente. The selected poetry of Vincent Huidobro. Edited, with an introduction, by David M. Guss. Translated from the Spanish by David M. Guss *et al.* New York: New Directions, 1981. 234 p.: bibl.

Fine introduction for English speakers. Several translators and several levels of success. Many voices of translation not *necessarily* a drawback considering many voices of Huidobro. Generally accurate; it is perhaps playfulness that suffers most. Guss provides good editing and basic information about a poet long overdue in English.

6461 Kozer, José. The ark upon the number. Translated by Ammiel Alcalay. Merrick, N.Y.: Cross-Cultural Communications, 1982. 36 p.: ill. (Cross-Cultural review chapbook, 0271–6070; 28)

Poems of family and memory. One sees language in movement here— particularly verbs which are given new grammatical functions and semantic shadings. Translation is occasionally brilliant, occasionally disappointing. *En face.*

6462 Martí, José. José Martí, major poems: a bilingual edition. English translation by Elinor Randall. Edited, with an introduction, by Philip S. Foner. New York: Holmes & Meier Publishers, 1982. 173 p.: bibl.

Companion piece to *Our America: writings on Latin America and the struggle for Cuban independence.* Representative selection from five collections of Martí's poetry; chronology. Translations are accurate but not entirely successful; poems do not translate, do not survive, as well as Martí's prose. *En face.*

6463 Sosa, Roberto. The difficult days. Translated from the Spanish by Jim Lindsey. Princeton, N.J.: Princeton University Press, 1983. 82 p. (The Locket Library of poetry in translation)

These poems, published in Spanish as *Los pobres*, have been taken to task for being riddled by cliché. Poverty, want, loss, humility portrayed not with brilliance, but with quiet sincerity. Excellent translation. *En face.*

BRIEF FICTION AND THEATER

6464 Bombal, María Luisa. New islands and other stories. Translated from the Spanish by Richard and Lucia Cunningham. New York: Farrar, Straus, Giroux, 1982. 112 p.

Oneiric, poetic, magic are words most often used to describe Bombal's works. Collection includes title novella and four other brief pieces. Until recently, Bombal was often listed as one of "few" women novelists of Latin America. Corpus of her work is slight, perhaps "feminine," but memorable. Translation is slightly too formal, but generally pleasant.

6465 Carballido, Emilio. Orinoco! Translated from the Spanish by Margaret Sayers Peden (LALR, 11 : 23, 1983, p. 51–83).

6466 Chilean writers in exile: eight short novels. Edited by Fernando Alegría. Trumansburg, N.Y.: Crossing Press, 1982. 162 p.

The intent of this book is well served ("continuing the agonizing process of bearing witness without attempting weighty summations or conclusions"— Víctor Perera). Cruel and violent stories, not surprisingly—and several *are* short stories, not novellas. Kessler translations are particularly good.

6467 Cortázar, Julio. We love Glenda so much, and other tales. Translated from the Spanish by Gregory Rabassa. New York: Knopf, 1983. 145 p.

Last English-language collection published during Cortázar's lifetime. One story, "Moebius Strip," is an apt metaphor for the shape of many Cortázar stories: "a present that contained something that perhaps was time . . ." Rabassa has long association with Cortázar, which is readily apparent in the finesse of the translations.

6468 Griego y Maestas, José. *Cuentos*: tales from the Hispanic Southwest; based on stories originally collected by Juan B. Rael. Selected by and adapted in Spanish by José Griego y Maestas. Retold in English by Rudolfo A. Anaya. Illustrated by Jaime Valdez. Santa Fe: Museum of New Mexico Press, 1980. 174 p.: ill.

Fascinating tales that often resound with echoes from universal folk tales but are at same time specific to our North American Southwest, "the northern frontier of Latin America." Originally collected by Juan Rael and Aurelio M. Espinosa, engagingly translated here by Anaya. Problems of unrecognizable regionalisms are admirably handled in final glossary.

6469 Huerta, Alberto. Selections from *La Virgen de Guadalupe y otras cosas*. Translated from the Spanish by Charles P. Dietrick and Susan Diesenhouse (UCSD/NS, 8, 1982, p. 201–210)

Well translated stories by emerging Mexican short story writer. Selections are from *La Virgen de Guadalupe y otras cosas*, which won the 1977 Bellas Artes Gran Premio.

6470 *Latin American Literary Review.* Carnegie-Mellon University. Vol. 8, No. 16, Spring/Summer 1980– . Pittsburgh, Pa.

Special issue devoted to "Hispanic Caribbean Literature" and edited by Roberto González Echevarría who also wrote an excellent introduction that discusses creative and scholarly contributions to the field. Interesting combination of "clean" translations plus annotations allows reading for pleasure and, if desired, scholarly ends. Various translators, all, apparently, closely supervised. Model collection.

NOVELS

6471 Alegría, Fernando. The Chilean spring. Translated from the Spanish by Stephen Fredman. Pittsburgh, Pa.: Latin American Literary Review Press, 1980. 160 p. (Discoveries)

Moving novel by leading voice of Chilean literature in exile, now in good English translation. Specifically political and Chilean work that will touch any "who can compassionately identify with the victims of man's inhumanity to man" (Kessel Schwartz). English version deserves broader critical notice than it received.

Argueta, Manlio. One day of life. See item **5239.**

6472 Cabrera Infante, Guillermo. Infante's inferno. Translated from the Spanish by Suzanne Jill Levine with the author. New York: Harper & Row, 1984. 410 p.

Language as sex. Sex as language. George Steiner, among others, has written of irrefutable liaison between our sexual and linguistic conjugations, copulations, and ejaculations. Levine and author work well together (as in *Tres tristes tigres*) but the English is less a translation than a transformation.

6473 Costantini, Humberto. The gods, the little guys, and the police. Translated from the Spanish by Tony Talbot. New York: Harper & Row 1984. 230 p.

Constantini mixes Olympus and Buenos Aires in a fragmented, polivocal, serious/funny novel about the "dirty war." Satirically, yet sympathetically, he describes a group of artists (?) who are unsystematic subjects of reprisal. Difficult translation well done.

6474 Cortázar, Julio. The winners. Translated from the Spanish by Elaine Kerrigan. New York: Pantheon Books, 1984. 374 p.

Reissue in paperback of 1965 translation of Cortázar's first novel. This Latin American ship of fools preceded the landmark translation of *Hopscotch* (1966) and introduced Cortázar to North American audience. Fine translation.

6475 Donoso, José. A house in the country: a novel. Translated from the Spanish by David Pritchard and Suzanne Jill Levine. New York: Knopf, 1984. 352 p.

"Combination of literary grace, political urgency and an untethered imagination" (Charles Champlin), a "strange, beautiful and sinister novel" (John Butt), many critics believe this to be Donoso's masterpiece, superior even to *The obscene bird of night*. The narrative passages are beautifully translated; dialogue is less effective.

6476 Dorfman, Ariel. Widows. Translated from the Spanish by Stephen Kessler. New York: Pantheon Books, 1983. 146 p.

Author's plan was to publish this novel in a European language—to be "translated" into Spanish and thus outmaneuver censorship. Called a "sharply dramatic little novel" (Alan Cheuse), it is easy to see why it could not be published in contemporary Chile. Kessler's translation is good, preserving tone of original.

6477 Dourado, Autran. The voices of the dead: a novel. Translated from the Portuguese by John M. Parker. New York: Taplinger Pub. Co., 1981. 248 p.

A kind of Brazilian gothic set in Duas Pontes, far in the interior. Dourago has been compared to Faulkner for "the grip of the past on the present, regional history as fate and myth, inescapable family destinies" (Katha Pollitt). Translation is unpleasant to North American ears, relying heavily on British colloquial language.

6478 García Márquez, Gabriel. Chronicle of a death foretold. Translated from the Spanish by Gregory Rabassa. New York: Knopf, 1983. 120 p.

This novella was described as "a dreamlike detective story" (*New York Times*), "remarkable, graphic, and grisly" (*New York Magazine*), and "exquisitely harrowing" (*New York Times Book Review*), continuing García Márquez's phenomenal reception in English. The fact that "we can almost see, smell and hear García Márquez's Caribbean backwater and its inhabitants" (*San Francisco Chronicle*) is due to Rabassa's translation.

6479 Mujica Láinez, Manuel. The wandering unicorn. Foreword by Jorge Luis Borges. Translated from the Spanish by Mary Fitton. New York: Taplinger, 1983. 322 p., 2 p. of plates: tables.

A version of French folk legend of Melusine, this fictional memoir covers 800 years of adventure, pageantry, and history. Good translation of colorful, well researched novel.

6480 Ribeiro, Darcy. Maíra. Translated from the Portuguese by E.H. Goodland and Thomas Colchie. New York: Vintage Books, 1984. 353 p. (Aventura)

First novel by anthropologist, this "wistful evocation of a doomed culture" (Jim Miller) brings the exoticism of a distant (in time and space) Indian culture to the North American reader, along with confrontation between the mythic world of that culture and encroaching religious and social change. Smooth translation with good sense of place.

6481 Valenzuela, Luisa. The lizard's tail: a novel. Translated from the Spanish by Gregory Rabassa. New York: Farrar, Straus & Giroux, 1983. 279 p.

Loosely, a fictionalized biography. Valenzuela's gift for dark fantasy, dark humor, and dark sex are readily apparent in this satire, a "Baroque and parodistic fantasy centered on and in the mind of a nameless mad Sorcerer" (Allen Josephs). Rabassa's inventiveness and creativeness challenged in these convolutions of language.

6482 Vargas Llosa, Mario. Aunt Julia and the scriptwriter. Translated from the Spanish by Helen R. Lane. New York: Farrar, Straus & Giroux, 1982. 374 p.

"Admirable" translation by Helen Lane of this semi-autobiographical novel. According to Julie Jones, Vargas Llosa "justifies the incorporation of melodramatic material in serious literature by arguing that melodrama is real, is human."

ESSAYS, INTERVIEWS, AND REPORTAGE

6483 Anti-Yankee feelings in Latin America: an anthology of Latin American writings from colonial to modern times in their historical perspective. Edited by F. Toscano and James Hiester. Various translators. Washington: University Press of America, 1982. 297 p.: bibl.

Interesting idea: to make available in one volume, in English, principal Latin American writings with anti-US bias. Includes many important writers and undeniably important texts. Bibliography. Translations are, unfortunately, unacceptable and cannot convey literary qualities editors cite as one of their standards for inclusion.

6484 *Art on the* line 0277–7053. Curbstone Press. 1– . Willimantic, Conn., 1981– .

Monographic series. First three volumes noted below are very slim and interesting books, cohesive in subject matter and containing not easily accessible material. They are well translated and edited: brief essays and thoughts, and poetry that illustrate authors' political orientation. As pointed out in *Choice*, audience for the series falls somewhere between traditional categories: No. 1, Roque Dalton, *Poetry & militancy* (translated from the Spanish by James Scully, 1981, 53 p.); No. 2, César Vallejo, *The Mayakovsky case* (translated from the Spanish by Richard Schaaf, 1982, 50 p.); and No. 3, César Vallejo, *Autopsy on surrealism* (translated from the Spanish by Richard Schaaf, 1982, 40 p.).

6485 Borges, Jorge Luis. Seven conversations with Jorge Luis Borges. Interviewer, Fernando Sorrentino. Translation, additional notes, appendix of personalities mentioned by Borges. Translator's foreword by Clark M. Zlotchew. Troy, N.Y.: Whitston Pub. Co., 1982. 219 p.: appendix, bibl., indexes.

Conversations recorded in 1971. Some new insights. Elaborate but thorough and informative notes on multitude of works and authors mentioned in the interviews. Of great interest to translators: an appendix, "Borges in English," by Norman Thomas di Giovanni, describes the collaborative method that brought much of Borges into English. Also includes appendix of personalities mentioned by Borges.

6486 Cieza de León, Pedro de. The Incas. Edited, with an introduction by Victor Wolfgang von Hagen. Translated from the Spanish by Harriet de Onís. Norman: University of Oklahoma Press, 1981. 397 p.: bibl., facsims., fold. maps (1 col.), index, plates (part col.) (The Civilization of the American Indian series; v. 53)

Reedition of 1959 publication. First translated by an Englishman in 1709. This is de Onís at her best. Editing is exemplary and footnotes an education in themselves.

6487 Dorfman, Ariel. The empire's old clothes: what the Lone Ranger, Babar, and other innocent heroes do to our minds. New York: Pantheon, 1983. 225 p.: bibl.

These essays explore major cultural myths of our time as they appear in popular comic books and magazines, attempting to "map out their concealed social and political messages." Fred Moramarco found book "well-researched, well-argued," but would like it better were it "about half as long." Good translation.

6488 Mallea, Eduardo. History of an Argentine passion. Translated from the Spanish and with an introduction and annotations by Myron I. Lichtblau. Pittsburgh, Pa.: Latin American Literary Review Press, 1983. 184 p.: bibl. (Explorations)

Mallea's novels have not been widely translated into English but here, in a meticulous translation, is first publication of his essays in English by major student of his work. Well known to students of Latin American literature, this seminal essay posits his theory of Argentine reality/duality. Excellent annotations and bibliography.

6489 Neruda, Pablo. Passions and impressions. Edited by Matilde Neruda and Miguel Otero Silva. Translated from the Spanish by Margaret Sayers Peden. New York: Farrar, Straus, & Giroux, 1984. 396 p.: index.

6490 Paz, Octavio. The monkey grammarian. Translated from the Spanish by Helen R. Lane. New York: Seaver Books, 1981. 162 p.: ill.

Novel/critique of language in which "the world becomes language . . . [and] language is transformed into a world." Paz uses the figure of the indian monkey chief Hanuman, the monkey/gramma, to effect a reconciliation of writing and speech, going beyond Derridian deconstruction to arrive in Galta and find the synthesis of oppositions that characterizes all Paz's writing.

6491 Timerman, Jacobo. Prisoner without a name, cell without a number. Translated from the Spanish by Tony Talbot. New York: Knopf, 1981. 164 p.

One of the first voices out of Argentina to attract truly international attention to the "dirty war." Anthony Lewis called this reportage by an experienced newspaper publisher "the most gripping and most important book I have read in a long time" (see also *HLAS 43:6636*).

6492 Vasconcelos, José. The cosmic race/La raza cósmica. A bilingual edition with an introduction and notes by Didier T. Jaén. Los Angeles: Centro de Publicaciones, California State University, 1979. 108 p.: bibl.

Jaén discusses this controversial essay in the light of its scientific and philosophical shortcomings, placing it in the context of later essays that expounded many of the same ideas. Argues the essay not as "racist theory," but as "theory of development of human consciousness." Spanish text follows English translation. Accurate translation, but overly faithful to original in syntax and lexicon.

BIBLIOGRAPHY, THEORY, AND PRACTICE

6493 Bassnett-McGuire, Susan. Translation studies. London: Methuen, 1980. 159 p.: bibl.

Thesis of this study, "to demonstrate that translation studies is . . . a discipline in its own right: not merely a minor branch of comparative literary study, nor yet a specific area of linguistics . . ." Modified Steiner, through influence of Andrés Lefevre. Argues against paraphrasing of prose text—already judged inadequate in poetry—and for a theory of theater translation.

Bellini, Giuseppe. Bibliografia dell ispanoamericanismo italiano. See item **10**.

6494 Bly, Robert. The eight stages of translation, with a selection of poems and translations. Boston, Mass.: Rowan Tree Press, 1983. 107 p. (Poetics series; no. 2)

Practice, not theory, answering the question, What is it like to translate a poem? Interesting commentary by an experienced and controversial translator. Some 50 p. of translations *en face.*

6495 Corvalán, Graciela N.V. Latin American women writers in English translation: a bibliography. Los Angeles: Latin American Studies Center, California State University, 1980. 109 p. (Latin American bibliography series; 9)

Very valuable reference tool lists bibliographies, anthologies, general bibiography of women writers, and Latin American women writers in English translation. This bibliography should be updated at regular intervals and given wider distribution.

6496 Estudos de tradutologia. Delton de Mattos, editor. Brasília: Kontakt, 1981. 1 v.: bibls.

Nine essays by "young linguists who reveal a promising future in the area of translation theory," intended to address the need to gather together as many studies as possible on the subject, and to invest translation with the stature of an interdisciplinary discipline. Based in semiotics, sociolinguistics, and practical questions.

6497 Kelly, L.G. The true interpreter: a history of translation theory and practice in the West. New York: St. Martin's Press, 1979. 282 p.: bibl., ill., indexes.

Scholarly critique of historical and modern theory and practice. Reasoned analysis of translation and language theory, the function of translation, and approaches to the process, with emphasis on critical judgments. Following Steiner's historical divisions, Kelly places our age at "beginning . . . of fourth stage, whose essential mark is consolidation of theory."

6498 Murad, Timothy. *Los de abajo* vs. *The underdogs*: the translation of Mariano Azuela's masterpiece (AATSP/H, 65:4, Dec. 1982, p. 554–561)

Interesting analysis by scholar interested in translation as a tool of literary criticism. His comments are not directed toward pinpointing isolated mistranslations—as can be the case with "translation police"—but, rather, toward illustrating how a text may be changed or subverted through subtle, and not so subtle, shifts between the original and translated versions.

6499 Pérez Martínez, Herón. Elementos para una teoría de la traducción (UNL/H, 22, 1981, p. 101–113)

Author takes Vázquez Ayora to task for imprecision of terminology. Proposes that translation does not take place on the plane of language but, rather, on that of the text: "one translates texts." He notes some ideas that will be developed into a comprehensive theory.

6500 Rónai, Paulo. A tradução vivida. 2a. ed., rev. e aum. Rio de Janeiro: Editora Nova Fronteira, 1981. 210 p.: bibl., index (Coleção Logos)

Commentary and memories of a prodigally productive Brazilian translator (among others, 17 annotated volumes of Balzac's *La comédie humaine*). Incorporates his voluminous and valuable work on etymology, especially cognates, but goes beyond: practical questions (*renumeraciones*); Brazilian vs. Portuguese; translating poetry; problems of proper names. Broad interest.

6501 Santos, Agenor Soares dos. Guia prática de tradução inglesa: comparação semântica e estilística entre os cognatos de sentido diferente em inglês e em português. 2a. de ordem, rev. e consideravelmente aum. São Paulo: Editora Cultrix: Editora da Universidade de São Paulo, 1981. 509 p.: bibl.

Excellent practical guide focusing on inherent dangers in translating cognates. Brief introduction and explanations of approach, plus dictionary of cognates with clear and instructive examples of usages within context. Highly recommended.

6502 *Translation Review.* University of Texas at Dallas. Vol. 9, 1982– . Richardson.

Interview with Richard Howard. Articles on Merwin as translator poet; on translating Garciliano Ramos; translation as literary criticism; collective translation; review of bilingual dictionaries; book reviews.

6503 ——. ——. Vol. 10, 1982– . Richardson.

Articles on translation strategies and translating local color; translating from intermediary languages; and translating *haiku*.

Interview with Hiroaki Sato. Profile of two university presses. Reviews.

6504 ——. ——. Vol. 11, 1983– . Richardson.

Excellent issue. Guest editor, George Steiner. Focus on Greece. Three articles on translating Greek poetry, one on translating prose, one on translating from oral tradition. Interview with well-known translator from the Greek, Edmund Keeley.

6505 ——. ——. Vol. 12, 1983– . Richardson.

Articles on specific figures: Longfellow as translator; Jean Follain in translation; problems of translating Attila Jozsef; Baudelaire translations. Also translating concrete poetry, and interview with Kenneth Pike. Reviews.

6506 ——. ——. Vol. 13, 1983– . Richardson.

Interview with Wallace Fowlie. Paul Mann's response to Rainer Schulte on translation as literary criticism. Donald Frame's pleasures and problems of translations. Translation of Ortega's essay on translation. Reviews.

JOURNAL ABBREVIATIONS LITERATURE

AATSP/H Hispania. American Association of Teachers of Spanish and Portuguese. University of Cincinnati. Cincinnati, Ohio.

ACH/BHA Boletín de Historia y Antigüedades. Organo de la Academia Colombiana de Historia. Bogotá.

ACO/B Boletín de la Academia Colombiana. Bogotá.

AR Areito. Areito, Inc. New York.

ATSP/VH Vida Hispánica. Journal of the Association of the Teachers of Spanish and Portuguese. Wolverhampton, U.K.

AU/P Phylon. Atlanta University. Atlanta, Ga.

BNBD Boletín Nicaragüense de Bibliografía y Documentación. Banco Central de Nicaragua, Biblioteca. Managua.

BNJM/R   Revista de la Biblioteca Nacional José Martí. La Habana.

CAM   Cuadernos Americanos. México.

CBR/BCB   Boletín Cultural y Bibliográfico. Banco de la República, Biblioteca Luis-Angel Arango. Bogotá.

CDLA   Casa de las Américas. Instituto Cubano del Libro. La Habana.

CDLA/CO   Conjunto. Revista de teatro latinoamericano. Casa de las Américas *for the* Comité Permanente de Festivales. La Habana.

CH   Cuadernos Hispanoamericanos. Instituto de Cultura Hispánica. Madrid.

CLA/J   CLA Journal. Morgan State College, College Language Association. Baltimore, Md.

CM/D   Diálogos. Artes/Letras/Ciencias humanas. El Colegio de México. México.

CM/NRFH   Nueva Revista de Filología Hispánica. El Colegio de México. México. University of Texas. Austin.

CNC/A   Actualidades. Consejo Nacional de la Cultura. Centro de Estudios Latinoamericanos Rómulo Gallegos. Caracas.

COLOQ   Colóquio. Revista de artes e letras. Fundação Celouste Gulbenkian. Lisboa.

CONAC/RNC   Revista Nacional de Cultura. Consejo Nacional de Cultura. Caracas.

CPES/RPS   Revista Paraguaya de Sociología. Centro Paraguayo de Estudios Sociológicos. Asunción.

CRIT   Criterio. Editorial Criterio. Buenos Aires.

EC/M   Mapocho. Biblioteca Nacional, Extensión Cultural. Santiago.

ECO   Eco. Librería Bucholz. Bogotá.

EEHA/AEA   Anuario de Estudios Americanos. Consejo Superior de Investigaciones Científicas [and] Universidad de Sevilla, Escuela de Estudios Hispano-Americanos. Sevilla.

ESME/C   Cultura. Revista del Ministerio de Educación. San Salvador.

FIU/CR   Caribbean Review. Florida International University, Office of Academic Affairs. Miami.

HAHR   Hispanic American Historical Review. Duke University Press *for the* Conference on Latin American History of the American Historical Association. Durham, N.C.

HISP   Hispanófila. University of North Carolina. Chapel Hill.

HISPA   Hispamérica. Revista de literatura. Takoma Park, Md.

HR   Hispanic Review. A quarterly devoted to research in the Hispanic languages and literatures. University of Pennsylvania, Dept. of Romance Languages. Philadelphia.

IAA   Ibero-Amerikanisches Archiv. Ibero-Amerikanisches Institut. Berlin, FRG.

ICC/T   Thesaurus. Boletín del Instituto Caro y Cuervo. Bogotá.

ICP/R   Revista del Instituto de Cultura Puertorriqueña. San Juan.

IFH/C   Conjonction. Institut français d'Haïti. Port-au-Prince.

IGFO/RI   Revista de Indias. Instituto Gonzalo Fernández de Oviedo [and] Consejo Superior de Investigaciones Científicas. Madrid.

IILI/RI   Revista Iberoamericana. Instituto Internacional de Literatura Iberoamericana. Patrocinada por la Universidad de Pittsburgh. Pittsburgh, Pa.

IJ/JJ   Jamaica Journal. Institute of Jamaica. Kingston.

INDEX Index of Censorship. Writers & Scholars International. London.

IUP/HJ Hispanic Journal. Indiana University of Pennsylvania, Department of Foreign Languages. Indiana, Pa.

LALR Latin American Literary Review. Carnegie-Mellon University, Department of Modern Languages. Pittsburgh, Pa.

LARR Latin American Research Review. University of North Carolina Press *for the* Latin American Studies Association. Chapel Hill.

NMC/N Nicaráuac. Revista bimestral del Ministerio de Cultura. Managua.

NS NS NorthSouth. NordSud NorteSur NorteSul. Canadian journal of Latin American studies. Canadian Association of Latin American Studies. University of Ottawa. Ottawa.

PAN/ES Estudios Latinoamericanos. Polska Akademia Nauk [Academia de Ciencias de Polonia], Instytut Historii [Instituto de Historia]. Warszawa.

PCCLAS/P Proceedings of the Pacific Coast Council on Latin American Studies. University of California. Los Angeles.

PUC/L Lexis. Revista de lingüística y literatura. Pontificia Universidad Católica del Perú. Lima.

QIA Quaderni Ibero-Americani. Associazione per i Rapporti Culturali con la Spagna, il Portogallo e l'America Latina. Torino, Italy.

RCLL Revista de Crítica Literaria Latinoamericana. Latinoamericana Editores. Lima.

REVIEW Review. Center for Inter-American Relations. New York.

RIB Revista Interamericana de Bibliografía/Inter-American Review of Bibliography. Organization of American States. Washington.

RO Revista de Occidente. Madrid.

SBAT/RT Revista de Teatro. Sociedade Brasileira de Autores Teatrais. Rio de Janeiro.

SECOLAS/A Annals of the Southeastern Conference on Latin American Studies. West Georgia College. Carrollton. Kennesey Junior College. Marietta, Ga.

SU/V Vórtice. Stanford University, Department of Spanish and Portuguese. Stanford, Calif.

SUR Sur. Revista bimestral. Buenos Aires.

TEMBRAS Tempo Brasileiro. Revista de cultura. Rio de Janeiro.

UA/REH Revista de Estudios Hispánicos. University of Alabama, Department of Romance Languages, Office of International Studies and Programs. University.

UB/BH Bulletin Hispanique. Université de Bordeaux *avec le concours du* Centre national de la recherche scientifique. Bordeaux, France.

UBN/R Revista de la Biblioteca Nacional. Ministerio de Educación y Cultura. Montevideo.

UC/AT Atenea. Revista de ciencias, letras y artes. Universidad de Concepción. Concepción, Chile.

UC/RCL Revista Chilena de Literatura. Universidad de Chile, Departamento de Literatura. Santiago.

UCC/TL Taller de Letras. Universidad Católica de Chile, Instituto de Letras. Santiago.

UCLA/JLAL Journal of Latin American Lore. University of California, Latin American Center. Los Angeles.

UCLA/M Mester. University of California, Department of Spanish and Portuguese. Los Angeles.

UCLV/I Islas. Universidad Central de las Villas. Santa Clara, Cuba.

UCNSA/EP Estudios Paraguayos. Universidad Católica Nuestra Señora de la Asunción. Asunción.

UCSB/NS New Scholar. University of California, Committee on Hispanic Civilization [and] the Center for Chicano Studies. Santa Barbara.

UFP/EB Estudos Brasileiros. Universidade Federal do Paraná, Setor de Ciências Humanas, Centro de Estudos Brasileiros. Curitiba, Brazil.

UFSI/R UFSI Reports. Universities Field Staff International Inc. Hanover, N.H.

UH/RJ Romanistisches Jahrbuch. Universitat Hamburg, Romanisches Seminar, Ibero-Amerikanisches Forschungsinstitut. Hamburg, FRG.

UH/U Universidad de La Habana. La Habana.

UK/KRQ Kentucky Romance Quarterly. University of Kentucky. Lexington.

UK/LATR Latin American Theatre Review. A journal devoted to the theatre and drama of Spanish and Portuguese America. University of Kansas, Center of Latin American Studies. Lawrence.

UNAM/PP Punto de Partida. Revista bimestral. Universidad Nacional Autónoma de México, Dirección General de Difusión Cultural. México.

UNAM/RMCPS Revista Mexicana de Ciencias Políticas y Sociales. Universidad Nacional Autónoma de México, Facultad de Ciencias Políticas y Sociales. México.

UNAM/RUM Revista de la Universidad Nacional Autónoma de México. México.

UNC/R Revista de la Universidad Nacional de Córdoba. Córdoba, Argentina.

UNESCO/CU Cultures. United Nations' Educational, Scientific, and Cultural Organization. Paris.

UNION Unión. Unión de Escritores y Artistas de Cuba. La Habana.

UNL/H Humanitas. Universidad de Nuevo León, Centro de Estudios Humanísticos. Monterrey, México.

UP/A Apuntes. Universidad del Pacífico, Centro de Investigación. Lima.

UP/CSEC Cuban Studies/Estudios Cubanos. Univerity of Pittsburgh, University Center for International Studies, Center for Latin American Studies. Pittsburgh, Pa.

UPR/CS Caribbean Studies. University of Puerto Rico, Institute of Caribbean Studies. Río Piedras.

UPR/LT La Torre. Universidad de Puerto Rico. Río Piedras.

URSS/AL América Latina. Academia de la Unión de República Soviéticas Socialistas. Moscú.

USP/RIEB Revista do Instituto de Estudos Brasileiros. Universidade de São Paulo, Instituto de Estudos Brasileiros. São Paulo.

UT/RCEH Revista Canadiense de Estudios Hispánicos. Asociación Canadiense de Hispanistas, Universidad de Toronto. Toronto.

UTIEH/C Caravalle. Cahiers du monde hispanique et luso-brésilien. Université de Toulouse, Institut d'Etudes hispaniques, hispano-américaines et luso-brésiliennes. Toulouse, France.

UV/PH La Palabra y el Hombre. Universidad Veracruzana. Xalapa, México.

UY/R Revista de la Universidad de Yucatán. Méridad, México.

MUSIC

ROBERT STEVENSON, *Professor of Music, University of California, Los Angeles*

DURING THE INTERIM since preparation of the last Music section of *HLAS 44*, the Latin American musicological horizon has brightened considerably. Stanley Sadie's promise (see *HLAS 38:9018*) that *The New Grove dictionary of music and musicians* (London: Macmillan, 1980, 20 v.) would contain an unprecedented number of Latin American articles was amply fulfilled. No previous encyclopedia in any language had contained substantial articles on all nations belonging to the Organization of American States, on the more populous cities, on 250 recognized historical as well as contemporary composers, and on 70 dances, song-types, and instruments peculiar to Latin America. Thanks to the energy and decisiveness of the Latin American sub-editor, French-born Gerard Béhague presently heading the Music Department of the University of Texas, capitals such as Quito indeed garnered more space (131 lines) than cities in Spain of great historical importance (e.g., Seville: 83 lines).

The growing recognition that Latin America deserves ample space in any international lexicon was visible in even Aaron I. Cohen's *International Encyclopedia of Women Composers* (New York; London: R.R. Bowker, 1981) prepared by a team at Johannesburg, South Africa. In such unexpected compendia as *Sohlmans* five-volume encyclopedia published at Stockholm, as well as in German *vade mecums* such as the two-volume *Brockhaus Riemann Musiklexikon*, Latin America played an increasingly important role in the 1975–84 decade. Among general encyclopedias, the translated *Great Soviet Encyclopedia* (New York: Macmillan, 1973–82, 31 v.) appearing in installments, made available articles of prime interest on national musics (items **7128** and **7199**), as well as on such notables as Carlos Gomes and Heitor Villa-Lobos.

The number of erudite periodicals grew gratifyingly during the early 1980s and with newcomers such as: *Revista Musical de Venezuela* at Caracas (mid-1980); *Ars: revista da Escola de Música e Artes Cênicas da Universidade Federal da Bahia* at Salvador (1981); *Pauta* at Mexico City (Jan. 1982); and *Boletim da Sociedade Brasileira de Musicologia* at São Paulo (1983). Meantime, *Revista Musical Chilena* continued the cynosure of Latin American periodicals under the transcendental guidance of Luis Merino Montero and Magdalena Vicuña Lyon. *Heterofonía*, rated by José Vicente Torres as the best North American music periodical, continued to flourish under the editorship of that miracle worker, Esperanza Pulido Silva. The handsome *Latin American Music Review*, edited at the University of Texas by Gerard Béhague, provided a ready forum in all languages for articles chiefly of ethnomusicological import. In contrast, *Inter-American Music Review* founded at Los Angeles in 1978, concentrated on long historical studies translated into, or written in, English.

No historic Latin American epoch is in greater need of the continuing attentions of trained musicologists than the 19th century. True, a plethora of literature on national anthems already existed when Gilbert Chase's *A guide to the music of Latin America*, second edition was published (1962; reprinted in 1972, see *HLAS 26:2157*). Before 1945, the Argentine national anthem alone accounted for 28 items in Chase's bibliography. But even for so well documented an anthem as the Argentine *himno nacional* (composed in 1812 and adopted in 1813), new documentation correcting the dates of its composer, Blas Parera—birth year erroneously given as 1777 in *The New Grove* (vol. 13, p. 48) and death year wrongly stated as 1817 (vol. 1, p. 565)—surfaced for publication in the 1978 second edition of Vicente Gesualdo's *Historia de la música en la Argentina* (see *HLAS 44:7016*). If information on such a favorite topic as national anthems and their composers still remains sketchy and controversial for countries such as Bolivia, Ecuador, Paraguay, and Venezuela, small wonder that other aspects such as cathedral music at Santiago, Chile, religious music throughout São Paulo province, and musical activity in the leading Pacific port city became the subjects of needed studies by Samuel Claro-Valdés (see *HLAS 44:7057*), Antônio Alexandre Bispo (item **7054**), and Luis Merino Montero (item **7121**) in 1982 publications. The trend promises to continue with 19th-century studies in prospect by Claro-Valdés, Malena Kuss, Lapique Becali, Merino Montero, Sordo Sodi, Jorge Velazco, and others.

A most welcome edition of the Brazilian mulatto José Maurício Nunes Garcia's Christmas matinas of 1799 was published in full orchestral score in 1978 (see *HLAS 44:7026a*). Vernacular and Latin music from the Mexican colonial period appeared in 1981 and 1982 (items **7152** and **7183**). However, there is still a great need for a scholarly reedition of the operas of Carlos Gomes (1836–96), as well as of the operas, at least in facsimile of manuscript scores, of Gustavo E. Campa, Ricardo Castro, Felipe Gutiérrez Espinosa, José Angel Montero, Melesio Morales, Eleodoro Ortiz de Zárate, Aniceto Ortega, and Cenobio Paniagua. Only then will Latin America's 19th-century music receive the attention it deserves.

GENERAL

Aldunate del Solar, Carlos. La música en el arte precolombino. See *HLAS 45:252*.

7001 Algemene muziek encyclopedie.
Edited by J. Robijns and Miep Zijlstra. Haarlem, The Netherlands: De Haan, 1979–1982. 6 v.: bibl., music, photos, plates.

Andrés Sas Orchassal (b. Paris, 6 April 1900; d. Lima, 26 Aug. 1967) wrote or participated in the writing of the large Latin American articles (Argentina, Brazil, Chile, Cuba, Guatemala, Honduras, Mexico). Based at Lima, Sas lacked ready access to recent periodical and monographic literature. As a result, this leading Dutch encyclopedia is inferior—even for events preceding 1900. Not he but the editors are to blame for careless oversights reflected in wrong dates and names.

7002 Béhague, Gerard. Folk and traditional music of Latin America: general pros-

pect and research problems (The World of Music [International Music Council, Paris] 25:2, 1982, p. 3–18, bibl., photos)

Most Latin American ethnomusicology has concentrated on description and suffered from lack of theoretical focus.

7003 ———. Tango (*in* The New Grove dictionary of music and musicians. London: Macmillan, 1980, v. 18, p. 563–565, bibl., music, photo)

Encyclopedic summary of the vast literature. Blend of controversial origin theories, with most attention devoted to the tango in Argentina. Although Béhague regards Carlos Gardel (1887–1935) as an "extraordinary figure" allowing him 15 lines, *The New Grove dictionary* does not accord him a biographical article.

7004 Bellenger, Xavier. An introduction to the history of musical instruments in the Andean countries: Ecuador, Peru and Bolivia (The World of Music [International

Music Council, Paris] 25:2, 1982, p. 38–50, ill., map, photos)

Pre-Inca, Inca, Iberian, mestizo instrumental preferences.

7005 Blum, Joseph. Problems of salsa research (SE/E, 22:1, Jan. 1978, p. 137–149, bibl.)

Excellent insights into the prejudices that prevent Latin American music research from taking seriously the "music of the people," concentrating instead on Amerindian and Hispanic forms. "I urge the reader who is interested in Latin American culture, or curious about the word *salsa* to go directly to the (readily available) recorded works of Machito, Tito Puente, Celia Cruz, Pacheco Cortijo, Fajardo, Joe Cuba, Charlie Palmieri, Eddie Palmieri, and if he can find them the older works of Arsenio Rodríguez and Noro Morales . . . Hearing alone is believing."

7006 Brockhaus-Riemann-Musiklexikon: in 2 Bd. Edited by Carl Dahlhaus and Hans Heinrich Eggebrecht. Wiesbaden, FRG; Brockhaus, FRG: Mainz: Schott, 1978–1979. 2 v.: bibl., ill., music.

Not nearly as valuable for Latin American bibliographers as the two-vol. revision and enlargement of the 12th ed. of *Riemann Musik Lexikon* (see HLAS 38:9017), this biographical and subject lexicon was compiled by editors who attached more importance to Afro-Cuban expressions than to other Latin American strands.

7007 Cáceres, Abraham. Preliminary comments on the marimba in the Americas (*in* Essays in honor of George List [see item **7011**] p. 225–250, bibl., disc., music)

African slaves brought the marimba to the New World. The *marimba de arco* borrowed by the Indians of Central America, probably because similar to their own *tun*, developed along different lines from Colombian and Ecuadorian marimbas. Ecuador's Tsátchela and Capaya Indians borrowed not only the marimba but other instruments from the blacks. Central American music is basically homophonic with divisive rhythmic structure, whereas Colombian and Ecuadorian black music is more contrapuntal with additive rhythmic structure, and other elements characteristic of West African music.

7008 Claro-Valdés, Samuel. Música teatral en América (UC/RMC, 35:156, oct./dic. 1981, p. 3–20, bibl.)

Authoritative history of Baroque stage music in the Americas incorporates data from 37 publications and (most importantly) from Archivo General de Indias (*Indiferente General 1608*) and Biblioteca Nacional, Madrid (*Manuscrito 2943*). With his usual careful command of sources, Claro-Valdés summarizes all previously researched data and adds significant new findings concerning stage events with musical interludes at Quito (30 Sept. and 1 Oct. 1789) at Santo Domingo in Hispaniola (from 12 Nov. 1789 through 6 Jan. 1790) at San Felipe de Lerma, Salta, Argentina (5 Dec. 1789), and at Santa Cruz de la Sierra, Bolivia (from 4 Dec. 1789).

7009 Cohen, Aaron I. International encyclopedia of women composers. New York: R.R. Bowker, 1981. 597 p.: bibl., indexes, photos.

This much-touted but extremely unreliable encyclopedia includes 31 Argentines, 24 Brazilians, nine Chileans, 12 Cubans, 10 Mexicans, four Peruvians, five Venezuelans, and a smattering from Central America and Caribbean island countries. Concerning Teresa Carreño (1853–1917), most renowned woman pianist of her generation and a composer, Cohen makes the following typical wrong statements: born of Spanish parents, studied under Arthur (sic) Rubinstein, followed an operatic career until 1882. No biographical or bibliographical data concerning Latin American women in this encyclopedia can be accepted without verification. The 435 numbered bibliographic references (p. 577–585) follow no discernible order—neither alphabetic, chronological, nor any other.

7010 Doyle, John G. Louis Moreau Gottschalk, 1829–1869: a bibliography and catalog of works. Detroit: *published for the* College Music Society *by* Information Coordinators, 1983. 386 p.: disc., facsims., ill., indexes (Bibliographies in American music; no. 7)

During more than two decades since his doctoral dissertation, *The Piano music of Louis Moreau Gottschalk* (New York University, 1960), Doyle has assimilated the widest variety of new Gottschalk published and unpublished research and woven it into a superlative annotated bibliography that devotes most attention to the Caribbean and South American phases of Gottschalk's career and composition.

7011 Essays in honor of George List. Editors, Caroline Card *et al.* Bloomington: Ethnomusicology Publications Group, Indiana University, 1978. 298 p.: bibl., disc., ill., music (Discourse n ethnomusicology; 1)

Festschrift honoring former Director of Archives of Traditional Music and Professor of Folklore at Indiana University, retired in 1976. Contains four essays: Robert Friedman on Cuba; Abraham Cáceres on the Caribbean; Barbara Seit on Mexico; and Robert E. Fogal on Argentina.

7012 Geijerstam, Claes af. Spanskamerikansk musik (*in* Sohlmans musiklexikon [see item **7022**] v. 5, p. 438–439)

Useful survey of popular and folkloric genres by author of *Popular music in Mexico* (Albuquerque: Univ. of New Mexico Press, 1976, 201 p., originally Uppsala University dissertation).

7013 López, Raymond V. Twelfth Inter-American Music Festival: Washington, D.C. May 8–14, 1981 (IAMR, 3:2, Spring/Summer 1981,p. 209–211)

Works performed included composers from the following countries: 12, US; four, Brazil; four, Mexico; three, Argentina; two, Chile; two, Uruguay; one, Puerto Rico.

7014 Marco, Guy A. and **Sharon Paugh Ferris.** Information on music: a handbook of reference sources in European languages. v. 2, The Americas. Foreword by James Coover. Littleton, Colo.: Libraries Unlimited, 1977. 296 p.: indexes.

This bibliography should supersede Gilbert Chase's *A Guide to the music of Latin America.* Reviewed in *Notes* (3:4, June 1978, p. 881), *The Music Times* (London, 120:1634, April 1979, p. 310), and *Inter American Music Review* (3:1, Fall 1980, p. 113–114).

7015 Die Musikkulturen Lateinamerikas im 19. Jahrhundert. Edited by Robert Günther. Regensburg, FRG: Gustav Bosse Verlag, 1982. 464 p.: bibl., facsims., index, music, photos (Studien zur Musikgeschichte des 19. Jahrhunderts; Bd. 57)

Chile emerges as the best served na-

tion in this much-delayed anthology of scholarship on 19th-century Latin American music. Reviewed in *Inter-American Music Review* (5:2, Spring/Summer 1983). See individual entries under Argentina (Aretz, item **7028**; Lange, item **7035**), Bolivia (Mesa, item **7046**), Brazil (Lange, item **7070**), Caribbean (except Cuba by Flores; Lewin; Thompson, item **7095**), Chile (Claro Valdés; Merino, item **7121**; Pereira Salas, item **7123**), Mexico (Sordo Sodi, item **7177**), Uruguay (Lange, item **7198**), and Venezuela (Ramón y Rivera). Günther begins this anthology at p. 9–19 with an overview of the entire history of music in Latin America, *Die Musikkulturen im Lateinamerikas im 19. Jahrhundert Tendenzen and Perspektiven*, buttressed by a 128-item bibliography.

7016 Olsen, Dale A. Folk music of South America: a musical mosaic (*in* Musics of many cultures: an introduction. Edited by Elizabeth May. Berkeley: University of California Press, 1980 [i.e. 1983] p. 386–425, bibl., disc., film., ill., music)

Acceding to the wider definition of folk music current in Latin American parlance (almost anything popular), Olsen covers musical expressions tinctured with possible Amerindian influences, black African musical derivatives, as well as inevitable Spanish and Portuguese song- and dance-types current among less economically privileged South Americans. Again, space limitation drastically limits him. Quotations range from Nicolas Slonimsky (1945) to John Storm Roberts (1974). The book which contains this essay does not cover Mexico, the Caribbean, or Central America.

7017 ———. Symbol and function in South American Indian music (*in* Music of many cultures: an introduction. Edited by Elizabeth May. Berkeley: University of California Press, 1980 [i.e. 1981] p. 363–385, bibl., disc., film., ill., music)

Olsen deserves much praise as he was allowed only 23 p. to cover the indigenous music of an entire continent (e.g., seven p. are taken up with three ills., map, and 10 musical examples). A "particularly excellent article" (Jeromy Montagu) and "well presented" (Thomas Vennum, Jr.).

7018 Orrego-Salas, Juan. LASA y la música (UC/RMC, 36:158, julio/dic. 1982, p. 50–52)

The Venezuelan Antonio Estévez's *Concierto* and Carlos Chávez's *Sinfonía India* were played (during LASA's ninth national meeting, Indiana University, Oct. 1980). Gerard Béhague presided at session on "The Place of Music in Latin American Studies" and read paper at another on "Afro-Brazilian Traits in Selected Nationalist Works of Brazilian 20th-century Composers." Luis Merino also spoke on "Acario Cotapos: a Chilean composer in New York," and Gerald Benjamin on "Julian Carrillo's Contribution to the Music of the Future."

7019 Ramírez Salcedo, Carlos. Algunas consideraciones sobre la música folklórica (CCE/RA, 7, nov. 1981, p. 27–57, ill.)

Platitudes concerning "music as art," "music as science," "our integral definition of music," "some aspects of folkmusic," the "cultural value of music," and other generalized topics.

Ramón y Rivera, Luis Felipe. Fenomenología de la etnomúsica latinoamericana. See item **962.**

7020 Rosentiel, Léonie. The New World (*in* Schirmer history of music. New York: Schirmer Books, 1982, p. 832–946, bibl., ill., music)

Apart from a few lapses, such as the dates for Gutierre Fernández Hidalgo (ca. 1553–20), and Juan de Lienas (fl. 1550), these 110 p. include the best succinct survey of music in the Americas (especially to 1900) in a general history presently being marketed.

7021 Singer, Roberta L. Tradition and innovation in contemporary Latin popular music in New York City (LAMR, 4:2, Fall/Winter 1983, p. 183–202, bibl., music)

Research for this paper and for her PhD dissertation *"My music is who I am and what I do: Latin popular music and identity in New York City* (Indiana University, 1982) occupied Singer Aug. 1977 through Jan. 1980. Topics covered in this paper include: The Role of the Music Collectors; Musical Values and Concepts (e.g., clave, tradition and experimentation, pitch-timbre-rhythm complex-improvisation, Latin jazz). Notes contain definitions of *Latino, salsa,* and *típico* as used by performers. This informed essay assumes added value because the bibliography of serious studies of Latin urban popular expression remains all too tenuous.

7022 Sohlmans musiklexikon. Huvudred., Hans Astrand. 2., revid. o. utvidgade uppl. Stockholm: Sohlman, 1975–1979. 5 v.: bibl., ill., indexes, music.

Following current trends, *Sohlmans* includes individual country articles on Argentina, Brazil, Chile (Samuel Claro-Valdés), Cuba, Ecuador, Mexico (Carmen Sordo Sodi), Peru (César Arróspide de la Flor), and Venezuela of value directly proportional to the reputation of the writers. This lexicon also abounds in Latin American biographies.

7023 Stevenson, Robert. The Americas in European music encyclopedias: pts. 1–2 (IAMR, 3:2, Spring/Summer 1981, p. 159–207; 5:1, Fall 1982, p. 109–116)

Two-part history and criticism of New World coverage in English, French, and Portuguese music lexicons. Special attention given *The New Grove dictionary of music and musicians* (London: Macmillan, 1980, 20 v.). Includes alphabetical lists of articles by leading contributors.

7024 ———. Caribbean music history: a selective annotative bibliography with musical supplement (IAMR, 4:1, Fall 1981, p. 1–112, music)

See Donald Thompson's review in *Latin American Music Review* (4:2, Fall/Winter 1983, p. 282–286).

7025 ———. Isabel Aretz: composer (IAMR, 5:2, Spring/Summer 1983, p. 2–5)

Compositional career of the director of INIDEF (Instituto Internacinal de Etnomusicología y Folklore), b. Buenos Aires but since marriage resident in Venezuela with her husband Luis Felipe Ramón y Rivera.

7026 ———. Latin America in *Ilustración Musical Hispano-Americana* (IAMR, 3:2, Spring/Summer 1981, p. 151–158)

Latin American musical items of sufficient value to merit summary and evaluation in the present chronologically arranged survey, appear in *Ilustración Musical Hispano-Americana* (152 issues: 30 Jan. 1888–15 May 1894). Edited by Felipe Pedrell in Barcelona.

7027 Tallmadge, William H. Salsa anyone? (Sonneck Society Newsletter [Brighton, Mass.] 9:1, Spring 1983, p. 2–23, disc.)

Good introduction to current salsa, with valuable discography of 14 discs obtainable at time of writing from Disco Latin

Club (P.O. Box 132, Rutherford, N.J. 06060–0132). Tallmadge properly decries salsa's neglect in the journal *Popular Music and Society*, which in 24 issues included one article on Jamaican reggae, excluding every other popular musical expression from Latin America.

ARGENTINA

7028 Aretz de Ramón y Rivera, Isabel. La música del gaucho (*in* Die Musikkulturen Lateinamerikas im 19. Jahrhundert [see item **7015**] p. 37–63, bibl., facsims., ill., music)

Representative *cifras*, *milongas*, *décimas*, and *estilos* sung by Argentine plainsmen who herded cattle before 1881 were published (music and texts) in first book devoted to the nation's folklore, Ventura R. Lynch's *La provincia de Buenos Aires* (1883). Tonic-dominant harmony in major keys prevailed in the accompaniments strummed on five-course guitars. Typical texts portray the cowboy singer dying of love.

7029 Arizaga, Rodolfo. Crónicas americanas en la vida y muerte de Manuel de Falla (Revista Musical de Venezuela [Caracas] 3:6, enero/abril 1982, p. 49–71)

Minutely detailed account of Falla's life in Argentina from his arrival in Buenos Aires on 18 Oct. 1939 to his death in Alta Gracia on 14 Nov. 1946. Gossipy epilogue contains newspaper accounts of his funeral honors and of the Argentinian premiere of *Atlántida* (3 May 1963).

7030 Béhague, Gerard and **Isabel Aretz de Ramón y Rivera.** Argentina (*in* The New Grove dictionary of music and musicians. London: Macmillan, 1980, v. 1, p. 564–671, bibl., music, photos)

Section on art music contains erroneous statement that Blas Parera, composer of the Argentine national anthem, died in 1817 (d. Mataró, near Barcelona, 7 Jan. 1840), omits important data concerning first opera composed and mounted in Argentina, and is weak in other respects. Most recent item in the art music bibliography is Rodolfo Arizaga's 1971 encyclopedia (see *HLAS 36:4520*). The folk music section profits from in-depth coverage (two-thirds of the article) and a much fuller and more up-to-date bibliography.

7031 Estrella, Miguel Angel. Playing for the people (INDEX, 12:1, Feb. 1983, p. 11–15)

Impassioned interview with Argentine pianist (b. 1937, Tucumán province village). Studied at Buenos Aires national conservatory whose instruction he chararacterized as "mediocre, reactionary, and elitist, catering to the reactionary bourgeoisie." Later studied in Paris with Nadia Boulanger. Incarcerated at La Libertad prison in Uruguay, he emerged to play his first concert after being freed in Nicaragua.

7032 Ferrer, Horacio. El libro del tango: crónica & diccionario, 1850–1977. Buenos Aires: Editorial Galerna, 1977. 769 p.

Begins with highly laudatory biography of Horacio Ferrer (b. 2 June 1933, Montevideo), by Jorge Siejo and three other admirers (p. 11–17). Continues with chronicle of tango divided into seven epochs (i.e., 1850–80, 1880–95, 1895–1910, 1910–25, 1925–40, 1940–55, 1955–70) and with an alphabetically ordered biographical, topical, and geographical dictionary (p. 233–763). Lacking bibliographies, the biographical portion nonetheless gives exact birth and death dates, plus much other exact details that makes it a far more precise instrument for tango than Rodolfo Arizaga's *Enciclopedia de la música argentina* (1972) is for art music.

7033 Fogal, Robert Edwin. Traditional music and the middle class in Argentina: context and currents (*in* Essays in honor of George List [see item **7011**] p. 267–278, bibl.)

Whereas the elite had before 1920 looked to Europe for musical models, "gaucho music" was purveyed to Argentina's middle classes after the 1916 centennial as a symbol of the nation's identity. Shift toward learning guitar instead of piano, commercialization of "folklore," and radio stations' fostering mass media "folk music" reached an apogee in 1960s. Essay served as preliminary to Fogal's PhD dissertation, *Traditional music and the middle class: a case study of Mercedes, province of Buenos Aires, Argentina* (Indiana University, 1981, 378 p.).

7034 Fontana, Adriana. El órgano en el Argentina: época colonial y siglo XIX (Revista del Instituto de Investigación Musicológica Carlos Vega [Universidad Católica Argentina, Facultad de Artes y Ciencias Musicales, Buenos Aires] 5:5, 1982, p. 49–50)

Useful compilation of data on organs and organ building in Argentina from 1585 (Santiago de Estero), 1607 (Church of San Francisco, Córdoba), 1620 (Buenos Aires Cathedral), 1691–93 (fabrication of organs at Jesuit mission of Yapeyú staffed by Anton Sepp), to end of 19th century. Author uses data excerpted from Grenón, Furlong Cardiff, García de Loydi's *La Catedral de Buenos Aires* (1971) and Rodolfo Barbacci.

7035 Lange, Francisco Curt. La música en la Argentina del siglo XIX (*in* Die Musikkulturen Lateinamerika im 19. Jahrhundert [see item **7015**] p. 65–91)

Argentina's preeminent role in 20th-century Latin American music was spurred by a phenomenal influx of capable foreign-born musicians in previous century. They were of such varied origin as José Antonio Picasarri from Spain (uncle of Juan Pedro Esnaola, 1808–78); Esteban Massini and Santiago Massoni from Italy, by way of Lisbon and Rio; Mariano Pablo Rosquellas from Spain, via Rio; and Johann Heinrich Amelung from Germany. Thalberg, José Amat, Louis Moreau Gottschalk, José White, Claudio José Domingo Brindis de Salas, and Edelmiro Mayer exemplify the foreign-born of widely different provenance whose visits or residences stimulated developments after Rosas' fall. Native-born composers ranged from the first opera composer to levy national folklore, Francisco A. Hargreaves (1849–1900), to Zenón Rolón (1856–1902) of partially African descent, and the Berutti brothers, Arturo (1862–1938) and Pablo (1866–1914) of Italian descent. The French-trained Alberto Williams (1862–1952) founded a conservatory chain, a musical review, and published a plethora of his own works. Musical reviews were founded at Buenos Aires in 1853 (*El Semanario*), 1874 (*La Gaceta Musical*), 1882 (*Mefistófeles*), 1886 (*El Arte*) and later on, at an increasing rate. Music publishing firms, and concert and opera halls springing in profusion responded to the cultural interests of multiplying immigrants that beginning with British and continuing through French, German, and Italian waves, made Argentina the richest and most populous Spanish-speaking nation in South America—with all that riches imply for the development of art music. English summary.

7036 Pérez Bugallo, Rubén. Un caso de folklore urbano: las comparsas salteñas (Revista del Instituto de Investigación Musicológica Carlos Vega [Universidad Católica Argentina, Facultad de Artes y Ciencias Musicales, Buenos Aires] 5:5, 1982, p. 31–48, music, photos)

Minute description of carnival processions in Salta. Carnival songs are exclusively *vidalas*, always in 6/8 or 3/8, usually in major. Six collected by Carlos Vega in 1938 are shown in music notation, plus two collected in 1981. Author, representing Argentina's Instituto Nacional de Musicología, began collecting in Jan. 1979 and finished at end of 1983. Three Argentine provinces exhaustively toured thus far in search of oral traditional music are Tucumán and La Rioja by Isabel Aretz (publications in 1946 and 1978) and La Pampa by Ercilia Moreno Chá (two LPs, *Documental folklórico de la Provincia de la Pampa*, 1975).

7037 Reichardt, Dieter. Tango Verweigerungund Trauer: Kontexte und Texte. Frankfurt, FRG: Vervuert, 1981. 270 p.: bibl., disc., ill (some col.), music.

In this coffee table book, the first of its scope and ambition in German, p. 110–248 are devoted to tango texts (alphabetized by title) accompanied by parallel translations in German. Lutz Bernsau's 25 interpretive water colors and charcoals, reproduced luxuriously, intermingle with the texts. Much more interested in sociopolitical context than music, Reichardt contents himself with a minimum of biography (mostly in end notes). The tango-canción dominates his discussion. The three music items, all with text, shown in facsimile (p. 13, 25, 33) are *Mentira*, *Milonga sentimental*, and *Malevaje* (music by Francisco Pracánico, Sebastián Plana, Juan de Dios Filiberto). Lack of index seriously prejudices value of this lavish oversize volume.

7038 Sas, Andrés and J. Gansemans. Argentinië (*in* Alegmene muziek encyclopedie [see item **7001**] p. 124–127, bibl.)

This out-of-date, unreliable article, like that on Bolivia by Gansemans in the same volume (p. 386–387), does this luxurious lexicon no honor.

7039 Suárez Urtubey, Pola. La musicografía argentina en la proscripción: un documento en el Buenos Aires rosista (Revista del

Instituto de Investigacion Musicológica Carlos Vega [Universidad Católica Argentina, Facultad de Artes y Ciencias Musicales, Buenos Aires] 5:5, 1982, p. 7–30, music)

In this chapter from her unpublished book, *Antecedentes de la musicología en la Argentina: documentación y exégesis*, author studies writings on musical subjects by exiles: Miguel Cané (padre) who wrote on Bellini and operatic matters (1859–60); Domingo Faustino Sarmiento's prolific musical journalism largely dedicated in 1840s to Italian opera as heard in Santiago de Chile. To him musical education mattered chiefly as a civilizing influence. Also discusses the precocious guitarist-composer Francisco Cruz Cordero (1822–63).

7040 ———. Los primeros estudios etnomusicológicos en el área de Tierra del Fuego (Revista del Instituto de Investigación Musicológica Carlos Vega [Universidad Católica Argentina, Facultad de Artes y Ciencias Musicales, Buenos Aires] 4:4, 1981, p. 7–23, music)

Extracted from author's doctoral thesis (Universidad Católica Argentina), this is a useful compilation of observations on Fuegian music in publications antedating World War I. Of much more specific value are the publications of Charles Wellington Furlong, who visited Tierra del Fuego in 1907 and 1908 (Onas, Yámanas or Yaganes) and Robert Lehmann-Nitsche, both of whom made cylinder recordings. Furlong's, augmented by Martin Gusinde's recordings (1922–23), gave Hornbostel the aural data on which was based "Fuegian Songs" in *American Anthropologist* (July/Sept. 1936). Curt Sachs was misinformed in classing the Fuegians as utterly lacking in instruments of any kind. Fuegian songs and vocal style have musical characteristics utterly unlike those of other American Indian tribes known to Hornbostel.

Vega, Carlos. Apuntes para la historia del movimiento tradicionalista argentino. See item **976.**

7041 Vignati, M.E. Fuentes bibliográficas de la música aborigen argentina (Revista del Instituto de Investigación Musicológica Carlos Vega [Universidad Católica Argentina, Facultad de Artes y Ciencias Musicales, Buenos Aires] 3:3, 1979, p. 44–54)

Summary of chroniclers' and travellers' observations on aboriginal music in Argentina to 1800.

BOLIVIA

7042 Bauman, Max Peter. Music, dance, and song of the Chipayas, Bolivia (LAMR, 2:2, Fall/Winter 1981, p. 171–222, bibl., music, photos)

Listed as a Swiss investigator currently "assistant professor at Berlin's Free University in the Department of Comparative Musicology (West Germany)," author is elsewhere in this issue identified as the model ethnomusicologist responsible for the LP 12-inch disc with accompanying 36-p. explanatory booklet, *Música andina de Bolivia* (Lauro Records, LP LI/s-062, 1980). In the characteristic song of the Chipayas who live 200 km southwest of Oruro at 3800 m. above sea level, women vocalize textless melodies at "a very high range, with slurred pitches prominent and a predominantly descending melody line." Author discusses *sikus, pututu, guitarrillas*, and other instruments ("the playing of them with the exception of the llama bells, which the women ring as they dance, is reserved exclusively for men").

7043 Becerra Casanovas, Rogers. Reliquias de Moxos: danzas, música, instrumentos musicales y fiestas costumbristas del Beni, con un epílogo sobre los silvícolas sirionó y moré; el Mamoré y las sublevaciones indígenas contra los blancos. 2a. ed. La Paz: Editorial Casa Municipal de la Cultura Franz Tamayo, 1977. 325 p.: bibl., ill., music (Biblioteca paceña)

Author calls this lavish collection of his historical and ethnomusicological writings (supplemented by his transcriptions and original musical compositions) the second edition of his *Reliquias de moxos: tratado histórico sobre el origen y significado de las danzas y de la música beniana* (La Paz: Inti, 1959, 75 p.). Despite heterogeneous character of both compilations, the patient investigator can profit from them—especially the 1978 ed. (see Robert Stevenson's review in *Inter-American Music Review*, 5:2, Spring/Summer 1983).

7044 Béhague, Gerard and **Julia Fortún.** Bolivia (*in* The New Grove dictionary of music and musicians. London: Macmillan, 1980, v. 2, p. 871–876, bibl., ill.)

Art music occupies one page, folk the rest. Leading Potosí colonial composer (Antonio Durán de la Mota) not mentioned, nor any Bolivian 19th-century composers. Deficient bibliography.

7045 García Muñoz, Carmen. Aproximación a la obra de Juan de Araujo (Revista del Instituto de Investigación Musicológica Carlos Vega [Universidad Católica Argentina, Facultad de Artes y Ciencias Musicales, Buenos Aires] 4:4, 1981, p. 25–65, facsims., music)

With her accustomed mastery, author accompanies her transcriptions of the two villancios *Al llanto más tierno a 4* with harp (Ti Ti A Te, Arpa) and *Salga el torrilo hosquillo a 8* with continuo (Ti Ti A Te, Ti A Te B, Acompañamiento) with penetrating commentary. Her catalog lists 159 works by Araujo (85 with complete sets of parts, 72 with incomplete); six works are credited to Cuzco (Archivo del Seminario de San Antonio Abad), one to San Ignacio de Moxos church in Bolivia, the rest to the Biblioteca Nacional at Sucre. Thus far, García Muñoz has identified Sor Juana Inés de la Cruz as author of three texts set by Araujo (*Los que tienen hambre; Si Dios se contiene en el sacramento; Venid mortales, venid a la audiencia*) and Manuel de León Marchante as writer of another (*Zagalejos venid y notad*).

7046 Mesa F., José de and **Carlos Seoane U.** La música de Bolivia durante el siglo XIX (*in* Die Musikkulturen Lateinamerikas im 19. Jahrhundert [see item **7015**] p. 93–120, bibl.)

Written by art historian aided by contributor to *The New Grove dictionary* (London: Macmillan, 1980), this survey usefully compiles information from Nicolás Fernández Naranjo's *La vida musical en la Paz* (1948) from Mesa's own previous *La música en Bolivia* (1969) and from Stevenson's data on Bolivia in *The music of Peru* (1960).

7047 Seoane Urioste, Carlos. Música virreinal en Bolivia: la *Misa* de Zipoli y otras obras musicales (Revista Musical de Venezuela [Caracas] 5:6, enero/abril 1982, p. 33–48, music)

Reprinted from *Arte y Arqueología* (1975), journal edited by Teresa Gisbert de Mesa, essay contains analyses of two anonymous motets from Julia Elena Fortún's private collection, the second dated 1782 (*Sub tuum presidium a 4*, with continuo, E minor). Seoane U. also remarks on Zipoli's *Mass in F* copied at Potosí in 1784 and performed under his direction at the Paraninfo, Universidad de San Andrés, La Paz, 11 Dec. 1972. Among various mistakes, Seoane U. errs in supposing that Furlong Cardiff "discovered" the music archive at Sucre Cathedral or that Robert Stevenson "photographed" any of the music in that archive. Lamberto Baldi, who delivered his "revision" of Robert Stevenson's transcription of the Zipoli *Mass* to Ricordi Americana in Buenos Aires, transcribed none of it himself.

7048 ———. Música virreinal en Bolivia: la música de Zipoli y otras obras musicales (Revista Musical de Venezuela [Caracas] 3:7/8, mayo/dic. 1982, p. 125–147, music)

Discussion of *Credo* and *Sanctus* of Zipoli's *Mass* discovered in Sucre Cathedral music archive by Robert Stevenson, followed by marred section on Juan de Araujo (wrong year of death, wrong archival location of Araujo's *Los Negritos*), and author's transcriptions of two anonymous motets, *O vos omnes a 4* with continuo, in C minor (dated 1780), and *Sub tuum praesidium a 4* with continuo, in E minor. Due to errors in printing, the order of pages for the two motets should correctly read 137–138, 142, 141, 140, 139, 143, 146, 145, 144. This error-ridden article evinces no independent consultation of Sucre Cathedral capitular acts.

BRAZIL

7049 Appleby, David P. The music of Brazil. Austin: University of Texas Press, 1983. 208 p.: bibl., ill., index, music.

Author, professor of music at Eastern Illinois University, wrote PhD dissertation *A study of selected compositions by contemporary Brazilian composers* (Indiana University, 1956). His book consists of six chapters: 1) Music in the Colony; 2) The Bragança in Brazil; 3) The Awakening of Nationalism; 4) Folk, Popular and Art Music; 5) The Nationalist Composers; and 6) After *Modernismo*. Last two chapters carry more conviction than others. Throughout book reveals substantial defects (see Robert Stevenson's review in *Inter-American Music Review*, 5:2, Spring/Summer 1983).

7050 Azevedo, Luiz Heitor Corrêa de.
Heitor Villa-Lobos (*in* Sohlmans musiklexicon [see item **7022**] v. 5, p. 814, bibl.)
Encyclopedia article with abbreviated works list.

7051 ———. Music and musicians of African origin in Brazil (The World of Music [International Music Council, Paris] 25:2, 1982,p. 53–62, music, photos)
Author's summary: "If only a small fragment, perhaps a minimum, of African music has been preserved in Brazil, the musical genius of the black race has borne its fruits through the contributions of its musicians." Names five outstanding examples culminating in his own teacher José Paulo Silva (1892–1967), black as a Senegalese, doctor of laws, and music authority of the first rank.

7052 Béhague, Gerard. Rasgos afrobrasileños en obras nacionalistas escogidas de compositores brasileños del siglo XX (UC/RMC, 36:158, julio/dic. 1982, p. 53–59)
Survey of 2oth-century compositions by Nepomuceno, Villa-Lobos, Camargo Guarnieri, and José Siqueira, showing Afro-Brazilian influences.

7053 ———. Brazil (*in* The New Grove dictionary of music and musicians. London: Macmillan, 1980, v. 3, p. 221–244, bibl., maps, music, photos)
Art music occupies four columns, folk music the remainder of encyclopedia article (24 p.). All 36 music examples belong to folk section (which is divided into introduction, indigenous music, Luso-Brazilian folk music traditions, Afro-Brazilian folk music traditions). Art-music bibliography runs to 21 items, most recent being Béhague's *The beginnings of musical nationalism in Brazil* (Detroit: Information Coordinators, 1971, 43 p.) condensed from his PhD dissertation (see *HLAS 34:5023*). Folk music bibliography includes 66 items, most recent dating from 1977.

7054 Bispo, Antônio Alexandre. Die katolische Kirchenmusik in der Provinz São Paulo zur Zeit des brasilianischen Kaiserreiches, 1822–1889. Regensburg, FRG: Gustav Bosse Verlag, 180. 358 p., 74 p. of

plates: bibl., ill., index, music (Kölner Beiträge zur Musikforschung; Bd. 108)
Marking new heights in Brazilian music research, this exposé of Catholic church music life in São Paulo province (1822–89) reveals a plenitude of able chapelmaster-composers scattered at 95 named places, including for example Campinas, Cunha, Santos, and Teitê. Two composers whose resplendent orchestral Masses are excerpted in the music supplement are Elias Alvares Lobo (São Paulo, 9 Aug. 1834–15 Dec. 1901; biography and works analysis, p. 136–145) and Tristão Mariano da Costa (Itú, 6 June 1846–6 April 1980; life and works, p. 146–149). The African-descended Veríssimo Augusto Glória (1867–1952; pictured with two pupils at Tafel 5) amassed a large archive gathered during journeys throughout the hinterland. Immense wealth of names, dates, places, and pieces itemized in Bispo's inaugural dissertation (defended at Cologne before Heinrich Hüschen and Hans Schmidt 30 June 1979) proves especially welcome, because he has magisterially explored a stratum of 19th-century Brazilian musical life hitherto almost completely ignored by historians. Bispo (b. São Paulo, 17 March 1949) earned architect's diploma (São Paulo University, 1972) but also pursued music studies that in 1975 resulted in a stipend for musicological study at Cologne University. Nine years later, he was teaching in West Germany.

7055 ———. Tendências e perspectivas da musicologia no Brasil (Boletim da Sociedade Brasileira de Musicologia [São Paulo] 1:1, 1983, p. 13–52, bibl.)
Sociedade Brasileira de Musicologia (founded São Paulo, 29 Sept. 1981) initiated a new epoch in the scientific study of Brazilian musics. Bispo recalls prior organizations such as Sociedade Nova Difusão Musical (also founded São Paulo, 1969), Associação Brasileira de Folclore, and Centro de Pesquisa de Música Brasileira (dependent on São Paulo's Instituto Musical).

7056 ———. Traditionen des Weihnachtsfestkreises in Brasilien: Anmerkungen zur Musikerziehung (*in* Leichlinger Musikforum. Leichlingen, FRG: Musikschule der Stadt Leichlingen, 181, p. 18–28)
Instruments making Christmas music (pastoral and centered around the crêche) include not only trumpets, clarinets, and saxo-

phones, but also *pandeiros, maracas,* and other folk instruments.

7057 ———. Zur Rezeptionsgeschichte der Kirchenmusik in Brasilien (*in* Musices Aptatio: Collectanea Musicae Sacrae Brasiliensis. Roma: Sekretariat der CIMS, 1981, p. 11–28, facsims., music)

First facsimile shows opening of late 18th-century Bahia chapelmaster Theodoro Cyro de Sousa's *Cor meum,* as newly orchestrated by José de Luz Passos (ca. 1985); second facsimile shows beginning of *Credo* from Sigismund Neukomm's *Missa Solemnis* (1820) composed during Neukomm's Brazilian residence. Excellent essay documents both church music produced by European-born composers who were residents in Brazil during colonial epoch and influx of sacred music by European composers who were never in Brazil. Not only such already well-known facts as the performance of Mozart's *Requiem* (Rio, 1819) and the 1821 rehearsal of Haydn's *Creation,* but also numerous data on spread of lesser known composers' works are included in this seminal article.

7058 Brasil, Hebe Machado. Fróes: um notável músico baiano. Salvador: Empresa Gráfica da Bahia, 1976. 193 p.: bibl., ill., music.

Sílvio Deolindo Fróes (b. Salvador, Bahia, 26 Oct. 1864), was son of musically talented and trained German mother who married Brazilian lawyer. Studied engineering in 1882 at Rio but switched to music wth Miguel Cardoso. Studied with Widor in Paris, remaining in Europe until 1900s. In 1902–03 his songs were sung in Salle Henri Herz and Salle Pleyel. In 1906 he relocated in Bahia where he taught piano for 30 years. His compositions reached 20 opus numbers, opus 18 (1910) having succumbed to impressionism and whole tone scales. He died in Bahia (3 Dec. 1948), respected as the paramount local musician of his generation. Book contains 23 facsimiles of his engraved compositions.

7059 Diniz, Jaime C. Músicos pernambucanos do passado. t. 3. Recife: Universidade Federal de Pernambuco, 1979. 176 p., 48 p. of plates.

Documented biographies of 15 17th-century musicans and three 18th-century (last b. 1796) by premier investigator of Pernambucan music history. Prologue by Fran-

cisco Curt Lange. Reviewed by Castillo Didier in *Revista Musical de Venezuela* (2:5, sept./dic. 1981, p. 127–128).

7060 ———. Notas sobre o piano e seus compositores em Pernambuco: contribução ao I Ciclo de Música Pernambucana para Piano, de Salão e e Teatro. Recife: Edição do Coro Guarapes do Recife, 1980. 54 p.

Program notes for four recitals in the Teatro Santa Isabel at Recife (5, 12, 19, 26 May 1980), giving precious insight into local music history. Reviewed in *Inter-American Music Review* (3:1, Fall 1980, p. 109).

7061 ———. I [i.e. Primeiro] Ciclo de Música Pernambucana para Piano. Recife: Fundação de Cultura Cidade do Recife, 1980. 8 p.: ill.

Cycle included four women composers whose dates and activities Diniz records. Benedicto Raymundo da Silva (1859–1921), possibly the most important male composers programmed in series, was subject of Moacir Medeiros de Sant'Ana's monograph (Maceió: 1966).

7062 Efegê, Jota. Figuras e coisas do carnaval carioca. Apresentação de Artur da Távola. Rio de Janeiro: FUNARTE, 1982. 326 p.: ill., index.

Author, who published *Maxixe: a dança excomungada* (Conquista: 1974), and *Figuras e coisas da música popular brasileira* (Rio de Janeiro: FUNARTE, 1978–1980, 2 v.), throws light on scattered aspects of the Rio Carnival in series of 145 vignettes already previously published as newspaper articles. Topics range from "Carnival doesn't live solely on sambas and marchinhas, but also on valsas," to "At the carnival of 1862, the floor collapsed but the Zouaves guaranteed the continuation of the dance (i.e., although stage floor fell five handspans, dancers masked as Zouaves restored calm, and ball continued until classical final galop). Despite their readability, these vignettes would have to be carefully and individually studied in order to extract from them any orderly, chronological history of Rio Carnival music.

7063 Franchetti, Paulo and **Alcyr Pécora.** Caetano Veloso: seleção de textos, notas, estudos biográfico, histórico e crítico e exercícios. São Paulo: Abril Educação, 1981. 112 p.: bibl.

Caetano Emmanuel Vianna Telles

Veloso (b. Santo Amaro da Purificação, Bahia, 7 Aug. 1942) is the brother of the equally famous recorded popular music star Maria Bethânia. His biography (p. 11) includes marriage to Dedé Gadelha and his first LP *Domingo* in 1967. After forced months abroad in London (1969) and elsewhere for political activism, he returned to Brazil in 1971. In 1977 with Gilberto Gil, he took part in Festival de Arte e Cultura Negra in Nigeria and made the LP *Bicho*. In 1981 he made the LP *Outras Palavras*. Authors (both b. 1954) publish texts of 58 songs by Caetano Veloso transcribed from five LPs.

7064 Franco, Adércio Simões. Música folclórica (UV/L, 7, agosto 1980, p. 18–25, ill.)

After truisms concerning what constitutes folklore and folk music, author cites well known examples of folk influences in the works of Alexandre Levy, Alberto Nepomuceno, Oscar Lorenzo Fernandez, Francisco Mignone, and especially Villa-Lobos.

7065 Giffoni, Maria Amália Corrêa. Danças miúdas do folclore paulista. 2a. ed., ampliada. São Paulo: Livraria Nobel, 1980. 188 p.: bibl., ill., music.

Choreography, costumes, and music, for popular countryside dances collected throughout São Paulo state by University of São Paulo and Unviersidade Mackenzie trained folklorist. Simple piano arrangements provide *habanera* basses for the *ciranda*, *chapéu*, and other dances. Author groups dances by area in which recorded.

7066 Heitor Villa-Lobos (*in* Grote Winkler Prins Encyclopedie 9n 25 delen. Amsterdam: Elsevier, 1983, v. 23, p. 196, bibl.)

Better article than others of comparable length in English-language general encyclopedias. Includes works list and recent literature.

7067 Kiefer, Bruno. Villa-Lobos e o modernismo na música brasileira. Porto Alegre: Editora Movimento, 1981. 179 p.: bibl., ill. (Coleção Luis Cosme; v. 13)

How greatly if at all Villa-Lobos' creative career was shaped by the Week of Modern Art at São Paulo (11–18 Feb. 1922) is ostensible central concern of this generally unsatisfactory book. Ruth Gresh's review

thoroughly chastises this superficial study (see *Latin American Music Review*, 4:2, Fall/Winter 1983, p. 273–277).

7068 Lange, Francisco Curt. Algumas novidades em torno à atividade musical erudita no período colonial de Minas Gerais (LAMR, 4:2, Fall/Winter 1983, p. 247)

On 8 Aug. 1812, 31 Minas Gerais mulatto musicians solicited permission to unionize against the abusive demands of local clergy for free music. Heading their brotherhood (authorized 1 Sept. 1812) was a drummer named Floréncio José Ferreira Coutinho, who was regimental *mestre de música* in succession to Francisco Gomes da Rocha. On 20 May 1735, the Confraternity of The Blessed Sacrament in Our Lady of the Pillar Church at Ouro Preto, agreed that no other confraternity should have the use of an organ being bought for festival occasions, except by Blessed Sacrament confraternity's explicit permission. In 1778, organ was moved for the convenience of the musicians. Despite move, organ continued to need constant repairs. Consequently, this was not likely to have been the organ played by José Joaquim Emerico Lobo de Mesquita and Jerónimo de Souza Lobo at end of century.

7069 ———. La música colonial religiosa de la Capitanía General de Minas Gerais y su incorporación a la vida musical contemporánea (Revista Musical de Venezuela [Caracas] 5:6, enero/abril 1982, p. 11–32)

Paper includes numerous valuable precisions. When Lange began his Minas Gerais researches in 1944, very few 18th-century music manuscripts survived. Later copies (often defective and anonymous) abounded, but not originals. Chapelmaster posts in Minas Gerais Captaincy (1716–49) were held not by ecclesiastics but by laity, apparently always mulattos. For that matter, mulattos continued to monopolize music-making in Minas Gerais until well after independence. Music for festivals sponsored by confraternities belonged to the confraternities themselves, and not to individuals, and was archived at confraternity headquarters. Until 1780 most Minas Gerais works lack composer ascriptions. Even works such as the mulatto José Emerico Lôbo de Mesquita's lovely *Mass in E flat* (*Kyrie* and *Gloria*) took Lange infinite time and pains to reconstruct. When first performed at Rio in late 1958, it still lacked the later-found oboe and flute parts.

7070 ———. A música no Brasil durante o século XIX: Regência-Império-República (*in* Die Musikkulturen Lateinamerikas im 19. Jahrhundert [see item **7015**] p. 121–166)

Exhaustive essay written with Lange's usual masterful command, tracing developments to 1900 and composers active after 1800 (e.g., foreigners: Marcos Portugal, Sigismond Neukomm, Louis Moreau Gottschalk, and José Amat; Brazilians: Antônio Carlos Gomes, José Maurício Nunes Garcia, Francisco Manuel da Silva, Brasílio Itiberê da Cunha, Alexandre Levy, Leopoldo Miguez, Henrique Oswald, Alberto Nepomuceno, and Francisco Braga).

7071 Luiz Heitor Corrêa de Azevedo (*in* Brockhaus-Riemann-Musiklexikon [see item **7006**] v. 1, p. 276)

List of writings stops at 1970. In contrast with Pedro Humberto Allende, Isabel Aretz, Martha Argerich, Claudio Arrau, José Vicente Asuar—to go no farther than the letter A—this lexicon (item **7006**) omits a host of other Latin Americans of commensurate stature (e.g., Becerra Schmidt, Camargo Guarnieri, Francisco Curt Lange, Orrego-Salas, Manuel Ponce, Carlos Vega.).

7072 Mariz, Vasco. A canção brasileira: erudita, folclórica, popular. 3a. ed. Rio de Janeiro: Civilização Brasileira; Brasília: *em convênio com o* Instituto Nacional do Livro, Ministério da Educação e Cultura, 1977. 348 p.

The first ed. with this title, issued by Ministério de Educação e Cultura in 1959, grew out of *A canção de câmara no Brasil* (Pôrto: 1948) published three years after the author entered the Brazilian diplomatic service (see *HLAS 14:3366* and *HLAS 23:5716*).

7073 Neves, José Maria. Villa-Lobos, o choro e os choros. São Paulo: Musicália Cultura Musical, 1977. 92 p.

In this translated condensation of his thesis, *Les choros: synthèse de la pensée musicale de Villa-Lobos* (La Sorbonne, 1971), author traces relationships between popular *choro* and 14 by Villa-Lobos, which he analyzes individually. However, constant allusion to music examples that are absent from this booklet seriously compromises value of analyses.

7074 Peppercorn, Lisa M. Heitor Villa-Lobos (*in* Brockhaus-Riemann-Musiklexikon [see item **7006**] v. 2, p. 656, bibl.)

In contrast with the scandalously poor article on Carlos Gomes in this same lexicon (see item **7006**, v. 1, p. 485), Peppercorn's compresses considerable information into 43 lines, plus a 13-line bibliography.

7075 Pinto, Tiago de Oliveira. Considerações sobre a musicologia comparada alemã: experiências e implicações no Brasil (Boletim da Sociedade Brasileira de Musicologia [São Paulo] 1:1, 1983, p. 69–106, ill., music)

Invaluable rundown of German studies of Brazilian ethnic musics.

7076 Pontificia Universidade Católica do Rio de Janeiro. O ciclo do ouro: o tempo e a música do barroco católico. Pesquisa de Elmer C. Corrêa Barbosa. Assessoria no trabalho de campo, Adhemar Campos Filho, Aluízio José Viegas. Catalogação das músicas do século XVIII, Cleofe Person de Mattos. Rio de Janeiro: Ministério da Educação e Cultura, FUNARTE: Xerox, 1979. 454 p.: ill., music.

Cleofe Person de Mattos aided by Roberto Richard Duarte prepared entries for 18th-century liturgical works catalogued (p. 67–275) and culled from 11 archives. Reviewed in *Inter-American Music Review* (3:1, Fall 1980, p. 115–116).

7077 Sempé, Moacir Matheus. A música entre os Guaranis, antes do Jesuítas (*in* Simpósio Nacional de Estudos Missioneiros, 2nd, Santa Rosa, Brazil, 1977. Anais. Santa Rosa: Faculdade de Filosofia, Ciência e Letras Dom Bosco, 1978, p. 190–197, bibl.)

After a *catena* of musical allusions drawn from Jesuit and other missionary services, author concludes that truly autochthonous music, not beholden to European sources, fails to survive among Guarani indigenes—if indeed more than the kind of melodies recorded by Jean de Léry ever existed among them.

7078 Shatunóvskaya, Irina. Arte que hermana a los pueblos (URSS/AL, 1:61, enero 1983, p. 116–121, photos)

List of Latin American participants in the VII International Tchaikovsky Competition (Moscow, 23 June-9 July 1982). Brazilian cellist Antônio Meneses (age 25), who won gold medal in cello, studied at Stuttgart before winning prizes in prior competitions at Barcelona, Rio de Janeiro, and Munich.

7079 Siqueira, Baptista. Os Cariris do Nordeste. Rio de Janeiro: Livraria Editora Cátedra, 1978. 351 p.: bibl., ill., index, music.

Author's lack of formal ethnomusicological training prevents this ambitious book (ostensibly devoted to Cariri Indians of Northeastern Brazil) from being much more than a ramble. Reviewed in *Inter-American Music Review* (5:1, Fall 1982, p. 121–122).

7080 ———. Ficção e música. Rio de Janeiro: Folha Carioca Editora, 1980. 346 p.: bibl., ill., music.

Extremely useful compilation reproduces excerpts relating to music culled from 33 important Brazilian works of fiction published 1842–1923 (p. 21–104).

7081 Souza, José Geraldo. Os precursores das pesquisas etnomusicais no Brasil (Boletim da Sociedade Brasileira de Musicologia [São Paulo] 1:1, 1983, p. 53–67, music)

Concise 100-year survey of Brazilian writings on Brazilian folkloric and ethnomusicological topics, from Sílvio Romero's *Cantos populares do Brasil* (1883) to present.

7082 Tacuchian, Ricardo. Bandas: anacrônicas ou atuais? (Arte [Revista da Escola de Música e Artes Cênicas da Universidade Federal da Bahia, Salvador] 4, jan./março 1982, p. 59–77)

Brief survey of history of bands in Brazil, followed by assessment of current band movement in Rio de Janeiro state. In 1982, more than 60 bands participated in the 7th Congress of Rio de Janeiro state bands. Author teaches music history at Universidade Federal do Rio de Janeiro.

7083 Welch, James B. The organ in Brazil: pts. 1–3 (The Diapason [American Institute of Organbuilders, Des Plains, Ill.] 71:6, June 1980, p. 1, 6–7; 71:7, July 1980, p. 1, 14–15; 71:10, Oct. 1980, p. 16–20, bibl., ill.)

Historical aperçu by traveling organ professor reviewed in *Inter-American Music Review* (4:2, Spring/Summer 1982, p. 87–88).

THE CARIBBEAN (except Cuba)

7084 Agerkop, T. Surinam (*in* The New Grove dictionary of music and musicians. London: Macmillan, 1980, v. 18, p. 374–377, bibl., photos)

Encyclopedia article dealing solely with ethnic musics (Amerindians, Bush Negroes, rural and urban Creoles and blacks, East Indians, Javanese) to the complete neglect of European and Jewish settlers' art music achievements. Bibliography is correspondingly weak and partial.

Aho, William R. Sex conflict in Trinidad calypsoes, 1969–1970. See *HLAS 45:1040.*

7085 Caso, Fernando H. Héctor Campos Parsi en la historia de la música puertorriqueña del siglo XX. San Juan: Instituto de Cultura Puertorriqueña, 1980. 156 p.: bibl., ill., music.

Reworked Indiana University 1972 Master's thesis also briefly covers Jack Delano, Amaury Veray, and other contemporaries of Campos Parsi. Reviewed in *Inter-American Music Review* (4:2, Spring/Summer 1982, p. 91).

7086 Dancis, Bruce. Marley's ghost: reggae today (Mother Jones [Foundation for National Progress, San Francisco, Calif.] 7:10, Dec. 1982, p. 54–55, photos)

Among Jamaican groups reaching out for US acceptance, author favorably mentions Steel Pulse and Black Uhruru. In Jamaica itself, "toasting" in which vocalists sing/talk their lyrics over lengthy recordings is a favorite form of reggae, but "toasting" is not understandable outside the island. The purer the reggae messianic message, the less exportable it tends to become.

7087 Davis, Martha Ellen. Himnos y anthems—"coros"—de los "americanos" de Samaná: contexos y estilos (MHD/B, 10:16, 1981, p. 85–107, ill.)

Of the approximately 6,000 blacks who in 1824–25 were persuaded by African Methodist Episcopal Bishop Richard Allen to settle in Hispaniola (then ruled by black president Boyer of Haiti), only a remnant survived at Samaná when in 1928 Elsie Crews Parsons published "Spirituals from the 'American' colony of Samaná Bay, Santo Domingo" in *Journal of American Folklore* (41,

p. 525–528). After 1930, the preservation of the African Methodist Episcopal musical heritage in Samaná became progressvely more difficult. Likewise, the Iglesia Evangélica Dominicana has similarly lost most of its English langue heritage. Only at wakes, where old people sing, are hymns in English still sung. Forms part of author's (PhD, University of Illinois, 1976) ongoing series that began in *Boletín del Museo del Hombre Dominicano* (14, 1980, p. 165–198).

Davis, Martha Ellen. Voces del purgatorio: estudio de la salve dominicana. See item **1092.**

7088 Desroches, Monique. Validation empirique de la méthode sémiologique en musique: le cas de indicatifs de tambour dans les céremonies indiennes en Martinique (Yearbook of the International Folk Music Council [Urbana, Ill.] 11, 1980, p. 67–76, tables)

Revision of paper given at meeting of Society of Ethnomusicology (Montreal, 1979). Between 1854–83, 26,000 Asian-Indians (mostly Dravidians) were brought to Martinique to do tasks formerly assigned to black slaves. Author foresees extinction (ca. 1990) of their cult involving: 1) priest who addresses saints in Tamoul; 2) interpreter who translates into Creole; and 3) drummers. Includes tables of drum rhythms heard during animal sacrifice ceremonies.

7089 Dower, Catherine. Puerto Rican music following the Spanish American War, 1898: the aftermath of the Spanish American War and its influence on the musical culture of Puerto Rico. Lanham, Md.: University Press of America, 1983. 203 p.: bibl., index, music.

Uses book to refute Fernando Callejo's influential opinion that musical life declined after 1898. Topics of first six chapters: 19th-century musical tradition; economic and cultural regression; arrival of the Americans; George Cabot Ward and Puerto Rican society; public schools and music in the curriculum; musical activities in the island in the early 20th century. Next, she profiles 15 Puerto Rican musicians active in that period: Casimiro Duchesne (1850–1906); Angel Mislán (1862–1911); Julio Carlos de Arteaga (1865–1923); José Ignacio Quintón (1881–1925); Julián Andino (1854–1926); Fernando Callejo (1862–1926); Juan Ríos Ovalle (1867–

1928); Rafael Balseiro Dávila (1867–1929); Braulio Dueño Colón (1854–1934); Arístides Chavier (1867–1942); Amalia Paoli (1861–1942); Elisa Tavárez (1879–1960); Monsita Ferrer (1882–1966); Ramón Morlá (1875–1953); and Jesús Figueroa (1878–1971).

Folklore infantil de Santo Domingo. See item **1096.**

7090 Gilliam, Rita. The politics of reggae music. Kingston: J. Rodgers, 198? 12 leaves.

Racist attitudes in US are blamed for America's less than wholehearted espousal of reggae. "Through a unique relationship with Haile Selassie I, the believing Rastafarian has entered into a divine state of daughtership and sonship . . . The political leadership of Haile Selassie speech is sung over a heavy bassed beat by Bob Marley."

7092 Mancebo, Licinio. El Archivo Nacional de Música de la República Dominicana y su historia (HET, 13:68, enero/marzo 1980, p. 47–48)

Founded by presidential decree (15 Nov. 1968), the Dominican Republic National Music Archive has been directed since 1971 by Licinio Macebo, who here summarizes its activities.

7093 Mastrogiovanni, Antonio. II [i.e. Segunda] Bienal de Música Contemporánea en Puerto Rico (Revista Musical de Venezuela [Caracas] 2:3, enero/abril 1981, p. 71–74)

From 20 Aug. to 21 Sept. 1980, San Juan hosted 17 concerts of mostly avant-garde music by European and American composers.

7094 Sáenz Coopat, Carmen María. Respirar este aire es algo bien bonito (Boletín de Música [Casa de las América, La Habana] 86/87, enero/abril 1981, p. 15–22, plate)

In 1976, five University of Puerto Rico students, including Iván González, spokesman for them, began performing satires at small café-theaters. Group favored Puerto Rican independence and believed salsa was merely Cuban music several years old. Two of group's LPs have sold in excess of 135,000 copies. Their best selling disc includes their version of Nicolás Guillén's *La muralla* and songs by Mercedes Sosa. "To breathe this [Havana] atmosphere is something really pleasant"—is spokesman's phrase for article's title.

7095 Thompson, Donald. Nineteenth-century musical life in Puerto Rico (*in* Die Musikulturen Lateinamerikas im 19. Jahrhundert [see item **7015**] p. 327–332, bibl.)

First public concerts by visiting foreign virtuosos took place in 1827, first opera presentation (*Il barbieri di Siviglia*) in 1835. First permanent theater was inaugurated in 1832 (Teatro Municipal at San Juan). *Guarionex* (1856) was first opera by island-born composer Felipe Gutiérrez Espinosa. Manuel Tavárez, Juan Morel Campos, and Braulio Dueño Colón exemplified excellent native-born composers, who, however, cultivated less ambitious genres than opera. Includes Spanish language summary.

7096 Torre, Lola de la. Domingo Crisanto Delgado: 1806–1858, músico canario, organista en la Catedral de San Juan de Puerto Rico (Revista de Musicología [Madrid] 6:1/2, 1983, p. 529–540)

Domingo Crisanto Delgado (b. 1806) received his musical education at Cathedral of La Laguna, Tenerife. In Dec. 1821, he was employed as singer, Aug. 1826 as copyist, and April 1828 as assistant succentor. Studied harmony and composition with Miguel Jurado de Bustamante, La Laguna Cathedral chapelmaster, from 1826–28. During illnesses of next maestro de capilla, Manuel Fragoso, Delgado wrote needed cathedral music—an Ascensión psalm in 1831, music for the transfer of the bones of a former dean in 1832, etc. In Sept. 1834, he was appointed to teach the cathedral boys. Rivalry with Justo Sierra, who from 1835 taught the cathedral instrumentalists, may have impelled Delgado to quit La Laguna Cathedral in Sept. 1836. In Nov. 1836, he sailed for Puerto Rico, where he entered San Juan Cathedral as second succentor and substitute organist in 1837. From 1848 until his death in San Juan in 1856, he was principal organist. His compositions in the Museo Osuna, Tenerife, include a symphony (*Tempestad*); at the Santa Catalina Convent in La Laguna, 15 religious works; and at the Archivo General de Puerto Rico, another five sacred works, the latest (dated 1856) *Misa "La Providencia."* Includes catalog of compositions.

Warner, Keith Q. Kaiso!, the Trinidad calypso: a study of the calypso as oral literature. See *HLAS 45:1143.*

CENTRAL AMERICA

Acevedo, Jorge Luis. La música en Guanacaste. See item **1043.**

7097 Borgen, José Francisco. Letras y música de la canción folklórica (BNBD, 48, julio/agosto 1982,p. 89–91, ill.)

Paramount among popular Nicaraguan singer-composers is the physically not prepossessing Camilo Zapata, author of cattle song *El ganao colorao.* Trío Mominbó takes its name from *Monimbó,* widely diffused song by Erwin Krüger (b. León, Nicaragua). Krüger succumbs to Mexican mariachi influences. Cuban influences pervade *El pregón del paletero.*

7098 Brinton, Daniel G. Danzas y bailes de Nicaragua (BNBD, 48, julio/agosto 1982, p. 5–11, ill.)

Carlos Mántica A.'s translation of part of Brinton's preface to *The Güegüence: a comedy-ballet in the Náhuatl-Spanish dialect of Nicaragua* (Philadelphia: 1883).

7099 Brown, Charles T. A Latin American in New York: Alejandro Monestel (LAMR, 3:1, Spring/Summer 1982, p. 124–127, bibl.)

Monestel, the leading Costa Rican composer of his time, worked in US (1901–37). Based on author's PhD dissertation, *Alejandro Monestel, 1865–1950: his life and works* (Minnesota University, 1973), summary draws together best biographical data but lacks complete works list or thorough discussion of Monestel's music.

7100 Canciones corales de la América Latina (HET, 15:76, enero/marzo 1982, p. 51)

Album issued in 1981 by OAS's Performing Arts Division, No. OEA-009, contains on first side Costa Rican folk songs and arrangements. Outstanding among these is *La guaira morada* by Roberto Gutiérrez and Carlos López. Flip side contains folk and folkish songs credited to Bolivia, Brazil, Chile, Colombia, Cuba, Mexico, and Peru. Singers, all unpaid university students and day workers, belong to Coro de Cámara of Orquesta Sinfónica de Costa Rica.

7101 Cardenal Argüello, Salvador. Música indígena para marimba (BNBD, 48, julio/agosto 1982, p. 73–76, ill.)

Two-part article first published in *Cuaderno del Taller San Lucas* (3, 18 Oct. 1943, p. 82–83; 4, 4 Oct. 1944, p. 75–81) and annotated in *HLAS 9:1883* and *HLAS 11:1485.*

7102 Catálogo cronológico de las obras de Luis A. Delgadillo (BNBD, 48, julio/agosto 1982, p. 119–126, ill.)

No attempt is made to update or correct page-for-page unacknowledged reproduction of Pan American Union's *Compositores de América: datos biográficos y catálogos de sus obras* (v. 2, 1956, p. 42–49). Delgadillo died (20 Dec. 1961), five years after this Pan American Union's catalog of his works.

7103 Espinoza, Rudy. *Sinfonía No. 1* (BNBD, 48, julio/agosto 1982, p. 149–162, ill.)

Obviously first conceived for and at the piano, this 51-measure single movement (Allegro moderato, 4/4 chiefly)—scored for paired woodwinds, paired brass, strings, and a modest percussion section—lacks anything distinctly profiled. Movement bears more the character of an introduction.

7104 Flores, Bernal. La vida musical en Costa Rica en el siglo XIX (*in* Die Musikkulturen Lateinamerikas in 19. Jahrhundert [see item **7015**] p. 261–275, bibl., music, photos)

Manuel Mario Gutiérrez (1829–87), composer of national anthem; Alejandro Monestel (1865–1950), Central America's most published composer; and Julio Fonseca (1885–1950), were all native-born Costa Ricans. Population (growing from 50,000 to 300,000 during 19th century) could not sustain large-scale, long-lasting expensive music ventures. Nonetheless, the Costa Rican National Theater, opened in 1897, counts among the best in Latin America.

7105 Garfias, Robert. The marimbas of Mexico and Central America (LAMR, 4:2, Fall/Winter 1983, p. 203–228, bibl., ill., photos)

Noted ethnomusicologist and Dean of School of Fine Arts, University of California, Irvine, distinguishes between two families of

marimba, Colombian/Ecuadorian and Central American/Mexican. Against Marcial Armas Lara, Garfias favors Vida Chenoweth's postulate that the Central American marimba (like all other New World marimbas) traces its ancestry to Africa—but for mostly different reasons than hers. Drawings and photos of African congeners helpfully reinforce Garfias' arguments.

7106 Ibarra Mayorga, Salomón. Monografía del Himno Nacional de Nicaragua (BNBD, 48, julio/agosto 1982, p. 12–28, ill.)

Previously published by the Nicaraguan Ministerio de Relaciones Exteriores in 1955 (23 p.)—with reeditions in 1958 and 1964 (35 p.)—this monograph was written by author of the prize-winning 1918 text, officially adopted in 1939. Author declares the music to have been originally a psalm brought to León around 1789 by Ernesto or Anselmo Castinove, a Toledan friar. Shows samples of melodies used at other times in Nicaraguan history as national anthems (e.g., those adopted in 1889 and 1893).

7107 López Guerra, Tino. Managua (BNBD, 48, julio/agosto 1982, p. 92–93, ill.)

Verse-and-choral refrain song praising Nicaragua's capital as an earthly paradise. Melody harmonized in ubiquitous thirds. Leading tone treated as in Charles Gabriel's *Brighten the corner where you are*, which this *canción corrido* resembles in other respects.

7108 Monsanto, Carlos. Guatemala a través de su marimba (LAMR, 3:1, Spring/Summer 1982, p. 60–72, bibl.)

Mariano López Mayorical in his *La polémica de "La Marimba"* (Guatemala: Editorial José de Pineda Ibarra, 1978) compiled 120 recent newspaper clippings on the origin of the marimba—nationalists favoring Mayan rather than African origin.

7109 Orrego-Salas, Juan A. Luis (Abraham) Delgadillo (*in* The New Grove dictionary of music and musicians. London: Macmillan, 1980, v. 5, p. 335)

Nicaragua's leading composer's death date given as 1962, should read 20 Dec. 1961. *Baker's biographical dictionary* (1978, p. 397) provides a works list.

7110 Pallais, Azarías H. Recordando a Vega Matus (BNBD, 48, julio/agosto 1980, p. 35)

Flowery tribute to Vega Matus (1875–1937), native of Masaya, who studied composition at Guatemala City with Juan Aberle.

7111 Sas, Andrés and **J. Meel.** Guatemala (*in* Algemene muziek encyclopedie [see item **7001**] v. 4, p. 111–112, bibl., photo)

Despite skeleton bibliography (two items), this article like that on Honduras by same authors (same volume, p. 289) falls far below the standard of European-subject articles in this pretentious Dutch language lexicon (item **7001**).

7112 Stocks, Anthony. *Crecerás*: una canción de hamaca (IPGH/FA, 30, 1980, p. 117–120, ill.)

Author's Spanish translation and musical transcription (Idaho University) of lullaby sung by 10-year-old Cuna girl, Griselda María López (Tigre, San Blas, Aug. 1977) to two infants swinging in their hammocks. Rhythm transcribed as eighth- and quarter-notes with phrase-ending rests, melody as first five notes of E flat minor.

7113 *El Ternerito y El zopilote* (BNBD, 48, julio/agosto 1982, p. 87–88, ill.)

Two G major narrative songs (anonymous words and music) in alternating 6/8 and 3/4 (hemiolia), collected by Santamaría musician at Granada, Nicaragua. However, any nationalistic fervor that tries to make these songs uniquely Nicaraguan is belied by the transcriptions.

7114 Vega Miranda, Gilberto. Muestrario musical de la revista *Elite* (BNBD, 48, julio/agosto 1982, p. 36–50, ill.)

The five vocal and two instrumental selections here anthologized (originally published as musical supplements to undesignated issues of 1950s Managua society monthly *Elite*) include two blues (Alberto Ramírez G. and Paco Soto Carrión), danzón (Arturo Picado S.), two fox-trots (Luis F. Urroz and Gilberto Vega), tango (Humberto Arauz M.), and tango canción (Carlos Tunnermann), all crushingly commonplace.

7115 ———. Músicos nicaragüenses de ayer (BNBD, 48, julio/agosto 1982, p. 51–72, ill.)

Brief biographies of 41 musicians beginning with Chico Díaz Zapata (1812–82) and concluding with Arturo Picado (1888–1944). Extracted from author's *Breviario*

(1945–46) noted in *HLAS 13:2714*. Includes 24 music notations (three of which are complete pieces), eight portraits.

CHILE

Agosin, Marjorie. Bibliografía de Violeta Parra. See item **1071.**

7116 Bustos Valderrama, Raquel. El legado de Don Jorge Urrutia Blondel (UC/RMC, 36 :158, julio/dic. 1982, p. 3–5)

In 1981, Juan Amenabar R., Vicedecano of the Facultad de Artes, Universidad de Chile, bespoke the urgent need for rescuing and classifying the personal archives left by Chilean composers who have died during the last three decades. Urrutia Blondel (d. 5 July 1981) left such an archive that contains in addition to his own compositions, newspaper clippings beginning in 1922, criticisms that he wrote under the pseudonym "Dr. Clavecín," photographs, radio talks (1974–76) on Chilean music history, Easter Island material, 146 books, 476 music scores, and 120 editions of Chilean composers.

7117 ———. María Luisa Sepúlveda Maira: 1892–1958 (UC/RMC, 35:153/155, enero/sept. 1981, p. 117–140, bibl., music)

Pupil of Domenico Brescia (who taught successively at Santiago, Quito, and San Francisco), Sepúlveda was profiled in Otto Mayer-Serra's *Música y músicos de Latinoamérica* (1947).

7118 Letelier Llona, Alfonso. *Los Sonetos de la muerte* en su acontecer musical (UC/RMC, 35:153/155, enero/sept. 1981, p. 89–96, music)

Composer's analysis of his *Opus 18* (1943–48), for soprano and orchestra lasting 34 and a half minutes. Score preserved in Archivo de la Facultad de Artes, Universidad de Chile.

7119 Márquez, Andrés. When ponchos are subversive (INDEX, 12:1, Feb. 1983, p. 8–10, ill.)

In this interview, members of "Illapu," exiled Chilean folk group, discuss events leading to their expulsion in Oct. 1981. Singing political songs with *charango, zampoña* (panpipes), and *bombo* (drum) accompaniment, they performed (London, Sept. 1982) at cultural festival emphasizing solidarity with

El Salvador, Guatemala, and Chile. However, they feel isolated from their roots and not as creative as they were while in Chile.

7120 Massone, Juan Antonio. El sostenido dolor de *Los Sonetos de la Muerte* (UC/RMC, 35:153/155, enero/sept. 1981, p. 75–81)

Analysis of Gabriela Mistral's 13 sonnets of death, the first three of which were set by Alfonso Letelier Llona (1943–48) for soprano soloist accompanied by large symphonic orchestra. These three settings were successively premiered at Santiago Teatro Municipal (20 Nov. 1942; 25 Aug. 1944; and 26 Nov. 1948). First two sonnets were sung by Blanca Hauser, third by Teresa Yrarrázaval.

7121 Merino Montero, Luis. Música y sociedad en el Valparaíso decimonónico (*in* Die Musikkulturen Lateinamerikas im 19. Jahrhundert [see item 7015] p. 199–235, bibl.)

Merino utilized travel accounts, histories of theater life at Valparaíso, reminiscences, and contemporary newspaper accounts to document this superb study of 19th-century musical life in Valparaíso. The city had an active concert life; Protestantism flourished in Valparaíso and oratorio performances grew proportionately. Valparaíso bred both excellent performers and ambitous composers (e.g., Carlos Hucke). *Telésfora* (1846), Chile's first opera, was composed by Aquinas Ried (1810/15–1869), longtime Valparaíso resident who also authored valuable account of Mapuche music and dance. Adolfo Yentzen wrote the opera *Arturo*, as well as a Mass which premiered (Sept. 1869) in Valparaíso. Francisco Calderón, the most fecund Chilean composer of zarzuelas (b. Quillota, 1853) taught in Valparaíso, Tacna, and La Paz, and was later maestro de capilla at Cochabamba. Some of his salon pieces, which numbered more than 100, were published in Valparaíso. Also published a textbook, *Breve tratado de teoría de la música* (Valparaíso: Tipografía Nacional, 1888). In 1884 Pedro Cesari moved to Valparaíso, where he published a combined history and theory of music text in 1896. Also composed patriotic hymns and directed an 1895 Valparaíso performance of Handel's *Messiah*.

7122 Orrego-Salas, Juan A. and María Ester Grebe. Chile (*in* The New Grove dictionary of music and musicians. London: Macmillan, 1980, v. 4, p. 230–240, music, photos)

Art-music occupies two pages, folk the rest. Name of first opera composed in Chile misspelled, Bisquertt misspelled; *Juana La Loca* by Ortiz de Zárate never played at La Scala; no mention of Campderrós or Alzedo's activities. Emphasis on folk to the detriment of art-music runs parallel to other country articles in *The New Grove dictionary of music and musicians*.

Parra, Violeta. Cantos folklóricos chilenos. See item **1075.**

7123 Pereira Salas, Eugenio. La vida musical en Chile en el siglo XIX (*in* Die Musikkulturen Lateinamerikas im 19. Jahrhundert [see item **7015**] p. 237–259, photos)

An Academia Músico-Militar began popularizing military music in 1817. In 1826 the Sociedad Filarmónica sponsored the first attempt at a symphony orchestra. Manuel Robles (1780–1837) composed a national anthem replaced in 1828 by one composed by Ramón Carnicer (1789–1855). Italian opera invaded Chile in 1830 (and thereafter increasingly dominated high society tastes). National conservatory dates from 1849, Federico Guzmán (1837–85) was the most fecund and widely renowned Chilean composer of the century. Eleodoro Ortiz de Zárate and Remigio Acevedo Guajardo composed pioneer Chilean operas. Taste was broadened at the close of the century by Luis Arrieta Cañas' championing of Wagner and by oratorio performances.

7124 Santa Cruz Wilson, Domingo. Jorge Urrutia Blondel (UC/RMC, 35:156, oct./dic. 1981, p. 74–77)

Elected member of Instituto de Chile (1969/76) awarded the National Art Prize—Chile's highest distinction for a musician, Urrutia Blondel became the subject of an entire issue of *Revista Musical Chilena* (138). Recalls Urrutia Blondel's trajectory, beginning with 1924 membership in the Sociedad Bach. Necrology of more than ordinary literary as well as historical merit.

7125 Silva Solís, Mario. *In memoriam* Pablo Garrido Vargas: 1905–1982 (UC/RMC, 36:158, julio/dic. 1982, p. 126–127)

Garrido (b. 26 March 1905, Valparaíso; d. 14 Sept. 1982, Santiago). Funded Mackay

School Music Society comprising fellow students who played chamber works. Studied harmony, counterpoint, and composition with Edouard Van Dooren and Giuseppe Quintano. Founded string quartet and orchestra, beginning folklore studies, and taking interest in jazz's African roots (Antofagasta, 1926–29). During first Paris visit, studied with Andreas Liess. Visiting professor, University of Puerto Rico (1950–51). Apart from books listed in catalogs, he published two articles. His compositions were listed in *Composers of the Americas* (Washington, 9, 1963, p. 67–73).

7126 ———. Jorge Urrutia Blondel (UC/RMC, 36 :158, julio/dic. 1982, p. 6–46)

Meticulous catalog of 102 works (1919–80) by the 1976 national prizewinner (b. 17 Sept. 1905, La Serena; d. 5 July 1981, Santiago).

7127 Uribe Echevarría, Juan. Villancicos hispanos y chilenos (SCHG/R, 148, 1980, p. 7–67, ill., music)

Diffuse literary analysis of Baroque villancico texts printed in Spain, followed by author's analysis of what he considers Chilean offshoots. First three monodic villancicos shown as music examples are Christmas songs, whereas 16th-century secular-text villancicos set by Juan Vásquez and Enríquez de Valderrábano shown as concluding examples belong to the Renaissance courtly tradition.

7128 Valukin, E.P. Music of Chile (*in* Great Soviet Encyclopedia. New York: Macmillan, 1982, v. 29, p. 160)

Summary mentioning chief 20th-century composers but omitting paramount 19th-century composer, Federico Guzmán. Víctor Jara treated as martyr.

COLOMBIA

7129 Béhague, Gerard and **George List.** Colombia (*in* The New Grove dictionary of music and musicians. London: Macmillan, 1980, v. 4, p. 568–580, map, music, photos)

Persistent tendency to downplay all art-music developments in Latin American nations in favor of folk is again exemplified here where one and a half pages are devoted to art, the rest to folk. Art-music section is

marred by mistakes (first viceroy named in 1740, not 1566; Zorro, not Zorra). Folk section summarizes lifetime results obtained by best North American specialist in South American ethnomusicology. List took no interest in middlebrow urban popular music, leaving this important topic a no-man's land. All other folk music sections in Latin American articles published in *New Grove* omit or scarcely mention the music dear to the urban masses.

7130 Escobar, Luis Antonio. Hoja de vida y catálogo de sus obras. Bogotá: Josmar Impresores, 1982. 26 p.

Catalog of 179 works divided under instrumental and vocal categories, preceded by composer's abbreviated biography (b. 14 July 1925, Villapinzón, Cundinamarca). Escobar also lists 16 recordings and eight literary works.

7131 Stevenson, Robert. Bogotá (*in* The New Grove dictionary of music and musicians. London: Macmillan, 1980, v. 2, p. 849, bibl.)

For author's better article on this city (greater detail and richer bibliography), see *Die Musik in Geschichte in Gegenwart* (15, 1973, columns 893–895).

CUBA

7132 Afro-Cuban jazz (*in* Brockhaus-Riemann-Musiklexikon [see item **7006**] v. 1, p. 16)

Article mentioning bongo player Chano Pozo and Frank Grillo, typifies the interest taken by this lexicon (item **7006**) in everything Afro-Cuban (see individual articles on cha-cha-chá, mambo, rumba).

7133 Carpentier, Alejo. The Miracle of Anaquillé: an Afro-Cuban ballet (LALR, 8:16, Spring/Summer 1980, p. 55–62)

Translation of scenario written in 1927 for unproduced ballet by Amadeo Roldán. Carpentier's libretto for another Roldán ballet, *La rebambaramba* (also 1927), was commissioned by Serge Diaghilev but not produced because of his 1929 death in Venice. In 1930 Carpentier provided Alejandro García Caturla with the scenario for farce called *Manita en el suelo*. Carpentier's preface to present scenario documents Manuel M. Ponce's having written music for "a still unpublished choreographed piece by Mariano Brull." *The Miracle of Anaquillé* depicts American businessman whose efforts at imposing Wrigley's gum, ice cream sodas, and Rotarian religion on Cuban peasants are thwarted by chieftain of *náñigo* (African religious) group. Further to show American degradation, sailor dressed as bullfighter makes Spanish señorita go down on her knees before him.

7134 Crook, Larry. A musical analysis of the Cuban rumba (LAMR, 3:1, Spring/Summer 1982, p. 92–123, bibl., disc., music)

Penetrating analysis of all musical components. Concludes with *Una rumba en la bodega* transcribed (15 p.) from recording *Guaguancó afro-cubano* (Grupo Folklórico de Alberto Zayas, Panart LP-2055).

7135 Friedman, Robert. "If you don't play good they take the drum away:" performance, communication, and acts in Guaguancó (*in* Essays in honor of George List [see item **7011**] p. 209–224, bibl.)

Guaguancó is Afro-Cuban form of rumba performed primarily in urban areas of Cuba and Puerto Rico, as well as by immigrants in New York and other US cities. *Rumberos* perform it in their own or friends' homes, at religious ceremonies or parties after santería, and at formal public events such as theater concerts and community festivals. They learn their art through imitation of established *rumberos* who play the *segundo* and *tumba* (single headed drums tuned to different pitches). Time line is kept by *claves* (pieces of wood struck together) and/or *palitos* (wooden sticks). Consists of "a fixed repeated rhythmic pattern based on density of 16 pulses on which the overall structure of the music, speech, and dance is based."

7136 Gálvez, Zoila. Entrevista a la famosa cantante Zoila Gálvez [por Samuel Feijóo] (Signos [Biblioteca Martí, Santa Clara, Cuba] 26, sept./dic. 1980, p. 203–204, ill., plates)

African-descended coloratura soprano, Zoila Gálvez (b. 1902, Guanahay, Cuba). Her father's mother was born a slave in Gutiérrez Quirós family but displayed such early aptitude that she was taught to read. Singer's father became army captain and Cuba's first black alcalde. Father brought her to Havana at seven to become concert pianist, but she preferred to sing. Studied there with Tina Farelli and Arturo Bori, then studied in Milan (1921–24). Made local début at the Havana Teatro Nacional (1924). Sang on same program with Trío Matamoros and Gonzalo Roig's orchestra (1928). Sang Gilda in highly successful *Rigoletto* (Havana, 1938). Racial prejudice hampered her career in US. However, made New York Town Hall début and Carnegie Hall début with pianist Borislav Bazala and flutist Alberto Socarras (26 April 1953). By then, she was too old (49) for the Metropolitan. When interviewed (Aug. 1979), she was contract voice teacher at Havana's Teatro Musical.

7136a Inciarte, Rafael. Sones y conguitas de Guantánamo, Santiago, Manzanillo y Yateras (Signos [Biblioteca Martí, Santa Clara, Cuba] 26, sept./dic. 1980, p. 209–225, facsim., plate)

With the exception of one, all 33 transcribed songs are in major. Tonic alternating with dominant or dominant-seventh chords suffices for harmonization of everything in the collection. The omnipresent tags of 16th-note, 8th-note, 16th-note and/or 16th-note tied to first note in next beat, impart same rhythmic flavor, whether item be labeled *son*, *bachata*, *changüi*, *conga*, *conguita*, or *marcha*. Every item is noted in 2/4, with four-bar phrases as almost invariable norm. Without giving exact month and day, collector does give years when collected for a half dozen songs (e.g., *Yo soy carabalí* identified as a guaracha, *Cauterio oye el flamboyan* sung frequently in Guántanamo for 80 years, but to our ears sounding like a Puerto Rican plena). Collector himself was saxophonist who played at Santiago's 1938 Carnival.

7137 Kahl, Willi. Bolero (*in* The New Grove dictionary of music and musicians. London: Macmillan, 1980, v. 2, p. 870–871, bibl., music)

Cuban bolero "is duple-metre dance that exhibits closer relationships with the habanera and Afro-Cuban musical styles than with the Spanish bolero." Explanation that follows goes beyond same author's article on *bolero* in *Die Musik in Geschichte und Gegenwart* (2, 1952, columns 81–82).

7138 Lapique Becali, Zoila. Música colonial cubana en las publicaciones periódicas: 1812–1902. La Habana: Editorial

Letras Cubanas, 1979. 297 p.: bibl., ill., music (Colección Cubana)

Already known as author of "El Filarmónico Mensual" (see *HLAS 26:2219*), article republished in this book (p. 79–92)—Lapique Becali is a trained librarian. Pt. 1 is history of periodicals (p. 11–75). Pt. 2 lists them chronologically by first year of publication and gives titles of music published in them, but no assurance as to which music (all of salon type) is still extant. Consult authoritative review by Lester D. Brothers in *Latin American Music Review* (4:1, Spring/Summer 1973, p. 173–176).

7139 Nodal, Roberto. The sacred drums of the Lucumí (FIU/CR, 7:2, April/June 1978, p. 20–23, ill.)

Lucumí (Yoruba) came to Cuba from African area lying between Niger River and Nigeria-Dahomey border, bringing their pantheon with them. Cuba *batá* drums which are constructed in three sizes (e.g., *Iyá*, largest stands 30 in.) "are used only in religious ceremonies," and must be consecrated in elaborate ceremony. Sometimes players "have to play for almost three hours without interruption" during possession rituals. Sacred drums (which must be periodically fed with mixture of chicken or rooster carcass and aguardiente) "cannot be stretched and tuned by the use of fire." Drummers must be adult men of proven virility who learn their techniques by lengthy and exacting apprentice system. Author of this popularized article, identified as "anthropologist with the University of Wisconsin-Milwaukee," leans heavily on Fernando Ortiz.

7140 Orovio, Helio. Diccionario de la música cubana: biográfico y técnico. La Habana: Editorial Letras Cubanas, 1981. 442 p.: ill., music, photos.

First Cuban music dictionary—product of 10 years' labor—includes definitions of such familiar terms as *bolero, cha-cha-chá, contradanza, danzón, guaracha, mambo, rumba,* and *son* that frequently are buttressed by musical examples. Includes sections on seven schools of music (p. 133–135), 45 orchestras (p. 268–287), eight music periodicals (p. 323–325), and 10 theaters (401–405). Helpful photographs. Biographies include: Desi Arnaz, Machito = Frank Grillo, Benny Moré, Chano Pozo, and Damaso Pérez Prado, but not serious music cultivators,

such as Alberto or Jorge Bolet, Juan Antonio Camara, Luis Casa, Aurelio de la Vega, Julián Orbón, and others of greater or lesser fame entered in Otto Mayer-Serra's *Música y músicos de Latinoamérica* (México: 1947). Gilbert Chase gets appreciative article but not Joaquín Nin-Culmell. This dictionary (self-avowedly of unequal value) profiles present powers such as Harold Gramatages and Argeliers León with all due respect in lengthy articles. Articles on colonial personalities range from passable (e.g., Esteban Salas, Ignacio Cervantes) to minimal (e.g., Pablo Desvernine, Antonio Raffelín, Serafín Ramírez, Gapar Villate, José White). Why does Trinidadian José Manuel Jiménez merit 28 lines whereas Nicolás Ruiz Espadero's only 32? Information on Ernesto Lecuona is scattered and censors all politically unwelcome facts. Articles lack bibliographies. For this reason if none other, Mayer-Serra must be constantly consulted in conjunction with Orovio. Although published (and printed) in 1981, this dictionary takes no account of new data in Zoila Lapique Becali's 1979 work (item **7138**) concerning Juan Lino Fernández de Coca, Juan de Dios Alonso, etc. For bibliographer's comment, see item **89a.**

ECUADOR

7141 Béhague, Gerard. Ecuador (*in* The New Grove dictionary of music and musicians. London: Macmillan, 1980, v. 5, p. 829–834, bibl., music, photos)

Art music occupies one page of this five-page article, folk music the rest.

Belzner, William. Music, modernization, and westernization among the Macuma Shuar. See *HLAS 45:1407.*

Parducci Z., Resfa. Instrumentos musicales de viento del litoral ecuatoriano prehispánico. See *HLAS 45:825.*

7142 Schechter, John. *Corona y baile:* music in the child's wake of Ecuador and Hispanic South America, past and present (LAMR, 4:1, Spring/Summer 1983, p. 1–80, bibl., music, photos)

According to author, who taught at Syracuse University in 1983, "this article is revised version of one chapter of his doctoral dissertation, *Music in a Northern Ecua-*

dorean Highland Locus: Diatonic Harp, Genres, Harpists, and Their Ritual Function in the Child's Wake, The University of Texas at Austin, May 1982, UMT Publication No. 8217936." He did his research (Sept. 1979-Sept. 1980) "under the sponsorship of HEW Fulbright-Hays, and with institutional assistance from the Instituto Nacional de Antropología e Historia, Quito, and the Instituto Otavaleño de Antropología, Otavalo." Examines all layers of child-wake ceremony—at which harping and singing form a significant part.

MEXICO

7143 Bellinghausen, Karl. El tesoro de los diamantes de vidrio (HET, 15:78, julio/sept. 1982, p. 26–29, facsims.)

Tesoro de la música polifónica en México (vol. 2) appearing 1982 under CENIDIM's auspices, 30 years after vol. 1 of the *Tesoro* edited by Jesús Bal y Gay, contains Robert Stevenson's transcriptions published 1974 with the title *Seventeenth-century villancios from a Puebla convent archive transcribed with optional added parts for ministriles* (see HLAS 38:9175). Changes in 1982 reissue on superior paper involve suppression of "optional added parts for *ministriles*" (which have been replaced with rudimentary keyboard realizations of the unfigured basses by Felipe Ramírez Ramírez, organist). Because not acquainted with Lima 1974 publication, Ramírez Ramírez remained unaware of copyright infringement until after *Tesoro* (vol. 2) started circulating.

7144 Benjamin, Gerald R. Una dueda cultural saldada: la contribución de Julián Carrillo a la música del futuro (UC/RMC, 36:158, julio/dic. 1982, p. 60–71, disc., music)

Explanation of Carrillo's 13th-sound contributions, including notation. Lists of his musical and theoretical works, and of his recordings to be obtained from Dolores Carrillo Flores, Santísimo 25, San Angel, México 20, DF.

7145 Brennan, Juan Arturo. El primer disco de la UAM [i.e. Universidad Autónoma Metropolitana-Iztapalapa]: pt. 1 (Pauta [Universidad Autonóma Metropolitana, México] 5, enero 1983, p. 136–138, photos)

Recorded between 3–6 Oct. 1982 in Teatro del Fuego Nuevo, México, and issued in early Dec. 1982, the album entitled *Música mexicana de hoy* contains chamber size works by Joaquín Gutiérrez Heras, Julio Estrada, Mario Lavista, Manuel Enríquez, Gerardo Tamez, Antonio Navarro, Francisco Núñez, and Eduardo García de León. Performing artists were Cuarteto Da Capo and Dúo Castañón-Bañuelos.

7146 Campos, Rubén M. Manuel M. Ponce (HET, 15:79, oct./dic. 1982, p. 6–7, photo)

Already in early youth, Ponce preferred writing comprehensible music that could be loved by the masses. Article originally appeared in *Revista Cultura* (1917).

7147 Carrizosa, Selvio. Novena Feria y Festival Nacional de la Guitarra en Morelia (HET, 15[i.e. 14]:76, enero/marzo 1982, p. 36–38)

Fair and National Guitar Festival at Morelia (8–11 Aug. 1981) culminated by visit to Paracho, Morelia, where Félix Manzanero from Spain gave seminar on guitar making. At Morelia Hiram Dordelly from CENIDIM and Carmen Sordo Sodi lectured; Leopoldo Téllez (cello), and Selvio Carrizosa (lute, vihuela, guitar) were among performers. Morelia activities were concentrated at nearly renovated Teatro Ocampo (where youthful guitarists played programs) and daringly up-to-date Teatro José María Morelos.

7148 14 [i.e. Catorce] compositores españoles de hoy. Coordinador, Emilio Casares Rodicio. Oviedo, Spain: Arte-Musicología, Servicio de Publicaciones, Universidad de Oviedo, 1982. 478 p.: bibl., disc., ill. (Ethos; 9 Música)

In 1975 Carlo Cruz de Castro wrote 15-minute speaking piece, *Mixtlitlan* (meaning "mysterious region" or "between clouds" in Náhuatl), for narrator, 20-voice mixed chorus, brass, string bass, piano, and assorted percussion that was premiered at Mexico City (5 Dec. 1978). Present book contains further data on the cooperative Spanish-Mexican festivals of contemporary music. For further data on Cruz de Castro, who with the Mexican pianist-composer Alicia Urreta founded series in 1943, see *Inter-American Music Review* (5:1, Fall 1982, p. 125–126).

7149 Dallal, Alberto. Loie Fuller en México (IIE/A, 50:2, 1982, p. 297–307, ill.)

Fuller (b. Fullersburg, Ill., 1862) gained international fame dancing *Serpentine* (1891), *Butterfly* (1892), *Salomé* (1895), and *Fire Dance* (1895). Arriving at Mexico City (12 Jan. 1897) accompanied by her mother, she created a sensation at the Teatro Nacional.

7150 Díaz Du-Pond, Carlos. Cincuenta años de ópera en México: testimonio operístico. México: UNAM, Instituto de Investigacones Estéticas, 1978. 326 p., 32 leaves of plates: ill. (Estudios y fuentes del arte en México; 36)

Anecdotal account of leading stage director's opera experiences in US and Mexico. Studded with stars' names, this breezy book desperately needs an index. For review, see *Inter-American Music Review* (5:1, Fall 1982, p. 118–121).

7151 Driskell, Joy. La fiesta musical en Yucatán (UY/R, 140:24, marzo/abril 1982, p. 35–46)

Jaranas, which are 6/8 or 3/4 dances derived from Spanish jota, enliven every Yucatán urban or rural fiesta. When the band leader shouts *bomba*, the male pays versified compliment to his female partner. Reversion rite *El Torito* jarana closes the Saturday dance before a Sunday bullfight. *La cabeza de cochino*, another *jarana* encountered in all five communities investigated by the author, celebrates the festival patron saint. Instrumental melodies although based on the diatonic scale are played on "out-of-tune" European-type instruments. Melodic intervals from scale step in fifth thereby gain local flavor.

7152 Estrada, Julio. El espacio de la música (IIE/A, 50:2, 1982, p. 309–313)

Multiple-choir splendors by Giovanni Gabrieli (1553/6–1616) were made possible by spatial arrangements in St. Mark's, Venice. Mexico City-native Francisco López Capillas (1605/10–1674) wrote for four choirs stationed in four corners of Mexico City Cathedral. Among 19th-century composers, Berlioz exploited space in works such as his *Requiem* (Op. 5, 1837). Estrada suggests that contemporary Mexican composers might consider spacing their performers. Not only can performers be separated widely but they also can move about to advantage during musical events.

7153 Estrada Gutiérrez, Juan B. *et al.* Rectificación de algunos organistas mexicanos (HET, 15:79, oct./dic. 1982, p. 40–42)

Six leading Mexican organists deny Felipe Ramírez Ramírez's claims to having inaugurated the organ in Auditorio Nacional, having initiated popular organ concerts, having given first impetus to restoration of historic cathedral organs, and having pioneered in researching Mexican viceroyal epoch music.

7154 Fesperman, John T. Organs in Mexico. Photos by Scott Odell. Raleigh, N.C.: Sunbury Press, 1980. 109 p., 25 leaves of plates: bibl., ill., index, photos.

Valuable information concerning historic Mexican organs is flawed for lack of a thorough bibliography and insufficient command of the Spanish language. For review, see *Inter-American Music Review* (4:2, Spring/Summer 1982, p. 86–87).

7155 Gradante, William. "El Hijo del Pueblo:" José Alfredo Jiménez and the Mexican *canción ranchera* (LAMR, 3:1, Spring/Summer 1982, p. 36–59, bibl.)

José Alfredo Jiménez, composer of popular hits "Ella," "El Jinete" (*huapango*), "Yo," "Cuatro Caminos," "Sucedió en la Barranca," "El Cobarde," and "Que Suerte la Mía," (b. Dolores Hidalgo, 19 Jan. 1926). Three years later the widow Carmelita Sandoval moved with her four children to the capital. Further biographical details include the composer's having "enjoyed" much greater royalty earnings than even Agustín Lara.

7156 Halffter, Cristóbal. Ausencia y presencia de Rodolfo Halffter en la música española (HET, 15:77, abril/junio 1982, p. 6–8, photo)

Rodolfo Halffter, uncle of the writer, dealt a blow to Spanish music with his settlement in Mexico, because he was the "best prepared member of the Spanish generation of 1927."

7157 Iglesias Alvarez, Antonio. El piano de Rodolfo Halffter (HET, 15:77, abril/junio 1982, p. 9–16)

Summary and evaluation of piano works, preceded by biographical summary.

7158 ———. Rodolfo Halffter: su obra para piano. Madrid: Editorial Alpuerto, 1979. 358 p.: bibl., disc., ill., music.

Valuable study of Rodolfo Halffter's piano oeuvre, preceded by authoritative biography. For review, see *Inter-American Music Review* (5:1, Fall 1982, p. 123–125).

7159 López, Raymond Valencia. Manuel M. Ponce visto por un profesor norteamericano de ascendencia mexicana (HET, 15:79, oct./dic. 1982, p. 30–35, photos)

Topics covered: how to acquire books, articles, printed music, records; reasons for slow diffusion of Ponce's works in US. Author, brilliant pianist and organist, teaches Mexican music history at East Los Angeles College, Monterey Park, Calif.

7160 México. Secretaría de Educación Pública. Instituto Nacional de Bellas Artes. Centro Nacional de Investigación. Documentación e Información Musical. Tesoro de la música polifónica en México. t. 3, Tres obras del Archivo de la Catedral de Oaxaca. Transcribed and edited by Aurelio Tello. México: 1983. 98 p.: bibl., facsim., music.

Transcriber (b. Cerro del Pasco, Perú, 1951) is Coordinator of Musicological Research at CENIDIM, Mexico. Reproduced from informal and miniscule hand copy, present volume contains Manuel de Zumaya's *Villancico a 7* with violins, clarín, and continuo; Juan de los Reyes' *Magnificat a 7* with violins, *bajones*, *clarín*, and organ; and Juan Mariano Mora's *Misa de Sacris Solemniis* (not *Solemnis*, as misspelled by editor; other misspellings occur). Volume, prepared in evident great haste, is reviewed in *Inter-American Music Review* (5:2, Spring/Summer 1983).

7161 Otero, Corazón. Manuel M. Ponce y la guitarra. México: Fondo Nacional para Actividades Sociales, 1981. 226 p., 38 p. of facsimiles: bibl., disc., photos.

Valuable introduction to best known segment of Ponce's compositions contains copious data on his associations with his prime promoter, Andrés Segovia. For review, see *Inter-American Music Review* (5:1, Fall 1982, p. 126–127).

7162 Pahlen, Kurt. Rodolfo Halffter en la música de su tiempo (HET, 15:77, abril/junio 1982, p. 24–36)

Rambling appreciation (showing scant personal acquaintance with Halffter's works), eked out with tedious *obiter dicta* on other chief 20th-century composers.

7163 Parker, Robert L. Carlos Chávez: Mexico's modern-day Orpheus. Boston, Mass.: Twayne Publishers, 1983. 166 p.: bibl., disc., ill., index, music (Twayne's music series)

Aided by composer's daughter Anita Chávez, Parker—lifetime student of Chávez's works and presently assistant dean of Music School, University of Miami (Florida)—provides excellent introduction to Chávez's oeuvre (solo compositions, chamber music, vocal works, symphonies and concertos, final orchestral works, dramatic works), preceded by biographical chapter and followed by concluding summary chapter. Clara Meierovich enthusiastically reviewed this valuable book in *Heterofonía* (16:83, oct./dic. 1983, p. 53–54).

7164 Pulido, Esperanza. Consideraciones acerca de la obra lírica de Lan Adomián (HET, 16:83, oct./dic. 1983, p. 12–16, ill., music)

Adomián, at 71 received Guggenheim in composition, finished only one opera, *La mascherata*. Libretto by Alberto del Pizzo, Italian residing in Mexico, deals with failed coup against a Latin American president involved in an extramarital affair that ends with his mistress being strangled.

7165 ——. Elisa Osorio de Saldívar (HET, 15[i.e. 14]:76, enero/marzo 1982, p. 49)

After her husband's death, Elisa Osorio de Saldívar began coordinating his almost finished 2000-typewritten-page *Bibliografía de musicología y musicografía mexicana* which represented three decades of intense preparation. His legacy of colonial tablature (organ, cittern, guitar) ranked as the best in Latin American private possession. He collected sheet music, concert programs, newspaper clippings, stamps with musical associations, and letters.

7166 ——. El Festival Cervantino (HET, 13:70, julio/sept. 1980, p. 13–17)

Four Mexican and two foreign symphony orchestras (Filarmónica of Mexico City, Sinfónica Nacional, Sinfónica de Guanajuato, Sinfónica de Xalapa, Leipzig Gewandhaus and Philadelphia) participated in Eighth Festival Cervantino, Guanajuato, May 1980. Festival featured two opera companies (New York City and Antwerp), excellent chamber music, seven ballet companies, nine soloists including galaxy of theatrical, folkloric, and popular music stars. Héctor Vasconcelos, son of José Vasconcelos, directed the festival—equal of which in expense or audience will not soon be seen again.

7167 ———. Liga de Compositores de México (HET, 15[i.e. 14]:76, enero/marzo 1982, p. 47)

Counteracting ignorance of foreigners who unjustly bewail lack of present-day creative activity in Mexico, each of the following 18 members of the Liga de Compositores has had one or more works published by Editorial Ricordi & Co.: Miguel Alcázar, Emmanuel Arias, Salvador Contreras, Guillermo Flores Méndez, Marta García Renart, Juan Helguera, Mario Kuri Aldana, Raúl Ladrón de Guevara, Armando Lavalle, Sergio Ortiz, José Pomar, Luis Sandi, Mario Stern, Enrique Santos, Simón Tapia Colman, Roberto Téllez Oropeza, Leonardo Velázquez, Jesús Villaseñor.

7168 ———. Mexican women in music (LAMR, 4:1, Spring/Summer 1983, p. 121–131)

Traces women's participation in music from Sor Juana Inés de la Cruz to present. Composers mentioned include Emiliana de Zubeldía, María Teresa Prieto, María Grever, Consuelo Velázquez, Alida Vázquez, Alicia Urreta, María García Renart, and Lilia Vázquez. Also studies singers, pianists, and musicologists.

7169 ———. Música mexicana (HET, 15[i.e. 14]:76, enero/marzo 1982, p. 43–44)

In order to reach a wider public than *Ediciones Mexicanas de Músicas* specializing in vanguard publications, Liga de Compositores (Dolores 2, Zona Postal 1) began publishing easier music in more generally accessible styles. Works issued 1980–82 include: Miguel Alcázar, *Suite para Guitara*; Juan Helguera, *Homenaje a Silvestre Revueltas para Guitarra*; Raúl Ladrón de Guevara, *Preludio y Minueto para Guitarra*; Sergio Ortiz, *Trío para Oboe, Clarinete y Fagot*; Luis Sandi, *Sinfonía Mínima para Cuerdas* (14 p.); Enrique Santos, *Fantasía para Piano*; Mario Stern, *Pequeño Ostinato para Soprano, Clarinete, Viola y Violoncello*; Leonardo Velásquez, *Siete Piezas Breves para Piano*; Jesús Villaseñor, *Tripartita para Piano*. In 1982, Universidad de Veracruz sponsored more adventurous works in Colección Yunque de Mariposas: Salvador Contreras, *Sonatina No. 1 para Piano* (in

three short movements); Manuel de Elías, *Dos Piezas para Clarinete Solo* (*Imago* without bar-lines, *Pieza de Cámara No. 6*) and *Sonata No. Uno para Piano*; Manuel Enríquez, *Imaginario* for organ (aleatoric); Francisco González, *Inducción* for woodwind quartet accompanying lead clarinet; Mari Juri Aldana, *Tres Preludios para Piano*; Mario Lavista, *Gama* for one or two flutes in C (aleatoric); Mario Stern, *Vals para Piano* (continuous alternation of various meters); Jesús Villaseñor, *Aledebarran* for guitar solo (constant meter changes).

Robb, John Donald. Hispanic folk music of New Mexico and the Southwest: a self-portrait of a people. See item **1121.**

7170 Romero, Jesús C. Historia del Conservatorio Nacional de Música: pt. 2 (HET, 15[i.e. 14]:76, enero/marzo 1982, p. 56–69)

The Conservatorio Nacional's faculty of 14 included Agustín Caballero as director, Aniceto Ortega for composition professor, Tomás León for piano, Luis Muñoz Ledo for music history and bibliography, Alfredo Bablot for esthetics, Eduardo Liceaga for acoustics, Cristóbal Reyes for wind instruments, and Amado Michel for *solfège*. By error, the traditional date given for inauguration of the National Conservatory has been 16 Jan. 1866. This mistake stems from Melesio Morales' *Reseña que leyó a sus amigos . . . Febrero de 1906* (México: Imprenta del Corazón de Jesús, 1907, p. 3). Error was repeated in Eduardo Liceaga and Antono García Cubas' *Breve reseña de la fundación del Conservatorio* (p. 35–38) written 40 years after Dr. Romero's essay (here partially reprinted) was first published in *Nuestra Música* (1, July 1946). For pt. 1, see HLAS 44:7099.

7171 Russell, Craig H. Santiago de Murcia: the French connection in Baroque Spain (Journal of the Lute Society of America [Manhattan, Calif.] 15, 1982, p. 40–51, bibl., music)

Murcia, widely known in 18th-century Mexico, completed in 1732 a guitar anthology entitled *Passacalles y obras* that emigrated to Mexico, where it was bought for the British Library. Both *Passacalles* (and Murcia's *Resumen* for 1714/1717) draw heavily on French guitar sources. *Passacalles* incorporates 22 dances by Campion and 15 by Le Cocq.

7172 Saldívar, Elisa Ororio Bolio de. Educadores del jardín de niños mexicano. Prólogo de Luz María Serradell. México: Talleres Gráficos de la Editorial del Magisterio Benito Juárez, 1980. 563 p.: bibl., index, ports.

This superlative biographical dictionary of 76 20th-century Mexican kindergarten educators (mostly women, but some men) includes fully documented lives of musicians—pianists primarily (see p. 53, 105, 133, 219, 293, 315, 325, 357, 373, 411, 431, 445, and 477). As a document for Mexican cultural history, this compilation is invaluable.

7173 Saldívar y Silva, Gabriel. Refranero musical mexicano y un apéndice de refranero general usado en canciones. México: Universidad Autónoma Metropolitana, Dirección de Difusión Cultural, Departamento Editorial, 1983. 181 p. (Molinos de viento; 16)

Pt. 1 consists of alphabetical list of music-related words that occur prominently in proverbs, pt. 2 is an alphabetized vocabulary of key words in well-known Mexican songs. Key words serve somewhat as subject index to songs in which they occur.

7174 Sas, Andrés. Mexico (in Algemene muziek encyclopedie [see item **7001**] v. 6, p. 302–303, photos)

Wrong dates and misspellings of names of Mexicans riddle this out-of-date article that despite author's death (Lima, 26 Aug. 1967), could have been easily updated from other lexicons.

7175 Seitz, Barbara. The Mexican *corrido* (in Essays in honor of George List [see item **7011**] p. 251–266, bibl.)

Mexican corrido differs from Spanish romance because of its preference for major mode, repetitive tonic-dominant harmony, and stereotyped fast 6/8 rhythmic formulas. So far as text pages, Mexican corridos began with reference to performance situation, identification of principals in the narrative by place, date, and name. They close with the chief actors' farewell, followed by the performer's leavetaking. In the middle comes a core of narrative detail, interspersed with comments on events narrated. Corridos are commonly performed by two men singing in parallel thirds or sixths and accompanying themselves on guitars. Harp and/or mariachi accompaniment may be added.

7176 Sheridan, Guillermo. Olavarría y Ferreri, Domec, Justo Sierra: Wagner rico de colores (Pauta [Universidad Autónoma Metropolitana, México] 2:7, julio/sept. 1983, p. 42–65, map, photos)

Wagnerian excerpts were performed as early as 10 Oct. 1864, but no operas were performed until *Lohengrin* (18 Nov. 1890). In addition to pasting together what Enrique de Olavarría's *Reseña histórica del teatro en México* contains, author of this aperçu of Wagner's music in Mexico to 20 Feb. 1911 adds comments by Gustavo E. Campa and Justo Sierra.

7177 Sordo Sodi, Carmen. La música mexicana en la época del Presidente Benito Juárez (in Die Musikkulturen Lateinamerikas im 19. Jahrhundert [see item **7015**] p. 299–315, bibl., ill., music)

Résumé of Mexican musical life (1840–72) stresses data extracted from periodicals *La Orquesta*, *La Madre Celestina*, and *El Siglo XIX*. Topics include: theaters, composers of operas and zarzuela (e.g., Cenobio Paniagua, Melesio Morales, Aniceto Ortega); cultural societies and music instruction (e.g., national conservatory); Angela Peralta's preeminence as diva and her opera company; corrido, jarabe, other folkloric types. The 12 music examples began *La Cucaracha*, *Jarabe Tapatío*, *Los Enanos* and continue with such universally known favorites as *El Atole*, *El Perico*. All 12 are in major mode (even *Adiós Mamá Carlota*), three are in 2/4 time, the rest in 3/4 or 6/8.

7178 Spierer, Leon. El Concierto para Violín y Orquesta de Halffter (HET, 15:77, abril/junio 1982, p. 17–23, music)

Detailed analysis of Rodolfo Halffter's violin concerto (Op. 11, 1939–40), buttressed by 5 p. of musical excerpts. Author is fervent admirer and performer of work, which he ranks among leading violin concertos of last four decades.

7179 Stevenson, Robert. Aztec music (in The New Grove dictionary of music and musicians. London: Macmillan, 1980, v. 1, p. 760–761, bibl., ill.)

Survey article, cued to early chroniclers' accounts and recent ethnohistory studies in German, Spanish, and English.

7180 ———. Carlos Chávez's Los Angeles connection (IAMR, 3:2, Spring/Summer 1981, p. 133–150)

Chávez's correspondence with John Vincent (23 Feb. 1950–15 Jan. 1974) documents this article. Also available in Spanish in *Heterofonía* (Mexico, 15:1[76] p. 3–19).

7181 Swan, Christopher. The music of Mexico is the cry of a land whipsawed by change (Christian Science Monitor [Boston] 17 Feb. 1984, p. B1 and B32)

Contrasts activities of three composers: 1) Julio Estrada teaching at University of California, San Diego "because he cannot find the technology in financially ravaged Mexico to develop his advanced theories;" 2) Mario Lavista who edits musical magazine *Pauta* and whose advanced works are published by Ediciones Mexicanas de Música; and 3) Manuel Enríquez who is "the country's leading composer." Alberto Alva, head of National Conservatory is quoted as saying that "Mexico's largest music school cannot afford instruments for its pupils." Gerard Béhague says that "Composers will not be as productive as in better times. The select few will have the limelight."

7182 Taibo, Paco Ignacio. La canción obrera mexicana de 1915 a 1937: antología (CEHSMO, 5:18, enero 1980, p. 6–17)

Texts culled from five cancioneros (1915–37) are in this collection of militant workers' songs. However, tunes, frequently specified, include Jaime Nunó's music for Mexican national anthem, Rouget de Lisle's *Marseillaise*, Sebastián Yradier's *La Paloma*, and an excerpt from Verdi's *Nabucco*. *La Adelita* is only anonymous Mexican popular song specified for any of the texts. Only three of the seven cancioneros levied by author were published in Mexico, others at Buenos Aires, Barcelona, or Los Angeles.

7183 Two Mexico City choirbooks of 1717: an anthology of sacred polyphony from the Cathedral of Mexico. Transcribed and edited by Steven Barwick. Carbondale: Southern Illinois University Press, 1982. 165 p.: facsims.

Barwick traces lives of Mexico City Cathedral composers (1585–1730). Also painstakingly analyzes 1717 manuscripts from which music in pts. 1–2 were transcribed. Except for one work each by Antonio Rodríguez de Mata (d. 1642), Francisco López Capillas (d. 1674) and Antonio de Salazar (d. 1715), 15 Latin liturgical works in present volume are by the native of Mexico City,

Manuel de Zumaya = Sumaya (d. Oaxaca, 1755). Zumaya's *Adiuvanos*, with which volume begins, requires five-voice choir, rest of his works a four-voice. His teacher, Salazar, wrote superb eight-voice *O sacrum convivium* (p. 134–144) which is only double-choir work in this edition.

7184 Varela-Ruiz, Leticia. Die Musik im Leben der Yaqui: Beitrag zum Studium der Tradition einer mexikanischen Ethnie. Regensburg, FRG: Gustav Bosse Verlag, 1982. 271, 167 p.: bibl., disc., ill., music (Kölner Beiträge zur Musikforschung; Bd. 127)

In this published version of doctoral dissertation done under Robert Günther's supervision at Cologne University, author (native of Sonora where Yaqui live) exhaustively discusses not only autochthonous but also acculturated songs, instruments, rituals, and dances.

7185 Velazco, Jorge. Juan Bosco Correro (HET, 15[i.e. 14]:76, enero/marzo 1982, p. 23–26, photos)

Juan Bosco Correro Morales (b. Mexico City, 25 June 1934; d. 19 July 1981) was trained as organist by his father. Later teachers were Pedro Michaca, Alfonso de Elías, Carlos del Castillo, and especially National Conservatory organist (and musicologist) Jesús Estrada. Beginning in 1953 he served as Hammond representative in Mexico. During next 28 years, he toured nationally and internationally, recorded (Miguel Bernal Jiménez's *Concertino* for organ and orchestra, the signature of Radio Universidad), and from 1967 played harpsichord in the four-member Collegium Musicum Barrocum. With his five children and wife he formed a recorder group that before his fatal illness, toured Mexico with a Baroque repertory.

7186 ———. El pianismo mexicano del siglo XIX (IIE/A, 50:2, 1982, p. 205–239, ill.)

Piano dominated music in Mexican homes during 19th century, to detriment of chamber music and art song. Salon music was published at Mexico City (handsomely engraved at Leipzig or elsewhere) by Melesio Morales (1838–1908), Julio Iturate (1845–1905), Ernesto Elorduy (1854–1913), Felipe Villanueva (1862–93), and Ricardo Castro (1866–1907). Velazco's own keyboard excellence inspires him into giving gratifying researched account of century's chief piano pedagogues, concert artists, and program builders.

First keyboard arrangement (p. 208) simplifies Beethoven's *String trio*, Op. 8 (published Vienna, 1797), polacca movement.

7187 ———. Rodolfo Halffter (HET, 15:77, abril/junio 1982, p. 38–41, bibl., photo)

Halffter reached Mexico as member of Junta de Cultura del Gobierno Español. Mexicans who studied with him at Conservatorio Nacional included such lights as Luis Herrera de la Fuente, Mario Lavista, Eduardo Mata, and Héctor Quintanar. In 1946, was appointed director of *Nuestra Música*. He established first Mexican contemporary ballet company, La Paloma Azul, that produced not only his *La Madrugada del Panadero* but also ballets by Silvestre Revueltas and Blas Galindo. Monday evening concerts, which were his idea, stimulated many youthful composers to write works performed more often well than badly.

7188 Vidal Rivero, Miguel. La trayectoria de arte musical y poesía de la orquesta típica yucalpetén (UY/R, 24:141/142, mayo/agosto 1982, p. 73–78)

Consists of 40th anniversary tribute to regional orchestra (founded 12 April 1942) with Daniel Ayala Pérez as first director of 29-member ensemble (including five violins, one cello, one salterio, four marimbas, one flute, one clarinet, two percussion, and 14 guitars, latter doubling as singers).

PARAGUAY

7189 Aretz, Isabel. Paraguay (*in* The New Grove dictionary of music and musicians. London: Macmillan, 1980, v. 14, p. 175–178, bibl., music, photos)

Encyclopedia article dealing mostly with indigenous and folk expressions. Art music deemphasized.

7190 Gómez-Perasso, José Antonio and **Luis Szaran.** Anguá parará. Asunción: Estudios Folklóricos Paraguayos, 1978. 77 p.: ill., music (Estudios folklóricos paraguayos; 1:1)

Band called *Peteke* that plays in honor of San Roque, second patron of Pirayu Calle and Pororó (684 inhabitants in 1962), consists of pair of drums (cedar wood, the open end covered with dog, goat, or deer skin) and reed flutes (five finger holes, end hole). Illustra-

tions show six players (two are drummers). Musical appendix shows eight E Major flute and drum pieces, all fast 6/8. Melodies, except for the penultimate starting on sixth degree, use none except first five degrees of E Major and leading tone beneath first degree. All end on the tonic.

7191 Los Mensajeros del Paraguay (HET, 15[i.e. 14]:76, enero/marzo 1982, p. 51)

Album OEA-006 with above title was released in 1981 by OAS' Performing Arts Division, Efraín Paesky, Director. Four Paraguayan singers—Mario Agustín Llanes, Director, María Vecca, Zararías P. Olmedo, and Blas Velázquez (the last, *requintista*)—perform polkas, *guaranías*, and *paraguayas* (accompanying themselves with harp, guitar, and a *requinto*).

PERU

7192 Arróspide de la Flor, César. José Bernardo Alcedo (*in* The New Grove dictionary of music and musicians. London: Macmillan, 1980, v. 1, p. 228–229, bibl.)

Peruvian national anthem composers' treatise, *Filosofía elemental de la música*, is incorrectly listed as having been published at Lisbon and misleadingly summarized. No workslist.

7193 ———. Peru (*in* Sohlmans musiklexikon [see item **7022**] v. 5, p. 40–41, bibl., music)

Survey of music in Peru since independence by dean of Peruvian musicographers (b. Lima, 3 Jan. 1900).

7194 Béhague, Gerard and **Isabel Aretz.** Peru (*in* The New Grove dictionary of music and musicians. London: Macmillan, 1980, v. 14, p. 557–566, bibl., music, photos)

Béhague wrote the art music portion (3 columns), divided into pre- and post-1821 sections; Aretz, the folk music (14 columns). All four archaeological instruments pictured on p. 560 are in European collections.

7195 Mastrogiovanni, Antonio. Edgar Valcárcel (Revista Musical de Venezuela [Caracas] 2:3, sept./dic. 1981, p. 83–90)

Biography and analysis of Valcárcel's prize winning *Hanac Pachap* for children's choir, mixed adult choir, and symphony orchestra.

7196 Turino, Thomas. The charango and the *sirena*: music, magic, and the power of love (LAMR, 4:1, Spring/Summer 1983, p. 81–119, bibl., photos, music)

Author (doctoral student in ethnomusicology, University of Texas, Austin) did his *charango* research in southern Peru (1981–82). Among *campesinos* in Canas province, "the charango is used almost exclusively by young, single men in courting activities, and the instrument is viewed as an essential tool for winning a girl." Pt. 2 of article argues that "the strict association of the *sirena* with stringed instruments seems to be original for Latin America . . . The musician can partake of the *sirena*'s power only through the medium of the charango."

7197 Vega, Carlos. Colección de música popular peruana: pt. 2 (Revista del Instituto de Investigación Musicológica Carlos Vega [Universidad Católica Argentina, Facultad de Artes y Ciencias Musicales, Buenos Aires] 3:3, 1979, p. 12–43)

Continuation and conclusion of Vega's posthumous essay on the Martínez Compañón collection, begun in the 1978 annual issue of this *Revista*.

URUGUAY

7198 Lange, Francisco Curt. La música en el Uruguay durante el siglo XIX (*in* Die Musikkulturen Lateinamerikas im 19. Jahrhundert [see item **7015**] p. 333–343)

After 1851, Italian operas were performed in Montevideo within two or three years of their European premieres. Teatro Solís (inaugurated 25 Aug. 1856 with *Ernani*) became focus of Uruguayan concert and operatic life. Louis Moreau Gottschalk, who spent nine months at Montevideo, was but one of many world-famous celebrities who spent time there. Lange thoroughly covers musical organizations, performers, pedagogues, and composers.

7199 Mikhailov, Dzh. K. Music of Uruguay (*in* Great Soviet encyclopedia. New York: Macmillan, 1981, v. 27, p. 682, bibl.)

Competent article mentioning chief composers and landmarks.

7200 Salgado, Susana. Cluzeau-Mortet: tesis de musicología. Montevideo: A. Monteverde, 1983. 521 p.: bibl., ill.

Published version of thesis (defended 19 Aug. 1965, Universidad de la República, Facultad de Artes y Ciencias) describes life (92 p.) and offers piece-by-piece analysis (313 p.) of the compositions of Luis Cluzeau-Mortet (b. Montevideo, 16 Nov. 1889; d. 28 Sept. 1957). Although 11 photographs are inserted before p. 43, book lacks any facsimile of Cluzeau-Mortet's musical manuscripts or any reproductions of his 58 printed works (mostly songs and piano pieces).

7201 Zorrilla de San Martín, Cochonita. Momentos musicales: autobiografía de Florencio Mora. Montevideo: Talleres Gráficos Bouzout, 1978. 63 p., 12 leaves of plates: ill., index.

Widow's compilation of autobiographical fragments by a Chilean-born violinist, Florencio Mora, who studied at Brussels in Eduardo Fabini's class (1882–1950). After further European study and concertizing, Mora married and settled in Uruguay. For review, see *Inter-American Music Review* (5:1, Fall 1982, p. 123).

VENEZUELA

7202 Abreu, José Antonio *et al.* Pablo Casale (Revista Musical de Venezuela [Caracas] 2:5, sept./dic. 1981, p. 105–108)

Necrology of twice winner of Venezuela's Premio Nacional de Música (d. Caracas, age 75, 6 Aug. 1981). Tributes by seven Venezuelans to Italian-born opera conductor, violinist, and pedagogue who arrived in Caracas in 1948.

7203 Aretz de Ramón y Rivera, Isabel. L'ancienne musique européenne orientale au Vénézuela (Folio Musica [Filharmonia Pomorska, Bydgoszcz, Poland] 1:1, 1983, p. 11–16, bibl.)

Improvised three-part polyphony sung around altars in Venezuelan countryside houses resembles improvised Georgian folk polyphony. *Utoroyó* (inverted reed clarinet) of Goajira Peninsula Indians (Venezuela) resembles Bulgarian *joró*.

7204 ———. Indigenous music of Venezuela (The World of Music [International Music Council, Paris] 25:2, 1982, p. 22–35, bibl., music)

Yanomani group, Piaroas, Yekuanas, Guajibos Waraos, Goajiros perform as many types of music as there are different indigenous languages. Aretz magisterially summarizes salient traits of each indigenous enclave.

7205 Castillo Didier, Miguel and Giovanni D'Amico Ujich. Organos venezolanos del siglo XIX (UC/RMC, 36:158, julio/dic. 1982, p. 72–104, bibl., ill.)

Venezuela's earliest organ builders were the French Claudio Febres, active at Caracas 1710–11, and Nicolas de Clermon at work there in 1727 and during next half-century. With admirable documentation and considerable attention to specific organs (shown in plates are Cathedral de la Asunción, Margarita, San José de Tiznados; Parroquia de San Sebastián de los Reyes). Authors carry organ-building history to arrival of seven Cavaillé-Coll organs in Venezuela (1870–90). In 1881–82, Caracas Cathedral received its 22-rank Cavaillé-Coll, for many decades largest in the capital.

7206 D'Amico Ujcich, Giovanni and Miguel Castillo Didier. Un Cavaillé-Coll en la Emerita Augusta Americana: algunos órganos de los Andes venezolanos (Revista Musical de Venezuela [Caracas] 3:7/8, mayo/dic. 1982, p. 13–82, bibl., photos)

Mérida Cathedral Schmelzer-Laukuff two-manual pipe organ contracted by Archbishop Acacio Chacón in 1958 and inaugurated in 1960, is sixth organ in cathedral's history. Fifth was a Cavaillé-Coll (1877–1967). Other Cavaillé-Coll organs inaugurated in the Caracas parishes were: San José, 1889; Santa Teresa, 1884; El Valle, ca. 1890; San Francisco, ca. 1888–89; and Caracas Cathedral, 1897. Latter instrument is now in Cathedral of Los Teques. Authors, who are fastidious scholars, also discuss with all possible detail other organs in old Venezuelan Andean churches. Their endnotes and bibliography are done with great care and are mines of futher data. However, their enthusiasm for Venezuelan organ history is not matched by a present-day pipe organ movement in Venezuela.

7207 Eichhorn, Johannes. La pianista venezolana Teresa Carreño, 1853–1917 (Revista Musical de Venezuela [Caracas] 5:6, enero/abril 1982, p. 147–152)

Written in 1965 by an admirer of Carreño, resident in East Berlin, article tells

of author's discovery of her 1906 cylinder recording of Chopin's *Ballade*, Op. 23.

7208 Faïnshteïn, M. Sh. Teresa Carreño's Russian visits (IAMR, 3:2, Spring/Summer 1981, p. 121–123)

Translation of article in *Latinskaîa Amerika* (1, Jan. 1980, p. 124–128) giving details of Carreño's visits to St. Peterburg (Nov. 1896) and Moscow (Nov. 1899).

7209 Hernández López, Rhazés et al. In memoriam (Revista Musical de Venezuela [Caracas] 2:3, enero/abril 1981, p. 105–124)

Necrologies of Eduardo Plaza Alfonso (Caracas, 1911–80), Eduardo Lira Espejo (Santiago de Chile, 1912-Caracas, 1980), and José Clemente Laya Morales (Caracas, 1813–81).

7210 José Angel Lamas y su época. Walter Guido, editor. Caracas: Biblioteca Ayacucho, 1981. 15 p., 364 p. of music: bibl., ill.

Orchestrally accompanied choral works (Lamas' *Popule meus* and *Miserere*; J.M. Olivares' *Stabat mater*; and Cayetano Carreño's *In monte Oliveti*) from Venezuela's best musical epoch, preceded by biobibliographical introduction.

7211 Lira Espejo, Eduardo. Carmen Teresa de Hurtado Machado (Revista Musical de Venezuela [Caracas] sept./dic. 1981, p. 108–110)

In memoriam tribute to singer and pedagogue (d. Caracas, 19 Aug. 1981).

7212 ———. Teresa Carreño: estrella errante (Revista Musical de Venezuela [Caracas] 3:7/8, mayo/dic. 1982, p. 83–92)

The remains of Carreño (b. Caracas, 22 Dec. 1853; d. New York, 12 June 1917) were returned to Caracas in 1938 and reinterred in the Venezuelan Panteón Nacional (9. Dec. 1977) in ceremony attended by President Carlos Andrés Pérez and other high ranking Venezuelan dignitaries. Only one other woman's remains are buried in Panteón Nacional: Luisa Cáceres de Arismendi (1799–1866).

7213 Mambretti, Mabel. Venezuela (*in* Sohlmans musiklexikon [see item 7022] v. 5, p. 775, bibl.)

Author of this survey article (b. 1942) classes herself with younger Venezuelan generation that includes conductor Yannis Ionnidis (b. Athens, 8 June 1930) and electronic composer Alfredo del Monaco (b. Caracas, 29 April 1938).

7214 Milanca Guzmán, Mario. *El Cojo Ilustrado,* 1892–1915: una investigación hemerográfica (Revista Musical de Venezuela [Caracas] 5:6, enero/abril 1982, p. 73–143, facsim.)

Between 15 April 1906 and 1 July 1909 "the best Venezuelan fortnightly" included 38 musical supplements, the contents of which are here tabulated and analyzed. *El Cojo Ilustrado* began with issue dated 1 Jan. 1982, including from its first year articles on musical matters and reviews of musical events. Best represented Caracas-born composer in musical supplements is Reynaldo Hahn (1874–1947) with four items. Most pieces are salon piano or parlor vocal works by Europeans ranging from Godard and Massenett to Chaminade. However, supplements also contain a *Toccata* by J.S. Bach (15 Nov. 1908) and a few substantial works by Schumann and Chopin.

7215 ———. Eduardo Richter: 1874–1912 (Revista Musical de Venezuela [Caracas] 3:7/8, mayo/dic. 1982, p. 151–228, ill., music)

Native of Caracas trained in youth as pianist and violinist, Eduardo Richter was 37 years old at his death (20 Aug. 1912). At the instigation of Caracas newspaper, *El Tiempo,* two concerts were organized to raise money toward purchase of a house for Richter's widow and children. First in Teatro Municipal (31 Aug. 1912) enlisted 40 music performers. Second (14 Dec. 1912) under auspices of Venezuelan President Juan Vicente Gómez, began with orchestral selection, and continued with the play, *El prólogo de una drama* by José Echegaray and the zarzuela with music by Manuel Nieto, *La tela de Araña.*

7216 Plaza, Juan Bautista. Don Bartolomé Bello: músico (Revista Musical de Venezuela [Caracas] 2:5 , sept./dic. 1981, p. 71–79, notes)

Documented biography of Andrés Bello's father, who was appointed a Caracas Cathedral musician (28 June 1774), and who also graduated as bachelor of civil law from University of Caracas, and who five years later was advanced to the degree of *licenciado* by the University of Santo Domingo.

7217 Stevenson, Robert. Isabel Aretz: composer (IAMR, 5:2, Spring/Summer 1983, p. 2–5)

Compositional career (with annotated catalog of works) of the director of INIDEF (Instituto Interamericano de Etnomusicología y Folklore), who was born in Buenos Aires but transferred residence to Venezuela upon marriage to Luis Felipe Ramón y Rivera.

JOURNAL ABBREVIATIONS MUSIC

BNBD Boletín Nicaragüense de Bibliografía y Documentación. Banco Central de Nicaragua, Biblioteca. Managua.

CCE/RA Revista de Antropología. Casa de la Cultura Ecuatoriana, Núcleo del Azuay. Cuenca.

CEHSMO Historia Obrera. Centro de Estudios Históricos del Movimiento Obrero Mexicano. México.

FIU/CR Caribbean Review. Florida International University, Office of Academic Affairs. Miami.

HET Heterofonía. Revista musical bimestral. México.

IAMR Inter-American Music Review. Publisher, Robert Stevenson. Los Angeles, Calif.

IIE/A Anales del Instituto de Investigaciones Estéticas. Universidad Nacional Autónoma de México. México.

INDEX Index to Censorship. Writers & Scholars International. London.

IPGH/FA Folklore Americano. Instituto Iberoamericano de Geografía e Historia, Comisión de Historia, Comité de Folklore. México.

LALR Latin American Literary Review. Carnegie-Mellon University, Department of Modern Languages. Pittsburgh, Pa.

LAMR Latin American Music Review. University of Texas. Austin.

MHD/B Boletín del Museo del Hombre Dominicano. Santo Domingo.

SCHG/R Revista Chilena de Historia y Geografía. Sociedad Chilena de Historia y Geografía. Santiago.

SE/E Ethnomusicology. Wesleyan University Press *for the* Society for Ethnomusicology. Middletown, Conn.

UC/RMC Revista Musical Chilena. Universidad de Chile, Facultad de Artes. Santiago.

URSS/AL América Latina. Academia de Ciencias de la URSS (Unión de Repúblicas Soviéticas Socialistas). Moscú.

UV/L Logos. Universidad del Valle, Departamento de Humanidades. Cali, Colombia.

UY/R Revista de la Universidad de Yucatán. Mérida, México.

PHILOSOPHY: LATIN AMERICAN THOUGHT

JUAN CARLOS TORCHIA ESTRADA, *General Secretariat, Organization of American States*

COMO ANTICIPARAMOS EN EL *HLAS 44* (p. 611) por razones de espacio esta sección se limitará, en adelante, a la bibliografía sobre el pensamiento latinoamericano, bien que tomando la expresión en términos muy amplios, que van desde interpretaciones muy generales de América Latina en su conjunto, hasta estudios sobre filósofos y corrientes, pasando por trabajos que, aunque no estrictamente filosóficos, ilustran sobre el efecto de las ideas en la sociedad. Se trata, en realidad, del material que antes se incluía en las subsecciones "Filosofía Latinoamericana" e "Historia de las Ideas." Por lo tanto, no tendrán asientos con descripción de contenido las obras y artículos de autores latinoamericanos que se ocupen de filosofía en general (digamos, sobre Kant o la filosofía antigua, o sobre filosofía de la historia o teoría del conocimiento). Este material será cubierto, en forma panorámica, en la introducción. Se iguala así esta sección de la Historia, donde se recoge la producción sobre historia de América Latina, pero no lo que historiadores latinoamericanos escriben sobre historia europea, por ejemplo.

El incremento en la producción filosófica latinoamericana en los últimos 40 o 50 años ha sido extraordinario. En la medida en que este *Handbook* pueda ser muestra de ese hecho, basta comparar la primera sección de Filosofía publicada en 1940 (ver *HLAS 5*, p. 418–427) con los volúmenes más recientes.[1] La situación justifica disponer ya—como lo sugirió oportunamente Jorge J.E. Gracia—de un instrumento bibliográfico especial para la producción filosófica latinoamericana, inexistente a pesar de su obvia necesidad, y cuya función trató de suplir la sección de Filosofía de este *Handbook* hasta el número anterior, en la medida de lo posible. Una empresa de esta naturaleza debiera ser labor mancomunada de universidades o institutos de investigación latinoamericanos.

Ahora bien, dejando de lado el aspecto práctico del *Handbook* y pasando al significado del hecho, debe decirse que, con ser importante, ese incremento cuantitativo no es lo esencial, pues resulta, en realidad, de un cambio de actitud, de una intensificación del interés por la filosofía, y de la voluntad de cultivarla cada vez con mayor rigor profesional. La consecuencia práctica de ese giro ha sido la existencia de mayor número de Facultades o Escuelas de filosofía y de Institutos de Investigación, y un aumento en la cantidad y calidad de las revistas y publicaciones filosóficas. En este sentido, lo que ha ocurrido en los últimos 40 o 50 años en el campo de la filosofía latinoamericana ha producido un cambio mayor que el verificado desde el siglo XVI hasta fines del siglo XIX.

Cuando estos últimos 40 o 50 años se vean en perspectiva histórica, la fecha de 1940, que usamos en forma puramente simbólica para señalar el comienzo de la nueva etapa, se contará entre las que representan un giro importante. Las anteriores habían sido: el abandono de la escolástica para dar lugar al ingreso pleno de la filosofía moderna, a comienzos del siglo XIX; la difusión del positivismo en el tramo final de ese mismo siglo; y los inicios de la superación del positivismo apenas entrado el siglo actual. Esas líneas divisorias no son, por supuesto, rígidas.

La llamada etapa de superación del positivismo, representada por los nombres ilustres de Vaz Ferreira, Alejandro Korn, Enrique Molina, Alejandro Deustua, Antonio Caso, José Vasconcelos, etc., es el comienzo de la madurez filosófica latinoamericana, porque en ella la filosofía comienza a ser cultivada por sí misma. La acción de esas figuras proporcionó las bases para que en la cuarta década del siglo se iniciara el período que antes mencionábamos, caracterizado por hacer del ejercicio de la filosofía algo cada vez más profesional y riguroso.[2]

Es interesante—pero de ninguna manera es casual—que la fecha en que la Filosofía se incorpora al *Handbook* (1940) coincide con los comienzos de la etapa de intensificación filosófica a que nos estamos refiriendo.

Para establecer la distancia entre 1940 y esta penúltima década del siglo, tomemos un solo aspecto, utilizando las palabras de Risieri Frondizi en la nota introductoria del *HLAS 5*: "Ademá de la falta de buenas ediciones de los clásicos, otra deficiencia que creemos debe señalarse es la carencia, en toda América Latina, de una revista estrictamente filosófica. No faltan, por cierto revistas con títulos pretenciosos pero desgraciadamente el contenido no está de acuerdo con el título. En general los artículos de carácter filosófico se publican en revistas literarias que frecuentemente carecen del menor sentido de jerarquía intelectual" (p. 420). El juicio puede ser excesivamente severo, pues no era Frondizi hombre de circunloquios diplomáticos, pero lo importante es el hecho. Al respecto interesa señalar que un año después de publicado el *HLAS 5* aparecería en México la revista *Filosofía y Letras* y, dentro de la misma década o al comienzo de la siguiente, *Cuadernos de Filosofía* en Buenos Aires, la *Revista de Filosofía* en Chile y la *Revista Brasileira de Filosofia* en São Paulo, sin pretender una lista exhaustiva. Ese proceso continúa, con altibajos de apariciones y desapariciones, hasta hoy, en que publicaciones como *Revista Latinoamericana de Filosofía*, *Crítica*, *Escritos de Filosofía*, *Dianoia*, *Revista Venezolana de Filosofía*, *Análisis Filosófico*, etc., tienen muy alto nivel de calidad. El contraste con los hechos observados por Frondizi es muy grande. Las dificultadas que hoy confrontan las revistas filosóficas latinoamericanas—salvo excepciones—se deben a problemas económicos o a la inestabilidad de las instituciones, pero no a la carencia de personas con excelente formación para llenar sus páginas.[3]

Como consecuencia de lo anterior, esta introducción se dividirá habitualmente en dos partes: la primera dedicada a comentarios generales sobre los estudios que formarán la bibliografía propiamente dicha; y la segunda, en la que se señalarán las principales publicaciones filosóficas latinoamericanas que hayan llegado a nuestro conocimiento.

1. ESTUDIOS SOBRE EL PENSAMIENTO LATINOAMERICANO

El material recogido en esta sección autoriza a afirmar que la actividad monográfica, espositiva y crítica sobre el pensamiento latinoamericano se mantiene, se manifiesta en casi todos los países y abarca tanto nombres consagrados como autores menos divulgados. Su temática es, pues, variada, excepto en casos de recordación conmemorativa o en fenómenos excepcionales, como el de José Carlos Mariátegui en los últimos años. Y, como es natural, la historiografía no puede dejar de ser un espejo de las diferentes posiciones filosóficas e ideológicas, tanto en preferencias temáticas como en juicios de valor.

Sobre el persistente tema del pensamiento latinoamericano—el sentido de su historia, su valor, su carácter auténtico o dependiente, etc.—encontramos en esta entrega varias manifestaciones, pero sobre todo dos libros de importancia: el de Miró Quesada, *Proyecto y realización del filosofar latinoamericano* (item 7521), y el de Auturo A. Roig, *Teoría y crítica del pensamiento latinoamericano* (item 7528). El primero es continuación de una obra anterior, *Despertar y proyecto del filosofar latinoamericano* (ver *HLAS 40:9474*). El segundo pone de lleno a Roig, autor de una vasta obra historiográfica, en el plano de la especulación sobre el campo que cultiva. Obras de lectura obligada cualquiera sea la posición de quien las lea, no podrían resumirse en este comentario; pero puede decirse que ambas renuevan el tema—que viene de lejos—a la luz de nuevas circunstancias: la de Miró Quesada, por efecto de la "tecnificación" actual de la filosofía latinoamericana; la de Roig, en consonancia con el clima que crea la filosofía de la liberación—tomada la expresión en sentido muy amplio. (De Roig puede verse también *Filosofía, universidad y filósofos en América Latina* [item7526]). Dentro de este mismo tema, quisierámos llamar la atención sobre dos útiles artículos: el de Guillete Sturm "Dependencia y Originalidad en la Filosofía Latinoamericana" (item 7511), y el de Mario Sambarino, "Sobre la Imposibilidad de Fundamentar Filosóficamente una Etica Latinoamericana" (item 7532). Ambos son más analíticos que entusiastas del americanismo filosófico. Por último, se conectan con este tema dos panoramas generales: una recopilación preparada hace tiempor por José Gaos y ahora reeditada, *Antología del pensamiento de lengua española en la edad contemporánea* (item 7503), y el examen que Ricardo Maliandi hace en "Trayectoria y Sentido de la Etica en el Pensamiento Latinoamericano" (item 7519).

América Latina en general, no sólo su pensamiento, es un constante tema de interpretación. La literatura sobre este asunto es abundante. En esta entrega debemos señalar dos obras destacadas: *Situaciones e ideologías en Latinoamérica* (item 7529), del gran historiador argentino José Luis Romero, fallecido en 1977, e *Identidad, tradición, autenticidad: tres problemas de América Latina*, de Mario Sambarino (item 7531). La primera contiene trabajos de interpretación histórica. La segunda es un análisis filosófico. Desde el punto de vista marxista, trata la cuestión nacional en América Latina el libro de Ricaurte Soler, *Clase y nación: problemática latinoamericana* (item 7533), en tanto José Aricó estudia el pensamiento de Marx sobre América Latina (item 7504).

Trabajos de índole monográfica o crítica que cubren toda la región son los de Gregorio Weinberg sobre la Ilustración (item 7539) y de Hugo Biagini sobre el Primer Congreso Pedagógico Interamericano (item 7506).

La filosofía de la liberación es un sector del pensamiento latinoamericano que continúa activo. Precisamente se titula *Filosofía de la liberación* el trabajo más importante entre los de esa dirección que aquí se recogen, y del cual es autor Enrique Dussel (item 7509). Aunque exceden el campo de lo propiamente filosófico, ciertas discusiones actuales en torno a la teología de la liberación interesan para el panorama ideológico latinoamericano por su marcado tono secular (items 7502, 7514, 7516, y 7525).

En cuanto a historiografía sobre el pensamiento mexicano se destacan dos trabajos: una minuciosa crítica al historicismo de José Gaos, de Mario Sambarino (item 7553), y un excelente ensayo sobre Vasconcelos, de Enrique Krauze (item 7547). También hay buenos trabajos sobre Leopoldo Zea, por María Elena Rodríguez Ozán (item 7552); sobre Morelos, de A. Churruca Peláez (item 7544); y sobre Ignacio Ramírez, por David Maciel (item 7548).

De la no muy nutrida bibliografía aquí reunida sobre Centroamérica y Panamá, destacamos el libro de García Laguardia sobre José Cecilio del Valle (item 7557).

Sobre el resto de la zona del Caribe hay que señalar una excelente obra: *Main currents in Caribbean thought* de Gordon Lewis (item **7565**). "Haitian Social Thought in the 19th Century," de Bellegard-Smith, es también de gran utilidad (item **7563**).

Como en el número anterior, en éste se recogen varios trabajos sobre Andrés Bello. El libro de Arturo A. Roig que vincula la obra de Bello al campo de la semiótica (item **7579**), y el artículo de Arturo Ardao sobre la iniciación filosófica de Bello (item **7569**) merecen especial mención.

Ya hemos señalado en otra oportunidad el interés que recientemente se ha despertado en Ecuador por la historia de las ideas. Notamos ahora la aparición de una nueva edición, ampliada, de la obra de Arturo A. Roig comentada en *HLAS 44:7536* (item **7583**). Otros escritos de interés son el estudio de Rodolfo Agoglia sobre "Montalvo, Mera y el Romanticismo" (item **7580**), una obra colectiva sobre Espejo (item **7582**), y un artículo sobre la física de Juan Bautista Aguirre (siglo XVIII), de Terán Dutari (item **7585**).

Una vez más debemos llamar la atención sobre la abundancia de la literatura en torno a José Carlos Mariátegui. De 26 entradas correspondientes a Perú, 19 son escritos de o sobre Mariátegui, o vinculados a su obra. Debe recordarse también que en México se elaboró una buena antología de González Prada (item **7600**).

En el caso de Bolivia se destacan una obra sobre Tamayo (item **7612**), de Albarracín Millán (item **7612**), y la de Guillermo Francovich, *Los mitos profundos de Bolivia* (item **7613**). En el de Chile, el buen libro de Subercaseaux sobre José Victorino Lastarria (item **7619**).

Brasil es hoy en día uno de los países que mayor atención prestan a la historia de su propio pensamiento. Es de reciente creación el Centro de Documentação do Pensamento Brasileiro (Salvador, Bahia), que ha publicado un catálogo de su biblioteca (item **7621**), un valioso *Indice da Revista Brasileira de Filosofia: 1951–1980* (item **7631**) y una bibliografía de Silvestre Pinheiro Ferreira (item **7641**). En sendas compilaciones de textos básicos aparecieron: *A filosofia política positivista*, con introducciones de Antonio Paim (item **7626**) y *Corrente eclética na Bahia*, también con introducción del mismo autor (item **7623**). Entre las obras de conjunto se destaca *O humanismo brasileiro*, de Vamireh Chacon (item **7622**), y entre las instrumentales, la *Bibliografia filosófica brasileira: 1808–1930*, preparada por Antonio Paim (item **7637**). La obra de mayor aliento entre las incluidas sobre Brasil es el volumen colectivo *As idéias políticas no Brasil*, que puede considerarse un verdadero acontecimiento (item **7630**). Mencionaríamos por último buenas obras sobre autores individuales: Reale (item **7636**) y Alberto Torres (item **7642**).

En el caso de Argentina hay que señalar, en primer lugar, la aparición de un nuevo panorama general de las manifestaciones filosóficas en ese país, del que son autores Luis Farré y Celina Lértora Mendoza (item **7652**). Además de su obra filosófica personal, Farré había publicado, en 1950, *Cincuenta años de filosofía en la Argentina*. Celina Lértora es una distinguida investigadora de la filosofía colonial en su país. En cuanto a estudios sobre autores, se destaca el homenaje que la Sociedad Interamericana de Filosofía ha rendido a Francisco Romero, en un volumen en el que han colaborado autores de América Latina, Estados Unidos y Europa (item **7646**). Se ha continuado con la publicación del epistolario de Coriolano Alberini, y la revista *Cuyo*, de Mendoza, ha dedicado artículos a Ismael Quiles, V. Fatone, M.A. Virasoro, E. Pucciarelli, L. Farré y C.A. Erro, entre otros. Macedonio Fernández ha sido objeto de atención por parte de Hugo Biagini (item **7647**), y Alejandro Korn por parte de E. Anderson Imbert y Daniel Zalazar (item **7645 y 7666**), en tanto Mario Casalla estudia la estética del poeta y novelista Leopoldo Marechal (item **7649**).

Aunque no centralmente vinculada al pensamiento latinoamericano, no puedo dejar de mencionarse la *Histoire de la philosophie espagnole* (Université de Toulouse-Le Mirail, 1983), del destacado hispanista francés Alain Guy, a quien se deben valiosos trabajos sobre el pensamiento español e hispanoamericano. Una característica de este obra es que la mitad de su extensión está dedicada al siglo XX, conteniendo por lo tanto una gran riqueza de información sobre ese período.

2. BIBLIOGRAFIA FILOSOFICA RECIENTE

En materia de ediciones de clásicos, Juan David García Bacca ha comenzado la edición en español de las obras de Platón, en traducción suya. Auspician esta empresa de largo aliento la Presidencia de la República de Venezuela y la Universidad Central de ese país. El primer volumen contiene los siguientes diálogos: *Carmides, Lisis, Eutifrón, Apología, Critón, Fedón* y *Menón*.

La Universidad Simón Bolívar (Caracas) ha comenzado la publicación de una Biblioteca de la Antigüedad Clásica, en ediciones bilingües. Conocemos dos volúmenes: de Marco Tulio Cicerón, *Lelio: sobre la amistad*, traducción y notas de Angel J. Cappelletti (1982), y de Tito Lucrecio Caro, *De la naturaleza de las cosas*, traducción de Lisandro Alvarado con estudio preliminar del propio Cappelletti (1982). Guillermo Malavasi ha recopilado y traducido textos de *El ente y la esencia*, de Santo Tomás, que en segunda edición publicó en 1981 la Editorial de la Universidad de Costa Rica. *Doctrina espïritual de Bossuet* es una edición bilingüe con traducción de Angélica Berho y Juan Terán, que en 1981 fue publidaca por la Universidad Nacional de Tucumán. El prólogo y las notas son del mismo Terán. Una destacada labor es la realizada por Ezequiel de Olaso con su edición de *Escritos filosóficos* de Leibniz (Buenos Aires: Editorial Charcas, 1982). Las notas de esta edición son del propio Olaso y de Roberto Torretti, y las traducciones de éstos y de Tomás E. Zwanck. Las bibliografías, notas y referencias, así como los índices—en conjunto en valioso aparato crítico—dan particular mérito a esta obra y la singularizan en el medio de habla española. Por último, Eduardo Vázquez, profesor venezolano bien conocido por sus trabajos sobre Hegel y Marx, ha traducido, del segundo, la *Crítica del derecho del estado hegeliano* (Caracas: Universidad Central de Venezuela, 1980).

Como siempre, la labor crítica es la más abundante, y en algunos casos asume características de alta calidad. Entre la monografías dedicadas a un solo autor destacamos: Daniel Herrera Restrepo, *Los orígenes de la fenomenología* (Bogotá: Universidad Nacional de Colombia, 1980); Néstor García Canclini, *Epistemología e historia: la dialéctica entre sujeto y estructura en Merleau-Ponty* (México: UNAM, 1979); Denis L. Rosenfield, *Política e liberdade em Hegel* (São Paulo: Editora Brasiliense, 1983); Marly Bulcao, *O racionalismo da ciência contemporánea: uma análise da epistemologia de Gaston Bachelard* (Rio de Janeiro: Edições Antares, 1981); Roberto Machado, *Ciência e saber: a trajetória da arqueologia de Michel Foucault* (Rio de Janeiro: Edições Graal, 1981); José Ignacio López Soria, *De lo trágico a lo utópico: sobre el primer Lukács* (Caracas: Monte Avila, 1979); Otto Maduro, *La cuestión religiosa en el Engels pre-marxista: estudio sobre la génesis de un punto de vista en sociología de las religiones* (Caracas: Monte Avila, 1982) y anteriormente, del mismo autor, *Marxismo y religión* (Monte Avila, 1977); Francisco García Bazán, *Neoplatonismo y Vedânta: la doctrina de la materia en Plotino y Shánkara* (Buenos Aires: Depalma, 1982), parte de una obra más amplia; García Bazán es autor también de *Gnosis: la esencia del dualismo gnóstico* (2a. ed., 1978) y *Plotino y la gnosis* (1980). Otros trabajos de índole monográfica: Martha S. Mateo, *Razón y sensibilidad en la ética de Kant* (Universidad Nacional de Tucumán, 1981); Rodolfo Cortés del Moral, *Hegel y la ontología de la historia* (México: UNAM, 1980); Antonio Ramos Gómez Pérez, *El análisis sobre la usura en la "Suma Teológica" de Tomás de Aquino* (México: UNAM, 1982); Francisco Alvarez, *El pensamiento de Ortega y Gasset* (San José: Editorial Costa Rica, 1981); Virginia E. López Domínguez, *La concepción fichteana del amor* (Buenos Aires: Sudamericana, 1982).

Otras obras críticas son reunión de estudios y ensayos. En un volumen titulado *Ciencia jónica y pitagórica* (Caracas: Equinoccio, 1980), Angel J. Cappelletti reúne trabajos sobre Anaximandro, Alcmeón de Crotona y Diógenes de Apolonia, entre otros. *Vigilia y utopía: problemas de la filosofía contemporánea* (Universidad Autónoma de Guadalajara, 1980), de Osvaldo Ardiles, es un conjunto de artículos sobre temas contemporáneos, de un autor enrolado en la filosofía de la liberación. Marilena de Souza Chauí, en *Da realidade sem mistérios ao mistério do mundo* (São Paulo: Brasiliense, 1981), reúne ensayos sobre Espinoza, Voltaire y Merleau-Ponty. La Universidad de Carabobo (Valencia, Venezuela: 1981) ha publicado la obra de Ezequiel de Olaso, *Esceptismo e Ilustración: la crisis pirrónica de Hume y Rosseau*, que consta de tres trabajos, centrados en la distinción entre esceptismo "pirrónico" y escepticismo "académico." Ensayos sobre Sartre y Hegel, además de "Ideologia, Ciência e Poder" y "Filosofia e Realidade Nacional" se encuentran en Gerd A. Borheim, *O idiota e o espírito objetivo* (Porto Alegre: Globo, 1980). *Marx: lógica e política* (São Paulo: Brasiliense, 1983), de Ruy Fausto, es un conjunto de artículos sobre temas marxistas. En *Conocimiento y tradición metafísica* (Quito: Ediciones de la Universidad Católica, 1981), Julio Terán Dutari se confirma en su posición tomista mediante "estudios gnoseológicos" sobre Bergson, Heidegger, Husserl, Hegel, Kant y Santo Tomás. Aunque obra de crítica, es destacable por el enfoque personal *Ensayos sobre la dialéctica: estudios sobre la dialéctica en Hegel y Marx*, de Eduardo Vásquez (Caracas: Universidad Central de Venezuela, 1982). Por la misma Universidad y en el mismo año apareció *Compromisos y desviaciones: ensayos de filosofía y literatura* de Juan Nuño, autor proclive al estilo polémico.

En parte ensayo crítico y en parte análisis personal de temas es el conjunto de trabajos que Cástor Narvarte ha recogido en *Problemas de método y teoría* (Santiago: Universidad de Chile, 1980). *Gramsci*, de Carlos Nelson Coutinho (Porto Alegre: L&PM, 1981), es una combinación de estudio general con presentación de textos.

Tiene fecha de 1979 la publicación del vol. 2 de las *Actas* del IX Congreso Interamericano de Filosofía, que se realizó en Caracas. Este volumen está dedicado al tema general de "Las Tendencias Actuales de la Filosofía en el Continente Americano," subdividido en los siguientes temas especiales: "Filosofía de la Ciencia y Filosofía Analítica;" "Filosofía de la Praxis;" y "Filosofía Fenomenológica y Existencial."

Algunas obras son contribuciones a una determinada disciplina. Por ejemplo, de importancia para la filosofía de la lógica es *Ensaio sobre os fundamentos da lógica*, de Newton C.A. Da Costa (São Paulo: Editora HUCITEC: Editora da Universidade de São Paulo, 1980). Junto con Francisco Miró Quesada, el autor es uno de los principales representantes latinoamericanos en este campo.

Existe en la actualidad, en América Latina, particular interés por la filosofía del lenguaje. Alguna obras aparecidas últimamente en ese dominio son: Carlos Vogt, *Linguagem pragmática e ideológica* (São Paulo: HUCITEC: Fundação de Desenvolvimento da UNICAMP, 1980); Tomás Segovia *et al.*, *El lenguaje: problemas y reflexiones actuales* (Universidad Autónoma de Puebla, 1980); Humberto Giannini, *Desde las palabras* (Ediciones Nueva Universidad, 1981). Cid Seixas, *O espelho de Narciso: livro 1, Linguagem, cultura e ideologia no idealismo e no marxismo* (Rio de Janeiro: Civilização Brasileira; Brasília: Instituto Nacional do Livro, 1981); Emilio Garroni, *Re-conocimiento de la semiótica* (México: Editorial Concepto, 1979); Raul Landim Filho y Guido Antônio de Almeida, organizadores, *Filosofia da linguagem e lógica* (São Paulo: Edições Loyola; Rio de Janeiro: Pontifícia Universidad Católica, 1980).

Debe recordarse también: Héctor O. Ciarlo, *Crítica de la razón poética* (San Juan: Universidad de Puerto Rico, 1982).

El Padre Ismael Quiles, S.J., ha reeditado su *Introducción a la filosofía*, como vol. 3 de sus *Obras* (Buenos Aires: Depalma, 1983). En 1981 publicó *Persona y sociedad, hoy* (Editorial Universitaria de Buenos Aires y Centro Editor Argentino), que recoge conferencias basadas en sus obras anteriores *La persona humana* y *Más allá del existencialismo*.

Por último, otras obras van marcando etapas en el pensamiento personal de un autor. Así, *Verdade e conjetura* (Rio de Janeiro: Editora Nova Fronteira, 1983), es la última obra del filósofo brasileño Miguel Reale. Se trata de una teoría del "pensamiento conjetural," tema, a nuestro juicio, de la mayor relevancia para la teoría de la filosofía, y que el autor desarrolla como camino de fundamentación de la metafísica. Esta obra en cierto centido continúa una anterior, *Experiencia e cultura* (1977), con la que Miguel Reale pasó de la filosofía del derecho, donde ya había ganado un sólido lugar, a la fundamentación de una teoría del conocimiento como "teoría general de la experiencia," que finalmente apunta a la "fundação de um novo humanismo que saiba conciliar os valores objetivos da ciência como os da subjetividade criadora." Esta última obra está basada en amplias referencias al movimiento filosófico del siglo XX.

Por su parte, *Ratio Technica* (Caracas: Monte Avila, 1983), de Ernesto Mayz Vellenilla, conforma una trilogía con *El dominio del poder* (1982) y *El sueño del futuro*, de próxima aparición. La meditación de Mayz Vallenilla se organiza en torno al tema contemporáneo de la técnica y su efecto en el mundo moderno, para buscar la raíz de la respuesta en un teoría de la existencia humana donde al *afán de poder*, que es fuente de la *ratio technica*, se contrapone "una antagónica vertiente existenciaria: el *amor* o *eros*." Arturo Ardao, en *Espacio e inteligencia* (Caracas: Equinoccio, 1983), recoge una serie de trabajos que señalan una persistente meditación sobre el problema del espacio, no tanto en su concepción físico-matemática como en su relación con el hombre y su existencia. Para el espacio así considerado, Ardao augura una intensidad de pensamiento semejante a la que dio lugar, en la filosofía contemporánea, el problema del tiempo. Algunos de los trabajos recogidos son: "Relaciones entre el Espacio y la Inteligencia," "La Antropología Filosófica y la Espacialidad de la Psique," "Crisis de la Idea de Historia como Geo-Historia" y "Praxis y Espacio Exterior."

La bibliografía contenida en revistas filosóficas sobrepasa el espacio de esta introducción. Contienen buenas contribuciones la *Revista Latinoamericana de Filosofía* (Buenos Aires), que acaba de cumplir 10 años de aparición ininterrumpida; la *Revista Brasileira de Filosofía* (São Paulo); la *Revista Venezolana de Filosofía*; *Escritos de Filosofía* (Academia Nacional de Ciencias de Buenos Aires) que dedica cada número a una tema especial, siendo los últimos: No. 4: Técnica; No. 5: Tiempo, I y No. 6: Razón, I; *Reflexão* (Universidade Católica de Campinas); la *Revista de*

Filosofía de la Universidad de Costa Rica; etc. La lista está lejos de ser exhaustiva y, por supuesto, deja fuera las numerosas revistas generales y universitarias que acogen artículos filosóficos.

NOTAS

1. Si se excluyen las traducciones, el número de artículos y libros recogidos en el *HLAS 5* apenas sobrepasa los 50. El promedio de entradas de la sección en los *HLAS 38, 40, 42, 44* fue casi siete veces aquel número; o puesto de otra manera: aquella cantidad inicial es a lo sumo el 15 por ciento del promedio de asientos que contienen los *HLAS 38 a 44.*

2. Dentro de ese medio siglo se pueden distinguir etapas, pero ahora nos interesa solamente atenernos a las grandes líneas.

3. Lo anterior no prejuzga sobre cómo se verá ese cambio cuando pueda ser visto en perspectiva, pues eso dependerá de las coordenadas de valor que se apliquen para juzgar. Sospechamos, por ejemplo, que los resultados serán diferentes según que el valor más alto se ponga en la pureza técnica de la filosofía o en la función operante del pensamiento sobre la realidad social. Pero aquí no nos interesa realizar un ejercicio de profecía, sino señalar el hecho de la mencionada expansión, para los efectos prácticos de este *Handbook,* ante todo, y para captar su significado dentro del proceso histórico de la filosofía latinoamericana.

GENERAL

7501 Abellán, José Luis. La idea de América: origen y evolución. Madrid: Ediciones Istmo, 1972. 246 p.: bibl., ill. (Colección Fundamentos; 23)

Obra rica, no recogida anteriormente en este sección, escrita desde el punto de vista del pensamiento español y con gran simpatía por los temos americanos. El contenido va más allá de lo que indica el título, y desde varios ángulos se intenta una interpretación general de América Latina. Concluye con una útil cronología.

7502 Andrade Filho, Francisco Antônio de. Igreja e ideologias na América Latina, segundo Puebla. São Paulo: Edições Paulinas, 1982. 317 p.: bibl. (Igreja dinâmica)

Tesis de maestría. Aunque muy crítico del Documento de Puebla, puede ser útil para una idea general del proceso de compromiso de la Iglesia Católica en América Latina, con especial referencia al problema de la ideología.

7503 Antología del pensamiento de lengua española en la edad contemporánea. Introducción y selección de autores y textos de José Gaos. Culicán, México: Universidad Autónoma de Sinaloa, 1982. 2 v. (lvi, l397 p.): bibl.

Esta obra se publicó originalmente en 1945, dato no señalado en la presente edición. Es probablemente la única que incluye autores de habla española de ambos lados del Atlántico. Conserva gran parte de su valor a pesar del tiempo transcurrido.

7504 Aricó, José. Marx y América Latina. Lima: Centro de Estudios para el Desarollo y la Participación, 1980. 179 p.: bibl. (Serie Debate)

El título del libro debe entenderse en el sentido de lo que Marx pensó sobre América Latina. El problema del autor es por qué ese pensamiento fue escaso e inapropiado. Aunque bien informado, el trabajo se resiente por una exposición que pudo tener mejor secuencia.

7505 Bartley, Russell H. Acerca de la historia de las corrientes ideológicas en la latinoamericanística (URSS/AL, 1:61, enero 1983, p. 31–37)

Es, en realidad, una denuncia a la promoción de los estudios latinoamericanos en Estados Unidos, por considerarla "neocolonialista."

7506 Biagini, Hugo E. Educación y progreso: Primer Congreso Pedagógico Interamericano. Buenos Aires: Academia Nacional de Ciencias, Centro de Estudios Filosóficos (CINAE), 1983. 110 p.: appendix, bibl.

Trabajo prácticamente exhaustivo sobre el Congreso que se menciona en el subtítulo, que se llevó a cabo en Buenos Aires en 1882. Incluye bibliografía y apéndice documental.

7507 Briceño Guerrero, José M. Europa y América en el pensar mantuano. Caracas: Monte Avila Editores, 1981. 221 p. (Colección Estudios)

Ensayo de una filosofía de la historia europea de signo aristocrático-ultramontano, y de América como *paideia* de Europa.

7508 Cerutti Guldberg, Mónica. La filosofía en Latinoamérica como intervención en la política y en las ciencias (UNAM/L, 14, 1981, p. 177–189)

Consideraciones de apoyo a una filosofía de la liberación, basadas en autores franceses contemporáneos como Foucault y Althusser, entre otros.

Chiaramonte, José Carlos. Supuestos conceptuales en los intentos de periodización de la historia latinoamericana. Ver item **1758.**

7509 Dussel, Enrique D. Filosofía de la liberación. Bogotá: Universidad Santo Tomás, Centro de Enseñanza Desescolarizada, 1980. 240 p.: ill., indexes.

El autor se propone que la obra sea una introducción a la filosofía de la liberación. Es, también, una síntesis sistemática de lo que Dussel ha producido personalmente sobre ese tema, pero la exposición es más directa y menos erudita que en sus obras anteriores, como corresponde al propósito de la presente.

7510 García Regueiro, Ovidio. Ilustración e intereses estamentales: la versión castellana de la *Historia* de Raynal (*in* Coloquio Ilustración Española e Independencia de América, Bellaterra, Spain, 1978. Homenaje a Noël Salomon: Ilustración española e independencia de América. Edición preparada por Alberto Gil Novales. Barcelona: Universidad Autónoma de Barcelona, 1979, p. 165–205)

Detallado estudio de la libre traducción (incompleta) que el Duque de Almodóvar hizo de la *Histoire philosophique et politique des établissements et du commerce des européens dans les deux Indes*, con cotejo a dos columnas de various pasajes y análisis de los motivos de las variantes. De interés en general para la Ilustración española. Ver la reseña del historiador en item **1823.**

7511 Gillette Sturm, Fred. Dependencia y originalidad en la filosofía iberoamericana (UNAM/L, 14, 1981, p. 191–212)

Contribución de un autor norteamericano a un discutidísmo problema de la filosofía latinoamericana. Ofrece útiles distinciones sobre las nociones de "Iberoamérica," "originalidad" y "filosofía." Trabajo de lectura aprovechable.

7512 González Alvarez, Luis José. Etica latinoamericana. Bogotá: Universidad Santo Tomás, Centro de Enseñanza Descolorizada, 1978. 228 p.: bibl. (Filosofía a distancia)

Obra de introducción. En lugar del esquema clásico de un manual, intenta introducir a una ética *desde* América Latina, en función de sus problemas (principalmente sociales) y con el instrumento que ofrece la filosofía de la liberación.

7513 González Casanova, Pablo. América Latina: las críticas a las ciencia sociales y las tareas inmediatas (CSUCA/ESC, 21, sept./dic. 1978, p. 209–223, bibl.)

Quien se interese por la sociología "comprometida," políticamente participante o aun simplemente politizada de América Latina, y por la crítica a la llamada sociología científica, encontrará útil la información y la bibliografía. La posición del autor es de abierta simpatía a la sociología como forma o parte del compromiso político.

Halperin-Donghi, Tulio. "Dependency theory" and Latin American historiography. See item **1908.**

7514 Idígoras, José L. La liberación en Puebla (RCPC, 36:172/173, julio/dic. 1981, p. 18–36)

Defiende el documento emanado de la Conferencia Episcopal de Puebla, señalando que acogió el tema de la liberación y sus concomitancias teológicas y eclesiales, pero a la vez puntualizó los excesos a que ese tema dio lugar desde la anterior Conferencia de Medellín.

7515 Intelectuales, poder y revolución. Prólogo, selección y notas de Gabriel Careaga. 3a. ed., corregida y aumentada. México: Ediciones Océano, 1982. 285 p.: bibl., ill.

Interesan para esta sección: Daniel Cossío Villegas, "El Intelectual Mexicano y la Política" y Juan Marsal, "Los Intelectuales Mexicanos, el PRI y la Masacre de Tlatelolco."

7516 Kloppenburg, Boaventura. La Iglesia Popular en Puebla y su contexto (RCPC, 36:172/173, julio/dic. 1981, p. 48–71)

Las tendencias de Teología de la Liberación y de Iglesia Popular son consideradas antes, durante y después de la Conferencia Episcopal de Puebla (1979). La impresión del autor es que todo continuó como si Puebla no hubiera acontecido.

7517 Kossok, Manfred. Notas acerca de la recepción del pensamiento ilustrado en América Latina (*in* Coloquio Ilustración Española e Independencia de América, Bellaterra, Spain, 1978. Homenaje a Nöel Salomon: Ilustración española e independencia de América. Edición preparada por Alberto Gil Novales. Barcelona: Universidad Autónoma de Barcelona, 1979, p. 149–157)

Como lo indica el título, se trata de notas (preguntas, planteo de cuestiones). Son, sin embargo, perspicaces y útiles.

7518 Ladunsans, Stanislaus. Uma visão panorâmica da criatividade filosófica, hoje, na América Latina (PUC/V, 28:109, março 1983, p. 24–34)

Visión de la historia y el presente de la filosofía latinoamericana. El punto de vista tomista y católico del autor lo lleva a construir uma imagen histórica que posiblemente no reconozcan como propia los que no pertenenecen a su misma orientación filosófica.

Lancha, Charles. El ideal unionista latinoamericano de Bolívar y Martí. Ver item **1888.**

7519 Maliandi, Ricardo. Trayectoria y sentido de la Etica en el pensamiento latinoamericano (Separata de Cuadernos Salmantinos de Filosofía [Universidad Pontificia de Salamanca, Spain] 5, 1978 [i.e. 1979] p. 359–375)

Util, amplio y bien elaborado panorama de la ética en el pensamiento filosófico latinoamericano (ver *HLAS 42:7584*).

7520 Matyoka de Yeager, Trudy. Positivismo latinoamericano: Zea y después de Zea (RCPC, 26:172/173, julio/dic. 1981, p. 94–98)

El tema es la historiografía sobre el positivismo y sus problemas. La obra de Zea no es tan central en el artículo como sugiere el título. Contiene datos útiles, pero no logra concretarse en una tesis clara y definida.

7521 Miró Quesada Cantuarias, Francisco. Proyecto y realización del filosofar latinoamericano. México: Fondo de Cultura Económica, 1981. 220 p.: bibl. (Colección Tierra firme)

Obra muy importante, que debe considerarse conjuntamente con otra anterior del autor: *Despertar y proyecto del filosofar latinoamericano* (ver *HLAS 40:9474*). En la presente se propone mostrar que existen ya, y desde muy recientemente, algunas manifestaciones filosóficas latinoamericanas de calidad que no desmerecen de lo que se produce en los mejores centros mundiales. La selección de autores incluidos para estudio puede dar lugar a observaciones, como inevitablemente ocurre con toda selección. Pero esta obra, y la anterior mencionada más arriba, son de examen inevitable para meditar sobre la historia y la naturaleza del pensamiento filosófico latinoamericano.

7522 Morandé, Pedro. Ritual y palabra: aproximación a la religiosidad popular latinoamericana. Lima: Centro Andino de Historia, 1980. 79 p.: bibl.

Enfoque de revaloración de la religiosidad popular, tema desde el cual se critica la Teología de la Liberación y su tendencia secularizante. Frente al cristianismo puro como "religión de la palabra" (revelada), la religiosidad popular es considerada "cúltica," por ser una mezcla de cristianismo y creencias precolombinas.

Morse, Richard M. La cultura política iberoamericana de Sarmiento a Mariátegui. Ver item **1775.**

7523 O Novo socialismo francês e a América Latina. Organizado por Hélgio Trinidade e Fernando Henrique Cardoso. Tradução dos textos de Cleuza Vieira Vernier. Rio de Janeiro: Paz e Terra, 1982. 185 p.: bibl. (Coleção O Mundo, hoje; v. 37)

Preparado com motivo del triunfo socialista de Mitterrand en Francia, y orientado en ese sentido. De este volumen interesa para esta sección el artículo de F.H. Cardoso, "A América Latina e o Socialismo na Década de 80."

7524 Reacsos, Nelson. La filosofía latinoamericana: un proyecto político y un principio de acción (UNAM/L, 14, 1981, p. 169–176)

Consideraciones metodológicas y programáticas para fundamentar un pensamiento que, en términos amplios, haría parte de la filosofía de la liberación. El siguiente es un párrafo típico: "A Latinoamérica no le queda otro camino que una filosofía revolucionaria, que termine con la explotación, la dependencia, el colonialismo . . ."

7525 Richard, Pablo. La Iglesia latinoamericana entre el temor y la esperanza: apuntes teológicos para la década en los años 80. Prólogo, Gustavo Gutiérrez. San José: Departamento Ecuménico de Investigaciones, 1980. 103 p. (Colección Testimonios)

Se reiteran las tesis clásicas de la Teología de la Liberación, quizá radicalizadas en sus aspectos de politización secular. Más interesantes son las comparaciones entre la Teología de la Liberación latinoamericana y otras variantes "progresistas" de la Teología europea, hechas en el primero de los artículos incluidos en el libro.

7526 Roig, Arturo Andrés. Filosofía, universidad y filósofos en América Latina. México: Universidad Nacional Autónoma de México, Coordinación de Humanidades, Centro Coordinador y Difusor de Estudios Latinoamericanos, 1981. 271 p.: bibl. (Nuestra América; 4)

El autor se ha destacado por su intensa labor sobre historia de las ideas en América Latina. En este libro recoge numerosos estudios anteriores, entre ellos algunos dedicados al tema de la historia de las ideas en general y al problema de la filosofía latinoamericana.

7527 ———. La "Historia de las Ideas" y sus motivaciones fundamentales (Revista de Historia de las Ideas [Casa de la Cultura Ecuatoriana, Centro de Estudios Latinoamericanos de la Pontificia Universidad Católica del Ecuador, Quito] 4, 1983, p. 151–166)

Muestra que el movimiento de "Historia de las Ideas," como fenómeno latinoamericano, tiene una trayectoria histórica con varias etapas, vinculadas éstas a distintas situaciones filosóficas (y a factores extrafilosóficos). La utilidad del trabajo reside en el trazado de ese cuadro histórico, que sin duda facilita la meditación epistemológica e histórica sobre lo que en América Latina se denomina "Historia de las Ideas." Señala que a lo largo de todo el proceso la "Historia de las Ideas" ha estado vinculada a una intención "de revalorización de lo iberoamericano."

7528 ———. Teoría y crítica del pensamiento latinoamericano. México: Fondo de Cultura Económica, 1981. 313 p.:

bibl. (Colección Tierra firme)

Podría caracterizarse esta obra como perteneciente en general a la orientación propia de la filosofía de la liberación. Sin embargo, ni está en el centro de ella, ni tiene su aliento polémico, ni por lo tanto su tono a veces casi agresivo y "contestatario." Sin pérdida de su propia personalidad, tiene rasgos que la emparentan con la modalidad de pensamiento y expresión de Leopoldo Zea. Varios de los artículos habían sido publicados anteriormente, pero el conjunto forma aquí un todo orgánico. En el fondo, se trata de una búsqueda filosófica de la identidad latinoamericana, no sólo en su ser, sino también en su posible hacer y su programa de realizaciones. Es también un intento de afirmar esa identidad, frente a variadas subestimaciones, propias y ajenas. Con este libro el autor pasa de la historiografía sobre el pensamiento latinoamericano a la "filosofía de la historia" de América Latina.

7529 Romero, José Luis. Situaciones e ideologías en Latinoamérica. Ensayos compilados por Luis Alberto Romero. México: Universidad Nacional Autónoma de México, Coordinación de Humanidades, Centro Coordinador y Difusor de Estudios Latinoamericanos, 1981. 244 p.: bibl. (Nuestra América; 2)

Excepto sus libros *El pensamiento político de la derecha latinoamericana* y *Latinoamérica: las ciudades y las ideas*, esta obra contiene todo lo escrito por José Luis Romero sobre América Latina. El acierto de esta edición reside en haber sido J.L. Romero uno de los mayores historiadores latinoamericanos y uno de los más lúcidos intérpretes de Latinoamérica.

Ronan, Charles E. Francisco Javier Iturri, S.J. and Alcedos' *Diccionario geográfico*. See item **2629.**

7530 Rubio Angulo, Jaime. Producción filosófica latinoamericana (PUJ/UH, 10:14, marzo 1981, p. 111–117)

A pesar de la amplitud del título, las noticias contenidas en este artículo se refieren a autores involucrados en la filosofía de la liberación o cercanos a ella.

7531 Sambarino, Mario. Identidad, tradición, autenticidad: tres problemas de América Latina. Caracas: Centro de Estudios Latinoamericanos Rómulo Gallegos, 1980.

326 p.: bibl. (Colección Enrique Bernardo Núñez; 2)

Es éste uno de los libros más serios y de mayor exigencia filosófica entre los que tratan el frecuentado tema del título. No es tanto una obra de tesis como de análisis, que al desbrozar el campo conceptual elegido sienta las bases para una más fructífera discusión del asunto.

7532 ———. Sobre la imposibilidad de fundamentar filosóficamente una ética latinoamericana (Fragmentos [Centro de Estudios Latinoamericanos Rómulo Gallegos, Departamento de Investigaciones, Caracas] 8, sept./dic. 1980, p. 1–10)

Argumentación destinada a mostrar que no tiene sentido teórico hablar de una "ética latinoamericana," ni siquiera desde el ángulo de una "ética de la situación."

7533 Soler, Ricaurte. Clase y nación: problemática latinoamericana. Barcelona: Fontamara, 1981. 143 p.: bibl. (Colección Ensayo contemporáneo)

Tratamiento de la cuestión nacional, con énfasis en la realidad de las clases sociales, desde un punto de vista marxista. La segunda parte estudia la idea de la unidad hispanoamericana, especialmente en Lucas Alamán y Justo Arosemena.

7534 Sotelo, Ignacio. América Latina: un ensayo de interpretación. Madrid: Centro de Investigaciones Sociológicas, 1980. 171 p.: bibl. (Colección Monografías: no. 27)

La perspectiva desde la que se realiza la interpretación es sociológica. Los principales temas tratados son la historia del pensamiento social latinoamericano, el desarrollo reciente de la sociología en Latinoamérica, el tema de la dependencia y el militarismo.

Soto Cárdenas, Alejandro. Influencia de la independenca de los Estados Unidos en la constitución de las naciones latinoamericanas. Ver item **1898.**

7535 Tanzi, Héctor José. El pensamiento europeo y su influencia en la emancipación americana (PAIGH/H, 92, julio/dic. 1981, p. 99–126)

La tesis del trabajo es que Rousseau y la Ilustración francesa no fueron necesarios para fundamentar la ideología de la Independencia, pues las fuentes españolas habrían

sido suficientes. La "demostración" se hace, principalmente, en base a elementos declarativos de documentos oficiales. Ver la reseña del historiador en item **1899.**

7536 Trinidade, Hélgio. El tema del fascismo en América Latina (IEP/REP, 30, nov./dic. 1982, p. 111–141)

El tema del trabajo es: /Hasta qué punto puede hablarse de *fascismo* en América Latina? Examinando los regímenes de Vargas en Brasil y Perón en Argentina, el autor repasa una larga serie de opiniones sobre el particular. Se inclina a negar "la existencia de regímenes políticos fascistas en América Latina," aceptando sin embargo "la presencia de movimientos fascistas limitados a los años treinta."

7537 Utopía y revolución: el pensamiento político contemporáneo de los indios en América Latina. Estudio introductorio, selección y notas de Guillermo Bonfil Batalla. México: Editorial Nueva Imagen, 1981. 439 p.: bibl. (Serie interétnica)

Antología cuya intención es señalar la existencia de un movimiento y un pensamiento políticos propios de las poblaciones indígenas. Se incluyen "ideólogos" indios y textos de las organizaciones indígenas. La introducción del compilador: "Utopía y Revolución: el Pensamiento Político Contemporáneo de los Indios en América Latina," es muy útil.

7538 Vidal Muñoz, Santiago. La filosofía y la Historia de las Ideas en Iberoamérica (CH, 386, agosto 1982, p. 274–297, bibl.)

Campea en todo el trabajo—de dificultosa expresión—un sentido integralista en la concepción del hombre. Consecuentemente, preconiza una Historia de las Ideas que vaya más allá de lo intelectual en sentido restringido e incluya valores, creencias, etc.

7539 Weinberg, Gregorio. The Enlightenment and some aspects of culture and higher education in Spanish America (Studies on Voltaire and the Eighteenth Century [Voltaire Foundation, Taylor Institution, Oxford, England] 167, 1977, p. 491–522)

Panorama de la influencia de la Ilustración en las ideas, las ciencias y la enseñanza superior, con especial referencia a los cambios que provocó en dicha enseñanza.

MEXICO

7540 Adame Goddard, Jorge. El pensamiento político y social de los católicos mexicanos, 1867–1914. México: Universidad Nacional Autónoma de México, Instituto de Investigaciones Históricas, 1981. 273 p.: bibl. (Serie de historia moderna y contemporánea; 15)

De 1867–92 se extiende, según el autor, una etapa tradicionalista y "conservadora." En el período 1892–1914 estudia las doctrinas del "catolicismo social," posiblemente lo más interesante del volumen. Buena monografía, con útil lista de fuentes consultadas.

7541 Andrés Molina Enríquez. Toluca: Gobierno del Estado de México, 1979. 106 p.: port. (Serie José Antonio Alzate y Ramírez. Colección Testimonios del Estado de México; 16)

Con las ideas expresada en sus obras *Los grandes problemas nacionales* (1909) y *La revolución agraria en México* (1934), Molina Enríquez contribuyó de hecho a la Revolución Mexicana. Esta obra recoge una serie de breves trabajos sobre él, más bien de divulgación y homenaje.

7542 Cardiel Reyes, Raúl. La filosofía política del México actual. México: Universidad Nacional Autónoma de México, Coordinación de Humanidades, 1980. 77 p.

Se trata de una exposición breve pero precisa. Su objeto es determinar las fuentes conceptuales de la Revolución Mexicana. Según el autor, la Revolución no fue tal por imponer ideas nuevas, sino por armar un programa para la acción, y estableció las bases de una democracia social.

7543 Carr, Barry. Marxism and anarchism in the formation of the Mexican Communist Party: 1910–1919 (HAHR, 6 3:2, May 1983, p. 277–305)

Detallado recuento de los orígenes del Partido Comunista Mexicano, especialmente de la tensión entre los elementos anarcosindicalistas y los adherentes al marxismo.

7544 Churruca Peláez, Agustín. El pensamiento insurgente de Morelos. Prólogo de Ernesto de la Torre Villar. México: Editorial Porrúa, 1983. 241 p., 8 leaves of plates: ill.

Obra muy apoyada en los escritos de Morelos, que pone en relación su pensamiento—especialmente el religioso y teológico—con su actuación y su época.

7545 Cueva, Hermilo de la. José Vasconcelos: semblanza y pasión otoñal. México: B. Costa-Amic Editor, 1976. 165 p.

Escrito con admiración por quien fuera médico personal de Vasconcelos. Libro de naturaleza más bien anecdótica.

7546 Guillén, Pedro. Jesús Silva Herzog, Isidro Fabela, José Vasconcelos. México: Universidad Nacional Autónoma de México, 1980. 228 p.

Ensayos biográficos y de apreciación valorativa sobre tres maestros mexicanos. Escritos con simpatía hacia ellos.

Herrejón Peredo, Carlos. Hidalgo: la justificación de la insurgencia. Ver item **1987.**

7547 Krauze, Enrique. Pasión y contemplación en Vasconcelos: pt. 2 (Vuelta [México] 7:79, junio 1983, p. 16–26, bibl.)

Ensayo brillante sobre la personalidad y la acción de Vasconcelos.

7548 Maciel, David. Ignacio Ramírez, ideólogo del liberalismo social en México. México: Universidad Nacional Autónoma de México, 1980. 220 p.: bibl.

Muy buena monografía, que llena un vacío historiográfico. Concebida como "biografía intelectual," relaciona el pensamiento y la significación de Ramírez (1818–79) con el clima histórico. Bien elaborados el ensayo bibliográfico y la bibliografía propiamente dicha.

7549 Moreno, Roberto. La ciencia de la Ilustración mexicana (EEHA/AEA, 32, 1975, p. 25–41)

Utilizando conceptos de Basalla y Kuhn, concluye que la labor científica de Humboldt en México constituye un nuevo "paradigma." El artículo trata primordialmente de la etapas en que puede dividirse el estilo de trabajo científico en el México del siglo XVIII. Ver la reseña del historiador en item **2005.**

7550 Neira, Hugo. En torno a Octavio Paz (Socialismo y Participación [Centro de Estudios para el Desarrollo y la Participación (CEDEP), Lima] 12, dic. 1980, p. 71–79)

Ensayo sobre *El laberinto de la soledad.*

7551 Noriega, Alfonso. Francisco Severo Maldonado, el precursor. México: Universidad Nacional Autónoma de México, Coordinación de Humanidades, 1980. 282 p., 1 leaf of plates: bibl. ill.

Obra de difusión, pero oportuna, sobre un tema poco conocido. Sitúa al autor en el contexto de las ideas iluministas y destaca su contribución al conocimiento de la realidad mexicana. Sacerdote mexicano, Maldonado (1755–1832) entra igualmente en el campo de las ideas filosóficas, políticas y económicas.

Prieto Castillo, Daniel. El arte y el anarquismo mexicano. Ver item **403.**

Rodríguez Ozan, María Elena. La enseñanza de la historia de las ideas en México. Ver item **2272.**

7552 ———. El proyecto asuntivo en la obra de Leopoldo Zea (UNAM/L, 14, 1981, p. 161–168)

Util resumen de lo que podría denominarse la filosofía de la historia de América Latina que Leopoldo Zea ha desarrollado en sus obras de pensamiento personal.

7553 Sambarino, Mario. El historicismo personalístico de José Gaos. Caracas: Centro de Estudios Latinoamericanos Rómulo Gallegos, 1982. 40 p. (Cuadernos)

Reconoce el carácter ineludible que tiene el problema del historicismo y lo examina cuidadosamente en Gaos. El estilo de crítica rigurosa que representa es encomiable. (El estudio se había concluido en 1976).

Schmidt, Henry C. The Mexican intellectual as political pundit, 1968–1976: the case of Daniel Cosío Villegas. See item **2282.**

Suárez Iñiguez, Enrique. Los intelectuales en México. Ver *HLAS 45:8090.*

7554 Valadés, J.C. Precursores del socialismo antiautoritario en México (CEHSMO, 6:21, enero 1981, p. 25–30, photos)

Los hechos narrados, referentes a las primeras organizaciones obreras en México, ocurrieron en la segunda mitad del siglo XIX. Se indica al comienzo que este artículo apareció en *La Protesta* (Buenos Aires), en 1928, y nunca había sido antes reproducido en México.

AMERICA CENTRAL

7555 Alfaro, Ricardo J. El pensamiento de Ricardo J. Alfaro. Estudio introductorio y antología, Carlos Manuel Gasteazoro. Panamá: Presidencia de la República, 1981. 413 p.: bibl. (Biblioteca de la cultura panameña; t. 10)

Contiene una antología del diplomático, político e historiador R.J. Alfaro (1882–1971) y una cronología de su vida y de los acontecimientos contemporáneos.

Andrews, Patricia A. El liberalismo en El Salvador a finales del siglo XIX. Ver item **2376.**

7556 DeWitt, Donald L. Educational thought in Panama: the pedagogical movement of the 1920s (UPR/CS, 17:1/2, April/July 1977, p. 134–145)

Sobre las ideas pedagógicas de los principales educadores panameños de las dos primeras décadas del siglo.

7557 García Laguardia, Jorge Mario. Ilustración y liberalismo en Centroamérica: el pensamiento de José Cecilio del Valle. México: Departamento Editorial de la Universidad Nacional Autónoma de México, 1982. 81 p.

Util y bien informada exposición de las ideas de José Cecilio del Valle, especialmente de su formación dentro del pensamiento ilustrado.

7558 Kuhn, Gary G. El positivismo de Gerardo Barrios (RCPC, 36:172/173, julio/dic. 1981, p. 87–88)

Breve nota sobre la presidencia de Barrios (1858–63) y su clima de ideas.

7559 Leiva Vivas, Rafael. Vigencia del sabio Valle. Ciudad Universitaria Rodrigo Facio, Costa Rica: Editorial Universitaria Centroamericana, 1980. 442 p.: bibl. (Colección Rueda del tiempo)

Biografía de José Cecilio del Valle, 1780–1834 (ver también item **7557**).

7560 Miró, Rodrigo. El ensayo en Panamá (APL/B, 3, 1982, p. 9–28)

Introducción a una antología del ensayo en Panamá. El género, tomado aquí en términos amplios, es siempre fuente de expresiones que van más allá de lo literario y entran en el campo de la historia de las ideas.

7561 El Pensamiento contemporáneo costar-ricense. San José: Editorial Costa Rica, 1980. 1 v.: bibl. (Biblioteca Patria; 18)

Se trata de pensamiento político. Se recogen, en forma antológica, textos de representantes del "neoliberalismo" (entre otros, Brenes Mesén y García Monge) y del "socialcristianismo" (casi exclusivamente el ex-Presidente Calderón Guardia y el Arzobispo Sanabria Martínez).

7562 Woodward, Ralph Lee, Jr. Pensamiento científico y desarrollo económico en Centroamérica: 1860–1920 (RCPC, 36:172/173, julio/dic. 1981, p. 73–86, graphs, tables)

Se muestra la relación entre la adhesión a la forma científica de pensamiento (característica del positivismo) y el desarrollo material (lo que en el título se denomina "desarrollo económico") durante la época estudiada. Síntesis útil. Ver la reseña del historiador en item **2447**.

CARIBE INSULAR

7563 Bellegarde-Simth, Patrick. Haitian social thought in the 19th century: class formation and Westernization (UPR/CS, 20:1, March 1980, p. 5–33)

Extenso trabajo, con nutrida información sobre un tema poco frecuentado. Se tiende a poner las ideas en relación con el ambiente histórico y con similares situaciones en el resto de América Latina.

7564 Franco, Franklin J. Historia de las ideas políticas en la República Dominicana: contribución a su estudio. Santo Domingo: Editora Nacional, 1981. 1 v.: bibl., port.

El autor considera el campo de estudio elegido como descuidado por la historiografía y aun por la enseñanza. Es un panorama general, que llega hasta la actualidad, pero que será seguido por un segundo volumen.

7565 Lewis, Gordon K. Main currents in Caribbean thought: the historical evolution of Caribbean society in its ideological aspects, 1492–1900. Baltimore, Md.: Johns Hopkins University Press, 1983. 375 p.: bibl., index. (Johns Hopkins studies in Atlantic history and culture)

Decrito el contenido por el propio autor como: "a descriptive and critical analysis of the total complex of ideas, sentiments, outlooks, attitudes, and values that, in the fullest sense of the word, constitute the ideology of the groups that have figured in the Caribbean story," se trata de una valiosa e imprescindible obra de historia intelectual. Es interesante señalar que una de las tesis del autor es que los elementos ideológicos extraños terminaron por ser adaptados a la realidad de la región, dándole un carácter propio, que es lo que reiteradamente se ha afirmado en el caso de América Latina en relación con las ideas europeas.

López Váldez, Rafael L. Ideario social de Don Fernando Ortiz. Ver *HLAS 45:8185*.

7566 Morán Arce, Lucas. Ser o no ser, o, La angustia existencial puertorriqueña. San Juan: L. Morán Arce, 1982. 120 p.

Reflexiones sobre la búsqueda de la identidad cultural en Puerto Rico, desde bases raciales e históricas, y tomando en cuenta diversas interpretaciones de autores locales.

7567 Toledo Sande, Luis. Ideología y práctica en José Martí. La Habana: Editorial de Ciencias Sociales, 1982. 299 p. (Colección de estudios martianos)

Los artículos que tratan de las ideas más generales o "filosóficas" de Martí son: "Anticlericalismo, Idealismo, Religiosidad y Práctica en José Martí" y "Pensamiento y Combate en la Concepción Martiana de la Historia." Otros tratan de Martí y la mujer, la creación intelectual y la masonería. El enfoque es marxista-leninista—por lo menos en lo declarativo.

VENEZUELA

7568 Ardao, Arturo. Bello y la filosofía lainoamericana (CONAC/RNC, 43:249, abril/dic. 1982, p. 91–111)

Sitúa a Bello en el actual problema de la existencia y sentido de la filosofía latinoamericana, agregando una oportuna comparación con Alberdi. Excelente artículo.

———. Del mito Ariel al mito anti-Ariel. Ver item **5098**.

7569 ———. La iniciación filosófica de Bello: su *Análisis ideológica* de los tiempos verbales (*in* Bello y Caracas [see *HLAS 44:5121*] p. 329–390)

Fundamental estudio de *Análisis ideológica de los tiempos de la conjugación castellana*, obra primeriza de Bello aunque publicada en 1841, como momento hacia su *Gramática de la lengua castellana* y su *Filosofía del entendimiento*. El análisis va desde consideraciones sobre filosofía y gramática en la historia de la filosofía hasta la relaciones con Condillac y Destutt de Tracy y un estudio detallado de la obra en cuestión. Este artículo apareció parcialmente en *Revista Nacional deCultura* (Caracas, 241, 1979).

7570 Brewer-Carias, Allan R. Algunos aspectos de la concepción del Estado en la obra de Andrés Bello (CONAC/RNC, 43:249, abril/dic. 1982, p. 162–192)

Extensa exposición de la idea del Estado, su funcionamiento y sus poderes, en Bello.

Caballero, Manuel. La sección venezolana de la Internacional Comunista: un tema para el estudio de las ideas en el siglo XX venezolano. Ver item **2913**.

7571 Dessau, Adalbert. Ideas directrices y significación histórica del pensamiento filosófico de Andrés Bello, 1781–1865 (RCLL, 7:16, 1982, p. 41–66)

Artículo que merece atención, tanto en lo que se refiere a Bello y su vinculación con el pensamiento de la Ilustración, como en sus consideraciones sobre el desarrollo histórico de la filosofía en América Latina en general. La posición marxista habitual en el autor se limita aquí a ciertas afirmaciones que no son centrales a su trabajo de interpretación.

7572 Flores F., Sergio and **Juan Saavedra A.** Bello y la ciencia histórica: una tradición vigente (SCHG/R, 149, 1981, p. 7–20)

Sobre la influencia de Bello en los autores que constituyen el comienzo de la historiografía nacional en Chile.

7573 Krebs, Ricardo. Proyecciones del pensamiento histórico de Andrés Bello (CONAC/RNC, 43:249, abril/dic. 1982, p. 267–296)

Expone las ideas de Bello sobre la ciencia histórica (en oposición a la concepción de Lastarria) y sobre la "filosofía de la historia" de América de dicho pensador. Por último, trata de su influencia sobre la historiografía chilena.

Marta Sosa, Joaquín. Nueva civilización, nueva revolución. Ver *HLAS 45:6267*.

7574 Mieres, Antonio. Ideas positivistas en Gil Fortoul y su *Historia*. Caracas: Ediciones de la Facultad de Humanidades y Educación, Instituto de Estudios Hispanoamericanos, Universidad Central de Venezuela, 1981. 275 p.: bibl.

Examen de la *Historia constitucional de Venezuela* (1907–09), de Gil Fortoul, especialmente de las ideas básicas que la informan, de sesgo positivista.

7575 Moreno Davis, Julio César. Andrés Bello como filósofo (APL/B, 3, 1982, p. 54–63)

Breve exposición de la influencia del empirismo inglés en Bello.

***Pensamiento político* venezolano del siglo XIX.** Ver item **2930**.

7576 Ramírez, Rafael. La intelectualidad impotente: crítica de la obra de Ludovico Silva. Caracas: Universidad Central de Venezuela, Facultad de Ciencias Económicas y Sociales, División de Publicaciones, 1981. 181 p.: bibl. (Colección Libros)

Minuciosa polémica contra la interpretación del marxismo (especialmente en lo que se refiere al concepto de ideología) del autor venezolano Ludovico Silva, realizada desde una posición supuestamente marxista ortodoxa. (Sobre Ludovico Silva, ver *HLAS 36:5230–5231; HLAS 40:9710;* y *HLAS 42:7526*).

7577 Ramis, Pompeyo. Veinte filósofos venezolanos: 1946–1976. Mérida, Venezuela: Universidad de Los Andes, Consejo de Publicaciones, 1978. 273 p.: bibl.

Obra de exposición, de estructura simple, que intencionalmente utiliza abundantes citas de los autores tratados. Entre estos últimos se encuentran: García Bacca, Granell, Núñez Tenorio, Ludovico Silva, Riu, Mayz Vallenilla, Cappelletti, Nuño, etc.

Reyes de Viana, Celia and **Celia I. Viana Reyes.** José Enrique Rodó, "genio" educador iberoamericano. Ver item **5127**.

7578 Rodríguez, Simón. Inventamos o erramos. Caracas: Monte Avila Editores, 1980. 225 p.: bibl. (Biblioteca de utopías)

Antología de escritos de Simón

Rodríguez, preparada por Dardo Cúneo, de quien es el ensayo preliminar.

7579 Roig, Arturo Andrés. Andrés Bello y los orígenes de la semiótica en América Latina. Quito: Ediciones de la Universidad Católica, 1982. 90 p. (Serie Cuadernos universitarios; no. 4)

Busca desentrañar, de la *Filosofía del entendimiento,* los contenidos que contribuirían a una "prehistoria" de la semiótica en América Latina. Dentro del mismo tema hay oportunas referencias a Simón Rodríguez y el romanticismo latinoamericano.

ECUADOR

7580 Agoglia, Rodolfo Mario. Montalvo, Mera y el romanticismo (Revista de Historia de las Ideas [Casa de la Cultura Ecuatoriana; Centro de Estudios Latinoamericanos de la Pontificia Universidad Católica del Ecuador, Quito] 2:4, 1983, p. 63–71)

Analiza las relaciones de Juan Montalvo (1832–89) y Juan León Mera (1832–94) con el romanticismo y el historicismo, y reivindica el carácter americano de la obra de ambos.

7581 Malo González, Hernán. La filosofía en el Ecuador republicano (*in* Arte y cultura, Ecuador: 1830–1980. Coordinación del proyecto, Carlos Paladines. Fernando Tinajero Villamar et al. Quito: Corporación Editora Nacional, 1980, p. 69–83 [Libro del sesquicentenario; 2])

Panorama general pero, más que nada, reivindicación del valor de la filosofía en el Ecuador.

7582 Paladines, Carlos *et al.* Eugenio Espejo: conciencia crítica de su época. Quito: Centro de Publicaciones, Pontificia Universidad Católica del Ecuador, 1978. 369 p.: bibl.

Contiene cinco trabajos de various autores sobre Eugenio de Santa Cruz y Espejo (1747–95): tres de carácter biográfico y dos que analizan su pensamiento. Los dos últimos son: Carlos Paladines, "El Pensamiento Económico, Político y Social" y Samuel Guerra Bravo, "El Itinerario Filosófico de Espejo." Contiene bibliografía.

7583 Roig, Arturo Andrés. Esquemas para una historia de la filosofía ecuatoriana.

2a. ed. Quito: Ediciones de la Universidad Católica, 1982. 195 p.: bibl. Ver *HLAS 44:* 7563.

Se agrega un capítulo: "La Historia de las Ideas y la Historia de la Filosofía Latinoamericanas: el Despertar de una Tarea en el Ecuador."

7584 ———. Momentos y corrientes del pensamiento utópico en el Ecuador (UNAM/L, 1981, p. 51–69)

Se refiere al pensamiento "utópico" en Eugenio Espejo, pero también a otras manifestaciones durante el siglo XIX, entre ellas Juan Montalvo y su vinculación con el socialismo utópico. (Sobre el "milenarismo" en José de Valdivieso, mencionado por el autor, ver *HLAS 44:7590*).

7585 Terán Dutari, Julio. La *Física* de Juan Bautista Aguirre, ante el segundo centenario de la *Crítica* de Kant (Revista de Historia de las Ideas [Casa de la Cultura Ecuatoriana; Centro de Estudios Latinoamericanos de la Pontificia Universidad Católica del Ecuador, Quito] 2:4, 1983, p. 15–47)

La utilidad de este trabajo consiste en la exposición de ciertas ideas generales del jesuita ecuatoriano J.B. Aguirre (1725–86), extraídas de sus escritos sobre "física." Aparentemente el autor estaría por publicar una traducción de la *Physica ad Aristotelis mentem* (1758), del propio Aguirre.

PERU

Adorno, Rolena. Bartolomé de las Casas y Domingo de Santo Tomás en la obra de Felipe Waman Puma. Ver item **5029.**

7586 Alarco, Francisco. La psicoterapia dinámica y José Carlos Mariátegui (Revista de la Universidad Católica [Pontificia Universidad Católica del Perú, Lima] 5, agosto 1979, p. 83–107)

Mezcla de análisis técnico y mensaje político, afirma el valor de los escritos de Mariátegui para la psicología dinámica.

7587 *Allpanchis Phuturinqa*. Instituto de Pastoral Andina. Vol. 14, No. 16, 1980- . Cusco, Perú.

Número dedicado a "Mariátegui y el Mundo Andino." Contiene: Robert Paris, "J.C. Mariátegui y el Modelo del 'Comu-

nismo' Inca;" Carlos Franco, "El Nacionalismo Andino;" J. Tamayo Herrera, "Mariátegui y la *Intelligentsia* del Sur Andino;"
M. Arroyo Posadas, "La Correspondencia de J.C.
Mariátegui a Jauja;" Manuel Marzal, "La
Comunidad Indígena y su Transformación
según Castro Pozo."

7588 Aricó, José. Mariátegui y los orígenes
del marxismo latinoamericano (Socialismo y Participación [Centro de Estudios
para el Desarrollo y la Participación Lima] 5,
dic. 1978, p. 13–42)
Aunque es parte de la extensa polémica que se ha desarrollado en torno al autor
de los *Siete ensayos*, es uno de los trabajos
más abarcadores sobre el Mariátegui político.
Parte de reconocer en el marxismo un carácter crítico y problemático. Se concibió como
introducción a un conjunto de escritos de diversos autores. Ver la reseña del historiador
en item **2948.**

7589 Bieber, León Enrique. En torno al origen histórico e ideológico del ideario
nacionalista populista latinoamericano: gestación, elaboración y vigencia de la concepción aprista de Haya de la Torre. Berlin:
Colloquium Verlag, 1982. 85 p.: bibl., index
(Bibliotheca Ibero-Americana; Bd. 30)
Obra de carácter monográfico. La tesis
principal es que el origen de la doctrina
aprista residió en la polémica de Haya de la
Torre con los miembros de la Tercera Internacional, y no en factores de la realidad histórica e ideológica propia de América Latina.
La forma en que el autor excluye esos factores hace prever críticas a su tesis, de parte
de los estudiosos del tema.

7590 Bustamante, Cecilia. Intelectuales
peruanas de la generación de José
Carlos Mariátegui (Socialismo y Participación [Centro de Estudios para el Desarrollo
y la Participación, Lima] 14, junio 1981,
p. 107–119)
Además de recordar a la autora franco-
peruana Flora Tristán, expone la obra y la acción de Dora Mayer (1868–1959), Madga
Portal (1901) y María Wiesse de Sabogal
(1892–1964), entre otras. Muy útiles indicaciones bibliográficas. Ver la reseña del historiador en item **2964.**

7591 Chang-Rodríguez, Eugenio. Poética
y marxismo en Mariátegui (HISPA,
34/35, 1983, p. 51–67)

El contenido no responde plenamente
al título. Quizá lo más útil sea la apreciación
de Mariátegui como crítico literario.

7592 Choy, Emilio *et al.* Lenin y Mariátegui: estudios. 2a. ed. Lima: Empresa
Editora Amauta, 1980. 255 p. (Biblioteca
Amauta)
Artículos de varios autores, no tanto
de estudio como de valoración positiva de
ambos personajes. De entre las varias interpretaciones que existen sobre el marxismo
de Mariátegui, en esta obra se tiende a in-
cluirlo dentro del marxismo-leninismo.

Estado de las ciencias sociales en el Perú. Ver
HLAS 45:8221.

7593 Falcón, Jorge. Educación y cultura en
Lenin-Mariátegui. Lima: Empresa Editora Amauta, 1981. 190 p.: bibl.
Varios trabajos sobre Mariátegui, de un
autor prolífico en el tema.

7594 ———. Mariátegui y la Revolución
Mexicana y el estado anti-imperialista.
Lima: Empresa Editora Amauta, 1980. 95 p.:
bibl.
Contiene un trabajo sobre la interpretación de la Revolución Mexicana por Mariátegui y tres bibliografías que ilustran sobre
el interés de Mariátegui en dicha Revolución
(ver *HLAS 44:7586–7587*).

7595 Flores Galindo, Alberto. La agonía de
Mariátegui: la polémica con la Komin-
tern. 2a. ed. Lima: Centro de Estudios y Promoción del Desarrollo, 1982. 157 p.: bibl.
(Serie Estudios)
No se limita al relato de la polémica
entre Mariátegui y su grupo y la Tercera Internacional, sino que analiza los temas en
que se centra la diferencia, especialmente el
carácter nacional que Mariátegui quiere dar
al socialismo. Esta segunda edición difiere de
la primera en los anexos, que son de hecho
notas o artículos.

7596 ———. Un viejo debate: el poder (Socialismo y Participación [Centro de Estudios para el Desarrollo y la Participación,
Lima] 20, dic. 1982, p. 15–41)
Repasa la polémica de Haya de la Torre
con Mariátegui sobre los medios de acceso al
poder. Reproduce en anexo ocho cartas de
Haya, siete de las cuales fueron envidadas a
Eudocio Ravines entre 1926–29.

7597 Franco, Carlos. Del marxismo euro-
céntrico al marxismo latinoamericano.
Lima: Centro de Estudios para el Desarrollo y
la Participación, 1981. 112 p.: bibl. (Textos de
contrapunto; 1)
Se describe y comenta el pensamiento
de Marx sobre los países hoy llamados "peri-
féricos," pensamiento que pasó por dos etapas:
una "eurocéntrica" y otra más respetuosa de
las diversidades mundiales. Se muestra cómo
Haya de la Torre y Mariátegui pensaron esas
cuestiones reconociendo la peculiaridad de
América Latina y utilizando el marxismo
como un instrumento. Quiere ser una contribución a los orígenes del pensamiento de
izquierda en Latinoamérica.

7598 ———. Mariátegui-Haya: surgimiento
de la izquierda nacional (Socialismo y
Participación [Centro de Estudios para el
Desarrollo y la Participación, Lima] 7, sept.
1979, p. 11–44)
Trabajo extenso y detallado. Después
de señalar las características que definirían a
la "izquierda nacional," desarrolla su tesis
central: pese a sus diferencias, Haya de la
Torre y Mariátegui coinciden en ser los fundadores, entre 1920–30, de la izquierda nacional en el Perú. Ver la reseña del historiador
en item **2973.**

7599 García Salvattecci, Hugo. Sorel y
Mariátegui. Prólogo, Luis Alberto
Sánchez. Lima: E. Delgado Valenzuela, 1979?
276 p.: bibl.
Libro de abundante argumentación,
que presenta un Mariátegui más soreliano
que marxista. Luis Alberto Sánchez le pone
un prólogo elogioso y coincide con sus tesis.
Ambos, es de suponer, serán discutidos por
las otras vertientes de la interpretación de
Mariátegui. En cualquier caso, el libro,
aunque no es una monografía técnica im-
pecable, es de lectura no prescindible, por
concentrarse intensamente en un deter-
minado y válido aspecto.

7600 González Prada, Manuel. Textos: una
antología general. Prólogo, selección y
notas de Jorge Ruedas de la Serna. México:
Secretaría de Educación Pública: Universidad
Nacional Autónoma de México, 1982. 283 p.:
bibl. (Clásicos americanos; 13)
Antología muy oportuna y útil. Contiene textos de los siguientes libros: *Páginas
libres; Horas de lucha; Prosa menuda; El*

tonel de Diógenes; y *Bajo eloprobio.* Se
agrega un buen prólogo, indicaciones bibliográficas y una cronología.

7601 Interdonato, Francisco. El ateísmo en
el mundo actual: estudio aplicado al
Perú. Lima: Iberia, Industria del Offset, 1968.
381 p.: bibl.
Examina al ateísmo o "no creencia" en
el Perú en función de las opiniones de autores
filosóficos y escritores peruanos. Pero esto es
sólo parte del enfoque general del ateísmo en
el mundo moderno.

7602 Kossok, Manfred *et al.* Mariátegui y
las ciencias sociales. Lima: Empresa
Editora Amauta, 1982. 117 p.: bibl. (Serie
conmemorativa 50° aniversario de la muerte
de J.C.M. Biblioteca Amauta)
El mejor trabajo de este volumen es el
de tema más circunscripto: Antonio Melis,
"Presencia de J.G. Frazier en la Obra de
Mariátegui." Otros autores son: Manfred
Kossok, Anatoly Shulgovsky, R. Prado Re-
dondez y Kinichiro Harada.

7603 Luna Vegas, Ricardo. Mariátegui y el
Perú: de ayer, de hoy y de mañana.
Lima: Ediciones Rincón Rojo, 1981. 164 p.
Ensayos periodísticos breves, de di-
vulgación, pero en muchos casos acalorada-
mente polémicos, como respecto de José
Aricó (ver item **7588**), Vargas Llosa y Luis
Alberto Sánchez y otros apristas peruanos.

7604 Mariátegui, José Carlos. Obras. Selección, Francisco Baeza. Prólogo,
Enrique de la Osa. La Habana: Casa de las
Américas, 1982. 2 v. (Colección Pensamiento
de Nuestra América)
Se recogen numerosos escritos de
Mariátegui, pero no hay indicación alguna
sobre el plan y la organización de la obra, ni
siempre se señala cuánto se incluye y cuánto
se omite. Enrique de la Osa escribe con simpatía un largo prólogo en que se resume la
vida y la acción de Mariátegui.

7605 ———. La Revolución Mexicana ante
el pensamiento de José Carlos Mariátegui. Compilación y prólogo de Manuel
González Calzada. México: Consejo Editorial
del Gobierno del Estado de Tabasco, 1980.
96 p., 1 leaf of plates: ill.
Contiene diversos artículos de Mariátegui sobre México (en especial sobre la
situación política de la época), publicados en

las revistas peruanas *Mundial* y *Variedades*, entre 1922–30.

7606 Mariátegui en Italia. Bruno Podestá, editor. Giovanni Casetta *et al.* Traducción del italiano, Raúl Crisafio. Lima: Empresa Editora Amauta, 1981. 144 p.: bibl. (Serie conmemorativa 50° aniversario de la muerte de J.C.M. Biblioteca Amauta)

Obra aprovechable para el investigador, más allá de las obvias simpatías que la animan. La introducción de Bruno Podestá es seguida de una bibliografía de Mariátegui en italiano. Siguen trabajos de Malcom Silvers (muy útil), Robert Paris, G. Casetta y A. Melis.

Mires, Fernando. Los indios y la tierra: o como concibió Mariátegui la revolución en el Perú. Ver item **2997**.

Ortega, Julio. Crisis, identidad y cultura en el Perú. Ver item **5419**.

7607 El Pensamiento fascista, 1930–1945. José de la Riva-Agüero *et al.* Selección y prólogo de José Ignacio López Soria. Lima: Francisco Campodónico: Mosca Azul Editores, 1981. 254 p.: bibl. (Biblioteca del pensamiento peruano; 1)

Acertadamente dice el autor de esta compilación que se ocupa de un tema descuidado por la historiografía. Se recogen textos de Riva Agüero y Ferrero Rebagliati, así como otros de publicaciones periódicas, y aun escritos puramente propagandísticos. La oportuna nota introductoria desbroza el camino y señala aspectos que requieren mayor estudio. Buena contribución a la historia de las ideas.

7608 El Pensamiento indigenista. Selección, prólogo y bibliografía, José Tamayo Herrera. Lima: Francisco Campodónico: Mosca Azul Editores, 1981. 210 p.: bibl. (Biblioteca del pensamiento peruano; 2)

La idea de esta antología es muy oportuna. El prólogo del compilador es ilustrativo sobre el tema. Contiene bibliografía. Los textos corresponden al período 1867–1957, sin pretensiones de exhaustividad. Entre los autores representados están González Prada, Villarán, Valcárcel y Gamaliel Churata.

Pike, Frederick B. Peru's Haya de la Torre and archetypal regeneration mythology. See item **3006**.

7609 Quijano, Aníbal. Reencuentro y debate: una introducción a Mariátegui. Lima: Mosca Azul Editores, 1981. 117 p.: bibl.

Este libro, que parte de una posición definida del autor en el "socialismo revolucionario," y que en gran parte entra al discutidísimo tema de la verdadera naturaleza del marxismo de Mariátegui, hallará sin duda encontradas opiniones y variados contradictores; pero no es ni hagiográfico ni dogmático, y conviene que esté en la bibliografía de todo estudioso de Mariátegui. Entre otras cosas, señala la necesidad de una visión de Mariátegui en función de su completa evolución intelectual.

7610 Remond, Walter. Una defensa de la América intelectual: apologías por pensadores peruanos del siglo XVII (UNAM/L, 14, 1981, p. 213–237)

Interesante trabajo que muestra dos cosas: 1) la queja del que practicaba la filosofía en América ante la falta de reconocimiento por parte de los europeos; y 2) el hecho de que el "americano" no sentía entonces estar haciendo una filosofía distinta de la europea, sino que se identificaba dentro de un solo y único movimiento filosófico. Las conclusiones se extraen de prólogos y prefacios a varias obras de filosofía del siglo XVII peruano.

Skirius, John. The interpenetration of some ideas and images in González Prada's prose. See item **5132**.

7611 Trazegnies Granda, Fernando de. La idea de derecho en el Perú republicano del siglo XIX. Lima: Pontificia Universidad Católica del Perú, Fondo Editorial, 1980. 383 p.

Intento de historia intelectual. Las concepciones del derecho en el Perú del siglo XIX se ponen en estrecha relación con la realidad político-social. El resultado es un proceso de "modernización tradicionalista," forjado por las clases dominantes. Trabajo útil a pesar de las modestas declaraciones del autor.

Valcárcel, Luis E. Memorias. Ver item **3019**.

Wise, David. Indigenismo de izquierda y de derecha: dos planteamientos de los años 1920. Ver item **3024**.

BOLIVIA

7612 Albarracín Millán, Juan. Filosofía boliviana del siglo XX. v. 1, El pensamiento filosófico de Tamayo y el irracionalismo alemán. La Paz: Akapana, 1981. 147 p.: bibl., indexes.

Expone las ideas del pensador boliviano, especialmente en su relación con Nietzsche, Fichte y Goethe.

7613 Francovich, Guillermo. Los mitos profundos de Bolivia. La Paz: Editorial Los Amigos del Libro, 1980. 211 p. (Enciclopedia boliviana)

Contribuye a la interpretación de la realidad boliviana mediante el análisis de tres "mitos," que corresponden, respectivamente, a la época precolombina, a la colonia y a la independencia. En torno a ese tema central se comentan también otros aspectos de la cultura boliviana.

7614 González M., René. Breve historia de las ideas políticas en el mundo y en Bolivia. Sucre, Bolivia: Librería-Editorial Tupac Katari, 1982. 213 p.: bibl., ill.

El mayor interés del libro reside en la segunda parte, que es una síntesis de las ideas políticas en Bolivia.

CHILE

Bello y Chile: Tercer Congreso del Bicentenario. Ver item **5103.**

Castedo, Leopoldo. Chile en tiempos de Bello: la organización de la libertad. Ver item **3068.**

Gazmuri Riveros, Cristián. Notas sobre la influencia del racismo en la obra de Nicolás Palacios, Francisco A. Encina y Alberto Cabero. Ver item **3089.**

———. La idea de decadencia nacional y el pensamiento político conservador chileno en el siglo XX. Ver *HLAS 45:6308.*

Jaksić, Iván. Philosophy and university reform at the University of Chile: 1842-1973. See item **3101.**

Krebs, Ricardo. Proyecciones del pensamiento histórico de Andrés Bello. Ver item **3103.**

7615 Ossandón, Carlos A. Alejandro Venegas y las posibilidades de un pensamiento nacional (RFL, 5:9/10, enero/dic. 1979, p. 153–170)

Venegas (1871–1922), pensador chileno, autor de *Sinceridad: Chile íntimo en 1910,* es analizado aquí con la intención de extraer consecuencias para un posible pensamiento nacional.

7616 Pensamiento teológico en Chile: contribución a su estudio. v. 1, Epoca de la Independencia Nacional, 1810–1840. Edición de Juan A. Noemi C. José Arteaga Ll. *et al.* Santiago: Universidad Católica de Chile, 1978. 1 v.: bibl., index (Anales de la Facultad de Teología, 0069–3596; v. 27, cuaderno 2)

Inventario analítico de la literatura teológica chilena en el período estudiado, que incluye tanto la teología sistemática como los escritos "que tratan acerca de las realidades en que está involucrada la fe cristiana." Buena contribución, con amplia bibliografía.

7617 Ruiz, Carlos. Notes on authoritarian ideologies in Chile (NS, 6:11, 1981, p. 17–36)

Estudia el pensamiento nacionalista y autoritario de las primeras décadas del siglo XX en Chile, especialmente el de Jaime Eyzaguirre. Lo pone en relación con la sociedad contemporánea y sostiene que el pensamiento de esa época resurge en la fundamentación ideológica del actual gobierno chileno. Ver la reseña del historiador en item **3132.**

Salcedo-Bastardo, J.L. Bello y los "simposiums" de Grafton Street. Ver item **1896.**

Salinas Campos, Maxmiliano A. El laicado católico de la Sociedad Chilena de Agricultura y Beneficiencia, 1838–1849: la evolución del catolicismo y la Ilustración en Chile durante la primera mitad del siglo XIX. Ver item **3135.**

7618 Schnepf, Ryszard. Ideas de Ignacy Domeyko (PAN/ES, 8, 1981, p. 143–168)

Rasgos biográficos y de pensamiento de un científico polaco emigrado a Chile en el siglo XIX. Ver la reseña del historiador en item **3140.**

7619 Subercaseaux S., Bernardo. Cultura y sociedad liberal en el siglo XIX. Santiago: Editorial Aconcagua, 1981. 325 p.: bibl. (Colección Bello) Buena monografía sobre José Victorino Lastarria (1817–88).

Presenta sus ideas y su obra literaria combinadas con el clima intelectual, político y social de la época en Chile. Agrega al final de cada parte del libro una cronología. Util bibliografía.

Universidad de Chile. Facultad de Filosofía, Humanidades y Educación. Instituto Profesional de Santiago. Departamento de Bibliotecología. Bio-bibliografía de la filosofía en Chile desde el siglo XVI hasta 1980. Ver *HLAS 45:25.*

BRASIL

7620 Borheim, Gerd A. Filosofia e realidade nacional (Encontros com a Civilização Brasileira [Rio de Janeiro] 19[3]: 1, jan. 1980, p. 93–112)

El tema es la relación entre la universalidad de la filosofía y su posible carácter nacional. El autor lo reconduce al problema de la cultura y de las diferencias culturales. Concluye examinando el caso del positivismo y el del neotomismo en Brasil. No se desprende una conclusión definida.

7621 Cataloga de obras filosóficas. Salvador: Centro de Documentaçao do Pensamento Brasileiro, 1983. 156 p.

Se trata del catalogo de la Biblioteca del centro, en lo que se refiere a filosofía en el Brasil.

7622 Chacon, Vamireh. O humanismo brasileiro. São Paulo: Secretaria de Estado da Cultura: Summus Editorial, 1980. 272 p.: bibl.

Conjunto de valiosos ensayos, algunos de los cuales han sido recogidos anteriormente en otros *Handbooks.* Tratan de algunos aspectos de la historia de las ideas en Brasil, precedidos de un trabajo sobre la relación entre la Sociología del Conocimiento y la Historia de las Ideas.

7623 Corrente eclética na Bahia. Introdução e notas, Antônio Paim. Pesquisa, Anna Maria Moog Rodrigues *et al.* Rio de Janeiro: Pontifícia Universidade Católica: Conselho Federal de Cultura: Editora Documentário, 1979. 108 p.: bibl. (Textos didáticos do pen-

samento brasileiro; v. 9. Coleção Documenta/Brasil; 12)

Reproduce artículos aparecidos en periódicos y revistas que representan la influencia del eclecticismo en Bahía. Buena contribución documental, parte de una valiosa colección.

7624 Côrtes, Paulo Campos. A concepção filosófica de Tobias Barreto. Rio de Janeiro: Gráfica Olímpica Editora, 1980. 47 p., 4 p. of plates: ill.

Exposición breve y elogiosa. Destaca el mérito de Miguel Reale en revalorar a Tobias Barreto.

7624a Faedrich, Nelson Boeira *et al.* RS [i.e. Rio Grande do Sul], cultura e ideologia. Porto Alegre: Mercado Aberto, 1980. 167 p.: bibl. (Série Documenta; 3. História)

De esta publicación destacamos "O Rio Grande de Augusto Comte," estudio sobre el positivismo en Rio Grande do Sul.

7625 Filosofia no Brasil: desafios. Campinas: Pontifícia Universidade Católica de Campinas, 1980. 153 p.: bibl. (Reflexão; 17)

De los artículos de este número, tres se refieren a la filosofía en Brasil: A.J. Severino, "O Papel da Filosofia no Brasil: Compromisos e Desafios Atuais;" O.A. Pegoraro, "Política da Filosofia no Brasil;" y C. Marcondes Cesar, "Vicente Ferreira da Silva e o Pensamento Sul-Americano."

7626 A Filosofia política positivista. Introdução, Antônio Paim. Rio de Janeiro: Pontifícia Universidade Católica, 1979. 2 v.: bibl. (Textos didáticos do pensamento brasileiro; vol. 14–15. Coleção Documenta/Brasil; 13–14)

Estos dos volumenes continúan una excelente colección, cuyo plan, según entendemos, quedó interrumpido. Se dedican a las manifestaciones del "castilhismo" en Rio Grande do Sul (fines de siglo XIX y comienzos del XX). Los textos llevan presentaciones de Celina Junqueira e introducciones de Antonio Paim.

7627 Gomes, Eduardo Rodrigues. Campo contra cidade: o ruralismo e a crise oligárquica no pensamento político brasileiro, 1910–1935 (UMG/RBEP, 56, jan. 1983, p. 49–96)

Resumen de una Tesis de Maestría. Se estudia el pensamiento de autores como

Alberto Torres y Oliveira Vianna, entre otros, quienes critican la estructura latifundista del campo brasileño. El agrarismo se considera "modernizante" y no reacción conservadora de *élites* rurales. Se señalan las razones sociales y políticas que se tuvieron para defender ese tipo de agrarismo.

7628 Guimarães, Aquiles Côrtes. Momentos do pensamento luso-brasileiro. Rio de Janeiro: Tempo Brasileiro, 1981. 96 p.: bibl.

Ensayos sobre el pensamiento filosófico en Portugal y Brasil. Interesa especialmente: "A Filosofia Portuguesa na Fase Aurea do Eclecticismo Brasileiro: 1850–1880."

7629 Höffling, Luciana M.G. Reflexões a influência positivista no pensamento brasileiro (Reflexão [Instituto de Filosofia e Teologia da Pontificia Universidade Católica da Campinas (PUCC), São Paulo] 7:22, jan./ abril 1982, p. 15–26, bibl.)

Pasa, en efecto, revista a la vastísima influencia del positivismo en el Brasil, en sus diversos aspectos.

7630 As Idéias políticas no Brasil. Coordenador, Adolpho Crippa. Colaboradores, João Alfredo de Souza *et al.* São Paulo: Editora Convivio, 1979. 2 v. (270, 303 p.): bibl.

Esta valiosa obra colectiva sigue a otra, de la misma editorial y del mismo coordinador: *As idéias filosóficas no Brasil* (ver *HLAS 42:7578*). Algunos de los colaboradores son destacados especialistas, como Nelson Saldanha, R.S. Maciel de Barros, Ubiratan B. de Macedo, A.C. Villaça, Antônio Paim, Paulo Mercadante, Vamireh Chacon, etc.

7631 Indice da *Revista Brasileira de Filosofia*: 1951–1980. Salvador: Centro de Documentação do Pensamento Brasileiro, 1983. 120 p.

Este útil *Indice* va precedido de una reseña histórica de la *Revista* y del Instituto Brasileiro de Filosofía, institución que la creó y aún la publica.

7632 Leite, A. Roberto de Paula. Notas sobre a história das idéias filosóficas no Brasil: pt. 1 (IHGSP/R, 76, 1980, p. 346–354)

Primera parte de un artículo sobre el tema. Además de afirmar que en Brasil (y en general en América Latina) hubo adaptación de ideas filosóficas europeas, traza algunos rasgos de la filosofía colonial.

7633 Macedo, Silvio de. Pontes de Miranda: uma visão poliédrica de sua obra (IHGA/R, 36, 1980, p. 101–133)

Estudio monográfico sobre Pontes de Miranda (n. 1892), científico, filósofo y jurisconsulto brasileño.

7634 Macedo, Ubiratan. Ortega y Gasset e a cultura brasileira (MEC/C, 10:35, julho/dez. 1980, p. 35–39)

Excelente ensayo que en breve espacio da una clara idea de la influencia de Ortega en autores brasileños (algunos poco conocidos en el resto de Latinoamérica). El largo predominio positivista en Brasil pudo impedir una mayor absorción y adopción del pensamiento orteguiano. Estima que todavía podría haber campo en el país para asimilar el raciovitalismo del autor español.

Mangabeira, João. Idéias políticas de João Mangabeira. Ver item **3612**.

Marinho, Joaquim Saldanha. O Rei e o Partido Liberal. Ver item **3616**.

7635 Miguel Reale na UnB [i.e. Universidade de Brasília]: conferências e comentários de um seminário realizado de 9 a 12 de junho de 1981. Brasília: Editora Universidade de Brasília, 1981. 175 p.: ports (Coleção Itinerários)

Interesante publicación que reproduce un simposio en el cual varios autores analizan aspectos del pensamiento del destacado filósofo brasileño del Derecho, Miguel Reale. Se incluyen también las respuestas de Reale y una auto-exposición filosófica de dicho autor. De interés historiográfico es "Miguel Reale e a Filosofia Brasileira," de Antônio Paim.

Montenegro, João Alfredo de Souza. O liberalismo conservador de Cairu. Ver item **3630**.

Moraes, Evaristo de. As idéias fundamentais de Tavares Bastos. Ver item **3632**.

7636 Müller, Alzira Correia. Fundamentação da experiência em Miguel Reale. São Paulo: Edições GRD; Brasília: *em convênio com o* Instituto Nacional do Libro, Ministério da Educação e Cultura, 1981. 131 p.: bibl.

Exposición del pensamiento filosófico de Reale, centrado principalmente en el problema de la experiencia y sus consecuencias gnoseológicas, previa colocación de ese pensamiento en el medio y la época en que se originó. Al final, encuentra oportuna la comparación de Reale con Ortega y Gasset.

Nabuco, Joaquim. Joaquim Nabuco: política. Ver item **3637.**

Nabuco de Araújo, José Thomaz. O Centro Liberal. Ver item **3638.**

7637 Paim, Antônio. Bibliografia filosófica brasilera: 1808–1930. Salvador: Centro de Documentação do Pensamento Brasileiro, 1983. 96 p.

Muy oportuna contribución bibliográfica que completa la correspondiente a 1931–77 (ver *HLAS 42:7591*). Ambas son producto de la destacada labor de Antônio Paim.

7638 ———. Gonçalves de Magalhães e o apogeu do ecletismo brasileiro (IBF/ RBF, 32:127, julho/set. 1982, p. 253–267)

Sitúa a Gonçalves de Magalhães en relación con el eclecticismo francés del siglo XIX. Las principales obras del autor brasileño se publicaron entre 1858–80. La más conocida es *Fatos do espírito humano* (1858).

Paiva, Vanilda Pereira. Paulo Freire e o nacionalismo desenvolvimentista. Ver *HLAS 45:4567.*

7639 Queiroz, Suely Robles Reis de. Aspectos ideológicos da escravidão (IPE/EE, 13:1, 1983, p. 85–101)

Muy útil para el conocimiento de la ideología esclavista en Brasil. Las fuentes son principalmente discursos parlamentarios.

7640 Ribeiro Júnior, João. A Ilustração brasileira (Reflexão [Instituto de Filosofia e Teologia da Pontifícia Universidade Católica de Campinas (PUCC), São Paulo] 7:22, jan./abril 1982, p. 5–14, bibl.)

El título puede dar lugar a equívoco. "Ilustración brasileña" es denominación propuesta por Maciel de Barros para el período 1870–90. El artículo trata, por lo tanto, del positivismo en Brasil.

7641 Silvestre Pinheiro Ferreira, 1769– 1846: bibliografia e estudos críticos. Salvador: Centro de Documentação do Pensamento Brasileiro, 1983. 59 p.

Contiene: 1) bibliografía de libros y artículos de Pinheiro Ferreira; 2) bibiografía de escritos sobre él; y 3) cinco artículos críticos sobre Pinheiro Ferreira, de los que son autores J.J. Lopes Praça, Cabral de Mon-

cada, Delfim Santos, A Braz Teixeira y A. Paim (sobre Pinheiro Ferreira, ver *HLAS 34:5154* y *HLAS 40:9450*).

7642 Simões Neto, F. Teotonio. Repensando Alberto Torres. São Paulo: Editora Semente, 1981. 224 p. (Coleção Revelações)

Sitúa y expone las ideas políticas de Alberto Torres (1865–1917), de tendencia nacionalista, considerado por Farias Brito como el fundador de la filosofía política en Brasil. Atribuye a su pensamiento político la propuesta de "un Estado democrático, abierto a la participación, 'laico,' federal, con separación entre los poderes, con autonomía de la sociedad, la cual tiene asegurados sus derechos políticos, civiles y sociales."

7643 Staudt, Leo Afonso. Notas introdutórias sobre o estudo da história da filosofia no Brasil (PUC/V, 26:104, dez. 1981, p. 422–428, bibl.)

Consideraciones y noticias generales, que sin embargo ilustran sobre el grado de avance en el interés por el pensamiento filosófico en Brasil. También son indicio del efecto logrado por la posición inspirada por Miguel Reale y Antônio Paim, entre otros.

ARGENTINA

7645 Anderson Imbert, Enrique. Alejandro Korn y el positivismo (IILI/RI, 48: 118/119, enero/junio 1982, p. 369–376)

Sobre el juicio de Korn acerca del positivismo, su teoría del "positivismo autóctono" y su interpretación de lo que él consideraba las tres generaciones positivistas argentinas. El autor conoció de cerca a Korn. El artículo debe ponerse en relación con el de Daniel Zalazar (item **7666**).

———. Alejandro Korn y la generación del 80. Ver item **5095.**

7646 Ardao, Arturo *et al.* Francisco Romero, maestro de la filosofía latinoamericana. Caracas: Sociedad Interamericana de Filosofía, 1983. 181 p.: bibl.

Con motivo de cumplirse, en 1982, los 20 años de la muerte del filósofo argentino Francisco Romero, la Sociedad Interamericana de Filosofía organizó el presente volumen de homenaje. Su contenido es el siguiente: prólogo de E. Mayz Vallenilla; Arturo Ardao, "La idea de Inteligencia en Romero;" Angel J.

Cappelletti, "Francisco Romero y el Espiritualismo Latinoamericano del Siglo XIX;" Risieri Frondizi, "Valor y Trascendencia;" Jorge Gracia, "Romero y la Individualidad;" Alain Guy, "Francisco Romero, Philosophe de l'Esprit;" William Kilgore, "The Ethics of Francisco Romero;" F. Miró Quesada, "Reportaje a Francisco Romero;" J.C. Torchia Estrada, "Romero y Brentano: la Estructura de la Historia de la Filosofía;" Leopoldo Zea, "Romero y la Normalidad Filosófica Latinoamericana."

7647 Biagini, Hugo E. Macedonio Fernández y su ideario filosófico. Buenos Aires: Instituto de Literatura Argentina Ricardo Rojas, Universidad de Buenos Aires, 1982. 16 p.

Expone el difícil pensamiento de Macedonio Fernández y señala su condición de adelantado de ciertos rasgos postpositivistas en plena vigencia del positivismo.

7648 ———. La temporalidad en las ideas argentinas: preclasificación bibliográfica del siglo XX (RFL, 5:9/10, enero/dic. 1979, p. 199–215)

Bibliografía de libros y artículos de autores argentinos que, directa o indirectamente, tratan del tema de la temporalidad.

Cantraine, Philippe. Borges filósofo y la filosofía de la existencia: la conciencia, la existencia y el tiempo. Ver item **5576.**

7649 Casalla, Mario C. La estética de Leopoldo Marechal: un ejemplo de apropiación nacional de la cultura universal (RFL, 5:9/10, enero/dic. 1979, p. 3–27)

Para el autor, lo universal y lo nacional no son incompatibles. Defiende por eso la posibilidad, para el pensamiento y la cultura en general, de un "universal situado." La obra de Marechal, *Descenso y ascenso del alma por la belleza*, sería un ejemplo de aquella posibilidad, y con tal intención es estudiada en este artículo.

7650 Caturelli, Alberto. El conocimiento desde y del pensamiento argentino (*in* Ser y no ser de los argentinos: sociología para nosotros. Fernando N. Cuevillas *et al.* Buenos Aires: Ediciones Macchi, 1979, p. 349–380)

Se divide en dos partes: 1) reseña histórica, desde la colonia hasta la actualidad, muy apretada pero incluyendo prácticamente todos los nombres vinculados a la filosofía;

2) información institucional (Facultades, revistas, etc.). Muy visible la simpatía hacia el pensamiento cristiano.

7651 Epistolario: Coriolano Alberini. Edición de Diego F. Pró. Mendoza, Argentina: Universidad Nacional de Cuyo, Facultad de Filosofía y Letras, Instituto de Filosofía, 1981. 2 v.: bibl.(Colección de historia de la filosofía argentina. Serie documental; 4)

Continuación del epistolario de Alberini. Contiene cartas de filósofos y escritores argentinos y americanos, de figuras políticas, historiadores y sociólogos. Diego Pró tuvo a su cuidado las notas aclaratorias.

7652 Farré, Luis and **Celina A. Lértora Mendoza.** La filosofía en la Argentina. Buenos Aires: Editorial Docencia-Proyecto CINAE, 1981. 241 p., 2 p. of plates: ill. (Colección Interacción educativa)

Tras sensatas consideraciones metodológicas y un panorama equilibrado de la época colonial, el siglo XIX recibe un breve tratamiento y la mayor extensión del libro se dedica a las manifestaciones filosóficas desde el positivismo en adelante. Este enfoque es legítimo en tanto la obra se ocupa de lo filosófico en sentido estricto, sin entrar en el campo más general de lo que se entiende por "Historia de las Ideas." Cumple así su mayor función en el período desde fines del siglo XIX hasta la actualidad. La parte contemporánea se trata también según disciplinas filosóficas y señalando aspectos institucionales (Congresos, revistas, etc.). En el capítulo final, de conclusiones generales, se destaca— entre otros juicios susceptibles de aprobación o no según el lector de que se trate— la firme pertenencia de los autores a la orientación "profesional" de la filosofía latinoamericana, es decir, críticos de las posiciones "americanistas."

7653 Fernández, María Angela. Planteo ontológico de la libertad en Miguel Angel Virasoro (UNCIF/C, 13, 1980, p. 41–61)

Trabajo expositivo sobre la libertad en el filósofo argentino.

7654 Gabrielides de Luna, Angélica. El pensamiento del Doctor Luis Farré (UNCIF/C, 13, 1980, p. 169–226, bibl.)

Aunque nacido en España (1902), Luis Farré desarrolló toda su actividad filosófica en Argentina. Esta exposición recorre su obra crítica y de pensamiento personal. Contiene bibliografía.

7655 García Bazán, Francisco. Vicente Fatone y la filosofía de la religión en la Argentina (UNCIF/C, 13, 1980, p. 25–40)
Fatone es visto como fenomenólogo de la religión, especialmente a la luz de su último libro, *El hombre y Dios* (1955).

7656 García Losada, Matilde J. El existencialismo de Erro en su concreción como filosofía nacional (UNCIF/C, 13, 1980, p. 227–244)
Sobre el tema de lo nacional argentino y de lo latinoamericano en Carlos Alberto Erro. Separada de este artículo (p. 257–265) hay una ficha biobibliográfica de este autor.

7657 Guerrero, César H. Las ideas flosóficas en San Juan. Prólogo de Diego F. Pró. San Juan, Argentina: Ediciones Agon, 1982. 105 p.: bibl.
El título denota más de lo que el libro contiene. Más exacta es la descripción del prologuista: "antecedentes históricos de la cultura filosófica en la Provincia de San Juan."

7658 Lucero, Ignacio T. La filosofía política y de la historia de José M. Estrada (UNCIF/C, 13, 1980, p. 135–167)
Trabajo panorámico y de exposición sobre José Manuel Estrada (1842–94), historiador católico argentino.

McLynn, F.J. The political thought of Juan Domingo Perón. See item **3294.**

Olaso, Ezequiel de. Las ideas ilustradas de Manuel José de Lavarden en el *Discurso* de 1778: una contribución al estudio de la influencia del Padre Feijóo en el Río de la Plata. Ver item **2791.**

7659 Ossandon, Carlos A. El concepto de "normalidad filosófica" en Francisco Romero (CH, 385, julio 1982, p. 92–105)
La principal bondad de este artículo es que no solamente expone la noción de "normalidad filosófica," puesta en circulación por Francisco Romero, sino que la analiza, critica y le da mayor elaboración como categoría historiográfica.

7660 Pérez de Watt, Haydée O. Aproximación al pensamiento filosófico de Eugenio Pucciarelli (UNCIF/C, 13, 1980, p. 63–133, bibl.)
Es posiblemente el trabajo más pormenorizado que se le ha dedicado hasta ahora a Pucciarelli. Contiene bibliografía de este autor hasta 1973.

7661 Pró, Diego F. La doctrina del hombre en la filosofía insistencial (UNCIF/C, 13, 1980, p. 7–23)
Exposición de la trayectoria filosófica del Padre Ismael Quiles, hasta la etapa de su filosofía "insistencial" (ver item **7662**).

Quentin-Mauroy, Dominique. J.B. Alberdi, 1810–1884, et la formation de la conscience nationale argentine. See item **3327.**

7662 Quiles, Ismael. Autorretrato filosófico. Buenos Aires: Ediciones Universidad del Salvador, 1981. 143 p.: bibl.
Mezcla de *Selbstdarstellung* y autobiografía filosófica, con bibliografía y antología. Esencial para conocer el pensamiento del Padre Quiles.

7663 Romero, José Luis. Las ideologías de la cultura nacional y otros ensayos. Selección, Luis Alberto Romero. Postfacio por Tulio Halperín-Donghi. Buenos Aires: Centro Editor de América Latina, 1982. 236 p. (Serie complementaria: sociedad y cultura; 3. Capítulo. Biblioteca argentina fundamental; 151)
Reproduce artículos que aparecieron en su obra anterior, *La experiencia argentina*, excepto uno titulado "Campo y Ciudad: las Tensiones entre Dos Ideologías." Esta edición tiene también un postfacio de Tulio Halperín-Donghi: "José Luis Romero y su Lugar en la Historiografía Argentina."

7664 Rougès, Alberto. Las jerarquías del ser y la eternidad. Prólogo, María Eugenia Valentié. Tucumán, Argentina: Universidad Nacional de Tucumán, 1981. 135 p.: ill. (Publicaciones de homenaje a Alberto Rougès; t. 1)
Se trata de otra reedición de la obra fundamental de Rougès, originalmente publicada en 1942. Lleva una comprensivo prólogo de María Eugenia Valentié.

Seguí, Juan Francisco and Bartolomé Mitre. Polémica sobre la Constitución. Ver item **3349.**

Tondo, Américo A. La eclesiología de los Doctores Gorriti, Zavaleta y Agüero. Ver item **3363.**

7665 Torchia Estrada, Juan Carlos. Un texto inédito de Francisco Romero (UCR/RF, 20:51, junio 1982, p. 3–4)
Reproduce, con una introducción, una conferencia de Francisco Romero sobre el problema de la historia en el positivismo, de 1960, y hasta ahora inédita.

Winston, Colin M. Between Rosas and Sarmiento: notes on nationalism in peronist thought. See item **3374**.

7666 Zalazar, Daniel. Alejandro Korn y la Generación del 80 (*in* On the centennial of the Argentine Generation of 1880. Edited by Hugo Rodríguez Alcalá. Riverside: University of California, Latin American Studies Program, 1980, p. 96–114)

Sitúa a Korn dentro de la llamada "Generación del 80," discutiendo los límites y el contenido de esa generación. Uno de los aspectos más interesantes de este trabajo es la indicación de que las severas críticas que Korn dirigió a los hombres del 80 pudieran vincularse a sus sentimientos religiosos, que lo habrían llevado a coincidir, en ese aspecto, con la oposición católica al laicismo de la mencionada generación.

URUGUAY

7667 Echenique, Carlos A. Las ideas pedagógicas del Dr. Francisco A. Berra y su aporte al americanismo filosófico. Montevideo: Barreiro y Ramos, 1981. 127 p.: bibl., ill.

Exposición de las ideas pedagógicas de Berra (1844–1906), quien actuó en Uruguay y Argentina.

JOURNAL ABBREVIATIONS
PHILOSOPHY

APL/B Boletín de la Academia Panameña de la Lengua. Panamá.

CEHSMO Historia Obrera. Centro de Estudios Históricos del Movimiento Obrero Mexicano. México.

CH Cuadernos Hispanoamericanos. Instituto de Cultura Hispánica. Madrid.

CONAC/RNC Revista Nacional de Cultura. Consejo Nacional de Cultura. Caracas.

CSUCA/ESC Estudios Sociales Centroamericanos. Consejo Superior de Universidades Centroamericanas, Confederación Universitaria Centroamericana, Programa Centroamericano de Ciencias Sociales. San José.

EEHA/AEA Anuario de Estudios Americanos. Consejo Superior de Investigaciones Científicas [and] Universidad de Sevilla, Escuela de Estudios Hispano-Americanos. Sevilla.

HAHR Hispanic American Historical Review. Duke University Press *for the* Conference on Latin American History of the American Historical Association. Durham, N.C.

HISPA Hispamérica. Revista de literatura. Takoma Park, Md.

IBF/RBF Revista Brasileira de Filosofia. Instituto Brasileiro de Filosofia. São Paulo.

IEP/REP Revista de Estudios Políticos. Instituto de Estudios Políticos. Madrid.

IHGA/R Revista do Instituto Histórico e Geográfico de Alagoas. Maceió, Brazil.

IHGSP/R Revista do Instituto Histórico e Geográfico de São Paulo. São Paulo.

IILI/RI Revista Iberoamericana. Instituto Internacional de Literatura Iberoamericana *patrocinado por la* Universidad de Pittsburgh. Pittsburgh, Pa.

IPE/EE Estudos Econômicos. Universidade de São Paulo, Instituto de Pesquisas Econômicas. São Paulo.

MEC/C Cultura. Ministério da Educação e Cultura, Directoria de Documentação e Divulgação. Brasília.

NS NS NorthSouth/NordSud/NorteSur/NorteSul. Canadian journal of Latin American studies. Canadian Association of Latin American Studies. University of Ottawa.

PAIGH/H Revista de Historia de América. Instituto Panamericano de Geografía e Historia, Comisión de Historia. México.

PAN/ES Estudios Latinoamericanos. Polska Akademia Nauk (Academia de Ciencias de Polonia), Instytut Historii (Instituto de Historia). Warszawa.

PUC/V Veritas. Pontifícia Universidade Católica do Rio Grande do Sul. Porto Alegre.

PUJ/UH Universitas Humanística. Pontificia Universidad Javeriana, Facultad de Filosofía y Letras. Bogotá.

RCLL Revista de Crítica Literaria Latinoamericana. Latinoamericana Editores. Lima.

RCPC Revista del Pensamiento Centroamericano. Centro de Investigaciones y Actividades Culturales. Managua.

RFL Revista de Filosofía Latinoamericana. Ediciones Castañeda. San Antonio de Padua, Argentina.

SCHG/R Revista Chilena de Historia y

Geografía. Sociedad Chilena de Historia y Geografía. Santiago.

UCR/RF Revista de Filosofía de la Universidad de Costa Rica. San José.

UMG/RBEP Revista Brasileira de Estudos Políticos. Universidade de Minas Gerais. Belo Horizonte, Brazil.

UNAM/L Latinoamérica. Anuario de estudios latinoamericanos. Universidad Nacional Autónoma de México, Facultad de Filosofía y Letras, Centro de Estudios Latinoamericanos. México.

UNCIF/C Cuyo. Anuario de historia del pensamiento argentino. Universidad Nacional de Cuyo, Instituto de Filosofía. Mendoza, Argentina.

UPR/CS Caribbean Studies. University of Puerto Rico, Institute of Caribbean Studies. Río Piedras.

URSS/AL América Latina. Academia de Ciencias de la URSS (Unión de Repúblicas Soviéticas Socialistas). Moscú.

INDEXES

ABBREVIATIONS AND ACRONYMS

Except for journal acronyms which are listed at: a) the end of each major disciplinary section, (e.g., Art, Film, History, etc.); and b) after each serial title in the *Title List of Journals Indexed*, p. 639.

a.	annual
ABC	Argentina, Brazil, Chile
A.C.	antes de Cristo
ACAR	Associação de Crédito e Assistência Rural, Brazil
AD	Anno Domini
A.D.	Acción Democrática, Venezuela
ADESG	Associação dos Diplomados de Escola Superior de Guerra, Brazil
AGI	Archivo General de Indias, Sevilla
AGN	Archivo General de la Nación
AID	Agency for International Development
a.k.a.	also known as
Ala.	Alabama
ALALC	Asociación Latinoamericana de Libre Comercio
ALEC	*Atlas lingüístico etnográfico de Colombia*
ANAPO	Alianza Nacional Popular, Colombia
ANCARSE	Associação Nordestina de Crédito e Assistência Rural de Sergipe, Brazil
ANCOM	Andean Common Market
ANDI	Asociación Nacional de Industriales, Colombia
AP	Acción Popular
APRA	Alianza Popular Revolucionaria Americana
Ariz.	Arizona
Ark.	Arkansas
ASA	Association of Social Anthropologists of the Commonwealth, London
ASSEPLAN	Assessoria de Planejamente e Acompanhamento, Recife, Brazil
Assn.	Association
Aufl.	Auflage (edition, edición)
AUFS	American Universities Field Staff Reports, Hanover, N.H.
Aug.	August, Augustan
aum.	aumentada
b.	born (nacido)
BBE	Bibliografia Brasileira de Educação
b.c.	indicates dates obtained by radio-carbon methods
BC	Before Christ
bibl(s).	bibliography(ies)
BID	Banco Interamericano de Desarrollo
BNDE	Banco Nacional de Desenvolvimento Econômico, Brazil
BNH	Banco Nacional de Habitação, Brazil
BP	before present
b/w	black-and-white
C14	Carbon 14
ca.	circa
CACM	Central American Common Market
CADE	Conferencia Anual de Ejecutivos de Empresas, Peru
CAEM	Centro de Altos Estudios Militares, Peru
Calif.	California

CARC	Centro de Arte y Comunicación
CARICOM	Caribbean Common Market
CARIFTA	Caribbean Free Trade Association
CBD	central business district
CD	Christian Democrats, Chile
CDI	Conselho de Desenvolvimento Industrial
CEBRAP	Centro Brasileiro de Análise e Planejamento, São Paulo
CECORA	Centro de Cooperativas de la Reforma Agraria, Colombia
CEDAL	Centro de Estudios Democráticos de América Latina, Costa Rica
CEDE	Centro de Estudios sobre Desarrollo Económico, Univ. de los Andes, Bogotá
CEDEPLAR	Centro de Desenvolvimento e Planejamento Region, Belo Horizonte, Brazil
CEDES	Centro de Estudios de Estado y Sociedad, Buenos Aires; Centro de Estudos de Educação e Sociedade, São Paulo, Brazil
CEDI	Conselho Ecuménico para Documentação e Informação, Brazil
CEESTEM	Centro de Estudios Económicos y Sociales del Tercer Mundo, Mexico
CELADE	Centro Latinoamericano de Demografía
CEMLA	Centro de Estudios Monetarios Latinoamericanos, Mexico
CENDES	Centro de Estudios del Desarrollo, Venezuela
CENIDIM	Centro Nacional de Información, Documentación e Investigación Musicales, Mexico
CENIET	Centro Nacional de Información y Estadísticas del Trabajo, México
CEPADE	Centro Paraguayo de Estudios de Desarrollo Económico y Social
CEPA-SE	Comissão Estadual de Planejamento Agrícola, Sergipe, Brazil
CEPAL	See ECLA.
CERES	Centro de Estudios de la Realidad Económica y Social, Bolivia
CES	constant elasticity of substitution
cf.	compare
CFI	Consejo Federal de Inversiones, Buenos Aires
CGE	Confederación General Económica, Argentina
CGTP	Confederación General de Trabajadores del Perú
ch., chap.	chapter
CHEAR	Council on Higher Education in the American Republics
Cía.	Compañía
CIA	Central Intelligence Agency
CIDA	Comité Interamericano de Desarrollo Agrícola
CIDE	Centro de Investigación y Desarrollo de la Educación, Chile
CIE	Centro de Investigaciones Económicas, Buenos Aires
CIMI	Conselho Indigenista Misioneiro, Brazil
CIP	Conselho Interministerial de Preços
CIPCA	Centro de Investigación y Promoción del Campesinado, Bolivia
CLACSO	Consejo Latinoamericano de Ciencias Sociales, Secretaría Ejecutiva, Buenos Aires
CLASC	Confederación Latinoamericana Sindical Cristiana
CLE	Comunidad Latinoamericana de Escritores, Mexico
cm	centimeter
CNI	Confederação Nacional da Industria, Brazil
Co.	company
COB	Central Obrera Boliviana
COBAL	Companhia Brasileira de Alimentos
Col.	collection, colección, coleção
Colo.	Colorado
COMCORDE	Comisión Coordinadora para el Desarrollo Económico, Uruguay
comp.	compiler
CONCLAT	Congresso Nacional de Classe Trabalhadora, Brazil
CONDESE	Conselho de Desenvolvimento Econômico de Sergipe, Brazil

Conn.	Connecticut
COPEI	Comité Organizador Pro-Elecciones Independientes, Venezuela
CORFO	Corporación de Fomento de la Producción, Chile
CORP	Corporación para el Fomento de Investigaciones Económicas, Colombia
corp.	Corporation
corr.	corregida
CP	Communist Party
CPDOC	Centro de Pesquisa e Documentação, Brazil
CRIC	Consejo Regional Indígena del Cauca, Colombia
CUNY	City University of New York
CVG	Corporación Venezolana de Guayana
d.	died
DANE	Departamento Nacional de Estadística, Colombia
DC	developed country; Demócratas Cristianos, Chile
d.C	después de Cristo
déc.	décembre
Dec.	December
Del.	Delaware
dept.	department
depto.	departamento
dez.	dezembre
dic.	diciembre
disc.	discography
DNOCS	Departamento Nacional de Obras Contra as Sécas, Brazil
Dr.	Doctor
Dra.	Doctora
DRAE	*Diccionario de la Real Academia Española*
ECLA	Economic Commission for Latin America
ECOSOC	UN Department of Economic and Social Affairs
ed(s).	edition(s), edición(es), editor(s)
EDEME	Editora Emprendimentos Educacionais, Florianópolis, Brazil
Edo.	Estado
EEC	European Economic Community
EFTA	European Free Trade Association
e.g.	*exempli gratia* (for example)
ELN	Ejército de Liberación Nacional, Colombia
ENDEF	Estudo Nacional da Despesa Familiar, Brazil
ESG	Escola Superior de Guerra, Brazil
estr.	estrenado
et al.	*et alia* (and others)
ETENE	Escritório Técnico de Estudos Econômicos do Nordeste, Brazil
ETEPE	Escritório Técnico de Planejamento, Brazil
EUDEBA	Editorial Universitaria de Buenos Aires
EWG	Europaische Wirtschaftsgemeinschaft. *See* EEC.
facsim(s).	facsimile(s)
FAO	Food and Agriculture Organization of the United Nations
FDR	Frente Democrático Revolucionario, El Salvador
Feb./feb.	February, febrero
FEDECAFE	Federación Nacional de Cafeteros, Colombia
fev.	fevreiro, février
ff.	following
FFMLN	Frente Farabundo Martí de Liberación Nacional, El Salvador
FGTS	Fundo do Garantia do Tempo de Serviço, Brazil
FGV	Fundação Getúlio Vargas
FIEL	Fundación de Investigaciones Económicas Latinoamericanas, Argentina

film.	filmography
fl.	flourished
Fla.	Florida
FLACSO	Facultad Latinoamericana de Ciencias Sociales, Buenos Aires
fold.	folded
fol(s).	folio(s)
FRG	Federal Republic of Germany
FSLN	Frente Sandinista de Revolución Nacional, Nicaragua
ft.	foot, feet
FUAR	Frente Unido de Acción Revolucionaria, Colombia
Ga.	Georgia
GAO	General Accounting Office, Washington
GATT	General Agreement on Tariffs and Trade
GDP	gross domestic product
GDR	German Democratic Republic
GEIDA	Grupo Executivo de Irrigação para o Desenvolvimento Agrícola, Brazil
Gen.	General
GMT	Greenwich Meridian Time
GPA	grade point average
GPO	Government Printing Office
h.	hijo
ha.	hectares, hectáreas
HLAS	*Handbook of Latin American Studies*
HMAI	*Handbook of Middle American Indians*
Hnos.	hermanos
IBBD	Instituto Brasileiro de Bibliografia e Documentação
IBGE	Instituto Brasileiro de Geografia e Estatística, Rio de Janeiro
IBRD	International Bank of Reconstruction and Development
ICA	Instituto Colombiano Agropecuario
ICAIC	Instituto Cubano de Arte e Industria Cinematográficas
ICCE	Instituto Colombiano de Construcción Escolar
ICE	International Cultural Exchange
ICSS	Instituto Colombiano de Seguridad Social
ICT	Instituto de Crédito Territorial, Colombia
IDB	Inter-American Development Bank
i.e.	*id est* (that is)
IEL	Instituto Euvaldo Lodi, Brazil
IEP	Instituto de Estudios Peruanos
IERAC	Instituto Ecuatoriano de Reforma Agraria y Colonización
III	Instituto Indigenista Interamericano, Mexico
IIN	Instituto Indigenista Nacional, Guatemala
ill.	illustrations(s)
Ill.	Illinois
ILO	International Labour Organization, Geneva
IMES	Instituto Mexicano de Estudios Sociales
Impr.	Imprenta, Imprimerie
in.	inches
INAH	Instituto Nacional de Antropología e Historia, Mexico
INBA	Instituto Nacional de Bellas Artes, Mexico
Inc.	incorporated
INCORA	Instituto Colombiano de Reforma Agraria
Ind.	Indiana
INEP	Instituto Nacional de Estudios Pedagógicos, Brazil
INI	Instituto Nacional Indigenista, Mexico
INIT	Instituto Nacional de Industria Turística, Cuba

INPES/IPEA	Instituto de Planejamento Econômico e Social, Instituto de Pesquisas, Brazil
INTAL	Instituto para la Integración de América Latina
IPA	Instituto de Pastoral Andina, Univ. de San Antonio de Abad, Seminario de Antropología, Cuzco, Peru
IPEA	Instituto de Pesquisas Econômico-Social Aplicadas, Brazil
IPES/GB	Instituto de Pesquisas e Estudos Sociais, Guanabara, Brazil
IPHAN	Instituto de Patrimônio Histórico e Artístico Nacional, Brazil
ir.	irregular
ITT	International Telephone and Telegraph
Jan./jan.	January, janeiro, janvier
JLP	Jamaican Labour Party
JUCEPLAN	Junta Central de Planificación, Cuba
Kan.	Kansas
km	kilometers, kilómetres
Ky.	Kentucky
l.	leaves, hojas (páginas impresas por una sola cara)
La.	Louisiana
LASA	Latin American Studies Association
LDC	less developed countries
LP	long-playing record
Ltda.	Limitada
m	meters, metros
m.	murió (died)
M	mille, mil, thousand
MAPU	Movimiento de Acción Popular Unitario, Chile
MARI	Middle American Research Institute, Tulane University, New Orleans
Mass.	Massachusetts
MCC	Mercado Común Centro-Americano
Md.	Maryland
MDB	Movimiento Democrático Brasileiro
MDC	more developed countries
MEC	Ministério de Educação e Cultura, Brazil
Mich.	Michigan
mimeo	mimeographed, mimeografiado
min.	minutes, minutos
Minn.	Minnesota
MIR	Movimiento de Izquierda Revolucionaria, Chile
Miss.	Mississippi
MIT	Massachusetts Institute of Technology
MLN	Movimiento de Liberación Nacional
mm.	millimeter
MNC's	multinational corporations
MNR	Movimiento Nacionalista Revolucionario, Bolivia
Mo.	Missouri
MOBRAL	Movimento Brasileiro de Alfabetização, Brazil
MOIR	Movimiento Obrero Independiente y Revolucionario, Colombia
Mont.	Montana
MRL	Movimiento Revolucionario Liberal, Colombia
ms.	manuscript
msl	mean sea level
n.	nacido (born)
NBER	National Bureau of Economic Research, Cambridge, Mass.
N.C.	North Carolina
N.D.	North Dakota
Neb.	Nebraska

neubearb.	neubearbeitet (revised, corregida)
Nev.	Nevada
n.f.	neue Folge
N.H.	New Hampshire
NIEO	New International Economic Order
NIH	National Institutes of Health, Washington
N.J.	New Jersey
N.M.	New Mexico
no(s).	number(s), número(s)
NOSALF	Scandinavian Committee for Research in Latin America
Nov./nov.	November, noviembre, novembre, novembro
NSF	National Science Foundation
N.Y.	New York
N.Y.C.	New York City
OAS	Organization of American States
Oct./oct.	October, octubre
ODEPLAN	Oficina de Planificación Nacional, Chile
OEA	Organización de los Estados Americanos
OIT	*See* ILO.
Okla.	Oklahoma
Okt.	Oktober
op.	opus
OPANAL	Organismo para la Proscripción de las Armas Nucleares en América Latina
OPEC	Organization of Petroleum Exporting Countries
OPEP	Organización de Países Exportadores de Petróleo
OPIC	Overseas Investment Corporation
Or.	Oregon
ORIT	Organización Regional Interamericana del Trabajo
out.	outubre
p.	page(s)
Pa.	Pennsylvania
PAN	Partido Acción Nacional, Mexico
PC	Partido Comunista
PCR	Partido Comunista Revolucionario, Chile and Argentina
PCV	Partido Comunista de Venezuela
PDC	Partido Demócrata Cristiano, Chile
PDS	Partido Democrático Social, Brazil
PEMEX	Petróleos Mexicanos
PETROBRAS	Petróleo Brasileiro
PIMES	Programa Integrado de Mestrado em Economia e Sociologia, Brazil
PIP	Partido Independiente de Puerto Rico
PLANAVE	Engenharia e Planejamento Limitada, Brazil
PLANO	Planejamento e Assesoria Limitada, Brazil
PLN	Partido Liberación Nacional, Costa Rica
PNAD	Pesquisa Nacional por Amuestra Domiciliar, Brazil
PNM	People's National Movement, Trinidad and Tobago
PNP	People's National Party, Jamaica
pop.	population
port(s).	portrait(s)
PPP	purchasing power parities
PRD	Partido Revolucionario Dominicano
PREALC	Programa Regional del Empleo para América Latina y el Caribe, Organización Internacional del Trabajo, Santiago, Chile
PRI	Partido Revolucionario Institucional, Mexico
PROABRIL	Centro de Projetos Industriais, Brazil

Prof.	Professor
PRONAPA	Programa Nacional de Pesquisas Arqueológicas, Brazil
prov.	province, provincia
PS	Partido Socialista, Chile
pseud.	pseudonym, pseudónimo
pt(s).	part(s), parte(s)
pub.	published
PUC	Pontificia Universidad Católica, Rio de Janeiro
PURSC	Partido Unido de la Revolución Socialista de Cuba
q.	quarterly
rev.	revisada, revised
R.I.	Rhode Island
s.a.	semiannual
SALALM	Seminar on the Acquisition of Latin American Library Materials
sd.	sound
s.d.	*sine datum* (no date, sin fecha)
S.D.	South Dakota
SDR	special drawing rights
SELA	Sistema Económico Latinoamericano
SENAC	Serviço Nacional de Aprendizagem Comercial, Rio de Janeiro
SENAI	Serviço Nacional de Aprendizagem Industrial, São Paulo
SEPLA	Seminario Permanente sobre Latinoamérica, México
Sept./sept.	September, septiembre, septembre
SES	socio-economic status
SESI	Serviço Social de Industria, Brazil
set.	setembre
SIECA	Secretaría Permanente del Tratado General de Integración Centroamericana
SIL	Summer Institute of Linguistics
SINAMOS	Sistema Nacional de Apoyo a la Movilización Social, Peru
S.J.	Society of Jesus
s.l.	*sine loco* (place of publication unknown)
s.n.	*sine nomine* (publisher unknown)
SNA	Sociedad Nacional de Agricultura, Chile
SPVEA	Superintendência do Plano de Valorização Econômica de Amazônia, Brazil
sq.	square
SSRC	Social Sciences Research Council, New York
SUDAM	Superintendência de Desenvolvimento da Amazônia, Brazil
SUDENE	Superintendência de Desenvolvimento do Nordeste, Brazil
SUFRAME	Superintendência da Zona Franca de Manaus, Brazil
SUNY	State University of New York
t.	tomo(s), tome(s)
TAT	Thematic Apperception Test
TB	tuberculosis
Tenn.	Tennessee
Tex.	Texas
TG	transformational generative
TL	Thermoluminescent
TNEs	Transnational enterprises
TNP	Tratado de No Proliferación
trans.	translator
U.K.	United Kingdom
UN	United Nations
UNAM	Universidad Nacional Autónoma de México
UNCTAD	United Nations Conference on Trade and Development
UNDP	UN Development Programme

UNEAC	Unión de Escritores y Artistas de Cuba
UNESCO	UN Educational, Scientific and Cultural Organization
Univ.	university, universidad, universidade, université, universität
uniw.	uniwersytet
UP	Unidad Popular, Chile
URD	Unidad Revolucionaria Democrática
URSS	Unión de Repúblicas Soviéticas Socialistas
US	United States
USIA	US Information Agency, Washington
USSR	Union of the Soviet Socialist Republics
UTM	Universal Transverse Mercator
v.	volume(s), volumen (volúmenes)
Va.	Virginia
viz.	*videlicet* (that is, namely)
vol(s).	volume(s), volumen (volúmenes)
vs.	versus
Vt.	Vermont
W. Va.	West Virginia
Wash.	Washington
Wis.	Wisconsin
Wyo.	Wyoming
yr(s).	year(s)

TITLE LIST OF JOURNALS INDEXED

Journals that have been included in the *Handbook* as individual items are listed alphabetically by title in the *Author Index*, p. 703.

Abside. Revista de cultura mexicana. México. (A)

Actualidades. Consejo Nacional de la Cultura, Centro de Estudios Latino-americanos Rómulo Gallegos. Caracas. (CNC/A)

Administrative Science Quarterly. Cornell Univ., Graduate School of Business and Public Administration. Ithaca, N.Y. (CU/ASQ)

Affari Esteri. Associazione Italiana per gli studi di politica estera. Roma.

Afro-American Music Review. Detroit, Mich.

Agricultural History. Agricultural History Society. Washington. (AHS/AH)

Alero. Univ. de San Carlos. Guatemala.

Alfa. Univ. de São Paulo, Faculdade de Filosofia, Ciências e Letras. Marília, Brazil. (FFCLM/A)

Allpanchis. Instituto de Pastoral Andina. Cuzco, Perú. (IPA/A)

Amazonía Peruana. Centro Amazónico de Antropología y Aplicación Práctica. Lima. (CAAAP/AP)

América Indígena. Instituto Indigenista Interamericano. México. (III/AI)

América Latina. Academia de Ciencias de la URSS [Unión de Repúblicas Soviéticas Socialistas]. Moscú. (URSS/AL)

América Latina. Centro Latino-Americano de Pesquisas em Ciências Sociais. Rio de Janeiro. (CLAPCS/AL)

American Anthropologist. American Anthropological Association. Washington. (AAA/AA)

American Antiquity. The Society for American Archaeology. Menasha, Wis. (SAA/AA)

American Ethnologist. American Ethnological Society. Washington. (AES/AE)

American Historical Review. American Historical Association. Washington. (AHA/R)

American Jewish Archives. The American Jewish Archives. Cincinnati, Ohio. (AJA)

American Journal of Public Health and the Nation's Health. The American Public Health Association. Albany, N.Y. (APHA/J)

American Neptune. The American Neptune, Inc. Salem, Mass. (AN/AN)

American Speech. Columbia Univ. Press. New York. (AMS)

Américas. Organization of American States. Washington. (OAS/AM)

The Americas. A quarterly publication of inter-American cultural history. Academy of American Franciscan History. Washington. (AAFH/TAM)

Anais. Arquivo Histórico do Rio Grande do Sul. Pôrto Alegre, Brazil.

Anais do Museu Paulista. São Paulo. (MP/AN)

Anales. Administración del Patrimonio Cultural. San Salvador.

Anales de Antropología. Univ. Nacional Autónoma de México, Instituto de Investigaciones Históricas. México. (UNAM/AA)

Anales de Arqueología y Etnología. Univ. Nacional de Cuyo, Facultad de Filosofía y Letras. Mendoza, Argentina. (UNC/AAE)

Anales de la Sociedad de Geografía e Historia de Guatemala. Guatemala. (SGHG/A)

Anales de la Universidad Central del Ecuador. Quito. (UCE/A)

Anales de la Universidad de Cuenca. Cuenca, Ecuador. (UC/A)

Anales del Instituto de Investigaciones Estéticas. Univ. Nacional Autónoma de México. México. (IIE/A)

Anales del Instituto Nacional de Antropología e Historia. Secretaría de Educación Pública. México. (INAH/A)

Anales del Museo Nacional David J. Guzmán. San Salvador. (MNDJG/A)

Análisis. Cuadernos de investigación. Lima. (ANA)

Andén para la Cultura. Ediciones Candilejas. Córdoba, Argentina.

Annales: économies, sociétés, civilisations. Centre national de la recherche scientifique *avec le concours de la* VIᵉ Section de l'Ecole pratique des hautes études. Paris. (AESC)

Annales de démographie historique. Société de démographie historique. Paris.

Annals. Organization of American States. Washington. (OAS/A)

Annals of the Southeastern Conference on Latin American Studies. West Georgia College. Carrollton. (SECOLAS/A)

Anthropological Linguistics. A publication of the Archives of the Languages of the World. Indiana Univ., Anthropology Dept. Bloomington. (IU/AL)

Anthropos. Anthropos-Institut. Freiburg, Switzerland. (AI/A)

La Antigua. Univ. de Santa María La Antigua, Oficina de Humanidades. Panamá. (USMLA/LA)

Antropología. La Paz.

Antropología Andina. Cusco, Perú.

Antropología e Historia de Guatemala. Instituto de Antropología e Historia de Guatemala. Guatemala. (IAHG/AHG)

Antropológica. Fundación La Salle de Ciencias Naturales, Instituto Caribe de Antropología y Sociología. Caracas. (FSCN/A)

Anuario. Instituto de Investigaciones Históricas Dr. José Gaspar Rodríguez de Francia. Asunción.

Anuario. Univ. Central de Venezuela, Instituto de Estudios Hispanoamericanos. Caracas. (IEH/A)

Anuario. Univ. Michoacán de San Nicolás de Hidalgo, Escuela de Historia. Morelia, México.

Anuario Bibliográfico Ecuatoriano 1976 y 1977 y Bibliografía Ecuatoriana. Univ. Central del Ecuador, Biblioteca General, Editorial Universitaria. Quito.

Anuario Bibliográfico Uruguayo de 1978. Biblioteca Nacional. Montevideo.

Anuario Colombiano de Historia Social y de la Cultura. Univ. Nacional de Colombia, Facultad de Ciencias Humanas, Depto. de Historia. Bogotá. (UNC/ACHSC)

Anuario de Estudios Americanos. Consejo Superior de Investigaciones Científicas [and] Univ. de Sevilla, Escuela de Estudios Hispano-Americanos. Sevilla. (EEHA/AEA)

Anuario de Estudios Centroamericanos. Univ. de Costa Rica. Ciudad Universitaria Rodrigo Facio. (UCR/AEC)

Anuario de Historia del Derecho Español. Instituto Nacional de Estudios Jurídicos. Madrid. (INEJ/AHD)

Anuario de Letras. Univ. Nacional Autónoma de México, Facultad de Filosofía y Letras. México. (UNAM/AL)

Anuario Musical. Barcelona.

Apollo. London.

Apuntes. Univ. del Pacífico, Centro de Investigación. Lima. (UP/A)

Araisa. Anuario del Centro de Estudios Latinoamericanos Rómulo Gallegos. Caracas. (CELRG/A)

Arbor. Madrid. (ARBOR)

Archiv für Völkerkunde. Museum für Völkerkunde in Wien und von Verein Freunde der Völkerkunde. Wien, FRG. (MVW/AV)

Archivo Artigas. Comisión Nacional Archivo Artigas. Montevideo.

Archivo Ibero-Americano. Los Padres Franciscanos. Madrid. (PF/AIA)

Archivos del Folklore Chileno. Santiago.

Archivum Franciscanum Historicum. Firenze, Italy. (AFH)

Archivum Historicum Societatis Iesu. Rome. (AHSI)

Areíto. Areíto, Inc. New York. (AR)

Arizona and the West. Univ. of Arizona. Tucson. (UA/AW)

The Art Bulletin. College Art Association of America. New York.

Art Journal. College Art Association of America. New York.

Arte. Revista da Escola de Música e Artes Cênicas, Univ. Federal da Bahia. Salvador, Brazil.

Artes de México. Revista bimestral. México. (ARMEX)

Asclepio. Consejo Superior de Investigaciones Científicas, Instituto Arnau de Vilanova de Historia de la Medicina, Archivo Iberoamericano de Historia de la Medicina y Antropología Médica. Madrid. (CSIC/A)

Asien, Afrika, Lateinamerika. Deutscher Verlag der Wissenschaften. Berlin.

Atenea. Revista de ciencias, letras y artes. Univ. de Concepción, Chile. (UC/AT)

Aula. Univ. Nacional Pedro Henríquez Ureña. Santo Domingo. (UNPHU/A)

B.B.A.A. Boletín Bibliográfico de Antropología Americana. Instituto Panamericano de Geografía e Historia, Comisión de Historia. México. (BBAA)

Barroco. Minas Gerais, Brazil.

Beiträge zur Romanischen Philologie. Rütten & Loening. Berlin. (BRP)

Belizean Studies. Belize Institute of Social Research and Action [and] St. John's College. Belize City. (BISRA/BS)

Berichte zur Entwicklung in Spanien, Portugal, Lateinamerika. München, FRG. (BESPL)

Bibliografía Histórica Mexicana: 1976-1978. El Colegio de México, Centro de Estudios Históricos. México.

Bibliographie d'articles des revues. Institut des hautes études de l'Amérique Latine. Centre de documentation. Paris.

Bibliography of the English-Speaking Caribbean. Books, articles and reviews in English from the arts, humanities, and social sciences. Iowa City, Iowa.

Boletim. Instituto Histórico, Geográfico e Etnográfico Paranaense. Curitiba. Brazil.

Boletim Bibliográfico. Biblioteca Mário de Andrade. São Paulo. (BMA/BB)

Boletim Bibliográfico da Biblioteca Nacional. Biblioteca Nacional. Rio de Janeiro.

Boletim da Cidade do Recife. Prefeitura Municipal do Recife, Conselho Municipal de Cultura. Recife, Brazil.

Boletim da Sociedade Brasileira de Musicologia. São Paulo.

Boletim Informativo e Bibliográfico de Ciências Sociais. Associação Nacional de Pós Graduação e Pesquisa em Ciências Sociais. Rio de Janeiro.

Boletim Informativo SIP: Anuário. Instituto Nacional do Cinema. Rio de Janeiro.

Boletín. Academia de Historia del Cauca. Popayán, Colombia.

Boletín. Museo Arqueológico de la Serena, Chile.

Boletín. Museo del Oro [and] Banco de la República. Bogotá. (MOBR/B)

Boletín. Provincia de Santa Fe. Ministerio de Gobierno. Archivo General de la Provincia. Santa Fe, Argentina.

Boletín Americanista. Univ. de Barcelona, Facultad de Geografía e Historia, Depto. de Historia de América. Barcelona. (UB/BA)

Boletín Bibliográfico. Banco Central de Nicaragua. Managua.

Boletín Bibliográfico. Biblioteca del Congreso Nacional. Sección Procesamiento. Santiago.

Boletín Cultural y Bibliográfico. Banco de la República, Biblioteca Luis-Angel Arango. Bogotá. (CBR/BCB)

Boletín de Antropología Americana. Instituto Panamericano de Geografía e Historia. México.

Boletín de Artes Visuales. Anuario. Organización de los Estados Americanos, Secretaría General. Washington.

Boletín de Ciencias Económicas y Sociales. Univ. Centroamericana José Simeón Cañas, Depto. de Economía. San Salvador.

Boletín de Ciencias Políticas y Sociales. Univ. Nacional de Cuyo, Facultad de Ciencias Políticas y Sociales. Mendoza, Argentina. (UNC/BCPS)

Boletín de Coyuntura Socioeconómica. Univ. del Valle, División de Ciencias Sociales y Económicas, Centro de Investigación, y Documentación Socioeconómica. Cali, Colombia.

Boletín de Estudios Latinoamericanos. Centro de Estudios y Documentación Latinoamerica nos. Amsterdam. (CEDLA/B)

Boletín de Filología. Univ. de Chile, Instituto de Filología. Santiago. (UC/BF)

Boletín de Historia y Antigüedades. Academia Colombiana de Historia. Bogotá. (ACH/BHA)

Boletín de Información. Centro Interamericano de Artesanía y Artes Populares (CIDAP). Cuenca, Ecuador.

Boletín de la Academia Chilena de la Historia. Santiago. (ACH/B)

Boletín de la Academia Colombiana. Bogotá. (ACO/B)

Boletín de la Academia de Ciencias Políticas y Sociales. Caracas. (ACPS/B)

Boletín de la Academia Hondureña de la Lengua. Tegucigalpa. (AHL/B)

Boletín de la Academia Nacional de Historia. Buenos Aires. (ANH/B)

Boletín de la Academia Nacional de Historia. Quito. (EANH/B)

Boletín de la Academia Nacional de la Historia. Caracas. (VANH/B)

Boletín de la Academia Norteamericana de la Lengua Española. New York. (ANLE/B)

Boletín de la Academia Panameña de la Lengua. Panamá. (APL/B)

Boletín de la Biblioteca Nacional. Lima. (PEBN/B)

Boletín de la Facultad de Derecho y Ciencias Sociales. Univ. Nacional de Córdoba. Córdoba, Argentina.

Boletín de la Real Sociedad Geográfica. Madrid. (RSG/B)

Boletín de Música. Casa de las América. La
Habana.

Boletín del Archivo General de la Nación.
Managua.

Boletín del Archivo General de la Nación.
Secretaría de Gobernación. México.
(MAGN/B)

Boletín del Archivo Histórico. Congreso de la
República. Caracas.

Boletín del Archivo Histórico de Jalisco.
Guadalajara, México.

Boletín del Archivo Histórico de Miraflores.
Caracas.

Boletín del Departamento de Investigación de
las Tradiciones Populares. México.

Boletín del Instituto de Historia Argentina y
Americana Emilio Ravignani. Facultad de
Filosofía y Letras, Universidad Nacional de
Buenos Aires. (IHAAER/B)

Boletín del Instituto Riva-Agüero. Pontifica
Univ. Católica del Perú. Lima. (IRA/B)

Boletín del Museo del Hombre Dominicano.
Santo Domingo. (MHD/B)

Boletín del Sistema Bibliotecario de la
UNAH. Universidad Nacional Autónoma
de Honduras. Tegucigalpa.

Boletín Histórico. Fundación John Boulton.
Caracas. (FJB/BH)

Boletín Informativo para Asuntos Migratorios
y Fronterizos. Comité de Servicio de Los
Amigos, Centro de Información para Mi-
gración y Desarrollo. México.

Boletín Informativo Trotskysta. Tendencia
Cuartainternacionalista. Organización
Trotskysta Revolucionaria. Lima.

Boletín Nicaragüense de Bibliografía y Documentación. Banco Central de Nicaragua,
Biblioteca. Managua. (BNBD)

Brasil Açucareiro. Instituto do Açúcar e do
Alcool. Rio de Janeiro. (IAA/BA)

Brasile: "Cinema Novo" e Dopo. Quaderni
della Mostra Internazionale del Nuevo
Cinema. Venezia, Italy.

Brigham Young University Studies. Provo,
Utah. (BYU/S)

Britain and Latin America. An annual review
of British-Latin American relations. Latin
American Bureau. London.

Bulletin. Société suisse des américanistes.
Geneva. (SSA/B)

Bulletin de la Sociéte d'histoire de la Guadeloupe. Archives départementales *avec
le concours du* Conseil général de la
Guadeloupe. Basse-Terre, West Indies.
(SHG/B)

Bulletin de l'Académie des sciences humaines et sociales d'Haiti. Port-au-Prince.
(ASHSH/B)

Bulletin de l'Institut français d'études andines. Lima. (IFEA/B)

Bulletin des études portugaises et bresil-
iennes. Institut français de Lisbonne *avec
la collaboration de* Etablissements français d'enseignement supérieur, Instituto de
Alta Cultura, et du Depto. Cultural do Itamarati. Lisbon. (BEPB)

Bulletin d'information. Association des ar-
chivistes, bibliothecaires, documentalistes
francophones de la Caraïbe, Section Haïti.
Port-au-Prince.

Bulletin hispanique. Univ. de Bordeaux *avec
le concours du* Centre national de la recherche scientifique. Bordeaux, France.
(UB/BH)

CCS Current Awareness Service. Caribbean
Community Secretariat. Information and
Documentation Section. Georgetown,
Guyana.

CENIDIM. Boletín informativo. Centro Nacional de Investigación e Información Musical Carlos Chávez. México.

CLA Journal. Morgan State College, College
Language Association. Baltimore, Md.
(CLA/J)

Cadernos DCP. Univ. Federal de Minas
Gerais, Faculdade de Filosofia e Ciências
Humanas, Depto. de Ciência Política. Belo
Horizonte, Brazil. (UFMG/DCP)

Cahiers Césairiens. Pennsylvania State Univ.,
French Dept. University Park.

Cahiers des Amériques Latines. Paris.
(CDAL)

Cahiers du cinéma. Paris.

Canadian Journal of History/Annales Cana-
diennes d'Histoire. Journal of History Co.,
Ltd. Saskatoon, Canada.

Canadian Psychiatric Association Journal.
Ottawa.

Canadian Review of Studies in Na-
tionalism/Revue canadienne des études
sur le nationalisme. Univ. of Prince Edward
Island. Charlottetown.

Caravelle. Cahiers du monde hispanique et
luso-brésilien. Univ. de Toulouse, Institut
d'études hispaniques, hispano-americaines
et luso-brésiliennes. Toulouse, France.
(UTIEH/C)

Caribbean Quarterly. Univ. of the West Indies. Mona, Jamaica. (UWI/CQ)

Caribbean Review. Florida International
Univ., Office of Academic Affairs. Miami.
(FIU/CR)
Caribbean Studies. Univ. of Puerto Rico, In-
stitute of Caribbean Studies. Río Piedras.
(UPR/CS)
Caribbean Studies. Univ. of the West Indies.
Mona, Jamaica. (UWI/CS)
Caribe. Univ. of Hawaii, Dept. of European
Languages and Literatures. Honolulu.
El Caribe Contemporáneo. Univ. Nacional
Autónoma de México, Facultad de Ciencias
Políticas y Sociales, Centro de Estudios
Latinoamericanos. México.
Caricom Perspective. Caribbean Community
Secretariat. Georgetown, Guyana.
Casa de las Américas. Instituto Cubano del
Libro. La Habana. (CDLA)
Casa del Tiempo. Univ. Autónoma Metro-
politana, Dirección de Difusión Cultural.
México.
Casas Reales. Museo de las Casas Reales.
Santo Domingo.
Centro Latinoamericano de Economía Hu-
mana. Montevideo. (CLAEH)
Christian Science Monitor. Boston.
Church History. American Society of Church
History, Univ. of Chicago. Chicago, Ill.
(ASCH/CH)
Ciência e Cultura. Sociedade Brasileira
para o Progresso da Ciência. São Paulo.
(SBPC/CC)
Ciencia y Sociedad. Instituto Tecnológica.
Santo Domingo.
Ciencia y Tecnología. Editorial Universidad
de Costa Rica. San José.
Cine Cubano. La Habana.
Cine Olho. São Paulo.
Cinejornal. Embrafilme. Rio de Janeiro.
Cinema. Fundação Cinemateca Brasileira.
São Paulo.
Cinéma. Paris.
Cinema BR. São Paulo.
Cladindex. Resumen de documentos
CEPAL/ILPES. Organización de las Na-
ciones Unidas, Comisión Económica para
América Latina (CEPAL) [and] Centro
Latinoamericano de Documentación Eco-
nómica y Social (CLADES). Santiago.
Clio. Academia Dominicana de la Historia.
Santo Domingo. (ADH/C)
Colección Documental de la Independencia
del Perú. Comisión Nacional del Sesqui-
centenario de la Independencia. Lima.

Colóquio. Fundação Calouste Gulbenkian.
Lisboa. (COLOQ)
Communications. École des hautes études en
sciences sociales, Centre d'études trans
disciplinaires. Paris. (EHESS/C)
Comparative Political Studies. Northwestern
Univ., Evanston, Ill. [and] Sage Publica-
tions, Beverly Hills, Calif. (CPS)
Comparative Studies in Society and History.
An international quarterly. Society for the
Comparative Study of Society and History.
The Hague. (CSSH)
Computers for the Humanities. Amsterdam,
The Netherlands.
Comunicações e Artes. Univ. de São Paulo,
Escola de Comunicações e Artes. São
Paulo.
Comunidad. Revista de la U.I.A. Cuadernos
de difusión cultural. Univ. Iberoamericana.
México. (UIA/C)
Conjonction. Institut français d'Haïti. Port-
au-Prince. (IFH/C)
Conjunto. Casa de las Américas for the Com-
ité Permanente de Festivales. La Habana.
(CDLA/CO)
Construtura. Univ. Católica do Paraná.
Curitiba, Brazil.
Controversia: Para el Examen de la Realidad
Argentina. México.
Convivium. Revista bimestral de inves-
tigação e cultura. Editora Convívio. São
Paulo.
Creación & Crítica. Lima.
Criterio. Editorial Criterio. Buenos Aires.
(CRIT)
Critica d'Arte. Studio Italiano di Storia
dell'Arte. Vallecchi Editore. Firenze, Italy.
(CA)
Cuaderno del Centro de Estudios Inter-
disciplinarios de Fronteras Argentinas.
Buenos Aires?
Cuadernos Americanos. México. (CAM)
Cuadernos de Filosofía. Univ. de Buenos
Aires, Facultad de Filosofía y Letras.
Buenos Aires. (UBAFFL/C)
Cuadernos de Filosofía. Univ. de Buenos
Aires, Facultad de Filosofía y Letras.
Buenos Aires. (UBAFFL/C)
Cuadernos de Filosofía. Univ. de Concep-
ción, Instituto Central de Filosofía.
Concepción.
Cuadernos del Consejo Nacional de la Uni-
versidad Peruana. Lima.
Cuadernos del Instituto Nacional de Antropo-
logía. Secretaría de Estado de Cultura y

Educación, Dirección General de Institutos de Investigación. Buenos Aires. (AINA/C)

Cuadernos del Seminario de Historia. Pontificia Univ. Católica del Perú, Instituto Riva-Agüero. Lima. (PUCP/CSH)

Cuadernos del Sur. Univ. Nacional del Sur, Instituto de Humanidades. Bahía Blanca, Argentina. (UNS/CS)

Cuadernos Hispanoamericanos. Instituto de Cultura Hispánica. Madrid. (CH)

Cuadernos Hispanoamericanos. Revista mensual de cultura hispánica. Centro Iberoamericano de Cooperación. Madrid.

Cuadernos Políticos. Revista trimestral. Ediciones Era. México. (CP)

Cuadrante. Centro de Estudios Regionales. Tucumán, Arg. (CER/C)

Cuban Studies / Estudios Cubanos. Univ. of Pittsburgh, Univ. Center for International Studies, Center for Latin American Studies. Pittsburgh, Pa. (UP/CSEC)

Cultura. Ministério da Educação e Cultura, Diretoria de Documentação e Divulgação. Brasília. (MEC/C)

Cultura. Ministerio de Educación. San Salvador. (ESME/C)

Cultura. Revista del Banco Central del Ecuador. Quito. (BCE/C)

Cultura. Revista del Ministerio de Educación. San Salvador. (ESME/C)

Cultures. United Nations Educational, Scientific and Cultural Organization. Paris. (UNESCO/CU)

Current Anthropology. Univ. of Chicago, Ill. (UC/CA)

Cuyo. Anuario de historia del pensamiento argentino. Univ. Nacional de Cuyo, Instituto de Filosofía. Mendoza, Argentina. (UNCIF/C)

Davar. Revista literaria. Sociedad Hebraica Argentina. Buenos Aires. (SHA/D)

Debates en Antropología. Pontificia Univ. Católica del Perú, Depto. de Ciencias Sociales. Lima. (PUCP/DA)

Denver Quarterly. Univ. of Denver. Denver, Colo.

Desarrollo Económico. Instituto de Desarrollo Económico y Social. Buenos Aires. (IDES/DE)

Desarrollo y Sociedad. Univ. de Los Andes, Facultad de Economía, Centro de Estudios sobre el Desarrollo Económico (CEDE). Bogotá. (CEDE/DS)

The Developing Economies. Institute of Developing Economies. Tokyo. (IDE/DE)

Diacritics. A review of contemporary criticism. Cornell Univ., Dept. of Romance Studies. Ithaca, N.Y. (CU/D)

Diálogos. Artes/Letras/Ciencias Humanas. El Colegio de México. México. (CM/D)

Diánoia. Univ. Nacional Autónoma de México, Centro de Estudios Filosóficos. México. (UNAM/D)

Diapason. American Institute of Organbuilders. Des Plains, Ill.

Dispositio. Univ. of Michigan, Dept. of Romance Languages. Ann Arbor.

Documentos de Arquitectura Nacional y Americana. Univ. Nacional del Nordeste, Depto. de Historia de la Arquitectura. Resistencia, Argentina.

El Dorado. Univ. of Northern Colorado, Museum of Anthropology. Greeley.

Eco. Librería Bucholz. Bogotá. (ECO)

Económico. Ministerio de Economía y Finanzas. Montevideo.

Ecuador: Bibliografía Analítica. Banco Central del Ecuador. Centro de Investigación y Cultura. Cuenca.

Educação Hoje. Faculdade de Filosofia, Ciências e Letras de Palmas, Brazil.

La Educación. Organization of American States, Dept. of Educational Affairs. Washington. (OAS/LE)

Ele, Ela. Rio de Janeiro.

Encontros com a Civilização Brasileiro. Editora Civilização Brasileira. Rio de Janeiro. (ECB)

Encuentro: Selecciones para Latinoamérica. Centro de Proyección Cristiana. Lima.

English Journal. East Lansing, Mich.

Ensaios de Opinião. Rio de Janeiro.

Escritos de Filosofía. Academia Nacional de Ciencias, Centro de Estudios Filosóficos. Buenos Aires.

Escritura. Teoría y crítica literaria. Univ. Central de Venezuela, Escuela de Letras. Caracas. (UCV/E)

Esquire. New York.

Estrategia. Instituto Argentino de Estudios Estratégicos y de las Relaciones Internacionales. Buenos Aires. (IAEERI/E)

Estudios Andinos. Univ. of Pittsburgh, Latin American Studies Center. Pittsburgh, Pa. (UP/EA)

Estudios Atacameños. San Pedro de Atacama, Chile.

Estudios Contemporáneos. Univ. Autónoma de Puebla, Instituto de Ciencias, Centro de Estudios Contemporáneos. Puebla, México.

Estudios de Cultura Maya. Univ. Nacional Autónoma de México, Centro de Estudios Mayas. México. (CEM/ECM)

Estudios de Cultura Náhuatl. Univ. Nacional Autónoma de México, Instituto de Historia, Seminario de Cultura Náhuatl. México. (UNAM/ECN)

Estudios de Historia Moderna y Contemporánea de México. Univ. Nacional Autónoma de México. México. (UNAM/E)

Estudios de Historia Novohispana. Univ. Nacional Autónoma de México, Instituto de Investigaciones Históricas. México. (UNAM/EHN)

Estudios Fiscales. México.

Estudios Latinoamericanos. Polska Akademia Nauk [Academia de Ciencias de Polonia], Instytut Historii [Instituto de Historia]. Warszawa. (PAN/ES)

Estudios Paraguayos. Univ. Católica de Nuestra Señora de la Asunción. (UCNSA/EP)

Estudios Sociales. Corporación de Promoción Universitaria. Santiago. (CPU/ES)

Estudios Sociales Centroamericanos. Consejo Superior de Universidades Centroamericanas, Confederación Universitaria Centroamericana, Programa Centroamericano de Ciencias Sociales. San José. (CSUCA/ESC)

Estudos Baianos. Univ. Federal da Bahia, Centro Editorial e Didático, Núcleo de Publicações. Bahia, Brazil. (UFB/EB)

Estudos Brasileiros. Univ. Federal do Paraná, Setor de Ciências Humanas, Centro de Estudos Brasileiros. Curitiba, Brazil. (UFP/EB)

Estudos Econômicos. Univ. de São Paulo, Instituto de Pesquisas Econômicas. São Paulo. (IPE/EE)

Estudos e Pesquisas em Administração. Univ. Federal de Paraíba, Curso Mestrado em Administração. João Pessoa, Brazil.

Estudos Históricos. Faculdade de Filosofia, Ciências e Letras, Depto. de História. Marília, Brazil. (FFCLM/EH)

Estudos Ibero-Americanos. Depto. de História, Pontifícia Univ. Católica do Rio Grande do Sul. Pôrto Alegre. (EIA)

Estudos Leopoldenses. Faculdade de Filosofia, Ciências e Letras. São Leopoldo, Brazil. (FFCL/EL)

Ethnicity. New York.

Ethnohistory. Journal of the American Society for Ethnohistory. Buffalo, N.Y. (ASE/E)

Ethnology. Univ. of Pittsburgh, Pa. (UP/E)

Ethnomusicology. Wesleyan Univ. Press for the Society for Ethnomusicology. Middletown, Conn. (SE/E)

Etnía. Museo Etnográfico Municipal Dámaso Arce. Olavarría, Argentina. (MEMDA/E)

Etnohistoria y Antropología Andina. Museo Nacional de Historia. Lima.

Etnologia Polona. Warsaw.

Etudes hispano-américaines. Univ. de Haute Bretagne, Centre d'études hispaniques, hispano-américaines et luso-brésiliennes. Rennes, France. (UHB/EHA)

Europe. Revue littéraire mensuelle. Paris.

Excelsior. Diorama de la cultura. México.

Explicación de Textos Literarios. California State Univ., Dept. of Spanish and Portuguese. Sacramento.

FEM. Publicación femenina. Nueva Cultura Feminista. México.

Fénix. Biblioteca Nacional. Lima. (FENIX)

Film Quarterly. Univ. of California. Berkeley.

Filme Cultura. Ministério de Educação Cultural, Embrafilme [Empresa Brasileira de Filmes]. Rio de Janeiro. (MEC/FC)

The Florida Historical Quarterly. The Florida Historical Society. Jacksonville. (FHS/FHQ)

Folia Histórica del Nordeste. Instituto de Historia, Facultad de Humanidades, Univ. Nacional del Nordeste, Instituto de Investigaciones Geohistóricas. Resistencia, Argentina.

Folia Humanistica. Ciencias, artes, letras. Editorial Glarma. Barcelona. (FH)

Folio Musica. Filharmonia Pomorska. Bydgoszcz, Poland.

Folklore Americano. Instituto Panamericano de Geografía e Historia, Comisión de Historia, Comité de Folklore. México. (IPGH/FA)

Folklore Annual. Austin, Tex.

Foreign Language Index. Public Affairs Information Service. New York.

Foro Internacional. El Colegio de México. México. (CM/FI)

Fragmentos. Centro de Estudios Latinoamericanos Rómulo Gallegos, Depto. de Investiga ciones. Caracas.

Franciscanum. Revista de las ciencias del espíritu. Univ. de San Buenaventura. Bogotá. (USB/F)

Fund og Forskning i det kongelige samlinger. Copenhagen.

Futurable. Fundación Argentina Año 2000. Buenos Aires.

Gaceta de Cuba. Unión de Escritores y Artistas de Cuba. La Habana. (UEAC/GC)

The Geographical Magazine. London. (GM)

The Geographical Review. American Geographical Society. New York. (AGS/GR)

Geosur. Asociación Sudamericana de Estudios Geopolíticos e Internacionales. Montevideo.

Geschichte und Gesellschaft. Zeitschrift für Historische Sozialwissenschaft. Univ. Bielefeld, Fakultät für Geschichtswissenschaft. Bielefeld, FRG. (UB/GG)

Guatemala Indígena. Instituto Indigenista Nacional. Guatemala. (GIIN/GI)

Guías y Catálogos. Archivo General de la Nación. México.

Hablemos de Cine. Lima.

Handbook of Latin American Art. New Haven, Conn.

Heterofonía. Revista musical bimestral. México. (HET)

Hispamérica. Revista de literatura. Takoma Park, Md. (HISPA)

Hispania. American Association of Teachers of Spanish and Portuguese. Univ. of Cincinnati, Ohio. (AATSP/H)

Hispania. Revista española de historia. Instituto Jerónimo Zurita, Consejo Superior de Investigaciones Científicas. Madrid. (IJZ/H)

Hispanic American Historical Review. Duke Univ. Press for the Conference on Latin American History of the American Historical Association. Durham, N.C. (HAHR)

Hispanic Journal. Indiana Univ. of Pennsylvania, Dept. of Foreign Languages. Indiana, Pa. (IUP/HJ)

Hispanic Review. A quarterly devoted to research in the Hispanic languages and literatures. Univ. of Pennsylvania, Dept. of Romance Languages. Philadelphia. (HR)

Hispanófila. Univ. of North Carolina. Chapel Hill. (HISP)

Historia. Revista-Libro trimestral. Buenos Aires.

Historia. Univ. Católica de Chile, Instituto de Historia. Santiago. (UCCIH/H)

Historia Crítica. Revista de la Carrera de Historia. Univ. Nacional Autónoma de Honduras. Tegucigalpa.

Historia Mexicana. El Colegio de México. México. (CM/HM)

Historia Obrera. Centro de Estudios Históricos del Movimiento Obrero Mexicano. México. (CEHSMO)

Historia Paraguaya. Anuario de la Academia Paraguaya de la Historia. Asunción. (APH/HP)

Historia y Cultura. Museo Nacional de Historia. Lima. (PMNH/HC)

The Historian. A journal of history. Phi Alpha Theta, National Honor Society in History. Univ. of Pennsylvania. University Park. (PAT/TH)

Histórica. Pontificia Univ. Católica del Perú, Depto. de Humanidades. Lima. (PUCP/H)

Histórica. Univ. Autónoma del Estado de México, Instituto de Investigaciones Históricas. México. (UAEM/H)

Historical Reflections/Reflexions Historiques. Univ. of Waterloo, Dept. of History. Waterloo, Canada.

Históricas. Univ. Nacional Autónoma de México, Instituto de Investigaciones Históricas. México.

Historiografía Rioplatense. Instituto Bibliográfico Antonio Zinny. Buenos Aires.

Historiografía y Bibliografía Americanista. Escuela de Estudios Hispano-Americanos de Sevilla. Sevilla. (EEHA/HBA)

History Today. Longman Group, Ltd., Periodicals and Directories Division. London.

Hojas Universitarias. Revista de la Fundación Univ. Central. Bogotá. (HU)

L'Homme. Revue française d'anthropologie. La Sorbonne, l'École pratique des hautes études. Paris. (EPHE/H)

Horizontes. Revista de la Univ. Católica de Puerto Rico. Ponce. (UCPR/H)

Humanidades. Pontificia Univ. Católica del Perú, Facultad de Letras. Lima. (PUC/H)

Humanitas. Boletín ecuatoriano de antropología. Univ. Central del Ecuador, Instituto de Antropología. Quito. (UCEIA/H)

Humanitas. Univ. de Nuevo León, Centro de Estudios Humanísticos. Monterrey, Mex. (UNL/H)

Humboldt. Revista para o mundo ibérico. Ubersee-Verlag. Hamburg, FRG. (HUMB)

Ibero Americana. Scandinavian Association for Research on Latin America (NOSALF). Stockholm. (NOSALF/IA)

Ibero-Americana Pragensia. Univ. Carolina de Praga, Centro de Estudios Ibero-Americanos. Prague. (UCP/IAP)

Ibero-Amerikanisches Archiv. Ibero-Amerikanisches Institut. Berlin, FRG. (IAA)

Iberoromania. Max Niemeyer Verlag. Tübingen, FRG.

Ideas y Valores. Revista del Instituto de Filosofía y Letras. Univ. Nacional. Bogotá. (UN/IV)

Ideologies & Literature. A journal of Hispanic and Luso-Brazilian literatures. Univ. of Minnesota, Institute for the Study of Ideologies and Literature. Minneapolis. (IL)

Inca. Centro de Estudiantes de Arqueología. Lima.

Index on Censorship. Writers & Scholars International. London. (INDEX)

Index Translationum. UNESCO, International Institute of Intellectual Cooperation. Geneva.

The Indian Historian. American Indian Historical Society. San Francisco, Calif.

Indiana. Beiträge zur Volker-und Sprachenkunde, Archäologie und Anthropologie des Indianischen Amerika. Ibero-Amerikanisches Institut. Berlin, FRG. (IAI/I)

Indiana Folklore. Bloomington.

Indice de Artículos de Publicaciones Periódicas en el Area de Ciencias Sociales y Humanidades. Instituto Colombiano para el Fomento de la Educación Superior (ICFES). División de Documentación e Información. Bogotá.

Indice de Ciências Sociais. Instituto Universitário de Pesquisas do Rio de Janeiro (IUPERJ). Rio de Janeiro.

Información Documental Costarricense y Centroamericana. Univ. de Costa Rica. Instituto de Investigaciones Sociales. San José.

Informaciones. Univ. Nacional de Asunción, Escuela de Bibliotecología. Asunción.

Informações sobre a Indústria Cinematográfica Brasileira. Embrafilme. Rio de Janeiro.

Insula. Madrid. (INSULA)

Inter-American Economic Affairs. Washington. (IAMEA)

Inter-American Music Review. R. Stevenson. Los Angeles, Calif. (IAMR)

Interciencia. Asociación Interciencia. Caracas. (AI/I)

Interior. Revista bimestral. Ministério do Interior. Brasília.

International History Review. Univ. of Toronto Press. Toronto.

International Journal of American Linguistics. Published by Indiana Univ. *under the auspices of the* Linguistic Society of America, American Anthropological Association, *with the cooperation of the* Joint Committee on Native Languages. Bloomington. (IU/IJAL)

International Review. United States Dept. of Housing and Urban Development, Office of International Affairs. Washington.

Inti. Univ. of Connecticut, Dept. of Romance Languages. Storrs. (INTI)

Investigaciones y Ensayos. Academia Nacional de la Historia. Buenos Aires. (ANH/IE)

Islas. Univ. Central de las Villas. Santa Clara, Cuba. (UCLV/I)

Istmo. Revista del pensamiento actual. México. (ISTMO)

Jahrbuch für Geschichte von Staat, Wirtschaft und Gesellschaft Lateinamerikas. Köln, FRG. (JGSWGL)

Jamaica Journal. Institute of Jamaica. Kingston. (IJ/JJ)

Jamaican Historical Review. The Jamaican Historical Society. Kingston. (JHS/R)

Jeune cinéma. Paris.

Journal de la Société des américanistes. Paris. (SA/J)

Journal of American Folklore. American Folklore Society. Austin, Tex. (AFS/JAF)

Journal of Anthropological Research. Univ. of New Mexico, Dept. of Anthropology. Albuquerque. (UNM/JAR)

Journal of Belizean Affairs. Belize City. (JBA)

Journal of Caribbean History. Univ. of the West Indies, Dept. of History [and] Caribbean Universities Press. St. Lawrence, Barbados. (UWI/JCH)

A Journal of Church and State. Baylor Univ., J.M. Dawson Studies in Church and State. Waco, Tex. (BU/JCS)

Journal of Commonwealth & Comparative Politics. Univ. of London, Institute of Commonwealth Studies. London. (ICS/JCCP)

Journal of Developing Areas. Western Illinois Univ. Press. Macomb. (JDA)

Journal of Economic History. New York Univ., Graduate School of Business Administration *for the* Economic History Association. Rensselaer. (EHA/J)

Journal of Ethnic Studies. Western Washington State College, College of Ethnic Studies. Bellingham.

Journal of European Economic History. Banco de Roma. Roma.

Journal of Family History. Studies in family, kinship and demography. National Council on Family Relations. Minneapolis, Minn. (NCFR/JFH)

Journal of Historical Geography. Academic Press. London.

Journal of Information Science, Librarianship and Archives Administration. United Nations Educational, Scientific and Cultural Organization. Paris. (UNESCO/JIS)

Journal of Inter-American Studies and World Affairs. Sage Publication *for the* Center for Advanced International Studies, Univ. of Miami. Coral Gables, Fla. (SAGE/JIAS)

Journal of Interdisciplinary History. The MIT Press. Cambridge, Mass. (JIH)

Journal of Latin American Lore. Univ. of California, Latin American Center. Los Angeles. (UCLA/JLAL)

Journal of Latin American Studies. Centers or institutes of Latin American studies at the universities of Cambridge, Glasgow, Liverpool, London and Oxford. Cambridge Univ. Press. London. (JLAS)

Journal of Negro History. Association for the Study of Negro Life and History. Washington. (ASNLH/J)

Journal of Peasant Studies. Frank Cass & Co. London. (JPS)

Journal of Popular Culture. Bowling Green, Ohio.

The Journal of San Diego History. San Diego Historical Society. San Diego, Calif. (SDHS/J)

Journal of Social and Political Studies. Council on American Affairs. Washington.

Journal of Social History. Univ. of California Press. Berkeley. (UCP/JSH)

Journal of Spanish Studies: Twentieth Century. Kansas State Univ., Dept. of Modern Languages. Manhattan. (JSSTC)

Journal of the Barbados Museum and Historical Society. Barbados. (BMHS/J)

Journal of the Folklore Institute. Indiana Univ. Bloomington. (IU/JFI)

Journal of the History of Ideas. City College. New York. (JHI)

Journal of the Lute Society of America. Manhattan, Calif.

Journal of the West. Los Angeles, Calif. (JW)

Journalism Quarterly. Association for Education in Journalism *with the cooperation of the* American Association of Schools, Depts. of Journalism [and] Kappa Tau Alpha Society. Univ. of Minnesota. Minneapolis. (AEJ/JQ)

Kaie. National History and Arts Council of Guyana. Georgetown. (NHAC/K)

Karukinka. Instituto de Investigaciones Históricas de Tierra del Fuego. Buenos Aires.

Kentucky Romance Quarterly. Univ. of Kentucky. Lexington. (UK/KRQ)

Kriterion. Revista da Faculdade de Filosofia da Univ. de Minas Gerais. Belo Horizonte, Brazil. (UMGFF/K)

Labor Information Bulletin. Organization of American States. Inter-American Commission of Women. Washington.

Language. Journal of the Linguistic Society of America. Waverly Press, Inc. Baltimore, Md. (LSA/L)

Lateinamerika. Univ. Rostock. Rostock, FRG. (UR/L)

Latin American Digest. Arizona State Univ., Center for Latin American Studies. Tempe. (ASU/LAD)

Latin American Indian Literatures. A new review of American Indian texts and studies. Univ. of Pittsburgh, Dept. of Hispanic Languages and Literatures. Pittsburgh, Pa. (UP/LAIL)

Latin American Literary Review. Carnegie-Mellon Univ., Dept. of Modern Languages. Pittsburgh, Pa. (LALR)

Latin American Music Review. Univ. of Texas. Austin. (LAMR)

Latin American Perspectives. Univ. of California. Riverside. (LAP)

Latin American Research Review. Univ. of North Carolina Press *for the* Latin American Studies Assn. Chapel Hill. (LARR)

Latin American Theatre Review. A journal devoted to the theatre and drama of Spanish and Portuguese America. Univ. of Kansas, Center of Latin American Studies. Lawrence. (UK/LATR)

Latinoamérica. Anuario de estudios latinoamericanos. Univ. Nacional Autónoma de México, Facultad de Filosofía y Letras, Centro de Estudios Latinoamericanos. México. (UNAM/L)

Latinamericanist. Center for Latin American Studies, Univ. of Florida. Gainesville.

Letras. Univ. Nacional Mayor de San Marcos. Lima. (UNMSM/L)

Letras de Hoje. Pontifícia Univ. Católica do Rio Grande do Sul, Centro de Estudos da Lingua Portuguesa. Pôrto Alegre, Brazil.

Les Lettres romances. Univ. catholique de Louvain, Fondation universitaire de Belgique. Louvain, Belgium. (UCL/LR)

Lexis. Revista de lingüística y literatura. Pontificia Univ. Católica del Perú. Lima. (PUC/L)

Libros al Día. Caracas.

Lingua. North-Holland Publishing Co. Amsterdam. (LINGUA)

Língua e Literatura. Univ. de São Paulo, Depto. de Letras, Faculdade de Filosofia, Letras e Ciências Humanas. São Paulo. (USP/LL)

Logos. Revista de la Facultad de Filosofía y Letras, Univ. de Buenos Aires.

Logos. Univ. del Valle, Depto. de Humanidades. Cali, Colombia. (UV/L)

Lotería. Lotería Nacional de Beneficencia. Panamá. (LNB/L)

Louisiana History. Univ. of Southwestern Louisiana, Louisiana Historical Association. Lafayette.

Luso-Brazilian Review. Univ. of Wisconsin Press. Madison. (UW/LBR)

Man. A monthly record of anthropological science. The Royal Anthropological Institute. London. (RAI/M)

Mapocho. Biblioteca Nacional, Extensión Cultural. Santiago. (EC/M)

Mariner's Mirror. Society for Nautical Research. Sussex, United Kingdom.

Marxist Perspectives. Transaction Periodicals Consortium. Rutgers Univ. New Brunswick, N.J. (RU/MP)

Megafón. Centro de Estudios Latinoamericanos. Buenos Aires.

Mélanges de la Casa de Velázquez. Paris.

Mensário do Arquivo Nacional. Ministério da Justiça, Arquivo Nacional, Editoração e Expediente, Divisão de Publicações. Rio de Janeiro. (MAN)

El Mercurio. Santiago de Chile.

Mester. Univ. of California, Dept. of Spanish and Portuguese. Los Angeles. (UCLA/M)

México: Artículos Clasificados. Univ. Nacional Autónoma de México. Facultad de Ciencias Políticas y Sociales. Centro de Documentación. México.

Mexicon. Aktuelle Informationen und Studien zu Mesoamerika. Internationale Gesellschaft für Mesoamerika-Forschung (IGM). Berling, FRG.

Meyibó. Univ. Nacional Autónoma de México, Centro de Investigaciones Históricas [and] Univ. Autónoma de Baja, Centro de Investigaciones Históricas. México.

Military History of Texas and the Southwest. Military History Press. Austin.

Millenium. London School of Economics. London.

Missionalia Hispanica. Instituto Santo Toribio de Mogrovejo [and] Consejo Superior de Investigaciones Científicas. Madrid. (ISTH/MH)

Modern Language Journal. The National Federation of Modern Language Teachers Associations [and] Univ. of Pittsburgh. Pittsburgh, Pa. (MLTA/MLJ)

Modern Language Notes. Johns Hopkins Univ. Press. Baltimore, Md. (MLN)

Modern Language Review. Univ. of Guyana, Dept. of Modern Languages. Georgetown.

Montalbán. Univ. Católica Andrés Bello, Facultad de Humanidades y Educación, Institutos Humanísticos de Investigación. Caracas. (UCAB/M)

Mother Jones. Foundation for National Progress. San Francisco, Calif.

Mundo Nuevo. Instituto Latinoamericano de Relaciones Internacionales. Paris. (MN)

Música Sacra. Editora Vozes. Petrópolis, Brazil. (MS)

Die Musik in Geschichte und Gegenwart. Kassel. Wilhelmshöhe, FRG. (MGG)

NS NorthSouth NordSud NorteSur NorteSul. Canadian journal of Latin American studies. Canadian Association of Latin American Studies. Univ. of Ottawa. (NS)

The National Bibliography of Barbados. Public Library. Bridgetown.

National Geographic Magazine. National Geographic Society. Washington. (NGS/NGM)

Natural History. American Museum of Natural History. New York. (AMNH/NH)

Ñawpa Pacha. Institute of Andean Studies. Berkeley, Calif. (IAS/ÑP)

Die Neue Rundschau. S. Fischer Verlag. Frankfurt. (NR)

New Mexico Historical Review. Univ. of New Mexico [and] Historical Society of New Mexico. Albuquerque. (UNM/NMHR)

The New Scholar. Univ. of California, Committee on Hispanic Civilization [and] Center for Chicano Studies. Santa Barbara. (UCSB/NS)

New Scholasticism. Catholic Univ. of America, Catholic Philosophical Association. Washington.

Nexos. Sociedad de Ciencia y Literatura, Centro de Investigación Cultural y Científica. México.

Nicaráuac. Revista bimestral del Ministerio de Cultura. Managua. (NMC/N)

Niterói. Revista brasiliense. Ciências, letras e artes. Academia Paulista de Letras. São Paulo.

Norte Grande. Revista de estudios integrados referentes a comunidades humanas del Norte Grande de Chile, en una perspectiva geográfica e histórico-cultural. Univ. Católica de Chile, Instituto de Geografía, Depto. de Geografía de Chile, Taller Norte Grande. Santiago. (UCC/NG)

North Dakota Quarterly. Univ. of North Dakota. Grand Forks.

Notes et études documentaires. Direction de la documentation. Paris. (FDD/NED)

Noticias Culturales. Instituto Caro y Cuervo. Bogotá. (ICC/NC)

Nova Americana. Giulio Einaudi Editora. Torino, Italy. (GEE/NA)

Nuestra Historia. Centro de Estudios de Historia Argentina. Buenos Aires. (CEHA/NH)

Nueva Narrativa Hispanoamericana. Adelphi Univ., Latin American Studies Program. Garden City, N.Y.

Nueva Revista de Filología Hispánica. El Colegio de México [and] the Univ. of Texas. México. (CM/NRFH)

L'Oeil. Revue d'art mensuelle. Nouvelle sedo. Lausanne, Switzerland. (OEIL)

Orbis. Bulletin international de documentation linguistique. Centre international de dialectologie générale. Louvain, Belgium. (CIDG/O)

Orbis. A journal of world affairs. Foreign Policy Research Institute, Philadelphia, Pa. *in association with the* Fletcher School of Law and Diplomacy, Tufts Univ., Medford, Mass. (FPRI/O)

The Pacific Historical Review. Univ. of California Press. Los Angeles. (UC/PHR)

Pájaro de Fuego. Sequals Editora. Buenos Aires.

La Palabra y el Hombre. Univ. Veracruzana. Xalapa, México. (UV/PH)

El Palacio. School of American Research, Museum of New Mexico [and] Archaeological Society of New Mexico. Santa Fe. (SAR/P)

Past and Present. London. (PP)

Patrimonio Histórico. Instituto Nacional de Cultura, Dirección del Patrimonio Histórico. Panamá. (INC/PH)

Pauta. Univ. Autónoma Metropolitana. México.

Peasant Studies Newsletter. Univ. of Pittsburgh, Center for International Studies [and] Dept. of History. Pittsburgh, Pa. (UP/PSN)

Pensamiento Económico. Organo oficial de divulgación. Colegio Hondureño de Economistas. Tegucigalpa. (CHE/PE)

Pesquisas: História. Univ. do Vale do Rio dos Sinos, Instituto Anchietano de Pesquisas. São Leopoldo, Brazil.

Philologica Pragensia. Academia Scientiarum Bohemoslovenica. Praha. (ASB/PP)

Philosophica. Rijksuniversiteit. Gent, The Netherlands.

Phylon. Atlanta Univ. Atlanta, Ga. (AU/P)

Planindex. Resumen de documentos sobre planificación. Organización de las Naciones Unidas. Comisión Económica para América Latina (CEPAL). Centro Latinoamericano de Documentación Económica y Social (CLADES). Santiago.

Plantation Society. Univ. of New Orleans. New Orleans, La.

Ploughshares. A journal of the arts. Massachusetts Council on the Arts. Cambridge.

Point of Contact. New York Univ., Ibero-American Language and Area Center. New York.

Polémica. Univ. de Carabobo, Dirección de Cultura. Valencia, Venezuela.

Política y Espíritu. Cuadernos de cultura política, económica y social. Santiago. (CPES/PE)

Positif. Paris.

Presença Filosófica. Sociedade Brasileira de Filósofos Católicos. São Paulo.

Proceedings of the American Philosophical Society. Philadelphia, Pa. (APS/P)

Proceedings of the Pacific Coast Council on Latin American Studies. Univ. of California. Los Angeles. (PCCLAS/P)

Proceso. Huancayo, Peru.

Publicaciones. Univ. de San Juan, Instituto de Investigaciones Arqueológicas. San Juan, Argentina.

Publications of the Modern Language Association of America. New York. (PMLA)

Pucará. Univ. de Cuenca, Facultad de Filosofía, Letras y Ciencias de la Educación. Cuenca, Ecuador.

Punto de Partida. Revista bimestral. Univ. Nacional Autónoma de México, Dirección General de Difusión Cultural. México. (UNAM/PP)

Quaderni Ibero-Americani. Associazione per i Rapporti Culturali con la Spagna, il Portogallo e l'America Latina. Torino, Italy. (QIA)

Quaderni Storici. Istituzioni agrarie nel decollo industriale. Facoltà di Economia e Commercio, Istituto di Storia e Sociologia. Ancona, Italy. (QS)

Quarterly Review of Film Studies. Redgrave Publishing Co. Pleasantville, N.Y.

Red River Valley Historical Journal. Red River Valley Historical Assn. Durant, Okla.

Reflexão. Instituto de Filosofia e Teologia, Pontificia Univ. Católica da Campinas (PUCC). São Paulo.

Relaciones. Estudios de historia y sociedad. El Colegio de Michoacán. Zamora, México. (CM/RE)

Relaciones de la Sociedad Argentina de Antropología. Buenos Aires. (SAA/R)

Res Gesta. Facultad de Derecho y Ciencias Sociales, Instituto de Historia, Univ. Pontificia Católica Argentina. Rosario.

Research Center for the Arts Review. Univ. of Texas. San Antonio.

Research in African Literatures. Univ. of Texas Press. Austin.

Review. Center for Inter-American Relations. New York. (REVIEW)

The Review of Politics. Univ. of Notre Dame. Notre Dame, Ind. (UND/RP)

Revista Aleph. Manizales, Colombia.

Revista Argentina de Administración Pública. Instituto Nacional de la Administración Pública. Buenos Aires.

Revista Brasileira de Biblioteconomia e Documentação. Federação Brasileira de Associações de Bibliotecários. São Paulo.

Revista Brasileira de Cultura. Ministério da Educação e Cultura, Conselho Federal de Cultura. Rio. (CFC/RBC)

Revista Brasileira de Economia. Fundação Getúlio Vargas, Instituto Brasileiro de Economia. Rio de Janeiro. (IBE/RBE)

Revista Brasileira de Estudos Políticos. Univ. de Minas Gerais. Belo Horizonte, Brazil. (UMG/RBEP)

Revista Brasileira de Filosofia. Instituto Brasileiro de Filosofia. São Paulo.(IBF/RBF)

Revista Brasileira de Folclore. Ministério da Educação e Cultura, Campanha de Defesa do Folclore Brasileiro. Rio. (CDFB/RBF)

Revista Brasileira de Lingüística. Sociedade Brasileira para Professores de Lingüística. São Paulo. (SBPL/RBL)

Revista Brasileira de Política Internacional. Instituto Brasileiro de Relações Internacionais. Rio de Janeiro. (IBRI/R)

Revista Canadiense de Estudios Hispánicos. Asociación Canadiense de Hispanistas, Univ. of Toronto. Toronto. (UT/RCEH)

Revista Centroamericana de Economía. Univ. Nacional Autónoma de Honduras, Programa de Postgrado Centroamericano en Economía y Planificación del Desarrollo. Tegucigalpa.

Revista Chicano-Riqeña. Gary, Ind.

Revista Chilena de Antropología. Santiago.

Revista Chilena de Historia y Geografía. Sociedad Chilena de Historia y Geografía. Santiago. (SCHG/R)

Revista Chilena de Literatura. Univ. de Chile, Depto. de Literatura. Santiago. (UC/RCL)

Revista Civilização Brasileira. Editora Civilização Brasileira. Rio de Janeiro. (RCB)

Revista Coahuilense de Historia. Colegio Coahuilense de Investigaciones Históricas. Saltillo, México.

Revista Colombiana de Antropología. Ministerio de Educación Nacional, Instituto Colombiano de Antropología. Bogotá.

Revista de Antropología. Casa de la Cultura Ecuatoriana, Núcleo del Azuay. Cuenca. (CCE/RA)

Revista de Antropología. Univ. de São Paulo, Faculdade de Filosofia, Letras e Ciências Humanas [and] Associação Brasileira de Antropologia. São Paulo. (USP/RA)

Revista de Atualidade Indígena. Mina Gráfica Editora. Brasília.

Revista de Biblioteconomia de Brasília. Univ. de Brasília, Associação dos Bibliotecários do Distrito Federal e Departamento Biblioteconomia. Brasília.

Revista de Ciencias Sociales. Univ. de Costa Rica. San José. (UCR/RCS)

Revista de Ciencias Sociales. Univ. de Puerto Rico, Colegio de Ciencias Sociales. Río Piedras. (UPR/RCS)

Revista de Comunicação Social. Ceará, Brazil.

Revista de Crítica Literaria Latinoamericana. Latinoamericana Editores. Lima. (RCLL)

Revista de Cultura Brasileña. Embajada del Brasil en España. Madrid.

Revista de Dialectología y Tradiciones Populares. Centro de Estudios de Etnología Peninsular, Depto. de Dialectología y Tradiciones Populares, Consejo Superior de Investigaciones Científicas. Madrid. (CEEP/RD)

Revista de Economía Latinoamericana. Banco Central de Venezuela. Caracas. (BCV/REL)

Revista de Estadística y Geografía. Secretaría de Programación y Presupuesto, Coordinación General de los Servicios Nacionales de Estadística, Geografía e Informática, Dirección General de Estadística. México.

Revista de Estudios Agro-Sociales. Instituto de Estudios Agro-Sociales. Madrid. (IEAS/R)

Revista de Estudios Hispánicos. Univ. of Alabama, Dept. of Romance Languages, Office of International Studies and Programs. University. (UA/REH)

Revista de Estudios Políticos. Instituto de Estudios Políticos. Madrid. (IEP/REP)

Revista de Filosofía de la Universidad de Costa Rica. San José. (UCR/RF)

Revista de Filosofía Latinoamericana. Ediciones Castañeda. San Antonio de Padua, Argentina. (RFL)

Revista de Historia. Univ. de Concepción, Instituto de Antropología, Historia y Geografía. Concepción, Chile.

Revista de História. Univ. de São Paulo, Faculdade de Filosofia, Ciências e Letras, Depto. de História [and] Sociedade de Estudos Históricos. São Paulo. (USP/RH)

Revista de Historia. Univ. Nacional de Costa Rica, Escuela de Historia. Heredia. (UNCR/R)

Revista de Historia Americana y Argentina. Univ. Nacional de Cuyo, Facultad de Filosofía y Letras, Instituto de Historia. Mendoza. (UNC/RHAA)

Revista de Historia de América. Instituto Panamericano de Geografía e Historia, Comisión de Historia. México. (PAIGH/H)

Revista de Historia de las Ideas. Instituto Panamericano de Geografía e Historia [and] Editorial Casa de la Cultura Ecuatoriana. Quito. (IPGH/RHI)

Revista de Historia del Derecho. Buenos Aires.

Revista de Historia Militar. Servicio Histórico Militar. Madrid. (SHM/RHM)

Revista de Indias. Instituto Gonzalo Fernández de Oviedo [and] Consejo Superior de Investigaciones Científicas. Madrid. (IGFO/RI)

Revista de Información Científica y Técnica Cubana. Academia de Ciencias de Cuba. Instituto de Documentación e Información Científica y Técnica. La Habana.

Revista de la Academia Boliviana de Ciencias Económicas. Cochabamba, Bolivia.

Revista de la Biblioteca Nacional. Ministerio de Educación y Cultura. Montevideo. (UBN/R)

Revista de la Biblioteca Nacional José Martí. La Habana. (BNJM/R)

Revista de la Escuela de Comando de la Fuerza Aérea Argentina. Buenos Aires.

Revista de la Facultad de Derecho. Univ. Autónoma de México. México. (UNAM/RFD)

Revista de la Historia del Derecho. Buenos Aires.

Revista de la Junta de Estudios Históricas de Mendoza. Mendoza, Argentina. (JEHM/R)

Revista de la Junta Provincial de Historia de Córdoba. Archivo Histórico Monseñor P. Cabrera. Córdoba, Argentina. (JPHC/R)

Revista de la Sociedad Bolivariana de Venezuela. Caracas. (SBV/R)

Revista de la Mexicana de Historia Natural. México. (SMHN/R)

Revista de la Universidad. Univ. Nacional Autónoma de Honduras. Tegucigalpa. (HUN/RU)

Revista de la Universidad Católica. Pontificia Univ. Católica del Perú. Lima.

Revista de la Universidad Complutense. Madrid. (RUC)

Revista de la Universidad de Costa Rica. San José. (UCR/R)

Revista de la Universidad de México. Univ. Nacional Autónoma de México. México. (UNAM/RUM)

Revista de la Universidad de Oriente. Santiago, Cuba. (UO/R)

Revista de la Universidad de Yucatán. Mérida, Mex. (UY/R)

Revista de la Universidad del Zulia. Maracaibo, Venezuela. (UZ/R)

Revista de la Universidad Nacional de Córdoba. Dirección General de Publicaciones. Córdoba, Argentina. (UNC/R)

Revista de Letras. Univ. de Puerto Rico en Mayagüez, Facultad de Artes y Ciencias. Mayagüez. (UPRM/RL)

Revista de Musicología. Madrid.

Revista de Occidente. Madrid. (RO)

Revista de Oriente. Univ. de Puerto Rico, Colegio Universitario de Humacao. Humacao. (UPR/RO)

Revista de Política Internacional. Instituto de Estudios Políticos. Madrid. (IEP/RPI) Revista de SINASBI. Información Científica y Tecnológica de Archivos y de Estadística e Informática, Comisión Coordinador del Sistema Nacional de Servicios de Bibliotecas e Información. Caracas.

Revista de Teatro. Sociedade Brasileira de Autores Teatrais. Rio de Janeiro. (SBAT/RT)

Revista del Archivo General de la Nación. Buenos Aires.

Revista del Archivo General de la Nación. Instituto Nacional de Cultura. Lima. (PEAGN/R)

Revista del Archivo Histórico del Guayas. Guayaquil, Ecuador. (AHG/R)

Revista del Instituto de Antropología. Univ. Nacional de Tucumán. San Miguel de Tucumán, Arg. (UNTIA/R)

Revista del Instituto de Cultura Puertorriqueña. San Juan. (ICP/R)

Revista del Instituto de Investigación Musicológica Carlos Vega. Univ. Católica Argentina, Facultad de Artes y Ciencias Musicales. Buenos Aires.

Revista del México Agrario. Confederación Nacional Campesina. México. (CNC/RMA)

Revista del Museo Nacional. Casa de la Cultura del Perú, Museo Nacional de la Cultura Peruana. Lima. (PEMN/R)

Revista del Pensamiento Centroamericano.

Centro de Investigaciones y Actividades Culturales. Managua. (RCPC)

Revista do Arquivo Municipal. Prefeitura do Município de São Paulo, Depto. Municipal de Cultura. São Paulo. (AM/R)

Revista do Instituto de Estudos Brasileiros. Univ. de São Paulo, Instituto de Estudos Brasileiros. São Paulo. (USP/RIEB)

Revista do Instituto de Filosofia e Ciências Humanas. Univ. Federal do Rio Grande do Sul. Pôrto Alegre. (IFCH/R)

Revista do Instituto do Ceará. Fortaleza, Brazil. (IC/R)

Revista do Instituto Histórico e Geográfico Brasileiro. Rio. (IHGB/R)

Revista do Instituto Histórico e Geográfico de Alagoas. Maceió, Brazil. (IHGA/R)

Revista do Instituto Histórico e Geográfico de São Paulo. São Paulo. (IHGSP/R)

Revista do Instituto Histórico e Geográfico Guarujá/Bertioga. São Paulo. (IHGGB/R)

Revista do Museu Paulista. São Paulo. (MP/R)

Revista dos Tribunais. São Paulo.

Revista Eme-Eme. Estudios dominicanos. Univ. Católica Madre y Maestra. Santiago de los Caballeros, República Dominicana. (EME)

Revista Española de Antropología Americana: Trabajos y Conferencias. Univ. de Madrid, Facultad de Filosofía y Letras, Depto. de Antropología y Etnología de América. Madrid. (UM/REAA)

Revista Española de Lingüística. Editorial Gredos. Madrid.

Revista Geográfica. Instituto Geográfico Militar del Ecuador, Depto. Geográfico. Quito. (IGME/RG)

Revista Geográfica. Instituto Panamericano de Geografía e Historia, Comisión de Geografía. México. (PAIGH/G)

Revista Hispánica Moderna. Columbia Univ., Hispanic Institute in the United States. New York. (HIUS/R)

Revista Histórica. Museo Histórico Nacional. Montevideo. (UMHN/RH)

Revista Iberoamericana. Instituto Internacional de Literatura Iberoamericana *patrocinada por la* Univ. de Pittsburgh, Pa. (IILI/RI)

Revista Interamericana de Bibliografía [Inter-American Review of Bibliography]. Organization of American States. Washington. (RIB)

Revista Latinoamericana de Filosofía. Centro de Investigaciones Filosóficas. Buenos Aires. (CIF/RLF)

Revista Letras. Univ. Federal do Paraná, Setor de Ciências Humanas, Letras e Artes. Curitiba, Brazil. (UFP/RL)

Revista Lotería. Lotería Nacional de Beneficencia. Panamá. (LNB/L)

Revista Mexicana de Ciencias Políticas y Sociales. Univ. Nacional Autónoma de México, Facultad de Ciencias Políticas y Sociales. México. (UNAM/RMCPS)

Revista Mexicana de Sociología. Univ. Nacional Autónoma de México, Instituto de Investigaciones Sociales. México. (UNAM/RMS)

Revista Musical Chilena. Univ. de Chile, Facultad de Artes. Santiago. (UC/RMC)

Revista Musical de Venezuela. Caracas.

Revista Nacional de Cultura. Consejo Nacional de Cultura. Caracas. (CONAC/RNC)

Revista Nacional de Cultura. Ministerio de Cultura y Educación, Secretaría de Estado de Cultura. Buenos Aires.

Revista Paraguaya de Sociología. Centro Paraguayo de Estudios Sociológicos. Asunción. (CPES/RPS)

Revista/Review Interamericana. Univ. Interamericana. San Germán, Puerto Rico. (RRI)

Revista Universidad de Medellín. Centro de Estudios de Posgrado. Medellín, Colombia. (UM/R)

Revista Universitaria. Anales de la Academia Chilena de Ciencias Naturales. Univ. Católica de Chile. Santiago. (UCC/RU)

Revista Venezolana de Filosofía. Univ. Simón Bolívar [and] Sociedad Venezolana de Filosofía. Caracas. (USB/RVF)

Revolución y Cultura. Publicación mensual. Ministerio de Cultura. La Habana. (RYC)

Revue d'histoire économique et sociale. Editions Marcel Rivière *avec le concours du* Centre national de la recherche scientifique. Paris.

Revue française d'histoire d'outre-mer. Société de l'histoire des colonies françaises. Société française d'histoire d'outre-mer. Paris.

Revue historique. Presses universitaires de France. Paris. (PUF/RH)

Ritmo. La Plata, Argentina.

Ritmo. Revista del Conservatorio de Música Juan José Castro. México.

Romanistisches Jahrbuch. Univ. Hamburg, Romanisches Seminar, Ibero-Americanisches Forschungsinstitut. Hamburg, FRG. (UH/RJ)

Saeculum. Jahrbuch für Universalgeschichte. München, FRG. (SJUG)

SECOLAS Annals. Kennesaw College, Southeastern Conference on Latin American Studies. Marietta, Georgia.

SELA en Acción. Secretaría Permanente del Sistema Económico Latinoamericano, Oficina

San Marcos. Lima.

Santiago. Univ. de Oriente. Santiago de Cuba.

Sapientia. Organo de la Facultad de Filosofía. Univ. Católica Argentina Santa María de los Buenos Aires. Buenos Aires. (UCA/S)

Sarance. Instituto Otavaleño de Antropología. Otavalo, Ecuador.

Savacou. Caribbean Artists Movement. Kingston.

Science and Society. New York. (SS)

Scientific American. Scientific American, Inc. New York. (SA) de Información. Caracas.

Screen. London.

La Semana de Bellas Artes. México.

Semestre de Filosofía. Univ. Central de Venezuela. Caracas.

Semiosis. Seminario de Semiótica, Teoría, Análisis. México.

Separata de Cuadernos Salmantinos de Filosofía. Univ. Pontificia de Salamanca. Salamanca, Spain.

Série de História. Coleçao Museu Paulista, Univ. de São Paulo, Brazil.

Signos. Biblioteca Martí. Santa Clara, Cuba.

Signos. Estudios de lengua y literatura. Univ. Católica de Valparaíso, Instituto de Literatura y Ciencia del Lenguaje. Valparaío, Chile. (UCV/S)

Signs. Journal of women in culture and society. The Univ. of Chicago Press. Chicago, Ill. (UC/S)

Síntesis Informativa Iberoamericana. Instituto de Cultura Hispánica. Centro de Documentación Iberoamericana. Madrid.

Smithsonian. Smithsonian Institution. Washington.

Social and Economic Studies. Univ. of the West Indies, Institute of Social and Economic Research. Mona, Jamaica. (UWI/SES)

Social Science Quarterly. Univ. of Texas, Dept. of Government. Austin. (UT/SSQ)

Socialismo y Participación. Centro de Estudios para el Desarrollo y la Participación (CEDEP). Lima.

Sonneck Society Newsletter. Brighton, Mass.

South Atlantic Bulletin. South Atlantic Modern Language Association. Chapel Hill, N.C.

Southern California Quarterly. Historical Society of Southern California. Los Angeles. (HSSC/SCQ)

Southern Folklore Quarterly. Univ. of Florida *in cooperation with the* South Atlantic Language Association. Gainesville. (UF/SFQ)

Southwestern Historical Quarterly. Texas State Historical Association. Austin. (TSHA/SHQ)

Staden-Jahrbuch. Beiträge zur Brasilkunde. Instituto Hans Staden. São Paulo. (IHS/SJ)

Statistical Bulletin of the OAS. Organization of American States. General Secretariat. Washington.

Status. São Paulo.

Studi di Letteratura Ispanoamericana. Milano.

Studia. Revista semestral. Centro de Estudos Históricos Ultramarinos. Lisboa. (CEHU/S)

Studies in Comparative International Development. Rutgers Univ. New Brunswick, N.J. (RU/SCID)

Studies in Latin American Popular Culture. New Mexico State Univ., Dept. of Foreign Languages. Las Cruces.

Studies in the Anthropology of Visual Communication. Society for the Anthropology of Visual Communication. Washington.

Studies in the Social Sciences. West Georgia College. Carrollton.

Studies on Voltaire and the Eighteenth Century. Voltaire Foundation, Taylor Institution. Oxford, England.

Suplemento Antropológico. Univ. Católica de Nuestra Señora de la Asunción, Centro de Estudios Antropológicos. Asunción. (UCNSA/SA)

Sur. Revista semestral. Buenos Aires. (SUR)

Taller de Letras. Univ. Católica de Chile, Instituto de Letras. Santiago. (UCC/TL)

Temas Económicos. Univ. de Antioquia, Facultad de Ciencias Económicas, Depto. de Economía. Medellín, Colombia.

Tempo Brasileiro. Revista de Cultura. Rio de Janeiro. (TEMBRAS)

Terra Ameriga. Associazone Italiana StudiAmericanistici. Genova, Italy. (AISA/TA)

Texto Crítico. Univ. Veracruzana, Centro de Investigaciones Lingüístico-Literarias. Xalapa, México.

Thesaurus. Boletín del Instituto Caro y Cuervo. Bogotá. (ICC/T)

Thesis. Nueva revista de filosofía y letras. Univ. Nacional Autónoma de México, Facultad de Filosofía y Letras. México.

Tiemporeal. Simón Bolívar Univ. Caracas.

Tiers monde. Problèmes des pays sous-développés. Univ. de Paris, Institut d'étude du dévellopement économique et social. Paris. (UP/TM)

La Torre. Univ. de Puerto Rico. Río Piedras. (UPR/LT)

Trabajos y Comunicaciones. Univ. Nacional de La Plata, Depto. de Historia. La Plata, Argentina. (UNLP/TC)

Tradición Popular. Univ. de San Carlos de Guatemala, Centro de Estudios Folklóricos. San Carlos. (USCG/TP)

Tradiciones de Guatemala. Univ. de San Carlos de Guatemala, Centro de Estudios Folklóricos. Guatemala. (USCG/TG)

Tramoya. Univ. Veracruzana. Xalapa, México.

Transactions of the Institute of British Geographers. London.

Trans/Form/Ação. Faculdade de Filosofia, Ciência e Letras de Assis. Assis, Brazil.

Translation Review. Richardson, Tex.

Trimestre Económico. Fondo de Cultura Económica. México. (FCE/TE)

Trinidad and Tobago National Bibliography. Central Library of Trinidad and Tobago [and] Univ. of the West Indies Library. Port-of-Spain.

UFSI Reports. Universities Field Staff International Inc. Hanover, N.H. (UFSI/R)

Unesco Journal of Information Science, Librarianship and Archives Administration. United Nations Educational, Scientific and Cultural Organization. Paris. (UNESCO/JIS)

Unión. Unión de Escritores y Artistas de Cuba. La Habana. (UNION)

Universidad. Univ. de Antioquia. Medellín, Colombia. (UA/U)

Universidad. Univ. Nacional del Litoral. Santa Fe, Argentina. (UNL/U)

Universidad de La Habana. La Habana. (UH/U)

Universidad Nacional de Colombia. Revista de extensión cultural. Medellín.

Universidad Pontificia Bolivariana. Medellín, Colombia. (UPB)

Universitas Humanística. Pontificia Univ. Javeriana, Facultad de Filosofía y Letras. Bogotá. (PUJ/UH)

Universo. Univ. Autónoma de Santo Domingo, Facultad de Humanidades. Santo Domingo. (UASD/U)

Urban Anthropology. State Univ. of New York, Dept. of Anthropology. Brockport. (UA)

Veritas. Revista. Pontifícia Univ. Católica do Rio Grande do Sul. Pôrto Alegre, Brazil. (PUC/V)

Via. A new literary magazine. Univ. of California, Office of Student Activities. Berkeley. (VIA)

Vida Hispánica. Journal of the Association of the Teachers of Spanish and Portuguese. Wolverhamptom, U.K. (ATSP/VH)

Vórtice. Stanford Univ., Dept. of Spanish and Portuguese. Stanford, Calif. (SU/V)

Vozes. Revista de cultura. Editora Vozes. Petrópolis, Brazil. (VOZES)

Vuelta. México.

Wari. Ayacucho, Peru.

Washington Review. Washington.

Western Folklore. Univ. of California Press for the California Folklore Society. Berkeley. (CFS/WF)

The Western Historical Quarterly. Western History Association, Utah State Univ. Logan. (WHQ)

The World of Music. International Music Council. Paris.

YaxKin. Instituto Hondureño de Antropología e Historia. Tegucigalpa. (YAXKIN)

Yearbook of the International Folk Music Council. Urbana, Ill.

Yucatán: Historia y Economía. Revista de análisis socioeconómico regional. Univ. de Yucatán, Centro de Investigaciones Regionales, Depto. de Estudios Económicos y Sociales. Mérida, México.

Zacatecas. Anuario de historia. Univ. Autónoma de Zacatecas, Depto. de Investigaciones Históricas. Zacatecas, México.

Zeitschrift für Ethnologie. Deutschen Gesellschaft für Völkerkunde. Braunschweig, FRG. (DGV/ZE)

Zeitschrift für Kulturaustausch. Institut für Auslandsbeziehungen. Berlin, FRG. (IA/ZK)

Zeitschrift für Missionswissenschaft und Religionswissenschaft. Lucerne, Switzerland. (ZMR)

Zeitschrift für Romanische Philologie. Tübingen, FRG. (ZRP)

Zona Franca. Editorial Trazón. Caracas.

SUBJECT INDEX

1946. Archivo Municipal de Ocoyoacac (Mexico), 48. Archivo Nacional (Chile), 76. Archivo Parroquial de Zacualpán de Amilpas (Mexico), 1914. Argentina, 64–65. Atlacomulco de Fabela (Mexico), 2061. Barbados, 45. Bolivia, 2613, 2739, 3049. Brazil, 46. Carrizal (Mexico), 2157. Central America, 85, 2335. Dominican Republic, 7092. Ecuador, 2614, 2616. Europe, 2335. Latin America, 74. Mexico, 1947, 2127, 2239–2240, 2286, 2301. Spain, 67a. Union of the Soviet Socialist Republics, 2286. United Kingdom, 2324. United States, 2335. Venezuela, 2637.

Arciniega, Claudio de, 368.

Arciniega, Germán, 5021.

Arenas, Reinaldo, 5269, 5348.

Aretz, Isabel, 7025, 7217.

Arévalo Martínez, Rafael, 5260.

ARGENTINA. *See also Chaco; Falkland Islands; Latin America; names of specific cities and provinces; Patagonia; Rio de la Plata; South America; Southern Cone; Tierra del Fuego.*
Art, 311, 322, 324, 417–426.
Bibliography, 13, 20, 65, 94, 420, 3167, 3222, 3298, 3306, 3331, 7648.
Folklore, 967–977, 3175.
History, 20, 3169, 3173, 3176, 3179, 3187–3188, 3236, 3257, 3271, 3289, 3320, 3353, 3370–3371.
  Ethnohistory, 1663, 1743.
  Colonial Period. *See Viceroyalty of Peru; Viceroyalty of Rio de la Plata.*
  Independence Period, 2873–2874, 2877, 2882–2887, 2889a, 2893.
  19th Century, 3088, 3151–3152, 3154–3157, 3160, 3164–3165, 3170, 3174, 3180, 3183–3186, 3189–3191, 3196–3197, 3199, 3201, 3210–3211, 3216–3217, 3223, 3225, 3230–3231, 3234, 3246, 3250, 3252, 3258–3260, 3262, 3264, 3273–3274, 3295, 3298, 3303, 3306–3307, 3318, 3321, 3327, 3333, 3337, 3339–3342, 3348–3350, 3352, 3358, 3368, 3444, 5128a, 5509, 5529.
  20th Century, 3088, 3151, 3153, 3158–3159, 3161, 3163,-3167, 3172, 3183, 3193, 3195–3196, 3198, 3200, 3202–3206, 3217–3219, 3221–3222, 3223–3224, 3226, 3232–3233, 3238–3239, 3247–3248, 3251–3252, 3255, 3260, 3262, 3264, 3269–3270, 3272–3274, 3276, 3284–3285,

3287–3288, 3290–3292, 3294, 3296–3297, 3299–3301, 3310, 3313–3314, 3316–3317, 3319, 3324, 3326, 3338, 3343, 3346, 3351, 3360, 3364–3365, 3367. 3369, 5540.
Language, 4506, 4523, 4531–4532, 4554, 4558, 4581.
Literature, 94, 5091, 5095, 5100, 5107, 5119, 5128a, 5138, 5611, 5865, 5870, 5880, 6491.
  Drama, 5893, 5902–5904, 5918, 5924, 5929, 5933, 5935, 5946, 5948, 5953, 5978, 6018, 6021, 6024.
  Poetry, 5109, 5513, 5539, 5627, 5643–5644, 5648, 5656–5657, 5659, 5669, 5677–5678, 5698, 5703–5704, 5708–5711, 5728–5729, 5731, 5738, 5742, 5749–5750, 5757, 5761, 5774, 5786, 5848, 5853, 5872.
  Prose Literature, 5092, 5105–5106, 5108, 5112, 5508–5551, 5569–5613, 5729, 6467, 6473–6474, 6479, 6481, 6488.
Music, 7003, 7011, 7028–7041.
Philosophy, 3363, 5095, 5576, 5591, 7645–7666.

Argentina and Brazil Relations, 3307, 3355.

Argentina and Chile Relations, 3347.

Argentina and Italy Relations, 3339.

Argentina and Spain Relations, 2787.

Argentina and United Kingdom Relations, 3194–3195, 3232–3233, 3304.

Argentina and United States Relations, 1886, 3195, 3232, 3365.

Arguedas, Alcides, 5364, 5369a.

Arguedas, José María, 5364, 5398–5399, 5403–5405, 5409–5410, 5417–5418, 5420–5422, 5424, 5426–5427.

Argüello, Santiago, 5863.

Arica, Chile (city). History, 2708, 2752, 3086.

Aricó, José, 7603.

Arinos, Afonso, 6317, 6370.

Arlt, Roberto, 5598, 5605.

Armed Forces. *See Military.*

Arosemena, Florencia H., 2380.

Arosemena, Justo, 2442, 7533.

Arreola, Juan José, 5193.

ART (items 251–517). *See also Aesthetics; Architecture; Art Criticism; Art under specific countries and regions; Artists; Colonial Art; Crafts; Folk Art; Graphic Art; Jewelry; Magic Realism; Modern Art; Painting; Photography; Pottery; Precolumbian Art; Sculpture.* Bibliography, 2, 27, 380–381, 384, 420. Congresses, 259, 266, 284. History, 264, 281. Museums, 318, 322,

Literature.
Prose Literature, 6445.
Barbosa, Rui, 3682, 3692.
Barceló, Alberto, 3245.
Barnet, Miguel, 5310.
Barreto, Paulo. *See Rio, João de.*
Barrett, Rafael, 5613a.
Barrett, Tobias, 7624.
Barrios, Gerardo, 7558.
Barros, Maciel de, 7640.
Basadre, Jorge, 2983, 2999.
Bastidas, Micaela, 2688.
Batlle y Ordóñez, José Pablo Torcuato, 3413, 3418, 3423, 3430.
Battle of Chacabuco (1817), 3144.
Battle of Concepción (1882), 3129.
Battle of Huamachuco (1883), 3126.
Battle of Tacna (1880), 3117.
Bautista Muñoz, Juan, 2493.
Belgrano, Manuel, 2876–2877.
Belief and Customs. *See also Festivals; Folk Medicine; Folklore; Religion; Religious Folklore; Rites and Ceremonies; Voodoo.* Argentina, 969, 972. Bolivia, 983. Borderlands, 1104. Brazil, 1007, 1035, 4592. Chile, 1076. Dominican Republic, 5833. Guatemala, 1052. Paraguay, 1129. Peru, 1137. Saint Lucia, 1089. Trinidad, 1098.
BELIZE. *See also Central America; Latin America.*
Bibliography, 108.
History, 2328.
19th Century, 2381, 2401, 2406.
20th Century, 2382, 2401.
Language, 6441.
Literature.
Prose Literature, 6434.
Bell, Lindolf, 6391.
Bello, Andrés, 1879, 2815, 3066, 3068, 3083, 3103, 3136, 4582, 4584, 5096, 5099, 5101–5103, 5110, 5115, 5117, 5128, 5134, 5998, 7568–7573, 7575, 7579.
Bello, Bartolomé, 7216.
Belo Horizonte, Brazil (city). Art, 502.
Beluche, Renato, 2848.
Belza, Manuel Isidoro, 3051.
Benavides de Peña, Paquita, 2958.
Bendfeldt Rojas, Lourdes, 5261.
Benedetti, Mario, 5839, 6002.
Benítez Rojo, Antonio, 5335, 5351.
Benson, Nettie Lee, 105.
Berra, Francisco A., 7667.
Bertonio, Ludovido, 1579.
Betancourt, Rómulo, 2910, 2936.
Bianco, Enrico, 481.

Bianco, José, 5583.
BIBLIOGRAPHY (items 1–111). *See also Archives; Bibliography under specific subjects; Biography; Books and Book Dealers; Dissertations and Theses; Libraries and Library Services; Library Science; Manuscripts; National Bibliographies; Periodicals; Printing; Publishers and Publishing Industry; Reference Books.*
Bilingualism. *See also Language and Languages; Linguistics.* Argentina, 4506. Code-shifting, 4628. Jamaica, 4628. Latin America, 4515.
Biography. *See also Bibliography; Genealogy; History; names of specific individuals; names of specific occupations; Reference Books.* Argentina, 92, 3332, 3373, 3375. Bolivia, 3044, 3051. Brazil, 68, 90, 3455, 3472, 3476, 3495, 3530, 3537–3538, 3543, 3557, 3676, 7059, 7063. Central America, 2410. Chile, 3133, 3144, 3148. Cuba, 7140. Dominican Republic, 5340. El Salvador, 2421. Guatemala, 335, 2405. Latin America, 95, 7006, 7022. Latin Americanists, 96. Mexico, 1977, 2183, 2277, 7546. Nicaragua, 2387, 2450. Panama, 2388. Peru, 2953–2954. Uruguay, 69a. Venezuela, 309, 2848, 5437. Viceroyalty of New Spain, 1923. Viceroyalty of Peru, 2687.
Bioy Casares, Adolfo, 5570, 5594.
Bishops. *See also Catholic Church; Clergy.* Argentina, 2893. Latin America, 1767, 1802, 1883. Rio de la Plata, 2797. Viceroyalty of New Granada, 2664. Viceroyalty of Peru, 2709.
Black Carib (indigenous group), 1050.
Blacks. *See also Anthropology; Maroons; Mulattoes; Negritude; Race and Race Relations; Slavery and Slaves.* Belize, 2382, 6434. Brazil, 1776, 3490, 3508, 6196, 6280, 6313, 7051. Chile, 2748. Costa Rica, 5673. Cuba, 2551, 5312, 5824. Haiti, 1776. History, 1810. in Literature, 5434, 5801, 5824, 6196, 6313, 6417, 6430. Latin America, 1810, 2593, 7007. Panama, 1070, 2310, 2380a, 5667. Peru, 2862. Rio de la Plata, 2777, 2779. South America, 5801. Venezuela, 5434. West Indies, 6417, 6430.
Blanco, Andrés Eloy, 5846.
Blanco, José Félix, 2828.
Blest Gana, Alberto, 5097, 5116a.
Bobadilla, Francisco de, 1868.
Bogle, Paul, 2550.
Bogotá, Colombia (city). History, 2660. Music, 7131.

tionships; Sociology; Youth. Brazil, 1016. Colombia, 1081. Viceroyalty of New Spain, 1966.

CHILE. See also Andean Region; Easter Island; Latin America; names of specific cities and provinces; Patagonia; South America.
Art, 307, 310, 323, 325, 427–428.
Bibliography, 18.
Folklore, 18, 1071–1080.
History, 2751, 2987, 3053, 3055, 3062, 3069, 3072, 3075, 3081, 3086, 3089, 3091, 3096, 3099, 3103, 3108, 3118–3119, 3137.
Ethnohistory, 1655, 1693, 1742.
Colonial Period. See also Viceroyalty of Peru. 2627, 2745–2752, 3112.
Independence Period, 2815, 2870–2871, 2889.
19th Century, 2749, 3054, 3057, 3063, 3065–3068, 3070–3071, 3073–3074, 3076, 3079–3080, 3083, 3085, 3087–3088, 3092–3093, 3095, 3097, 3100–3102, 3104–3107, 3111–3112, 3116–3117, 3120, 3122, 3124–3131, 3133–3136, 3938–3141, 3143–3150, 3264, 7619.
20th Century, 3056–3061, 3064–3065, 3067, 3072a, 3076–3078, 3080, 3088, 3090, 3092–3093, 3097–3098, 3101–3102, 3106–3107, 3113, 3115–3116, 3121, 3123, 3125, 3132–3134, 3142–3143, 3145–3149, 3264.
Language, 4538.
Literature, 7118, 7120.
Drama, 5892, 5905, 5930, 5955.
Poetry, 5076, 5671, 5715, 5717, 5724–5725, 5753–5754, 5769, 5787, 5793–5794, 5832, 5833–5837, 5854, 6460, 6471, 6489.
Prose Literature, 5097, 5116a, 5481–5507, 6464, 6466, 6475–6476, 6487.
Music, 1071–1072, 1074–1075, 1080, 7116–7128.
Philosophy, 3078, 3140, 7615–7619.
Chile and Europe Relations, 3063.
Chile and Peru Relations, 2987.
CHILOE (island). See also Chile. Folklore, 1073.
Language, 4524.
Chimango, Antônio, 6335.
Chimú. See also Precolumbian Civilizations. 1697.
Chinese. in Cuba, 2559. in Mexico, 2190.

Chiquitos, Bolivia (prov.). History, 3048.
Chiriguano (indigenous group), 1601.
Choquehuanca, José Domingo, 2864.
Church History. See also Catholic Church; Churches; Clergy; Colonial History; History; Inquisition; Missions; Monasticism and Religious Orders; Protestant Churches. Argentina, 3177, 3363, 3371. Bibliography, 17. Brazil, 3593, 3639. Chile, 3057–3058, 3104, 3142. Costa Rica, 2315, 2385. Cuba, 2491, 2506. Ecuador, 2616. Latin America, 1752, 1759–1760, 1767, 1794, 1825, 1841a, 1843, 1883, 1912, 7502. Mexico, 1920, 1956a, 1964, 2013, 2061, 2210, 2217. Nicaragua, 2338. Paraguay, 3393. Peru, 2623, 2692, 2694, 2698–2699, 2710. Puerto Rico, 2587. South America, 2831. Uruguay, 3371. Venezuela, 2637, 2650. Viceroyalty of New Granada, 2660, 2663. Viceroyalty of New Spain, 1547, 1828, 1949, 1971, 2023. Viceroyalty of Peru, 2626, 2685, 2711. West Indies, 2538.
Churches. See also Architecture; Catholic Church; Church History; Protestant Churches. Brazil, 470, 493. Dominican Republic, 326. Mexico, 349, 358, 363, 365, 370. Panama, 332–333, 336. Peru, 373, 376. Puerto Rico, 328.
Cícero, Father, 1013
Cieza de León, Pedro de, 1708, 2723, 5069.
Cimarrons. See Maroons.
Cities and Towns. See also City Planning; Colonization; International Migration; Land Settlement; Land Use; Sociology; Urbanization. Brazil, 3450, 6333. Colombia, 2651. History, 2436, 3450. in Literature, 6333. Panama, 2436. Peru, 1638. Venezuela, 2638, 2645. Viceroyalty of New Spain, 1921. Viceroyalty of Peru, 2717.
City Planning. See also Architecture; Cities and Towns; Housing; Land Use; Regional Planning; Urbanization. Brazil, 502, 509, 512. Chile, 428. Dictionaries, 4567. Ecuador, 431. History, 1811. Latin America, 1811. Mexico, 389.
Clark, Lygia, 486.
Clavijero, Francisco Javier, 1977.
Clergy. See also Bishops; Catholic Church; Church History; Monasticism and Religious Orders. Argentina, 2757. Chile, 2871, 3058, 3067, 3130. Cuba, 2491. Latin America, 2851. Rio de la Plata, 2767. Viceroyalty of New Spain, 1949, 2013, 2023.
Cluzeau-Mortet, Luis, 7200.

nal Migration; Migrant Labor; names of specific ethnic groups and nationalities; Ports. Argentina, 3250, 3272–3273, 3277–3278, 3297, 3309, 3331, 3357, 3444, 5112. Azores/Brazil, 3518. Brazil, 1761, 3556, 3591, 3600, 3617, 3622, 3626, 3643, 3647–3648. Chile, 3063. Costa Rica, 2443. Cuba, 1761. Ecuador, 2678. Haiti/Cuba, 2590. Latin America, 1761, 1779, 1845, 1912. Mexico, 2094, 2270, 2295. Mexico/United States, 2201, 2285. Paraguay, 3387. Peru, 3000, 3003, 3025. Puerto Rico, 2536. Trinidad, 2504. United States, 2084. Uruguay, 3444. Venezuela, 2931, 2939. Viceroyalty of New Granada, 2666.

Encomiendas. *See also Colonial History; Labor and Laboring Classes; Treatment under Indigenous Peoples.* Ecuador, 1615. Latin America, 2621. Paraguay, 1654. Peru, 1667. Rio de la Plata, 2805. Venezuela, 1731. Viceroyalty of New Spain, 2054. Viceroyalty of Peru, 2732.

Enlightenment. *See also History; Philosophy.* Brazil, 7640. Central America, 7557. Latin America, 7510, 7517, 7539. Mexico, 7549, 7551.

Enríquez, Manuel, 7181.

Ercilla y Zúñiga, Alonso de, 5033, 5049, 5055, 5076.

Errázuriz, Crescente, 3067, 3112.

Erro, Carlos Alberto, 7656.

Escobar, Luis Antonio, 7130.

Espejo, Eugenio. *See Santa Cruz y Espejo, Francisco Javier Eugenio.*

Espionage. Brazil, 3588.

Espírito Santo, Brazil (city). Folklore, 993.

Espírito Santo, Brazil (state). Art, 503. Folklore, 1004, 1035. Literature, 6322.

Esteves Sagué, Miguel, 3234.

Estorino, Abelardo, 5959.

Estrada, José Manuel, 7658.

Estrada, Julio, 7181.

Estrella, Miguel Angel, 7031.

Ethics. *See also Crime and Criminals; Philosophy.* Latin America, 7512, 7519, 7532.

Ethnic Groups and Ethnicity. *See also names of specific groups; Race and Race Relations.* Amazonia, 1614. Andean Region, 1688–1689. Aztec, 1552. Brazil, 1581. Guatemala, 2370. Latin America, 1826, 1903. Mesoamerica, 1566. Peru, 2962. Rio de la Plata, 2804. Trinidad, 2543. United States, 2083, 2094. Viceroyalty of Peru, 1586.

Ethnography. *See also Ethnohistory.* Southern Cone, 1692.

ETHNOHISTORY (items 1501–1750). *See also Archaeology; Ethnohistory under names of specific countries and regions; Ethnography; History; Indigenous Peoples; names of specific indigenous groups; Precolumbian Civilizations.* Congresses, 1530. Definition, 1682. Study and Teaching, 1508.

Ethnomusicology. *See also Folk Music; Folklore; Indigenous Music; Music.* Brazil, 7081. Latin America, 962. Peru, 7196. Tierra del Fuego, 7040.

Excavations. *See also Archaeology; Historic Sites.* Chichén Itzá (Mexico), 274. Ecuador, 1636. Guatemala, 337. Mesoamerica, 272, 274. Palenque (Mexico), 1975. Peru, 376.

Expeditions. *See also Discovery and Explorations; Explorers.* Argentina, 3153. Rio de la Plata, 2796, 2803. Southern Cone, 1692. Spanish, 1814. Tierra del Fuego, 3109. to Brazil, 3569.

Explorers. *See also Conquistadors; Discovery and Exploration; names of specific explorers; Travelers.* Borderlands, 2039.

Eyre, Edward John, 2531.

Eyzaguirre, Jaime, 3132, 7617.

Fabela, Isidro, 7546.

Fajardo, Miguel, 5632.

FALKLAND ISLANDS. *See also Argentina; Argentina and United Kingdom Relations.* Bibliography, 72. History, 2765, 3235.

Falla, Manuel de, 7029.

Fallas, Carlos Luis, 5262.

Family and Family Relations. *See also Children; Households; Kinship; Marriage; Sociology.* Brazil, 3458, 3558. Chile, 3072, 3106. Guatemala, 2369. Mexico, 2165. Rio de la Plata, 2784. Viceroyalty of New Spain, 1936, 1943, 1992.

Fanelli, Antonio María, 2767.

Fantastic Literature. *See also Literature; Magic Realism; Prose Literature under specific countries.* Argentina, 5547, 5583. Mexico, 5178. Peru, 5416.

Farias, Cordeiro de, 3570.

Farré, Luis, 7654.

Fatone, Vicente, 7655.

Feminism. *See also Women.* Brazil, 3675, 6368. Latin America, 5122. Mexico, 2230. Peru, 3009. South America, 3253.

Brazil, 514, 4602, 6267, 6329, 6360. in
Literature, 6329. Rio de la Plata, 2766a,
5126, 5729.
Gê (indigenous group), 1000.
Gelman, Juan, 5848.
Genealogy. *See also Biography; History.* Inca,
1617.
Geographical Names. *See also Geography;
Names.* Argentina, 1690. Ecuador, 1612.
Latin America, 1862, 4565. Mexico, 1528,
4563. Náhuatl, 1551. Nicaragua, 4548.
Geography. *See also Boundary Disputes; Ge-
ographical Names; Historical Geography;
Maps and Cartography; Social Sciences.*
Andean Region, 1732. Bibliography, 2056.
Borderlands, 2056. Ecuador, 2619.
Guatemala, 2359. Venezuela, 2650. Vice-
royalty of New Spain, 1951.
Geology. *See also Earthquakes; Minerals and
Mining Industry; Petroleum Industry and
Trade; Science.* Bibliography, 29. Brazil, 29.
Germans. in Argentina, 3309. in Brazil, 3591,
3617, 3639, 6054.
Gil Fortoul, José, 5125, 7574.
Giorgi, Bruno, 483.
Girondo, Oliverio, 6344.
Gironella, Alberto, 390.
Glória, Veríssimo Augusto, 7054.
Godoy, Manuel de, 5562.
Godoy Cruz, Tomás, 2881.
Goeldi, Oswaldo, 491.
Goiás, Brazil (state). Art, 449. History, 3501,
3535, 3571, 3656.
Gold. *See also Jewelry; Minerals and Mining
Industry; Silver.* Brazil, 3448. Colombia,
263. Mesoamerica, 277. Peru, 262. Vice-
royalty of Peru, 2720.
Goldemberg, Isaac, 5025.
Gómez, Juan Vicente, 2919.
Gómez, Laureano, 2900.
Gómez Carrillo, Enrique, 5819.
Gómez de Avellaneda y Arteaga, Gertrudis,
5113, 5122.
Gómez Farías, Valentin, 2118.
Gómez Sánchez, L., 5950.
Gongorism, 5080.
Gonzaga Cuevas, Luis. *See Cuevas, Luis
Gonzaga.*
González, Gregorio, 2707.
González, Jesús María, 2138.
González Delvalle, Alcibiades, 5949.
González Echeverría, Roberto, 5362.
González Prada, Manuel, 5132, 7600.
Gorostiza, Carlos, 5948, 5978, 5981.

Gottschalk, Louis Moreau, 7010, 7198.
Goya, Francisco, 5562.
Grandjean de Montigny, Auguste Henri Vic-
tor, 504.
Graphic Arts. *See also Art; Painting; Print-
ing.* Argentina, 419. Brazil, 472, 485, 491.
Colombia, 430. Latin America, 379. Mex-
ico, 398, 402.
GREATER ANTILLES. *See also Caribbean
Area; Cuba; Dominican Republic; Haiti;
Jamaica; Puerto Rico; West Indies.*
Folklore, 1087–1100.
GRENADA. *See also Caribbean Area; Com-
monwealth Caribbean.*
History.
Colonial Period, 2497.
19th Century, 2528.
20th Century, 2589.
Groussac, Paul, 5119, 5587.
Guadalajara, Mexico (city). Art, 353.
Guadalajara, Mexico (state). History, 2032.
GUADELOUPE. *See also Caribbean Area;
West Indies.*
History, 2460, 2466, 2481, 2498, 2499.
Colonial Period, 2505.
19th Century, 2566.
Language, 4632.
Guamán Poma. *See Poma de Ayala, Felipe
Huamán.*
Guanajuato, Mexico (state). History, 1985.
Guaraní (indigenous group), 1129, 1134–1135,
1587, 1634, 1661, 1668, 1716, 2795, 2806,
2810, 3514, 7077.
GUATEMALA. *See also Central America;
Latin America; names of specific cities
and departments.*
Art, 296–303, 331, 334–335, 337,
409–410.
Bibliography, 91.
Folklore, 1047, 1049–1059, 1062, 1064,
1066–1067, 5241.
History, 1762, 2308, 2326–2327, 2330,
2336, 2405.
Ethnohistory. *See also Mesoamerica.*
1521.
Colonial Period. *See also Audiencia of
Guatemala; Viceroyalty of New Spain.*
2337, 2342, 2344, 2346–2349, 2359,
2362, 2364–2369, 2373.
19th Century, 2379, 2386, 2409, 2411,
2428, 2430, 2448.
20th Century, 2430, 2445, 2448.
Language, 4559.
Literature, 1057, 5241, 5261.

Lezama Lima, José, 5330, 5349, 5353, 5850, 5858, 5887.

Liberalism. *See also Political Philosophy; Political Science; Social Sciences.* Brazil, 3632, 3638. Central America, 7557. Costa Rica, 7561. Cuba, 5129. Ecuador, 2944. El Salvador, 2376. Latin America, 1769. Mexico, 2100. Peru, 2955.

Liberation Theology. *See Philosophy of Liberation.*

Libraries and Library Services. *See also Archives; Bibliography; Education.* 380. Barbados, 45. Brazil, 19, 46–47b, 58, 61, 97. Chile, 44. Congresses, 41. History, 44. Latin America, 41, 63, 380. North America, 252.

Library Science. *See also Bibliography; Information Science; Libraries and Library Services.* Brazil, 42, 47. Caribbean Area, 40. Congresses, 41. Latin America, 40–43, 62. Study and Teaching, 43. Venezuela, 99.

Lima, Alceu Amoroso, 6317, 6351.

Lima, Jorge de, 5800.

Lima, José Pereira, 3595.

Lima, Peru (city). Art, 376. History, 1960, 2715–2717.

Lima Barreto, Afonso Henrique de, 6302.

Lincovsky, Cipe, 5978.

Linguistics. *See also Bilingualism; Language and Languages; Sociolinguistics.* Bibliography, 4509. Brazil, 4591. Congresses, 4514. Cuba, 4510. Dictionaries, 4568. Methodology, 4608. Theory, 6496.

Liniers y Bremond, Santiago Antonio María de, 2885.

Lira, José Ramón, 3094.

Lira Espejo, Eduardo, 7209.

Lisboa, Antônio Francisco, 464.

Lispector, Clarice, 6358, 6368, 6372.

Literacy and Illiteracy. *See also Education.* History, 1545. Mesoamerica, 1545. Mexico, 1545.

Literary Criticism. *See also Authors; Literature; names of specific authors; Prose Literature; Modernism; Negritude; Romanticism; Semiotics; Structuralism; Surrealism.* Andean Region, 5359, 5364. Argentina, 5095, 5106–5107, 5109, 5112, 5130–5131, 5539, 5569–5613, 5848, 5853, 5872. Barbados, 6445. Bolivia, 5365, 5367, 5369–5370, 5641, 5856. Brazil, 6153, 6191, 6200, 6239, 6252, 6260, 6271, 6273, 6316–6399. Caribbean Area, 5323, 5346, 5873, 6439, 6450. Central America, 5259. Chile, 5116a, 5793–5794, 5817,

5834–5835, 5837, 5854. Colombia, 5371–5371a, 5373–5384, 5495–5507, 5810, 5859, 5867, 5878. Costa Rica, 5789, 5830. Cuba, 5098, 5121, 5134a, 5308, 5310–5311, 5313, 5318–5320, 5324, 5327, 5330, 5332, 5334, 5336–5338, 5342, 5344, 5349–5357, 5796, 5815, 5823, 5825–5826, 5838, 5840, 5850, 5858, 5860. Dominican Republic, 5133, 5329, 5797, 5833. Ecuador, 5385, 5388, 5390–5393, 5682, 5813. Guatemala, 5260, 5819. Haiti, 6420–6421, 6427. History, 6336. Honduras, 5266. Jamaica, 6442, 6448. Latin America, 5003, 5012–5013, 5015, 5017, 5019–5020, 5026–5027, 5080–5081, 5104, 5110, 5265, 5319, 5360, 5363, 5617, 5790, 5799, 5811. Martinique, 6428. Mexico, 5116, 5184–5236, 5821, 5842, 5844–5845. Nicaragua, 5263, 5792, 5822, 5828–5829, 5831, 5869. Paraguay, 5614–5617, 5655, 5808. Periodicals, 5265. Peru, 5120, 5132, 5134b, 5394, 5396–5400, 5402–5431, 5798, 5843. Puerto Rico, 5111, 5795, 5852. Rio de la Plata, 5120. Theory, 5006. Trinidad, 6449. Uruguay, 5618–5626, 5809, 5816, 5827, 5839, 5841. Venezuela, 5433–5434, 5437–5438, 5441, 5443–5444, 5446, 5788, 5805, 5814, 5846–5847, 5849, 5851, 5855. West Indies, 6419, 6429, 6447.

Literatura de cordel. *See also Books and Book Dealers; Folk Literature; Folklore; Literature; Poetry.* 1003, 1008, 1010–1013, 1017, 1020–1021, 6346, 6361. Bibliography, 961, 966. Brazil, 1026–1028, 1030–1031, 1033–1034, 1040. History, 1031.

LITERATURE (items 5001–6506). *See also Authors; Ballads; Books and Book Dealers; Drama; Fantastic Literature; Folk Drama; Folk Literature; Humanism; Journalism; Language and Languages; Legends; Literary Criticism; Literatura de cordel; Magic Realism; Modernism; Poetry; Prose Literature; Romanticism; Semiotics; Structuralism; Surrealism; Translations of Latin American Literary Works; Vanguardism; Wit and Humor.* Bibliography, 10, 5022, 5201, 5326, 5433, 5613a, 5623, 6357, 6425. Congresses, 5279. Dissertations and Theses, 67. History, 5009, 5013, 5024, 5027, 5085, 5105, 5259, 5317, 5368, 5500, 6319. Periodicals, 94, 5073, 5084, 5192, 5290, 5293–5294, 5305, 5344, 5366, 5401, 5861, 5873, 5882, 5884–5885, 6394, 6431–6432. Theory, 6327, 6332.

Livestock. *See also Agriculture; Animals; Cattle Trade.* Brazil, 3446.

Llanos. Venezuela, 2642.

Lloréns Torres, Luis, 5795.

Lobo, Elias Alvares, 7054.

Local Government. *See also Cities and Towns; Political Science; Public Administration.* Bibliography, 31. Brazil, 31. Mexico, 2014. Viceroyalty of New Granada, 2668.

Logging. *See Forests and Forest Industry.*

Lopes Neto, J. Simões, 6360, 6398.

López, Carlos Antonio, 3388, 3398.

López de Gómara, Francisco, 5054.

López de Gómara, Justo S., 5953.

López Pumarejo, Alfonso, 2903.

López Rega, José, 3369.

Lorenzo, Bartolomé, 5074.

Louisiana, United States (state). *See also Borderlands.* History, 2509.

Lunfardo. *See also Language and Languages; Spanish Language.* 4523.

Lynch, Patricio, 3105.

Lyra, Carlos, 6289.

Machado, Luciana Maria do Rosario, 3557.

Machado de Assis, 6334, 6357, 6367, 6369, 6373.

Madero, Francisco Indalecio, 2192, 2224, 2262.

Magalhães, Domingos José Gonçalves de, 7638.

Magalhães, Juracy Montenegro, 3610.

Magaña, Sergio, 5999.

Magariños Cervantes, Alejandro, 5140.

Magic Realism. *See also Fantastic Literature; Literature; Prose Literature; Surrealism.* Bibliography, 5028. Mexico, 5224.

Magloire-Saint-Aude, Clément, 6420.

Maldonado, Alonso, 1596.

Maldonado, Francisco Severo, 7551.

Maldonado, Ricardo, 5631.

Maldonado, Uruguay (dept.). History, 3432.

Malinche, 5088.

Mallarmé, Stéphane, 5850, 5876.

Mangabeira, João, 3612.

Manuscripts. *See also Archives; Bibliography; Codices.* Guatemala, 2357. Huarochirí, 1645, 1735. Mesoamerica, 1512, 1516. *Runa yndio ñiscap,* 1649. Viceroyalty of New Granada, 2662. Viceroyalty of New Spain, 1542, 1838, 1848. Viceroyalty of Peru, 1708.

Maps and Cartography. *See also Geography.* Aztec, 1574.

Maranhão, Brazil (state). Bibliography, 1039. Folklore, 1023, 1039. History, 3468.

Marechal, Leopoldo, 5577, 7649.

Margil de Jesús, Antonio, *Fray,* 2365.

Mariátegui, José Carlos, 2948, 2971, 2973, 2992, 2997, 3001, 3019, 5394, 7586–7588, 7591–7599, 7602, 7605–7606, 7609.

Marimba. *See also Music.* 7007, 7105, 7108.

Marinello, Juan, 5328.

Marinetti, Filippo Tommaso, 5806.

Maritime History. *See also History; Merchant Marines; Military History; Pirates; Shipwrecks.* Andean Region, 1683. Argentina, 2876. Brazil, 3449, 3540, 3575, 3646. Chile, 3080. Latin America, 1754, 1813, 1829, 2848. Mesoamerica, 1683.

Markets. *See also Business; Commerce; Economic History; Food and Food Industry.* Andean Region, 1639. Audiencia of Quito, 2674. Bolivia, 1592.

Marley, Bob, 7086.

Mármol, Américo. *See Bonilla, Manuel Antonio.*

Mármol, Miguel, 5264.

Maroons. *See also Blacks; Slavery and Slaves.* Cuba, 5287. Dominican Republic, 2461. Haiti, 2461–2462. Panama, 2310. Peru, 2862.

Maroto, Rafael, 3144.

Marqués, René, 5795, 6012.

Márquez Rodríguez, Alexis, 5279.

Marquiegui, Juan Guillermo de, 2873.

Marriage. *See also Family and Family Relationships; Kinship; Sex and Sexual Relations.* Chile, 3107. Inca, 1589. Mesoamerica, 1520. Peru, 2985. Viceroyalty of New Spain, 1962, 1983, 2515.

Mars, Jean Price. *See Price-Mars, Jean.*

Martí, José, 39, 1788, 1888, 2471, 5029a, 5121, 5134a, 6462, 7567.

Martí, Mariano, 2650.

Martínez Bustos, Juan, 3128.

Martínez Estrada, Ezequiel, 5570, 5605.

Martínez Vegazo, Lucas, 2732.

MARTINIQUE. *See also Caribbean Area; West Indies.*

Language, 6413.

Literature.
Poetry, 6413, 6422, 6428.

Music, 7088.

Marx, Karl, 7504.

Marxism. *See also Communism and Communist Parties; Political Philosophy; Socialism and Socialist Parties.* Latin

zil, 3497, 3516. Jamaica, 2565. Latin America, 1803–1804. Mexico, 349, 2051, 2154. Venezuela, 2635.

Missiones, Argentina (prov.). History, 2813.

Missions. *See also Catholic Church; Church History; Missionaries; Monasticism and Religious Orders; Protestant Churches.* Borderlands, 2038, 2043, 2047. Brazil, 3514, 3526. California, 2038, 2043. Central America, 2383. Mexico, 2155. Rio de la Plata, 2759, 2769, 2778, 2789, 2795. Venezuela, 2634–2635, 2639.

Mistral, Gabriela, 5834, 5836, 7118, 7120.

Mitre, Bartolomé, 3190, 5105.

Modern Art. *See also Art; Photography.* Argentina, 417–418, 420, 422, 425. Bibliography, 380. Brazil, 482, 486–487, 489, 510. Chile, 427. Cuba, 412, 415. Dominican Republic, 412. Ecuador, 432–433. Latin America, 380. Mexico, 399. Venezuela, 436–437, 445.

Modernism (literature). *See also Literary Criticism; Literature; Poetry; Prose Literature.* Brazil, 6330, 6350, 6394, 7067. Guatemala, 5819. Latin America, 5629, 5802. Mexico, 5215. Nicaragua, 5863. Paraguay, 5637. Periodicals, 6394.

Molina, Enrique, 425.

Molina Enríquez, Andrés, 7541.

Molinari, Diego Luis, 3361.

Monasticism and Religious Orders. *See also Augustinians; Catholic Church; Church History; Clergy; Confraternities; Dominicans; Franciscans; Jesuits; Missionaries; Mormons; Religion.* Argentina, 3184, 3257. Belize, 2401. Brazil, 3459. Caribbean Area, 2485. Ecuador, 2945. Guatemala, 2362. Latin America, 1852, 5048. Mexico, 2199. Peru, 3017. South America, 1834. Venezuela, 2636. Viceroyalty of New Spain, 1828, 1929, 2003. Viceroyalty of Peru, 2625, 2689.

Monestel, Alejandro, 7099, 7104.

Monetary Policy. *See also Banking and Financial Institutions; Economic Policy; Fiscal Policy; Public Finance.* Argentina, 3318.

Montalvo, Juan, 5957, 7580, 7584.

Montejo, Eugenio, 5851.

Montenegro, Carlos, 5343.

Montero, Alvero, 5635.

Monterrey, Mexico (city). History, 2076.

Montes de Oca, Marco Antonio, 5886.

Montevideo, Uruguay (city). History, 3417, 3443.

Monti, Ricardo, 5989.

Montt, Manuel, 3079.

Mora, Florencia, 7201.

Morazán, Francisco, 2410.

Morejón, Nancy, 5824.

Morelos, José María, 2101, 7544.

Morelos, Mexico (state). Art, 265. History, 2002, 2081, 2129, 2147, 2177.

Morelos y Pavón, José María, 1984.

Moreno, Mariano, 2885–2886.

Mormons. *See also Monasticism and Religious Orders.* Mexico, 2154–2155.

Mortality and Morbidity. *See also Death; Demography; Population.* Brazil, 3624. Guatemala, 2379. Mexico, 2000.

Mortuary Customs. *See also Anthropology; Archaeology; Belief and Customs; Death; Rites and Ceremonies.* Brazil, 1002. Ecuador, 7142.

Moscote, José D., 2433.

Mota, Mauro, 6251.

Mujica Láinez, Manuel, 5585.

Mulattoes. *See also Race and Race Relations.* Brazil, 7069.

Multinational Corporations. *See also Business; Commerce; Foreign Investments; Foreign Trade; Industry and Industrialization; International Economic Relations.* Latin America, 2407.

Muñoz Marín, Luis, 5299a.

Murals. *See Painting.*

Murena, H.A., 5581.

Museums. *See also Museums under Art.* Maritime, 1813. Mexico, 265, 273.

MUSIC (items 7001–7217). *See also Composers; Dance; Ethnomusiciology; Folk Music; Indigenous Music; Marimba; Music; Music under Festivals; Musical Instruments; Musicians; Opera; Popular Music; Religious Music; Salsa; Singers; Tango.* Bibliography, 7010, 7014, 7024, 7076. Dictionaries, 7001, 7006, 7009, 7022–7023, 7140. History, 7020. Periodicals, 7026, 7114, 7138. Study and Teaching, 7039, 7055, 7075.

Musical Instruments. *See also Music.* Andean Region, 7004. Argentina, 7034. Brazil, 7056, 7083. Cuba, 7139. Mexico, 7154, 7186. Venezuela, 7205–7206.

Musicians. *See also Artists; Composers; Ethnomusicology; Folk Music; Music; Popular Music.* Afro-Brazilian, 7051. Argentina, 7031. Brazil, 7059, 7063, 7068, 7078. Cuba, 89a, 7132, 7140. Dictionaries, 7140. Latin America, 7078. Mexico, 7153,

7185. Nicaragua, 7115. Puerto Rico, 7089. Uruguay, 7201. Venezuela, 7207–7208, 7215–7216.

Mutabaruka, 6443.

Mutis, Alvaro, 5859, 5867.

Myths and Mythology. *See also Archaeology; Folk Literature; Folklore; Legends; Narratives; Religion; Symbolism.* Andean Region, 1637, 1649, 1734. Aztec, 1517, 1550. Brazil, 986, 1034. Ecuador, 1643–1644. El Salvador, 1069. Guaraní, 1134–1135. Guatemala, 5241. Inca, 1619, 1735. Mataco, 970. Maya, 1510. Mesoamerica, 1556. Mexico, 5199, 5209. Peru, 1735, 3006. Quechua, 1735, 1738. Taino, 5302. Toba, 1133. Paraguay, 1134–1135.

Nabuco, Joaquim, 3585, 3637, 3692.

Naipaul, V.S., 6439, 6450.

Nalé Roxlo, Conrado, 5990.

Names. *See also Geographical Names; Linguistics; Sociolinguistics.* Ecuador, 1612. Latin America, 1581. Quechua, 1737.

Nardone, Benito, 3424.

Nariño, Antonio, 2852.

Narratives. *See also Folk Literature; Folklore; Legends; Literature; Myths and Mythology.* Argentina, 958, 969, 973, 977. Bolivia, 980–981. Borderlands, 1101, 1109. Brazil, 987, 1000, 1003, 1008, 1022, 1036. Colombia, 1083. Ecuador, 958, 1084, 1086. El Salvador, 1069. Guatemala, 1053, 1055–1056. Haiti, 1091, 1093, 1100. Inca, 1673–1674. Latin America, 958. Mexico, 1113, 1116, 1123. Náhuatl, 1113. Peru, 1086, 1139–1140. Quichua, 1086. Saint Vincent, 1087. Study and Teaching, 1056. West Indies, 1095.

Narváez, Francisco, 435, 443.

Natá, Panama (city). History, 2311.

National Bibliographies. *See also Bibliography.* Brazil, 5–6. Costa Rica, 4. Dominican Republic, 3. Haiti, 7.

National Characteristics. *See also Anthropology; Cultural Identity; National Patrimony; Nationalism.* Andean Region, 7587. Argentina, 7663. Brazil, 7620. Latin America, 2842, 7501, 7531. Puerto Rico, 7566.

National Identity. *See Cultural Identity; National Characteristics; Nationalism.*

National Patrimony. *See also Cultural Policy.* Brazil, 478. Mexico, 345, 353. Peru, 374.

Nationalism. *See also Foreign Policy; Inter-*national Relations; National Characteristics; Nativistic Movements; Political Science.* Andean Region, 1672. Argentina, 3166, 3243, 3329, 3374, 7656. Bolivia, 3045, 5449. Brazil, 3586, 6328. Caribbean Area, 2606. Central America, 2306. Chile, 3078, 3091, 3143, 7617. in Literature, 6328. Latin America, 1777, 2827, 3329. Mexico, 2086, 2097, 2162, 2291. Panama, 2442. Peru, 1665, 2947, 3019, 3026, 5429. Philosophy, 7617, 7656. Puerto Rico, 2480, 2576.

Nativistic Movements. *See also Indigenous Peoples; Nationalism; Religion.* Andean Region, 1593, 1726. Peru, 2984.

Natural History. *See also History; Science.* Mexico, 1570–1571.

Natural Resources. *See also Ecology; Fish and Fishing Industry; Forests and Forest Industry; Minerals and Mining Industry; Petroleum Trade and Industry.* Viceroyalty of New Spain, 2010.

Nava, Pedro, 6396.

Nayarit, Mexico (state). Folklore, 1105.

Negritude. *See also Blacks; Literary Criticism; Literature.* 5801, 5824. Haiti, 6418, 6427. Peru, 3006. West Indies, 6417.

Nejar, Carlos, 6252.

Nel Gómez, Pedro, 429.

Neri, Rafael José, 5279.

Neruda, Pablo, 5737, 5832, 5854.

Nervo, Amado, 5842.

NETHERLANDS ANTILLES. *See also Caribbean Area; Saint Martin.*
Bibliography, 2474.
History, 2464, 2474.

Netto, José Antônio, 3521.

New Mexico, United States (state). Art, 295. History, 2040, 2044, 2054.

Newspapers. *See also Freedom of the Press; Journalism; Mass Media; Periodicals.* Argentina, 3223. Brazil, 3609, 3635. Ecuador, 2853. Indexes, 81. Paraguay, 3407. Peru, 2977. Uruguay, 3419. Venezuela, 2935.

NICARAGUA. *See also Central America; Latin America; names of specific cities.*
Art, 253, 408.
Bibliography, 5863.
Folklore, 1046.
History, 2312, 2331, 2333.
  Colonial Period. *See also Viceroyalty of New Spain.* 2333, 2338, 2354.
  19th Century, 2374–2375, 2377, 2387, 2450.
  20th Century. *See also Nicaraguan Rev-*

Positivism. *See also Phenomenology; Philosophy; Religion.* Argentina, 7645, 7647, 7665. Brazil, 7624a, 7626, 7629, 7640. Central America, 7558. Latin America, 7520. Venezuela, 5125, 7574.

Postal Service. Argentina, 3181. Chile, 3134, 3145. Mexico, 2091. Paraguay, 3401.

Potosí, Bolivia (dept.). Folklore, 983.

Pottery. *See also Archaeology; Art; Crafts; Folk Art.* Brazil, 446, 448. Guatemala, 300, 302. Mesoamerica, 278. Mexico, 290, 362, 1108, 1126. Peru, 306. Venezuela, 256, 340.

Precolumbian Architecture. *See also Archaeology; Architecture; Historic Sites; Precolumbian Civilizations.* Inca, 260. Maya, 1529. Mesoamerica, 267, 274.

Precolumbian Art. *See also Archaeology; Art; Folk Art; Precolumbian Civilizations; Precolumbian Sculpture; Precolumbian Textiles.* Andean Region, 1613. Baja California, 271. Chavín, 257. Colombia, 263. Congresses, 259, 266. Costa Rica, 254. History, 264. Latin America, 261, 264, 286. Mesoamerica, 255, 275–276, 278. Mexico, 266. Nicaragua, 253. Peru, 262. Venezuela, 256.

Precolumbian Civilizations. *See also Archaeology; Aztec; Chimú; Ethnohistory under specific countries and regions; Inca; Indigenous Peoples; Maya; Olmec; Precolumbian Architecture; Precolumbian Art; Precolumbian Trade.* Chavín, 257. Costa Rica, 254. Ecuador, 1644. Latin America, 286. Peru, 2615.

Precolumbian Sculpture. *See also Precolumbian Art; Sculpture.* Huasteca, 269. Maya, 268. Mesoamerica, 267, 270, 273.

Precolumbian Textiles. *See also Precolumbian Art; Textiles and Textile Industry.* Argentina, 311. Mesoamerica, 272.

Precolumbian Trade. *See also Archaeology; Commerce; Precolumbian Civilizations.* Borderlands, 2050. Peru, 1660.

Prescod, Samuel J., 2546.

Presidents. *See also Dictators; Kings and Rulers; names of specific presidents; Politicians; Statesmen.* Argentina, 3161, 3197, 3248. Bolivia, 3044, 3049, 3051. Brazil, 3615. Colombia, 2900, 2903–2904. Guatemala, 2405. Honduras, 2437. Mexico, 2093, 2244, 2264. Panama, 2380a. Peru, 2958. Venezuela, 2910, 2936.

Price-Mars, Jean, 2568.

Printing. *See also Bibliography; Books and Book Dealers; Graphic Arts; Publishers and Publishing Industry.* Brazil, 452. Ecuador, 2853.

Protestant Churches. *See also Church History; Missions; Monasticism and Religious Orders; Religion.* Argentina, 3177. Costa Rica, 1769. Cuba, 2575. Latin America, 1752, 1770. Mexico, 2063.

Proverbs. *See also Folk Literature; Folklore; Literature.* Argentina, 972. Brazil, 988, 1014. Chile, 1077. Haiti, 1091, 4625. Latin America, 4570. Quichua, 1086. Paraguay, 1131. Patagonia, 967. Uruguay, 1146, 4518.

Public Administration. *See also Bureaucracy; Military Governments; Political Science; Public Policy.* Brazil, 3479.

Public Enterprises. *See also Business; Public Works.* Venezuela, 2914.

Public Finance. *See also Economic History; Economics; Finance; Fiscal Policy; Monetary Policy; Taxation.* Argentina, 3325. Brazil, 3546. Chile, 3065. Congresses, 2621. Ecuador, 2677. Guatemala, 2386. History, 2621. Venezuela, 2621.

Public Health. *See also Diseases; Medical Care; Nutrition.* History, 1805. Latin America, 1805. Panama, 2397–2398.

Public Opinion. *See also Freedom of the Press; Political Science.* Spain, 1893. United Kingdom, 2468. United States, 2083.

Public Policy. *See also Cultural Policy; Economic Policy.* Mexico, 2173. United States, 2238.

Public Works. *See also Public Enterprises.* Caribbean Area, 40. History, 2116. Latin America, 40. Mexico, 2116. Panama, 2397–2398.

Publishers and Publishing Industry. *See also Bibliography; Books and Book Dealers; Censorship; Periodicals; Printing.* Brazil, 452, 3461. Dominican Republic, 100.

Pucciarelli, Eugenio, 7660.

Puebla, Mexico (city). History, 1976.

Puebla, Mexico (state). Art, 352, 362. History, 1565, 2109.

Puerto Ricans. *See also Hispanic Americans.* 81.

PUERTO RICO. *See also Caribbean Area; Greater Antilles; United States.* Art, 328. Folklore, 1090. History, 2455–2456, 2458, 2480, 5299a. 19th Century, 2520, 2522, 2532, 2534,

Cuba, 5129. Ecuador, 7580. Latin America, 7579. Venezuela, 5118.
Romero, Francisco, 7646, 7659, 7665.
Romero, José Luis, 3164, 3263, 7663.
Romero, Mariela, 5970.
Romero, Ricardo, 402.
Romero, Silvio, 6334.
Romero, Tomas Antonio, 2771.
Rosa, João Guimarães, 6376.
Rosas, Juan Manuel José Domingo Ortiz de, 3157, 3164, 3333, 5128a.
Rossy y Calderón, Manuel F., 2570.
Rousseau, Jean Jacques, 1889.
Roza, José Ignacio de la, 2883.
Rubber Industry and Trade. *See also Agricultural Industries; Forests and Forest Industry.* Brazil, 3694.
Rubião, Murilo, 6377.
Ruggiero, Juan Nicolás, 3245.
Ruiz, Manuel, 5272.
Ruiz de Alarcón, Hernando, 1527.
Rulfo, Juan, 5025, 5184, 5187a, 5193, 5196, 5204, 5219, 5221, 5226, 5229, 5233.
Rural Sociology. *See also Peasants; Sociology; Urbanization.* Bolivia, 3040. Mexico, 2129, 2158, 5225. Peru, 5470.

Sábato, Ernesto, 5602, 5608, 5610.
Sabino, Fernando Tavares, 6149, 6393.
Sabogal, Maria Wiesse de, 7590.
Sacrifice. *See also Religion.* Mesoamerica, 1511.
Sáenz, Manuela, 2818.
Sahagún, Bernardino de, 1502, 1504–1505, 1547, 2001, 2009.
SAINT KITTS. *See also Caribbean Area; Commonwealth Caribbean.* History.
Colonial Period, 2497.
19th Century, 2528.
SAINT LUCIA. *See also Caribbean Area; Commonwealth Caribbean.* Folklore, 1089.
SAINT MARTIN. *See also Caribbean Area; Netherlands Antilles.* History, 2464.
SAINT VINCENT. *See also Caribbean Area; Commonwealth Caribbean.* Folklore, 1087.
Sainz, Gustavo, 5188, 5216, 5227, 5236.
Salcedo, Dominican Republic (prov.). History, 2477.
Salgado, Plínio, 3667.
Salsa (music). *See also Popular Music.* 7005, 7021, 7027.

Salta, Argentina (prov.). Literature, 5008. Music, 7036.
Salvador, Brazil (city). History, 3487.
San Andrés de Pica, Chile (city). History, 3062.
San José, Costa Rica (city). History, 2332, 2385.
San Juan, Argentina (prov.). History, 2883. Philosophy, 7657.
San Luis, Argentina (prov.). History, 2800.
San Martín, José de, 2816, 2880, 2883, 2889, 2892.
Sánchez, Luis Alberto, 7603.
Sandinistas. *See also Nicaragua under Political Parties.* 5237, 5245.
Sandino, Augusto César, 2374–2375, 2384, 2399, 2434, 2441, 5244, 5246, 5654.
Santa Anna, Antonio López de, 2093, 2139, 2141.
Santa Catarina, Brazil (state). Art, 513, 516. History, 3449, 3457, 3471. Literature, 6324.
Santa-Cruz, Mariscal Andrés de, 3049.
Santa Cruz Pachacuiti Yamqui, Juan de, 1607, 1738, 5038.
Santa Cruz y Espejo, Francisco Javier Eugenio, 7582, 7584.
Santo Domingo, Dominican Republic (city). Art, 327, 329.
Santa Fe, Argentina (prov.). History, 2875, 3250.
Santa Marta, Colombia (city). History, 339.
Santamaría, Francisco Javier, 2143.
Santiago, Chile (city). History, 2750, 3108, 3119, 3127, 3137. Language, 4538.
Santiago, Dominican Republic (city). Art, 326.
Santiago, Guatemala. *See Antigua, Guatemala (city).*
Santiago del Estero, Argentina (city). History, 2790.
Santiago del Estero, Argentina (prov). History, 3328. Language, 4581.
Santo Domingo, Dominican Republic (city). History, 2493. Language, 4539.
Santos, Eduardo, 2907.
Santos Vargas, José, 2869.
Santos Zelaya, José, 2377.
São Luís do Maranhão, Brazil (city). Art, 501. History, 501.
São Paulo, Brazil (city). Art, 507–508, 511, 515. Folklore, 1011. History, 507, 515, 3643, 3649, 3671. Literature, 6310.
São Paulo, Brazil (state). Folklore, 997, 999, 1014, 1030, 7065. History, 3446–3447, 3476, 3493, 3495, 3590. Music, 7054, 7065.

Sardá, Josep, 2859.
Sarduy, Severo, 5324, 5336, 5338.
Sarmiento, Domingo Faustino, 3333, 5100, 5106–5107, 5605.
Sawkins, Santiago, 2552.
Schlappriz, Luís, 472.
Schmid, P. Martín, 2778.
Science. *See also Astronomy; Geology; Natural History; Technology.* Brazil, 4610. Dictionaries, 4610. Mexico, 2152, 2175. Spain, 1814. Viceroyalty of New Spain, 2005.
Scorza, Manuel, 5416, 5431.
Sculpture. *See also Aesthetics; Art; Precolumbian Sculpture.* Brazil, 466, 483, 496. Ecuador, 342. Guatemala, 331. Mexico, 354, 357, 361, 392, 396. Nicaragua, 408. Panama, 336. Peru, 306, 371. Venezuela, 435, 442, 444.
Sebreli, Juan José, 5581.
Semiotics. *See also Literary Criticism; Structuralism.* Argentina, 5602. Peru, 5395. Venezuela, 7579.
Sendero Luminoso, 5430.
Sepúlveda Maira, María Luisa, 7117.
Sergipe, Brazil (state). History, 3558, 3688.
Sette, Mário, 6399.
Sex and Sexual Relations. *See also Human Fertility; Marriage; Sociology.* Bibliography, 21. Inca, 1589, 1673–1674. Latin America, 21. Mesoamerica, 1541. Viceroyalty of New Spain, 1936, 1956, 1983.
Shamanism. *See also Folk Medicine; Religion.* Ecuador, 1711. Venezuela, 1610.
Shipwrecks. *See also Maritime History.* Viceroyalty of New Spain, 1958.
Shrines. *See also Religion.* Peru, 1696, 1707.
Sierra Gorda, Mexico (region). History, 2106.
Sierra O'Reilly, Justo, 2133.
Sigaud, Eugênio de Proença, 484.
Sigüenza y Góngora, Carlos de, 5044, 5053.
Silva, Ludovico, 7576.
Silva Herzog, Jesús, 2257, 7546.
Silva Lezaeta, Luis, 3093.
Silver. *See also Gold; Jewelry; Minerals and Mining Industry.* Latin America, 1818. Mexico, 2077. South America, 2622. Spain, 1871a. Spanish Colonies, 1871a. Viceroyalty of Peru, 2720.
Sinaloa, Mexico (state). History, 2161.
Sinán, Rogelio, 5258.
Singerman, Berta, 6018.
Singers. *See also Music; Musicians.* Cuba, 7136. Paraguay, 7191. Venezuela, 7211.
Siqueiros, David Alfaro, 382.

Sivers, Yegor, 2391.
Slavery and Slaves. *See also Abolition of Slavery; Blacks; Colonial History; Labor and Laboring Classes; Maroons; Sociology.* Barbados, 2463. Brazil, 1005, 3466, 3474, 3486, 3488, 3496, 3508, 3510, 3512–3513, 3515, 3520, 3528, 3530, 3532, 3541, 3558, 3565, 3567, 3573, 3580, 3583, 3604, 3618–3620, 3624, 3641, 3674, 3681–3682, 7639. Caribbean Area, 1791, 2452, 2473, 2489, 2500–2502, 2507, 2528, 2557. Congresses, 1791. Cuba, 2533, 2554, 2559, 5985. Dominican Republic, 2461. Grenada, 2497. Haiti, 2461, 6426. Jamaica, 2465, 2558, 2565. Latin America, 1801, 1827, 1872, 1900, 3512, 4571. Mexico, 3486. North America, 1770. Panama, 2310, 2343. Philosophy, 7639. Portugal, 3512. Puerto Rico, 2518–2519, 2553, 5985. Rio de la Plata, 2798, 2814. Saint Kitts, 2497. South America, 1770. Venezuela, 2643. Viceroyalty of New Granada, 2653–2654, 2662. Viceroyalty of Peru, 2684. West Indies, 2538.
Soares de Moura, Raul, 3660.
Soccer War (1969). *See Honduras/El Salvador under Boundary Disputes.*
Social Classes. *See also Elites; Labor and Laboring Classes; Nobility; Poor; Social History; Social Structure; Sociology.* Argentina, 3165. Aztec, 1539. Brazil, 1040, 3542, 3680. Cuba, 2454, 2588. Ecuador, 2941. Haiti, 7563. Latin America, 283, 7533. Mexico, 2160, 2211, 2258, 2296, 5148. Peru, 2963, 2975. Puerto Rico, 2536. Rio de la Plata, 2808. Spanish Colonies, 1869. Viceroyalty of New Spain, 1921, 1960.
Social History. *See also History; Labor and Laboring Classes; Poor; Social Classes; Social Structure; Sociology; Urbanization.* Argentina, 3164, 3215, 3231, 3260, 3264, 3356, 3366. Barbados, 2508. Bolivia, 5365. Borderlands, 2044. Brazil, 502, 3482, 3510, 3523, 3568, 3648, 3659, 3670, 3696. Chile, 2751, 3059, 3072a, 3076, 3082, 3089, 3264. Ecuador, 2678. Haiti, 2521. History, 2617. Latin America, 1785, 1802, 1839, 1844–1846, 2109. Mexico, 1915, 1918, 1922, 2020, 2024, 2057, 2060, 2109, 2174, 2223. Paraguay, 2763. Patagonia, 3244. Peru, 2706. Puerto Rico, 2541. Rio de la Plata, 2776. Study and Teaching, 2109. Tierra del Fuego, 3110. Uruguay, 3264, 3411, 3415–3416.

AUTHOR INDEX

Caputo, Sara de Astelarra, 3195
Carballido, Emilio, 5900, 5928, 5966, 6465
Carbonell, Abel, 2896
Card, Caroline, 7011
Cardenal, Ernesto, 5831
Cardenal Argüello, Salvador, 7101
Cárdenas, Carmelo Oscanoa de, 990
Cárdenas, Lázaro, 2286
Cárdenas A., Renato, 4524
Cárdenas Ayaipoma, Mario, 2690
Cárdenas de la Peña, Enrique, 2181
Cárdenas Paravicini, Elvira, 3035
Cárdenas Ruiz, Manuel, 2488
Cárdenas Tabies, Antonio, 1073
Cárdenas Timteo, Clara, 88
Cárdich, Samuel Armando, 5469
Cardiel Reyes, Raúl, 7542
Cardim, Luís Henrique, 6288
Cardoso, Ciro Flamarion S., 1801
Cardoso, Fernando Henrique, 7523
Cardoso, Geraldo, 3486
Cardoso, Ivan, 510
Cardoso, Onelio Jorge, 5274–5276
Cardoza y Aragón, Luis, 385
Cardozo, Efraim, 2762
Cardozo, Flávio José, 6155
Cardozo, Lubio, 6013
Careaga, Gabriel, 7515
Carelli, Mario, 6321
Carías Lindo, Erasmo, 5681
Carib, 6441
Caride, Vicente P., 419
Carilla, Emilio, 5081, 5109
Carlos Fuentes: a critical view, 5189
Carlos Magno, Paschoal, 6209
Carlyle, Thomas, 3399a
Carmack, Robert M., 1516, 1543
Carmagnani, Marcello, 1755, 1965, 3196
Carneiro, Edison, 3487
Caro, Miguel Antonio, 5110
Carón, Carlos María, 5516
Carpentier, Alejo, 5277–5279, 5316, 7133
Carr, Barry, 2182, 7543
Carranza Coronado, Ramiro, 2896, 2908
Carrasco, David, 1517
Carrasco Delgado, Sergio, 3067
Carrasco M., Iván, 5790
Carrasco Pizana, Pedro, 1518–1522
Carrasquilla, Juan, 1602
Carrazzoni, Maria Elisa, 505
Carreira, Liberato de Castro, 3546
Carrera, Mario Alberto, 5967
Carrera Andrade, Jorge, 5682
Carrera Damas, Germán, 1785, 2822, 2825
Carrera Gómez, Susana, 4525

Carril, Bonifacio de, 3197–3198
Carrillo Azpéitia, Rafael, 2073
Carrillo-Herrera, Gastón, 5832
Carrillo y Pérez, Ignacio, 348
Carrión, Benjamín, 5387, 5845
Carrión, Carlos, 5463
Carrizosa, Selvio, 7147
Carrocera, Buenaventura de, 2634–2635
Carrol, Glenn R., 3223
Carstensen, Fred V., 2074
Cartas baianas, 1821–1824: subsídios para o
    estudo dos problemas da opção na indepen-
    dência brasileira, 3453
Cartas diplomáticas: Eusebio Ayala, Vicente
    Rivarola; Guerra del Chaco, 3381
Carter, Shiela, 5833
Carvalho, Age de, 6210
Carvalho, Antônio Morais de, 6211
Carvalho, Carlos, 6285
Carvalho, José Antônio, 503
Carvalho, José Murilo de, 3547–3548
Carvalho, Luiz Seráphico de Assis, 482
Carvalho, Mario Bezerra de, 4610
Carvalho Neto, Paulo de, 954, 1048, 1084
Carynnyk, Deborah B., 1523
La Casa cusqueña, 372
Casal, Lourdes, 5683
Casal, Pío, 2386
Casalla, Mario C., 7649
Casares Rodicio, Emilio, 7148
Casas Dupuy, Rosario, 5006
Casasola, Gustavo, 2183
Casasola, Miguel V., 2183a
Casaus, Víctor, 5304
Cascudo, Luís da Câmara, 991
Case, Robert, 2075
Casetta, Giovanni, 7606
Caso, Fernando H., 7085
Cassá, Roberto, 2573
Cassou, Jean, 5242
Castagnino, Raúl Héctor, 5791, 5902
Castañeda, Paulino, 1802
Castañeda Delgado, Paulino, 1966
Castañeda León, Luisa, 1136
Castedo, Leopoldo, 3068, 3076
Castedo-Ellerman, Elena, 5968
Castellanos, Alfredo, 3415
Castellanos, Joaquín, 3199
Castelli G., Amalia, 2691
Castellón, Hello, 1147
Castelo Branco, Renato, 6036
Castillero Calvo, Alfredo, 332–333
Castillo, Abel Romeo, 2853
Castillo, Gustavo del, 1916
Castillo, Otto René, 5684

Matyoka de Yeager, Trudy, 7520
Maunez-Vizcarrondo, Santiago, 5291
Maurício, Augusto, 3621
Mauricio, Julio, 5893, 5929
Mauricio Salazar, Abraham, 291
Mauro, Frédéric, 3622–3623
Mauroy, Dominique Quentin. *See* Quentin-
Mauroy, Dominique.
Maya, Carlos, 1939
Mayer, Enrique, 1667
Mayo, Carlos, 3300
Mayo, John, 1891
Mayo, Osvaldo, 3300
Mayorga, Wilfredo, 5930, 5998
Mayorga Santana, Ramiro, 3113–3114
Maza, Francisco de la, 5071
Mazo, Gabriel del, 3301
Mazzotti, José A., 5733
Medeiros, Manoel da Costa, 3467
Medeiros, Paulina, 5597
Medin, Tzvi, 2235
Medina, Alvaro, 414
Medina, Enrique, 5535
Medina, José Ramón, 5439, 5849
Medina Vidal, Jorge, 5841
Medrango García, José Luis, 363
Meel, J., 7111
Megale, Nilza Botelho, 1015
Megenney, William W., 4571
Meier, Matt S., 30
Meireles, Cecília, 6164–6165, 6240
Meireles, José Dilermando, 6166
Meireles, Mario Martins, 3468
Meisel R., Adolfo, 2662
Mejía Sánchez, Ernesto, 5174, 5931
Mejía Vellajo, Manuel, 5734
Mejía Zúñiga, Raúl, 2118
Mejías, Hugo A., 4572
Melendes, Joserramón, 5735
Meléndez, María J., 2418
Meléndez Chaverri, Carlos, 2352
Melgar Bao, Ricardo, 2991
Melia, Bartolomeu, 1668
Melid, Bartomeu, 3393
Melis, Antonio, 2992, 5598
Mellado de Hunter, Elena, 4549
Mello, Antônio Carlos de, 6117
Mello, Frederico Pernambucano de, 3469
Mello, Gustavo Bandeira de, 6167–6168
Mello, José Antônio Gonsalves de, 3489, 3491
Mello, Melilo Moreira de, 6118
Mello, Oliveira, 6370
Mello, Thiago de, 6241
Mello, William Agel de, 4615

Mello Júnior, Donato, 474
Mello Sobrinho, Cláudio, 4597
Melo, Gladstone Chaves de, 4603
Melo, Jerônimo Martiniano Figueiria de, 3625
Melo, Maria do Carmo Barreto Campello de, 6242
Mélo, Veríssimo de, 1016
Melo Neto, João Cabral de, 6243–6244
Memória de Ilhéus: edição comemorativa do centenário de sua elevação á idade, 3470
Memorias inéditas del censo de 1931, 2594
Mencía, Mario, 2595
Mendelson, José, 3302
Mendes, Mariam Garcia, 6313
Méndez, Luz María, 2749
Méndez de la Vega, Luz, 5736
Méndez-Domínguez, Alfredo, 86
Méndez Rodenas, Adriana, 5336
Mendieta y Núñez, Lucio, 5842
Mendiola Quezada, Vicente, 358
Mendive, Carlos L., 5563, 5965
Mendizábal de Roel, Margarita, 1140
Mendoza, Cristóbal, 2826
Mendoza L., Gunnar, 2869
Mendoza Meléndez, Eduardo, 2993
Menegus Bornemann, Margarita, 2236
Menéndez, Iván, 2237
Menéndez Díaz, Conrado, 4511
Meneses, Carlos, 5414
Meneses, Guillermo, 5477
Menezes, Eduardo Diatahy B. de, 1017
Menezes, Emílio de, 6395
Menjivar Rieken, Gloria, 1069
Menotti, Emilia Edda, 3161
Menotti del Picchia, Paulo, 6060
Los Mensajeros del Paraguay, 7191
Mensajes de los Gobernadores de Córdoba a la Legislatura, 3303
Meo Zilio, Giovanni, 5242
Mercader, Martha, 5536–5537
Merheb, Alice Inês Silva, 1018
Mérida, Carlos, 398
Merino de Zela, E. Mildred, 1141
Merino Montero, Luis, 7121
Merrell, Floyd, 5415
Merrim, Stephanie, 5337
Mesa, Carlos E., 1669, 1843, 2663
Mesa, José de, 342, 375
Mesa F., José de, 7046
Mesoamérica, 2322
Mesoamérica: directorio y bibliografía, 1950–1980, 86
Mestre Ghigliazza, Manuel, 2107
Mexican immigrant workers in the U.S., 2238

Turcato, Teresinha, 6182
Turcios, Froylán, 5266
Turino, Thomas, 7196
Turner, E. Daymond, Jr., 5072
Turner, Ethel Duffy, 2294
Turner, Frederick C., 3276
Turner, Mary, 2558–2559
Turnier, Alain, 2483
Turrent, Jaime, 5179
Turu, Danielle, 2560
Tutikian, Jane, 6142
Tutino, John, 2030, 2156
Twinam, Ann, 2669
Two Mexico City choirbooks of 1717: an
    anthology of sacred polyphony from the
    Cathedral of Mexico, 7183
Tyler, Daniel, 2157
Tyrakowski, Konrad, 2031, 2102

Ugarte, María, 329
Ulacia, Manuel, 5778
Ulloa y Sotomayor, Alberto, 3018
Umpierre, Luz María, 6020
Unceín Tamayo, Luis Alberto, 1873
Unger, David, 6452
United States. Department of State, 2561
United States relations with Mexico: context
    and content, 2295
Universidad Central de Venezuela, *Caracas.*
    Taller de Historia del Movimiento Obrero
    en Venezuela, 2937
Universidad de San Carlos de Guatemala.
    Facultad de Humanidades. Escuela de Bib-
    liotecología, 91, 1047
The University of Dayton Review, 5073
University of Texas, *Austin.* Institute of
    Latin American Studies, 96
Unruh, Vicky Wolff, 5428
Unveiling Cuba, 5305
Urbano, Henrique, 1733–1734
Uribe, Eloisa, 392
Uribe Echevarría, Juan, 1080, 7127
Urbina, Leandro, 5913
Urioste, George L., 1649, 1735
Urquiza Almandoz, Oscar F., 3366
Urrutia de Stebelski, Cristina, 1940
Urteaga, Augusto, 2254
Urton, Gary, 1529
Usandizaga y Mendoza, Pedro María de, 4557
Uslar Pietri, Arturo, 2647, 5445
Usui, Mikito, 107
*Utopía y revolución: el pensamiento político
    contemporáneo de los indios en América
    Latina,* 7537
Uzcátegui, Emilio, 2944

Valadés, J.C., 7554
Valcárcel, Carlos Daniel, 2721
Valcárcel, Luis E., 3019
Valda Cortés de Viaña, Aurora, 5366
Valderrama, Mariano, 3020
Valdés, Hernán, 5494
Valdivieso, Jaime, 5858
Valdman, Albert, 4627
Valencia Espinoza, Abraham, 1736
Valencia López, Raymond. *See* López,
    Raymond Valencia.
Valencia Vega, Alipio, 3051
Valenzuela, Luisa, 6481
Valero, Roberto, 5356
Valiente, Teresa, 1737
Valladares, Clarival do Prado, 461, 470, 492
Valladares, Luiz Fernando, 6275
Vallarino, Roberto, 5779
Valle, Alúsio P., 6143
Valle, Gerson, 6276
Valle de Siles, María Eugenia del, 2738
Vallée, Lionel, 1738
Vallejo de Paredes, Margarita, 1088, 5268,
    5890
Valukin, E.P., 7128
Vamos Szabo, Emmerich, 3145
van den Berg, Hans. *See* Berg, Hans van den.
van Oss, Adriaan C. *See* Oss, Adriaan C. van.
van Steen, Edla. *See* Steen, Edla van.
Van Young, Eric, 1953, 2032
van Zantwijk, Rudolf. *See* Zantwijk, Rudolf
    van.
Vance, Birgitta, 4558
Vanderwood, Paul J., 405, 2158
Vangelista, Chiara, 3196, 3689
Vanni, José Miguel, 3367
Vanzolini, Paulo Emílio, 6277
Varas, Jaime, 2562
Varela Marcos, Jesús, 1873a
Varela-Ruiz, Leticia, 7184
Vargas, Alvaro Rocha, 3481
Vargas, José María, 433, 2682, 2945
Vargas, Oscar René, 2331
Vargas, Vilma, 5814
Vargas, Virginia, 2978
Vargas Llosa, Mario, 5242, 5429–5430, 5473,
    6482
Vargas Lugo, Elisa, 321
Varner, Jeannette Johnson, 1874
Varner, John Grier, 1874
Varón, Rafael, 1739, 2733
Vasconcellos, Marcos de, 6183
Vasconcellos, Marilus Moreira, 6075
Vasconcellos, Sylvio de, 6184
Vasconcelos, José, 6492